Seeking Our Past

Seeking Our Past

An Introduction to North American Archaeology

SECOND EDITION

SARAH W. NEUSIUS
Indiana University of Pennsylvania

G. TIMOTHY GROSS
Ecology and Environment, Inc., and University of San Diego

New York   Oxford
OXFORD UNIVERSITY PRESS

Oxford University Press is a department of the University of Oxford.
It furthers the University's objective of excellence in research, scholarship,
and education by publishing worldwide.

Oxford   New York
Auckland   Cape Town   Dar es Salaam   Hong Kong   Karachi
Kuala Lumpur   Madrid   Melbourne   Mexico City   Nairobi
New Delhi   Shanghai   Taipei   Toronto

With offices in
Argentina   Austria   Brazil   Chile   Czech Republic   France   Greece
Guatemala   Hungary   Italy   Japan   Poland   Portugal   Singapore
South Korea   Switzerland   Thailand   Turkey   Ukraine   Vietnam

Copyright © 2014, 2007 by Oxford University Press

Published by Oxford University Press
198 Madison Avenue, New York, NY 10016
www.oup.com

Oxford is a registered trademark of Oxford University Press.

ISBN: 978-0-19-987384-5

Printing number: 9 8 7 6 5 4 3 2 1
Printed in the United States of America
on acid-free paper

For my students, who continue to keep me searching for ways to explain my passion for North American archaeology, and for Phil, Ginny, and Ben, whose support allows me to pursue this passion.

—SWN

For my family—my daughter, Jennifer, my late father, George, and my late mother, Marlo, and for the students who have used this book in my classes and made so many helpful comments.

—GTG

Contents

CHAPTER 9 Foragers and Villagers of the Southwestern Mountains, Mesas, and Deserts 262

Definition of the Area 263
The Environments of the Southwest 264
ANTHROPOLOGICAL THEMES: TOPIC 9.1 Thematic Research Questions in Chapter 9 267
Climatic Change 267
Hunters and Foragers 267
Paleoindian 267
Early and Middle Archaic 268
Late Archaic 270
Farmers and Villagers 271
Anasazi (Ancestral Pueblo) 272
Mogollon 276
ISSUES AND DEBATES: BOX 9.1 Interpreting the Chaco Phenomenon 277
CLUES TO THE PAST: EXHIBIT 9.1 Fantasies on Clay: Mimbres Pottery 280
Hohokam 282
Patayan 285
Sinagua 286
Reorganization, Aggregation, and Conflict in Late Prehistory 286
New Arrivals 289
Chapter Summary 290
Suggestions for Further Reading 291
Other Resources 291
Case Study: Casas Grandes at the Edge of the Southwestern and Mesoamerican Worlds **Paul E. Minnis and Michael E. Whalen** 292

CHAPTER 10 Bison Hunters and Horticulturists of the Great Plains 299

Definition of the Area 300
The Environment 300
Climatic Change 303
ANTHROPOLOGICAL THEMES: TOPIC 10.1 Thematic Research Questions in Chapter 10 304
Paleoindians on the Plains 304
Plains Archaic 304
Late Archaic Developments 306
The Woodland Period on the Great Plains 307
CLUES TO THE PAST: EXHIBIT 10.1 Hide Scrapers 311
Plains Village Traditions 313
Late Prehistoric Bison Hunters of the Northern Plains 316
ISSUES AND DEBATES: BOX 10.1 Historic Period Ethnicities and the Archaeological Record 318
The Protohistoric Period and European Contact 319
Chapter Summary 321
Suggestions for Further Reading 321
Other Resources 321
Case Study: Investigations at Double Ditch Village, a Traditional Mandan Earthlodge Settlement **Stanley A. Ahler and Phil R. Geib** 322

CHAPTER 11 Foragers and Farmers of the Eastern Woodlands Heartland 331

Definition of the Area 332
The Environment of the Interior Eastern Woodlands 333
Climatic Change 335
ANTHROPOLOGICAL THEMES: TOPIC 11.1 Thematic Research Questions in Chapter 11 336
Paleoindians 335
Archaic Foragers 336
Archaic Material Culture 337
Subsistence, Settlement, and Sedentism 339
Trade, Mound Building, and Mortuary Treatments 342
Woodland Mound Builders 344
Early and Middle Woodland Material Culture 345
Subsistence and Settlement in the Early and Middle Woodland 346
Early and Middle Woodland Mound Building, Ceremonial Life, and Interaction 347
CLUES TO THE PAST: EXHIBIT 11.1 Stone Platform Pipes 351
The Late Woodland 352
Mississippian Societies 355
Mississippian Material Culture 356
Mississippian Households and Communities 357
Mississippian Subsistence and Economies 357
Mississippian Sociopolitical Systems 358
The Fort Ancient Tradition 361
ISSUES AND DEBATES: BOX 11.1 How Big and Powerful Was Cahokia After All? 362
The Protohistoric Period and European Contact 364
Chapter Summary 365
Suggestions for Further Reading 366
Other Resources 366
Case Study: Mouse Creek Phase Households and Communities: Mississippian Period Towns in Southeastern Tennessee **Lynne P. Sullivan** 367

SENECA

Iroquois

Student CD Contents

Preface

We have been immensely gratified by the response of students and professors to the first edition of *Seeking Our Past*. On the whole, both students and professors have been appreciative of our efforts to present the archaeology of North America in an up-to-date and thorough but accessible way. We still believe that North America's past is fascinating and fun to learn about, and we are still troubled that the stories of this continent's past based on archaeology are poorly known by those who live here. We also remain convinced that placing these archaeological stories within the context of the field of contemporary North American archaeology is the best way to create a resource for today's instructors and students. As archaeologists and instructors, however, we both have been doing archaeology, reading about archaeology, and teaching North American archaeology using *Seeking Our Past* since the first edition came out in 2007. Our experiences have led us to new ideas about how to present the subject. While the first edition went a long way toward embodying our vision, it was not perfect, and a number of our colleagues and students have provided helpful suggestions. Moreover, archaeologists have been adding to our understanding of the North American past since we stopped our research for the first edition. Thus, we are pleased to have the opportunity to update this text. We want it to remain as current as possible, and we hope to improve on its success in assisting students and instructors in exploring North American archaeology.

OUR APPROACH

We have retained the approach taken in the first edition and readers will still find the following:

- A culture area approach, because as flawed as the concept is when projected into the archaeological past, it is still how North American archaeology organizes itself. As a result, culture areas provide novices with the context for further study.

- Case studies written by the primary researchers juxtaposed with culture area summaries as a way of enriching discussion around the problems North American archaeologists investigate, the methods they use, and the data they generate. Eight bonus case studies are found in Section D on the Student CD and may be substituted or added to assigned readings.

- Coverage of both history and prehistory, because bridging the gulf between pre-historic and historic archaeology is essential to properly telling Native American, Euroamerican, and other histories on this continent, and because in contemporary CRM practice archaeologists need to be conversant in both subfields.

- Treatment of archaeological ethics throughout the book, because all students of archaeology should be made aware of the diverse constituencies and viewpoints that affect contemporary archaeology as well as of issues in archaeological stewardship and education.

- Treatment of contemporary archaeological practice especially of the nature of cultural resource management, because the discipline, as well as the career possibilities, in archaeology has changed dramatically in recent decades.

- The inclusion of feature boxes that help make the text more readable and concepts more accessible while integrating with the chapter narrative:

    - *Faces in Archaeology* in Part 1 that profile archaeologists as we introduce the discipline
    - *Anthropological Themes* in Part 2 (new in this edition) that summarize the broad research questions to which culture area archaeology contributes
    - *Clues to the Past* in Part 2 that discuss specific artifacts, features, or structures and clarify how archaeologists work from the material record to interpret the past
    - *Issues and Debates* in all chapters that treat both scholarly and ethical debates in order to enrich classroom discussion

- *Bonus Faces in Archaeology* are found on the Student CD in Section E, while *Bonus Issues and Debates* are included in Section F of the Student CD.

- Pedagogical aids including an extensive glossary, chapter openings that are designed to engage students, chapter summaries, lists of suggestions for further readings for each chapter, and discussion questions for each case study. The Student CD also includes Section H, Exploring Further, which provides links to related websites and suggestions of sites and museums to visit, and Section I, which provides students with learning objectives, study questions and self quizzes for each chapter. A new addition to the Student CD is Section J, which discusses issues of style for students preparing written work.

- An Instructor's Guide, which provides sample syllabi, chapter outlines, suggested test questions, and PowerPoint images, is also available to instructors through OUP.

WHAT'S NEW IN THE SECOND EDITION?

We have retained much of the organization and content of the first edition. A major goal of our revisions has been to update the content and a second goal has been to streamline its presentation. There are several substantial revisions to this edition:

- We have reduced redundancy by consolidating discussion of Paleoindians from the culture area chapters (Chapters 4–12) to Chapter 3, and expanding on it.

- We have enhanced the treatment of historical archaeology by removing discussion of the culture areas after the Contact or early Colonial periods, and moving some of this material to a completely new chapter (Chapter 13) that covers North American historical archaeology thematically.

- We have reduced redundancy and streamlined the treatment of the Eastern Woodlands culture areas by reorganizing this material into two chapters instead of three. The new Chapter 11 covers the interior Eastern Woodlands in both the Southeast and the southern Midwest, while the new Chapter 12 discusses archaeological knowledge of the northern and coastal parts of the Eastern Woodlands including Florida. These chapters should be considered together because these divisions are artificial.

- A number of changes have been made with respect to case studies:
    - In the interests of streamlining, we no longer have a case study associated with Chapter 2, and the case study "It Takes a Team: Interdisciplinary Research at the Koster Site," by Michael Wiant and Sarah Neusius, has been moved to Section D, Bonus Case Studies, on the Student CD.
    - Because of the reduction in Eastern Woodlands chapters from three to two, we also have made the case study "The Hopeton Earthworks Project: Using New Technologies to Answer Old Questions," by Mark Lynott, a Bonus Case Study available on the Student CD.
    - A new case study has been written for the new Chapter 13 on historical archaeology: "Community Archaeology: Understanding the Contexts of Archaeological Practice," by Carol McDavid and Christopher Matthews.
    - The case study for Chapter 3 has been rewritten, Torben Rick has been added as a second author, and the title has been changed to "Paleocoastal Occupations of California's Northern Channel Islands" in order to take into account new findings in this exciting research area.
    - Significant updates have been made to "Deep-Site Excavation at Gatecliff Shelter," by David Hurst Thomas, in Chapter 8 and to "A New History of Maize-Bean-Squash Agriculture in the Northeast," by John Hart, in the new Chapter 12. Minor edits have been made to a few of the other case studies in this text and on the Student CD.

- Several changes also have been made in *Issues and Debates* feature boxes:
    - Chapter 3's "Why Is the Kennewick Case So Significant?" has become a Bonus Issue and Debate in Section F of the Student CD. It has been replaced in Chapter 3 with the more current feature box "Debating the Solutrean Hypothesis."
    - The feature box "How Far Did the Vikings Get?" which was in Chapter 4 in the first edition, has been moved to Chapter 13, where it fits with thematic discussion of European contact. It has been replaced in Chapter 4 with "*Kwäaday Dän Ts'inchi*: British Columbia's Ice Man."
    - The feature box in the first edition's Chapter 11 on the Southeast, "Ridges, Aisles, and the Map of Poverty Point" has been moved to Section F, Bonus Issues and Debates, on the Student CD due to the reduction in the number of Eastern Woodlands chapters.
    - We also have reduced the number of *Issues and Debates* feature boxes in Chapter 14 and moved "Can Academia Train Archaeologists for the Twenty-first Century" to Section F, Bonus Issues and Debates, on the Student CD.

- Changes in the *Clues to the Past* feature boxes are as follows:
    - Due to the reduction in the number of Eastern Woodland's chapters, the feature box "Design Motifs and Artifacts of the Southeastern Ceremonial Complex" that was in the first edition's Chapter 11 on the Southeast has been dropped and some of the information in it has been added to the text.
    - A new feature box, "Modified Bone, Tooth, and Antler from a Florida Wet Site," has been written for the new Chapter 12.
    - The feature box "Iron Furnaces" that was in Chapter 13 in the first edition has been incorporated into the new Chapter 13 on historical archaeology.

- The four *Faces in Archaeology* profiles in Part 1 have been streamlined and updated.

- We have added a short feature box to Chapters 3–13 titled *Anthropological Themes.* These feature boxes remind students of the broad anthropological research questions listed in Chapter 2 and locate relevant discussions in each chapter.

- New chapter openings have been written for Chapter 7 on California and for the new Chapter 12 on the Northern and coastal parts of the Eastern Woodlands. The chapter opening for the first edition's Chapter 7 has been moved to Chapter 13, and the historical archaeology related chapter openings from the first edition's Chapter 11 and Chapter 13 have been dropped and partially incorporated into the text of Chapter 13.

- In response to reviewer comments, the extensive references now appear in the main text and have been converted to American Antiquity style, as have the in-text citations.

- Section H on the Student CD has been thoroughly checked and updated. Some recommendations have been deleted and new websites and places to visit have been added.

- Section J, "Writing Term Papers About Archaeology," has been added to the Student CD because we find that our students benefit from guidance concerning writing the papers we assign.

BASIC ORGANIZATION

As the table of contents indicates, this text still is divided into three unequal parts. In Part 1 we introduce the discipline of North American archaeology in two chapters. The first chapter introduces the field. The case study associated with this chapter is of a large CRM mitigation project, which may be a type of archaeology beginning students have not encountered previously. Chapter 2 introduces North American environments and the standard concepts utilized in organizing discussions of the North American past.

Part 2, which is the bulk of this text, covers the body of knowledge archaeologists have generated about the culture history and lifeways of the North American past. Chapter 3 discusses the peopling of the continent and Paleoindian adaptations. Chapters 4–12 introduce the archaeology of the ten culture areas commonly recognized for North America. We combine the Arctic and the Subarctic culture areas. In order to reduce redundancy, the Eastern Woodland's two culture areas, Southeast and Northeast, are not treated separately. Instead we look first in Chapter 11 at the interior Eastern Woodlands where agricultural economies and substantial sociocultural complexity developed, and then in Chapter 12 at the northern and coastal parts of the eastern Woodlands where both dependence on agriculture and sociocultural complexity was more variable. Each of the chapters has a case study, and collectively these introduce the wide variety of research topics North American archaeologists explore.

Part 3 consists of Chapter 14, which reconsiders anthropological themes and discusses the importance of archaeological stewardship. It also suggests what research topics promise to be important in the future and takes note of how the discipline and its techniques are changing. There is no case study in this final chapter.

The Student CD includes bonus materials that instructors and students may find useful substitutes or additions to the printed text. Each bonus feature further illustrates the archaeology discussed in one or more chapters. We also have included sections on the history of North American archaeology and on field and laboratory methods. For additional ideas about where these bonus sections might be incorporated, look for the CD symbol in the margin of the text.

The Student CD also includes other resources that students may find useful. In Section H, Exploring Further, we list links to websites concerning North American archaeology as well as places students and instructors might want to visit. In Section I we provide a student study guide that includes chapter learning objectives, study questions, and other study aids. In Section J we provide students with advice about writing term papers including how to make in-text citations and format reference lists.

ACKNOWLEDGMENTS

There are many people to thank for assistance in the development of this revision. We certainly want to thank all the case study contributors for their willingness to share their expertise in this book. Those who contributed in the first edition have reconsidered their case studies, providing minor and more substantial revisions. We especially thank Torben Rick, Carol McDavid, and Chris Matthews, who have provided new material for this edition. In addition, we thank our colleagues profiled in the *Faces in Archaeology* sections—James Judge, Robert Kelly, Linda Mayro, Lynne Sebastian, and Julie Stein—for their continued involvement and input on updating their profiles. Without these people this text wouldn't be the resource it is.

We especially appreciate as well those colleagues who have communicated with us concerning ways we could improve the text:

- Stephen Black, Texas State University

- Barbara Borg, College of Charleston

- Joseph Diamond, SUNY–New Paltz

- Robert Hard, University of Texas–San Antonio

- Curtiss Hoffman, Bridgewater State College

- Lewis Messenger, Hamline University

- Barb Roth, University of Nevada–Las Vegas

- Larry Zimmerman, Indiana University–Purdue University Indianapolis

In addition, Madonna Moss from the University of Oregon gave us extensive comments that were exceedingly helpful and forwarded two graduate student reviews from a class that used the first edition. David Carlson from Texas A&M also provided us with detailed comments, and was kind enough to provide the information in Table 2.2, updating our information on radiocarbon calibration. Others too numerous to accurately remember have made less formal but still helpful comments about *Seeking Our Past*. We have tried to take into account the suggestions of all these reviewers in our revision, and even when we have not done so, we are grateful for the attention and thoughtfulness of each reviewer.

Several colleagues helped us with illustrations for the first edition that we are still using, and for this edition, we thank Eleanor King, Kennetth Sassaman, Bruce Smith and Bill Marquardt for assistance with new photos.

We are grateful as well to the students who have been in our own classes in North American archaeology since 2007. They have provided important feedback about this text even when they were not aware they were doing so, and their reactions have been on our minds as we have made revisions.

Of course, though they are not mentioned specifically here, we also remain grateful to the long list of colleagues, students, and others who helped us produce the first edition of *Seeking Our Past*. Without them the book would not have been produced in the first place, and so could not have been revised.

We especially want to thank our OUP editor for the second edition, Sherith Pankratz, for her enthusiasm and patience, as well as Cari Heicklen and Caitlin Greene, Sherith's assistants, for her help with tasks large and small as we have completed this project. We are also grateful for the staff of talented people at Oxford who produced this revised edition, especially Marianne Paul, Production Editor.

At Indiana University of Pennsylvania, graduate student Lydia DeHaven put the references in EndNote and then transformed them into the correct American Antiquitystyle, while graduate student Angela Jaillet helped redraw some of the projectile point figures and graduate student Jon Libbon did much of the initial research on permissions needed for this edition.

Gross thanks his colleagues at Affinis, especially CEO Mike Busdosh; his colleagues at Ecology and Environment, Inc.; his colleagues at San Diego State University and the University of San Diego, especially Aana Cordy-Collins and Jerome Hall; and the board of trustees, members, and staff of the San Diego Archaeological Center for encouragement and assistance throughout this process. Of course, his daughter's support and encouragement were immeasurably important, as was that of Patty Kemp.

Neusius thanks Linda Dreischalick, Department of Anthropology Secretary, and her staff of student workers for their support as she tried to balance this project with the demands of teaching, advising and research. Finally, she is grateful for the counsel, support, and friendship of Phil Neusius, who, despite his own demanding responsibilities, has been willing to juggle schedules and put up with her distraction once more so she could complete these revisions.

Contributors

STANLEY A. AHLER, deceased

ANTHONY T. BOLDURIAN, Professor, Department of Anthropology, University of Pittsburgh at Greensburg

CORY DALE BRETERNITZ, Senior Archaeologist, PaleoWest Archaeology

DALE R. CROES, Professor, Department of Anthropology, South Puget Sound Community College and Adjunct Faculty, Department of Anthropology, Washington State University

BOYCE N. DRISKELL, Director, Archaeological Research Laboratory, University of Tennessee

JON M. ERLANDSON, Executive Director, Museum of Natural and Cultural History, University of Oregon

BEN FITZHUGH, Associate Professor, Department of Anthropology, University of Washington

RHONDA FOSTER, Tribal Historic Preservation Officer, Cultural Resources Department, Squaxin Island Tribe

PHIL R. GEIB, Anthropology Department, University of New Mexico

SARA GONZALEZ, Department of Anthropology, Vassar College

G. TIMOTHY GROSS, Cultural Resource Specialist, Ecology and Environment, Inc, and University of San Diego

JOHN P. HART, Director, Research and Collections Division, New York State Museum

KENT G. LIGHTFOOT, Professor, Department of Anthropology, University of California at Berkeley

MARK LYNOTT, Supervisory Archaeologist, Midwest Archaeological Center, National Park Service, U.S. Department of the Interior

CHRISTOPHER N. MATTHEWS, Associate Professor of Anthropology, Hofstra University

CAROL MCDAVID, Executive Director, Community Archaeology Research Institute, Inc. (CARI)

PAUL E. MINNIS, Professor, Department of Anthropology, University of Oklahoma

DARREN MODZELEWSKI, Boalt Law School, University of California at Berkeley

SARAH W. NEUSIUS, Professor, Department of Anthropology, Indiana University of Pennsylvania

LEE PANICH, Department of Anthropology, Santa Clara University

OTIS PARRISH, Member of the Kashia Band of Pomo Indians of the Stewarts Point Rancheria

L. MARK RAAB, Adjunct Professor of History and Geosciences, University of Missouri-Kansas City

TORBEN C. RICK, Curator of North American Archaeology, Department Of Anthropology, National Museum of Natural History, Smithsonian Institution

CHRISTINE K. ROBINSON, MA, RPA

LARRY ROSS, Cultural Resource Specialist, Cultural Resources Department, Squaxin Island Tribe

TSIM SCHNEIDER, Department of Anthropology, University of California at Berkeley

ELIZABETH M. Scott, Assistant Professor, Department of Sociology and Anthropology, Illinois State University

SARAH C. SHERWOOD, Environmental Studies, Sewanee: The University of the South

LYNNE P. SULLIVAN, Curator of Archaeology, Frank H. McClung Museum, University of Tennessee

DAVID HURST THOMAS, Curator, American Museum of Natural History

RENEE B. WALKER, Associate Professor, Department of Anthropology, State University of New York College at Oneonta

MICHAEL E. WHALEN, Professor, Department of Anthropology, University of Tulsa

MICHAEL D. WIANT, Director, Dickson Mounds Museum

ANDREW YATSKO, CNRSW Archaeologist, Environmental Operations and Planning, Naval Facilities Engineering Command, Southwest

LARRY ROSS, Cultural Resource Specialist, Cultural Resources Department, Squaxin Island Tribe

TSIM SCHNEIDER, Department of Anthropology, University of California at Berkeley

ELIZABETH M. SCOTT, Assistant Professor, Department of Sociology and Anthropology, Illinois State University

SARAH C. SHERWOOD, Environmental Studies, Sewanee: The University of the South

LYNNE P. SULLIVAN, Curator of Archaeology, Frank H. McClung Museum, University of Tennessee

DAVID HURST THOMAS, Curator, American Museum of Natural History

RENEE B. WALKER, Associate Professor, Department of Anthropology, State University of New York College at Oneonta

MICHAEL E. WHALEN, Professor, Department of Anthropology, University of Tulsa

MICHAEL D. WIANT, Director, Dickson Mounds Museum

ANDREW YATSKO, Senior Archaeologist, Cultural Resources Program, Naval Facilities Engineering Command, Southwest

PART ONE

Introducing North American Archaeology

CHAPTER 1

The Nature and Practice of North American Archaeology

Everybody has heard of Indiana Jones. This adventuresome Hollywood archaeologist is always getting himself into and out of scrapes in exotic locales while saving unique and mysterious artifacts from being put to evil uses. Indiana Jones is part of popular Western culture: he speaks to our yearning for the exotic and the mysterious, and he makes us laugh. Indiana Jones is immensely entertaining.

Of course, Indiana Jones is fictional. His adventures bear very little resemblance to actual archaeological work. Yet journalists often introduce stories about archaeology with references to Indiana Jones. The following headlines appeared as we wrote this book: "Robotic Indiana Jones to Penetrate Pyramid," "An Internet 'Indiana Jones' Receives AIA Award for Excellence in Undergraduate Teaching," and "University Archaeologist Brings Indiana Jones to Life." These are articles about serious archaeologists and archaeology in which the character created on film by Harrison Ford is merely a device to catch the interest of the reader. Then, having seduced people into reading further, the journalist begins the real story.

Admittedly Indiana Jones is a common point of reference and also great fun, but we think real archaeology is interesting in itself. It is unfortunate that archaeology is seldom taught in school and that only a few Americans have easy access to a public museum with archaeological exhibits. Books about archaeology rarely make the best-seller list, although mysteries with archaeologists as characters (see Chapter 10) seem to be quite common. Television, particularly the Discovery Channel and PBS, probably has raised archaeology's profile. However, little of this material focuses on the archaeology of the United States and Canada. Thus, perhaps unsurprisingly, even most Americans who have learned something about archaeology know nothing about North America's archaeological past. Indeed, one public opinion survey found most Americans unable to name important archaeological sites within the United States (Ramos and Duganne 2000:16).

What we hope to do in this text is to provide you with many reference points for North American archaeology and to change and deepen your understanding of what archaeology is, erasing any perception that our continent's past is not as interesting as the past of other lands. To us, the past of North America is varied, fascinating, and even mysterious, and our discipline is dynamic and exciting. Most of all, we hope reading this book persuades you of the need to preserve America's archaeological past. Preserving our heritage is an important challenge for the increasingly multicultural societies of North America in the twenty-first century.

THE SCOPE OF THIS BOOK

You can easily find several different definitions of **archaeology** by consulting a dictionary or by finding the word in a textbook glossary. Most likely these definitions will have several common features. They will use words like "past," "ancient," and "prehistoric" because the word *archaeology* itself has as its root *archaeo*, which means old. Literally, archaeology is the study of the old. However, a good definition must include the idea that archaeologists use physical evidence to learn about the past. No one can study the past directly, but archaeologists can analyze the material traces of past people and places and consider what they can tell us. Archaeologists collect **artifacts**, objects made or modified by humans, and **ecofacts**, natural materials that have been used by humans. We also record traces of past structures, fires, pits, and refuse dumps (Figure 1.1). We study these material remains, as well as the ways in which they are distributed in space and time; these are our clues to the past—our data. These data collectively are called the **archaeological record**. Thus, we say that archaeologists study the past through the examination of the archaeological record.

Such a general definition catches most of what all archaeologists have in common; but the definition is still not entirely satisfactory because it does not indicate what it is about the past that archaeologists are trying to find out. In fact, this is precisely what distinguishes different types of archaeologists, and it is the source of the variety of definitions for archaeology that you may encounter. Some archaeologists would stress that archaeologists study human lifeways, but other archaeologists might promote the idea that archaeology documents the history of material culture. The theoretical and methodological reasons for these various definitions are beyond the scope of this book. Our choice is to define archaeology as the study of past human behavior and culture through the analysis of material remains. Our definition is in keeping with an American tradition of archaeology because this is a book about the archaeology of North America.

Most of this book considers the body of knowledge archaeologists have generated concerning the past cultures of this continent. It introduces the variability in past ways of life and the record of culture change. We present consensus viewpoints on the past, illustrating the evidence for archaeologists' ideas through case studies of real archaeological projects. The fact is that there is too rich a literature about the North American past for an introductory text such as this one to be complete. Our goal is not to be an encyclopedia, but instead to make this body of knowledge comprehensible, whether a reader is satisfied with an introduction or intends to pursue the field further.

This text is primarily about what archaeologists think happened during the North American past, but it also introduces the practice of North American archaeology. This is because it is hard to understand the conclusions archaeologists have drawn, and impossible to evaluate them critically, without knowing how the data were derived. Thus, in this chapter and the next, we review how North American archaeologists do archaeology. This introduction also is not exhaustive, but we do introduce critical vocabulary and suggest the scientific context for studying this continent's past. The CD that accompanies the book offers more information about both the history of North American archaeology (Student CD, Section A) and the methods used by contemporary archaeologists (Student CD, Sections B and C). We encourage those who have little background in archaeology to explore these sections.

In addition, we have tried throughout this book to give a sense of what it is actually like to be an archaeologist today. You may be surprised to learn that North American archaeologists work in a variety of settings— in universities and museums but also in private businesses and government agencies. Moreover, since archaeologists are only one group of twenty-first-century stakeholders with an interest in North America's past, we must confront a number of public relations and ethical issues in our work. Finally, serious threats to the record of America's past exist in modern society. Not only can we destroy the evidence of the past as our cities grow and our use of the landscape changes, but some people are interested in artifacts largely for their market value. These contemporary realities affect the practice of North American archaeology in many ways. If you envision archaeologists as laboring primarily in the dusty reaches of museums and labs, you are likely to find these other aspects of contemporary archaeology particularly surprising.

One last note about scope is that when we say "North America," we are referring mainly to the continent north of central Mexico. In this book, we use **culture areas** (e.g., Kroeber 1963), geographical regions within which there is a general similarity of culture, to

FIGURE 1.1 One way in which archaeologists discover the traces of the past is through excavation, such as the test excavations being conducted at the Fleming site in Pennsylvania by students enrolled in field school at Indiana University of Pennsylvania.

discuss the archaeology of North America. The areas that we treat usually are grouped in North America culturally, while the cultures of central and southern Mexico typically are placed in a unit known among anthropologists as Mesoamerica (Figure 1.2), which also is delineated from South America and the Circum-Caribbean. This does not mean that there has been no contact between the cultures of Mexico and North America, but cultural contrasts, both ethnographic and archaeological, are clearly evident to anthropologists.

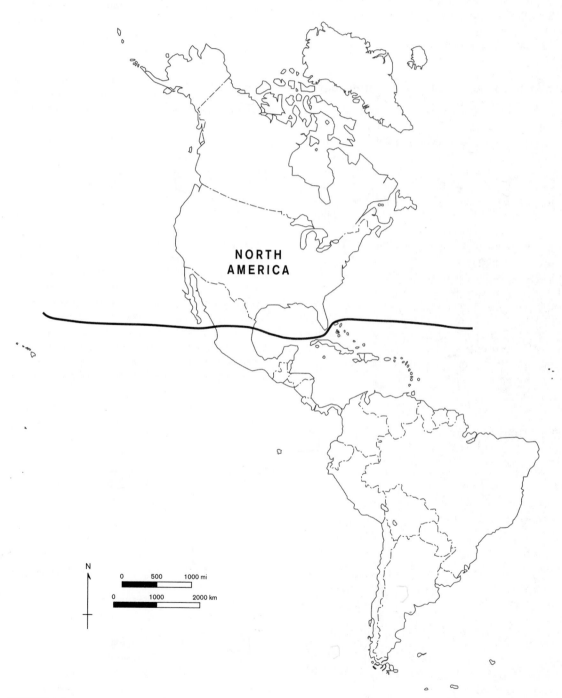

FIGURE 1.2 The cultures of North America are grouped by anthropologists into a North American culture area as shown.

WHAT IS NORTH AMERICAN ARCHAEOLOGY?

In one sense, North American archaeology is simply the archaeology done within the culture areas of North America. However, most North American archaeologists also are guided by the principles of Americanist archaeology, an approach that developed largely in the United States but is practiced elsewhere as well. Three aspects of this approach are important to understanding it.

North American Archaeology Is Anthropology

At most North American universities and colleges, courses in North American archaeology are offered by an anthropology department. The American tradition is to see archaeology as a type of **anthropology**, the holistic study of the physical, cultural, and social aspects of humans in all times and places. The subfields of anthropology (Figure 1.3) are archaeology, **cultural anthropology**, which studies recent humans and their cultures through description of observed human behaviors, **linguistic anthropology**, which examines human language, and **biological anthropology**, which studies both human biological evolution and human biological diversity. Chances are that the department providing your course also offers courses in these other areas of anthropology. As the holistic and comparative study of humans, anthropology is concerned with humans in both the past and the present. As the social science that has most often studied non-Western societies, it is natural that anthropology incorporates the archaeological study of preliterate prehistoric people.

There also are historical reasons for the Americanist inclusion of archaeology within anthropology. Like other Western sciences, anthropology developed as Europeans encountered new areas, peoples, and cultures from the fifteenth century onward. Europeans needed to explain the newly apparent diversity among humans. In North America, anthropological scholarship naturally focused on American Indians. Thus as anthropologists tried to understand the diversity of Native inhabitants, they framed many questions about the human settlement and history of this continent. To illustrate, one anthropologist might study contemporary Indian cultures that were assumed to be vanishing while at the same time exploring the artifacts and ruined structures of these Indians' ancestors. Yet the same anthropologist, in other contexts, might be interested in recording native language or in describing the physical appearance of people. In this way, archaeology became inextricably linked with other studies of Native Americans. The legacy of this approach is still felt by North American archaeologists. Indeed, most of us consider ourselves to be anthropologists. Graduate students in anthropology may focus on archaeology, but, with a few exceptions, they take their degrees in anthropology.

The historical inclusion of archaeology within anthropology leads to an important distinction between North American and European archaeology. In Europe, archaeologists, who may be more likely to see archaeology as a type of history, have studied their own ancestors. American archaeologists, who usually have been of European descent, most often have studied somebody else's ancestors. This is not a trivial matter. Among other things, it means that North American archaeology, like all anthropology, has its roots in the colonial encounter as well

FIGURE 1.3 Archaeology is one of the four subdisciplines of anthropology.

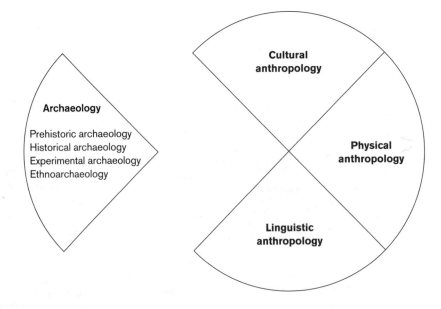

Archaeology

Prehistoric archaeology
Historical archaeology
Experimental archaeology
Ethnoarchaeology

Cultural anthropology

Physical anthropology

Linguistic anthropology

as in the ideologies of the dominant American culture. For example, the nineteenth-century concept of **manifest destiny**, which held that Americans were destined to displace North America's Native inhabitants, also affected early anthropological ideas about American Indians.

Fortunately, such viewpoints have become outdated, in part because the archaeological record has revealed the complexity of the past. The discussion in Box 1.1 gives some idea of how early misconceptions such as these were overturned as archaeological evidence mounted.

ISSUES AND DEBATES

BOX 1.1

Who Were the Mound Builders?

One of the great stories of the coming of age of North American archaeology is the Mound Builder debate that developed during the nineteenth century. This story illustrates both how preconceptions can influence scholarship and how careful data collection and analysis can lead scientists to discard erroneous ideas.

When the first American traders, surveyors, and speculators came over the Appalachian ridges into the Ohio country during the eighteenth century, they were amazed by what they found. **Mounds**, enclosures, and other earthworks dotted the landscape. As more and more land west of the mountains was explored and settled, it became obvious that these earthen constructions were not isolated phenomena. In all, hundreds of thousands of mounds and earthworks in many sizes and shapes once existed. The largest mound we know of, Monks Mound (Figure 1.4), located in the broad floodplain of the Mississippi River east of St. Louis, rises more than 98 feet (30 m) and covers nearly 14 acres at its base (Milner 1998). However, Monks Mound was only one of at least a hundred mounds of various kinds at this site. The earthworks at Newark, Ohio, include octagonal, circular, and rectangular enclosures laid out with geometric precision. The Great Enclosure at Newark has a diameter of 1200 feet (365 m) and encloses 30 acres (12 hectares) (Woodward and McDonald 2002:189). The better-known stone circle at Stonehenge, with its diameter of 330 feet (100 m), would fit three times into this space

FIGURE 1.5 The Serpent Mound winds across a ridge top in Adams County, Ohio.

with room to spare! There also are **effigy mounds**, constructed in the shape of animals, such as the Serpent Mound in Ohio (Figure 1.5). Even the earlier conical burial mounds can be quite impressive. For example, Grave Creek Mound, located on the floodplain of the Ohio River in Moundsville, West Virginia, is at least 62 feet (19 m) tall and contains an estimated 1.2 million cubic feet (34,000 m³) of dirt (Hemmings 1984).

As the Ohio country was settled by European Americans, these constructions were sometimes ignored and obliterated, sometimes marveled at, and sometimes the stimulus for romanticism. Some of the earliest scholars such as Thomas Jefferson, whose many interests included archaeology, and Albert Gallatin, senator from Pennsylvania and secretary of the Treasury under Jefferson and Madison, concluded that the mounds must mean that American Indians once had been culturally sophisticated (Kennedy 1994). However, most European Americans believed that the tribal people they knew as fairly mobile, lacking in material possessions, and at least as dependent on wild food sources as on their garden products could not have had the knowledge to build these impressive earthworks. Instead, they credited a more sophisticated people with the constructions they were finding. Thus, by the early nineteenth century, the idea that a now extinct race of people

FIGURE 1.4 The largest extant mound is Monks Mound, located at the Cahokia site, Collinsville, Illinois.

who built mounds once existed in the midcontinent made sense to most people. Even scholars often accepted the idea that the Mound Builders had been a different people from the Indian tribes in the area.

Speculations identified the Mound Builders as wandering Hindus, the lost tribe of Israel, or migrating Mexicans. In some versions, the Amerindians came later and annihilated the Mound Builders, while in others the Mound Builders abandoned North America and migrated to Mexico, where they built the great Mexican civilizations. Various hoaxes, such as stone tablets supposedly bearing alphabetic scripts, were also perpetrated in support of the "lost race" stories (Feder 2002). No matter the details, the idea of a lost race fed the romantic imagination of nineteenth-century Americans. Of course, stereotypes and racist assumptions also were at work. For example, some argued that Native Americans were too lazy and disorganized to have done the work required to build the mounds.

Fortunately, at the end of the nineteenth century, a resolution of the Mound Builder debate based on evidence became possible. In 1881 the federal government through the Bureau of American Ethnology of the Smithsonian Institution funded an expedition designed to determine who the Mound Builders had been. Hired to head this undertaking was a scientist named Cyrus Thomas. Before pursuing his interests in ethnology and archaeology, Thomas had been a lawyer, a Lutheran minister, and an entomologist. He had helped found the Illinois Natural History Society and was associated with John Wesley Powell in this endeavor. Powell is well known for his explorations of the Grand Canyon, but he is also notable for his directorship of the Bureau of American Ethnology. When Congress insisted that the then large sum of $5000 annually be spent on mound exploration, Powell turned to Thomas for help (Muller 1996).

What makes Thomas such a good example of a scientist, albeit a late nineteenth-century one, is that he let the empirical evidence guide his conclusions about the Mound Builders. By his own admission, he began his work believing that a distinct mound-building race had once existed. However, by the time he wrote his report (Thomas 1894), the overwhelming empirical evidence yielded by his investigations had changed his mind. Thomas made a systematic study of approximately 2000 mounds and earthworks in 21 states

over a seven-year period. The linkages to American Indians in artifacts and in burial treatments were obvious, and Thomas concluded that the mounds were built either by the very Indians that Europeans first encountered or by their ancestors. He also found that there was no evidence that the Mound Builders had migrated from Mexico or elsewhere. Thomas's report not only settled the identity question to his own satisfaction, but it convinced the growing archaeological community. Archaeologists turned their attention to documenting the details of the mound-building past rather than to speculating about origins.

Today, most Americans know very little about these mounds (Figure 1.6). Lacking knowledge of what Cyrus Thomas established more than a century ago, modern Americans might even be tempted to believe that aliens built the Serpent Mound, as some have claimed. Nevertheless, today's antidote to becoming mired in speculations is the same as Thomas's—look at the evidence and draw your conclusions accordingly. The Mound Builder controversy has long been settled, but its twofold lessons remain valid: that American Indians built the mounds and that our stereotypes can mislead us when we do not consider the evidence carefully.

For an example of current research on the Mound Builders, see the case study by Mark Lynott, "The Hopeton Earthworks Project: Using New Technologies to Answer Old Questions," on your CD, Section D.7.

FIGURE 1.6 Saul's Mound, at Pinson Mounds in Pinson, Tennessee, is part of a large complex of earthworks and mounds that the public can visit.

Although more recent archaeologists have seen Native American culture as equal to European and other cultures, a focus on generalizing about cultures rather than on specific histories has resulted in some devaluing of native cultures (Trigger 2006:315–316). Archaeologists also may have too easily accepted the idea that native culture vanished and was destroyed by the advancing dominant culture. An uncritical acceptance of this idea can

lead to the dismissal of contemporary Native American culture as irrelevant as well as to the notion that the archaeologist is the only valid authority on past Native American culture. With such a mind-set, archaeologists can think of their work as a service to the descendants of early Americans and to society at large. While this idea of what archaeology is about may be well-meaning, it is more than a little patronizing.

In reality, there is both continuity and disjunction between contemporary Native American cultures and the diverse cultures of North America's past. There was not an abrupt break between the Prehistoric and the Historic periods. Instead, there have been a wide variety of cultural results spanning the centuries of interaction. This means that denying contemporary Native Americans direct input into the scientific story of their ancestors narrows our understanding of the past. It also may lead archaeologists to ignore Native American sensibilities about burials and artifacts. Unfortunately, Native Americans historically have had good reason to distrust archaeologists, and there has been considerable contention over the management of Indian **cultural resources** as Native people have asserted their rights more forcefully in recent decades (Watkins 2003). Relationships between archaeologists and Native Americans still need improvement, but there is a much greater sensitivity to native concerns among today's archaeologists (Wilcox 2010). What this will mean for the future of the discipline remains to be seen, but it is clear that new understanding does not involve a rejection of the anthropological character of North American archaeology. In fact, some have seen greater involvement with Native Americans as a rediscovery of archaeology's roots in a more holistic and culturally relative anthropology.

North American Archaeology Considers Itself a Science

A second point about North American archaeology is that, like other fields in anthropology, it is a social science. If the idea that archaeology is a science seems questionable, remember that the nature of science often is misunderstood. The most significant point to consider about science is that it is primarily a way of investigating our world. Individual sciences have very different methods, but they have in common a general way of proceeding (Thomas 1998:44–47). You may have seen formulations of the **scientific method** when studying other sciences (Figure 1.7). In summary, this method provides a means of investigating interactions between things in the natural, observable world. It begins with examining and thinking about what has been observed and proceeds with the formulation of hypotheses about relationships between natural phenomena. Then, new observations of the natural world provide tests for hypotheses. New data are summarized and examined to see whether they are consistent with the ideas and assumptions originally held. They may cause a scientist to change his or her ideas or they may not. In the former case, we can say the hypothesis was disproved; in the latter, we can say it was confirmed. Findings may contribute to general theories, which, in turn, can lead to new hypotheses and further testing. Scientific investigation is considered fruitful if it causes new questions to be raised and new hypotheses to be formed.

Archaeology is a science because it follows these procedures. Archaeologists can explore ideas about the past by examining artifacts, fire pits, and house foundations. We cannot directly observe the past, but we can directly observe traces of what happened in the past. By checking and cross-checking our observations, drawing conclusions about what they mean, and then forming new hypotheses for further testing our ideas in new studies, we can build up an understanding of the past. Of course, we may draw incorrect conclusions; but because we are engaged in a process of

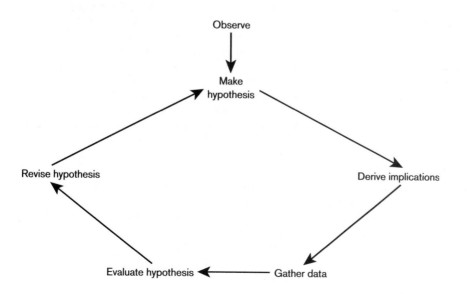

FIGURE 1.7 Simplified representation of how the scientific method proceeds.

hypothesis testing, new data should eventually lead to a revision of wrong ideas.

Archaeologists have long been concerned with being rigorous and scientific in their procedures, but it is true that ideas about what qualifies as "scientific" have varied among archaeologists in different times and places. There was a period during the 1960s and immediately thereafter when some archaeologists thought that using the scientific method, more or less rigidly defined as illustrated in Figure 1.7, was the only valid means of exploring the past. Such a method of study was supposed to lead archaeologists to the truth about the past, while earlier archaeological attempts to be scientific were understood as being limited to description or speculation. The position that there is one right way to do science—one rigid scientific method—is a form of **scientism**, a more general view that there is only one way to acquire valid knowledge about the natural universe. Most contemporary archaeologists are far more flexible, and today the viewpoints of some theorists of the 1960s seem overly simplistic.

Contemporary archaeologists are more aware that our individual perspectives and experiences as modern people affect both the questions we ask and the assumptions we make about meaning. We also recognize that nonarchaeologists also have ideas about the past that should not be ignored. There may be several viewpoints or stories to be told, resulting in a richer understanding overall. Some archaeologists explicitly try to include a humanistic approach in their investigations, seeking out more personal and individualistic assessments of the past as well (e.g., Spector 1993). A few archaeologists even have argued that we cannot obtain an objective understanding of the past at all, though this view certainly is not held by all North American archaeologists. It also would be incorrect to say that the majority of North American archaeologists have given up the quest to be scientific or have abandoned the basic procedures of hypothesis testing outlined earlier. As with all anthropology, the goal remains increasing knowledge about people. Hypothesis testing still is a powerful means of working on this endeavor, even though archaeologists are learning to question their own biases and to incorporate a range of perspectives about the past.

North American Archaeology Contributes to History

The characterization of archaeology as anthropology and as a science may be new to you. You may have thought of archaeology as much more like history than anthropology. It certainly is true that archaeology can contribute to historical understanding of any period in the past. While there are some things that we cannot learn from artifacts and other material traces of humans, there also are ways in which archaeological studies can enhance a purely historical understanding.

First, precisely because much of archaeology focuses on non-Western and preliterate peoples, it provides different perspectives on what happened in the past from those due to history. For example, Native Americans can be understood as "people without history" (Wolf 1982). This doesn't mean that Native Americans had no history before Europeans came to North America. Except where it specifically intersects with the story of literate Westerners, however, the story of the Native American past is not part of standard histories of humanity. Recognizing the limitations of the strictly historical perspective, archaeologists have sought to add to knowledge of human history by describing and explaining cultures not covered in the written records of the past. There are of course valid nonarchaeological stories of the North American past, such as those told by descendants, themselves that contemporary archaeologists are finding enrich understanding as well.

Second, even in the case of historical archaeology, our discipline contributes in ways that history cannot. Interest in North American **historical archaeology** is considerable today, (Deagan 1982; Kelly 2005). Broadly historical archaeology is the archaeological study of people who made written records, but in practice historical archaeologists usually focus on the archaeology of European expansion and the interactions with indigenous populations that resulted (Deetz 1996:4). When the focus is on the lives and cultures of indigenous peoples following European contact the historical contribution is obvious. Even when a great deal of historical study has been completed, the written records do not necessarily contain a complete picture of the past. As any historian knows, diaries, descriptions of events, and other documents are written from a particular point of view and can conceal nearly as much as they reveal. The artifacts and the remains of historic buildings explored by archaeologists provide different and sometimes startling information about the past. Archaeology can verify and amplify the story told in documents. It can piece together the details that chroniclers of earlier times neglected to mention. It can provide information about social classes or ethnic groups who have received scant attention in written documents. In this sense, as Charles Orser has written, "archaeology opens narrow thresholds to the past across which historians, relying on written words alone, typically cannot traverse" (Orser 1996:11). Working together, archaeologists and historians can develop a richer understanding of the past. In Chapter 13 we address the many contributions historical archaeology has been making.

You can gain more insight into the nature of North American archaeology from reading Section A of the Student CD. This section also provides some insight into archaeological theory and debate. The historical context out of which this field developed contributes to an understanding of the Americanist approach just outlined, and it introduces the individuals who developed techniques and theories important in this field. The case study in Section D.1 of the Student CD illustrates the changing nature of archaeological practice during the twentieth century.

THE NORTH AMERICAN ARCHAEOLOGIST

Another way to understand the field of archaeology is to explore the biographies of some of its practitioners. Although questions about North America's peoples and their past began to be asked as soon as Europeans discovered the continent, it was not until the end of the eighteenth century and the beginning of the nineteenth century that anyone systematically investigated the antiquities of this continent. Even then, investigations such as Thomas Jefferson's into a Virginia mound were rare. Moreover, although careful description and cataloging became commonplace in the latter half of the nineteenth century, archaeology remained a hobby or sideline. Museum jobs for archaeologists began to be available after 1890, and the first graduate programs in archaeology and anthropology were established as American universities were developed in the early twentieth century. It was at this time that professional societies also began to form and new archaeological methods were developed that required training, while a growing body of data about our past also had to be mastered. Archaeology became an academic discipline within anthropology during these years. Arthur Parker (Student CD, Section E.1) stands as one example of an early twentieth-century archaeologist whose career spanned the development of the discipline of archaeology in North America.

FACES IN ARCHAEOLOGY   PROFILE 1.1

W. James Judge, Professor and Director of the Chaco Project

Question: What do the central Rio Grande valley of New Mexico, Fort Lewis College in Durango, Colorado, and television's *Beavis and Butt-Head* have in common?
Answer: Jim Judge.

Jim Judge (Figure 1.8), who retired from teaching in 2001, began his professional career at the University of New Mexico. His doctoral research was on the early human occupations of the middle Rio Grande valley of New Mexico. That work, completed in 1970 and published in 1972, is still an important discussion of the nature of the earliest occupations of the Southwest. After completing his doctorate, Judge took a position at Colorado State University, later returning to the University of New Mexico as a professor.

Judge joined the Chaco Project, a cooperative effort between the National Park Service and the University of New Mexico, as a research archaeologist in 1974, after having designed and implemented a sample survey of the canyon as a contractor through the university. He served as director of the project from 1977 to 1985. As discussed in Chapter 9, Chaco Canyon was a major regional exchange system between AD 900 and AD 1150. The Chaco Project set about the task of intensive study of the Chaco system. These investigators amassed an archive of previous published and unpublished work, conducted surveys, excavated key sites, and used **remote sensing** to study the area. The project also included studies of past environments in Chaco Canyon and the surrounding area. The Chaco Project was instrumental in increasing our understanding of the Chaco system and was important in focusing southwestern archaeologists on regional interaction

FIGURE 1.8 Archaeologist James Judge at Chaco Canyon.

systems. The project produced or contributed to many important reports and research papers. Judge coauthored the report on the survey of the canyon and coedited a volume comparing the **Hohokam** and Chaco regional systems.

After leaving the Chaco Project, Judge directed the Fort Burgwin Research Center, a research arm of Southern Methodist University located near Taos, New Mexico. In 1989 the center hosted the Society for American Archaeology's Taos Anti-looting Conference, bringing together over 70 participants to discuss methods of preventing **relic hunters** from destroying sites. Judge's participation in this conference is one reflection of his interest in preservation of the archaeological record.

In 1990 Judge moved to Fort Lewis College in Durango, Colorado, where he has held the position of professor emeritus since his retirement. Having taught field schools in his previous positions, he continued this interest at Fort Lewis, with investigations at two pueblos that made up part of the community surrounding the Lowry Ruin, a Chacoan outlier located near Cortez, Colorado. One of Judge's interests is electronic publication of archaeological results, and the report on one of these field school excavations, Puzzle House, is published on the Internet (http://www.fortlewis.edu/anthro/puzzlereport/).

Over the years, Judge has taught introductory courses in anthropology and archaeology, as well as courses in southwestern archaeology, field techniques, laboratory methods, and evolutionary archaeology. In addition to his Paleoindian and Chacoan research, he had an interest in settlement patterns, predictive modeling, and remote sensing in archaeology. Judge has received awards for his teaching and his research and has published extensively. He is a member of the Preservation Technology and Training Board, a group of professionals who provide advice to the National Center for Preservation Technology. He is also on the board of directors for the Archaeological Conservancy and the steering committee for the Chaco Digital Initiative (http://www.chacoarchive.org), a web page bringing together information on Chacoan archaeology. Judge has also served on the Society for American Archaeology Governmental Affairs Committee and is an adviser for the GIS program at Fort Lewis College.

The career of Jim Judge illustrates a successful pursuit of research in a particular area carried out from different universities sequentially. It also demonstrates an interest in new and developing technologies like remote sensing and electronic publishing. Finally, Judge's time with the Chaco Project illustrates a fruitful collaboration between a government agency and an academic institution. Not only did that collaboration produce volumes of new information about the past in the Chaco region, information that continues to provide data for scholarly publications, but it also provided management information for the Park Service and information for the interpretation of the Chaco system to the public.

But where, you might be wondering, does *Beavis and Butt-Head* come into the picture? Well, in addition to the accomplishments just outlined, this archaeologist is the proud father of Mike Judge, creator of *Beavis and Butt-Head* and the hit series *King of the Hill*.

Contemporary North American archaeologists still can be found working in museums, and many more are employed in universities. In fact, the university is the primary work setting for one of us (Neusius). Today, most archaeologists have careers that include several different work settings over their course. Profile 1.1 offers one example of an archaeological career centered in academic settings.

The varied work settings for today's archaeologist are attributable to the transformation of North American archaeology, beginning during the 1970s, by the development of **cultural resource management (CRM)**. CRM is an applied form of archaeology done in response to various laws that require archaeological investigations as part of federal and state programs. In the United States and in Canada, there is a history of government involvement with archaeological sites dating back to the nineteenth century, when the U.S. government sponsored investigations of mounds and explorations of the American West. Several large government-funded archaeological projects during the mid-twentieth century also established the government's role in archaeology within the United States (Neumann et al. 2010). The first piece of U.S. legislation involving archaeological sites was the Antiquities Act of 1906, which protected historic or prehistoric remains on federal lands and made it possible for the president to establish national monuments. Following this came a whole series of acts supporting the concept that archaeological sites, as well as historic buildings, are cultural resources for the public, and asserting that it is the responsibility of the government to protect them (Table 1.1). Cultural resources are sites, buildings, and artifacts that are significant to understanding of the past and thus are irreplaceable.

Today, anyone who plans to study North American archaeology must become familiar with an elaborate framework of laws affecting archaeological practice. In the United States, it is virtually impossible to move forward with any undertaking of the federal government or permitted or funded by it without considering whether the activity contemplated will affect important cultural resources.

TABLE 1.1 Significant U.S. Federal Legislation Related to North American Cultural Resources

Native American Graves Protection and Repatriation Act of 1990 (NAGPRA)	Protection of Native American graves and cultural materials uncovered on federal and tribal land; requires the inventory and, when requested, the return of skeletal, funerary, and other sacred items to federally recognized Native American tribes by any federal or federally funded institution
Abandoned Shipwreck Act of 1987	Allows for the protection and recovery of shipwrecks and underwater sites and encourages state management of underwater cultural resources
Archaeological Resources Protection Act of 1979	Stiffens penalties for looting or damaging of sites on federal and tribal lands; requires uniform regulations for treatment of archaeological resources on such lands with respect to permitting and penalties
Archaeological and Historic Preservation Act of 1974	Requires avoidance of the loss of archaeological data and allows agencies to spend a portion of their budgets to recover data being threatened
National Environmental Policy Act of 1969	Requires all federal agencies to specify the impact of their undertakings on cultural as well as natural resources
National Historic Preservation Act of 1966 (amended 1976 and 1980)	Protection of significant cultural resources through the National Register; provides a mechanism for integrating state agencies into the process through the Advisory Council on Historic Preservation and State Historic Preservation Offices; Sections 106 and 110 are particularly important in stipulating the assessment and management of cultural resources
Department of Transportation Act of 1966 Section 4(f) (amended 1968)	Requires any transportation project that will affect a National Register–eligible resource to avoid or minimize effects on that resource
Reservoir Salvage Act of 1960	National Park Service given the authority to administer the salvaging of archaeological resources threatened by the construction of dams and reservoirs (preceded by Smithsonian Institution River Basin Surveys and various Works Progress Administration programs)
Historic Sites Act of 1935	Provides for the designation of National Historic Landmarks; allows archaeological survey before site destruction
Antiquities Act of 1906	Protection for archaeological sites on federal land; penalties for looting

Many state laws mirror federal legislation in protecting cultural resources potentially affected by state projects. For example, the **California Environmental Quality Act (CEQA)**, passed in 1970, was one of the first state laws calling for archaeological impact studies. Because of this long history, California has a large number of CRM firms, and state agencies like CALTRANS (California's Department of Transportation) and the various state parks have large CRM staffs as well. CEQA compliance is administered at the local level. Many California jurisdictions require archaeologists to belong to the **Register of Professional Archaeologists (RPA)**, an organization of archaeologists dedicated to promoting standards and ethics among archaeologists. As a result, California has more members on the register than any other state. Recently, several other states have been adding the RPA requirement.

Both the number of jobs available to North American archaeologists overall and the percentage of these jobs found outside universities and museums have greatly increased as CRM has developed (Zeder 1997). One of us (Gross) teaches part time and is employed part time by a private firm from which he does CRM archaeology as well. Neumann, Sanford, and Harry (2010:1) estimate that nearly 80 percent of archaeologists are employed in the private or government sectors. Altschul and Patterson (2010) use a variety of data sources to estimate that in 2008, there were around 7350 archaeologists employed in CRM technical activities in the United States, an estimate a little higher than a 2005 SAA survey of its memberships concluded. These authors also estimate that annual expenditure in 2008 on CRM archaeology may have been as high as $500 million. Regardless of the statistic it is clear that CRM now plays an important role within the discipline and many academics are involved in one way or another in CRM-funded projects as well. These changes originally generated some mutual disdain between CRM and academic archaeologists, but we think the tensions are mellowing as the field continues to develop. See Section F.1 on the Student CD for additional perspective on these two types of contemporary archaeology. You also can get an impression of what a career in CRM is like from Profile 1.2.

As Profile 1.2 indicates, Lynne Sebastian is a woman who has risen to the top of her profession. During the mid-twentieth century, despite the accomplishments of some renowned women archaeologists, there was a definite bias against women in the field. This began to change in the 1970s (Patterson 1995), and current data on gender distribution suggest that archaeology is no longer so heavily dominated by men. One survey (Zeder 1997) found that while under 40 percent of the professional archaeologists were female, a little more than 50 percent of the students were. Moreover, the highest proportions of females were in the younger cohorts, and the proportion of professional women tended to decrease as age increased. It is unclear whether these young women will remain in the profession, perhaps encountering a glass ceiling that keeps them from promotion, or whether they will choose other careers as they mature. A survey done in 2005 found that women were being

---

FACES IN ARCHAEOLOGY   PROFILE 1.2

Lynne Sebastian, Archaeologist and Historic Preservationist

Lynne Sebastian's career provides one example of a contemporary archaeologist who has chosen to work outside academia. As the president of the Society for American Archaeology from 2003 to 2005, Sebastian (Figure 1.9) can be seen as one of today's most prominent North American archaeologists. It is notable that she is only the fifth woman to become president of the SAA, but it is even more significant that she is the first president whose career has been spent solely in cultural resource management.

Sebastian did not pursue archaeology until she was in her thirties, after she had already earned a bachelor's degree in English and secondary education and a master's degree in

FIGURE 1.9 Lynne Sebastian at Chaco Canyon.

English literature. When she was an undergraduate student, she was interested in classical archaeology and Egyptology, but her mother convinced her that it would be more practical to be a teacher. When Sebastian graduated from college trained to teach high school English, however, there was a teacher surplus. She took secretarial jobs and then found work as an editor of archaeological publications at the Museum of Anthropology of the University of Michigan. Eventually, she began doing copyediting for *American Antiquity*, the journal of the Society for American Archaeology, while she worked on her master's in English literature at the University of Utah. She credits the professors with whom she came in contact at that time with opening up the world of anthropology and archaeology for her. Upon coming to see that archaeology provides a way to understand human culture and behavior, she decided to pursue archaeology rather than literary criticism.

After taking some anthropology and archaeology classes at the University of Utah and getting some field training, Sebastian worked for the Dolores Archaeological Program (see Student CD, Section D.5.) Sebastian entered graduate school at the University of New) Mexico in 1980 and became interested in the archaeology of Chaco Canyon in northwestern New Mexico, which was then being studied for the National Park Service (NPS) by New Mexico professor Jim Judge, whose career was highlighted in Profile 1.1. Although she did not work on the NPS Chaco Project, Sebastian explored political leadership in the Chaco system for her doctoral dissertation. While obtaining her doctorate, Sebastian worked for the University of New Mexico's Office of Contract Archaeology, a CRM unit based at the university. Through this latter job, Sebastian gained practical background in excavation, analysis, and report writing. She feels fortunate to have had the chance to work on several large contract projects during those years. Because these were full-time projects, several times she took a term off from graduate school, but the fieldwork was interesting and challenging. In fact, she loved this work so much that she discarded any notion of pursuing a career in academia.

Sebastian's career took another turn in 1987 when she began a job as Deputy State Historic Preservation Officer for New Mexico. Part of this job's attraction was that it provided benefits, unlike the CRM project work that both she and her husband, another archaeologist, had been doing. Although she missed archaeological field-work and analysis at first, once again a new world was opened to her. This time it was the world of historic preservation, which involves far more than review of archaeological contract reports. She also found herself consulting with Native American tribes and government agencies, educating the public, and working to lessen threats to the archaeological record. She was good at putting people together to solve preservation problems, and this important work was satisfying. Although she began her employment with the state with the idea that the job would be temporary, she stayed 12 years. From her original position, she was named State Archaeologist and then promoted to **State Historic Preservation Officer (SHPO)**, which meant that she had responsibility for all facets of New Mexico's historic preservation program. She became a voice for archaeology in the National Conference of State Historic Preservation Officers (NCSHPO) and also grew active in the Society for American Archaeology, serving on the Public Education Committee and as secretary of the organization.

By the mid-1990s, Sebastian expected that she had made her last career move. In 1999, however, caught in political cross fire, she abruptly lost her job. Despite an outcry from the preservation community, there was no going back. Sebastian's career had taken another turn, and she landed in the private sector working first for Statistical Research, Inc., a company that provides services in CRM and historic preservation in the Southwest and along the West Coast, and, since 2002, for the SRI Foundation. The SRI Foundation is a not-for-profit organization that seeks to enrich society by fostering and improving the practice of historic preservation. As Director of Historic Preservation Programs, Sebastian teaches continuing professional education workshops and provides technical assistance to agencies and private industry clients on compliance with federal historic preservation laws. She also carries out research on best practices in CRM and serves as an expert witness on historic preservation and cultural resource issues. Sebastian feels very fortunate to be finishing out her career in an organization that allows her to make use of many skills that she has acquired in her varied experiences over the past 40 years.

The career of this committed CRM professional suggests that being an archaeologist can lead to rewarding work in government and private companies as well as in universities and museums. Clearly, there is an important place for archaeologists in broader fields such as historic preservation. Indeed, accomplishments like Sebastian's earn as much professional respect as more traditional archaeological pursuits. See the Student CD, Section E.2, for another example of a career in CRM archaeology.

---

paid less than men, but the causes of the apparent gender gap are unclear because the women surveyed generally were at earlier stages in their careers than the men (Association Research, Inc. 2005). Certainly the number of women in the field has been growing, but only more assessment over the next few decades will establish whether gender equality is increasing within archaeology.

Advances made by women in the field of archaeology not withstanding, surveys show that there is very little ethnic diversity among Americanist archaeologists. Zeder (1997) found that 89 percent of her survey respondents were of European American ancestry. This number does not include Canadians, who objected to being classified as European American. Zeder estimates that only about 2 percent of American archaeologists have a non–European American ancestry. This is a startling figure, especially since the populations most North American archaeologists study are not European American, and scholars today

agree that individuals' personal social experience cannot help but affect their understanding of the past. No wonder that professional organizations like the SAA are actively trying to expose students of other ethnicities to archaeology.

Avocational Archaeology

Avocational archaeologists are people who lack formal education in anthropology and archaeology and are not paid for work that they do in the field. Avocational archaeologists can work alone, through avocational societies like the Mid-Columbia Archaeological Society in Washington State, or through organizations like Crow Canyon Archaeological Center (Figure 1.10) and Earth Watch, which take paying participants on archaeological projects. Avocational archaeologists vary in the diligence with which they report their work, but many are very conscientious. In fact, we know about the location of many sites

FIGURE 1.10 Volunteers from Crow Canyon Archaeological Center excavating an Ancestral Pueblo site.

across the country thanks to the work of avocationals. There are even avocational societies with journals, like the *Pacific Coast Archaeological Society Quarterly*, that not only report the projects conducted by the society but also include papers by professional archaeologists. Others, like the Society for Pennsylvania Archaeology, which publishes the *Pennsylvania Archaeologist*, include both amateurs and professionals as members.

It is important to make the distinction between legitimate avocational archaeologists and relic hunters or **pothunters**, however. Avocational archaeologists observe good archaeological procedure and are careful to keep records of where materials are found. Many work closely with professionals. Some avocational societies have developed certification programs, often in association with colleges or museums. Ethical avocational archaeologists do not do archaeology primarily to add to their personal collections; rather, they are interested in learning about the past and its people. They make sure that the artifacts and records of their work are properly maintained, and they help record and preserve sites in the areas in which they live. Relic hunters, on the other hand, generally dig sites for the artifacts, paying little attention to the locations of finds. They heedlessly destroy the archaeological record to get a few more items for their trophy cases or for the black market in antiquities. You can read more about the destructive nature of such activities in the opening sections of Chapters 6 and 11. In Chapter 14

we discuss efforts to deter destructive behaviors especially in Box 14.1.

Native Americans and Other Descendant Populations

As touched on earlier in this chapter, an important aspect of the contemporary archaeological scene in North America is the growing involvement of Native Americans, whether as collaborators and informants in archaeological projects or as full partners in investigations (e.g., Dongoske et al. 2000). A number of tribes have developed cultural heritage programs that involve archaeological investigations. An **indigenous archaeology** in which Native people themselves control the course of archaeological studies is developing (Watkins 2000, 2003). Progress has been slow, however: many Indians still distrust archaeologists and some archaeologists are still resistant to the loss of control that full collaboration entails.

However, besides the growing political savvy and power of Native Americans, two circumstances help ensure that indigenous involvement is a real trend, likely to change archaeological practice and enrich archaeological understanding of the past. First, today's North American archaeologist is aware that archaeology does not hold the only viable view of the past. The **postmodernist** critique of science has made archaeologists reluctant to cloak ourselves in science and more concerned with how experience and social context influence people's ideas of the past. Within North American archaeology, these ideas have been expressed especially in what is known as **postprocessualism** (see Student CD, Section A, for discussion of this theoretical approach and its significance).

Second, laws now bind archaeologists to respect the concerns of descendant populations. For example, the Native American Graves Protection and Repatriation Act of 1990 (**NAGPRA**) stipulates consultation with descendants in the event of the discovery of new burials. This law also requires the notification of descendants and possible return of human remains and grave goods held in museums. What should happen to **culturally unaffiliated human remains (CUHR)** for whom specific descendant populations are not clear continues to be an area under debate as well. The regulations for **Section 106** of the **National Historic Preservation Act (NHPA)** require consultation with Native Americans and other descendants in a wide variety of CRM projects in the United States. Moreover, it is now possible for tribes to conduct their own CRM studies on tribal lands, which means that today some archaeologists actually work for Native American tribes.

Archaeological collaboration with Native Americans is evident in several places in this text. See the case study by Rhonda Foster, Larry Ross, and Dale Croes, "Archaeological/Anthropological–Native American Coordination: An Example of Sharing the Research on the Northwest Coast of North America," in Chapter 5, and "Cultures in Contact at Colony Ross," by Kent Lightfoot et al., the case study in Chapter 7, for examples of archaeological projects that have involved direct native input. The discussions in Sections F.3 and F.4 of the Student CD also are relevant.

Of course, other descendant populations may be affected by archaeology. The same aspects of contemporary archaeology that have been promoting cooperation with Native Americans also have led to involvement with other ethnic groups. See Chapter 13's case study, "Community Archaeology: Understanding the Contexts of Archaeological Practice," by Carol McDavid and Christopher Matthews, for examples of archaeology done with African American communities. One example of the complexities involved in such interactions is provided in Box 1.2.

ISSUES AND DEBATES   BOX 1.2

Politics and Scholarship in the Investigation of New York City's African Burial Ground

The middle of Manhattan seems an unlikely place for a major archaeological discovery. It's not that there hasn't been a long history of human habitation, or even that the majority of that history already has been documented by written records (Cantwell and Wall 2001). Rather, it seems logical to assume that construction and development in Manhattan as the city grew have obliterated most of the earlier uses of this land. Realistically, how likely is it that intact cultural remains lie beneath the streets and tall buildings with their subbasements that now cover the island? In 1989, when the General Services Administration (GSA) announced plans to build a large federal office complex in lower Manhattan, few people anticipated the discovery of any significant remains. Nevertheless, following the procedures set out by various CRM laws, the project had to begin with research on the history of the site, including a determination of what if any archaeological materials might be preserved beneath the ground.

The initial researchers found that the lots on which the federal building was to be constructed included the city's dedicated African Burial Ground. Although most people think of slavery as part of the history of the Southeast, the Dutch began to bring African slaves to New Amsterdam in 1626, and it is

believed that just before they left the colony, 40 percent of the population consisted of enslaved Africans. The British continued to practice slavery, primarily because they needed the labor provided by slaves to run the thriving port and city. Thus, at the time of the American Revolution, New York had the second highest number of enslaved Africans of any colonial city (Harrington 1996). Beginning in 1697, applicable law forbade the burial of Africans in the New York's churchyards, and a spot then located away from the populated area was designated for the burial of Africans. Until 1790, when the expanding city grew into and over the area, thousands of free and enslaved Africans as well as some poor white people and possibly prisoners of war captured by the British during the American Revolution were buried there (Cantwell and Wall 2001:281).

However interesting and historically significant the proposed construction site was, it seemed unlikely that two centuries of development and construction in lower Manhattan had left any of the original burials intact. Still, a careful record search suggested that if remains had been left undisturbed, they would be beneath a small alley that had been laid out in the 1790s. Thus, test excavations in this area were recommended, and they were begun in 1991, even as the larger project got under way. Everyone was in for a surprise, including the archaeologists. Not only were intact burials found beneath the alley, but it became clear that a deep layer of landfill had been dumped over the burying ground at the beginning of the nineteenth century so that, in fact, a good deal of it lay undisturbed, well beneath the probing of nineteenth- and twentieth-century construction projects. Eventually, over 400 human burials were uncovered at the site. What to do with this find and the excavated human remains was not settled without major controversy.

Historians, archaeologists, and preservationists knew that a tremendous amount of information about the lives of Colonial period Africans could be gained from the recovery of the newly discovered graves and their contents. Research into the origins of the African slaves, their state of health, their retention of African culture, the work they did, and a host of other anthropological and biological matters could be explored. Yet retrieving this kind of information would mean very slow and painstaking work in the midst of a major construction site, and years of careful, detailed laboratory analysis of the finds. It would mean the expenditure of a large sum of money and the loss of millions more due to construction delays. Perhaps unsurprisingly, the GSA wanted to find the simplest and quickest way to remain in compliance with the law and get on with the construction of the office complex. The pressure on the archaeologists and the forensic anthropological team they had brought in to speed up their excavation, even to cut corners, was enormous. They were working 12-hour days, seven days a week, trying to maintain careful procedures but still satisfy their client, the GSA. This project had turned into a nightmare, but what they were discovering was terribly important!

Yet, neither the GSA nor, initially, the archaeologists had reckoned with another aspect of the significance of the African Burial Ground: its importance to African Americans interested in their slave heritage. Many African Americans saw the cemetery, remote and rude as it had been, as having belonged to their ancestors; it was one place Africans could congregate, and certainly it had been a place of ritual significance as well. Moreover, its discovery afforded an opportunity to tell the story of the people as well as to honor their memory.

Predictably, conflict and misunderstanding erupted. Led by New York City's first African American mayor, David Dinkins, the African American community became increasingly assertive. They insisted that their ancestors buried at this spot had been discriminated against during their lives, and now, the GSA and the archaeologists were going to discriminate against them after death by not developing a new and thorough research design, by not exercising enough respect and care in their work, and by not properly curating and studying the recovered remains. Dinkins and others wanted African American archaeologists and scholars to be in charge so that the sacred and social significance of the site would not be overlooked, and they wanted a memorial to their ancestors. It became a classic American media circus. The GSA tried to stand firm; politicians up to the congressional level got involved; and prominent African American scholars inserted themselves into the situation. The original archaeological firm resigned.

Eventually, out of this chaos, people arrived at solutions that were largely beneficial to everyone. The GSA agreed to build only the office tower originally contemplated, not an adjacent four-story structure. Here, excavation was stopped and an estimated 200 burials left intact in the ground. A new, larger archaeological firm with experience in the excavation of African burials completed the excavation of exposed materials, and then the excavation was stopped. African American biological anthropologists and other scholars from Howard University in Washington, DC, one of America's top historically black universities, took over the analysis of the human remains and graves. As a result, we have learned a tremendous amount, especially about the health and living conditions of these early African Americans; in addition, the history of Northern slavery during the Colonial period has been illuminated. Finally, an on-site memorial was eventually built and the site became a National Monument in February 2006. In the fall of 2003, after years of careful study at Howard University, the human remains were reinterred with the pomp and circumstance befitting the people on whose backs, both in life and in death, the great city of New York was built.

Looking back, we might express regret—that politics and the media exacerbated a difficult situation—or we might say that it simply takes clout to achieve the preservation of cultural resources in our society today. We might consider it unfortunate that activist ethnic communities can determine the course of scientific projects, or we might consider involvement and respect for descendant communities to be the only ethical course. We might say that it was unfair that the hard work of the original archaeologists was not deemed adequate, or we might say that this story proves the need for minority scholars. We might bemoan the information lost to construction or even in leaving some human remains undisturbed, or we might celebrate the information eventually gained (Blakey and Rankin-Hill 2004; Medford 2004). There are many possible perspectives. Nevertheless, it is clear that modern archaeological research does not take place in a social vacuum, nor is it so esoteric that only archaeologists care. It also should be clear that great archaeological finds can still be made, even in unlikely places. We all stand to learn about our past, provided we can sort out the complexities of the modern contexts within which archaeology is done.

Other Stakeholders

A wide variety of people who are not archaeologists including scholars in allied fields like history interact with archaeologists in a diverse way. Among these people are museum educators, teachers, historic preservationists, and other specialists in cultural tourism with whom today's archaeologists collaborate in developing curricula, exhibits, and public programs. One widely recognized ethical responsibility for today's archaeologist is the interpretation of our results and the promotion of preservation of archaeological resources to the public. Both those with whom we collaborate in interpreting the past and the public itself have legitimate interests and concerns that must be kept in mind. These other perspectives can only enrich our understanding of the past.

The potential contribution of private **collectors**, those who accumulate artifacts and art for personal enjoyment and financial gain, is harder to determine. Archaeologists may disagree about the private collection of artifacts. Most believe that any buying and selling of artifacts only fuels the looting of sites and the dispersion of artifacts that together might be informative. Some private collectors have come into possession of very important artifacts and are willing to share information about these artifacts with archaeologists. These individuals may maintain that their activities actually protect artifacts from languishing unseen and unused in museums, universities, and other repositories. Archaeologists generally do not believe these are valid arguments, but some are more willing than others to use private collections in the pursuit of what happened in the past.

AN OVERVIEW OF THE ARCHAEOLOGICAL PROCESS

Professional archaeologists make their living by studying the things that people left behind. From these we learn what happened in the past—how people made their living, how they arranged themselves and their settlements on the landscape, how they governed themselves, how they interacted with one another, how they died, and how their loved ones treated them after they died. Archaeologists study artifacts, ecofacts, features, and their patterned relationships in the ground or on the ground surface, to make inferences about the past. This is true for all archaeologists, but the goals and sources of funding for research investigations conducted by academics and for cultural resource management studies are somewhat different.

Projects conducted by colleges, universities, and museums look at the past for answers to specific research questions. Most archaeologists work within the

FIGURE 1.11 Field school students at the Mary Rinn site learning to set up excavation units. They learned excavation techniques as part of research concerning the Late Prehistoric period in western Pennsylvania.

framework of **conservation archaeology** and regard archaeological sites as irreplaceable resources that should be preserved, as opposed to excavated if at all possible. As a result, archaeological sites are considered too important to be sacrificed to student training alone, and field school excavations (Figure 1.11) also explore important research questions about the past. Academic research projects are generally funded by grants, although student fees and the institution's budget may also make contributions to the costs of the research. Grants are made by federal agencies such as the National Science Foundation or the National Park Service and by private foundations like the National Geographic Society and the Wenner-Gren Foundation. Numerous small grants are made by states and other organizations as well. The granting process generally requires a detailed proposal that explains the **research design** or what the project intends to find out and the justification for the work proposed. Specific research questions are stated, and the plan for gathering the necessary data is presented.

As indicated earlier, government agencies, like the U.S. Forest Service and the Army Corps of Engineers as well as consulting firms under contract to agencies or private clients, also perform archaeological studies. These studies are done as part of the environmental permitting process, often in conjunction with **Environmental Impact Statements (EISs)**, which assess the environmental impacts of a proposed undertaking. These documents are required by laws designed to ensure that before issuing permits for land-altering activities, governments have considered archaeological sites, historical structures, and **traditional cultural properties (TCPs)**, places that have a special meaning to members of an ethnic group or community. Federal agencies are also required to inventory and manage the archaeological sites and historical properties on lands they own. Local laws relating to historic properties may be just as important to the protection of archaeological sites as federal legislation, especially in densely populated areas coping with urban sprawl.

These CRM studies are funded either by the governmental agency doing the land-modifying project or by the entity requesting the federal permit. Although governmental agencies perform archaeological studies for their projects, private companies or university research divisions conduct much of the CRM archaeology done today. These companies contract with the agency doing the work or with the private company seeking the permit. Contracts are often awarded through a competitive bid process, with cost to the client most often (but not always) the major factor in the award decision. This chapter's case study, "The Pueblo Grande Project: An Example of Multidisciplinary Research in a Compliance Setting," by Cory Breternitz and Christine Robinson, illustrates the nature of a large CRM project.

Archaeological investigations involve both fieldwork and laboratory analyses. Fieldwork may start with searching records about known site locations followed by finding new **archaeological sites**. An archaeological site is any location at which there are material remains of the human past. Sometimes this discovery is fortuitous, but often sites are found as part of an **archaeological site survey**, a field program that systematically locates, identifies, and records sites (Figure 1.12). The various techniques that can be employed in finding sites systematically are described in the Student CD, Section B. During the survey, artifacts are often collected from the surface of the sites or are picked up as **isolated artifacts**, items not found on archaeological sites.

When sites are thought to contain information relevant to research questions or when they are likely to be destroyed by anticipated activities, they are excavated. Testing may be used to determine if sites are worthy of extensive excavation, and **geophysical**

prospecting may be conducted. Geophysical prospecting is the use of such special techniques as **ground-penetrating radar (GPR)**, which provide subsurface information without excavation. These techniques allow archaeologists to target their excavations more precisely, and they reduce both the labor expended in excavation and the destruction of sites. Full-scale excavations still are required when site destruction by development is inevitable. During excavation, artifacts and other remains are collected, their positions in the site soils are recorded, features are explored, and the site is documented. The Student CD, Section B, provides more description of the specific techniques used in excavation.

Excavation is not the end of the process, however; it is actually the beginning. Following fieldwork, the finds are cleaned and **cataloged**, that is, inventoried and assigned unique numbers that associate each item with the location at which it was found. Only then can materials be analyzed. Analysis involves the study of the recovered artifacts and ecofacts (Figure 1.13) according to archaeological **typologies**, which are archaeological systems of classification or, when appropriate, biological systems of classification. Analysis also involves the dating of objects, the determination of how they were used, and in some instances sourcing, which involves determining where an item originated. Studies of the spatial distribution of sites, artifacts, ecofacts, and features also may make use of **Geographical Information System (GIS)**, which retrieves, stores, and manipulates geographic data. In archaeology, GIS can be used to compare site distributions against environmental information and also to analyze the location

FIGURE 1.12 Field crew surveying in parallel transects on Otay Mesa near the Mexican border in California.

FIGURE 1.13 A lithic analyst records information about the attributes of projectile points.

of features and artifacts at a site. Section C of the Student CD provides more information about analytical procedures commonly used by archaeologists.

The final step in the laboratory phase of archaeological investigations is packaging artifacts and ecofacts for **curation**. Curating archaeological materials is more than just storing them. In proper curation facilities (Figure 1.14), artifacts and other archaeological materials are stored under conditions that keep them from deteriorating, but they are also available for use in public education and for future study by archaeologists as new techniques are developed. The long-term curation of collections, which may allow later reanalysis even after a site is destroyed, is particularly important. At least three of our case studies illustrate the use of collections. These are "Weaponry of Clovis Hunters at Blackwater Draw," by Anthony Boldurian (Student CD, Section D.3), "Mouse Creek Phase Households and Communities: Mississippian Period Towns in Southeastern Tennessee," by Lynne Sullivan (Chapter 11), and "A New History of Maize-Bean-Squash Agriculture in the Northeast," by John Hart (Chapter 12), all of which utilized existing collections to conduct significant research. Unfortunately, as explained in "The Curation Crisis" (Student CD, Section F.2, today, there are more collections than there are places, space, and funding to care for them. This is a problem that the archaeological community is debating and seeking to resolve.

When research is completed, archaeologists are obligated to share the information they have acquired with

FIGURE 1.14 Artifacts at the Hopewell Culture National Historical Park in Ohio are carefully stored so that they can be studied by researchers or used in exhibits.

other archaeologists, agency managers, their clients, and the public. This is done in a variety of ways. Research grants and CRM contracts require reports from research archaeologists at the end of the project and may require progress reports throughout the course of the work. The results of the investigations may be published in monographs or articles in scholarly journals. Sometimes the results of cultural resource management reports are published, but most often they languish in the storehouses of agencies and state clearinghouses as part of the vast, unpublished **gray literature**. The problem of how to provide access to the information in the gray literature remains a great concern to North American archaeologists. Archaeologists also increasingly recognize an obligation to share their findings with the public, and popular articles, public talks, web presentations, and even videos aimed at the public rather than the scholarly community are becoming more common.

FIGURE 1.15 Archaeologists built this reconstruction of the framework supporting a Late Prehistoric Monongahela house in conjunction with Pennsylvania Archaeology Month public programs, but they also clarified their understanding of such structures and their construction in the process.

Other Ways to Learn About the Past

Fieldwork and laboratory analysis are not the only ways archaeologists learn about the past. When available and relevant, historical records are consulted. **Ethnohistory** is a field allied with archaeology. It is the use of historical documents, ethnographic accounts, linguistic data, ecology, and archaeology to provide insight into recent cultures. This multidisciplinary approach is often used to document sacred sites and traditional cultural properties for consideration in the planning of development projects. **Ethnoarchaeology** also helps archaeologists build understanding of the patterns discernible in the archaeological record. In ethnoarchaeology, the researcher observes living people to see how their behavior creates the archaeological record. Researchers also may try to duplicate features of the archaeological record to better archaeological understanding of that record (Figure 1.15) using replicative studies or **experimental archaeology**.

Both ethnoarchaeology and experimental archaeology contribute to the development of **middle-range theory**—theory that is aimed at understanding the meaning of patterning in the archaeological record. Experimental archaeology is part of two case studies in this text: "Weaponry of Clovis Hunters at Blackwater Draw," by Anthony Boldurian (Student CD, Section D.3), and "A New History of Maize-Bean-Squash Agriculture in the Northeast," by John Hart (Chapter 12).

CHAPTER SUMMARY

In this chapter we have introduced the nature of North American archaeology and its contemporary practice. The most important points that have been made can be summarized as follows:

- Archaeology is the study of past human behavior and culture through the study of material remains. North American archaeology is a type of anthropology as well as a type of science that contributes to scholarly understanding of the past, but it differs from historical research because it focuses on material remains.

- The field of North American archaeology did not develop as a profession until the early twentieth century, after which archaeologists worked mostly in museum or university settings. Since the 1970s, however, many have been employed in cultural resource management positions either in the government or in the private sector.

- There are many stakeholders in North America's past besides archaeologists and allied scholars. These include avocational archaeologists, Native Americans and other descendant populations, educators and their students, and even relic hunters and collectors. Professionals must take each of these groups into account as they work to understand our past.

- Archaeological investigations in both academic and CRM settings may involve archaeological surveys, excavations, laboratory analyses, cataloging of collections, curation of collections, and report writing. Archaeologists also use ethnohistorical research, ethnoarchaeological investigations, and experimental archaeology to understand the past of North America.

SUGGESTIONS FOR FURTHER READING

For more information on the nature of archaeology and its methods:

Kelly, Robert L., and Thomas, David Hurst
    2011 *Archaeology*, 6th ed. Wadsworth Cengage Learning, Belmont, California.

For a classic source on the history of American archaeology:

Willey, Gordon R., and Jeremy A. Sabloff
    1993 *A History of American Archaeology*, 3rd ed. W. H. Freeman, San Francisco.

For more information on specific archaeological field methods:

Hester, Thomas R., Harry J. Schafer, and Kenneth L. Feder
    2008 *Field Methods in Archaeology*. Left Coast Press, Walnut Creek, California.

For more information on specific methods of archaeological laboratory analysis:

Sutton, Mark Q., and Brooke S. Arkush
    2007 *Archaeological Laboratory Methods: An Introduction*, 4th ed. Kendall/Hunt, Dubuque, Iowa.

For more on CRM archaeology:

King, Thomas F
    2008 *Cultural Resource Laws and Practice*, 3rd ed. AltaMira Press, Lanham, Maryland.

Neumann, Thomas W., Robert M. Sanford, and Karen G. Harry
    2010 *Cultural Resources Archaeology: An Introduction*, 2nd ed. AltaMira Press, Walnut Creek, California.

For more on archaeological curation:

Sullivan, Lynne P., and S. Terry Childs
    2003 *Curating Archaeological Collections: From the Field to the Repository*. Archaeologist's Toolkit 6. AltaMira Press, Walnut Creek, California.

OTHER RESOURCES

Sections H and I of the Student CD supply web links, places to visit, additional discussion questions, and other study aids. The Student CD also contains a variety of additional resources. See, in particular, "A Brief History of North American Archaeology" (Section A), "Archaeological Fieldwork" (Section B), "Archaeological Laboratory Analysis" (Section C), "Interpreting the Ripley Site: A Century of Investigations," by Sarah Neusius (Section D.1), "Arthur Parker, Archaeologist and Museologist" (Section E.1), "Linda Mayro, Pima County Cultural Resources Manager" (Section E.2), "What Do Professors and CRM Archaeologists Think of Each Other?" (Section F.1), and "The Curation Crisis" (Section F.2).

CASE STUDY

A great deal of contemporary North American archaeology is done in the context of cultural resource management as **compliance archaeology**—archaeological investigations performed to meet the requirements of laws and regulations rather than as basic research. Although this means that location and scope are dictated by the parameters of the overall project, it also means that archaeological investigations are conducted in places such as growing urban areas that otherwise might not be excavated. In this case study, the construction of an expressway in Phoenix required testing of the highway right-of-way. The project area went through a portion of Pueblo Grande, a large Hohokam village ruin that the City of Phoenix maintains as a cultural park. As you will learn in Chapter 9, *Hohokam* is the name archaeologists have given to the major cultural tradition that developed in

southern Arizona well over a thousand years ago. Testing of the right-of-way revealed an unexpected number of features including human burials dating to the Hohokam Classic period. These burials had to be removed and then rapidly returned to the Native American descendants. Although some of the original topics of interest could not be explored, multidisciplinary analyses have yielded important insights into the health of Classic period Hohokam people and into the environment in the Phoenix Basin just prior to the disappearance of this culture from southern Arizona around 600 years ago. As you read this case study, pay particular attention to the steps in the CRM process and to the surprises the archaeologists received as the project unfolded. Ask yourself, as well, if we would know what we now do about the Hohokam and their demise if CRM investigations had not been required.

THE PUEBLO GRANDE PROJECT

An Example of Multidisciplinary Research in a Compliance Setting

Cory Dale Breternitz and Christine K. Robinson

PUEBLO GRANDE IN A MODERN CONTEXT

In 2004 Phoenix, Arizona, surpassed Philadelphia as the fifth largest city in the United States. Rapid growth in the city and in the greater metropolitan area has been occurring for the past two decades. The increase in population has led to a building boom that includes housing, commercial development, and the necessary infrastructure to support greater numbers of people. As a result of federal, state, and other publicly funded projects, southern Arizona in general and the Phoenix metropolitan area in particular support some of the largest and oldest private CRM consulting firms in the country. Major freeway construction projects in the 1980s in the Phoenix metropolitan area provided the start-up opportunities for many private archaeology consulting firms, such as Soil Systems, Inc. (SSI), that assist state and federal agencies in reaching compliance with state and federal historic preservation legislation (Roberts et al. 2004). The number of CRM companies registered to do business in Arizona reflects the number of compliance-based projects that are being undertaken every year in one of the fastest growing states in the country.

The Phoenix Basin is defined geographically by linear mountain ranges typical of the Basin and Range Province, which includes all of southern Arizona,

Nevada, southern Oregon, and southeastern California. The three largest rivers in southern Arizona all converge in the western Phoenix Basin. The Santa Cruz River flows into the Gila River just south of the basin, and the Salt River joins the Gila River in the western margins of the Phoenix Basin. Prior to the construction of dams in the early twentieth century, the Gila and Salt rivers provided the Arizona Sonoran Desert with a year-round water supply (Figure 1.16). Ironically, the historic occupation of the Phoenix Basin and the founding of the largest cities in Arizona did not become possible until dams had been built to control the Gila and Salt rivers. For over a millennium, control and management of the available water supply in the Sonoran Desert has been the key element to survival in this harsh and fragile landscape. A reliable water supply continues to be most important in accommodating future growth and in maintaining a sustainable population.

Visitors to the Phoenix metropolitan area today see an urban oasis supporting over 1.5 million people surrounded by an arid, seemingly inhospitable desert landscape. Yet, Phoenix has thousands of acres of green grass, palm trees, parks, lakes, and canals. One-third of Arizona's population resides in Maricopa County. Yet strikingly, other than the artificial lakes and canals, there is no apparent natural water source. The contrast between the artificial urban oasis and the

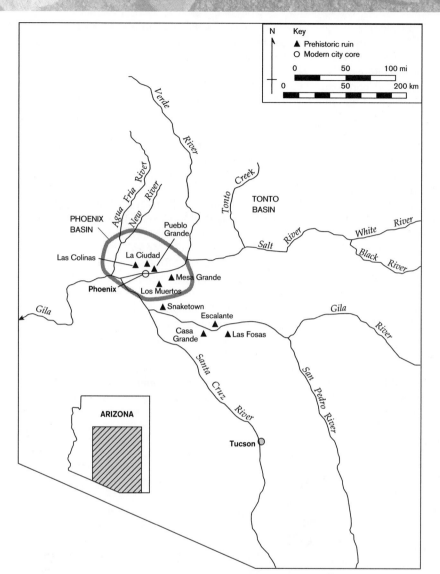

FIGURE 1.16 Locations of Pueblo Grande and other major Hohokam sites in central Arizona.

surrounding desert gives the impression that day-to-day survival could not have been possible without modern amenities. Visitors and long-time residents alike are amazed to learn that the Phoenix Basin and the Salt and Gila River valleys supported one of the most successful and technologically advanced prehistoric societies in pre-Columbian North America.

The Hohokam culture thrived in southern Arizona for over a thousand years and included large villages with thousands of permanent residents. The Hohokam built public architecture, including large artificial **platform mounds**, **ball courts**, and multistoried **great houses**, and controlled an extensive trade network for the exchange of exotic and utilitarian goods. This society owed its existence to over a thousand miles of well-engineered irrigation canals that harnessed, controlled,

and distributed the most highly valued commodity—water. The sophisticated network of canals invented and engineered by the Hohokam distributed domestic and agricultural water to thousands of prehistoric residents in the Phoenix Basin and irrigated tens of thousands of hectares of agricultural land between 1500 and 600 years ago (AD 500–1400). Today, urban sprawl and agricultural fields largely cover evidence of the Hohokam. To the untrained eye there is little visible evidence for the Hohokam remaining in southern Arizona, yet the Sonoran Desert is dotted with thousands of archaeological sites consisting of adobe compounds, platform and trash mounds, ball courts, and over a dozen great houses.

The most famous Hohokam site is Casa Grande National Monument in Coolidge, Arizona, on the Gila River

40 miles (65 km) south of Phoenix. Casa Grande was the first archaeological monument to be designated by Congress and is protected by the National Park Service. Unlike the more famous Ancestral Pueblo culture in the Four-Corners and Colorado Plateau region of northern Arizona, represented by dozens of archaeological sites in the National Park System, the Hohokam culture is underrepresented by parks and monuments and is largely unknown to the general public.

At the headgates of the largest canal system in the Phoenix Basin, Canal System 2, was Pueblo Grande, or Big Town, one of the largest and longest-lived Hohokam village sites (Figure 1.17). Pueblo Grande was occupied for nearly 800 years. At its greatest extent, the village covered nearly 1 square mile (2.59 km²) and had over a thousand permanent residents. Prominent southwestern archaeologists have studied Pueblo Grande for more than a century. The first archaeological work at Pueblo Grande occurred in the late 1800s, when Adolph Bandelier visited the site and Frank Hamilton Cushing conducted the first excavations. Early scholars observed the site before the expansion of agriculture, industry, and urbanization in later decades destroyed most of the surface features. Pueblo Grande was then described as an extensive area of small mounds and ruins on the north side of the Salt River, dominated by a large platform mound and a multistory adobe tower, the Great House (see Downum and

Bostwick 1993). The Pueblo Grande mound is one of the largest monumental mounds in the western United States, and the Great House was one of a handful of similar Hohokam structures, of which only the one at Casa Grande National Monument remains today.

Omar Turney and Frank Midvale, who mapped the extensive Hohokam canal systems throughout the Phoenix Basin in the 1920s through 1940s, recognized the prominence of Pueblo Grande. It is primarily through the efforts of Turney and Midvale that we know the extent of the Hohokam irrigation system and the many sites along these miles of canals that now lie buried beneath metropolitan Phoenix. By the 1920s, the Great House at Pueblo Grande had been destroyed, but the City of Phoenix succeeded in preserving the mound by establishing a cultural park that eventually grew to include over 100 acres (40 hectares) in the southern part of the site. The foresight on the part of the city has preserved the most visible features of the site. The rest of Pueblo Grande has remained in private hands and been subjected to urban development.

Between the 1920s and mid-1980s, excavations at Pueblo Grande were carried out by several researchers, mostly in and around the platform mound and the area to the west of the mound. Although these efforts were conducted for a variety of purposes and were not part of an integrated research plan, they resulted in the excavation

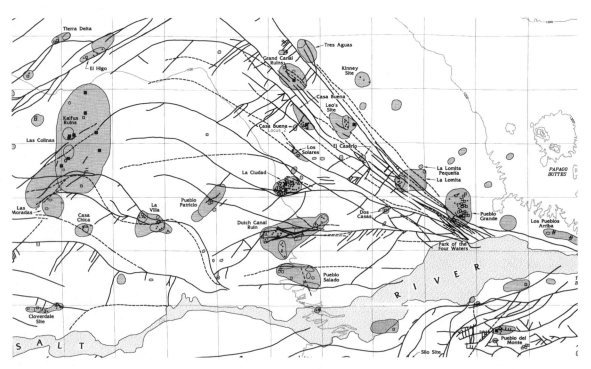

FIGURE 1.17 Canal system 2 with Pueblo Grande at its head is just part of the extensive system of canals built by the Hohokam in the Phoenix Basin.

and study of at least 400 houses and burials, a ball court, several trash mounds, and irrigation features. These efforts also resulted in a basic understanding of the construction and use history of the mound and helped establish that the southern part of the site was occupied from before 1200 BP (see Chapter 2 for discussion of dating conventions in archaeology). The mound itself belongs to a later part of the sequence (for summaries, see Bostwick and Downum 1994; Downum and Bostwick 1993).

Today, Pueblo Grande is at the intersection of major transportation corridors, which include freeway interchanges, important surface transportation arteries, a transcontinental railroad, and the sixth busiest passenger and freight airport in the country. This location has placed Pueblo Grande at the center of commercial development and has had major impacts on this significant cultural resource. Ironically, it is this concept of a central place that created Pueblo Grande originally. Pueblo Grande's location at the head of the largest prehistoric canal system, which provided domestic and irrigation water to numerous large villages and thousands of prehistoric residents downstream, allowed Pueblo Grande to become prominent in the Hohokam settlement and social systems.

In the early 1980s, planners in Phoenix realized that an urban freeway system was needed to accommodate increasing population growth. The Arizona Department of Transportation (ADOT) was the state agency responsible for constructing the freeway system throughout the Phoenix Basin. The aptly named Hohokam Expressway was designed to connect urban freeway corridors to Sky Harbor International Airport, which is less than a mile from Pueblo Grande. As a state agency, ADOT must comply with the Arizona Antiquities Act and is required to evaluate and mitigate any impacts to cultural resources that might result from any construction project. The Hohokam Expressway was to be constructed through a portion of Pueblo Grande adjacent to the city-owned park. The preferred alignment would cut a north-to-south swath through the site and destroy approximately 20 percent of the eastern edge of Pueblo Grande.

ADOT asked for proposals for the **mitigation** of the information loss that would be incurred at Pueblo Grande when the freeway was constructed. Qualified archaeological firms including our company, Soil Systems, Inc., prepared technical proposals for a **data recovery program** that was to be reviewed and approved by ADOT, the State Historic Preservation Officer, and the City of Phoenix. A research design that posed questions to be addressed with the data and artifacts recovered by the excavations was required. SSI's data recovery plan also had a public education and outreach component, outlined the field and laboratory methods to be used, discussed the company's qualifications to undertake the job, and named the key personnel who would be part of the research team. The results of the project had to be published, and all artifacts and data recovered during the excavations and subsequent analysis, including all photographs, maps, field notes, and analytical data, were to be permanently taken care of at the Pueblo Grande Museum.

IMPLEMENTING A RESEARCH DESIGN AND WORK PLAN IN AN URBAN ENVIRONMENT

SSI was awarded the contract for the archaeological data recovery at Pueblo Grande in 1987. Since only a few **sherds** were visible on the modern ground surface, and it was unclear if there were any subsurface deposits, the first stage of the fieldwork was to conduct systematic testing of the entire project area. Testing began with the excavation of 398 systematic backhoe trenches, each 10 meters (33 ft.) long throughout the entire freeway corridor, supplemented by 206 judgmental trenches. Systematic trenches were placed at set intervals, while judgmental trenches were placed where project archaeologists suspected important remains might be found. This allowed us to quantify the types and condition or degree of disturbance (**integrity**) of the prehistoric deposits in the project area. One of the initial questions centered on the preservation of any houses, burials, or pits (features). What, if anything, was left in the project area, and what was the condition of any found items? Were there any data to recover, or had the buildings and feedlots that covered the freeway corridor destroyed everything? Many, including ADOT, suspected that most of the prehistoric features in the project area had been destroyed. The results of the backhoe trenching showed numerous prehistoric features, including hundreds of human burials. Another surprise was that the features that were present dated almost exclusively to the Classic period (800–550 BP).

Despite extensive excavations at other Hohokam sites in the Phoenix area, largely associated with other ADOT freeway projects, very few features dating to this part of the Hohokam sequence had been investigated. Because the Classic is the last major period of the Hohokam occupation, Classic period remains at any Hohokam site tend to be the closest to the modern ground surface. Consequently, these remains are usually the first to be destroyed by modern development. Because the Hohokam Expressway project area contained prehistoric features that dated almost exclusively to the Classic period, and because there were so many burials, a major shift in the data recovery field strategy was required. Very little was known about the Classic period in the Phoenix Basin. Besides, the burials had to be recovered, which meant sampling was replaced by nearly 100 percent recovery of remains.

At the conclusion of the testing phase, SSI had a good understanding of what types of prehistoric features were present and their distribution across the project area. Nevertheless, the excavation phase of the Pueblo Grande Project required innovation because so many features were distributed over such a large area. A stripping bucket was specially developed that consisted of a toothless backhoe bucket nearly 4 feet wide (1.22 m), attached to the arm of a backhoe. This allowed the backhoe operator to remove a 4-foot-wide swath of overburden in a highly controlled manner, sometimes only a few inches at a time. An archaeologist monitored all stripping of the overburden, and when nearly 80 acres had been stripped, the tops of buried features lay exposed, increasing excavation and mapping efficiency. Areas that contained stratified deposits were stripped multiple times. Once all the exposed features had been excavated and recorded, they were stripped away to expose any underlying features.

This methodology revealed clusters of habitation architecture, including pithouses and aboveground adobe structures surrounded by encircling adobe walls (Figure 1.18). These clusters of habitation structures, referred to as compounds by students of the Hohokam, were called habitation areas. Clusters of inhumation and cremation burials were found adjacent to each habitation area. These burial clusters were referred to as burial groups. Fourteen habitation areas and 17 burial groups were identified in the Hohokam Expressway project area. Scattered throughout the project area and associated with the habitation areas and burial groups were hundreds of undifferentiated pit features, **borrow pits**, roasting pits, and trash deposits (Figure 1.19).

The Pueblo Grande Project research design initially developed by SSI (Foster 1994) addressed site structure, socioeconomic organization, and interaction patterns by emphasizing **households**—archaeological remains reflecting family units that had lived together and cooperated economically. Other research goals included paleoenvironmental reconstruction, the examination of mortuary patterns, and **bioarchaeological** or human bone analyses. In many respects, the research goals were successfully met. The excavations demonstrated that the site underwent a dramatic expansion after 850 BP (AD 1100), during the Classic period.

However, we had mixed success obtaining data to address some questions. Most significantly, households proved to be largely unworkable as units of analysis. The long, continuous site occupation, which included ongoing use, remodeling, and modification, left relatively few unmixed and undisturbed contexts other than burials. Enormous quantities of discarded artifacts accumulated over the centuries left large amounts of temporally mixed deposits and a low proportion of nonburial features that had temporally recognizable contents reflecting specific behaviors. Very few houses with intact, associated artifact **assemblages** were encountered, probably because houses were routinely cleaned out before being abandoned, so that the bulk of artifact assemblages from houses consisted of refuse that washed into the empty structures. Nonetheless, some observations about changes in site structure over time were possible. We were able to identify groupings of houses or habitation areas and associated burial groups that reflected social entities larger than households, and these socially related groups could be compared across a large part of the site.

Another set of unforeseen problems related to burials. We didn't anticipate the poor condition of the human

FIGURE 1.18 Overview of Pueblo Grande during the Hohokam Expressway Project, showing work on architecture.

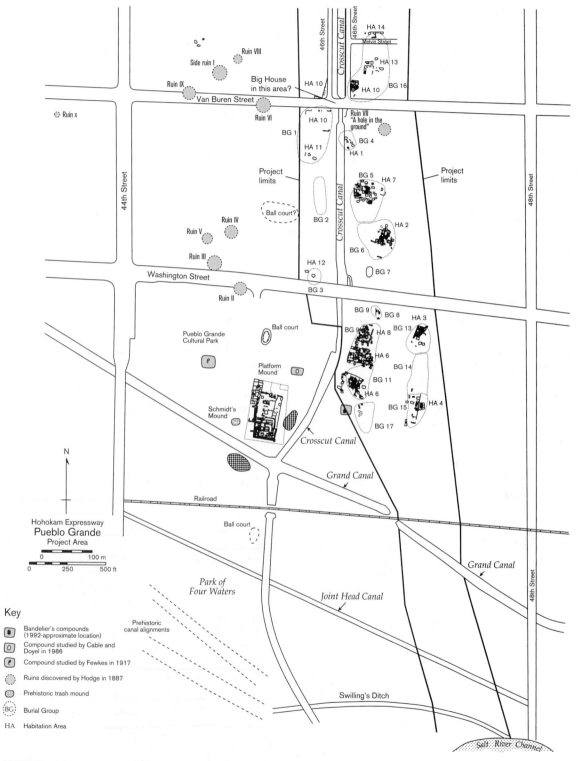

FIGURE 1.19 Distribution of habitation areas and burial groups in the Hohokam Expressway Project area and their relation to known features at Pueblo Grande.

(Data from Soil Systems, Inc. Computer cartography by GEO-MAP, Inc., 1982.)

remains, and osteological analysis was conducted only after the remains were removed to the laboratory. As a result, the collection of measurements and observations of some types was limited because the bone further deteriorated after it was removed from the ground. Because of an accelerated schedule of **repatriation**, or return of remains to the Native American descendants, the remains were reburied before we could conduct dental analyses that would have assessed the cultural affiliation of the burial population. On the other hand, the bioarchaeological research team did complete some analyses on the human remains and so was able to make observations about aspects of nutrition and health.

To successfully accomplish an urban archaeological project of the magnitude of the Pueblo Grande Project, SSI enlisted the assistance of many outside consultants and experts. We established a peer review team consisting of experts in Hohokam research to review all aspects of the fieldwork, analysis, and interpretation. SSI also hired several experts for the analysis and interpretation of specific artifact classes such as shell artifacts, **obsidian** sourcing, argillite sourcing, analysis of faunal (animal) bone, turquoise sourcing, pollen analysis, human osteology, and mortuary patterns. Throughout the course of the five-year project, SSI met with the multidisciplinary research team members in the field and at our office to discuss the results. This allowed all project team members to interact and to question, debate, and discuss analytical results. Thus, each analyst was able to become familiar with the results of the other analysts. Everyone kept in touch with the big picture that was developing and provided input into the overall research. By maintaining a flexible research strategy, we were able to refocus the research goals of the project to accommodate the data that were being recovered. As the project developed, the concepts of environmental degradation, poor health, and nutritional stress of the Classic period Hohokam population at Pueblo Grande became the focus of our research.

PUEBLO GRANDE DURING THE CLASSIC PERIOD

The Pueblo Grande Project resulted in the complete excavation of over 40 acres of the site, including 807 burials, over 300 houses, and more than 1600 other prehistoric features, the vast majority of which dated to the Classic period. Project results were reported in a multivolume report series (Breternitz 1994), an edited synthetic volume (Abbott 2003), an award-winning doctoral dissertation (Abbott 2000), peer-reviewed articles, and numerous topic-specific technical reports, conference papers, and master's theses. The project cost over

$4.5 million and was the largest, single study of a major Hohokam village to date. It also revolutionized our understanding of the Hohokam Classic period.

We now know that the Classic period was a time of many changes for the Hohokam (Abbott 2003). These changes were manifested in architecture, ceramics, trade and exchange, burial practices, and sociopolitical organization. At Pueblo Grande there was as much change during the 250-year Classic period, as in the previous 400-year transition from Sedentary to Classic. During the Classic period at Pueblo Grande, we defined the Soho phase as lasting between 800 BP and 650 BP (AD 1150–1300), and the Civano phase, which lasted a relatively short period of time, no longer than 100 years between 650 BP and 550 BP (AD 1300–1400). A Polvorón phase (600+ to 525 or 500 BP/AD 1350+ to 1425 or 1450) is also identifiable at Pueblo Grande.

During the Soho phase, population at Pueblo Grande increased over that of the preceding Sacaton phase (Abbott 2003). We have attributed this increase to the immigration into Pueblo Grande of peoples living elsewhere in the Phoenix Basin (Van Gerven and Sheridan 1994). During this period of aggregation and population increase, health, subsistence, and the availability of natural resources appear to have been in decline in comparison to the previous periods (Kwiatkowski 1994; Van Gerven and Sheridan 1994). The aggregation of population at Pueblo Grande during the Soho phase related in part to a general degradation of the local environment brought about by 600 years of intensive use of the Phoenix Basin by the Hohokam (Kwiatkowski 1994). Things began to go badly for the Hohokam living at Pueblo Grande during the Soho phase. During the Civano phase, things got worse.

We noted the appearance of compound architecture and changes in exchange networks, artifact assemblages, and burial practices occurred during the Civano phase. Pithouses arranged around courtyard groups gave way to the construction of compounds—aboveground adobe structures surrounded by enclosing walls. Platform mounds and ball courts were abandoned, and great houses appeared at some of the larger primary Hohokam centers in the Salt and Gila River valleys. The Pueblo Grande data suggest that the appearance of compounds of pithouses and surface structures enclosed by adobe walls during the Civano phase coincided with a population decline both in actual numbers of people living at the site and in their general health. Compound architecture may have been an attempt by the Hohokam to establish physical boundaries between their closest neighbors because resources had become so scarce.

To reconstruct the Classic period environment surrounding Pueblo Grande, our research team used contemporary and historical information to approximate the prehistoric plant communities within a

5-kilometer radius (3.1-mile) of Pueblo Grande during the Classic period. This **carrying-capacity** model was developed independently of the human remains and architectural data to arrive at estimates of the population that could be supported by historically important native plant resources. Our results suggested that the peak population at Pueblo Grande would have been closer to thousands of people than to tens or hundreds of thousands (Kwiatkowski 1994). Population estimates generated from architectural and human remains data supported the notion that the maximum population at Pueblo Grande during the Classic period did not exceed 1000 to 1500 people (Mitchell 1994a, 1994b).

The residents of Pueblo Grande probably lived through a number of droughts and floods, including flooding events in the late part of the sixth century BP (late AD 1300s). If the stream flow model developed by researchers at the University of Arizona (Nials et al. 1989) is correct, during this century the Hohokam of the Salt River valley experienced both droughts and floods of a magnitude greater than at any other period in the past 1200 years. These major droughts and floods would have had a disastrous effect on the canal system. Floods and droughts also would have affected the natural resources along the riverbanks and floodplain, which would have served as potential backup resources for crop failures.

Our carrying-capacity study indicates that during the Classic period, the residents of Pueblo Grande may have been living with little or no buffer against natural disasters such as floods and droughts. These catastrophes would have been most detrimental to the success and surpluses of both cultivated and natural resources. Years of exploitation by sedentary populations of the natural resources for food, fuel, and shelter, as well as heavy use of the land available for irrigated agriculture during the Classic period, eventually began to erode any buffers that may have existed during earlier periods. Combined with population aggregation into fewer and larger settlements, such as Pueblo Grande, these factors produced serious problems.

Faunal remains recovered from Pueblo Grande included aquatic species including muskrat, beaver, and fish (James 1994). The presence of these animals is significant because until recently, few prehistoric specimens of muskrat, beaver, or fish had been identified from any Hohokam sites. The quantity of muskrat at Pueblo Grande represents the largest number of specimens recovered to date from a single Hohokam site (James 1994). The muskrat remains showed signs of charring, and they occurred in contexts that indicated that the animals were being consumed as food. Muskrat is considered a starvation food, and the increased use of muskrat as a food source between the early and the late Classic suggests growing subsistence stress among the inhabitants (James 1994).

Fish remains accounted for over 25 percent of the total faunal assemblage. In fact, fish was second in importance only to rabbit as a food resource at Pueblo Grande. The size of the fish represented in the collections decreased markedly from the Early to Late Classic, suggesting that by the Late Classic period at Pueblo Grande, only relatively small fish were available. Possible explanations for this decrease include overexploitation in the vicinity of the site (James 1994), degradation of the local riverine microenvironment, or a combination of both.

Deer remains from Pueblo Grande are few and are represented by finished artifacts, such as awls and hairpins. This suggests that during the Classic period, deer bone was brought into the site as finished artifacts rather than as a source of edible animal protein. The deer bone recovered from Classic period contexts does not appear to have been acquired by hunting, and the lack of deer remains also probably results from environmental degradation and overexploitation by the Hohokam of that time (James 1994; Kwiatkowski 1994). Based on the animal remains from Pueblo Grande, animal protein available to the Classic period Hohokam consisted almost exclusively of meat from rabbits, fish, and rodents.

Pollen and **flotation** samples from Pueblo Grande, which provide information on plant materials in the deposits, indicate that maize was an important food source (Miller 1994). Trace-element analysis of the human remains indicates that maize may have played a greater role in the diet of Late Classic inhabitants than that of Early Classic inhabitants and that protein was less available during the Late Classic period (Jones and Sheridan 1994). The proportion of corn to wild plant remains increases during the Late Classic. That is, native plant remains were less abundant in the Late Classic pollen and flotation samples, which further supports the notion of a general deterioration of the environment surrounding Pueblo Grande and a decrease in native plants. During the Late Classic, the Hohokam may have become more dependent on corn as a primary subsistence resource because native plant resources were in decline and of limited availability. Animal protein was limited to rabbits, fish of decreasing size, and aquatic rodents. Corn was becoming the primary source of nutrition, so that *any* impact on the successful corn crop yield, such as droughts, floods, or malfunction of the canal system, or failure to maintain it, would have had a disastrous effect on an already precarious food supply, which provided only limited protein.

The analysis of over 800 inhumations and cremations recovered from Pueblo Grande provided an unprecedented glimpse into the lives of the Classic period Hohokam. We were not limited to architectural and material culture data; we had access to the stories of the people who actually lived and died at Pueblo Grande. Despite the many accomplishments of the Hohokam, analyses of the health and nutrition of the Classic period Pueblo Grande population paint a bleak picture and support many of the conclusions arrived at independently by the paleoenvironmental and subsistence studies.

The rate of mortality among the Pueblo Grande Hohokam was high. The mean life expectancy of a newborn was only slightly more than 15 years, and the modal age at death was birth (Van Gerven and Sheridan 1994). This means that although the most frequent age at death was 15, half the children born at Pueblo Grande did not survive to see their first birthday. The data indicate that 66 people per 1000 died each year. Simply to maintain the population with so many deaths would have required a comparable birthrate, which would be higher than any birthrate observed in the world today. It appears, then, that the Pueblo Grande Hohokam population was either in decline or dependent on immigration to maintain its numbers (Van Gerven and Sheridan 1994). Immigration to Pueblo Grande during the Early Classic period probably maintained a relatively stable population. During the Late Classic, however, immigration was probably not a significant factor, and the population at Pueblo Grande began a steady decline. Adding to the difficulty of everyday survival, the demographic data indicate that relative to producers, there would have been a large number of consumers under 15 years of age, and a handful over 50. This situation would have placed a heavy burden on the young adult population.

During the Late Classic period, severe conditions appear to have affected almost everyone. Infant mortality remained stable, but for individuals beyond age 10, there was an 8 percent reduction in mean life expectancy during the Late Classic (Van Gerven and Sheridan 1994).

Ninety-nine percent of the Pueblo Grande burials that could be studied had been nutritionally stressed over the course of their lives (Van Gerven and Sheridan 1994). The average Pueblo Grande child experienced nutritional stress for 33 months during its first 84 months (7 years) of life. Iron deficiency anemia is the most common nutritional deficiency in the world today. Among Pueblo Grande individuals, extensive iron deficiency anemia was observed in both sexes and across all ages, and an 18 percent increase in iron deficiency anemia was observed between the Early and Late Classic periods (Van Gerven and Sheridan 1994).

Analyses also showed differences between males and females at Pueblo Grande. Females were consuming more plant resources, whereas males had greater access to animal protein, such as it was. The lack of animal protein, combined with high reproductive demands, would have aggravated female dietary stress and increased the likelihood of death for females during the reproductive years. Between the Early and Late Classic periods, there was a general decrease in the amount of animal protein consumption, combined with an increased reliance on corn as opposed to native plant resources (Jones and Sheridan 1994). All the lines of evidence lead to the conclusion that the people of Pueblo Grande experienced dietary stress that worsened over time.

The Hohokam maintained a stable and impressive culture in the Sonoran Desert for over a thousand years. However, the human remains, paleoenvironmental reconstructions, and subsistence data collected by the Pueblo Grande Project indicate that by the late Classic period, the Pueblo Grande Hohokam were experiencing dire problems: nutritional and reproductive stresses that severely diminished their numbers. By the end of the Late Classic period, the struggle was lost and the Hohokam all but disappeared from the archaeological record. Although there is now some evidence that the Salt River valley may never have been completely abandoned, the essence of the Hohokam culture disappeared. Thus the Late Classic period marks the physical, social, and economic decline of these people and perhaps the physical environment they had once so successfully exploited.

The Pueblo Grande Project was sponsored by the Arizona Department of Transportation, contract 87-53.

DISCUSSION QUESTIONS

1. What is Pueblo Grande, and why is it a significant cultural resource? What can archaeologists infer from the site's location and from the presence of great houses, ball courts, and platform mounds?

2. Why were the excavations and analyses described here conducted? Did the project's origins affect what archaeology was done?

3. Why weren't the archaeologists very successful in using the household as the basic unit of analysis? Does this deviation from the original research design mean that the information obtained was not useful?

4. What kinds of evidence for environmental deterioration and nutritional stress during the Hohokam Classic period were recovered from the Pueblo Grande Project? Why do archaeologists pursue multiple lines of evidence through multidisciplinary research like that described here?

CHAPTER 2

Culture and Environment in North America's Past

In a hole in the ground there lived a hobbit. Not a nasty, dirty, wet hole, filled with the ends of worms and an oozy smell, nor yet a dry, bare, sandy hole with nothing in it to sit down on or to eat: it was a hobbit-hole, and that means comfort.

—Tolkien

With these words, J. R. R. Tolkien begins his well-known book *The Hobbit*, drawing us into the Shire of the hobbits and the fantastic world of which it is a part. Fantasy writers like Tolkien create imaginary places and creatures with their prose. Tolkien's vivid accounts of hobbit holes, the Shire, and the Misty Mountains enable us to picture these places and their inhabitants, and the *Lord of the Rings* movies reinforce what we have imagined about the land of the hobbits and their friends.

The world of North America's past also is a place we must imagine and in a sense recreate through archaeology. To understand North American archaeology, one needs to cultivate a perspective on this world both culturally and environmentally. In the archaeologist's mind's eye, the land of the past spreads out peopled with cultural groups, and telling of long-ago events and perhaps forgotten places that are fascinating if not in the same way as Tolkien's fictional Middle Earth. The past of North America that archaeologists seek is elusive because the archaeological record is incomplete, but it still can capture our curiosity. Unlike the world Tolkien describes, North America's past stretches over thousands of years during which landscapes and characters have changed again and again. Discovery of the evidence for even one small portion of this past can draw people into an endlessly intriguing intellectual exploration.

While we cannot claim Tolkien's gift for engaging description, this text provides archaeological glimpses of America's past. This chapter, as the second of our background chapters, provides specific information that will promote a better understanding of this continent's past. We have discussed some highlights of the nature and practice of North American archaeology; we now turn to what archaeologists and other scientists understand about the geography of the past, to archaeological conventions for talking about the past, and to the broad themes of North American archaeological research. This material is designed to help readers keep their bearings in the remaining chapters of this text.

NORTH AMERICAN CULTURE AREAS

As noted in Chapter 1, a culture area is a geographic area within which ethnic groups tend to have similar cultural traits. It has long been assumed that such areas result primarily from adaptation to similar environmental circumstances. Thus, culture areas tend to be closely related to physiographic regions within North America. For example, the Great Plains roughly corresponds to the Plains culture area recognized by anthropologists.

The concept of culture areas developed among North American anthropologists at the end of the nineteenth century as a means of organizing the large quantity of American Indian data that was being generated. Instead of arranging museum collections by the type of article being displayed, anthropologists wanted to use cultural information in grouping cultures together. Because it was then believed that American Indians did not have long histories, geographically based cultural areas made sense (Holmes 1914). Clark Wissler (1926) and Alfred Kroeber (1963) expanded on the concept by identifying centers from which cultural traits spread outward. Kroeber attempted to systematically define culture areas by using trait lists and examining similarity between groups of traits. Although originally ethnographic in nature, these areas have long been used by archaeologists for studying the past as well.

Thinking about Native Americans, whether past or present, in terms of culture areas has become convention because it is useful in describing diverse Indian cultures. We use them in this book for convenience in presenting the large amount of information we cover. The boundaries of culture areas are not rigidly fixed. Throughout history there have been contacts and influences across the boundaries between areas. Moreover, despite considerable similarity in cultural traits, the human groups located within a given culture area have differed as well. Cultural areas cannot be rigidly applied particularly when we extend them over time.

It is apparent by now that we use the terms "Indian" and "Native American" interchangeably. We also will use an array of tribal and archaeological culture names. Which terms are correct? Why are there multiple terms? Box 2.1 addresses these issues.

What Culture Areas Are Commonly Recognized?

Although various researchers have recognized slightly different culture areas for North America, today anthropologists commonly recognize ten areas (Figure 2.1). With a few exceptions, the chapters in this text correspond to these culture areas.

We combine discussion of two culture areas, the Arctic and Subarctic culture areas, including most of Canada and Alaska as well as Greenland, in Chapter 4. The division between these areas is essentially defined by the northerly extent of forests. These two culture areas encompass a very large region in which a variety of Eskimo and American Indian cultures were found at European contact. Traditionally, these people have supported themselves through hunting and collecting wild marine, riverine, and terrestrial resources. Arctic and Subarctic people were first contacted by the Norse about 1000 years ago, while the French, the British, and eventually Russians and Americans began arriving about 500 years ago. Especially in the interior and extreme north, traditional lifeways persisted into the twentieth century.

A third culture area, the Northwest Coast, is introduced in Chapter 5. This narrow culture area is located along the Pacific coast of North America from northern California to southern Alaska. Native peoples in this area long relied on the sea and on fish such as salmon that spawn in the area's rivers. They developed cultures that were complex economically, socially, and politically. Russian, Spanish, and British traders began to enter this culture area during the eighteenth century, and Americans followed in the nineteenth. These Europeans brought disease and considerable social disruption to the Native inhabitants. Historically, lumbering and fishing were important pursuits.

Inland from the Northwest Coast in both Canada and the United States, anthropologists have defined the Plateau culture area, which we discuss in Chapter 6. As in the culture areas mentioned already, people living here were hunter-gatherers who used a variety of resources including salmon, land mammals such as bison and elk, and roots. They developed a number of different cultural patterns, each of which shows the influence of an adjacent culture area. Plateau cultural groups were not contacted until Lewis and Clark passed through the region in 1805, but European diseases preceded actual European Americans by at least 25 years. British and a few

What Are You Called? Names and Politics

The name *Indian* comes from Columbus's search for a route to the Indies and his assumption that the people he encountered were "Indians." Many descendants of the people who were living in the Americas when Columbus bumped into the West Indies resent being called Indian. Some prefer to be designated Amerind, Native American, or First Nation (common in Canada). Others, however, find nothing offensive in the term "Indian." An elder from a southern California tribe expressed this when addressing the San Diego Archaeological Center Board. Paraphrasing, she said, "I've been an Indian for all of my 65 years. My father was an Indian and his father was an Indian. I don't know where you get off changing what we are called." Because there is no clear consensus, we shall generally use Native American, First Nation, or Indian.

Many living tribes have been called by names other than their own name for themselves. Explorers often assigned names to one tribe based on what other tribes called them rather than what they called themselves. The Spanish called the people living near the present town of Yuma, on the Colorado River, Yumans, apparently based on the name used by the Tohono O'odham. The "Yumans" called themselves Quechan and prefer to be called that today. The Tohono O'odham were called Papago for many years, based on the name the Spanish gave them. In Chapter 4, "Eskimo" is used sparingly because the people in Canada find that term offensive and prefer to be called Inuit. However, "Inuit" is not appropriate for all those formerly designated Eskimo, especially peoples of Alaska like the Yup'ik, who don't seem to be uncomfortable with the more general name.

Not only are Indians reclaiming their names for themselves, but they are also reclaiming their names for the landscape. Mt. McKinley is often referred to by its Koyukon Athabascan name, Denali, and the National Park that includes the mountain is also called Denali. In 2010 the Canadian government officially changed the name of Queen Charlotte Islands to Haida Gwaii, a name the Haida people had been using since the 1980s.

Not all tribes have reasserted their names for themselves, however. For example, the Navajo call themselves Diné, and many tribal offices use that name, but the official term is "the Navajo Nation."

In addition, some Native American groups express discomfort with what archaeologists call the archaeological groups they discuss. To be able to communicate with one another and with the public about what they are learning, archaeologists have had to devise names for ancient cultural traditions. For example, in the Southwest, we do not know what the people who built Cliff Palace at Mesa Verde, or Snaketown, in present-day Arizona, called themselves. As you will learn in Chapter 9, we commonly recognize four general, geographically distinct traditions—the Mogollon, the Patayan, the Hohokam, and the Anasazi. The name **Mogollon** comes from the Mogollon Mountains in New Mexico, and the mountains were named for a Spanish governor of the Province of New Mexico. **Patayan** comes from a Walapai word meaning "old people." "Hohokam," which comes from the Pima language, is said to refer to people who have disappeared or vanished. Emil Haury (1976:5) says his Pima workers explained to him that *hohokam* actually means "all used up." **Anasazi** is derived from a Navajo term that, like Hohokam and Patayan, was thought to mean old people or ancestors. Often "Anasazi" is translated as "enemy ancestors," an appellation some modern Pueblo people find offensive. **Ancestral Pueblo** has been offered as an alternative name, but this is not altogether satisfactory because the Mogollon also are almost certainly ancestral to at least some of the modern Pueblos. Since, however, most of the published literature still uses "Anasazi," we use the term sparingly, alongside "Ancestral Pueblo."

Throughout North America, there is an abundance of names and terms for the diverse peoples of the past as well as for their present-day descendants discussed in this text. It also is important to note that how we discuss the past, even beyond the names, can influence how we understand it. For instance if we describe people as having vanished and sites as abandoned, we tend to overlook the continuities with descendant populations that more nuanced vocabulary may enable. To learn about archaeology is to become familiar with many of these terms, and to develop sensitivity to the wishes of the descendants.

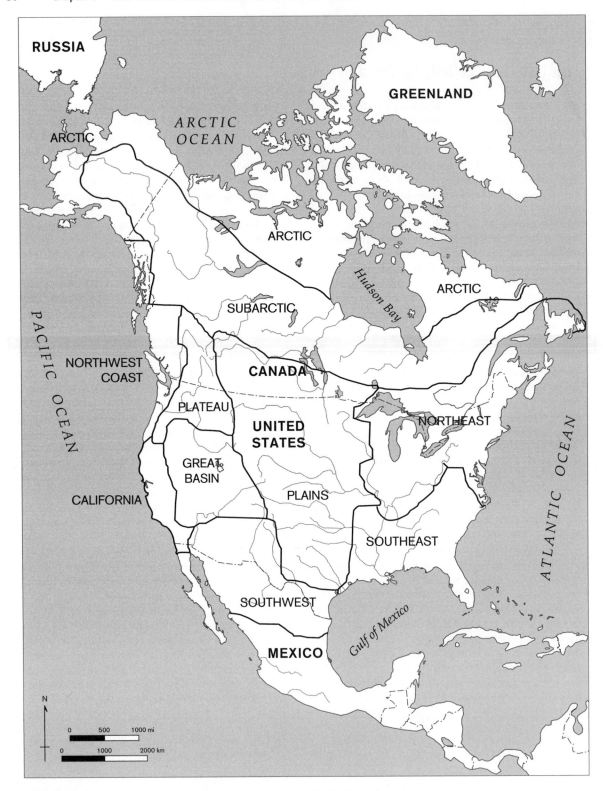

FIGURE 2.1 Ten culture areas have traditionally been recognized for North America.

American traders established themselves on the plateau as the nineteenth century progressed, and native groups eventually lost most of their land base.

Diversity in human adaptation was well developed in the **California culture area**, which includes a little of the northern part of Baja California as well as most of the present state of California. We discuss this area in Chapter 7, noting that while some people were organized into small groups of hunter-gatherers, fairly complex sociopolitical groups did develop, and some small-scale experimentation with horticulture occurred as well. Native Californians were first contacted by the Spanish in the sixteenth century, but the Spanish missions were not established until the eighteenth century. California was a province of Mexico for a short time during the nineteenth century and became part of the United States in 1848, when the famous gold rush developed. Russians also established trading posts in California. Each incoming group brought disease and serious cultural disruption to native populations. Particularly during the American period, native populations were annihilated and lifeways destroyed as miners and other settlers entered the area.

In Chapters 8 and 9, we discuss the two culture areas of the desert West. The first of these is the **Great Basin culture area**, which corresponds to the large area between the Sierra Nevada in eastern California and the Rocky Mountains. Environmentally, this area includes large deserts that are in some places interspersed with forested mountain ranges and lakes. Most Great Basin's inhabitants were hunter-gatherers, although some groups experimented with agriculture. Generally these cultural groups were not affected by European Americans until the middle of the nineteenth century, although trappers and traders had entered the area earlier. After this, fencing by ranchers as well as the construction of dams disrupted native subsistence practices significantly.

The second desert culture area is the **Southwest**, introduced in Chapter 9. Although deserts do occur here, the mountainous areas of the Southwest are relatively well watered and heavily forested. Many southwestern peoples developed agriculture, although most supplemented their subsistence with hunting and gathering. By the early sixteenth century, hunter-gatherers including ancestral Navajo and Apache had entered the northern Southwest area. Shortly thereafter, in the mid-sixteenth century, Spanish explorers arrived from Mexico and began establishing towns, forts, and missions. Although the Spanish were ousted in the 1680s by a native revolt, they returned before the end of the seventeenth century. During the nineteenth century, Mexico and then the United States took control. Historic period settlers were ranchers, farmers, and miners.

Chapter 10 introduces the **Plains culture area**, which extends through the midsection of North America from southern Canada all the way to central Texas. This vast area is grassland, although the topography and elevation, the amount of water, the types of grasses, and the animal resources available vary considerably. This area was home both to nomadic bison hunters and to more settled horticultural groups, who may have hunted bison seasonally or not at all. Spanish explorers first entered the southern Plains during the sixteenth century, while British fur traders came into the northern Plains. The biggest impact on Plains Indian lifestyles came from the reintroduction of the horse after European contact. Although horses had existed in North America, they became extinct by the end of the Pleistocene. Another important development was the spread of smallpox by the early 1800s, decimating Plains Indian populations, especially the less nomadic villagers of the river valleys. As American farmers and ranchers settled on the Plains, military conflicts developed between native populations and the settlers.

The ninth and tenth commonly identified culture areas are the **Southeast** and the **Northeast**, which encompass the Eastern Woodlands of the continent. These areas are discussed together in Chapters 11 and 12. Although hunter-gatherer as well as horticultural adaptations characterized residents of these regions, prior to the arrival of Europeans many of the people of the interior Eastern Woodlands were sedentary, and lived in complex polities with well-developed social hierarchies. The archaeological story of these peoples including those of southern Midwest and all but the coastal portions of the Southeast is the focus of Chapter 11. The de Soto expedition in the 1540s affected the balance of power among these groups and spread disease that decimated several formerly large Indian chiefdoms. Native populations were further disrupted as Europeans colonized these regions. After the passage of the **Indian Removal Act of 1830**, the Indians of these areas also were subject to forced removal, although some escaped into isolated areas. Europeans and Americans utilized the land of the Southeast to produce agricultural commodities for cash and export. Of course, this system was supported by a massive influx of African slaves. Even after the Civil War, much of this culture area remained agrarian.

The rest of the Eastern Woodlands including coastal areas, the northern Great Lakes region, the Mid-Atlantic, New England and the Canadian Maritime Provinces are covered separately in Chapter 12. Here mixed fishing, hunting, and gathering, and in some areas horticulture, usually formed the subsistence base. In some instances, sedentism, social ranking, and organization into complex polities developed, even where agriculture was not possible, but in others they did not. European fishermen were exploiting the waters off the Northeast coast even before 1500, but the people of these areas began to be affected by Spanish, French, British, and Dutch arrivals during the sixteenth century. Many native populations migrated, resettled, or were exterminated in wars and other conflicts. Nevertheless, native populations also remained on reservations within this area or assimilated into the general population of farmers and tradespeople, so that even here there is cultural continuity with the past. Eventually, parts of the Mid-Atlantic and New England became the center for much of the early industrial development in the United States.

NORTH AMERICAN ENVIRONMENTS

Biomes and Habitats

The concept of culture area subsumes both environmental and cultural attributes of geographic areas. Thus, before discussing archaeological concepts about culture, we must survey the diversity of North American environments. Kroeber (1963:13) argued that vegetation patterns provide the most useful basis for further understanding the environmental features of North American culture areas. We prefer a more ecological approach that focuses on interactions between physiography, vegetation, and animals. North America includes many diverse **habitats**. In the language of ecologists, a habitat is an area of land with physical characteristics that affect and are modified by living organisms such as plants and animals. **Communities** of interrelating plants and animals develop in habitats, and at the largest scale we call these aggregations of organisms **biomes**. Humans are both part of these biomes and users of the resources available in them. **Ecotones** are communities that are transitional between biomes or among their biotic communities. Archaeologists have been particularly interested in human association with ecotone communities, sometimes arguing that it is the high resource density and diversity of these regions that attract people to them.

Figure 2.2 shows the general location of the major North American biomes before historical times. This map assumes that it is possible to generalize about communities that develop when areas are left undisturbed for long periods of time. However, within these biomes, there always has been much local variation. Ecosystems also are dynamic and changing by their nature: plants and animals in biotic communities influence one another and can modify the characteristics of the community as a whole. Climatic change (see later

in this chapter) can affect environmental characteristics dramatically, but subtler interactions between species always are taking place.

Eight broad biomes are usually recognized within North America (Shelford 1963). The **tundra** is the treeless biome of the North American and European Arctic (Figure 2.3). In North America, tundra is found at latitudes 57° or more north, although it also is found in the northern Rocky Mountains above the **tree line**.

Forested biomes include the **coniferous forest** (Figure 2.4), a second biome of great areal extent in North America, stretching across Canada and extending southward into the United States in the continent's mountain chains. The **moist temperate forest biome** of the northern Pacific Coast also is dominated by coniferous trees, but ecologists consider this to be a separate, third biome. This biome is located at lower elevations than mountain coniferous forest and is adjacent to the Pacific coast extending from central California northward to southern Alaska.

Anotherforest biome, the **temperate deciduous forest biome** (Figure 2.5), is found south of the coniferous forest in most of the eastern part of the continent from the Great Lakes area to the Gulf of Mexico, including the northern two-thirds of the Florida Peninsula. It also extends from the Atlantic Ocean westward to the Mississippi River in the north and to the south, across it into the Ozark Mountains. Within this vast forested biome, there is much variation within forests, particularly as one travels from north to south.

Grasslands occur in North America at high elevations as alpine meadows above timberline, and they also occur as openings in the temperate deciduous forest. However, the greatest extent of grasslands on this continent is the **temperate grassland biome** that stretches from Alberta southward into northern Mexico and from the margins of the forest on the east all the way to the Rocky Mountains. Temperature extremes vary considerably within this vast grassland: only a few months of the year are frost free in the north, whereas there is no frost at all in the south. Rainfall also is variable within these grasslands, from about 40 inches (101.6 cm) annually in areas on the east to about 12 inches (30.5 cm) annually in the western regions. Importantly, except in the eastern portions, more precipitation evaporates annually than is acquired in rainfall. Thus, an important distinction can be made between the tall grass and mixed grassland from approximately longitude 100° west–east to the margins of the temperate deciduous forest and the short-grass grassland west from approximately the same longitude to the foot of the Rocky Mountains (Figure 2.6). Other areas of grassland occur west of the Rockies stretching to the coastal ranges in California, and a mesquite grassland occurs in southern Arizona, southern New Mexico, southwestern Texas, and portions of northern Mexico.

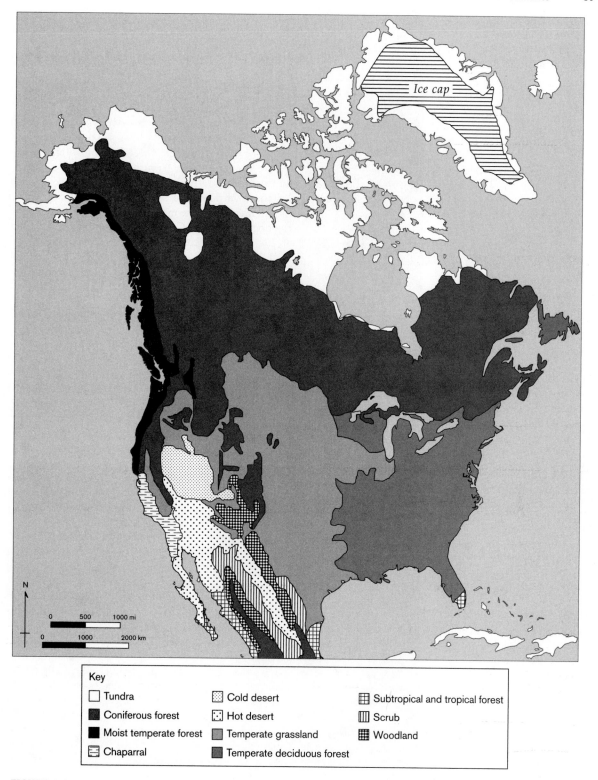

FIGURE 2.2 The major North American biomes before the Historic period.

FIGURE 2.3 Arctic tundra on Baffin Island. House remains are visible on the far side of the stream.

FIGURE 2.4 Coniferous forest covers vast portions of Canada and North America's mountains.

FIGURE 2.5 The temperate forest that covers much of the eastern part of North America contains many distinct forest communities. The pre-European climax forest in Pennsylvania would have had less brushy undergrowth than appears in this modern area of regrowth.

a

b

FIGURE 2.6 An important subdivision within North America's grasslands is between the (a) tall-grass prairie, found east of the 100th meridian, and (b) the short-grass areas that characterize the western Great Plains.

FIGURE 2.7 Chaparral covers these slopes, with riparian vegetation in the valley bottom and some pine trees in the distance.

There are three other large biomes of importance in North America. In northern Baja California, southern California, and north into central Oregon, biotic communities adapted to arid conditions are grouped into the **chaparral biome** (Figure 2.7). Both sclerophyll vegetation with thick, water-retaining leaves and woodland with grassy ground cover typify this biome. The biotic communities of the Great Basin in western Utah, most of Nevada, south central Oregon, southwestern Wyoming, and some of eastern California can be grouped together as the **cold desert biome** (Figure 2.8a). This area is a desert because much of the ground surface is bare, but it becomes cold in the winter, with mean January temperatures ranging between 29 and 39°F. In contrast the **hot desert biome** of North America is confined to the Southwest, California, and the states of northern Mexico (Figure 2.8b). These deserts have very hot summer temperatures, and rainfall ranges between 3.5 and 13 inches (8.9–33 cm) annually.

Other biomes and communities also occur in North America. These include a southern coniferous forest in the high mountains of northern Mexico, which is dominated by species of pine, and the subtropical and tropical forests in southern Florida. Communities representative of the latter biomes are found in areas that are close to sea level, receive at least 50 inches (127 cm) of rain annually, and very rarely experience frost.

It is also important to note that river systems are a major environmental feature on this continent. Figure 2.9 shows the major river drainages and lakes of North America, although there are many thousands of lakes smaller streams and lakes not shown. Keep in mind that plant and animal communities at the margins of rivers, streams, and lakes often are distinct. These are ecological edges in which plants and animals from several habitats are found. Of course, resources of the ocean are important environmental features of coastal environments. As in lake margins and river floodplains, a number of habitats may be found close together, adjacent to the ocean, giving the coast the high diversity and density of plants and animals that is found in ecological edges. On both the east and west coasts, **anadromous fish**, which seasonally spawn in fresh water but spend much of their lives in the ocean, were important additions to the available resource base. Examples of such fish are salmon, alewife, and smelt.

Finally, waterfowl migrations are an important seasonal feature in a number of areas of North America. We can recognize several major migratory flyways that bring birds south across much of North America in the winter and north again during the summer months. There is an east coast flyway, a Mississippi River flyway, a central flyway on the Plains, and a Pacific flyway that includes some parts of the Rocky Mountains. The numbers of birds that migrate through these pathways are monumental today and may have been greater in the past.

The Climate of North America

Climatologists also have developed a series of classifications for the North American continent. They base

a

b

FIGURE 2.8 The desert biomes of the American West include (a) the cold desert biome and (b) the hot desert biome.

these on empirical data concerning temperature and precipitation. The classifications recognize a number of climatic zones, including a polar zone far to the north, a boreal zone stretching across Canada and generally corresponding to the coniferous forest biome, a variety of temperate and dry zones in what today is the continental United States, as well as a subtropical humid zone in the Southeast.

Various airflows control North American climatic regimes (Lydolph 1985:203–209). An arctic airstream originates in the polar area and moves south into interior North America. A tropical airstream flows north into the United States. Meanwhile, the Pacific maritime airstream is characterized by a northern flow out of Asia and, south of this, an airflow from the subtropical eastern Pacific. The relative positions of these airstreams are responsible for climatic fluctuations on a seasonal and annual basis, although there also are upper airflows that affect North American weather (Figure 2.10).

The Rocky Mountain chain forms a more or less continuous north–south obstacle for air masses and is a

dominant feature in North American climate. East of the Rockies, air masses are not blocked by topography, and the climatic regime, based on seasonal variation in air mass dominance, is relatively simple (Bryson and Hare 1974). The amount of moisture generally decreases from the Atlantic Coast westward to the western portion of the Great Plains, which lie in the **rain shadow** of the Rocky Mountains. A boundary between humid and dry climates, mirrored in the distribution of tall-grass as opposed to short-grass prairies, can be recognized at approximately the 100th meridian. North of southern Saskatchewan and Alberta, where the grassland stops and coniferous forests begin, this distinction is not clear because of the cooler overall temperatures.

It is much more difficult to generalize about the climate of North America from the Rocky Mountains westward, as the various mountain ranges and the basins between them disrupt and affect air masses in complex ways. However, temperature and moisture are still largely affected by flows of cold air from the north and by warmer, westerly airflows that drive out

FIGURE 2.9 The many lakes, rivers, and other bodies of water as well as their shorelines of North America have always been important features of the resource base.

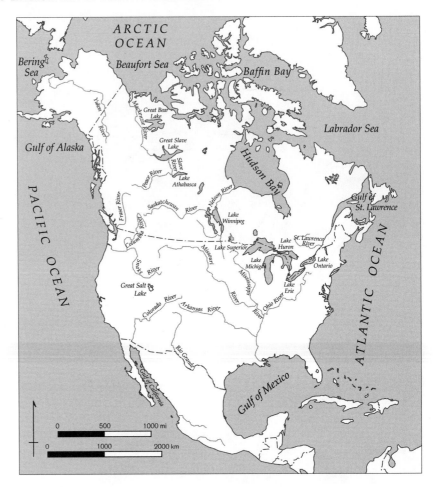

the cold air. The tropical airflow from the Gulf of Mexico tends to invade only the southern portions of the West in the summer months, when it brings much needed rainfall.

The west coast itself has a relatively mild, temperate climate even into southern British Columbia, where average January temperatures may be above freezing. More importantly, seasonal changes in temperature are less pronounced than in the rest of the continent because of the effects of ocean currents. However, there is a moisture gradient such that southern California is dry year-round and northern British Columbia and southern Alaska are wet year-round. In between, northern California is wet only in the winter, while Washington State and southern British Columbia are dry only in the summer (Bryson and Hare 1974:7–8).

This brief description of North American environment and climate provides an introduction to the continent's ecological diversity. Archaeologists are interested in this environmental information because it helps the contexts of human cultures over time and across space. Contemporary archaeologists use a variety of interdisciplinary methods to reconstruct past environments as discussed in Box 2.2.

Human Impact on North American Habitats and Landscapes

It is very common to think of North America prior to the arrival of Europeans as unspoiled, natural land. In this view, Euro-American culture is blamed for spoiling the vast wilderness of this continent. The biomes we have discussed, which Shelford (1963) argued were essentially pre-European, have undergone gradual environmental degradation culminating in the industrial period with massive pollution. However, the idea of a pristine pre-Columbian wilderness is not strictly accurate.

Native Americans should be seen not as passive constituents of the environment but as dynamic actors in past ecosystems. Archaeologists are increasingly aware of this latter point, but descriptions of native manipulation of plants, animals, and landscape are

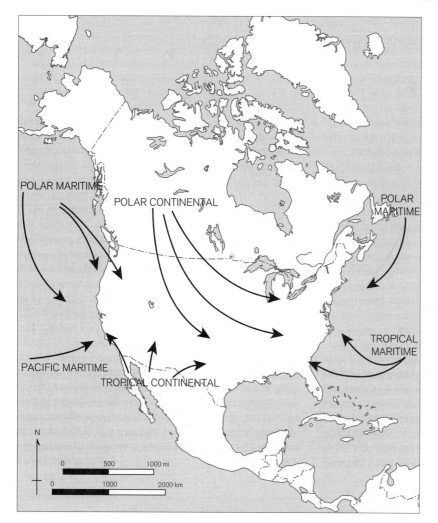

FIGURE 2.10 North America's climate is controlled largely by the airflows shown, which originate in polar regions, flow out of the tropics, or develop over the Pacific Ocean.

Is Environmental Reconstruction an Ancillary Study?

Most people think the central activities of archaeology are the excavation of sites and the interpretation of their artifacts; the reconstruction of hunting and butchering practices or the delineation of past environments is seldom seen as central to archaeology. This chapter's description of North American environmental features and climatic change may seem somewhat beside the point. As anthropologists, however, archaeologists today have a holistic interest in culture and behavior. Information about site distributions and material culture, is necessary to document the cultures and cultural

change in an area. In addition, however, we hope to reconstruct how people lived and why their behavior changed. Understanding the environmental context in which behavior occurred doesn't explain everything about culture change, but it does provide one important perspective on human behavior.

Thus, archaeological interest in human subsistence and in human interactions with plants, animals, and landscapes has developed directly out of the desire to know how people actually lived in the past. Mid-twentieth-century developments in anthropological theory, especially in

cultural ecology, the study of interactions between human societies and ecosystems, also have been influential. The result is that contemporary archaeology is hardly ever just about sites, features, and artifacts. Ecofacts are just as important. The analysis of subsistence remains is a normal part of excavation projects, as is the delineation of the geological setting of sites and local environmental features. Today's archaeological undertaking is likely to be highly interdisciplinary, involving specialists with expertise in geology, botany, zoology, and other sciences. Some of these specialists have their primary training in archaeology, while others have specialized in a related science such as geology.

The various interdisciplinary fields are covered in courses in archaeological methods. We mention a few fields here. First, **palynology** is important to reconstructing past environments. Palynologists study fossil pollen extracted from soil samples collected at archaeological sites or at other locations where sediments are known to be old. Ideally, they sample locations in which pollen has been deposited year after year for long periods of time and for which **stratigraphy** can provide temporal information. On the basis of counts of pollen grains of various types, palynologists reconstruct the plant life of a region at a given time in the past. Since the distance that pollen grains are likely to travel and the amount of pollen produced vary among plants, interpretation can be a complicated matter.

Geoarchaeologists also can contribute to the reconstruction of environment. These archaeologists reconstruct the depositional characteristics of sites and identify the natural processes involved in site formation by evaluating sediments and stratigraphy. This kind of research cannot help but aid in the reconstruction of past environments. For example, knowing whether sediments were deposited by wind or by water provides important information about an area's environmental history.

Ethnobotanists, who study plant remains from archaeological sites, and **zooarchaeologists** (Figure 2.11), who study animal remains from archaeological sites (see Student CD, Section D.6), are concerned both with reconstructing human subsistence and diet and with interpreting past environmental conditions. Because the plant and animal parts recovered from excavations represent species with habitat preferences, their presence in a collection can be considered evidence of those habitats in the vicinity of a site. For example, the presence of hickory nut shells and wild turkey bones in an archaeological site most likely indicates that mixed deciduous

forests were present nearby. It is also true, of course, that some plants and animals are traded into an area, and in any given area, humans select only some of the species for use.

A wide variety of other indicators also can provide environmental clues. For example, the varying widths of tree rings indicate changes in moisture and temperature, and **packrat middens**, the accumulations left where packrats have hoarded food, provide a partial list of plant species in the immediate area. In addition, tiny land snails, which are very sensitive to microenvironmental factors such as vegetation and moisture, can be found in sediment columns, providing important information. Archaeologists also can reconstruct vegetation by studying hard, nearly indestructible silica particles found in plant cells. These particles, called **opal phytoliths**, have distinctive shapes, which can, in many cases, be used to identify the plant from which they came. Unfortunately, this kind of study is complicated because a single plant species can produce phytoliths of different kinds in different parts of its structure.

All these interdisciplinary methods make important contributions to contemporary North American archaeology. Although they are sometimes called "ancillary studies," with the implication that they are supplementary to the main archaeological analyses, it is difficult to imagine modern archaeologists being able to investigate the myriad subjects that interest them without data from such research. Arguably, the palynologist, geoarchaeologist, ethnobotanist, or zooarchaeologist is as important to archaeological research today as the lithic or ceramic analyst. Together, teams of archaeologists build a more complete understanding of the past than would be possible for any researcher alone.

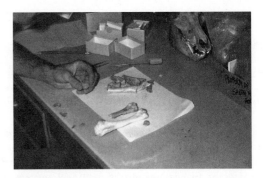

FIGURE 2.11 A zooarchaeologist compares a turkey bone fragment with a comparative specimen that is complete, while other fragments of bone from the same provenience remain be identified.

not commonly available outside anthropology and geography. Nonindustrial people can modify their environments by clearing land for houses and villages, burning vegetation to promote the growth of seed plants or to promote suitable browse for large mammals, and overhunting certain species of game, causing their disappearance. Gradual deforestation of land as wood for fuel is acquired, terracing of fields to promote water retention, and irrigating of land to improve the water supply to cultivated crops are other practices that alter the habitat. The North American ethnographic and archaeological records document the existence of these and other practices among Native Americans (Doolittle 2000; Minnis and Elisens 2000). Moreover, Native Americans should not be understood simplistically as people who lived in harmony with their environment. This is a modern myth, which serves us in critiquing the dominant American society; it is a contemporary version of the "noble savage" image (Krech 1999).

Nevertheless, pre-Columbian modifications of the landscape were very different from those that occurred after European contact. As ecological historians (e.g., Cronon 1983; Crosby 1994; Silver 1990) remind us, the ecological consequences of European arrival were complex. Europeans did not simply deforest the land or deplete populations of beaver; they brought different systems of living on the land, which changed habitat distributions subtly at first, and later dramatically. Whereas Indians often affected the landscape in ways that promoted certain species of animals and plants or certain habitat types, like old field habitats left by shifting cultivators, some European settlers, from their first arrival, looked at North America in terms of the commodities it provided rather than as a place to subsist. The establishment of the fur trade, the concept of permanent rather than shifting cultivation of fields, and the relatively rapid depopulation of native settlements were among the many factors that worked together to transform the aboriginal landscape in colonial times. Eventually, of course, the shift from an agrarian to an industrial economy, accompanied by major increases in human population size, had dramatic impacts on North American habitats. Lumbering, the growth of a variety of industries, the impoundment of rivers, the growth of cities, and many other factors must be considered in any environmental history of this continent.

Paleoclimatic Change

Because cultural change may result from environmental change, archaeologists must consider the role of climatic change in the composition of North American habitats. The most significant climatic change with continent-wide effects was the **Pleistocene** or Ice Age. In popular movies, the Ice Age is depicted with vast expanses of ice and snow, large and fearsome animals like mammoths and saber-toothed cats, and humans who huddle under skins in caves and rockshelters sometimes venturing out at great risk to hunt mighty beasts. The reality was that the environment was highly variable during the Pleistocene, as were human adaptations to it. Many parts of North America were not glaciated at all; but, nonetheless, the Pleistocene biotic communities may have been quite different from those we can observe today. A good understanding of North America's Ice Age environments is important to archaeologists because this is when humans first entered the continent. The Pleistocene usually is dated from 1.8 million until approximately 10,000 years ago, but human entry into the Americas does not seem to have occurred until the end of this epoch, within the last 25,000 years or less.

During the Pleistocene epoch, large, thick glaciers expanded southward over much of the Northern Hemisphere. However, within the Pleistocene, there were major fluctuations in climate. Parts of the Pleistocene that were colder are called **glacials**, and parts that were warmer are called **interglacials**. Periods of glaciation within the Pleistocene are given different names in Europe and in the United States. In North America, the last period of glaciation is called the **Wisconsin glaciation**. It is believed to have begun before 100,000 years ago and to have ended around 10,000 years ago. However, the exact timing is complicated to reconstruct, and understanding remains incomplete (Pielou 1991). The climatic and geologic epoch following the Pleistocene, which began 10,000 years ago and continues in the present, is called the **Holocene**. Many scientists have made the point that the Holocene is not much different in warmth, or so far in length, from one of the interglacials that have occurred at other points in the Pleistocene. This means that, hard as it is to imagine, the Ice Age may not be over at all!

During the cold peaks of the Ice Age, the outline of the North American continent was different. The massive glaciers that formed during the Ice Age captured enough of the earth's water to lower the level of the oceans, exposing areas of land, now under water (Figure 2.12). For example, a large area of dry land, called **Beringia**, connected Siberia and Alaska during the Ice Age. Different land configurations affected ocean currents and the gradients of rivers, resulting in significant habitat change. Other changes were more subtle. Normally, rain and snow that is absorbed into rivers and lakes eventually returns to the oceans, but during the Pleistocene this water remained trapped in the ice of glaciers, changing the ratio between two

FIGURE 2.12 During the Pleistocene, massive ice sheets covered much of North America. This map shows the continent as the Cordilleran and Laurentian ice sheets began to part. Now-submerged areas of Beringia and the coastlines were exposed at this time (after Meltzer 1993:13).

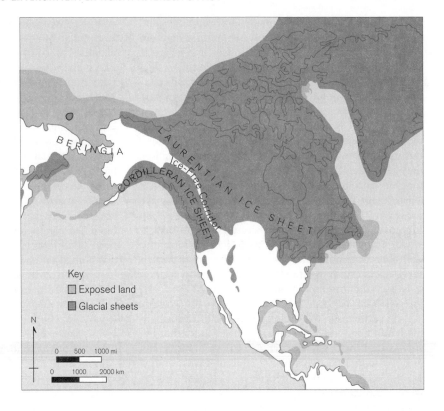

forms, or isotopes, of the oxygen in the oceans' waters. Thus in comparison to the atmosphere, seawater contains proportionately more of the heavier isotope, ^{18}O, than of the more common form of oxygen, ^{16}O. The capture of rain and snow in glaciers prevents the oxygen contained in these waters from returning to the oceans and rebalancing the isotopic. This means that an indirect measure of the degree of glaciation is the ratio between the isotopes ^{18}O and ^{16}O found in the contents of ocean sediments (Bennett and Glasser 1996:13–14).

At the peak of the Wisconsin glaciation, nearly 20,000 years ago, the combined ice sheets were much greater in extent than those in Europe, covering an area about the size of Antarctica. However, much of Alaska was not glaciated during the Ice Age. Warm ocean currents from the south kept coastal and interior Beringia free of ice. Farther south, there were two North American ice sheets during the Wisconsin glaciation (Figure 2.12). One of these, the **Cordilleran ice sheet**, expanded over the northern Rocky Mountains, while the second, the **Laurentian ice sheet**, formed to the east over Hudson Bay and eastern Canada. These ice sheets formed when the snow that fell during the winter failed to melt away during the summer, and as this happened year after year, the snow was compacted into ice. However, over time ice domes

built up at the center of the ice sheet and squeezed the underlying ice outward, causing growth in the ice sheet's areal extent. If the sheet reached a region in which summers were warm enough to melt the ice at the glacial margins, the spread of the glacier stopped. Thus, as temperatures fluctuated during the Wisconsin glaciation, the edge of the ice sheets advanced and retreated. These ice sheets sometimes touched and, when the glaciers shrunk, sometimes were separated. Refugia, where animals and plants adapted to nonglacial climates survived, also probably existed along both coasts throughout the Wisconsin glaciation.

During the Ice Age the biomes of North America generally were shifted southward. However, because of the complexity of temperature fluctuations and of ice sheet advances and retreats, there is room for debate about what vegetation looked like on a local level. Much of the area immediately in front of the ice must have been characterized by **permafrost** and tundra vegetation. However, evidence suggests that in some places coniferous forest also existed (Pielou 1991:84). Different biotic communities probably filled adjacent areas in a kind of patchwork. Dryness most likely prevented the development of forests in most areas of the western part of North America, except for a narrow area just south of the ice. Mammoths, mastodons, dire wolves, and saber-toothed cats were only some of the now extinct Ice Age mammals that roamed North America. As today, the biotic communities of the Pleistocene were so diverse, and interrelated in such complex ways, that they are best discussed at the local level.

Archaeologists have been very interested in what happened environmentally as the ice began to shrink because there were most certainly populations of human foragers in North America at this time. Several millennia of warming during which there were glacial retreats and advances preceded the recognized Pleistocene–Holocene boundary at around 10,000 years ago. As the ice melted, sea levels rose; but at first the great ice sheets decreased in thickness rather than extent. This meant that for a time, as coastlines were drowned, the area of ice-free land in North America actually got smaller (Pielou 1991:167). Another aspect of postglacial change was that as the thickness of the ice decreased, the earth's crust that had warped under the weight of massive layers of ice began to rebound. This resulted in an **isostatic** change in which the land rose in relation to the sea. Since, however, this process of rebounding took some time, when the ice first melted, the exposed land surface was actually lower than sea level in some places. Thus, the ocean flooded these areas, forming large inland seas such as in the valley of the St. Lawrence River. Large proglacial lakes also formed in the middle of the North American continent as the Cordilleran and Laurentian ice sheets receded. For example, the Laurentian ice sheet shrank toward the east northeast, but the elevation of the Great Plains rose toward the west, as it still does today. This pattern of shrinkage and elevation meant that the large volume of water melting off the glacier sometimes became trapped between the ice edge and the rising land. In other areas, meltwaters cut massive river channels for the drainage of the proglacial lakes.

The Beringian land bridge was progressively submerged and the Bering Strait widened as the ice melted. As this happened, the climate of the land on either side became moister and milder, and the vegetation changed from arctic herbs and low grasses to a more shrubby tundra dominated by dwarf and shrub birches. The largest animals, such as the mammoths and bison of Ice Age Beringia, were reduced in numbers, but elk and other species that could adapt their diets to eating the shrubs flourished. Along the coast, sea mammals migrated northward, and conditions improved for humans (Pielou 1991:208–210). There were actually many migrations of animal and plant species at this time. Overall, the transformation as climate warmed was more complicated than just a northward shifting of biomes. Forest composition as well as location changed after the Pleistocene; in fact, in some places several communities developed in succession (Pielou 1991:229–232).

If you live in a part of North America that was glaciated, you probably know that many glacial features are still present on the landscape. These features affect the modern environment in many ways. For example, in much of the Upper Midwest, there are numerous **kettle holes** or lakes, where stagnant ice blocks were left isolated, eventually becoming overlain and surrounded by glacial deposits of various sorts. When the ice finally melted, a depression was formed that has filled with water. These kettle lakes often are associated with **glacial kames**, which are mounds and ridges that represent deposition of outwash from melting glaciers. This topography influences the biotic communities that develop. For example, landscapes dotted with small lakes and kames have a great deal of ecological diversity.

During the Holocene, climate has not remained constant either. A particularly important climatic interval during the mid-Holocene is called the **Hypsithermal Interval**, or sometimes the **Altithermal**. This was a period of warmer and, in some places, drier climate than we have today. The Hypsithermal lasted at least 3000 years, and in the center of North America it peaked about 7000 years ago. In general, biotic communities shifted northward or upward in elevation during the Hypsithermal. However, there is some variation in the timing of the Hypsithermal, and not surprisingly there also are regional differences in the precise effects.

A second climatic episode that has interested North American archaeologists is the **Little Ice Age**. Climate began to deteriorate after 650 years ago, but the coldest period from 400 to 100 years ago (AD 1550–1850) profoundly affected cultural events in Europe (see Brian Fagan 1999). North American archaeologists also have sought connections among changing human settlement patterns, subsistence practices, and the Little Ice Age. In reality, small oscillations in climate have been occurring throughout the Holocene. Just prior to the Little Ice Age, there was a warm period, sometimes called the Medieval Warm period because it stretched between AD 900 and 1300. Although not as profound as the Hypsithermal, its changes certainly did affect North American environments.

Events like El Niño and La Niña are alterations in climate on an even smaller scale. El Niño and La Niña (more formally, the El Niño Southern Oscillation, or ENSO) are an interannual oscillation in which the atmosphere and the ocean of the tropical Pacific interact and affect the climate of large portions of the globe including North America. During El Niño years, conditions in the southern United States are wetter than normal, but conditions in western Canada and the northwest and north central United States are drier. In La Niña years, the reverse conditions prevail, so that the southern United States is dry and the northwest and north central parts of the continent are wet (D'Aleo 2002). A weaker North Atlantic Oscillation may affect the northeastern parts of North America (Fagan 1999).

There is much to consider about past environments, but this brief introduction may help explain the fascination some archaeologists have with the environmental context for the sites they study. As introduced earlier, one of the interdisciplinary fields that contributes to this understanding is geoarchaeology. In Profile 2.1, we describe a career in this type of archaeology.

FACES IN ARCHAEOLOGY   PROFILE 2.1

Julie Stein, Archaeologist and Geoarchaeologist

Julie Stein (Figure 2.13) is an archaeologist whose interests have led her into the interdisciplinary field of geoarchaeology. Convinced that archaeologists need to better understand sediments and stratigraphy, Stein has done much to make geoarchaeology more widely appreciated. She is a professor of anthropology at the University of Washington in Seattle though her career has included stints as curator of archaeology and executive director at the Burke Museum of Natural History and as divisional dean of research for the College of Arts and Sciences. In 1999, she received the Rapp Award from the Geological Society of America (GSA) for her contributions to the field of geoarchaeology.

As an undergraduate at Western Michigan University, Stein pursued anthropology, but while taking her first archaeological field school in 1972, she discovered her passion when she realized how the beach deposits and glacial tills containing the site being excavated fascinated her. After discussions with her introductory geology professor, she began to identify a way to combine both

geology and archaeology. As she tells it, it was her undergraduate professors' insistence that she attend the meetings of the GSA that really helped her define professional goals. At the GSA Stein discovered she wasn't the only one to see the potential of combining archaeology and geology. She was able to meet many of the small group of geologists and archaeologists developing the field of geoarchaeology at that time.

Eventually, Stein was offered a three-year fellowship in an interdisciplinary graduate program at the University of Minnesota. Although her master's thesis was a geoarchaeological study at a Bronze Age site in Greece, she was most interested in North American archaeology. Thus, for her doctorate, she became involved with the Shell Mound Archaeological Project (SMAP), which was then exploring shell mounds located along the Green River in Kentucky. Stein may be best known for her work on the cultural and noncultural histories of **shell middens** in Kentucky and, later, along the Northwest Coast. *Deciphering a Shell Midden* (Stein 1992) is a basic reference for archaeologists working in this kind of context.

Stein received her doctorate in 1980 and began an appointment at the University of Washington. At a time when geoarchaeology was marginal, she persuaded faculty at the University of Washington that her geoarchaeological expertise would be an asset to the school's program in anthropology and archaeology. Since then, geoarchaeology has become more mainstream within archaeology.

Throughout more than 20 years at the University of Washington, Stein has remained an advocate for the importance of geoarchaeology. She has been active in professional societies in both archaeology and geology, and she helped found the Geoarchaeology Interest Group of the Society for American Archaeology. Included in her list of research consultations is work in Peru, Belize, and the Marianas, but most of her research has been in North America. Besides continuing work on shell mounds in various locations, Stein has consulted with both historic and prehistoric archaeologists working at Monticello in

FIGURE 2.13 Julie Stein.

Virginia, at Cape Addington in Alaska, and at Fort Jefferson, Wickliffe Mounds, and Big Bend in Kentucky; she has even helped look for Lewis and Clark's privies in Oregon.

Closer to home, she has developed expertise in Northwest Coast archaeology, directing a series of excavations in the San Juan Islands. Among these, her Vashon Island Project was noteworthy for its involvement of the public. Her most recent project, with graduate student Amanda Taylor, has dated the occupational history of 80 shell midden sites on islands off the coast of Washington. It took years of perseverance and countless talks at community centers and small historical museums to obtain permissions from sixty landowners, Washington State's Office of Archaeology and Historic Preservation, and Native American tribes. The resulting radiocarbon dates allow archaeologists to at long last address significant questions about the rise of social complexity and territoriality. The key to this research was using shell instead of charcoal, made possible because Stein and others calculated the fluctuating marine correction factor using paired shell and charcoal dates. Determining when people occupied various islands has taken over 10 years, but these data are invaluable. Stein also was asked to analyze the sediments adhering to the Kennewick skeletal remains, which are among the oldest human remains in North America (see "Why Is the Kennewick Case So Significant?" in Section F.4 on the Student CD).

Stein has put much energy into teaching and mentoring students, but she also has been deeply involved in the proper curation of the Burke Museum's archaeological collections, including many collections the museum was maintaining for the National Park Service and tribes in the region. She believes that the skills she developed as an interdisciplinary archaeologist have paid off for her as an administrator. Recently, Stein has become the Executive Director of the museum. This new position allows her to focus on the meaning and goals of natural history museums in the twenty-first century. Communities are asking museums to use the collections in new and innovative ways, as well as for exhibits and programs that bring us together so we can learn from one another. Today, Stein's expertise as a geologist, her experience with public archaeology, and her classroom teaching experience allow her to communicate across these diverse audiences as she faces the challenges of being a natural history museum director.

THE SYSTEMATICS OF NORTH AMERICAN CULTURE HISTORY

Now that you know something about North American environment and climate, we can discuss systematics, that is, the classificatory schemes and conceptual units that archaeologists use to study past cultures. Thus far we have introduced only one concept that is in wide use—the concept of culture areas. This concept, however, does not incorporate information about temporal change. Cultural change is a topic of great interest to archaeologists. This has been true especially since the early part of the twentieth century, when a **culture history** paradigm developed in archaeology (see Student CD, Section A). Culture history is the ordering of artifacts and other cultural phenomena into a sequence over time and in space. However, it is more than a simple chronology. Culture history offers an account of how cultural phenomena have changed. Prior to the early twentieth century, North American archaeologists did not articulate this goal very clearly because they assumed that there was little time depth to human occupation of this continent. However, as more was learned, delineating culture history became an important focus of archaeological work. Although in the latter part of the twentieth century, archaeologists rejected the notion that cultural historical formulation was the ultimate goal of archaeology, an area's culture history remains the baseline from which other questions about the past can be addressed.

To construct culture histories, archaeologists need units of analysis with which to order cultural items. For example, archaeologists group the artifacts they find into types based on a set of attributes that they consider important (see Student CD, Section B). These attributes may be stylistic/morphological, functional, or technological. For the construction of culture history, archaeologists construct **temporal types** that are believed to have temporal significance. In a sense, these types are like **index fossils** in paleontology. Their presence is indicative of a particular time frame during which they are known to have been made by a particular cultural group. The temporal meaning of these types is determined through stratigraphic analysis, direct dating, and comparison with other sites of known age. For example, imagine future archaeologists finding iPods at several sites. Once they had determined that this item of material culture wasn't associated with contexts that predate the twenty-first century, they would be able to use the presence of iPods as an indicator of when sites were inhabited.

After types having temporal significance have been identified, patterning and clustering of types is examined. In this work, archaeologists try to separate sites into **components** by using **stratification** or other indicators. A component is a culturally unique part of a particular site, often thought to represent a single occupation by a group of people or at least repeated occupations by the same social group. Some sites have only one component; others have many. The assemblage of artifacts from each component can then be assumed to represent a distinct community's activities at a particular point in time.

Comparisons of assemblages provide an understanding of patterning in space and time, allowing for a regional perspective on culture history. A **phase** is a grouping of similar components at multiple sites in a region. Types of artifacts, features, the spatial plan, and other attributes of these components are similar. Yet they also are distinct from the characteristics of other components elsewhere. The relationships between phases, sites, and components are illustrated in Figure 2.14. The phase is the basic unit of regional archaeological analysis, corresponding loosely to a culture. Archaeologists try to assign assemblages from various sites to one phase or another, and thus place them in regional cultural history.

Sometimes archaeologists also want to link phases or types that seem to be related. American archaeologists use two terms, **horizon** and **tradition**, to make such linkages. As initially defined, the horizon marks traits and assemblages whose distribution in space suggests a rapid spread over a broad area (Willey and Phillips 1958:33). In contrast, traditions have to do primarily with temporal continuity in technology or material culture (Willey and Phillips 1958:37).

These units of classification allow archaeologists to construct regional culture histories. But what about broader, continent-wide patterns in North America's past? Similarities in traditions and horizons may indicate some pre-Columbian evolutionary stages (Willey and Phillips 1958). A **culture stage** is a general level of cultural development as defined by formal attributes. The focus in stage definition has been on technological and economic aspects of cultural development. Traditionally, for all of the Americas, five basic stages have been suggested for pre-Columbian times. These were the Lithic stage, for which stone tools were the main evidence; the preceramic hunting and gathering Archaic stage; the Formative stage, in which agriculture and social ranking first appeared; the Classic stage, when the first American civilizations appeared, and the post-Classic stage after the collapse of these first civilizations. Only the first three stages have been considered evident in North America, while the Classic and post-Classic have been applied to civilizations that developed in Mesoamerica and South America.

Archaeologists still use these designations to refer to North American culture history to some extent. However, the idea that broad patterns of cultural evolution can be found across the continent is no longer widely accepted. First, there is now so much variation evident in the cultural sequences known for North America, that reference to such patterns seems to obscure more than it clarifies. In addition, theoretical support for once popular neo-evolutionary models has lessened (see Student CD, Section A). Contemporary archaeologists prefer to use periods of time to subdivide the long record of humans in North

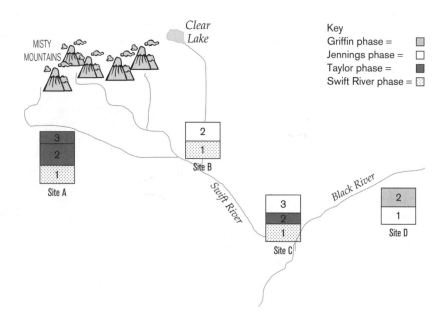

FIGURE 2.14 Hypothetical map illustrating the relationships between components and phases for four excavated sites with various components numbered 1, 2, or 3 at each site and shaded to indicate the regional phase (Griffin, Jennings, Taylor, or Swift River) to which each component has been assigned.

America. Instead of the Lithic stage, archaeologists now more commonly recognize a **Paleoindian period** in which the first human cultures developed and flourished in North America. These first inhabitants of North America were hunter-gatherers who used stone and bone tools to acquire and process the wild resources available throughout the continent. Arguing against a continent-wide stage, however, there may have been great variation in how mobile people were, in the types of wild resource they utilized, and even in their social organization. This period begins when humans first settled in North America and extends to approximately 10,000 years ago. As we will discuss in Chapter 3, when the Americas were settled and by whom is a matter of great debate. In addition, the end of this period varies a little among culture areas. Some archaeologists, like Bob Kelly (highlighted in Profile 2.2), are particularly interested in Paleoindians, and throughout the continent fascinating new data are emerging.

FACES IN ARCHAEOLOGY

PROFILE 2.2

Robert Kelly, Archaeologist and Professor

Like many archaeologists, Bob Kelly (Figure 2.15) is fascinated by hunter-gatherers. He has studied archaeologically known **foragers** and conducted ethnoarchaeological research among living foragers.

Bob Kelly has been interested in archaeology for as long as he can remember. As a child growing up in New England, he loved Sir Leonard Wooley's book *The Young Archaeologist*. He also loved the outdoors, and during the early days of the environmental movement in the 1960s, he imagined a kinship with those who lived off the land, especially American Indians. This encouraged Kelly's interest in the past people of North America, and when he learned of a scholarship in 1973 to participate in an archaeological excavation, he jumped at the chance to apply. He was awarded the scholarship, and that summer, at 16, he participated in his first excavation, at Gatecliff Shelter (see "Deep-Site Excavation at Gatecliff Shelter, Nevada" by David Hurst Thomas in Chapter 8). He returned several times to the Gatecliff excavation, and his pursuit of archaeology as a career was determined.

After only three years in high school, Kelly entered Cornell University where he studied anthropology and archaeology. He continued to work in the Great Basin, serving as a field supervisor on various projects. He excavated shell middens and burials mounds on St. Catherines Island, Georgia, and spent a semester excavating an Inca site in Chile. After graduating in 1978, Kelly went to the University of New Mexico for his master's degree and then in 1980 to the University of Michigan for his doctorate, which he earned in 1985. Throughout his graduate work, he focused on the archaeology of Great Basin hunter-gatherers. His dissertation research, funded by the American Museum of Natural History, explored the subsistence and settlement patterns of western Nevada's Carson Sink and Stillwater Mountains through survey and excavation.

Since graduate school, Kelly's career has taken a traditional academic track. He taught briefly at Colby College in Maine before moving to the University of Louisville in Kentucky, where he taught between 1986 and 1997. At Louisville, he had a heavy academic load, teaching classes on archaeological methods, North American archaeology, Native Americans, hunter-gatherer ecology, and both cultural and physical anthropology as well as archaeological field school. Kelly also shouldered major administrative responsibilities, serving his department as coordinator of the archaeology program and, for five years, as chair. Kelly spent the 1988–1989 academic year on a research fellowship at the School of Advanced

FIGURE 2.15 Bob Kelly doing archaeological fieldwork.

Research in Santa Fe, New Mexico. Out of this research came his book *The Foraging Spectrum* (1995), which explores both anthropological theory about foragers and the diversity of hunter-gatherer behavior, exploding many stereotypes in the process. A second edition is now in the works.

That work interested Kelly in researching foragers ethnographically. In addition, he was looking for an opportunity to do fieldwork with his wife, cultural anthropologist Lin Poyer. The opportunity arose during the summers of 1993, 1994, and 1995, when the two collaborated on ethnoarchaeological work among the Mikea in Madagascar, maize and manioc horticulturalists and seasonal foragers. This fieldwork was continued by Bram Tucker, then a graduate student from the University of North Carolina and now a professor at the University of Georgia.

A move to the University of Wyoming in 1997 gave Kelly more opportunity to pursue his archaeological interests, this time on the High Plains and in the Rocky Mountains. While his teaching load was reduced, he still served as department head for four years, and in 2000 and 2003 as president-elect and then president of the Society for American Archaeology. As mentioned earlier (see Lynne Sebastian, Profile 1.2), this professional service position is a sign of high professional stature but demands much time and energy. Here he experienced new aspects of archaeology, working on a controversial court case concerning Paleoindian skeletal remains, the effect of the World Trade Center disaster on archaeology (there were large collections in one of the subbasements, and the SAA offered its help in the recovery of human remains), and the effect of the war in Iraq on antiquities.

Currently, Kelly is concentrating on Paleoindian foragers at the Pleistocene–Holocene boundary. He has reinvestigated the Pine Spring site, where archaeological work in the 1960s had suggested that there were Paleoindian materials in association with extinct fauna. He has also studied rockshelters in Wyoming's Bighorn Mountains to understand why the fluted points associated with earlier Paleoindians (see Chapter 3) are rarely found in North American rockshelters. That work has led to an interest in climate change and human population dynamics. Bob Kelly's successful balancing act incorporating teaching, research, and service exemplifies the academic path in archaeology. His consistent fascination with hunter-gatherers, in both the past and present, also illustrates that archaeologists are anthropologists. In both ways, his career provides an important perspective on contemporary North American archaeologists.

An Archaic stage may be recognized by archaeologists, but most also have ceased to treat this as a formal stage (Emerson and McElrath 2009). Like Paleoindians, Archaic cultures had hunter-gatherer economies, although these postglacial ones may have been more centered on the use of a broad variety of resources in a local area (Figure 2.16). Originally, the Archaic was distinguished from the later Formative by what was missing from the Archaic. Cultural traits that were absent were agriculture, settled villages, burial mounds or earthworks, and pottery, all of which were associated with Formative cultures. However, we now know that each of these traits was not entirely absent among people considered Archaic. In addition, in some parts of North America, people never developed agriculture but did become sedentary villagers, with social and economic differentiation. On the other hand, in the Great Basin and in many parts of the Subarctic, where people almost always lived in small foraging bands, the entire cultural sequence after Paleoindians can be considered Archaic. These exceptions make it difficult to talk about a continent-wide Archaic stage, and indeed, the variability among Archaic Societies apparently was great (Emerson et al. 2009). The now more commonly designated **Archaic period** follows the Paleoindian, beginning about 10,000 years ago and extending until between 3000 and 2000 years ago. You will see some variation in this date range as we discuss each culture area, and along the Pacific Coast, the term Archaic often is not used at all.

North American archaeologists generally do not use the concept of a Formative stage. West of the Rockies, except in the Southwest culture area among people like the Hohokam discussed in Chapter 1's case study, agriculture did not play a major economic role. However, settled life and the development of social hierarchies often did. Along the Pacific Coast, **complex hunter-gatherers**, who developed social ranking, had hereditary chiefs, and lived in large, settled communities, are found in the later pre-Columbian times. Here archaeologists are far more likely to simply designate Early, Middle, and Late periods, abandoning the traditional terminology altogether. East of the Rocky Mountains, archaeologists generally designate a **Woodland period** beginning between 3000 and 2000 years ago. Woodland variants have been recognized in the Plains, Midwest, Great Lakes, Northeast, Mid-Atlantic, and Southeast culture areas.

Still more recent settled agriculturalists, including the Mississippians of the Midwest and the Southeast, the Iroquoians of the Northeast, and the Plains Village groups of the Missouri River valley were farmers who

FIGURE 2.16 Artist's conception of life during the Middle Archaic at the Black Earth site in southern Illinois, showing the broad range of food items (deer, turtle, fish, crayfish, nuts, and water lily roots) utilized by Archaic people.

lived in settled villages, although their sociopolitical organization varied. Convention is to separate these cultural phenomena from Woodland complexes. The later groups are sometimes called **Late Prehistoric**, but generally they are simply referred to by their culture name directly.

Of course, European exploration and settlement marks the beginning of a **Historic period**, for which there are written records and many complex cultural changes. This period cannot be seen as part of the stage sequence proposed by earlier archaeologists at all, but the interactions between Native peoples and Europeans as well as the political and industrial development of the United States and Canada are important topics of contemporary archaeological research.

Other Important Concepts

Archaeologists also use many general anthropological concepts. One very commonly employed set of terms concerning human sociopolitical organization consists of Elman Service's (1962) concepts of the **band**, the **tribe**, the **chiefdom**, and the **state**. This simple classification scheme helps us examine the various ways interrelationships among groups within a society are managed and controlled in the process of making a living. However, as formulated they imply an evolutionary progression from simple to complex sociopolitical organization that is outdated and seldom strictly intended in contemporary archaeological discourse.

You should know that reference to a band level of organization means that people lived in small, mobile groups of related people among whom there was little differentiation in power and wealth and who relied on **reciprocity**, or the sharing of food, tools, and labor among social equals as means of economic exchange. These people formed an **egalitarian society**. You should also know that a tribe is a larger group of people, often living in a village without well-developed governmental structures, but divided into kinship groups such as **clans**, which may collectively own the land on which crops are grown. In the classic formulation, tribal people are food producers. However, some pre-Columbian North American groups that depended on hunting and gathering or had mixed economies were organized in this manner. In addition, **big men**, individuals who enjoy higher status and power owing to their entrepreneurship and their skillful use of social obligation, may exist within tribes, though the applicability of this term to past Native American societies is debatable.

The same can be said about the concept of chiefdoms, which are a type of organization in which kinship is an important organizing feature, but families and lineages as well as individuals have differential access to resources and labor, and variable amounts of power and prestige although true classes are lacking. In other words, people live in a **ranked society,** In the classic formulation the key to the chiefdom system is the production of some agricultural or other surplus, which is redistributed by those in power. Other models of how power and authority can be distributed may be more useful in understanding North American polities (Butler and Welch 2006; Hegmon 2005). For example, the contrast between hierarchy and **heterarchy**, or ranked versus network systems, may be important when studying variable North American societies. Ritual knowledge as well as wealth may confer prestige in some societies, and it has been argued that this was true among many past North Americans. In fact, it has been argued that neo-evolutionary ideas about chiefdoms have inhibited the full exploration of the many kinds of polities created by Native Americans in the past (Pauketat 2007).

There has also been debate about whether the concept of a state, a large, autonomous political unit having a centralized government and containing many communities, can be applied to pre-Columbian North America. Don't confuse this concept with the states of the United States such as Pennsylvania or California. In anthropology, the concept refers to a type of sociopolitical organization, in which people are **stratified** or divided into social classes based on differences in wealth and power while political offices have permanent reality apart from the individual incumbents. Certain Mississippian polities of the Eastern Woodlands may have had some characteristics of the state, but this is not accepted by all archaeologists working in these contexts (Butler and Welch 2006).

It is important to remember that although all the typologies mentioned here provide archaeologists with useful terminology, the concepts are abstractions, and exceptions will always be found. Sometimes it is variation rather than types that is most useful in trying to understand and explain change. Types are tremendously useful when we try to answer the questions of what, when, and where; but clues to how and why things are more likely to come from looking at cases that don't easily fit into types. If you encounter some of this terminology when reading about North American societies, try to think critically about how it is being used and what is being implied.

THEMES IN THE STUDY OF NORTH AMERICA'S PAST

So much happened in North America's past and so many fascinating cultures and places catch our interest, that it is very easy to lose sight of the big picture. Yet, for meaningful understanding of North American archaeology, one must have a sense of both the developments in the various culture areas and of the ways in which the North American archaeological record can inform the study of broad anthropological questions about the nature and history of humans as a whole.

In this text, we suggest that most North American archaeological research can be seen as contributing to the study of eight thematic questions about the North American past, each of which contributes still broader issues in the history of humans. These thematic questions are listed in Table 2.1 and discussed briefly here; each is addressed by the information provided in Part 2, and we will return to them in Chapter 14.

First, one of the most fascinating things about humans is that we can be found so widely around the globe, while many other species are much more restricted in their distribution. Although it is clear that modern humans evolved in the tropics, modern humans eventually settled all the continents except Antarctica. The settlement of North America is part of the history of this dispersion. Most scholars agree that the settlement of the Americas occurred relatively late in the human story, no earlier than 25,000 years ago. A variety of questions concerning the nature of human migratory behavior and the timing of key cultural developments, such as the hunting of large game animals and boat building, can be addressed by using North American evidence. We examine these issues in more depth in Chapter 3 as the second part of this book begins. Besides the case study "The Paleocoastal Occupations of Northern California's Channel Islands" by Jon Erlandson and Torben Rick (in Chapter 3), "Eel Point and the Early Settlement of Coastal California: A Case Study in Contemporary Archaeological Research" by L. Mark Raab and Andrew Yatsko (Student CD, Section D.4) is directly relevant to these issues.

Second, the main reason that humans have been so successful in global colonization is that we are a highly adaptable species that uses culture to adjust to the varying circumstances encountered during migration and settlement. Thus we are able to live in environments that would be uninhabitable were we dependent on biology alone. There is a tremendous amount of evidence about

TABLE 2.1 Thematic Research Questions in North American Archaeology
1. How and when did the original settlement of North America occur?
2. How have humans adapted to the diverse environments of North America and to climatic change over time?
3. How, when, and where did food production develop in North America?
4. How, when, and where did sociopolitically complex, internally differentiated cultural systems develop in North America?
5. What ethnic identities can be identified and historically traced in North America's past?
6. What movements of human populations can be documented in the North American past after the continent's initial settlement?
7. How did settlement by Europeans and culture contact between Native Americans and Europeans transform North American cultural and natural landscapes?
8. How did the United States and Canada develop into global and industrial powers?

the diverse ways people have used culture to survive in North America. Hunter-gatherer strategies in particular can vary in a wide variety of ways. Archaeologists often recognize a continuum between foragers who move residentially as a group when resources are depleted, and **collectors** who move less frequently, establishing longer-term camps and sending out foraging parties to acquire resources and bring them back to the main camp for the everyone's use (Binford 1980). Two case studies on the student CD are most closely related to hunter-gatherer adaptations : "It Takes a Team: Interdisciplinary Research at the Koster Site," by Michael Wiant and Sarah Neusius (Section D.2), and "The Dust Cave Archaeological Project: Investigating Paleoindian and Archaic Lifeways in Southeastern North America" by Renee Walker et al. (Section D.6). Part 1's case study, "The Pueblo Grande Project: An Example of Multidisciplinary Research in a Compliance Setting" by Cory Breternitz and Christine Robinson considers issues of adaptation among agriculturalists. Many examples of horticultural and agricultural adaptations also are provided in Part 2.

A third significant question in anthropology is when, how, and why humans shifted to the production of their own food. This transition is widely recognized as one of the most important points in the human story: it not only changed how people acquired food and what they ate, it had social consequences of great importance. Although stereotypical views of Native Americans may suggest otherwise, experiments with farming occurred in southern California and the Great Basin, and the majority of populations inhabiting the Southwest, the Plains, and the Eastern Woodlands became farmers. Moreover, the transition to food production was not necessarily an abrupt one, and many North American hunter-gatherers managed the resources they utilized in highly sophisticated ways (Minnis and Elisens 2000). For example, along the Northwest Coast, exploitation of marine resources involved construction of clam gardens that fostered clam growth (Isabella 2011).

In fact, one of the important archaeological discoveries since flotation (see Student CD, Section C) became routine in archaeology is that groups in the interior parts of the Eastern Woodlands domesticated a variety of native plants as long ago as the Archaic period. This development provides an important example of the independent shift to food production in a temperate forest region. In addition, throughout the culture areas noted previously, later adoption of tropical cultigens, notably maize and beans, has provided insights into the diffusion of farming across diverse environments. Material relevant to the shift to food production can be found primarily in discussions of later pre-Columbian groups contained in

Chapters 9 to 12. Chapter 12's case study by John Hart, "A New History of Maize-Bean-Squash Agriculture in the Northeast," describes recent archaeological findings about how and when agricultural systems centered on the cultivation of maize, beans, and squash came into existence in the Northeast.

A fourth overarching research question addressed by anthropologists is when, where, and how complex sociopolitical systems developed among humans. In other words, how did chiefdoms (ranked) and states (stratified) come into being? As used by anthropologists, "complexity" refers to the existence of social hierarchies and/or various mechanisms for integrating large groups of people. There were a variety of North American pre-Columbian groups organized into complex polities, and the archaeological record (Figure 2.17) contains considerable evidence concerning the early stages of sociopolitical complexity. These developments occur in coastal areas among hunter-gatherers as well as among agriculturalists. Anthropologists have found that sociopolitical complexity is much more common among food-producers than among foragers, but this only makes the North American cases of complex hunter-gatherers all the more fascinating and important. In addition, very interesting nonhierarchical forms of complexity, or heterarchy, may also have existed in some Native American societies. The topic of developing complexity is addressed in each of our culture area chapters. Sociopolitical complexity also is addressed directly in the case study by Ben Fitzhugh, "From Sites to Social Evolution: The Study of Emergent Complexity in the Kodiak Archipelago, Alaska" (Chapter 4), and later in "Chumash Complexity" (Box 7.1).

Fifth, anthropologists are fascinated with human cultures and the groups that share them, and North American archaeology has much to contribute in this respect. Unfortunately, it is not necessarily a simple matter to recognize ethnic groups in the past. **Ethnicity** is based on identification with an ethnic group and is an elusive, dynamic, and nonmaterial property. Of course, there are material expressions of the sense of belonging to a particular group. People of different ethnicities may dress differently, cook differently, and use distinctive decorative motifs or styles in the artifacts they make. Ideally, archaeologists identify these material correlates of ethnicity in the archaeological record using the systematic concepts introduced in the preceding section of this chapter. However, as Section A of the Student CD explains, perceptions about what archaeological units mean have changed over the last century. Archaeologists have moved from a fascination with ordering these units in culture histories to a focus on behavior, activities, and the processes of culture change and, now, to investigating the possibility of multiple

FIGURE 2.17 The main plaza at Moundville in Alabama. Like many others considered Mississippian by archaeologists, this large site includes a large open plaza with regularly spaced, flat-topped mounds indicating community planning, labor mobilization, and ritual activity suggestive of sociopolitical complexity.

potential histories of North America's past based on various ethnic traditions, gender, and differences in power, wealth, and prestige.

Regardless, the problem of identifying ethnic or cultural groups in the past, and telling something about their lifestyle, remains an important theme in North American archaeology. Today's recognition that one of archaeology's contributions is helping marginalized groups recapture their history has made ethnic identification more important. NAGPRA also has made identification of ethnicity a requirement in the disposition of human remains. Unfortunately identification of ethnicity over many generations can be challenging. Archaeologists have been most successful in identifying specific ethnicities in the very late pre-Columbian, Protohistoric, and Historic periods. Reference to this theme can be found throughout Part 2 of this text. Ethnicity is directly addressed in Box 10.1, "Historic Ethnicities and the Archaeological Record," and in "Ethnicity and Class in Colonial Foodways," by Elizabeth Scott (Student CD, Section D.8).

A sixth closely related topic, population movements and migrations, is of great interest to North American archaeologists today. Both episodes of depopulation and the sudden appearance of new human groups in an area are are relevant to understanding cultural causation and human history. Historical questions about past population composition and movement also are significant to modern descendant groups. Such issues are addressed in a number of places in Part 2, but most directly in discussions of late

pre-Columbian migrations in Chapters 8 and 9 as well as in Box 12.1, "Iroquoian Origins," and in "The Dolores Archaeological Program: Documenting the Pithouse-to-Pueblo Transition" by Sarah Neusius (Student CD Section D.5).

A seventh topic, culture contact, similarly interests anthropologists. One of the greatest historical stories of culture contact has to do with the European global exploration beginning in the fifteenth century. North American archaeology has a great deal to contribute to understanding of this dynamic period. Historical records recount events and developments from the perspective of European settlers, but the archaeological record helps show that what actually happened was much more complex. At the very least, there are alternative perspectives on the encounter that make clear the active role of Indians in structuring contact and its aftermath. In the fifteenth and sixteenth centuries, future European dominance was hardly a given, and the common perception that replacement of native populations was inevitable should be questioned. As we mentioned in Chapter 1, it is also true that many native ethnicities have survived into the present, greatly transformed but nevertheless testaments to the persistence of early cultural traditions. While we cannot trace the history of all Native peoples, Chapters 4 through 12 contain some discussion of the Protohistoric and early Historic changes. Chapter 13, on historical archaeology, also touches on related later developments in North America's past. The case study in Chapter 7, "Cultures in Contact at Colony Ross," by

Kent Lightfoot et al., also provides insight into a little-known colonial encounter on the Pacific Coast.

Finally, from an anthropological perspective, another great transition in the human story is the relatively recent development of global capitalism and the industrial state. This transformation in human culture also involves much more than a technological change and has had important economic, demographic, social, and political consequences. Moreover, this transformation is ongoing in many parts of the globe today. The stories of European colonization, the slave trade, nation building, immigration, and industrial development in the United States and Canada during the Historic period are directly associated with this transition. At the very least, historical archaeology can enrich understanding of these processes. However, because of its focus on the material record, archaeology also is particularly well suited to other tasks: the exploration of the lives of those about whom there is little written record, and the investigation of topics such as the impact of mass production and the development of industrial technology. Each of our chapters looks at this range of topics in its section on the Historic period. In addition, Exhibit 13.1, "Iron Furnaces," directly addresses one part of the early industrial record.

Much of the excitement of North American archaeology comes from the different examples it provides about the questions listed in Table 2.1. What makes a piece of archaeological evidence most interesting may be what it contributes to discourse about one of them. Keep these themes in mind as you read about the North American culture areas in the rest of this text.

A WORD ABOUT DATES AND DATING

As discussed in Section C of the Student CD, archaeologists use several dating techniques. The two most important methods of **absolute dating** used in North America are **radiocarbon dating** including **AMS dating**, based on measurements of carbon isotopes in organic materials, and **dendrochronology**, based on analysis of tree rings. In addition to learning about these techniques, however, it is necessary to understand the variety of conventions for reporting dates, which can be confusing to beginning students.

It might seem most sensible to report dates in BC/AD (before Christ/anno Domini [in the year of the Lord]) as is common in the calendar used popularly today. Those who object to the religious connotations of BC/AD propose the designations BCE/CE (before the common era/of the common era). In areas such as the Southwest, for which dendrochronology is well established, BC/AD dates often are used because

this method produces dates in calendar years. A second instance in which AD dates commonly are used is in writing about historical archaeology, where calendar dates may actually appear in written records. However, for most North American archaeologists absolute dates have been obtained through radiometric dating. Understanding these dates is a little more complicated.

First of all, saying that something happened 1000 years ago would seem to be a straightforward statement, but precisely what "1000 years ago" means in calendar years will be different in the year of publication of this text and 50 years later. This may not be a great problem when the span of years is large or when the author is not far removed in time from the reader, but it obviously makes a difference for the scientist wishing to be precise. Reporting radiocarbon dates relative to the year AD 1950, the approximate year of the invention of this technique, is the archaeological convention for resolving this problem. Thus, when you see a date of 1000 BP, or 1000 years before present, it will always mean 1000 radiocarbon years before AD 1950 no matter when you are reading the date.

Second, because there has been fluctuation in the amount of atmospheric carbon-14 (^{14}C), there is not a direct correspondence between a radiocarbon year and a calendar year. Especially for longer time spans, the discrepancy may be significant, and it is important for archaeologists to mark dates as calibrated by using "cal BP" (or even "cal BC/AD") when they have adjusted them. For example, 928 cal BP is roughly equivalent to an uncorrected date of 1000 BP, and 13,887 cal BP is roughly equivalent to 12,000 BP (Table 2.2). (Another suggestion is that BP be used for calibrated and bp for uncalibrated dates.) However, radiocarbon dates can be calibrated in several ways by using tree-ring or other date estimates, and calibration curves almost certainly will continue to be adjusted as we learn more about these fluctuations and refine other dating techniques (Reimer et al. 2009). Thus, scholarly journals often ask that dates simply be reported in uncalibrated radiocarbon years, to ensure that they are comparable.

A third issue with the radiocarbon dates is that the dates obtained are approximations. A date obtained from a particular radiocarbon sample will be reported as a date range rather than a single date in years BP. For example, it might be given as the date 1000 ±50 BP to indicate that the true date most likely falls between 1050 BP and 950 BP or cal AD 899 and 1162 based on current calibration curves (Reimer et al. 2009). This means that dates such as 1000 BP are obvious simplifications of complex data.

All of this is more than bewildering to novices; it presents a problem for authors of books like this

TABLE 2.2 Comparison of Uncalibrated and Calibrated Radiocarbon Dates

Uncalibrated Years BP	Calibrated Years BP	Calibrated Years AD/BC
500	524	AD 1,426
1,000	928	AD 1,022
1,500	1,382	AD 568
2,000	1,950	0 BC
2,500	2,568	618 BC
3,000	3,211	1,261 BC
3,500	3,825	1,875 BC
4,000	4,505	2,555 BC
4,500	5,133	3,183 BC
5,000	5,730	3,780 BC
5,500	6,294	4,344 BC
6,000	6,824	4,874 BC
6,500	7,426	5,476 BC
7,000	7,840	5,890 BC
7,500	8,345	6,395 BC
8,000	8,861	6,911 BC
8,500	9,521	7,571 BC
9,000	10,197	8,247 BC
9,500	10,738	8,788 BC
10,000	11,395	9,445 BC
10,500	12,459	10,509 BC
11,000	12,882	10,932 BC
11,500	13,344	11,394 BC
12,000	13,837	11,887 BC
12,500	14,770	12,820 BC
13,000	15,525	13,575 BC
13,500	16,721	14,771 BC
14,000	17,012	15,062 BC
14,500	17,650	15,700 BC
15,000	18,233	16,283 BC
15,500	18,680	16,730 BC
16,000	19,211	17,261 BC
16,500	19,559	17,609 BC
17,000	20,233	18,283 BC
17,500	20,657	18,707 BC
18,000	21,466	19,516 BC
18,500	22,174	20,224 BC
19,000	22,510	20,560 BC

Courtesy of David L. Carlson (based on Intcal09).

one who wish to provide understandable and comparable dates throughout many chapters. We considered several possible ways of resolving the problem and found none of them to be perfect. In the end, we have used BP dates except for the Historic period. In Chapter 9, on the Southwest culture area and in a few other places where they may be helpful, we provide BC/AD dates in parentheses. We also provide approximate calibrated dates as well as BP dates in the timelines provided for Chapters 3 to 12. Our goal has been to make the dates we use clear and comparable.

CHAPTER SUMMARY

This chapter has introduced background information about North American environments and cultures as well as archaeological systematics that will be helpful in understanding what archaeologists have learned about the human past in this part of the world. The following points were made:

- The diverse cultures found in the North American continent commonly have been organized into ten culture areas, including the Arctic, the Subarctic, the Northwest Coast, the Plateau, California, the Great Basin, the Southwest, the Plains, the Southeast, and the Northeast.
- North American environments also are diverse and can be divided into several macroscale biomes, while North American climate is largely controlled by the interaction of arctic, tropical, and Pacific airstreams.

Nevertheless, climate changes and human induced changes must be taken into account when considering the human past in this continent.
- Archaeologists use a variety of conceptual units and typological devices in studying the North American past especially temporal types, components, phases, horizons, traditions, and cultural periods.
- Key research questions relate the study of North America's past to broader themes in the anthropological study of humans. These involve settlement of the continent, human adaptation to diverse environments, the development of food production, the development of sociopolitical complexity, the identification of ethnicity, the migration of human populations, post-Columbian culture contact, and the development of globalization and industrialization.

SUGGESTIONS FOR FURTHER READING

For a classic description on the culture areas of North America:

Kroeber, Alfred L.
  1963 *Cultural and Natural Areas of Native North America*, 4th ed. University of California Press, Berkeley.

For more information about North American environments:

Ubelaker, Douglas H. (editor)
  2006 *Environment, Origins, and Population. Handbook of North American Indians, Vol. 3, William C. Sturtevant, general editor, Smithsonian Institution*, Washington, D.C.

For more on the various interdisciplinary methods used by archaeologists:

Pearsall, Deborah M.
  2000 *Paleoethnobotany: A Handbook of Procedures*. Academic Press, New York.

Reitz, Elizabeth, and Elizabeth Wing
  1999 *Zooarchaeology*. Cambridge University Press, Cambridge.

Sobolik, Kristin D.
  2003 *Archaeobiology*. The Archaeologist's Toolkit 5, Larry J. Zimmerman and William Green, series editors. AltaMira Press, Walnut Creek, California.

Stein, Julie, and William Farrand (editors)
  1999 *Sediments in Archaeological Context*. University of Utah Press, Salt Lake City.

For a readable account of environmental change associated with the end of the Wisconsin glaciation:

Pielou, E. C.
  1991 *After the Ice Age: The Return of Life to Glaciated North America*. University of Chicago Press, Chicago.

For information on the impact of Native Americans on their environment:

Minnis, Paul E., and Wayne J. Elisens
  2000 *Biodiversity and Native America*. University of Oklahoma Press, Norman.

For other views on the North American past:

Pauketat, Timothy R., and Diana Di Paolo Loren (editors)
  2005 *North American Archaeology*. Blackwell, Malden, Massachusetts.

For more on archaeological dating:

Nash, Stephen E.
  2000 *It's About Time: A History of Archaeological Dating in North America*. University of Utah Press, Salt Lake City.

OTHER RESOURCES

Sections H and I of the Student CD supply web links, places to visit, additional discussion questions, and other study aids. The Student CD also contains a variety of additional resources. Particularly relevant resources include "A Brief History of North American Archaeology" (Section A) and "Archaeological Laboratory Analysis" (Section C). "It Takes a Team: Interdisciplinary Research at the Koster Site" (Section D.2) and "The Dust Cave Archaeological Project: Investigating Paleoindian and Archaic Lifeways in Southeastern North America" (Section D.6) nicely illustrate interdisciplinary investigations of human adaptations, and "Ethnicity and Class in Colonial Foodways" (Section D.8) is an example of zooarchaeological analysis.

PART TWO

The North American Past

CHAPTER 3

Peopling of the Americas

E very American schoolchild learns that when Christopher Columbus and his expedition arrived in the Caribbean in October 1492, Columbus assumed that he had found some outer islands of the Asian mainland and, thus, a route around the world. It is clear from the journal of Columbus's first voyage that he was searching for Asian commodities and people. Finding these would have confirmed his belief that the West Indies were part of Asia. However, America was not Asia, and once this was realized, it raised the question of who the people living in America actually were. Thus opened a chapter in both human mythmaking and scientific debate that remains unfinished today.

Tales and ideas about where Indians came from are plentiful. One idea was that the New World was first settled by merchants from Carthage, an ancient city in North Africa established by great seafaring traders, the Phoenicians. According to Aristotle, Carthaginian merchants sailed out into the Atlantic and found an uninhabited island, but explorations ceased when the Carthaginian Senate banned all travel to the island (Huddleston 1967:17). Another idea, which was suggested very early by Europeans, is that Native Americans originally were the inhabitants of the lost continent of Atlantis. In this tale, as Atlantis sank, the Atlanteans escaped to the previously uninhabited American continents, diversifying into many tribes and nations. Of course, the story of Atlantis itself is a parable told by Plato in relating a discussion between Socrates and his students concerning the perfect society (Feder 2002:178–188). You may also have heard of various ideas that American Indians are the descendants of the lost tribes of Israel or of other peoples mentioned in the Bible. For example, there is a biblical reference to King Solomon's navy visiting a place called Ophir, which either was already inhabited or then was settled by some of the men in Solomon's navy (Huddleston 1967:33–47). Of course, the Book of Mormon, based on golden tablets Joseph Smith said he found in New York State, also links the American Indians to biblical lands. It details a history of several migrations from Palestine to America before the time of Jesus, and identifies the American Indians as Lamanites, who defeated related mound-building emigrants, called the Nephites (Williams 1991:159–167).

These tales reflect efforts to make sense of New World peoples previously unknown to Europeans. Many early scholars thought the original settlers must have been forgotten by their homeland contemporaries, but could be accounted for in European religious or classical writings. The earliest explanations represent efforts to integrate the Americas and their inhabitants into European cosmological assumptions. In the prescientific sixteenth-century world of Europeans, the presence of people in the Americas had to be reconcilable in this way. As for the Book of Mormon, its story of the Lamanites fits quite well with nineteenth-century myths about the Mound Builders (see Box 1.1). Modern culture has produced attempts at explanation such as Goodman's (1982) claim that the Garden of Eden was in California and that all human life originated there, or the various claims of von Däniken (e.g., 1970) for alien rather than Native American origins for some of the more spectacular traces of the past. Each of these efforts probably tells us more about the writer's worldview than about the settlement and origin questions that interest archaeologists.

Like all people, Native Americans themselves also have origin stories. These stories are significant in many ways, and anyone who plans to pursue North American archaeology is encouraged to explore them for cultural insights. Like Judeo-Christian creation accounts, Indian stories are meant to explain the place of humans in the universe, the origins of animals, landmarks, social customs, and people themselves, and to provide lessons concerning right behavior. Sometimes they contain information useful to tracking the history of the people who tell them, and some people take them quite literally; but they are sacred stories, not scientific accounts of the past (Archambault 2006).

Another tradition of explanation by Europeans also began during the sixteenth century, soon after Columbus's voyages. In this tradition, scholars used their experience of American Indians and their observations of Indian artifacts, physical characteristics, and behaviors to answer origin questions. Early scholars noticed the physical similarities between American Indians and Asians and concluded that the Indians' ancestors had migrated from Asia. Even before the Bering Strait was found, some (e.g., Acosta 1963 [1604]) suggested that America was connected to Asia in the unexplored far north. Subsequently, as Western science matured and stressed empirical data, a scientific approach to the problem was developed.

North American archaeology, of course, belongs to this latter tradition. Through the discovery and excavation of sites, through the material remains we recover, and through interdisciplinary studies of past environments, archaeologists have tried to address the settlement of the Americas. Our research has been formulated to address the how, when, and where of migration. Using many kinds of evidence, archaeologists have constructed various scenarios. The state of archaeological knowledge on the settlement of the Americas is the topic of this chapter. Reading and studying this chapter should provide a general orientation to archaeological viewpoints. You may also want to explore Native American origin stories, beginning with those indicated in this chapter's "Suggestions for Further Reading."

Archaeologists have identified a large number of early North American sites that provide information about the settlement of this continent (Figure 3.1). Nevertheless, there is still debate about how, when, and from where human entry into the Americas occurred, not to mention interest in the adaptive strategies of these first Americans.

EARLY IDEAS ABOUT SETTLEMENT

Early North American anthropologists took an essentially "flat view" of the Native American past. Generally, they did not believe a great deal of time could have passed since people arrived on this continent. The idea of an ancient human past anywhere in the world did not develop until after 1859, when the coexistence of humans with the fossil remains of extinct animals in Europe was established (Grayson 1983). The Paleolithic period, stretching back long before biblical times into the Ice Age, became increasingly well documented in Europe. In North America, however, there was a general consensus that the Indians had not been here more than three or four thousand years.

Nevertheless, during the latter half of the nineteenth century, some people claimed to have evidence supporting the idea of an American Paleolithic. For example, in the 1870s, Dr. Charles Abbott, a physician whose farm was near Trenton, New Jersey, was

---

ANTHROPOLOGICAL THEMES   TOPIC 3.1

Thematic Research Questions in Chapter 3

As we pointed out in Chapter 2, it is easy to lose sight of the big picture when considering the diverse cultures and histories of North America. It is obvious that the first theme listed in Table 2.1 (How and when did the original settlement of North America occur?) is the main topic of this chapter and its case study. It may be less clear that many sections, especially the section entitled "Paleoindian Adaptations" and this chapter's case study, are directly relevant to the second theme listed in Table 2.1 (How have humans adapted to the diverse environments of North America and to climatic change over time?) as well.

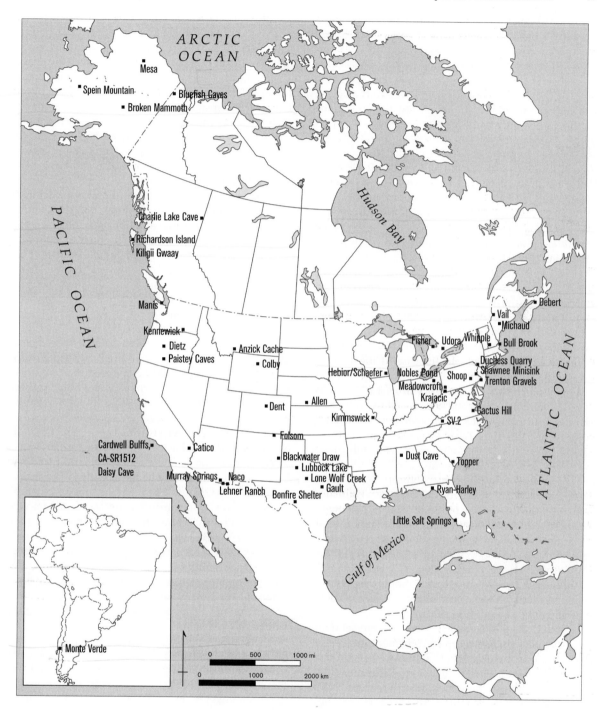

FIGURE 3.1 Locations of early North American sites mentioned in Chapter 3. See Figure 3.10 as well.

convinced that crude artifacts he had recovered came from Ice Age gravel deposits. Abbott interested scholars in his finds and published his claim widely. The similarity of Abbott's **"paleoliths"** to European Paleolithic artifacts was the primary support for assigning them to an early human presence. For a time, the Trenton gravels and the tools found there were thought to be legitimate evidence of the Ice Age presence of humans in North America. Other, even less plausible finds also were considered possible indications of Ice Age humans at this time (Williams 1991:116–129). However, the evidence for an early human presence in North America had not been critically evaluated.

Some influential anthropologists questioned the data. William Henry Holmes of the Smithsonian Institution established that similarities in form to Paleolithic tools from Europe were not sufficient by themselves to document human presence during the Ice Age. In addition, the stratigraphic context of an artifact would have to be unambiguously glacial. In case after case, Holmes found that the deposits did not date to the Ice Age or that the artifacts could be considered more recent ones that had intruded into glacial deposits by other means. In the case of the Trenton gravels, he argued that the artifacts actually were more recent Indian quarry refuse—**preforms** for more sophisticated tools—that had been moved by rodents or erosion and incorporated into older deposits. By the first few decades of the twentieth century, the archaeological consensus concerning possible Paleolithic tools was with Holmes (Adovasio and Page 2002).

A second Smithsonian anthropologist, Ales Hrdlička, also took up the role of debunker. Trained as a medical doctor and interested in skeletal pathology, Hrdlička often was consulted on discoveries of possible human bones in glacial context. He consistently argued that these bones could not represent Paleolithic or glacial humans because they did not resemble **Neanderthal** remains found in Europe. He also insisted that stratigraphic evidence concerning skeletal and other finds be carefully documented.

Both Holmes and Hrdlička were imposing and impressive individuals, who were vehement in their rejection of poor evidence and not afraid to intimidate less established scientists. In the end, their position was proved wrong, but not because they were wrong to reject the specific claims they reviewed. Holmes and Hrdlička established the rules of evidence archaeologists still use. To prove the early existence of humans in the Americas, we need objects that are unquestionably artifacts or human bones, as well as a context for these objects that clearly establishes the early date and the undisturbed nature of the deposits (Adovasio and Page 2002:99). For one reason or another, these criteria were not met prior to the late 1920s.

What changed the consensus was the discovery, near Folsom, New Mexico, of a stone spear point in clear association with the rib cage of an extinct species of bison (Figure 3.2). The Folsom site was discovered in 1908 by George McJunkin, an African American ranch foreman for the Crowfoot Ranch. Following a particularly heavy rainstorm that had resulted in flash floods, McJunkin was checking fencelines when he found that a newly cut gully had left a large gap beneath one section of fence, exposing several large bones. McJunkin was an amateur naturalist, and he saw that although the bones resembled modern bison bones, they were much larger. Over the years, McJunkin continued to remove bones from this bone bed, and he also made many unsuccessful efforts to interest others in what he was certain was an important fossil find.

However, shortly after McJunkin died in 1922, two men he had tried to interest in his find finally visited the spot, recovering a bag of bones. Both the men, Carl Schwacheim and Fred Howarth, were known locally for their interest in fossils. However, it was not until Howarth purchased an automobile in 1922 that the trip from their homes in Raton became an afternoon outing as opposed to a two-day trip (Preston 2002:16). Although quickly convinced that the bones they recovered came from an extinct animal, the two amateurs weren't positive whether it was an elk or a bison. In 1926 they traveled to Denver to bring some bones to Jesse D. Figgins, director of the Colorado Museum of Natural History (now known as the Denver Museum of Nature and Science). Figgins already had been involved in a dispute about early Americans at the Lone Wolf Creek site in Texas. Figgins had championed this find, while Hrdlička and others had rejected it because of the circumstances of the site's excavation (Meltzer 1991b:31–32).

Figgins was immediately interested in the Folsom finds. Excavations at the Folsom site began in the summer of 1926, and in July workers uncovered well-made spear points of the type archaeologists now call Folsom points in association with the bison bones. Unlike the "paleoliths" of Abbott and his contemporaries, these artifacts were far from crude and represented very sophisticated flaking techniques. Figgins wrote up the results of this excavation, claiming that the artifacts proved that the bison at the Folsom site had been killed by humans. He even visited Hrdlička in Washington with his finds. Hrdlička remained skeptical and urged Figgins to leave any future finds **in situ** until other scientists could review the context.

Renewing excavations at Folsom in the summer of 1927, workers found another spear point embedded in the sediments surrounding an articulated bison rib cage. This time Figgins directed them to leave the point in place until other scientists could confirm its location.

FIGURE 3.2 Spear point found in clear association with the ribs of an extinct bison at the Folsom site in New Mexico. This find left no doubt that humans had been in North America before the close of the Pleistocene.

Meanwhile, Figgins telegraphed Hrdlička and others inviting them to come see the discovery. Hrdlička's colleague Frank Roberts, who was already in the Southwest; Alfred Kidder, who was working at Pecos Pueblo in New Mexico; and Barnum Brown, a paleontologist from the American Museum of Natural History in New York who had found the first *Tyrannasaurus rex* skeleton, soon arrived. Under the leadership of Brown, the excavation uncovered 17 other spear points in association with the extinct bison remains, making it possible for each wave of scientists who visited to see Folsom points in direct association with bison bones as the excavation progressed (Meltzer 1991b:33). In 1928 the Pleistocene age of the sediments was established by the geologist Kirk Bryan of the U.S. Geological Survey, and from that time on there could be no doubt that humans were indeed associated with Ice Age fauna. Hrdlička's admonition to let the experts establish the validity of any potential early man finds had paid off, ironically refuting his own views on the subject.

After the Folsom finds had been recognized as clearly dating to the Ice Age, there was renewed searching for other early sites. Other bison-hunting groups were suggested by points of different types found at other sites (Fagan 1987:52), and before long, even older cultural assemblages were documented. Once again it wasn't a scientist who first suspected the significance of finds, this time in the vicinity of Clovis, New Mexico. There, in blowouts created by the winds of the Dust Bowl, a young Native American cowboy, James Ridgely Whiteman, found what he called "warheads" along with mammoth and bison bones. When Whiteman took Edgar Billings Howard, a researcher funded by the University of Pennsylvania Museum of Archaeology and Anthropology and the Philadelphia Academy of Sciences, to a place called Blackwater Draw near Clovis in 1932, the academic investigator immediately determined to excavate there the following summer. From 1933 to 1937, Howard excavated at Blackwater Draw. Here, another point type, originally called "generalized Folsom point" and now called the Clovis point, was first documented. In addition, Howard's work established that the hunters who made the Clovis points and associated tools hunted mammoths as well as other now extinct animals. Using an interdisciplinary approach that drew on geology and paleontology as well as archaeology, Howard was eventually able to demonstrate that Clovis points were located stratigraphically beneath Folsom points and that early mammoth hunting had been followed by focus on bison during Folsom times. See the case study in Section D.3 of the Student CD for a discussion of recent reanalysis of the lithic artifacts collected by Howard's team, and Exhibit 3.1 for information on these distinctive Paleoindian points.

CLUES TO THE PAST   EXHIBIT 3.1

Fluted Points: The Original American Invention?

Fluted **projectile points** are a classic example of a **diagnostic artifact**. Such archaeological artifacts are considered markers of particular cultural entities restricted in space and time. Thus, when such a diagnostic is found, it conveys temporal, spatial, and cultural meaning to archaeologists. In the case of fluted points, a Paleoindian presence and a terminal Pleistocene time frame are indicated. There are more than 11,000 documented fluted points from the continental United States alone. Not surprisingly, the distribution of these points is not even, and specific varieties of fluted points are still more restricted in spatial extent (Anderson and Faught 1998; Anderson et al. 2010). Given the traditional focus on Paleoindian kill sites from the Great Plains and the Southwest, it may be a surprise that the majority of fluted points come from the east, where large numbers have been found in the major river valleys and on either side of the Appalachian Mountains. Many of these points also are surface finds, but some have been found in datable stratigraphic contexts, and a number of varieties are recognized.

The Clovis point is the best known of the fluted point varieties, and it represents the earliest fluted point tradition. This point has a lanceolate form with a narrow blade, a concave base, and at least one major flute or flake taken from a prepared **platform** at the base up the center of the point. Fluting generally has taken place as the final step in the production of the point. Grinding on the base of the point also is common. Within the general Clovis designation, there is variation as shown in Figure 3.3 (bottom row). Some Clovis points exhibit **overshot flaking**, a trait also found in several Upper Paleolithic European assemblages. Overshot flaking results in thinning flake scars traversing the entire facial surface. In other Clovis points, flake scars from both sides instead meet at the middle. The sides of the point may be straight, slightly convex, slightly concave, or strongly concave and waisted. The degree of basal concavity also varies.

Folsom points (Figure 3.3, top row), which are found stratigraphically above Clovis at a number of Paleoindian sites on the Great Plains and in the Southwest, also are well known. Folsom points represent a very refined

technology in which the basal striking platform for fluting has been carefully prepared. As a result, fluting leaves a broad channel, well up into the point. In addition, the point often is broadest above the middle of the blade so that the tip looks a little "snub nosed," and the basal concavity may be deep enough to create straight ears at the sides of the base.

Some authorities recognize a **Full-fluted horizon** following Clovis that includes Folsom and other point types that are deeply indented at the base and have lengthy flutes (Anderson et al. 2010). These points are thought by some to mark adaptive changes associated with the onset of the **Younger Dryas** climatic episode, a cooler period that interrupted postglacial warming trends beginning at approximately 11,000 BP. However, the importance of this climatic episode is not clear (see Holliday and Meltzer 2010; Meltzer and Holliday 2010). An **Unfluted horizon**

FIGURE 3.3 Fluted points exhibit considerable variability in size and morphology: bottom row, Clovis points; upper row, Folsom points.

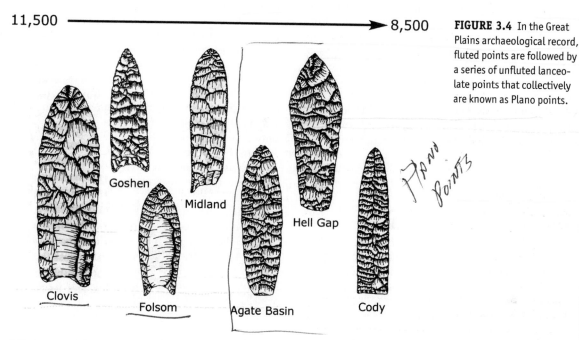

11,500 ———————————————➤ 8,500

Goshen

Midland

Clovis

Folsom

Hell Gap

Agate Basin

Cody

Plano Points

FIGURE 3.4 In the Great Plains archaeological record, fluted points are followed by a series of unfluted lanceolate points that collectively are known as Plano points.

follows the Full-fluted horizon and is characterized by various lanceolate, but unfluted points as well as by some slightly notched forms with beveled bases.

This sequence is best known on the Great Plains, where archaeologists have recognized a sequence of Paleoindian points that begins with Clovis and is followed by Folsom and later by unfluted, but still lanceolate varieties of points grouped together as the **Plano complex** (Figure 3.4). In the Eastern Woodlands, the Full-fluted horizon is represented by Redstone, Cumberland, Gainey, and Barnes points and Folsom points are generally found only at the western margins of the woodlands. A variety of Late Paleoindian unfluted points, particularly from the Southeast, also are known.

Farther west, fluted points, sometimes called **Western Clovis**, have been found in western Washington, southern British Columbia, the Columbia and Snake River basins, California, the Great Basin, and the Basin and Range country of the Southwest (Willig 1991). Most of these western fluted points are surface finds, but some occurring in stratigraphic contexts have been dated between 10,500 BP and 7500 BP and thus postdate Clovis on the Great Plains. Besides this, these Western Clovis points are often found on the same sites with points usually assigned to the **Western Stemmed Point tradition**, 11,000 BP to 7000 BP (Dixon 1999) that are not fluted at all.

As mentioned elsewhere in this chapter, the earliest fluted points in Alaska are younger or contemporaneous with fluted points south of the ice sheets. Most of these Alaskan points exhibit multiple flutes or basal thinning flakes and have been dated to no earlier than 10,500 BP.

Fluted points also have been found in Alberta, but dated after 10,500 BP. Triangular, basally thinned points found in this area also may be associated with fluting (Carlson 1991b). This part of interior Canada may well have been colonized from the south as the first people at sites like Charlie Lake Cave in British Columbia were hunting bison in what was then a more open environment (Fladmark et al. 1988).

Archaeologists are particularly interested in exploring the question of how fluting of points developed. Because fluted points are not found outside North and Central America and seem to be later in the north than in the south, we might argue that they are an American invention. Fluted projectile points probably began to be made as terminal Pleistocene hunters with a **blade** and **biface** technology adapted to changing postglacial environments, but under what specific circumstances? Several have proposed that the density and diversity of point types in the Southeast means fluting began there (Bryan 1991; Mason 1962; Stanford 1991). However, other archaeologists argue that a review of the radiocarbon record indicates that Clovis people rapidly colonized North America from the North (Hamilton and Buchanan 2007). Besides this, the technological variation among fluted points remains important to investigate. What is its significance? Finally, these points were just part of a toolkit that included other tool forms (see Figure 3.14), and the entire toolkit is important for understanding Paleoindian lifestyles even though fluted points are the diagnostic indicators of Clovis and many later Paleoindians.

Absolute dating methods such as radiocarbon had not been developed when the Folsom and Clovis discoveries were made. Thus, archaeologists did not know when these cultures had existed in terms of dates. Nevertheless, they thought the Ice Age had ended about 10,000 years ago and that at this time various types of large game animals had become extinct. On this basis, they soon designated Clovis and Folsom people as Paleoindians, Ice Age inhabitants of the Americas. We will discuss Paleoindian culture at the end of this chapter, after considering the complicated problem of how and when first settlement of the Americas actually occurred.

THE CLOVIS-FIRST SCENARIO

Following the recognition of Folsom and Clovis, many more sites were found to contain evidence of associations between these or similar point types and large game. In addition, similar points were found throughout much of North America, and sequences of point styles were established in some regions. After radiocarbon dating had been invented, in the late 1940s, archaeologists were able to confirm that many of these contexts did date to the end of the Ice Age or the beginning of the Holocene. Clovis sites were shown to date to a very short period of time, from 11,500 BP to 10,900 BP, and a recent reevaluation of the dates has suggested that the actual date range may be as small as 11,050 BP to 10,800 BP (Waters and Stafford 2007). Despite claims for older sites and deposits, for many years the professional consensus was that the **Clovis culture** represented the first human occupation of the Americas. This was because in the majority of proposed **Pre-Clovis** cases, further analyses showed either the dating, the stratigraphy, or the human origin could not be verified.

For example, the Calico site in California's Mohave Desert briefly enjoyed fame because Louis Leakey, renowned for his early hominid finds in Africa, supported its authenticity. Located above what once was the Pleistocene Lake Manix near Yermo, California, and possibly dated between 50,000 and 100,000 years ago (Mueller 2005), Calico was investigated by archaeologist Ruth "Dee" Simpson from the San Bernardino County Museum. Taken to the site while visiting California on a lecture tour, Leakey eventually identified a small number of artifacts among the many broken pieces of stone recovered. He also designated a particular concentration of rocks as a possible hearth. However, Vance Haynes, a geologist from the University of Arizona, who eventually examined many of the Pre-Clovis sites, pointed out that an interglacial **alluvial fan** like the Yermo fan is not a good source of

materials on which to base a claim for ancient humans. Such fans as deposits of sand, gravel, and mud often contain naturally broken rocks, some of which may superficially resemble crude human artifacts. Moreover, when careful comparisons were made between these "flaked" stones and unquestionable artifacts, the Calico site items appeared even less like artifacts. It also became clear that the supposed hearth actually was a natural cluster of rocks that appeared hearthlike only after partial excavation of the area. For all these reasons, Haynes concluded that Calico was not a valid Pre-Clovis site, and most archaeologists today concur with him (Adovasio and Page 2002:38–141; Meltzer 1993:63–65, 2009:98–100).

Many sites and artifactual finds have been considered and then rejected as Pre-Clovis in origin since the 1930s. Solid evidence for a Pre-Clovis human occupation in the Americas has been hard to come by. Solid evidence after all must include irrefutable evidence for humans, recovered from an undisturbed context, as well as unambiguous dating before Clovis times. These criteria only make sense, but they have been hard to satisfy.

Until recently, many archaeologists simply concluded that Pre-Clovis settlement did not happen. As a result, they developed a model of the human settlement of the Americas that revolved around Clovis being the first American culture. The **Clovis-First** scenario can be stated in four central propositions as follows:

1. *Humans did not enter the Americas until the very end of the Wisconsin glaciation and did not settle south of the ice sheets until about 12,000 BP, approximately the time we first find Clovis sites.*

2. *These first Americans were big-game hunters who followed large herd animals such as mammoths from Siberia into an unglaciated and productive Alaskan landscape before the Beringian land bridge (see Figure 2.12) was drowned.*

3. *Eventually, during the waxing and waning of the ice sheets associated with the end of the Wisconsin glaciation, the first Americans followed their prey down an **ice-free corridor** between the Cordilleran and Laurentian ice sheets into North and South America.*

4. *Once south of the ice, the big-game hunters were able to exploit a pristine niche without competition from other human residents, which allowed them to multiply rapidly and spread widely, as indicated by the wide distribution of Clovis and other Paleoindian sites.*

The Clovis-First scenario also became associated with a proposal by Paul Martin (1973) that early Americans were such efficient hunters of mammoths, horses, giant bison, and other **megafauna** that they figured in the

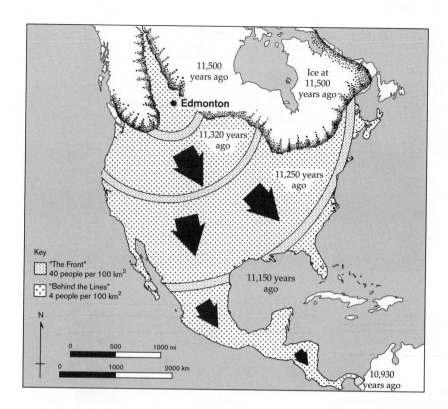

FIGURE 3.5 Martin's model of how, once an ice-free corridor had opened up, Paleoindians who were big-game hunters could have moved rapidly through North America, pushing their prey to extinction while quickly populating the continent.

extinction of these animals at the end of the Pleistocene. The question of why so many species of game became extinct at the end of the Pleistocene has been variously investigated and explained (Barnosky et al. 2004; Grayson 2001; Martin and Klein 1984). Martin's ideas are a version of the explanation known as Pleistocene overkill that human predation reduced these species' populations so greatly that they could no longer survive. However, Martin was quite specific about the timing of this human predation, suggesting that the first settlers of the Americas were highly specialized big-game hunters who arrived in eastern Beringia about 13,000 years ago and followed megafaunal herds down the ice-free corridor in western Canada as it opened, arriving in the Edmonton area about 12,000 years ago. From there they rapidly pushed south, exterminating herds until they reached Tierra del Fuego about 11,000 years ago (Figure 3.5). Mosimann and Martin (1975) also published a statistical simulation showing how hunter-gatherers could have moved so far, so rapidly.

Although Pleistocene overkill is not widely accepted by archaeologists today (Fiedel and Haynes 2004; Grayson and Meltzer 2003), the Clovis-First scenario benefited from Martin's overkill model. First, it cemented the notion that the first Americans were specialized big-game hunters, an assumption that subsequent data may call into question. Second, Martin showed how very rapid settlement within a little over a thousand years might have been possible for mobile,

highly specialized hunter-gatherers as was required by the Clovis-First scenario. Thus, although not strictly dependent on Martin's ideas, many elements of this scenario were bolstered by the incorporation of elements of the Pleistocene overkill model.

TOWARD A NEW CONSENSUS

For a long time, the Clovis-First scenario represented the archaeological consensus about the settlement of the Americas. Today, most archaeologists recognize that a more complicated story of early settlement is suggested by the current evidence. As a result, many new possibilities are being considered. Current investigations are focusing on when precisely the Americas were settled, on documenting the archaeology of Beringia, on which routes of entry people took, and on indications from various nonarchaeological data sources, especially genetics.

When Did People First Settle in the Americas?

As we have noted, many proposed candidates for Pre-Clovis sites have been rejected upon further investigation. However, there is an increasing amount of evidence for a human presence before 12,000 BP. Two key sites stand out as most important in shifting perspectives.

FIGURE 3.6 Today the remaining deposits at Meadowcroft Rockshelter are protected from the elements by a structure built into the hillside. Visitors are able to see the deposits from a viewing platform at the front of this structure.

The first of these is Meadowcroft Rockshelter, located in the Cross Creek drainage of extreme southwestern Pennsylvania near the small town of Avella. Meadowcroft Rockshelter is a stratified, multicomponent site with a long record of human use (Figure 3.6). Because of its careful excavation under the direction of James Adovasio, as well as the suite of radiocarbon dates obtained, Meadowcroft provides archaeological information of regional significance throughout the Holocene. However, the greatest significance of this site stems from the deposits in Stratum IIa that have early radiocarbon dates. If a conservative approach is taken and the various radiocarbon dates obtained from this **stratum** are averaged, the deepest cultural evidence dates to approximately 14,500 BP. These deposits were found beneath a major rockfall from the roof of the shelter. They contain a distinctive stone tool assemblage called the Miller complex, which is distinguished by small, **prismatic blades** that have been detached from small cores. Figure 3.7 shows the unfluted projectile point that is the **type specimen** for Miller lanceolate projectile points (Adovasio et al. 1999).

There have been two main criticisms of the Meadowcroft data. First, the small assemblages of plant and animal remains from Stratum IIa, which indicate the presence of a mixed coniferous/hardwood forest, are said to be inconsistent with a Pleistocene date. However, given that these ecofactual assemblages are very small samples, that the actual glacier probably was at least 100 miles (160 km) north of Meadowcroft during this early occupation, and that our understanding of the mosaic of habitats at the end of the Pleistocene is poor, Adovasio and others do not believe the critics' points are sufficient grounds for rejection of the radiocarbon dates.

FIGURE 3.7 The Miller lanceolate specimen type from Meadowcroft Rockshelter.

The second criticism has centered on whether the dates have been contaminated by the presence in the deposits of either coal or fossilized wood fragments called vitrite. Again, Adovasio points out that the upper part of the Meadowcroft sequence has never been questioned, nor has the reliability of his stratigraphic sequence. Redating by different radiocarbon labs has produced consistent results, and contaminants have not been found. Analyses of the sediments have produced no evidence of contamination from groundwater (Goldberg and Arpin 1999). In short, despite its critics Meadowcroft Rockshelter remains a probable Pre-Clovis site. This does not, however, set back the time of first human entry by many millennia, nor is the Miller complex of tools drastically different from later Paleoindian technologies.

A second site is even more significant to the Pre-Clovis case, though it is not in North America. Monte Verde is located on Chinchihuapi Creek, a tributary of the Maullin River, in south central Chile, approximately 500 miles (800 km) south of Santiago. It has been painstakingly investigated by an international research team headed by Tom Dillehay. At Monte Verde, an ancient campsite was buried in terrace deposits and covered by a layer of peat 6 to 12 inches (15–30 cm) thick.

Since the peat inhibited decay, preservation of normally perishable artifacts and ecofacts is outstanding. Excavators have recovered stone, bone, and wood artifacts as well as cordage fragments, mastodon bones, hide fragments, pieces of mastodon tissue, and a wide variety of plant remains. The remains of hearth features have also been found, along with a structure 22 yards (20 m) long, apparently made of wood and animal hides. A second wishbone-shaped structure is believed to have been used to process mastodon carcasses. In addition, a human footprint from a child or teenager has been preserved in clay apparently brought in to line the hearths. Whatever its dates, Monte Verde is an unusual and important site because of its preservation.

There are two possible use surfaces in Stratum MV-7 at Monte Verde beneath the layer of peat. Because the older surface (dated to 33,000 BP) has not been extensively exposed and investigated, the researchers do not make claims for Pre-Clovis use of Monte Verde on this basis. Instead, they focus on the younger use surface, designated MV-2, which contains the bulk of the materials, including the structural remains. This use surface has been dated to between 12,700 BP and 12,300 BP. Although these dates are only slightly more than a millennium older than those for the Clovis sites in North America, Monte Verde is much farther south. Assuming that humans entered the Americas via Beringia, they must have begun their migration long before its occupation, and much more than a millennium before Clovis.

Of course, Monte Verde also has had its critics. Both the dating and the artifact analysis have been questioned. Yet the validity of the dating just cited (12,700–12,300 BP) was settled to most archaeologists' satisfaction in 1997 after a site visit by a panel of experts. Among those examining the site were skeptics and Pre-Clovis proponents. Although a much heralded consensus from this visit was that the upper cultural surface at Monte Verde was indeed more than 12,000 years old and did break the Clovis barrier, subsequent criticism of the Monte Verde research has led to some backtracking by some Clovis-First proponents. Much was made of supposedly muddled procedures in excavation and analysis (Fiedel 1999a), but most archaeologists do not accept the conclusion that the Monte Verde evidence has been invalidated. In 2008, two AMS dates (12,290 ±60 BP and 12,310 40 BP) obtained from seaweed found in sediment samples from structure floors further confirmed the site's Pre-Clovis age (Dillehay et al. 2008).

In fact, there is other evidence from South America that corresponds well with the Monte Verde findings (e.g., Sandweiss et al. 1998). A wide human distribution in South America by 11,000 years ago is indicated. The diversity of early locations and subsistence evidence suggest that big-game hunting was not the sole means of subsistence. This might indicate that humans had a long time to settle into South American environments or that there were multiple migration waves from the north. There also have been claims for much earlier human occupation in South and Central America. These sites either have been rejected by most archaeologists as invalid or have not yet been investigated thoroughly. Investigating South American data remains of central importance to solving the puzzle of the human settlement of the Americas (Kelly 2003).

Besides Meadowcroft Rockshelter and Monte Verde, several other sites may indicate a Pre-Clovis human presence in North America. Several of these are still under scrutiny, but they add to the emerging picture of a widely dispersed, low human population prior to 12,000 BP. Among these are the following sites:

1. *The Bluefish Caves are located southwest of the Old Crow Basin in the Yukon. Here possible bone tools have been suggested to mark Pre-Clovis human entry. The stone tools from these caves appear to be similar to assemblages at other early Alaskan sites but are not firmly dated. The AMS technique has been used to date a split caribou tibia that may be a fleshing tool at 24,800 BP and a mammoth bone flake and its parent core to 23,500 BP (Cinq-Mars and Morlan 1999).*

2. *The Topper site is located on the Savannah River in South Carolina. Microblades, flakes, **burins**, and small cores, but no bifaces, have been found in a distinct stratum beneath a layer containing Clovis artifacts. This Pre-Clovis stratum was dated to 16,000 to 15,000 years ago by **optically stimulated luminescence (OSL)** (Adovasio and Page 2002). Older radiocarbon dates (ca. 50,000 BP) from still deeper levels of this site were reported in the fall of 2004, but the tools associated with that period are not believed to be truly artifacts by some authorities (Powell 2004).*

3. *The Cactus Hill site is located in a sand dune on the Nottaway River in Virginia. Two different archaeological teams have found a distinct stratum beneath deposits containing Clovis artifacts at this site. In this lower stratum, investigators have found stone tools and a charcoal concentration, as well as a hearth. Radiocarbon dates on the charcoal concentration and on the hearth, respectively, are 16,670 ±730 BP and 15,070 ±70 BP (McAvoy and McAvoy 1997). The artifacts include small blades and lanceolate, unfluted points or knives representing a core and blade technology that may have affinities to the assemblage from Stratum IIA at Meadowcroft Rockshelter (Adovasio and Page 2002:267).*

4. *The Shaefer and Hebior sites are part of an archaeological complex called **Chesrow**, located in southeastern*

Wisconsin. Mammoth bones at these sites exhibit evidence of human butchering, while a variety of lithic artifacts including unfluted lanceolate points made from local quartzite have been recovered. Bone collagen subjected to AMS testing has yielded a date of 12,310 ±60 BP for Shaefer and dates of 12,480 ±60 BP and 12,520 ±50 BP for Hebior (Overstreet and Stafford 1997). Other Chesrow sites have yielded only possibly butchered mammoth bones, but two periods of mammoth carcass utilization at ca. 13,500 BP and ca. 12,500 BP, respectively, are now proposed (Adovasio and Pedlar 2004; Overstreet 2004).

5. *The Little Salt Spring site*, a freshwater **cenote**, or limestone solution pit is located near Charlotte Harbor in southwestern Florida (Figure 3.8). The shell of an extinct tortoise impaled with a sharpened wooden stake was found on a ledge within the cenote. A bone from the tortoise dated to 13,450 ±190 BP, and the stake itself dated to 12,030 ±200 BP (Clausen et al. 1979).

6. *The Manis site is* located on Washington State's Olympic Peninsula. Here the tip of a bone projectile point was found embedded in the rib of a mastodon. Two dates from this site place it at 12,000 ±310 BP and 11,850 ±60 BP (Gustafson et al. 1979) (Figure 3.9).

7. *The Paisley Caves are* dry caves located in southern Oregon near what once was the shoreline of a Pleistocene lake. The lowest levels within these caves represent the Late Pleistocene and have yielded apparently human **coprolites** containing genetic markers associated with founding Native American populations (see later in this chapter). AMS dates for at least three of the coprolites by different laboratories produced dates greater than 12,000 BP (Gilbert et al. 2008).

8. *Site SV-2 (44SM37),* located near Saltville, Virgina, is one of several significant paleontological and

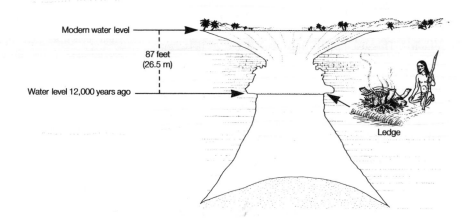

FIGURE 3.8 Artist's conception of the sinkhole at Little Salt Spring in which a speared tortoise shell was found on a submerged ledge.

Modern water level

87 feet (26.5 m)

Water level 12,000 years ago

Ledge

FIGURE 3.9 Archaeologist working on mastodon bone at the Manis site in Sequim, Washington. Note the use of a water hose in the excavation.

archaeological sites in the Saltville valley. Modified and used bone items have been found in association with a few crude sandstone tools, and from the lowest levels of this site a musk-ox tibia has been AMS dated to 14,510 +80 BP (McDonald 2000).

Given this evidence, most archaeologists now think Clovis was not first, though many questions remain. Most important among these is the question of whether current evidence simply pushes the timing of first human settlement back a few thousand years or requires entry prior to the coldest part of the last glacial epoch known as the last glacial maximum (LGM). The LGM occurred between 20,000 BP and 18,000 BP. As just indicated, with the exception of Bluefish Caves in the Yukon, possible Pre-Clovis sites in North America do not predate the LGM. However, it may be unlikely that routes south either along the coast or through the ice-free corridor would have been open to humans early enough to allow for the human occupation of Meadowcroft Rockshelter at 14,500 BP, of the Topper and Cactus Hill sites between before 15,000 BP, or of Monte Verde in Chile by 12,500 BP (Madsen 2004). This would mean that a human population had to exist south of the glaciers in North America prior to the LGM. Archaeologists need much more archaeological and environmental evidence from both northeastern Asia and the Americas to be able to reliably sort out the most probable sequence of events, and it is certainly premature to propose a new scenario that will account for all the data.

What Does the Beringian Archaeological Record Contribute?

Despite recent suggestions of a Northern Atlantic route of entry (see Box 3.1, "Debating the **Solutrean Hypothesis**"), it is most probable that humans first entered the Americas via northeastern Asia and Alaska. This is the case whether or not the first migrants were terrestrially focused large-game hunters, as was presumed in the Clovis-First model, or coastally adapted foragers, as has been suggested more recently. Given the timing at the end of the Ice Age, these populations came through interior or coastal Beringia, the vast area of land between Asia and Alaska exposed by the lowering of sea level during glacial periods (see Chapter 2). Scientists once thought that Northeast Asia was too cold and harsh for human hunters until the very end of the Pleistocene. They also thought that humans did not develop boats or inhabit the coasts of North Asia until quite recent times. However, both these assumptions are no longer accepted by most scholars.

Recent work indicates that humans were in central Siberia at the site of Nepa by about 35,000 BP to 30,000 BP (Meltzer 2009:20), and there are other sites in Siberia that also have yielded similar pre-LGM dates (Kuzmin and Keates 2005). Similarly sites in the Aldan River valley of the Sahka Republic including Irkine 2 and Ust-Mil 2 have produced dates between 36,000 BP and 27,000 BP (Goebel 2004). The site of Yana, located at 70° north in extreme western Beringia has yielded a date of 27,000 BP (Pitulko et al. 2004) (Figure 3.10).

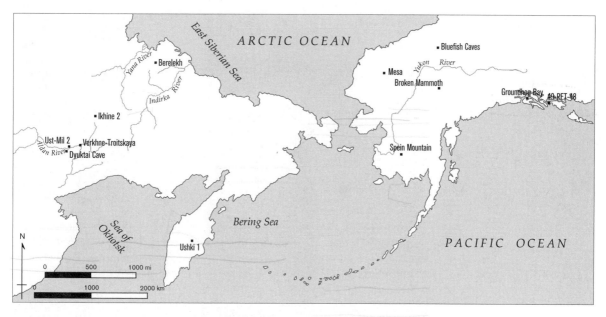

FIGURE 3.10 Beringia, showing the location of Beringian sites mentioned in Chapter 3.

However, it is not clear that humans remained in these regions during the peak of glaciation between 20,000 BP and 18,000 BP, and a number of scholars have argued for a recolonization of far northeastern Asia after the LGM (Goebel 2004). Central Siberian sites apparently dating after the LGM and a number of sites in the Sakha Republic that are grouped together as the **Dyuktai tradition** (Diuktai culture) date to as early as 16,000 BP. These provide evidence of post LGM settlement of Northeastern Asia. Farther north and east in the Sakha Republic and in Kamchatka and Chukotka, areas we might properly call western Beringia, the oldest known sites are younger. Dates suggest use of the Berelekh site located along a tributary of the Indigirka River, which drains into the East Siberian Sea in the northern part of the Sakha Republic around 14,000 BP. The site has been long known as a mammoth cemetery of paleontological significance; the archaeological component, which is spatially distinct from the mammoth bone accumulations, was first recognized in the 1970s (Mochanov and Fedoseeva 1996b). Other important sites, Ushki 1 and 5, are located along the shore of Ushki Lake in the Kamchatka River valley, Kamchatka (Dikov 1996). The lower layer at Ushki I produced a radiocarbon date of 13,980 ±146 BP (Dikov 1996), but these sites may be even younger, dating between 11,000 and 10,000 BP, suggesting a relatively late recolonization of western Beringia (Goebel 2004).

One important question archaeologists ask is, how similar are early artifact assemblages and human adaptations in both continents? Can connections be traced across Beringia? A critical distinction in early stone tool assemblages may help us sort out connections with American assemblages. In Beringian cultural assemblages, there are stone tools and also some worked bone tools. Two different ways of making stone tools are represented (Figure 3.11). First, people flaked or chipped cores of rock into bifacial points, as

FIGURE 3.11 Examples of tools found in Dyuktai Cave: (a) wedged-shaped microblade core, (b) microblades, (c) base of bifacial knife, (d) bifacial knife, (e) biface, and (f) side scraper. (Adapted from Mochanov and Fedoseeva 1996a, Figures 3.5 and 3.6.)

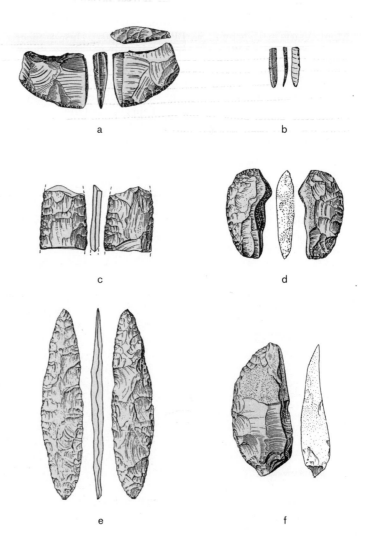

a

b

c

d

e

f

well as other bifacial tools and blades that could be made and used in various ways. Assemblages include blade cores, blades, bifaces, scrapers, and other tools as well as worked bone and ivory rods. This blade and biface technology bears some resemblance to North American Paleoindian technologies including Clovis. Second, archaeologists also have recovered **microblades**, made from small cores of rock and then then set into slits cut into bone or antler spears (see Exhibit 4.1). Microblades have been made from flakes or from pebbles or cobbles, resulting in a **wedge-shaped core**. Interestingly, microblade technology was not part of the Clovis and other Paleoindian manufacture of stone tools in most of North America, but did spread into Alaska and down the coast early in the Holocene (see Chapter 4).

In eastern Siberia and western Beringia, some of the assemblages from prior to the LGM seem to follow the first technological pattern as do the later tool assemblages from Berelekh and the lowest layers at Ushki-1. At Ushki-1 small bifacial stemmed points also have been found. In contrast the Dyuktai tradition stone tool technology is characterized by wedge-shaped cores, microblades, scrapers, and burins as well as bifacially worked tools, including projectile points and knives. These tools have been found in association with remains of mammoths and other large Pleistocene game. Some of the mammoth bone and ivory has also been worked into tools. This kind of assemblage with microblades is also found in the upper layers at Ushki-1 and at other later sites in Siberia and Beringia.

The oldest sites in eastern Beringia, or Alaska, are more or less contemporaneous with Clovis sites farther south. Among these, several central Alaskan sites located along the Tanana River have yielded reliable radiocarbon dates. The Broken Mammoth site has been shown to have four cultural zones with the stratigraphically lowest of these called Cultural Zone IV having a date range of 11,800 BP to 11,000 BP. Cultural Zone III at Broken Mammoth dates to between 9300 BP and 10,300 BP (Yesner 2007). Swan Point, also in the Tanana river valley, is multicomponent, with the oldest materials at the site having been dated to 11,660 BP and slightly younger deposits dated at 10,230 ±80 BP. Other important sites have been found in the Nenana River valley, a major tributary of the Tanana River that originates in the Alaska Range. The most important of these is Dry Creek, a deeply stratified site for which the stratigraphy has been well dated by a series of radiocarbon samples. Here the oldest component (Component I) has a radiocarbon date of 11,120 ±85 BP, while the overlying Component II is dated at 10,690 ±250 BP (Hamilton and Goebel 1999; West 1996a).

Archaeologists recognize two early tool traditions in these central Alaskan sites (Figure 3.12). One is known as the **Nenana complex** and is a blade and biface industry that lacks microblades. The complex contains Chindadn points or knives, which are thin, teardrop-shaped bifaces. The second complex, the **Denali complex** has obvious similarities to the Dyuktai tradition in Siberia and western Beringia. This assemblage includes wedge-shaped cores, microblades, and burins. Similar tool assemblages, which include microblades, have been found in Alaska well into the Holocene, and have been called collectively the **Paleoarctic tradition**. Some radiocarbon dates suggest that tool traditions in which wedge-shaped cores, microblades, and burins figure prominently were preceded in Alaska by an older blade and biface industry. However, closer consideration of the site assemblages may suggest an even more complicated and regionally variable sequence (Hamilton and Goebel 1999), and there are site sequences that indicate a reverse in this order (Bever 2006).

As indicated in Exhibit 3.1, it appears that fluted points were not made in Alaska before they were made to the south and that some technological differences distinguish Alaskan fluted points and those found farther south (Clark 1991). Fluting and perhaps other technological traits traditionally associated with Paleoindians probably first developed south of the ice sheets in North America, and then were brought northward as the Ice Age ended. Two key Alaskan sites with technological affinities to Clovis are Spein Mountain, which is located in the Kuskokwim River drainage of southwestern Alaska, and the Mesa site, located on the northern side of the Brooks Range in Arctic Alaska.

Although fluted points from the Mesa site have not been found associated with bone, **blood residue analysis** indicates that some of them were used to kill or butcher large mammals, including mammoths (Loy and Dixon 1998:21). The Spein Mountain site has only one AMS radiocarbon date (10,050 ±90 BP) obtained from charcoal found in a soil sample, but it is an important site because of the lanceolate projectile points recovered there are reminiscent of Paleoindian point styles found farther south (Ackerman 1996a). The Mesa site appears to have been a hunting station where hunters made and resharpened their stone tools while watching game movements below the mesa on which the site is located. A series of AMS radiocarbon dates from hearth features found at this site range between 11,700 BP and 9700 BP, with the majority of dates postdating 10,500 BP. Tools found at the Mesa site, which include fluted points, also appear to be similar to Paleoindian tools found farther south (Kunz and Reanier 1996). Note that these

FIGURE 3.12 Nenana (a–i) and Denali complex (j–o) artifacts: (a, b) bifaces, (c, d) blades, (e–g) end scrapers, (h, i) perforators, (j, k) bifaces, (l) burin, (m) microblade core, and (n, o) microblades.

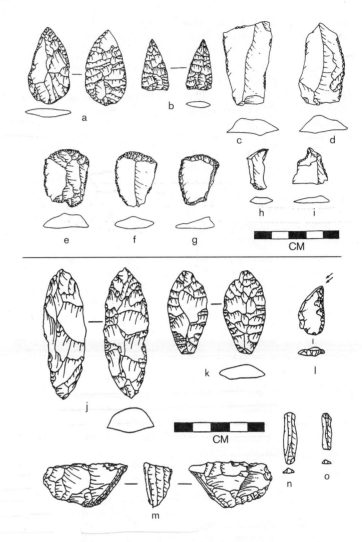

dates do not significantly predate the Clovis culture (11,050–10,800 BP).

Besides the tool assemblages, subsistence assemblages occasionally give archaeologists a glimpse of the adaptive strategies of the first humans in this area. The faunal assemblage from the Broken Mammoth site in central Alaska is surprisingly diverse and includes fish, small mammals, and waterfowl as well as larger animals like bison and elk. Yesner (2007) believes that even the larger mammals were taken through encounter strategies rather than drives and suggests that there were seasonal differences in which animals were targeted reflected in the different layers at the site.

The possibility of an early coastal entry via the southern shore of Beringia also cannot be dismissed. It is now clear that at least by 50,000 BP, people were able to cross to Australia by boat. In addition, evidence of coastal adaptations by generalized foragers in several places during the last 40,000 years increases the plausibility of the argument for settlement of the Americas in this manner. Maritime foragers were in the Japanese islands at least between 28,000 and 20,000 BP (Ikawa-Smith 2004), and some scholars suggest a route north across lands exposed by lowering of the sea in what today is the Sea of Okhotsk to Kamchatka peninsula and then through Beringia into southern Alaska (Madsen 2004). Once again, however, archaeological evidence for this possible colonization is lacking.

As more and more systematic archaeological work has been done in Beringia on both continents, a better picture of early human use of this area is being gained. However, it still appears that much of Beringia was not inhabited by humans until the terminal Pleistocene and early Holocene. These findings remain puzzling in the light of Pre-Clovis findings farther south.

What Routes of Migration Were Used?

Two potential routes of entry have been most favored by archaeologists (Figure 3.13). As noted already, the Clovis-First scenario assumed that the First Americans moved south into North America through an ice-free corridor that opened between the two North American ice sheets in Canada. This open corridor would have stretched south from the Yukon through portions of the Northwest Territories, Alberta, and southern Saskatchewan. However, for most of the Ice Age this route would have been blocked by glaciers. Only during interglacials and as glaciation came to an end would the Cordilleran and Laurentian ice sheets have retreated away from each other, opening unglaciated areas. The gap between glaciers would have had to be large for vegetation, large herbivores, and human hunters to enter the corridor. There has been considerable geologic and climatological investigation of when an ice-free corridor traversable by human hunters and their prey might have existed. The current viewpoint is that this corridor was not truly open between about 22,000 BP, as the last glacial advance developed, and

about 14,000 BP. Certainly, a corridor would have been open to hunters around 11,500 BP if entry did not occur until then, but it would also have been a possible route south before 22,000 BP if humans arrived that early.

Although there have been a number of proposed Pre-Clovis sites in western Canada, these sites have eventually been rejected for one reason or another. For example, at Varsity Estates, near the city of Calgary, Alberta, possible artifacts such as choppers, cores, scrapers, and gravers have been reported from glacial till deposits believed to be more than 21,000 years old. However, most archaeologists suspect a natural origin for these objects. Other sites indicate Terminal Pleistocene interaction between humans and megafauna already present in North America prior to the LGM (McNeill et al. 2004). Bluefish Caves in the Yukon may mark the northern end of the corridor and, as noted earlier, may provide evidence of human presence in Pre-Clovis times. However, sites in the corridor to the south have provided no indication of pre-12,000 BP occupation (Wilson and Bums 1999). We don't know whether earlier sites have been deeply buried, were

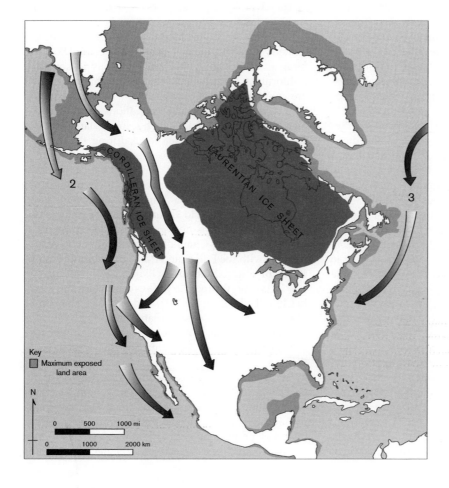

FIGURE 3.13 Possible routes of human entry into North America: (1) traditionally accepted ice-free corridor route, (2) coastal route along the West coast, and (3) recently proposed route across the northern Atlantic.

destroyed by subsequent glacial advances or retreats, or never existed in the first place. Only much more serious deep-testing programs can hope to improve understanding of these issues.

A second route along the west coast of North America has also been proposed. In this view, the first settlers followed the South Alaskan coast and then the Pacific Coast of North America and eventually Central and South America. These people would have been coastally adapted generalized foragers with boats who did not penetrate the interior of the continent until they were south of the ice. Fladmark (1979, 1983) maintained that there were small, ice-free pockets along the Pacific Coast that could have served as refuges for humans even during glacial periods. Proponents of this route have argued either for very early entry before the LGM when the southern coast of Alaska would have been blocked by massive glaciers (Gruhn 1994) or for much more recent use of this route, as warming began perhaps 14,000 years ago (Dixon 1999).

Until recently, most archaeologists have not taken this idea seriously, in part because the idea of intrepid big-game hunters migrating through a windswept, ice-free corridor seemed compelling (Mandryk 2004). As long as Clovis-First was the prevailing model, it was thought that the first migrants were terrestrially focused big-game hunters while the coasts were thought to have been largely uninhabited until Holocene times. The coastal route theory was also questioned because of the lack of evidence for early sites in this region.

Now that there is increasing acceptance of Pre-Clovis occupation of the Americas, the coastal route is being reexamined. Dixon (1999) has proposed that a revised coastal model provides the best fit for the data. Specifically, he proposes that the initial human colonization of the Americas began about 13,500 BP, when generalized foragers used boats to travel along the southern coast of Beringia and then southward into the Americas. Making use of a coastal–intertidal biome found along the entire Pacific Coast, these people moved rapidly southward before the glaciers of the continental interior had melted. Dixon proposes that interior areas were inhabited more gradually over the next few thousand years, and that coastal foragers also rounded the tip of South America and came north again before the midcontinents were settled. In Dixon's model, Clovis comes at the end of the migratory sequence after about 11,500 BP. Although this entry model is speculative, some archaeologists think it fits the data we now have better than the formerly popular idea of an ice-free corridor route.

First, there are now a few sites that suggest movement along the coast at an early date. An early date of

10,180 ±800 BP also has been obtained from the Ground Hog Bay site located near Juneau, Alaska, but this date, which does not conform to other radiocarbon dates obtained from the site, may not be reliable (Ackerman 1996b). Carbon isotopic studies of human remains from 49-PET-408, a site on Prince of Wales Island in Alaska, also suggest a largely marine diet at 9200 BP (Dixon 1999).

Leaf-shaped bifaces and other artifacts possibly related to the Nenana complex in Alaska or to the Western Stemmed Point tradition found the cave sites on Haida Gwaii (formerly the Queen Charlotte Islands) of British Columbia indicate that humans were present here by at least 10,600 BP (Fedje and Mackie 2005). Related maritime adaptations have been documented beginning at approximately 9500 BP at the Kilgii Gwaay and Richardson Island sites in the southern Queen Charlotte Islands. The earliest portions of these sites lack microblade technology. Interdisciplinary research also indicates that there may have been unglaciated portions of the continental shelf in Hecate Strait, which lies between the Queen Charlotte Islands and the mainland throughout much of late Pleistocene. Between 15,000 BP and 12,000 BP this area was not glaciated and supported a diverse herb and dwarf shrub vegetation (Fedje and Mathewes 2005).

Certain early sites along the Pacific Coast of the United States provide evidence for generalized coastal foragers. The most important cluster is in southern California, where several sites on the Channel Islands are more than 10,000 years old (see this chapter's case study, "Paleocoastal Occupations of California's Northern Channel Islands" by Jon Erlandson and Torben Rick). Lowered sea level during the Ice Age meant that what today are separate islands were a single, exposed landmass. The remains of pygmy mammoths have been recovered here, and some researchers have suggested an association with stone tools and hearths. However, careful sediment and other analyses have not supported this contention. Occupation of the Channel Islands that is contemporaneous with the Full-fluted tradition beginning about 10,500 BP is apparent at sites like Daisy Cave.

Of course, the recovery of seaweed at Monte Verde in Chile (Dillehay et al. 2008) and evidence from other coastal South America sites (Sandweiss et al. 1998) also indicate early maritime adaptations. However, one basic problem with investigating the coastal route theory is that much of the Pleistocene age coastline was drowned as sea level rose owing to the melting of the ice sheets. It is highly unlikely that we will find sites representing Late Pleistocene occupation of the continental shelf, although we might find sites slightly inland or perhaps on coastal islands. A simulation by Surovell (2003) also questions whether a model of coastal foragers who eventually moved inland can explain the population distribution of Paleoindians at 11,000 BP.

A third idea about routes of entry is discussed in Box 3.1. Dennis Stanford and Bruce Bradley have suggested that we rethink a route of entry westward from Europe across the Atlantic that was suggested by some early archaeologists (e.g., Renaud 1931). They propose that the first migrants have come westward by boat, skirting the margins of the North Atlantic ice. This route of entry might explain the presence of more indications for Pre-Clovis occupation in eastern than western North America as well as apparent similarities between Upper Paleolithic stone tool tradition called Solutrean and Clovis tool technology. This idea has received considerable attention especially in the popular press, but, as discussed in Box 3.1, many archaeologists dismiss this proposal as well.

ISSUES AND DEBATES   BOX 3.1

Debating the Solutrean Hypothesis

One of the most perplexing aspects of the peopling of the Americas is the question of how humans got here in first place. As we've indicated, evidence for the actual route of entry has been very limited. Most scholars have assumed that an entry through Beringia must have taken place. The key debate has been whether the route southward was through an ice-free corridor or along the coast. However, recently Dennis Stanford and Bruce Bradley (Bradley and Stanford 2004; Stanford and Bradley 2002) suggested that it was time to revisit an old idea that the first settlers came from Europe. They reminded archaeologists of early observations (e.g., Greenman 1963; Renaud 1931) that beautifully made fluted Clovis points and other Paleoindians artifacts resemble artifacts made in Europe during the Upper Paleolithic. Specifically the leaf-shaped, sometimes stemmed projectile points of the **Solutrean culture** (22,000–18,000 BP) found in France, Portugal, and Spain seem similar technologically to Paleoindian points. In the spirit of "thinking outside the box," these archaeologists have suggested that we rethink the possibility of a route of entry westward from Europe across the Atlantic. Focusing research solely on a Beringian entry point, they argue, has been unproductive. Rejecting the dogma of Beringian entry may explain some of the puzzling aspects of Pre-Clovis and Clovis data.

Bradley and Stanford's Solutrean or North Atlantic hypothesis is based on several key points. First, they argue that Clovis technology is distinctive and well developed enough to have had a precursor. Specifically they believe that the two basic flaked-stone technologies of Clovis, bifacial thinning and large blade production, are sophisticated enough that they couldn't have just developed randomly. Yet they argue that Beringian archaeology, which they characterize as dominated by microblade and wedge-shaped core technologies, has not produced evidence of an appropriate precursor, nor even located sites old enough to have been Clovis precursors. Instead they see both any Alaskan fluted points and the blade and biface Nenana assemblages in Alaska as coincident with or younger than Clovis culture to the South.

Second, Stanford and Bradley are struck by the similarities between Clovis technology and the technologies of the Solutreans (Figure 3.14). They say that the most important similarity is in the technique of bifacial thinning known as overshot flaking. Both Clovis and Solutrean tools exhibit this technique in which flakes are struck so as to cross from one side of the biface to the other, resulting in bifaces that are thin and flat as well as large thin flakes that were used to make other tools. Pressure flaking, heat-treating of stone to improve its flaking quality, basal thinning, margin grinding to dull the edges for hafting, and even some fluting are other attributes of Solutrean stone tools that these scholars find reminiscent of Clovis. Other tool types such as distinctive scrapers and an occasional burin also seem to be similar, and bone projectile points and other items of bone, antler, and ivory have been found in both Solutrean and Clovis assemblages. Recent discovery of small stones engraved with geometric patterns at the Gault site in Texas also resemble similar Upper Paleolithic artifacts from Europe .

A third argument made by Stanford and Bradley is that the distribution of Pre-Clovis sites such as Meadow-croft, Cactus Hill, and sites in Florida is primarily in the eastern part of North America. Arguing that the Pre-Clovis technology evident at is obviously transitional between Solutrean and Clovis technologies, they envision that Solutrean hunters came inland from the Atlantic coast of North America during Pre-Clovis times. They also claim that the oldest Clovis sites are from Southeast with younger dates for Clovis being in the West.

Finally, Stanford and Bradley contend that it is plausible that Solutrean hunters began to exploit the

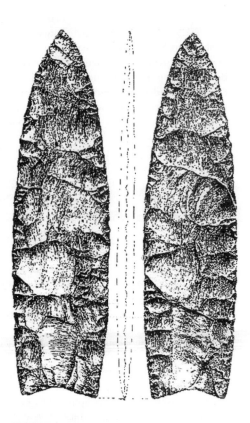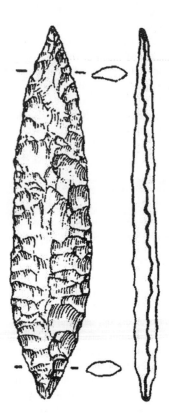

FIGURE 3.14 Some scholars see technological similarities between Solutrean points like the one on the right and Clovis points like the one on the left as evidence of European origins for Clovis.

Subarctic marine life zone during the LGM. This life zone is particularly rich in sea mammals, birds, and fishes, and if positioned close to northern Spain and Portugal in Solutrean territory, it is probable that Solutrean hunters would have learned to exploit its resources. Ultimately they see Solutrean hunters adapting to a coastal marine economy and following the ice-edge habitat, located much farther south during the LGM, into North America. These hunters then became the Pre-Clovis people of eastern North America.

The Solutrean hypothesis has received popular attention (e.g., BBC 2004; Discovery Channel), perhaps because it is an intriguing idea to some that Europeans rather than Asians were the first inhabitants of North America. This idea links well with a number of perplexing biological indicators of connections to Europeans such as narrow faced skeletons like Kennewick (see CD Section F. 4) and rare genetic markers at first thought to only be found in Europeans (see later in this chapter). Unfortunately, it's possible to look at the Solutrean hypothesis in a superficial way and even to derive simplistic racial implications from it. As might be expected, the popular renderings of this idea do not do justice to the arguments set forth by Stanford and

Bradley, nor do they take into account the very real fact that the majority of archaeological scholars have found fault with this hypothesis.

A number of researchers have pointed out what they find to be flaws in Stanford and Bradley's reasoning (e.g., Straus 2000, Straus et al. 2005). Arguments made against the Solutrean hypothesis usually center on several key observations. First, critics usually argue that the technological similarities including the use of overshot flaking between Solutrean and Clovis assemblages need not be attributed to ancestor-descendant relationships, but could be due to similar adaptations to similar environments or to the availability of high quality lithic raw materials instead. Although Stanford and Bradley do list a series of traits that they expect to find in lithic assemblages that are transitional between Solutrean and Clovis, some of these such as pressure flaking and heat-treating were used rather widely by stone tool makers in the past, and nearly all are found among at least some other archaeological cultures. Moreover, many aspects of Solutrean technology are not found in Clovis assemblages or found only rarely. Bone tools and both portable and nonportable art are of great importance in Solutrean contexts, but besides the engraved limestone pieces recovered at the Gault site, there is nothing comparable in Clovis contexts. In short, to many archaeologists Stanford and Bradley make too much of the technological similarities between Clovis and Solutrean technologies.

Second, critics point out that there is a significant time gap between the end of the Solutrean culture at 17,000 BP and the beginning of Clovis, roughly 6000 years later. It is true that Pre-Clovis sites in the Americas date to this gap, but then it is in Pre-Clovis technology rather than in Clovis technology that the closest correspondence to Solutrean might be expected and sought. Unfortunately, there is much less evidence for Pre-Clovis technologies than for Clovis and such comparisons are difficult to make except in a general sense.

Third, as we discuss elsewhere in this chapter, both characteristics of craniofacial morphology and lineage markers in mtDNA were once thought to be indicative of European traits. If this were true, it would bolster the case for a North Atlantic route of entry. However, as study of these non-archaeological indicators has proceeded, it is much less clear that either of these requires European descent at all. At the moment, the biological evidence is viewed as arguing for an Asian origin for Native American populations.

A fourth point also made by critics of the Solutrean hypothesis is that even though the archaeology of Beringia has not been well developed, Stanford and Bradley are incorrect to argue that there are no possible antecedents to Clovis represented in assemblages from this area. Straus, Meltzer, and Goebel (2005) have shown that many of the characteristics that are considered by Stanford and Bradley to be important for linking Solutrean with Clovis assemblages are also found in Beringian and Siberian lithic complexes.

Finally, there is really no evidence of Solutrean marine mammal hunting or adaptation to the ice edge. There is evidence of Solutrean use of coastal resources such as shellfish, but the actual fish remains recovered from Solutrean sites are riverine or anadromous species rather than ocean fish. Marine mammal remains are lacking except for some seal flipper phalanges, and though some cave art may represent seals, it is confined to Solutrean sites adjacent to the Mediterranean and does not depict seal hunting. There also has not been much exploration of how productive the ice edge in the North Atlantic actually was during the LGM. In sum, this aspect of the Solutrean hypothesis is purely speculation (Straus, Meltzer, and Goebel 2005).

Of course, speculation formulated into alternative hypotheses has an important place in archaeological science. Archaeologists do not know how the Americas were settled and by what routes, and there is certainly a great deal of room for testing all the possible routes of entry and the assumptions associated with them. The debate over the Solutrean hypothesis has focused attention on key topics. One of the most important of these is how to interpret technological similarities and differences (Collins 2005). When can archaeologists attribute them to adaptive convergence, and when are they more likely to indicate cultural descent? Another key topic is the evidentiary requirements for drawing conclusions about human migrations. These are both classic archaeological questions that the debate over the Solutrean hypothesis has stimulated. Whether or not we reject this hypothesis, we should be glad for the debate it has generated.

A final possibility is that there were several migrations into the Americas and that these came from different places rather than always from Asia. Some of the evidence for early settlement could be explained if by recognizing multiple migrations and possibly routes (Faught 2008). This would mean that there were several source populations for American Indians though the best way to explore this may be to explore biological rather than archaeological evidence.

Insights from Nonarchaeological Data

Cultural remains are not the only materials that provide scholars with an understanding of the settlement of the Americas. Human remains are also important sources. Not surprisingly, there have been some claims of Pre-Clovis human remains from North America, but AMS dating has established that they probably all date after 11,000 BP (Taylor et al. 1985).

However, a number of other human skeletal remains have been reliably dated between 11,000 and 8000 years ago. Although this database is small and some of the material is fragmentary, it does allow preliminary investigation of the biological features of the earliest Americans. Comparison of the characteristics of these skeletons with the skeletons of present-day Native Americans and also with the characteristics of Asian and other populations may shed light both on where migrants came from and on their route of entry. In fact, such comparisons are fascinating and puzzling. This is because the dimensions of the face and cranium of at least some of these earliest Americans differ in significant ways from those of modern-day Native Americans (Steele and Powell 1994, 2002). The **Kennewick skeleton** (see CD Section F.4) is one of the examples, but there are others. As a group, the crania older than 8500 BP are less like modern northern Asians and modern Native Americans in certain characteristics than we might expect. Specifically, the braincase is narrower and longer than that generally found among modern North Asians and Native Americans. However, it is wider and shorter than the norm for modern South Asians and Europeans. These earliest Americans also seem to have had faces that were intermediate in terms of the width of the face and of the nasal aperture.

Interpreting these observations is a complicated matter. These distinctive craniofacial features may be telling us something about the populations that first settled the Americas, and to this end there has been recent study of possible craniofacial types (Jantz and Owsley 2001; Neves and Hubbe 2005). For example, the earliest Americans, now sometimes called **Paleoamericans** rather than Paleoindians (Bonnichsen and Turnmire 1999), could have migrated from different populations and regions than the ancestors of the majority of modern Native Americans did. If this is the case, there were at least two migrations from at least two separate source populations into the Americas. However, there is evidence that craniofacial features can change in response to environmental change, cultural practices, and isolation of populations so that attributing the differences in these features to different source populations alone is at best overly simplistic (Roseman and Weaver 2004). It might instead be that the craniofacial differences we observe between modern Native Americans and the few skeletons we have of the earliest Americans result from normal processes of inheritance, genetic drift, mutation, and interaction between populations over the last 10,000 years. It is important to remember that it is difficult enough to use craniofacial features to distinguish modern human populations, let alone try to project those into the past in order to discover ancestor-descendant relationships.

A variety of other biological characters have been explored in modern Native American populations based on the assumption that Native Americans should be more like other modern populations also descended from the source population or populations for the first American migrants. Sometimes these characters can also be studied in archaeological specimens. Most important among these studies has been investigation of dental and mitochondrial DNA (**mtDNA**) characteristics.

Dental characteristics have been carefully evaluated by comparing both modern and prehistoric Native American specimens with the teeth of other human populations. A large number of tooth crown and root traits have been shown to vary in consistent ways between populations. For example, both **shovel-shaped incisors** and three-rooted first lower molars are rare among Europeans but commonly found among Asians and Native Americans. In contrast, **Carabelli's cusp**,

an extra reduced cusp or tubercle sometimes found on the upper molars, is much more common among people of European descent than among other populations (Figure 3.15) (Turner 1983).

Christy Turner's evaluation of dental data indicates little dental variation among Native American populations, although the greatest variability characterizes northern populations, as would be expected if settlement of the Americas occurred recently and proceeded north to south. In addition, all Native American populations appear to be more closely related to Asian populations than to those from Europe or Africa. These data also led Turner to argue that Native Americans result from three separate migrations out of northern Asia. Turner believed these to be (1) a Paleoindian migration that, based on dental traits, originated in North Asia and was responsible for most American Indian populations, (2) a later Aleut-Eskimo migration also starting in North Asia, and (3) a third migration of the ancestor of Na-Dene-speaking groups of western North America.

Turner identified the dental pattern found among Native Americans and North Asians as **Sinodont** and

FIGURE 3.15 Dental characteristics that occur in differing frequencies in populations of Asian and Native American as opposed to European descent.

Shovel-shaped incisor

Non-shovel-shaped incisor

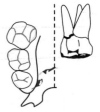

Carabelli's cusp on an upper first molar

Three-rooted lower first molar

Two-rooted lower first molar

contrasts it with a South Asian pattern he calls **Sundadont**. Thus, Turner argued strongly for a single ancestral population that was located in North Asia, perhaps in eastern Siberia. Turner tended to accept the Clovis-First scenario, arguing that Native American Sinodonts have been diverging from North Asian Sinodonts since approximately Clovis times (Greenberg et al. 1986; Turner 1983, 1994).

Turner's interpretation also corresponded with some linguistic analyses, notably those of Joseph Greenberg (Greenberg, 1987; Greenberg et al. 1986), who has proposed that all Native American languages cluster into three groups: a large Amerind group, an Aleut-Eskimo group, and a Na-Dene group. Obviously these fit perfectly with Turner's idea of three waves of migration into North America. Greenberg has accumulated a vast amount of data on Native American languages; however, his methods are somewhat controversial. Other linguists (e.g., Goddard and Campbell 1994) believe that there are many more linguistic groupings among Native American languages and argue for more detailed linguistic analyses. Moreover, recent molecular studies indicate that the tripartite division proposed by these researchers does not correspond with the genetics of Native Americans at all. In fact, the data indicate either widespread genetic exchange across linguistic difference or shared languages in spite of genetic differences (Meltzer 2009:163).

In the last two decades a great deal of new genetic data has been brought to bear on the problem of Native American origins. Most studies have been of modern populations, although an increasing number of ancient DNA (aDNA) studies are providing important information as well. These studies have identified markers in the mitochondrial (mtDNA), which is inherited only from one's mother, and the Y chromosome DNA, which does not recombined during sexual reproduction (non-recombining Y, or NRY). Markers of a person's maternal lineage are evident in the mtDNA, and for males the NRY indicates the paternal lineage. People who share markers can be grouped together into genetic lineages called **haplogroups** and their branches, or **haplotypes**. Haplogroups that are found in both Asian and American populations and also were the sources of haplotypes found only in the Americas are considered founding haploppgroups or lineages. There are five founding haplogroups that have been found by studying the mtDNA of contemporary Native Americans (haplogroups A, B, C, D, and X) along with haplotypes for each of these (Schurr 2004; Schurr et al. 1990). An additional haplogroup (M) was recognized recently in mid-Holocene aDNA (Malhi et al. 2007), and there may yet be other founding mtDNA haplogroups that are no longer present among modern Native American populations but were in earlier

populations. NRY haplogroups and haplotypes also have been recognized by studies of the Y chromosome (haplogroups C, P, Q, and R) (Schurr 2004).

Approximately 97 percent of Native Americans can be placed in haplogroups A–D based on mtDNA. **Haplogroup X**, which is much rarer than the other lineages found among contemporary Native Americans, was originally thought to reflect linkage to European populations as well as possible support for the Solutrean hypothesis (see Box 3.1). Although haplogroup X might indicate recent admixture with modern European Americans, differences between European and Native American haplogroup X characteristics argue against this interpretation. Haplogroup X also has been found in populations from the Altai region of Central Asia and farther east in Asia (Derenko et al. 2001). Since it now appears that haplogroup X is present, if rare, throughout Eurasian populations, finding it among Native Americans does not necessarily mean it came from Europeans after all.

Studies of the distribution of the founding haplogroups and haplotypes provide many clues concerning the settlement of the Americas. There is a rapidly growing body of data and a wide variety of interpretations, which makes it difficult to identify consensus viewpoints. Nonetheless, several summary points can be made.

First, the source populations for Native Americans must be sought in Asia. More specifically a region extending from the Altai Mountains to southeastern Siberia and northern China is the most likely source area for Native American populations. Somewhat broader source areas may be suggested by the known distribution of haplogroup X, and NRY evidence may indicate a source population in south-central or eastern Siberia as well (Schurr 2005). Nevertheless, genetic studies support the long-standing assumption that the Americas were populated by people from Northeast Asia rather than elsewhere.

Second, although some genetic studies have concluded that as many as three initial migrations into the Americas could have taken place, there may be somewhat more support for a single initial migration among geneticists (Schurr 2004). One recent study of Asian and American mtDNA concluded that the ancestors of Native Americans paused in Beringia long enough for the divergence of American haplotypes before continuing southward, then moved rapidly to populate areas throughout the Americas, diverging and interacting from there and even, in small numbers, back migrating to Asia (Tamm et al. 2007). These conclusions are, however, about the initial founding human population. Later migrations are certainly possible, and nearly all researchers agree that Eskimo-Aleut and Athapaskan or Na-Dene peoples migrated in the Americas later in time.

Third, a variety of estimated ages for the various founding lineages derived from modern mtDNA and NRY range from the pre-LGM period to the end of the Pleistocene. Molecular age estimates are based on assumptions about mutation rates in various portions of the DNA as well as other assumptions concerning numbers of founding lineages, so age calculations must be understood as estimates that may yet be refined or proven incorrect. In general, molecular data provide divergence date estimates between 35,000 BP and 15,000 BP (Schurr 2004, 2005) in concert with a Pre-Clovis migration. The dating for the Eskimo-Aleut and Na-Dene migration is estimated between 10,000 BP and 5,000 BP by geneticists. Ancient DNA occurrences of haplogroups and haplotypes is yet again another matter, and because we do not have skeletons of great age or aDNA from very many skeletons, the oldest findings are in skeletons younger than 10,000 BP.

Finally, the current dates of divergence for the founding haplogroups and haplotypes strongly suggest a coastal route of entry as the ice-free corridor would not have been open prior to approximately 12,000 BP. Fix (2005) has developed a simulation for the dispersal of the five founding haplogroups via a coastal migration route using expected and observed frequencies of these lineages in various populations.

These genetic studies are interesting and significant, but the data and interpretations they generate are not panaceas. As with other puzzling areas, these data raise as many questions as they answer, and there is room for much more study, especially of aDNA. Genetic results must be considered in conjunction with archaeological, geological, and other evidence. It is only then that they become truly useful.

In summary, although there is not the sort of consensus once represented by the Clovis-First position, most archaeologists do accept a Pre-Clovis human presence in the Americas. As a result of this acceptance, attention has turned to the possibility of a coastal route of entry, and new evidence concerning this route is being generated. It seems most likely that only small numbers of people were in the Americas before Clovis times. It also seems most likely that the Pre-Clovis period began after the LGM, only a few thousand years before Clovis. Nonarchaeological as well as archaeological data seem to generally support these conclusions. However, the archaeology of Beringia is still in its infancy and cannot be said to fully support the Pre-Clovis position. It remains a puzzle that deserves much archaeological attention. There are still many other unknowns concerning the settlement of the Americas. Related to these are questions concerning the nature and diversity of early human adaptations in the Americas.

PALEOINDIAN ADAPTATIONS

The first Paleoindian discoveries, reviewed at the beginning of this chapter, have strongly conditioned archaeological understanding of the nature of Clovis and Folsom adaptations. The association of stone tools and extinct fauna not only established the greater time depth of humans in the Americas, but suggested that the First Americans were hunters of large game such as mammoth and bison. As more kill sites were discovered on the Plains and in the Southwest, the concept of Paleoindians as big-game hunters became established in archaeological thinking. The close similarity among Clovis points from all parts of the continent reinforced the idea that the Clovis culture was a single, continent-wide adaptation. Moreover, the Pleistocene overkill model seemed to explain how specialized big-game hunters could have rapidly colonized the entire continent. As a result, the traditional viewpoint has been that cultural differentiation among Paleoindians was largely a temporal phenomenon with the earliest people focused on the exploitation of now extinct megafauna and later Paleoindians relying on more modern game herds. Other aspects of these Paleoindian adaptations were thought to include short-term use of camps and high mobility, small group size, the use of high-quality raw materials, often obtained at a distance, and sophisticated stone-working techniques.

Acceptance of a Pre-Clovis presence in the Americas has led to rethinking models and the accumulation of more data has changed perspectives concerning Paleoindian lifestyles. Archaeologists no longer envision a single lifestyle for the continent's first inhabitants. Today both regional and temporal variations among Paleoindians are assumed, and the challenge is to document the diversity of lifeways. The body of data on these lifeways is growing steadily.

Temporally, we can subdivide the Paleoindian period into Pre-Clovis, Clovis, and Later Paleoindian subperiods. The end of Clovis seems to be closely related to the onset of the Younger Dryas climatic interval, a period of major cooling that interrupted the warming trend at the end of the Wisconsin glaciations. At least in New England and the Canadian Maritime Provinces, the end of the Younger Dryas may also be associated with the end of the fluted point era (Newby et al. 2005). One recent hypothesis concerning environmental change and Paleoindian subperiods has recently caught archaeologists' attention. Noting that a calcium-rich black stratigraphic layer often has been identified immediately above Clovis deposits, some researchers have proposed that an extraterrestrial impact over northern North America at this juncture caused major environmental changes, the final demise of Pleistocene megafauna, and a demographic collapse in Clovis populations (Firestone et al. 2007). Exploration of this hypothesis has generally discounted it (Buchanan et al. 2008; Holliday and Meltzer 2010), but it does present a fascinating proposition that is leading to much more attention being paid to the environmental specifics of the Younger Dryas (Toner 2010).

Regional contrasts in dating, technology, and adaptations also are evident, and this is reflected in some variability in subperiod designations across the continent. Summary information concerning some of the oldest archaeological sites in North America's ten culture areas is presented in Table 3.1 in order to provide you with a sense of the Paleoindian record across the continent.

TABLE 3.1 Examples of Paleoindian Sites and Data from North America's Ten Culture Areas

Culture Area	Dates of Oldest Sites	Site and Tradition Names and Locations	Artifact Assemblages	Other Information
Arctic	24,800 BP	Bluefish Caves, Yukon	Possible bone artifacts	
	11,000 BP	Nenana complex, Central Alaska	Core and blade technology, Chindadn points, no microblades	Diverse fauna remains, both large and small game, as well as waterfowl and some fish
			Microblades, wedge-shaped microblade cores, bifacial tools, burins	Blood residue from large mammals including mammoths
	11,000–8,000 BP	Denali complex, Central Alaska	Fluted points	
	11,700–9,700 BP	Mesa site, Northern Alaska		
Subarctic	10,000–7000 BP	Northern Cordilleran complex	Leaf-shaped points, prismatic blades, no microblades	
			Microblades	
		Northwest Microblade tradition		
Northwest Coast	12,000 BP	Manis site, Sequim, Washington	Bone point embedded in mastodon rib	Mastodon bones may show disarticulation by humans
			Leaf-shaped bifaces	
	10,600 BP	Queen Charlotte Islands,	Leaf-shaped bifaces, scrapers, unifaces, cobble choppers, gravers, spokeshaves	
	9500–8900 BP	Kingii complex	Kingii toolkit plus microblades	
	8900–5000 BP	Moresby tradition		

TABLE 3.1 (*Continued*)

Culture Area	Dates of Oldest Sites	Site and Tradition Names and Locations	Artifact Assemblages	Other Information
Plateau		Richey-Roberts Clovis Cache, East Wenatchee, Washington	Clovis points, bifacial and unifacial stone tools, and bone rods	Blood residue from bison, deer, members of the rabbit family, and humans
				Fauna dominated by bison, along with elk, deer, and pronghorn
	11,500 BP	Marmes Rockshelter	Human cremations	
	9000–7800 BP	Windust and Cascade phases	Lanceolate and Leaf-shaped points, cobble tools, bifaces, scrapers, gravers, burins, bola stones, edge ground cobbles, bone points, needles, awls, and beads	
California	15,800–11,380 BP	Tulare Lake, Central Valley	Human bones, Clovis-like points from surface bifaces, projectile points, eccentric crescents, shell beads, bone bipoints, or fish gouges	
	13,000–8000 BP	Northern Channel Island sites	Fluted obsidian points	Woven seagrass, cordage shellfish and fish, sea otter, seal, seabirds
	12,000–11,000 BP	Borax Lake		
	10,000–8500 BP	San Dieguito	Leaf-shaped points and knives	
Great Basin	12,000 BP	Paisley Caves		Human coprolites
	11,000–10,000 BP	Tule Springs, Nevada	Charcoal and artifacts	Extinct species
	11,700–8500 BP	Gypsum Cave		Ground sloth dung
	11,000–8000 BP	Owl Cave, Idaho	Folsom and Plano points	Mammoth, bison, camels,

(*Continued*)

TABLE 3.1 (*Continued*)

	11,600- 10,300 BP	Jaguar Cave, Idaho	Plano points	Extinct mountain sheep, domestic dogs
	11,500–10,500 and later	Connley Cave No. 4B, Smith Creek Cave, Sunshine Locality	Western Stemmed point varieties, crescents	
Southwest	40,000 BP??	Pendejo Cave?		Fingerprints and human hair
	10,900 BP	Sandia Cave, New Mexico	Single-shouldered projectile points (integrity issues)	
			Clovis Points, scrapers, knives, chopper	Mammoth bones
		San Pedro Valley Clovis		
	8500–8000 BP	Surface finds of Clovis and Folsom		
		Cody complex		
Great Plains	19,000–15,600 BP?	La Sena and Shaffert sites, Medicine Creek, Nebraska	Mammoth bones with fracture patterns possibly made by humans	
		Numerous Clovis sites	Clovis points, prismatic blades, bone and ivory rods, gravers, scrapers, engraved cobbles, caches	
	11,050–10,900BP			Mammoths, bison, other extinct megafauna, other animals
			Folsom points	
				Bison, large and small mammals, birds, fish
		Numerous Folsom sites	Agate Basin, Hell Gap, Cody complex, Allen, and other unfluted lanceolate points	Bison kills
	10,900–10,200 BP			
		Unfluted Plano complex		
	10,500–8000 BP			

(Continued)

TABLE 3.1 (*Continued*)

Culture Area	Dates of Oldest Sites	Site and Tradition Names and Locations	Artifact Assemblages	Other Information
Southeast	16,000 years ago	Topper site, South Carolina	Artifacts beneath Clovis layer	
	16,700–15,000BP	Cactus Hill, Virginia	Small blades, unfluted lanceolate points	
			Modified and used bone, crude sandstone tools	
	14,510 BP	SB-2, Virginia	Wooden Stake driven through tortoise shell	Musk-ox tibia
			Suwanee (unfluted) points	
	13,500–12,000 BP	Little Salt Spring, Florida		Extinct tortoise
	13,130–9450 BP	Page-Ladson, Ryan-Harley, Florida	Clovis points, Gainey points in Northeast	Underwater sites, mastodon stomach contents, turtle, deer, fish
			Folsom, Cumberland, and Redstone	
			Dalton	
	12,000–10,900 BP	Numerous Clovis finds and a few dated sites	Dalton, Quad, Hardaway	Cemetery site
		Full Fluted points and sites		Waterfowl, white-tailed deer, hackberry seeds, hickory nuts
	10,800–10,500 BP	Sloan site, Arkansas		
	10,500–10,000 BP	Dust Cave, Alabama		
Northeast	14,500 BP	Miller complex, Meadowcroft Rockshelter, Pennsylvania	Small prismatic blades, small cores, Miller unfluted lanceolate point	Diverse faunal assemblage
			Butchered mammoth carcasses, unfluted lanceolate points, other stone tools	
		Chesrow complex, Wisconsin	Gainey (fluted) points, bone rods	Mammoth utilization

(*Continued*)

TABLE 3.1 (*Continued*)

12,500 BP			
		Gainey (fluted) points	
	Sheriden Cave, Paleo-Crossing, Ohio		Associated extinct fauna
11,000–10,400 BP	Debert, Nova Scotia, Vail, Maine, Bull Brook, Massachusetts	Fluted points, scrapers, knives	
	Shawnee-Minisink, Pennsylvania	Unfluted Lanceolate points	Caribou utilization??
11,000–10,500 BP	Varney Farm, Maine		
			Fish and seeds
10,900 BP			
9400–9000 BP			

Pre-Clovis Subperiod

Given the small number of sites, it is not surprising that archaeologists still know very little about Pre-Clovis adaptations. The most reasonable assumption is that these people were generalized foragers who used a variety of resources. Some may have hunted large game animals, while coastal peoples most certainly would have depended on fish, shellfish, and other marine and littoral resources. The well-preserved remains at Monte Verde in Chile include a chunk of mastodon meat, but also evidence for utilization of a variety of plant and animal resources including seaweed and shellfish (Dillehay et al. 2008). Unfortunately, there are no equivalently well-preserved Beringian and North American Pre-Clovis sites that allow us to test these assumptions.

Human interaction with now extinct megafauna, especially mammoths and mastodons, is indicated in various contexts dating to Pre-Clovis times. Data often come from studies of animal bone taphonomy rather than artifacts. For example, Johnson (2005) has studied the human damage to mammoth bones (e.g., cut marks and impact fractures) recovered from thirteen Pre-Clovis sites located within the Great Plains Biome. She concludes that within North American grasslands, generalized Pre-Clovis foragers both hunted mammoths and scavenged carcasses for food and for bone and tusks. Another suggestion based solely on paleontological finds of mammoths and mastodons in deposits of aquatic origins has been that the earliest Americans were caching parts of carcasses in ponds in order to preserve the meat (Fisher 2004). Some of the sites that Johnson considers are associated with the proposed Pre-Clovis Chesrow complex of southeastern Wisconsin (Overstreet 2004, 2005), which, besides apparently butchered mammoth bones, has yielded unfluted bifaces as well as flakes. Overstreet suggests that this complex is part of an Initial Eastern Biface tradition of Pre-Clovis age that in southeastern Wisconsin is associated with exploitation of tundra habitats at the margins of glacial ice.

Clovis Subperiod

In contrast to the situation for Pre-Clovis, there is a large body of data for the Clovis period. Although much can still be learned about this part of the Paleoindian record as well, a much fuller picture of Clovis adaptations has been emerging in recent years. Besides Clovis points, the Clovis toolkit includes bone points with beveled ends, bone and ivory foreshafts for spears, bone **shaft wrenches,** large bifaces, prismatic blades, blade cores, end and **side scrapers,** and **gravers,** as well as more expedient tools (Figure 3.16).

Important sites like the Gault Site in Central Texas, which was a quarry, a workshop, and a campsite are adding to archaeological understanding of Clovis lithic technology (Waters et al. 2011). The large numbers of artifacts recovered from this site establish that Clovis flintknappers used separate reduction trajectories for making blades and for making projectile points and other bifacial tools.

FIGURE 3.16 Clovis toolkit showing large biface, two Clovis points, a stone blade, a bone shaft wrench probably used for straightening spear shafts, a bone foreshaft, a wedge, a scraper, and other stone artifacts.

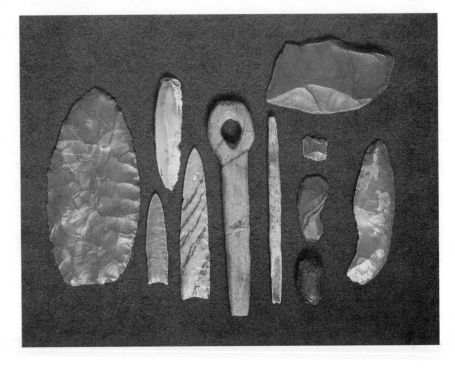

Researchers now argue for some regional diversity in Clovis era lithic technology and tradition. For example, in the Northwest, the **Windust phase** may overlap with Clovis and continue beyond it (Bonnichsen and Turnmire 1999), and a Western Stemmed Point tradition may coexist or even precede Clovis in the Great Basin and Snake River plain (Bryan and Touhy 1999). Beck and Jones (2010) even argue that the first human inhabitants in areas of the West between the coast ranges and the Rocky Mountains were actually people who migrated in from the West Coast. These migrants lacked Clovis technology and made large, contracting stemmed points indicative of the Western Stemmed Point tradition instead. Clovis populations with their highly distinctive technology arrived later from either the southern Plains or the Southeast according to these researchers.

Models of Clovis lifestyles have often drawn on the idea that Clovis people were entering pristine landscapes, devoid of other humans. One very influential proposal was that Paleoindians were not like any ethnographically known recent hunter-gatherers because they were not "place oriented." Instead of foraging within a known territory, they focused on terrestrial fauna, some of which was on the move, often in unknown terrain. This meant that they relied on their knowledge of animal behavior as well as their hunting technology, that they did not store resources, and that they moved often in response to seasonal and year-to-year fluctuations in resource availability. These attributes of the earliest Americans would have changed over time as the resource structure altered, human population levels grew, and territoriality developed (Kelly and Todd 1988).

Although the acceptance of a Pre-Clovis human presence means that North America was not uninhabited when Clovis people arrived, the existing human population was certainly small. If we assume that the rapid spread of Clovis technology is not the result of diffusion among preexisting populations, but evidence of an actual migration of people, models of colonization have some relevance. Clovis people were unusual in this respect, and modern analogues are lacking (Meltzer 2004, 2009; see also Barton et al. 2004). Archaeological analogues also are rare, though Ellis (2008) compares Clovis and other fluted point makers with the people of the Arctic Small Tool tradition that spread across the Arctic between 4000 BP and 3500 BP, finding similar technological attributes designed for flexibility and rapid tool production.

There is certainly evidence from Clovis sites for the traditional model of Clovis hunters as specialized big-game hunters. Mammoth remains have been found at a number of dramatic Clovis kill sites in the Southwest (Figure 3.17) and on the Great Plains. For example, at Blackwater Draw (see Student CD, Section D. 3), there are remains from six mammoths

FIGURE 3.17 Excavations at the Naco site in Arizona where a Clovis mammoth kill site was uncovered.

apparently killed when they came to the spring for water. At the Dent site in Colorado, 11 mammoth cows and one mammoth bull, possibly driven over a bluff and later dispatched, have been found in association with Clovis points. Other sites, including Naco, Murray Springs, and Lehner Ranch in southern Arizona and the Colby site in northern Wyoming, also contain mammoth bones in association with Clovis points. Clovis bison kill sites do also occur (Bement and Carter 2010). Waguespack and Surovell (2003) explored evidence for diet breadth from 33 Clovis sites spanning much of North America, concluding that a model of specialized hunting of large game supplemented with some use of small game fits the data best.

On the other hand, as Kornfeld (2007) points out, the impression that Paleoindians were specialized big-game hunters depends to a large extent on the available database. As this database has expanded, even on the Great Plains, the idea that Paleoindians were big-game specialists has been reexamined. For example, Hill (2007) examined prey body size in 60 Paleoindian sites in the Great Plains and the Rocky Mountains, concluding that environmental setting did affect hunting strategies even though large game dominated faunal assemblages. He found that more diverse hunting strategies were evident in Paleoindian sites located in alluvial valley and mountain foothill settings as opposed to those located in the grasslands of the High Plains.

Other evidence suggests both locational and seasonal variety in Clovis as well as in later Paleoindian adaptations. For example, large-game kill sites are almost completely restricted to the Great Plains and the Southwest. The Kimmswick site located in eastern Missouri, where Clovis is directly associated with mastodon remains, is atypical for eastern Paleoindian sites (Graham et al. 1981). A growing body of evidence suggests that many if not most Paleoindians had a more generalized strategy that may well have varied seasonally. At the Broken Mammoth site in Alaska, Yesner (2007) infers that there was seasonal variability in animal use, noting the diversity of animals in the faunal assemblage. A partial list of species recovered includes bison, elk, caribou, moose, mountain sheep, hare, marmot, beaver, otter, fox, and wolf, as well as swans, geese, ducks, and some fish. Even at Lubbock Lake, a Clovis site in Texas where mammoth, horse, camel, and bison appear to have been exploited, many smaller mammals were also utilized. These include jackrabbit, muskrat, and wild turkey, as well as ducks, geese, and turtles (Johnson 1977). Similarly, at the Gault site in Texas and at related Clovis components on the Southern Plains, fish, amphibians, reptiles, birds, and small mammals as well as mammoth, horse, and bison have been recovered (Collins 2007).

Much Paleoindian evidence from the Eastern Woodlands is from surface finds of fluted points

(Brennan 1982; Meltzer 1988) or from quarry sites (Lepper and Meltzer 1991), but where sites have been found and efforts made to collect a full range of subsistence remains, the results do not suggest specialization on big game (see Levine 1997). For example, at Shawnee Minisink, a stratified site near the Delaware Water Gap, occupied nearly 11,000 years ago, the first Paleoindian encampment seems to represent late summer or early fall harvesting of fish, berries, and other fruits, as well as tool production and maintenance activities (Dent 2002, 2007). One consideration of Paleoindian presence in the Maritime Provinces of Canada suggests that Late Paleoindians on what now is Prince Edward Island were beginning to exploit various coastal and marine resources (Keenlyside 1991). In New England, Paleoindians may have been attracted to proglacial lakes and rivers from which waterfowl and other resources rather than megafauna might have been obtained (Dincauze and Jacobson 2001).

For the Eastern Woodlands as a whole, David Meltzer (Meltzer 1988; Meltzer and Smith 1986) proposed that two subsistence–settlement patterns developed among the earlier makers of fluted points. He argued that in the Southeast, which was never glaciated and throughout the Pleistocene supported complex forests with a mix of deciduous and coniferous trees and both boreal and temperate zone resources, specialized hunting of large game would not have made ecological sense. Instead, generalized foraging by small residential groups should be expected. In contrast, deglaciated regions to the north, where tundra and spruce parkland predominated at the end of the Pleistocene and beginning of the Holocene, specialized, sometimes communal, hunting of game such as caribou from large base camps may have been a reasonable strategy.

This model may be useful. Several large sites in the Great Lakes area that consist of a series of discrete artifact clusters are believed to represent communal base camps from which the hunting of caribou herds took place (Storck 1984). For example, at the Fisher site, located in Ontario, 19 artifact concentrations were found over approximately 55 acres. Located adjacent to glacial Lake Algonquin, the site probably afforded an excellent view of the surrounding spruce parkland in which caribou herds would have been found. The positioning of sites like the Vail site, located in a narrow valley in western Maine through which caribou herds presumably would have migrated, also reinforces archaeologists' ideas that Northeastern Paleoindians were caribou hunters. Caribou bones have been recovered from the Whipple site in New Hampshire, the Bull Brook site in Massachusetts, the Michaud site in Maine, the Udora site in Ontario,

and elsewhere. Split caribou bone has also been found at the Dutchess Quarry Cave in New York State (Funk et al. 1970).

Although it is true that these sites could represent a series of repeated uses by small, highly mobile bands of Paleoindians, some archaeologists believe communal hunts were being conducted. Careful restudy of Bull Brook, a large Paleoindian site located in eastern Massachusetts, supports the idea that this site represents a large aggregation of people, perhaps from different bands, during a single occupation rather than repeated reuse by one or more small bands as we might traditionally expect (Robinson et al. 2009). Seeman (1994) used the similarity in raw materials and refits of flakes across clusters at the Nobles Pond site in Ohio to determine that this site was an aggregated camp rather than the result of repeated short-term visits by small groups.

West of the Great Plains, evidence for a big-game hunting focus also is lacking in Paleoindian sites (Dixon 1999). Because the largest concentrations of fluted points and western stemmed points are along the shorelines of former lakes that dried up after the Pleistocene, some have proposed that Paleoindians in the Far West exploited a variety of fish and waterfowl resources as well as small and large game. Along the California coast, early people certainly used coastal resources in Clovis and later times (see this chapter's case study and Bonus Case Study Section D.4 on the student CD by L. Mark Raab and Andrew Yatsko, "Eel Point and the Early Settlement of Coastal California: A Case Study in Contemporary Archaeological Research").

The idea that Paleoindians were highly mobile hunter-gatherers who lived in small social groups has been based on variety of lines of evidence. Clovis and later Paleoindian sites are fairly widely dispersed, and they seldom contain evidence of **midden** deposits or permanent structures. Consider, for example, the Shoop site in Pennsylvania, where concentrations of lithic debris are dispersed in clusters about 33 feet (10 m) in diameter along a ridge from which game movements may have been visible (Figure 3.18) (Witthoft 1952). Similarly, the Debert site in Nova Scotia has been interpreted as the locus of short-term encampments used to monitor the movements of game (MacDonald 1968).

Other evidence for a high degree of mobility is the fact that Paleoindian tools found together in the same site often are made from a variety of raw materials, some of which have been transported long distances from their sources. Although exchange between different groups of Paleoindians has been proposed as one mechanism for the movement of lithic materials to sites far from natural outcroppings

FIGURE 3.18 Artist's conception of Paleoindians hunting caribou.

(Hayden 1982), most archaeologists believe Paleoindian hunters procured the raw material themselves. Often they initially made large bifaces or tool blanks, which were kept for later use (Ellis 2008; Meltzer 1984–1985). The selection and transport of high-quality raw materials is one aspect of the evidence that Paleoindians were master flintknappers as well. They clearly knew what stone was good to flake and went to some lengths to obtain it.

A number of spectacular artifact caches of Clovis origin also have been found. These caches are concentrations of artifacts including well-made Clovis points, blades, and other bone and stone artifacts. One idea about these caches is that they were burial offerings, as suggested by the Anzick cache, near Wilsall, Montana: over 100 artifacts were covered with red ocher, a pigment traditionally associated with the mortuary practices of Native Americans. Burning and destruction of artifacts left in caches may also indicate a ritual nature to such features (Deller et al. 2009). Another idea, however, is that mobile Paleoindian hunters were simply storing valuable, but heavy, raw materials at these locations.

On the other hand, there is some evidence that Paleoindians even during Clovis times may have

had territories through which they moved. This interpretation has been used by Pinson (2011) to explain the structure of the Dietz site, a Great Basin Clovis and Western Stemmed Point tradition site located in Oregon. The site is composed of many discrete activity areas reflecting repeated use, but the lithic raw materials come from an area not greater than 120 km, or a four- to five-day walk. Smith (2010) used X-ray fluorescence analysis of the raw materials in Paleoindian stone artifacts to demonstrate that the early inhabitants of the Great Basin probably had discrete foraging territories as well. Although these territories were larger than the territories of later people, Smith argues that there were at least two foraging territories in the western Great basin during Paleoindian times.

Archaeologists also have argued that at least some Paleoindians' mobility was conditioned by the distribution of lithic raw materials. In effect Paleoindians were tethered to the lithic materials they depended upon (Gardner 1977, 1983). Several eastern Paleoindian sites have been interpreted as quarry-related base camps or workshops. It is assumed that these sites appear large compared with hunting camps because of repeated use of the quarry rather than because many people used them at once (Lepper and Meltzer 1991).

Late Paleoindian Subperiod

There also is a large and growing body of data on post-Clovis or Late Paleoindian adaptations. Regional diversity in subsistence, mobility, and settlement is certainly evident in this material. In addition, there are several thoroughly excavated and analyzed sites from this period that give us a better window on how humans adjusted to local environments at the very end of the Pleistocene and beginning of the Holocene. Three examples illustrate these sorts of studies and what they have been teaching us.

Reinvestigation of the Folsom site in New Mexico has given us a clearer picture of this historically important kill site (Meltzer 2006). Meltzer concludes that there is no evidence of a camp as well as a kill site, although given the fact that the Folsom hunters killed and processed 32 bison, a camp that has subsequently been destroyed may have existed. The kill most likely represents a single encounter kill made in the Fall by a nonresidential group of hunters who transported both meat and bone when they left the site after extensive butchering. The stone used to make the tools found at the Folsom site suggests movement through a 90,000 km^2 area in the Piedmont and Plains of Colorado. This site supports the classic model of highly mobile, large-game Paleoindians, as do many other Great Plains Folsom and Plano kill sites (e.g., Wilmsen 1974). On the other hand, not all bone bed sites are kill sites. Recent reanalysis using GIS and zooarchaeological techniques at Bonfire Shelter in Texas has suggested that it was merely a processing site, rather than a bison jump or kill site (Byerly et al. 2005).

Consider the Allen site, located in the Medicine Creek valley of southern Nebraska, in contrast (Bamforth 2007). This site was used by small groups of Paleoindians repeatedly as a campsite over the millennia between 11,000 BP and 8500 BP, and is near to two other special purpose Paleoindian sites in the same drainage. Individual episodes of occupation at the Allen site were probably short, and perhaps got shorter and shorter over time. These camps were usually used during the warmer months of the year. The faunal assemblage from this site is very diverse and indicates that people camping here utilized animals from open uplands, areas close to the creek and the creek itself, hunting bison and later deer and antelope, but also taking small game like rabbits and prairie dogs, while gathering mussels and catching fish as well. The presence of grinding stones indicates the probable consumption of seeds, although ethnobotanical assemblages are not available. Although the raw materials used in groundstone implements from the site appear to have come from some distance away, nonlocal raw material is nearly completely lacking from the flaked lithic assemblage, and Bamforth concludes that the Allen site's inhabitants moved regularly within a small region of the west-central Great Plains.

The Ryan-Harley site located along the Wacissa River in northern Florida is a third post-Clovis campsite, but one with very well preserved bone remains. There are no radiocarbon dates, but the presence of unfluted Suwanee points generally establishes its cultural and chronological affiliation. The small faunal assemblage, including fish, amphibians, birds, reptiles and both extinct and modern mammal species, is highly varied. Extinct species include tapir, horse, mastodon, tortoise, and muskrat. This site establishes the survival of megafauna into the Younger Dryas in the Southeast when it is thought to have become extinct elsewhere in North America. In addition, it documents Paleoindian utilization of wetland or swampy areas (Dunbar et al. 2005).

Other sites from the Late Paleoindian period as well are providing archaeologists with similarly detailed windows on variable human adaptations at this time. This chapter's case study provides information concerning human use of the Pacific coast at this time at Daisy Cave. On the Student CD (Section D.6) you will find a case study concerning Dust Cave, a site in northwestern Alabama whose deepest levels date to the Late Paleoindian subperiod. Here the high usage of waterfowl and other birds, the reliance on both terrestrial and aquatic resources, and the richness and diversity of animal usage all present a very different subsistence picture than that of the Paleoindian specialized on large game usage (see also Walker 2007). Kuehn also found an association between aquatic habitats and Late Paleoindian sites as well as evidence for generalized foraging in his review of five sites from Wisconsin (Kuehn 2007). Thus, it is increasingly clear that regionalization and diversity in human adaptations characterized post-Clovis Paleoindians.

In conclusion, although the data remain imperfect, more is being learned about Paleoindian adaptations. Traditional models associated with the dominance of the Clovis-First scenario have been largely discarded, and detailed studies of key sites are enriching our understanding (Figure 3.19). Most archaeologists agree that many Paleoindians were not specialized big-game hunters at all but were instead generalized foragers who exploited big game at times. Both temporal and regional variation in adaptation is now widely recognized. Other topics, such as those that take us beyond subsistence and settlement into investigations of social dynamics, are

FIGURE 3.19 Excavation of the Gault site in Texas. This is one of the sites now providing new insights about the variability in Clovis adaptations.

also being addressed (e.g., Chilton 2004). Hints of ritual activities at Paleoindian sites, such as the recovery of intentionally deposited raven skeletons in Paleoindian deposits at Charlie Lake Cave in British Columbia (Driver 1999), are receiving renewed attention (see Meltzer 2009:316–318). Like the many remaining questions concerning human entry into the Americas, Paleoindians lifestyles continue to captivate archaeologists and new questions are raised as more data has been gathered.

CHAPTER SUMMARY

This chapter has introduced archaeological views about the early settlement of North America as well as many of the questions that remain for archaeologists. It also has sketched in the lifestyles of the people who first settled the Americas. The most important points made in this chapter can be summarized as follows:

- Although early scholars did not believe that humans had been in the Americas for more than a few thousand years, after the discovery of a fluted projectile point embedded in the rib cage of an extinct bison at the Folsom site in northeastern New Mexico, viewpoints changed. A scenario known as Clovis-First had as its central proposition the position that humans did not settle the North American continent until after 12,000 BP when big-game hunters followed herds of large game south through an ice-free corridor between the glaciers, spreading rapidly across the continent thereafter.

- Today, most archaeologists accept the Pre-Clovis presence of humans in the Americas, although only a few sites are believed to date before 12,000 BP, and these are only a few millennia older but still after the last glacial maximum. A great deal of exciting research has resulted from these changing perspectives. Questions concerning the dating of first human entry, the evidence for early settlement of Beringia, the possible routes of entry, and the implications of nonarchaeological data including that derived from study of DNA all are being actively explored. However, a detailed new consensus has not been reached.

- Archaeologists once thought all Paleoindians had similar big-game hunting lifestyles, but new data have led to rethinking traditional models of Paleoindian adaptation. Today, diversity in tool assemblages, subsistence, mobility, and settlement patterns across regions as well as seasonal and long-term temporal contrasts all are being explored.

SUGGESTIONS FOR FURTHER READING

For a good start in gaining familiarity with Native American origin and other stories:

Erdoes, Richard, and Alfonso Ortiz
   1997 *American Indian Myths and Legends*. Pimlico Press, London.

For thoughtful and readable summaries of the topics covered in this chapter:

Dixon, E. James
   1999 *Bones, Boats and Bison: Archaeology of the First Colonization of Western North America*. University of New Mexico Press, Albuquerque.

Meltzer, David
   2009 *First Peoples in a New World: Colonizing Ice Age America*. University of California Press, Berkeley.

For an accessible summary of the implications of South American evidence on the settlement of the Americas:

Dillehay, Thomas D.
   2000 *The Settlement of the Americas: A New Prehistory*. Basic Books, New York.

For a highly individualistic account of the search for the First Americans emphasizing the Meadowcroft Rockshelter case:

Adovasio, James M., with Jake Page
   2002 *The First Americans: In Pursuit of Archaeology's Greatest Mystery*. Random House, New York.

For a collection of some of the classic articles about Paleoindian archaeology:

Huckell, Bruce B., and J. David Kilby (compilers)
   2004 *Readings in Late Pleistocene North America and Early Paleoindians: Selections from American Antiquity*. Society for American Archaeology, Washington, D.C.

OTHER RESOURCES

The Student CD (Sections H and I) gives web links, additional discussion questions, and other study aids. The Student CD also contains a variety of additional resources. Particularly relevant resources include case studies "Weaponry of Clovis Hunters at Blackwater Draw" (Section D.3), "Eel Point and the Early Settlement of Coastal California: A Case Study in Contemporary Archaeological Research" (Section D.4), and "The Dust Cave Archaeological Project: Investigating Paleoindian and Archaic Lifeways in Southeastern North America" (Section D.6).

CASE STUDY

The nature of Paleoindian adaptations has been debated by archaeologists. Traditional models of Paleoindians as hunters focused on large terrestrial mammals have been questioned as archaeologists have found sites other than the kill sites of the Great Plains and Southwest that contain evidence for a more diversified subsistence and lifestyle. Around the world, we now know that human use of coastal environments has a much longer history than once thought.

Evidence that some Paleoindians used coastal resources has encouraged the perspective that a coastal route of entry into the Americas was possible.. This case study discusses several sites that demonstrate seafaring and coastal foraging by Paleoindians on California's Northern Channel Islands. As you read, consider the implications of these island sites for routes of human entry into the Americas and the diversity of Paleoindian adaptations.

PALEOCOASTAL OCCUPATIONS OF CALIFORNIA'S NORTHERN CHANNEL ISLANDS

Jon M. Erlandson and Torben C. Rick

Research on California's Channel Islands is helping to change views about the colonization of the Americas, the antiquity of maritime adaptations, and the nature of the earliest peoples of the Pacific Coast. The initial migration of humans into the Americas was long seen as a terrestrial enterprise, with hunters trekking across the frigid plains of Beringia, through a newly deglaciated "ice-free corridor" leading to the vast central plains of North America. In this Clovis-First model, the First Americans arrived in the New World about 13,000 years ago and spread rapidly through uninhabited interior regions leaving scattered Clovis points, kill sites, and campsites to mark their presence. North American coastlines were thought to have been settled thousands of years later, after large game were hunted out of interior regions and people slowly adapted to the supposedly less productive resources (shellfish, etc.) of coastal zones. Thus, the Pacific Coast was largely irrelevant to the initial colonization of the New World and early cultural developments in North America. This story fit with contemporary anthropological theory that saw seafaring and maritime adaptations as very late developments in human history (see Erlandson 2001).

Recent data from Africa and the Pacific Rim challenge these models, showing that anatomically modern humans (*Homo sapiens sapiens*) settled some African coastlines at least 160,000 years ago, and spread out of Africa along Asia's south coast roughly 70,000 years ago, colonizing Australia by boat about 50,000 years ago and several archipelagoes of the western Pacific between about 45,000 and 15,000 years ago. Such discoveries, along with new doubts about the availability of the ice-free corridor route at key times, have pushed the Pacific Coast to the forefront of the debate about how and when the Americas were first colonized. The coastal migration theory (Fladmark 1979)

and an ecological correlate known as the kelp highway hypothesis (Erlandson et al. 2007) also gained credibility in recent years, as two occupation sites near the Pacific Coast of South and North America—Monte Verde in Chile (Dillehay et al. 2008) and Paisley Caves in central Oregon (Gilbert et al. 2008)—were identified and dated to 14,000 or more years ago, roughly a millennium before Clovis peoples roamed the interior.

Off the California Coast, early sites on San Miguel and Santa Rosa islands are also showing that Paleoindians colonized offshore islands by about 13,000 years ago (Erlandson et al. 2011; Johnson et al. 2002; Rick et al. 2001). At least seven Paleocoastal sites have now been dated between about 13,000 cal BP and 11,300 cal BP (Rick and Erlandson 2011), along with dozens of sites dated between about 10,200 and 8,000 years ago. These sites have produced a wealth of information about early maritime peoples along the Pacific Coast, including evidence that Paleocoastal peoples were seafarers with a diverse marine-based economy and sophisticated maritime technologies. In this case study, we summarize our recent findings at these Paleocoastal sites and the dynamic geography of the Northern Channel Islands near the end of the Pleistocene.

ENVIRONMENTAL SETTING

Located between about 20 and 42 km off the California Coast, the Northern Channel Islands have been separated from the mainland for millions of years. During the last glacial, however, when sea levels were 120 to 60 meters below present, the Northern Channel Islands of San Miguel, Santa Rosa, Santa Cruz, and Anacapa were joined together as a single island known as **Santarosae**. Twenty thousand years ago, the east end

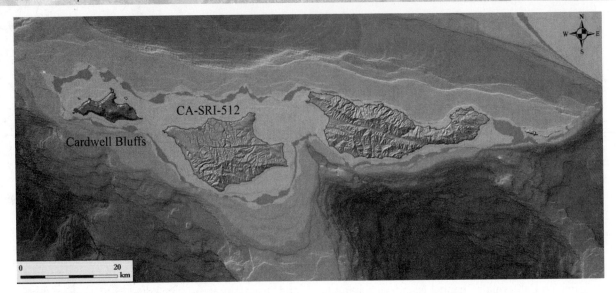

FIGURE 3.20 Archaeological locations discussed in the text and approximate shorelines at 12,000 and 10,000 cal BP.

of Santarosae was only about 6 to 8 kilometers from the mainland. Pygmy mammoths (*Mammuthus exilis*) roamed the island at the time, and a cooler and moister climate supported extensive conifer forests. As sea levels rose rapidly after the end of the last glacial, roughly 70 percent of Santarosae was flooded as it broke into a series of islands and islets (Kennett et al. 2008) (Figure 3.20), the coniferous forests shrunk to small relict communities, and the diminutive mammoths disappeared forever. For understanding the peopling of the Americas, rising seas and coastal erosion are particularly problematic as they have flooded the ancient coastlines and coastal lowlands where early maritime peoples would have spent most of their time.

Today San Miguel and Santa Rosa islands, part of western Santarosae Island in the Terminal Pleistocene, are relatively small islands (37 and 217 km², respectively) sculpted by the sea, with ancient marine terraces forming extensive central tablelands separated from the coast by steep escarpments. Other than the pygmy mammoths, a vampire bat, and small rodents, the first humans who landed on Santarosae found no terrestrial mammals endemic to the island.

Today the coastlines of San Miguel and Santa Rosa islands are a mix of rocky shores and sandy beaches, but rocky coastlines were probably more abundant prior to historical overgrazing and severe erosion of island dune fields. Although terrestrial resources are limited, the ocean surrounding the islands is extremely productive. The upwelling of cool, nutrient-laden ocean waters supports rich plankton blooms and extensive kelp forests that feed complex marine food webs offering a diverse array of shellfish, fish, marine mammals,

and seabirds. More than 150,000 seals and sea lions haul out on island beaches each year, and whales, dolphins, and porpoises are also common in Santa Barbara Channel waters. Sea otters (*Enhydra lutris*) were also common until their local eradication in the mid-1800s by commercial hunters engaged in the historic fur trade.

CULTURAL BACKGROUND

For thousands of years prior to European contact, San Miguel and Santa Rosa were home to the Island Chumash people and their ancestors. Occupying coastlines from Malibu to San Luis Obispo, the coastal Chumash are known for their high population densities, sociopolitical complexity, and elaborate maritime technology—including the *tomol*, or plank canoe (Arnold 2001; Rick 2007). The evolution of this sophisticated seafaring culture was the product of millennia of cultural adaptation to the Channel Islands and broader Santa Barbara Channel area. Archaeological data also demonstrate that Paleoindian peoples first explored the landscapes and seascapes of the Channel Islands by boat at least 13,000 years ago. Due to the difficulty of tracing ethnicity through such deep time, we don't know for certain if today's Chumash people are descended from these Paleocoastal peoples, but it is entirely possible.

Over the years, scholarly views about when the Channel Islands were first settled have changed significantly. Some early archaeologists believed the islands were colonized relatively late, in part because one of the earliest well-documented archaeological cultures of the adjacent mainland, the Millingstone complex, is not found on the islands. In the 1960s, in contrast, Phil Orr (1968) of the Santa Barbara Museum of Natural History argued that humans first settled the Channel Islands more than 40,000 years ago, where they hunted mammoths for tens of thousands of years, and left Pleistocene fire pits and shell middens as proof of their presence. Even now, no clear association of human artifacts with mammoth remains has been found and most archaeologists have rejected Orr's claims for a pre-Clovis occupation of the islands.

One of Orr's early localities withstood the test of time: the Arlington Springs site, where a few leg bones of "Arlington Man" were found eroding from a canyon wall over 11 meters (37 feet) below the surface. Orr (1962, 1968) dated charcoal associated with these bones to about 10,000 ^{14}C years, an age equal to about 12,000 calendar years after calibration. More recent research, conducted in consultation with Chumash elders, including AMS ^{14}C dating of small samples of purified bone collagen from the Arlington Man skeleton, suggests that he died on Santarosae Island nearly 13,000 years ago (Erlandson et al. 2008; Johnson et al. 2002). These dates indicate that Paleoindians used boats to reach the Northern Channel Islands at the same time that Clovis hunters roamed the Great Plains. Unfortunately, the lack of diagnostic artifacts or other occupational debris at Arlington Springs has prevented any firm conclusions about the adaptations of Arlington Man or his potential relationships to Clovis peoples or other cultural traditions.

On San Miguel Island, a low-density shell midden at Daisy Cave dated to roughly 11,500 years ago hinted at a maritime adaptation for early Paleocoastal peoples but also produced no diagnostic artifacts among the few chipped stone artifacts recovered (Erlandson et al. 1996; Rick et al. 2001). What we do know is that during more than a century of archaeology and artifact collecting, no Clovis or other fluted points have ever been found on California's Channel Islands.

DEFINING THE NATURE OF EARLY PALEOCOASTAL ADAPTATIONS ON SANTAROSAE

Identifying coastal sites occupied by Pleistocene peoples is particularly challenging due to the effects of rising postglacial seas, coastal erosion, and related landscape changes. To locate Paleocoastal sites on the remnants of Santarosae, we have focused our efforts on searching geographic features (caves, freshwater springs, and tool-stone outcrops, etc.) that may have drawn early maritime peoples away from submerged coastlines that can lie as much as 8 to 10 kilometers offshore. This strategy has been highly successful, facilitating the identification of at least six new Terminal Pleistocene sites on San Miguel and Santa Rosa islands that are producing a wealth of information about the technologies, adaptations, and lives of Santarosae's Paleocoastal people.

One key locality is a large site complex at Cardwell Bluffs on eastern San Miguel, situated in an extensive cobble field that contains beach-rolled nodules of chert that early Paleocoastal peoples used to make stone tools. Here, hundreds of chipped stone bifaces have been recovered on eroded surfaces, often closely associated with the remnants of at least five shell midden loci that mark camps used by Paleoindians while they were quarrying, stone working, and retooling hunting equipment (Erlandson et al. 2011). AMS ^{14}C dates on marine shells and charcoal from these middens indicate that the quarry/workshop/campsites were occupied between about 12,200 cal BP and 11,300 cal BP, among the earliest shell middens in North America.

The diagnostic artifacts from the Cardwell Bluffs sites include scores of leaf-shaped bifaces and biface preforms, most of them broken during production, as well as dozens of delicately made stemmed points with prominent barbs or serrations, and numerous chipped stone **crescents** (Figure 3.21). Given the lack of sizable endemic land mammals, the stemmed points must have been used primarily in aquatic hunting and fishing activities. The function of the crescents, similar to lunate artifacts found in early sites scattered throughout California and the Great Basin, is more enigmatic, but many archaeologists believe they served as transverse projectile points used in hunting birds (Erlandson et al. 2011). Although most of the artifacts from the Cardwell Bluffs sites seem to be related to hunting, faunal remains from the middens come solely from shellfish harvested from rocky shores (abalones, mussels, crabs, chitons, turban snails, etc.) that were located two kilometers or more away from the sites when they were occupied.

Several sites of similar age have been found on Santa Rosa Island recently (Rick and Erlandson 2011), including two deeply stratified sites that have produced similar stemmed points and crescents but very different faunal assemblages. The best documented of these is CA-SRI-512W, dated to about 11,700 cal BP and located roughly a kilometer from Arlington Springs. Discovered during a coastal survey by the authors in 2008, the site is embedded in a **paleosol** (a buried soil) sealed beneath up to 2.5 meters of essentially sterile alluvium. The site has produced scores of small stemmed and barbed projectile points (Figure 3.22), along with numerous crescents and flake tools, just a few larger biface preforms, two bone tool fragments,

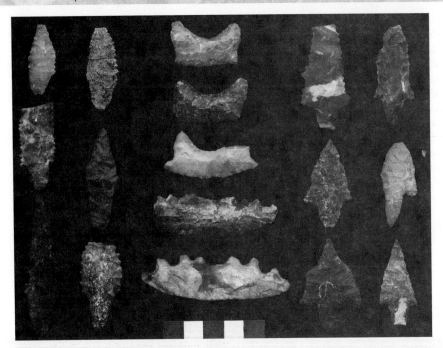

FIGURE 3.21 Chert projectile points from Cardwell Bluffs Sites (CA-SMI-678 and CA-SMI-679, adapted from Erlandson et al. 2011). Center column = five eccentric crescents (top to bottom: SMI-679-39, -214, -67, -5, and -341). Left columns = Amol points (top to bottom, column 1: 678-58, 679-24, 679-256; column 2: 678-722, 679-28, 678-38). Right columns = Channel Island Barbed points (column 4, top to bottom: 679-255, 679-216, 679-300; column 5: 679-215, 678-101, 678-86). SMI-678-722 was found in situ within shell midden stratum dated to ~12,240–11,750 cal BP.

FIGURE 3.22 Paleocoastal artifacts from CA-SRI-512W on Santa Rosa Island (adapted from Erlandson et al. 2011). Channel Island Barbed points at left and three crescents in center column are from slope below eroding A6 paleosol; sawn red ocher, abraded bone tool fragments (upper right), projectile points, and crescents at right were found in situ in test units. (Photo by J. Erlandson.)

and a large piece of sawn red ocher. The faunal remains associated with these artifacts are dominated by the remains of waterfowl (mostly geese) and seabirds, with smaller amounts of marine mammal and fish bone. The presence of several species of migratory geese suggests that the site may have been occupied primarily during winter. Unlike the Cardwell Bluffs sites, no shellfish remains have been found at CA-SRI-512W. Our reconstruction of the local paleogeography suggests that the site was about 5 to 6 km from the open coast at the time it was occupied, but it may have been situated near an extensive marsh formed as rising seas inundated the lower reaches of Arlington Canyon (Erlandson et al. 2011).

Together, Arlington Springs, Daisy Cave, the Cardwell Bluffs sites, CA-SRI-512W, and other early Paleocoastal sites suggest that seafaring Paleoindians settled Santarosae Island by Clovis times and developed a diversified maritime economy during the Terminal Pleistocene. The presence of stemmed points, crescents, and leaf-shaped bifaces at the sites seems to link these early island peoples technologically to lake- and marsh-side sites of the **Western Pluvial Lakes tradition** across the American Far West. A single obsidian flake found at CA-SRI-512W supports this notion as its geochemistry shows that it was obtained from a volcanic flow located in the southern Sierras nearly 350 km to the east (Erlandson et al. 2011).

LATER PALEOCOASTAL LIFEWAYS: A VIEW FROM DAISY CAVE

The Daisy Cave site consists of a narrow fissure-like cave, a small rock shelter located just outside the cave mouth, and a dense shell midden deposited on the slope below (Erlandson et al. 1996). The cave is one of the few places on San Miguel fully sheltered from the strong northwesterly winds that buffet the island for much of the year. The rocky shoreline below the site is rich in shellfish, and a mosaic of kelp forest, rocky reef, and sandy bottom habitats just offshore support a variety of fish, marine mammals, and seabirds. Because offshore waters drop off relatively steeply, the cave was also relatively close to the coast throughout the Holocene. The combination of shelter and proximity to the sea attracted people to Daisy Cave for at least 11,500 years, although the earliest well-documented occupation was relatively ephemeral.

A chronology anchored by over 50 ^{14}C dates shows that Daisy Cave was also occupied multiple times during the Early, Middle, and Late Holocene. The most extensive midden deposits are associated with Late Paleocoastal occupations dated between about 10,000 cal BP and 8600 cal BP. The deepest sequence of stratified midden layers was found along the drip line of the rock shelter, where the Paleocoastal strata accumulated as amalgamations of cultural debris, wind-blown sediments, pebbles and cobbles derived from the weathering of the conglomerate cave walls, and the remains of animals (gulls, owls, mice, etc.) that used the cave over the millennia. Protected from rain and runoff inside the drip line, these materials are intermixed with bird guano deposited by cormorants and other seabirds that still nest and roost at the site.

The salty seabird guano pickled the cultural debris, leading to extraordinary preservation of shell, bone, and woven artifacts in the Early Holocene strata.

Between about 10,000 cal BP and 8600 cal BP, Daisy Cave was occupied multiple times by Paleocoastal peoples. A diverse array of stone, bone, shell, and other artifacts were recovered from these late Paleocoastal strata, along with thousands of animal bones and shells. Scores of chipped stone tools were recovered, including numerous flake tools, a few biface fragments, and abundant tool-making debris. Most of the chipped stone tools are expedient types made on flakes or chunks that were minimally retouched or utilized. A few projectile points or bifaces were found, however, including one crescent and one stemmed and barbed point (Figure 3.23a and b).

Numerous shell beads were also recovered from the Paleocoastal strata, all made from purple olive (*Olivella biplicata*) shells with their tops (spires) removed to facilitate stringing (Figure 3.23c). Similar *Olivella* beads have been found in other early sites along the California Coast, as well as early interior sites where they indicate long-distance trade with coastal peoples. The earliest specimens from Daisy Cave are among the oldest shell beads found in North America.

Also found in the late Paleocoastal strata were several small **bipoints**, or fish gorges made from bird and mammal bone (Figure 3.23d). These bone gorges—the oldest known fishhooks in the Americas—with a line tied around them just off center and wrapped with bait, were used to catch a variety of fish in rocky reef or kelp forest habitats. Unlike most barbed hooks, which catch fish by piercing their mouth or lip, bone gorges were designed to be swallowed by a fish, catching in their throat when the gorge toggled as the line was jerked.

Most extraordinary of all were more than 1500 woven sea grass (*Phyllospadix* sp.) artifacts found in the Paleocoastal strata. Most of these botanical artifacts were pieces of cordage, but a few woven items and several bundles or clumps of unwoven sea grass were also found. The two most complete basketry fragments are pieces of twined sea grass bundles (Figure 3.23e) that retain several finished edges. The function of these objects is not certain, but they may be sandal fragments—possibly toe flaps that would have covered the top of the foot (Connolly et al. 1995). If so, the **provenience** and width of the most complete specimen suggest that it was probably worn by a child about 8600 years ago. About 1500 pieces of cordage include several different types and many knotted specimens. In the field, cordage was found in discrete concentrations we hoped might be fragments of nets or other woven structures. Despite meticulous

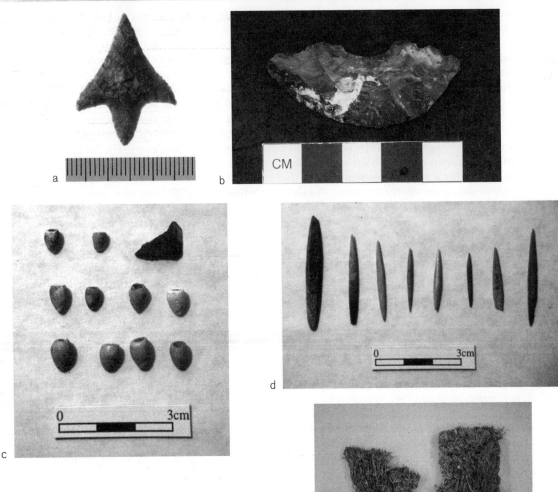

FIGURE 3.23 Artifacts from Daisy Cave (a) barbed point (b) notched "eccentric crescent" tool; (c) shell beads (whole olive scale), ready for stringing; (d) assorted bone bipoints, or fish gorges; and (e) twined sea grass bundles (fragments of basketry).

excavation, however, we recovered hundreds of small and unconnected pieces of cordage that appear to be the debris and "cutoffs" left over from the manufacture of cordage, maintenance of fishing nets, and other activities.

The Paleocoastal strata were also extremely rich in faunal remains, especially marine fish and shellfish, but also the bones of sea otter, pinnipeds, and seabirds. The shellfish were dominated by California mussels, black abalones, turban snails, and other species from rocky intertidal habitats. Over 27,000 fish bones from at least 18 types of fish were recovered, but these were dominated by surfperch (Embiotocidae), rockfish (*Sebastes* spp.), cabezon (*Scorpaenichthys marmoratus*), and California sheephead (*Semicossyphus pulcher*), relatively small fish found near shore in rocky coast and kelp forest habitats (Rick et al. 2001). Dietary reconstructions for the Early Holocene strata suggest that shellfish and small fish made up roughly equal amounts of the meat eaten by the site occupants, but the presence of seal, sea otter, and seabird bones show that the Paleocoastal peoples at Daisy Cave harvested a wide range of marine resources as much as 10,000 years ago.

SUMMARY AND CONCLUSIONS

The submergence of coastlines around the world by rising postglacial sea levels has made early coastal sites difficult to find. On the Northern Channel Islands, our systematic search of caves, springs, and other natural features that drew people inland from now-submerged shorelines has resulted in the identification and dating of more than 50 sites occupied between about 13,000 and 8000 years ago. The earliest of these sites show that maritime Paleoindians had settled islands off the Pacific Coast when Clovis and Folsom peoples roamed interior regions of North America (Erlandson et al. 2008). These and other research findings have forced a reevaluation of traditional terrestrial models for the Pleistocene colonization of the Americas, transforming the Pacific Coast from an area peripheral to Paleoindian studies to one central to current theories about the peopling of the New World.

The Paleocoastal assemblages from the Channel Islands also raise questions about a common assumption of archaeologists applying optimal foraging theory to coastal peoples. In modeling or interpreting the behavior of hunter-gatherers, archaeologists often assume that large animals are more productive for humans to pursue than small game and that evidence for the exploitation of smaller animal and plant resources signal an intensification of human subsistence. At Cardwell Bluffs, Daisy Cave, and other early shell middens of the Santa Barbara Channel region, however, faunal evidence suggests that the subsistence of some of the earliest maritime peoples was relatively eclectic, focused on smaller shellfish, birds, and fish as well as marine mammals. This is clearly evident at Cardwell Bluffs and Daisy Cave, where small turban snails and mussels dominate the earliest assemblages. This suggests that intertidal shellfish—which can often be easily collected in large quantities—were among the most productive resources for Paleocoastal peoples. As a result, the highly productive marine habitats of California's Channel Islands attracted Paleocoastal peoples for at least 13,000 years.

DISCUSSION QUESTIONS

1. What has been found at Paleocoastal sites on California's Channel Islands, and how old are they?
2. Why are these sites so important? What implications are there for modeling the settlement of the Americas?
3. How did postglacial sea level rise affect the Channel Islands and the setting of these Paleocoastal sites? What challenges do such problems pose for archaeologists trying to understand the deep history of coastal migrations and adaptations?
4. Having read about these Paleocoastal sites, do you think archaeologists need to modify their traditional arguments that it is more productive for hunter-gatherers to pursue large game than collecting of shellfish or catching fish? Why or why not?

CHAPTER 4

Foragers of the North

An archaeologist, wearing a jacket and rubber boots, kneels next to a marine biologist on the shoreline of a small inlet. They are tabulating data on oil coverage and damage in a sampling area they have set up. As they work, the biologist from another team is frantically trying to get their attention, for she has seen something alarming—a huge Alaskan brown bear, running across the beach right at her two colleagues. The archaeologist hears his name and looks up the beach. He stands, sees the bear closing in, and taps the biologist on the shoulder. They both know these bears can be dangerous, but neither has had the bear training session promised when they took the job. They try to control the sense of panic that threatens to overwhelm them as they decide whether to run or take some other course of action. The bear, which actually had been chasing salmon down the creek that flowed next to them and had not noticed the people, suddenly sees them. It stops, puzzled for a second at these tall creatures standing out on the treeless shore, and after taking a few halting steps toward the humans, turns instead to wander back to the other side of the low beach ridge to fish in a small pool.

Breathing a sigh of relief, the experts return to examining the oil-soaked shoreline. For the rest of the morning the humans and the bear cautiously check each other out, while tending to their own business. But why is the archaeologist looking for damaged archaeological sites along the Alaskan shore? His team is part of the massive response to the 1989 Exxon *Valdez* oil spill.

Archaeologists were very much a part of the activity after the Exxon *Valdez* disaster, one of the worst oil spills in U.S. history. Twenty-four archaeologists were employed as part of the cleanup team. They cooperated with state and federal officials, as well as native corporations that had cultural resource responsibilities, and they developed a program to identify archaeological sites on the shoreline that were either soaked with oil or threatened with damage as a result of the cleanup.

One heartening result of this work was the finding that the oil did little damage to materials in the archaeological sites, because the portions of sites affected were subject to wave erosion, and the fragile materials from these parts of the sites had already been destroyed by wave action. Because of the cultural resource identification program and a coordinated program of sensitizing cleanup workers to the value of cultural resources (as well as the legal protections that apply to the sites and artifacts), damage from cleanup was less than it might have been otherwise. There was some disturbance to shoreline deposits, and, unfortunately, there were two documented acts of vandalism to sites.

As damaging to other aspects of the environment as the oil spill was, ironically the site identification program enhanced our knowledge of area archaeology. In the process of assessing the archaeological sites, many previously unrecorded sites were added to the archaeological site inventories. Synthesis of the data has contributed important new information to our understanding of this part of the Arctic and Subarctic (Wooley and Haggarty 1995).

This is not the first time oil has played a role in the development of northern archaeology. The construction of the Trans-Alaska Pipeline from the North Slope oil fields to the port of Valdez required archaeological study to clear the right-of-way. Surveys were conducted by the University of Alaska and Alaska Methodist University in the late 1960s and early 1970s. Archaeologists had to work in very remote places to conduct the first really large-scale cultural resource management project required by federal law. Over 330 sites were recorded, and $2.2 million was spent on a project that provided important information on this 800-mile (1290 km) transect across Alaska.

These oil-related projects have revealed that there are many cultural resources within the vast Arctic and Subarctic culture areas covered in this chapter. Because of the remoteness as well as the low density of human populations, many of these sites are unrecorded. Thus large oil-related CRM projects like those mentioned here have been a boon to the archaeological study of the area.

DEFINITION OF THE AREA

This chapter discusses the archaeology of the North, including most of Alaska and the northern part of Canada. This broad area encompasses both the Arctic and the Subarctic culture areas, but there are some good reasons to discuss these areas together (Figure 4.1).

The Arctic extends from the Kenai Peninsula along the Alaska coast to the Bering Sea, taking in the Aleutian Islands and those in the Bering Sea. As the land turns east, the Arctic includes the coast and adjacent tundra of the Yukon and the Northwest Territories, the northern islands, most of **Nunavut**, parts of northern Quebec, the Labrador coast, and

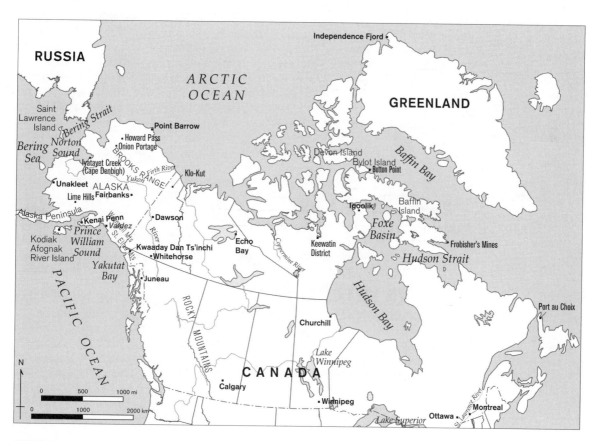

FIGURE 4.1 The Arctic and Subarctic culture areas showing the locations of sites mentioned in Chapter 4.

TABLE 4.1 Introduction to Arctic and Subarctic Culture History

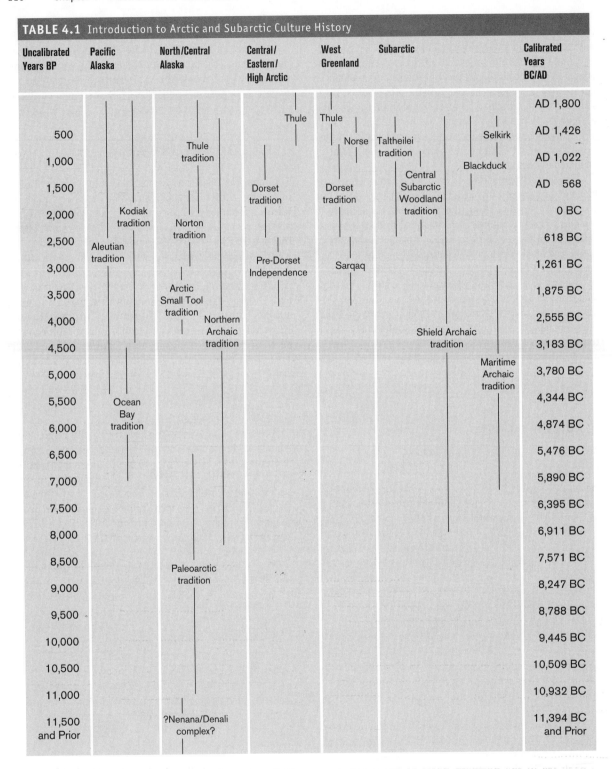

Uncalibrated Years BP	Pacific Alaska	North/Central Alaska	Central/ Eastern/ High Arctic	West Greenland	Subarctic	Calibrated Years BC/AD
						AD 1,800
500			Thule	Thule	Taltheilei tradition — Selkirk	AD 1,426
1,000		Thule tradition		Norse	Blackduck	AD 1,022
1,500			Dorset tradition	Dorset tradition	Central Subarctic Woodland tradition	AD 568
2,000	Kodiak tradition	Norton tradition				0 BC
2,500	Aleutian tradition					618 BC
3,000			Pre-Dorset Independence	Sarqaq		1,261 BC
3,500		Arctic Small Tool tradition				1,875 BC
4,000		Northern Archaic tradition				2,555 BC
4,500					Shield Archaic tradition	3,183 BC
5,000					Maritime Archaic tradition	3,780 BC
5,500	Ocean Bay tradition					4,344 BC
6,000						4,874 BC
6,500						5,476 BC
7,000						5,890 BC
7,500						6,395 BC
8,000						6,911 BC
8,500						7,571 BC
9,000		Paleoarctic tradition				8,247 BC
9,500						8,788 BC
10,000						9,445 BC
10,500						10,509 BC
11,000						10,932 BC
11,500 and Prior		?Nenana/Denali complex?				11,394 BC and Prior

Greenland. The Subarctic lies inland from the Arctic, including interior Alaska and Canada south of the Arctic from the Alaska border through the Yukon Territory, the Northwest Territories, and part of northern Alberta, Saskatchewan, and Manitoba, as well as the areas north of the St. Lawrence River and the Great Lakes, with the exception of southern Ontario and southern Quebec.

The physiographic boundary between the Arctic and the Subarctic is essentially the tree–line—the area where the tundra gives way to coniferous forest to the south. The July 50°F (10°C) isotherm, a line indicating areas of similar temperature, and the southern extent of permafrost, the condition of the ground being frozen at depth all year long, also form reasonable boundaries for the Arctic (Stager and McSkimming 1984:27–28). From a cultural point of view, the line separating the Inuit and Eskimo from other Indian or First Nation groups defines the boundary between the Arctic and the Subarctic (Damas 1984:1). To the south, the Arctic borders the Northwest Coast in Alaska. The Subarctic borders the Plateau, the Plains, the Midwest and Upper Great Lakes, and the Northeast (Helm 1981; Stager and McSkimming 1984:27; Willey 1966:410–411). The cultural chronologies for the Arctic and the Subarctic are outlined in Table 4.1.

THE ENVIRONMENT

Arctic

The Arctic is a land of harsh cold, with little diversity in plant and animal species. There is little soil, and the growing season is short. Precipitation is slight, and high winds help shape a plant life that is low growing, hugging the ground. The terrain varies from west to east, with Alaska having rugged mountains in the south and a tundra plain in the north. Included in the highlands are volcanic mountains that have been active within the last 200 years. Across Canada the tundra continues, with ample signs that the area was covered by glacial ice in the past. Although precipitation is low in this area, it is poorly drained, so boggy conditions prevail in many areas. In Greenland, the coastal strip that concerns us here is generally steep, sloping from the sea to the ice-capped mountains (Dumond 1987).

Sea ice is a prominent feature of the Arctic environment. During the winter months, sea ice reaches land throughout most of the Arctic, and in the summer, the pack ice in the northern parts of the Arctic can reach land at times. Ice can persist in sheltered bays into the summer, and the northern Arctic islands are usually surrounded (Stager and McSkimming 1984).

The sea in the Arctic provided marine mammals—whales, seals, and walruses—all of which were hunted. Fish like Pacific salmon or the arctic char were important anadromous fish that were taken where they were available. Land animals available included caribou, polar bear, musk ox, fox, and arctic hare.

Subarctic

Physiographically the Subarctic varies from east to west. The Canadian Shield is a vast area where bedrock hills are spread among valleys and bogs. Thin soils lie over crystalline bedrock. The Cordillera, which includes the northern end of the Rocky Mountains, is an area of mountains and valleys that separate the shield from the Yukon Plateau. This is a region of rugged relief, and its vegetation zones vary with altitude on the mountain ranges. The Yukon, Kuskokwim, and Tanana plateaus are a complex of hills, low mountain ranges, valleys, and plateaus that make up the central part of Alaska and parts of the adjoining Yukon Territory and British Columbia. The Yukon and Kuskokwim rivers are prominent features of this area, which, unlike the Canadian Shield, was little affected by the glaciers. Beyond the plateaus of central Alaska are found high, glaciated mountains including the Wrangell, Alaska, and Aleutian ranges. Generally, the mountains slope steeply into the sea (Gardner 1981).

Forest characterizes the Subarctic, although the area also includes transition to the tundra of the Arctic. Coniferous trees like white spruce, black spruce, and tamarack are common, and balsam fir and jackpine are also important. Much less common, but important to the inhabitants of the area, are broadleaf trees like poplar, aspen, and birch (Gardner 1981:12–13). The birch was important as a source of bark for making canoes and containers.

Terrestrial animals were important in the economy of peoples living in the Subarctic. Large game like caribou and moose were most important to people living here, but mountain goat, Dall sheep, elk, bison, musk ox, and deer also were present. Small mammals included snowshoe hare, beaver, woodchuck, hoary marmot, muskrat, porcupine, and arctic ground squirrel. Birds of economic importance in the past were species of grouse, goose, and duck, while salmon and many other fish were available in the rivers (Gillespie 1981).

Climatic Change

The most important climatic changes in the harsh environments of the North certainly have been those associated with glaciation, as discussed in Chapters 2 and 3. Later environmental changes certainly also affected

ANTHROPOLOGICAL THEMES   TOPIC 4.1

Thematic Research Questions in Chapter 4

As we pointed out in Chapter 2, the North American archaeological record provides significant evidence for several broad anthropological themes. Archaeologists working in the Arctic and Subarctic culture areas address at least three of the themes listed in Table 2.1, and we touch on other themes less directly. Table 4.2 helps you locate relevant sections of this chapter for each theme, although as you become more familiar with the archaeology of the Arctic and Subarctic culture areas, you will discover more specific research questions and issues as well.

TABLE 4.2 Research Themes for the Arctic and Subarctic

Research Question	Particularly Relevant Sections
How have humans adapted to the diverse environments of North America and to climatic change over time?	Discussions of the various Archaic traditions, the Arctic Small Tool tradition, and the later cultures of the Arctic and Subarctic
What ethnic identities can be identified and historically traced in North America's past?	Discussions of the Thule in the Arctic and of later cultures in the Subarctic
What movements of human populations can be documented in the North American past after the continent's initial settlement?	Discussion of the Thule migration into the High Arctic

the Arctic and Subarctic. The Medieval Warm period (ca. 1050–650 BP) was a time of warmer climate when sea ice appears to have been reduced. This would have allowed greater sea travel and better whaling conditions, as bowhead whales changed their migration routes. The Little Ice Age (ca. 400–100 BP) may well have affected Arctic populations in a variety of ways. Many scholars believe this episode was responsible for the demise of the Norse settlement in Greenland (see Box 13.1), and increases in the amount of sea ice probably impeded the migration of bowhead whales in Arctic Canada. This, in turn, almost certainly had an effect on the native communities that depended on whale hunters for much of their subsistence.

EARLY CULTURES

The Arctic and Subarctic are critical areas for understanding the early cultures of the New World. Assemblages with fluted points are found in Alaska, but generally do not predate Clovis assemblages farther south. As we discussed in the preceding chapter, the earliest well-dated materials from Alaska represent the Nenana and Denali complexes, which are characterized by contrasting technologies. The Nenana complex includes blades, bifaces, and Chindadn points. The Denali complex, in contrast to the Nenana, includes microblades and is part of the Paleoarctic tradition,

which has similarities to early Siberian assemblages. Microblades are important in early assemblages from the western portions of the Subarctic as well as the Arctic. The earliest archaeological assemblages in the western Subarctic are assigned to the **Northwest Microblade tradition**, which may also be subsumed under the Paleoarctic.

ARCHAIC

By 8000 BP archaeologists see the beginnings of the Archaic period, but its manifestations vary considerably from place to place within the Arctic and Subarctic. In the interior, the **Northern Archaic tradition** developed, and on the Pacific Coast maritime cultures, the **Ocean Bay**, **Kodiak**, and **Aleutian traditions**, appear. In the eastern Subarctic, the **Shield Archaic** and the **Maritime Archaic** are commonly recognized traditions.

The Northern Archaic

Originally based on material from the site of Onion Portage site on the Kobuk river in Alaska, the Northern Archaic tradition includes a variety of assemblages that have been found in sites from the interior of Alaska and west of the MacKenzie River in northwestern Canada. As originally defined, this tradition was distinguished largely on the basis of side-notched

CLUES TO THE PAST

EXHIBIT 4.1

Microblades

Archaeologists define blades as flakes that are at least twice as long as they are wide. Generally, they are also parallel sided, and they are produced in small numbers during flaking activities like biface manufacture. When larger numbers of blades are found, it is usually concluded that they were struck from specialized cores. Blades are part of the Clovis toolkit, for example.

As the name indicates, a microblade is a small blade, generally less than 20 mm (¾ in.) long and 5 mm (¹³/₆₄ in.) wide. In addition to parallel sides, a microblade generally has one or more ridges (edges of the scars from the removal of previous flakes) on the **dorsal surfaces**. Microblade cores were made on flakes or bifaces that were set up to allow a number of microblades to be struck from them, usually from a single platform. Such cores were normally about the size of a book of matches and could yield several dozen small, sharp microblades. This technology is a good way to get the largest possible cutting edge out of a small piece of quality raw material. But what good is a cutting edge if the blade is too small for a person to hold?

Actually, the small, sharp blades were very useful. Prehistoric toolmakers fitted microblades into slots cut into bone or wood and glued them in side by side so that the length of the razor-sharp edge of the finished implement was not limited by the size of the individual blades (Figure 4.2). These composite tools included knives and projectiles, and although slotted bone shafts have been recovered in places like Lime Hills, Cave 1 (Ackerman 1996c:471, Fig. 10-7), they have more often been weathered away, leaving only the tiny slivers of sharp stone behind.

Although they appear in several areas of North America, including at the Poverty Point site in Louisiana (Student CD, Section F.6), in many Middle Woodland sites in eastern North America, and along the California coast, microblades are particularly important in the Arctic and Subarctic, as well as in the northern parts of the adjoining Northwest Coast and Plateau. Furthermore, microblade technology provides a tangible link between North American cultures and those of Asia, where the technology appeared earlier. Microblades are found in sites from the Ural Mountains, which divide Europe and Asia, into central British Columbia (Goebel et al. 2000).

The cores of microblade technology are wedge shaped and distinctive. Other characteristic by-products of blade manufacture include **crested blades** (*lames à crêtes* is the name given them in the French literature on lithic technology), blades removed from the face of the core that remove a ridge created by flaking (West 1996b:305), and **core tablets** removed from the top of the core to form or rejuvenate a platform. Microblades appear to have been made by pressure rather than by freehand percussion or indirect percussion from a punch rested on the platform and struck by the hammer (West 1996b:305).

Microblades appear first in the western part of their range, in the Transbaikal area of Asia, and dates become more recent as they moved east. At the Studenoe-2 site in the Transbaikal area, they are dated to between 18,000 BP and 17,000 BP, and at the Bering Strait they date to about 10,000 BP (Goebel et al. 2000). Microblades and wedge-shaped cores are linked to early migrants in the Arctic, although these people may have been preceded by others who did not make microblades (see Chapter 3).

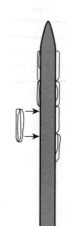

FIGURE 4.2 Composite tool made by using microblades.

---

projectile points and the absence of microblades and microblade cores. Other bifacial stone tools, various scrapers, and other implements also are associated with it. The **Pallisades** (6000–4500 BP) and the **Portage** (4500–4100 BP) **complexes** were recognized at Onion Portage, distinguished primarily by the appearance of leaf-shaped points in the Portage. Artifacts associated with these complexes include convex based side-notched points, unifacial knives, and large numbers of **end scrapers**, as well as notched pebbles that may have been hafted for use as axes (Figure 4.3) (Anderson 1968, 2008; Dumond 1987). Apparently,

FIGURE 4.3 Artifacts from the Portage and Pallisades complexes: (a) knife, (b) projectile point, (c) end blade, (d) beaked tool, and (e) adze blade.

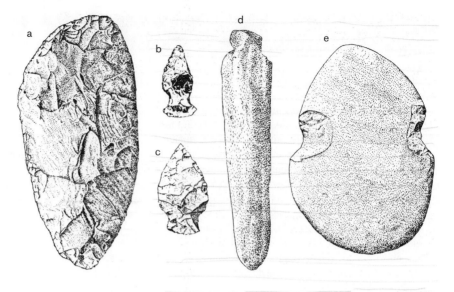

Northern Archaic spread south and eastward over time (Workman 1998).

Since the Northern Archaic was defined in the 1960s, a number of sites which have both side-notched points and microblades have been found. It appears that there is some diversity in Archaic toolkits at this time in the area where the Northern Archaic is found, apparently linked to diversity in subsistence activities. Subsistence appears to have been focused on caribou (Esdale 2008). Bison were hunted in the southern Yukon as well (Workman 1998:568).

The Shield Archaic

After the glaciers retreated from the Canadian Shield, people from the northern Plains moved into this area. This movement started about 8000 BP and is marked by finds of Agate Basin points at sites that include camps in the Keewatin District. The occurrence of these camps at known caribou crossings (places where caribou were concentrated while crossing rivers) suggests that the abundant herd animals may have been what attracted people to move here. Archaeologists believe the Shield Archaic developed out of the Agate Basin (Wright 1981:87–88). As the glaciers continued to shrink northeastward, Shield Archaic groups expanded eastward all the way to the coast of Labrador, reaching there by about 2950 BP (Wright 1998). Thus, eventually, this cultural expression characterized a vast area in the boreal forest of Canada.

Scrapers, bifaces, and knives are characteristic of Shield Archaic assemblages (Figure 4.4). Early in the Shield Archaic, points tend to be lanceolate, but side-notched points become the most common at the end of the period. Millingstones, which are common in

Archaic contexts in other culture areas, are almost completely absent (Wright 1981:88–89). Unfortunately, the generally acidic soils of this region have destroyed most perishable artifacts and ecofacts. The resources of the northern boreal forests are dispersed. As a result, Shield Archaic groups were highly mobile, probably dividing into small family groups over the winter, and living in somewhat larger summer camps from which a variety of resources could be procured.

The Shield Archaic groups almost certainly represent the ancestors of the Algonquian-speaking peoples of the area in historical times. The emphasis on hunting and fishing seen in Shield Archaic sites continued with the Innu or Algonquians, as did the organization into small bands (Wright 1981:96).

Ocean Bay, Kodiak, and Aleutian Traditions

The Ocean Bay tradition or period (7000–3500 BP) is found on Kodiak Island. Similar material is found on the adjacent Alaska Peninsula and in much of Pacific Alaska, and it may be related to material from Anangula in the Aleutians. This tradition is significant for at least two reasons. First, Ocean Bay sites represent early maritime adaptations in the Pacific area of Alaska. Focus on the sea would persist here for many millennia, leading to a degree of sociocultural complexity uncommon among hunter-gatherers. These developments are discussed in this chapter's case study by Ben Fitzhugh, "From Sites to Social Evolution: The Study of Emergent Complexity in the Kodiak Archipelago, Alaska." Second, tools made of ground slate, a raw material of great importance in several parts of the Arctic and Subarctic, appear in this early tradition. These tools contrast with the chipped stone tools we have been discussing thus far.

FIGURE 4.4 Artifacts of the Shield Archaic, including bifaces, scrapers, and projectile points.

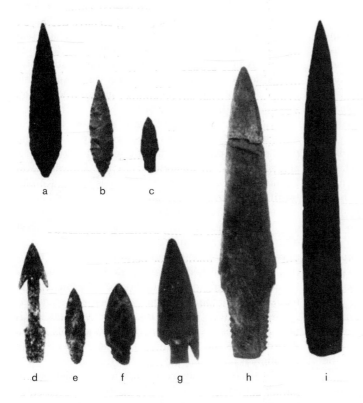

FIGURE 4.5 Ground and flaked tools of the Ocean Bay tradition: (a–c) flaked projectile points, (d) harpoon head, (e) flaked point, (f) knife or blade, (g) blade, (h) ground slate projectile point or blade, (i) ground slate blade.

a   b   c

d   e   f   g   h   i

The Ocean Bay tradition began about 7000 BP, with the introduction of ground slate tools to an inventory still dominated by flaked stone (Figure 4.5). The flaked stone includes percussion-flaked, leaf-shaped knives or projectile points; long, narrow, weakly stemmed percussion-flaked knives or projectile points; microblades; and scrapers. Although not common, bone harpoon heads (Figure 4.6) are found. These have grooves in their tips where a stone point or end blade could be fitted (Dumond 1987:57–59).

FIGURE 4.6 Schematic representations of the use of end blades and side blades in harpoon heads.

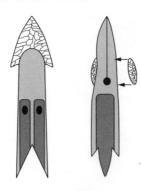

FIGURE 4.7 Kodiak tradition oil lamp from a site on the upper Naknek drainage of the Alaska Peninsula.

Based on the little bone that has been found and on the presence of the harpoon heads, archaeologists have deduced that the Ocean Bay people made their living by hunting sea otter, seal, sea lion, porpoise, and whale. Site locations are consistent with this way of life, but at least one site, located on the Afognak River, is so situated that salmon might have been taken during the summer migration.

On Kodiak Island at about 4500 BP, Ocean Bay develops into what has been variously labeled the Takli Birch phase, Ocean Bay II, or Chirikof Island's Old Islander phase. Characteristic of the **Takli phase** are slate lance or dart points, the oil lamp, and chipped stone tools that resembles earlier Ocean Bay tools. The oil lamp (Figure 4.7) was an open bowl used to hold oil rendered from the fat of sea mammals; a wick of moss placed in the oil was lit to provide both light and heat in Arctic dwellings. Although a bowl that may have served as an oil lamp was recovered from an early Ocean Bay tradition context, oil lamps are more common after 4500 BP. Ground slate is important in Takli stage assemblages, but the transverse knife called the *ulu* was not part of the toolkit (Dumond 1987).

Dwellings are indicated by patterns of postholes and what appears to be the depressed floor of a tent. Sea mammal hunting was important in the Takli phase, and bone harpoon heads continue to be found. Fishing probably also continued to be important, but evidence also exists for land mammal hunting in the form of broken land mammal bone. Takli sites are found in locations appropriate for these activities (Dumond 1987).

Following the Takli phase is the **Kachemak stage or period**, dated from 3500 BP to 1000 BP. Ground slate implements continue to occur in a variety of forms. However, the beginning of the process of making these tools differs from that in the preceding stage. In the Takli stage, ground slate tools were first shaped by sawing, while in the Kachemak stage chipping was the first step in ground slate tool production. Kachemak stage ground slate tools include the *ulu*. This is a transverse knife with a curved blade, and its handle mounted parallel to and opposite from the cutting edge. In Inuit and Eskimo culture these were "women's knives" used for a variety of cutting tasks, especially butchering animals taken in the hunt. Other forms of ground slate tool include knives and weapon blades (Figure 4.8).

Oil lamps are common in Kachemak sites, and some are highly decorated, especially toward the end of the stage. A variety of bone tools, including barbed harpoon heads, also occur. In addition to these harpoons, which are secured in the flesh of the wounded prey animal by barbs carved into the heads, the bone tool assemblage includes **toggling harpoon** heads (Dumond 1987). Toggling harpoons have heads that detach from the shaft and turn sideways in the prey animal. A line connected to the harpoon head allows the hunter to stay tethered to the prey (Figure 4.9). This critical development in sea mammal hunting technology improved the hunting success.

Labrets of stone and bone are also found in Kachemak sites. Similar to those worn by people who practice body piercing today, these prehistoric labrets are plugs that are inserted into the lip or cheek. Kachemak is followed by the Kodiak Island **Koniag tradition** or period of later prehistory discussed in the bonus case study by Ben Fitzhugh.

The Aleutian tradition, which is found to the west of the Kodiak tradition and begins about 5000 BP, also developed out of the Ocean Bay tradition. This tradition is distinguished from the Kodiak tradition by the absence of ground slate tools until very late. Flaked tools are common, and among these are stemmed points and knives (Figure 4.10). As in the Kodiak tradition, oil lamps are found, and the bone tools of the Aleutian tradition are similar to those of the Kodiak tradition.

Sea mammal bones are a common element in Aleutian tradition middens, but marine invertebrates like the sea urchin are also common in some sites. Marine fish like cod, halibut, sculpin, and greenling were important, as were both migratory and resident birds. Land mammals taken include foxes in the western Aleutians, and caribou and bear in the east. Sites of this tradition can be large coastal middens that people seem to have inhabited on a semipermanent

FIGURE 4.8 Implements of the Kachemak stage: (a) flaked slate blade, (b) ulu blade, (c) spear side-prong, (d) sawn bone tube, (e) bipointed bone (possibly a gorge), (f) fishhook shank, (g) fishhook barb, (h–i) flaked stone points, (j) bone arrowhead with slits for blades, (k) barbed dart, (l) toggle harpoon head, (m) carved bone, perhaps representing a seal, (n) notched ulu, (o) jet labret, (p) flaked stone drill, (q) chert wedge, (r) U-notched scraper.

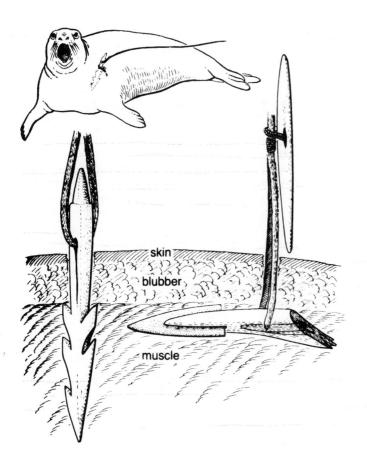

FIGURE 4.9 Action of barbed harpoon heads (left) and toggling harpoon heads (right).

FIGURE 4.10 Artifacts of the Aleutian tradition: (a–b) large flaked bifaces, (c–f) flaked projectile or lance points.

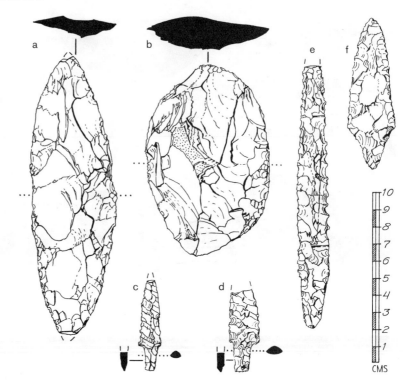

basis. This emphasis on marine resources probably was possible because sea level stabilized around 5000 BP, creating improved habitat for shellfish and fish along the shorelines (McCartney 1998).

About 500 BP ground slate *ulus* begin to make an appearance in the Aleutians. Some other traits appear to have spread into the area with the *ulu*, but most of the material culture remained the same. The Aleutian tradition people appear to have been the ancestors of the modern Aleuts.

Maritime Archaic

Use of sea resources also characterizes Archaic people located on the far northeast coast of North America. Here groups have been considered part of a Maritime Archaic tradition, which dates from about 7500 BP to 3000 BP. This tradition was first recognized based on a cemetery at the site of Port aux Choix in northwestern Newfoundland, and the Maritime Archaic is one of several Middle–Late Archaic traditions also of importance in the archaeology of the Northeast culture area (see Chapter 12). By 6000 BP, a northern branch of this tradition had spread from the Strait of Belle Isle north of Newfoundland, along the Labrador coast past the treeline (Tuck 1998). Eventually, around 3000 BP, the Maritime Archaic in Labrador disappears and people called **Paleoeskimos** by many archaeologists are in

evidence. The Paleoeskimos can be related to a new cultural tradition that first develops far to the west, the **Arctic Small Tool tradition**.

ARCTIC SMALL TOOL TRADITION

Between 4000 BP and 3900 BP, a new archaeological manifestation appears in northern Alaska, characterized by tools that are generally smaller than those of the preceding archaeological cultures. Originally called the **Denbigh Flint complex** from the discovery of such artifacts in a site on Cape Denbigh on the shore of Norton Sound, Alaska (Giddings 1964), it was renamed the Arctic Small Tool tradition after similar artifacts were found over a much greater area, eventually including the High Arctic from Alaska to Greenland. The people who made these tools were the first to colonize the Arctic Ocean coast.

The Arctic Small Tool tradition assemblages contain small, finely worked end blades and side blades that probably were mounted in bone projectiles (Figure 4.11). Microblades are also part of the assemblage, as are burins made on small bifaces. **Burin spalls** sometimes show evidence of use as engraving tools. Arctic Small Tool tradition assemblages may include **adzes** with polished bits and an interesting burinlike tool, with the bit created by grinding the area that

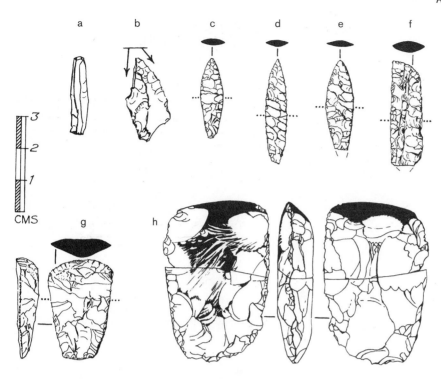

FIGURE 4.11 Artifacts of the Arctic Small Tool tradition: (a) microblade, (b) burin, (c–e) projectile points, (f) side blade, (g) scraper, and (h) adze blade with the bit polished.

would normally be the burin spall scar (the scar of the long flake that creates the burin tip on standard burins). Oil lamps are not present at the beginning of the tradition but are incorporated into it by the end. Bone needles, bone or antler foreshafts for projectiles (probably arrows, indicating use of the bow and arrow), and small bone harpoon heads round out the kinds of artifact found at Arctic Small Tool tradition sites, although these organic items are known only from the eastern part of the range of the tradition. This pattern is attributed to poor preservation of organic materials in the Alaskan sites explored so far (Dumond 1984b:74, 1987).

The separation of the Paleoarctic materials from the Arctic Small Tool tradition occupations at key sites by layers containing artifacts of the Northern Archaic indicates that the development did not occur in Alaska but most likely resulted from a migration out of Siberia. The Arctic Small Tool tradition is not found in the Aleutians, where the Aleutian tradition is thought to have continued until historical times. The evidence clearly suggests two different migrations of people into the Americas (Dumond 1984b:74–75).

Houses have been reported from a number of the Alaskan sites, including Onion Portage and Howard Pass, and at Brooks River in the upper Naknek drainage. Fourteen houses have been at least partially excavated at Brooks River, and all appear to be roughly square and about 4 meters (13 ft.) across (Figure 4.12). They were partially dug into the prehistoric ground surface, and a sloping entry ramp led into the house from the side. A fire area, sometimes ringed with rock, occupied the center of the house floor. In one case there appears to be four postholes around the hearth that may have served as roof supports. Rectangular slab structures in some of the houses are associated with fire-altered rock and may have been used for **stone boiling**. The fill of some of the structures indicates that the roofs were probably sod. Though hunting caribou seems to have been the primary occupation at many of the Arctic Small Tool sites, at least a few on the Alaska Peninsula appear to be situated in such a way as to have taken advantage of summer salmon runs.

Independence and Pre-Dorset

The Arctic Small Tool tradition spread out of Alaska throughout the High Arctic all the way to Greenland. In the eastern part of the Arctic two phases are recognized—**Independence** and **Pre-Dorset**. The Independence sites are the earliest sites in the extreme northern Arctic, with occupation at Independence Fjord in the far north of Greenland occurring between 4000 BP and 3700 BP. The Independence artifacts are similar to those found in the Alaskan sites of the Arctic Small Tool tradition, with microblades, small burins, small side and end blades, and end scrapers. Implements are, overall, slightly larger in the eastern

FIGURE 4.12 Plan of an Arctic Small Tool tradition house from the Brooks River, Alaska.

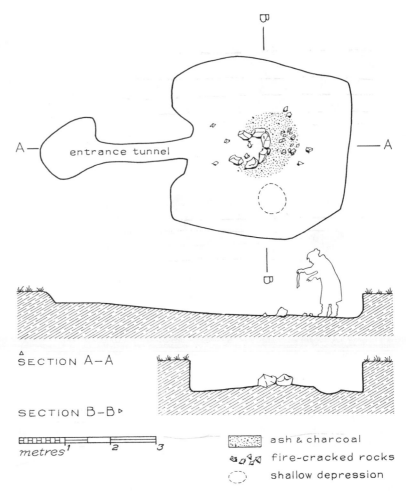

SECTION A—A

SECTION B—B ▷

metres 1 2 3

▨ ash & charcoal
▨ fire-cracked rocks
◌ shallow depression

sites, and tapering stems are found on many of the end blades (Figure 4.13). The edges of flaked tools are often serrated (Dumond 1987).

Unlike most of the Alaskan sites, preservation of organic materials is good on many of the Independence sites. Bone arrowhead fragments and barbed, non-toggling harpoons have been recovered. The harpoons come from Devon Island in the Arctic Archipelago. They are not found in Greenland sites, where faunal remains indicate an emphasis on hunting musk ox. At Independence sites, people also made needles, suggesting the manufacture of tailored clothing.

The Greenland sites appear to represent both summer and winter habitations. Sites inferred to have been summer residences have areas paved with flagstone that would have provided outside work areas. Sites thought to be winter camps have pits for caching food. Houses tend to be elliptical rings of rock with parallel lines of vertical rock slabs defining the **midpassage**, an area that cuts the house in half (Figure 4.14). In the center of the midpassage is usually a square,

slab-lined hearth. Because there is no evidence of roofing material like sod, these structures appear to represent the remains of tents, probably of musk ox hide. We know that the houses were not built of snow, like later Inuit houses, because the open indoor fires would have given off significantly more heat than the flames of small oil lamps. Whatever the construction of the superstructure, these houses must have been substantial enough to shelter people during the long winters of the north. The northern Greenland winter is marked by 2½ months of total darkness (Dumond 1987; McGhee 1996:50). The Independence sites are farther north than those in Alaska. Some of the Greenland sites are within 700 kilometers (435 miles) of the North Pole (Dumond 1987).

Postdating the Independence material, although sometimes treated at a regional variant, is the material known as Pre-Dorset. This material is found in northeast Canada north of Hudson Bay, in the Hudson Straits, and in the Foxe Basin, as well as in parts of Greenland south of where the Independence materials

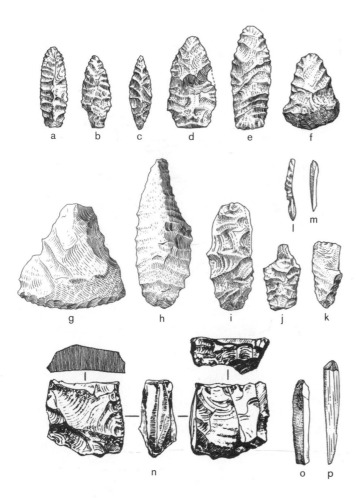

FIGURE 4.13 Artifacts of the Independence culture.

are found. In Greenland, it is known as the **Sarqaq (Saqqaq) culture** (Dumond 1987).

The tools from Pre-Dorset sites differ from those found in Independence sites. Burins and scrapers included in these assemblages indicate the working of bone, antler, and ivory. Burins have ground tips, and burinlike tools with ground rather than flaked faces are found. End blades that are bipointed, thin, and slender were made for use on arrows, and bows appear to have been similar to the small and recurved type the Eskimo used in historical times. People used harpoon heads with open sockets for hunting seal and walrus, while beluga and narwhal may have been hunted as well (Figure 4.15). Lance heads of antler were also open socketed and had grooves for both side and end blades. Dogs apparently helped in the hunt, as their remains are found in the Pre-Dorset levels at Igloolik (Maxwell 1984:361).

The artifacts of the Sarqaq sites are predominantly stone tools, since organic materials are not preserved at most of the sites. Stemmed and bipointed end blades for arrows are common, and many of these have serrated edges. Some of the arrow points have partially ground faces. End and side blades for larger lances are also found, but harpoon end blades are not recovered. Perhaps self-tipped harpoons of bone or antler were used. Spalled burins with ground tips occur, along with scrapers of various types. Large knives with pointed or rounded tips and triangular transverse knives were used for cutting. Soapstone lamps provided light and heat during Sarqaq times. Microblades are part of the Sarqaq collections, but they are relatively rare (Fitzhugh 1984:536). The Sarqaq assemblages resemble those of Alaska at the same time period, though artifacts tend to be somewhat larger, but they differ from other eastern Arctic assemblages (Dumond 1987).

Recent analysis of DNA from human hair that was recovered from permafrost at Qeqertasussuk, an archaeological site at Disko Bay, Greenland, has shed light both on the individual who grew the hair and on the human migrations into the New World. Radiocarbon dated to 4170–3600 calyrBP (corrected for local marine reservoir effect), the genome of the

FIGURE 4.14 Independence house illustrating the midpassage (top: viewed from above).

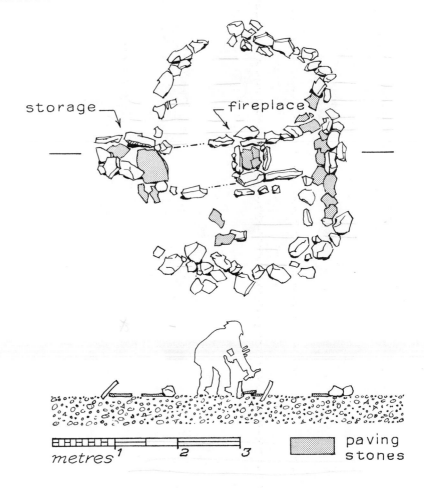

FIGURE 4.15 Pre-Dorset harpoon heads.

representative of the population in which they lived, the genomic data indicate that the individual is closely related to northeast Asian populations but is not related to Inuit or modern Native American populations, indicating an independent migration from Asia (Rasmussen et al. 2010).

LATER CULTURES OF THE ARCTIC: DORSET, NORTON, AND THULE

Dorset (2500–800 BP)

Certainly derived from the Arctic Small Tool tradition, and often considered part of it, is the **Dorset tradition**. This Paleo-Eskimo tradition developed in the eastern Arctic and is marked by the disappearance of both the bow and arrow and stone drills (McGhee 1996:142–144), and by the rarity of dog remains (Dumond 1987). Harpoon heads with closed sockets (until late in the Dorset tradition, when open sockets reappear), rectangular soapstone lamps, side-notched end blades, slate

individual has been reconstructed. The genetic profile indicates the individual was dark skinned, had dark hair, was prone to balding, and had dry ear wax. Metabolic adaptations to cold are also indicated. Keeping in mind that a single individual may not be

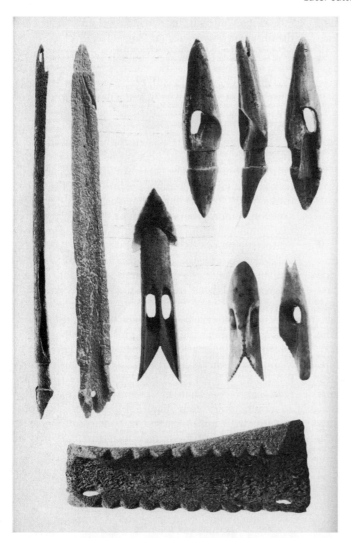

FIGURE 4.16 Dorset
artifacts: (left) lance blade, (center) harpoon head with chipped stone end blade, (upper right and right center) harpoon heads, (bottom) ice creeper.

knives, and polished burinlike tools (Figure 4.16) are characteristic of the Dorset tradition (Dumond 1987; McGhee 1996:131).

The preservation of organic material is excellent in many Dorset sites, so we have insights into the perishable culture of these people. In addition to closed-socket harpoon heads, archaeologists have found other bone, ivory, antler, and horn artifacts, including broad bone knives that resemble tools used by recent Inuit people to cut snow into the blocks from which their domed snow houses are constructed. Bone artifacts identified as sled shoes indicate the presence of sleds, an important means of transport for the Inuit. Since, however, there are no dog remains and no artifacts resembling Inuit dog harness hardware, it is likely that humans powered the sleds. Another type of Dorset perishable artifact identified by comparison to Inuit objects is the **ice creeper**, a flat bone or ivory item

having pointed projections carved into one side. The Inuit strapped similar gear to the bottoms of their feet to give them traction on the ice. Needles of bone and ivory bear witness to the continued presence of tailored clothing. In some Dorset sites the needles even are accompanied by actual fragments of hide clothing (Dumond 1987; McGhee 1996:144–145).

Dorset people appear to have occupied sites for longer periods of time than their predecessors, based on greater accumulations of the bones of their prey. The makeup of the bone refuse indicates that sea mammals, especially seals, were playing a larger role than caribou in the diet (Dumond 1987). At winter Dorset settlements people built substantial houses with sod coverings. These houses were rectangular, 4 to 5 meters (13–16 ft.) across, excavated up to half a meter (1.6 ft.) deep, and they had midpassages. The midpassages in these houses lacked charcoal in the central box, as stone lamps provided light and warmth. The occurrence of snow knives suggests the presence of snow houses, and clearly demarcated deposits of artifacts and bone, as would be left when such houses melted, support this inference (Dumond 1987; McGhee 1996:131). Tent rings (rock circles) also sometimes occur in association with midpassage houses; probably the tents were summer homes.

Toward the end of the Dorset tradition a new type of structure—the **longhouse**—was built (Figure 4.17). These structures, which were 6 to 7 meters (20–23 ft.) wide and from 10 to 40 meters (33–131 ft.) long, were outlined either with vertically set slabs of rock or with large boulders. The outlining walls are up to a meter (3 ft.) high. Since no roofing materials have been found in these structures, they probably were not roofed. It also is hard to imagine roofing such a large structure with the meager building materials available in the Dorset environment. There is little habitation debris near these structures, and there is no evidence of fires having been built in most of them, although they usually have a line of hearths outside the structure. The longhouses may not have served as dwellings; instead, they may have been enclosures in which related groups built their shelters at times when people came together in larger groups, perhaps for social or ceremonial activities (McGhee 1996:207).

 One striking thing about the Dorset culture is its portable art (Figure 4.18). Although art is not common in comparison to utilitarian items from Dorset sites, the organic preservation at Dorset sites has led to the recovery of carvings in wood, ivory, antler, and bone. Human beings were the most common subject of Dorset carvings, followed by sea mammals, bears, birds, caribou, fish, weasels, and a few other creatures. Sea mammals, of course, represented food, but bear figures appear to have been part of a ceremonial aspect of Dorset life. Some bear figurines have been found that appear to have been amulets buried with an individual (Dumond 1987). Bears are often depicted as if they were flying or floating, and are also often embellished with straight lines that suggest the animal's skeleton. Among the human depictions are miniature masks, again hinting at ceremonial activity. The site of Button Point on Bylot Island, north of Baffinland, yielded two life-size masks. Button Point also had human and animal figures carved in wood; splinters of wood had been inserted in small slits carved in the objects.

The masks, the bears, and the wooden figures with slits and splinters suggest the presence of shamanism, which is highly developed in Inuit and Eskimo culture. Many of the carvings suggest spirit animals or transformation, a theme also indicated by an interesting type of artifact—"**shaman's teeth**." These are depictions of mouths with teeth (Figure 4.18, center), including exaggerated canines, carved in bone, some of which have the marks of the human teeth that once clasped

FIGURE 4.17 The remains of a Dorset longhouse.

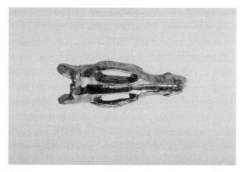
a

b

c

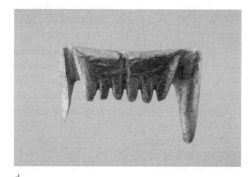
d

e

FIGURE 4.18 Dorset portable art: (a) floating/flying bear, (b) pair of swans, (c) miniature mask, (d) shaman's teeth, (e) killed human figure.

them (Dumond 1987; Maxwell 1984:366–367; Taylor and Swinton 1967).

There is a correlation in Dorset toolkits between raw materials for stone tools and the function of the tool. Toolmakers usually chose quartz crystal for making microblades, colored cherts for making scrapers and harpoon end blades, jade for polished chisel-like tools for carving bone and ivory, and slate for other ground tools. Trade moved materials throughout the Dorset world, allowing people to make their tools from the appropriate material even if it did not occur in their local territory. Traded materials included stone for tools, especially jade and the related materials **nephrite** and jadeite, but also copper from the Coppermine River valley and iron from meteorites found in northwestern Greenland. The iron was used in some end blades for harpoons and to make other tools (McGhee 1996:139–140).

Dorset sites are restricted to the central and eastern Arctic and the eastern Subarctic, getting as far east as Greenland and as far south as Newfoundland (Renouf and Bell 2009). What became of the Dorset, who declined in numbers and eventually largely disappeared from the eastern Arctic by 1150 BP, remains a topic of debate. Two other groups colonized the Arctic around the time of the Dorset decline, the Thule (see later in this chapter) and the Vikings, or Norse (see Chapter 13). Possible explanations usually have focused on the Thule migration into the area, especially since Thule sites sometimes overlie Dorset sites, but these seem to represent reoccupation of already abandoned sites (Agger and Maschner 2009). Some Dorset people may have assimilated into Thule populations in places like Greenland (Appelt and Gulløv 2009). There also is no evidence of violence between these groups. However, the legends of the Inuit descendants of the Thule concerning the Tunit who once lived in Inuit territory, not always peacefully, may be applicable (McGhee 1996:211–212). The Tunit are portrayed as having prepared the land for humans by locating productive hunting spots and building the lines of cairns that directed caribou to the waiting hunters. Arguments that the Thule were simply better adapted to the warmer Arctic conditions of the Medieval Warm period that began around 1000 years ago, outcompeting the Dorset because of their superior technology, may have some merit. However, reconsideration of the timing of the Thule migration, which will be discussed next, suggests to some researchers that the Dorset were already in decline before the Thule arrived. Agger and Maschner (2009) have recently suggested that disease brought by the Norse, with whom the Dorset certainly had contact (Sutherland 2009), could have been a major factor in Dorset decline as well.

Norton Tradition (3000–1200 BP)

While the Dorset people were occupying the central and eastern Arctic, and even a little before the Dorset, the Norton tradition developed in the western Arctic. The **Norton tradition** is a series of three recognized cultures, the **Choris**, **Norton**, and **Ipiutak** (Table 4.1). The tool assemblage of the Norton tradition is similar to that of the preceding Arctic Small Tool tradition, especially the Denbigh Flint material, but also included ceramics and oil lamps, at least among the Choris and the Norton peoples.

The Choris culture (3000–2500 BP), the earliest of the Norton tradition, is found in northern Alaska north of the Bering Strait. Choris flaked stone tools are very similar to Denbigh materials from the Arctic Small Tool tradition, both in form and in execution. Points, knives, and side blades, as well as chipped and ground burins, and flake knives, all show continuity with earlier forms. New point styles, chipped adze blades, and burin spalls struck from irregular flake cores appear over time. At about the same time, **feather-tempered pottery** appears. The surface of the pottery may be **cord-marked**, bearing impressions left from the use of a cord-wrapped paddle, or stamped or incised with linear designs (Anderson 1984:85–86). The pottery is well made and appears to have come to Alaska as part of a developed technology. Asia is the most likely source for the ceramic industry (Anderson 1968). Among the Choris artifacts are lanceolate points (Figure 4.19) that resemble Scottsbluff and Angostura points, Paleoindian points of the Plains. On the Plains these points date much earlier than do the Choris materials, and the relationship, if any, is still unclear (Anderson 1968, 1984:87).

Oval Choris houses have been found measuring about 13 by 7 meters (42 × 24 ft.). The details of construction of the houses are not clear from the sediment stains and postholes. At Onion Portage an interesting arrangement of structures, perhaps tents, was found surrounding and connected through passageways to a central oval structure that was dug into the ground. A stone hearth was found in the central structure and stone-lined hearths warmed the surrounding structures. The artifacts in the central structure differed from those found in the structures located around it. The round structures had evidence of food preparation and the working of hides, whereas the central structure had evidence of the manufacture of hunting implements and wood carving. These differences may suggest a division of labor similar to that of the modern Eskimo, with the central structure activities being like those of Eskimo men and the other activities such as food preparation and hide working being like the activities of Eskimo women (Anderson 1984:86–87).

The Norton complex, apparently derived from the Choris, appears about 2500 BP and occurs from the Alaska Peninsula to the Firth River in northwestern Canada (near the Alaska–Canada border) (Dumond 1987:106). The use of checked stamped designs on pottery suggests continuity with Choris (Figure 4.20).

FIGURE 4.19 Choris lanceolate points.

FIGURE 4.20 Fragment of Norton pottery.

The use of ceramic and stone lamps is also carried over from Choris. Stone tools include end and side blades, knives, ground burinlike tools, scrapers, and notched net sinkers. Ground slate knives were also part of the Norton toolkit. Caribou hunting, sealing, and net fishing for salmon was done at least at the southern end of the Norton range. Whaling is also indicated (Anderson 1984:87–88; Dumond 1987).

Dwellings for the Norton people were generally square, dug into the ground about 0.5 meter (1.6 ft.), and had short entryways, although there is considerable variability in the Norton structures. One structure excavated at Unakleet is 8 by 12 meters (26 × 39 ft.) and appears to have been essentially a men's house similar to the Eskimo *kazigi*. That this structure is

larger than others, and had predominantly artifacts that are associated with men in Eskimo culture, support this identification (Dumond 1987).

About 2000 BP the Ipiutak complex can be defined. It shares a number of traits with the Choris and Norton complexes but lacks both lamps and pottery. In addition, houses with entry ramps, ground slate tools, and evidence of the pursuit of whales are found in Ipiutak. The Ipiutak complex is especially well known for its art, much of which comes from burials. People made elaborate carvings of animal and human figures, as well as linked chains and pretzel-like objects (Figure 4.21). Utilitarian objects like harpoon socket pieces and snow goggles are also elaborated with incised geometric designs. The style of the art is

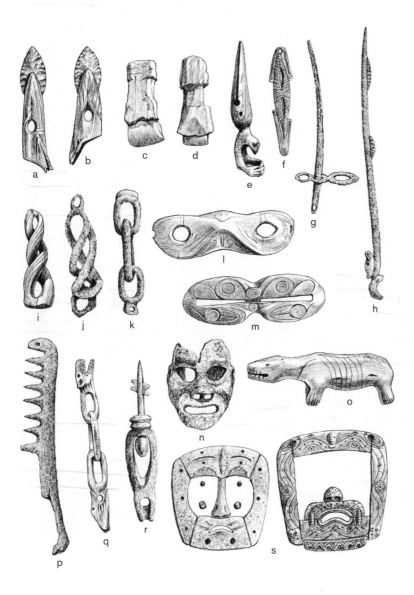

FIGURE 4.21 Ipiutak art: (a–b) harpoon heads, (c–d) bone adze heads with slate blades, (e–f) ivory carvings or ornaments, (g–h) ivory daggers, (i–j) ivory swivel and open-work carvings, (k) ivory ornamental linked object, (l–m) ivory snow goggles, (n) human effigy of antler, (o) ivory polar bear effigy (p–q) ivory implement and ornament (r) swivel, (s) ivory masklike carvings.

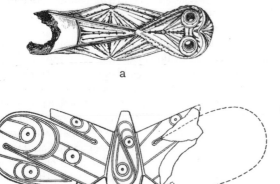

a

b

FIGURE 4.22 Okvik (a) and Old Bering Sea (b) style artifacts. The Okvik piece is a decorated ivory object and the Old Bering Sea item is a "winged object." Note the differences in the style of decoration.
(Adapted from Willey 1966:Figures 7.8 and 7.12.)

reminiscent of Scytho-Siberian art found to the west (Anderson 1984:88–89).

Thule (2000 BP to Modern Times)

The **Thule tradition** developed out of the Norton tradition in the islands of the Bering Strait beginning about 2000 BP. Perhaps people or influences from Asia also were responsible for this tradition. The hallmark of this culture is a new technology for hunting sea mammals, particularly whales, in open water, and it produced a successful occupation that ultimately spread from Alaska through the eastern Arctic all the way to Greenland. The Thule people are the direct ancestors of the Inuit; their culture also diffused southward into the area of Pacific Eskimos.

The **Old Bering Sea** and **Okvik cultures** are the earliest expression of the Thule tradition. These people lived on Saint Lawrence and adjacent islands, as well as on the Asian coast. The tools of these two groups are quite similar, and the distinction between them is based on decorative art styles. Although some archaeologists have suggested that the Okvik style is older than the Old Bering Sea, Dumond (1987:119) treats them as

contemporary cultures that developed at about the same time that Ipiutak sites were being created on the Alaskan mainland (also Ackerman 1984:108). The styles are characterized by differences in the design elements used (Figure 4.22) (Collins 1937).

During the Okvik/Old Bering Sea times (2200–1250 BP), ground stone artifacts, particularly polished slate, were common. These included projectile points, adzes, *ulus*, and lanceolate ("men's") knife blades. Chipped stone was present in the form of end blades, side blades, knives, and drills; whale bone, antler, and ivory artifacts took a number of forms. Drills, needles, awls, needle cases, hide scrapers, picks, mattocks, harpoon heads, foreshafts, sockets, counterweights (called "winged objects" based on their appearance), and harpoon butt ice picks are all part of the bone/antler/ivory part of the toolkit. Harpoons were complicated multicomponent objects as suggested by Figure 4.23. Cooking pots and lamps were made of pottery that was marked with linear or check designs. The earliest pottery of this period was tempered with fiber, but a shift occurs to gravel temper later (Ackerman 1984:108; Dumond 1987).

The Okvik/Old Bering Sea people made their living hunting sea mammals. They were hunted from the ice edge, but the presence of mouthpieces and plugs of the type used by modern Eskimos for floats to be attached to harpoon lines indicates hunting on open water as well. The large open boat called an **umiak** was introduced at this time. Harpoon shaft ice picks suggest the practice of winter hunting for seals at their breathing holes. This practice, documented in historical times, involved patient waiting at a breathing hole for the seal to appear, harpooning the seal, and using the ice pick to enlarge the hole in the ice to allow removal of the animal. People also hunted on land with the bow and arrow. Fish were caught by hooks or were speared. Humans powered sleds that were used to transport materials, and from kayak parts and models of kayaks we know that closed boats were in use (Ackerman 1984:108; Dumond 1987).

The **Birnik culture** (2200–1250 BP) is evident on the northern Alaska coast, but some sites are found in Siberia as well, and it may represent a migration of people from Northeast Asia through the Bering Straits into northwest Alaska (Mason 2009). These people

FIGURE 4.23 Schematic of a harpoon.

hunted sea mammals (possibly including whales) in open water from kayaks and umiaks. A distinctive flat toggling harpoon head, usually made of antler, characterizes the culture. Sleds were improved, though the lack of harness parts suggests that dogs were still not being used to pull them. Pottery lamps and other items were marked with circles and spirals impressed into its surface (Dumond 1987).

Birnik people made houses that were square and measured 10 to 13 feet (3–4 m) across. The houses had driftwood or whalebone superstructures and were entered through a passageway. Floors were lined with planks, and a sleeping platform was constructed along the rear wall. The entire affair was covered with sod for insulation (Dumond 1987).

It is probably from the Birnik that the **Thule culture** (1050–400/250 BP) itself developed. The Thule culture is indicated by a complex range of specialized tools seen among the historical Eskimo and Inuit. These included hunting gear such as arrows, spears, and harpoon heads (both toggling and barbed) made of bone, antler, or ivory, and stone implements, as well as mouthpieces for floats. The proportion of ground stone in the artifact assemblage rose to approximately 50 percent of the stone tools (Dumond 1987:136), and these included end blades, double-edged knives, and *ulus*, as well as labrets. People made gravel-tempered as opposed to fiber-tempered ceramics, and their pots were shaped like flowerpots rather than in the globular forms made earlier.

Recent DNA studies confirm the connection between the Birnik and the Thule migrants into the eastern Arctic. However, they also suggest that there is a discontinuity between Birnik populations and Western Thule populations, raising new questions about the movement and interaction of people of various ethnicities in northern Alaska as Thule culture first developed (Hollinger et al. 2009).

The evidence from material culture suggests that the Thule expanded quite rapidly from northern Alaska through the eastern Arctic, all the way to Greenland. The umiaks, capable of carrying a large number of people, their gear, and even their dogs, allowed for rapid movement. The ability to go into the open ocean to hunt whales, including the largest Arctic whale, the bowhead, meant that large stores of food could be amassed for getting the village through the winter, and winter villages of subterranean pithouses are present at a number of locations dating to Thule times. Dogsleds first appear during this time, as indicated by specialized harness hardware including swivels and buckles and the remains of ladderlike sleds (Dumond 1987; McGhee 1984). Snowshoes have also been found in Thule culture sites (Dumond 1984a:101).

It has long been argued that the Thule were following their principal prey, bowhead whales, as they expanded. The distribution of a particular type of hunting artifact, the **Sicco-type harpoon head** (Figure 4.24), is a marker for this early expansion. Sicco-type harpoon heads are found from Point Barrow, Alaska, through the islands of the High Arctic to Thule, the place in northwestern Greenland after which the culture was named. As the Thule adapted to the Canadian Arctic, they left small winter villages of pithouses, but also used domed snow houses. Typical houses were similar to the Birnik houses, but they were round or oval and lined with boulders. Because driftwood was scarce in the Canadian Arctic, people made the superstructure of whale bones instead. Stones lined the floor rather than planks, and stone was used to pave the sleeping platform at the rear of the house (McGhee 1984:369–372).

Pauketat and Loren (2005:20) point out that the differing social histories of the Dorset and Thule peoples may help explain the Thule expansion. Following Whitridge (1999), they suggest that gender divisions and the nature of the cultural experience, as well as the nature of corporate groups, are important in understanding the replacement of the Dorset by the Thule people. However, the extent and nature of contact between Thule and Dorset populations throughout the Eastern Arctic is still debated.

Robert McGhee, originally a proponent of the climate-change explanation, now argues for the development of a robust trade in Arctic commodities such as fur and ivory for iron ultimately from China. He suggests that the development of efficient methods for hunting bowhead whales and the adoption of the sinew-backed Mongol-style bow that persisted in the Arctic into historical times were important in the development of Thule. McGhee believes that the

FIGURE 4.24 Sicco-type harpoon head.

Thule, having a strong dependence on iron (and other metals) for cutting and engraving tools, were drawn to the meteoritic iron of the eastern Arctic and the copper from the Coppermine River area. In addition, the potential for the trade in metals with the Norse settlers in Greenland, who would have been eager for furs and ivory in exchange, drew them farther east. Viewing Thule migration as even more rapid and not occurring until the twelfth or thirteenth centuries, he argues that the areas to the south were not populated by the Thule at first (McGhee 2005:120–124). Recent work exploring the difficulties of radiocarbon dating Thule, based on choosing the appropriate marine reservoir correction and the potential for contamination from marine animal fats, has questioned the timing of the Thule occupation (Friesen and Arnold 2008). In general, redating of sites using contemporary understanding of the **marine reservoir effect** supports the notion that the Thule migration may not have been associated with the onset of the Medieval Warm Period at all (McGhee 2009).

Between 800 BP and 700 BP, the Thule began to expand into the southern Arctic Archipelago, and farther to the Hudson Bay and mainland coast. Somewhat later they moved down into the coast of Labrador. As they moved into the areas away from the bowhead whale migration routes to places where these large creatures were not available, they began to emphasize other foods. Caribou, fish, and ring seal became the staples. Following this broadening of the food spectrum, people of the Thule culture were able to move farther south yet, into the Barren Grounds, where caribou hunting and fishing sustained them (McGhee 1984:373–375).

A number of foods were pursued in addition to the whales. Seals and walrus were hunted from kayaks, using the **atlatl** and barbed darts. Birds were hunted in the same way, but multipronged darts were used. Winter ice hunting of seals continued as well. Land animals were hunted using the recurved bow and arrow. Arrowheads were made of antler. Prey species included caribou, musk ox, bear, and smaller mammals. Bolas were used, probably to hunt birds, and fish were speared using leisters (fish spears with three prongs) or were caught on lines equipped with composite fishhooks or gorges (McGhee 1984:370–371).

The Thule were certainly the ancestors of the historical Inuit, and the continuity in material culture is striking. This is seen particularly in the bone, antler, wood, and ivory material—material that is preserved in the dry and frozen Arctic. Organic material usually disintegrates in archaeological soils because of the action of bacteria. To survive, bacteria need moisture, warmth, and oxygen. Oxygen is in good supply in the Arctic, but moisture and warmth are seriously lacking.

We shall see in later chapters how other conditions such as intense dryness or oxygen deprivation in water-logged sites also can preserve perishable artifacts.

LATER CULTURES OF THE SUBARCTIC

Although the people of the Subarctic seem to have persisted in essentially Archaic lifeways until the Contact period, archaeological work in this area has defined a number of archaeological complexes besides the Archaic ones noted earlier. Most of these refer to Late Prehistoric developments after approximately 1000 BP, but after about 2100 BP, a **Central Subarctic Woodland culture**, possibly associated with a new emphasis on wild rice gathering, appeared. This cultural development is coincident with the appearance of **Laurel culture** ceramics in the central Subarctic of northern Ontario, Manitoba, and eastern Saskatchewan. These ceramics, which are characterized by coarsely tempered conoidal pots (Figure 4.25), are also found to the south, where burial mounds and other characteristics suggest they have affinities with Middle Woodland developments in the Midwest and Upper Great Lakes (see Chapter 12). This first Subarctic pottery does not appear until between 2150 BP and 2050 BP. Other than the pottery, however, subsistence and settlement practices generally resembled those of the Shield Archaic (Pilon 1996, 1998).

Late Prehistoric, or Terminal, Woodland complexes also have been defined for the interior Subarctic. The **Blackduck culture**, found in the boreal forests from the north shore of Lake Superior west into Manitoba, north to the lowlands around Hudson Bay, and as far east as western Quebec, is a ceramic complex that first appears around 1450 BP. Blackduck also has some Plains affinities and is still evident in the Historic period. Archaeologists believe that this culture is the ancestral culture for many of the Ojibwa bands in this

FIGURE 4.25 Central Subarctic Woodland pottery.

area historically. A related, somewhat later culture recognized by archaeologists, the **Selkirk culture**, is evident beginning about 1050 BP. Selkirk is believed to be ancestral to the historical Cree.

The later prehistory of the northwestern Canada is called the **Taltheilei tradition** (Gordon 1998), within which a series of projectile points can be defined beginning about 2600 BP and continuing into the Contact period. These people apparently were caribou-hunting ancestors of the historical Dene. Athapaskan archaeology in the Subarctic is particularly well represented at the Klo-kut site in the Middle Porcupine drainage of the Yukon. This site, which has deposits dating back to about 1200 BP, reflects

continuity in occupation from these earliest deposits to the historically known Athapaskan-speaking Kutchin. Subsistence at this site seems to have been constant through time; the people hunted caribou herds, intercepting them as they migrated north in the late spring and early summer. While there is some change through time in stone tools, the quality of bone and antler tools, and the use of birch bark, the basic pattern can still be traced into the Historic period (Morlan 1973).

As discussed in Box 4.1, First Nations sometimes have a great interest in archaeological finds. This is particularly the case when they involve the discovery of human remains.

ISSUES AND DEBATES   BOX 4.1

Kwäaday Dän Ts'inchi: British Columbia's Ice Man

In 1999 an emergency meeting of elders and members of the Champagne and Aishihik First Nations was called to decide what should be done about some human remains that were found in British Columbia. In August of that year three hunters walking above tree line in Tatshenshini-Alsek Park found much of the body of a person melting out of the glacier there. The remains were recovered by a team of specialists with the consent of the First Nations, and First Nations individuals participated in the recovery, including saying appropriate words of respect before the operation began. The elders and members of two groups must have had a dilemma on their hands. Many traditional Native American and First Nations people have a strong belief in respecting the dead by reinterring any discovered burials or cremations as soon as possible, if they cannot simply be left where they are at the time of discovery. It was also clear that this individual had the potential to provide important information about the past, including details of the last days of his life. What was ultimately decided was there should be study of the remains but that it should be done with the consent and supervision of the Champagne and Aishihik First Nations. They also gave the individual a name—*Kwäaday Dän Ts'inchi*—"long ago person found" in their language (British Columbia Ministry of Forests, Lands, and Natural Resource Operations 2011).

Found associated with the body or nearby were parts of a walking stick, an iron-bladed knife (the iron could have been obtained by trade from the north, ultimately originating in Asia, as discussed earlier in this chapter, or from contact with European explorers), an atlatl, and a bag containing dried salmon and leaves. The torso was

found lying on a robe made of gopher or arctic ground squirrel pelts.

Radiocarbon dates were obtained for artifacts accompanying *Kwäaday Dän Ts'inchi*, as well as from his bones. The artifacts yielded dates of different ranges, suggesting the glacier may have covered a site that was used for some period of time. Although the initial dates suggested an age of 550 years, the best interpretation of the data indicates he died between AD 1670 and 1850 (Richards et al. 2007). Pollen in the stomach also suggests *KwäadayDän Ts'inchi* died in mid-July or August (Mudie et al. 2005).

One of the most interesting findings about *Kwäaday-Dän Ts'inchi* is what we know about his diet. It appears that in his last days he left the coast, as indicated by bits of coastal crustacean and plants in his well-preserved digestive tract. Isotopic analysis indicated a diet dominated by marine resources but with a change to more terrestrial resources late in his life (Richards et al. 2007). Further study of the lipids in bone and skin tissues yielded a strong marine signature for the bones but not for the skin. Since the skin results are believed to relate to only the last three weeks of life, these findings suggest that *KwäadayDän Dan Ts'inchi* altered his diet away from marine foods at the very end of his life (Corr et al. 2008).

Nearly 250 individual First Nations people from British Columbia, Yukon, and Alaska volunteered blood samples for DNA analysis to explore genetic relations to *KwäadayDän Ts'inchi*. Based on mitochondrial DNA, 17 matches to living people were found. Of these 17 individuals, 15 identified themselves as members of the Wolf Clan. Establishing this connection, including identification of the ancestor as probably a member of the Wolf

Clan, resulted in considerable interest and pride among the First Nations, especially because it reinforced stories from local oral history (*Leader-Post* 2008).

After sampling was finished, the First Nations claimed the body and cremated it in 2001. They returned the ashes to near where he had been found (Gray 2001). Thus there are two sides of the remarkable story of *KwäadayDän Ts'inchi*. It is one of First Nations' cooperation with archaeologists and other scientists, but also of respect for the remains of an ancestor. Both insight into the lifestyle of this individual and knowledge of his connections to contemporary people were gained.

EUROPEAN CONTACT

As we have already indicated, contact between Artic peoples and European peoples began around AD 1000 (950 BP) when the Norse entered the eastern Arctic. Norse colonies, the Eastern and Western Settlements, were established on the southwest coast of Greenland. These colonies are believed to have persisted until approximately AD 1450 (500 BP). The impact of the Norse on the peoples of this area is only beginning to be understood (Sutherland 2009) but as we've mentioned previously both Dorset and Thule populations most likely had some contact with the Norse. See Box 13.1, "How Far Did the Vikings Get?" for further discussion of the Norse in North America.

After, the Norse European exploration of the Arctic ceased until the end of the sixteenth century, and European fishermen began to visit the waters off the eastern Subarctic coast not long after. The British mariner Martin Frobisher began to search for the fabled Northwest Passage, a hoped-for water route from the Atlantic to the Pacific, in 1576. He was followed by many other explorers, some of whom are mentioned in Chapter 13. These events did little to alter native lifeways in the Eastern Arctic, and in some areas through the nineteenth century some native groups of the Arctic had yet to encounter Europeans.

At European contact there was a distinction between the peoples of the Arctic and those of the Subarctic. The Arctic people were the Inuit or Eskimo, and the Aleut; they spoke separate but related languages that can be grouped into the Eskimo–Aleut linguistic family (Woodbury 1984). The peoples of the Subarctic were Indian people who were distinct from the Inuit and Eskimo. They spoke two kinds of languages, the Athapaskan in the west and the Algonquian in the east. The Athapaskan languages were related to the Navajo and Apache languages of the Southwest, as well as to languages in the Plateau, the Northwest Coast, and California. Athapaskans such as the Kutchin, Tanana, Ahtena, and Ingalik of today occupied the interior of Alaska, while the Canadian Athapaskans included the ancestors of the Tutchone, Slavey, Dogrib, Chipewyan, Beaver, and Carier (Krauss and Golla 1981). The Algonquian speakers included groups ancestral to the Cree, Montagnais, and Naskapi in the north and the Ojibwa in the south. The Ojibwa, clustered around the Great Lakes, and thus, extended southward into the Northeast culture area (Rhodes and Todd 1981).

The story of European exploration in the Arctic and Subarctic is a fascinating tale of adventure and hardship, though beyond the scope of this chapter. Besides seeking the Northwest Passage, Europeans saw this vast region primarily in terms of what could be extracted from it: furs, whale oil, fish like cod, and even minerals. They were not interested in settlement per se, although many European powers did establish settlements along the coasts, and between the late seventeenth and the early nineteenth centuries, traders penetrated deep into the interior. Archaeological excavations can reveal much about these early settlements and outposts.

CHAPTER SUMMARY

This chapter discussed what we have learned about the archaeology of the Arctic and Subarctic culture areas. The treatment should open the way to a more detailed exploration of these fascinating areas. Points of particular importance are as follows:

• The Archaic period begins by 8000 BP, and its manifestations vary considerably within the Arctic and Subarctic. On the Pacific Coast we see the Ocean Bay, Kodiak, and Aleutian traditions and the beginnings of the exploitation of sea resources, as well as the early use of ground slate implements. In the western Sub-arctic the Northern Archaic tradition appears to represent generalized foragers who made side-notched points but no microblades. In the eastern Subarctic, the Shield Archaic and the Maritime Archaic are commonly recognized traditions.

- Between 4000 BP and 3900 BP, the Arctic Small Tool tradition, characterized by finely worked end blades and side blades, microblades, adzes with polished bits, and burinlike tools, developed in the western Arctic, probably in Siberia. The Arctic Small Tool tradition spread east from Alaska through the Canadian Arctic all the way to Greenland, where there are two phases: Independence and, later, Pre-Dorset.
- Derived from the Arctic Small Tool tradition, the Dorset tradition (2500–800 BP) developed in the eastern Arctic. Dorset sites lack evidence of the bow and arrow and of the stone drill, but bone is well preserved in these sites, revealing a rich bone tool industry and striking bone carvings. The Dorset disappeared around 800 BP, probably replaced quickly by Thule people, who were spreading east out of Alaska during the Medieval Warm period.
- The Norton tradition, including the Choris, Norton, and Iputiak cultures, signals the beginnings of material culture much like that used by the historical Inuit, with ceramics and specialized hunting equipment appearing. About 2000 BP, the Thule tradition developed out of the Norton and spread eastward. Hunting of sea mammals, particularly the bowhead whale, was very important, and the specialized boats of the Historic period, the umiak and the kayak, are both present, as is the dogsled. Ultimately the Thule expanded in the southern Arctic, reaching all the way to Hudson Bay.
- Several late cultures have been defined for the Subarctic, including the Central Woodland culture (after ca. 1000 BP), marked by Laurel ceramics, and the Blackduck and Selkirk cultures, which are thought to have developed into the historical Ojibwa and Cree, respectively. In northwest Canada, the Taltheilei tradition associated with Athapaskans has been defined.

SUGGESTIONS FOR FURTHER READING

For a classic treatment of the archaeology of the Arctic:

Dumond, Don E.
   1987 *The Eskimos and Aleuts*, 2nd ed. Thames and Hudson, London.

For an account of Arctic archaeology written for the general public and emphasizing the Dorset way of life:

McGhee, Robert
   1996 *Ancient People of the Arctic.* University of British Columbia Press, Vancouver, British Columbia.

For two volumes that cover the prehistory of the Canadian Arctic and Subarctic up to 1450 BP:

Wright, James V.
   1995 *A History of the Native Peoples of Canada*, Vol. I. Mercury Series, Paper 152, Archaeological Survey of Canada. Canadian Museum of Civilization, Ottawa.

Wright, James V.
   1999 *A History of the Native Peoples of Canada*, Vol. II. Mercury Series, Paper 152, Archaeological Survey of Canada. Canadian Museum of Civilization, Ottawa.

For a discussion of the archaeology, ethnography, and history of exploration of the Arctic:

McGhee, Robert
   2005 The Last Imaginary Place: A Human History of the Arctic World. Oxford University Press, Oxford.

OTHER RESOURCES

Sections H and I of the Student CD give web links, additional discussion questions, and other study aids. The CD contains a variety of additional resources.

CASE STUDY

Although they were consistently hunter-gatherers, the peoples of the Arctic and Subarctic varied considerably in their cultural adaptations. This isn't surprising, given the vast region encompassed and the many environmental circumstances within these culture areas. As this chapter has demonstrated, time adds another dimension to this variability over which archaeologists have traced many changes. Along the Pacific Coast of Alaska, hunter-gatherer societies with a maritime subsistence base eventually developed aspects of sociocultural complexity usually associated with agriculturalists. These include sedentism, social ranking, chiefs, endemic warfare, and differential accumulation of wealth and prestige. Contemporary Native Alaskans have become increasingly interested in reclaiming this heritage, and they often have asked archaeologists to help them document it. This case study shows how changing site characteristics and distributions discovered through archaeological survey and some excavation on Kodiak Island were used to evaluate a model of growth in social complexity among hunter-gatherers. This work provides a good example of how archaeologists can use information on settlement to test their ideas about what happened in the past. As you read this case study, pay attention to the research process, noting how the data were generated and how they were related to the expectations derived from the model.

FROM SITES TO SOCIAL EVOLUTION

The Study of Emergent Complexity in the Kodiak Archipelago, Alaska

Ben Fitzhugh

Mention Alaska, and most Americans who have not been there are likely to conjure up images of ice and snow, polar bears and walruses, and Eskimos in igloos. Alaska has its share of these (with the exception of igloos, or snow houses, which were primarily a winter dwelling of the Canadian Arctic Inuit cultures), but Alaska is much more varied and diverse than its stereotypes. From the frozen and tundracovered north country along the Arctic Ocean and interior north of the Arctic Circle, to the vast boreal forests of the central interior and southeastern coasts, to the treeless Alaska Peninsula and volcanic islands of the Aleutians, Alaska presents a complex landscape full of challenges and opportunities that have helped shape unique cultural adaptations and social traditions throughout the Holocene.

Alaska has a 12,000-year legacy of hunting, fishing, and gathering cultures. The earliest known archaeological evidence is found in the interior mountain regions and dates to the terminal Pleistocene, when people in the area were perhaps still hunting megafauna like mammoths, as well as smaller game, fish, and birds. The oldest coastal occupations date between 9000 and 10,000 years ago and are found around the North Pacific Rim of southern and southeastern Alaska. By contrast, the colder coastal plains and ice-bound coastlines of the Bering Sea and Arctic Ocean were not occupied until 4500 years ago. The variation in colonization histories of the different Alaskan landscapes (coastal and interior, forested and tundra, mountains and plains) and the cultural trajectories that unfolded on them make this region one of the most intriguing for studying hunter-gatherer adaptation and social evolution.

While in graduate school, as I began looking for a place to begin my research career, I focused on Alaska's legacy of hunter-gatherer adaptation and evolution for two reasons. First, I was fascinated by maritime hunter-gatherer culture and its development, and Alaska was a great place to study that. Second, the development of relatively complex hunter-gatherer groups around much of Alaska's coasts, in the absence of agriculture, provided an interesting context for the study of emergent complexity. For decades, anthropological archaeologists had assumed that agriculture was a necessary and sufficient stimulus for cultural complexity—ranked and stratified societies with socioeconomic classes, economic specialization, monumental architecture, organized military, and so on. In common models of social evolution, hunter-gatherers were the baseline, the evolutionary origins *away from which* more complex cultures evolved! Accordingly, existing hunter-gatherers were viewed as marginal populations living where agriculture could not flourish, and surviving, perhaps easily, perhaps desperately (depending on the model), in a constant state of dependency on nature. By contrast, the coasts of Alaska, especially its Pacific coasts, from the Aleutian Islands to the Southeast Panhandle, saw the development of cultural groups with a suite of relatively complex characteristics such as social ranking with powerful chiefs, endemic warfare, slavery, wealth accumulation, competitions for prestige, and at least in Southeast Alaska, monumental houses and totem poles (part of the broader Northwest Coast cultural tradition). These characteristics are well established in the ethnohistoric and ethnographic literature of the region

(Townsend 1980). Something about adapting to the coastal environments seemed to encourage the development of the kind of complexity seen in southern Alaska. I wanted to understand this. While several anthropologists had approached this kind of question from the perspective of comparative ethnography, few had used archaeological evidence to document actual trajectories of hunter-gatherer social evolution over the long term. That became the goal of my first major research project.

GETTING STARTED

Research questions are important, but they don't do much good without a place to study them. Finding a place to conduct research is particularly challenging at the beginning of one's career, without a solid basis on which to select a research area. I was fortunate to spend three summers working on field projects in different parts of Alaska as an undergraduate and early graduate student. The first of these projects, in 1987, was on a fabulous **wet site** in the Kodiak Archipelago (Figure 4.26) (Jordan and Knecht 1988). On that project I gained familiarity with the generous archaeological record of the region and the growing enthusiasm of the local people to learn more about their archaeological heritage. In the summer of 1992 I returned to Kodiak to make contacts and explore possible research locations for my Ph.D. dissertation. I soon learned that the village of Old Harbor, in southeast Kodiak, was interested in having someone inventory the archaeological resources of their region. I jumped at the chance.

It is helpful to consider the historical context of this opportunity and why the residents of a small Alaskan village were eager to support my archaeological research. To do this, we need to take a brief detour to explore the history of Native–white interactions over the past 200 years. Of course, Native Alaskans had controlled their own fate for millennia prior to Russian contact in the mid-eighteenth century. From contact until 1867, when the territory was sold to the United States for pennies an acre, Russia controlled the southern Shelikof Strait and Alaskan territories—including Kodiak, which had been the location of the first Russian settlement and colonial headquarters. Russians had been mainly interested in sea otter pelts, and the occupation was primarily entrepreneurial in spirit. Native Alaskans in the Aleutians and around the Gulf of Alaska were drawn into this enterprise both willingly and unwillingly as hunters and support personnel for the Russian colonists. Over the decades, disease ravaged the area, killing 75 percent or more of the native population during the Russian occupation. Orthodox missionaries came in after initial contact and defended native rights to humane treatment and wages. They brought Orthodox Christianity to southern Alaska, where it remains a staple of native belief today. And ultimately Native Alaskans were recognized by the Russian Empire as citizens.

With the transfer of possession, the U.S. government took a markedly different approach. Following policies established to "manage" Native Americans elsewhere in the country, the federal government treated the Alaskans as conquered subjects, not making them citizens until 1924 when all aboriginal descendants in the United States were granted U.S. citizenship. As lucrative natural resources were discovered in the territory, Native use of the land came increasingly into conflict with resource extraction by outsiders. The lack of a legal basis for the dispossession of Native Alaskans of their land became critical with the discovery of oil fields in North Alaska and the birth of a plan to build a pipeline south to Prince William Sound. To settle the legal issues once and for all, in 1971 the United States formally acknowledged Native Alaskan land rights with the passage of the **Alaska Native Claims Settlement Act (ANCSA)**. This historic legislation awarded large tracts of ancestral lands across Alaska to regional and village native corporations established to manage them (Mitchell 2001).

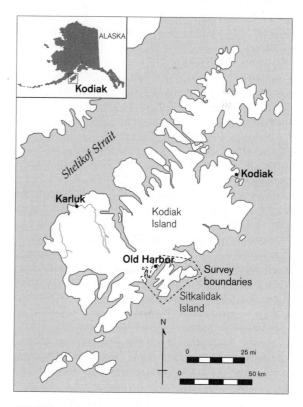

FIGURE 4.26 The Kodiak Archipelago, showing the location of Sitkalidak Island.

While not without its own problems, ANCSA signaled a turning point for Alaska Natives. The law came after more than a century of institutionalized cultural suppression born of racism, a rush by outsiders to exploit the "natural" wealth of Alaska (furs, gold, fish, oil, etc.), and assimilation policies that collectively discouraged native language, culture, and identity. Social, economic, and educational policies of the early twentieth century left many native communities physically, psychologically, and spiritually depressed (Pullar 1992). High rates of alcoholism and suicide were symptomatic of a broader loss of control over subsistence resources, limited access to newly introduced market economies, and a social environment that privileged Euro-American values and history. In this context, native heritage was suppressed and devalued. Many identified more with Russian than indigenous ancestry. The passage of ANCSA, and the change in political climate it signaled, finally gave Native Alaskans a basis on which to reclaim their heritage and assert positive cultural identities as Native Alaskans. In an effort to reconnect with their precolonial past and heal the social and psychological damage of the preceding century, many native groups began to develop cultural heritage programs that sought to document their past through study of archaeology, oral history, language, and traditional knowledge.

Archaeological research in the 1970s and 1980s was one of several sources of data used to establish ANCSA land claims, and on Kodiak, this research raised awareness among Natives and non-Natives alike of the rich Alutiiq past. In the 1980s, excavations at the phenomenal Karluk wet site produced amazing examples of the perishable art, tools, and textiles. With these discoveries, the Alutiiq Cultural Center (later the Alutiiq Museum and Archaeological Repository) was formed to foster exploration of the archaeological history and cultural heritage of the Alutiiq people. The study of archaeological sites and artifacts became a focal point for cultural revival.

In this context, different village corporations on Kodiak were interested in gaining archaeological databases of their own and promoting archaeological investigations in their respective regions. The Old Harbor Native Corporation (OHNC) had sponsored previous archaeological work at the location of the event, in 1784, that had initiated the Russian conquest of Alaska: the attack on Kodiak Island. Two years later, OHNC approved my offer to conduct an archaeological survey of their ANCSA land (primarily Sitkalidak Island: see Figure 4.26), throwing in unsolicited funding to assist in the effort. I also received financial support from the National Science Foundation, the Wenner-Gren Foundation, and the University of Michigan, where I attended graduate school at the time. The Alutiiq Culture Center in the town of Kodiak was instrumental with logistical support. I began fieldwork in June 1993 with a crew of three, a small motorboat ("skiff" in Alaskan terminology), and assorted camping and archaeological gear. The project lasted three summers.

WHAT DID THE SITKALIDAK ARCHAEOLOGICAL SURVEY PROJECT DO?

In a general sense all archaeological surveys are variations on a common theme. Archaeologists look at maps, select areas to investigate—often through some more or less formal strategy—and then go looking around, trying to find the remnants of human activities, sometimes soliciting help from locals with intimate knowledge of the area. When **archaeological deposits** (sites) are identified, they must be located on maps so they can be found again. And in most surveys, some attempt is made to discern cultural material that will provide clues to the age and kinds of activities performed at a given location. Sometimes surface site maps are drawn and small excavations are made to better understand the history of site occupation.

Some surveys are geared to finding "good sites" or "significant sites" to excavate or protect from destruction, and no explicit effort is made to use the data generated to answer regional-scale questions. Other surveys have more analytical and synthetic goals, seeking information on the distribution of sites across a landscape and, from that, occupation history at a regional scale. Site testing and excavation can then be used to add clarity and detail to the regional picture. While less detailed information about any single site can be gleaned from a survey analysis, the results give us a more comprehensive understanding of changes in settlement and land use patterns. Eventually, survey and excavation data become complementary, allowing archaeologists to synthesize the regional patterns and local details into a more representative model of past cultural systems and their change.

While the Old Harbor Native Corporation's primary goal was to protect sites by listing them and noting their distributions on a map, my research interests compelled me to make the survey more synthetic (hence more comprehensive). Kodiak has long been rich in sea life such as fish, sea mammals, seabirds, and shellfish and relatively poor in terrestrial resources. The primary terrestrial game, grizzly bear, fox, land otter, and weasel, were hunted for furs and occasionally for food, but were relatively unimportant. This explains the observation that most archaeological deposits around Kodiak are close to shore. Within the study area shown in Figure 4.26, therefore, I decided to survey most intensively around the coasts, where marine-oriented hunter-gatherers would have conducted most of their land-based activities. We also surveyed all rivers large enough to support salmon runs, but looked less intensively at steep slopes and mountaintops in this relatively rugged region.

The survey took three summers of roughly three months each. In the first season and continuing through the project, the primary goal was **reconnaissance**—searching for sites, describing them, mapping their location, and sketching their size and appearance. Finding the sites involved a combination of looking for house depressions, lush vegetation, and eroding shell midden and using soil probes and **shovel test pits** to dig for archaeological evidence. Once a site was discovered, we also dug small test pits or cleaned off eroding bluffs to describe the stratigraphy and to collect representative artifacts, faunal samples, and charcoal for radiocarbon dating. In the second summer, we also opened up larger test excavations at two sites to improve our understanding

of poorly known time periods (Figure 4.27). The final season was spent excavating a third site with students from the Old Harbor School and wrapping up the reconnaissance in areas that had not yet been visited.

Upon completion of the fieldwork, we had documented 150 archaeological sites distributed in age from 7500 to 50 years ago. These sites ranged from small, short-lived campsites and activity areas to large sod house villages. Prior to our work, fewer than 40 sites had been recorded for this area and most were relatively recent—and conspicuous—such as large village sites. As a result, this project added considerably to what was known about the variety of past settlement types and land uses in the region. Using this new information to understand the evolution of Kodiak societies and emergent complexity required countless hours of analysis back in the lab. Before discussing the results of these analyses, we must consider the theoretical model that was developed to guide research and analysis.

FIGURE 4.27 Test excavations conducted by the Sitkalidak Archaeological Survey.

FRAMING THE RESEARCH QUESTIONS

Philosophers of science have long noted that the development of scientific knowledge involves both the generation of ideas and the evaluation of ideas with evidence. This leads to a bit of a chicken-and-egg problem—do you start by generating ideas or by collecting information? Science is an ongoing process that tacks back and forth between these two activities. And one of the hardest parts of becoming a scientist is deciding where to jump into the cycle. It is generally accepted that in formal research, the articulation of a set of research questions and ideas about their possible solution usually precedes the collection of data. And that's how I got started.

As already noted, my big research questions related to the evolution of "complex hunter-gatherers" or the relatively more coordinated and ranked or even hierarchical hunter-gatherers seen around the North Pacific. This topic was too general to guide specific research, and it was necessary to develop a series of more focused questions and hypotheses relating to expected sequences of events. I did this by constructing a model or scenario outlining what I thought might have been the processes guiding Kodiak social evolution. To do this, I used two sources of information: a half-century of prior archaeological research in the area, which provided a reasonable culture history for the region, and a rich history of anthropological theory.

CULTURE HISTORY

The culture history was worked out for Kodiak in a series of projects beginning in the 1930s. Since the late 1960s, we have understood Kodiak archaeology in a series of four periods (Ocean Bay, Kachemak, Koniag, and Historic) (Clark 1984). The Ocean Bay period began sometime before 7000 years ago (calibrated to calendar years) and lasted for about 3500 years. This period is defined by chipped stone tools (including core-and-microblade technology in the first 2000 years), yielding gradually to ground slate tools late in the period (Clark 1979, 1982; Steffian et al. 2002). Slate is a common raw material in the Kodiak Archipelago, and grinding slate into projectile points and knives may have been an adaptation to the abundant local material and/or an innovation that improved the success of sea mammal hunting. Slate tools tend to shatter upon entry into prey and would have been effective in disabling swimming animals. Limited evidence of organic tools and fauna suggests that people were active maritime foragers from the beginning of the period. They used bone hooks to catch fish and barbed bone harpoon points to hunt sea mammals, most likely from boats, though we have no direct evidence of the kinds of boats used. The Ocean Bay period is also notable for the predominance of floors coated in **red ocher**, an iron pigment. Small pithouses make their appearance in the late Ocean Bay period. These were constructed of sod walls and floors sunk partially into the ground. From the earliest times, small pecked and ground stone lamps were used with sea mammal oil, presumably to light dark quarters during the long winter nights.

The Kachemak period, beginning around 3500 years ago, is defined primarily by the addition of new tool types and the loss of core-and-blade technologies. Continuities in technology suggest that this was a local development, not a population replacement (Clark 1996). Among the new tools were toggling harpoon heads, ground slate ulus or semicircular knives, and plummet-shaped sinker stones. Notched stone sinkers, made for holding down nets, had been used in the late Ocean Bay period but became much more prevalent in the Kachemak. The first aggregations into villages are observed during the Kachemak period. Late in the period, after about 500 BC, we also see increased use of bodily ornamentation with labrets and other jewelry (Steffian and Saltonstall 2001), the decoration of large lamps with relief carvings of human, animal, and abstract figures, and the development of a mortuary tradition that appears to relate to mummification and ancestor worship (Simon and Steffian 1994).

The Koniag period also appears to represent continuity with previous occupations, though this conclusion remains somewhat controversial (see Fitzhugh 2003:53–54). The period witnesses the expansion of houses from small single-roomed dwellings to multifamily units with a large main room surrounded by smaller side chambers (Figure 4.28). Excavations of Koniag period houses at the New Karluk wet site uncovered elaborate objects indicative of status competition, warfare, ceremonialism, gambling, and shamanism (Jordan and Knecht 1988). Large multiroomed houses were packed close together in this large village, with clear evidence of permanent occupation over 600 years. These finds and other evidence from Koniag period archaeological sites support ethnohistorical accounts made in the early years of the Russian occupation on Kodiak; these accounts suggest that village chiefs and "rich men" controlled resources, became powerful through trade and warfare, owned war-captive slaves, and threw potlatch feasts to honor their houses, villages, and guests. As noted earlier, the political domination of Russians and later Euro-Americans after 1784 changed Alutiiq society dramatically.

THE MODEL

The culture history revealed through archaeological study around Kodiak suggests a number of changes in the organization of hunter-gatherer societies through this 7500-year sequence, ending with the relatively complex social, political, and economic organization of the Late Koniag. Some of the more significant changes included increased residential permanence or sedentism, economic intensification and increased emphasis on seasonal food storage, and the development of a competitive social structure that encouraged status competition, trade in prestige valuables, and endemic warfare. These are some of the same developments that have been implicated in the emergence of social hierarchy in agricultural societies. My goal was to account for how and why these changes occurred on Kodiak, and to do that, I needed a model (Fitzhugh 2003:101–132). Here are some of the core features.

Drawing primarily on ideas from ecological anthropology, I suggested that the Kodiak sequence could be understood as a series of behavioral and organizational changes generated by people trying to adapt to their dynamic and changing physical and social environment. Early on, the Kodiak region was largely empty of people, and immigrants would have benefited from residential flexibility. They should have targeted the most profitable game, which would have included the sea mammals and large fish that give more calories for the effort and also generate secondary products such as skins and bone for tools. To facilitate residential flexibility, tools and facilities should have been portable. As population began to grow, small groups would have broken off, occupying new territories around the archipelago. This should have led to a gradual increase in the concentration of people around the islands and eventually to a restriction on mobility. At the same time, hunting and fishing by an increasingly dense population should have eventually caused a decline in the success rates as certain slowly reproducing species became overharvested. This is more likely for sea mammals and really large fish like halibut than it is for schooling fish like salmon and herring, and shellfish.

As more people put pressure on the available resources, technologies should be developed to try to counter the declining success in hunting and fishing. The more successful innovations would be those that reduced the costs of catching and processing smaller species, which come in denser concentrations and are rapid reproducers. Schooling fish would have been among the most attractive targets for these intensified technologies. Nets that could capture large numbers of fish and processing tools and techniques that could increase the rate of cleaning them would allow people to raise their overall return rates. With higher overall return, it would be possible to store the spring, summer, and fall catch of schooling fish for use in the lean, cold, and dark winter months.

With the successful innovation of intensive foraging/processing technologies, like nets and *ulus*, people could afford to aggregate during winter months, eating stored foods and socializing. Winter villages should form and become more permanent, and overall population densities should continue to increase. But again, with higher population densities, people also lose some ability to move around freely. The emphasis on storage for lean periods would reduce the incentive to share stores, increasing the importance of the concept of private property, which typically is alien to small

Kachemak houses

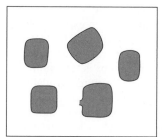

10 mi

Koniag houses

FIGURE 4.28 Kachemak and Koniag houses.

and mobile hunter-gatherer groups. And the higher population densities would also increase levels of competition over the most stable and productive resource patches. With more sedentary residence, people could also claim ownership of particular resource patches, and defend them.

Ethnographic research has shown that people in all human societies, even the most egalitarian, engage in political competition to one degree or another. Where people tend to depend more or less equally on one another for survival, this competition is minimized in favor of cooperative adaptive strategies. And when interdependence becomes less equal, competitive strategies become more pronounced. This is the situation expected when people become more densely packed onto a landscape, and when their vital resources are excludable and vary in reliability. Then some people are better off than others. Those lucky or shrewd enough to control the better hunting and fishing locations need to work hard to defend their privileged access. They can do this by establishing alliances with other elites and attracting subordinates to help control the resource. Allies and subordinates are also potential challengers, and so effort must be expended on appeasing these populations. Feasts and food giveaways are a common way of solidifying alliances and attracting subordinates. The ability to give away food and other goods sends a message of affluence and strength to recipients and bystanders. Symbols of power in the form of exotic and nonutilitarian products and labor-intensive crafts and monuments (all part of a new prestige economy) emerges to signal elite access to alliances and subordinate labor. Warfare, from local skirmishes to organized long-distance raids, provides a context for warriors to gain status and for kin groups or villages to demonstrate their strength to allies and competitors. Slaves captured in raids raise the labor potential of successful warriors and chiefs and increase their ability to compete for prestige in feasts and giveaways.

At this point the model brings us to a state reminiscent of social organization and interaction at European contact throughout the North Pacific from northern California to the Aleutian Islands. Ecological characteristics prevented elites from expanding control beyond the areas of one or a few villages, and yet some commanded sizable local populations. Wealthy and powerful chiefs and rich men (and women) sat at the top of a social system in which individuals were ranked both through inheritance and through achievements in life. Others measured their status by their genealogical proximity to elites and/or through their participation in the household activities of more or less powerful families. Slaves occupied the lowest category, though they could be freed or marry into free families, and earn higher status in time.

RESULTS OF THE SITKALIDAK ARCHAEOLOGICAL SURVEY

It is important to remember that models are plausible accounts, not actual descriptions of events. Models are useful to the extent that they make sense of existing observations and simultaneously call our attention to new observations that can be made to support or contradict aspects of the model's account. Thus to turn a model into a scientific tool, we must draw from it archaeological predictions that do not simply refer to the information we used to create the model in the first place, which would create a logically circular argument.

The model I developed included a series of archaeological predictions for the Ocean Bay, Kachemak, and Koniag time periods. Some of these predictions could be evaluated with data from the Sitkalidak Archaeological Survey, and others could not. The model generated expectations about the nature of site size, permanence, location, and density on the landscape, as well as differences in habitation structures, artifacts, and faunal remains. I shall discuss a few broad lines of evidence.

As expected, Ocean Bay sites in the Sitkalidak survey were universally small, most with thin deposits and little apparent investment in fixed structures. Extended excavations at one of these sites suggests that red ocher floors are the remnants of aboveground tent facilities, perhaps with earth holding down the tent edges (Figure 4.29). This general observation, supported by other early Ocean Bay excavations around Kodiak, is significant because tents are portable structures in which the investment made in construction is not lost when the group moves to a new area—a sign of residential flexibility. A different kind of flexibility is indicated by the location of Ocean Bay sites, themselves. All ten Ocean Bay sites located on the coast were sited in strategic locations halfway between exposed outer-coast and protected inner-bay locations. This allowed residents the daily choice of foraging near home or traveling to the outer coast or inner bays, depending on the weather and expectation of resource availability. Thus, Ocean Bay peoples appeared to select camps that gave them the greatest number of options, and they were prepared to move those camps when local resources flagged. Artifacts from the Ocean Bay sites suggested a focus on hunting and processing.

By contrast, the Kachemak settlement pattern suggested a significant change in the nature and intensity of site occupations. Kachemak sites were found both in the midbay locations and in the inner-bay and river areas. This shift is consistent with the development of a more intensive summer salmon fishery. Recall that net sinkers and *ulu* processing knives become abundant

FIGURE 4.29 Red ocher floor (marked by string), indicating the previous location of an Ocean Bay tent site.

in this time period. The largest salmon streams discharge into the inner-bay zones, making these prime locations for salmon fishing in summer. By this time, semisubterranean sod houses, first built in the late Ocean Bay period, were well established. This signals increased investment, at the expense of portability. Sod houses take considerable labor to construct and are not designed to be moved, suggesting more permanent occupation of territories and the anticipation of continued future use of constructions. Also as seen in other archaeological studies around Kodiak, significant village aggregations are first seen in the Kachemak period. Villages occur in midbay locations, suggesting a continued interest in maintaining foraging flexibility when the people were not targeting fish in rivers. These sites are more heavily developed, with thicker deposits, clay-lined storage pits, and other features. In many of the early Kachemak sites, recent excavations by other archaeologists have also shown massive fish processing and smoking facilities, indicative of the new focus on food storage. The early part of the Kachemak period was also a time of increased cold and wet climate (Mann et al. 1998). Low winter temperatures would have lasted longer, and increased storminess would have hampered maritime foraging in winter, increasing the importance of storage.

Indications of social competition are seen in the Sitkalidak settlement patterns starting in the late Kachemak period, around 1200 years ago. Small defensive sites made up of single house features on top of defendable promontories and small islands begin to appear at this time. The ones we found were inside Sitkalidak Strait and suggest localized skirmishes between competing families. Later, during the Koniag period, defensive

sites grew to include as many as 50 house pits, situated strategically around the outsides of Sitkalidak Island and along the strait, apparently for defense against nonlocal marauders. Artifacts from the Kachemak sites show a general decline in emphasis on hunting and an increase in fishing and processing tools. Ornaments such as labrets and other decorative pieces also increase in importance, suggesting greater attention to social display and competition. These new emphases become most important in the following Koniag period.

The end of the Kachemak and Koniag periods witnesses another significant expansion of the settlement system. Village sites grow larger and are primarily located in an area previously unsettled: the outer-coast zone. This shift appears to relate to the expansion of both whale hunting in open water and political competition. Locating villages in exposed coasts allowed villagers access to whale migration routes and, significantly, greater visibility of whales and approaching enemies. The largest villages were often located adjacent to large defensive sites. As mentioned previously, house size expanded in this period to include multiple side rooms and large central rooms. Measurements of house areas from Kachemak and Koniag sites around Sitkalidak also showed an increase in the variability of house areas in Koniag times. This development, which is expected when some families become larger and more powerful than others, provides our first indication of significant social differentiation. Larger houses supported larger extended families, more slaves, and more storage of food and other goods. Larger central rooms enabled wealthy families to host neighbors and allies in gift-giving potlatch feasts. Interestingly, while hunting tools decline in proportion to other tool types on average in the Koniag period, they are strongly represented on defensive sites.

These findings were generally supportive of the model. While the Sitkalidak survey was unable to recover preserved faunal material from sites older than Koniag, additional support comes from a study of faunal remains from sites around the Kodiak Archipelago. In his dissertation research on faunal collections from other areas around Kodiak, Robert Kopperl (2003) showed that sea mammals and codfish were under increased pressure toward the end of the Ocean Bay period just prior to the shift to intensive net fishing, processing, and storage. Other results of the Sitkalidak survey and more recent research suggest revisions of the model.

One of the biggest mysteries at the present time is an apparent drop in human population (number of sites and site sizes) during the late Ocean Bay and early Kachemak. The model had anticipated population increase with the ability to feed more people as more efficient fishing and processing technologies were developed. One possible explanation is that the colder climate imposed such harsh conditions that even with the more effective fishing technologies, populations suffered for centuries. A more likely explanation is that the archaeological evidence for the early Kachemak period is poorly represented and people were actually doing well, but living in areas that have been less thoroughly investigated. Recent research suggests that people might have moved onto the larger rivers elsewhere in the archipelago. Sea-level fluctuations might also have obliterated some coastal sites from this time.

CONCLUSION

The Sitkalidak Archaeological Survey contributed new information to help us understand how maritime hunter-gatherers on Kodiak become more economically, socially, and politically complex. Many questions remain. For example, we still don't understand why political competition and emergent inequalities took more than 2000 years to develop after the shift to intensive fishing

practices. Perhaps it just took that long for conditions to grow so crowded that some people could not survive the bad resource years without assistance from those controlling the more productive commodities.

It is also important to recognize that the complexity that occurred around Kodiak was much less pronounced than that seen in some other areas, such as Mesoamerica, the southeastern United States, and the Andes. Indeed, some archaeologists question the use of the term at all for these hunter-gatherer groups. What the Sitkalidak Archaeological Survey project succeeded in showing is that social evolution occurs in hunter-gatherer history, just as it does among food producers. There probably are limits to the degree of hierarchy and political centralization that hunter-gatherer elites can accomplish. Because of their greater productivities and shelf-lives, agricultural resources are often significantly more alienable from producers. This allows agricultural elites to manipulate food surpluses to a greater extent than is possible for hunter-gatherer elites. This also means that hunter-gatherer commoners often retain relatively more autonomy than peasants in some agricultural economies. It would, however, be a grievous mistake to assume that all hunter-gatherer societies were necessarily egalitarian. This research adds to a growing number of studies that show the error of such thinking.

To the Alutiiq students and Old Harbor community, this research has helped to flesh out a more detailed picture of the archaeological heritage of their region. The project itself included students from the Old Harbor School. After each season of fieldwork, the broader community turned out for exhibitions of artifacts and discussions of project results. And the Old Harbor Native Corporation is now actively protecting the archaeological sites on its land with the help of maps and inventories produced by the project. As the twenty-first century begins, the Alutiiq people of Kodiak have their eyes set firmly on the future. The archaeological past provides a benchmark, a historical record of some 7500 years, that dwarfs the most recent and often tragic 200 years since Russian contact.

DISCUSSION QUESTIONS

1. Why was archaeological work done on Sitkalidak Island in the first place? How well did Fitzhugh's research interests and goals fit with the OHNC's interest in documenting its heritage?

2. In the model outlined in this case study, what role do population growth and pressure have? What other factors help explain the changes expected?

3. How well do the data about site size, location, and density, as well as about structures, storage pits, and artifacts,

fit expectations of the model? What do you think should be investigated further?

4. Do you think that agriculture is a necessary precursor to any significantly greater complexity than that observed in the ethnographic and late archaeological record for Kodiak? Why or why not? Is increasing cultural complexity inevitable or beneficial to members of a society? Be prepared to justify your opinion.

CHAPTER 5

Paths to Complexity on the Northwest Coast

I magine walking through the Makah Cultural and Research Center (MCRC) galleries past baskets, whaling gear, house planks, fishing tackle, and dugout canoes. A wooden ramp leads into a plank house built inside the gallery. Walking up the ramp, you pass whale bones that have been carefully aligned. Inside the plank house, you immediately notice the aromas: cedar and dried fish. As your eyes adjust to the light, you begin to see, arrayed around the edges of the house, the living areas of several families. The items each family used are there sitting as if just abandoned: baskets, bentwood boxes, fishhooks of wood, clubs, and harpoons with blades ground out of thick mussel shell. The fish smell comes from dried and smoked salmon stored in the rafters for safekeeping.

The house in the museum is a replica of a house at Ozette, an extraordinary archaeological site on Washington's Olympic Peninsula not far from Neah Bay, the home of the MCRC. Ozette is extraordinary in several ways. First, it is a village site where mudslides buried houses under layers of mud. The site stayed wet over the centuries, excluding the oxygen needed by the organisms that destroy perishable archaeological materials. As a consequence, items of wood and fiber, seldom found in dry sites, were preserved. Second, the excavation techniques were very different from the shovel, trowel, brush, and screen methods one generally associates with archaeology. At Ozette, as at most wet sites, excavation was carried out by using water hoses, ranging from fire hoses to remove overburden (the sediments and soils that lie on top of the archaeological deposits) to garden hoses fitted with nozzles that gave a fine and delicate spray. Finally, Ozette was excavated at a time when relations between archaeologists and Indians in most parts of the country were at best strained, with some research undertakings marred by almost violent confrontations between Native Americans and archaeological field crews. In this turbulent time, Ozette was excavated by archaeologists at the invitation of the Makah Tribal Council and with full cooperation of the tribe (Erikson et al. 2002; Kirk and Daugherty 2007:104). Tribal members participated in all stages of the project, from excavation to conservation (a special problem for the water-saturated artifacts from the site) to curation of the collections, ultimately at the Makah Cultural and Research Center.

The artifacts in the museum's plank house are replicas made by Makah artisans: the actual artifacts from Ozette are in the galleries, too, displayed in cases that help keep them well preserved. Modern Makah also built the plank house. They split the planks and assembled the house outside to allow the boards to weather appropriately. They held a number of social events and salmon bakes in the building before disassembling it and rebuilding it in the Cultural Center as part of the displays. The dugout canoes are also replicas, made by Makah carvers directed by elders who had memories of canoe making. The reawakening of traditional art forms like carving and basket making, required to make the replicas of the Ozette artifacts, is just one way in which this site and its excavation touched the members of the Makah tribe.

In 1970, when storm waves cut into the terrace at Ozette and spilled planks and artifacts from the original house out onto the beach, it was the Makah who contacted Richard D. Daugherty of Washington State University. The site had been tested years earlier, but the threat of destruction of this part of the site prompted the excavations, which lasted until 1981. Not only did the Makah Tribe request the excavations, but they were partners in the process all the way along. As the excavations began to yield artifacts, the elders identified them and explained how they were used and what they meant to Makah life.

The organization of both the exhibits and the archaeological collections further reflects the success of the Makah Tribe in taking possession of its heritage. In the galleries of the MCRC are many displays with labels in Makah and English. Photos of Makah people are seen throughout the hall, and their voices are heard. Makah people staff the museum, give the tours, and run the educational programs, which include programs in language preservation that date back to the 1960s. The artifacts from Ozette and nearby Hoko River are stored in the collections management portion of the MCRC, not according to archaeological classifications, but by Makah linguistic classes. Further, because Makah society was based strongly on gender divisions, there are classes of items that were strictly men's items, others that were strictly women's, and a class that was appropriate for either gender. Cultural rules prohibited members of one gender from handling some items associated with the other gender, and thus the Makah have developed curation rules that specify which items may be handled by male staff, which can be handled by female staff, and which can be handled by either. Clearly Makah cultural traditions permeate the MCRC in many ways, both in the public areas and behind the scenes.

The Ozette excavations were truly a remarkable collaboration between archaeologists and Indian people. The archaeologists understood the material they were excavating better than would have been possible without the Makah elders there to identify and explain the artifacts. The Makah found a new enthusiasm for their old material culture and validation for many of their beliefs about the past. The MCRC continues to be a thriving museum and a central part of Makah life, and archaeologists continue to learn from the Ozette artifacts. Ozette is just one of many places in the Northwest Coast where such collaboration can be fruitful for all parties.

DEFINITION OF THE AREA

The Northwest Coast archaeological area is defined on the basis of the Northwest Coast culture area and encompasses a strip of land running from Yakutat Bay in Alaska on the north, down along the coasts of British Columbia, Washington State, and Oregon, to end in northern California at Cape Mendocino (Ames and Maschner 1999:17; Matson and Coupland 1995:19–20; Suttles 1990a:1). The crest of the coastal mountains and Cascade Range defines the eastern edge of the area, so the area encompasses the Puget Lowlands and its Oregon expression, the Willamette valley (Figure 5.1).

The Subarctic borders the Northwest Coast on the north, and there was some influence from that area. The Plateau lies to the east of the southern portion of the Northwest Coast, and is sometimes lumped with it in discussions. California is the southern neighbor of this area. Anthropologists and archaeologists have developed several different schemes for dividing the Northwest Coast into subareas. There are considerable differences as one proceeds from north to south, and for this discussion we will use a simple scheme of Northern subarea, Central subarea, and Southern subarea, following Ames and Maschner (1999:19).

A number of different chronological sequences have been developed for different regions of the Northwest Coast. We use the general chronology (Table 5.1) presented by Ames and Maschner (1999:Figure 7) to organize our discussions.

THE ENVIRONMENT

The landscape of the Northwest Coast consists of elements arranged generally in north-to-south strips of territory—the continental shelf, the Outer Mountains, the coastal lowlands, and the Inner Mountains (Ames and Maschner 1999:44). The continental shelf is the broad area of relatively shallow water between the coast and the deeper water to the west. In some areas, such as the coasts of Washington and Oregon, the shelf is exposed and forms a broad coastal plain. The Outer Mountains rise abruptly to the east of the continental shelf/coastal plain and include the mountains of Alaska's Alexander Archipelago, the coastal mountains of British Columbia's islands, the Olympic Mountains

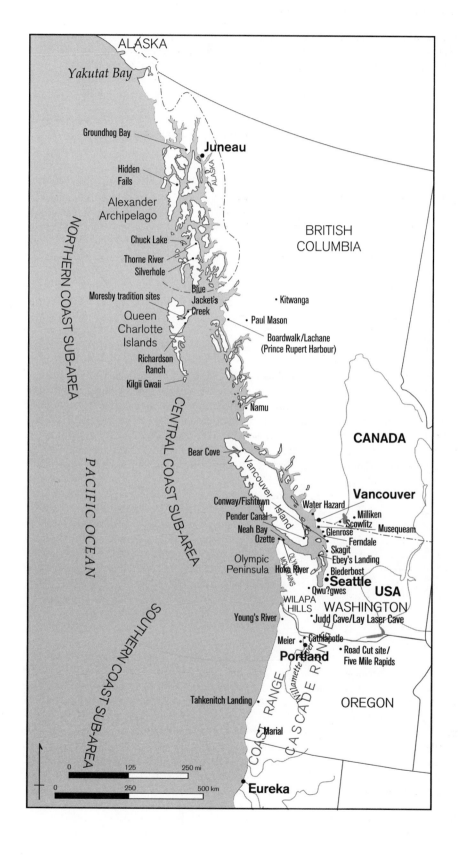

FIGURE 5.1 The Northwest Coast culture area, showing the location of sites mentioned in Chapter 5.

TABLE 5.1 Introduction to Northwest Coast Culture History

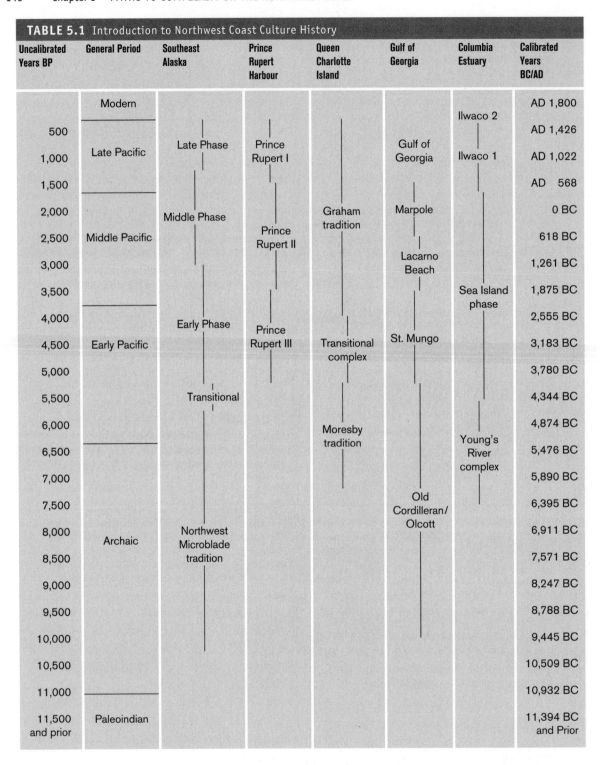

Uncalibrated Years BP	General Period	Southeast Alaska	Prince Rupert Harbour	Queen Charlotte Island	Gulf of Georgia	Columbia Estuary	Calibrated Years BC/AD
	Modern					Ilwaco 2	AD 1,800
500							AD 1,426
1,000	Late Pacific	Late Phase	Prince Rupert I		Gulf of Georgia	Ilwaco 1	AD 1,022
1,500							AD 568
2,000		Middle Phase		Graham tradition	Marpole		0 BC
2,500	Middle Pacific		Prince Rupert II				618 BC
3,000					Lacarno Beach		1,261 BC
3,500						Sea Island phase	1,875 BC
4,000		Early Phase					2,555 BC
4,500	Early Pacific		Prince Rupert III	Transitional complex	St. Mungo		3,183 BC
5,000							3,780 BC
5,500		Transitional					4,344 BC
6,000				Moresby tradition		Young's River complex	4,874 BC
6,500							5,476 BC
7,000							5,890 BC
7,500					Old Cordilleran/ Olcott		6,395 BC
8,000	Archaic	Northwest Microblade tradition					6,911 BC
8,500							7,571 BC
9,000							8,247 BC
9,500							8,788 BC
10,000							9,445 BC
10,500							10,509 BC
11,000							10,932 BC
11,500 and prior	Paleoindian						11,394 BC and Prior

of the Olympic Peninsula, Washington's Willapa Hills, and the Coast Ranges of Oregon and California. In some areas the Outer Mountains form the coastline and there is no coastal plain. In these areas the shore rises steeply and is not particularly hospitable. The coastal lowlands are partially submerged by Puget Sound, and in the south they form the Puget–Willamette Lowland, including the Willamette valley. To the east of the coastal lowlands are the Inner Mountains, primarily the Cascade Range.

The coastline is variable, with the central coast presenting a jumble of islands and inlets, many stretching inland for quite a distance. This has the effect of increasing the amount of coastline for this stretch of coast. Both to the north and the south of the island and inlet areas are stretches of relatively straight coast, broken only by a few bays and **estuaries** (Suttles 1990a:16).

The major rivers in the Northwest Coast, which run east–west, include the Columbia and the Fraser rivers, each draining substantial areas and extending east out of the Northwest Coast. Many of the rivers, especially those along the Oregon coast and the Olympic Peninsula, have relatively small drainage areas. A major exception is the Willamette River, which flows north through Oregon in the lowland between the coastal mountains and the Cascade Range and empties into the Columbia River. These rivers and their tributaries have important runs of anadromous fish, including steelhead and varieties of salmon that were very important in the development of the distinctive Northwest Coast way of life, at least in some areas. Eulachon, or candlefish (Figure 5.2), is a small anadromous fish that has high oil content and was also a major element of the Northwest Coast pattern. Anadromous fish were important because they entered the rivers and streams in great numbers at predictable times during the year and could be harvested in a number of ways.

The ocean also provided important resources. Shellfish were collected from the shores and estuaries, and coastal wetlands provided plant foods, waterfowl, and terrestrial animals that live along the wetlands. Fish were also taken in the nearshore waters and in estuaries. Puget Sound is a particularly rich shallow-water environment (Ames and Maschner 1999:44–45). Sea mammals, including sea otters, seals, and sea lions, could also be taken along the coast. Some Northwest Coast peoples like the Makah practiced whaling, hunting whales (including grays and humpbacks [Huelsbeck 1994]) from large dugout canoes. The recent reinstatement of traditional whaling in Makah culture has been very controversial among environmentalists (Dark 1999).

The Northwest Coast is essentially a rain forest, but a temperate one. Dominant trees include western hemlock, Sitka spruce, and Douglas fir, though their distribution is complex. One forest tree, western red cedar, provides a critical construction material in many areas of the Northwest Coast for items as diverse as dugout canoes, houses, bentwood boxes, and baskets (see Box 5.1). Although the forests dominated the

FIGURE 5.2 Eulachon on a drying rack.

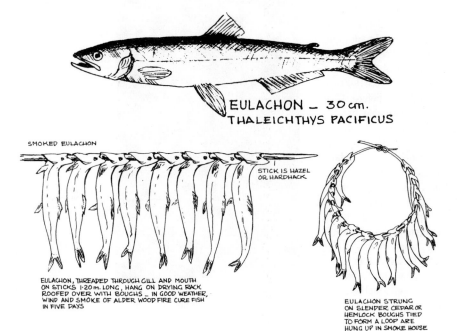

EULACHON — 30 cm.
THALEICHTHYS PACIFICUS

SMOKED EULACHON

STICK IS HAZEL OR HARDHACK

EULACHON, THREADED THROUGH GILL AND MOUTH ON STICKS 1·20 m. LONG, HANG ON DRYING RACK ROOFED OVER WITH BOUGHS — IN GOOD WEATHER, WIND AND SMOKE OF ALDER WOOD FIRE CURE FISH IN FIVE DAYS

EULACHON STRUNG ON SLENDER CEDAR OR HEMLOCK BOUGHS TIED TO FORM A LOOP ARE HUNG UP IN SMOKE HOUSE

ISSUES AND DEBATES   BOX 5.1

How Many Old Scarred Trees Do We Need?

The Indian and First Nation peoples of the Northwest Coast used forest products heavily for everything from dugout canoes to planks for house construction to bark for making basketry and cordage. Often these products were harvested from living trees, leaving visible scars. It is these trees, trees with evidence of use by Native people in the past, that are called **culturally modified trees**, or CMTs (Figure 5.3). The trees can be living or they can be standing deadwood, but they have value both to the Native people and to archaeologists. If you don't know what to look for, however, you can walk right past them without even noticing.

Culturally modified trees can often be dated by using dendrochronology. Their distribution, dating, and the type of modification (e.g., house plank harvest, bark stripping) provide the archaeologist with intimate knowledge of how people used the land in the past. One study for the Gifford Pinchot National Forest in Washington State found correlations between CMTs and trails, camps, huckleberry patches, and huckleberry processing sites, and it provided information on huckleberry patch management and continuity of culture in the area (Eldridge 1997:3–4). For First Nation and Native Americans, these trees are both tangible remains of their heritage and proof that their ancestors made use of particular areas. In an age of reawakening of old ways, the trees show where materials once were gathered and provide silent testimony to past technologies.

CMTs receive some protection by governments in Canada and the United States; for example, they are routinely recorded on cultural resource surveys. In addition, there have been attempts to inventory some large areas outside the development process. In British Columbia, a province that has a very large number of CMTs, the Heritage Conservation Act protects those modified before 1846 (Eldridge 1997:5). Other protections are available for trees modified after 1846, and many First Nation people are of the opinion that all CMTs should be preserved: these organic artifacts demonstrate use of specific areas of land and can be seen as support in land claim cases.

The controversy surrounding CMTs basically entails the questions of how many should be preserved in any area and whether preservation efforts should be allowed to impact local logging and development. The debate is ongoing, with litigation and legislation changing the playing field. Preservation of every CMT would preclude much development and certain economically important pursuits such as logging. Should we preserve all the CMTs? And if not, which ones and how many should we preserve?

In any event, trees die (and many CMTs are already dead), and they decay. Thus from the long-term viewpoint any preservation is only temporary. This is a hard issue, and one that will take some time to resolve.

Modified trees are present in many forms. In areas that were logged in the late nineteenth and early twentieth centuries, stumps with the notches cut for springboards (boards the loggers stood on to saw through the tree with crosscut saws) survive, sometimes in large numbers. In the Rocky Mountains and Sierra Nevadas, where aspen trees grow, Hispanic and Basque sheepherders in the same time span left "aspen art," or **arborglyphs** (Thurman 2001). These range from simple signatures or initials to elaborate depictions of camp scenes or people. In other areas, unmodified trees can be historic, spurring preservation battles. In California, where eucalyptus trees were imported in the 1800s and planted on farms and ranches, there is often debate about preserving the groves of trees as part of the historical cultural landscape, if not the last remnant.

From a strictly archaeological point of view, these tree resources can be documented and will provide information about the past. The real question is one of heritage value. Should we preserve these bits of the past, or is it too costly to do so? The debate continues, and the ultimate answers will depend on how we value the past.

FIGURE 5.3 Culturally modified tree.

Thematic Research Questions in Chapter 5

As we pointed out in Chapter 2, the North American archaeological record provides significant evidence for several broad anthropological themes. Archaeologists working in the Northwest culture area address at least three of the themes listed in Table 2.1, and we touch on other themes less directly. Table 5.2 helps you locate relevant sections of this chapter for each theme, although as you become more familiar with the archaeology of the Northwest Coast, you will discover more specific research questions and issues as well.

TABLE 5.2 Research Themes for the Northwest Coast

Research Question	Particularly Relevant Sections
How have humans adapted to the diverse environments of North America and to climatic change over time?	Discussions in the sections on Earliest Occupations, the Archaic, and the Pacific Period
How, when, and where did sociopolitically complex, internally differentiated cultural systems develop in North America?	Discussion in the sections on the Early, Middle, and Late Pacific periods as well as in the section on the Modern Period
What ethnic identities can be identified and historically traced in North America's past?	Discussion in Exhibit 5.1, "Basketry and Cordage," and in the case study by Foster, Ross, and Croes, "Archaeological/Anthropological–Native American Coordination"

landscape, there were also prairies or open grasslands in parts of the Puget Lowlands and the Willamette valley. The forests provided plant foods like berries, and corms or bulbs were also collected. The productivity of the forests decreases from south to north; thus, plant foods were generally more important in the southern Northwest Coast (Ames and Maschner 1999:46). Deer, wapiti or elk, mountain sheep, and mountain goats were hunted on the land.

Climatic Change

Pleistocene glaciers covered large areas in the Northwest Coast, particularly the northern and central portions. Land immediately adjacent to the Pacific Ocean in Washington, Oregon, and northern California was not glaciated, however. The glaciers started melting between 14,000 and 15,000 years ago, and by 12,000 years ago the entire coast was ice free (Ames and Maschner 1999:48–49; Carlson 1990:60). In Chapter 2, our discussion of the process of deglaciation and its effects pointed out not only that sea level rose as water from melting glaciers returned to the sea, but that isostatic changes cause the land, which had been deformed by the weight of the great ice sheets, to spring back. In the Northwest Coast, this meant the flooding of areas of the continental shelf that had been exposed during the height of the glacial periods. Because of isostatic rebound, some areas that are

under water today were actually exposed for a time after glaciation as the land rose faster than the sea level. Other areas that are currently dry also were dry land during the glaciation but flooded as the glaciers melted because the land did not rebound as fast as sea levels rose. The story of sea level rise, isostatic rebound, and coastal flooding during the first several millennia of the Holocene is a complicated one (Ames and Maschner 1999:50–51).

EARLIEST OCCUPATIONS

The earliest occupations of the area have been discussed in Chapter 3. As mentioned, 49-PET-408 provides evidence of the use of marine resources by 9200 BP. Another important early site that indicates use of fish is Kilgii Gwaii on Ellen Island in southern Haida Gwaii (formerly Queen Charlotte Islands). This site is in the intertidal zone today, but was on the shore when occupied. Rising sea level drowned the site after about 100 years of use, preserving it and creating a continually wet environment that preserved organic artifacts. Among these are wooden wedges that foreshadow later use of split wood on the Northwest Coast. Shellfish, fish bone, and sea mammal bone indicate a maritime orientation, although terrestrial animals are also present, including the remains of bear (Moss 2011:63–64).

ARCHAIC

Northwest Microblade Tradition

The oldest Archaic materials in the area consist of the two contrasting patterns, a northern one focused on microblades and a southern one with connections to the adjacent Plateau. The Northwest Microblade tradition is sometimes called the Paleoarctic tradition to emphasize the connections with the north. Found from the Alaska Panhandle to the area south of Vancouver Island in British Columbia, it is characterized by sites that produce microblades, as well as the cores from which they were struck, pebble tools, and flakes. Bifaces are very rare in these sites.

Ground Hog Bay 2, located on Alaska's Chilkat Peninsula, has dates ranging from around 9200 BP to 4200 BP for the earliest strata. Wedge-shaped microblade cores, microblades, scrapers, cobble choppers, blade cores, and flake cores are all found in these strata (Figure 5.4). This site is also one of the few to have bifaces associated with microblades (Ackerman 1996b:426–429).

Other sites with microblade assemblages include Hidden Falls in southeast Alaska (dated to about 9000 BP: [Davis 1996:421]), Thorne River (ca. 9000 BP), and Chuck Lake (ca. 8200 BP). Of these, Chuck Lake is particularly important for the animal remains found there, which include shellfish, fish, and land mammals (Ames and Maschner 1999:68).

Among the numerous sites in British Columbia that have produced microblades are those of the **Moresby tradition** on the Queen Charlotte Islands (7500–5000 BP), the Paul Mason site on the Skeena River (5000–4300 BP), and the stratified site of Namu in Fitzhugh Sound. Roy Carlson (1991a) dates the microblade assemblage at Namu to between 8000 BP and about 5200 BP. This southern microblade site also has evidence of bifaces, suggesting some influence from the south.

Because of the nature of the microblade cores found there, Ackerman (1996c:429) suggests that Ground Hog Bay 2 and Hidden Falls represent the spread of microblade technology from interior Alaska, with roots in the Denali complex (see Chapter 3). He attributes the other microblade sites to a spread of this technology from the south.

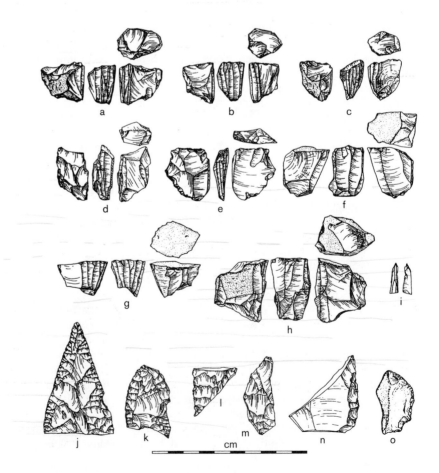

FIGURE 5.4 Artifacts for Groundhog Bay site 2: (a–d, f–h) wedge-shaped microblade cores, (e) burin, (i) microblade with a graverlike tip, (j–m) biface fragments, and (n, o) side scrapers.

One of the most interesting aspects of the archaeology of the Northwest Coast is the presence of saturated archaeological sites in which normally perishable artifacts of wood and fiber are preserved. The earliest basketry from a Northwest Coast site is from waterlogged deposits at the Silver Hole site on Prince of Wales Island in Alaska. Radiocarbon dated to 5945 BP, this basket exhibits characteristics similar to those found in historical Tlingit–Haida basketry, suggesting to Dale Croes (1997) a degree of cultural continuity from the Microblade tradition into modern times.

Old Cordilleran Tradition

The other major Archaic tradition on the Northwest Coast is characterized by stemmed leaf-shaped points and pebble tools and is called **Old Cordilleran** or sometimes the **Pebble Tool tradition**. First described for the Plateau (Chapter 6), Old Cordilleran (Figure 5.5) material occurs on the central and southern portions of the Northwest Coast as well. Matson (1976) attributes artifacts from the oldest strata at the Glenrose Cannery site, located on the Fraser River, to the Old Cordilleran. These deposits dated between about 8500 BP and 5500 BP and produced 11 antler wedges, an antler punch, and a barbed bone point, as well as numerous cobble tools. Only a few leaf-shaped points and knives were recovered (Matson and Coupland 1995).

Other sites with similar assemblages and dates include the Milliken site (Borden 1961), about 80 miles (130 km) up the Fraser from Glenrose, and Bear Cove (Carlson 1979) on the northern end of Vancouver Island (Matson and Coupland 1995:78). The Milliken site dates to about 9000 BP, and Bear Cove to about 8000 BP. In Washington, sites grouped under the term **Olcott** produced material considered to be part of the Old Cordilleran, primarily from surface contexts. The Ferndale site on the Nooksack River is a dated site with Olcott material, and the date of 4180 ±20 BP is a minimum date for the end of the occupation there (Matson and Coupland 1995:78). Olcott material is generally assigned dates between 5000 BP and 9000 BP. Similarly, Layser Cave and Judd Peak Rockshelter in the Cascades south of Mount Ranier yielded collections with both microblades and stemmed bifaces reminiscent of points from the Plateau (see Chapter 6). These deposits date to between 7700 BP and 5500 BP (Kirk and Daugherty 2007:86–88). Much of the material from these sites is heavily patinated and includes leaf-shaped points (Cascade points), knives, and pebble tools (Matson and Coupland 1995:78).

One of the most important Old Cordilleran sites is the Dalles Roadcut site at Five Mile Rapids on the Columbia River, on the border between the Northwest Coast and the Plateau. Excavated in 1953 by Luther Cressman (Cressman et al. 1960), this site yielded leaf-shaped points and pebble tools, but burins, bola stones, and edge-ground cobbles were also recovered in sediments that date to approximately 9000 BP to 7500 BP. Large quantities of salmon bone were recovered from these levels, as well, and the bone of birds such as cormorants, bald eagles, and condors were also found. Work by Virginia Butler at the site confirms that

FIGURE 5.5 Old Cordilleran artifacts from various sites in British Columbia: (top row, from left) three leaf-shaped bifaces, a flaked scraper, two microblade cores; (center row) snubnose scraper, four microblades; (bottom row) two pebble tools (the one on the right came from an intertidal site, as indicated by the barnacle near the flaked edge). The pebble tool with the barnacle is 4.4 inches (11.4 cm) wide.

humans butchered the fish. Five Mile Rapids was a historically known fishing spot for Indians along the Columbia River, and the site deposits indicate considerable time depth for fishing in the area.

The Tahkenitch Landing and Marial sites extend the range of the Old Cordilleran south. Tahkenitch Landing, dated to between 8000 BP and 3000 BP, is located near Coos Bay in Oregon. The artifacts recovered from the oldest layers at the site are sparse and do not indicate a particular cultural affiliation. The faunal assemblage is rich, however, with remains of mammals, birds, and fish. Although most of the fish could have been collected from estuaries, the Pacific hake would most likely have been collected from offshore. The Marial site, on the Rogue River, is located 80 miles (130 km) from the coast. Radiocarbon dates for the portions of the site that produced leaf-shaped points and cobble tools of the kind associated with the Old Cordilleran ranged from 8560 BP to 5850 BP (Matson and Coupland 1995:79–80).

In summary, Archaic sites in the Northwest Coast suggest that there was greater cultural diversity on the coast at this time than at any time afterward. Due to the small number of sites, some researchers suggest populations were small and mobile, exploiting large territories and moving frequently. Subsistence remains are sparse at most sites, but there are indications of the use of terrestrial and marine foods. These early northwesterners harvested shellfish, fish, and sea mammals from the ocean. There is also evidence that they hunted large mammals, especially at inland sites. Salmon, a mainstay of later diets, also was exploited during this period, as indicated by the quantities of salmon bone from The Dalles Roadcut site at Five Mile Rapids.

PACIFIC PERIOD

Ames and Maschner adopt the name **Pacific period** for the period after the Archaic on the Northwest Coast. Chartkoff and Chartkoff (1984) first described this period in California to recognize the development of complexity in that area's prehistory (see Chapter 7). Ames and Maschner (1999:87) see general similarities between developments in California and the Northwest Coast. During the Pacific period, which Ames and Maschner (1999:Figure 7) divide into Early, Middle, and Late subperiods, the traits that set the Northwest Coast apart as a culture area developed. Populations grew, becoming sedentary with the cyclical occupation of permanent village sites. Houses at least partially dug into the ground appeared first, but ultimately the cedar plank house became the preferred dwelling style. Although there is evidence of the use of aquatic resources from the earliest occupations of

the area, the economy began to be focused on them. In many areas this meant salmon, but shellfish, sea mammals, and fish of other types were also important. Storage of fish and other resources became important, and population densities increased to levels unparalleled in most other parts of North America. Woodworking, a necessary technology for house construction, became a major industry, and the people produced cedar canoes, storage boxes, clubs, and art. Indeed, the distinctive Northwest Coast art style developed during this period as well. Evidence from burials, village organization, and house size indicate an increasing complexity in social organization, with the development of both an elite class of nobles and a class of slaves.

Early Pacific Period

The Early Pacific period, which extends from 6400 BP to 3800 BP, saw the disappearance of microblade cores and the introduction of a variety of bone and antler tools. Microliths were made, but a **bipolar technology** now allowed use of small nodules of stone; other types of flaked stone, including projectile points and cobble tools, also are found. The bone tools included unilaterally and bilaterally barbed harpoons, bone points, awls, and punches, and antler wedges (Figure 5.6) became more common than they were in the Archaic. One reason for the greater abundance of bone and antler tools in the Early Pacific period is that many of the sites are shell middens, an excellent environment for the preservation of bone.

At Namu this period starts with a diverse economy, but in Namu 3 (6000–5000 BP), considerable amounts of shell accumulated, indicating an increase in the people's use of shellfish. Salmon were also more heavily used than in the prior levels. In Namu 4 (5000–4000 BP), subsistence remains indicate a diversification in resource use, although fishing also increased a bit. Herring was used heavily during the entire period. Hunters and fishers took sea mammals (seal and sea otter), rockfish, and cod (Ames and Maschner 1999:137–138). Throughout the coast, people seemed to have had a diversified economy, but seafood played an important part. **Isotopic analysis** of bone from 90 Early Pacific and early Middle Pacific period burials indicates that 90 to 100 percent of the protein the individuals consumed was from the ocean (Ames and Maschner 1999:138).

Ground stone tools also began to replace chipped stone in many areas. Ground slate points were probably used as tips for harpoons but also could have been used on spears or as knives (Figure 5.7). **Celts** are another type of ground stone found during this period. Associated with woodworking, these artifacts probably served as the blades for adzes. Ground stone mauls, used for

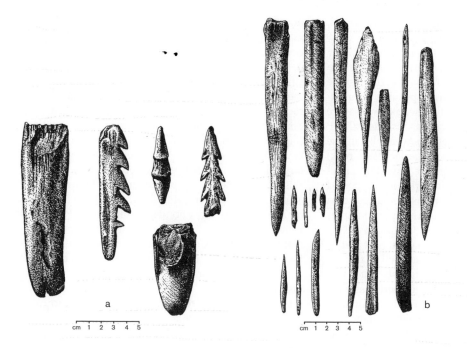

FIGURE 5.6 Early Pacific period bone and antler tools from the St. Mungo site: (a) wedges and points and (b) points, a needle, and other tools.

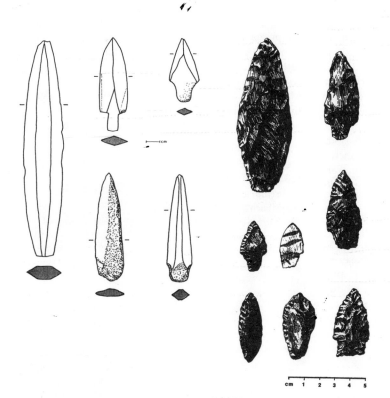

FIGURE 5.7 Early Pacific period ground and flaked points.

driving the bone and antler wedges in splitting wood, are also part of some Early Pacific period assemblages.

Burials are common during this period, and they provide considerable important information. In addition to the isotopic analyses mentioned earlier, grave goods and the patterning of burials provide information on the relative status of the people who were buried in the middens. Burials occur as early as 5400 BP at Namu, and by 4500 BP, cemeteries were also in use on the Queen Charlotte Islands (Blue Jacket's Creek) and in the Gulf of Georgia (Pender Canal). A small portion of the individuals in cemeteries of this period had distinctive wear on their teeth, as well as patterns of tooth loss that the wearing of labrets caused (Ames and Maschner 1999; Matson and Coupland 1995). Labrets are seen in later periods as symbols of status, and the distribution of labret wear, as well as the circumstances of some of the burials, suggests that it was an indicator of status in the Early Pacific period as well. Because labret wear was restricted to adults and was split equally between men and women, it may well have been a mark of **achieved status**, which results from an individual's accomplishments, rather than **ascribed status**, which is based on the circumstances of an individual's birth.

Graves also provide evidence about violence experienced by individuals during their lives. Skeletons with evidence of trauma have been found in a number of sites. The types of trauma include depressed skull fractures of the sort clubs would cause, injuries to the face and front teeth, and breaks in the forearm that are called parrying fractures because they tend to be incurred when a person uses the arms to fend off an attacker who is armed with a club. Decapitated skeletons are also found in some sites of this period. These data suggest conflict between groups, a conclusion that is further supported by southeast Alaskan sites, which around 4200 BP were built in defensible locations such as bluff tops (Lambert 2002).

Many of the patterns found in the ethnographic cultures of the Northwest Coast are foreshadowed in the Early Pacific period. Although the subsistence base is broad, there are signs of an increase in emphasis on coastal and riverine resources. Bone and antler implements became more common, though this may be due in part to better preservation, and ground stone became important. It is in the Middle Pacific period that the patterns really begin to resemble the ethnographically recorded lifestyle of the Northwest Coast.

Middle Pacific Period

The Middle Pacific period, in which sea level generally was stabilized, is dated between 3800 BP and 1800/1500 BP. In parts of the Pacific Northwest,

however, tectonic adjustments of the land after the glacial ice had melted caused the coast to sink and the ocean to flood some areas.

The food quest is marked at this time by intensification of certain activities, especially fishing. New methods of obtaining fish appear in the archaeological record. These include extensive use of nets, as evidenced by the common occurrence of net sinkers (Figure 5.8), an artifact type that was rare before the beginning of the Middle Pacific period. Although a few large fish weirs have been located that date to before this period, they are found over a wide area by the Middle Pacific period (Moss 2011:91–92) (see this chapter's case study by Rhonda Foster, Larry Ross, and Dale R. Croes, "Archaeological/Anthropological–Native American Coordination: An Example of Sharing the Research on the Northwest Coast of North America," for a discussion of a more recent fish trap). Fish weirs consist of stakes driven into the mud of the intertidal zone to direct fish, and ultimately, to catch them (Moss 2011:37–38).

Another important development in this period is the development of storage boxes. These bentwood boxes (Figure 5.9) are made from a plank of cedar that has been scored and bent into a rectangle. A wooden bottom is sewn on, and a lid is fitted to the box. Seams are waterproofed. In ethnographic times these were the primary storage devices, although items were also stored in baskets and allowed to hang in the house rafters. The boxes first appear in the archaeological record as coffins (Ames and Maschner 1999:140; Martindale and Marsden 2003:26), but it is inferred that they were being used for storage at the same time. Storage is a critical aspect of the Northwest Coast

FIGURE 5.8 A girdled stone (top) and a perforated stone. Such artifacts, believed to have been used as net weights, are found in sites of the Middle Pacific period and later.

FIGURE 5.9 Bentwood box recovered from the Late Pacific period at Ozette. Although many were found buried by mud on the floors of Ozette's houses, these wooden artifacts are first found in Middle Pacific contexts.

pattern, with the large population densities dependent on stored foods.

It appears that populations grew substantially during this period. Ames and Maschner (1999:55, Figure 4) indicate that populations on the southern Northwest Coast grew rapidly between 4500 BP and 3200 BP, peaking at 3000 BP. In the north there was a period of growth before the Middle Pacific period, but another period of rapid growth occurred at 3200 BP, with the highest populations levels attained at 3000 BP. This assessment of population growth is based on numbers of radiocarbon dated sites as indicators of population. Modeling of population on the Northwest Coast by Dale Croes and Steven Hackenberger (1988) supports this general trend.

Rectangular houses make their appearance during this period. These are probably the earliest plank houses, made by securing planks split from cedar logs to posts sunk in the ground. The planks could be removed and set up on another framework at another site, facilitating some residential mobility. At the Paul Mason site, rectangular houses are present between 3450 BP and 2950 BP, and they are arranged in two rows just as they were in villages known ethnographically. Another early site with houses arranged in rows was the Boardwalk site at Prince Rupert Harbour. Located on the lower Fraser River, the Katz site has a two-row arrangement, but the structures are pit houses (Hanson 1973).

The northern part of the Northwest Coast appears to have experienced an increase in violence. Prince Rupert Harbour provides the best evidence of this, with a high proportion of the burials from this time period showing signs of violence ("parry" fractures and depressed skull fractures), primarily to males (Cybulski 1992; Matson and Coupland 1995:233–234). Weapons (Figure 5.10) are also present in the Prince Rupert Harbour sites, including stone and bone clubs, ground slate daggers, and bipointed ground stone artifacts (Fladmark et al. 1990:234). Evidence of trauma and violence is much less common on the southern coast (Lambert 2002:215). Moss (2011:128–129) cautions

that patterns of warfare recorded ethnographically for the Northwest Coast cannot safely be projected back in time, however, or be seen as characteristic of the entire region.

Social ranking developed during this period, with strong evidence by 1500 BP (500 BC). There is evidence that both individuals and villages were ranked. Individual differences in status are indicated by cranial deformation in the south and by the wearing of labrets in the north. Labret wear in the Middle Pacific period is restricted almost solely to males, and the labrets were larger than before. Burial patterns are also important indicators of status. Grave goods are found in relatively few burials, with exotic items, rare items, and the apparent work of specialized artists such as copper artifacts particularly concentrated in a few burials. Young individuals are among those with grave goods, indicating that status now was ascribed rather than achieved. There are also possible indications of the practice of slavery during this period. An anomalously low ratio of women in the burial population at the Prince Rupert Harbour sites and the presence of beheaded burials, burials in positions that differed from the norm, and burials with evidence of scalping have been pointed to as evidence of slavery, although the case is far from strong. Another line of evidence perhaps suggesting status differentiation is the knob-topped hats from Hoko River, discussed shortly.

Art objects from the Middle Pacific period are few, and most of them have been found in the Gulf of Georgia region, starting in the Locarno Beach phase (Ames and Maschner 1999:104). These include carved clubs, carved stone bowls, and a carved wood atlatl fragment. Known as the Skagit atlatl because it was found near the mouth of the Skagit River, the fragment is carved of yew wood in an elaborate representation of a creature poised above a human face (Figure 5.11). The oldest carved wood from the Northwest Coast is a mat creaser from the Hoko River site that has stylized birds forming its handle (Figure 5.12). The beginnings of the elaborate Northwest Coast art style are foreshadowed in the small sample of pieces from this period, and by the Marpole phase, sites often yield carved zoomorphic items that are well within the style (Ames and Maschner 1999:105).

Wet sites provide a glimpse at perishable artifacts during the Middle Pacific period. In the Prince Rupert Harbour area, the Lachane site has saturated deposits that date to between 2500 BP and 1600 BP (Matson and Coupland 1995:231). Artifacts include wood boxes and bowls, wedges, chisel and adze handles, and canoe paddles, as well as basketry and cordage. Croes (1997) sees continuity between the basketry styles at the site and historical Tsimshian basketry.

FIGURE 5.10 Bone clubs recovered from Prince Rupert Harbour. Specimen on the left dates to circa 2500 BP, while the others are more recent.

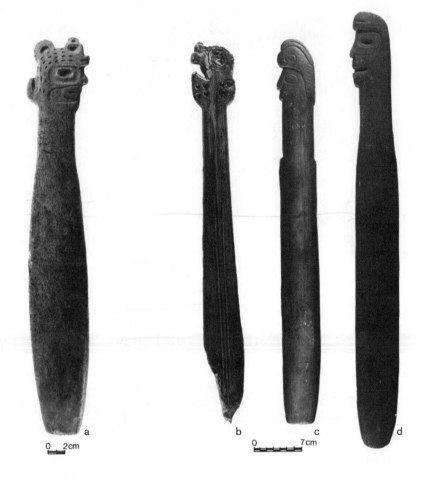

Hoko River (Croes 1995) is a wet site located on the Strait of Juan de Fuca on Washington's Olympic Peninsula. The site complex includes saturated deposits, an adjacent dry site, and a rockshelter. The wet site and its adjacent dry occupation date to between 3000 BP and 2500 BP. The artifacts accumulated on a growing river bar, with the wet components remaining saturated. The carved item shown in Figure 5.12 was one of these artifacts. Other perishable items recovered include both bentwood fishhooks and **composite fishhooks** made of several pieces (Figure 5.13). A wide variety of baskets were also found, including large open-weave pack baskets, small fine-weave baskets, flat bags, and medium to large baskets interpreted as storage baskets. Basketry hats, tule mats, cordage, wooden wedges, a variety of pointed wooden items (including barbed projectile points), wooden floats for fishing line, the base to a fire drill, and a wooden comb were also found, along with the debris from woodworking, including split wood and wood chips. A fragment of split western red cedar may be a piece of a small bentwood box, but this is far from certain. Unmodified stones were found with lines attached

in various ways. These are interpreted as net anchor stones, but they differ from stone anchors recognized at other Northwest Coast sites in that the stones themselves have not been modified. Artifacts identified as anchors at sites without the level of preservation found at Hoko River generally either have grooves ground or pecked into them or have biconical holes drilled in them. Croes (1995:177–180) says that the Hoko anchor stones would not be recognized as artifacts if they were found without the lines attached to them.

The hats from the site are of particular interest. They are conical and have knobs on the top (Figure 5.14). This style of hat was an indicator of high status in the ethnographic period, and the finding of such headgear in the Hoko River wet deposits offers tantalizing evidence for the possible presence of status differentiation during the Middle Pacific period. Exhibit 5.1 discusses some of the other kinds of information archaeologists get from normally perishable artifacts.

Microliths, primarily of quartz, were found both in the wet site and in the dry deposits. In the wet site many of the microliths were found in cedar handles (Figure 5.15). Most of the microliths were of bipolar

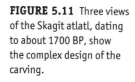

FIGURE 5.11 Three views of the Skagit atlatl, dating to about 1700 BP, show the complex design of the carving.

FIGURE 5.12 This artifact, recovered from the Hoko River wet site, is the oldest example of carving from the area.

spalls off quartz pebbles collected near the site. Jeff Flenniken (1981) replicated the manufacture and hafting of these tools and demonstrated they could be used efficiently as knives for cleaning fish. A few true microblades of crystal quartz were recovered as well.

Replication has been an important part of the Hoko River project, and important information has come from replicating fishhooks and using them. Ricky Hoff (1980) replicated hooks and fishing tackle and conducted fishing experiments in consultation with Makah elders. Experiments both in the open sea and at the Seattle Aquarium provided data on the kinds of fish that could be taken with hooks of different kinds. The bentwood hooks appear to have been used for taking Pacific cod. This conclusion is supported by the fishbone from Hoko River. The composite hooks, on the other hand, were probably used on bottom fish like flounder and sculpin (Croes 1995:99–104).

Late Pacific Period

The Late Pacific period begins after the Middle Pacific period at 1800 BP to 1500 BP and continues until European exploration of the Northwest began in the

eighteenth century AD. Between 800 BP and 650 BP (AD 1150–1300), the climate was warm and dry, while the cooling of the Little Ice Age between 600 BP and 100 BP (AD 1350–1860) variously affected the Northwest Coast. It is during this period that the patterns of the ethnographic period really became evident in Northwest Coast sites.

A major change in technology occurred during this period, namely the replacement of flaked stone tools by bone, antler, and ground stone tools. The tools in use during the Late Pacific period are very much like those of the Historic period. This change is most marked on the south and central coast because farther north flaked tools were not particularly important during the entire Pacific period.

Subsistence activities appear to have intensified during the Late Pacific. Salmon are important in many areas, but other resources were locally important, in some cases almost replacing salmon in the local menus. Storage, however, was a critical aspect of the economy throughout the area. One aspect of subsistence intensification is the greater use of nearshore and offshore organisms. Halibut was an important fish in some areas where salmon were not present in sufficient

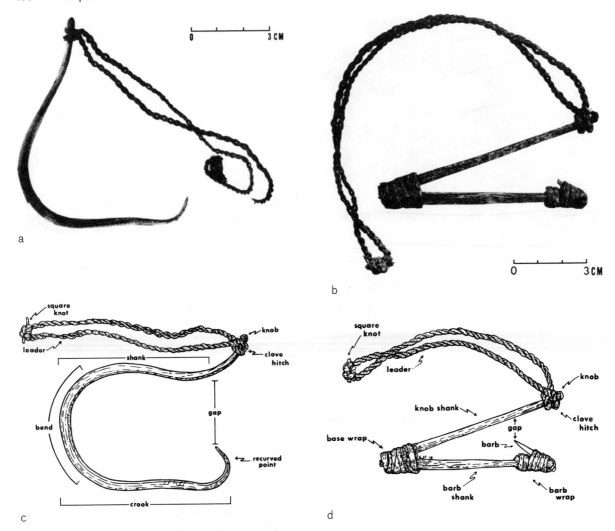

FIGURE 5.13 Bentwood (left) and composite (right) fishhooks from the Hoko River wet site.

numbers to be a staple. Schooling fish such as cod and herring were caught in quantity, and smelt were also important. Whaling was practiced in areas of exposed coast, and other sea mammals, especially fur seals, were also taken (Ames and Maschner 1999:145). Fishing was accomplished in a number of ways, including the use of a wide variety of nets, weirs and traps, and fishing tackle with hooks, weights, and lines. Toggling harpoons were used in whaling and in hunting seals.

Bent wooden boxes continued to be made and used for storage. These boxes were watertight and could be used for boiling food, as well as for storing it. As documented at Ozette, baskets were also used for storage.

Ames and Maschner (1999:95) suggest that population in the Northwest reached a peak during the Late Pacific period, between 900 BP to 1000 BP. Following

this peak there was a decline in populations, with Modern period populations being somewhat smaller.

Remains of houses are more common in Late Pacific period sites, especially those dating after 500 BP. As discussed in the opening section of this chapter, whole houses were preserved at Ozette. The site shed light on the methods of construction and repair of plank houses, and it provided insight into the organization of material inside the house. The lessons from Ozette are discussed at the end of this section. Other houses from this period include those from the Meier site near Portland, Oregon. Based on excavation of over a third of the houses, this village appears to have been occupied for about 400 years, from AD 1400 to 1830, indicating considerable continuity in house use. Village arrangement in rows was well established at this time, and in many villages some houses were

FIGURE 5.14 Example of a knobbed whaler's hat, worn in this eighteenth-century depiction of Macuina, a Nootka chief.

noticeably larger than the others, suggesting ranking of households.

People continued to make many woodworking tools. These included wedges for splitting planks, as well as adzes of various sizes for hewing the timbers. Chisels are also found and were used in wood carving. Adze blades were commonly made from ground stone, but ground shell blades were also made. The blades were fitted into wooden handles. These woodworking tools were used to make houses, but were also used in the manufacture and decoration of bentwood boxes and canoes. Carved wood dugout canoes (Figure 5.17) were critical in fishing, whaling, and in transportation of people and goods. New tools (Figure 5.18), including pile drivers for placing wooden posts, were added to the toolkit during this period.

The evidence for social ranking changes in the Late Pacific period, when midden burial ceases all along the coast. Apparently historical practices of placing the dead in areas away from the village, often leaving the body exposed on a platform or in a tree, had been established. In the Fraser River area and in the Willamette valley, some burials were made in specially constructed mounds. Significant effort went into the construction of the Scowlitz mounds on the Fraser River, and the presence of quantities of grave goods in one mound suggests that some individuals controlled considerable wealth and labor. The distribution of

FIGURE 5.15 Hafted microlith in place in the deposits at the Hoko River wet site.

CLUES TO THE PAST   EXHIBIT 5.1

Basketry and Cordage

Perishable materials are preserved in archaeological sites only in rare instances. In the Arctic the cold arid conditions sometimes preserve wood, bone, antler, ivory, hide, and fiber, including basketry and cordage. In the Northwest Coast area as in Florida, perishable items are most often preserved in wet sites, where the saturated conditions deprive destructive organisms of oxygen they need to live (see also Exhibit 12.1. "Modified Bone, Tooth, and Antler from a Florida Wet Site"). In the Great Basin and the Southwest, perishable items are preserved in arid settings in dry caves. These settings provide a glimpse at items not normally preserved for archaeologists to study. Basketry and cordage have proved to be particularly interesting artifact types.

Basketry can be made by a number of different techniques, but **twining**, **plaiting**, and **coiling** are the most common (Figure 5.16). Twined and plaited baskets have two kinds of elements—**warp** and **weft**. The warp elements run lengthwise in the basket, and weft elements run perpendicular to the warp. In twined baskets the weft elements are crossed over between the warp elements, and in plaiting the warp and weft are simply interwoven. In coiling, a foundation of material is coiled, and each coil is sewn to the adjacent coils to hold the basket together. For cordage the fibers can be twisted up to the right

(**Z-twist**) or up to the left (**S-twist**). In addition, the twisted strands can be combined into cordage of two, three, or more plies by braiding or by twisting, again using the Z- or S-twist.

There are, then, a number of alternative methods of achieving the finished basketry or cordage product, be it a storage basket or twine for tying things together. In addition to the different techniques, there is also considerable variability in raw materials that can be used. The choices of a basket or cordage maker in producing the finished product are conditioned to a large part by the way the person learned the craft, generally from relatives. For that reason, there tend to be general similarities within groups, and the products of a particular set of craftspeople can be contrasted with the work of others. In short, basketry and cordage styles carry information about the group that made the artifacts, and, because methods of manufacture (the choices made in producing the basket or cordage) change through time, the products can be used as time markers as well.

In the Northwest Coast, with the extraordinary number of wet sites with good preservation, basketry has been used to explore the development of ethnicity through time. Croes (1995:116–132) used attributes such as basket base construction technique, hat construction

FIGURE 5.16 Techniques of basketry construction: (a) plaiting, (b) twining, (c) coiling, plan view, and (d) coiling, detail of stitching.

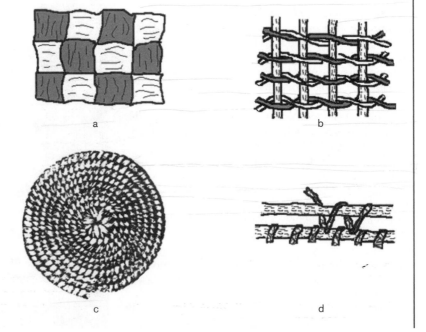

techniques, ways in which handles were attached, and **selvage** or edge-finishing type to compare basketry from wet sites along the Northwest Coast. He found that the perceived division between northern and southern areas has considerable time depth (Croes 1997). He also concluded that the distinct regions of the Northwest Coast have differed from one another for at least 3000 years, and that there is considerable continuity in ethnic groups and their territories over that time (see this chapter's case study). Interestingly, the preserved basketry suggests ethnic differences in areas that had been lumped into a single archaeological unit based on stone, bone, and shell artifacts (Croes 1995:132).

Basketry construction techniques are important in other areas, as well, as we explain in connection with the

Great Basin (Chapter 8) and the Southwest (Chapter 9). One of the hallmarks of the **Fremont culture** in the Great Basin is a distinctive type of coiled basket, and the types of basket made help to define the cultural periods in the Southwest. Indeed, the spread of **Numic speakers** in the Great Basin has been investigated by examining the distribution of basketry (Adovasio and Pedler 1994).

Likewise, cordage studied by Croes (1995:148–151) shows patterns similar to the Northwest Coast baskets, indicating ethnic continuity over time. Cordage is seen as an ethnic marker in other areas as well, including the Northeast, where the cordage used to treat the surfaces of pots may help determine ethnicity (Maslowski 1996; Petersen 1996). As one might suspect, though, considerable research remains to be done on this topic.

FIGURE 5.17 Quileute Chief Charlie Howeattle uses his hand adze while preparing to add a piece to the dugout canoe he has fashioned from a red cedar log.

mounds, with some villages having associated mound complexes and others not having them, suggests that villages may have been ranked relative to one another, complementing the ranking of individuals (Ames and Maschner 1999:190–194).

Evidence of warfare increased during the Late Pacific period. Burials provide indications of increased violence and the spread of high levels of conflict throughout the Northwest Coast. Some villages are clearly built in defensive locations such as at the top of

FIGURE 5.18 Late Pacific period woodworking tools.

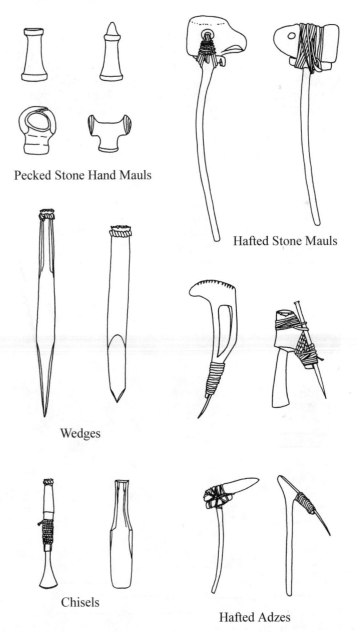

Pecked Stone Hand Mauls

Hafted Stone Mauls

Wedges

Chisels

Hafted Adzes

bluffs, and refuges with temporary shelters built inside fortifications (walls and ditches) were located near some villages in southern British Columbia and northern Washington. Moss and Erlandson (1992) document a number of defensive sites for this period from southeast Alaska as well. Fortified villages were also found on the northern Northwest coast. Maschner (1997) suggests that the rise of defensive locations and fortifications is a result of the replacement of hand-to-hand confrontations in combat with a new technology: the bow and arrow.

The distinctive Northwest Coast art pattern was fully developed in the Late Pacific period, although there are generally fewer art objects in many areas because the practice of burying the dead in middens ceased. Fewer burials mean fewer grave goods, and consequently fewer art objects for some parts of the coast. Carved bone, stone, and antler items are recovered from several sites (Figure 5.19). Carved stone bowls have come from sites along the lower Columbia. Figurines of clay also are found in the lower Columbia area, the only ceramic artifacts in the Northwest Coast

FIGURE 5.19 Stone bowls from the Gulf of Georgia area.

area. There are numerous examples of wooden art from Ozette.

Ozette provides many lessons about aspects of Northwest Coast culture. One of the most sobering aspects of the excavations for archaeologists is that over 90 percent of the artifacts recovered from the house excavations were perishable and would not have survived at a normal site. The houses were shed roof plank houses that range from 69 by 36 feet to 56 by 33 feet (21 × 11 m to 17 × 10 m). Each house had from six to ten hearth areas that probably indicate the locations of specific families in the house, though the entire population of the house may have used some of the hearths. The spatial arrangements of artifacts reflected ethnographic patterns and indicated where high-status occupants lived, as shown by the distribution of ceremonial paraphernalia and whaling equipment (Kirk and Daugherty 1978:94). Differences in size and distribution are clues to status differences between the houses, as well as within them (Matson and Coupland 1995:266–267). A study of shellfish use at the Ozette houses examined the distribution of different species. Patterning indicated that different houses were acquiring shellfish from different portions of the coast, suggesting household ownership of resources (Huelsbeck 1989). Knob-topped hats of the type discussed earlier for Hoko River were also found at Ozette.

A number of the items from the Ozette houses were decorated. Two house planks carved with whale designs, for example, apparently were parts of decorative screens. The handles of wood-carving tools were themselves carved into designs that included human and animal heads. A bowl (Figure 5.20) was carved in human form with the legs at one end and the head, complete with a braid of human hair attached at the other. One of the most spectacular objects was a carving of a whale fin that was decorated with over 700 inlaid sea otter teeth (Figure 5.21).

In summary, the major trends in the development of Northwest Coast culture during the Pacific period are population growth and grouping into large households, the intensification of the use of the ocean's resources, and development of ranking of individuals, households, and perhaps even villages. There is regional variation in such details of culture as basketry

FIGURE 5.20 Hardwood bowl carved in the form of a man replete with a braid of human hair.

FIGURE 5.21 A whale fin effigy carved of red cedar and inlaid with 700 sea otter teeth.

and art styles, and in the emphasis in food-getting activities, but many strong similarities unite the area. There have been many attempts to link the archaeological cultures of the area to the First Nation peoples who inhabit it today, people whose ancestors were present when the explorers arrived. Evidence of relationships stretching back into the Archaic period demonstrates considerable continuity in the locations of groups over time.

MODERN PERIOD

The **Modern period** on the Northwest Coast is marked by voyages of exploration. These journeys began in AD 1741 with Vitus Bering's Russian expedition, which reached southern Alaska. The discovery of sea otters was the impetus for the Russian exploitation of the area from the north. In 1774 and 1775 Spanish sailors explored the coast north of their foothold in California. Another notable voyage was that of James Cook, who sailed north to the Gulf of Alaska. These voyages paved the way for the period of fur trade expeditions (Suttles 1990c).

When the Modern period began, this region was (and still is) home to the Tlingit, Tsimshian, Wakashan (e.g., Haida, Heiltsuk or Bella Bella, Nuu-chah-nulth or Nootka, and Makah), Salishan (e.g., Nuxalk or Bella Coola, Squamish, Samish, Lummi, Clallam, and Lushootseed), and Penutian (e.g., Chinook, Multnomah, Yaquina, Kallapuya, and Lower Umpqua) peoples, as well as some Athapaskan peoples like the Klatskanie, Upper Umpqua, and the Tolowa (Thompson and

Kinkade 1990). Ames and Maschner (1999:13) describe these people as "the most socially complex hunting and gathering societies known on earth." Based on the ethnographic record, these societies had rigid, ranked social classes, usually composed of a small group of nobles, a larger group of commoners, and, at the bottom of the social heap, slaves, who were essentially property. The peoples of the Northwest Coast also achieved some of the highest population densities anywhere in North America outside central Mexico and California (see Chapter 7).

Recently, at least some archaeologists have begun to view the issue of complexity, including the utility of the term "complex hunters and gatherers," differently. Moss (2011:32–39), for example, argues that the peoples of the Northwest Coast were actually food producers. She notes that a subsistence emphasis on fishing is different in important ways from one on hunting terrestrial animals and gathering plants. Johnsen (2004:4–5) suggests that manipulation of the salmon streams and rivers influenced yield and characterized the people as "salmon ranchers." Clam gardens were apparently created in some areas as well, by building rock walls to retain sand and increasing available clam habitat (Harper et al. 1995), and some dogs were specially bred for their wool (Schulting 1994). Moss (2011:39–43) also points to cultivation of plants such as camas, and notes that tobacco introduced from outside the area was clearly cultivated. Berry yields may have been encouraged through techniques that included fertilization and burning. Potatoes found as cultigens among Northwest Coast peoples were thought to have been a result of early contact with explorers. Genetic analyses

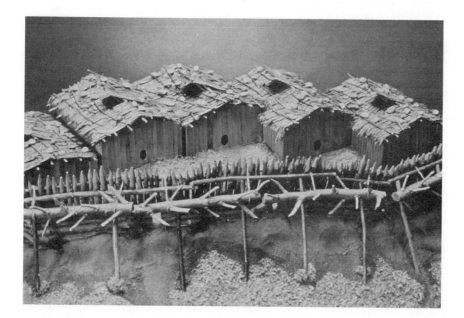

FIGURE 5.22 Model of Kitwanga Fort by Arthur Price and Dr. George F. MacDonald. The fortifications surrounded five plank houses.

suggest instead that some are related to South American varieties, suggesting a coastal trade or contact scenario as a possible explanation (Zhang et al. 2010). This certainly presents an interesting line for future research.

The Modern period is well represented in the archaeological record of the Pacific Northwest. Many sites have components dating to this time, often indicated by the presence of goods received by the villagers as part of the fur trade. Excavations have tended to focus on the nature of changes brought about by contact. Examples include Fladmark's (1973) excavation of an early Modern period house at the Richardson Ranch site in the Queen Charlotte Islands. He found that the house differed from the houses described for the historical Haida of the area. He was also able to show that argillite was being carved prior to the Historic period, refuting the notion that Haida carvings of this soft black stone started after the Europeans arrived. The village of Cathlapotle, located in the Wapato valley along the Columbia River not far from Portland, Oregon, was excavated in the early 1990s; the work was sponsored by the U.S. Fish and Wildlife Service, the Chinook Tribe, and Portland State University. The village had been visited by the Lewis and Clark expedition on March 29, 1806, and there are descriptions of the village

from that encounter. The excavation exposed plank houses that range in size from 200 by 45 feet to 60 by 30 feet (61 × 14 m to 18 × 9 m). Glass trade beads serve as a marker of deposits from the Modern period, and the excavations document the replacement of bone tools with metal tools after contact. The data from the excavation are served as the basis for the reconstruction of a Chinook plank house at an interpretive center built near the site (Ames and Maschner 1999:12; Friends of the Ridgefield National Wildlife Refuge 2012).

The excavation of a fortified site on the middle Skeena River in British Columbia is another example of investigation of Modern period deposits. Kitwanga Fort (Figure 5.22), excavated in 1979 by George MacDonald, provides information about conflict after the commencement of the fur trade. Although established before European contact, the fort was occupied throughout the eighteenth century. The site was associated with the trade trail system along the Skeena River that moved eulachon oil from the coast to the interior. Excavation provided details about the construction of the site, revealing, for example, that houses had large storage pits and escape hatches. The fort has been rebuilt and is now a Canadian National Historic Site (Ames and Maschner 1999:215; MacDonald 1989).

CHAPTER SUMMARY

In this chapter we have summarized the development of the distinctive cultures of the Northwest Coast, which prehistorically was one of the most densely populated and socially complex areas of North America. The following points are particularly important:

- Two contrasting patterns form the earliest well-documented material of the Archaic period: the Microblade tradition and the Old Cordilleran tradition. The Microblade tradition is found in the northern part of the Northwest Coast from southern Alaska to Vancouver Island in British Columbia. Sites of this tradition have, in addition to microblades and microblade cores, pebble tools and flakes. The Old Cordilleran is found in the southern part of the area, as well as in the Plateau, and is marked by leaf-shaped bifaces (including Cascade points) and cobble tools. There appears to be an area of overlap in southern British Columbia and Washington State, where sites have produced both bifaces and microblades.

- The Pacific period (6400–175 BP) was a time of developing sociocultural complexity, significant population growth, the establishment of permanent villages with houses (first pithouses and then cedar plank houses). The economy became increasingly focused on aquatic resources, and woodworking became very important.

- In the Modern period the Northwest Coast was home to a variety of tribal groups. These peoples had rigid, ranked social classes ranging from nobles at the top through commoners to slaves. They had some of the highest population densities anywhere in North America except central Mexico and California (see Chapter 7). Many groups appear to have been in essentially the same location since the Archaic.

SUGGESTIONS FOR FURTHER READING

For summary discussions of the archaeology of the Northwest Coast area:

Ames, Kenneth M., and Herbert D. G. Maschner
  1999 *Peoples of the Northwest Coast: Their Archeology and Prehistory.* Thames and Hudson, London.
Matson, R. G., and Gary Coupland
  1995 *The Prehistory of the Northwest Coast.* Academic Press, San Diego.
Moss, Madonna L.
  2011 *Northwest Coast: Archaeology as Deep History.* Society for American Archaeology, Washington D.C.

For a frank and moving museum ethnography of the Makah Cultural and Research Center:

Erikson, Patricia Pierce, Helma Ward, and Kirk Wachendorf
  2002 *Voices of a Thousand People: The Makah Cultural and Research Center.* University of Nebraska Press, Lincoln.

For a popular treatment of the archaeology of the state, including the Northwest Coast and the Plateau areas:

Kirk, Ruth, and Richard D. Daugherty
  2007 *Archaeology in Washington.* University of Washington Press, Seattle.

For good discussions of the prehistory of the area, as well as ethnographic and historical information on the Northwest Coast:

Suttles, Wayne (editor)
  1990 *Northwest Coast.* Handbook of North American Indians, Vol. 7, William C. Sturtevant, general editor. Smithsonian Institution, Washington, D.C.

For a collection of papers addressing the archaeology of the north coast of British Columbia with reference to native collaboration:

Cybulski, Jerome S.
  2001 *Perspectives on Northern Northwest Coast Prehistory.* Archaeological Survey of Canada Paper 160, Mercury Series, Canadian Museum of Civilization, Ottawa.

OTHER RESOURCES

The Student CD, Sections H and I, gives web links, additional discussion questions, and other study aids. The Student CD also contains additional resources. Early coastal occupations that may provide some perspective on the maritime cultures of the Northwest Coast and comparisons with the inhabitants of Qwu?gwes described in the this chapter's case study are discussed in the case study in Section D.4 "Eel Point and the Early Settlement of Coastal California: A Case Study in Contemporary Archaeological Research".

CASE STUDY

As we have made clear in a number of places, North American archaeologists increasingly work directly with Native Americans when sites and artifacts are discovered and investigated. The relationship has not always been easy, but with experience, cooperative efforts are increasingly productive. Along the Northwest Coast, the presence of wet sites with truly remarkable preservation provides archaeologists with a chance to study artifacts such as nets, baskets, and wooden implements that seldom are preserved. These sites also can give tribes a greater sense of their links with the past and become a focus of tribal heritage preservation efforts.

Today many tribes have their own cultural resource management programs, staffed by archaeologists who conduct comprehensive CRM, and skilled tribal craftsmen often can recognize recovered artifacts and share insights into their use that enrich everyone's understanding of past practices.

In this case study, a cultural resources director who also holds an appointment as **Tribal Historic Preservation Officer (THPO)**, the tribe's CR specialist (archaeologist), and a college professor describe their collaboration. Based on a formal cooperative agreement between the tribe as a government and the college as a state entity, the authors have cooperated in the uncovering of a remarkable wet site and nearby fish trap. Each party gives us unique insights about the finds themselves and about the value of their collaboration. In order to keep different perspectives clear, personal narratives are italicized in this case study while coauthored sections are in roman type. As you read about what these researchers have found, pay attention to the contrasting perspectives each author brings to the investigations. What are the elements that have made this collaboration so successful?

ARCHAEOLOGICAL/ANTHROPOLOGICAL–NATIVE AMERICAN COORDINATION

An Example of Sharing the Research on the Northwest Coast of North America

Rhonda Foster, Larry Ross, and Dale R. Croes

The conflict, over who "owns" the past—scientists or tribes—does not need to happen. Both groups have equal legal and other claims to be involved. If scientific technical skills and tribal cultural expertise are shared, an equal partnership can be forged that produces the best all-around results. This case study, which exemplifies how the formalized, 50/50 sharing of the research has expanded both the scientific and cultural outcomes in the Pacific Northwest, is from both tribal and scientific archaeological points of view. We describe how the Squaxin Island Tribe and South Puget Sound Community College arrived at a formal cooperative agreement that helped set the stage for developing (1) a tribal cultural resources department, (2) the first full-scale investigation in the region of a site that contains a wet (waterlogged) component, (3) outreach CRM training through online classes at the community college, and (4) interpretation of the site for the public at the tribe's new museum. Working together, respecting each other's needs, archaeologists and tribes can create the scientific and cultural results they both require.

(Cultural Resources Department-CRD): *More than a decade ago, the Elders of Squaxin Island Tribe determined the importance of protecting our cultural resources and recording our history so that we could both teach our history to our people and correct the inaccuracies that were written about us by scientific professionals. The outcome was to* *create a cultural resources department that would allow us to manage our cultural sites within our traditional area and to build a tribal museum. The main goal of the tribe was for staff in the Cultural Resources Department (CRD) to obtain the skills necessary to manage cultural sites. Not only did we learn the skills required in archaeology, we were gifted with an archaeologist with whom we could build a trust relationship. Later we hired our own archaeologist. In the tribe's opinion this was rare.*

What we came to realize while learning archaeology is that large portions of our culture were not being addressed by any professional archaeologist. It always amazed the tribe that the outside world viewed our past as dead and long gone, and ignored our traditional cultural properties. Archaeologists have often ignored tribes during their quest to make a "big find," and when they did, they portrayed themselves to the public as the experts about the cultures of the peoples who inhabited those sites. In native societies this is extremely rude and unimaginable. You must understand that there is very little trust by tribes of professional anthropologists and archaeologists who do not have the skills to work with tribes to conduct comprehensive cultural resource management. In addition, it is important for the tribe to manage their cultural resources themselves, as this strengthens the connection between us and our ancient past and our ancestors, and helps us to continue our culture into the future with our children.

(Dale Croes): *As a wet site archaeologist on the Northwest Coast of North America, I typically have worked in partnership on projects with Native Americans. Initially, I worked with the Makah Tribe as a graduate student at the Ozette Village wet site, and later I directed the Hoko River wet site (Croes 1995, 1999). However, no formal cooperative agreement was signed between Washington State University, where I went to graduate school, and the Makah government for those projects. The formal cooperative agreement [with the Squaxin Island Tribe] creates the foundation for the relationship between tribes and archaeologists on two main levels. First, it sets an immediate foundation for trust that rapidly promotes the sharing of scientific technical training and cultural expertise of the tribe—expertise that is particularly important for well-preserved wet site work. Second, with the president of my state institution and the chairman of the tribe's government signing, we can point to the agreement to justify taking the time needed (as part of our regular duties) to work together as a 50/50 team on important projects. In this case, our agreement led to the discovery of the wet site on Mud Bay and to the follow-up scientific and cultural interpretation of the ancient nets, baskets, fish traps, and woodworking tools found there (see full agreement published in Foster and Croes 2002).*

We worked together to initiate the first ever field course in archaeology (Anthropology 280) at South Puget Sound Community College. A local property owner, longtime Washington secretary of state Ralph Munro, had urged Croes to visit his beach on the southern tip of Puget Sound near Olympia, to look at a shell midden site and see what it might represent. A record search at the State Historic Preservation Office revealed that this site had never been recorded. The decision was made to conduct a summer field class at the site as a training tool for students. Normally, the tribe neither condones nor encourages excavations, and it was never the tribe's intent to be involved with one. However, shortly after the start of the summer testing program we found something that led the tribe to reconsider its position about excavating at that location. The find was a twisted cedar bough rope fragment, discovered in a wet portion of the site. The students had been using a screw auger (3 in., 7.6 cm), driven to a depth of 20 cm (7.87 in.), every 5 meters (15 ft.) across a 5 by 5 meter gridded site area.

A test square measuring 1 by 1 meter (3.3 × 3.3 ft.) was dug in 5 cm (2.5 in.) increment **levels** in this area to explore the deposits. The water table was reached at a depth of 50 cm. While using a fine stream of water to uncover delicate wood and fiber, Croes noticed that a small section of two-strand cedar bark string was being exposed. He called to Foster, who was screening, that a string was being found, and he privately hoped more would be there. The string quickly turned into a large section of preserved gill net. Croes knew it was

certainly a wet archaeological site, and Foster knew it was a gift from the ancestors! As the cedar bark gill net was discovered (Figure 5.23), the tribe, recognizing that this gift could be lost forever if not protected, decided to support the decision to excavate.

(CRD): *Guided by the Creator and through our ancient ancestors, we were gifted with irreplaceable artifacts used hundreds of years ago. Our link, our culture, and our future were all incorporated at this site we now called Qwu?gwes (Quot-Qwass), which means "a place to come together, share, and gather" in Lushootseed, our traditional Salish language.*

We began comanaging the investigations of this ancient but unrecorded Squaxin Island Tribe shell midden and possible village on Mud Bay. The testing demonstrated that the site complex was much larger than anticipated. It was a shell midden 100 meters (330 ft.) long, and it included a possible living area where plank longhouses may have stood, a freshwater spring, an activity/food-processing area next to the housing, and a waterlogged, buried, intertidal shell midden area in front of the freshwater spring.

(Croes): *Almost anyone could recognize that we had found a fiber net, but through the cultural expertise of the tribal members, we learned what the net was made of, how it had been made, and how it had operated as a salmon gill net. We also learned how and why it probably had come to be located in this intertidal area—through the ambition of an overenthused youth.*

With careful hydraulic excavation—using water and fine-adjust hose nozzles—we were able to recover approximately 18 square meters (60 ft.²) of cedar bark gill net, which was placed in a polyethylene glycol preservation solution and taken to the lab at the college for conservation.

The need for our team to become officially organized for this and other efforts to preserve cultural material, protect cultural sites, and train cultural resource technicians rapidly expanded. Under the guidance of the CRD, we formulated our cooperative agreement so that we had a formal understanding between our governments, signed by the heads of each entity, which clarified our responsibilities to each other's programs. Therefore, our state community college institution of higher education, our state archaeological regulatory institution (the Office of Archaeology and Historic Preservation), and the Tribal Council were brought together to sign the agreement on May 31, 2000 (Foster and Croes 2002). The State Historic Preservation Officer, the president of South Puget Sound Community College, and the chairman of the Squaxin Island Tribe gave speeches on forming the team and looking forward to a partnership that allowed for true comprehensive cultural resource management well beyond Mud Bay, to cover the tribe's entire traditional area.

FIGURE 5.23   (a) Cedar bark gill net as first exposed in midden. (b) Section of the net after cleaning in the lab for preservation.

Then these leaders signed the cooperative agreement clearly outlining our responsibilities as tribal and state representatives. We believe this is the first such formal agreement in the country, and that it could serve as a model for others (Foster and Croes 2002). Now, whenever we have a need to cooperate on a project, we can point to this agreement to justify our working together, and the regulatory agency, the State Historic Preservation Officer, has a commitment to come to our aid if needed. Our agreement does not guarantee smooth coordination, but it does provide a formal commitment to be available to work together on mutually beneficial projects.

EXAMPLES OF SCIENTIFIC AND CULTURAL APPROACHES AT THE QWU?GWES WET SITE

To demonstrate the results of sharing the research between the college and the tribe, as well as the value in general of wet site explorations on the Northwest Coast to the tribes of the region, we will present the scientific approach to the analysis of fiber and wood artifacts from the site complex followed by the CRD's cultural approach to the analysis of the same artifacts. This shows the contrast and benefit of an equal partnership and ownership of research. This arrangement is particularly beneficial for studying waterlogged areas at

shell midden sites, which contain the 90 to 95 percent of the ancient Northwest Coast material culture lacking in other sites (see also Foster and Croes 2004). We will briefly discuss the cedar bark gill net, the upbay fish trap area, and the woven basketry.

The Gill Net

(Croes): *Once we began finding the fiber net, we were faced with the task of archaeologically recovering and preserving a sizable section of it. The tribal weavers immediately recognized the fiber to be from the inner bark of the western red cedar* (Thuja plicata), *and Foster, as a fisherperson, observed the web size and identified the probable function as a gill net for small salmon species (see her discussion later).*

I will follow through a common scientific descriptive and comparative analysis of the Qwu?gwes net. The identification of [the artifact] as a net was primarily through visual inspection, where a series of knots was established to create a web with consistent sized openings. Like all other reported Northwest Coast wet site ancient nets, the Qwu?gwes net is made of string gauge cordage tied into a net with square knots (sometimes called reef knots and/or, if collapsed, lark's head knots)(Figure 5.23). The square knot is a no-slip knot, and therefore very practical for nets. Also, square knots in western nets are typically said to be tied by hand, without using a netting needle (Ashley 1944:64–65). The cordage was twisted using two strands, and most of the cordage's single elements were twisted to the left (L, or clockwise) and plied together with a right-directed twist (R, or counterclockwise). This forms a Z lay. Z lay is also the main type recorded for twisted 2+-strand cordage at most other Northwest Coast wet sites.

Nets have been found at many other presently reported Northwest Coast wet sites. The oldest net so far dates to approximately 5000 years old (^{14}C dating) from the Lanaak wet site (49 XPA 78) on southern Baranof Island, southeastern Alaska (Bernick 1999). Therefore, netting is a very ancient technology along the Northwest Coast.

All ancient Northwest Coast wet site nets are of string gauge cordage and tied with square knots. Other characteristics vary widely, from materials used to number of elements used in making the net strings to size of mesh. The uses also vary from smaller mesh dip nets to larger web gill nets.

(CRD): The net was made from cedar bark and measured as a 5-inch (13 cm) stretch mesh, which was measured in three separate locations the day of the discovery while it was still wet. In our traditional area this type of gill net was used to fish for the smaller species such as coho, blueback, and steelhead. It is important to have a gill net in addition to a fish trap, as gill nets allow a fisherman to go where the salmon are. There are several ways to fish using this gill net including using it with a landline, drifting, and to round-house or beach-seine a school of salmon.

When we started removing the gill net in layers, it was immediately evident to me that there was something out of the ordinary. Hundreds of salmon jaws were still in the net. No fisherperson in their right mind would leave salmon in a gill net, even today. For one person to hand-make a cedar gill net would take over 8 months. Salmon left in the net would rot the net out very rapidly. Something had happened that was not usual. The possibilities are:

1. A major disaster took place which covered up the gill net or caused our ancestors to leave in a hurry

2. The net was being used and got caught on a snag underwater, which would require the fisherman to cut the net, leaving a portion of the net underwater and unreachable.

3. It is normal for a young person to ask an elder if there is any abandoned gill net nobody wants that they could use for practice. Some young person, although he or she had participated in many fishings, might have been overwhelmed by catching more salmon than anticipated, and lost or broken the net. Most fishermen could read a run, determine the amount of net to let out, and harvest only what the family could process, but I have witnessed teenagers get in over their heads, sink a boat, sink a net, and lose a lot of equipment.

The Fish Trap

(Croes): On the other side of the point from the Qwu?gwes site at the mouth of a stream is a well-preserved, waterlogged, cedar stake, intertidal fish trap. To properly record this large structure, which consisted of over 440 stakes crossing in two perpendicular directions across the cove, we needed to do extensive mapping. We all agreed that we needed a detailed map of each stake's location and elevation before we sampled any stakes. To do this, I made arrangements for the college survey class to map the entire area, including the possible ancient village and shell midden/waterlogged site areas, and the fish trap. For this complex mapping task, the students used Professor Michael Martin's CADD/Survey program and the Hewlett Packard 48 Total Station, with a programmed Survey GX Card. The objective was to compile a complete set of generated maps that chart, categorize, classify, and visually document the entire area (Figure 5.24).

The resulting fish trap maps show the contour of the inlet, the shoreline, and the position of each of the visible fish trap stakes. Fish trap A contains the positions of 108 visible stakes, and fish trap B contains the positions of 332 visible stakes across the channel of the inlet.

With these maps completed, we decided that students would remove a fish trap stake every 5 meters and replace that stake with a visibly mapped and labeled modern stake. These sampled stakes would be placed in conservation. The recovered stakes were photographed (with stake map number) before excavation, excavated and cleaned, photographed in position, removed, measured, and photographed on all sides before being taken to the lab. Now stabilized, they are displayed in the new Squaxin museum.

Removal of the stakes allowed us to see how the stakes were manufactured. Each stake is a split cedar post approximately 10 × 10 cm (4 × 4 in.) in cross section, and the bases are sharpened for placement. Some of the stakes' points were cut with a metal axe, as seen through the sharp angled cuts. These are thought to be possibly later, post-Contact period, replacement stakes. In the central "door" area, where there are double rows of stakes and the remnants of split plank that slid between these rows, we found stakes that appeared to be adze cut—less sharp angled, followed by splitting off sections of wood (Figure 5.24). To determine whether this was an ancient structure, we submitted a sample from the outer ring of an adzed stake for radiocarbon dating. This sample returned a calibrated date of 470 years old, removing any doubt that the fish trap was constructed before the Contact period (Figure 5.24).

(CRD): Herding schools of salmon takes talent, so the fish traps were used in conjunction with one another. The side trap was used first, as it is very similar to a natural back eddy, whose slower water the salmon love to rest and pool up together in. The trap's door would be opened to catch as many chum and/or chinook salmon as needed or was possible. Once the side trap was full, or held the amount of salmon needed, the door to the side trap would be shut. Then the door

a   b

FIGURE 5.24 (a) Mapping in the fish trap stakes. (b) Students remove a mapped stake and point to adze cut area at bottom—this stake was found by radiocarbon dating to be 470 years old.

to the main fish trap would be opened to allow the remainder of the school to go upstream or be caught.

Numerous stone choppers have been found at these traps. They are perfect to use on chum salmon, which to the Squaxin people are the strongest spirited salmon, as they are determined, independent, and they will not give up. Therefore, the nets for catching chum have to be replaced much sooner than any other gear. The cedar posts used to make the fish trap would last much longer than a net, and would be the ideal way to catch a chum. When the salmon are caught in the trap, the whole village would be excited. To the Squaxin Island people, this is the best time of year.

The Basketry

(Croes): So far, three main types of basketry have been found at the Qwu?gwes site: (1) cedar bark checker-weave matting, (2) open-twined, small to large "pack" baskets of cedar splints, and (3) fine twill and checker-plaited ornamental basketry.

(CRD): Cedar splints open-weave baskets: When the tribe realized a portion of basket was exposed, and knew a basket would be excavated the following day, invitations were sent to "The People." In addition, other tribal groups were encouraged to be a part of bringing out the baskets. Tribal basket weavers were present to identify, interpret, and teach about the designs, materials, and weaving techniques (Figure 5.25). To not be allowed to participate while so-called experts were studying and interpreting your culture would have been a violation to all humankind. This would

have been disrespectful, and it was something to shy away from. Distrust prevents positive communication, and without communication how can anyone present a comprehensive theory, interpretation, or view of any culture?

The two baskets excavated that day were made of cedar splints (from roots or boughs). The design, although not complete, is a statement by the weaver, and sometimes explains which family is represented. These types of baskets are utilitarian, made to haul heavy items. We call them pack baskets. The handles were woven in a special way to handle heavy loads, and a strap could be used to tie to the handles if using it as a burden basket (Figure 5.26). Most clam baskets were built to hold at least 50 pounds [23 kg]. They needed handles such as the ones on these baskets, because the basket was lifted and moved many short distances while collecting oysters or clams.

Cedar bark checker and fine twill basketry: Cedar was the main wood and fiber used to make tools, clothing, containers, etc. for "The People." The fragmented cedar bark weave could have once been either a mat or basket bottom. Whatever was made of the cedar bark strips, the process to thin and cut these small identical pieces took skill.

(Croes): With this growing basketry database, I conducted an initial and preliminary basketry attribute presence/absence comparative analysis with other ancient basketry collections from Northwest Coast wet sites to begin to see what degrees of similarity to them might be demonstrated by this new southern Puget Sound wet site. These "pack" baskets are distinctive because of the way they were constructed, with the distinct open twining, the looped

a   b

FIGURE 5.25 (a) Sumiko Yashado helping to recover pack baskets with water excavation. (b) Tribal basket weavers Rhonda Foster (left), Lynn Foster (center), and Barbara Henry (right) discuss the composition of an ancient Squaxin basket.

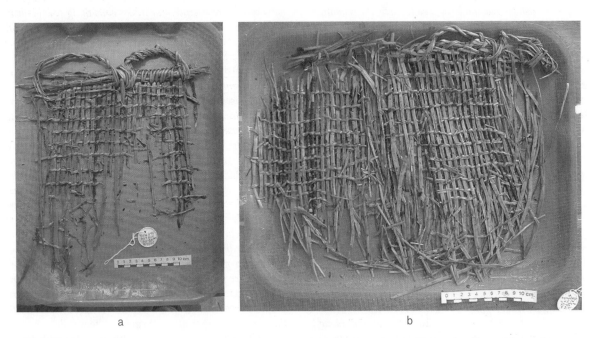

a   b

FIGURE 5.26 Two open-twined cedar pack baskets found one on top of the other. Note double loop handles and decoration applied by leaving bark on certain warp elements. The basket on the right is in full round.

rim, and especially the double-looped opposing two-strand cordage handles and elaborate topstitching (Figure 5.26). Qwu?gwes clustered with two other recent (within last 1000 years) Lushootseed language area wet sites, Fishtown *and Conway; however these Lushootseed area sites are about 150 miles [240 km] north of Qwu?gwes on the Skagit River Delta. Though baskets do not speak, I am sure the weavers of these baskets shared an ancient tradition of Coast*

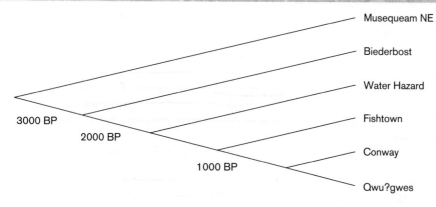

FIGURE 5.27 Slanted cladogram derived from Gulf of Georgia–Puget Sound wet site basketry attributes (modes) creating a phylogenesis tree of Coast Salish basketry styles and proposed ethnic linguistic interconnections for 3000 years (based on PAUP software) (see also Croes et al. 2005).

Salish Lushootseed teachings and learning in terms of basketry traditions.

In comparison to the typical Northwest Coast stone and bone artifacts, wet site basketry is a better signal of lines of ethnicity. They indicate who the people were who carefully passed on the complex family basketry traditions from generation to generation. We have seen these styles change, but still statistically relate in style through thousands of years in different major linguistic regions established along the Northwest Coast (Croes 1995). This signaling of ethnicity follows a process called phylogenesis, demonstrating an ethnic identity style passed exclusively through a cultural group from one generation of family to the next. In our traditionally Coast Salishan region, we have documented at least 3000 years of Salishan basketry phylogenesis different from other areas and demonstrating part of their deep-rooted heritage. Figure 5.27 is a phylogenetic branching chart through time, representing ancient Coast Salish wet sites including Qwu?gwes. Few of us can point to specific evidence of at least 3000 years of our cultural identity. Now, with well-preserved wet site archaeology, several major Northwest Coast ethnic groups, including the Squaxin Island Tribe, whose oral history documents this, can point to scientific proof of at least 3000 years of their identity through basketry styles.

REVIEW OF QWU?GWES SITE EXPLORATIONS

(Croes): We have provided a preliminary summary of three categories of wood and fiber artifacts from the Qwu?gwes wet site. I have considered these items from a "scientific" analysis approach and the tribe has provided the cultural knowledge passed down by multiple generations of its people. These approaches have proven to be complementary, and have provided everyone a much better understanding of the more complete material culture common to waterlogged sites.

(CRD): All cultural sites are important to the Tribe. We now categorize them as archaeological or traditional cultural properties that include spiritual, burial, sacred, and gathering sites. It is important to stress that the tribe looks to these sites as a connection to our ancestors, who have instilled in us values that are different from modern societies. Very few people understand that the Native people who embrace the Earth, Creator, and all living things, are also the first natural scientists of the land, always striving to work with our surroundings, being a part of, not conqueror of, the things we hold as sacred and give "continuous thanks" for. The Squaxin Island Tribe embraces science (archaeology) as a base platform to build on, but recognizes the importance of including the people and their knowledge of their culture. When this happens, it is what the Cultural Resources Department calls comprehensive cultural resource management, which is much richer and more comprehensive than just basic archaeology.

(Croes): Wet sites are important to archaeological analysis, since they contain the vast majority of items once deposited in any Northwest Coast or other site. They also have been found dating to some of the earliest time periods known on the Northwest Coast—recent discoveries of ancient cordage, possible basketry and wooden wedges on the southern Queen Charlotte Islands, British Columbia, Canada, date to over 9400 years old.

For some time we have investigated Northwest Coast wet sites, but they have yet to be a central focus of Northwest Coast archaeology. More and more tribes have encouraged archaeologists to start moving their focus in this direction to best understand the rich heritage of this region. Possibly it will be the tribes' interests in the preservation of their material culture that will require archaeologists to shift their training into working with the Native peoples to locate and properly investigate wet sites in any part of the Americas.

ADDITIONAL TRIBE–COLLEGE COOPERATIVE EFFORT FOCUSES

Several other equally important outcomes have resulted from the cooperative agreement. For a full detailing of these efforts, see Foster and Croes (2002, 2004). Such actions, which will contribute to the future of archaeology and comprehensive cultural resource management in our region and all of North America, include the following:

- The Squaxin Island Tribe Cultural Resources Department, established to comanage all the cultural resources of interest to the tribe within the 2.5 million acres of the tribe's traditional area.

- College-based and accredited outreach training programs, developed and conducted online with tribes and agencies.

- Ongoing archaeological field school training at South Puget Sound Community College (Anthropology 280, 12 credits) and research at the Qwu?gwes cultural site complex (2000–2004).

- Opportunities for students from the community college to work with CRD, the Squaxin Island Museum Library and Research Center, and tribal members on various cultural resource management activities, giving students personal experience in working with a tribe and a better understanding from tribal members about their culture.

- Coordination with the new Squaxin Island Museum Library and Research Center (see http://www.squaxinisland.org/) in developing public outreach and exhibits.

Larry Ross, former civil engineer and environmental specialist with the state Department of Transportation and a former student of anthropology at South Puget Sound Community College and anthropology graduate of Washington State University, now works full time as the cultural resource specialist for the CRD. He has participated in all aspects of the cooperative agreement and adds his personal perspective of his work with the Squaxin Island Tribe:

(Larry Ross): *During my time as a student at South Puget Sound Community College and later as an employee of the tribe, I have seen what an effective tool the cooperative agreement has been to provide a framework for cooperation. As a student, I got to know and work with tribal members during the summer field school I attended at Qwu?gwes. Tribal members and students learned archaeological skills, got to know each other, and shared the experience of discovery. We students were exposed to the culture we were studying through interaction with people from that culture. For example, as basketry and cordage fragments were found, tribal weavers who were there could identify the materials used, why those materials were chosen, how the item had been made, and its use. In some cases, such as with cedar bark cordage, they would demonstrate how to make it.*

The cooperative agreement continues to provide opportunities for tribal members to connect with their culture and to teach others about it. It also provides training that will help them and the tribe to more directly co-manage the cultural resources within their traditional area for the future. Students have opportunities to work with the CRD doing research, conducting field surveys, and hopefully, gaining a personal connection with tribes that will influence their later careers to be more than just about science.

CONCLUSION

We believe we have shown not only an example of how a tribe and a scientific anthropology unit can work in sharing research, but also a general direction in which American archaeology and anthropology is headed. With tribes participating in the responsibilities of managing the cultural resources in their traditional areas, anthropologists and archaeologists will more and more have to work directly with Native peoples in pursuing their own research interests. If the desire of each party is to protect the cultural resources and share the research, an effective way to formalize that goal together is to establish a formal cooperative agreement that is signed by the heads of each of the entities (not by the cultural resource manager of the tribe or an anthropologist at the college, but by their respective institutional heads). An agreement signed at that level can provide the best validation, authorization, justification, and foundation of trust to pursue these important cultural resource management goals as a formal team. For a full discussion of these efforts and a copy of the agreement, see Foster and Croes (2002).

DISCUSSION QUESTIONS

1. Who is sharing the research in the collaboration described here? What knowledge and skills do each of the parties bring to their work together?

2. The authors argue that having a formal agreement between the tribe and the college as a representative of the state has been important to the successful collaboration. Do you agree that a less formal agreement between Foster and Croes as individuals would have been less effective? Why or why not?

3. Why are archaeologists so interested in wet sites like Qwu?gwes, and why is it important that they seek the cultural expertise of tribal members? Why would tribes want to participate in excavations at such sites?

4. What was learned by comparing attributes in the Qwu?gwes basketry with those in basketry from other sites along the Northwest Coast? What makes this information significant to archaeologists and also to the tribe?

CHAPTER 6

Rivers, Roots, and Rabbits:
The Plateau

Members of an archaeological field crew once knocked on the door of a house overlooking the Snake River in Washington. They were arriving at a party hosted by a man who had showed up at their field camp a few days before, proclaiming himself the "local archaeologist." Although the guests had been told a bit about what to expect, they were not prepared for what they would see in the basement recreation room. The walls were covered with frames full of arrowheads, knives, and spear points neatly mounted on black velvet backgrounds. Some were arranged in artful patterns. Other frames held beads of several types of marine shells traded from the Pacific Coast. On the mantle over the fireplace were two human skulls, stained green by the copper ornaments that had been included in their graves. Another skull, flanked by the host's favorite stone tools and bits of green, corroded copper, looked up from inside the glass-topped coffee table in front of the large, comfortable sofa. The host seemed proudest of a work in progress in the recreation room, for he visibly enjoyed showing everyone where he was covering his air conditioner ducting with notched cobble net weights.

Unfortunately, collections like this are all too common on the Plateau, particularly along the Columbia and Lower Snake rivers. There is a long tradition of looting sites for the artifacts they contain. Many of the large village sites yield spectacular numbers of arrowheads and fancy ground stone objects like the clubs called "slave killers," which are often carved in animal shapes. In the past there was a lucrative market in material from these sites, and a simple Internet search will show that such items still bring a good price. Indeed, the host of the party offers material for sale on the web, still proclaiming himself an archaeologist.

Stories about the relic hunters abound. A book on Columbia River archaeology published in 1959 describes this type of collecting and illustrates something of the lore of the old-time relic hunters (Strong 1959:149–152). The author reports that collectors working a site on the Deschutes River could expect to find a thousand points in a week and that one individual had collected 600 points from a 3 square foot (0.28 m²) area of the site. Indeed, a collector with fewer than 5000 arrowheads was considered "just a dabbler" (Strong 1959:150). Collecting points replaced the sale of fruit for at least one orchard owner living along the Columbia during the Depression. The book also introduces a character known as Arrowhead Charley, a legendary collector who worked the river banks for 35 years. He is said to have found over 150,000 points during his career, and he kept the very best ones for sale in case of emergency, thinking of them as his bank account.

There are also stories about relic hunters dynamiting sections of the river bank at old Indian villages and washing the sediment through sluice boxes, following the earlier practice of hydraulic gold miners. The wooden troughs had slats nailed across the bottom so that the sands and silts washed through and the heavier items like stone tools were caught by the bars and could be picked out. Another story comes from the town of Umatilla, Oregon. When John Day Dam was being built, the town was in the path of the floodwaters. Between 1965 and 1966 the Corps of Engineers jacked up a number of the buildings and moved the town to higher ground (Umatilla Chamber of Congress 2004). A large village had once been located on the original site of Umatilla, and once the buildings had been moved, relic hunters started digging in the old town. Rangers were sent to patrol the site to prevent vandalism, but, so the story goes, the relic hunters were not easily dissuaded. They avoided the daytime patrols simply by coming at night, using the old foundations as access points from which to tunnel into the site like miners. They worked by lantern light and put tarps up over the tops of the foundations to keep their activities from being detected.

With almost industrial relic hunting going on, it is not surprising that vandalism has destroyed many important parts of the area's archeological record. This type of relic hunting, which destroys so much information about the past, is not, after all, archaeology. Not everyone with an interest in artifacts in the area is a collector, however. Groups like the Mid-Columbia Archaeological Society have come together to help preserve the past. Members are supposed to sign a code of ethics that prohibits relic hunting, and when they conduct excavations it is with the proper permits and under the supervision of trained archaeologists. One marvelous example of their work is Bateman Island near Richland, Washington. This island was a major pithouse village and was described in the journals of the Lewis and Clark expedition. By the 1960s the site had been heavily picked over by collectors, and unfilled pits were everywhere. There appeared to be no undisturbed portion of the site left to excavate scientifically. The Mid-Columbia Archaeological Society arranged to have the asphalt road that ran across the site taken up, revealing an undisturbed swath across some important deposits on the site. These avocational workers excavated the roadbed and their work is the only record we will ever have of undisturbed deposits at this important site. Through the cooperation of amateurs and professionals, we can still learn important things about the Plateau culture area's past.

DEFINITION OF THE AREA

The Plateau (Figure 6.1) is an in-between culture area: it lies between the Cascade and British Columbia Coast ranges on the west and the Rocky Mountains on the east. Culturally it is in between the Northwest Coast on the west and the Plains on the east, and between the Great Basin (and a small portion of California) on the south and the Subarctic on the north. It is defined as most of the area drained by the Fraser River in the north and the Columbia River in the south, although part of the Snake River, a tributary of the Columbia, is included in the Great Basin (D. Walker 1998b:1; Willey 1966:396). The coastal portions of both rivers are included in the Northwest Coast. The modern states and provinces covered by the Plateau include the interior of southern British Columbia, eastern Washington, northern Idaho, western Montana, northeastern Oregon, and a band that extends from central Oregon a short way into California. Although there are a number of traits that came to the Plateau from elsewhere during the ethnographic period, there is good archaeological and historical evidence that the cultures of the Plateau are, indeed, an independent development (Willey 1966:396). Prior to the 1960s one of the main archaeological research topics in the Plateau was establishing the timing and history of the initiation of the Plateau pattern, as seen in the ethnography of the area. The chronology that has been developed is outlined in Table 6.1.

THE ENVIRONMENT

The terrain of the Plateau is quite varied, ranging from the mountains that form its eastern and western borders to the flats of the Columbia Basin and the Fraser and Thompson plateaus. The Fraser Plateau is the lowland around the upper Fraser River and varies from flat to rolling topography. South of it, along the Thompson River, is the Thompson Plateau, which is actually a series of low ridges and the valleys in between, except where streams have cut deep valleys. The relief in this area has been affected by glaciation, with the ridges becoming rounded and the valleys filling up with glacial till (Chatters 1998).

The Okanagan Highland, which straddles the border between British Columbia and Washington, is also a series of ridges, again sculpted by glacial ice into a terrain of rolling north–south hills and small plateaus, although some peaks in the area reach heights of 5000 feet (1500 m). The Columbia Basin covers much of central and eastern Washington, with fingers extending into Oregon along the Deschutes River and into Idaho between the Spokane and Snake rivers. Made up

FIGURE 6.1 The Plateau culture area, showing the location of sites mentioned in Chapter 6.

primarily of horizontal layers of basalt that escaped from ancient volcanic vents, the basin has a topography of flat to rolling hills, although the Yakima Folds form a series of low ridges on the west side. Loess, or windblown silt, covers much of the Columbia Basin,

and one area of it has been cut by a number of old drainage features resulting from periodic floods caused when glacial Lake Missoula drained catastrophically. This region of the basin has been given the graphic name the Channeled Scablands (Chatters 1998).

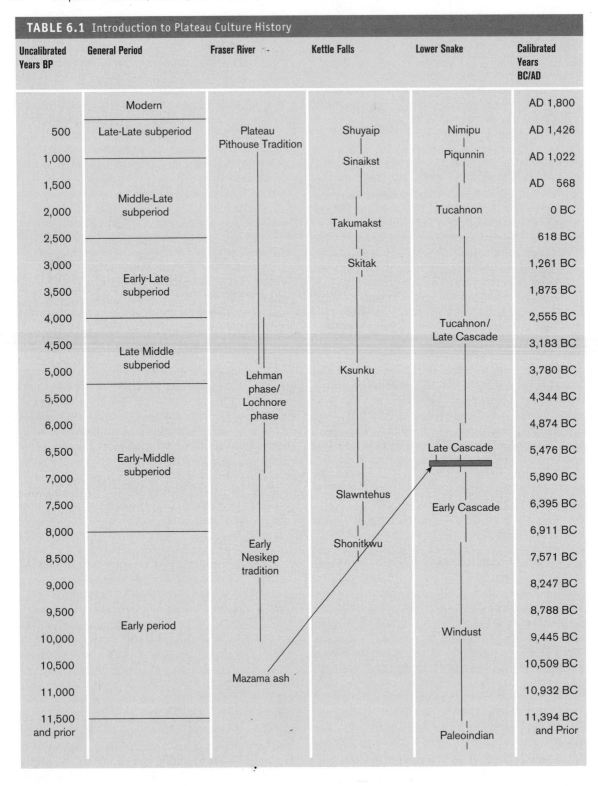

TABLE 6.1 Introduction to Plateau Culture History

Uncalibrated Years BP	General Period	Fraser River	Kettle Falls	Lower Snake	Calibrated Years BC/AD
	Modern	Plateau Pithouse Tradition	Shuyaip	Nimipu	AD 1,800
500	Late-Late subperiod		Sinaikst	Piqunnin	AD 1,426
1,000					AD 1,022
1,500	Middle-Late subperiod			Tucahnon	AD 568
2,000			Takumakst		0 BC
2,500					618 BC
3,000	Early-Late subperiod		Skitak		1,261 BC
3,500					1,875 BC
4,000				Tucahnon/ Late Cascade	2,555 BC
4,500	Late Middle subperiod				3,183 BC
5,000		Lehman phase/ Lochnore phase	Ksunku		3,780 BC
5,500					4,344 BC
6,000					4,874 BC
6,500	Early-Middle subperiod			Late Cascade	5,476 BC
7,000					5,890 BC
7,500			Slawntehus	Early Cascade	6,395 BC
8,000					6,911 BC
8,500		Early Nesikep tradition	Shonitkwu		7,571 BC
9,000					8,247 BC
9,500					8,788 BC
10,000	Early period			Windust	9,445 BC
10,500					10,509 BC
11,000		Mazama ash			10,932 BC
11,500 and prior				Paleoindian	11,394 BC and Prior

In Oregon south of the Columbia are the High Lava Plains, a relatively flat volcanic landscape with lava tubes, old volcanic craters, and cinder cones (Sanders 1999). The plains are nearly a mile above sea level, and only the westernmost portion of this physiographic region is in the Plateau culture area. South of that is a section of the Basin and Range province, discussed further in Chapter 8. This western portion of the Basin and Range province in Oregon and farther south in northern California is the home of the Klamath and the Modoc. Culturally this area is part of the Plateau. Finally, in the northeast corner of Oregon is a series of mountain ranges called the Blue Mountains. These are ranges of folded rock with valleys like the Grand Ronde and the Wallowa valley in between. The Snake River has cut a deep gorge through the eastern part of this area called Hells Canyon (Chatters 1998).

The Cascade and Coast ranges receive a good deal of rain, as do the higher peaks of the Rocky Mountains. The Blue Mountains also receive more rainfall than the areas around them, owing to their elevation. The Plateau is considerably drier than the surrounding highlands, however, because the western mountains create a rain shadow throughout most of it. The major water sources are the rivers that flow through the Plateau. The Fraser and Columbia rivers and their tributaries, like the Thompson and the Snake, drain most of the Plateau. The Klamath River system, which includes Upper and Lower Klamath lakes, is the major river for the southernmost Plateau. The Columbia Basin has almost no surface water away from the rivers (Chatters 1998).

Not only do the rivers provide water, they also provided one of the critical subsistence resources—anadromous fish. Plateau species include chinook, coho, sockeye, chum, and pink salmon, steelhead trout, and Pacific lamprey. The fish runs varied in the abundance of fish, the size of particular runs, and the particular species that were available from place to place (Schalk 1978), but the timing of the runs was predictable enough to permit people who were prepared for the return of the fish to harvest sizable catches, at least in the good years. Of these, chinook salmon, sockeye salmon, and steelhead trout were the most important species prehistorically on the Plateau. Large waterfalls serve as obstacles in the migration of the fish, and they prevent anadromous fish from reaching much of the eastern Plateau. The catches of fish were generally much larger on the downstream portions of the rivers, decreasing with distance upstream (Chatters 1998). In addition to fish, the rivers provided freshwater shellfish. The freshwater pearl mussel, the western ridge mussel, and several species of the floater, or *Anodonta*, have been recovered from archaeological sites in the Plateau (Lyman 1980).

A wide range of vegetation types is found in the Plateau, ranging from shrub steppe and grassland steppe in the lower-lying areas to forests and alpine meadows in the mountains. Xeric (dry) montane forest and mesic (moderately moist) montane forest, with fir trees, cedar, hemlock, and pine, are more common in the northern portions of the Plateau and in the mountains. Grassland steppe is found on the Fraser Plateau and, along with shrub steppe, dominates the Columbia Basin. Some areas of woodland transition association, an open forest of pine with some oaks, occur around the Columbia Basin, and juniper is added to this association in the Lava Highlands and in the Klamath/Modoc area of the far southern Plateau (Chatters 1998).

Many mammals were available in the various habitats of the Plateau, including elk, moose, caribou, deer, bison, mountain sheep, mountain goat, and pronghorn. Moose and caribou are common only in the north, although moose are found in the Rocky Mountains and the northern Cascade Mountains. Bison historically ranged into some of the mountain valleys in the eastern Plateau, but they are found in archaeological sites in the Columbia Basin (Schroedl 1973). Mountain goats are restricted to the mountains and generally are found above tree line. Deer (both white-tailed and mule deer) are found throughout the area in suitable habitats, as are mountain sheep. Elk occur in the mountains and in adjacent grasslands, while pronghorn are restricted to the driest portions of the Plateau. Rabbits are another significant resource, with both jackrabbits and cottontails being important (Chatters 1998).

Climatic Change

Glaciers covered much of the northern Plateau and capped the mountain ranges in the Pleistocene. By 11,000 BP, the ice was gone. Chatters (1998:42–46) describes climate change through five broad periods. The trend in climate is one of postglacial aridity from 11,000 BP to 9500 BP, followed between 9500 BP and 6400 BP by moister conditions in the northern Plateau but greater aridity in the Columbia Basin. Between 6400 BP and 4500 BP there was a period of cooling across the Plateau. The cooling culminated in the period between 4500 BP and 2800 BP, with wetter conditions occurring in this time range as well. The period from 2800 BP to the present has been one of warming.

One geological aspect of the region that may have affected resources was the heavy volcanic activity of the region. The area is part of the volcanically active area that rings the northern Pacific, and the major eruption of Mount St. Helens in 1980 is but one in a

FIGURE 6.2 Volcanic ash strata at the Gore Creek site in the South Thompson River valley, British Columbia, showing two white bands of volcanic ash. The lower thin band is Mount Mazama ash (7000–6700 BP), while the upper thicker band dates to the eruption of Mount St. Helens that occurred about 3200 BP.

long string of events. The eruption of **Mount Mazama**, the name given to the volcano that stood where Crater Lake is today, spread volcanic ash over a wide area of the Plateau. Often visible as a separate stratum in Plateau archaeological sites (Figure 6.2), this layer of ash provides a time marker in the stratigraphic sequence—strata above the ash postdate the eruption, and those

below the ash predate it. The explosion of Mount Mazama, and, therefore, the age of the ash layers found in archaeological sites, is dated to somewhere between 7000 BP and 6700 BP. The ash layer is thickest close to Crater Lake and gets thinner with increasing distance, but it is a handy reference strata throughout much of the Plateau. Other volcanic ashes, which can be distinguished from one another on the basis of chemical and optical characteristics, occur in more limited ranges and are generally thinner than Mazama ash. Where they are available and have been independently dated, however, they too can be used as time markers. In addition to the use of volcanic ash as a chronological marker, there is debate in the archaeological literature about the effect the ash fall may have had on populations living in the area about 7000 years ago (see Box 6.1).

A general series of periods has been developed for the entire Plateau, although its subregions may have patterns that vary from the periods in this scheme. The sequence starts with the **Early period**, from 11,500 BP to 8000 BP. This is followed by the

---

ISSUES AND DEBATES   BOX 6.1

Volcanoes and Human Settlement

May 18, 1980. I (GTG) am lying in a sleeping bag camped in west central Idaho at the Washington State University Anthropology Department Pig Roast. It's 8:20 in the morning when my wife, my dog, and I are awakened by what sounds like two sonic booms. We scratch our heads because we can't recall the last time we heard a sonic boom in this area, but don't think too much more about it as we get up, socialize a bit, and then pack to return to Pullman, Washington. We get home in the early afternoon and find ourselves standing on the front lawn of our little rental house with our neighbors (flintknapper Jeff Flenniken and his wife and son), watching an ominous line of dark clouds roll toward us from the west. My wife says, "If I didn't know better, I'd think we were watching a Texas squall line and I'd be looking for a tornado shelter." Young Josh Flenniken says, "Maybe it's something from the volcano." We pat Josh on the head and say "Sure" as we wander back into the house. Though we had been following the news of the rumblings and spewings foreshadowing an eruption of Mount St. Helens, none of us had listened to the news that day. If we had, we would have realized the sonic booms we heard all the way over in Idaho were the sounds of the eruption and that the roiling black clouds were volcanic ash that was to

float down on Pullman later that afternoon, covering everything with a concretelike grayish-white powder. It got so dark that the birds began to sing, as they do at dusk.

None of us knew what effect the ash would have on us, but soon everyone in Pullman and most of the rest of eastern Washington was wearing a painter's mask around town. We avoided driving because we feared the fine glass shards of the ash would destroy car engines. School was closed the next day; the stores quickly sold out of painter's masks, and people generally stayed inside. Many worried that supply trucks would not be driving the ash-strewn roads, and the stores sold out of beer!

Volcanism is nothing new in the Northwest. As we discuss in this chapter, volcanic ash layers are often encountered in archaeological and geological profiles. Ash layers from Mount Mazama are used as stratigraphic markers throughout the Plateau, as well as in the northern Great Basin (see David Hurst Thomas's case study in Chapter 8, "Deep-Site Excavation at Gatecliff Shelter, Nevada"). Other volcanoes also have distinctive ashes that can be identified; Glacier Peak ash has been cataloged, as has ash from earlier eruptions of Mount St. Helens. Knowing that the Plateau has been covered in ash a number of times in the past, a natural question is: "What effect did the ash fall have on the people living there?"

The area around Fort Rock Cave in the part of Oregon included in the Northern Great Basin was abandoned after the Mazama eruption. Fort Rock Cave is closer to Mount Mazama than are most parts of the Plateau, and its eruption in the seventh millennium BP coincided with the beginning of a long dry period that might well have led to depopulation of the area even without the volcanic ash. On the other hand, in the Southwest (Chapter 9), the dark-colored, coarse ash or cinders from the eruption that created Sunset Crater are seen as increasing agricultural productivity by holding solar heat and providing mulch.

In the Plateau, an extreme view is that widespread volcanic ash would have made the area uninhabitable. The argument is that the rain of ash would have killed off fish, especially the all-important salmon. It then would have taken a long time for the runs to recover to a point that salmon could again be a mainstay of the diet. It also has been argued that the ash might have hurt plant foods, not only affecting people directly but exerting the indirect effect of reducing the animal populations that fed on the plants—animals like deer, pronghorn, and rabbit. According to an alternative view, recovery from the ash fall would have been rapid, with little effect on prehistoric populations.

The Mount St. Helens eruption provided a test for the arguments in this debate, as scientists had the chance to monitor recovery from the event. Although the area around the volcano itself initially was devastated, plant life returned relatively quickly. Farther away, there was little effect on vegetation or wildlife, and fish runs recovered much more quickly than many had expected (Figure 6.3).

Mount St. Helens rumbled again from 2004 through the end of 2007, sending up small (actually tiny in comparison to the 1980 eruption) bursts of steam and ash and pooling lava in the crater. The mountain is currently quiet. With these changes, we are reminded that volcanism may have shaped some of the past events in the areas covered in this chapter.

FIGURE 6.3 Recovery of vegetation 14 years after the 1980 Mount St. Helens eruption.

ANTHROPOLOGICAL THEMES   TOPIC 6.1

Thematic Research Questions in Chapter 6

As we pointed out in Chapter 2, the North American archaeological record provides significant evidence for several broad anthropological themes. The archaeology of the Plateau is especially relevant to two of these themes as listed in Table 2.1, and we touch on other themes less directly. Table 6.2 helps you locate relevant sections of this chapter for each theme, although as you become more familiar with the archaeology of the Plateau, you will discover more specific research questions that archaeologists can pursue.

Table 6.2 Research Themes for the Plateau

Research Question	Particularly Relevant Sections
How have humans adapted to the diverse environments of North America and to climatic change over time?	Discussions concerning the Early, Middle, and Late periods
How, when, and where did sociopolitically complex, internally differentiated cultural systems develop in North America?	Discussions of the Late Period

Middle period, from 8000 BP to 4000 BP, which is divided into the Early Middle period (8000–5300 BP) and the Late Middle period (5300–4000 BP). The **Late period** then extends from 4000 BP to AD 1720, with three subdivisions—the Early Late period (4000–2500 BP), the Middle Late period (2500–1500/1000 BP), and the Late Late period (1500/1000 BP to AD 1720) (Chatters and Pokotylo 1998). These periods are shown in Table 6.1.

EARLY PERIOD

Projectile points are common elements for this period, and they vary temporally and spatially. Early in the period, before 9000 BP, Windust and related points are found (Figure 6.4). These are lanceolate points that were shouldered and stemmed or unstemmed, often with indentations or notches in the base. Leaf-shaped Cascade points are the points found almost exclusively between 9000 BP and 7800 BP, after which they are found alongside large side-notched points called Northern Side Notched and corner-notched points called Bitterroot. A Cascade point was reported to be embedded in the hip of the Kennewick skeleton (see Chapter 3) (John Fagan 1999). These point types are important in distinguishing the cultural phases for the Lower Snake River developed by Frank Leonhardy and David Rice (1970). In their scheme, the Windust points were characteristic of the Windust phase and the Cascade points of the **Cascade phase**. The Cascade phase could be divided into an early part with only Cascade points and a late part when the notched points are found as well. Leonhardy and Rice's phases have been very important in the development of the archaeology of the Lower Snake River and the Mid-Columbia region.

Other artifacts commonly found during this time are cobble tools, bifaces, scrapers, gravers, burins, and bola stones. Some sites have also yielded bone points, needles, bone awls, edge-ground cobbles, beads, and antler wedges. Millingstones are found at a few sites, as are anvil stones, abraders, and antler flakers (Ames et al. 1998:103).

Marmes Rockshelter, located on the Lower Snake River, is a very important site for this period and for subsequent periods in the prehistory of the Columbia Basin. The site was excavated beginning in 1962 as part of the cultural resource management efforts for Lower Monumental Reservoir. Three years later, work was assumed to be finished, but Roald Fryxell, geologist for the Washington State University team that excavated the site, had a geological test trench cut in the floodplain in front of the shelter. The discovery of burned bone at 14 feet (4 m) below the ground surface led to continued excavation that lasted until the area was flooded by the reservoir in 1969. Efforts had been made to buy additional time by constructing a coffer dam to keep water away from the site, but this measure ultimately proved to be ineffective.

FIGURE 6.4 Early Plateau projectile point forms: top row, Windust phase points; bottom row, Cascade phase points.

The site created quite a stir at the time of its investigation, and preliminary reports indicated that the site contained much information. Unfortunately, only preliminary reports and some specialized studies were published. Lack of a solid report on the site was a serious problem and an embarrassment for the archaeological community until 2004, when the final report for the project was published (Hicks 2004). The initiative for completing the report came from the Confederated Tribes of the Colville Reservation, and contracts were let to perform studies on the materials and to bring together the notes. Ultimately the remains of five individuals were discovered in what had been a single cremation, dated to about 11,500 BP. An additional five burials were found, and these included grave goods like *Olivella* beads, points, and bifaces (Ames et al. 1998:105; Ames and Maschner 1999:125; Kirk and Daugherty 1978:36–38).

There is regional variation in the material recovered at Plateau sites from the Early period. The few sites from Northern Plateau generally have small assemblages with microblades and flake tools. As noted earlier, microblades occur in the northern Northwest Coast in early sites, as well as in the Arctic and Subarctic (Chatters and Pokotylo 1998:74). In the Southern Plateau, most sites of the Early period appear to be short-term habitation sites marked by small, low-density artifact deposits lacking microblades. In the Wells Reservoir and at Kettle Falls, there is evidence of structures built on the ground surface with floor areas of 118 to 162 square feet (11–15 m²). At Wells Reservoir, hearths were found outside the structures but not inside, suggesting that these areas were primarily for sleeping (Ames et al. 1998:106; Chatters and Pokotoylo 1998:74). Evidence of another structure was found at the Paulina Lake site in southern Oregon. This structure had pine support posts, and rocks outlined a cleared area with a hearth in the center. Radiocarbon dates on the posts average 9490 BP. The floor space inside the structure is estimated to have been about 13 by 16 feet (4 × 5 m) (Tveskov and Connley 1997). There is a tendency for assemblages to contain more expedient tools toward the end of the period.

MIDDLE PERIOD

Early Middle Subperiod (8000–5300 BP)

Continuity with the Early period marks the Early Middle subperiod, as many elements carry forward. In the Northern Plateau the Nesikep tradition represents people who used a foraging strategy to hunt deer and elk (Chatters and Pokotylo 1998:74).

Microblades and wedge-shaped cores are found, along with corner-notched points, scrapers, antler wedges, bone points and needles, and red ocher. Animal remains from Nesikep tradition sites include deer, elk, salmon, steelhead trout, and birds, as well as freshwater mussels (Pokotylo and Mitchell 1998:83–84). Pithouses are absent (Stryd 1998). The **Lochnore phase**, apparently representing the replacement of local populations by Salishan speakers from the coast, follows in the Northern Plateau. This migration is attributed to the coastal people following salmon up the river as the salmon runs became more developed after the melting of the glacial ice. Lochnore sites date to the same period as some of the later Nesikep tradition sites (Lehman phase), suggesting a period of coexistence, if the linguistic interpretations are correct (Chatters and Pokotylo 1998:74; Pokotylo and Mitchell 1998:83–84).

In the Southern Plateau there is a simplification of technology at this time, although microblades are found in much of the upper middle Columbia, suggesting influences from the north. Tools generally became more expedient during this time, and some items, like needles, apparently were no longer made. Animal remains vary and appear to reflect the most abundant resource or the resource that gave the greatest yield for the effort required to get it. In some areas deer were the dominant resource, but fish, rabbit, and shellfish dominate at other sites. The use of roots as food appears to have increased throughout the period, and the **hopper mortar** and pestle were introduced (Figure 6.5), replacing millingstones and edge-ground cobbles. On the eastern edge of the Plateau, large concentrations of fire-altered rock mark the location of earth ovens (Figure 6.6) beginning around 6400 BP, and there is direct evidence of camas use by 5500 BP.

In the Early Middle subperiod, a burial pattern known as the **Western Idaho Burial complex** is recognized. Defined by Pavesic (1985) based on material from collectors and museums and data from limited professional excavation, the Western Idaho burial complex is an elaborate set of burials made away from habitation sites. Internments of multiple semiflexed or **flexed burials** are sometimes accompanied by what may be cremated remains. Grave goods include large, distinctive leaf-shaped bifaces called **turkey-tail points**; the name comes from notches at one end (Figure 6.7) (see later, Figure 11.8 as well). Also accompanying the burials are large unnotched bifaces, caches of obsidian blanks and preforms, and large side-notched points. The use of red ocher is common, and *Olivella* shells, crystals of a mineral called specular hematite, and pipes are also found. Pavesic suggests that many of the items found in graves of this complex were made especially for burial ceremonies because

FIGURE 6.5 Drawing of a hopper mortar in use.

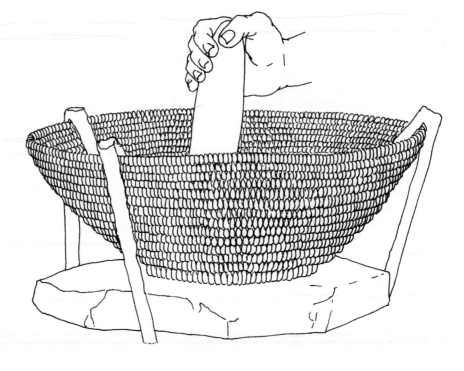

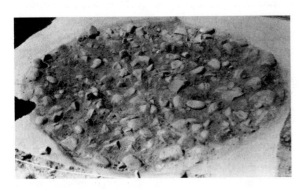

FIGURE 6.6 Earth oven probably used in processing roots.

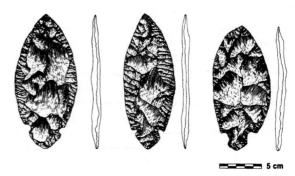

FIGURE 6.7 Turkey-tail bifaces from the Western Idaho burial complex.

they are larger than their presumed function requires and show almost no wear on the biface edges. The presence of shell from the Pacific coast indicates long-distance trade (Pavesic 1985). The burial pattern is dated to between 6000 BP and 4000 BP (Roll and Hackenberger 1998:129).

Late Middle Subperiod (5300–4000 BP)

During the Late Middle period people began to settle down in some of the best locations, places that were close to resources that could be collected during all seasons of the year. This is indicated by the appearance of sites with at least one **pithouse** (see Exhibit 6.1), generally close to the steppe–forest margins. Indeed, this change in mobility was the major difference between the Early and Late Middle subperiods, as artifact technologies continue relatively unchanged. Houses at these sites are variable in size, both within and between regions. For example, houses along the South Thompson River range from 10 to 15 feet (3–4.5 m) in diameter, while on the Lower Snake River they were between 23 and 30 feet (7–9 m), and in southwestern Idaho they were between 13 and 20 feet (4–6 m). Round, oval, and rectangular forms are known.

CLUES TO THE PAST

EXHIBIT 6.1

Pithouses

One of the distinctive characteristics of the Plateau is the occurrence of large villages of pithouses. Pithouses are not, however, restricted to the Plateau. Houses with floors excavated below ground level provided winter homes in the Arctic (Chapter 4), and on the Northwest Coast they precede the plank houses (Chapter 5). Pithouses also occurred in many of the other areas discussed in this text, and they are especially important in California and in the Southwest. Just exactly what is a pithouse?

As the name implies, pithouses are houses built in pits. Generally, a pit the size of the desired house floor is excavated, and then a framework is built and covered to roof the structure. The pits can be shallow, perhaps only a few centimeters, or as deep as several meters. The walls of the pit often serve as at least part of the walls of the houses, although some houses are built within the pit rather than incorporating the pit into their structure. Where wood is scarce, builders used other material, such as whalebone in the Arctic and on California's Channel Islands.

Some pithouses have substantial roofs, often supported by large posts inside the house. These houses were usually entered through a hole in the roof that also served as a chimney, letting the smoke from the hearth escape. Pithouses with roofs that were not substantial enough to support a person's weight were generally entered from the side. In areas of extreme cold in the Arctic, people used tunnels for entry and these tunnels often sloped to below the floor level to make a sink for cold air and keep the heated air of the house inside.

The superstructures of pithouses can be conical, as in Figure 6.8, or domed; in the case of very deep pithouses, the roof can be flat and flush with the ground surface. Internal features like benches, platforms, and storage pits are found on the floors of some pithouses.

The earliest evidence of pithouses in western North America comes from southwestern and south central Wyoming (Ames 2000), where Larson (1997) has discussed 45 structures from 28 sites, with the oldest dating to between 8400 BP and 7700 BP. The oldest dates for pithouses in

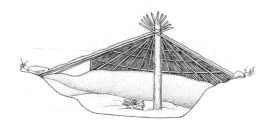

FIGURE 6.8 Reconstruction of a Plateau pithouse. (After Leonhardy and Rice 1970.)

the Plateau come from a period between 7500 BP and 4600 BP at the Johnson Creek, Hatwai, and Givens Springs sites (Ames 2000).

Pithouses probably were built for a number of reasons, but heat conservation is certainly one possibility. Pithouses, especially the deeper ones, use the insulating properties of the soil to retain warmth. Many have evidence of earth or sod coverings over the roofs that would further have served to keep heat in. Indeed, development of pithouses is generally seen as a signal in the archaeological record of a decrease in a group's mobility. This is because the effort in constructing a pithouse—digging the pit, obtaining the wood or other material for the roof structure, and covering the framework with some material like hides, tule mats, thatch, earth, or sod—represents a substantial investment in labor and materials. A study by Patricia Gilman (1987:541–542), which looked at ethnographic evidence of pithouse use around the world, concluded that most people who have used pithouses in recent times have done so primarily in the winter. However, there is evidence that specific pithouses were used at other times. For example, Larson (1997) suggests that the Wyoming pithouses in her study were used residentially in the summer and then as storage during the rest of the year (Ames 2000).

Although pithouses may seem unusual to our modern sensibilities, they were efficient, functional homes for many North Americans of the past.

During the Late Middle subperiod, the diversity of animal bone in the sites is the greatest of any time in Plateau prehistory. Resources varied from place to place, however. In areas like the Lower Snake River, people ate deer and roots, primarily, while large mammals and freshwater mussels were important in the upper reaches of the Middle Columbia River. Salmon may have been more important in the north (Chatters and Pokotylo 1998:75–76).

Salmon storage is suggested, at least at one site in the Northern Plateau called the Baker site. At this site archaeologists found small, circular pits inside three excavated pithouses (Stryd and Rousseau 1996:196). Isotopic analysis of human bone from the Northern Plateau indicates that diets consisted of almost 49 percent marine foods (Chatters and Pokotylo 1998:76). Stryd and Rousseau see the Late Middle subperiod as marking the beginning of the **Plateau Pithouse tradition**, a pattern understood to be very similar to the ethnographic pattern for the area. Further, they see the period as a time of logistic mobility in which people brought resources in to the residential site rather than moving themselves to the resources (Stryd and Rousseau 1996:198). The same kind of evidence for salmon storage is not found in the Southern Plateau, however, suggesting that populations there did move to resources, but less frequently than in earlier periods.

Shell artifacts and obsidian are more common than in earlier times at some sites during the Late Middle period. This suggests the possibility that people increased trade as a means of buffering the natural fluctuation in availability of resources. Desirable trade goods could have been acquired during times when resources were relatively more abundant and traded away in exchange for food at times of relative local food scarcity. Such a buffering mechanism could have been important in allowing the reduced mobility apparent at this time (Chatters and Pokotylo 1998:76).

Pithouse settlements suggesting sedentism become rare after 4500 BP, and there appears to have been a major population reduction in the Southern Plateau (Chatters and Pokotylo 1998:76). Archaeologists assume that areas like the Eastern Plateau saw relatively high mobility throughout the Middle period. Thus the end of the sedentary pithouse sites probably marked a return to a more mobile lifestyle throughout the Plateau. Although most of the settlement in the Middle period was in low-elevation settings, at the end of the period (ca. 4500 BP) there is some evidence in the Eastern Plateau of the use of high elevations for limited collecting, probably of pine nuts (Chatters and Pokotylo 1998:76).

LATE PERIOD

It was during the Late Period (4000 BP to AD 1720) that the ethnographic pattern of the area really took form. This period is divided into three subperiods, while the coming of the horse to the Plateau, which brought many changes to Plateau societies, marks the end of the period.

Early Late Subperiod (4000–2500 BP)

The general trend in the Early Late subperiod throughout most of the Plateau is toward storage-based economies and toward a collector strategy (Binford 1980). This means the establishment of long-term base camps, intensive use of key resources such as salmon, and storage.

In the Eastern Plateau, although use of roots intensified, mobile hunting appears to continue. Based on radiocarbon dating of features thought to be camas ovens, Thoms (1989:444) sees the time between 3500 BP and 2500 BP as having heavy root use, with a falloff in use after this time, followed by increases in the next subperiod. Fish may have become more important in the Eastern Plateau at this time as well, because notched pebbles thought to be net sinkers (Figure 6.9) become common on some sites there (Chatters and Pokotylo 1998:76–77).

Elsewhere on the Plateau a shift toward the collector strategy is more apparent. Sites with clusters of pithouses become common again after a 500-year period when they were scarce. Storage pits are often associated with these pithouses; pithouses tend to be deeper and larger than before, and earth ovens also are frequently found at pithouse sites. Reuse of pithouse depressions (see this chapter's case study by G. Timothy Gross, "The Miller Site: Four Seasons of Backwards Archaeology on Strawberry Island") and increases in the density of the associated artifacts suggest greater settlement permanence. In addition to the pithouse sites, specialized resource extraction camps appear in the archaeological record, supporting the inference that people were practicing a collector strategy. Fish, roots, game, and freshwater mussels were obtained at such camps (Chatters and Pokotylo 1998:76–77).

Salmon appears to have become more readily available at this time because of cooler and moister climatic conditions. Large game animals, on the other hand, probably were less available because forest cover

FIGURE 6.9 Notched cobble net weights.

increased. Increases in salmon use are indicated on the Columbia, Fraser, and Thompson rivers, both by high densities of salmon bone in sites and by isotopic analysis of human skeletons from this subperiod, which indicate that more than half the protein in the diets came from marine sources (Chatters and Pokotylo 1998:76–77). Along the Lower Snake River an increase in net weights and **harpoon valves** (Figure 6.10) in artifact inventories indicates fishing, although fish bone is only the third most common type of bone in the faunal assemblages from sites of this time, and deer dominate these collections. Deer clearly was important, but artifact assemblages do not contain large quantities of projectile points; instead they have large numbers of cobble tools, fishing-related artifacts, and milling equipment (hopper mortar bases and pestles) (Ames et al. 1998:112).

Trade items are less common in this subperiod, and stone tools are generally made of locally available materials, often of low quality. Regional styles of projectile points develop. A notable exception to the lack of trade items is the recovery of **steatite** beads and nephrite adzes (Figure 6.11) in the Upper and Middle Columbia River areas. These artifacts originated in the Fraser River area (Chatters and Pokotylo 1998:76–77; Hayden and Schulting 1997).

Middle Late Subperiod (2500–1000 BP)

The Middle Late subperiod saw expansion of territories and coalescence of populations into large pithouse villages, especially in the lower reaches of the larger rivers. There is also growing evidence for social inequality and for intergroup violence. Trade increases again, possibly fed by a need for prestige items to reinforce the social hierarchy.

Although most Plateau people continue to focus on salmon fishing, root crops became more important at this time. In the north, large earth ovens in highland sites indicate an increase in the use of roots. In the valleys of the Columbia and Snake rivers, people ventured out into uplands and into the arid Columbia Basin. During

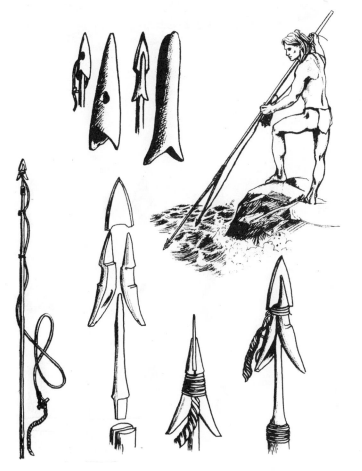

FIGURE 6.10 Harpoon valves and reconstructions of their use.

FIGURE 6.11 Nephrite adze.

this time the Columbia Basin saw a boom in bison population, which may have attracted people to these arid lands, as indicated by mass bison kill sites (Schroedl 1973). Highland camps often have hopper mortar bases, suggesting processing of roots. Antler digging stick handles (Figure 6.12) are first found in the Plateau at this time. Camas roasting in the Eastern Plateau declined during the Middle Late period, however, perhaps because of drying of the meadows where the roots are found (Chatters and Pokotylo 1998:77–78; Roll and Hackenberger 1998:132). The bow and arrow was adopted at this time, becoming established in the south between 2400 BP and 2100 BP, but not until 1500 BP in the north (Chatters and Pokotylo 1998:78). This is marked by the appearance of smaller points (arrowheads) in the archaeological record of the area (Figure 6.13).

Large pithouse villages, with the individual houses generally smaller than in preceding periods, were built in the lower reaches of the major rivers. Over 100 pithouses were built at some of these sites (Figure 6.14). Pithouse settlements are found in the Middle Columbia and in Hells Canyon along the Snake River by the end of this period. Chance and Chance (1985) note an increase in salmon fishing at Kettle Falls.

An increase in the territory traveled by people in the course of their expeditions to resource camps may have contributed to an increase in both the quality and the diversity of tool raw materials. Either people extracted raw materials from new geological sources while traveling, or they increased the frequency of contact and trade with other groups. Trade goods increase at sites during this period, especially at the large population centers. Carved steatite, antler, and whalebone, as well as **dentalium shells** (sometimes incised), shell disk beads, pipes, stone clubs, whalebone clubs (Figure 6.15), and exotic materials like nephrite and

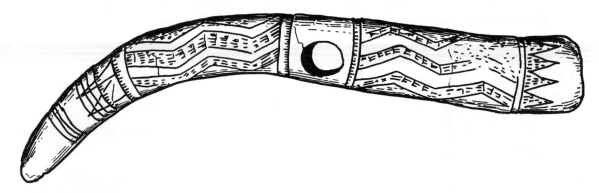

FIGURE 6.12 Antler digging stick handle.

FIGURE 6.13 Arrowpoints from the Miller site.

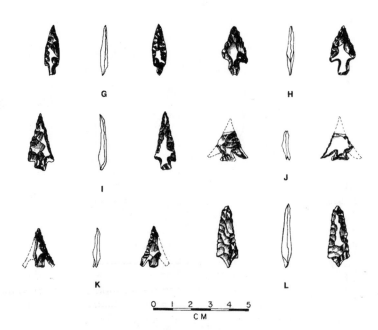

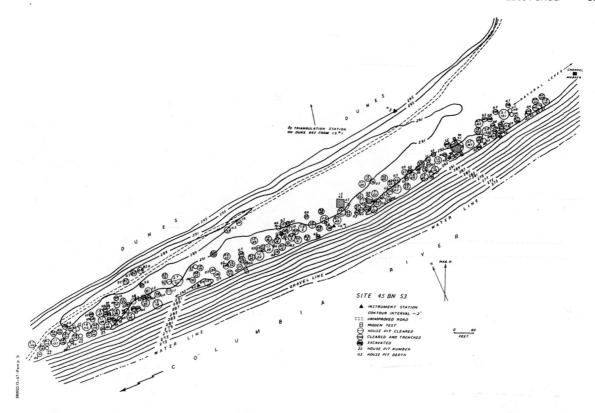

FIGURE 6.14 Map of site 45 BN 53, a Late period pithouse village site near Umatilla, Washington; circles represent former pithouse locations; 40 feet (scale) = 130 meters.

obsidian were important in this trade (Chatters and Pokotylo 1998:78; Hayden and Schulting 1997). Many of the elaborately carved items display art styles similar to those of the Northwest Coast, and raw materials also show similarities. Some sites, such as Wakemap Mound on the Columbia and the village sites of the Middle Fraser River valley, were located at important points on trade routes, and their inhabitants may have been trade specialists (Chatters and Pokotylo 1998:78).

It appears that social inequality fueled the expansion of trade, with elite members of society reinforcing their positions through the display of luxury items. Toward the end of the Middle Late subperiod, some sites have a few houses that are larger than the majority, suggesting the presence of elite households. Elaboration of some burials also occurs, and there are concentrations in the occurrence of exotic trade items, again suggesting the presence of elite individuals. Violence also is evident in this period. The occurrence of projectile points embedded in human bone indicates conflict, as do fortified sites and the location of sites on islands, which are hard to attack (Chatters and Pokotylo 1998:78–79). People built storage facilities

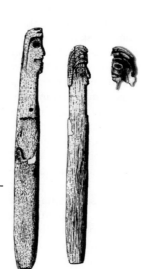

FIGURE 6.15 Whalebone clubs recovered from Plateau sites: left and center, artifacts from the Kamloops area of British Columbia; right, artifact was recovered from The Dalles.

in caves, also suggesting a defensive strategy relating to the critical stored resources. People may have marked their territories both with the distinctive rock art and with the large cemeteries that appear in this subperiod.

FIGURE 6.16 Keatley Creek, a pithouse village along the Fraser River; circular depressions mark former pithouse locations.

Late Late Subperiod (1000 BP to AD 1720)

The Late Late subperiod represents continuity with the Middle Late subperiod, but there are a few important changes. There appears to have been a decline in population at the beginning of this subperiod. Village size decreased, and the differences among individuals in burial treatment disappeared, for the most part. Hayden and Ryder (1991) note that the decline in the villages along the Fraser River in the Lillooet area may have been due to a natural disaster—a landslide on the Fraser that prevented the normal running of salmon. Among the Lillooet area villages is Keatley Creek (Figure 6.16). Population size appears to have increased in the Upper Columbia River area. The Arrow Lakes–Slocan valley area, which had been abandoned during the preceding subperiod, had village sites again. Camas-roasting features increased in the Calispell valley in the Eastern Plateau at this time as well (Chatters and Pokotylo 1998:79).

As in most areas, the history of the ethnographic pattern of people on the landscape has been an important research topic. Movements of people during the Late Late subperiod established Historic period territories and ethnic configurations, although the earlier Lochnore phase apparently represented a movement of Salish people from the coast into the Plateau. The Athapaskans appear to have moved into the Chilcotin Plateau after 600 BP, as indicated by changes in house form, settlement pattern, and artifacts. Numic speakers probably entered the Southern Plateau around 1000 BP. Later, in historical times, plank houses in the area of The Dalles indicate an expansion there of the Chinook (Chatters and Pokotylo 1998:80).

MODERN PERIOD

The Protohistoric or Modern period begins with the introduction of non-Indian influences on the peoples of the Plateau. Although the end of the Late period is set at AD 1720, non-Indian influences really start to have an effect between the years 1600 and 1750. These influences included epidemic diseases, trade goods, the coming of missionaries, and the coming of the horse. Most of the Indians living in the Plateau in the Historic period spoke languages of one of two families. Speakers of Interior Salish, a close linguistic relative of Coast Salish on the Northwest Coast, were found in the Northern Plateau. The Salish speakers include the Shuswap, Lillooet, Thompson, Okanagan, Colville, Sanoil-Nespelem, Kalispel, and Coeur d'Alene. The Southern Plateau was home to Sahaptins, including the Nez Perce, Yakima, and Umatilla. At the western edge of the area along the Columbia River there was a small area of Chinookan language groups such as the Wasco and Wishram. In southern Oregon and into northern California the Klamath and Modoc spoke closely related Klamath languages. In the north are Athapaskans like the Kootenai. Finally, the Cayuse and the Molala spoke language isolates without known affinities (Kinkade et al. 1998; Willey 1966:397).

Epidemic diseases were devastating to Plateau populations. The epidemics may have started as early as the 1500s, based on discontinuities in the archaeological record at some sites. The first epidemics probably came from the coast as sailors brought communicable diseases to the people of the Northwest

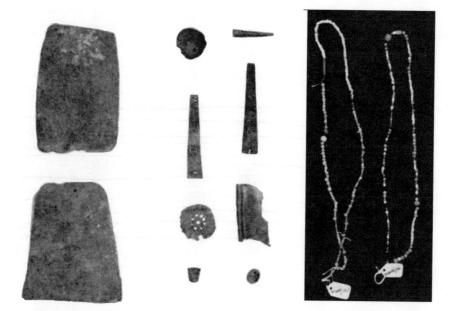

FIGURE 6.17 Historic period trade items from the Plateau.

Coast, who passed them along to the interior peoples (Campbell 1989). Smallpox was one of these diseases, and it hit the Plateau a number of times, the final epidemic occurring in 1853. The mobility of the Plateau peoples and their extensive kin and trade ties encouraged the spread of epidemics throughout the region (Walker and Sprague 1988). The widespread fatalities due to the epidemics led to changes in burial patterns, with some elaboration of grave goods. New styles of interment included canoe burials, burials in cedar cists, burials in fenced enclosures, and burials in log enclosures. Cremation also became more common, and in some cases, a horse was sacrificed at an individual's grave site (Walker and Sprague 1988)!

European and Asian trade goods (Figure 6.17), observed among Plateau groups by the Lewis and Clark expedition in 1805, are found in late archaeological sites in the region. These include artifacts like blue glass beads, Spanish coins, and copper kettles. These items became important commodities in Plateau trade. Trade centers on the Plateau were sites of trade fairs that brought people from distant places. The major trading locations, like The Dalles and Kettle Falls, had been important in trade prehistorically as well. In historical times, Plateau people traded well outside the Plateau, participating in trade with Spanish settlements in New Mexico, for example, and with trade centers on the Upper Missouri River. There are even documented expeditions of Walla Walla, Cayuse, and Yakima to the Central

valley of California, where they obtained slaves, beads, metal goods, and bows in exchange for horses, buffalo robes, dried salmon, and dentalium shells (Walker and Sprague 1988).

One factor that contributed to the long-range trade in this period and had a major effect on lifestyles in parts of the Plateau was the introduction of the horse. Horses descended from stock originally brought to the Spanish settlements in New Mexico moved north along existing trade routes and arrived in the Southern Plateau in the 1700s. The Plateau people, especially the Cayuse, Nez Perce, Palouse, and some Yakima, adopted the horse readily, increasing their mobility considerably. Lewis and Clark reported huge herds of horses owned by Plateau groups, and historical reports attribute approximately 20,000 horses to the Cayuse, Umatilla, and Walla Walla tribes in the mid-nineteenth century (Walker and Sprague 1988).

Not only did the horse provide greater mobility, it also allowed heavier loads to be transported. This led to an increase in warfare, as mounted combatants had a strong advantage over people on foot, and raiders on horseback could strike over longer distances. As raiding from the Plains became more common, warfare developed along the lines of the Plains tribes, with war chiefs and warrior societies. Although tribes of the eastern periphery of the Plateau had occasionally traveled over the mountains to hunt buffalo before the horse, the horse allowed such trips to become more common and more productive (Walker and Sprague 1988).

CHAPTER SUMMARY

In this chapter we have introduced the prehistoric and early historical archaeology of the Plateau. The archaeology of the Plateau received much attention lately as a result of the discovery of the Kennewick skeleton in 1996 and the ensuing legal battles over its ultimate disposition. The following points about the Plateau are important:

- The Old Cordilleran tradition (9000–7500 BP) was characterized by leaf-shaped bifaces, cobble tools, burins, and bola stones. Large quantities of fish bone at the Roadcut site on the Columbia indicate that fishing was well established at this time. Some Early period sites in the northern Plateau have produced microblades.
- The Middle period (8000–4000 BP) continues trends established in the Early period and is typically divided into an Early Middle period and a Late Middle period. One basic distinction is that Late Middle period groups seem to have been more sedentary, relying more heavily on salmon. After 4500 BP there was a decrease in population, and the remaining people seem to have been more mobile again.
- The Late period extends from 4000 BP to AD 1720 and is the period in which historical patterns are fully developed. The Late period is usually divided into Early, Middle, and Late subperiods. During the Early Late period, clusters of pithouses again become common, and there is evidence for an increase in the permanence of settlements as well as a collector strategy. In the Middle Late period, populations came together in large pithouse villages (some with over 100 pithouses), and group territories expanded, especially in the lower reaches of the major rivers. The evidence suggests that social ranking and intergroup conflict occurred at this time, and trade increased. Patterns established in the preceding period continue in the Late Late period (1000 BP to AD 1720), although populations declined and villages became smaller over much of the area.
- The Modern period is marked by the coming to the Plateau of non-Indian influences. These include epidemic disease, the horse, Euro-American trade goods, and missionaries. All these factors had important effects on the people of the Plateau, but the horse became particularly important, allowing increases in mobility, and some of the Plateau people moved seasonally to the Plains to hunt bison.

SUGGESTIONS FOR FURTHER READING

For an introduction that includes much useful information about Plateau archaeology:

Aikens, C. M.
   1993 *Archaeology of Oregon.* U.S. Department of the Interior, Bureau of Land Management, Oregon State Office, Portland.

For excellent summaries of the prehistory of the various regions of the Plateau:

Walker, Deward E., Jr. (editor)
   1988 *Plateau.* Handbook of North American Indians, Vol. 12, William C. Sturtevant, general editor, Smithsonian Institution, Washington, D.C.

For a recent collection of articles on Plateau prehistory that discusses complexity and new chronological information:

Prentiss, William C., and Ian Kuijt (editors)
   2004 *Complex Hunter-Gatherers: Evolution and Organization of Prehistoric Communities on the Plateau of Northwestern North America.* University of Utah Press, Salt Lake City.

For the long-awaited report on the excavations at a very important Plateau site:

Hicks, Brent A. (editor)
   2004 *Marmes Rockshelter: A Final Report on 11,000 years of Cultural Use.* Washington State University Press, Pullman.

For an accessible description of a large pithouse village and the issue of emerging sociocultural complexity:

Hayden, Brian
   1997 *The Pithouses of Keatley Creek: Complex Hunter-Gatherers on the Northwest Plateau.* Harcourt Brace College, Fort Worth, Texas.

For important discussion of the Plateau and other portions of British Columbia:

Carlson, Roy L., and Luke Dalla Bona (editors)
   1996 *Early Human Occupations in British Columbia.* University of British Columbia Press, Vancouver.

OTHER RESOURCES

The Student CD, Sections H and I, supplies web links, additional discussion questions, and other study aids. The Student CD also contains additional resources. Pithouses, emphasized in Exhibit 6.1 and in the following case study, were also used by the earliest inhabitants of the Dolores River valley in southwestern Colorado, as described in Section D.5, "The Dolores Archaeological Program: Documenting the Pithouse-to-Pueblo Transition."

CASE STUDY

As indicated in this chapter, the people of the Plateau often lived in villages consisting largely of a series of pithouses, and sites containing multiple telltale depressions from these structures are common. Since differences among pithouses and their contents both between and within sites can have chronological, social, or ethnic significance, the careful study of houses and house contents is warranted. The following case study describes how the erosion of several pithouses located on an island in the Snake River in Washington State brought archaeologists to a large pithouse village. Initially investigations were limited to documenting the contents and nature of the pithouses actually being eroded by river waters.

Over the course of several field seasons, however, the focus of research changed to investigating the nature of the whole site. The increase in scope has allowed the U.S. Army Corps of Engineers to better manage this important archaeological resource. It also has shown that there were several occupations of this site, as well as greater variability within pithouse villages than archaeologists once thought. Experimental archaeology has shown as well how people at this site processed antelope for marrow, providing insights into Plateau adaptations in general. As you read this case study, pay particular attention to the three different occupations. How and why are they different?

THE MILLER SITE

Four Seasons of Backwards Archaeology on Strawberry Island

G. Timothy Gross

A barge loaded with wheat lumbers down the Snake River, powered by the pushboat behind it. The barge rides low in the water, and the two craft send a V-shaped wave or wake out through the channel of the river, now a reservoir backed up behind McNary Dam. The spreading wave hits the cobble apron that surrounds the upstream end of Strawberry Island and climbs the short distance to the sand and silt bank that sits atop the apron. Next the wave hits the soft sediments of the bank, ripping a little more away from the already undercut base, and a piece of the bank crashes down on the cobbles below. The lapping of the reservoir waters against this block of sediment slowly removes the sands and silts, leaving behind rocks and bits of broken bone. Some of the rocks are blocky, jagged, and blackened from heat; others are flakes; one or two are cobble choppers. The bone is mostly pronghorn, but a few fish vertebrae may be seen as well. In the newly exposed section of bank there is visible a gently curving band of charcoal, making a thin black smile in the tan sands and silts. This band marks the floor of a pithouse.

When a survey team from Washington State University (WSU) visited Strawberry Island in 1975, they found the beaches of the upper end of the island littered with artifacts and the sand and silt banks showing stratified deposits. They noted the presence of over 100 depressions thought to represent the former sites of pithouses. They also noted that, in addition to damage from barge wakes, the island had been vandalized by relic hunters. They recommended that measures be taken to protect the banks from erosion and noted that a mapping and testing project was slated for 1976 (Cleveland et al. 1977:34–36). That project was the beginning of the four field seasons that I will discuss in this case study. I joined the project in 1977 as a crew chief and was the field director for the last two seasons (Schalk 1983:v).

Strawberry Island is located in the Snake River about 5 miles (8 km) upstream from the confluence of the Snake and the Columbia, not far from Columbia Park, where Kennewick Man was found (see Section F.4 on the Student CD). This area in general is known as the Pasco Basin and is one of the driest parts of the Plateau. The river is no longer free-flowing in this stretch, as the construction of McNary Dam on the Columbia River created Lake Wallula, which includes this portion of the Snake. A channel that is flooded most of the time by reservoir waters, but was dry except during floods before the dam was built, bisects the island. Strawberry Island Village, also known as the Miller site, occupies the portion of the island that is upstream from this channel. The site was first recorded as part of the Smithsonian River Basin Survey in 1948, and excavations were conducted in 1951 (Osborne and Crabtree 1961) as part of the salvage work connected with the construction of McNary Dam.

The 1951 project on Strawberry Island recorded 131 depressions on the surface of the Island that were thought to represent house pits. Seven were excavated in some fashion. A square measuring 5 by 5 feet (1.5 × 1.5 m) was excavated in four of the depressions, two adjacent depressions were excavated with a trench that intersected both, and one additional depression was excavated intensively with a block of 19 of the 5 by 5 foot squares.

BACKWARDS ARCHAEOLOGY

When I talk about the excavations at Strawberry Island, I often joke that we excavated the site backwards. By that I mean that we started by taking a very fine look at small parts of the site and extended operations each field season, putting the previous season's work into a little broader context each year, until in the last year we sampled space across the island to see how the areas we had been excavating fit in. This was not a result of backwards thinking by the archaeologists; instead, it reflected the evolution of the attitude of the project sponsors, the U.S. Army Corps of Engineers, toward archaeology and toward their legal responsibilities. This evolution mirrors changes that took place across the country, signaling the change from a **salvage approach** for federal agency archaeology to one that focuses on managing the resources. That is, rather than doing no more than what was needed to save any resources that were threatened by projects or their long-term effects, the agencies began to develop understandings of sites and their contexts, trying to preserve those that were truly important.

The initial WSU project in 1976, directed by Greg Cleveland with Richard D. Daugherty serving as principal investigator, created a map of the site showing all the visible depressions. The map was made by a combination of aerial photography and land surveying.

White crosses were placed in each depression that could be recognized, and aerial photographs were taken. A transit survey was also undertaken, not only to locate the depressions but also to set up **datum points** for the construction of a grid system. The detailed map that resulted showed the location of 133 depressions (Figure 6.18). Each of the depressions was assigned a number, though it was later discovered that the WSU numbering system differed from that used by Osborne and Crabtree (1961).

Excavation during the first field season was confined to trenches in three contiguous depressions on the southeast side of the island (also referred to as the left bank, in keeping with the convention of referring to the banks as if the viewer was looking downstream). Items within the trenches were point plotted (mapped in three dimensions) in the hope that the vertical distributions would indicate the location of house floors both in the field maps and in computer mapping that followed the field season. This was deemed appropriate excavation strategy because floors were very hard to define in the sandy sediments of the island. Plotting each individual item encountered was a time-consuming process, but it resulted in detailed information about sections of house pits. Provisions in the contract restricted excavation to areas that were being lost to erosion. The Corps of Engineers saw their responsibility as limited to saving what was being destroyed (Cleveland et al. 1977; Cleveland 1978a).

The 1977 the excavation was again restricted to areas being eroded. Again under Cleveland's supervision, excavation continued in two of the house pits

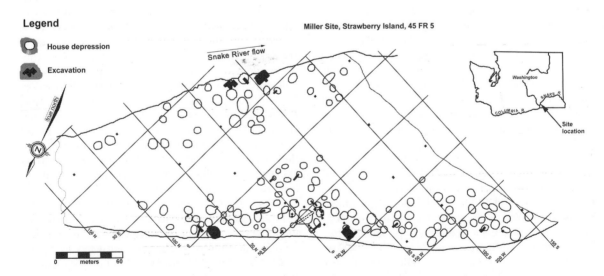

FIGURE 6.18 Map of the Miller site showing the depressions and the location of excavations.

FIGURE 6.19 Excavation in progress on Strawberry Island pithouses.

For each depression chosen in this way, a trench was laid out from the rim of the depression on the north side to the center of the depression. Depending on the size of the depression, these trenches were 5 to 7 meters (16 to 23 ft.) long. Each trench was excavated using standard 10 cm (4 in.) levels. This exercise allowed us to explore the range of variation in depression types.

By the 1979 field season, in which Schalk assumed the role of principal investigator as well as project director, we had some idea of the range in variation in depressions and had detailed data on the contents of some depressions, including piece-plotted provenience on material in several pithouses. We also had some information on the space between houses on the site from the two area excavations that had been conducted. We knew as well that depressions in the right-bank cluster exhibited some structure in their distribution, with groups of depressions appearing to be clustered together, perhaps forming compounds. In the final year of the project we designed one last sample so that we could put the existing data into a larger context. In this sample, excavations were laid out on a grid at 25 meters (82 ft.) intervals on the north–south axis and 50 meters (164 ft.) on the east–west axis. Each excavation on the grid was a 1 by 1 meter (3 × 3 ft.) test unit excavated to the sterile cobble basement stratum of the island. In the 1979 excavation we also examined spatial variability by selecting one of the pithouse clusters and excavating 29 small 1 by 1 meter units in it. The final task was carrying one of the open area excavations begun in 1978 down to the cobble layer.

Thus what we did was the reverse of what is often done. Generally, the first stage of an excavation is designed to provide information about the structure of the entire site, and subsequent areas for detailed excavation are selected based on the results of the initial sampling. In the Strawberry Island case, owing to the Corp of Engineer's interpretation of their responsibilities, we were restricted at first to detailed excavation; only at the end of the project could we do the sampling across the site that allowed us to establish a context into which to fit our detailed information. This sequence of events reflects changes that were happening nationwide in cultural resource management. In the early days of federal archaeology, with the notable exception of some projects run by the National Park Service, most federal archaeology was considered to be salvage work, aimed at rescuing some data from sites that were disappearing, owing to such federal actions as dam building. Ultimately federal archaeology in many agencies took on an active role in managing the resources under government jurisdiction, a task that

investigated in 1976 (**piece plotting** artifacts in the third had been completed in 1976), and excavations were begun in a depression on the right bank of the island (Figure 6.19). Excavation in some open areas between depressions was also begun in 1977. The trenches that allowed examination of stratification were excavated with a backhoe, which had been transported in a surplus military landing craft, and passed through the boat lock in Ice Harbor Dam, located just upstream from Strawberry Island.

In 1978 Randall Schalk took over as project director. He received permission from the Corps of Engineers to excavate in areas of the island beyond those that were eroding. Excavation that year continued in the open areas, and a new sample of depressions was designed. Upon evaluating the variability in the kinds of depression seen on Strawberry Island, Schalk noted first of all that there were two clusters of depressions, one on the right bank and one on the left. Further, the depressions varied both in size and in shape. Some of the depressions were round, while others were elliptical. Creating a chart of the possible attributes, Schalk noted which combinations on the chart had already been examined by the WSU program. He then went to Osborne and Crabtree's report and noted the types they had examined. With WSU and the Smithsonian's River Basin excavations considered, it was easy to tell from the chart which combinations of attributes had not been sampled. All the possibilities for the unsampled combinations were listed, and examples were chosen with the aid of a table of random numbers until at least one of each combination had been picked for further work.

FIGURE 6.20 Schematic profile of a depression on the Miller site showing the difference between saucer-shaped and steep-walled pithouses.

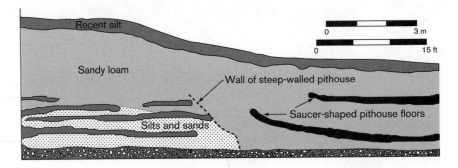

called for information beyond the identification of what was being destroyed. The responsibility of federal agencies to manage their resources, rather than merely reacting to proposed impacts, is now part of the law: a 1980 amendment to the National Historic Preservation Act (NHPA) outlines these responsibilities in **Section 110**.

Beginning with the initial excavations in 1976, the Strawberry Island project was funded on a year-to-year basis. Accordingly, a report was supposed to be prepared after each field season. The 1976 and 1977 field reports (Cleveland et al. 1977, 1978a) were prepared, but the Corps of Engineers ruled that a spate of high-priority contracts from the federal agency to Washington State University took precedence over the preparation of reports for the 1978 and 1979 field seasons. As Schalk began working on the combined report on the last two field seasons (Schalk 1983), it became apparent that there were more data than could be adequately reported with the available budget and that additional analyses were needed to make the existing data fully useful. Although a request was made to the Corps of Engineers for the additional funding to carry out a full reporting of the excavation, no such monies could be obtained. The final report on the 1978 and 1979 seasons (Schalk 1983) summarizes what was done and provides some analysis and synthesis, but there are no detailed discussions of individual excavation units or areas, and little tabular presentation of data by excavation area. Nonetheless, the project has contributed considerably to the understanding of Lower Snake–Mid-Columbia archaeology, as we shall see.

WHAT WE LEARNED

Three occupations have been documented, although the earliest is represented by material from the bottom of only one trench, at the meeting of the sands and silts and the cobble base of the island. Items found at the contact include a few fire-altered rocks, cobble tools, three projectile points, siliceous flakes, shell fragments, and a sliver of bone (Mierendorf 1983:47). This contact is dated in a different part of the site at 2472 ±110 BP.

The first major occupation of the Miller site is in the group of house pits on the right bank of the island. Most of the pithouses in this large cluster appear to have been built over a very short time. These pithouses, with a single date of 1395 ± 80 BP, were deep, and steep pit walls were indicated by truncation of the bedded natural sands and silts of the island (Figure 6.20).

The final village occupation was a series of saucer-shaped pithouses that were built on both banks of the island. A number of radiocarbon dates indicate that this occupation started about 600 BP and ended around 200 BP. This later date is reinforced by the complete absence of historical trade goods, which are so common on Contact period sites in the area.

One of the important aspects of the analysis carried out for this project is the use of replication. Jeff Flenniken (1977, 1978) studied the lithic material from the site and described four main modes of flaked stone tool production. The first system he describes, based on experimental manufacture of artifacts and comparison of the resulting artifacts and **debitage** to those found in the excavation, is the production of flaked tools by means of a biface reduction technique. Raw materials for this system were generally cherty materials and obsidian, and they were often collected as cobbles. Flakes were heat-treated prior to further reduction. The second system was the reduction of pebbles or large flakes through bipolar reduction into flat flakes that were either used as produced or worked into arrow points. The raw materials were essentially the same for this system, but the cores may have been heat-treated prior to flake removal. The third system is the production of oval flake tools from basalt, quartzite, and granite cobbles, probably picked up along the cobble beaches of the island. The flakes (Figure 6.21a, b), which were excellent

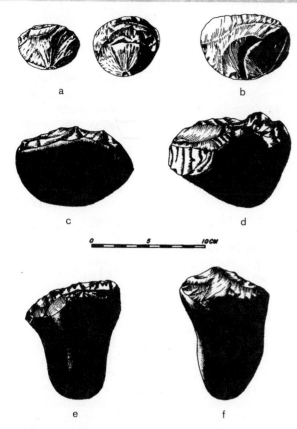

a   b

c   d

0   5   10 CM

e   f

FIGURE 6.21 Flaked tools from the Miller site: (a, b) flake knives and (c, d, e, f) cobble choppers.

knives without any further modification, were produced by a block-on-block technique in which a thin, oval cobble was held between the thumb and fingers and struck on the edge against a stationary anvil stone. Generally a single oval flake would result. The final system was the production of cobble choppers. This was accomplished by freehand percussion on basalt cobbles. Relatively thin cobbles were selected, and a few flakes were removed unifacially from one end to produce a steep working edge. Such tools are common on sites in the area (Figure 6.21c, d).

Many of the cobble choppers recovered in excavation were bifacial, and they show varying signs of wear, from unused edges to edges that are a band of crushed and pockmarked stone with the remnants of flake scars behind them (Figure 6.21e, f). This kind of wear indicates considerable battering and may have resulted from the use of an anvil stone to process materials. The crushing would be a result of contact between the chopper and the anvil. Flenniken believes that the bifacial cobble choppers started out as unifacial

tools and that the flake scars on the other face were acquired during use, as the tools accidentally struck the anvil with enough force to detach a flake. Although these choppers were almost certainly multipurpose tools, one activity represented in the archaeological record at Strawberry Island Village was the processing of long bones from large mammals like pronghorn for the marrow they contain. That is one of the activities that Cleveland (1977) and Flenniken (1977) explored in greater detail through replication.

To test whether marrow extraction was a reasonable explanation for the cobble choppers, often heavily worn, the anvil stones with their pockmarked surfaces, and the quantities of splintered long bones, Cleveland contacted Fish and Game departments throughout the Northwest. The Department of Fish and Game in Wyoming was able to provide two dead pronghorns, which were shipped to Pullman for experimental purposes. Cleveland's goals were to understand the food value of marrow and meat from pronghorns, to see whether marrow extraction produced the kinds of splintered bone found at the site, and to see whether the process of butchering and marrow extraction produced the same kinds of wear patterns seen in the archaeological record on replicated ovate flake knives and the cobble choppers. The meat and marrow weight yields were used to estimate the nutritional yield of pronghorns.

Flenniken (1977:100–101) summarizes the observations made on the use of the cobble choppers. He notes that unmodified cobbles were unsuitable for marrow extraction. The rounded surfaces slipped off the greasy bone, and if enough force was used to break the bone with the cobble, the bone shattered, driving tiny bone splinters into the marrow. Removal of a flake or two from the edge of the cobble provided the edge necessary to fracture the bone without shattering it, leaving the marrow tube to be picked out, relatively bone free. The edges of the choppers incurred pockmark wear from hitting the anvil stone as well as the bone, which damaged the tool edge and the anvil surface. Sometimes, when contact was made with the anvil, flakes were driven off the chopper. These could be distinctive, having pockmarked platforms. In the experiments, cobble choppers that started out as **unifaces** became bifacial through the process of contact flake removal. With sufficient use, pockmarks obliterated the flaked edge of the tool. The ovate flake knives made by Flenniken's third technological system were used in the butchering process. The wear patterns on the cobble tools and on the ovate knives used in the experiment matched those on the archaeological specimens.

The bone from the site did, indeed, match the bone from the experiments well enough to support the inference that people had been able to collect marrow by breaking bones. The ends of bones and portions of bone, like the scapula, were also used to provide marrow. In many cases these bones were broken to expose the spongy bone (cancellous tissue), and this was probably boiled to provide a rich broth. Evidence of both kinds of marrow extraction was found in houses at the Strawberry Island village.

What were the houses like at Strawberry Island? The earlier houses were deep pithouses (20–28 in., or 30–50 cm deep) with abrupt sides. They tended to be smaller than the later houses, but had sizable post-holes. Beyond the postholes there is no evidence of the nature of the superstructure. Later houses were shallower and had saucer-shaped floors that lacked postholes. Again, the nature of the superstructure is unknown. There is a patterning in the distribution of artifacts around and within the structures. Around the structures immediately outside the house is a ring of debris that appears to be trash associated with the occupation of the house. Often called the **midden ring**, this area contains discards that are as-sumed to be contemporaneous with the living floors. The use zone within the house is another matter. In the earlier, steep-walled houses, the floors are ephemeral, and little debris is associated with them. Relatively thick and dark deposits suggesting a greater intensity of use, on the other hand, mark the saucer-shaped floors. Interestingly, however, no traceable compact floors can be found in Strawberry Island's pithouses, since the sediments in which they were made were so sandy.

The identification of animal remains from the site provided the material for Deborah Olson's master's thesis (Olson 1983) and yielded some important infor-mation. Three classes of animals—rabbit, pronghorn, and salmon and related fish (salmonids)—dominated the bone collections from the site. The rabbit class of bones includes both jackrabbit and cottontail, though jackrabbits are by far the more common. Deer and elk bones are found in the collections, but both are much less common than pronghorn. The salmonids are dif-ficult to identify more specifically from the parts that were preserved at the Miller site, but the species repre-sented probably include chinook salmon, which ap-pears to be the most common type, as well as sockeye salmon, coho salmon, and steelhead trout. Bones from fish of the sucker family were also recovered. Other animals noted in smaller numbers are ground squirrel, mouse, beaver, dog, coyote, black bear, weasel, and river otter, along with unspecified reptiles, birds, and snakes. Interestingly, no bison bones were identified in all the collections, though cow/bison-sized bone frag-ments were recovered from the beach and from the surface of the island. These are most likely modern

cow, however, unrelated to the prehistoric occupation of the site.

Faunal remains were compared across the island, and an important pattern emerged—a strong associa-tion between types of faunal remains and types of houses. Steep-walled houses are associated with faunal assemblages that have salmonids as the most common element. The houses with saucer-shaped floors, on the other hand, are dominated either by pronghorn or by rabbit. Schalk and Olson conclude a discussion of the faunal remains by saying:

> To our knowledge, this is the first demonstration in the Plateau of a recurrent association between archi-tectural forms and faunal assemblages. It is also the first reported occurrence on the Columbia Plateau of a Late Prehistoric residential site in which pronghorn is the dominant ungulate in the faunal assemblage. (Schalk and Olson 1983:107)

Cleveland (1978b:37–40) reviewed the evidence for pronghorn hunting and concluded that the pronghorn found at the Miller site probably were caught in large communal game drives. This conclu-sion was based on the age structure of the pronghorn in the assemblage. The presence of individuals that were six to eight months old at the time of death (based on the characteristics of their mandibles) both rein-forces this conclusion and points to late fall or winter as a time for the hunts. The distribution of faunal re-mains suggests that whole animals were distributed to the individual houses, a pattern consistent with communal hunting (Schalk and Olson 1983:103–104). If individual hunters had procured individual animals, it is expected, based on ethnographic meat-sharing patterns, that portions of animals would have been distributed rather than whole animals.

Schalk reconstructs the occupation of the island and examines the differences between the two major periods of use. The first occupation was that of the right bank, where deep, steep-sided pithouses were built, probably around 1400 BP. The number of depres-sions on the right bank suggests that the population of that early occupation would have been large, "possibly numbering in the hundreds" (Schalk 1983:139). Most of these features do not show signs of reuse, although a few contained multiple floors. Schalk suggests that there was an occupational hiatus, perhaps caused by unfavorable climatic conditions, although there is some evidence for reuse of some of the right-bank pit-houses by a smaller group of people after the initial building of the pithouses.

The second major occupation, from 600 BP to 200 BP, was the one associated with the saucer-shaped floors, and it occupied both the right and left banks. Stratigraphic evidence, both in the fill of the depressions and in the open areas, indicates some accumulation of natural sediment between the two occupations. These houses were larger and tended to occur along the river's edge, contrasting with the earlier occupation, which spread into the center of the island. Schalk also notes that the houses of the earlier occupation of the right bank form groups or clusters, while the later houses are more scattered. The occurrence of clusters of houses into compounds suggests the existence of some sort of group organization at a level higher than the individual household in the earlier pithouse occupation. This tantalizing suggestion is just one of the many avenues for further research that can be pursued with data from this project.

The patterning in faunal remains has already been mentioned, with the early, steep-walled houses having faunal assemblages dominated by salmonids and the later occupation having either rabbit or pronghorn as the dominant animal. Schalk does not think that fish use decreased, however; instead, he suggests that it actually increased in the later occupation. It is the nature of the use that is seen to have changed, with a greater reliance on stored salmon—fish that were caught and dried at a location away from the village—leading to the lower relative numbers of fish bones.

Schalk explains the changes as resulting from an imbalance between population and resources. Basically, arid conditions that set in after the right-bank occupation ended caused a scarcity of terrestrial resources. As noted at the beginning of this case study, the Pasco Basin is one of the most arid parts of the Plateau, so drying would have been particularly severe there. Since similar droughts had occurred prehistorically without leading to similar changes, Schalk suggests that the number of people had grown during relatively good times and that the region was so heavily populated that prior solutions to environmental stress, involving increased movement of groups of people over larger territories, were not feasible. With the larger populations restricting the ranges over which people could hunt and gather food, the alternative was to intensify efforts to collect a specific resource. Migrating fish populations were the resource for which increased effort would have paid off. Such a "quantum increase" in fishing, Schalk suggests (1983:146), led to longer stays in residential bases, and the period of use of the later pithouses on the island was longer, explaining the greater quantities of artifacts associated with these house floors.

Two trends are seen in the artifact assemblages that support the foregoing explanation of change. First, the bipolar reduction system is more common in the later pithouses, indicating a more frugal use of the raw material, since this technique provides more cutting edge per unit of rock than freehand percussion. This

scenario is consistent with a reduction in mobility and territory size, accompanied by fewer opportunities to collect raw materials, since previous sources now lay beyond the boundaries of the smaller home range. Both projectile points and ovate flake knives are also more common in the later occupation. This is consistent with a greater emphasis on hunting pronghorn and rabbit to supplement the diet of stored fish that probably formed the staple for the occupation of Strawberry Island Village.

IMPACTS OF THE PROJECT

Although the level of reporting for the Strawberry Island Project is not as thorough as we would like, the work at the Miller site has made some substantial contributions to Plateau prehistory. The site is used as evidence for the formation of large pithouse villages in the Southern Plateau (e.g., Ames 2000; Ames et al. 1998). It also marks a change in the way Plateau prehistory was addressed. Prior to the Strawberry Island Project, Plateau developments were seen as primarily additions to a static cultural base. New artifact types appeared in the record and projectile points changed through time, but the adaptation was seen as relatively constant. The Miller site, which allowed comparisons between occupations that were about 800 years apart, showed that there were also changes in the relative proportions of materials in assemblages, and that there was important, previously unexplored variability. Adaptations were not static but changed in response to such factors as increased aridity and population growth.

Strawberry Island illustrates another point as well. The collections from the Strawberry Island Project still exist at Washington State University. Clearly, there is a great potential for further study of those collections to address important questions raised in the original analyses and questions that have arisen as our understandings of regional prehistory have grown. Further, the ready availability today of techniques like AMS dating means that samples that could not be dated back in 1979 can be dated today. This should allow testing the reconstruction of two occupations and refined dating of the early occupation at the contact between the cobbles and the sands on the island. The site has been protected since the end of the excavations. Riprap has been placed around the banks of the island to shield them from further damage. Productive new research that adds substantially to the study of Plateau prehistory can be accomplished with the existing collections, and the site remains for further research when questions requiring new excavation arise.

DISCUSSION QUESTIONS

1. Why was the Miller site excavated backwards? How and why did the excavation strategy change over the course of the project? What's the difference between salvaging and managing archaeological resources?

2. When was the Miller site inhabited, and what periods in Plateau culture history does it represent? What was the basis for concluding that there were three distinct occupations of the site?

3. What evidence leads to the conclusion that the inhabitants of this site were extracting marrow from pronghorn bones? How did people apparently obtain the marrow?

4. Contrast the evidence for subsistence practices in the two pithouse occupations. Can you think of other ways to interpret the lack of fish in the later pithouses? How might you test Schalk's ideas about what was happening?

CHAPTER 7

Diversity and Complexity in California

I t's a warm, sunny day in the San Pasqual valley just north of San Diego. A group of about 20 people sit in a circle around a large blue tarp that is littered with bits of rock. All of the people in the circle are watching as one of their number balances a large tabular rock on his thigh, raises his right hand, and then brings it down, delivering a sharp blow with the rock in his hand to the rock on his thigh. A large piece of rock breaks off and falls to his feet. He repeats the process several times, explaining what he is doing as he takes piece after piece of the rock on his thigh. He finally stops, sets the large rock, now quite a bit smaller, aside, and the others crowd in to select some of the pieces he has produced. The people return to their seats and begin breaking pieces off the rocks they have chosen.

This scene is repeated year after year at the annual Flintknapping Workshop held at the San Diego Archaeological Center, a nonprofit archaeological curation and education facility (see Student CD, Section F.2). Though the majority of participants in the workshop are college students, they range from junior high school students to retirees. Each has his or her own reason for attending, but they share a curiosity about how stone tools were made. Some will go on to use replication, the making of duplicates of artifacts recovered from archaeological sites, to both see how they were made and to experiment with ways in which they could have been used, in their research, while others will make stone tools as a hobby, and a number will have their curiosity satisfied with this single class.

Archaeologists use experimental studies like flintknapping to better understand the past. By matching not only the end product, say a particular kind of projectile point, but also the kinds and amounts of debitage, we gains insights into the operation of technology in the past. These experiments allow exploration of the qualities of rock being chosen for tool production and may provide insights into why certain raw materials were traded long distances. Archaeologists sometimes are confronted with flaked materials that do not match anything found naturally. Experiments with heat treatment of rock have in some cases demonstrated that these items are local rock that has been heat treated or baked, changing not only the physical appearance but the flaking qualities of the rock. Replicative studies also including the recreation of wear patterns.

In wear pattern studies, replicas of the tools are made and used under controlled conditions to perform tasks. Different tool replicas are used for a certain time or a certain number of strokes to cut hard materials such as bone, soft material such as hides or grasses, and intermediate materials such as wood. Microscopic examination of the damage to the edges provides a reference matching with archaeological items.

Wear pattern studies are not limited to flaked stone tools, however. One interesting project carried out at the San Diego Archaeological Center was funded by the National Science Foundation and looked at wear patterns on ground stone. For this study a local archaeologist made sets of millingstones—grinding slabs and accompanying handstones, grinding basins and handstones, and mortars and pestles—out of three different materials. Handstones were paired with bases of the same material and were used to grind three different materials—small seeds, acorns, and clay. Center staff and volunteers did some of the experimental grinding, but much of it was done by the public. The center hosted grinding days during which people volunteered to use the grinding tools to process the various raw materials. Local Kumeyaay and Luiseño individuals, schoolchildren, college students, and other interested people ground their allotted materials on the replicated millingtstones for specified time periods. The primary result was a library of wear patterns associated with different tool raw materials and ground materials by grinding tool type for comparison with prehistoric specimens. The comments from the volunteer grinders also proved useful in understanding the use of the tools.

Replicative studies have a long history in California, the area discussed in this chapter.

DEFINITION OF THE AREA

The California archaeological culture area (Figure 7.1) does not exactly match the modern political boundaries of the state, although it includes most of California's territory. Portions of the northwest corner of the state were considered in Chapter 5 on the Northwest Coast area, and parts of northeastern California were covered in Chapter 6 on the Plateau area. The arid Mojave Desert and the areas east of the Sierra Nevada are part of the Great Basin presented in Chapter 8. Further, the California archaeological area extends down into Mexico to below Ensenada in Baja California, although this area and the adjacent parts of southern California could be considered with the Southwest (Chapter 9) because ceramics and rudimentary stone architecture, both southwestern traits, are found there. However, the area has sufficient Californian traits to legitimately be included in the California culture area.

Researchers have proposed often-contradictory time schemes for various regions of California, and,

because of the regional diversity, there have been few attempts to discuss chronological periods for the area as a whole. In their 1984 synthesis of California archaeology, Joseph L. and Kerry Kona Chartkoff (1984:15–16) discuss the area's archaeology in terms of three major periods: Paleoindian, Archaic, and Pacific. These terms are used in other areas and have essentially the same meaning in California as elsewhere. The Pacific period was defined to reflect the level of complexity attained by cultures in the Late Prehistoric and Historic periods: it was akin to that of the agricultural Pueblo or Woodland and Mississippian people elsewhere, but it was based on a hunting and gathering economy (Chartkoff and Chartkoff 1984:16). As we saw in Chapter 6, some archaeologists working along the Northwest Coast also recognized the Pacific period as being useful. This scheme, along with those for subregions in California, is presented in Table 7.1.

THE ENVIRONMENT

Both the state of California and the archaeological culture area are characterized by environmental diversity, with differing environments often being found in relatively close proximity. In the San Diego area, for instance, it is possible to start at the beach or San Diego Bay and drive east through the coastal plain, the chaparral-covered foothills that grade into oak forests in the mountains, and finally into very arid desert, all in less than 2 hours or 60 miles (100 km). Although diversity is the key, the environment can be broken down into three major regions: the coast, the Central valley, and the Sierra Nevada.

One of California's most striking features is its long coast, with its sandy beaches, rocky cliffs, bays, lagoons, and estuaries. Traveling inland from the coast, one finds either the mountains of the Coast Ranges or coastal plains of varying widths. The Coast Ranges parallel the coast from Point Conception north and are divided into the North Coast Ranges and the South Coast Ranges by San Francisco Bay. At Point Conception the Transverse Ranges reach the ocean. Their offshore extension is seen in the Northern Channel Islands (Santa Cruz, Santa Rosa, San Miguel, and Anacapa). South of the Transverse Ranges is the broad Los Angeles Basin, and the Peninsular Range. Sandy beaches are found primarily in the south, although cliffs occur all along the coast. Bays, estuaries, and lagoons provided salt marsh vegetation, while the coastal plain and the Coast Ranges had coastal sage scrub, chaparral, and oak woodlands, as well as some native grasslands. From Monterey north, coastal redwood forests are found. Shellfish and ocean fish,

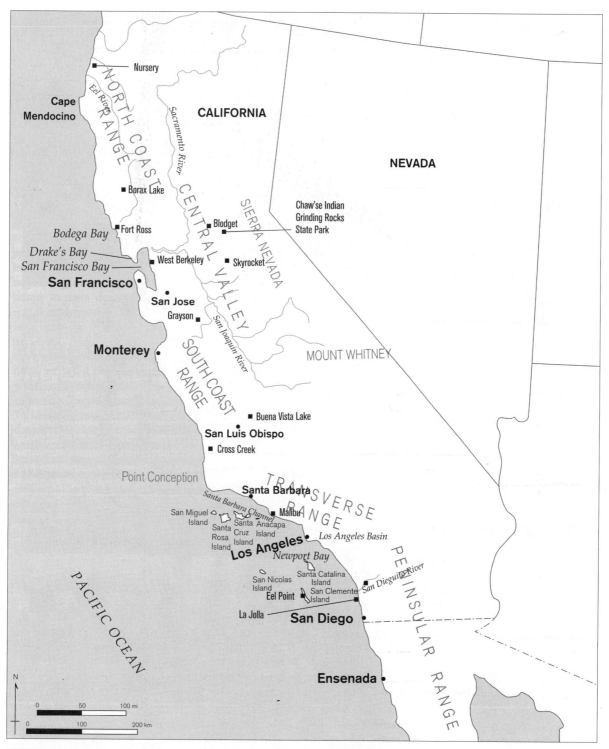

FIGURE 7.1 The California culture area, showing the location of sites mentioned in Chapter 7.

TABLE 7.1 Introduction to California Culture History

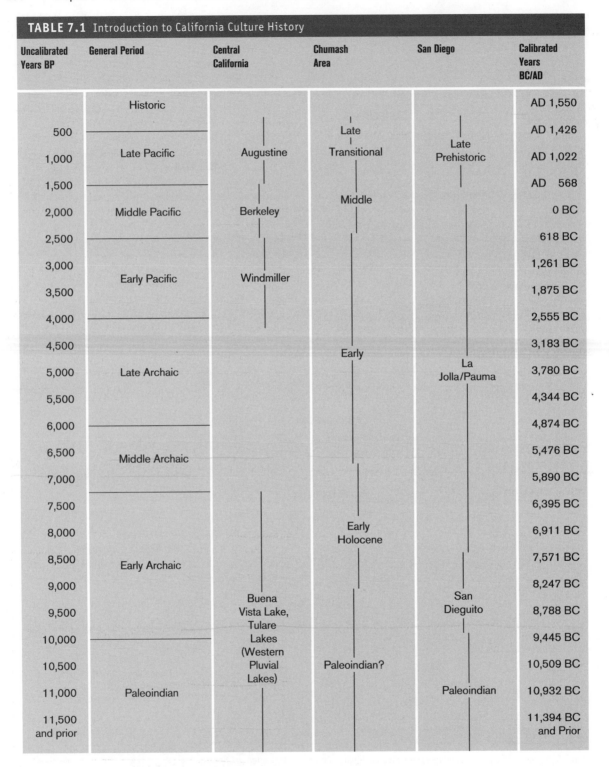

Uncalibrated Years BP	General Period	Central California	Chumash Area	San Diego	Calibrated Years BC/AD
	Historic				AD 1,550
500			Late		AD 1,426
1,000	Late Pacific	Augustine	Transitional	Late Prehistoric	AD 1,022
1,500					AD 568
2,000	Middle Pacific	Berkeley	Middle		0 BC
2,500					618 BC
3,000					1,261 BC
	Early Pacific	Windmiller			
3,500					1,875 BC
4,000					2,555 BC
4,500			Early		3,183 BC
5,000	Late Archaic			La Jolla/Pauma	3,780 BC
5,500					4,344 BC
6,000					4,874 BC
6,500	Middle Archaic				5,476 BC
7,000					5,890 BC
7,500					6,395 BC
8,000			Early Holocene		6,911 BC
8,500	Early Archaic				7,571 BC
9,000				San Dieguito	8,247 BC
9,500		Buena Vista Lake, Tulare Lakes (Western Pluvial Lakes)			8,788 BC
10,000					9,445 BC
10,500			Paleoindian?		10,509 BC
11,000	Paleoindian			Paleoindian	10,932 BC
11,500 and prior					11,394 BC and Prior

as well as sea mammals in some places, were important foods.

East of the Coast Ranges lies the long, broad, fertile Central valley. This relatively flat valley is a sediment-filled basin that runs 400 miles (645 km) north–south, and is as wide as 95 miles (155 km) in places. Major rivers drain the Central valley, the Sacramento on the north and the San Joaquin on the south. These rivers and their tributaries host major runs of anadromous fish. Vegetation in the Central valley includes marshes, grasslands, oak woodlands, and oak parkland where oaks are found on grassy hills.

The foothills of the Sierra Nevada ranges mark the eastern edge of the Central valley. The mountains rise relatively gently, but their eastern side is quite steep. This is because they are fault-block mountains. Mount Whitney, in the Sierra Nevada, is the highest point in the United States south of Alaska, at 14,497 feet (4419 m). Oak woodlands, pine forests, and areas of alpine meadow are all found in the Sierra Nevada, as are isolated groves of giant sequoias.

Climate and Climatic Change

California's climate, like its topography, is variable. The south is sunny much of the time, but fog is common along the coast and in the Central valley. Rainfall is heavier in the north than in the south, and periods of extended drought are not uncommon in southern California. Air temperatures along the coast are affected by the ocean, which serves to stabilize temperatures, lessening the extremes recorded inland.

Past climates in California have exerted important influences on the past inhabitants of the state, although the effects of some climatic events are the center of heated debate among archaeologists. The most important changes were associated with the end of the Pleistocene. As mentioned in Chapter 2, a warming trend was accompanied by a rise in sea level, which had the effect of drowning large areas of the coastal plain.

This rising sea level flooded river valleys on the mainland, in many areas creating lagoons that were very productive environments for early Archaic peoples. As sea level stabilized, the lagoons began to accumulate silt, which eventually choked them, leaving mudflats rather than open water. Where the rising sea met highlands, sea cliffs were cut. Old middens preserved in some coastal areas have strata that slant shoreward, stopping abruptly at an eroded cliff face. This indicates that in the past, shell mounds extended well out beyond the current cliff level. Thus considerable archaeological evidence has been lost to sea cliff erosion. Changes in the coastline

---

ANTHROPOLOGICAL THEMES   TOPIC 7.1

Thematic Research Questions in Chapter 7

As we pointed out in Chapter 2, several broad anthropological research questions can be addressed by North American archaeologists. The archaeology of the California is especially relevant to three of these themes as listed in Table 2.1, and we touch on other themes less directly. Table 7.2 helps you locate relevant sections of this chapter for each theme although as you become more familiar with the archaeology of the California, you likely will discover additional research questions related to them.

Table 7.2 Research Themes for California

Research Question	Particularly Relevant Sections
How have humans adapted to the diverse environments of North America and to climatic change over time?	Discussions in the sections on Foragers and on the Pacific Period, especially the subsection on Pacific Period Lifeways
How, when, and where did sociopolitically complex, internally differentiated cultural systems develop in North America?	Discussion of the Pacific Period and especially Box 7.1, "Issues and Debates: Chumash Complexity"
What ethnic identities can be identified and historically traced in North America's past?	Discussion in Box 7.1, "Issues and Debates: Chumash Complexity," and the chapter case study, "Cultures in Contact at Colony Ross"

must be taken into account, then, in reconstructing the lifeways of ancient coastal inhabitants.

EARLY CULTURES

In Chapter 3, we touched on early human presence in California. Although there have been claims for very early occupations such as at the Calico site, there is no currently accepted evidence for Pre-Clovis use of this culture area. On the other hand, as indicated in Chapter 3's case study "Paleocoastal Occupations of California's Northern Channel Islands," there is growing evidence of early paleocoastal occupations that date as early as Clovis. There also are fluted point sites in the North Coast Range and in the Central Valley. The **San Dieguito complex** of Southern California also represents early human occupation by 10,000 BP.

FORAGERS: THE ARCHAIC PATTERN

With the changes at the end of the Pleistocene (ca. 10,000 BP), people began to adapt to warmer and drier conditions and the loss of many of the resources that originally attracted people to the area. This is when the Archaic pattern developed. As in other areas of the North America, the California Archaic has been understood as a reaction to changing resources in which people broadened their food base, incorporating hard seeds that could not be processed without specialized grinding equipment. It is because these grinding implements are such a hallmark of the Archaic in California that the period in southern California is often referred to as the **Millingstone horizon** (Wallace 1955).

Coastal

Along the California coast from San Luis Obispo south into Baja California are found sites assigned to the Millingstone horizon, the Archaic expression along the southern California coast. The site of Cross Creek in San Luis Obispo County may indicate that this way of life dates back to 9900 BP, but the Archaic is generally thought to have started about 8500 BP or later. Since sea level rose after the disappearance of the continental glaciers at the end of the Pleistocene, many of the sites of the early Archaic peoples are underwater today or have been eroded away by wave action. Only the tantalizing remnants at Cross Creek and on the Channel Islands provide glimpses of what the earliest Archaic adaptation was like. Sites increase in number as time goes on, and a picture of Archaic development emerges.

The **La Jolla complex** (8500–2000 BP), known from sites in southern California and northern Baja California, is an example of the Millingstone horizon. The La Jolla complex, originally called the Shell Midden people by Malcolm J. Rogers, is marked by sites along the coast containing considerable amounts of shell, along with relatively simple flake and cobble tools, as well as **manos** and **metates**. Manos are handheld grinding stones, and metates are the bases on which manos were used to grind seeds or other material. Some sites have yielded flexed burials, and cemeteries have been found at some of the larger sites. Inland Archaic sites in the San Diego area have some characteristics in common with the La Jollan sites, but have a greater range of flaked stone tools, many not made from cobbles. They also lack shell. These sites, which have been given the name **Pauma complex** in the northern part of San Diego County, are not common, although in many cases inland Archaic occupations may go unnoticed because of mixing with later components.

On the Santa Barbara coast and the adjacent Channel Islands, various observers have defined a number of phases, but a simple scheme of Early, Middle, and Late periods commonly is used today. Chester King's (1990) chronological studies of beads provide a large part of the basis for these periods. The Early period is equivalent to the Archaic and part or all of the Early Pacific period. At the beginning of the Early period the archaeology is much like the La Jolla, but with **extended burials** with red ocher. In contrast to the La Jolla, some pithouses have been found in Early period sites. Later in the Early period people used mortars and pestles and had relatively fewer millingstones or metates. Projectile points were also more common on later in the Early period as well, and sites were closer to the ocean and had flexed burials.

Central California

In the San Francisco Bay area and in the Central valley, the earliest Archaic times are poorly represented in the archaeological record. This probably is because San Francisco Bay did not exist as a body of water at the end of the Pleistocene. Rising seas of the early Holocene began to flood the lowlands behind the Coast Ranges, forming an ever-growing bay fringed by productive marshlands. Many of the earliest sites in the Bay area may be underwater today. In the Central valley there has been very active deposition of sediments in the floodplains of the Sacramento and San Joaquin rivers, also probably burying most Archaic sites. Deposits at the Grayson site in Merced County include small mortars, pestles, millingstones, and simple shell beads and are thought to date to between 5250 BP and 4550 BP (Moratto 1984:191). Sites at Buena

Vista Lake (Ker-39 and Ker-60) also have some material that may be germane to this time. The lower levels of these two sites produced millingstones and manos, and extended burials were found at one of them. The Skyrocket site, excavated in the 1990s as data recovery associated with mining operations, is a stratified site on the eastern edge of the southern Central valley that provides a long record of human occupation in the area. Millingstones found there may date back to 9200 BP (Fagan 2003:86–88). At the very end of the Archaic and the beginning of the Pacific period the **Windmiller pattern**, which will be discussed further shortly, developed.

Northern Coast

On the northern California coast from San Francisco Bay to the Klamath River a Middle to Late Archaic occupation known as the **Borax Lake tradition** is found. The hallmark for this tradition is the Borax Lake point, a distinctive projectile point with a square stem (Figure 7.2). Little excavation has been conducted at Borax Lake tradition sites, and the original work at Borax Lake is the best known. Recent excavation at the Nursery site in Humboldt County documents the presence of the Borax Lake tradition on the coast (Humboldt State University 2004). This tradition is represented in the archaeological record by manos and metates, scrapers, scraper planes, knives, and bifaces of other kinds (Chartkoff and Chartkoff 1984:111–113). Mortars and pestles are found in the later part of the pattern, and a few polished stone items known as **charmstones** (Figure 7.3) have also been recovered from Borax Lake tradition sites (Bennyhoff and Fredrickson 1994:24).

Settlement Pattern

Archaic settlement patterns have been best delineated for southern California. Millingstone horizon sites are found along the coast and are usually situated on high ground such as bluffs and marine terraces (Erlandson 1994:258). The choice of high ground for sites may represent a real trend in occupation, or it may be that the sites on high ground are the only ones readily available to archaeologists. Sites at lower elevations may have been flooded, eroded by the sea, or buried under alluvial fill. People of the Millingstone horizon preferred to settle near the lagoons and estuaries that formed as the rising sea flooded river and stream mouths at the beginning of the Holocene, and many coastal lagoons are ringed with a large number of Millingstone horizon sites. The productivity of these lagoons would have been considerable first as open-water systems with lush salt marshes around the shores and

FIGURE 7.2 Borax Lake point.

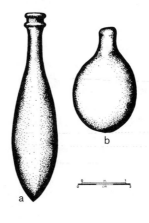

FIGURE 7.3 Borax Lake charmstones: (a) plummet-shaped and (b) bulb-shaped. (Old 7.5)

b

a

schools of fish and open-water shellfish (like scallops). These marshes would have attracted seasonal flights of birds migrating along the coast as well. Over time, the streams, whose mouths were flooded to form the lagoons, carried sediment from the uplands they drained and began to fill these bodies of water. As mudflats formed, these also became productive habitats, being colonized by clams that burrow into the soft mud.

Ultimately, though, many small bays and estuaries were closed off from the open ocean or were filled with silt and ceased to be useful as resource areas for humans. Later Archaic populations adjusted to this change by moving to the open coast or to permanent bays and wetlands like San Diego Bay. The larger coastal sites probably served as seasonal base camps, with inland sites being occupied at least part of the year. In the southern part of the California coast, Jon Erlandson (1994:258–259) sees a highly mobile existence for the early Archaic populations, with relatively small groups occupying the sites. In the Santa Barbara and San Luis Obispo areas, on the other hand, he believes people at this time were semisedentary, moving from large coastal sites to a variety of seasonal camps.

Subsistence

The Early Archaic people probably had a very diverse diet, gathering from a wide variety of environments. Along the coast, shellfish were very important, supplemented by seeds and land animals. Interestingly, the remains from early sites indicate that fish were not favored resources. The presence of millingstones, which begin to be found in sites dated to between 8000 BP and 9000 BP, is evidence of the importance of seeds. Seeds and shellfish complemented each other in the diets of coastal people, with shellfish being high in protein and low in calories, while seeds provided the carbohydrates and calories needed for good health (Erlandson 1991). In inland areas such as northwestern California, hunting of large game was important early, combined with collection of hard seeds.

In the Middle Archaic there is considerable evidence of a rise in importance of hunting throughout California, and on the Channel Islands there is an increase in fishing activity (Hildebrant and McGuire 2002). Acorns, which are so important to the later people of California, were probably first used in the early Archaic. Evidence from the Skyrocket site in the foothills of the Sierra Nevada suggests that acorns may have been a supplementary food as early as 8500 BP, but mortars and pestles used to process them in quantity are not common until between 6000 BP and 5000 BP (Erlandson 1994:262; Fagan 2003:209).

Population Density

Populations at the beginning of the Archaic appear to have been small: few sites have been found, and their size generally was small. Population grew throughout the Archaic, with the pace of growth increasing significantly with time. Erlandson (1994:258) notes that population increased considerably in the Early and Middle Archaic (9500–6000 BP)—perhaps as much as ten times. Late Archaic populations continued to grow.

COMPLEXITY: THE PACIFIC PERIOD

Nature of Complexity

The Pacific period marks the transition from the Archaic to more complex lifeways. As noted earlier, this California post-Archaic pattern is seen by many archaeologists as equivalent to post-Archaic developments elsewhere in North America. Developments during this period ultimately led to the populations of Native Americans encountered by the explorers and colonists. The post-Archaic people of California achieved complexity not by adopting agriculture but by adopting a few stable foods and focusing their economic activities on them (Chartkoff and Chartkoff 1984:147). These strategies led to higher population levels in some parts of California than were reached on the Northwest Coast—indeed, the highest population densities recorded in North America north of Mexico. The large populations were organized by settlement with hereditary leaders. Trade was important and extensive, and helped support the leaders. The appearance of luxury items, along with the development of notions of ownership of property, led to inequality, with some families and individuals having more access to resources than others. These changes were almost certainly a reaction to imbalances between growing populations and the available resources, and these imbalances, in turn, were often caused by changes in climatic conditions. The specific nature of the climatic changes is one of the hotly debated topics in California archaeology.

Coastal

In coastal southern and central California the beginning of the Pacific period is called the Middle period, based primarily on changes in bead and ornament styles. The patterns seen in the Middle period have their roots in the late Archaic, but sites from this time show a more focused economy. In the Santa Barbara region the emphasis was on hunting land animals and procuring marine mammals, while farther south acorns and other hard seeds were the focus. Shellfish remained important along the coast, and fishing increased. Sites are marked by the presence of mortars and pestles, as well as an increase in projectile points over earlier occupations (Warren 1968). Trade goods become more important than in earlier sites. Traded material includes shell, steatite, and obsidian (Chartkoff and Chartkoff 1984:165–166).

The Middle period was followed by the development of Late period cultures. In the Santa Barbara region this is marked by the occurrence of small arrowheads, the mortar and pestle, and a wealth of ground stone artifacts (Figure 7.4). There is an elaboration of artifacts of many types, and shell inlay was applied to bowls, pipes, and pestles (Figure 7.5). Engraving was used to enhance the appearance of stone items. There also is clear evidence of extensive use of marine resources, including fish and sea mammals.

In the Late period people made the *tomol*, or plank canoe, that was so important to the Chumash and Gabrilino, although there is a suggestion that boat manufacture may date back much further in the Channel Islands area (see Section D.4 on the Student CD).

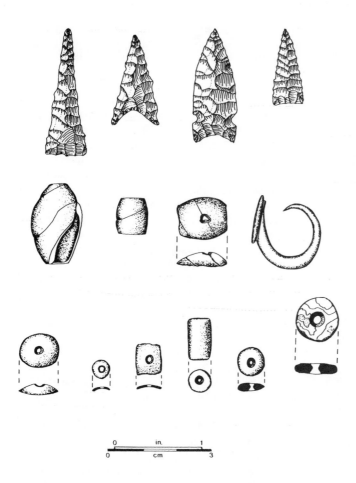

FIGURE 7.4 Santa Barbara Middle period artifacts: (top row) projectile points; (middle row) whole *Olivella* shell bead, *Olivella* barrel bead, split and punched *Olivella* bead, fishhook; (bottom row) various disk and tube beads.

The use of the plank canoe, which could be used in ocean waters, made the development of interdependent economic systems on the islands and the mainland possible. The nature of the rise and maintenance of complexity among the Chumash is currently a topic of debate, as discussed in Box 7.1.

There also is considerable evidence for the development of status differentiation or social ranking among the people of the Late period. As discussed in Box 7.1, much of the evidence comes from cemeteries and the differential distribution of rare items in cemeteries.

Farther south on the coast and in the adjacent foothills and mountains archaeologists have defined the **Cuyamaca** and **San Luis Rey complexes** for the Late period. These are seen as the ancestors of the modern Kumeyaay and the Luiseño, respectively. Sites of these complexes have brownware ceramics (Figure 7.6), as well as triangular and side-notched arrowheads. Mortars are common, as are metates and manos for processing hard seeds. Ceramics seem to have a longer history with the Cuyamaca complex, given the wider variety of forms, including not only **ollas** and bowls, but also

FIGURE 7.5 Carved and inlaid artifacts: (top) flanged stone pestles; (bottom) sandstone bowl with appliqué of beads in asphalt.

trays, pipes, rattles, pottery anvils (used in shaping the paddle-and-anvil pottery), and effigies of various kinds. People of both complexes cremated their dead, in contrast to the Archaic practice of flexed burial. Cremation and ceramics probably originated to the east and were adopted first by the Cuyamaca complex peoples and then by those of the San Luis Rey complex.

ISSUES AND DEBATES   BOX 7.1

Chumash Complexity

When the Spanish explorers and missionaries first encountered the people of the Santa Barbara Channel, they
found one of the most populous areas in North America. As
many as a thousand people lived in villages, each one
composed of groups of houses, the largest being reserved
for the head chief, or *wot*; there were sweathouses dug
partially into the ground, as well as an enclosed ceremonial area, a gaming area, storehouses, and a cemetery
(Grant 1978:510). The Chumash sailed the waters of the
channel in unique canoes made by splitting planks from
driftwood logs, shaping them, sewing them together, and
using natural asphalt caulking to seal the seams (Gamble
2002). The people used these *tomols* for fishing, for hunting sea mammals, and for traveling to the Channel Islands.
The islands were linked to the mainland communities
through intricate webs of trade and marriage relationships. Villages on Santa Cruz Island specialized in the
manufacture of beads from California purple olive shell
(*Olivella biplicata*). Villages on the island controlled the
quarries where chert was mined to produce thin bladelets
used in drilling the beads, as well as the production of
those drills (Arnold 1992). Shell beads served as a kind of
money throughout southern and central California (Grant
1978:516).

The Chumash also made trade items, including stone
bowls and tubular pipes. They excelled in basketry, producing water bottles, trays, storage baskets, and other
forms. Stone mortars and pestles were finely made, and
prestige items such as raptor talon pendants, bone rings
and tubes, and shell beads of many kinds were produced
for the upper crust of Chumash society.

The ethnographic record provides evidence of both
elite families and commoners, and the archaeological
record reinforces this social ranking. Recent analysis of
patterning within cemeteries indicates both differential
distributions of prestige items among burials and spatial
segregation of high-status burials within the cemeteries.
These findings point to differences in access to status
items, and, therefore, differences in social class. The discovery that very young individuals were buried with elaborate grave goods indicates that status was inherited, since
the children had not lived long enough to have distinguished themselves (Gamble et al. 2001).

Archaeologists working in the Chumash area liken
the social organization of the area to that of a simple
chiefdom, and there is evidence that some *wots*, or chiefs,
presided over regions containing multiple villages. Some
villages had subchiefs as well. The *wot* inherited his or her

position and was responsible for administering resource
areas controlled by the village, for accumulating and dis-
tributing surplus food and other material, for organizing
ceremonies and feasts, and for warfare. The chiefs were
drawn from a larger elite or noble class in Chumash society
(Erlandson and Rick 2002).

Not only were resource areas controlled by the *wots*,
but members of the noble class also owned the *tomols*.
Since tomols represented a substantial investment in time
and materials, only wealthy members of the upper class
could afford to commission their construction. Arnold
(1992:71) has estimated that the construction of a *tomol*
required between 180 and 540 person-days. Members of
the Brotherhood of the *Tomol* owned and manufactured
these plank canoes, and membership in the group crosscut
localized villages (Gamble 2002:312).

It is clear, then, that the Chumash were complex
hunter-gatherers. They epitomize trends we see in
California for hereditary leadership, ownership of resources,
development of social classes, and large, semisedentary
to sedentary populations. Just when this complex organization developed and why are subjects of considerable
debate among archaeologists.

Chester King (1990), in a seminal study of beads and
other materials associated with burials, developed a sequence of bead types that is widely used in southern
California. He also suggested that the Chumash developed
steadily for over 7000 years, with the hallmarks of complexity developing by the end of the Early period, around
2550 BP. Arnold and O'Shea (1993) criticized King's work
for the assumption that the meaning of artifacts, particularly shell ornaments, could be projected 7000 years
into the past. Arnold (1992) instead believes that the
development of chiefdoms was a relatively late phenomenon, occurring between 800 BP and 650 BP. She sees
this development as a result of individuals exploiting economic hard times brought on by the elevated sea surface
temperatures that reduced the productivity of the ocean
in the Santa Barbara Channel. Individuals would have
stepped in to organize labor in the production of shell
beads, as well as the quarrying and manufacture of the chert
drills necessary to manufacture the beads. The beads,
made almost exclusively on the islands, could have been
traded to the mainland for food. On the mainland they
became currency that was intricately woven into the complex exchange relationships developing there (King 1976).

Two important studies by Lynn Gamble (Gamble et al.
2001, 2002) support King's position, to a degree. Gamble

(2002) looked at the development of the *tomol* and its antiquity, concluding that the plank canoe technology was at least 1300 years old in the Santa Barbara Channel area. To the extent that canoes were owned, this dating bolsters King's position of early development of social hierarchies. In another study with Phillip Walker and Glenn Russell (Gamble et al. 2001), patterns at the historic and prehistoric cemeteries at Malibu were interpreted as suggesting the presence of ascribed status in the Middle period, again supporting King's conclusions.

Although agreeing with Arnold on the timing of changes, Raab and Larson (1997) argue that the period of higher sea surface temperatures noted by Arnold was not a time of reduced marine productivity, but rather a relatively bountiful time. They find evidence for extended and severe droughts during this period, however. These authors argue that the droughts, associated with the Medieval climatic anomaly, caused populations to concentrate at areas with reliable water. The concentration of population led to the development of fixed territories, increases in intergroup conflict, and ultimately to the development of the leadership hierarchy, in their view.

Using oxygen isotope measurements with fine resolution, combined with archaeological data, Kennett and Kennett (2000) reexamined the relationship between climate and culture change in the Northern Channel Islands. Their data indicate change beginning at 1650 BP and accelerating after 650 BP. They agree with Raab and Larson that marine productivity at this time was high and that drought was a problem. They also note that fluctuations in land resources would have been quite unpredictable.

Finally, in a recent treatment of the problem, Erlandson and Rick (2002) note the difficulty in identifying specific indicators of a chiefdom level of complexity in the archaeological record. Instead of looking for hallmarks of complexity, they focused on the development of specific traits known in historical Chumash society. These traits include elaboration of material culture, development of village layout, and specific architectural forms and burial practices. They conclude that Chumash development was both gradual and punctuated by sudden bursts of change. They note a key transition at about 3450 BP and another between 1450 BP and 550 BP. They also highlight the variability within the Chumash adaptation.

The timing and explanation of the development of complexity among the Chumash is important not only for California studies, but also for the general understanding of complex hunter-gatherers. Thus, Chumash complexity will continue to be a topic of considerable debate contributing to the larger anthropological dialog for some time.

FIGURE 7.6 Southern California ceramic vessels.

Central California

The Windmiller pattern in the Central valley, especially the Sacramento Delta area, is recognized as early as 5000–6000 BP and lasts until 2500 BP (Arnold and Walsh 2010:94–96). It also marks the earliest well-known occupation of the area. The Windmiller pattern is known mostly from excavation of cemeteries on clay knolls that rise above the floodplain of the delta. Windmiller burial patterns were quite elaborate, with graves including red ocher. Burial goods or offerings were present with most burials, and they include mortars, shell beads and ornaments, and ground charmstones (Figure 7.7). Most burials are extended and were placed

FIGURE 7.7 Windmiller pattern artifacts: (a–f) projectile points, (g) millingstone, (h) mano, (i) mortar, (j) pestle, (k) ground stone pipe bowl, (l) charmstone, (m–s) shell ornaments, and (t–x) bone implements.

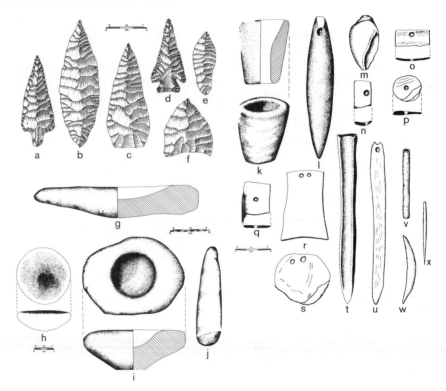

in the grave on their backs, although occasional flexed burials and even cremations are found. Windmiller sites include large numbers of baked **clay cooking balls**, which are thought to have substituted for rock in stone boiling, since the delta lacked ready supplies of rock for this purpose. Bone remains indicate that people hunted deer, elk, pronghorn, rabbit, and water birds, and the large number of projectile points from Windmiller sites underscores the importance of this hunting. Salmon and other fish were taken with fish spears or hooks. Ornaments are well developed, and throughout the Central valley periods are defined in part on the basis of differences in shell and stone beads, pendants, and jewelry of other types. One interesting use of shell was an appliqué effect created by affixing shell beads to objects with **asphaltum**. Obsidian, shell, quartz crystals, alabaster, asphaltum, and other exotic materials indicate that the people who occupied the Windmiller sites participated in well-developed trade networks (Moratto 1984:201–207).

Berkeley pattern sites, which follow Windmiller, have more mortars and pestles; bone artifacts are more common and are found in greater variety; and there are large projectile points that exhibit diagonal flaking, as well as specific forms of beads and ornaments. Manos and metates, on the other hand, are rare. Burials are flexed and are generally accompanied by fewer artifacts. The Berkeley pattern (Figure 7.8)

was defined in the San Francisco Bay area at the West Berkeley site, and it appeared in that area about 4000 BP. It spread into the Delta region by about 2500 BP (Moratto 1984:209–211, 278). A decrease in projectile points relative to millingstones suggests that the collecting and processing of plants was becoming more important in the economy (Bennyhoff and Fredrickson 1994:23).

Recent work on the shell mounds of the area indicate an complex history with the sites starting out as villages in which the normal discard of shell, bone, rock, and ash led to the creation of mounding, which was accelerated by the importation of earth and rock in early Berkeley times (4000–2500 BP) to keep the villages above the rising bay waters. That this course was taken is explained by some archaeologists as keeping ties with the ancestors who were buried in the basal levels of the village and with the ceremonial spaces that had been defined. Mounds, which would have been visible on the landscape, could also have served to reinforce claims to territories. The later years of the Berkeley pattern saw a proliferation of mounds, with mound clusters of four to six being anchored by early mounds nearer the water. This is a sign of population growth (Arnold and Walsh 2010:69–73; Lightfoot 1997).

The final pattern in the Delta area, the **Augustine pattern**, is characterized by the presence of well-shaped

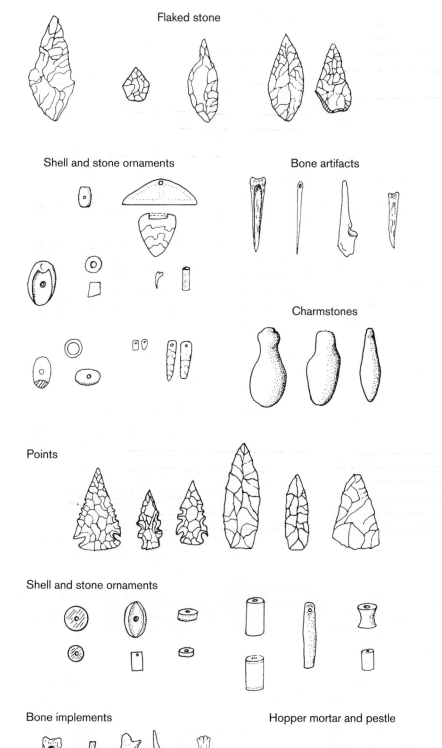

Flaked stone

Shell and stone ornaments

Bone artifacts

Charmstones

FIGURE 7.8 Berkeley pattern artifacts from the Napa District; scales variable.

Points

Shell and stone ornaments

Bone implements

Hopper mortar and pestle

FIGURE 7.9 Augustine pattern artifacts from the Napa District; scales variable.

mortars and pestles, small projectile points, numerous shell artifacts, worked bone (including awls for coiled basket making), charmstones, and polished stone pipes (Figure 7.9). Fishing equipment is more abundant than in earlier contexts, but it is not common. New to the fishing gear is the harpoon. Burial practices change in the Augustine pattern. Flexed burials occur, but cremation is also found. Grave pits as well as grave artifacts were often burned. Fishing increased during Augustine times, but acorns were still the staple (Bennyhoff and Fredrikson 1994:23). The Blodget site, an important Augustine pattern and Historic period Miwok site, has produced evidence of a well-developed pottery-making industry (Moratto 1984:213).

Shell mounds were generally not occupied by people carrying the Augustine pattern, but they were used for ritual and burial purposes. It appears that bay resources dwindled and populations turned inland, expecially to the exploitation of acorns, but the mounds were still important in their ritual systems (Arnold and Walsh 2010:74–75; Lightfoot and Lubby 2002).

North Coast

On the North Coast there are similarities to the Delta sequence. In the Eel River region, for instance, materials known as the **Shasta aspect** of the Augustine pattern are found. Artifacts from this time include Gunther barbed points, hopper mortars, manos and metates, bifaces of chert, charmstones, and spire-lopped *Olivella* beads. Semisedentary winter villages were located in lowland settings, and camps occupied by portions of the village population in other seasons have been found in the uplands (Fredrickson 1984).

PACIFIC PERIOD LIFEWAYS

Settlement Pattern

A variety of site types characterizing the Pacific period are found in the archaeological record. These include permanent villages, seasonal camps, and specialized resource extraction sites (quarries for acquiring materials for stone tools, weirs in rivers to help with catching fish, etc.), and rock art sites. Trading sites also developed that facilitated the exchange of goods and were important parts of the networks that connected various populations in prehistoric California. Specialized sites replaced the more generalized camp sites of the Archaic period. In some areas, such as the Santa Barbara Channel and the Central valley, populations became sedentary, occupying the same spot for generations, while elsewhere people became semisedentary, splitting their time between permanent village sites and seasonal camps of various kinds. The increase in the permanence of villages led to the formation of defined cemeteries in many areas (Chartkoff and Chartkoff 1984:205–218). Many sites of this period also are marked by the presence of **bedrock milling features** (see Exhibit 7.1).

Subsistence and Social Organization

The key to the economies of the Pacific period was the intensified pursuit of specific resources: what has been called a focal economy. Acorns were the staple plant food almost everywhere in California, but other important foods included hard seeds, especially of large-seeded grasses, anadromous fish, and marine resources such as fish and sea mammals. Focusing on these resources allowed populations to grow, but whether and

---

CLUES TO THE PAST   EXHIBIT 7.1

Bedrock Milling Features

If you ever hike in California's mountains you will be likely to turn a corner and come upon a boulder covered with holes. These are bedrock milling features, which Indians used for grinding seeds or other material. Bedrock milling features come in several different forms, ranging from conical holes, called mortars, to oval basins. Mortars are associated with the processing of large seeds such as hulled acorns, which can be pulverized into flour by pounding

with a cylindrical pestle. The basins are essentially metates worn into bedrock and would have been used with a mano to grind smaller hard seeds (Figure 7.10).

Bedrock milling features are found in many parts of North America where suitably hard rock crops out at the surface. They are particularly common in California and adjoining states, as well as in the Southwest. West Texas has a number of recorded bedrock milling sites as well.

Ethnographically, they are primarily known from California, Oregon, and the Southwest.

Mortars were used in the processing of acorns to make them edible, and ethnographic descriptions for Sierra Nevada groups identify shallow mortars as "starter mortars" in which initial pounding was done, with deeper mortars used to finish the processing (McCarthy et al. 1985). Following the grinding, the flour had to be treated to remove the bitter-tasting tannic acid (the same chemical used to tan leather). This was usually done by placing the meal in a shallow basket set over a bed of sand. Water was poured through the meal to dissolve the acid and carry it away. The flour was deemed ready when it no longer tasted bitter.

The acorn meal could be cooked as a gruel, left to set up as a gelatinous cake (like grits left to cool in the pan), made into a bread, or added to stews as a thickener. Because the acorn stored so well, it was a staple food, and the mortar was important in its efficient use. The earliest mortars were shallow depressions in rocks. These depressions were not deep enough to contain the acorns during pulverization, so basketry hoppers (conical baskets without bottoms) were glued to the mortars edges to keep the acorns under control. Archaeological evidence for this practice has been found in the form of mastic (usually asphaltum) adhering to shallow mortars.

Bedrock mortars are generally found where suitable bedrock occurs in areas that have oak trees. They are often near water. In California they are concentrated in the Sierra Nevada but are also common in northeastern California, in the Monterey area, and in the mountains and foothills of southern California. Some bedrock milling is even reported from the Channel Islands (Meighan 2000:63). Granite is the most common bedrock used for milling, but mortars, basins, and slicks are found on just about any type of hard rock outcrop including schist, limestone, volcanic rock, and hard sandstone. The largest concentration of bedrock mortars in North America is preserved in the Sierra Nevada northeast of Stockton in Chaw'se Indian Grinding Rock State Historic Park. There, in an area of grasslands and oak forest, are found 1185 bedrock mortars on marbleized limestone. Wherever these bedrock milling features occur, they can tell archaeologists important things about the lifestyles of the past.

FIGURE 7.10 Bedrock milling features (mortars and grinding basins) on a granite boulder near Lakeside, San Diego County, California.

FIGURE 7.11 Large basketry granary.

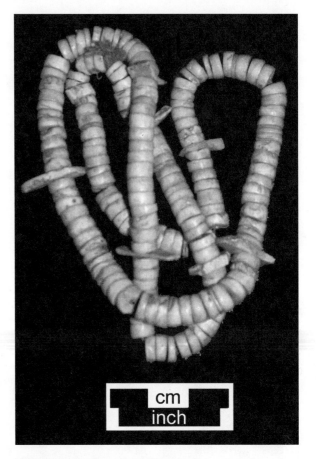

FIGURE 7.12 Late period shell beads.

to what extent most of these foods were used depended on the people's ability to store them.

Acorns are abundant when they ripen, and because of the oils they contain, they store very well. A prominent feature of most villages in California in the Pacific period would have been acorn granaries, structures designed for storing large quantities of nuts. These were often large, basketlike constructions coiled out of willow or other brush and set on posts (Figure 7.11). They were furnished with lids, and each granary would hold many bushels of acorns. In the desert areas of the South Coast, where mesquite and screwbean took the place of acorns, such granaries were used to store these staples as well. In the far south of the state, large ceramic vessels were also made to store seeds. On rivers and streams in which they were available, anadromous fish were dried and stored just as on the Plateau (Chapter 6) and Northwest Coast (Chapter 5).

The increase in population led to the development of hereditary leadership. Such systems most likely evolved as individuals demonstrated their abilities to lead and to acquire surpluses, as well as to be successful at trading with other groups for goods not available in the home territories. Before long, however, talented leaders developed systems under which they could pass their positions of primacy on to family members. Unsurprisingly, the families that controlled the leadership also had greater access to material goods. Luxury goods such as shell beads (Figure 7.12) became symbols of wealth, and these served as money in the Santa Barbara Channel and in the San Francisco Bay area and Central valley. On Santa Cruz Island, the production of shell beads, along with the control of the chert needed to make the drills used in their manufacture, formed the basis for a complex chiefdom, as discussed in Box 7.1.

Trade became critically important during this period. Large networks developed to move shell beads, obsidian for toolmaking, asphaltum, and steatite, as well as food items. These networks served to bolster the leadership hierarchies, and they provided critical raw materials; but they also served as a hedge against hard times, as luxury goods could be traded for food when local harvests were sparse.

The leadership structure and the trade networks may also have served to control violence, to a degree. Early in the Pacific period, roughly between 1950 BP and 1050 BP, many, though not all, of the cemeteries investigated contain individuals who bear signs of violence, including broken bones and arrowheads embedded in the bone. Evidence of violence has been recovered particularly from the San Francisco Bay area and from the Santa Barbara region (Arnold and Walsh 2010:37, 72). Resource shortages, probably caused by droughts, may have led to widespread fighting among groups over productive areas. Later in the Pacific period, there are fewer signs of trauma in burials (Fagan 2003:32–33).

Population Density

Populations grew dramatically during the Pacific period. Not only are more sites of this period found, but many of the sites are very large. Villages in the

Santa Barbara Channel area, as well as those in the San Francisco Bay area, which produced massive shell mounds on the shore, and in the Central valley, grew to considerable size, with accessory sites used seasonally and for special resource procurement.

The linguistic diversity of California has long fascinated archaeologists, and many attempts have been made to tie archaeological complexes to specific linguistic groups. (Figure 7.13). Two language stocks, the Penutian and the Hokan, dominated the state, but a number of other language stocks were represented as well. Penutian, related to languages on the Plaeau, was found throughout much of the central part of the area, both in the Central valley

and along the central California coast. The Miwok, Yokut, Wintun, Coastanoan, and Maidu all spoke Penutian languages. The Hokan stock included groups scattered around the margin of the Penutians, such as the Kumeyaay of southern California, the Shasta, Yana, Yahi, and Pomo of northern California, and the Esselen and Salinan of the central California coast. This distribution has led to the notion that Hokan was earlier in California than Penutian and was displaced by the latter. The Yukian language was made up of two languages, Yuki and Wappo, which were found north of San Francisco Bay and form a language isolate, showing relations to no other languages. The Wailaki and Kato in northwestern

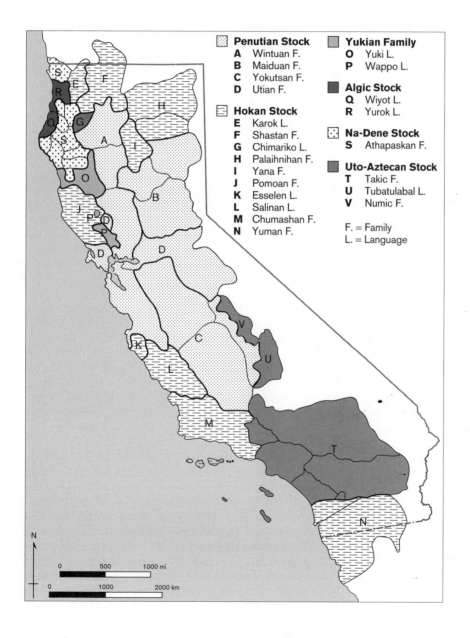

FIGURE 7.13 Language stocks and language families of the California area.

California represented the Athapascan family of the Na-Dene stock, related to languages in Canada and in the Southwest. Finally, the Luiseño, Cahuilla, Tongva, and Cupeño of southern California were representatives of the Uto-Aztecan family, which has linguistic relatives in the Great Basin (Numic, see Chapter 8) and in the Southwest (see Chapter 10).

The various linguistic reconstructions for the area are too complex to discuss in detail here, but an example from recent work illustrates the point. Looking at the presence of loan words that appear to be Uto-Aztecan in origin among inhabitants of the central California coast, DNA data that suggest affiliation of skeletal material from archaeological sites in the San Joaquin valley with Uto-Aztecan speakers, and distribution of physical types, Sutton (2009) offers a new interpretation of the origins of the Takic speakers of Southern California. He argues that the ancestors of the Tongva and related groups occupied the southern San Joaquin valley and were displaced by the Penutian movement into the valley. They moved into the Los Angeles basin to become the Tongva. He further argues that the language spread south and east to people who biologically were Yuman and differentiated into Luiseño, Cahuilla, and Cupeño relatively recently.

PREHISTORIC ARCHAEOLOGY IN CALIFORNIA TODAY

We have already discussed NAGPRA and how it permeates the practice of American archaeology today. California archaeologists had a history of resolving burial issues with Native Americans before NAGPRA became law, however, and California Indians are very active in the repatriation process. For example, the **California Native American Burial Act**, passed in 1982, requires involvement of the Native American community in determining the fate of human remains discovered in the state by archaeologists or by anyone else.

Several California reservations have responded to the pace of development and to the demands of NAGPRA by hiring archaeologists or, as in the case of the Pechanga Band in southern California, establishing a cultural resource department. The Barona Reservation led the way in the establishment of the Kumeyaay Cultural and Repatriation Committee (see Student CD, Section F.3).

EUROPEAN CONTACT AND COLONIZATION

Despite earlier exploration of Baja California and present-day Arizona by the Spanish, the exploration period in California really starts with the voyage of Portuguese-born João Rodrigues Cabrilho (known often as Juan Cabrillo). In 1542 Cabrilho led the first European expedition to see San Diego Bay, sailed through the Channel Islands, and reached at least as far north as Cape Mendocino (Chartkoff and Chartkoff 1984:252–253). Succumbing to injuries sustained in a skirmish with the Indians on San Miguel Island, Cabrilho died and was buried on the island. His explorations and those to follow brought knowledge of California to European attention, and left a few trade goods among the Native Americans encountered, but had little effect that can be seen in the archaeological record.

British privateer Sir Frances Drake, who sailed the California coast as part of his circumnavigation of the globe in 1579, stopped in a convenient bay to repair his ships. This bay was probably Drake's Bay, north of San Francisco. A brass plaque found in the area in 1934 bore an inscription claiming the land for Britain. Drake's records mention such a plaque, but the 1934 find has been demonstrated to be a hoax. European goods have been recovered from archaeological middens in the Drake's Bay area, and they may be items obtained by the local Miwok during Drake's stay. Other European and Asian artifacts from Marin County middens are probably from wrecks of the Spanish galleons in the late sixteenth century.

As in the Plateau, contact with Europeans not only brought exotic goods like glass beads, china, and iron, but also diseases. Indeed, epidemic diseases from Europe for which the Indians had no natural immunity spread well ahead of the European explorers, so that smallpox and other illnesses probably reduced the population of California substantially prior to the first encounter of many Native Americans with the explorers and missionaries. One estimate is that disease had reduced California's Native American population by two-thirds prior to the arrival of the Spanish missionaries. Since this loss of population must have had a substantial effect on the social organization and the subsistence activities of the Indians, the cultures described by the explorers may not closely resemble those that existed only a century before their coming.

Colonization began in California in 1769, when a land expedition from Baja California reached San Diego and established a fort, or presidio, and a mission. The goal of Spanish settlement was to protect Spain's interest in the Crown's claim to the land, given both Russian and English forays into the area. In addition, the Catholic Church sent missionaries to convert the Indians to Christianity and to get them settled at the missions. Twenty-one missions were established stretching north to just south of San Francisco, and these were protected by four presidios (Figure 7.14). We use the Spanish mission archaeology of California as an example in Chapter 13 as well. In addition to the Spanish, Russia claimed land in California, establishing a colony at Fort Ross, north of San Francisco, in 1812. The archaeology of this colony is discussed in this chapter's case study by Lightfoot et al. ("Cultures in Contact at Colony Ross").

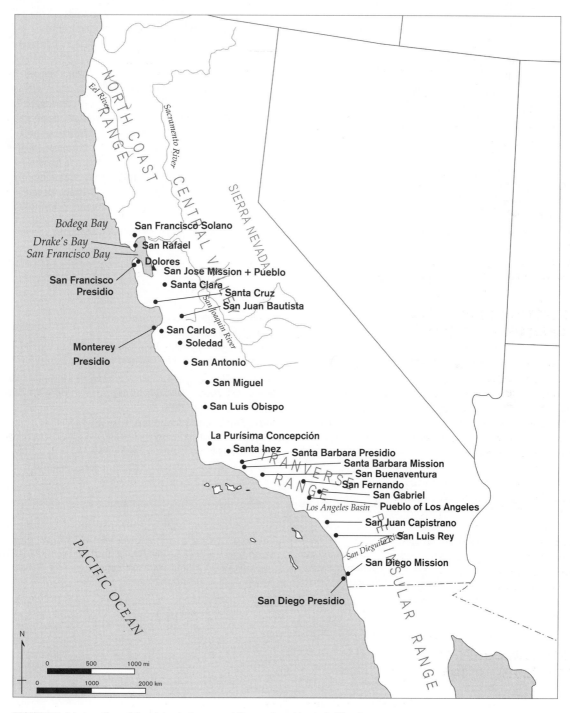

FIGURE 7.14 Location of Spanish missions, presidios, and pueblos in California.

CHAPTER SUMMARY

Like the environment of the state, the archaeology of the California archaeological area is diverse. The following points summarize the prehistory of the area as presented in this chapter:

- As in other areas, the Archaic in California represents an adaptation to diverse resources. In southern California the Archaic is often collectively called the Millingstone horizon, as exemplified by the La Jolla complex (8500–2000 BP) in the San Diego area. In the Santa Barbara region the Archaic is encompassed in the Early period. In central California, materials from Buena Vista Lake and the Skyrocket site represent the Archaic. The Borax Lake tradition, with distinctive Borax Lake points, along with millingstones, is an Archaic expression in northern California.

- The Pacific period was defined to recognize the complexity of the later pre-Columbian peoples of California—a level of complexity normally associated with the production of crops rather than with hunter-gatherers. Regardless of area in California, the Pacific period is marked by population growth, the establishment of permanent settlements, extensive trade, social ranking, and ownership of productive resources. The Chumash culture epitomizes this in the Santa Barbara area. The Windmiller, Berkeley, and Augustine patterns, and related manifestations, represent this period in the San Francisco Bay area.

- The exploration of California by Europeans began in 1542, and contact brought both trade goods and disease to the people of this culture area. Colonization by both the Spanish and the Russians began in the late eighteenth and early nineteenth centuries.

SUGGESTIONS FOR FURTHER READING

For a summary of California archaeology written primarily for the nonarchaeologist:

Chartkoff, Joseph L., and Kerry Kona Chartkoff
  1984 *The Archaeology of California.* Stanford University Press, Stanford, California.

For the most recent summary treatment of California archaeology:

Fagan, Brian
  2003 *Before California: An Archaeologist Looks at Our Earliest Inhabitants.* Rowman & Littlefield, Lanham, Maryland.

For the classic text on California archaeology:

Moratto, Michael J.
  1984 *California Archaeology.* Academic Press, Orlando, FL. Reprinted in 2004 by Coyote Press, Salinas, California.

For a collection designed to update the status of California archaeology in the 20 years following the classic Chartkoff and Chartkoff (1984) and Moratto (1984) works:

Jones, Terry L., and Kathryn A. Klar (editor)
  2007 *California Prehistory: Colonization, Culture, and Complexity.* Alta Mira, Lanham, Maryland.

OTHER RESOURCES

The Student CD, Sections H and I, supplies web links, additional discussion questions, and other study aids. The Student CD also contains additional resources. Early coastal occupations in California are discussed in "Eel Point and the Early Settlement of Coastal California: A Case Study in Contemporary Archaeological Research" (Section D.4). Section F.3, "A Local Reaction to NAGPRA: The Kumeyaay Cultural and Repatriation Committee," is particularly relevant to this chapter as well.

CASE STUDY

When thinking about the European colonization of California, it is easy to forget that Russia as well as Spain was a colonial power along this part of the Pacific Coast. Yet Russians competed for trade well south of Alaska, establishing a colony, called Colony Ross, north of what today is San Francisco. Here the Russian-American Company rather than the Spanish had considerable effect on Native people, as detailed in this case study about the Fort Ross Archaeological Project. The fort community was multiethnic, including Alaskan Natives, Coast Miwok and Kashaya Pomo Indians, and Russians. This case study describes a collaborative program between the Fort Ross State Historic Park, the Kashaya Pomo Tribe, California State Parks, and the University of California at Berkeley that focuses on the impact of Russian colonialism on the Native peoples of this area. Because of their collaboration with Kashaya Pomo elders, the archaeologists were able to develop low-impact strategies for gathering data primarily by using geophysical testing as well as traditional excavation. They also are major contributors to changes in the interpretive program at Fort Ross through their work on a Kashaya Pomo interpretive trail and a digital website that will make the native story at Colony Ross more widely accessible. As you read this case study, reflect on the example it provides of how archaeologists now try to incorporate diverse stakeholders in their work. How does this context change the story that gets told?

CULTURES IN CONTACT AT COLONY ROSS

Kent G. Lightfoot, Sara Gonzalez, Darren Modzelewski, Lee Panich, Otis Parrish, and Tsim Schneider

For thousands of years before the coming of Europeans, Kashaya Pomo and Coast Miwok peoples inhabited the coastal lands north of San Francisco Bay. Like many other California Indians, they were hunter-gatherers who harvested wild plants and animals from the sea and land for food, medicine, clothing, housing material, and ceremonial regalia. Villages nestled along protected coastal embayments and ridge tops of the Northern Coast Ranges mountains contained tule-thatched or redwood bark houses, ceremonial structures (round houses), sweat houses, dance enclosures, and extramural cooking and work areas. Large villages served as the political centers for broader communities of dispersed family groups who would come together for periodic dances, ceremonies, initiation rites, and feasts.

With the founding of Colony Ross in 1812 by the Russian-American Company (RAC), a mercantile enterprise licensed by the tsar of Russia, life would change forever for the Kashaya Pomo and the Coast Miwok. The Russian merchants placed the primary administrative center of the colony, which they called the Ross settlement, in the heart of Kashaya Pomo territory, and they chose Bodega Harbor in Coast Miwok country to be the principal port facility (Port Rumiantsev) (Figure 7.15). The Russian-American Company came to California to profit from the exploitation of the region's natural bounty. The mercantile

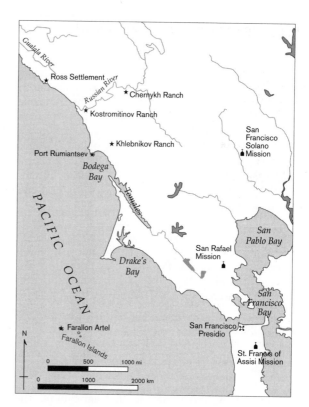

FIGURE 7.15 The location of Colony Ross showing Russian settlements and ranches.

enterprise harvested sea mammals, primarily sea otters and fur seals, to fuel the lucrative maritime fur trade that supplied sea mammal pelts to China, Europe, and the United States, primarily for use as robes, fur trim, and other clothing accessories. The Russian merchants attempted to grow wheat, barley, and other crops, and to raise livestock at Colony Ross to feed other RAC colonies in the North Pacific (Aleutian Islands, Kodiak Island, Prince William Sound, etc.), which experienced periodic food shortages. The Ross settlement also served as a manufacturing center for the production of goods (timber, bricks, metal utensils, and tools) that were shipped to the other North Pacific colonies and also traded to the Franciscan missionaries in **Alta California** for foodstuffs grown in the extensive mission complexes.

FORT ROSS ARCHAEOLOGICAL PROJECT

Today the historic Ross settlement and its nearby environs comprise the Fort Ross State Historic Park. The Fort Ross Archaeological Project is examining the culture history of the Kashaya Pomo people and the long-term implications of their encounters with the first mercantile colony in California. Members of the collaborative research team include archaeologists and rangers from California State Parks, faculty and students from the University of California at Berkeley, and elders and tribal scholars from the Kashaya Pomo Tribe. The collaborative team is investigating how the Kashaya Pomo negotiated the mercantile colonial program introduced by the Russian-American Company that exposed local hunter-gatherers to a pluralistic, international workforce and to a market economy.

Company managers recruited eastern Europeans, Native Siberians, Creoles (people of mixed Russian and native ancestry), and Native Alaskans—primarily from Kodiak Island and Prince William Sound—to live and work at Colony Ross. The Native Alaskans brought their sophisticated maritime technology (*baidarkas*, or skin kayaks, carved harpoon points, compound fish hooks, etc.) to Colony Ross to harvest commercially sea otters and fur seals by the thousands, and to hunt other sea mammals, seabirds, and fish for food. The managers also recruited nearby Kashaya Pomo and Coast Miwok Indians to work as seasonal laborers in shipbuilding, brick making, and agriculture. The Indians were hired for specific tasks (e.g., harvesting wheat, tending livestock), with compensation negotiated on a case-by-case basis; the merchants paid the Native people "in kind" for their services, usually with food, tobacco, beads, and clothing.

RESEARCH QUESTIONS

The historical circumstances surrounding Colony Ross help to shape the questions asked by the Fort Ross Archaeological Project. Our current focus is to understand better the cultural practices and social interactions of the Kashaya Pomo and Coast Miwok people who lived and worked in a mercantile social setting and to compare their experiences to other Native Californians who were incorporated into European (as well as Mexican and American) colonial institutions of other kinds (e.g., missions, presidios, pueblos, ranchos). Some aspects of the history of the Russian colony are well known because RAC employees and other European visitors kept detailed records and personal journals. From these historical documents, archaeologists are able to learn important details about how life at Colony Ross was organized. Yet historical documents often only give one side of the story, leaving out others. In the case of Colony Ross, most documents describe the colonial situation from a European point of view. Because of our interest in the Kashaya Pomo and Coast Miwok who lived and worked at Colony Ross, we used careful and critical readings of these documents, alongside inferences drawn from the archaeological record of the colony, to generate conclusions about how Colony Ross differed from other colonial endeavors in California. Documents and archaeology are also employed to examine how Native American groups negotiated the constraints that the Russian colony imposed on their traditional lifeways.

One of the interesting things we learned from the history of Colony Ross is that it differed significantly from contemporaneous European colonies. During the period in which the Russian-American Company operated its mercantile outpost in northern California, the coastal regions to the south were being actively colonized by Spain (see Figure 7.14). Although Spain had ruled parts of Central and South America for centuries, the first Spanish colonists did not arrive in Alta California until 1769 (Costello and Hornbeck 1989). In much of the New World, Spain's colonial empire was based on three interrelated institutions: **presidios, pueblos**, and missions. In other words, the Spanish relied upon soldiers, civilian colonists, and missionaries to maintain control of their colonies. In Alta California, Spain's main colonizing agents were Franciscan missionaries. Although the missionaries themselves worked to convert Native peoples to Christianity, both the archaeological and historical records suggest that their role in the larger colonial framework was much broader.

In Alta California, the mission period lasted from roughly 1770 through the 1830s. The Franciscan padres, under the leadership of Junípero Serra, founded a chain of 21 missions that ran along the Pacific coast as far north as San Francisco Bay. The Spanish brought localNpeople to the missions, and additionally forced groups from outlying areas to relocate to mission sites. At the missions, tightly controlled social practices were intended to "civilize" Native Californians by converting them to both Christianity and European lifestyles. Native Californians who lived at the missions were also forced to grow crops and raise livestock for trade and to supply other parts of Spanish California. Poor living conditions at the missions exacerbated the spread of disease, and several devastating epidemics struck the native populations of the California missions. Within the framework of Spanish colonialism, the missions provided the colonies with cheap labor and cleared the territory of an uncontrolled indigenous population (Jackson and Castillo 1995; Milliken 1995).

From historical sources and from the archaeological record, we know that at Colony Ross, the relationships between the Russian-American Company and Native Alaskans and Native Californians were structured very differently. Colony Ross was a multicultural community in which certain ethnicities held greater and lesser status, but no real attempt was made on the part of the Russians to eradicate native cultural practices. Russian colonialism, however, was driven by profit, and this is manifested in the Russians' dealings with native groups (Dmytryshyn et al. 1989; Tikmenev 1978). In the eighteenth century, Russian traders moved across Siberia and Alaska, physically coercing Native peoples into the colonial workforce in relentless pursuit of furs and skins. In Alaska, the Russian traders treated the local indigenous populations so poorly that eventually the tsar was forced to intervene on their behalf. But by the time the RAC founded its colony in California, the company's policies toward native groups had softened, and its leaders even signed treaties with some of the Native Californians. The land incorporated into the Ross Colony was territory already claimed by Spain, and these treaties served to legitimize the Russian claim to what is now the Sonoma County coast. For the Coast Miwok and Kashaya Pomo groups who lived in the area, the Russians represented the lesser of two colonial evils, and the treaties were likely signed in the hope that a Russian presence in the area might prevent the expansion of the Spanish mission system into their homelands.

During the early years of the colony, relations between the Russians and their indigenous neighbors were relatively benign. Allied against the Spanish, the RAC and local native groups coexisted without much conflict; indeed, the area around the colony became a refuge for Indians fleeing the Spanish missions farther south. Yet as the Native Alaskan hunters rapidly decimated the otter population, the Russian colony intensified its agricultural and manufacturing programs. These undertakings required a large amount of labor, and often Native Californians who were prisoners of the Russians were forced to work for the colony. In the early 1820s the Russians, like the Spanish, began to mount armed raids into the countryside to capture Native Californians to be used as laborers. Demand for labor increased again in the 1830s with the establishment of three outlying ranches that were designed to increase the agricultural output of the colony, and relations with local native groups deteriorated (Lightfoot et al. 1991).

Unlike the Spanish, who hoped to assimilate Native peoples into new societies based on a European ideal, the Russian managers of Colony Ross simply wanted to turn a profit. Although certain individuals within the RAC advocated for the fair treatment of Native Californians, the company's policies toward Nnative groups were driven by economic, rather than religious or governmental, concerns. The contrasting aims of the Spanish and Russian colonies are clearly demonstrated in California, both historically and archaeologically. These differences are also reflected in the histories and experiences of the various indigenous groups whose members were forced to negotiate the complex colonial worlds of the late eighteenth and early nineteenth centuries.

COLLABORATION WITH NATIVE AMERICANS

In addition to historical documents and the archaeological record, a third crucial source of information on the history of the Colony Ross region derives from the descendants of the Kashaya Pomo people on whose land the Russians established the Ross settlement. The once extensive tribal territory of the Kashaya, which included the Gualala River to the north and extended south of the Russian River, has shrunk to the 40-acre Stewarts Point Reservation located about 15 miles (24 km) north of the Fort Ross State Historic Park. About 600 Kashaya Pomo live in northern California today, and while many work in nearby cities and towns, they return to the reservation for the seasonal cycle of dances, feasts, and ceremonies. Consultation with Kashaya Pomo elders provides an avenue for incorporating their oral traditions into the research and interpretation program of the Fort Ross Archaeological Project (Figure 7.16). The development of our collaborative partnership with the Kashaya Pomo has benefited from the hindsight of decades of encounters between archaeologists and Native people—relationships that have witnessed dramatic changes over the past 35 years in North America (Downer 1997).

FIGURE 7.16 Consultation between archaeologists and Kashaya Pomo elders at the Fort Ross State Historic Park, June 2004.

In the 1960s and 1970s, during the height of **processualism** in North American archaeology, collaborative research with Native Americans was more the exception than the rule. Most archaeologists either ignored or passively listened to the concerns of Native people with respect to the protection of ancestral sites. The civil rights movement of the 1960s, however, gave Native Americans a platform to assert their inherent rights as sovereign tribes and to find ways to more readily protect and manage their cultural property and resources.

Native advocacy led to the passage of several laws either directly or indirectly calling for archaeologists and other officials wishing to conduct research on federal or Indian land to *consult* with tribal people about proposed research. Some of these laws are the Native American Graves Protection and Repatriation Act of 1990 (NAGPRA), the **Archaeological Resources Protection Act of 1979** (**ARPA**), and the National Historic Preservation Act of 1966 (NHPA). Additionally, most states including California have their own versions of these federal laws. For example, the California Environmental Quality Act (1970) requires consultation with affected tribes before and during archaeology done on state land. As a consequence of these legislative actions, laws now exist that protect sacred sites by mandating consultation before any archaeological research can be conducted.

These and several other federal and state laws have affected archaeological practice on both federal and nonfederal land. Furthermore, in concert with federal and state laws requiring consultation, many Native Californian groups have developed procedures for the management, protection, and preservation of sites and ancestral territories, as well as guidelines for recording and studying archaeological sites. Many of these practices are being incorporated into the method and theory of North American archaeology. In 1994 members of the Society for American Archaeology met to discuss moral and ethical issues surrounding the archaeology of Native people in America. This resulted in the adoption of a code of ethics that acknowledges the rights and beliefs of Native people (Lynott and Wylie 1995). The overall consequences are significant; archaeologists are developing more innovative ways in which to gather data, to analyze and curate archaeological materials, and to interact and work with stakeholders and descendant communities. While these indigenous archaeologies are still developing in the context of North American archaeology (Watkins 2000), projects such as the one at Colony Ross illustrate that consultation and collaboration with local Native people can lead to meaningful, insightful, and exciting conclusions.

The Fort Ross Archaeological Project has benefited from consultation with the Kashaya Pomo in two significant ways. One is in the incorporation of native oral histories and oral traditions that inform us about the culture history, cultural practices, and worldviews of the Kashaya Pomo people. By incorporating indigenous voices into archaeological projects, we can gain a better understanding of the experiences of the ancestral communities that created and lived at many of the archaeological sites of the region (Echo-Hawk 1997). Stories and memories handed down from one generation to another provide a window into the past for examining traditional technology and lifeways (e.g., hunting and gathering practices, ceremonies, village organization) and for obtaining insights into their entanglements with foreign colonists. Native consultation also provides important insights into contemporary Kashaya perspectives on colonialism and the maintenance of native cultural practices and language retention. The Fort Ross Archaeological Project incorporates native narratives in the study of pre-contact archaeological remains, as well as historic sites that witnessed encounters between Kashaya and Native Alaskans, Creoles, Russians, and others.

It is the judicious use of native oral histories and oral traditions, in combination with archival documents and archaeology, that provides the most powerful approach, outside a time machine, for investigating the past. The integration of multiple lines of evidence from documentary, oral, and archaeological sources, which comprises the holistic study of historical anthropology, provides a more balanced and inclusive view of history. Each source can contribute a somewhat distinctive historical perspective from the vantage of people of varied cultural backgrounds and homelands. This kind of multisourcing approach is critical in the study of pluralistic social contexts such as Colony Ross. Specifically, we employ native oral traditions, ethnohistoric records from European visitors to the northern California coast, ethnographic information about the Kashaya Pomo, maps of the region, and archived photographs of cultural landscapes and family members, all of which present unique lines of evidence on the history of the Kashaya coast.

The second significant contribution of Natives' participation in the Fort Ross Archaeological Project is in the theory and method of our archaeological practice. Collaboration with Kashaya elders has emphasized the need to protect and preserve ancestral archaeological remains. This has led to a concerted effort to develop low-impact or less intrusive methods of investigating archaeological places in the Fort Ross State Historic Park. Archaeological methods are employed to limit the amount of excavation, especially in the initial "testing" phases. Excavation by nature is a destructive activity; but it provides necessary information on site stratigraphy and the context of artifactual remains.

Our field program attempts to maximize information about the spatial organization of sites based on surface and near-surface investigations before subsurface testing takes place. We attempt to develop an increasingly detailed picture of the site structure before any significant excavation work is begun. As the site structure comes into focus, and potential house structures, midden areas, and workplaces take shape, we work with Kashaya participants to develop plans for "surgical strikes" where limited excavation may take place that will be most useful for evaluating our research questions and understanding site histories. This field program also tells Kashaya elders what they need to know about archaeological procedures to make informed decisions about where investigations should be prohibited for spiritual or other reasons.

We employ a multiphased field program that begins with the least intrusive methods. Surface pedestrian survey is undertaken in areas with limited ground cover to detect archaeological sites and to define site boundaries. Detailed topographic maps of the site surface are then produced, followed by geophysical survey, and the systematic surface collection of artifacts. We use geophysical survey methods to search for anomalies belowground that may be produced by cultural features or artifacts. **Magnetometers** measure sub- and near-surface magnetic anomalies, while other instruments measure the electrical conductivity or resistance subsurface deposits. Cultural features that retain moisture or alter the flow of electricity through the subsurface matrix may be detected by means of these low-impact methods, thus providing a tentative picture of site structure prior to subsurface investigation (A. J. Clark 1990).

The low-impact approach was recently employed in the study of the Metini Village, a Kashaya village that dates to the Russian and post-Russian occupation of the region and may also predate Colony Ross (Lightfoot et al. 2001). Kashaya Pomo oral tradition emphasizes the sacredness of this place; the center of the site is dominated by a large surface depression that is the remains of a round house used for ceremonies and religious practices. Following a "ritual blueprint" for the investigation of the Metini Village Project, archaeological crews adhered to specific Kashaya cultural practices (Parrish et al. 2000). For example, women field workers were not allowed to work within the sacred village area during their menstrual periods, nor could they cook or do any kitchen chores at camp. We defined the boundaries of the village through surface pedestrian survey, mapped the topographic features of the site, employed a Geometrics G-858 cesium gradiometer and a Geonics EM-38 electromagnetic conductivity instrument to search for subsurface anomalies, and completed a systematic collection of surface materials from 4 percent of the site's surface. The completion of this multiphased surface investigation resulted in a series of overlay maps that showed the topography, subsurface anomalies, and artifact distributions across Metini Village—spatial information that was used by archaeologists and Kashaya elders to place several excavation units measuring 1 meter by 1 meter (3.281 ft. × 3.281 ft.) in strategic places across the site.

The benefits of the low-impact approach extend beyond site investigation, accountability to various stakeholding communities, and publication of a site report. Research designs with limited but strategically placed excavation units have implications for the collection and curation of archaeological materials. The smaller assemblages of artifacts produced from low-impact studies take pressure off crowded curation facilities and artifact repositories. Furthermore, the recovery of fewer materials addresses the unease of many Indian communities about the curation of ancestral remains in museums and curation facilities. Finally, the use of low-impact field methods and limited collection of archaeological materials leaves sites in condition for any future excavations that may be desirable when improved technologies become available.

PUBLIC OUTREACH AND EDUCATION

Collaboration with Kashaya Pomo elders and tribal scholars has also led to renewed emphasis on public outreach programs that highlight Kashaya culture history and the people's encounters with foreign colonists. In the past decade the importance of public outreach and education in archaeology has developed into a dynamic and emerging enterprise. Whereas 20 years ago outreach typically meant posted signs on trails in state or national parks indicating the precious nature of the archaeological record, today the presentation and representation of cultural heritage occupies a significant portion of archaeological research programs. This growth is witnessed in the creation of countless interpretive centers, in public archaeology days held during a field season and, importantly, in the various educational outreach programs run by local, state, and national society organizations, government offices, academic departments, and even research teams themselves (Stone and Planel 1999). The importance of outreach is further enshrined in the Society for American Archaeology's Principles of Archaeological Ethics document that consistently stresses the importance of accountability to the public through eight ethical principles concerning stewardship, accountability, commercialization, public outreach and education, intellectual property, public reporting and publication, records and preservation, and training and resources (Lynott and Wylie 1995). And as training programs begin to offer more courses in ethics and to instruct their students in education and outreach, archaeological interpretive programs and outreach efforts will likely become mandatory components of research projects.

Considering archaeology's accountability to its multiple publics, the Fort Ross Archaeological Project, in collaboration with the Kashaya Pomo Tribe and California State Parks, will embark on the creation of the Kashaya Pomo Interpretive Trail at Fort Ross State Historic Park. Currently, the park consists of an interpretive center and at its core, a dominating reconstruction of the Russian stockade and enclosed buildings (Figure 7.17). Although the park has a well-developed interpretive program run by California State Parks and the Fort Ross Interpretive Association, the pure physicality of the stockade and the less developed interpretive plan for cultural sites outside the stockade emphasizes the park's elite Russian past (Parkman 1996/1997). This is a framework that minimizes the role of the Kashaya, as well as those of Native Alaskan, Coast Miwok, and Creole descent, in the creation of the park as a heritage site.

Every interpretive program must decide to tell its audience a finite number of stories, or narratives, and this interpretive trail is no different. To represent the full scope of Colony Ross's past, the interpretive trail must focus on representing the diversity and complexity of the park's multiple histories and find a way for people to literally step outside the stockade and experience different aspects of the region's cultural heritage. The role of collaboration has been especially important in this process, and the Kashaya people's modern connection to the site was instrumental in selecting specific narratives for the trail and in conceiving of the

FIGURE 7.17 Fort Ross: the proposed interpretive trail will take park visitors outside the reconstructed Ross stockade complex into the nearby landscape.

appropriate methods and means of representation. Thus the trail will not focus solely on the Russian period of occupation. Instead, it will lead visitors physically and mentally away from the imposing stockade and allow them to consider the Kashaya heritage and the multiethnic community that once defined Ross.

With the trail, we have the opportunity to tell a complicated and intriguing history that features the Kashayas' deep past at the park (ca. 6000–8000 years ago), the foundation of a multiethnic colony oriented around fur hunting and agricultural production, and the region's subsequent occupation by Mexican and American ranchers. Segmenting these stories in coherent trail segments will take planning and coordination. Thus the trail itself comprises two loops, each of which will feature a different aspect of the park's history. The West Loop will wind itself along the coast and through the Kashayas' prehistoric past, featuring the oldest sites in the park, and will cover a wide range of topics such as views of the landscape, folklore, and subsistence practices. In contrast, the East Loop will provide a tour through the fort that accentuates the history of colonial encounters between the Kashaya and Colony Ross's multiethnic colonists, exposing the public to the entirety of the historic Ross settlement. Each trail stop incorporates archaeology, native oral traditions, European firsthand accounts, historical photographs and illustrations, site maps, and other forms of documentation to provide comprehensive overviews of the natural and cultural heritage of the region. Archaeological sites such as lithic scatters, cupule rocks, which bear small pecked concavities, and shell middens may be used in on-site interpretation. The critical combination and presentation of diverse lines of evidence offers a unique context within which to construct and present indigenous perspectives on the archaeological record to the public.

It is the overall intention of the Kashaya Pomo Interpretive Trail to create interpretations that reflect the multiethnic heritage of Fort Ross as well as native perspectives on this heritage. Extensive collaboration between Kashaya Pomo and archaeologists contribute to native perspectives in all aspects of archaeological research and resulting interpretations (Dowdall and Parrish 2003). In the interpretive project, the incorporation of native oral traditions, Kashaya participation in the interpretive process, historical photographs and documents, and Kashaya interpretations of artifacts and the landscape will complement archaeological evidence and will be used to construct native-infused perspectives on the archaeological record at Ross. This critical combination of diverse lines of evidence is viewed as an essential part of the process of creating multivocal and native-inspired interpretation of Ross's heritage (Lightfoot et al. 1998).

Unfortunately, the degree to which any interpretive trail can convey its messages is constrained by the medium of trail signposts and accompanying materials: they are costly and nondurable, and the format prohibits the imparting of extensive interpretation. Therefore, in addition to the signposts and panels, brochures, guided tours, public lectures, and "archaeology days" will supplement the proposed interpretive program, providing additional outlets for interaction between project staff, local communities, and park visitors (Figure 7.18).

The impact of the trail upon people's understandings of Ross also is limited by the ability of various publics to visit the park in its isolated location, or physically walk the trail. Development of a website as an extension to the current interpretive trail program both overcomes these limitations and provides an opportunity to reach out to and interact with a wider audience. Digital interpretive environments combine the ability to use multiple media to construct interpretations within a format of increased accessibility, interactivity, and reflexivity between multiple audiences—real and virtual. Although access to the technology poses certain ethical problems, a digital Kashaya Pomo Interpretive Trail can serve as an alternative point of access for audiences otherwise unable to visit the park in person, as well as an enhanced educational tool for teachers, students, and others interested in the park. As archaeologists attempt to grapple with issues of accountability, education, outreach, and collaboration, the use of digital interpretive environments for archaeological interpretation has great potential for satisfying these ethical and moral requirements.

FIGURE 7.18 Guided tour for park visitors of the proposed Kashaya Pomo Interpretive Trail during the initial phase of testing possible interpretive scenarios, June 2004.

CONCLUSION

The Fort Ross Archaeological Project exemplifies a collaborative research program that is holistic, broadly comparative, and focused on change over time. We draw inferences from a number of different sources, including native oral traditions, historical records, and archaeological research. The knowledge gained from these investigations is used to achieve a better understanding of the social contexts of the pluralistic mercantile endeavor of Colony Ross, and to examine the experiences of Native Californians who lived there against the backdrop of other indigenous peoples who witnessed colonialism firsthand elsewhere in the world. The daily practices and social relations of the Kashaya Pomo and Coast Miwok people who lived and worked at Colony Ross are additionally examined diachronically, that is, through prehistory to the present. In close collaboration with members of the Kashaya Pomo Tribe and the California State Parks, the Fort Ross Archaeological Project strives to practice archaeology that meets the demands and expectations of a diverse array of stakeholders including Native peoples, academics, archaeologists, and the general public.

DISCUSSION QUESTIONS

1. Who were the Native people affected by the Russians at Colony Ross? How did the colonization efforts of the Russians differ from those of the Spanish? How do you suppose these differences ultimately affected Natives?

2. How has consultation with the Kashaya Pomo changed the program of archaeological work at Fort Ross? What advantages and disadvantages do you see?

3. Why should archaeologists be concerned with the nature of public outreach at Fort Ross? Do you agree that the new interpretive trail should focus on representing "the diversity and complexity of the park's multiple histories"? Explain.

4. Compare and contrast this case study with the one in Chapter 5. How do the archaeologists and Native people in these case studies illustrate new trends in the practice of archaeology?

CHAPTER 8

Mobility, Flexibility, and Persistence in the Great Basin

I t's a hot summer evening in the mid-1940s at the Wendover Air Base gunnery school. The airmen, tired from a hard day's training for World War II combat duty, are casting about for something to fill the time until lights out in this remote part of the western Utah. Some of them wander to the new base club, built in a cave in the side of a mountain. Base personnel have leveled the floor, poured a concrete dance floor, installed a jukebox, and put in a full bar. Here the airmen drink and dance and laugh, most of them not noticing the dim figures of mounted people painted on to the walls. It is quite likely that none of them suspect what lies beneath their feet, for excavations of the cave (named Jukebox Cave by its excavator) later yielded preserved basketry and other artifacts from a long human occupation. The airmen were literally dancing on the past without knowing it.

Archaeological sites are not always evident to the general public without the help of trained interpreters. It is not uncommon, for instance, for a consulting archaeologist to visit a property with an owner who plans to develop it but has learned that an archaeological survey is first required. "I've lived on this property for 30 years," the owner often says, "and I never found any Indian stuff." In some cases the archaeologist can actually bend over and pick up a flake or sherd for the inspection of an owner who had not recognized an artifact in plain sight. In other cases, the sites are found during survey. As we have seen, however, it is quite possible for people to walk (or dance) over archaeological sites without knowing it. That is one reason for the loss, each year, of many archaeological sites—they are bulldozed into oblivion simply because people did not know they were there.

Caves like Jukebox Cave are emblematic of Great Basin archaeology. In the course of their everyday lives, people who took refuge from the region's heat in caves and rockshelters left behind artifacts, and deposits grew. Since many of the caves are dry, items left in them remained dry as well. The lack of moisture prevents the decay of wood, fiber, hide, and other natural materials not usually found in archaeological sites.

Dry cave sites have produced a wealth of material that allows insight into past lifeways. Duck decoys fashioned out of tule stalks hint at hunting practices on the ancient lakes that filled the desert basins at times in the past. Atlatl throwing boards, darts, and foreshafts show the articulation of pieces not obvious when only stone hooks, points, and throwing board weights are recovered. Flaked knives hafted into handles provide insight into the use of these tools. Coprolites, which are preserved feces, even tell us about the contents of specific prehistoric meals, and some caves contained many, many coprolites. Feather and rabbit skin blankets, leather pouches with their contents still together, snares, and rabbit nets all would have disappeared from open sites. Another interesting class of artifacts found in dry caves are **quids**. These are masses of chewed fiber, often of yucca, that were spit out in the caves and still often preserve the tooth marks of the person who had chewed them. Whether they were chewed for their nutritional value, as part of fiber extraction, or as a precursor to chewing gum is not known. Preserved textiles also are particularly important. As we saw in Chapter 5 (Exhibit 5.1), manufacturing techniques can provide evidence of cultural contact and affiliation. For this reason much attention has been paid to basketry and cordage in the Great Basin.

The excavation of dry caves has made critical contributions to the understanding of the past in the Great Basin. Indeed, Danger Cave, located in the vicinity of Jukebox Cave and excavated at the same time by Jesse D. Jennings (1957) of the University of Utah, provided the basis for the definition of the **Desert culture**, one of the main interpretive frameworks for Basin prehistory for many years, and one that had far-reaching implications for the study of the archaeology of the entire West. It's a good bet that those airmen at Jukebox Cave had no idea what marvelous information lay in the dust beneath their feet.

DEFINITION OF THE AREA

The Great Basin occupies the area between the Sierra Nevada and the Rocky Mountains (Figure 8.1). The heart

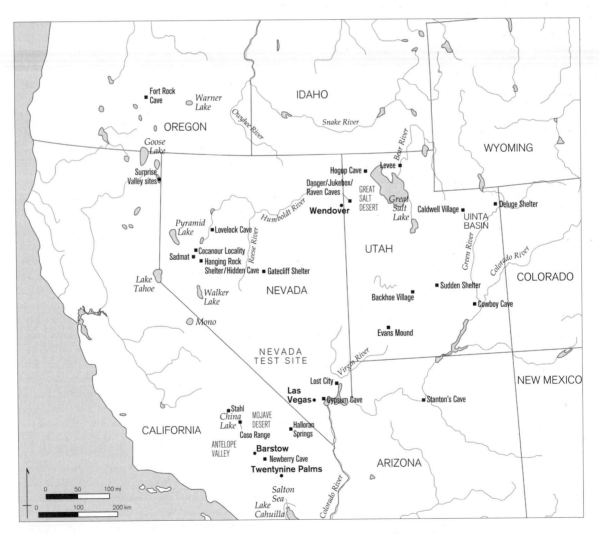

FIGURE 8.1 The Great Basin culture area showing the location of sites mentioned in Chapter 8.

of this area is the hydrographic Great Basin, which is an area of internal drainage where all streams and rivers end in lakes or playas within the basin itself. This area covers most of the states of Utah and Nevada. The cultural Great Basin encompasses a larger area, including parts of Oregon and Idaho, eastern California, western Colorado, and western Wyoming that drain into rivers that ultimately reach the sea (D'Azevedo 1986:1; Jennings 1986:114). Culturally the area is bounded by the Plateau on the north, California on the west, the Southwest on the south, and the Plains on the east. Contact with these regions and influences from them occur with varying degrees of intensity throughout the prehistory of the area.

There are a number of regional chronologies, and these often fail to match. In Table 8.1 we present regional timelines, along with a basinwide set of periods offered by Jesse Jennings, albeit reluctantly, knowing, as he did, the level of variability present both in the record and in archaeologists' interpretation of that record. In this chapter we will use very broad periods to organize the discussions. Since except for the agricultural adaptation of the Fremont culture, the Great Basin exemplifies what archaeologists once called the Archaic stage (see Chapter 2) from nearly the beginning of human occupation, we shall focus on the Archaic.

THE ENVIRONMENT

The Great Basin is a region of great variation in landform and climate. High mountains overlook deep valleys, often with broad, arid floors. As noted earlier, the heart of the region is the vast area of internal drainage—an area where rivers do not flow to the sea but end in lakes or playas. Lakes like Great Salt Lake, Pyramid Lake, Humboldt Lake, Mono Lake, and Walker Lake result from this pattern of internal drainage, and they are mere remnants of huge lakes that filled large parts of the basin at the end of the Pleistocene (as well as other, even earlier times). Among these large bodies of water called **pluvial lakes** (Figure 8.2) were Lake Bonneville, a lake that included much of northwestern Utah, and Lake Lahontan in western Nevada. To the south in the Mojave Desert portion of the region, Lake Mohave filled playas along the Mojave River.

Like the ethnographic Great Basin, the archaeological Great Basin extends beyond the boundaries of the hydrographic Great Basin, into areas drained by the Snake River, the Pitt River, and the Colorado River. Uniting the area, however, is the general topography of mountain ranges and intervening basins (the Basin and Range province). The occurrence of mountain ranges and adjacent valleys leads to increased environmental diversity, for there is variability within each valley

based on elevation, as well as variation among valleys. Within a valley the contrast between the often-dry valley floor and the mountain slopes is great, with the mountains being relatively more moist, sometimes supporting forests and subalpine meadows. The local and regional variability leads to patterns of associations between landforms, plants, and animal populations that are relatively predictable; and the ethnographic and archaeological records suggest that the inhabitants of the Basin understood these patterns well.

Vegetation is also variable. In the north the valleys are covered with cold desert vegetation (Figure 8.3) characterized by saltbush and sagebrush; in the south (Figure 8.4), warm desert vegetation is dominated by creosote. Grasslands are found in the north on the Snake River Plain, and combinations of sagebrush and grassland cover foothills. Mountain range vegetation is zoned by elevation, with piñon–juniper forests on the lower slopes, followed by the scrub oak zone, the ponderosa pine forest, the aspen forest, the spruce and fir forest, and the alpine herb zone above the tree line in the southern mountains. Northern ranges go from sagebrush to piñon–juniper, to sagebrush again, and then to open conifer forests; the alpine herb zone is less common in the north (Harper 1986).

Water is, of course, a critical resource in the deserts of the Great Basin. Water is found in the lakes mentioned earlier and the rivers that feed them, but significant areas of marsh in the basins today were lakes in the Pleistocene. Although such marshlands were limited in distribution, they were very productive areas, yielding rushes, grasses, and succulent plants that provided important food resources (Harper 1986).

Lake Cahuilla, located in the California culture area west of the Colorado River, is a lake with a particularly interesting history that contrasts with climatically controlled lakes of the Great Basin. The Pleistocene lakes of the Great Basin formed with higher rainfall or cooler temperatures resulting in an accumulation in the basins of more water than had evaporated. In contrast, Lake Cahuilla appeared and disappeared over the millennia as a result of slight changes in the Colorado River levees and in the course of the river, which sent the water into the Imperial valley and ultimately into the Salton Trough, landforms that are below sea level. When the river again changed course, returning to the channel that took it to the Sea of Cortez, the water supply for Lake Cahuilla was cut off, and the lake began to shrink through evaporation, ultimately disappearing (Mehringer 1986:36–37; Wilke 1978). Today, southern California's Salton Trough is home to the Salton Sea, a lake that appeared in the early twentieth century as a result of levee failure during railroad construction along the Colorado River.

TABLE 8.1 Introduction to Great Basin Culture History

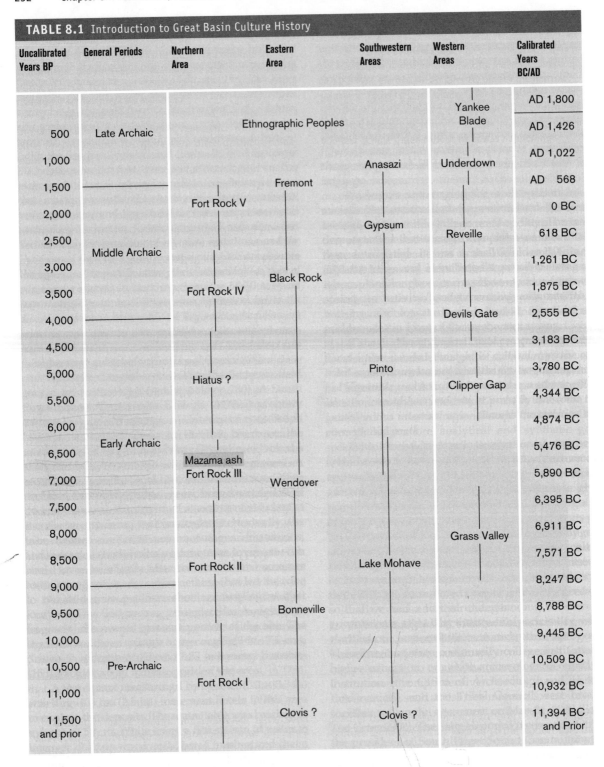

Uncalibrated Years BP	General Periods	Northern Area	Eastern Area	Southwestern Areas	Western Areas	Calibrated Years BC/AD
					Yankee Blade	AD 1,800
500	Late Archaic	Ethnographic Peoples				AD 1,426
1,000					Underdown	AD 1,022
1,500			Fremont	Anasazi		AD 568
2,000		Fort Rock V				0 BC
2,500				Gypsum	Reveille	618 BC
3,000	Middle Archaic					1,261 BC
3,500		Fort Rock IV	Black Rock			1,875 BC
4,000					Devils Gate	2,555 BC
4,500						3,183 BC
5,000		Hiatus ?		Pinto		3,780 BC
5,500					Clipper Gap	4,344 BC
6,000						4,874 BC
6,500	Early Archaic	Mazama ash				5,476 BC
7,000		Fort Rock III	Wendover			5,890 BC
7,500						6,395 BC
8,000					Grass Valley	6,911 BC
8,500		Fort Rock II	Lake Mohave			7,571 BC
9,000						8,247 BC
9,500			Bonneville			8,788 BC
10,000						9,445 BC
10,500	Pre-Archaic					10,509 BC
11,000		Fort Rock I				10,932 BC
11,500 and prior			Clovis ?	Clovis ?		11,394 BC and Prior

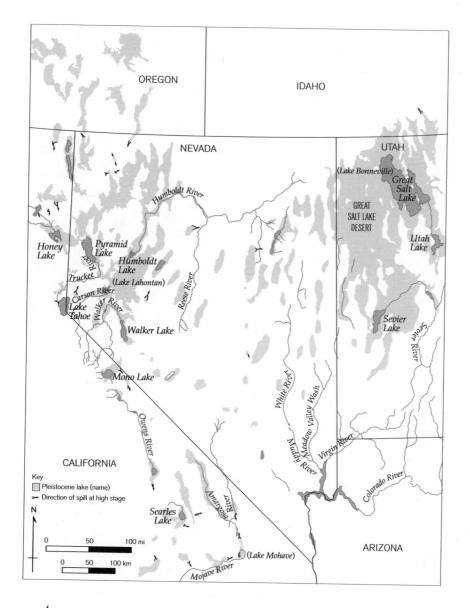

FIGURE 8.2 Pluvial lakes of the Great Basin.

OREGON

IDAHO

NEVADA

UTAH

(Lake Bonneville)

Great Salt Lake

GREAT SALT LAKE DESERT

Humboldt River

Honey Lake

Pyramid Lake

Humboldt Lake

(Lake Lahontan)

Truckee River

Carson River

Lake Tahoe

Walker River

Reese River

Walker Lake

Utah Lake

Sevier Lake

Sevier River

Mono Lake

White River

Owens River

Middy River

Meadow Valley Wash

Virgin River

CALIFORNIA

Key

☐ Pleistocene lake (name)

➤ Direction of spill at high stage

N

Searles Lake

Amargosa River

Colorado River

ARIZONA

0   50   100 mi

0   50   100 km

(Lake Mohave)

Mojave River

FIGURE 8.3 Vegetation of the Northern Great Basin, northern Utah.

Animal populations vary with the vegetation, and the aridity often leads to low population densities. Small mammals, jackrabbit, deer, elk, pronghorn, and mountain sheep can be found in various Great Basin environments, while bison once ranged into its northeastern part (Harper 1986). Fish and clams were available in rivers and some lakes, and ducks and other waterfowl were also found in the lake and marsh environments. Some reptiles, such as the desert tortoise and the chuckwalla, a large lizard, were sizable enough to have been important foods. Additionally, insects, such as caterpillars of the Pandora moth, crickets, and grasshoppers, were abundant enough to be collected as food. The larvae and pupae of a brine fly were abundant in some lakes in the west central Great Basin, and they were also collected (Fowler 1986).

Climatic Change

Changes in environment have long been a research topic in the Great Basin, where the Altithermal has often been used to explain gaps in the archaeological record. Climatic studies have been part of major excavations, particularly in recent years, and a wealth of climatic data abounds, ranging from preserved plant material in fossil packrat middens to fossil pollen in lakes and marshes to tree rings of bristlecone pine in the White Mountains, which provide a long and

FIGURE 8.4 Vegetation of the Southern Great Basin.

detailed record of precipitation and temperature. Humans, by leaving debris in the dry caves, also contributed to the environmental record, and the study of plant parts, pollen, and bone from these sites has made significant contributions to our understanding of how past environments in the Great Basin changed over time.

The classic three-part scheme of Ernst Antevs (1948) divided postglacial time into **Anathermal,** a cool and moist period from 9000 BP to 7000 BP, Altithermal, a drier and warmer period from 7000 BP to 4500 BP, and **Medithermal,** the develpment of conditions like the present day starting about 4500 BP. This nomenclature was often applied simplistically by archaeologists, with the Altithermal often being blamed for apparent hiatuses in the archaeological record.

One recent change in vegetation also is particularly interesting. This is the relatively rapid change in the character of the vegetation of the valleys and foothills. At contact with European Americans, these areas had more grasses and much less brush than they do now, and this change began within a few decades of the newcomers' arrival. It turns out that this change is due to suppression of fires that once periodically swept portions of the Great Basin. Many of these fires had been set by the Indians to keep the land open (Harper 1986:52–53). This example of the intimate environmental knowledge acquired by the original residents of the Great Basin also demonstrates that even hunter-gatherers can alter habitats, albeit on a smaller scale than is seen in the changes wrought by more recent industrialized societies.

EARLY CULTURES: THE PRE-ARCHAIC

Like the surrounding culture areas, there is sparse, scattered evidence for the earliest occupation of the Great Basin, primarily in the form of isolated fluted points. Many areas have also yielded the bones of extinct animals, but there are almost no provable associations between these fossils and human artifacts. As discussed in Chapter 3, Western Stemmed points found here and in other portions of the West are believed by some archaeologists to be contemporaneous or earlier than fluted points (Beck and Jones 2010). There is also evidence that discrete foraging territories were already established for Great Basin Paleoindian populations.

ARCHAIC

Danger Cave Sequence and the Concept of the Desert Culture

When the University of Utah Summer Archaeological Field Schools resumed in 1949 after a hiatus during World War II, a young archaeologist named Jesse Jennings took his students to the Wendover area along the Utah–Nevada border. He excavated Jukebox Cave, discussed in the opening to this chapter, as well as Raven Cave and Danger Cave. This excavation and the subsequent analysis and reporting of the project in 1957 would have a long and important role

ANTHROPOLOGICAL THEMES

Thematic Research Questions in Chapter 8

As pointed out in Chapter 2, there is a macro-scale anthropological big picture from which we can view North America's past. This is certainly true for the Great Basin, and you will find in this chapter material directly relevant to at least three of the broad research questions discussed in Chapter 2 and listed in Table 2.1. We touch on other themes less directly. Table 8.2 helps you locate relevant sections of this chapter for each theme. Reading these sections likely will suggest more specific questions and issues as well.

TABLE 8.2 Research Themes for the Great Basin

Research Question	Particularly Relevant Sections
How have humans adapted to the diverse environments of North America and to climatic change over time?	Discussions of the Archaic and of the Fremont as well as Exhibit 8.1, "Rabbit Nets," and discussion in the case study, "Deep Site Excavations at Gatecliff Shelter, Nevada"
What ethnic identities can be identified and historically traced in North America's past?	Discussions in the section titled "Numic Peoples and Their Spread"
What movements of human populations can be documented in the North American past after the continent's initial settlement?	Discussions in the section titled "Numic Peoples and Their Spread"

in the study of Great Basin archaeology and would help shape understanding of the prehistory of the entire West.

Located on a shore of ancient Lake Bonneville on the western edge of the Great Salt Desert, Danger Cave represented occupations ranging back to 11,000 BP. The cave had a wide mouth, but the entrance had been choked with more than 14 feet (4 m) of deposits so that it appeared to be only a shallow rockshelter. Jennings recognized five periods of occupations in the strata that had artifacts (Figure 8.5). Unlike caves excavated earlier, Danger Cave was a site where people lived, not just a place where they cached things. Indeed, much of the cultural fill of the cave was chaff from pickleweed, a plant that was gathered for its edible seeds. Because people lived in Danger Cave, it provided evidence for a much greater range of activities and a more detailed picture of the inhabitants' lifeways than did caves used primarily for storage (Jennings 1957).

Evidence for the earliest human use of the cave came from sands that overlay gravels from Lake Bonneville. These sands had hearths, millingstones, a lanceolate point, and cordage. The artifact inventory became richer in subsequent levels, yielding over a thousand whole and broken millingstones, numerous manos and flaked tools, bone, basketry, cordage, bone

tools, food bones, and plant material. From the assemblage at the Wendover cave sites, Jennings developed the concept of the Desert culture (Jennings 1957).

Looking at the artifacts and their distributions in Danger Cave and, at the same time looking at Julian Steward's (1938) ethnographic work with Numic speakers of the Basin, Jennings saw continuity in adaptation. He noted changes in the artifacts over time in the deposits, to be sure, but he felt the basic cultural adaptation, the Desert culture, remained the same. From this base, which he saw going back in time 11,000 years, he postulated a widespread basic Archaic stage culture not only in the Great Basin, but throughout the West. He saw connections with the **Cochise tradition** of the Southwest (see Chapter 9), materials from the Plateau, and even the San Dieguito material of California (Jennings 1964:166–169).

The Desert culture was a focal point of much subsequent research, and it became the primary lens through which the prehistory of the Great Basin was viewed. Objections began to be raised, however, as people found exceptions to the patterns suggested by the Desert culture model, and as archaeologists began to better appreciate both the spatial and temporal diversity of the Great Basin's past. Eventually even Jennings (1973), in an article titled "The Short Useful Life of a Simple

FIGURE 8.5 Stratigraphy of Danger Cave with the location of radiocarbon dates (years BP). Note the difference in the vertical and horizontal scales.

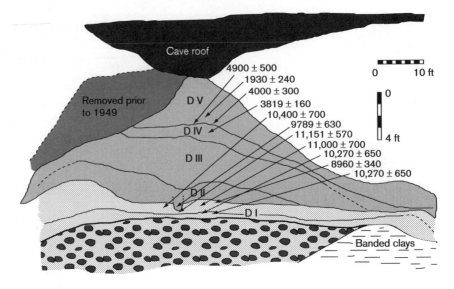

Hypothesis," abandoned the idea, although Great Basin archaeologists still refer to a **Desert Archaic**.

Hogup Cave (Aikens 1970), also in the Great Salt Desert of Utah, had deposits that were even deeper than those at Danger Cave. Pickleweed was a major food at Hogup Cave between 8400 BP and 3200 BP too, and although large game animals like bison, pronghorn, desert sheep, and deer were all represented in the bones found at the site, rabbits and rodents made a much greater contribution to the diet. Marshes near the site provided not only habitat for pickleweed, but also attracted waterfowl that were hunted by the inhabitants of the cave. After 3200 BP, hunting larger game became more important as rising lake levels flooded the marsh environments near the cave. Hogup Cave contains a record that continues to the Historic period and figures heavily in understanding Great Basin prehistory, but the picture provided by Hogup Cave, Danger Cave, and the other important cave sites shows only part of the Great Basin's past.

Beyond the Desert Culture Concept

Archaeologists now believe that cave sites, though providing important glimpses of the Great Basin's past, do not tell the whole story of the Desert Archaic. Large-area surveys were initiated to examine the inventory of site types within defined regions, often valleys. For example, surveys of Surprise valley in northeastern California documented a range of site types over a period of 6000 years (O'Connell 1975). The earliest occupation, the **Menlo phase** (6500–4500 BP), produced evidence of semisubterranean pithouses in valley sites, suggesting substantial base camps. From

lakeshores to the mountains, temporary camps that could have been used by groups moving out from the base camps were found in a variety of settings. Artifacts from Menlo sites include millingstones and distinctive projectile points (Northern Side Notched and others), mortars with conical depressions and pointed pestles for use in them, and stone pendants. Bone indicates that large mammals—sheep, antelope, deer, and even bison—were hunted. These findings contrasted with the picture of Great Basin life based on cave excavations.

Other important regional surveys have included work in Nevada by David Hurst Thomas. His investigations in the Monitor valley and the Reese River valley have provided insights into changes in settlement pattern and in subsistence over time (Thomas 1988; Thomas and Bettinger 1976). Thomas discusses the project in the Monitor valley and the role of the excavations at Gatecliff Shelter in this chapter's case study, "Deep-Site Excavation at Gatecliff Shelter, Nevada."

Cultural resource management studies also have required study of areas outside the cave sites favored by archaeologists of the mid-twentieth century. Considered together, this newer body of work provides some understanding of variability within the Desert Archaic.

Western Basin and Adjacent California

Following the poorly represented Fluted Point tradition occurrences, and in some cases overlapping with them, Stephen Bedwell (1973) has included a widespread number of complexes in the Western Pluvial Lakes tradition. This concept, based on Bedwell's work in the

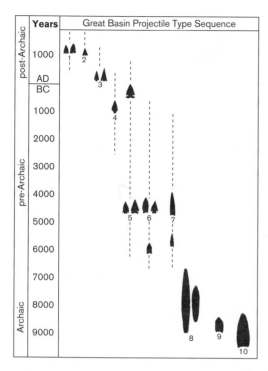

FIGURE 8.6 Great Basin projectile points and their distribution in time: (1) Desert Side Notched series, (2) Cottonwood Triangular, (3) Rose Springs–Eastgate series, (4) Gypsum Cave, (5) Elko series, (6) Pinto series, (7) Humboldt series, (8) Haskett, (9) Folsom, and (10) Clovis.

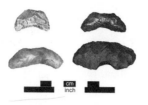

FIGURE 8.7 Lunate crescents from the Mojave Desert.

cave sites and have not even been found with any sign of hafting mastic like pine pitch.

Bedwell (1973) believed the Western Pluvial Lakes tradition to represent the remains of adaptations focused on lake side or river resources generally associated with the Pleistocene lakes, but others see this adaptation as a generalized one focusing on hunting (Warren and Crabtree 1986:184). Some archaeologists consider the Western Pluvial Lakes tradition to be Paleoindian, based on the assumed hunting emphasis. Others, pointing to both the dates and the presence of milling equipment in at least some sites, consider it to be Early Archaic. Generally, however, the Early Archaic in the Great Basin is assigned to the time after the drying of the lakes.

The **Pinto period** represents the Early Archaic in the southwestern Great Basin and is dated from 7000 BP to 4000 BP. This period occurred just after the great pluvial lakes in the Great Basin dried up. Pinto period sites contain assemblages that include Pinto points (Figure 8.6), leaf-shaped bifaces, and scraper forms that resemble those of the earlier Western Pluvial Lakes tradition, which is generally seen as being ancestral to the Pinto period complexes. Some Pinto period sites have produced a few Lake Mohave and Silver Lake points, reinforcing the perceived continuity. Drills and gravers are added to the assemblage, along with manos and shallow basin metates at some sites. At the Stahl site in California's Owens valley, excavators found a deep midden and postholes in patterns that suggest houses. Basin metates were common at the Stahl site (Harrington 1957).

In the Lahonton Basin a number of Early Archaic sites are found. The Cocanour locality on the Humboldt Sink is a site where the evidence of two structures were found. The remains of these structures are shallow circular depressions having diameters between 8 and 11 feet (2.4–3.4 m). Pinto points, millingstones, bifaces, scrapers, and choppers were found associated with the houses (Stanley et al. 1970). This was a residential site, based on the houses (Elston 1986). Lovelock Cave, Hanging Rock Cave, Hidden Cave, and many other cave sites of the area were used during this period sporadically, when water was available in the lake basin (as it was at various periods); they seldom were residential sites, but rather served as burial and cache sites (Elston 1986:140).

Fort Rock valley, includes the San Dieguito complex discussed in Chapter 7, the **Lake Mohave complex**, **Death Valley I**, and similar materials like the Sadmat site in Nevada and the Haskett locality in Idaho. It is dated to a period from 12,000 BP to 7000 BP. Sites and artifacts from the various complexes are generally found around the margins of pluvial lakes like Lake Mohave or Lake Lahonton, although the distribution of points associated with this tradition indicates their use in other environments as well.

Artifacts associated with the Western Pluvial Lakes tradition include stemmed points like the Lake Mohave, Silver Lake, and Haskett types (Figure 8.6), leaf-shaped bifaces, a variety of scrapers, and at some sites, milling equipment. At Fort Rock Cave a distinctive kind of sagebrush sandal, one of which was dated to 10,200 BP (8200 BC ± 250), is found with material assigned to the Western Pluvial Lake tradition. Crescentics are also associated with this period. These are generally lunate or crescent-shaped, bifacially flaked artifacts (Figure 8.7). Although they have been suggested to be transverse-mounted arrow points used to stun small game like birds, they have not been found hafted in any of the dry

Hidden Cave provides an excellent example of a cache cave site, though its most recent investigator, David Hurst Thomas, makes a point of doing away with the notion of a "typical site" because of the variation inherent in Great Basin prehistory (Thomas 1985). The site produced evidence of tool caches, food caches, and a huge number of human coprolites. The tool caches held things that were used in seasonal activities near the shelter, eliminating the need to cart the items around during moves to various other resource locations. Food caches helped even out the availability of food. Most plant foods and some animal foods are available only at certain times, but when they are available, they may be abundant. Other parts of the year can be lean, so collecting storable food beyond immediate needs and caching it makes sense. Evidence for caching was actually found in the coprolites, some of which had remains of foods that are available either at different times of the year or at different locations, indicating transport and storage. The quantity of coprolites found in the cave suggested the practice documented among the Indians of Baja California called the "second harvest." Since seeds can pass through the human digestive system undigested, human coprolites can be a reserve of seeds, assuming they can be found. By intentionally depositing feces in the dry environment of the cave, the people at Hidden Cave (and elsewhere) may have maintained an emergency food reserve in the seeds contained in coprolites (Thomas 1985). The coprolites from Hidden Cave provided an important glimpse into the diet in the region. They contained evidence of people having eaten fish, birds, cattail seeds and shoots, piñon nuts, and bulrush seeds (Elston 1986:141; Thomas 1985.).

The Middle Archaic is dated to between 4000 BP and 1500 BP. In the Mojave Desert and the southwestern Great Basin, this is called the **Gypsum period**. The beginning of the Middle Archaic was also the beginning of the **Little Pluvial**, a moist period that filled some desert basins with lakes, but the end of the period was more arid. The Gypsum period was a time of intensive occupation in the Mojave Desert, and subsistence activities became more diverse. Millingstones became more common, and the mortar and pestle also appear during the Gypsum period. Points (Figure 8.6) during this time include the Elko Eared, Elko Corner Notched, Gypsum Cave, and Humboldt Concave Base points (Warren and Crabtree 1986).

Newberry Cave, located east of Barstow in the Mojave Desert, has important deposits that bear on this period. The site produced radiocarbon dates on artifacts ranging from 3765 ±100 BP to 2970 ±250 BP. Excavations at the site produced Elko, Gypsum Cave,

and other points, many of them hafted in dart foreshafts. Also found in the cave were rocks with colored powder adhering to them; probably these had been used to grind and mix pigment derived from red and green stones found in the deposits. Crystals of quartz and calcite, fire drills, sandals, cordage, leather, and sinew were also recovered. **Split-twig figurines** were also found at the site, and pictographs decorate the walls of the cave with design elements primarily representing quadrupeds. Based on the preponderance of hunting gear combined with these other indicators, investigators conclude that the site was used in hunting ritual (Davis and Smith 1981).

The split-twig figurines (Figure 8.8) are found in a much wider area than just Newberry Cave. They have been recovered from at least 16 sites in northern Arizona, Nevada, Utah, and California. The oldest are about 4000 years old and come from Stanton Cave in the Grand Canyon. At Newberry Cave they dated to about 3000 BP, and in Cowboy Cave, Utah, they date to about 500 BP (AD 1455). The figurines were made by splitting a twig and forming the resulting pieces into the stylized image of a quadruped. Sometimes the figurines have a stick piercing them that may have been intended to represent a spear, reinforcing the notion they were used in hunting ritual. Rock art depicting quadrupeds, particularly mountain sheep, is common over much of the same region, with California's Coso Range having a particularly rich set of panels (Figure 8.9). Much of this rock art was made at the same time as the figurines. It has been suggested that there was a connection between the two. Because of their wide distribution, it may be that these figurines spread as part of a shamanistic ritual even across cultural lines. The rock art may be a related aspect of the same ritual system (Warren 1984:417–419).

Elsewhere in the western Basin, hunters of the Middle Archaic stashed duck decoys in Lovelock Cave (Figure 8.10). In the Lahontan Basin a distinctive kind of basketry, called Lovelock wickerware, first appears. Lovelock wickerware baskets were most often conical burden baskets used to carry quantities of material, and they often had places for **tumplines** to be attached (Adovasio 1986:197). The burden baskets were important in gathering piñon and in transporting materials over long distances. There is evidence that people in some parts of the western Great Basin decreased their range of mobility at this time (Elston 1986:142–143). In the Fort Rock region, for example, the Middle Archaic saw a dramatic increase in the use of local obsidian over obsidian brought in from a distance, suggesting that people were spending more time in the area (Jenkins et al. 1999).

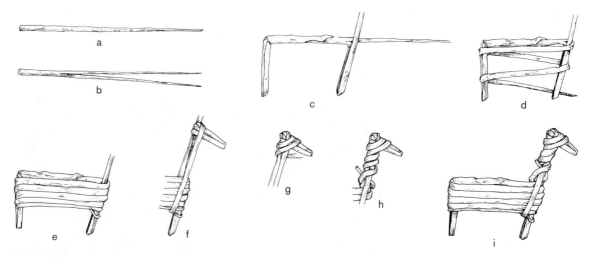

FIGURE 8.8 Split-twig figurine construction steps, based on examples from Etna Cave.

FIGURE 8.9 Sheep depicted in rock art from the Coso area, California.

FIGURE 8.10 Lovelock Cave cache that contained 11 duck decoys.

The Late Archaic, or Late Prehistoric, spans the time from the end of the Middle Archaic (about 1500 BP) to European contact. In the southwestern Great Basin this encompasses the **Saratoga Springs period** (1500–800 BP) and the **Shoshonean period** (800 BP to contact). The Saratoga Springs assemblages resemble those of the preceding Gypsum period, but the projectile points become smaller at about this time. This most likely reflects use of the bow and arrow instead of the atlatl. Rose Springs and Cottonwood Triangular points are the most common. Millingstones also continued to be important.

Different regions of the southwestern Great Basin exhibit influences from their neighbors. Influence from Southwestern groups of the lower Colorado River region is seen in the areas of the Mojave Desert south of the Mojave River. North of the Mojave River and in southern Nevada, **Virgin Branch Anasazi** interaction is evident. As we will discuss in Chapter 9, Ancestral Pueblo or Anasazi people were agriculturalists of the northern Southwest. They occupied parts of the Great Basin at some points in time as shown by sites like Lost City in Nevada. In the Mojave Desert the Ancestral Pueblo influence is seen in sherds found in sites and in their presence at the turquoise mines at Halloran Springs (Figure 8.11) between 1300 BP and 1100 BP. Other Southwesterners, the **Hakataya**, controlled them

FIGURE 8.11 Turquoise mines at Halloran Springs, California.

from 1100 BP to 700 or 800 BP until the Southern Paiutes used them (Warren and Crabtree 1986:191).

Desert Side Notched points and brownware pottery mark the Shoshonean period. In southern Nevada this period follows the Virgin Branch (Ancestral Pueblo) occupations of the area. Assemblages in the northern Mojave Desert include large triangular knives, millingstones with unshaped manos, mortars and pestles, incised stones, slate pendants, and shell beads. Trade with the Pacific Coast is apparent, and large village sites in the Antelope valley and along the upper Mojave River appear to owe their existence to their position on trade routes (Sutton 1980; Warren and Crabtree 1986:191–192).

In the northwestern Great Basin the Late Archaic is marked by Rose Springs and Eastgate points, again indicating the replacement of the atlatl by the bow and arrow. Subsistence became more diverse, with more types of resource being used and more ecological zones being exploited. Rabbit and other small game, along with plant food, became more important in the diet than larger animals. A change in lithic technology accompanied the change in projectile points, with the emphasis shifting from biface reduction and quarried raw materials to one that focused on expedient production of flakes and simple flake tools from locally available raw materials. Lovelock wickerware became less popular during this period.

Interpretation of the numerous styles of projectile points recovered from sites is an important issue in the archaeology of the western Great Basin. Box 8.1 discusses the use of points as time markers and explains why some have urged caution in the application of this practice.

Eastern Great Basin

The prehistory of the eastern Great Basin has been divided into five periods. The **Bonneville**, **Wendover**, and **Black Rock periods** all come before 1500 BP, when the Fremont culture, which is discussed shortly, spreads over the area. The final period is the Shoshonean, which follows the Fremont in the eastern Great Basin. Cave sites like Danger Cave (Figure 8.13), Hogup Cave, Sudden Shelter, and Deluge Shelter contribute greatly to our knowledge of the prehistory of the area.

The Bonneville period (11,000–9500 BP) is represented by remains at only a few sites. The lowest levels of Danger Cave, for instance, are assigned to this period. Although the artifacts associated with this period are sparse, some affinities are noted to the Western Pluvial Lakes tradition based on the occurrence of stemmed points resembling in deposits dated between 10,000 BP and 11,000 BP. It has been suggested that the Bonneville period may represent a transition between the big-game hunting of the Paleoindian period and the plant-oriented subsistence of the Desert Archaic in the area (Aikens and Madsen 1986:154).

The Wendover period (9500–6000 BP) is better known than the Bonneville, being represented at more sites. Sites from this period occur over a wide range of environmental zones, and a mobile existence at sites that change with the season is inferred. Plant

ISSUES AND DEBATES

BOX 8.1

Projectile Points and Time

Our discussion of the Archaic cultures of the Western Great Basin has necessarily referred to projectile points of many types. These artifacts are important to archaeologists because they are believed to be diagnostic of different periods in the past. However, there is controversy about whether projectile points really can be used as time markers. The crux of this debate concerns contentions by master flintknapper and replicator Jeff Flenniken and his associates that the use life of various Great Basin projectile points include breakage and repair. They maintain that this scenario makes possible the transformation of a point from one of the temporally sensitive types to another. In use experiments conducted by Flenniken (Flenniken and Raymond 1986; Flenniken and Wilke 1989), flintknappers made various common types of Great Basin projectile points, used them and broke them, and then repaired them, noting their morphological trajectories. These authors concluded that it was quite possible for a point to start out as one type and become transformed into another type through breakage and repair. For example, the Elko point, generally seen as a hallmark of the Middle Archaic, can be reworked into a Pinto point, which is generally assigned to the Early Archaic (Figure 8.12). Knowing this, it is easy to anticipate problems with chronologies inferred on the basis of projectile points alone.

Nevertheless, as the Gatecliff Shelter case study in this chapter makes clear, Thomas is a proponent of projectile point chronologies. Indeed, one of the reasons he sought out a site like Gatecliff Shelter was to establish chronological control for the surface sites he had been finding on survey. Thomas (1986a) wrote a reply to Flenniken, and others have also defended the use of points as time markers (Bettinger et al. 1991). They argue that although it is possible to transform one point type into another through breakage and repair, the temporal value of points has been demonstrated time and time again at stratified Great Basin sites like Gatecliff Shelter, Danger Cave, and Hogup Cave.

The debate has focused attention on **artifact use lives** and has led archaeologists to look for signs of reworking. Many points that might have been considered atypical can now be placed at the end of a breakage and repair trajectory. The debate has also led archaeologists to examine the criteria used in defining various projectile point types (e.g., Basgall and Hall 2000; Vaughn and Warren 1987; Warren 2002) with an eye toward making those definitions more secure.

The debate may be far from over, as replicative experiments continue, but the bottom line is that most Great Basin archaeologists continue to find projectile points useful in dating sites and components in sites. Indeed, Justice (2002) has published a large volume on projectile points of California and the Great Basin, including discussions of chronology.

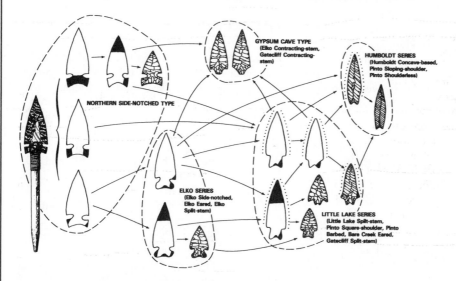

FIGURE 8.12 The Flenniken hypothesis: a model of the transformation of points from one type to another through breakage and repair.

FIGURE 8.13 Members of an archaeology class exiting Danger Cave, Utah.

foods were important in the diet, as seen both in the plant remains preserved in dry caves (the layers of pickleweed chaff found in Danger and Hogup Caves) and in the presence of seeds and pollen in coprolites (Aikens and Madsen 1986:155; Fry 1976; Kelso 1970). Plant-processing equipment includes manos and metates, and basketry for transport and storage is quite common in the dry cave sites (Aikens and Madsen 1986:154–155).

A wide range of animals were taken, including deer, pronghorn, mountain sheep, elk, and bison, as well as birds and small mammals. The atlatl was used to bring down large game, Projectile points from this period include Pinto, Humboldt, Northern Side Notched, and Elko types (Aikens and Madsen 1986:155–156). During the Wendover period in Hogup Cave there was a strong correlation between cordage, netting, and the bones of rabbits and hares, suggesting that the practice of using nets in rabbit drives was an old one in the Great Basin (Aikens and Madsen 1986:155) Incised and painted stones are found in some sites, and there is also jewelry made from Pacific Coast shells. Exhibit 8.1 introduces an important perishable artifact type often preserved in the dry caves of the eastern Great Basin.

During the Black Rock period (6000–1500 BP), Danger Cave apparently continued to be occupied, but many new sites were being established as well, and often in upland areas that previously had been used infrequently (Aikens and Madsen 1986:157–158). Changes in the degree to which plant and small-animal resources were used at different places in the region also have been noted. The period begins with a trend toward

drying of the environment, but later more moist conditions prevailed. Adjustments to these changing conditions in site location and in activities at sites probably explain the new patterning in site distributions.

Points from the Black Rock period are Elko and Gypsum Cave types. By the end of the period, Rose Springs and Eastgate points replace the larger types, signaling the appearance of the bow and arrow. Following the Black Rock period, the area was occupied by the Fremont.

THE FREMONT

Fremont is the name given to a set of archaeological phenomena that occur relatively late in the prehistory of the eastern Great Basin and disappear before the coming of European Americans. The Fremont sites, which exhibit a great deal of regional diversity, occur in a 900-year span between 1600 BP and 700 BP (AD 400–1300) (Marwitt 1986:161), although most of the sites found are between 1300 BP and 800 BP (AD 700–1200) (Barlow 2002:65). Sites attributed to one or another of the Fremont variants are found from southern Idaho in the north as far south as the Colorado River, and from northwestern Colorado across the Colorado Plateau and into the Great Basin to eastern Nevada (Barlow 2002:65).

A number of characteristics set the Fremont apart from earlier and later cultures of the area, and to some extent from their neighbors. The Fremont grew maize to varying degrees, and a particular type of maize, **Fremont dent corn**, occurs on Fremont sites. Plain

CLUES TO THE PAST

EXHIBIT 8.1

Rabbit Nets

The principle behind the fishing nets of the Pacific Northwest is not hard to grasp, but how would you catch rabbits in a net? In the fall, when jackrabbits were especially abundant and fat from their summer feeding, Indians of the Great Basin, such as the Washo, used to take long nets and stretch then across flats (Downs 1966:27). We know this because archaeologists have used ethnographic information to reconstruct how the nets recovered from sites like Hogup Cave were used.

A rabbit net, which was made from string about the thickness of kitchen twine (Figure 8.14), was about as tall as a tennis net is high. The net was staked to the ground, the top edge held up with stakes or bushes, and it was often deployed in a **V**. Half the people would stand at the end of the flat or valley opposite the net and start moving toward the net, where the other half was waiting. As the people moved toward the net, they made noise and beat the brush, scaring the rabbits so that the animals ran away from the noise and toward the net. Inevitably, many rabbits became entangled in the net, and some of the waiting people would kill them with clubs (Downs 1966:27; Wheat 1967:59).

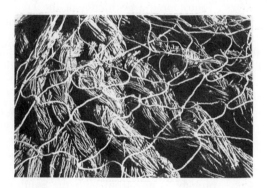

FIGURE 8.14 Paiute rabbit net spread over net coiled for storage.

Although the making of a net was a very time-consuming activity, the drive technique could be used to harvest a large number of rabbits in a short time. The rabbits would then be cleaned and generally split in half to be dried and stored. Rabbits were also cooked up for immediate feasting. Large numbers of people gathered for rabbit hunts, and the feasting could go on for days, until the population of rabbits was depleted. These large drives, at least among the Washo, were organized by a hereditary leader called the "rabbit boss" (Downs 1966:27).

Rabbit nets were very finely made. First, string was made, often from Indian hemp (Wheat 1967:59), although the Washo used cord made from sage (Downs 1966:27). The string, which would consist of these two plies twisted together (Wheat 1967:55–59), was knotted into a net designed so that the openings were just large enough for a rabbit's head to fit through—the rabbit's ears usually prevented the creature from backing out. Kroeber (1925:572) describes the Washo rabbit nets as having a 3-inch (8 cm) mesh and being approximately 1.5 to 2 feet (ca. 0.5 m) high. A historic net owned by Captain Wasson of the Walker Lake Paiutes was over 300 feet (100 m) long, although it was cut in half at his death and divided between his two daughters (Wheat 1967:59).

Besides food, the rabbits caught in nets provided another important commodity—their skins. These were cut into strips while fresh, and the strips curled as they dried, producing a fur-covered cord that was woven into blankets.

The archaeological record of the Great Basin indicates that such nets have a long history. Fragments of netting are found in many of the dry cave sites, and a whole specimen was found by early guano hunters in Lovelock Cave, and specimens have been recovered from dry caves in the Southwest as well. Thus we can surmise that rabbits were hunted in a similar manner for many millennia and over a large area. The recovery of these artifacts reminds us again how much we may be missing in archaeological sites at which good preservation is lacking.

gray ceramics are also characteristic of the Fremont, although some of the vessels are decorated with appliqué designs, and some are painted. Projectile points of the Fremont are small and vary from region to region. Basketry has been recovered from Fremont sites, and a technique of coiling called **one-rod-and-bundle coiling** (Figure 8.15) is associated with the Fremont. There is a distinctive kind of metate called the **Utah metate** (Figure 8.16) that has a trough grinding

surface and a flat shelf at one end. An art style that depicts broad-shouldered anthropomorphic figures with elements of clothing and adornment such as headdresses, necklaces, and earrings is also associated with the Fremont. These humanlike figures are found as clay figurines and as rock art (Figure 8.17). Finally, moccasins made in a distinctive style are found at some Fremont sites. Made from skin from the forelegs of deer or antelope, these moccasins are

FIGURE 8.15 One-rod-and-bundle basketry technique.

FIGURE 8.16 Utah metate from a San Rafael Fremont site.

cut in such a way that the **dew claws** of the animal are on the sole of the moccasin (Barlow 2002:65–66; Marwitt 1986:161).

Hamlets with pithouses and aboveground architecture, often of adobe, are part of the Fremont settlement pattern (Figure 8.18), although caves were also used both for habitation and for storage. Some Fremont sites have storage pits, and multiroom surface structures have been found. There is considerable variability in site size, with the largest sites having multiple pithouses or numbers of surface rooms. Other sites may consist only of storage structures, artifact scatters, or the distinctive rock art.

Although maize is present at Fremont sites, in some areas it appears to have made only a minor contribution to the diet, whereas in other areas it was a staple. The evidence for focus on maize includes the presence of irrigation ditches for fields near some sites, the common occurrence of maize cobs in middens, and the presence of Utah metates, which are often associated with very well worn manos. In addition, isotopic analysis indicates large quantities of maize in the diet. The analysis of human skeletal material from Backhoe Village, Evans Mound, and Caldwell Village suggests maize in the diet at levels similar to those found in the remains of the Anasazi to the south (Barlow 2002:67–68). However, in other Fremont sites hunting or gathering of plant foods appears to have been more important than maize cultivation.

Differences in the importance of maize are just one way in which variation is evident among Fremont sites. There is some temporal change within Fremont, consisting of the appearance of decorated and corrugated ceramics, a shift in pithouse form from round to rectangular, and the appearance of surface structures, all trends seen in the Southwest as well. However, the major variability in Fremont sites is regional (Barlow 2002:69). Five regional variants are recognized: **Uinta, San Rafael, Parowan, Sevier,** and **Great Salt Lake** (Figure 8.19) based on the degree of dependence on maize, types of architecture used, village size, and the types of ceramics, points, and bone tools found. Some researchers reserve the term "Fremont" for the first two, which occur on the Colorado Plateau east of the Wasatch Range, referring to the other three—all found west of the Wasatch in the eastern Great Basin—as Sevier (Marwitt 1986:163). Choosing to emphasize the similarities and relationships, we shall refer to all these groups as Fremont.

The borders of the regional variants are poorly defined. The various regions tend to grade into one another, and in the south the boundary with the **Kayenta Branch Anasazi** (see Chapter 9) is very indistinct. Some sites share Kayenta and San Rafael Fremont traits to such an extent that they can be classified as either (Marwitt 1986:170).

Both the origins and the ultimate fate of the Fremont are enigmatic. The occurrence of maize, ceramics, and architecture led some early archaeologists to consider the Fremont as simply an extension of the Southwest. Dates for the beginning of the Fremont vary, ranging from near 1600 BP (AD 400) in the north to around 1200 BP (AD 800) in the south. The dates in the north are early enough to preclude Anasazi influence as a possible explanation. Maize cultivation and pottery among these groups must have had another origin.

Most archaeologists today see the continuity of many elements between the Archaic and the Fremont, as well as important differences between the Anasazi and the Fremont (e.g., in the nature of the ceramics), as evidence of a Great Basin origin for the Fremont. Influences probably came from both the Southwest and from the Plains. Marwitt (1986:163) notes that distinctive Fremont traits, including the one-rod-and-bundle coiled basketry, Fremont hide moccasins, anthropomorphic figurines, and incised stones, all predate the appearance of the full constellation of Fremont material culture, in a few cases by several millennia. In Hogup Cave, for example, Fremont is recognized at after 1550 BP, when maize, pottery, and other Fremont items are found added to the existing Archaic inventory (Marwitt 1986:162–163).

Aikens (1966) proposed a Plains origin for the Fremont, seeing them as Athapaskan people who moved into northern Utah and, through influences

FIGURE 8.17 Fremont anthropomorphs as depicted in petroglyphs (top) and figurines from the Old Woman site in Utah (bottom).

from the Southwest, developed the Fremont pattern. Madsen (1979), on the other hand, believes that the Fremont may represent regional developments of different groups of Archaic Basin people who wound up sharing the Fremont traits through trade and contact or through the spread of a religious cult that encompassed the area. Madsen (1979:721) views the shared elements in the larger Fremont area as "superficial" and would divide this set of sites into a Sevier culture, a Fremont culture, and perhaps, a third as yet unnamed culture in the north.

What became of the Fremont also is a puzzle. Although some archaeologists have argued that the Fremont gave rise to the Numic speakers of the Great Basin, there is evidence that contradicts this suggestion. There is a distinct discontinuity in both basketry styles (one-rod-and-bundle basketry disappears with the Fremont) and in ceramics between the Fremont and the later Numic populations (Adovasio 1986:204; Madsen 1986:208). These data suggest replacement of people rather than development of the Fremont into the Numic peoples. Thus what became of the Fremont is unknown.

FIGURE 8.18 Snake Rock site, Utah: beneath a plan of the site are profiles of the relative vertical positions of the features in Strata 1 and 2.

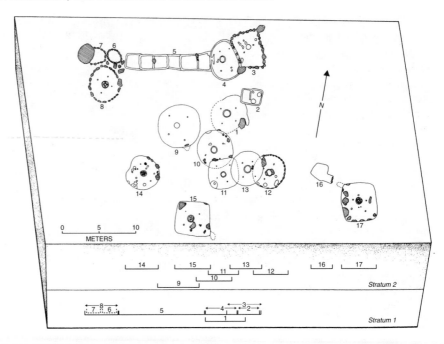

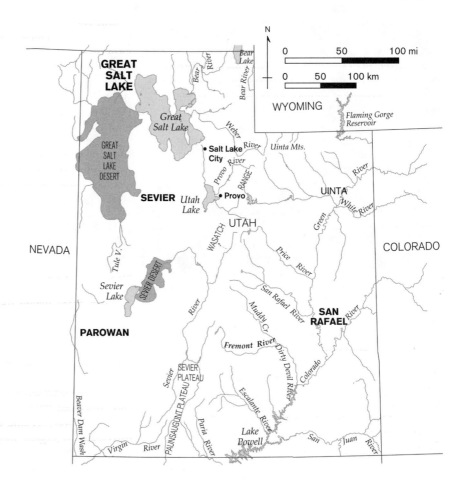

FIGURE 8.19 Location of Fremont variants.

NUMIC PEOPLES AND THEIR SPREAD

Post-Fremont times in the eastern Great Basin are assigned to the Shoshonean period because of the dominance of groups ancestral to Shoshone as well as the linguistically related Paiute and Ute. The Shoshonean period is also recognized as the end of the Late Archaic or Late Prehistoric in the western Great Basin. Distinctive brownware pottery is associated with Shoshoneans.

These Shoshonean or Numic-speaking groups occupied nearly the entire Great Basin when Europeans began to arrive. Since there seems to be a cultural discontinuity between these groups and archaeologically known groups in many areas, one long-standing problem confronting Great Basin archaeology has been explaining this **Numic spread**. Questions still debated include where Numic speakers came from, when they came, and why they dispersed.

Most archaeologists believe that the Numic speakers expanded recently and rapidly, having originated at the southwestern margins of the Great Basin beginning about 950 BP, but reaching the height of the expansion in the eastern Great Basin only after the disappearance of Fremont cultures. One of the primary pieces of evidence for this conclusion has been the fanlike distribution of Numic language branches in the Great Basin, with each branch forming a wedge that was narrowest in southeastern California (Figure 8.20). If longer periods of time had passed since the dispersal, this distribution should not be so clear. However, explaining why and how the dispersal happened has been difficult.

Three basic scenarios have been proposed. Bettinger and Baumhoff (1982) suggested that Numic speakers had a highly successful subsistence strategy based on resource generalization, and that they essentially outcompeted earlier Archaic peoples. However, both the Numic spread itself and the distinctive nature of Numic adaptive strategies have been difficult to demonstrate archaeologically (Bettinger 1998). A second scenario sees the Numic movement into the Basin as a result of their being more aggressive than the earlier people they replace (Sutton 1986). A third scenario has speakers of Numic languages moving into the central Basin about 5000 BP and expanding both to the east and the west as deteriorating climatic conditions made marsh-based adaptations in the west and Fremont agriculture in the east untenable, leading to abandonment (Aikens 1994). Resolving the issues concerning the distribution of Numic languages remains an important research topic, and has ramifications for the present Native American inhabitants of the area, particularly in the area of repatriation and the right to control human remains from the region. Indeed, a 2003 Ph.D. dissertation points out that at least some modern Numic speakers see themselves as descendants of people who always inhabited the Great Basin. The archaeologists' arguments about Numic spread are seen by these people as being insulting and unsupported, and their use to deny current Indian residents of the Great Basin their heritage (Brewster 2003).

PROTOHISTORIC

The Great Basin was one of the last areas of the United States to be fully explored, and the post-contact population has always been relatively light, making it possible for the Native Americans to continue some semblance of their original lifeways later than was possible in most other parts of North America. Nearly all these peoples spoke Numic languages, as we have just discussed (Miller 1986:98). The lone exception was the Washo, who spoke a language probably of the Hokan family found in California. The Washo apparently had been in contact with their Numic neighbors long enough to have accepted a number of loan words and also to have adopted some structural characteristics of the Numic languages (Jacobsen 1986:108–109). The Numic speakers include the Northern, Southern, and Owens valley Paiute, the Northern Shoshone, the Eastern and Western Shoshone, the Mono, and the Kawaiisu.

Early contact between Europeans and Native Americans was largely restricted to some explorations into portions of the Great Basin by Franciscan priests searching for routes to Alta California and to illegal trade (e.g., trafficking in human slaves) with Spanish colonists to the south. However, by the time exploring parties reached the area in the 1770s, the people of the Basin had already been exposed to some European influences indirectly through contact with their neighbors. From the Plains, especially, the people of the Basin had encountered the horse. While some groups in areas where the environment was suitable for keeping horses took to these animals as transportation in much the same way as the people of the Plains, others saw the horse in a different light. People who lived in areas where the vegetation was too sparse to graze horses saw the animals not as transportation, but as food. These different reactions to the horse changed the power dynamics in the Great Basin, with tribes adopting the horse benefiting while others were weakened (Malouf and Findlay 1986).

Contact with other Europeans increased as British and American traders entered the Great Basin from other directions seeking furs. More and more people traversed the region traveling on overland trails to California as well. Conflicts between Native inhabitants and these newcomers were sometimes hostile, but

FIGURE 8.20 Distribution of Numic speakers.

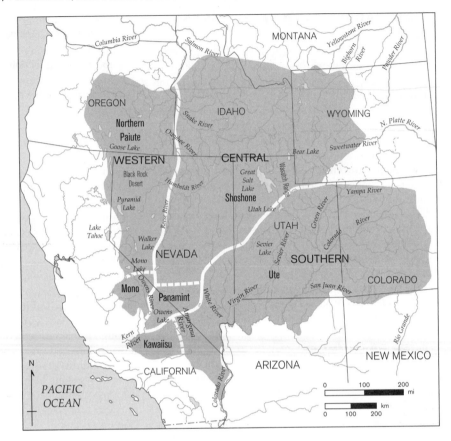

far more serious were the impacts of the fur trade on fragile but productive habitats and on the ability of Native people to persist in traditional subsistence practices. However, it was not until after the Treaty of Guadalupe Hidalgo in 1848 that great change began in the Great Basin. The Mormon migration into the region, beginning in 1847, brought the first real settlers, and the archaeology of early Mormon settlement can be significant (e.g., Ferg and Wilhelm 2005). The Mormons made serious attempts to get along with the people already living in the Great Basin, but as the number of church members grew, they could not help but affect the human and environmental balance of the area. Shortly non-Mormons also came in large numbers, either heading to California or establishing cattle ranches in the Basin.

CHAPTER SUMMARY

This chapter has introduced the archaeology of the Great Basin. Although hunting and gathering adaptations persisted through the millennia with only a short interruption from the Fremont, there still was important cultural variation in this area's past. This introduction provides background for further exploration. The main points made in this chapter are as follows:

- The Desert Archaic is a name frequently applied to the hunter-gatherers of the Great Basin whose lifeways persisted with relatively minor changes over millennia.

However, differences between the western and eastern Great Basin cultural sequence are notable.

- The Fremont culture of the eastern Great Basin (1600–700 BP) represents people who experimented with growing maize, built pithouses and above-ground storage rooms, made plain gray pottery, and used the one-rod-and-bundle coiling technique to create basketry. Regional variants within Fremont reflect differences in the level of dependence on maize as well as contrasts in material culture. Both the origins and the disappearance of Fremont are poorly understood.

- Numic-speaking or Shoshonean people inhabited most of the Great Basin in the Late Prehistoric period

and when Europeans began to arrive. The reasons behind the distributions of these people throughout the Great Basin are controversial and have been much debated, but they remain poorly understood.

SUGGESTIONS FOR FURTHER READING

For discussions of the archaeology as well as material on the environment, history, and ethnographic peoples of the Great Basin:

D'Azevedo, Warren L. (editor)
> 1986 *Great Basin*. Handbook of North American Indians, Vol. 11, William C. Sturtevant, general editor, Smithsonian Institution, Washington, DC.

For a recent introduction to the past peoples of the Great Basin:

Simms, Steven R.
> 2008 *Ancient Peoples of the Great Basin and Colorado Plateau*. Left Coast Press, Walnut Creek, California.

The classic paper by Julian Steward that provided the ethnographic model for the Desert culture concept is still in press:

Steward, Julian
> 1938 *Basin-Plateau Aboriginal Sociopolitical Groups*. Bureau of American Ethnology Bulletin 120, Washington, D.C. (Reprinted by the University of Utah Press, Salt Lake City.)

For a paper on the eastern Great Basin by one of the founders of Great Basin archaeology:

Jennings, Jesse D.
> 1978 *Prehistory of Utah and the Eastern Great Basin*. Anthropological Paper 98, University of Utah.

OTHER RESOURCES

Sections H and I of the Student CD provide web links, additional discussion questions, and other study aids. Section G contains additional resources. It is particularly interesting to compare Gatecliff Shelter, the subject of this chapter's case study, with an early cave

site in a very different setting, described in the bonus case study "The Dust Cave Archaeological Project: Investigating Paleoindian and Archaic Lifeways in Southeastern North America" (Section D.6 of the Student CD).

CASE STUDY

Caves and rockshelters have long been important in Great Basin archaeology because when deeply stratified, these sites contain a long record of use by various hunting and gathering groups. In addition, the arid climate of the high desert sometimes preserves usually perishable artifacts, providing archaeologists with unusual information unavailable elsewhere. Thus, caves and rockshelters in the Great Basin have the potential for preserving a record of environmental change that can parallel the cultural sequence. Such places are "dream sites" for the committed archaeologist. Gatecliff Shelter, located in Monitor valley of Nevada, is a well-known site in the central Great Basin that has provided important information on chronology and projectile point change as well as lifeways in the ancient Desert West. This site, which has been used as an example in other textbooks (e.g., Thomas 1998), provides insights into the nature of the archaeological record in this part of North America. This case study also illustrates how archaeologists find and excavate sites, and more than a little about why they choose the strategies they do. As you read this case study, think about what it took to find and excavate Gatecliff. Would you have the persistence to conduct this kind of research?

DEEP-SITE EXCAVATION AT GATECLIFF SHELTER, NEVADA

David Hurst Thomas

My interest in Gatecliff Shelter arose from a much broader project examining prehistoric land-use patterns in the central Great Basin (Nevada). Based on a close reading of the available ethnohistory, we conducted two large-scale regional surveys (in the Reese River and Monitor valleys), each of which relied entirely on surface remains—picking up artifacts and plotting their distribution (Thomas 1983a, 1983b, 1988; Thomas and Bettinger 1976). While these surveys provided valuable insights into ancient mobility and subsistence patterns, surface archaeology requires key assumptions about cultural chronology and about paleoenvironmental conditions. This is why we were seeking a site with deeply stratified deposits: to provide independent verification of our chronological and paleoenvironmental assumptions.

Here, I will focus on how we found Gatecliff Shelter, how we excavated the site, how we defined the stratigraphy, how we defined the time markers contained there, and how we reconstructed the human activities that played out inside Gatecliff Shelter during the last 6000 years.

GOOD OLD GUMSHOE SURVEY

We found Gatecliff through a fortunate combination of happenstance, hard work, and trial and error. James O'Connell calls the process "gumshoe survey," probably because such rudimentary archaeological reconnaissance closely resembles detective work: set out a problem, get some leads, track them down, and, if you're fortunate, you crack the case. In archaeology, "cracking the case" can mean turning up just the right site to answer a question that's bothering you. This is precisely how we found Gatecliff Shelter.

At the time, I was a graduate student at the Davis campus of the University of California, supporting my doctoral fieldwork by conducting archaeological field schools. The summer was taken up doing "systematic archaeological survey"—basically mapping and collecting the archaeological stuff that we could find on the ground surface in the Reese River valley. While the so-called surface survey was going well, we badly needed to check our findings against the kind of data you get only from excavating buried sites, such as caves or deep trash deposits. Although we looked everywhere, we never could seem to find the right place to dig. It was frustrating.

As it turned out, we eventually found the very deep cave site we were seeking—a place with great stratigraphy and plenty of archaeological stuff buried inside. While I'd like to be able to tell you about the sophisticated research strategy we designed to find Gatecliff Shelter, the truth is that we just lucked into it. Toward the end of our first field session in Reese River, we assembled the crew for steak dinners in the nearby town of Austin, Nevada. When our waitress politely inquired who was in charge and somebody pointed to me, she told me about her husband, a mining geologist who had prospected the western mountains for 40 years. Mr. Peer told me of a cave—over in Monitor valley, a dozen miles east of Austin.

He had not been there in years, but the details were fresh in his mind. He sketched a map on his business card. Although Mr. Peer remembered exactly where the cave was relative to the canyon, but he was not sure exactly which canyon. I stashed the card in my shirt, and thanked him for the tip.

It required lots of looking to find that cave, up and down each side canyon in Monitor valley, working our way slowly northward. After a week of this we came to Mill Canyon, just the next one on the list, with no greater potential than the ten canyons we had already combed. There was a cliff face nearly a half-mile long, and we became more and more discouraged as we moved up canyon, scanning each small alcove for pictographs. Finally, only one section remained to be inspected, where the black cherty formation was swallowed up beneath the alluvial Mill Canyon bottomland. We saw a dim shadow near the bottom, but a dozen similar shadows had been just that—shadows.

The paintings were not visible until we crawled into the mouth of the cave. There they were, just as Mr. Peer had said a year before: small human figures, painted in red and yellow pigments. On the other wall were cryptic motifs in white and black. And, yes, the roof had caved in years before. Half the floor was buried beneath tons of chert. One boulder would have dwarfed the pickup we had left in the canyon.

So we dug a small test pit, 50 centimeters (20 in.) on a side, and I scraped away the rocks and rat dung with my favorite Marshalltown trowel. We dug through the afternoon, taking notes and measuring artifacts. We finally stopped, armpit deep, when I could no longer reach the bottom of the test pit. It was a pretty meager haul: several pieces of broken bone, a few of them charred, and a dozen stone flakes, probably debris from resharpening stone knives or projectile points. Not exactly treasure, but we knew that at least one flintknapper had paused here to ply his craft. Still we were disappointed. The rock art already spoke of the occasional prehistoric visitor. We were looking for something more.

Across the sagebrush campfire that night our small crew assayed the finds. The rock art was neat; only two similar sites were known in the central Great Basin. The stones and bones were suggestive enough, but the shelter seemed hardly the deep site we had hoped for all year. The deposits were maybe 2 or 3 feet deep, and the strata probably jumbled. People had most likely dug storage pits, cleared bedding areas, and scooped out fire hearths in there for centuries. It probably had stratigraphy like most desert caves, which are so jumbled that they look as though they have been rototilled. At best, our test pit results were borderline.

As it turned out, we were wrong about this site, which we eventually called Gatecliff Shelter (after a local geological formation). The site came to dominate my archaeological life for more than a decade. The prehistoric deposits were not a few feet deep, as I had

initially thought. Gatecliff turned out to be 40 feet (12 m), deep, apparently the deepest rockshelter in the Americas. The strata were also not mixed, as I had first feared. Over the millennia, the shelter had been inundated again and again by flash floods. The surging waters laid down thick layers of mud, forming an impenetrable cap of rock-hard silt. This flooding occurred at least a dozen times, stratifying the deposits into horizontal "floors."

Gatecliff had what textbooks (including my own) describe as "layer-cake stratigraphy." The shelter had been occupied for much longer than the past few centuries, as I had thought at first. Gatecliff was old, at least 7000 years old, as radiocarbon dating would later establish. The sediments also contained ample evidence about the past environments of Monitor valley.

After finishing graduate school, I took a job at the American Museum of Natural History in New York City, where I convinced the museum to dispatch five major field expeditions to Gatecliff Shelter. More than 200 people helped excavate the site over the years. The National Geographic Society supported part of the fieldwork and prepared an educational film about the site. The society also wrote a book about our excavations at Gatecliff. The *New York Times* and the *New Yorker* magazine published stories about Gatecliff. There was coverage on television and radio. A U.S. congressman even became involved in the struggle to preserve the site. Gatecliff Shelter was decidedly on the map.

A VERTICAL EXCAVATION STRATEGY

It's electrifying to find a site like Gatecliff, but the "discovery" was only the beginning. Our excavation strategy and tactics evolved dramatically as we learned more about the site and its potential.

We began with two simple test pits dug the same year we found the site. From day one, we wanted to learn two things: how long people had used Gatecliff Shelter, and whether the buried deposits could tell us about the human chronology of the region. These two questions were clear-cut, and so was our fieldwork. Our earliest excavation strategy was vertical, designed to supply, as expediently as possible, a stratified sequence of artifacts and ecofacts associated with other potentially datable materials.

Like most archaeologists, I dig "metrically" in typically 1-meter squares. There is, of course, a minimum size in such exploratory soundings: squares much smaller than 1 by 1 meter (3.28 × 3.28 ft.) would squeeze out the archaeologists, and larger units are overly destructive (and too time-consuming).

Test pits tend to be quick and dirty, particularly because they must be excavated "blind," without knowing what stratigraphy lies below. Nevertheless, even in test pits, archaeologists must maintain three-dimensional control of the finds: the x axis (front to back), the y axis (side to side), and the z axis (top to bottom). This is why archaeologists dig square holes. Provided the sidewalls are kept sufficiently straight and perpendicular, excavators can use the dirt itself to maintain horizontal control on the x and y axes by measuring directly from the sidewalls. As test pits deepen, however, the sidewalls may start sloping inward, cramping the digger and biasing the measurements. Field archaeologists call these sloppy pits "bathtubs"—decidedly bad form.

What about vertical control? At Gatecliff, we dug test pits in arbitrarily imposed 10-centimeter (3.9 in.) levels. Everything of interest—artifacts, ecofacts, soil samples, and so forth—was kept in separate level bags; we had one bag for each 10-centimeter level. The z dimension for each level was usually designated according to distance below the ground surface: level 1 (surface to 10 cm below), level 2 (10–20 cm below), and so forth.

Excavation procedures vary widely, depending on the stage of excavation, the nature of the deposit, and the impulse of the archaeologist in charge (remember, digging is perhaps still as much craft as science). Because they are so small, test pits are often dug by trowel (rather than by shovel), maintaining a horizontal working surface. Dirt is scooped into a dustpan, dumped into a bucket, then carried off-site for a closer look.

The test pits told us that Gatecliff Shelter warranted a closer look, and we returned the next year for just that reason. The site was divided into a 1-meter grid system, oriented along the long axis of the shelter. We assigned consecutive letters to each north–south division and numbered the east–west division. By this method, each excavation square could be designated by a unique alphanumeric name (just like Bingo—A-7, B-5, and the ever-popular K-9). The east wall of the "7-trench," so named because it contained units B-7 through I-7, defined a major stratigraphic profile, a vertical section against which all artifacts, features, soil and pollen samples, and radiocarbon dates were correlated.

A vertical datum was established at the rear of the shelter. For all on-site operations, this single datum point was arbitrarily designated as zero. All site elevations from this point on were plotted as "x centimeters below datum." Then, using an **altimeter** and a U.S. Geological Survey topographic map, we determined the elevation of this datum point to be 2319 meters (7607 ft.) above sea level; today we might use satellite-driven technology to provide such controls.

All archaeological features—fire hearths, artifact concentrations, sleeping areas, and the like—were plotted on a master site map, and individual artifacts found in situ were plotted in three dimensions. All fill was first carefully troweled, then passed outside the cave for screening; artifacts and ecofacts found in the screen were bagged by stratigraphic or arbitrary level. Field notes at this stage were kept by individual excavators in bound, graph paper notebooks. Good field notes record everything, whether or not it seems important at the time. Depending on the nature of the site (and the stage of excavation), field notes can either be taken "formless" or recorded on specific unit-level forms, with precise categories defined for each kind of necessary information.

At this stage, we were looking primarily for change through time. At Gatecliff, this meant looking for key time-sensitive artifacts to be grouped into temporal types, which would enable us to place previously undated archaeological contexts into a meaningful sequence as we excavated. Laboratory work subsequently tested these preliminary field hypotheses, what geologists call their "horseback correlations."

The vertical excavation strategy is a deliberately simplified scheme designed to clarify chronology. Although this strategy blurs much of the complexity in the archaeological record, it can be justified for these initial temporal aims.

UNLOCKING THE STRATIGRAPHY AT GATECLIFF SHELTER

By the end of our fourth field season, our major strata-trench had reached a depth of 9 meters (30 ft.) below the ground surface, generating a stratigraphic profile that illustrates some of the quandaries involved in the workaday archaeological situation.

During our first three seasons at Gatecliff, I recorded and interpreted the Gatecliff stratigraphy myself. Drawing upon my somewhat limited classroom training in geology, soil science, and microstratigraphy, I drew and described the gross stratigraphy. This master profile served as the major descriptive device throughout the excavations.

As the field season wound down, it became clear that Gatecliff was too complex for me to continue the geological interpretation. This is not unusual in archaeology. On small-scale digs, archaeologists must often cover all the bases, from stratigrapher to photographer, from engineer to camp cook. But as the operation expands, specialists must be recruited to take over selected aspects. The trick is for an archaeologist to recognize the critical line separating flexibility from irresponsibility.

At Gatecliff, I was in danger of crossing that fine line, so we soon arranged for four experienced Great

Basin geologists to join the team. Although all had somewhat different ideas—and some rather heated debates took place—the diversity fostered a better overall interpretation of the stratigraphic column.

In the course of a decade, we had exposed a remarkably well-stratified profile, more than 40 feet (12 m) deep, spanning the last 7000 years. The Gatecliff profile resulted from a complex interplay of natural and cultural factors. The master stratigraphy demonstrates how deposits of two very different kinds resulted from each set of processes. The thin dark levels (such as those numbered 9, 11, and 13) are living surfaces, or cultural horizons. Each dark horizontal band represents a single campsite. The 16 cultural horizons occurred as the result of human habitation, and these surfaces contain the fire hearths, broken stone tools, grinding slabs, flakes, food remains, and occasional fragments of basketry and cordage. This stratigraphy allowed us to analyze material culture on a horizon-to-horizon basis at Gatecliff, allowing us to define "time markers" that are invaluable for dating other sites (especially surface sites). We were also able to record patterning of these artifacts on each floor, which allowed us to reconstruct the activities that had occurred on each living surface.

But what makes Gatecliff so unusual is that living surfaces were capped by sterile, noncultural layers of purely geological origin. After the excavation was finished, we divided up the Gatecliff profile into a sequence of 56 geological strata: layers of more or less homogeneous or gradational sedimentary material, visually separated from adjacent layers by a distinct change in the character of the material deposited.

Some strata, such as 2, resulted from small ponds that occasionally formed at the rear of Gatecliff Shelter (Figure 8.21). The pond water acted as a sink for wind-blown dust particles, which settled out as finely laminated silts. Other strata, such as 8, consist of coarser sediments grading from gravels at the bottom to fine sand silts at the top. Apparently, the ephemeral stream flowing in front of Gatecliff Shelter occasionally flooded and coursed through the shelter. The water of such flash floods would first deposit coarse sediments such as pea-sized gravels. As the water's velocity diminished, its carrying capacity decreased, and the particles deposited were smaller. Finally, when the water slowed, the tiniest silt particles would cap the stream deposits. Such floods occurred several times throughout the 7000 years of deposition at Gatecliff, and each time the previous occupation surface was immediately buried. When the inhabitants returned to Gatecliff, they thus lived on a new campsite, separated from the previous one by as much as 2 feet of sterile alluvial sediments.

Fifty-six such depositional strata were stacked up inside Gatecliff. Here is how we described one stratum

at Gatecliff (evident at the bottom of the master stratigraphy):

Stratum 22, Rubble: Angular Limestone Clasts, Charcoal Firepit, And Baked Area At Top, Somewhat Churned Into The Underlying Silty Top Of Stratum 23. Maximum Thickness 50 Cm On The Southwest Pile And Formed Continuous Layer Up To 15 Cm Thick In Eastern Parts Of Excavation, But Was Discontinuous Elsewhere. Almost As Voluminous As Stratum 17, The Top Was About {Min}4.85 M On The Southwestern Pile And Ranged From {Min}5.50 To {Min}5.30 M Elsewhere, And Its Bottom Was About {Min}5.30 M In The Southwest Corner, {Min}5.35 M In The Master Profile, And {Min}5.32 M In The Present Excavation.... Stratum 22 Was Deposited By Gradual Accumulation Of Roof Fall And Talus Tumbling Over The Shelter Lip Between 5250 And 5100 Years Ago. Stratum 22 Was Called Gu 6R-74 In The Field And Contained Cultural Horizon 14.

Several important points can be made about Stratum 22 at Gatecliff. Note, for instance, the detail of description. Exact depths are given relative to a central-site datum point, arbitrarily assigned a zero value of 0.0 meter. (Actually, as noted earlier, the Gatecliff datum is 2319 meters [7606 ft.] above sea level.) When paired with our horizontal grid system, these arbitrary elevations document the exact configuration of each geological stratum.

Each geological term is sufficiently well defined to permit geologists who have never visited Gatecliff to understand what Stratum 22 looked like. Note also how we separate such descriptions from our interpretation. This way, others can use our data to make their own assessments (disagreeing with us, if they wish). Geoarchaeologists sometimes use the term "stratification" to refer to the physical layers in a site, reserving "stratigraphy" for the geoarchaeological interpretation of the temporal and depositional evidence.

Forty-seven radiocarbon dates were processed on materials from Gatecliff (Table 8.3), and four of these dates were available from Stratum 22. This information, combined with the added radiocarbon evidence from adjacent strata, allowed us to estimate that Stratum 22 was laid down between about 5250 and 5100 years ago.

Other strata at Gatecliff provided different clues to help date the site. Stratum 55, near the very bottom of the site, contained an inch-thick lens of sand-sized volcanic ash (**tephra**), fragments of crystal, glass, and rock once ejected into the air by a volcanic eruption. Not discovered until the last week of the last field season, the tephra was indistinct, mixed with the

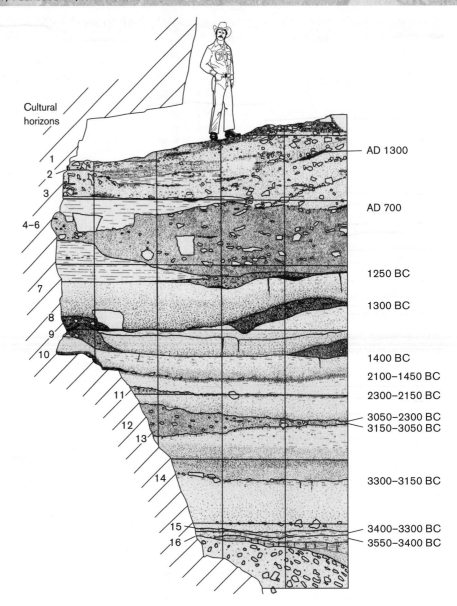

FIGURE 8.21 Stratigraphy in Gatecliff Shelter. In this scale, the standing figure is exactly 6 feet (1.83 m) tall, and each grid square is 1 meter across.

Cultural horizons

1
2
3
4–6
7
8
9
10
11
12
13
14
15
16

AD 1300

AD 700

1250 BC

1300 BC

1400 BC
2100–1450 BC
2300–2150 BC

3050–2300 BC
3150–3050 BC

3300–3150 BC

3400–3300 BC
3550–3400 BC

cobbles and rubble of Stratum 55. In the laboratory, the late Jonathan O. Davis, one of our geologists and a leading expert on the volcanic ashes of the American West, confirmed that this ashy deposit was Mount Mazama ash. When this mountain in the Oregon Cascades blew up 6900 years ago, it spewed out 11 cubic miles of pumice and related materials; the caldera formed by the Mazama explosion now contains Crater Lake. The Mount St. Helens eruption in 1980 was a cherry bomb in comparison. The prevailing winds, coupled with the force of the explosion itself, carried Mazama ash across the western United States. Wherever the ash settled out, it created

a "marker bed." **Tephrochronology** has become a valuable tool for dating sites in volcanically active areas. When Davis identified the Mazama ash at the bottom of Gatecliff, we had a critical, independent check on the largely radiocarbon-derived chronology at Gatecliff, and so we knew that Stratum 55 must be 6900 years old.

In truth, I am not certain whether I would have recognized the volcanic ash at the bottom of Gatecliff. At Mummy Cave (Wyoming), near Yellowstone National Park, the excavators confused the thin layers of Mazama ash with wood ash; the important tephra lens was later recognized under the microscope.

TABLE 8.3 Physical Stratigraphy of Gatecliff Shelter

Stratum	Soil	Nature of Deposit	Field Designation	Cultural Association	Radiocarbon Dating (years)	
					Age	Date
1	S-1	Rubble	GU 14	Horizons 1–3	0–1250 BP	AD 700–present
2		Sand and silt	Upper GU 13		1250 BP	AD 700
3	S-2	Rubble	Part of GU 12	Part of Horizon 4	1250–1350 BP	AD 600–700
4		Sand and silt	GU 13 and GU 12 silt		1350 BP	AD 600
5	S-3	Rubble	Part of GU 12	Parts of Horizons 4–6	1350–3200 BP	600
6		Sand and silt	GU 11		3200 BP	1250 BC
7		Rubble	GU 11 and GU 10R	Horizon 7	3250–3200 BP	1300–1250 BC
8		Sand and silt	GU 10		3250 BP	1300 BC
9		Rubble	GU 9R	Horizon 8	3300–3250 BP	1350–1300 BC
10		Sand and silt	GU 8 A and B		3300 BP	1350 BC
11		Rubble	GU 7R	Horizon 9	3400–3300 BP	1450–1350 BC
12		Sand and silt	GU 7		3400 BP	1450 BC
13		Rubble	6 Living Floor	Horizon 10	4050–3400 BP	2100–1450 BC
14		Sand and silt	GU 5 Silt		4050 BP	2100 BC
15		Rubble	Part of GU 5		4100–4050 BP	2150–2100 BC
16		Sand and silt	Part of GU 5		4100 BP	2150 BC
17		Rubble	GU 4	Horizon 11	4250–4100 BP	2300–2150 BC
18		Silty sand	GU 3		4250 BP	2300 BC
19		Sand and rubble	GU 2	Horizon 12	5000–4250 BP	3050–2300 BC
20	S-4	Silt and clay	GU 1A	Horizon 13	5100–5000 BP	3150–3050 BC
21		Sand and silt	GU 1 and GU 7-74		5100 BP	3150 BC
22		Rubble	GU 6R-74	Horizon 14	5250–5100 BP	3300–3150 BC
23		Silt	GU 6-74 and GU 5-74		5250 BP	3300 BC
24		Rubble	GU 4R-74	Horizon 15	5350–5250 BP	3400–3300 BC
25		Silt	GU 4-74		5350 BP	3400 BC
26		Rubble	GU 3R-74	Horizon 16	5500–5350 BP	3550–3400 BC
27–29		Silts	GU 3A-74		5500 BP	3550 BC
30		Sand	GU 3B-74		5500 BP	3550 BC
31		Rubble	GU 2R-74		5700–5500 BP	3750–3550 BC
32		Fine sand and silt	GU 2-74			

(Continued)

TABLE 8.3 *(Continued)*

Stratum	Soil	Nature of Deposit	Field Designation	Cultural Association	Radiocarbon Dating (years)	
					Age	Date
33		Fine sand and silt	GU 12-76, GU 1–78, and GU 1-74			
34		Sand	GU 2-78			
35		Rubble	GU 3R-78			
36		Silty medium sand	GU 3-78			
37		Sand and silt	GU 4-78 and GU 11-76			
38		Silt and fine sand	GU 5-78			
39		Rubble	GU 6R-78 and GU 10-76			
40		Sand	GU 6-78 and GU 9-76			
41		Sand	GU 7-78			
42		Sand and silt	GU 8-78 and lower GU 9-76			
43		Rubble	GU 9R-78 and GU 8-76		6250–5700 BP	4300–3750 BC
44		Sand	GU 9-78			
45		Sand	GU 10-78			
46		Rubble	GU 11R-78			
47		Sand and silt	GU 11-78			
48		Rubble	GU 12R-78			
49		Sand and silt	GU 12-78			
50		Silt	GU 13-78			
51		Sand and silt	GU 14-78			
52		Rubble	GU 15-78			
53		Sand	GU 16-78			
54		Rubble	Basal Rubble 1 [BR 1]		6900–6250 BP	4950–4300 BC
55		Rubble and tephra	Basal Rubble 2 [BR 2]		6900 BP	4950 BC
56		Rubble	Basal Rubble 3 [BR 3]		7100–6900 BP	5150–4950 BC

Fortunately, the Mazama tephra at Gatecliff was instantly recognized by Jonathan Davis. Both cases highlight the importance of having specialists work on-site, during excavation.

GATECLIFF PROJECTILE POINTS AS TIME MARKERS

Geologists proposed the law of superposition rather early in the game, in 1669! But fossils did not become a worthwhile tool for geological correlation until much later, during the early nineteenth century. Whereas eighteenth-century archaeologists commonly applied the principles of superposition to their excavations, we had to wait nearly two centuries to learn—once again from geologists—how the index fossil concept might make human artifacts useful tools in dating archaeological sites.

As noted earlier, the stratigraphy of Gatecliff Shelter looks like a huge layer cake stacked 40 feet high. Geology's law of superposition tells us that, all else being equal, the oldest artifacts will lie at the bottom, with later artifacts showing up progressively higher in the stratigraphic column. The Gatecliff deposits thus provide extraordinary temporal control over the past 7000 years. We can plot the vertical distribution of the more than 400 classifiable projectile points from Gatecliff Shelter (note that additional types were required to classify the entire Gatecliff collection).

Look at the sharp stratigraphic differences evident on Figure 8.22. All the Desert Side Notched and Cottonwood Triangular points occurred in the uppermost part of Gatecliff Shelter. The Rosegate series points were found in slightly older strata; Elko points are older than this, and Gatecliff points older still. Because 47 radiocarbon dates were available to date the geological sequence at Gatecliff, it was possible to assign the following time ranges to each category:

Desert Side Notched: post-AD 1300

Cottonwood Triangular: post-AD 1300

Rosegate series: AD 500–1300

Elko Corner Notched: 1500 BC–AD 500

Gatecliff Contracting Stem: 2500–1500 BC

Each time similar points are found in undated contexts, we receive a clue (a hypothesis, really) to their time of manufacture.

A related issue emerges here about the nature of archaeological data. Keep in mind that data are not objects. Data are observations made on objects, and the point typology from Gatecliff illustrates this principle. Using a series of formal attributes (weight, distal shoulder angle, and so forth), we grouped the individual

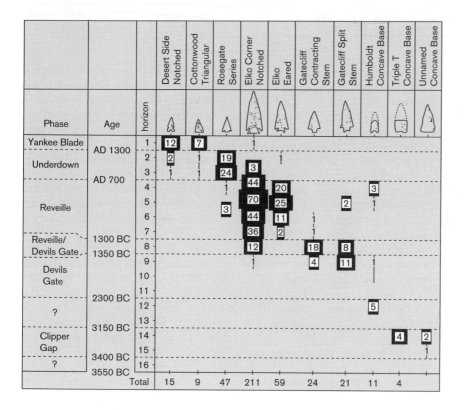

FIGURE 8.22 Projectile point distribution by depth. The horizontal dimension (frequency) is plotted on a logarithmic scale, which dampens the effect of differential sample size.

Gatecliff artifacts into morphological types, each a hypothesis to be tested against independent temporal data. But our "independent" data—the datable context of each point inside Gatecliff Shelter—were merely other observations made on the same objects from which we had derived the initial hypothesis. Because formal attributes are autonomous relative to context, the criterion of independence holds, and so the test is valid.

This principle is critical to archaeology. Hypotheses (even simple ones like time markers) need continual testing. We should never become too comfortable with our "verified" hypotheses. Even without lifting a shovel, we can refine the Gatecliff chronology in several ways. Why not measure the microscopic **hydration rim** on each obsidian projectile point? This would give us an independent age estimate. Some points still have hafting sinew adhering to the base. Why not use the new accelerator technology to radiocarbon-date these fibers? Here would be another independent estimate of age. Both tests elicit more data without requiring more objects. This is one reason for the importance of well-curated museum collections as research tools, enabling scientists of the future to generate new data from old objects.

Although critical to archaeology, time markers have distinct limitations. Archaeology can proceed with its initial objective—establishing cultural chronologies—only by making simplifying assumptions, and this is what we did with the projectile point chronology defined for Gatecliff Shelter. Never mind (for now) what the artifacts mean—we care only whether they change through time. As a result, some first-rate time markers were discovered at Gatecliff.

We have paid a price to find our time markers. Although we now know that Desert Side Notched and Cottonwood Triangular points postdate AD 1300, much ignorance remains. Why should two morphological types exist simultaneously? Are two social groups living at Gatecliff in the post-1300 time period? Are Desert Side Notched points designed for hunting bighorn, whereas Cottonwood points are for rabbits? Are Cottonwood points really for "war arrows," left unnotched so that they cannot be pulled out once lodged in an enemy's flesh? Or perhaps the difference is technological: could the Cottonwood Triangular points be unfinished, intended to be later notched (and thereby becoming Desert Side Notched points)? These guesses are hypotheses at present untested.

The master stratigraphic sequence (and the dozens of radiocarbon dates available from that column), allowed us to successfully define the cultural sequence of Gatecliff Shelter. But our vertical excavation strategy had also left us with a series of extremely steep and hazardous sidewalls. Even though the excavation was stairstepped downward to minimize these sidewalls, the sheer verticality of the site made it dangerous. Change was clearly in order, both conceptually and logistically.

A HORIZONTAL EXCAVATION STRATEGY

Gatecliff Shelter held potential far beyond mere chronology. Establishing cultural chronology is only archaeology's first objective; our early excavations amply demonstrated that Gatecliff could make useful contributions to paleoethnographic objectives as well. Several stratigraphic units contained short-term, intact occupational surfaces, and the remaining excavations at Gatecliff concentrated on the spatial distributions within these key stratigraphic units.

As we transcended our chronological objectives, we also shifted our digging strategy. We began looking beyond the modal aspects of culture to view things as part of the overall cultural matrix. In other words, the focus moved from the when and where to the more elusive what. Viewed in this manner, digging mine shafts becomes inappropriate. Culture in the broader sense embraces the structural elements basic to adaptive and ideational aspects, rather than merely aggregates of functional traits that happen to be shared. The paleoethnographic approach requires looking at the interrelationships among artifacts, waste debris, cultural features, and cave walls. We must understand what activities took place, not just which artifacts were deposited.

The tactics required to pursue paleoethnography likewise change, sometimes radically. With the stratigraphy suitably defined, extensive vertical sections were no longer necessary, and we concentrated on opening entire living surfaces simultaneously. The cultural lenses at Gatecliff were slowly excavated by hand, with thicker stratigraphic units removed in arbitrary 10-centimeter levels. Exposing the living floors proceeded more slowly than had the previous vertical excavations, and excavators were instructed to recover and map all artifacts in situ. Features were screened separately, and flotation samples were retained for laboratory processing. Significant debitage scatters were plotted, as were concentrations of bone and other artifacts. The excavated deposits were then placed in buckets and carried to the screening area (Figure 8.23), where they were passed through one-eighth-inch screens, and as before, artifacts missed by the excavators were saved, along with all fragments of chippage and bone.

The horizontal strategy required significantly more control within contemporary stratigraphic units.

FIGURE 8.23 Gatecliff Shelter during excavation.

A single crew chief took excavation notes for the entire site at this point (rather than having individual excavators do it, as before). Three-dimensional data were transferred to site notebooks, and living floor maps were plotted for each surface at the time of the excavation. A single excavator was assigned to each 2-square-meter unit, and all artifacts, features, and large ecofacts were plotted onto the large-scale living floor maps. Since then, sophisticated computer-driven systems have been developed to assist in piece-plotting objects on living surfaces.

The intrasite patterning of artifacts and ecofacts at Gatecliff is heavily size sorted. Smaller, lighter items tend to be fumbled or otherwise discarded in a "drop zone," whereas larger, heavier items are commonly "tossed" outside the central zone of the campsite. This means that, all else being equal, debris will tend to accumulate in concentric zones, centering in the central hearth area. On most of the horizons at Gatecliff Shelter, the smallest debris was found in a distinct drop zone at the rear of the shelter. Larger debris was discarded in a "toss zone" near the mouth of the shelter.

The Horizon 2 pattern is unique at Gatecliff Shelter because the central garbage heap took up most of the enclosed area, leaving virtually no room to construct hearths, create sleeping areas, or establish a specialized area of manufacture and tool repair, as we observed on most of the Gatecliff horizons.

We could plot three dozen fire hearths on the various living surfaces at Gatecliff Shelter. Although most horizons are spatially independent from the others, the hearths were built in a distinctive "hearthline," approximately 13 feet (4 m) from the rear wall. Even though the shape of Gatecliff Shelter changed markedly throughout its occupation period, this hearthline–rear wall distance remained virtually constant, as did intrasite zonation. In other words, as Gatecliff Shelter became larger, the hearths move farther inside the site in a predictable, linear fashion. So positioned, these small hearths offered several advantages: a distinct work zone was defined between the hearthline and the rear wall. Such placement, somewhat inside the drip line, protects the fires from precipitation and windy gusts, the smoke venting outside. In effect, each hearth created a relatively warm and smoke-free "rear room," a heated work and sleep area of nearly constant size between 160 and 215 square feet(15 and 20 square meters). The rear wall effectively functioned as a heat sink, warming the inner part of the shelter with only a small fire.

The exception was Horizon 2 (occupied about AD 1300), which showed an almost total reverse of the drop zone/toss zone pattern. For one thing, Horizon 2 lacks a definable hearthline; in fact, Horizon 2 lacks hearths of any kind. And rather than having debris increasing in size toward the drip line, in Horizon 2 the debris accumulated in the middle of the site. This central dump zone contained the partially articulated, field-butchered carcasses of about two dozen bighorn sheep; assorted butchering implements were discarded near the edges of the bone mass.

Overall, we think that Gatecliff Shelter functioned mostly as a short-term field camp, visited by all-male task groups who were exploiting a logistic radius too far to allow them to return at night to their base camp.

WHY DID PEOPLE CHOSE GATECLIFF SHELTER?

But Gatecliff Shelter was still just a single site in a huge landscape, and we literally spent dozens of year combing these desert mountains for other sites to put Gatecliff into its regional and human context.

We now understand that Gatecliff Shelter is surrounded by hundreds of bighorn hunting facilities. For thousands of years, sheep hunters worked the very highest reaches of the Toiyabe, Toquima, and Monitor mountains. Like the sheep, hunters began spending parts of their summers higher up, and at first, the bighorn must have been unaccustomed to two-legged predators. Although their atlatls could drop a sheep at 40 feet., the hunters soon found the long vistas of low sagebrush to be harshly unforgiving. They soon learned that the bighorn almost always spotted them first.

The bighorn knew that the deep canyons, flowing steams, perpendicular bluffs, and steep slopes of the tablelands provided them escape cover, often in the thick bristlecone and limber pine timber. When startled, sheep usually ran downslope for a short distance, then circled around and headed right back to the safety of the mountain. So the alpine hunters tipped the odds in their favor by building rock blinds and short walls, precisely placed to intercept the sheep as they completed their half circles. This vast array of hunting facilities survive today, not far from Gatecliff Shelter, typically next to game trails and along the tops of steep rock chutes, narrow talus slopes, and cirques—any place where an uphill-charging bighorn emerged from areas of constricted escape cover. Hunting blinds also cluster near breaks in the rimrock, where the sheep were naturally funneled.

Alpine hunters spent days, even weeks away from their families, and they engineered exclusive Man Caves that suited their hunting lifestyle. Gatecliff Shelter was one of these, located halfway up Mill Canyon (at 7600 ft.). When they camped there, the hunters were already partway up the Toquima Range.

The hunters selected Gatecliff Shelter as their mountain hunting camp and ignored many other places. Although they didn't know the physics involved, they surely understood that Gatecliff could shelter them like no place else. In this shallow south-facing rockshelter, the summertime sunshine first reaches the back wall in mid-morning and disappears in mid-afternoon. The effect reverses in cold weather, when the rear wall of Gatecliff Shelter is bathed in the warming rays of the low winter sun. Gatecliff Shelter is a huge lithic heat sink, with solar energy absorbed during the hot summer months and released up to three months after the onset of cold weather. This place stayed fairly cool in the summertime and held heat in the winter. The sheep hunters of Monitor valley knew that—for sure.

Over a 4000-year span, the alpine hunters engineered the space inside Gatecliff Shelter in the repetitious and redundant ways of their ancestors. Many times, the alpine hunters started afresh when they walked onto a new sterile surface at Gatecliff. Since their last visit (or those of distant ancestors), flash floods had roiled and swirled inside, burying everything beneath sealed floors of thick, hard, graded beds of impenetrable silt. None of the tools, the fire hearths, the food bones or the bedding poked up above this floor. Time and time again, even without visual clues from those living at Gatecliff before, the sheep hunters built their firehearths in exactly the same special places. They slept in the same spaces. They reworked their gear while sitting in the same spots. They threw their trash into the fireplaces or far beyond.

The sheep hunters described their ordered space in words long lost, but archaeologists have their own language to describe the same thing. Beginning about 4100 BC, the hunters staying at Gatecliff Shelter began building their fire hearths along a clearly defined arc positioned 10 to 12 feet. from the rear cave wall. This *hearthline* (three dozen hearths spread across nine wholly independent superimposed cultural horizons) separated everything inside. Hunters slept in the heated chamber along the rear wall. The hearthline also size-sorted the artifact fragments, debitage, and artiodactyl bone fragments that were generated and discarded at Gatecliff. Smaller fragments defined a distinctive *drop zone* in the most sheltered part of the site. Everything larger (articular ends and long bone pieces, bulky hammerstones, production stage biface fragments, and large lithic scrap) went into the *toss zone* that splayed across the drip line and down the exposed apron at the front. Early stage lithic production and rough butchering took place outside the hearthline. This *drop zone/toss zone* configuration makes perfect sense today. As one Nunamiut hunter put it, "Who wants to sit down on a large bone?"

Over the millennia, the alpine hunters returned frequently to their well-engineered camp at Gatecliff Shelter. With just a couple of small fires, they quickly created a warm, dry, and smoke-free place to camp and work. Before heading up to the alpine hunting grounds, this is where they made things right—fixing the right tools, crafting the right game plan, and making things right with the mountain.

The planning began long before the first bighorn was spotted. The alpine hunters already knew the landscape by heart. They remembered the best sheep beds and game trails; years before, they'd set up their own soldier cairns, rock blinds, and beehive blinds in exactly the right places. They probably made a few preliminary scouting trips up the mountain, always hoping for a quick kill, but often just spooking the wary sheep into their escape cover. The hunters must have returned empty-handed to Gatecliff many times, hoping for better results in the morning. But each time, they knew more about the immediacy of the weather, the water, the trees, and the condition of the herd.

Each hunter crafted and maintained his individual toolkit, inevitably losing or breaking some of his best weaponry. High or low in the mountains, hunters replaced their spent and lost items as necessary, curating, and replacing as they could. The hunters also did their medicine. Some young boys, on their first hunt, might have scoffed at the rituals and taboos that seemed to keep them from taking full advantage of their skills. But the elders knew better, and through their practice, they showed how to maintain proper relationships with the animal spirits and with the mountain. They knew that if hunters fail to treat the spirits with respect, the sheep will not make themselves available and entire families will suffer. Some hunters enjoyed more power than others, with hallucinations they took as supernatural communications. Others had dreams that conferred a "power" to perform physical feats or to summon up game when none could be seen.

Alpine hunters probably painted the walls inside Gatecliff Shelter, and this rock art is described by T. Thomas (1983) while Koski, McKee, and Thomas (1973) analyzed the pigments. About two dozen of the millingstones and manos recovered there were stained with red, yellow, and white pigments, the earliest dating back to 3900–4100 BC. Half a dozen red-stained paint palettes turned up in strata dating 1500–1700 BC. These pigments seem identical to the goethite, lepidocrocite, and hematite that, when applied with a gypsum binder, created the anthropomorphic and counting-line pictograph images that cluster along the rear wall.

How many times did the hunters head out from Gatecliff Shelter with high hopes, to hunt the Mt. Jefferson tablelands and other alpine reaches across the backbone of the Toquimas? On successful days, their skill and planning and medicine paid off. If it was late in the day, they may have overnighted briefly near the hunting grounds, gutting and bleeding out the carcass, then disguising it with branches overnight, to keep away the magpies, ravens, and eagles. Maybe they moved the innards away, as a decoy for the coyotes. If the weather was brisk enough to cool the meat, maybe they hiked straight home.

They often carried field-dressed sheep to Gatecliff Shelter, where they lightened the load by discarding waste, then smoking and drying the meat over small fires at the rear of the shelter. Eventually, the hunters picked through their gear—carrying some and caching other things for later—then headed home with their prize. Each hunt brought its own challenges, and Gatecliff Shelter remained a place to get it right.

Even when the mountain and the sheep chose not to cooperate, the hunters never returned home empty-handed. Sometimes, they hefted packets of flaked stone bifaces (raw materials for making smaller stone tools). Sometimes, they toted bulky limestone cobbles from a faraway mountain, for making the best millingstones and manos. Sometimes, they returned with dried marmots and woodrats, always welcome delicacies at home.

So it was that alpine hunting grounds (like Mt. Jefferson) were always closely entwined with the best hunting camps (like Gatecliff Shelter), ensuring that the hunters would not disappoint with empty arms.

DISCUSSION QUESTIONS

1. Why was Thomas so interested in finding a site like Gatecliff? Explain why a site like Gatecliff is worth looking for when one is doing regional surveys.

2. Describe the vertical strategy employed at Gatecliff. What were the goals of this phase of excavation? Why was a horizontal strategy eventually employed, and how did it help meet other goals?

3. Does determination of chronology logically precede paleoethnography, as Thomas suggests? Can it be argued that either the chronological goals or the paleoethnographic goals mentioned are more important in archaeology?

4. How was Gatecliff Shelter used over the years? How has archaeology at Gatecliff and elsewhere in the region informed this interpretation?

CHAPTER 9

Foragers and Villagers of the Southwestern Mountains, Mesas, and Deserts

On a moonlit night a lone hiker makes her way up a winding sandstone canyon, miles from the nearest road. She stops to look at petroglyphs in the dim light, and then pushes on to her goal, a set of ruins in an alcove in the canyon. After making camp, Dr. Eleanor Friedman-Bernal struggles up a talus slope and takes a trail to one of the ruins, only to find that pothunters, thieves of time, had been digging at this isolated ruin, leaving the ground scattered with human bone. Dr. Friedman-Bernal makes her way to a small pool below the ruin and is surprised to find frogs tethered to pegs around the edge of the water. She is also surprised to hear the strains of a flute playing a Beatles tune, "Hey Jude," out in the desolate canyon country where she had expected to find no one.

This is the way Tony Hillerman (1988:1–10) opens his Navajo detective novel *A Thief of Time*. Dr. Friedman-Bernal has made the trek to this ruin to look for a particular kind of pottery with a distinctive design that she is certain will validate her reconstruction of population movement after the collapse of the Chaco system. She expects this find to make her reputation as an archaeologist. When her associates at Chaco Canyon become worried because she has not returned, Hillerman's heroes Lieutenant Joe Leaphorn and Officer Jim Chee become involved in the case. The unfolding mystery takes Leaphorn and Chee through more vandalized ruins and the black market in Anasazi pottery, and through the Chaco Canyon Cultural Center.

The canyons of the American Southwest, with their spectacular ruins, are popular settings for works of fiction, and archaeology is woven into these tales to varying degrees. Besides mysteries, some novels try to portray life in the ruined towns that we see on the ground today. Archaeology and archaeologists are included in these books, but with varying degrees of accuracy. When archaeologists are portrayed, most often they are depicted as lone researchers working on a big career-making or career-saving discovery. Like Dr. Friedman-Bernal, they search for a big find to prove a pet theory, to prove themselves right, and often to justify themselves and their unorthodox ideas. Generally, in fiction, the archaeologist seeks a specific significant artifact and knows when she or he has found it. There is the sense that these fictional archaeologists can go on to great fame as a result of their discoveries, and there is also a sense that the press will be drawn to report the great discoveries without much work on the part of the archaeologist.

No archaeologist would discount the role of discoveries in enhancing our knowledge of the past, but such discoveries are only one aspect of archaeological research. In reality, today's archaeology is quite different from the solo endeavor suggested by fictional accounts. It usually is a team effort involving many individuals, whether conducted as part of the CRM process or as academic research. Also, finding the sites, deciding which ones have important information to yield, and getting the artifacts out of the ground comprise only the beginning of the process. Cleaning, cataloging, and analysis are critical as well. Curation of the resulting collections usually isn't mentioned at all in popular books; yet the ability to return to old, curated collections with new questions is vital for the effort to expand knowledge about the past. Archaeologists write descriptive reports and prepare research articles to disseminate the results of their work, but they seldom become famous, and only occasionally do their finds attract the popular press.

Of course, fictional accounts do not set out to educate the public about archaeology; they use archaeology as an element of plot and setting designed to tell an interesting story and keep readers involved. While the details of the depictions of archaeologists may not be completely accurate,

the inclusion of archaeologists as characters certainly is. One idea that Hillerman and other novelists communicate well is that there is a lot of anthropology and archaeology to be done in the Southwest. This is a region rich in far more than breathtaking, arid landscapes. A variety of contemporary Indian, Hispanic, and Anglo cultures and a rich and visible archaeological heritage also attract scholars. Anthropologists and archaeologists have been studying this area since the nineteenth century and have learned much about its past. This chapter introduces what has been learned.

DEFINITION OF THE AREA

Anthropologists define the Southwest culture area to include the entire state of Arizona, the western portions of New Mexico, southwestern Colorado, the southern portions of Utah and Nevada, the Mexican state of Sonora, and portions of the states of Chihuahua and Durango in Mexico as well (Figure 9.1). However, much less archaeological research has been done in the Mexican portions of this culture area, and most of our discussion treats the portions in the United States. This is an area where agriculture often was practiced

FIGURE 9.1 The Southwest culture area, showing sites that are mentioned in Chapter 9.

prehistorically, in contrast to the areas surrounding it on the west, north, and east. Architecture of stone or adobe masonry is also found throughout the pre-Columbian Southwest, as is the production of pottery. Some anthropologists have included most of Utah and adjacent Colorado, home of the Fremont culture in the Southwest, but in this text we treat these areas as part of the Great Basin (Chapter 8). The Southwest culture area has a rich and varied archaeological past that can be broken down into periods of varying length for convenience in discussion (Table 9.1). The descendants of the various aboriginal groups evident in the archaeological record populate the Southwest today, some of them living in pueblos that have been occupied for centuries (Ortiz 1979). It is important for Southwestern archaeologists to keep in mind the linkages between the people we study and Native people living in the Southwest today.

THE ENVIRONMENTS OF THE SOUTHWEST

When you think of the Southwest, you may envision landscapes resembling those in Figure 9.2. In fact, the region contains a diversity of environments and habitats to which humans have always had to adjust. Formally, this culture area includes portions of three major physiographic regions: the Basin and Range province in the west, the Colorado Plateau in the north, and the southern Rocky Mountains in the east. In addition, at various times in the past, southwesterners also inhabited the western margin of a fourth physiographic province, the Great Plains. Elevational variation within the Southwest is extreme. In the basins of the western Southwest, elevations may be close to sea level, while the highest peaks of the southern Rocky Mountains can reach over 13,000 feet (3965 m). Much of the Southwest is a rugged land, but there are also broad valleys and flat mesa tops.

The overriding environmental feature for humans living in the Southwest is the arid climate. Availability of water always has been of central importance to southwesterners. In general, the western and southern portions of the Southwest are drier than the northern and eastern portions. Average annual precipitation can be as low as 5 inches (127 mm) in the western Basin and Range province but three times as high in the southern Rocky Mountains.

Average precipitation estimates are misleading, however, because the cyclonic storms that bring much of the Southwest's moisture vary in pattern. In some areas, winter precipitation that is not lost to runoff is more important than rainfall from short summer thunderstorms. In other areas, most of the rainfall is attributable to summer thunderstorms, which

sometimes are violent and localized. In addition, the mountains of the Southwest receive the precipitation that results when air masses carrying moisture are uplifted in their journey over the peaks. Mountain slopes on the windward side receive a great deal of moisture, while the slopes on the other side are in a rain shadow. Slight changes in the position of the jet stream or in prevailing wind patterns can result in significant reduction or increase in precipitation. Rivers and streams also cannot be discounted as important sources of water in the Southwest.

Perhaps counterintuitively, the dry climate does not mean that the area is uniformly hot; in fact, temperature is variable over the Southwest. Elevation has a great deal to do with this, with cooler temperatures being characteristic at higher elevations, especially at night and during the winter. Once again, this is a complicated matter. For example, in the steep-sided canyons and narrow valleys, the phenomenon called cold-air drainage results in the trapping of cold air at the bottom of the canyon, so that it actually is warmer higher up the canyon sides than at the bottom.

Plant and animal life is highly variable in the Southwest as well, though the resources nearly always are sparsely distributed. Deserts cover much of the Southwest, but along some of the larger rivers a riparian forest with cottonwood, willow, and cattail can be found. In mountainous areas (Figure 9.3) vegetation is broadly zoned by elevation, with grasses and brushy species mixing with scrub oak, piñon, and juniper at the lower elevations, and species such as ponderosa pine, Douglas fir, and aspen being found somewhat higher. In the southern Rocky Mountains, subalpine forests are dominated by Engelmann spruce and subalpine fir, while at the highest elevations, treeless meadows occur. The Colorado Plateau also supports zonation by elevation. Although piñon–juniper woodland is the most common type of vegetation, there are many areas of bare rock, and low elevations support sagebrush and grasslands; the highest elevations usually have conifers of various types.

Animal species density reflects these vegetational differences. Many Southwestern animals combine a nonselective diet with movement between multiple vegetational and physiographic zones. In general, large- and medium-sized animals are rarest in low-elevation, more desertic areas, while small animals, including a wide variety of rodents, are highly diverse in the same areas. Similarly, larger-bodied animals show much more diversity in the higher elevations of the Southwest. This generalization should not obscure the presence of a great variety of birds throughout the Southwest, especially in the better-watered and agricultural areas. Migratory waterfowl fly across the

TABLE 9.1 Introduction to Southwest Culture History

Uncalibrated Years BP	General Periods	Western	Southwestern Cultural Phenomena Southwestern	Northern	Southern	Calibrated Years BC/AD
	Historic			Pueblo Revolt		AD 1,650
500		Patayan tradition	Casas Grandes	Ancestral Pueblo tradition Sinagua tradition		AD 1,426
1,000	Regional traditions		Hohokam tradition Mogollon tradition			AD 1,022
1,500						AD 568
2,000	Late Archaic/ Early Agricultural					0 BC
2,500						618 BC
3,000						1,261 BC
3,500						1,875 BC
4,000						2,555 BC
4,500		Pinto tradition	Cochise tradition	Oshara tradition		3,183 BC
5,000						3,780 BC
5,500	Archaic				Chihuahua tradition	4,344 BC
6,000						4,874 BC
6,500						5,476 BC
7,000						5,890 BC
7,500						6,395 BC
8,000						6,911 BC
8,500						7,571 BC
9,000					Various Plano complexes	8,247 BC
9,500		Stemmed tradition				8,788 BC
10,000	Paleoindian					9,445 BC
10,500				Folsom		10,509 BC
11,000						10,932 BC
11,500			Clovis			11,394 BC
and prior	Pre-Clovis?		?????????			and Prior

FIGURE 9.2 Canyon
Country of the Southwest:
Arches National Park, Utah.

FIGURE 9.3 Typical forest
vegetation of the southern
Rocky Mountains.

ANTHROPOLOGICAL THEMES   TOPIC 9.1

Thematic Research Questions in Chapter 9

As we pointed out in Chapter 2, the North American archaeological record provides significant evidence for several broad anthropological themes. Many of these themes can be addressed with data from the Southwest culture area. You will find material directly relevant to at least five of the broad research questions discussed in Chapter 2 and listed in Table 2.1, and we touch on other themes less directly. Table 9.2 helps you locate relevant sections of this chapter for each theme although as you become more familiar with the archaeology of the Southwest, you will discover more specific research questions and issues as well.

TABLE 9.2 Research Themes for the Southwest

Research Question	Particularly Relevant Sections
How have humans adapted to the diverse environments of North America and to climatic change over time?	Discussions in the Archaic section and in the section on Farmers and Villagers
How, when, and where did food production develop in North America?	Discussion of the Late Archaic as well as the section on Farmers and Villagers
How, when, and where did sociopolitically complex, internally differentiated cultural systems develop in North America?	Discussion in the section on Farmers and Villagers, especially Box 9.1, "Interpreting the Chaco Phenomenon," as well as the section on Reorganization, Aggregation, and Conflict in Late Prehistory. This chapter's case study also is directly relevant to this theme.
What movements of human populations can be documented in the North American past after the continent's initial settlement?	Discussions in the sections on the Late Archaic, Reorganization, Aggregation, and Conflict in Late Prehistory, and New Arrivals

region annually, though not in the numbers found in other parts of the United States. Aquatic mammals like muskrats and beavers, as well as turtles and fish, can occur in significant numbers where water habitats are present, and snakes and lizards also are widely distributed.

There were other resources besides plants and animals in the ancient Southwest. Today the Southwest is known as a region rich in minerals, including copper, lead, coal, and uranium. In pre-Columbian times, the mountains of the Southwest were sources of fine-grained chert, turquoise, and obsidian traded within the region and beyond.

Climatic Change

Although the various factors that structure the region's environment can be outlined, a changing environment has been a constant in the Southwest. The bedrock geology and the generally arid conditions of this area haven't changed greatly during the time of human habitation, but climate has experienced both long- and short-term variation. Major climatic changes such as those associated with the Pleistocene and the beginning of the Holocene affected the precipitation regimes of the Southwest in complex and fascinating ways. In addition, seasonal and annual changes in factors such as precipitation and temperature, as well as erosional and depositional events, have affected Southwestern environments greatly over time. Human modifications to the environment have been important as well—at least since Southwestern peoples became farmers and began to live in significant population concentrations. For example, the processes of clearing land for fields and acquiring wood for fuel probably significantly altered fragile Southwestern environments on a local scale during pre-Columbian times. For all these reasons, archaeologists have given particular attention to the task of paleoenvironmental reconstruction in the Southwest.

HUNTERS AND FORAGERS

Paleoindian

Although Pre-Clovis sites, such as Pendejo Cave in southeastern New Mexico, have been proposed, reliable evidence for human presence in the Southwest does not predate the Clovis period. Evidence of Clovis hunters is based on surface finds and, most importantly on mammoth kill sites such as Naco, Lehner Ranch, and Murray Springs in southeastern Arizona (see Figure 3.17). In the eastern part of the Southwest, Folsom and other Paleoindian complexes follow Clovis, while in Arizona, the San Dieguito complex, discussed in Chapters 7 and 8, has been found in surface remains. The **Ventana complex** (Figure 9.4) from Ventana Cave has been associated with both San Dieguito and Folsom but is not considered to represent either (Haury 1950). Recently reported dates from Ventana Cave suggest that this material is early Holocene rather than Paleoindian (Huckell 1998). This redating is consistent with findings, in the western Southwest, of San Dieguito materials associated with the beginnings of the second period of foraging, the Archaic.

Early and Middle Archaic

The Southwestern Archaic period lasted from about 8000 BP to 1750 BP, but it is relatively poorly understood as researchers have focused most of their attention on the later, pottery-making, settled horticulturists. The Early and Middle Archaic, from approximately 8000 BP to 3500 BP (see Table 9.1), can be characterized by generalized foraging adaptations, high human mobility, and relatively low human population. These millennia encompass a climatic interval usually called the Altithermal (ca. 7000–4500 BP) in the Southwest (Antevs 1948:1955). During this time, unusually warm conditions prevailed. There is debate over whether this interval was warm and moist or warm and arid, and there is considerable evidence of local variation and perhaps seasonal in moisture during the Altithermal (Huckell 1996). Nevertheless, Southwestern Archaic

FIGURE 9.4 Ventana complex materials from Ventana Cave, Arizona: (a, b) projectile points, (c, d) flake knives, (e) curved knife, and (f, g) discoidal scrapers.

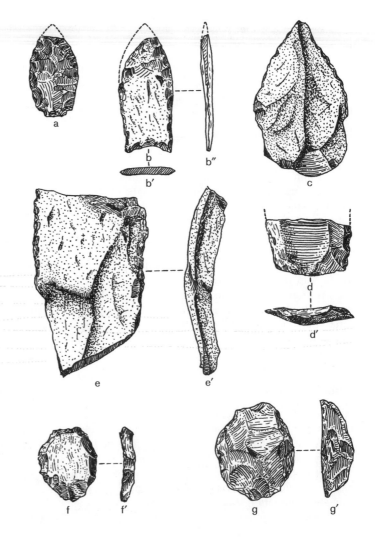

FIGURE 9.5 A Pinto point.

foragers had to cope with this warm period, and no doubt did so in a variety of ways that archaeologists are only beginning to comprehend. At the peak of the Altithermal some parts of the Southwest may have been largely abandoned while in others humans most likely were tethered to dependable water sources and less mobile.

Archaeologists have recognized regional variation in the Southwestern Archaic, developing culture history sequences for three to four regional traditions, named Pinto, **Oshara**, Cochise, and **Chihuahua** (Irwin-Williams 1979). The **Pinto tradition** (8000–1450 BP), found in the western portions of the Southwest, was originally described in the Pinto Basin of California. It is found primarily at surface sites in western and southern Arizona (including Ventana Cave), southern Nevada, and into southern California. Pinto points (Figure 9.5) are the hallmark of this tradition. Note that the Pinto period in the Great Basin ends at approximately 4000 BP before the Pinto tradition in the Southwest (see Chapter 8). The Oshara tradition (7450–1550 BP) is a long Archaic sequence defined for the northern Southwest. At the beginning of this sequence, the Jay phase, can be considered to be Late Paleoindian. The Jay projectile point resembles Late Paleoindian points from the Great Plains, but assemblages also include leaf-shaped knives that resemble San Dieguito material found in the western Southwest and California. As a result, there has been disagreement over whether Jay represents continuity with Paleoindian occupation of the northern Southwest or in-migration of a population from farther west. The Cochise tradition (9450–2150 BP) refers to the Archaic in the southwestern part of the Southwest, although it was originally applied more broadly. There is debate about the utility of this concept (Cordell 1997:109–111), but it is used by many archaeologists. The southeastern portion of the

Southwest has been seen as home to the Chihuahua tradition (7950 BP–1700 BP) (Beckett and MacNeish 1994). This tradition is not well understood; it shares similarities with both the Oshara and Pinto traditions, and yet has distinctive elements as well, particularly among the projectile points.

Many of the attributes that archaeologists can use to clearly distinguish the Archaic from the preceding Paleoindian period are technological. In the first place, ground stone implements occur in much higher frequencies after the Paleoindian. These include milling-stones, which were used to process the seeds that became of greater significance in the diet. Second, there were changes in the types of chipped stone implements being made. Projectile points from the Archaic tend to be smaller than those produced earlier, in the Paleoindian period. In addition, the side- and corner-notched morphology of the Archaic points reflects newer hafting techniques not used by Paleoindians, who made fluted or stemmed points. Alongside the projectile points was an array of other flaked stone tools, including scrapers, choppers, and knives of various kinds.

As with the Archaic elsewhere in the United States, the subsistence adaptation of Southwestern Archaic groups regardless of regional tradition can be referred to as a "broad-spectrum" adaptation. This term captures the notion that a very wide variety of plant and animal foods was consumed (Vierra 1994). Hunting of large game was an important part of the Archaic lifestyle, but added to this base were the trapping of small game and the gathering of wild seeds. Actually, the character of Archaic hunting and foraging probably was more complicated than this brief introduction allows. For example, researchers working with materials from Ventana Cave in southern Arizona have shown that the exploitation of small, locally available animals like the rabbit was highest prior to the middle of the Archaic and that selective hunting of larger game like deer began to increase in importance at this time (Szuter and Bayham 1989). Similar trends toward selectivity have been suggested for the use of plants in the San Juan Basin of the northern Southwest (Cordell 1997:120–121). In any case, ethnobotanical analysis at a variety of Archaic sites has resulted in the recovery of a wide variety of plant remains from Archaic contexts. These include ricegrass, dropseed, goosefoot, pigweed, hackberry, walnut, prickly pear, and other species. Storage of seeds to meet needs in winter is indicated by the presence of storage pits, especially in the northern part of the Southwest.

In their settlement patterns, Archaic hunter-gatherers were organized in small, mobile groups, following the blooming and ripening of plant resources. Groups in the northern part of the Southwest were probably more mobile than those in the south, where people would have been drawn to the valleys of the permanent rivers. Caves and rockshelters were frequently used as campsites, and many of these have remained dry since their occupation, preserving organic remains such as basketry, wood, and sandals (Figure 9.6). On the whole, Archaic sites tend to be fairly ephemeral because they were used only for short periods by a few people. However, simple houses are first seen in the Southwest at about 5150 BP. These houses are small, shallow pithouses, circular to oval in shape. Such structures may indicate that some people achieved a measure of sedentism even before agriculture was developed.

Late Archaic

The Late Archaic (ca. 3500–1750 BP) was a time of significant adaptive change that may correspond to the onset of more nearly modern, moister climate conditions. At this time, the larger numbers and sizes of sites suggest an increase in human population levels. This is also the period when many Southwestern hunter-gatherers incorporated the cultivation of crops into their subsistence, and some researchers (e.g., Huckell 1995, 1996) have proposed the use of the term **Early Agricultural period** instead of Late Archaic.

The record of early agriculture in the Southwest has dramatically improved in the last two decades, and new data have changed our perspectives on how Southwestern peoples became agriculturalists. Maize was first planted in the Southwest between about 4000 BP and 3500 BP, and early maize dates continue to accumulate as more research is conducted. Early dates have come from sites in the Mogollon Highlands of west central New Mexico and adjacent Arizona at sites

FIGURE 9.6 Yucca wickerwork sandals from Tularosa Cave, New Mexico.

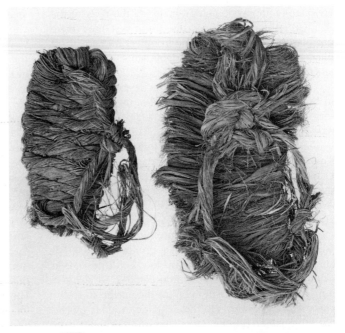

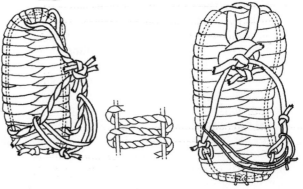

such as Bat Cave, where it is now believed to date to 3100 BP. In fact, there are more than 20 Southwestern maize dates older than 3000 BP (Vierra 2005). The oldest maize is from McEuen Cave in the Gila Mountains of southeastern Arizona, where dates cluster at or near 3700 BP. However sites in the Santa Cruz River valley including Las Capas and Clearwater also have maize dates of around 3700 BP. Mabry (2005) maps nearly 200 Late Archaic or Early Agricultural sites in southeastern Arizona. Along with maize, squash has been found in early contexts. Between 2500 BP and 2200 BP, other important cultigens including the common bean and the bottle gourd seem to have been cultivated, although not in the northern Southwest (Ford 1981). Human manipulation of native plants for seeds and fibers may also have begun during the Archaic as possibly domesticated amaranth has been recovered from Cerro Juanaqueña in northwestern Chihuahua (Mabry 2005).

Perhaps even more fascinating is the evidence for early water control and terracing in Late Archaic contexts. These include canals at various sites in the Santa Cruz River valley such as Las Capas and Costello-King. Early irrigation features dating as early as 3000 years ago have also been found near Zuni Pueblo in west central New Mexico (Damp et al. 2002). At Tumamoc Hill in the western Tucson basin, stone terrace walls are associated with maize and with Late Archaic projectile points. The most striking evidence of terracing is from Cerro Juanaqueña in Chihuahua, Mexico (Hard and Roney 2005). This site dates to approximately 3200 BP, and contains evidence of 550 terraces and 99 rock rings. Most of this construction is believed to have been done to create living surfaces and house platforms rather than for farming. Storage pits and dense assemblages of artifacts on constructed surfaces supports this interpretation.

Late Archaic villages are now known from southeastern Arizona. For example, in the Tucson basin there are Late Archaic pithouse villages like the Milagro site, which has a dozen or more pithouses and large quantities of maize apparently produced through floodplain farming. Another large site is the La Playa site located along the Rio Boquillas in Sonora, Mexico. This site covers approximately 12 square kilometers and includes low artificial mounds, dog burials, and hundreds of human burials many of which date to the Early Agricultural period (Carpenter et al. 2005). Marine shell from the Pacific also occurs in large quantities at this site, as does other evidence for long distance trade. Other Late Archaic habitation sites are smaller, but may well represent year-round occupations. For example, Damp (2007) identifies winter and summer houses as well as storage pits and hearths at Early Agricultural Period sites in the Zuni area.

The growing body of new evidence for the adoption of agriculture during the Late Archaic has led to a variety of explanatory models. The traditional model of a slow gradual adoption of agriculture by Southwesterners may apply in some areas where casual planting and tending of crops could easily be incorporated into a mobile, broad-spectrum adaptation. A successful crop would be harvested and stored like other seed, but an unsuccessful crop represented little lost effort. In other areas, however, people appear to rapidly have become dependent on maize and other domesticates, to have lived in more sedentary villages, and to have constructed a variety of features including canals and terraces that would have required substantial labor investment and social interaction. Some researchers argue that there is a discontinuity between Early and Middle Archaic Southwestern foragers and the Early Agricultural peoples of the Late Archaic that suggests in-migration of farming people bringing both the domesticates and the technology that allowed them to establish new lifestyles. Such a migration has been associated with the northward movement of Proto-Uto-Aztecan language speakers (Hill 2007) out of Mexico and into the Southwest, even though southward movement of this language group also has been envisioned. It has been argued as well that agriculture was brought rapidly onto the Colorado Plateau, where it quickly became the center of subsistence because of its productivity (Matson 2007). Recent work at Zuni tends to support this formulation for at least this part of the Plateau (Damp 2007). Additional evidence from the isotopes found in human bone collagen indicates that before 2300 BP people in northeastern Arizona were heavily dependent on maize (Coltrain et al. 2007).

We now realize that the first steps toward farming were more complicated and variable than has been thought traditionally. Obviously there is a great deal yet to be learned about the Late Archaic both in terms of diverse responses to environmental, technological, and social change and with respect to population movements. Because the origins of agriculture is a topic of such broad anthropological interest, current research on the earliest Southwestern farmers is especially significant.

FARMERS AND VILLAGERS

Traditionally, the people who inhabited the Southwest after approximately 1750 BP or AD 200 have received the most archaeological attention. Most of these Southwesterners were committed to agriculture and were settled into agricultural hamlets or villages. Their lifestyles did vary regionally, but they also had much in common. These farmers grew a variety of crops, especially the agricultural big three: maize, beans, and squash. Early maize was a type of popcorn called Chapalote popcorn, but after 1300 BP (AD 600) a new variety with larger kernels and fewer rows known as Maiz de Ocho began to be grown in the Southwest. This variety had more food energy and was easier to grind as well (Kantner 2004:67). Beans are particularly important because beans contain the amino acid lysine, which helps humans digest the protein available in corn. Moreover, while corn depletes the nitrogen in the soil in which it is grown, legumes like beans return nitrogen to the ground. Thus, these crops complement each other nicely, and it is no surprise that Native American farmers often grew them together.

Other cultigens were eventually grown in southern areas, where extensive canal systems were constructed for irrigation purposes (see Figure 1.17). Between 1650 BP and 1450 BP, these new crops, including cotton, sieva beans, jack beans, and cushaw squash, were adopted from Mexico. These cultigens can tolerate the high desert temperatures as long as they have enough water, and this was provided through irrigation. Other cultigens used in the area may have been locally domesticated because they are native southwestern plants. Examples are agave, which was used for its fibers as well as for food, amaranth, and little barley grass.

Economies were mixed and hunting continued, as did the gathering of wild plant foods. Farming actually opened up some new possibilities for both hunting and gathering, as crops attracted game animals that could be hunted in the gardens, and the cultivated fields were colonized by wild plants known as **ruderals**, which thrive in disturbed soils. Greens, roots, shoots, and seeds from ruderal plants were collected and possibly even nominally tended by Southwestern farmers. Hunting game attracted to the fields not only added to the meat portion of the diet, but also protected the crops by reducing the pests (Neusius 2008). The only domesticated animal in the Southwest besides the dog is the turkey. Turkeys were kept in pens at some sites and may have been raised as a source of feathers as well as food. However, domesticated turkey could be critical for survival, especially when game had been depleted (Rawlings and Driver 2010). In some places people also kept macaws and parrots imported from Mexico. These birds provided a source of colorful feathers for decorative and ceremonial uses.

Eventually farming and more sedentary lifestyles were associated with increased aggregation into larger settlements throughout the Southwest. This was not necessarily a slow and gradual process, because settlements grew both through births and by in-migration of people from other areas. The climate of the Southwest,

which often changed in ways that made areas more or less suitable for farming, sometimes led to abandonment of areas and migrations to more favorable locations.

A related trend is the elaboration of architectural features that served to unite or integrate members of the community. With the development of very large villages came a need to knit together the disparate households that made up the settlement into a cohesive unit. The increasingly larger multifamily dwelling structures that become common in the various parts of the Southwest can be understood as evidence of increased community integration. Archaeologists also have reasoned that large structures, accommodating activities that involved the whole community, such as dances, elaborate ceremonies, or ball games, helped foster common interests among the members of the various families or households.

The story of these changes is fascinatingly variable from region to region throughout the Southwest. However, archaeologists generally group the settled village dwellers of the Southwest in terms of four regional traditions: the Anasazi, the Hohokam, the Mogollon, and the Patayan. A fifth grouping, the Sinagua, has been variously considered part of each of these other traditions, and its affiliations remain poorly understood.

Anasazi (Ancestral Pueblo)

Archaeologists recognized the culture known as the Anasazi, or Ancestral Pueblo, before they could distinguish the other cultural traditions of the area (use of the terms Ancestral Pueblo and Anasazi was discussed in Chapter 2; see Box 2.1). The Ancestral Pueblo inhabited the Plateau country of the northern Southwest. They used the **coil-and-scrape technique** to make gray as well as black-painted, white and red-slipped ceramics, scraping away surface imperfections and thinning the walls as a vessel was constructed. Geometric and other designs were applied with black paint. Some gray pots had neck bands or were corrugated (Figure 9.7). Housing consisted of pithouses and masonry surface rooms of various kinds. In the later phases, the Ancestral Pueblo built the large pueblos and cliff dwellings for which the Southwest is so well known (Figure 9.8).

Subsistence was centered on growing maize, beans, and squash, but wild and ruderal plants and a variety of animals were part of the diet as well. Because of the limited growing season and the dramatic seasonal changes in the northern Southwest, storage of agricultural products was very important. We know

FIGURE 9.7 Anasazi grayware vessels from northern Arizona: (left) neck banded and (right) corrugated.

FIGURE 9.8 Spruce Tree House at Mesa Verde in winter.

that some features were used for storage because burning at some sites has left charred remains of stored maize and other foods while structures in dry caves have sometimes contained preserved maize cobs (with the kernels long ago gnawed off by rodents). In many parts of the Plateau, the agricultural cycle depended on sufficient soil moisture remaining after the snow melt to allow germination of the crops. Summer monsoonal rainfall would water these fields later in the growing season. In areas where rainfall was marginal for crop growth, **check dams** and water diversion structures were used to take advantage of runoff. Toward the end of the Ancestral Pueblo sequence, rudimentary canal irrigation was practiced, especially in the Rio Grande valley.

The **Pecos classification,** one of the first archaeological attempts at regional synthesis, as discussed in Section A of the Student CD (see especially Table A.1), was developed based on Anasazi sites, and a modified version is still used to order Ancestral Pueblo archaeology. Today this sequence starts with **Basketmaker** II around 1550 BP and ends with Pueblo V in the Historic period. Basketmaker II is preceramic and corresponds to the very end of the Archaic while Basketmaker III is the effective beginning of the Ancestral Pueblo per se. Pueblo I through Pueblo IV generally encompass the development of the first villages and then of larger communities. Many subregional phase schemes—**Mesa Verde, Chaco,** Kayenta, Virgin, and **Rio Grande branches**—have been developed to account for the specifics of cultural development in particular areas. Archaeologists usually prefer to use these schemes, which are too many and varied to present here, although they still make general references to the Pecos classification. Table 9.3 provides an example of the phase sequence for Chaco Branch Ancestral Pueblo. This branch is particularly interesting, as discussed later, because of the development of an unparalleled

regional system in Chaco canyon during Pueblo II times.

The development of Anasazi architecture has provided one of the key elements used in defining the Pecos periods and subregional phases for the Southwest. There was variation in the timing of changes, but the same trends are evident throughout the Ancestral Pueblo area. One of the most important developments early in the sequence is the **Pithouse-to-Pueblo transition,** generally occurring in Basketmaker III to Pueblo I times (see Bonus Case Study D.5 on the Student CD for an example). At this time, village layout changed from small groups of pithouses and storage rooms to arcs of room blocks with one or more pithouses located to the south. Basketmaker III communities were clusters of pithouses. These pitstructures had relatively standardized structure forms (Figure 9.9) with antechambers connected to the main chamber by a short passageway. Roofs were supported by posts. Fire pits are found in the center of the structures, and **wing walls** divided the main chamber. Deflectors, sandstone slabs set on edge, were placed between the opening of the passageway and the fire, presumably to divert air currents that came in through the passageway. Accompanying the pithouses are generally round, slab-lined surface rooms with **jacal** superstructures. These were presumably used for storage.

Pueblo I village plans changed to arcs of connected rectangular rooms with associated pitstructures and midden or trash disposal areas to the south. Construction went from slab-lined to jacal walls, with vertical sandstone slabs incorporated into the bottom of the walls, and finally to masonry walls. As rectangular rooms began to be built, a standard pattern began to emerge. This pattern was one of suites of three rooms: two small storage rooms in the back fronted by a surface habitation room, although it is likely that people used the plazas outside these room blocks for many

TABLE 9.3 Phase Sequences Chaco Branch Anasazi

Date			
BP	**AD**	**Chaco Canyon**	**Highlights**
550	1400		Chaco Canyon abandoned
600	1350		
650	1300	Mesa Verde	Use of cave sites and butte tops as well as other locations, economic interaction with Mesa Verde Anasazi
700	1250		
750	1200	Late Bonito	Population decline, but some new construction, imported ceramic types
800	1150		
850	1100	Classic Bonito	Construction of great houses and of soil and water control features, road system, height of Chaco's development
900	1050	(Pueblo II)	
950	1000		
1000	950	Bonito	Increased population, mostly small sites, but construction of some multistoried pueblos that later become great houses
1050	900	(early Pueblo II)	
1100	850		
1150	800	Pueblo I	Aboveground dwellings with associated proto-kivas and eventually kivas, more masonry architecture, increase in numbers of sites within the canyon as opposed to on its edges
1200	750		
1250	700		
1300	650		
1350	600	Basketmaker III	Sites with a few pitstructures used as dwellings found on mesatops
1400	550		
1450	500		

Based on Cordell 1997:Table 7.1 and 188–192.

activities. At the same time, the nature of pitstructures was changing; they were no longer exclusively dwellings but places for group activities and rituals. Although the wing walls and deflector continued to be present, the antechamber and passageway were replaced by a vertical **ventilator** connected to the pithouse by a horizontal, floor-level shaft. Larger villages were formed by adding groups of three-room suites and pithouses to the room blocks or by adding additional room blocks and pithouses.

These changes in architecture clearly signal increasing integration of people into communities. Activities and rituals that helped establish extra-familial relationships and identities and drew people together became more important. In this context oversized pitstructures, or proto-kivas, and eventually **kivas** can be assumed to be integrative facilities, based on analogy with modern Pueblos. The kivas lack wing walls, are circular, and are often lined with masonry. Roofs were cribbed, and masonry support structures, called pilasters, occurred regularly around the perimeter of the kiva on a raised bench. A small hole north of the fire pit is analogous to the

ceremonial hole that in modern kivas represents the entrance into the Lower World. This hole is called a **sipapu** and is found in earlier pithouses as well as in kivas. Large kivas or **great kivas** (Figure 9.10) sometimes were situated near room blocks, suggesting integration of various community segments on a larger scale.

In Pueblo II and later times, kivas were enclosed within the room blocks, possibly suggesting more restricted access to sacred space. This change is associated with the construction of large multistory, multiroom structures archaeologists call **great houses**. These appear first at Chaco Canyon, but eventually versions of these appear elsewhere as well. Some of the largest of these great houses have a complex history of additions or expansions that may suggest people's migrations into and away from various communities. The regional system centered at Chaco Canyon, sometimes called the **Chaco Phenomenon**, began to develop by about 900 BP in the Bonito phase (see Table 9.3) and persisted until approximately 650 BP (Judge 1991). The Chacoan system dominated much of the northern Southwest during these times, as shown by the roads

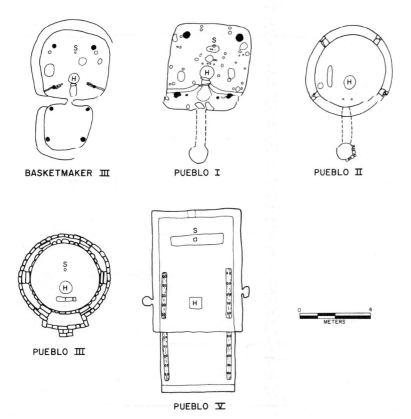

FIGURE 9.9 The changing plans of Anasazi pit structures from Basketmaker III pithouse to Pueblo V kiva: H, hearth; S, sipapu.

BASKETMAKER III

PUEBLO I

PUEBLO II

PUEBLO III

PUEBLO V

FIGURE 9.10 The great kiva at Chetro Ketl in Chaco Canyon, New Mexico.

and outlying settlements or great houses associated with it. Within the canyon itself a series of large great houses were constructed, but it is not clear exactly how these structures were used, nor is there consensus about the what Chaco represents in the first place, as discussed in Box 9.1.

One important feature of the Chaco system was the extension of Chacoan culture outside the canyon itself. A large number of great house communities with Chacoan traits are known from the Colorado Plateau. Elsewhere there are great kivas and other signs of Chaco's influence by about 850 BP in the twelfth century AD. As the influence of Chaco waned, some of these communities became important instead. Large communities developed south of Chaco in the Cibola region, west of Chaco in the Kayenta region and north of Chaco in the Mesa Verde area, but large population increases are not indicated in the Rio Grande region to the east. Developments in the Mesa Verde region to the north have been most extensively studied. Some archaeologists believe that Chacoan elites actually relocated to sites like Salmon and Aztec near Farmington, New Mexico (Lekson 2008). The series of great houses at Aztec represent one of the largest post-Chaco population concentrations, but it too declined after about 700 BP.

Certainly large numbers of people lived in the Mesa Verde region between about 850 and 650 BP, and many of these people aggregated in large communities especially after 750 BP. This is the period in which the large, well-known cliff dwellings of Mesa Verde such as the iconic Cliff Palace were constructed, but other large communities such as Sand Canyon Pueblo, west of modern-day Cortez, Colorado, were located on the edge of canyons rather than within the cliffs. Architectural features including masonry towers, some of which contain kivas are another feature of this period. Interestingly, social inequalities associated with exotic trade items and others signs of wealth are largely lacking.

The reasons for this change in settlement within the Mesa Verde region have been debated, but the combination of dense populations and changing environmental conditions most likely can be implicated. Another possibility that archaeologists have been exploring is the escalation of violence. While violence associated with political intimidation may have characterized the end of Chaco's influence, violence in the eighth century BP (thirteenth century AD) may well have resulted from competition for scarce resources, and population aggregations at this time would have been a logical response. Violence is suggested by humans remains with head wounds, burned structures, and signs of skeletons having been weathered and gnawed by animals rather than buried (e.g., Kuckelman et al. 2002).

As we discuss later, both social and environmental conditions probably contributed to the Ancestral Puebloan abandonment of the northern Southwest by the end of this century.

Mogollon

A second regional farming tradition is the Mogollon tradition. Archaeological sites recognized as Mogollon are found across southern New Mexico and west to the Verde River in Arizona, as well as in the Mexican states of Sonora and Chihuahua. The considerable variability in this large area is relatively poorly understood, although the **Jornada Mogollon** of the extreme southeastern Southwest can be distinguished from those in the Mogollon Highlands of Arizona and New Mexico. Mogollon ceramics, at the beginning of the sequence, are red- and brownwares made by the coil-and-scrape technology. Red-on-white and black-on-white pots were added to the ceramic repertoire with time. Pithouses are the primary form of architecture, but surface pueblos occur at the end of the Mogollon sequence.

A number of Mogollon regions and phase schemes have been proposed for the Mogollon, reflecting the regional variation in the tradition. These phases begin when the first pottery is made at approximately 1750 BP (AD 200) in all areas, but their details are beyond the scope of this summary. The Mogollon sequence is well known for the Mimbres valley of southwestern New Mexico. Here the phase sequence culminates in the Classic **Mimbres** phase 950–820 BP, during which sociocultural developments include aggregation into larger communities with some traits, suggestive of the Anasazi and limited social differentiation. After this time, many people in this area appear to have dispersed into small agricultural communities (Nelson 1999), but probably also contributed to new population aggregations elsewhere after 750 BP (AD 1200). To the west in the mountains of southeastern Arizona, the Mogollon sequence is different. Reid and Whittlesey (1997) call the end of this sequence the Mogollon Pueblo Period, dating it between 800 BP and 550 BP (AD 1150–1400) (Reid and Whittlesey 1997).

Dry farming was practiced by the Mogollon people. It involved the cultivation of maize, squash, beans, and cotton (Cordell 1997; Reid and Whittlesey 1997). Some check dams and other water control features have been noted. Subsistence depended more on hunting than appears to have been the case among either the Anasazi or the Hohokam. Deer, rabbits, rodents, and birds were all hunted. Piñon and acorns were among the collected foods. Based on evidence from cave sites like Tularosa Cave, the relative

ISSUES AND DEBATES

BOX 9.1

Interpreting the Chaco Phenomenon

Chaco Canyon always has been a place of great mystery to Americans. Here in the midst of the desolate country of northwestern New Mexico a small stream, the Chaco Wash, flows through a canyon lined by sandstone bluffs. It is a place not unlike other spots on the Colorado Plateau; yet in this canyon large multistory great houses lining the north bluff base or perching on the bluff tops stand as testaments to earlier use of the canyon at a surprising scale. As discussed in Section A of the Student CD, at the turn of the twentieth century Richard Wetherill was attracted to this spot, and he was joined in excavating and exploring Chaco's ruins by several notable archaeologists of his day. Archaeological interest in Chaco has continued for a century, and the public also has been drawn to the site. Today many people visit the Chaco Culture National Historic Park maintained by the National Park Service. Those who visit wonder how a place so empty and desolate today could have been the location for such significant constructions.

Of course, archaeologists have wondered more than most, and the investigations they have undertaken allow us to describe what is found at Chaco in considerable detail if not to fully explain what happened there. The dating of Chaco's many sites is now reasonably well established (see Table 9.3). There are many earlier sites, but most of the multistory great houses and other constructions that have attracted so much attention at Chaco are Pueblo II and early Pueblo III structures, built between approximately 1050 BP and 800 BP. After this period Chaco was in decline. Thus, the greatest cultural florescence at Chaco Canyon dates to a relatively short period of two and a half centuries (Sebastian 1992; Vivian 1990).

Of the great houses, Pueblo Bonito (Figure 9.11), with its D-shaped block of nearly 800 rooms, is the best known, but at least 10 other great houses also were built during this period: planned, multistoried masonry constructions containing enclosed plazas, many small kivas, and at least one great kiva as well. Some, including Pueblo Bonito, were expansions of earlier pueblos; but the rooms in the great houses also are larger than those found in smaller sites of the same period. In addition, features such as hearths, associated with domestic activities, are lacking in many parts of the great houses, suggesting that they weren't actually habitations, but public buildings perhaps used periodically. The numerous smaller pueblos dating to the period of greatest growth do appear to be habitations. These are single-story constructions with an

FIGURE 9.11 Pueblo Bonito, Chaco Canyon's best known great house.

average of 16 rooms, each of which is relatively small and has a low ceiling. They have unenclosed plazas and small kivas, although several of the sites may be associated with an isolated great kiva at Casa Rinconada on the south side of Chaco Wash. Chacoans also constructed water control and collection features such as diversion dams, canals, and headgates to catch rainfall runoff as it came down the side canyons.

The massive amount of construction at Chaco not only represents great expenditure of labor, but also the importation of massive amounts of timber from forests in places like the Chuska Mountains 75 kilometers away. Rare cylindrical vases containing traces of chocolate, copper bells imported from Mexico, macaw skeletons, turquoise, mica, marine shells, human effigy vases, painted tablets, and other exotic items have been found at Chaco. These items indicate a remarkable accumulation of trade items for the time period. Some of the material (e.g., turquoise) appears to have been manufactured locally into beads and pendants; but because much of this material was recovered in a small number of burials as well as in kiva offerings, the ritual significance of such items also should not be overlooked (Mathien 2001). Pottery, which may have been periodically dumped in great house refuse mounds in association with periodic gatherings, also occurs in Chaco's sites in unusually large amounts (Toll 2001).

One of the most intriguing aspects of the Chaco Phenomenon is the evidence for linkages between the sites in the canyon itself and the rest of the region. Not only did Chaco's inhabitants build roads within and around the canyon, but these roads extend for great distances within the region. In some instances, roads were actually cut into the sediments and bedrock or lined with boulders; other roads are simply slight swales marked by the removal

FIGURE 9.12 Chaco road segment.

of vegetation (Figure 9.12). Nevertheless, they are amazingly straight paths with uniform widths of about 30 feet (9 m) for major roads and about 15 feet (4.5 m) for secondary routes (Cordell 1997:320). These roads also are associated with signaling stations located on high points visible from the canyon's great houses. Moreover, the roads often lead to outlying great houses and communities located elsewhere in the San Juan Basin and beyond. Such outliers, even those found as far away as southeastern Utah, eastern Arizona, and southwestern New Mexico, also were planned communities with layouts similar to those found in Chaco Canyon itself. Recognition of the recurring pattern has fueled speculation concerning the nature of the regional system indicated by these arrangements.

In fact, the proper interpretation of the Chaco system is debated among archaeologists. Some of the oldest explanations noted the items of Mexican origin and attributed Chaco's development to trade with the Mexican civilizations far to the south. Beginning in the 1960s and 1970s, archaeologists most often viewed Chaco as the center of a chiefdom supported in part by a system of agricultural redistribution that arose in response to the stresses of population aggregation in such a harsh environment. In such models, great houses, whether at Chaco or at outlying locations, were first understood largely as storage facilities and the road system as the means of moving food and other goods about. The obvious emphasis on ritual at Chaco was viewed as a formal means of maintaining Chaco's control of the system. Still more recently, it has been proposed that Chaco was the venue for pilgrimage festivals through which the distribution of goods and services was regulated by Chacoans. This interpretation is supported by the evidence for ritual and for stockpiling in Chaco's great houses as well as by the indications that few people actually lived in these structures. The periodic refuse deposits of perhaps ritually broken

pottery at the Pueblo Alto great house also support this interpretation.

There certainly are problems with applying models of redistributive chiefdoms to the data on this regional system. Since the system's florescence actually is associated with a period of better climate, it is difficult to understand it as a response to environmental stress, and thus other models of political evolution are being explored. These tend to place more emphasis on the use of ritual and surplus to alter power relationships within human societies (e.g., Sebastian 1992). There is debate about how hierarchical the Chaco system actually was, although several particularly elaborate burials found at Pueblo Bonito may indicate social ranking. There are also differing viewpoints about how economic production was organized within it (see Cameron and Toll 2001). Some archaeologists have argued that Chaco lacked individual elites, illustrating, instead, a form of communalism in which labor and production were collectively managed. Other researchers (e.g., Lekson 1999) believe that archaeologists need to pay more attention to astronomically related aspects of ritual and cosmology in the Chacoan and subsequent systems of the Southwest like the Paquimé system highlighted in this chapter's case study by Paul E. Minnis and Michael E. Whalen, "Casas Grandes at the Edge of the Southwestern and Mesoamerican Worlds."

Regardless of how the Chaco system worked, its period of greatness was short. By 850 BP (AD 1100), Chaco began to decline. A few great houses were built, but they usually were smaller and less carefully constructed, and the plaza oriented great kivas are lacking. People may have consolidated their activities in the parts of the canyon close to Pueblo Bonito (Kantner 2004). As Chaco itself declined, population grew in other areas and Chacoan ideas seem to have been exported elsewhere in the Ancestral Pueblo world. What caused the end of the Chaco Phenomenon is as much a matter of debate as is its development, but there is evidence for drought that may have challenged Chaco's ritual leaders influence and control. Lekson (2005, 2008) argues that while Chaco was in control, the Pueblo world was mainly at peace, and that as it declined violence increased even as new centers ascended.

Despite more than a century of scholarly attention and debate as well as great improvements in the quality of the archaeological data, Chaco remains mysterious and fuels our imaginations. It stands as an icon of both archaeology's power to inform and archaeology's limitations and challenges, and for these reasons, scholars will continue to investigate its nature and significance.

dependence on cultivated food and gathered food fluctuated with time.

For much of the Mogollon sequence, settlements tended to be small, consisting of a few pithouses arranged in no particular pattern. Residentially mobile lifestyles may also have persisted. Pithouse designs changed over time (Figure 9.13). The earliest pithouses are D-shaped or round, generally have ramp entries on one side, and vary in size, in orientation with regard to cardinal points, and in type and arrangement of internal features. Roofs of these early pithouses were usually supported by a central post, and additional posts ringed the edge of the structure. Through time the pithouses became rectangular, with roofs supported by four posts. Between 1100 BP and 950 BP there was a tendency for pithouses to be lined with masonry. Ramp entries continue, but some pithouses had ventilator systems and roof entries like Ancestral Pueblo pithouses. Great kivas are found from the earliest occupations. At first these integrative structures are round or bean-shaped; then they become D-shaped between 1300–1100 BP, and later still these structures become rectangular.

Around 950 BP, in the Mimbres valley people constructed multiroom surface structures using un-shaped river cobbles and mortar. Buildings often began with just a few rooms, but additions made by succeeding generations could result in very large buildings, as large as 200 rooms. For example, at Swarts ruin, an earlier pithouse village was covered by six small room blocks, which were added to until there were two large room blocks flanking an open plaza (LeBlanc 1983). Unlike Ancestral Pueblo great houses, these buildings were clearly residential, but some of the rooms and perhaps some open plaza areas are believed to have had ritual functions. These large Mimbres sites are relatively rare; many more were small with fewer than ten rooms. While these large sites contain evidence of community integration and some trade in exotics including macaws from Mexico, it does not appear that truly regional systems developed here. Instead, communities remained autonomous, developing local mechanisms for social integration (Cordell 1997). The Mimbres people are best known for their pottery, which has highly stylized depictions of

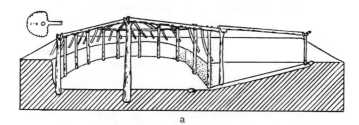

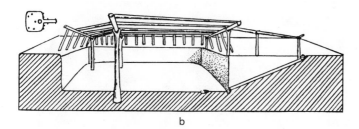

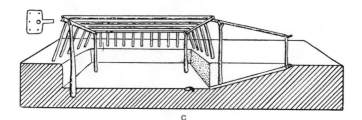

FIGURE 9.13 Suggested reconstructions of the superstructures of Mogollon pithouses: (a) ca. 1450–1250 BP, (b) ca. 1250–1050 BP, and (c) ca. 1050–950 BP.

CLUES TO THE PAST

EXHIBIT 9.1

Fantasies on Clay: Mimbres Pottery

Between 950 BP and 820 BP (AD 1000–1130), potters in the Mimbres valley of New Mexico, part of the Mogollon region, produced a distinctive black-on-white pottery. This Classic Mimbres pottery includes spectacular painted bowls with geometric and pictorial designs that are visually very appealing (Figure 9.14). The bowls have frequently been found in burials, often covering the head of the interred individual, and burials most often occur under the floors of rooms in the Mimbres pueblos. This association has led to massive destruction of Mimbres sites by relic hunters, sometimes using earthmoving equipment to explore for graves containing the precious pottery, which can command very high prices from international art collectors. Much of our ability to understand this fascinating pottery has been lost because of wanton destruction of the sites that held not only the pottery but also the keys to its role in Mimbres life.

Some have inferred that because Classic Mimbres pottery is black on white and bears some resemblance to Anasazi ceramics, the Mimbres were actually Anasazi who had occupied the Mogollon area. Mimbres Classic pottery differs from Anasazi pottery in some significant details, however, suggesting that it is a development from preceding Mogollon ceramic traditions. Most notably, Anasazi

pottery uses gray clay, whereas Mimbres pottery continues to use the brown clay that characterizes earlier Mogollon pottery. The black-on-white effect was achieved by applying black paint to a white **slip** that coated the brown clay.

Brody (1977) made an extensive study of designs on Mimbres pottery. He reported that while geometric forms are found on jars, ladles, and other household items, as well as on bowls, pictorial designs are limited to bowls. A number of different kinds of animal are depicted on these representational bowls, including antelope and bear, bats, birds of various kinds (including macaws and perhaps parrots), fish (some clearly representing species from the Pacific Ocean), and insects (Figure 9.15). Humans are also depicted, as are unidentifiable creatures that probably represent mythical figures. Included among these possible mythical figures are depictions that appear to represent the horned serpent, a theme found throughout the pre-Columbian Southwest, which is probably derived from Mesoamerica. Most of the bowls depict a single animal or human, but multiple figures were also painted on some bowls, and occasionally the depiction represents actions like hunting or dancing.

Although whole bowls are most often found with burials, there are strong indications that the ceramics

FIGURE 9.14 Mimbres depiction of a rabbit. Note the hole in the center of the bowl and the intricate geometric border.

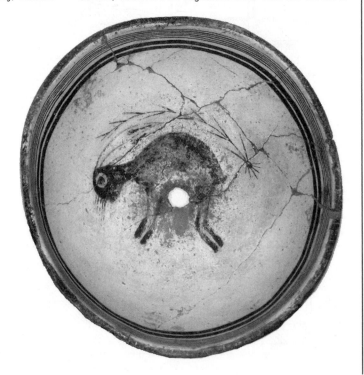

were in daily use and were not specifically made as grave offerings. Sherds of Classic Mimbres pottery are found in household refuse, indicating everyday use. Further, the whole vessels found with burials often have wear marks from dippers that were used to serve from the bowls.

Interestingly, the bowls found with burials almost always have a hole in them. These holes, generally punched from the outside of the vessel, are almost certainly part of the burial ritual.

Sourcing studies indicate that Mimbres pottery was made at numerous locations in the Mimbres area and that there was no particular craft specialization involved in its manufacture. Based on the nature of the activities depicted and on the observation that men are portrayed more often than women (though it is impossible to determine the gender of many of the human figures), it is suggested that men were important in painting the designs on the pottery, if not in the entire manufacturing process.

The beauty of Classic Mimbres pottery still speaks to us today, but it is perhaps unfortunate that it is so hauntingly beautiful. The price that such pots bring on the art market has led to destruction of the sites that could answer the myriad of questions about the role of this art in the lives of the Mimbres people and, perhaps, about the meaning of these enigmatic designs.

FIGURE 9.15 Mimbres depiction of fish.

animals and humans and was often found in burials (see Exhibit 9.1).

In the mountains of southeastern Arizona, Mogollon pithouse villages persist until approximately 800 BP. At sites like Bear Village in the Forestdale valley architectural features reflecting both Mogollon and Anasazi influences suggest that people with different background may have been residing together. This pattern is still clearer after 800 BP when surface buildings first are constructed by these western Mogollon people. At first surface pueblos were small, though great kivas were built with them. By 700 BP (AD 1200) larger pueblos were beginning to be built, and these late Mogollon people committed to sedentary agricultural lifestyles. After 650 BP (AD 1300), during the severe drought that affected much of the Southwest, large numbers of Ancestral Pueblo immigrants moved into the mountains, but before discussing these developments, additional regional traditions must be introduced.

Hohokam

The Hohokam occupied the low desert regions of Arizona. Archaeologists recognize red pottery or buff pottery decorated with red paint and manufactured using the paddle-and-anvil method as distinguishing characteristics of the Hohokam. Designs on the pottery include human and animal forms, as well as geometric patterns (Figure 9.16). Hohokam farmers built irrigation canals along the rivers, some of which were several kilometers long (see Figure 1.18). The Hohokam also planted **akchin** fields, which were watered by the floodwaters at the mouth of arroyos, and may have used other systems to retain water for cultivation as well (Masse 1991:210–211). Houses were jacal constructions in pits, and some massive adobe structures were built late in the Hohokam sequence (Cordell 1997). The Hohokam also built platform mounds and walled compounds. Hohokam artisans made a wide variety of jewelry, including shell jewelry made from materials obtained primarily from the Gulf of California, and participated in long-distance trading networks.

Cultural resource management studies have been especially important in developing our understanding of the Hohokam. With few exceptions, excavations prior to the advent of CRM focused on large sites with impressive features such as Snaketown, with its platform mounds, or Casa Grande with its great house. Cultural resource management required investigation of sites without the impressive features and helped flesh out the nature and range of variation in the Hohokam pattern. The case study by Cory Dale Breternitz and Christine K. Robinson, "The Pueblo Grande Project: An Example of Multidisciplinary

Research in a Compliance Setting," in Chapter 1, provides a good example of a CRM contribution to Hohokam archaeology.

As suggested by their impressive irrigation works, the Hohokam were highly successful farmers, who cultivated maize and five species of beans, as well as squash, bottle gourds, cotton, and several native plants such as little barley grass and amaranth. As noted previously, some of these cultigens required irrigation and were not adopted from Mexico until the period from 1650 BP to 1450 BP. The Hohokam also let chenopodium, tansy mustard, and maygrass grow in their fields, and they harvested these and other ruderal plants for their food value as well. Success in farming in the desert does not, however, mean that the Hohokam abandoned hunting and gathering. Like other Southwestern groups, the Hohokam supplemented their agricultural products with wild foods in season. Mesquite pods and cactus fruit, including that of the giant saguaro cactus, were particularly important. In addition, fish and shellfish were collected from the rivers and from the canals to supplement the diet. Hunting continued to be practiced as well, with some animals being taken in the fields. Small mammals such as jackrabbit, cottontail, and squirrel were most important, but bighorn sheep and deer were also killed.

Water was, indeed, critical to the Hohokam survival. This was reflected in their art (Haury 1976). Depictions of water-loving creatures are found in ceramic decoration, in carved stone, and in shell jewelry (Figure 9.17). Frogs and pelicans are particularly frequent subjects of the Hohokam artisans.

The Hohokam sequence has been divided into four subperiods: **Pioneer**, **Colonial**, **Sedentary**, and **Classic**

FIGURE 9.16 Hohokam red-on-buff ceramics: (a–c) jars and (d) cauldron.

a

b

c

d

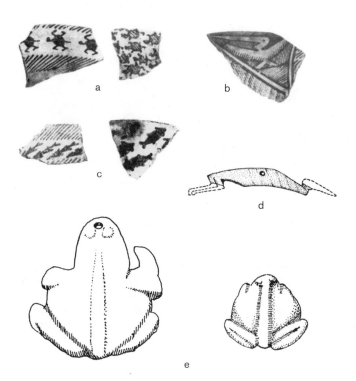

FIGURE 9.17 Hohokam representations of water-loving animals. (a) turtles, (b) pelican, (c) fish, (d) pelican effigy in shell, (e) frog effigies carved from whole shells.

TABLE 9.4 Hohokam Periods and Dates

Period	Dates	
	BP	AD
Classic	800–550	1150–1400
Sedentary	975–800	975–1150
Colonial	1175–975	775–975
Pioneer	1750–1175	200–775

(Table 9.4). Phase systems have been developed for the Gila and Salt River valleys around Phoenix, the Tucson Basin, and the intervening desert, reflecting differences in the paths of development in these areas. There has been considerable debate about the chronology of the Hohokam, with some researchers suggesting a beginning for the sequence as early as 2250 BP and others placing it as late as 1450 BP. Data from early agricultural sites now indicates that farming, villages, irrigation all predate the Hohokam. We now know that plain ware pottery was first made in the Hohokam area between approximately 1750 and 1550 BP (AD 200–400) and decorated pottery began to be made later (Reid and Whittlesey 1997). The consensus today is to begin the Hohokam sequence early in the Common Era.

Many elements of Hohokam culture are evident by the end of the Pioneer phase (1175 BP/AD 775). These include red-slipped and painted pottery, permanent villages, trash mounds capped with adobe, large irrigation systems, and ball courts. The earliest Hohokam settlements are clusters of pithouses, generally occurring in household groups. More accurately, the dwellings would be called houses built in pits: the walls of the house were separate from the walls of the pit (Figure 9.18). Some larger structures built at this time may have had communal purposes. The ball courts and capped mounds that appear at the end of the Pioneer period are presumed to have served the same kind of religious and integrative function in Hohokam society as great kivas did for the Anasazi and Mogollon. The ball courts are derived from farther south in Mexico. The structures, which today are marked by two long mounds defining an oval space with its floor lower than the surrounding desert, are believed to have been used in a ceremonial ball game. Craft items including pottery, carved stone bowls, stone palettes, figurines and shell jewelry all were being made in this period as well. Some of these items including the palettes and figurines were associated with human cremations.

The Colonial and Sedentary periods were times of cultural florescence for the Hohokam. Villages became more patterned and now consisted of groups of pithouse clusters, each of which seems centered on an

FIGURE 9.18 Hohokam house of the Sedentary period (Sacaton phase) from the site of Snaketown.

open courtyard. Over time, the population grew and communities became larger. Besides these courtyards, plazas, mounds, and ball courts all were common. Mortuary rituals and offerings were more elaborate, and archaeologists have recovered caches of deliberately destroyed stone effigies that may have been associated with death rituals. Artisans continued to craft finely made shell jewelry, figurines, stone bowls, and beads. These items appear in areas to the north and east, which were far removed from the core Hohokam areas around Phoenix and Tucson. Ball courts and cremated human remains also have been found elsewhere, suggesting the wide influence of the Hohokam. Thus, just as a regional system developed in Chaco Canyon, a high degree of regional integration developed among the Sedentary and Classic period Hohokam. This system centered in the Gila and Salt River basins near Phoenix but is thought to have extended over a much wider area.

Some very large villages such as Snaketown are found along the rivers. This site, located south of Phoenix, Arizona, was occupied from the Pioneer through the Classic periods (1650–550 BP) and had hundreds of pithouses, as well as trash mounds, formal platform mounds, and ball courts. Snaketown was situated on a canal system that stretched over 10 miles (16 km). Excavations at this site in 1934, followed by excavations in 1964, provided much of the basis for our early understanding of the Hohokam (Haury 1976).

The Classic Hohokam Period marks significant changes in Hohokam lifestyles, and it can be characterized as a period of reorganization following the collapse of true Hohokam culture in response to environmental change or population intrusion from other areas. Inmigration of Salado people has sometimes been used as an explanation, but other perspectives on the Salado, as discussed later, are more common today. Polychrome pottery also is associated with the end of the Classic Hohokam.

One change during the Classic period is settlement relocation and abandonment of some Hohokam areas. The new settlements involved the construction of walled compounds of adobe surface rooms. The adobe structures were not made of bricks as later adobes were; rather, they were built up by adding basketsful of mud to the growing walls. Multistory great houses of adobe were built at some sites. One Arizona site, Casa Grande, was four stories in height. Classic Hohokam sites also lack ball courts and feature formal platform mounds, level, sheer-sided, rectangular mounds that contrast with earlier low, capped, trash mounds because they were made by building an enclosing wall of adobe or stone and in-filling to create the platform. These platform mounds often had structures built on their tops as well. They were surrounded by walls that restricted access, and the recovery of ritual items in mound contexts may indicate a ceremonial function. Another possible interpretation is that these represent compounds for the elite to which commoners had only restricted access (Neitzel 1991:216). Hegmon (2005) has pointed out that in contrast to earlier Hohokam sites with ball courts to which everyone had access, access to these compounds was restricted, presumably to elites. Perhaps this indicates that elites were now in control of ritual aspects of Hohokam society, although the existence of elites is not universally accepted (Crown and Judge 1991:303). **Trincheras** or walled terraces on hilltops also appear in the Tucson basin and in Sonora during the Classic Period.

Patayan

The western Southwest is the home of the Patayan tradition, a diverse group of archaeological complexes found in the Colorado River valley and in the adjacent lands to the east and west. The Patayan tradition is less well known than the other Southwestern traditions. Most of the area of the Patayan tradition sites was occupied by Yuman speakers in the Historic period. There is a distinction made between the lowland Patayan, who lived along the Colorado River, and the upland Patayan. The upland Patayan includes considerable variability, though three general groups are recognized within this division: the **Cerbat** and **Cohonina** in northwestern Arizona, and the **Prescott** in west central Arizona.

One of the principal uniting themes of the diverse archaeological complexes considered under the name Patayan is pottery thinned by the **paddle-and-anvil technique**, in which the pottery finishing involves beating or pressing the coils used in construction until they are smoothed. In the lowland areas of the Arizona and California deserts, as well as the Colorado River valley, the pottery is primarily a buff ware (Figure 9.19), sometimes decorated with red paint. In the upland areas on both sides of the Colorado, brown pottery is found. Decoration of this pottery is generally confined to incised designs, and these are rare. Rock features are another hallmark of the Patayan. Such features include dry-laid masonry walls, earth ovens with considerable burned stone fill, and rock piles, often called trail shrines, along trails (McGuire and Schiffer 1982).

Little is known about Patayan settlement, at least along the Colorado River, because of the setting in which that settlement occurred. Settlements were apparently along the river during the growing season, and the areas where they were to be found have since been altered by flooding and by modern agriculture. Based on the Quechan and Mohave historical patterns, villages were probably scattered arrangements of jacal structures strung along the river terraces. These structures were generally rectangular, and both surface structures and pithouses occurred in the Historic period villages.

In the upland areas of the Cerbat, domed brush structures were built for houses, although rockshelters were frequently used as well. The Cohonina built a variety of structures in small settlements. Houses included pit structures and surface rooms that were constructed partly of rock.

Much less is known about Patayan subsistence than about that of the other southwestern traditions. The paucity of excavated sites makes reconstruction difficult. The historical pattern observed among the Quechan and the Mojave of the lower Colorado River appears to have some time depth and is the basis for present ideas about Patayan subsistence, at least along the river. Ethnographically, agriculture along the lower Colorado River was flood agriculture akin to that practiced by the ancient Egyptians along the Nile. Each spring the Colorado would overflow its banks, fed by snow melt from the Rocky Mountains. This flooding deposited a layer of rich topsoil onto the floodplain. The residual moisture allowed people to plant and raise crops in this soil. Away from the Colorado, rainfall farming was practiced, but in many areas hunting and gathering remained very important (Cordell 1997).

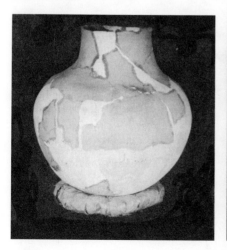 

FIGURE 9.19 Patayan ceramic jars: (a) vessel 12.6 inches (32 cm) tall and (b) vessel 13.2 inches (33.5 cm) tall.

Sinagua

The Sinagua, who were located in Arizona in the vicinity of Flagstaff and southward toward Phoenix, are an enigmatic cultural group about whom we understand surprisingly little. The people were farmers who built pueblo-style communities and made plain red- or brownware ceramics that were distinctive for being tempered with cinders or crushed volcanic rock. The paddle-and-anvil technique was used in making these ceramics. Sinagua sites date from approximately 1250 BP in the Flagstaff area, but they also have been found to the south in the Verde River valley (Reid and Whittlesey 1997). The mix of Sinagua traits has led archaeologists to consider these people closely related to the other southwestern traditions, especially the Anasazi and the Patayan, yet today there is a tendency to agree that whatever Sinagua represents, it is best treated as a unique cultural tradition.

The most important event in Sinagua history was the eruption of the volcano at Sunset Crater, which occurred in 866 BP (AD 1064), followed by additional eruptions over the next several hundred years. Although the first eruption buried many settlements in volcanic ash layers, the absence of human remains encased in this ash suggests that people had sufficient time to abandon their homes and flee.

In addition, although you might think this eruption would devastate farming in this area, there is considerable evidence that after the eruption people from many southwestern regions were actually attracted to the Flagstaff area. One theory is that the blanket of cinders worked as a sort of mulch, making the land more productive (Kamp 1998); but it is possible that supernatural powers were attributed to the volcano, and this drew people as well. Another possibility is that trade with other people simply increased at this time. In any case, after the eruption that created Sunset Crater, the Sinagua were influenced by the influx of ideas. Ceramics from several other areas, ball courts, and pithouses that seem to be a mix of Hohokam and Anasazi building styles all suggest this change. Several large sites date after the eruption, including the well-known Wupatki National Monument and cliff dwellings at Walnut Canyon National Monument, both of which can be visited today (Figure 9.20). Large and spectacular sites dating toward the end of the Sinagua sequence are found as well in the Verde valley, with the best known being the impressive five-story cliff dwelling called Montezuma's Castle. Most of the northern part of the Sinagua area was abandoned after about 650 BP, at about the same time the Anasazi left the Colorado Plateau. Thus, just like the people of the other major Southwestern traditions, the Sinagua were part of the population movements and reorganizations that took place after this time throughout the Southwest.

REORGANIZATION, AGGREGATION, AND CONFLICT IN LATE PREHISTORY

After the decline of Chaco (ca. 800 BP/AD1150), there were major relocations and settlement aggregations in the Puebloan world, as we have already indicated. We've seen as well that changes and developments

FIGURE 9.20 Wupatki National monument is one of the large Sinagua sites inhabited after the eruption of Sunset Crater.

among other Southwestern populations occurred at least by the century following this in other regional traditions. After this point in time, both pan-regional environmental stress from drought and large-scale population movements reflecting breakdown of regional traditions make it necessary to view the Southwest as a whole. Archaeologists are only beginning to understand the centuries between 750BP/AD 1200 and the arrival of the Spanish, but it is important to do so because in the developments of this period lie the origins of the historically known tribes of the Southwest (Gregory and Wilcox 2007).

Although tens of thousands of people lived in the northern part of the Southwest at 750 BP, by 650 BP a widespread abandonment of this area had taken place. Southwesterners had, of course, abandoned individual sites and valleys before as they responded to environmental and social change. One example is given in the case study in Section D.5 of the Student CD. Nevertheless, in this case the dislocation of human populations was particularly widespread. The Virgin Anasazi area of southeastern Nevada, the Kayenta Anasazi of northern Arizona, the Mesa Verde region of southwestern Colorado, the San Juan Basin of northwestern New Mexico, most of the Sinagua homeland, and some parts of the Mogollon Highlands were literally vacated by human populations at this time. You will note that this "great abandonment" corresponds with the end of the Fremont tradition in the eastern Great Basin as well (Allison 2010). This widespread abandonment has long been billed as one of the great mysteries of Southwestern archaeology, and archaeologists are still trying to understand what happened.

What is just as interesting about this period is that populations relocated and reorganized in several distinct areas that were important in late Southwestern prehistory and into the Historic period. One such area is the Rio Grande valley and areas near it in eastern New Mexico. Here pithouse villages and small pueblos characterize the archaeological record until after 650 BP, when a number of very large aggregated communities appeared. Many archaeologists believe that people from the Mesa Verde moved to this area at this time, although many of their cultural traditions were abandoned as they made this move (Lipe 2010). Ortman (2010) has proposed that the immigrants became the historically known Tewa speakers of the Rio Grande, but other researchers believe that the cultural developments and large populations also had roots in the Rio Grande area itself (Boyer et al. 2010).

Several other areas also seem to have received populations. The Western Pueblo areas of west central New Mexico and eastern Arizona experienced an influx of population. Sites in this area change from small pueblos to large aggregated communities beginning about 750 BP/AD 1200. These seem to suggest movement of populations from farther north and west out of the Virgin and Kayenta Anasazi areas into new areas. In the Tonto basin along the Salt River in central eastern Arizona, a case can be made that the mixing of various ethnic groups of Hohokam, Mogollon, and Anasazi origins at this time gave rise to the **Salado tradition**. These developments are associated with distinctive Gila and Tonto polychrome pottery (Figure 9.21) and the appearance of adobe compounds as well as platform mounds (Crown 1994; Dean 2000; Reid and Whittlesey 1997). Salado has been variously interpreted by archaeologists, some of whom have not seen it as a distinctive cultural tradition but an expression of Classic Period Hohokam culture. However, current interpretations tend to view Salado as a distinctive example of the complicated population movements and amalgamations that is dated between about 750 BP and 500 BP.

Perhaps the most significant development in the late prehistory of the Southwest occurred at Casas Grandes, or Paquimé, in northern Chihuahua, Mexico, where some affinities with the Mogollon tradition have been recognized and a population influx may have occurred after 650 BP. This chapter's case study is about recent work at Paquimé and associated sites. Now known to principally date to the period after 750 BP and to have been at its height more recently still, Paquimé has been interpreted as the center of its own regional system (e.g., Lekson 1999). Distinctive polychrome pottery may be diagnostic of this system. However, there is little agreement on the size and importance of the Paquimé polity, which is one reason it is necessary to establish the context for this large and impressive site, as described in the case study. Once thought to have Mesoamerican origins, Paquimé is interpreted by some contemporary researchers as linked to post-Chacoan developments in the Puebloan world (e.g., Lekson 2005).

Recent development of the Coalescent Communities Database, which contains data on known sites and site components with at least 13 rooms that date between 750BP/AD 1200 and 350 BP/AD 1600, is producing fascinating pan-Southwest perspectives on this period. Wilcox et al. (2007) have used this database to show the gradual contraction of aggregated human populations out of areas like the Four Corners and southern Arizona into a limited number of population centers such as Hopi, Zuni, Acoma, and the Rio Grande area where towns were located when the Spanish arrived. This sort of data analysis promises to help us understand the dynamics of population coalescence in late prehistory.

The causes of the abandonments, reorganizations, and large aggregations at this time are not fully

FIGURE 9.21 Gila polychrome sherds.

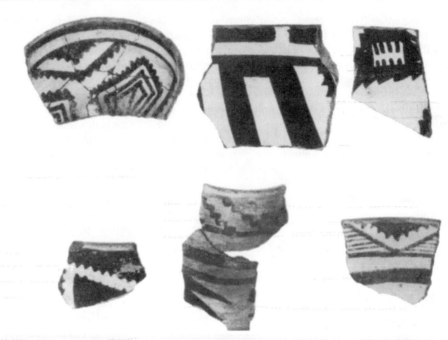

understood. Environmental factors may well have played a role in the abandonment of the northern Southwest. The villagers of this area may not have been able to survive droughts thought to have occurred here between approximately 674 BP and 651 BP (Varien et al. 1996), just as drought may have affected the Chacoan system earlier. Areas settled after the drought of the mid-seventh century BP may have had more favorable precipitation regimes. Perhaps the areas to the south and east into which populations moved were generally less risky because the summer rainfall was simply more reliable. However, some studies have indicated that the northern Southwest as a region probably could have supported a sizable population during these droughts even though local areas might have had to be abandoned (Van West 1996).

Moreover, the aggregated settlements that resulted elsewhere are not as easily explained by reference to the environment alone. One argument has been that warfare between towns and villages encouraged aggregation into defensive positions. Possibly scarcity of resources contributed to such conflict. Although there has been a tendency to see the peoples of the Southwest as peaceful, there always have been some Southwestern archaeologists who have attributed cultural historical changes to warfare. Recent discussions have recognized that there is evidence for intercommunity violence in the Southwestern record (e.g., Haas and Creamer 1993; LeBlanc 1999). There is little question that at least some violence, possibly even cannibalism (Turner and Turner 1999; White 1992), occurred in the

late prehistory of the Southwest. See "Was There Cannibalism in the Prehistoric Southwest?" (Section F.5 of the Student CD). For example, in the Gallinas area of New Mexico's Jemez Mountains, sites dated 750 BP to 650 BP include mass burials of skeletons with arrow tips embedded in the bones, a high percentage of burned habitation sites, and a large number of skeletons found unburied on the floors of burned structures (Cordell 1997:378). Even though it is not completely clear what role warfare might have played in the abandonments and aggregation of late prehistory, renewed interest and investigation of this topic promise that new insights will be forthcoming.

Finally, it should be noted that besides aggregation into very large sites, the end of the pre-Columbian period in the Southwest may also have been marked by new pan-regional mechanisms of integration. Casas Grandes has been interpreted as a center for religious pilgrimage (Fish and Fish 1999), and shamanic images on its pottery have been cited by some to suggest the presence of priest-shamans at the site (Van Pool 2003). One interpretation of Gila polychrome or Salado pottery is that it represents a religious ideology associated with fertility and water control. Crown (1994), who identifies images of parrots, snakes, horned serpents, eyes, the sun, and stars (Figure 9.22) as central symbols of this **Southwest Regional cult**, notes such images on polychrome pottery and in rock art from Mimbres times into the Late Prehistoric period. Studies of decorative styles and imagery may ultimately help archaeologists understand the late

FIGURE 9.22 Design motifs of the Southwestern Regional cult.

Another idea that might apply is that of heterarchy (Crumley 1995), in which relative equality is maintained by different villages based on power or superiority in different aspects of culture (e.g., military, vs. economic, vs. spiritual). Thus, the classic models of tribe versus chiefdom or egalitarian versus ranked, briefly introduced in Chapter 2, may not be easily applied to larger and more complex Southwestern societies after all.

NEW ARRIVALS

developments we have mentioned. Imagery of religious significance associated with the later development of the **Katchina cult** found among modern Pueblos has also been explored by archaeologists (Adams 1991).

Studies of late pre-Columbian and Protohistoric period Pueblo societies also have contributed to debate about hierarchy and inequality in significant ways. For example, it has been argued that Rio Grande pueblos at this time represent confederacies, in which relatively equal villages were allied, rather than chiefdoms.

Much of the northern Southwest had been abandoned by AD 1300, and an early explanation for the evacuation of this large area was the arrival of the Navajo, the Apache, and the Utes. It is clear today that the entrance of these peoples into the Southwest postdates the great abandonment, but authorities disagree about the timing and direction of the Navajo and Apache in-migration. One position holds that the earliest evidence for these tribes is in the **Dinétah phase** in the upper San Juan drainage that has been dated about 500 BP (e.g., Winter and Hogan 1992).

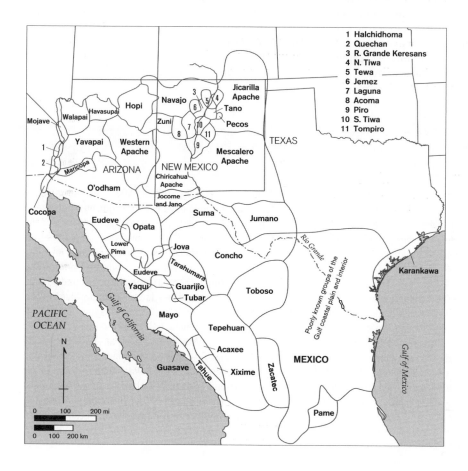

FIGURE 9.23 Historic groupings of Native people in the Southwest.

1 Halchidhoma
2 Quechan
3 R. Grande Keresans
4 N. Tiwa
5 Tewa
6 Jemez
7 Laguna
8 Acoma
9 Piro
10 S. Tiwa
11 Tompiro

Other archaeologists argue that these people first entered the Southwest from the Great Plains in the Historic period after the Pueblo Revolt of 1680 (e.g., Schaafsma 1996).

Navajo and Apache entered the Southwest as hunter-gatherers and developed territories north of and between the territories of the Pueblos of the time. These people continued to hunt and gather, but also began raiding the Pueblos for food. Archaeological sites indicate some experimentation, with settlement into pueblolike villages, and some agriculture was incorporated into the subsistence system (Towner 1996). The Utes also entered the northern Southwest about the same time as the Apache and Navajo, though most of their territory was in the Great Basin (see Chapter 8). Sites attributed by some to the Navajo and the Apache may in fact be Ute in origin. Because the Utes were highly mobile foragers, early Ute sites are difficult to detect in a landscape dominated by large and impressive Ancestral Pueblo ruins.

The other recent inhabitants of the Southwest all can be related to pre-Columbian peoples in the Southwest (Figure 9.23). The Pima and Tohono O'odham (formerly called Papago) of the Sonoran Desert occupy the territory where Hohokam sites are found, and they may be descended from the Hohokam. Close study of traditional native histories can help archaeologists sort out whether there was a hiatus after Hohokam (Teague 1993). These people speak languages from the Uto-Aztecan family and, in the Historic period, lived in **rancherias**, or settlements of dispersed houses, practicing a combination of farming and gathering. The Pueblo people of Arizona and New Mexico are clearly the descendants of the Ancestral Pueblo, although the Mogollon almost certainly made contributions to recent Puebloan populations as well. The Pueblos speak a diversity of languages, including languages of the Uto-Aztecan, Kiowa-Tanoan, and Keresen families, as well as Zuni, which is a language without close relatives. The Pueblos live in compact villages and practice irrigated and rainfall farming today, as they have in the historical past. The Mohave, Quechan, Cocopa, Maricopa, and various Pai groups (Yavapai, Walapai, Havasupai, Paipai) living along the lower Colorado River, Gila River, and adjacent upland areas are the successors to the Patayan. These people speak Yuman languages of the Hokan family. In the Historic period they made their living as floodwater agriculturalists along the Colorado River and its major tributaries, or practiced rainfall farming in the uplands.

Together, all of these people had to deal with the next newcomers: the Europeans. The Spanish arrived in AD 1540 with the Coronado expedition. Archaeologists and historians have had some success tracing the route of this expedition (Reid and Whittelsey 1997: 259–273). An archaeological site adjacent to Santiago Pueblo in New Mexico is thought to represent a campsite of the Coronado expedition during the winter of 1540–1541. Metal artifacts, one found in the chest of an individual, are thought to be bolt heads of Spanish crossbows (Espinoza-Ar 2005).

CHAPTER SUMMARY

This chapter has introduced the archaeological story of the Southwest culture area. We hope it has given a working perspective on the cultural context in which the well-known spectacular cliff dwellings of Mesa Verde developed, as well as on related aspects of the region's past. The main points made in this chapter are as follows:

- The peoples of the Southwestern Archaic were generalized foragers, but in the Late Archaic, as early as 3700 BP, maize and other plants began to be cultivated. In contradiction to traditional models of a slow addition of cultigens into the diet by mobile Archaic foragers, recent evidence suggests that some Late Archaic people lived in settled villages, used irrigation techniques, and were heavily dependent on corn and other crops.

- After approximately 1750 BP/AD200 several regional farming traditions have been recognized by archaeologists. These include the Anasazi or Ancestral Pueblo tradition of the northern Southwest, the Mogollon tradition of southern New Mexico, eastern Arizona, and northern Mexico, the Hohokam tradition of the deserts of the southern Arizona, the poorly understood Patayan tradition of the lower Colorado River valley and northwest Arizona, and the Sinagua tradition of north central Arizona.

- Early regional systems developed at Chaco Canyon in the Ancestral Pueblo area and among the Hohokam, where evidence of monumental architecture, long-distance trade, social differentiation, and other aspects of more complex societies have been found. However, the Chaco system was short-lived, declining after

800 BP/AD 1150, and the Hohokam also declined and dispersed after 550 BP, setting in motion new social dynamics.

- Late in the prehistory there were major population disruptions caused by environmental change as well as social conflicts, and people aggregated into new centers and variously participated in pan-regional economic and religious interactions. The depopulation of the northern Southwest and the growth and eventual decline of the regional system at Casas Grandes in northern Mexico both occurred at this time. Eventually historically known centers at Hopi, Zuni, and along the Rio Grande in north central New Mexico developed.

SUGGESTIONS FOR FURTHER READING

For a thorough introduction to the archaeology of the Southwest:

Cordell, Linda
  1997 *Archaeology of the Southwest*, 2nd ed. Academic Press, San Diego.

For a new perspective on the past in the Southwest:

Lekson, Stephen H.
  2008 *A History of the Ancient Southwest*. School for Advanced Research, Santa Fe.

For an interdisciplinary synthesis of the origins of one Southwestern tribe:

Gregory, David A., and David R. Wilcox (editors)
  2007 *Zuni Origins: Toward a New Synthesis of Southwestern Archaeology*. University of Arizona Press, Tucson.

For an accessible discussion of the Ancient Puebloan world:

Kantner, John
  2004 *Ancient Puebloan Southwest*. Cambridge University Press, Cambridge.

For a highly readable case study on a Sinagua site intended for undergraduates:

Kamp, Kathryn
  1998 *Life in the Pueblo: Understanding the Past Through Archaeology*. Waveland Press, Prospect Heights, Illinois.

For more detail on the research at Casas Grandes highlighted in the chapter's case study:

Whalen, Michel E., and Paul E. Minnis
  2009 *The Neighbors of Casas Grandes: Excavating Medio Period Communities of Northwest Chihuahua, Mexico*. University of Arizona Press, Tucson.

For discussion of the Hohokam at Pueblo Grande (also see Chapter 1's case study):

Abbott, David R. (editor)
  2003 *Centuries of Decline: The Hohokam Classic Period at Pueblo Grande*. University of Arizona Press, Tucson.

OTHER RESOURCES

Sections H and I of the Student CD supply web links, additional discussion questions, and other study aids. The Student CD also contains additional resources. Particularly relevant to this chapter are "The Dolores Archaeological Program: Documenting the Pithouse-to-Pueblo Transition" (Section D.5 and "Was There Cannibalism in the Prehistoric Southwest?" (Section F.5).

CASE STUDY

The pre-Columbian Southwest was the location of several large, aggregated Late Prehistoric sites. Understanding the nature and structure of the societies these sites represent is a major topic of research for Southwestern archaeologists. This case study describes investigations of the sociopolitical system centered in northern Mexico at the site of Casas Grandes, or Paquimé. Casas Grandes has been interpreted as a trading center that gained power from control of trade between the Mexican civilizations and Southwestern centers to the north. More recent interpretations have viewed this site as the powerful center of a Late Prehistoric regional system in the southern Southwest. Yet, as this case study indicates, until recently little research has been done to place this large site in the context of other sites in northern Mexico. Thus, we have known very little about the internal functioning of the Casas Grandes system. In some ways the work described here is quite basic because it is being done in an area about which so little is known. As you read this case study, think about how the kinds of information collected through survey and excavations at other related sites allow archaeologists to better understand Casas Grandes itself. What does this tell you about the nature of archaeology and about what makes a site important to archaeologists?

CASAS GRANDES AT THE EDGE OF THE SOUTHWESTERN AND MESOAMERICAN WORLDS

Paul E. Minnis and Michael E. Whalen

One of the major transformations among human groups was the development of complex societies. Such polities vary, but they are often characterized by the presence of cities, complicated economies in which individuals and families specialize in the production of specific goods, bureaucracies, monumental architecture, and rulers. The best-known examples of complex societies are the ancient states of the Near East, Mesoamerica, Asia, Africa, and South America. Yet, examples of complex societies are found throughout the world, including North America. Many factors must be examined in considering how such societies developed, as the matter is far from simple. For example, the rulers of early complex societies often exerted substantial influence over the local economy through tradition and taxation. At the same time, elites usually participated in a special economy involving the manufacture, distribution, and use of rare and exotic goods. Commonly, these goods were traded over long distances. Thus it is reasonable to ask how local and long-distance economies were related to the development of complexity.

The remains of one complex polity in North America were first visited by outsiders nearly four centuries ago. After an exhausting trek through what is now northern Mexico, an area that was thought to be a desolate hinterland, a small group of Spanish explorers led by Francisco de Ibarra entered an unusually lush valley in present-day Chihuahua, Mexico. Here they encountered the ruins of a spectacular town, Casas Grandes, or Paquimé (Figure 9.24), probably deserted not much more than a century before the Spanish explorers set foot there. The expedition's chronicler, Baltzar de Obregón, described in 1584 what the Europeans saw:

> There are many houses of great size, strength, and height. They are of six and seven stories, with towers and walls like fortresses for protection and defense against the enemies who undoubtedly used to make war on the inhabitants. The houses contained large and magnificent patios paved with enormous and beautiful stones resembling jasper. There are knife-shaped stones which supported the wonderful and big pillars of heavy timber brought from far away. The walls of the houses were whitewashed and painted in many colors and shades with pictures of the buildings. The structures had a kind of adobe wall. However, it was mixed and interspersed with stone and wood, this combination being stronger and more durable than boards. (translated by Hammond and Rey 1928)

Although Paquimé had been known as an unusually important site since Obregón's time, it was not until three and one-half centuries later that its grandeur revealed, during three years of excavation by the Joint Casas Grandes Project, a collaborative effort between the Amerind Foundation, a private research organization in Arizona, and Mexico's National Institute of Anthropology and History. This massive project mapped the site and excavated hundreds of domestic rooms, ritual features, and other contexts. Our work as well as other projects around Casas Grandes have added to and revised the pioneering research of the Joint Casas Grandes Project, especially of its director, Charles C. Di Peso.

FIGURE 9.24 Aerial view of Casas Grandes, or Paquimé, in Chihuahua, Mexico.
(Photo by Adriel Heisey.)

Any research is influenced by its historical context, and our work is no exception. Far northwestern Mexico is a poorly known area between two of the world's most intensively studied regions. Hundreds of archaeologists have studied thousands of archaeological sites for over a century to the north of Casas Grandes in the southwestern United States, where massive archaeological projects have been undertaken recently in compliance with cultural resource management statutes. To the south in Mesoamerica are the spectacular ruins of central Mexico, like the enormous ancient city of Teotihuacán and the Aztec capital of Tenochtitlán, as well as Mayan ruins still farther south. Relatively few Mexican archaeologists have devoted their lives to studying the less monumental remains in northern Mexico, and few North American archaeologists have crossed the border to work in a country with a different culture, language, and laws, as well as with fewer opportunities for research funding.

Consequently, the prehistory of northwestern Mexico is not as well known as that of adjacent regions, and this affects the research questions one can ask.

WHAT WAS KNOWN

Because of the Joint Casas Grandes Project, we know a great deal about this one site, an unusual situation in northwestern Mexico. Casas Grandes reached its height during the **Medio** (Spanish for "Middle") **period**, from approximately 750 BP to 500 BP (AD 1200–1450), when it was one of the largest communities in northern Mexico and the southwestern United States, with 1000 rooms and a population in the thousands. Not only large, this site was very influential, the center of a regional society bound together by a web of social, religious, cultural, and economic relationships.

Casas Grandes is at the far southern end of the Puebloan world, a large area centered on what is now New Mexico and Arizona. Modern Puebloan groups, such as the Hopi, the Zuni, and the pueblos around the Rio Grande in New Mexico, are the descendants of those who built many ancient communities. Like today's Puebloan peoples, their ancestors were not all exactly alike, and Casas Grandes is but one variation of a general Puebloan way of life. The site's overall appearance is more Puebloan than Mesoamerican in its unplanned layout. The domestic architecture of Casas Grandes consists of suites of contiguous aboveground rooms arranged in room blocks. Yet, Casas Grandes is different in other ways; the rooms are unusually large, sometimes in eccentric shapes, with very thick adobe walls, and some room blocks were more than two stories tall. Even the Mesoamerican-inspired ceremonial architecture, like ball courts and platform mounds, are not arranged in as orderly a manner as they often are at Mesoamerican centers.

Compared with other communities in the area, Casas Grandes has a far greater number of features suitable for ceremonies that would bring people together in shared rituals. Four types of ritual architecture are known: ball courts, platform mounds, feasting ovens, and ceremonial rooms. Ball courts usually have a flat I-shaped center, sometimes with embankments on either side. It is thought that ball courts in the Casas Grandes area and other parts of the southwestern United States, such as among the Hohokam to the northwest, were used to play a ball game with strong religious elements, as in Mesoamerica. Platform mounds probably hosted or marked important ceremonies, and enormous amounts of food to accompany public events were prepared in feasting ovens, some quite large (Figure 9.25). Various rooms throughout

FIGURE 9.25 Student standing inside excavated feasting oven at site 204.

the site had unusual artifact assemblages, leading Di Peso to interpret them as ceremonial rooms.

No doubt very important ceremonies took place at Casas Grandes, and Paul Fish and Suzanne Fish (1999) suggest that Paquimé may have been a pilgrimage destination for people outside the immediate area. A recent analysis of symbols on painted pottery from the Casas Grandes region suggested to Christine Van Pool (2003) that the leaders of Casas Grandes may have been shaman-priests whose sacred knowledge was a major source of their power.

In addition to being a religious center, Casas Grandes was also an economic powerhouse. While so much attention has been focused on exotic and rare goods, farming was its economic mainstay. Ever since Obregón's time, visitors have recognized that the river valley next to Casas Grandes was especially well suited for agriculture, with an unusually wide, fertile, and well-watered floodplain. This allowed the town to support a large population that ultimately grew to many times larger than the next largest communities. The farming productivity also facilitated surplus production, some of which may have been used by elites to help build their power and authority through giving feasts and other gifts.

Long-distance trade was important to Casas Grandes. Parrots, shell, and copper moved north, whereas turquoise was traded south. Parrots are especially significant. It appears that Casas Grandes learned how to raise scarlet macaws, a parrot native to the tropic forests of Latin America but not the high desert of Chihuahua. Most likely, Paquimé controlled if not monopolized trade in these parrots, whose feathers were prized by the ancient people of the North American Southwest. Both copper and shell artifacts ultimately came from west Mexico to the southwest. Charles Di Peso believed that Casas

Grandes was founded by long-distance traders, known in Mesoamerica as *pochteca*, to coordinate trade between the North American Southwest and Mesoamerica.

Regardless of how the Casas Grandes economy was specifically organized, much surplus flowed in, probably creating one of the wealthiest communities in the ancient North American Southwest. As you might expect, wealth was not distributed equally; some families or groups had access to more wealth than others. This is most clearly seen in several locations at Casas Grandes. Excavation crews located several rooms that must have been warehouses, each packed with special goods, such as raw minerals, magnificent painted pottery vessels, and especially shell, over a ton of it. Whether these caches were hoards of devotional offerings made by pilgrims or part of a more secular economy is not yet known, but the concentration of such goods is evidence of differential access to wealth at Casas Grandes.

Wealth accumulation probably was reserved for elites, small groups of people with greater power or prestige than others. Perhaps the term "rulers" overemphasizes the power they were able to exert over their fellow citizens. There are no obvious palaces or especially fancy housing, so the best evidence for social hierarchy comes from burials. John Ravesloot (1988) analyzed the 576 human burials recovered by the Joint Casas Grandes Project. While some individuals were interred with more grave goods than others, the most obvious characteristic indicating elites was burial location. Most people were buried in simple pits with a few grave goods. However, two burial clusters were uniquely placed. The most unusual was a group of three people buried in large ceramic vessels in tombs within a platform mound. No one else in Casas Grandes was accorded such a burial. Most likely these were very special people during their lives.

One could devote much effort to describing the spectacular site of Casas Grandes; Di Peso and his colleagues did … in eight dense volumes. The remarkable site has been designated as a **World Heritage Site** by UNESCO. The uniqueness of Casas Grandes extends beyond its fancy trade goods, abundant ritual architecture, and monumental apartment buildings. One example of what would seem to be of mundane interest should suffice to illustrate this point. This site probably has the most complicated intrasite water distribution system of any community in pre-Columbian North America. Water was drawn from a spring 6 kilometers (3.7 miles) from the community and sent via a master canal to a collection reservoir, complete with a settling basin, which then fed water through a series of smaller sinuous canals that snaked through the room blocks.

A second set of canals drained water away from the building, an important detail, since adobe walls are very vulnerable to water damage.

WHAT WE WANTED TO KNOW

For all the questions that remain about Casas Grandes—about its origin, dynamic history, social and political structure, and finally its demise—we now have a much better understanding than we did several generations ago. We know that for up to 250 years, it was one of the largest and most influential towns in the Puebloan world. Its leaders oversaw a thriving community of farmers with many artisans; it was a town that undoubtedly awed its neighbors. Fortunately, the careful work and detailed publications from the Joint Casas Grandes Project laid a strong foundation for future work.

But what should the future work be? That was the question facing us in the late 1980s. As tempting as the prospect might be, expending more major efforts on Casas Grandes did not seem like a good idea. After some reflection, it became clear that while we knew much about Casas Grandes itself, little was known about its regional context. How did Casas Grandes relate to the hundreds of Medio period villages and hamlets scattered about the International Four Corners, where Arizona, New Mexico, Chihuahua, and Sonora join? How could we understand the role of long-distance relationships, such as those with Mesoamerica, if at the same time we didn't understand the local relationships? Therefore, we began a long-term, multiphase project to address these concerns.

The results, however, are not just of interest for understanding Casas Grandes. This site represents but one example of the beginnings of complexity, a problem that is being studied by archaeologists worldwide. Examining Casas Grandes can, therefore, help build a comparative base to address this issue. For example, a number of scholars have begun to suggest that the simplest, complex polities control an area smaller than previously thought. That is, power in such societies was weaker and spottier than anticipated. Was this the situation between 750 BP and 500 BP in what is now northwestern Chihuahua?

WHAT WE ARE DOING

With these thoughts in mind, we began our field research in the summer of 1989. We hope the results of our research will be a systematic body of data allowing us to interpret the local setting of Casas Grandes. The work should also be useful for future generations of archaeologists, even if they use the data to disagree with our conclusions, just as we have used Di Peso's data to disagree with his interpretations.

Reconnaissance and Systematic Survey

The logical first research step was to conduct a reconnaissance survey in the region, a location that had not had a wide-ranging archaeological survey since the 1930s. In 1989 we conducted a short two-tiered field season. First, we visited archaeological sites in northwestern Chihuahua that were known, either from the early surveys or to local residents with whom we spoke. Needless to say, we could not record all the sites; rather we concentrated in four areas of varying distances from Casas Grandes. The idea was that Paquimé's power and influence may have varied with different distances from the center. We chose four areas, from directly around Casas Grandes up to more than 60 kilometers (37 miles) away. Reconnaissance surveys like this one are an excellent way to acquire quickly and cheaply a basic understanding of the archaeological landscape. However, such quick surveys usually produce biased data; large, highly visible, and unusual sites are more likely to be recorded. To enable us to better judge the representativeness of our reconnaissance survey data, it was necessary to fit in some systematic surveying. Thus we chose two areas west of Casas Grandes at the foothills of the massive Sierra Madre Occidental to be surveyed systematically.

Unlike reconnaissance survey, during systematic survey crew members walk parallel lines covering all terrain in the survey unit. This type of survey is an excellent data-gathering technique in semiarid environments, where crews can easily see artifacts and remnants of structures on the surface because trees are few and groundcover sparse. In this setting, shovel testing, to remove the surface vegetation that commonly occurs in locations like eastern North America, can be dispensed with.

We do have to face one unfortunate problem: massive looting of sites. Because of the demand for prehistoric relics, almost all Medio period sites have been looted by hand digging to recover ceramic vessels originally left as grave offerings. Most pots then end up north of the border in the United States. Much irreplaceable information is lost forever, but we collect what data we can.

During our first field season, we visited nearly a hundred sites, filling out site forms, making systematic collections of surface artifacts, taking photographs, and preparing maps. As is common with many countries having a rich archaeological record and a history of many important artifacts leaving the country,

Mexico prohibits removal of artifacts, so archaeologists must do basic artifact analyses in the field.

We were pleased that our first efforts in 1989 seemed to reveal some basic patterns. It seemed that sites within about a day's walk of Casas Grandes, an area we termed the core, were different from those farther away. For example, features such as ball courts and feasting ovens, of special importance for integrating the society, are far more abundant in the core than outside. Doughnut-shaped stones used as entrances to macaw pens, likewise, were far more common in the core area. We suspected that these patterns reflect tight control by Casas Grandes of communities within the core, whereas those more than a day's walk away (over 30 km, or a bit less than 20 miles), were relatively more independent. Despite the size and grandeur of Casas Grandes, its hegemony seemed to have been less extensive than anticipated.

The initial reconnaissance survey provided tantalizing patterns, but these were based on very small data sets. Fortunately, the National Science Foundation funded a large grant for a multiyear systematic survey. Our objective was to acquire a database large enough to support a proper evaluation of the hypotheses derived from the reconnaissance survey.

Despite the larger budget, we couldn't cover all of northwestern Chihuahua, so we needed to devise a research protocol to match our budget and research questions. Therefore, we worked in two major zones: the core zone within about 30 kilometers of Casas Grandes and what we termed the middle zone, centered on the San Pedro River about 60 kilometers north of Casas Grandes. The environments are not uniform within each study area, so from each zone we selected several similar survey areas, such as river valley and foothill settings, to help investigate the distribution of remains across the landscape.

Survey crews spent two long summer field seasons carefully and systematically walking over the survey locations, recording all archaeological remains encountered. By the end of this process, we had systematically covered over 200 square kilometers (80 miles²) and recorded about 450 sites, of which the majority dated to the Medio period. As with our initial survey, we mapped and photographed each site, filled out a form, and collected surface artifacts, mostly chipped stone and ceramics, but occasionally shell, turquoise, and other uncommon artifacts.

In general, we found that the patterns noted during the initial survey were replicated during systematic survey. Of course, the quality and variety of data were vastly better, and we continue to analyze these data. In addition, we now had data for the pre-Medio time periods, information we believe will be useful in research examining the origins of Casas Grandes. We published a number of articles about our results, but a book, *Casas Grandes and Its Hinterland: Prehistoric Regional Organization in Northwest Mexico* (Whalen and Minnis 2001b), was the major result of the systematic survey.

Excavation

Excavation can provide information to answer questions that can't be adequately addressed with survey data alone. But which sites should we study? The most efficient approach for our research since 1996, given our time and funding limits, was to excavate ancient communities that probably played different roles in the regional system (Whalen and Minnis 2009). Of course, much was already known about the center, Casas Grandes. We first decided to study the most common types of sites, hamlets where small groups lived in unremarkable communities. We chose two such sites having slightly different surface ceramic collections, which might indicate that they dated to slightly different times within the Medio period. Site 317 was small, and we excavated seven rooms and a small oven. Site 231 was a little larger, and here we had time to excavate about five rooms.

The next site studied, number 242, drew our attention when we first recorded it on reconnaissance survey. It had one of the largest and most elaborate ball courts outside of Casas Grandes itself (Figure 9.26). More importantly, it had the *only* platform mound we know of from a site other than Casas Grandes, which had about 18 platform mounds. The domestic mound also appeared different. On the basis of these characteristics, site 242 appeared to be an excellent candidate for study.

Unfortunately, we only had six weeks to test the site, and most of our efforts concentrated on the unusual domestic mound. As we suspected, excavation of a portion of the domestic mound revealed unusual architecture. Unlike the two villages we tested, which had small rooms and thin walls, the rooms at 242 were large and often more than simple rectangles. One room had 14 walls. Furthermore, the room walls were unusually thick. The domestic architecture of site 242, then, was more like Casas Grandes, 30 kilometers away, than like its neighbors. We have called the building form an "architecture of power" (Whalen and Minnis 2001a), and its presence, combined with the presence of the ball court and platform mound, suggests to us that this site was a secondary center within the Casas Grandes–dominated polity. Here agents or relatives of elites lived and held important ceremonies to help build and maintain the loyalty of outlying groups.

The three sites we tested through excavation are quite small, but there are larger sites in the Casas

FIGURE 9.26 Aerial view of the ball court at site 242.

FIGURE 9.27 Excavation of the floor of a room at site 204, La Tinaja.

Grandes area. While much smaller than Casas Grandes (200 rooms vs. 1000), they are still large by regional standards. The basic question for this phase of research regarded the role of large sites. Were they simply large communities, aggregations of families little different from the smaller villages, or were they structurally distinct, perhaps functioning like Casas Grandes?

Of two possible large sites to excavate, we chose the one that was more protected from looting. We had recently completed a three-season project at this site, number 204, or La Tinaja. A total of about 35 rooms from several different parts of the site were excavated, as were two feasting ovens, trash deposits, and the ball court (Figure 9.27). Our analysis suggests that there was a pre-Medio occupation and that the Tinaja site was most heavily occupied during the early part of the Medio period. This might suggest that the explosive growth of Casas Grandes occurred as it absorbed people from hinterland sites like La Tinaja. Our preliminary interpretation is that the Tinaja site was not a peer of Casas Grandes in the breadth and depth of its ritual importance.

More recently, our research has focused on the area right around Paquimé for comparison with our excavated sites father from the central site. During two seasons we excavated portions of a site (Site 315) about two kilometers from Casas Grandes. The quantity and quality of artifacts, and the type of architecture from this site suggest to us that it was the residence of influential or powerful people. Michael Whalen is now directing the excavation of another nearby site, again only two kilometers from Paquimé (Site 565), that promises to help us understand the end of the Medio period. Paul Minnis is currently studying farming and irrigation in the Rio Casas Grandes flood plain around Paquimé to better model the political ecology of the region.

Early during the excavation phase, we conducted a small study of prehistoric agricultural fields around Casas Grandes. Because of the low groundcover and the lack of Historic period farming that might have obliterated the remains of prehistoric fields, ancient rock walls (*trincheras*) built to retain soil and moisture, small canals, and rock pile fields can be seen on the surface. We had undertaken this study in anticipation of a future, larger-scale study of agriculture, but the results of our farming study helped interpret some of our excavation data. For example, the secondary center, site 242, is located next to a field system of nearly 100,000 square meters (25 acres), while the next largest field system was 8000 square meters (1.98 acres), with the average being about 2000 square meters (0.5 acre). It appears that the elites at 242 were controlling some basic food production, but for what? An analysis of ceramics from this site showed an unusually high frequency of large pottery jars with interior pitting. It is quite likely that this pitting is due to acids from the fermentation of corn beer, which probably was consumed during important festivals held at 242. This example simply demonstrates how important it is in archaeology to draw together data from multiple sources to construct as complete as possible an interpretation of the past.

WHAT STILL NEEDS TO BE DONE

In an area where little archaeological research has been conducted, there are so many questions to answer and topics to address. Our work focused on the landscape of power: how extensive was Casas Grandes' power and influence? We have argued that Casas Grandes exerted its strongest control within an unexpectedly small region, on the order of 30 kilometers. Beyond this core area, the influence of Casas Grandes was felt to lesser degree and in differing ways. Not unexpectedly, not everyone agrees with our interpretations. Some other scholars argue that Casas Grandes exerted more powerful and wide-ranging control (see various articles in Newell and Gallaga 2003; Schaafsma and Riley 1999).

How power is distributed across the landscape, our research focus, does not tell what the power was like. Power and control can come in many forms: economic, political, social, and religious. Much more research is needed to understand the exact nature of power in middle-scale polities. Van Pool's recent argument that the elites of Casas Grandes derived (some) power through manipulation of sacred knowledge is important. Does this suggestion conflict with ideas that emphasized the economic aspects of power, or are the two types of power complementary, and if so, were they both important in the development of Casas Grandes?

We must also consider what the Casas Grandes area was like before the Medio period. Both Di Peso and some more recent scholars believe that the Casas Grandes region was a sleepy backwater in the Puebloan world, and that Casas Grandes had few cultural antecedents in the area. We believe that our survey and excavation at the Tinaja site demonstrate that there was a larger pre-Medio population than previously thought and that there are clear connections between pre-Medio and Medio peoples. Unfortunately, the only excavation of pre-Medio sites in the area around Casas Grandes was conducted nearly a half-century ago. More needs to be done.

Until recently, Casas Grandes was discussed only in relation to the question of Mesoamerican–Southwest relationships. While our work emphasizes the local context of Casas Grandes, this region is still pivotal in addressing the issue of long-distance relationships. How were Mesoamerican symbols and religious structures used at Casas Grandes? How significant was trade between Casas Grandes and west Mexico? After all, Casas Grandes has more Mesoamerican goods and Mesoamerican-inspired symbols than any other site in the North American Southwest. Briefly, we think that Mesoamerican items, ideas, and icons were used by the local elites to help capture the loyalty of others and to help maintain their tenuous hold on power. Aspiring leaders used symbols and exotica known to have come from the great and powerful city to the south in an attempt to enhance their status among people in the region (Whalen and Minnis 2003). And it seems to have worked, but for only two centuries. Furthermore, understanding local and distant relationships in this case contributes to our understanding of the beginnings of civilization worldwide. The lesson, of course, is that we need to investigate our ancient past from many different approaches.

It is a cliché that research opens up as many questions as it answers, and our archaeological research in northern Mexico is no exception. New research not only provides fresh data but also directs us in more specific and productive ways of thinking about the distant past and about ourselves.

ACKNOWLEDGMENTS

Archaeological research is collaborative, involving many individuals and institutions. We have received funds from the National Science Foundation, the National Geographic Society, and the J. M. Kaplan Fund, as well as support from our home institutions, the University of Oklahoma and the University of Tulsa. Mexico's Instituto Nacional de Antropología e Historia, especially the Consejo de Arqueología and the Centro Chihuahua, courteously provided oversight and advice. Project crew members, most of whom were students from many different states and five different countries, are responsible for the quantity and high quality of our data. Finally, the people of northwestern Chihuahua—landowners, colleagues, officials, and friends—all contributed to our ability to conduct research for the past 14 years.

DISCUSSION QUESTIONS

1. What and where is Casas Grandes, or Paquimé? Why is this site important to archaeologists?

2. Why is relatively little known about the regional archaeology around Casas Grandes, even though this site has long been of interest? How does the approach taken by the authors help remedy this situation?

3. What indications are there of the complexity and power of the Casas Grandes system? Compare these patterns with what you have learned about the Chacoan system.

4. At the end of this case study the authors suggest some of the areas in which further research is needed. Which of these would you choose to investigate first, and how would you structure your research?

CHAPTER 10

Bison Hunters and Horticulturists
of the Great Plains

Like several other areas near western cities, Larimer County, Colorado, has a growing population. Communities like Fort Collins, Loveland, and Windsor, with close access to Interstate 25, and thus the Denver metropolitan area, have seen considerable growth in recent decades. The dry rangeland surrounding these communities is being transformed into suburban residential developments. In 1997 construction teams building one such development, River West in Windsor, made an unusual find. While grading for home sites and roads, they cut into a hillside and nicked the top of a large bed of bones about 18 feet (5.5 m) below the surface. Not that this interested the workers much; they had a job to do, and their work continued. Then someone who happened to volunteer at the Denver Museum of Nature and Science stumbled upon the exposed bones, which were mainly from bison. As their existence and possible significance became known, archaeologists at Colorado State University (CSU) were contacted to take a look (Dold 2003).

It turned out that this deeply buried, well-preserved bone bed is the result of a bison kill dating to about 2700 years ago. Despite later disturbance by scavengers and by runoff from thunderstorms, this is one of the largest kill site accumulations ever found. Although there may be as many as 300 bison represented here, the kill site apparently was used only once, when Plains Archaic hunters drove a herd of bison into a steep-sided arroyo and trapped them so that others could spear them from above. Given the age data from tooth eruption in bison calves studied so far, this kill appears to have taken place in the late summer or the early fall, when archaeologists speculate people were seeking meat to dry and store for the winter. Interestingly, large amounts of available meat may never have been processed at all, perhaps because so many animals were trapped. Also, there are two different projectile point styles, believed to be diagnostic of both local and nonlocal ethnic groups during the Late Archaic. This raises questions about whether people were cooperating in dispatching the bison or competing for the meat made available by the kill.

Excavation and analysis of this site by CSU archaeologists led by Dr. Larry Todd (Todd et al. 2001) was a major undertaking. The first problem, of course, was getting permission to excavate. Because the site was on private land, not to mention in the middle of a large construction site, archaeologists had no automatic right to work there. The property owner could proceed with development as he saw fit. Thus, an agreement had to be reached with the property owner that would not affect the construction plans. Fortunately, this was possible, and the site name, the Kaplan–Hoover site, honors the landowner and the owner of the cooperating construction company.

The physical excavation of the site was complicated by the nature of the deposits as well as by their location. While the excavation was under way a plastic shelter was erected over the site and heated in colder weather with portable propane heaters. Construction continued around the bone bed as the excavation took place. The site literally was a mass of bones, and there often was nowhere to stand or sit. Archaeologists ended up laying boards over the bone bed and working while lying prone on the boards, hanging over the bones. Just imagine how soon that must have become uncomfortable! Because bones the bones were fragile, recovery was a slow, painstaking process of brushing and picking with small bamboo sticks. Archaeologists also needed to record very detailed information about the position, orientation, and associations of each bone. This meant careful measuring and recording of data points that could later be analyzed. Once in the lab, bone reconstruction also required a long and careful process. The upshot of all these requirements was that the entire site could not be excavated. An area having a cross-sectional width of only 3 feet (ca. 1 m) has been excavated; but this small sample has yielded at least 10,000 bones and artifacts for study (Dold 2003).

The Kaplan–Hoover excavation was a very public undertaking. In part this was the result of its location and the circumstances of its discovery, but the archaeologists working there viewed it as an educational resource for the community as well as a research opportunity. Thus, they opened their excavation to the public. Schoolchildren, teachers, and many others saw the site under excavation and learned about archaeology and bison hunters in the process. The local chapter of the Colorado Archaeological Society, an organization through which amateurs can become involved in archaeology, developed a public outreach program that sought to present both archaeological and Native American perspectives on bison hunting, eventually creating a traveling exhibit about the site. The Kaplan–Hoover site was placed on the **National Register of Historic Places**, which lists and protects sites and buildings of significance in the United States. Once National Register designation was obtained, funding for its purchase and preservation became possible. This funding was obtained from the Colorado State Historical Fund, which receives monies from gambling tax revenues. Thus, although most of the site has been reburied, its long-term management is now assured. Cooperation among the homeowners' association for River West, the Town of Windsor, and archaeologists has been critical in the preservation plan for the site.

The story of Kaplan–Hoover illustrates the unfolding of one contemporary archaeological project. Through the cooperation of many people and the application of preservation laws, an important site that was threatened has been studied and preserved rather than destroyed. This story also introduces a type of site that has been found many times on the western Great Plains, although few known examples are as large as Kaplan–Hoover. On the Plains, bison hunting was an ancient and persistent way of life, and bison kill sites are a colorful aspect of its cultural remains. Indeed, the Historic period version of this pattern, involving equestrian pursuit of bison herds, often is taken as culturally emblematic of the Plains. Nevertheless, there is much more to the story of the human past on the Great Plains, as we shall see in this chapter.

DEFINITION OF THE AREA

The Plains culture area incorporates the people and places of both the tall-grass prairie and the short-grass high plains that stretch from the Saskatchewan River to the Rio Grande and east from the foothills of the Rocky Mountains to the upper Mississippi River valley (Figure 10.1). The area comprises southern Alberta, Saskatchewan, and southwestern Manitoba, the eastern portions of Montana, Wyoming, and Colorado, all of North Dakota, South Dakota, Nebraska, and Kansas, and major portions of Texas and Oklahoma, as well as small parts of eastern New Mexico, northwestern Missouri, and western Iowa, and most of Minnesota. This huge area excludes the Prairie Peninsula discussed in Chapter 12, as well as the intermontane grasslands found farther west, but otherwise corresponds roughly to the northern temperate grassland biome. The Plains culture area is routinely subdivided into five subunits: the Southern Plains, the Central Plains, the Northeastern Plains, the Middle Missouri, and the Northwestern Plains. These subareas are labeled in Figure 10.1, but boundaries for them are imprecise and are not drawn. In fact, as with all the culture areas we use in this text, the Plains culture area has been defined largely on the basis of historically known peoples. Since the nature and distribution of ethnic entities changed dramatically during the Historic period, it is important to remember that the boundaries of the whole culture area also are somewhat arbitrarily defined. Table 10.1 provides an outline of Plains culture history.

THE ENVIRONMENT

Most people think of the Great Plains as uniformly flat grasslands, but in fact the area exhibits considerable internal environmental variability. For instance, climate varies tremendously within the Plains. Near the eastern margins annual rainfall is over 39 inches (99 cm), while in eastern Colorado it is less than 14 inches (35.6 cm), and in some areas it is even lower. Much of the western Plains lies in the rain shadow of the Rockies, but at

FIGURE 10.1 The Great Plains culture area, showing sites that are mentioned in Chapter 10.

TABLE 10.1 Introduction to Great Plains Culture History

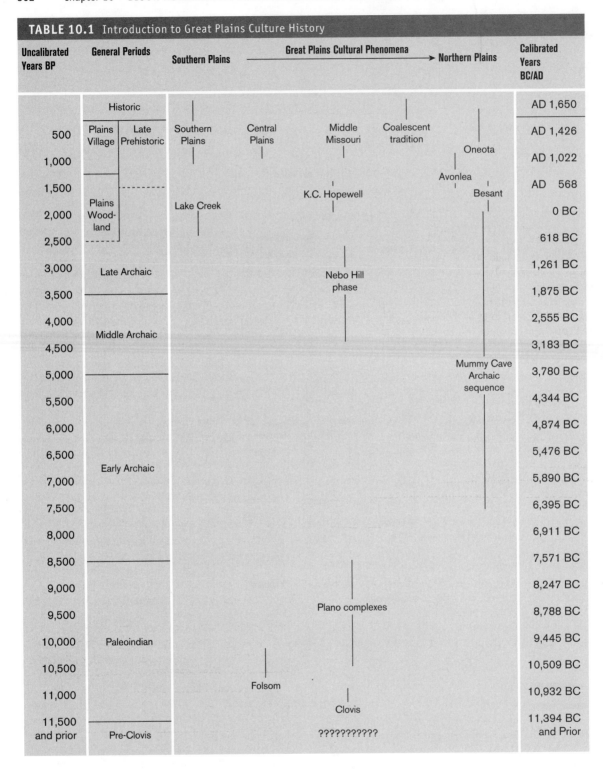

Uncalibrated Years BP	General Periods		Southern Plains	Great Plains Cultural Phenomena				Northern Plains	Calibrated Years BC/AD
	Historic								AD 1,650
500	Plains Village	Late Prehistoric	Southern Plains	Central Plains	Middle Missouri	Coalescent tradition			AD 1,426
1,000							Oneota		AD 1,022
1,500	Plains Wood-land				K.C. Hopewell		Avonlea	Besant	AD 568
2,000			Lake Creek						0 BC
2,500									618 BC
3,000	Late Archaic				Nebo Hill phase				1,261 BC
3,500									1,875 BC
4,000	Middle Archaic								2,555 BC
4,500									3,183 BC
5,000							Mummy Cave Archaic sequence		3,780 BC
5,500									4,344 BC
6,000									4,874 BC
6,500	Early Archaic								5,476 BC
7,000									5,890 BC
7,500									6,395 BC
8,000									6,911 BC
8,500									7,571 BC
9,000									8,247 BC
9,500					Plano complexes				8,788 BC
10,000	Paleoindian								9,445 BC
10,500				Folsom					10,509 BC
11,000									10,932 BC
11,500 and prior	Pre-Clovis				Clovis				11,394 BC and Prior
					???????????				

higher elevations, as in the Black Hills of South Dakota, there is more rainfall (Wedel and Frison 2001). From north to south there also is great difference in the length of the growing season. While killing frosts are almost totally lacking in Texas, on the Canadian Plains the growing season is only three months long.

The topography of the Plains also is not uniform, though overall there is a gentle drop in elevation from west to east. The land surface has been variously eroded and dissected over time, as well as modified by glaciers in the northern sections. A mantle of **loess**, fine windblown sediment derived from glacial outwash, blankets many areas as well. These deposits, which can be several feet thick, are thought to have been created when wind picked up and redistributed fine sediments left by glaciers.

Two main physiographic provinces have been identified (Fenneman 1931, 1938): the Central Lowlands province on the east and the Great Plains province to the west. The Central Lowlands province, a northern area that extends south to Iowa and includes the parts of the Plains in Minnesota and the eastern Dakotas, was glaciated recently. Similarly, only the northernmost parts of the Great Plains province like the Alberta Plains and the Missouri Plateau north of the Missouri River Trench were glaciated (see Figure 2.12). South of these areas in both provinces the land was unglaciated at least during the Wisconsin glaciations and older land surfaces have been eroding for longer periods of time.

The division between the tall-grass prairies to the east and the short-grass plains to the west occurs at approximately the 100th meridian. At present, most areas west of the 100th meridian do not receive more than 20 inches (50.8 cm) of rain annually, and this dryness helps determine what grass species can grow there. The boundary, however, has undoubtedly shifted in the past, just like the prairie–forest ecotone boundary on the east. Plains rivers incised into the landscape allow fingers of forest biomes to snake westward as well. Even farther west, canyons containing watercourses support species that require more moisture. These valleys are ecotones with relatively high species diversity. It also is true that distinct vegetation communities characterize particular locations within the Great Plains, such as the Sand Hills of western Nebraska and the Black Hills in South Dakota and Wyoming (Koch and Bozell 2003). The margin with the Rockies also is not abrupt, particularly in the Northwestern Plains, where mountains and their foothills interfinger with plains across a broad area.

Climatic Change

The cooler climate of the Late Pleistocene meant less evaporation of moisture on the Great Plains as well as less seasonal variation in temperature. In turn vegetation communities were quite different and some of the Plains was forested (Kay 1998b). The southern High Plains probably were a sagebrush grassland (Hall and Valastro 1995). However, the plant and animal communities of this period contained species not found together today and have no modern analogues.

The most significant environmental changes that have affected the human settlement of the Great Plains are those associated with the waning of the Wisconsin glaciation after its maximum at approximately 18,000 BP. In Alberta and northern Montana, the Laurentian and Cordilleran ice sheets parted as tempratures began to warm. This area is where the ice-free corridor (see Chapter 3) would have ended. As the Laurentian glacier shrank, complex and fundamental changes took place rapidly. One effect was that more drought-tolerant grasses became dominant, and large herbivorous species including mammoths were not able to survive. It is likely that reduction in habitat diversity and loss of more nutritious plant foods at the end of the Pleistocene were the critical factors in the demise of megafauna.

Another aspect of the northeastward retreat of the Laurentian glacier is the formation of large proglacial lakes. The most famous of these lakes is glacial **Lake Agassiz**, a giant lake that at one point or another, until it disappeared about 7500 years ago, inundated most of the area between the Rocky Mountains and the Lake Superior Basin and between South Dakota and Hudson Bay (Teller and Clayton 1983). As the ice sheet retreated toward Hudson Bay, drainage was blocked in every direction but south, trapping water between the rising land to the west and the glacier. Drainage first became possible through the Great Lakes, and finally the waters drained into the Tyrell Sea, which preceded Hudson Bay. As with all of North America's formerly glaciated areas, the landscapes of the northern parts of the Great Plains retain many glacial features, including the pothole lakes that dot the northeastern prairies.

We also know that the Great Plains climate continued to warm in the early through mid-Holocene. The mid-Holocene warm, dry period called the Altithermal (ca. 7000–4000 BP) was especially important on the Great Plains. On the east, the extent of the grasslands increased and prairie vegetation extended well into the Midwest. Prairie also expanded in Manitoba. In the western High Plains it became appreciably drier and warmer than it is today. Sometime between 4500 and 4000 years ago—sooner in some areas, later in others—essentially modern conditions began to develop on the Plains (Kay 1998b), although more minor climatic fluctuations have continued to occur.

ANTHROPOLOGICAL THEMES   TOPIC 10.1

Thematic Research Questions in Chapter 10

As we pointed out in Chapter 2, the North American arch-aeological record provides significant evidence for several broad anthropological themes. This is as true for the Great Plains as for other culture areas. You will find material directly relevant to at least four of the broad research questions discussed in Chapter 2 and listed in Table 2.1,

and we touch on other themes less directly. Table 10.2 helps you locate relevant sections of this chapter for each theme, although as you become more familiar with the archaeology of the Great Plains, you will discover more specific research questions and issues as well.

TABLE 10.2 Research Themes for the Great Plains

Research Question	Particularly Relevant Sections
How have humans adapted to the diverse environments of North America and to climatic change over time?	Discussions of the Archaic, Woodland, and Plains Village cultures as well as Late Prehistoric Bison Hunters
How, when, and where did food production develop in North America?	Discussion of Plains Woodland and Plains Village subsistence
What ethnic identities can be identified and historically traced in North America's past?	Discussion in Box 10.1, "Historic Ethnicities and the Archaeological Record"
What movements of human populations can be docu-mented in the North American past after the continent's initial settlement?	The discussion under Plains Village traditions, and of the Oneota on the Plains as well various Protohistoric

PALEOINDIANS ON THE PLAINS

Although Pre-Clovis human presence is not well estab-lished on the Great Plains, there are a few sites contain-ing mammoth and other extinct faunal remains with fracture patterns possibly made by humans. Without stone tools and reliable dates, debate will continue about the validity of these sites (Hofman and Graham 1998; Stanford 1999). In contrast, the presence of Clovis, Folsom, and Late Paleoindian people is well estab-lished. The Blackwater Draw and Folsom sites are located on the western margins of the Great Plains, and the stratified nature of key sites have allowed archae-ologists to develop a detailed Paleoindian projectile point sequence with Folsom following Clovis and various unfluted lanceolate points marking the Late Paleoindian period. Although the earliest Paleoindians hunted now extinct megafauna, bison hunting ways of life on the Great Plains began with Paleoindians.

PLAINS ARCHAIC

Paleoindian lifeways persisted on the Great Plains even after they had disappeared in other parts of North America. Archaeologists define the beginning

of the Archaic by using changes in projectile point morphology. On this basis, the Paleoindian period can be considered to end and the Archaic to begin at approximately 8500 BP when lanceolate projectile points were replaced across the Plains by a variety of notched forms.

There are several schemes for subdividing the millennia that follow this change, for although a hunt-ing and gathering way of life persisted in many parts of the Plains throughout the pre-Columbian past, a horticultural lifeway did develop along the river val-leys and in the prairies after approximately 2500 BP. This second type of lifestyle is designated the Wood-land, but calling everything after 2500 BP "Woodland" seems to deny the continuation of ancient patterns of hunting and gathering. The problem is one encoun-tered in many parts of North America after discovery of much greater diversity in human adaptations than had been envisioned in the traditional concepts of stages. In this chapter, we approach this problem by designating periods, while recognizing considerable variation from one part of the Plains to another (Table 10.1). This means that although we end the Archaic period at approximately 2500 BP to 1500 BP and follow it with **Plains Woodland** and Late Prehistoric we emphasize the arbitrariness of this ending. The dashed lines in Table 10.1 after 2500 BP and again at 1500 BP indicate that the end of the Archaic is difficult to fix precisely. Within the Archaic, we refer to the three traditional subperiods: Early Archaic (ca. 8500–5000 BP), Middle Archaic (ca. 5000–3500 BP), and Late Archaic (ca. 3500–2500/1500 BP), but we consider these designations largely arbitrary. Our approach doesn't completely resolve the difficulty just described, but we hope it simplifies variable adaptations in a way that is sensible for the novice student. If you pursue the archaeology of the Plains, expect to encounter different terminology and schemes (e.g., Vehik 2001).

The change to notched projectile points that marks the beginning of the Archaic has sometimes been interpreted as indicative of hunters adopting the atlatl, which is thought to require smaller darts and points than the thrusting spears of the Paleoindians (Frison 1998:151). A variety of projectile point forms have been recovered from datable, stratified deposits (Figure 10.2). For example, at Mummy Cave in northwestern Wyoming the Archaic strata, which are preceded by Paleoindian strata, have been dated from 7630 BP to 2050 BP (Frison 1991:Table 2.6) and the resulting sequencing for points has been widely used. The majority of Plains Archaic points are believed to have been dart points, but some Late Archaic points may be small enough to have served as arrow points. Distinctive notched or tanged knife forms with beveled edges also have been recognized in the Late Archaic (Figure 10.3), and on the southeastern edge of the Plains in Texas, these have been found in mortuary contexts (Broehm and Lovata 2004).

Archaic sites also contain more grinding implements than are found in Paleoindian sites. Grinding tools are considered evidence of increased emphasis on plant foods, notably seeds that must be ground to be digestible. Rock-filled pits, slab-lined hearths, and other fire pit features are common Archaic period features. These are believed to have been used to cook vegetables and other foods by heating the stones on a bed of coals, placing food wrapped in a green hide on top, and covering with earth or mulch to enable it to cook slowly. Processing of vegetable foods is inferred from the frequent association of grinding implements with these features. For example, at the Gore Pit site in southwestern Oklahoma, dated between 7000 BP and 6000 BP, several large circular basins containing burned rock, mussel shell, and some animal bone apparently were earth ovens. Late Archaic rock middens in central Texas are believed to have been used in processing desert plants like sotol and yucca (Vehik 2001:150).

There also is some indication of structure types during the Archaic. Circular pithouses with a single central post supporting a conical roof date as early as

FIGURE 10.2 Side-notched and corner-notched projectile points mark the beginning of the Archaic period on the Great Plains.

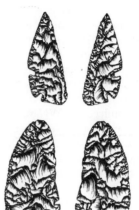

FIGURE 10.3 Late Archaic tanged knives; the specimens at the top have been worn and resharpened.

the end of the Early Archaic on the Northwestern Plains. For example, a well-preserved pithouse dated to 5300 BP to 3100 BP was found at the Medicine House site on the North Platte River in south central Wyoming. Pithouses, which continue to be found in Middle Archaic sites from this area, are thought to have been winter houses. In other Plains contexts, posthole patterns suggest other types of houses. Stone circles presumed to have been tipi rings also occur, but because these circles often have very little artifactual debris, they are difficult to date (Frison 2001). Neuman (2010) recently has suggested that winter tipi sites may have evidence of windbreaks as well.

In the Northwestern Plains of Wyoming, Montana, Alberta, and Saskatchewan, **medicine wheels**, or circular stone alignments with central cairns and radiating spokes, also are enigmatic. These apparently ritual or sacred constructions have captured the popular imagination, but they are not well understood. At least some of these constructions date to the Archaic, but they continue into the Late Prehistoric as well.

The subsistence constant for the Archaic on the Plains was, of course, the bison. The modern species of bison, *Bison bison*, evolved from larger Pleistocene bison species, *Bison antiquus* and *Bison occidentalis*, that have sometimes been found in Paleoindian sites. Bison provided meat, hides, and bones for tools and other purposes. Bison kills in late summer to fall would have provided animals with the most meat and fat. Archaeologists believe that Plains Archaic people cached surpluses of meat for their own use in winter. Bison were hunted both by individuals or small groups and communally by large numbers of people. The communal hunts have captured our imagination, but smaller kills probably also were frequent. We know that Archaic hunters drove bison into arroyo traps, parabolic sand dune traps, and artificial corrals, as well as off steep bluffs.

Many Archaic period sites help archaeologists understand the ways in which bison were hunted (e.g., Anderson et al. 1980; Todd et al. 2001). The Hawken site in the Black Hills of Wyoming represents an arroyo trap bison kill site used for several bison drives during the Early Archaic around 6400 BP. Nearly 300 projectile points have been recovered from this site. At the Middle Archaic Scoggin site in south central Wyoming, a corral was built to contain bison at the base of a steep talus slope. Archaeologists believe that hunters drove the bison down the slope and then, standing on the top, were able to pick off the bison before the animals could escape by charging back up the slope. Stone boiling pits outside the corral area probably were used to process the animals (Frison 1991b:193).

These dramatic bison kill and butchering sites captured the American imagination and led to stereotypes about Plains bison hunters. Like all stereotypes, there is some truth in such a characterization, but contrary to many depictions, the horse was not present until the Protohistoric period ,and bison was not the only resource utilized. Archaic people hunted bison on foot, and dogs were their only pack animals. They used other animal resources like deer, antelope, rabbit, prairie dog, birds, and even fish and freshwater mussels. Plant remains found in Archaic sites include acorns, various native seeds, fruits, and in some areas xerophytic edible plants like yucca and sotol. For example, at the Coffey site, north of Manhattan, Kansas, faunal remains from a series of encampments dating to 5270 to 5055 years ago include much bison but also deer, other mammals, fish, and migratory waterfowl, while archaeologists also have recovered plant remains from lamb's quarter, hackberry, bulrushes, grape, knotweed, and Solomon's seal.

Archaeologists have just begun to understand the great variability in Archaic adaptations across the Plains. Part of this variability is related to climatic change during the Archaic (e.g., Yansa 2007). The Early Archaic roughly corresponds to the mid-Holocene warm, dry period called either the Hypsithermal or Altithermal. While on the eastern and northern margins of the Plains this led to an expansion of grasslands, in the short-grass areas of the western Plains it may have meant conditions dry enough to reduce the amount of forage for bison and prevent the survival of other resources. Earlier archaeologists proposed that the western Plains were mostly abandoned during the Altithermal, but today we know that some people did continue to live on the Plains, perhaps exploiting mountain habitats at certain times of the year (Vehik 2001). Archaeological work at the High Plains Mustang Springs site, near Midland, Texas, revealed that foragers dug wells to obtain water during the Altithermal (Figure 10.4) (Meltzer 1991a). In better times, this site was at the location of a spring-fed pond, but after 6800 BP the spring failed, and humans who came there dug over 60 wells into the dry lake bed. Similar wells have been found at other Southern Plains sites including Blackwater Draw.

Other more local variability is even more poorly understood. Although the Archaic hunter-gatherers of the Plains were mobile hunter-gatherers, mobility, group aggregation, and seasonality strategies no doubt were diverse in this vast region. In the Southern Plains, particularly in drier periods, people may have camped near water sources, making forays into the surrounding region to obtain meat. Elsewhere a more cyclical pattern of nomadism probably obtained, with small bands having an approximate seasonal round that could be adjusted to seasonal and annual conditions. Group structure would have been flexible, so that during some seasons and in some places aggregations of bands took place, perhaps to cooperate in bison hunting and/or to find mates, share information, and exchange raw materials (Hofman 1989). Sites like the Early Archaic Spring Creek in southwestern Nebraska have been interpreted as base camps in such a system (Kay 1998a), but recent reanalysis of the faunal remains has led to an argument that the site was a bison processing site utilized only in the late summer or early fall (Widga 2004).

Late Archaic Developments

The Archaic way of life persisted for millennia. On the Canadian and Northwestern Plains, the Archaic can be considered to continue until approximately 1500 BP and to directly precede the Late Prehistoric (Frison 2001). In contrast, some Middle to Late Archaic complexes in the Central Plains already foreshadowed later Plains Woodland developments.

The most important of these is the **Nebo Hill phase** known from Kansas and Missouri near Kansas City. A distinctive Nebo Hill lanceolate point (Figure 10.5) has been known for some time. Although once thought to be a Paleoindian or Early Archaic point type because of its form, this point has been radiocarbon dated to between 4500 BP and 2600 BP, spanning the Middle to Late Archaic (Reid 1984). Other artifacts associated with this phase are bifacial hoes, bifacial gouges, rectangular and ovate manos, rectangular celts, and

FIGURE 10.4 Wells dug during the Altithermal by Archaic period foragers at the Mustang Springs site near Midland, Texas.

three-quarter-grooved axes (O'Brien and Wood 1998). Besides lithic artifacts, **fiber-tempered pottery**, untempered pottery, and ceramic human effigy fragments have been recognized in sites of this phase. Pottery with shredded fibers mixed through the clay (Kay 1998a:180) is the oldest pottery in the Plains culture area and as old as the oldest pottery in the Eastern Woodlands as well. Large sites of this phase are found in the uplands bordering the Missouri River, while smaller encampments have been found in the valleys of the Missouri's tributaries. Upland biface caches and burial mounds also are known. The chert in Nebo Hill burial mounds appears to be exotic, having come from central Missouri or farther away. In addition, one rolled copper bead and a lump of **galena** indicate some long-distance interaction. Subsistence information suggests that Nebo Hill people exploited deer, squirrel, bird, turtle, fish, nuts, and some native seeds, but no obvious cultigens have been found (Adair and Drass 2011). These developments foreshadow the next period in Plains prehistory.

THE WOODLAND PERIOD ON THE GREAT PLAINS

Despite the persistence of many aspects of the foraging way of life, archaeologists recognize a Woodland period on the Great Plains that begins when pottery, burial mounds, and sometimes horticulture began to be adopted by many Plains groups. Corner-notched projectile points may be another diagnostic for the Plains Woodland (A. M. Johnson and A. E. Johnson 1998). The nature and temporal extent of Plains Woodland are locally variable within the Great Plains, but may be apparent as early as 2500 BP and persist until 1150 BP or a little later and be subdivided into Early,

FIGURE 10.5 Nebo Hill
lanceolate points.

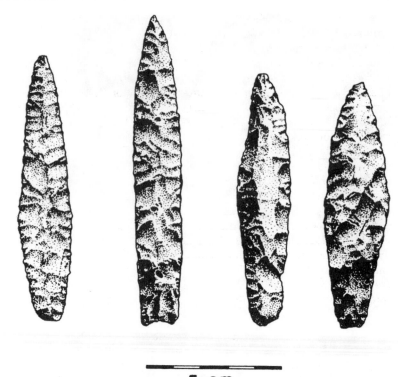

5 cm

Middle, and Late subperiods of approximately 500-year durations. These subperiods may be important locally, but are not discussed in the summary of the Woodland period that follows.

The first Woodland complexes are found in the Central Plains and the Northeastern Plains at approximately 2500 BP. In the Kansas City area, specimens of thick, stone-tempered pottery with geometric designs incised on the rim have been found in several sites that have been radiocarbon dated as early as 2495 BP. In northwestern Iowa, the first ceramics are dated to 2345 BP. In southwestern Minnesota, ceramics were made as early as 2150 BP (A. E. Johnson 2001). Such early developments are not found elsewhere on the Plains, but pottery, mounds, and sometimes horticulture have been dated after approximately 2000 BP in many areas of the Plains. Some authorities call the period after 2000 BP the **Ceramic period** (e.g., Adair 1988).

Woodland cultural developments were even more significant farther east, as Chapters 11 and 12 will make clear. Thus it seems most probable that such developments happened largely because of contact with people from the Eastern Woodlands. In addition, with the exception of the bow-and-arrow technology, each development is most common on the eastern margins of the Great Plains and in wooded river valleys that are most ecologically similar to areas to the east. In the Southern

Plains, Southwestern influences also are sometimes clear. Plains Woodland nevertheless has Plains roots, and many aspects of more ancient hunting and gathering lifeways persisted throughout the Woodland.

One example of issues related to the development of Plains Woodland can be found in the Kansas City area. As noted earlier, this is an area in which fiber-tempered pottery and burial mounds are known during the Late Archaic. Some of the Early Woodland pottery from this area is similar to Black Sand pottery made by Early Woodland people in western Illinois. While archaeologists have usually discounted the idea of actual migration from western Illinois to western Missouri at this time (e.g., O'Brien and Wood 1998), this has been due in part to the lack of a recorded sites with Black Sand pottery in between the two areas. This cord-marked, sand- and grit-tempered pottery often has rim nodes, exterior incising, punctuations or fingernail impressions and may be associated with distinctive lithic tools as well. Martin (2007) has recently reported new evidence for Black Sand pottery along the lower Missouri river east of Kansas City, suggesting that migration hypotheses may deserve renewed attention.

There are Middle Woodland connections between the Kansas City area and the Illinois River valley as well. After approximately 2000 BP, a complex known as **Kansas City Hopewell** is recognized by pottery with cord-wrapped stick impressions, dentate stamping, and eventually punctated, crosshatched, or plain rims suggestive of **Havana Hopewell** ceramics found in the lower Illinois River valley in the Midwest (Figure 10.6). Settlement patterns including large villages located on the stream bluffs as well as smaller camps occupied for shorter periods and burial mounds may be similar to those known from the Illinois River valley as well. The presence of horticulture similarly can be cited as reminiscent of the Middle Woodland farther east. Kansas City Hopewell mounds, located on the bluff tops near villages, have central stone tombs and also contain cremations, as well as **secondary** and **primary burials** much like Middle Woodland mounds in Illinois as well. Studies also show that while the chert used to make small Middle Woodland blades often came from central Missouri to the east, local clays generally were used to make pipes and figurines while copper implements are rare (Adair 1988). While earlier archaeologists did discuss a probable migration up the Missouri River from Illinois to Kansas City, more recently social interaction and sharing of knowledge and ideas have been seen as the most probable explanation for the similarities found (O'Brien and Wood 1998). However, Logan (2006) argues that this assumption is not supported by much evidence, and he believes there may have been a migration, which was then maintained through social interactions.

In the Kansas City area, as well as in the Great Plains altogether, the appearance of Woodland phenomena and its causes remain poorly understood. Much more data as well as more thorough analyses will be needed to sort out how and to what extent Woodland developments spring from local contexts as opposed to extra-regional influences. Origins aside, archaeologists have noted four significant developments during the Plains Woodland: the introduction of pottery throughout the Great Plains, the widespread adoption of the bow and arrow, the development of mound building or other group mortuary rituals, and the introduction of pre-maize horticulture into some group's economies.

a

b

c

FIGURE 10.6 Examples of Kansas City Hopewell pottery.

FIGURE 10.7 Typical Plains Woodland pot.

The development of pottery clearly represented a new and revolutionary way to carry, store, and cook foodstuffs. The pot shown in Figure 10.7 is representative of the type of ceramics Plains Woodland people made. One factor in adopting pottery may well have been increased sedentism, and this is probably why pottery was adopted later outside the valleys of the eastern prairies. These valleys were places where a living could be made without a great deal of mobility. After all, for nomadic peoples, heavy and breakable pots are not as efficient as skin bags. Pottery also represents changes in how food was cooked. The rock-filled pits, slab-lined hearths, and similar features of the Archaic were methods of indirect heating and cooking. Baskets covered with pitch could also be used to stone-boil food, but receptacles woven of organic materials are less likely to be preserved than ceramic pots. One of the advantages of pottery certainly was the ability to cook directly over a fire, and the sooted bottoms of pottery specimens indicate that cooking was done in this fashion. Careful studies of pottery technology over time show that potters gradually adjusted the thickness of pot walls and the size and character of the temper particles. This allowed them to cope with the thermal stresses of firing and cooking, while improving the thermal conductivity of the vessels (O'Brien and Wood 1998). Studies of pottery from the Middle Woodland Schultz site in Nebraska also suggest that pots were used for storage and transport as well as cooking of a variety of meat and plant foods. However, cooking of nuts and seeds, long assumed to have been of central importance to Woodland peoples, were not suggested by this particular study (Duddleson 2008).

The adoption of the bow and arrow, which was widespread by the Late Woodland but certainly began before this among some Great Plains people, also was significant. For example, in the Southern Plains, the Middle Woodland **Lake Creek focus** in the Texas and Oklahoma panhandles and adjacent areas represents a hunting and gathering lifeway associated with quartz- and limestone-tempered ceramics, brownware ceramics similar to Jornada Mogollon pottery in the Southwest, and corner-notched arrow points (Hofman and Brooks 1989).

You already may think of the bow and arrow as superior for hunting in comparison to the atlatl and dart. One advantage may be deeper penetration into the prey (Odell and Cowan 1986). Another could be that arrow points can be more easily hafted than dart points. Regardless, it has been argued that the adoption of the bow and arrow is correlated with more efficient hunting of game from bison to deer. Moreover, evidence from the Eastern Woodlands showing a high incidence of human skeletons with small points embedded in them suggests a possible correlation with increases in intergroup conflict beginning in the Late Woodland (O'Brien and Wood 1998:232).

Arrow points, recognized by their small size, may occur in earlier Woodland complexes, but they are more common after 1500 BP. For example, the **Keith complex**, which is found in sites extending from the prairies into western Kansas and Nebraska between the Platte and the Arkansas rivers, is an example of the Late Woodland in the Central Plains. Cord-roughened pottery tempered with calcite and small expanding stemmed or corner-notched points, often called Scallorn points, indicate this complex (O'Brien 1994). Another Late Woodland example is the **Avonlea phase** (ca. 1500–950 BP) on the Northwestern Plains, characterized by small, very finely made side-notched arrow points and **fabric-impressed ceramics**. Bison hunting was central to Avonlea subsistence, and many pound and jump sites are assigned to it. One of the best known is located in Alberta and has a colorful name, Head-Smashed-In. This jump site actually was used many times during the Archaic as well as the Late Prehistoric. It has been suggested that Avonlea represents Athapaskan migration into the area, but a much more complex reality in which groups of various ethnicities coalesced at this time seems more likely (Walde 2006).

The appearance of burial mounds and, in some areas of the Great Plains, **ossuaries** also must be considered an important Woodland development. Archaeologists generally assume that such formal disposal areas for the dead as mounds, cemeteries, and ossuaries are indicative of social groups with some measure of sedentism, or at least a territory of normal group use (e.g., Charles and Buikstra 1983). Mounds and other features provide reliable information on group membership because only those who belonged to a given group were buried in its dedicated mortuary places. These public monuments also symbolically mark the group's territory by their placement. Thus the appearance of burial mounds on the Plains during

Middle Woodland times could mean both that people were tied to particular territories if not sites and that their social relationships were formalized, most likely through such kinship structures as lineages. Some archaeologists also have argued that the mounds represent opportunities for public manipulation of labor and wealth to gain prestige and status. However, exotic items and prestige goods do not occur in great quantities in Plains Woodland contexts, and we cannot envision exchange at the scale found among Middle Woodland groups to the east (see Chapters 11 and 12). Nevertheless, some rare items are known from Plains Woodland sites, suggesting interregional trade networks did exist. For example, marine shell beads from a Pacific coast species of the snail *Olivella* have been identified from the Woodruff ossuary in Kansas (Hoard and Chaney 2010).

Perhaps the most interesting Woodland developments are in the area of subsistence. For most people living on the Great Plains, the Woodland period does not mark profound economic change. For example, the Woodland economy associated with the **Besant phase** of the Northwestern Plains beginning about 1850 BP centered on bison hunting. Sometimes designated as Late Plains Archaic because of their proficiency in bison hunting (e.g., Frison 1998), Besant people made grit-tempered, cord-roughened, undecorated ceramics,

FIGURE 10.8 Examples of the Besant projectile point.

and they also constructed burial mounds, at least in the Dakotas along the Missouri River bluffs, where archaeologists have designated a **Sonota Burial complex** (A. M. Johnson and A. E. Johnson 1998). The large and broad, corner-notched Besant point (Figure 10.8), as well as Besant ceramics, are found widely in the Northwestern Plains.

In the river valleys and prairies of the eastern Plains, however, horticulture, especially pre-maize gardening with native seed plants, developed during the Woodland. Although the ethnobotanical record is imperfect, in the Central Plains there is reliable evidence of the cultivated marsh elder from the Early Woodland and of other domesticates from Middle Woodland sites. Kansas City Hopewell people cultivated squash and marsh elder, but maize previously reported from the Trowbridge site has been AMS

CLUES TO THE PAST   EXHIBIT 10.1

Hide Scrapers

The scraper, a tool with a steep working edge used to scrape hides or wood, was made and used so often by the inhabitants of the Great Plains that it deserves further discussion. For example, at the Lashley Vore site in Oklahoma, which may have been the Wichita site visited by the French trader Jean Baptiste Bénard de la Harpe in 1719, Odell found that 30 percent of the tools were scrapers (Odell 2002). It is not unusual in Great Plains sites for scrapers to outnumber projectile points.

An important tool type throughout the past, scrapers usually were made from flakes or cores by further chipping or retouching to create the necessary steep edge. A scraper made from a flake required chipping on one face only. Such unifacial scrapers were made with the scraping edge on one side (side scrapers), on the end (end scrapers), or even on both the sides and the ends (**distolateral scrapers**). Unifacial end scrapers made from flakes are the most frequent type found on the Great Plains (Figure 10.9). They have one face

that is relatively flat. The other face is convex in cross section because of the steep retouch, which was done with percussion flaking or, in small specimens, with pressure flaking. Such a unifacial implement is called a plano-convex end scraper. The snub-nosed end scraper, another form, is triangular in outline, with the scraping edge made on the broader end (Lehmer 1971:75). Bone also was used as the scraper bit and, starting in the Protohistoric period, metal; but until then, stone scrapers were most common.

Plains end scrapers may have been held in the hand, particularly if they were large, but smaller ones probably were most often hafted to a wooden or bone shaft. Sinew was used to fix the stone to the shaft. Several haft styles would have been possible, but unfortunately the handles and the sinew have not been preserved often enough to allow an assessment of any variability. An antler scraper handle was found at the Kruse site in Kansas (Rohn and Emerson 1984).

FIGURE 10.9 Plains end scraper.

FIGURE 10.10 Scraping of a hide staked to the ground in one traditional Native American method of preparation.

Archaeologists can assess the function of scrapers by examining edge wear and breakage microscopically, but this has been done infrequently. At Lashley Vore, Odell found that hide scraping was the most frequent single type of wear on the stone tools (Odell 2002:252). Most archaeologists have simply assumed that scrapers were used to work the many hides obtained from bison and other animals. Hides were processed prior to use so that they did not rot and were pliable enough to be worked into clothing and other items. Most of us today do not know how to tan a hide, but there are many accounts of how Plains and other people processed hides. Once removed from the carcass, a hide must be scraped to clean off hair on the outer surface and any fatty tissue adhering to the inner surface. Hides probably were pegged on the ground or stretched on a frame before scraping (Figure 10.10). Tanning, which today may be done with chemicals, was first accomplished by mashing animal brains to release tannic acid and conditioners, and rubbing the paste into the hides. After tanning has rendered the hide soft and supple, it is soaked in water. Additional scraping and buffing of the hide and smoking it over a fire sealed the leather from moisture and made it usable.

Plains people used hides for clothing, for skin bags and other containers, and for tipi covers. Native Americans in the Middle Missouri area also made a kind of skin boat known as a **bullboat** (Ahler et al. 1991). After Europeans arrived in North America, Natives processed hides for trade as well as domestic uses. The trade in hides probably is related to the manufacture of larger numbers of scrapers, although this connection has been better documented in the Southeast (Cobb 2000) than on the Plains. Calculations of the ratio of scrapers to projectile points would be one simple measure archaeologists could employ to test this idea.

Just as hide processing was a universal activity, the presence of scraping tools in the Great Plains is ubiquitous. However, there is some variability in the types, the sizes, and the numbers of scrapers found across the Great Plains, and these differences have sometimes been helpful in distinguishing cultural complexes. In general, variability in scrapers has not been explored to the degree reached for projectile points or pottery vessels. In fact, consistent morphological categories for scrapers have not been employed. In contrast to projectile points, which were implements of the hunt and warfare, hide scrapers might be considered women's tools because ethnohistorically the processing of hides was a female activity. Women may have manufactured scrapers as well as used them. These gender implications have not been explored. Clearly, new areas of research concerning the apparently humble and domestic scraper may yet be possible.

dated to the post-Contact period (Adair and Drass 2011). Early Woodland sites in Iowa suggest that Northeastern Plains people were using domesticated sunflower by the Early Woodland, and had added little barley and knotweed by the Middle Woodland. Late Woodland additions to this complex were maygrass and tobacco (Adair 2003). It is clear that the adoption of horticultural strategies was variable across the Great Plains as a whole, but increased throughout the Woodland. Adair and Drass (2011) argue that during the Woodland pre-maize gardening occurred mostly in the eastern Plains among semisedentary groups living in the river valleys. No doubt the story of when and where Plains people began to grow crops is a complex and fascinating one that cannot be fully told without additional ethnobotanical sampling.

Although the Plains Woodland is not completely understood, it encompasses a fascinating time in which some Plains people began to make pottery, build burial mounds or construct ossuaries, use the bow and arrow, and some even experimented with horticulture. At the same time, other Plains people remained mobile hunter-gatherers following millennia-old lifeways.

PLAINS VILLAGE TRADITIONS

Beginning about 1150 BP, some of the Late Woodland people of the Great Plains began to commit more fully to horticulture. This may have been in response to contact with people to the East, but the specifics of such associations are still debated as discussed later. These societies, called **Plains Village** by archaeologists, were semisedentary with mixed economies in which both farming in the river bottomlands and seasonal bison hunting were important while other plants and animals were also utilized. Plains Village people often built **earthlodges**, which were timber-framed houses covered with a layer of earth (Figure 10.11), and these structures have a significant place in the oral traditions and cosmology of Plains Indians (Roper and Pauls 2005). Despite general similarities, some distinctions can be drawn between Plains Village adaptations in various parts of the Plains. Older lifeways, which did not include horticulture, also persisted where either aridity or a short growing season made it difficult to grow crops. Nevertheless, it is clear that in the Central Plains, the Middle Missouri, and some parts of the Southern Plains, the combination of horticulture and seasonal bison hunting led to a material richness and security that allowed larger and more permanent aggregations of people. Marked status differentiation did not develop, and a tribal social organization was maintained. Archaeologists have defined several traditions and many variants and phases for Plains Village based on pottery, house form, and other characteristics, but the broad traditions are most important for introductory students to know.

The **Central Plains tradition** includes Plains Village adaptations in the Central Plains between about 950 BP and 500 BP (AD 1000–1450), but is found first on the eastern margins of the Central Plains and then spreads westward. People generally made grit-tempered, cord-roughened, or smoothed surface vessels with vertical, flared, or **collared** rims, as well as plain, incised, or cord-impressed decorations. Their small arrow points were unnotched, side notched, or notched at both the side and the base (Wedel 2001:Table 1). Other characteristic artifacts include stone end and side scrapers, hoes made out of bison scapulae, split bone awls and other bone tools (Figure 10.12), as well as a variety of ground stone items. Square to rectangular house structures, often built below the ground surface, are found in unfortified clusters that may represent farmsteads or small hamlets rather than true villages (Roper 2007:56). Maize horticulture was part of the subsistence base, which can be characterized as an example of low-level food production (Smith 2001:27) in which domesticates contribute between 30 and 50 percent of the caloric intake. For example, excavations at the Mowry Bluff site (Wood 1969), an **Upper Republican phase** site of southern Nebraska, indicated a diverse subsistence base in which maize contributed approximately 30 percent of the diet, while bison

FIGURE 10.11 Reconstructed earthlodges located at On-A-Slant Village in North Dakota.

FIGURE 10.12 Bone artifacts of the Central Plains Village tradition.

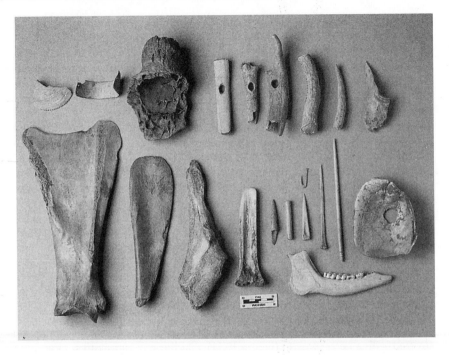

contributed about 10 percent, and deer and antelope together contributed another 10 percent. The other half of the diet came from other cultigens including sunflower, beans, and squash, as well as small game, birds, and fish, wild greens, seeds, nuts, and fruits (Nepstad-Thornberry et al. 2002).

The **Middle Missouri tradition** is a second Plains Village tradition that archaeologists date between about 1050 BP and 400 BP (AD 900–1550) (Winham and Calabrese 1998). It is found initially in the tall-prairie region of northwestern Iowa, southwestern Minnesota, and southern South Dakota, as well as along the Missouri River and its tributaries in North and South Dakota. Globular, grit-tempered pottery vessels were made by modeling and shaping with a paddle and anvil. People made triangular arrow points that were unnotched or side notched, end scrapers, drills, bifaces, a variety of ground stone items, bison or elk scapula hoes, bone and horn scoops, bone arrow-shaft wrenches, and many other bone tools as well as mussel shell beads and pipes of various types. Extra-regional trade is indicated by items made of exotic materials like copper from the Great Lakes, shell from the Gulf or Atlantic coast, as well as steatite from northern Wyoming and obsidian from the area of Yellowstone Park. People lived in villages, some of which were fortified by ditches and palisades, and they built rectangular structures including both houses and larger community buildings. People grew maize, beans, squash, sunflower, marsh elder, goosefoot, and other native seed plants as well as tobacco (Wood 2001:188).

The **Coalescent tradition** represents a third Plains Village tradition that traditionally was understood to represent a blending of the Central Plains and Middle Missouri traditions, but the first people of this tradition may actually have been immigrants from the Central Plains into South Dakota (Krause 2001). The Coalescent tradition begins at approximately 650 BP and continues into the Historic period. It is first evident in sites along the Missouri River in South Dakota between the mouths of the White and Bad rivers, but after about 500 BP (AD 1450), Coalescent people utilized a larger area, including locations outside the Missouri valley itself. Pottery was made with cord-roughened, simple stamped, or smoothed exteriors. Bone and lithic tools such as bison scapula hoes, bison skull scoops, split bone awls, snub-nosed end scrapers, diamond-shaped knives with beveled edges, and small triangular notched and unnotched projectile points are found in these sites. People in the Coalescent tradition initially constructed square or rectangular earthlodges, but after 500 BP houses became more circular. Early villages tend to be fortified, but later ones are not. Like other Plains Village people, Coalescent groups were horticulturists and bison hunters who supplemented their subsistence with generalized hunting and plant gathering. Ultimately Coalescent people became the historically known Mandan and Hidatsa tribes. This chapter's case study by Stanley A. Ahler and Phil R. Geib, "Investigations at Double Ditch Village, a Traditional Mandan Earthlodge Settlement," is about a Coalescent site that spans pre-contact through early historical times.

Plains Village societies also developed on the Southern Plains beginning around 1150 BP. **Southern Plains tradition** sites have plain and cord-marked pottery, as well as stone arrow points of various types and bone tools such as bison scapula hoes, bone digging sticks, and awls. Maize and beans have been documented in Southern Plains Village sites, but initially maize may have been the main tropical cultigen, supplemented by collection of native seeds (Bell and Brooks 2001:208). Squash has been poorly represented in Southern Plains sites, and beans are not present until approximately 750 BP (Adair and Drass 2011). Bison bone dominates the faunal assemblages that have been recovered, emphasizing the significance of bison hunting to Southern Plains Village people. Deer and small game were exploited too, and both fishing and harvesting of shellfish were minor parts of the economies (Brooks 1989). House structures seem to have varied from wattle and daub structures to ones made with stone slabs and formed into multiroom, single-story pueblos as in the **Antelope Creek phase** of the Texas panhandle (Figure 10.13). Interactions between Southern Plains village groups and the people of the Southwest through trade and sometimes actual population movements are a topic of considerable interest (Spielmann 1991).

Although sorting out the complex culture history of Plains Village societies continues to be an archaeological goal, contemporary Plains archaeologists are particularly interested in three key topics concerning Plains Village societies. First, it is important to recognize that although some native and occasionally tropical plants were grown during the Woodland, especially on the eastern side of the Plains, Plains Village phenomena represent an adaptive shift centered on addition of corn horticulture to the economy (Roper 2007). Contemporary use of flotation and water screening in excavations are adding to the evidence of this shift at a rapid rate. In the early part of the Plains Village sequence, people cultivated a variety of native seed plants including marsh elder, sunflower, goosefoot and possibly little barley, knotweed, and maygrass, all of which were cultivated by Eastern Woodland populations (Adair and Drass 2011). Growing these various crops, combined with hunting of game including bison and collecting of wild plant foods, is evident in the Middle Missouri, the Northeastern Plains, the Central Plains, and the Southern Plains, though the specific plants and sequences vary. Actual reliance on corn increased over time so that by historical times villagers had an economy based on seasonal bison hunting and farming corn, usually with less use of native cultigens. However, Nickel (2007) notes that the use of native seed plants persists at Mandan sites in the Middle Missouri area. It also is clear that besides communal bison hunting, Plains villagers

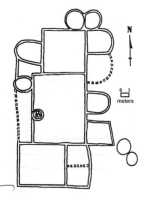

FIGURE 10.13 Plan of multiroom Antelope Creek phase structure showing Southwestern influence.

hunted and collected a very large list of animals for food and other purposes (Bozell et al. 2011). Understanding the specific patterns of plant and animal use involved in Plains Village adaptations at various times and places is important because these cases provide rare examples of low-level horticultural strategies.

A second area of great interest is documenting population movements and their effects on Plains village societies. The movement of people has long been of interest to Plains archaeologists. Although early simplistic explanations of culture change as the product of the in-migration of foreigners have been abandoned, this topic remains of great interest. There can be no doubt that the interaction between Plains Village populations and more distant cultural groups, as well as among different groups of Plains villagers, is key to understanding the history of the Great Plains. There are three points in the Plains Village record where population movements continue to be of particular research interest.

First, there is a long-standing tradition of understanding the origins of Plains Village traditions in the Central Plains and the Middle Missouri as a response to contact with or migration from Mississippian societies of the Midwest. For example, the **Steed–Kisker phase** (ca. 1000–650 BP), located along the Missouri River north of Kansas City, is noteworthy because of its **shell-tempered ceramics**, which have incised designs that resemble **Mississippian tradition** pottery from Cahokia, near St. Louis (see Chapter 12).

In a recent review of the origins of the Central Plains tradition, Roper (2007) points out that this development is an example of farming dispersal that fits best with models that see small groups or even segments of a population, such as marriage partners making the movement to new communities gradually and incrementally over many generations, rather than entire populations leaving one area and colonizing a new area. In this view, Midwesterners may have been responsible for introducing new farming lifeways into the Central Plains, but through alliances, marriage, and kin relationships these people merely became part of indigenous Central Plains communities so that the origins had local roots as well as extra-regional origins. The long history of ties between communities in the Kansas City area and those in Illinois mentioned in discussing the Woodland period supports this explanation, as does the time-transgressive spread of Plains Village lifeways up the rivers of the Central Plains. Similarly, Tiffany (2007) describes complicated processes involving trade and alliance between the indigenous people of the Missouri River trench, people of northwestern Iowa and Southwestern Minnesota, and Mississippians at Cahokia in Illinois in the development of the Middle Missouri tradition.

A second set of population movements documented in Plains Village archaeology is the movement of Central Plains villagers northward and eastward during the thirteenth century. By the early fourteenth century these people apparently were in South Dakota along the Missouri, where they are now known as the Initial Coalescent tradition. This shift may have been partially a response to climatic changes making horticultural lifeways less viable to the west and south, but the intrusion of people into the Middle Missouri area certainly would have led to interesting social dynamics. It may be that the immigrants were Caddoan speakers, like the Historic period Arikara and Pawnee, while the Middle Missouri tradition populations were Siouan speakers ancestral to the Mandan and Hidatsa (Bamforth 2006). As a result, alliances and intermarriage would have been less likely, and we can envision a very different migration model than that proposed earlier for the origins of the Central Plains tradition.

A third example of population interaction and movement involves the **Oneota**, a Late Prehistoric cultural tradition that developed out of Late Woodland populations in northern Illinois, Wisconsin, and eastern Iowa (see Chapter 12) (Henning 2005). Oneota economies were based on a mixture of hunting, gathering, and horticulture, and made shell-tempered pottery. Sites are seldom fortified, but enclosures and mounds are often found. The Oneota built longhouse-style structures rather than earthlodges. In the Red Wing region of Minnesota during the Oneota **Silvernale phase** (850–650 BP), the construction of pyramidal mounds, village fortifications, and some of the pottery designs may indicate direct linkages to Midwestern Mississippians (see Chapter 11). Oneota traded with early Plains Village populations (Henning 2007). However, sometime around 650 BP, Onetoa people began to establish villages on the Great Plains, where they may have dislodged some Central Plains tradition and some Middle Missouri tradition populations. Later Oneota migration onto the Plains began about 450 BP and continued into the Protohistoric period. The record

of interaction between migrant Oneota people, who appear to have been Siouan speakers, and Plains Village people is not fully understood (Ritterbush 2007), but some of these interactions may well have been violent.

In fact, the investigation of violence and warfare is a third area of current interest among Plains archaeologists. The population movements of the fourteenth century sometimes appear to have been marked by violence, and there are other points in the Plains Village record at which raiding may have taken place. Certainly the large aggregated villages of the Initial Coalescent often are fortified, and at this time, Middle Missouri groups withdrew into large, fortified communities near the mouth of the Heart and Cannonball rivers in North Dakota. Hostile relationships with other groups are indicated by the Crow Creek site, an Initial Coalesecent variant site in South Dakota (Figure 10.14). Here at least 486 skeletons, including remains of many partially dismembered and scalped individuals, were found in the fortification ditch (Willey 1990). The perpetrators of this massacre are not known with certainty, but might be Oneota or Middle Missouri tradition. Bamforth (2006) has explored the case for warfare in the Middle Missouri region concluding that Plains Village people often responded to drought-induced subsistence stress by raiding, but that other social factors may have been part of the impetus for violence between communities as well. One interesting finding is that violence sometimes precedes fourteenth-century population movements so that it cannot be exclusive attributed to intrusions of groups from outside the Middle Missouri.

LATE PREHISTORIC BISON HUNTERS OF THE NORTHERN PLAINS

In the Northwestern and Northeastern Plains, hunting and gathering persisted without horticulture throughout the Plains Village period. Beginning with the widespread adoption of the bow and arrow, bison hunting could be conducted even more easily. At this time, which most archaeologists begin at approximately 1500 BP and call the Late Prehistoric period, communal hunting reached its peak efficiency (Figure 10.15). All these northern adaptations are characterized by dependence on bison hunting, pottery making, and use of the bow and arrow. For example, many bison hunting camps and kill sites after 1150 BP are considered part of the **Old Women's phase**, which may represent the ancestors of the North Piegan, Blood, and Gros Ventre Indians. Other, more forest-oriented hunter-gatherers seem to have been located on the northeastern margins of the Great Plains. The Blackduck Culture (see Chapter 4) refers to people living in southwestern

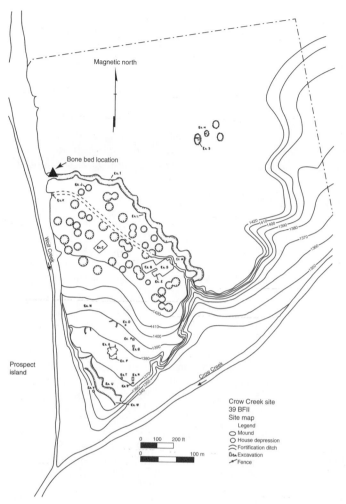

FIGURE 10.14 Plan of the Crow Creek site showing earthlodge depressions, the fortification ditch, and the location of the bone bed containing the remains of nearly 500 people.

FIGURE 10.15 Artist's conception of Late Prehistoric Plains bison hunters running bison into a chute and corral in which the animals could be more easily shot.

Manitoba who exploited fish and small game and may have collected wild rice, but also took bison by constructing buffalo pounds (Dyck and Morlan 2001). These are only a few of the archaeological entities recognized for the Late Prehistoric in the northern parts of the Plains.

Linkages with historically known tribes on Great Plains can often be surmised from the archaeological record of these Late Prehistoric and Plains Village groups (Hanson 1998; Schlesier 1994). Sometimes we can be fairly certain of this kind of connection, but as discussed in Box 10.1, this is not always the case.

ISSUES AND DEBATES   BOX 10.1

Historic Period Ethnicities and the Archaeological Record

Early ethnographies as well as the long and excellent ethnohistorical record from the Great Plains make the identification of linkages between archaeological sites and complexes and historically known ethnicities desirable. Establishing such anthropological linkages also can put more interesting detail into the bare bones and stones of archaeology. However, this task is not as simple as you might imagine.

Sometimes archaeological sites can be directly linked to ethnohistorical accounts. This is often true for the villages along the Missouri River in the northern Plains. Double Ditch Village, described in this chapter's case study, is one such place, having been inhabited by the Mandan Indians and recorded by Lewis and Clark in 1804. At the Knife River Indian Villages National Historic Site in North Dakota, Hidatsa Indian villages are documented as well (Ahler et al. 1991). Other more tenuous but widely accepted ethnic assignments include the correspondence of Apachean groups with the Protohistoric **Dismal River phase** of western Nebraska and western Kansas (Hofman 1989). In this case, however, precisely which Apache bands or subtribes might be responsible is a matter of dispute, as is the correspondence of Apachean people with other archaeological complexes (Hanson 1998). In still other cases, particularly among nomadic tribes that did not leave an extensive material record, archaeological sites have not been identified at all (Hanson 1998:461).

Despite its thematic importance within North American archaeology (see Chapter 2), the ethnic identity of the inhabitants of pre-Columbian archaeological sites is quite difficult to establish (Walde 2006). There are several reasons for this. First, the correspondence between ethnicity and archaeological cultures always is problematic. Ethnicity is an ideological and political matter of identity, while archaeological phases are constructed from similarities in material culture. Certainly people use items of material culture to symbolize their ethnic affiliation, but archaeological categories do not necessarily correspond to what

people themselves might have perceived and wished to convey.

Second, even a passing acquaintance with the history of the Great Plains points to tremendous change in the distribution and character of ethnic identities during the Protohistoric and early Historic periods. As a result, the tribes located in various areas in approximately 1800 were not necessarily those found in the same area throughout the pre-Columbian past. The arrival of the horse greatly affected both distributions and lifestyles, and cultural character changed dramatically within some ethnicities as well.

Third, although historical accounts are tremendously useful in understanding what happened as Europeans arrived on the Plains, they are fallible and incomplete. Names and designations for groups often are confusing because they fail to recognize ethnic differences perceived by Native peoples or neglect ethnic connections the people considered important (Syms 1985). This means that we cannot use the written record uncritically; careful scholarship is essential.

Fourth, other types of evidence of ethnic affiliation must be approached with a healthy skepticism as well. Historical linguistics, though very important to the problem of identifying ethnicities, is an area in which methodological concerns are much debated. **Glottochronology** has been of great interest to archaeologists because it provides an apparently objective and quantitative way to explore language differences, but it is less popular among linguists themselves. Also a number of researchers have attempted to use biological characters such as cranial morphology to distinguish ethnicity (e.g., Bass 1964; Ossenberg 1974). Once again the movement and mixing of populations add greatly to the complexity of such tasks. Moreover, ethnic groups are not necessarily biologically distinct, although there are usually some genetic and linguistic continuities within them.

In sum, the assignment of Historic period ethnicities to archaeologically evident populations is a highly complex research problem. It involves study of historical, archaeological, linguistic, and osteological data, and is therefore a holistic anthropological undertaking (Syms 1985). Nevertheless, when we can make accurate links, the results are rewarding. For example, it is possible to associate the Historic period Pawnee with archaeological sites located on the Republican River in Nebraska and Kansas (Wedel 1986). The Pawnee were one of the most populous historical groups in Nebraska during the nineteenth century, and we have available a good deal of observational material about their lifestyle. They were a loose confederacy of four subtribes, and the Kitkahahki, or Republican, band of Pawnee were located on the river of the same name. The Hill site, the Kansas Monument site, and site 14GE1 are documented in the early historical record, and Wedel has been able to draw a vivid picture of life in these villages from historical accounts and descriptions of the Pawnee (Wedel 1986:152–185).

It is always essential to examine the basis for identifications between ethnic groups and archaeological sites carefully. Extension of connections backward for many centuries or even for millennia (e.g., Schlesier 1994) is most problematic, but even during the Protohistoric and Historic periods it is not always reliable. Because we do know that archaeological populations generally represent the ancestors of historically known tribes, pursuit of possible direct linkages is a worthy undertaking if only because it underscores the more basic point that the Native American past is not completely disconnected from people in the present. Contemporary tribes and Native individuals have a real interest in identifications of these kinds, and when we can link to known tribes, we can enrich everyone's appreciation of the true history of cultures and interactions. Perhaps this is why an increasing number of archaeological accounts have been exploring such linkages (e.g., Odell 2002; Spector 1993).

THE PROTOHISTORIC PERIOD AND EUROPEAN CONTACT

Europeans arrived on the Plains from three directions. They came through New Mexico and Texas into the Southern Plains, through the drainages of the Mississippi River to the east, or across the Canadian prairies. The first contacts were in the Southern and Central Plains during the sixteenth century. Best known is the expedition of Coronado, who, after wintering at the pueblos along the Rio Grande in New Mexico, struck out to the east and north in 1541. Ultimately this expedition arrived at the settlement of Quivira in central Kansas, which probably was a Pawnee settlement (Wedel 1986). Farther north, contact was made with the Santee Sioux by the middle of the seventeenth century, and French traders reached the Pawnee from the east by 1700 (Swagerty 2001). These Europeans were followed by many more, although of course settlement of the Plains by people of European descent did not begin in earnest for several centuries.

The Europeans encountered a dynamic cultural landscape with many ethnicities and languages in which alliances changed and populations moved. The Historic period Plains tribes included farmers like the Mandan, Hidatsa, and Arikara in the Dakotas, and the Omahas, Iowas, Missouris, and Osages in Nebraska and Kansas. Other historically known tribes emphasized bison hunting and were more mobile. These included the Comanche, Wichita, and Kiowa in Oklahoma, Colorado, and Texas, and the Arapaho, Pawnee, Dakota, Cheyenne, Crow, and Gros Ventre farther north. Canadian Plains tribes were the Blackfeet, Assiniboin, Plains Cree, and

Plains Ojibwa. However, abandonments, relocations, and in-migration from the Woodlands were an important feature of the Protohistoric and Historic periods, and these groups had not necessarily inhabited the Plains for centuries. Groups originally located farther east were the Arikara, the Wichita, the Pawnee, the Cheyenne, the Crow, the Lakota and Dakota, the Assiniboin, the Cree, and the Ojibwa. In each case a complicated story of movement has been reconstructed.

A glance at what is known of Cheyenne relocations during historical times will quickly give a sense of how complicated the cultural geography could be. At the end of the seventeenth century the Cheyenne apparently lived in eastern Minnesota, but Sioux expansions during the early eighteenth century led to their relocation along the Sheyenne River. In their new territory, they established the fortified earth-lodge village archaeologists call the Biesterfeldt site (Figure 10.16) and adopted an essentially Plains Village lifeway (Wood 1971). Yet by the middle of the eighteenth century they had moved farther west again, edged out by the Plains Cree, the Plains Ojibwa, and the Assiniboin. This time they established themselves in the area of the Black Hills and became nomadic hunters. In this incarnation they are mentioned by Lewis and Clark in 1805. Thereafter the Cheyenne moved once again, being pushed west and south by the Teton Lakota (Swagerty 2001:256). The Cheyenne are just one tribe of many, and certainly all tribes did not undertake so many moves and transformations. However, the Cheyenne case does suggest the fluidity of Great Plains cultural geography during the Protohistoric and Historic periods.

FIGURE 10.16 Aerial shot of the Biesterfeldt site in southeastern North Dakota, looking southwest. Note circular earthlodge depressions and fortification.

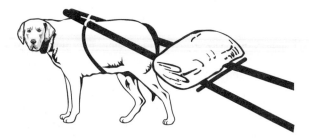

FIGURE 10.17 Dogs outfitted with travois were the primary pack animals of the pre-Columbian Great Plains.

Besides these kinds of relocations, three factors contributed profoundly to the cultural character of the Great Plains beginning in the Protohistoric period. The first of these was the introduction of the horse by Europeans. Although there once were native horses in North America, the American horse was extinct by the end of the Pleistocene. The pack animal of the pre-Columbian Plains Indians was the dog (Figure 10.17), which served secondarily as a food source when meat was scarce. Even in the early nineteenth century, Arikara families are reported to have had 30 to 40 dogs (Swagerty 2001:258). On the other hand, the introduction of the European horse, preadapted to the grasslands of the Plains and the long-distance movements of the tribes that lived there, brought a sort of revolution to the Plains. Horses impacted trade, mobility, the economy, intergroup relations, and internal social structures. Although the early explorers like Coronado had brought horses with them, there is no record of what happened to any horses still living when the expeditions left North America. By the mid-seventeenth century the Apaches may have been trading some

horses on the Plains, but it was not until the successful Pueblo Revolt in 1680–1692 that several thousand horses were confiscated by Native Americans. Most of these horses probably were traded onto the Great Plains. By the late eighteenth century a complex trade in horses was established. The extent to which various tribes could control or manipulate this trade affected both their economic and military fortunes.

Trade in European goods also transformed the Great Plains. The most important item of trade was the gun, since the tribes possessing firearms could dominate militarily. Thus guns affected alliances and political relationships among the tribes. In the mid-eighteenth century, guns were traded in the Plains for furs and hides. For trading partners the tribes had the British of the Hudson's Bay Company, working from Hudson Bay to the north, and French traders, traveling out from New France, or Louisiana. The Spanish were reluctant to allow trade in guns, which meant that New Mexico was not an early source of guns on the Great Plains (Binnema 2001). However, by the late eighteenth century, multiethnic **Comancheros** dealt in arms, ammunition, and Indian captives on the Southern Plains. In the Southern Plains the horse generally was adopted before the gun, while farther north the gun often came first.

Finally, as in so many areas of North America, contact with Europeans meant the spread of devastating diseases. Disease may well have traveled with trade items ahead of actual Europeans, and eventually depopulation was a major disrupting factor among the societies of the Great Plains. A number of epidemics occurred. The first well-documented case probably was a smallpox epidemic from 1687 to 1691 on the Southern Plains. By the early eighteenth century, the Arikara on the Missouri River may have been infected with measles, smallpox, and tuberculosis. A series of epidemics between 1734 and 1800 resulted in a major population decline across the Plains. Perhaps the worst epidemic was the smallpox epidemic of 1837–1838. The Mandan lost 95 percent of their already reduced population in that single year, and mortality was significant in many other tribes. Diseases continued to be devastating until the 1850s; they brought great suffering, but they also were the cause of migrations and changes in settlement patterns, as well as political breakdown and amalgamation (Swagerty 2001). This chapter's case study offers additional perspectives.

CHAPTER SUMMARY

This chapter has introduced the archaeological past on the Great Plains, demonstrating among other things that popular depictions of mobile bison hunters with horses do not apply to most of the past peoples of the Great Plains. The main points made in this chapter are as follows:

- The people of the Archaic period on the Great Plains (ca. 8500–2500 BP), which is first indicated by the appearance of notched projectile point styles, were hunter-gatherers who variously utilized bison and other animal and plant resources. In the Central Plains, several Middle and Late Archaic complexes with ceramics, burial mounds, and some use of plants that eventually were cultivated seem to foreshadow the Woodland.
- The first Plains Woodland complexes are found in the Central Plains at approximately 2500 BP, and pottery, mounds, and sometimes horticulture dated after 2000 BP occur more widely. Late Woodland complexes dated after approximately 1500 BP also show that the bow and arrow became prevalent at this time.
- Beginning around 1150 BP, semisedentary societies with mixed economies, called Plains Village by archaeologists, are evident on the Great Plains, and Central Plains tradition, the Middle Missouri tradition, the Coalescent tradition, and the Southern Plains traditions are recognized. Besides Plains Village, many the bison hunting societies of the Northeastern and Northwestern Plains are known from the Late Prehsitoric.
- The Protohistoric and early Historic periods on the Great Plains were particularly dynamic culturally, with some tribes reinventing themselves as they changed locations dramatically. In addition to the reintroduction of horses, the gun trade and the spread of devastating diseases like smallpox exerted transforming influences on Great Plains cultures during these periods.

SUGGESTIONS FOR FURTHER READING

For excellent summaries of Great Plains archaeology and ethnohistory:

De Mallie, Raymond J. (volume editor)
  2001 *Plains* (Pt. 1). Handbook of North American Indians, Vol. 13, William C. Sturtevant, general editor, Smithsonian Institution, Washington, DC.

Wood, W. Raymond (editor)
  1998 *Archaeology of the Great Plains.* University Press of Kansas, Lawrence.

For an excellent review of the Plains bison hunting lifestyle and the evidence for it:

Frison, George C.
  1991 *Prehistoric Hunters of the High Plains,* 2nd ed. Academic Press, San Diego.

For recent research on the archaeology of the Plains Villagers:

Ahler, Stanley A., and Marvin Kay (editors)
  2007 *Plains Village Archaeology: Bison-Hunting Farmers in the Central and Northern Plains.* University of Utah Press, Salt Lake City.

For a summary of the archaeology of Kansas:

Hoard, Robert J., and William E. Banks (editors)
  2006 *Kansas Archaeology.* University Press of Kansas, Lawrence.

For recent study of the nature of the earthlodge:

Roper, Donna C., and Elizabeth P. Pauls (editors)
  2005 *Plains Earthlodges: Ethnographic and Archaeological Perspectives.* University of Alabama Press, Tuscaloosa.

OTHER RESOURCES

Sections H and I of the Student CD provide web links, additional discussion questions, and study aids. The Student CD also contains a variety of additional resources, including the complete list of references as cited in this chapter.

CASE STUDY

Although the Indians of the Great Plains are most often associated with bison hunting, high mobility, and tipis, this chapter has shown that many inhabitants resided in villages in the river valleys for much of the year, relying on both horticulture and seasonal bison hunting for survival. In historical times, Arikara, Hidatsa, and Mandan Indians were aggregated into fortified settlements in the Missouri River trench. This case study describes the archaeological investigation of a village that was utilized by Mandan Indians and their ancestors. The investigations at Double Ditch Village were conducted both for research reasons and to provide information that could be used in the public interpretation of the site. They involved the collaboration of archaeologists and other specialists from a variety of institutions, incorporating geophysical techniques as well as excavation. For these reasons this case study provides a good example of the complexity of many contemporary archaeological projects. In addition, the research reveals that Double Ditch's inhabitants reconfigured the settlement several times, building four rather than two defensive ditches, mounding earth and planing off the village ground surface at various times. These findings raise new questions about how these transformations reflect changing social dynamics among the Mandan and other tribes. As you read this case study, ask yourself what the history of Double Ditch Village indicates about how people adjusted to the population relocations, outbreaks of intersocietal aggression, and epidemics of the Late Prehistoric, Protohistoric, and Historic eras on the Great Plains.

INVESTIGATIONS AT DOUBLE DITCH VILLAGE, A TRADITIONAL MANDAN EARTHLODGE SETTLEMENT

Stanley A. Ahler and Phil R. Geib

On the upper Missouri River, early summer days are 17 hours long, allowing much time for experimental field archaeology. On such a day in June 2003, when the prairie glowed orange in the hour before sunset, the silence was broken by the drone of a powered parachute crisscrossing high above Double Ditch Village. Two archaeologists in the steel cage hanging beneath the nylon canopy shot thermal infrared still and video images of the uneven, shadowed surface below them, recording patterns created by the remnant heat of the day. At the dawn of the twenty-first century, this ancient village was largely quiet except for occasional visitors who walked its surface and a small crew of archaeologists that briefly probed its secrets. Had aerial cameras been available 450 years ago, they would have recorded 1500 people living in a closely packed, heavily fortified settlement with adjoining gardens stretching far up and down the Missouri River floodplain. Over a few years, such cameras would have recorded many events that defined and reshaped the lives of the village residents, the ancestral Mandans. Corn planting and harvesting, bison hunting, feasting, and celebrations occurred in scheduled annual cycles. Less predictable but more momentous were influxes of foreign peoples to the ancestral Mandan homeland, episodes of intense warfare, and onslaughts by new, savage diseases such as smallpox that took one of every two lives on each appearance at the village.

By 750 BP, the ancestors of the historical Mandans occupied nearly the entire valley of the Missouri River in what is now South and North Dakota. Their lifeway, which archaeologists call the Plains Village tradition, centered on intensive hunting of the bison combined with cultivation of the tropical cultigens maize, beans, and squash; the people lived in villages composed of large bark- or earth-covered timber houses. By 550 BP, the ancestral Mandans had vacated the Missouri valley in South Dakota, coalescing in a smaller number of much larger, fortified settlements in North Dakota where the Cannonball and Heart rivers join the Missouri. By fifty years later, the ancestral Mandans were concentrated in a few large settlements near Heart River and Square Butte. Their village neighbors included ancestors of the Hidatsas upstream to the north and of the Arikaras downstream to the south. Several settlements near the Heart River were occupied without interruption until the late eighteenth century, when smallpox and warfare with the encroaching nomadic Sioux and Assiniboins drove the villagers farther upstream, where they emerged in written history as the Mandan tribe. Several sites are known as the traditional villages of the Mandans, and Double Ditch Village is one of at least seven such locations (Figure 10.18). In 1804–1805, several of the abandoned Mandan villages were observed by Meriwether Lewis and William Clark. On their expedition map they recorded Double Ditch as an "Old Indian Village Killed by The Sioux" (Moulton 1983:Map 28). Ethnographic information recorded early in the twentieth century indicates that Double Ditch was known to the Mandans as Yellow Earth

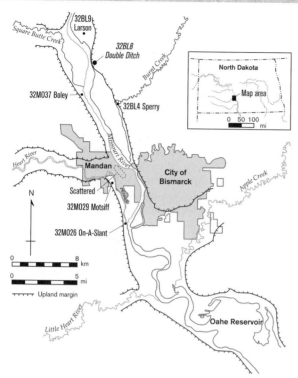

FIGURE 10.18 Double Ditch Village site location map showing traditional Mandan villages near the mouth of the Heart River, North Dakota.

FIGURE 10.19 Aerial photograph of Double Ditch Village, June 3, 1988.

Village (Bowers 1950:217, footnote 9) or Yellow Bank Village (Thiessen et al. 1979). The state of North Dakota purchased the site in 1936 for purposes of preservation and interpretation.

Double Ditch Village is today one of the most spectacular archaeological sites extant in North America. This is due to its large size (more than 20 acres), its commanding view of the Missouri valley both upstream and downstream, and its many internal surface features (Figure 10.19). Readily visible are a relatively complete inner fortification ditch and a portion of a concentric outer ditch (hence, the site name). The inner ditch has several small bastions, or outward projections along the fortification line. Within the area defined by this ditch are depressions in the ground that mark locations of about 33 circular earthlodges, 10 to 11 meters (33–36 ft.) in diameter, much like those built by the Mandans. The visible outer ditch lies about 60 to 70 meters (197–230 ft.) beyond the inner ditch. The surface in that area is irregular, and there are several basins, the largest of which are possibly borrow areas or plazas devoid of houses, and for these reasons, observers disagree on the number of lodge depressions between inner and outer ditches. A striking feature of the village is the more than three dozen earthen mounds, some of them huge, that lie at the perimeter of the settlement. Some mounds are just inside the second ditch; many more are outside it. Early archaeologists recorded the largest mounds as 3 meters (almost 10 ft.) high; today they are still at least 2 meters (6.6 ft.) high and no less impressive. Altogether, these mounds contain an estimated 6000 cubic meters (7850 yds.³) of fill. Based on test excavations in the mounds, this amount of fill also includes an estimated 1.6 million stone tools and tool fragments (arrow points, scrapers, used flakes, cores, etc.), more than 30,000 broken pottery vessels, and 142 metric tons (313,000 lbs.) of animal bone.

PREPARING FOR FIELDWORK AT DOUBLE DITCH

One hundred years ago, Double Ditch Village was a large and impressive archaeological site, but not necessarily unique regarding its appearance and internal features. Today, however, a site in this condition is rare on the Upper Missouri. Among the seven abandoned Mandan villages recorded by Lewis and Clark near the Heart River, Double Ditch is unusually well preserved. Two of the other six were obliterated before they could be accurately located; one has been incrementally and nearly completely destroyed; and three are now severely circumscribed and altered by cultivation, uncontrolled digging, and modern construction. Until the recent work at Double Ditch, not one of these sites had been extensively studied, and only one had been sampled using modern archaeological methods. Further underscoring the importance of Double Ditch Village, five man-made reservoirs have drowned 80 percent of the Missouri valley in the Dakotas (Lehmer 1971) and most of the hundreds of Plains Village sites contained therein. The region around Heart River was spared from flooding, but since the Heart region was bypassed by the salvage archaeology programs driven by reservoir construction, it has remained one of the least studied and least understood (Thiessen 1999). Thus, Double Ditch Village holds a key position. It lies at the heart of a little understood archaeological region that can document much of the prehistory and history of Plains Village peoples, and it is one of only a few large settlements sufficiently preserved for study in its spatial entirety.

In addition to the site's unusual size and condition, several other factors prompted recent investigations at Double Ditch Village. The village is a centerpiece among several archaeological sites preserved and managed by the state of North Dakota that range in age from Late Woodland to Historic. These sites are open to public visitation, and in the 1990s the State Historical Society of North Dakota (SHSND) began a systematic program of upgrading the interpretive and educational information available for these sites. For Double Ditch, existing information was meager, dating from excavations carried out in 1905 by two undergraduate students at Harvard University (Will and Spinden 1906). While their work was remarkable for its time—the first professional study of a Plains Village site in the Dakotas—the questions posed by the young archaeologists in 1905 were far different from those of today. In addition, the Lewis and Clark Bicentennial Celebration of 2004–2006 was expected to bring countless new visitors to the Missouri valley and North Dakota. Many visitors would be eager to learn about prominent sites such as Double Ditch, first recorded by Lewis and Clark and figuring clearly in the history of the Native peoples impacted by the Corps of Discovery and the events it foretold.

Sound interpretations and educational information are based on sound research, and the state of North Dakota provided special appropriations for new research at Double Ditch Village. New information has reached the public in several ways. Each major archaeological field season in 2002, 2003, and 2004 included an on-site interpretation program. Scheduled tour groups and drop-in visitors alike were met by interpreters who guided them through the site and explained the excavations in progress. The site is open to visitors throughout the year, and several movable interpretive displays allow self-guided tours. New information from current research is systematically input into updated versions of these displays. Results of research are summarized in technical reports that appear each year (e.g., Ahler 2004; Kvamme 2004). During the final two years of the project, new information will also be published in outlets for both public and scholarly audiences. In future years, project findings will be presented in museum exhibits at the North Dakota Heritage Center in Bismarck and in digital formats accessible via the Internet.

Like many modern archaeological endeavors, the Double Ditch program is a collaborative effort involving several partners. While much of the direct funding for the project has come from the state of North Dakota, many other entities have also provided support and have made "in-kind" contributions. Most of the archaeological staff members at the SHSND have been directly involved in the fieldwork. At the core of excavation programs in 2002 and 2003 were archaeological field schools involving 27 students from the University of Missouri–Columbia and the University of Kansas–Lawrence directed by W. Raymond Wood. The University of Missouri also supported a soil-coring program at the site directed toward graduate thesis research. Each summer from 2001 to 2004 experts in remote sensing led by Kenneth L. Kvamme at the University of Arkansas have conducted geophysical survey. At the request of the SHSND, the PaleoCultural Research Group (PCRG) has coordinated all research on the project. A nonprofit research and education organization with public membership, PCRG has drawn heavily on its members for volunteer field efforts and analytic studies. Twenty-six persons, including 16 PCRG members, have donated effort to the field program. For lab work conducted at its headquarters in Flagstaff, Arizona, PCRG has involved students majoring in anthropology at nearby Northern Arizona University, with some of the funding for student assistance provided through an arrangement with the university. Detailed studies of pottery, stone artifacts, faunal remains, botanical remains, radiocarbon samples, and trade artifacts are undertaken at the Flagstaff lab and at distant locations.

What are the specific research objectives at Double Ditch Village, and what are the methods for achieving these goals? Given the site size and visible features at Double Ditch, our broadest research objectives have been as follows:

1. *To understand the chronology of the site*

2. *To document in detail the structure of the site (positions of fortifications, earthlodges, basins, mounds, plazas, etc., as well as smaller features)*

3. *To reconstruct and explain changes in the community structure, or how and why the relationships of internal features and settlement size changed through time*

Another goal has been to learn about the social dynamics of the region during the history of the site, or how the early Mandan inhabitants of the village were affected by and interacted with people moving into the region and living in nearby areas. Social interactions at Double Ditch were complex and involved residents of other Mandan settlements at Heart River, eastern Hidatsa peoples migrating into the Missouri valley during the seventeenth century AD or perhaps earlier, several eastern groups such as the Sioux, who were pushing westward into Mandan territory to become nomadic bison hunters on the Great Plains, and European Americans moving westward who spread before them manufactured artifacts and deadly diseases previously unknown in North America. There are few precedents from modern Plains Village archaeology regarding "whole-village" investigations of sites as huge and complex as Double Ditch Village. One important model for Double Ditch research has been the study of large Hidatsa villages at the mouth of the Knife River (Ahler et al. 1991; Thiessen 1993). At Knife River, research was guided by detailed contour maps and by some of the first remote-sensing data from magnetic instrumentation to be applied on a whole-site scale.

At the start of the project, we held several assumptions regarding physical remains at Double Ditch Village. We assumed that the earthen mounds that ringed the village were heaps of refuse, and from the size of the mounds, we expected the village to have been lived in for two centuries or longer (established perhaps around 400 BP or AD 1550). Some evidence on the surface indicated that the inner ditch cut through existing features and was therefore the youngest fortification system in the site. From this we expected that the site had contracted in size through time, probably owing to depopulation due to disease, with the center of the village having been used the longest. The second, outer ditch would be the older one, defending a larger community, and the inner ditch more recent. Based on data from Hidatsa sites at Knife River, we expected refuse within the center of the village, beneath and around houses, to be 1 to 2 meters or more in thickness, owing to the long history of occupation and the effects of building repeatedly on the same location.

State-of-the-art remote-sensing technology played a major role in Double Ditch investigations. Since 1998 Kenneth Kvamme has had great success in applying a suite of methods including magnetic gradiometry, **electrical resistivity**, and ground-penetrating radar at village sites in the Dakotas (Kvamme 2003). Magnetic survey has proven the most useful remote-sensing method at many village sites where buried features lie near the ground surface. To collect magnetic data, a person carries a very sensitive magnetic gradiometer across the site along transects in measured spatial units, collecting 6400 or more readings from a survey block measuring 20 by 20 meters (22 × 22 yds.). Resulting data are displayed as patterns in gray-scale or as colors representing variations in magnetic intensity. From many previous applications at villages in the Dakotas, we knew that magnetic survey could pinpoint

the locations of hidden features such as underground storage pits subsequently filled with refuse, hearths and central fire pits within lodges, localized concentrations of refuse rich in rocks or organic matter, burned house floors and roof falls, and linear arrangements of sod and topsoil stacked along fortification ditches, as well as the ditches themselves (Kvamme 2003). We expected to document many if not all of these kinds of features at Double Ditch, and over the course of several years, we planned for remote sensing to map out details of the entire community not visible at the ground surface. The remote-sensing data would in turn be a tremendous boon to planning excavations.

A STAGED, MULTIYEAR PROGRAM

The approach to fieldwork and addressing the research goals has been staged, with the strategy for each new cycle of study adjusted according to results from recently completed work. This is a logical approach for complex archaeological sites, and a natural process for studies occurring over several years. Remote-sensing work was conducted over a four-year period from 2001 through 2004, with about 20 percent of the site surveyed during each of the first three seasons and the remaining 40 percent surveyed during 2004. Only a small hand-coring program, involving no excavation and focused on ground-truthing some of the first data from geophysical survey, was conducted in 2001. Progressively larger excavation programs involving field schools were conducted in 2002 (three weeks) and 2003 (five weeks), and a final five-week excavation and interpretive mapping program took place in 2004 involving a smaller field crew. In 2004, as this case study account was being drafted, the fieldwork of 2004 had just been completed, but much of the laboratory work was ongoing. In the two-year period after the 2004 field season, analytic studies were to be completed and all summary reports and publications for the project developed.

Remote sensing identified many unexpected features that proved important in all later work phases during the first field season (2001). Both magnetic and electrical resistance surveys revealed two large basins to be free of any detectable subsurface features. Follow-up coring with a simple tool called the Oakfield probe indicated that these basins were likely borrow locations from which large amounts of sediment, including all topsoil, had been removed. Several unexplainable linear anomalies, or patterns, were documented beneath the featureless surface near the village margin. Magnetic data and coring also documented large numbers of deep storage pits along the village margin where no indications of houses could be seen. Apparent rectangular houses (a form that predates the circular earthlodge) were documented near the village center. The greatest surprise came from coring these houses: artifact-bearing deposits within and around the houses were quite shallow, a half-meter (20 in.) or less in depth. This was quite contrary to the 2-meter-thick layer of debris found at other Late Plains Village sites, and it indicated *removal* of earth and refuse from the center part of the village.

With these 2001 findings, our attention was more focused during the next cycle of fieldwork. Coring studies in both the basins and residential areas indicated that the villagers had conducted large-scale earth-moving, and a new goal was to confirm and explain such activity. Because the core of the village appeared to lack deep stratified deposits, we shifted excavation focus to other locations that could provide long stratigraphic records. Unusual features had been discovered on the periphery of the village, in areas we had previously considered to lie beyond the limits of the settlement. Where was the village margin, and what was the purpose of the pits and linear features at what appeared to be the edge of the settlement?

The second round of remote-sensing fieldwork in summer 2002 yielded amazing discoveries. Late in the evening of the next-to-last day of geophysical survey, Ken and Jo Ann Kvamme asked the staff to assemble and prepare for a celebratory toast as they displayed the most recent composite magnetic map of the village. In the area mapped just that day along the village margin, well outside the ring of mounds, two remarkably regular, long curving lines marked the indisputable existence of two unsuspected fortification systems that lay well outside the outer visible ditch. The third ditch system appeared to connect several of the larger and outermost earthen mounds at the site, and the revealed portions of the outermost or fourth ditch system lay entirely beyond the mounds. The outermost ditch clearly included several large, squarish bastions that projected outward. The unexplained linear features on the village margin mapped the year before were now understood! The survey maps showed other unusual patterns, as well, including, in the nearly flat areas between the mounds and well outside the residential core of the settlement, large zones containing many pit features but no houses. A new series of presumed house depressions with rectangular form could also be seen in the north central part of the village.

A completely new picture of Double Ditch Village had suddenly appeared. The size of the fortified area in the settlement had mushroomed from 11 acres to more than 20 acres. Given the density of apparent houses within the inner ditch, a fortified area this large could have contained an estimated 190 earthlodges. Based on historical accounts of the number of people occupying a single lodge, this would imply a population of nearly 2000 people! The purpose of the large earthen mounds was suddenly of major interest. They no longer seemed to be merely trash heaps placed just outside the living area, but they appeared to bear some relation to placement of the fortifications. Perhaps they were intentionally constructed defensive features, closely integrated with ditches and palisades. And why were there no apparent houses outside the visible outer ditch? Had the village really consisted of 190 houses, or were the outer defenses designed to encircle pit storage zones or perhaps cemeteries? The bastioned fortifications appeared similar to systems at some villages dating 500 to 600 years ago, when rectangular houses were the norm. Was Double Ditch Village established at this time? If so, it would contain an unbroken three-century-plus record of Mandan cultural development.

The three-week round of excavation in 2002, following directly on the heels of the Kvammes's discoveries, could not begin to address all these questions. Paramount was developing a chronology for the site grounded in radiocarbon dating. The 1905 excavations had shown one of the largest mounds (Mound B) to be horizontally stratified, meaning that it had been built laterally, or outward from the village, in an accretional fashion. On the assumption that the mound was composed of trash built up over a few hundred years, the part of the mound laid down first could contain some of the oldest deposits in the site. In 1905 the Harvard students had dug a massive trench through this feature. We decided to use machinery to remove fill from their trench and efficiently sample mound contents along one wall (Figure 10.20). In addition, we needed to understand the two outermost, newly discovered fortification systems. What was their form, why did they have no surface expression, when were they constructed, and when were they abandoned and filled? Would the village contraction model hold up, with the outermost ditch being the oldest and the ditches to the interior being successively younger in age, until the site was abandoned around AD 1785? To answer these questions, we cut three sections across various parts of the outermost ditches, documenting them in profile and sampling their contents for artifacts and material that was datable by radiocarbon assay. In addition, we excavated parts of three isolated pits near the site periphery, wishing to learn the source of their fill, their purpose, and their age. Placement of the ditch and pit excavations was guided precisely by the magnetic survey maps.

Archaeological excavation is a destructive process. To minimize the loss of information, field workers not only record pages of information about what they see in the ground, they also apply artifact recovery methods that return even the smallest items of potential value to the lab. In the case of Double Ditch Village and many other Plains Village studies conducted since 1969, field

FIGURE 10.20 Excavation in progress during 2002 in the reopened Will and Spinden trench through Mound B. Diagram represents the Harvard students' cross section through Mound B: 5-foot increments on the scales represent about 1.5 meters; letters designate the strata recognized in the profile. (After Will and Spinden 1906:Plate XXX.)

recovery has involved water screening of nearly all excavated sediments over fine mesh (16-per-inch) window screen. This screening system assures recovery of not only large artifacts such as pottery and bison bones, but also thousands of small yet important items such as tiny stone flakes, bones of micromammals and fish, charred seeds, and tiny glass trade beads and small fragments of iron and copper that document the beginnings of contact and trade between Natives and European Americans.

The 2002 excavations provided their own surprises. As expected, Mound B proved to be stratified from one side to the other, but it was composed of not so much individual loads of trash as a homogenized mixture of earth and artifacts laid down in massive layers. Trade artifacts occurred throughout the mound, and pottery in the mound showed no measurable change from one side of the mound to the other. Together, this information indicated that Mound B was intentionally constructed from dirt hauled from elsewhere in the village (it was not a refuse heap, per se). Moreover, Mound B was built during a very short period of time, being constructed late in the history of the village, well after when trade artifacts first reached the region about 450 BP. The cleared-out trench also showed that those who had built the mound had borrowed away the ground beneath before the mound was constructed, and that the outer visible

ditch (Ditch 2) was dug at precisely the time Mound B was completed. The cross sections through the outer two fortification systems, Ditches 3 and 4, revealed them to be deep, narrow trenches, having sharp edges and no spoil dirt on either side. This was unusual for fortification ditches, which usually have rounded margins and spoil dirt thrown to the inside. Artifacts in Ditches 3 and 4 were clearly older than those in Mound B. Check-stamped pottery, a variety normally found only in sites dating 650–450 BP, was found in one storage pit near the village margin. This was another clue, in addition to apparent rectangular house depressions and bastioned fortifications, that the village may have been founded between 550 BP and 450 BP.

The 2003 and 2004 field seasons saw continuing and concluding geophysical surveys and a greater emphasis on excavation. These studies revealed much about the layout and dynamics of the community (Figure 10.21) and went a long way toward fulfilling several of our broader research goals. Remote sensing showed the outermost fortification system, now called Ditch 4, to include at least 10 large bastion loops. Ditch 4 generally lay well outside most of the earthen mounds, but it intersected four of the smallest of these features. Ditch 3, the next toward the interior, contained only three visible bastion elements and consisted, in places, of two closely spaced parallel ditch lines. Ditch 3

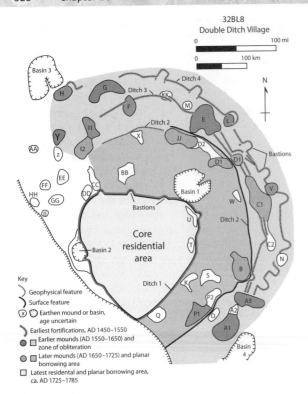

32BL8
Double Ditch Village

FIGURE 10.21 Double Ditch Village plan showing major features and change through time. Letters and Letter/Number combinations are used to label the mounds.

also appeared to be more intimately linked to some of the largest mounds on the village margin, with six or seven large earthen mounds lying along the line of Ditch 3. A portion of Ditch 2, the outer originally known ditch, was visible in magnetic data even where no evidence was visible on the surface.

Excavations in 2003 and 2004 focused on the mounds, a potential rectangular house, the outermost fortification ditch, and many pit features. We dug 15 deep test pits in 13 mounds. We wished to date each mound and learn whether it had been constructed rapidly from earth hauled over a short period of time, like Mound B, or in some other manner. Ultimately, we wished to know the chronological and functional relationships between the mounds and fortification systems. Seeking hard data about the earliest end of the village chronology, we sampled what appeared on the surface to be a rectangular house depression, one of several such features in the north central part of the site, and several pit features near the village margin, outside Ditch 2. We designed the outer ditch studies to clarify details of construction and chronology, building on the 2002 excavation data. A number of test pits targeted magnetic signals for storage pits

inside houses in the core of the village, inside Ditch 1. Here our goals were to sample the latest period of site occupation and to learn more about house-building and earthmoving activities near the village center.

The mound tests revealed more than we had expected. At four locations the tests exposed parts of open ditches directly beneath the mounds, clearly indicating that in many cases the ditches did not connect the mounds but, rather, the mounds had been built on top of fortification ditches no longer used for defense. But this relationship was not a simple one of mounds replacing ditches: it became clear that both ditches and mounds continued to be built late in the history of the settlement. At several mounds, stratigraphy showed that the surface *around* the mounds had been artificially lowered in some manner. The search for a rectangular house was unsuccessful. The rectangular depression between Ditches 1 and 2, thought to be a house location, proved to be a large, elongated borrow pit. The inhabitants had artificially truncated the entire area inside and around by digging out the earth and taking it away. Perhaps the depression marked a former rectangular house obliterated by borrowing.

Excavations within houses inside Ditch 1 and near the village core confirmed that this entire area had been planed off and borrowed away, as was the case at the location of the supposed rectangular house between Ditches 1 and 2. Floors of earthlodges in the village core lay only 20 cm (8 in.) below the present ground surface, and they rested directly on sterile sediment. The entire area within Ditch 2 had been subjected to what we call *planar borrowing*, or horizontally continuous earth removal over a large area, after which the dirt and artifacts were transported to the mounds or elsewhere. The villagers had removed the shallow parts of all except the latest earthlodges inside Ditches 1 and 2.

Excavations outside Ditch 2 and across Ditches 3 and 4 revealed that all traces of dwellings along with the upper parts of pit features and the ditch systems had been completely obliterated in that area. Only the lower parts of deeper features remained, with these overlain by a homogenized sediment layer containing small artifacts. This obliteration of the outer parts of the original settlement documents a severe, localized environmental impact resulting from activities of the villagers that continued after the dwelling area shrank and the outer part of the community was abandoned. It was only beneath mounds placed outside Ditch 2 that the old ground surface on which the village was settled was still preserved.

SUMMARY OF FINDINGS

Radiocarbon dating and artifact studies are ongoing as this is written, but several results bear mention. The earliest dates produced so far fall between 550 BP and 450 BP, and more dates from deepest and earliest contexts are expected to confirm that the community was founded around 500 BP (AD 1450). This founding date is consistent with the nature of the bastioned fortification system, the presence of check-stamped pottery, and many suggestions that rectangular houses once existed there. The three-century-long period of continuous occupation at Double Ditch makes the site a remarkable laboratory of continuing study of cultural change.

Stone artifacts from the excavations indicate a shift in geographic and presumed social connections outside the village during the history of the site. Early on, the villagers used Tongue River silicified sediment, a stone from near-local sources south of the village, and connections by travel or trade brought in quartzite and dendritic chert from distant sources far to the southwest, near the Black Hills in South Dakota and Wyoming. Later in time, the southern and southwestern connections faded, and people made heavier use of stone sources for Knife River flint and porcellanite to the west and northwest. This change in stone raw material use may reflect the influx of the nomadic Sioux into areas south and southwest of Double Ditch, as well as village alliances that shifted through time from the Arikaras who lived south of Double Ditch to the Hidatsas who lived to the north. We can easily organize pottery from the excavations into an "early" group and a "late" group. The contrast between groups is strong and suggests the sudden addition to the village pottery assemblage of ceramic products from one or two new social groups, a change occurring about 300 BP (AD 1650). This may imply a sudden increase in exchange with new, nearby peoples, or perhaps incorporation of foreign potters directly into the settlement. The cause underlying this abrupt change in pottery is a significant question for future research.

Figure 10.23 summarizes current knowledge regarding the internal dynamics of the settlement. The model of village contraction over time has been supported. Ditches 3 and 4 are clearly the oldest, with Ditch 4 likely dating between 550 BP and 450 BP (to be confirmed by more radiocarbon assays). Most if not all of the outer mounds are more recent than these two fortification systems, however, and it is clear that by perhaps 350 BP ditch systems 3 and 4 had been abandoned and several mounds had been built over them. Not all the mounds were constructed as rapidly as Mound B, but it is likely that several mounds were intentionally constructed as "strong points" or parts of village defenses. Based on historical data, wooden palisades or pickets consisting of closely spaced vertical posts were undoubtedly part of the village fortifications, but our excavations poorly documented the palisades. Several palisades may have linked to the large mounds or perhaps skirted around them, to complete the fortification system used after Ditches 3 and 4 were abandoned and some of the mounds were built.

After the outer mounds had been built, the village contracted to an area roughly demarcated by Ditch 2, and the process of obliteration of the older, abandoned, outer parts of the settlement began to occur. Degradation of the older perimeter of the original settlement continued until around 1785, when the village was abandoned. This "impact zone" around the settlement was probably devoid of vegetation and subject to erosion, and people may have located their garden plots and hobbled their horses there late in the history of the village. Planar borrowing and removal of earth for placement in mounds occurred throughout most of the area inside Ditch 2 and Ditch 1, and it may also have extended into the areas around some of the mounds. Based on the long period of mound construction beginning between 450 BP and 350 BP, several cycles of extensive earth removal may have occurred, continuing up until the time the village was abandoned. Such borrowing is a very unusual, labor-intensive activity, not well documented at any other Plains Village site. While one purpose of planar borrowing may have been to create mounds as elements in village defenses, this process of earth and artifact removal may also have functioned as a village-wide cleansing and renewal mechanism triggered by repeated and horrendous smallpox epidemics. One inescapable theme in the history of the site is that its population became continuously smaller over time. When the village residents threw up the palisade and dry moat that proved to be their last line of defense (Ditch 1), it protected a population that was only 20 percent the size of the village at its peak. The last ditch and palisade could not defend against the spotted demon that struck again in AD 1781–1782, nor against the Sioux who followed closely on the heels of the disease.

The Double Ditch Village Project is a testament to successful collaboration among several interested and dedicated parties. As with most archaeological studies, we have learned much more than we sought and many things we did not expect. Fortuitous discoveries are some of the finest rewards from planned and focused investigations. New investigative tools, such as closely coordinated remote-sensing and excavation studies, played a central role in the project. Without new methods to guide and direct the more conventional and indispensable forms of archaeological investigation, such as hand excavation, radiocarbon dating, and artifact studies, the cost of meeting the goals set for this project would have been prohibitive. While Double

Ditch Village is practically unique from the perspective of its preservation and complexity, the lessons we are learning there about how to approach Plains Village archaeology and how to interpret Mandan prehistory will be applied several times over at many other sites during the coming decades. The people of North Dakota are to be commended for supporting this exciting and informative study in archaeology.

DISCUSSION QUESTIONS

1. Why was the research described here undertaken? What were its goals? Who was involved?

2. Could as much have been learned about Double Ditch Village if the investigators hadn't done the geophysical studies they describe? Contrast the advantages and disadvantages of these techniques with those of traditional hand excavation.

3. Explain why these investigators came to believe that the mounds at Double Ditch Village were intentionally constructed rather than simply accumulations of refuse. What are the implications of this finding for what was happening at the village?

4. What might explain the changes in the raw materials used for making stone tools and in the types of pottery being made between the early and late parts of the occupation at Double Ditch Village? How would you investigate further?

CHAPTER 11

Foragers and Farmers of the Eastern Woodlands Heartland

In 1988 a heavy-equipment operator was borrowing dirt for a road construction project in southern Indiana when he encountered some spectacular artifacts. He collected the artifacts and took them home to Illinois. Next he contacted a well-known artifact collector from Indiana, sold the artifacts he had found for $6000, and showed the collector the site without obtaining permission from the landowner, the General Electric Company. Over the course of that summer, the artifact collector recruited helpers and proceeded to dig into what turned out to be a large, previously unrecognized Middle Woodland mound. Large quantities of artifacts were recovered, and some were later sold at an Indian relic show in Kentucky. Other collectors also removed artifacts from this site. Looting stopped only when security guards encountered looters on the property and required them to leave (Munson et al. 1995).

As word leaked out, it became clear that an important cultural resource had been harmed. Archaeologists concluded that the mound had not been recognized during the course of a preconstruction survey because it was so large that it looked like a natural ridge. Probable dimensions of 400 by 175 feet (120 × 50 m) by 15 to 20 feet (4.6 × 6.1 m) in height make this mound one of the five largest known Middle Woodland mounds. Efforts began to recover as many artifacts as possible. Eventually over 3000 artifacts from nine collections were returned. Among these artifacts were copper celts and panpipes, pearl and shell beads, finely made stone and bone tools, mica cutouts, and leather wrappings. Many of these items were truly rare and valuable. Archaeologists used these artifacts and their exploration of the mound itself to identify the site as Hopewell, dating it between 1850 BP and 1950 BP. They also concluded that those who constructed the mound participated in interregional exchange and ceremonialism with people as far away as southern Ohio (Seeman 1995). Yet, the internal structure of the mound, the actual positioning of artifacts, and the number of individuals that might have been buried in the mound could not be determined. Unfortunately, clandestine looting and sale of Indian artifacts for profit isn't unusual (see the opening of Chapter 6). Illegal pot hunting goes on all over the United States, destroying cultural resources and the information they could have provided.

Sometimes the sites damaged are highly significant, as was the case with the mound in Indiana, now called the GE Mound. What was different about the GE Mound case is that eventually five people were convicted under the Archaeological Resources Protection Act (ARPA) of 1979 (see Table 1.1), setting an important precedent for enforcement of this act's prohibition on interstate trafficking in artifacts.

The GE Mound was on property that was privately owned, and this was a critical issue in the court case. Whereas in some countries all known cultural resources are the property of the state, in the United States federal protections are not provided for cultural resources on private property unless federal funds or permits are involved. Under ARPA, however, it is illegal to sell, exchange, transport, or receive across state lines any artifacts that were obtained in violation of state or local law. State and local laws may or may not protect sites on private property. In Indiana, the excavation into the GE Mound would not have been illegal per se if permitted by the landowner. Some collectors maintain that General Electric at first gave tacit approval to the digging and collecting because the company did not immediately stop it (Gifford 1994). The looters of GE Mound admitted their actions, but they argued that ARPA was unconstitutionally vague and did not apply. The federal court did not find merit in the defendants' arguments, and the Supreme Court declined to review the decision.

The story of the GE Mound is instructive insofar as it reveals what different stakeholders in the past think about collecting and looting. Many archaeologists were outraged and strongly supported the prosecution of the looters. To an archaeologist, the looting of sites is fundamentally destructive to knowledge, while the sale of artifacts only encourages more looting. However, artifact collectors and some amateurs questioned the ARPA prosecution and thought the defendants were being made scapegoats for professional and landowner negligence. Prominent among their arguments were the claims that collecting and trafficking in antiquities is not truly harmful to anyone. Moreover, ignoring the contention that the GE Mound artifacts at issue were stolen property, the collectors argued that their rights to have artifact collections were being threatened. Native Americans were outraged primarily over the desecration of a burial site of their ancestors. Some Native Americans also were interested in what could be learned from the artifacts and mound. For others, however, the issue of respect for the ancestors outweighed any interest in obtaining knowledge about the past; these Native Americans successfully insisted on reburial of the recovered artifacts. The final stakeholder in the proceedings was the local public, which truly had its consciousness raised concerning the nature and value of local antiquities. There was tremendous growth in public concern for the local heritage, and a state law requiring an approved plan for all excavation into archaeological sites was not passed in 1989, after the looting of the GE Mound had come to light (Munson et al. 1995).

The GE Mound story reminds us that the archaeological record of the areas covered here includes the remains of some of the most spectacular pre-Columbian societies that existed in North America. Archaeologists are deeply interested in these past societies and their cultures, but so are many others, for different reasons. These interests can be destructive as well as benign. Deciding how to resolve competing perspectives fairly is important. Will we find ways to preserve resources and gain knowledge while respecting Native people, or will inadequate inventory of cultural resources, human greed, and a lack of legal protections result in the sweeping away of most of the traces of the past?

DEFINITION OF THE AREA

Chapters 11 and 12 cover the Eastern Woodlands of North America, which stretch from the margins of the Plains to the Atlantic Ocean across nearly a quarter of the continent. Two culture areas, the Northeast and the Southeast, have traditionally been recognized within the Eastern Woodlands (Figure 2.1). In this text we combine these areas because of the similarity of culture history, but focus first on the interior in this chapter and then cover the culture history of rest of the Eastern Woodlands in Chapter 12 (Figure 11.1). Because of the general environmental and cultural similarities throughout the East, it can be argued that the entire Eastern Woodlands should be treated as one cultural area. Organizing this material into two chapters allows us to focus first on the relatively spectacular developments of the interior Southeast and Midwest, where farming, mound building, and powerful chiefdoms were found in later pre-Columbian times. In the interior Eastern Woodlands stretching from the margins of the Great Plains to the Appalachian Mountains and from the southern Midwest to northern Louisiana, Mississippi, Alabama, and Georgia, there were broadly similar cultural sequences that archaeologists organize into the Paleoindian, Archaic, Woodland, and Mississippian (Table 11.1). We also have included the entire Mississippi valley in this chapter's discussion. Elsewhere in the Eastern Woodlands along the coasts, in southern Florida, in much of the Great Lakes, the Mid-Atlantic, New England, and southern parts of Canada the Mississippian tradition per se generally is lacking and the influence of interior Woodland cultures such as Hopewell less. Nevertheless the rich cultural histories of these areas are just as important, and in Chapter 12 we introduce them. However, as you read this chapter and the next, you should remember that there was interaction of people throughout the region, so these two chapters should be considered together. The locations of sites mentioned in this chapter are shown in Figure 11.1.

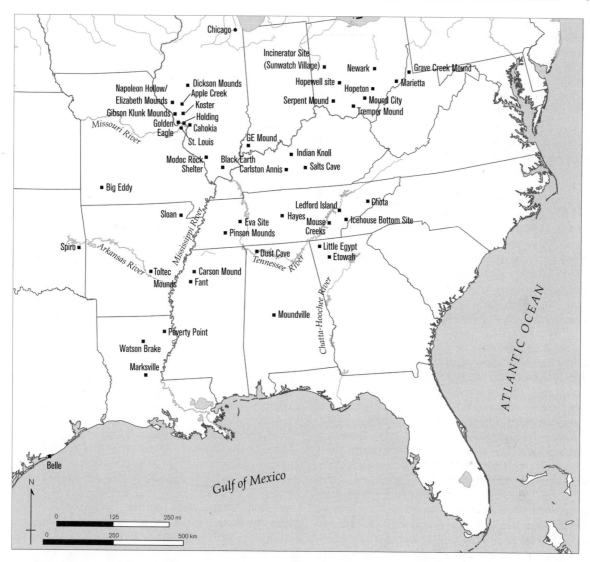

FIGURE 11.1 The interior Eastern Woodlands showing the locations of sites that are mentioned in Chapter 11.

THE ENVIRONMENT OF THE INTERIOR EASTERN WOODLANDS

The climate of the interior Eastern Woodlands is humid and mostly controlled by the interaction of Tropical, Pacific, and Polar air masses (Wright 2006). The southern interior has a subtropical climate with mild winters and hot and muggy summers punctuated by frequent thunderstorms. However, significant precipitation occurs in all seasons. There are distinct seasons, but snow and persistent freezing temperatures are rare. Farther north above 40° latitude the climate is classified as continental and generally summers are warm to hot while winters are cold. Mean temperatures in the coldest month, usually January, are below freezing and snowfall tends to be more common than rain in the winter.

Three physiographic divisions are important in the interior portions of the Eastern Woodlands: the Appalachian Highlands, the Interior Low Plateau, and the Central Lowlands Fenneman (1938). The Appalachian Highland is a complex mountain system with a number of distinct physiographic provinces. The Appalachian Plateau and the Ridge and Valley subprovinces mark the approximate eastern extent of the interior Eastern Woodlands on which we focus in this chapter. West of the Appalachian Mountain system in Tennessee and Kentucky is the Low Interior Plateau, where the

TABLE 11.1 Introduction to Interior Eastern Woodlands Culture History

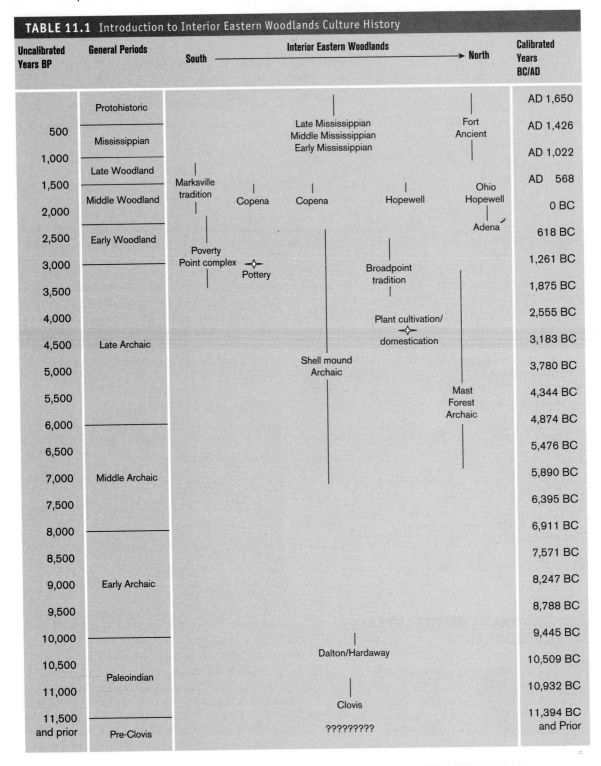

Uncalibrated Years BP	General Periods	Interior Eastern Woodlands					Calibrated Years BC/AD
		South → North					
	Protohistoric						AD 1,650
500			Late Mississippian		Fort Ancient		AD 1,426
	Mississippian		Middle Mississippian				
1,000			Early Mississippian				AD 1,022
	Late Woodland						
1,500		Marksville tradition				Ohio	AD 568
	Middle Woodland		Copena	Copena	Hopewell	Hopewell	
2,000							0 BC
						Adena	
2,500	Early Woodland						618 BC
3,000		Poverty Point complex			Broadpoint tradition		1,261 BC
		Pottery					
3,500							1,875 BC
4,000				Plant cultivation/ domestication			2,555 BC
4,500	Late Archaic						3,183 BC
5,000			Shell mound Archaic				3,780 BC
5,500					Mast Forest Archaic		4,344 BC
6,000							4,874 BC
6,500							5,476 BC
7,000	Middle Archaic						5,890 BC
7,500							6,395 BC
8,000							6,911 BC
8,500							7,571 BC
9,000	Early Archaic						8,247 BC
9,500							8,788 BC
10,000							9,445 BC
10,500			Dalton/Hardaway				10,509 BC
11,000	Paleoindian						10,932 BC
11,500 and prior			Clovis				11,394 BC and Prior
	Pre-Clovis		?????????				

underlying rocks dip gently northwestward into the Midwest. The Central Lowlands are areas north of the Interior Low Plateau generally covered with deposits left by the glaciers, and the primary agent that has shaped this part of the interior's topography is glaciation. Major river drainages such as the Mississippi and Ohio dissect the interior of the Eastern Woodlands providing additional topographic relief. The Ozark and Ouachita mountains are on the boundary between the Eastern Woodlands and the Southern Plains while the southern boundary of the interior falls in the northern part of the extensive Gulf Coastal Plain.

Most of the interior Eastern Woodlands naturally supported complex deciduous forests with a mix of trees and a wide variety of plant and animal resources. This forest is dominated by oak and hickory, but varies in its diversity and species richness depending on the specifics of soils, elevation, and moisture (e.g., Braun 1967; Shelford 1963). Portions of the interior in the north8ern Coastal Plain are dominated by pine forests with some deciduous trees. In modern times, many forests were cleared for agricultural activities, and even in the prehistoric past, clearings in the forests resulted from human settlement and farming (see later). In the Midwest, the Illinoian biotic province, or the **Prairie Peninsula**, naturally extends into the woodlands in a broad wedge stretching into into northern Indiana. Various tall-grass species dominate, but patches of oak-hickory forest may occur in the uplands, and the river valleys support a diverse deciduous forest. Aquatic resources are significant throughout the region, and migratory waterfowl pass through the area seasonally, tracking along the Mississippi flyway.

Climatic Change

Only the northern portions of the interior Eastern Woodlands were ever glaciated. The Wisconsin ice sheet extended southward to the approximate latitude of 37° north (see Figure 2.12), which means it covered areas in Missouri, Illinois, Indiana, Kentucky, and Ohio. The tremendously complex story of the ice sheet's retreat is partially written on the landscape in these areas, as it is for areas to the north and east covered in Chapter 12. However, since deglaciation had begun by at least 14,000 BP, ice was absent from all the areas covered in this chapter for most of the period of human habitation.

At the end of the Wisconsin glaciations, ecological communities were unlike any we know today, with very high diversity and mixes of species currently found in widely separated environments, as well as a mosaic of habitat types rather than the north-south zonation familiar today (Graham and Mead 1987; Wright 2006). Modern forest distributions took millennia to establish. Other aspects of the environment such as

drainage systems also did not resemble those today. As ocean levels rose, the coast underwent a complex process of drowning. The interaction of rising sea level, isostatic rebound, drainage patterns, and local topography in various parts of the Southeast resulted in significant environmental change in the Early Holocene. Farther north in the Midwest, lakes and rivers at first could not drain northeastward through the St. Lawrence River, so other drainage patterns through the Mississippi and Ohio valleys were established. Early in the Holocene the rivers of the area were cold, fast-flowing, often braided streams that were carrying large volumes of water. River regimes took millennia to stabilize (Baker 1983).

The mid-Holocene warming period, usually called the Hypsithermal in the Eastern Woodlands, also represented a period of significant change in forest cover (ca. 9000–2500 BP). Dry conditions around 7000 BP are particularly noteworthy. The most significant change in the Southeast was the disappearance of hardwood trees as dominants in some areas of the Coastal Plain. At this time various pine species became the dominants in these forests. The position of the Prairie Peninsula continued to shift eastward in the Midwest until about 7000 BP as well. After this date, the dry conditions waned and prairie vegetation retreated westward (King 1981; King and Allen 1977). Major change in river regimes and coastlines also occurred during the mid-Holocene as lower energy rivers with meander belts and aquatic habitats similar to those of the recent past developed. Following the mid-Holocene, after approximately 5000 years ago, essentially modern conditions prevailed throughout the interior Eastern Woodlands. However, this does not mean that minor oscillations in climate were not occurring.

Human populations also were responsible for altering habitats long into the past. We usually think of this happening when people shifted to fully agricultural economies within the last thousand years. This process, however, likely began on a small but perhaps locally significant scale (Wagner 2003). For example, in the Little Tennessee river valley, the record of pollen and plant remains suggests that human impact on the environment increased as soon as squash, gourd, and seed plants began to be cultivated, approximately 4000 BP. After this time, land clearing and other disturbances only increased (Delcourt et al. 1986). Of course, following European settlement, landscapes were even more significantly modified by human activities.

PALEOINDIANS

As discussed in Chapter 3, there is a large amount of evidence for occupation of the Eastern Woodlands by

ANTHROPOLOGICAL THEMES   TOPIC 11.1

Thematic Research Questions in Chapter 11

As we pointed out in Chapter 2, it is easy to lose sight of the big picture when considering the diverse cultures and histories of North America. This is certainly true for the interior of the Eastern Woodlands that is discussed in this chapter. However, you will find material directly relevant to at least four of the broad research questions discussed in Chapter 2 as listed in Table 2.1, and we touch on other themes less directly. Table 11.2 helps you locate relevant sections of this chapter for each theme. Reading these sections likely will suggest more specific questions and issues as well.

TABLE 11.2 Research Themes for the Interior Eastern Woodlands

Research Question	Particularly Relevant Sections
How have humans adapted to the diverse environments of North America and to climatic change over time?	Discussion of the Archaic, the Woodland, and the Mississippian cultures of the interior Eastern Woodlands
How, when, and where did food production develop in North America?	Discussions of subsistence and settlement in the Archaic, Woodland, and Mississippian periods
How, when, and where did sociopolitically complex, internally differentiated cultural systems develop in North America?	Discussion of mound building and interaction in the Archaic and Woodland periods as well as the section on the Mississippians and Box 11.1, "How Big and Powerful Was Cahokia After All?"
What ethnic identities can be identified and historically traced in North America's past?	Section on the Protohistoric and European Contact

Paleoindians. Probable Pre-Clovis sites, Clovis sites, and large numbers of Clovis and other fluted points as well as Late Paleoindian sites all are well represented in the archaeological record of the interior Eastern Woodlands. These data contribute significantly to many questions concerning the timing and nature of human settlement of North America as well as to archaeological understanding of the variability of human adaptations during the Paleoindian period. Research on both Pre-Clovis and other Paleoindian sites in the interior Eastern Woodlands is likely to continue to be important and productive.

ARCHAIC FORAGERS

The Eastern Archaic was originally defined as a stage of cultural development during which the people of the Eastern Woodlands were nomadic, egalitarian, generalized foragers who did not live in settled villages but moved within localized territories. These people also were characterized by the absence of pottery, cultivated crops, mounds and earthworks, and extensive long-distance trade (Ritchie 1932). In contrast, earlier Paleoindians were viewed as more specialized and more mobile hunters of game, while Woodland peoples were thought to have been more hierarchical in

sociopolitical organization, more sedentary, and to have made pottery, grown crops, built mounds, and developed long-distance trading networks.

These evolutionary formulations are no longer widely accepted, and the Eastern Archaic is more often treated simply as a period in time. However, implicit assumptions about Archaic peoples may still conform to the ideas of the stage concept, and there is still debate between those who take a generally evolutionary approach in conceptualizing the Archaic and those who see such an approach as constraining (Emerson and McElrath 2009). It is clear, however, that before 3000 BP, populations in some areas, such as the river valleys of interior Southeast and the Midwest, had developed many of the characteristics of the Woodland: settled villages, pottery making, horticulture, mound building and mortuary ceremonialism, as well as social differentiation. This means that there was much more variability in cultural sequences during the Archaic than early models can accommodate, and there has been growing interest in gaining a better understanding of what happened in diverse localities. Both interdisciplinary investigations at deeply stratified sites with good preservation (see the Bonus Case Studies on the CD, Section D.2 and Section D.6, for examples) and major CRM projects documenting settlement distribution have added to archaeological understanding in significant ways (Anderson and Sassaman 1996; Jefferies 1995a, 2008; McElrath et al. 2009).

The Archaic period in the interior Eastern Woodlands spans 7000 years, from approximately 10,000 BP to 3000 BP. Three Archaic subperiods typically are designated: Early Archaic (10,000–8000 BP), Middle Archaic (8000–5000 BP), and Late Archaic (5000–3000 BP). Some authorities, particularly in the Southeast, end the Middle Archaic and start the Late Archaic about a thousand years earlier (e.g., Bense 1994), and other schemes based on cultural traits have been proposed as well (e.g., Walthall 1980). Generally, however, Archaic subdivisions are not based on consistent cultural transformations across the Eastern Woodlands, but rather simply are useful means of dividing a long period of time about which archaeologists still have relatively limited information. Another approach now taken by some archaeologists is to avoid the Archaic terminology altogether and use Early, Middle, and Late Holocene periods (e.g., Anderson and Sassaman 2004; Sassaman and Anderson 2004). This last approach highlights significant climatic rather than cultural events.

Archaic Material Culture

Throughout the Eastern Woodlands, the terminal Paleoindian and beginning of the Archaic period often is marked by the appearance of unfluted points. The Dalton tradition (ca. 10,500–9900 BP) is defined on the basis of sites in southern Missouri, northern Arkansas, and southern Illinois (Goodyear 1982; Koldehoff and Walthall 2009). Based on point morphology, those who made Dalton points (Figure11.2) appear to be like other late Paleoindians in the Eastern Woodlands who did not make fluted points and were generalized foragers. At the Big Eddy site in Missouri, the Dalton horizon is clearly after the Clovis and Folsom layers and below the Early Archaic deposits.

As some Dalton sites in the Central Mississippi valley are large and possibly occupied year-round, more significant departure from Late Paleoindian lifeways is sometimes suggested. The Sloan site in Arkansas is one of the earliest cemeteries archaeologists have found anywhere in North America. Very large Sloan-style Dalton points made from raw material found only far to the north have been recovered at Sloan as well as in caches elsewhere. These have been interpreted as assertions of group identity that were used in social interactions (Sassaman 2005). Dalton tradition sites also contain stone adzes possibly used in canoe making as well as other woodworking (Figure 11.3). Such implements have not been common prior to the Dalton period, leading some researchers to argue that Dalton represents new types of adaptation that developed as the deciduous forests spread northward

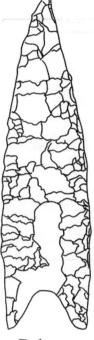

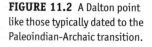

FIGURE 11.2 A Dalton point like those typically dated to the Paleoindian-Archaic transition.

Dalton

FIGURE 11.3 Dalton adzes believed to be some of the first woodworking tools used in the Eastern Woodlands.

(e.g., Koldehoff and Walthall 2009). In this interpretation, Dalton is a very early Archaic period adaptation.

A variety of lithic traits have been found to mark the Early Archaic as opposed to the Paleoindian period throughout the Eastern Woodlands. However, their significance in terms of human lifestyles can be debated. These characteristics are shown in Table 11.3. Greater quantities of bone tools may also mark the beginning of the Archaic.

Investigations at deeply stratified Archaic sites in the Eastern Woodlands Archaic have led to the development of chronologies based on technological change. The first efforts to develop an Archaic sequence of projectile points used sites in North Carolina's Piedmont (Coe 1964). A series of deep excavations in the Little Tennessee River valley, which were conducted in advance of the TVA's flooding of the Tellico Reservoir,

further clarified this sequence (Chapman 1975, 1977, 1985). Figure 11.4 illustrates some of the projectile point types that have been found in Archaic sequences in the interior Eastern Woodlands. Side-notched forms generally are followed by corner-notched forms and then by bifurcate forms. The later Middle Archaic is marked by the appearance of stemmed forms while Late Archaic forms often are stemmed as well, although some notched forms occur. Although this scheme has general validity, it is important to note that sequences in specific localities can be much more complex and variable.

TABLE 11.3 Lithic Traits Associated with the Paleoindian-to-ArchaicTransition in the Eastern Woodlands

1 Presence of notched and stemmed projectile points
2 Use of a wider range of lithic raw materials, including some that are harder to flake (e.g., quartzite, argillite, slate)
3 Predominant use of locally available stone, including cobbles from streambeds asopposed to exotic stone transported some distance
4 Less resharpening and other maintenance of chipped stone tools and more useof expedient stone tools, which are discarded after minimal use
5 Increase in ground and polished stone items, especially those associated withplant processing, woodworking, and fishing

---

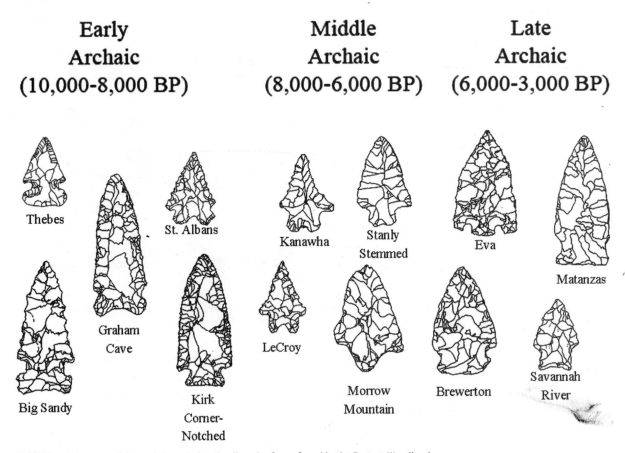

FIGURE 11.4 Some of the Archaic period projectile point forms found in the Eastern Woodlands.

Broad-bladed forms, sometimes considered representative of a Late Archaic **Broadpoint tradition**, also are important in the Late Archaic. There also are archaeological traditions based on projectile points and other attributes that have been suggested for the Middle to Late Archaic in the Northeast as a whole (Tuck 1978). One of these is the **Lake Forest Archaic**, associated with sites in the transitional forest of the Great Lakes and southern Canada, which are characterized by broad-bladed, side-notched points. Also apparently associated with deciduous forest sites farther south, with many narrow-bladed and stemmed projectile points, is the **Narrow Point tradition** or **Mast Forest Archaic** (see Figure 12.8). Whether these groupings are truly meaningful in terms of lifestyle isn't clear, but point types associated with both may be found in the interior of the Eastern Woodlands.

Other traits are also evident in Archaic period lithic assemblages. While Early Archaic stone tools are often described as formal and highly **curated**, like those of the Paleoindian period, archaeologists have noted that Middle Archaic lithics are more expedient. Moreover, fewer nonlocal raw materials are evident by Middle Archaic times (Amick and Carr 1996). Ground stone tools also increase in frequency and diversity during the Archaic as opposed to Paleoindian times. Finely made **bannerstones,** presumed to have been used as atlatl weights, are one example of Archaic tools made in this way (Figure 11.5).

Archaic sites contain many intriguing items of material culture besides lithics. Many bone tools have been found in Archaic sites. In Middle to Late Archaic contexts, especially in the southern Midwest and Midsouth, elaborately carved bone pins have been recovered (see Figure 11.6). In some parts of the areas covered in this chapter and the next copper implements dating to the Middle to Late Archaic have been found as well. These copper implements mark the beginning of a long-standing technology shared among the inhabitants of Eastern North America. Mining and working of native copper including the manufacture of ornaments as well as tools continued for many millennia into the Historic period (Levine 1999; Martin 1999).

Artifacts that represent the use of different methods of indirect cooking including clay cooking balls and perforated steatite slabs are found in Late Archaic sites in the lower Mississippi valley and elsewhere. The clay cooking balls, amorphous or shaped in a variety of forms, appear to have been heated in a fire and placed in pits or earth ovens to supply heat for the slow cooking of food. Steatite slabs, which archaeologists originally thought were net sinkers, most likely were used in a similar manner (Sassaman 1993). During the Late Archaic, trade with people of the Appalachian Piedmont where steatite can be quarried developed.

FIGURE 11.5 Bannerstones have central holes and come in a variety of shapes and raw materials; these specimens are presumed to have been atlatl weights.

Vessels as well as slabs were obtained. It is most likely that the first steatite vessels were receptacles for indirect cooking, rather than for use directly over fires.

The appearance of stone bowls is associated with what has been called the **container revolution** (Smith 1986). The first pottery in the Eastern Woodlands began to be manufactured during the Late Archaic in the Southeast at approximately 4500 BP. This fiber-tempered pottery is found in the Atlantic Coastal Plain and in Florida, and will be discussed in the next chapter. However, another early center of fiber-tempered pottery production lies along the middle Tennessee River in northern Alabama. This pottery is known as Wheeler ware. Some scholars have argued that changes in subsistence practices as discussed shortly required new food preparation techniques using bowls. Others have pointed out that both soapstone and pottery vessels may have been used in exchange networks and alliances as symbols of ethnic identity (Sassaman 1993, 1997).

Subsistence, Settlement, and Sedentism

Archaeologists working in the interior Eastern Woodlands have generated a wealth of faunal and floral data relevant to questions about subsistence and settlement change during the Archaic period (e.g., Simon 2009; Styles and McMillan 2009). During the Early Archaic and Middle Archaic, people apparently subsisted on a variety of resources and moved in small groups from campsite to campsite.

In fact, the relative diversity of plants and animals utilized in the Early Archaic is of particular interest. The faunal evidence from several Early Archaic sites (Styles and Klippel 1996; Styles and McMillan 2009) indicates that people were not focused on a few large-game resources; rather, they were generalized foragers who utilized a variety of animal resources. In the Middle Archaic, a narrowing of the faunal species being exploited indicates that people began to focus on procuring deer and fish. Similarly, at the Koster site in the Illinois River valley (see Student CD, Bonus Case Study D.2), Early Archaic faunal assemblages suggest

FIGURE 11.6 Carved bone pins from the Black Earth site in southern Illinois.

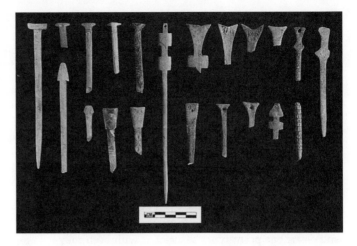

resource diversity, with shellfish, fish, birds, and mammals all being present. Small mammals like tree squirrels are surprisingly important as well. Later in the Middle Archaic, deer, shellfish, and fish predominate, suggesting more focal strategies as time went on (Neusius 1986b).

Some change in animal usage during the Middle Archaic may be attributable to warmer and drier climatic conditions associated with the opening of the forest canopy during the Hypsithermal, which would have favored edge-loving species like deer. At Dust Cave in northern Alabama, aquatic species become less significant during the Middle Archaic at the peak of the Hypsithermal, while edge-loving species such as deer, fox, rabbit, and skunk become more important (see Student CD, Bonus Case Study D.6). Subsistence change also may be associated with more logistical hunting and gathering as population levels increased.

Beginning as early as 7000 BP and continuing in the Late Archaic, greater usage of freshwater mussels and marine shellfish is reflected in the wide variety of shell mounds and rings throughout the East (Claassen 1996; Marquardt 2010; Marquardt and Watson 1983, 2005; Styles 1986). Besides shell mound sites along the coasts, discussed in Chapter 12, sites with large quantities of mussel shell cluster on the Tennessee River in Tennessee and Alabama, in the Nashville Basin, along the Green River in Kentucky, and along the Wabash River valley, although they are found throughout the areas covered in this chapter. The term **Shell Mound Archaic** has been applied to these sites. The best explanation for heavier use of mussels at this time is not that Archaic foragers had just discovered their edibility since some mussels have been found in earlier Archaic components. Instead, as rivers matured from fast-flowing, down-cutting streams to the more stable, slow-moving,

and meandering rivers we know today, habitats for large mussel beds became more frequent, and this resource increased in abundance and ease of exploitation. Of course, other aquatic fauna such as fish also were affected by these changes in the rivers, and their remains also are abundant in Archaic sites where flotation has been done.

However, as more data are gathered it has become clear that there was not one evolutionary trajectory of Archaic animal use, but regional variation that can be attributed to environmental conditions, mobility, demography, and other social factors. In addition, individual site records may not conform even to regional patterns. For example, the Hayes site in central Tennessee provides a particularly interesting Middle Archaic faunal assemblage. Deer, primarily procured in the fall, dominates the assemblage, with fish and aquatic turtles also being represented; the site, however, is a shell midden made up primarily of gastropods or snails rather than freshwater mussels. The researchers at this site believe the gastropods were collected as a food resource (Klippel and Morey 1986).

The primary Archaic plant foods for the interior Eastern Woodlands were nuts, including hickory nuts, acorns, pecans, walnuts, and to a lesser extent hazelnuts, chestnuts, butternuts, and beechnuts. These different types of nuts have varying nutritional compositions as well as collection, processing and storage requirements although they all mature in the fall (Scarry 2003). Other plant foods used by Archaic people were fleshy fruits, grains or seeds, wild beans, roots and tubers, and greens. There was both temporal and subregional variation in plant use during the Archaic. For example, seeds seem to have been less important in the diet during the Early Archaic than later, although people did eat fleshy fruits and greens when available

(Gremillion 1996, 2004; Simon 2009). It is important to note that differential preservation of relatively dense nutshell as opposed to other plant foods could be producing a biased picture of what resources were used.

Related topics of great interest to archaeologists have been population growth, settlement organization, and the development of sedentism during the Archaic. Simple counting of known site components suggests fairly stable population levels during the Early and Middle Archaic, with considerable population growth during the Late Archaic. This is a problematic way to measure population growth because it doesn't consider variation in site recording due to differential burial of old land surfaces or differences in site size. However, most archaeologists accept that human population levels were much larger at the end of the Archaic than at its beginning.

Early Archaic hunter-gatherers are believed to have lived in fairly small residential groups that moved frequently, camping in both upland and river valley locations. One common model for Early Archaic foragers is that they were organized into bands of closely related people that seasonally coalesced into **macrobands**. People who were part of a single macroband are thought to have foraged within a territory, such as a segment of a river valley. Beginning in the Middle Archaic, in areas where resources were abundant such as the major river valleys, this pattern of residential mobility may have given way to a strategy of logistical foraging from a base camp. Such base camps are even more common in the Late Archaic. Multi-seasonal villages may have been established, allowing collecting parties to go out to acquire specific resources, like deer. Among other things, the establishment of larger and more permanent settlements meant significant human modification of the surrounding habitats. However, living in larger, more permanent groups also meant a more complicated social environment. Some archaeologists argue that hints of the complex social systems of the Woodland period can be found in group integration within Middle and Late Archaic societies, although the evolutionary significance of this finding has been debated (e.g., Brown 1985; Sassaman 2005).

Perhaps the most important finding about Archaic Period subsistence has to do with the development of plant **domestication**, a topic that has international significance in the field of anthropology, as noted in Chapter 2. Although researchers are still piecing together the story, paleoethnobotanical studies of remains recovered through flotation (Chapman and Watson 1993) have established that the cultivation of domesticated plants began among the foragers of the Eastern Woodlands during the Archaic. This was not the cultivation of maize, beans, and squash that was so important to many Native Americans at European contact, but the cultivation of gourds and several weedy seed plants sometimes called the **Eastern Agricultural complex**. It has been proposed that the process of control and manipulation of these seed plants began in the Middle Archaic as the river valleys of the midcontinent were transformed into resource-rich locales (Smith 1992a). As the floodplains of these rivers matured, the floodplain habitat became more important to Archaic people. Repeated reuse of this habitat year after year may have created the kind of anthropogenic habitat favoring weedy seed plants that can rapidly colonize disturbed areas. In turn, these are precisely the plants that were eventually cultivated and domesticated. In upland areas, opening the forest canopy to promote nut production might also have favored the disturbed environment in which weedy seed plants thrive (Gardner 1997). It is likely that the first steps toward food production came about in different ways in different regions (Gremillion 1996).

Archaic people apparently were growing squash or gourds of the species *Cucurbita pepo* during the Middle Archaic. Rind fragments dated to at least 7000 BP have been found at the Koster site and at the Napoleon Hollow site in the lower Illinois River valley, and specimens dating to more than 5700 BP have come from the Carlston Annis site on the Green River in Kentucky. Other early squash specimens come from Pennsylvania and Michigan (Simon 2009), where they can be interpreted as evidence of human propagation because they are outside the currently known distribution of native wild gourds. Most archaeologists discount the possibility that the distribution of these native gourds used to be much greater than it is today (Decker-Walters 1993), in which case these finds would not represent human intervention. By the Late Archaic, however, remains of squashes with thickened rind and large seeds clearly indicate domestication of this type of squash. See the case study by John P. Hart, "A New History of Maize-Bean-Squash Agriculture in the Northeast," in Chapter 12 for more discussion of early cultivation of gourds and other squashes.

Archaic foragers domesticated three other weedy seed plants that naturally colonize disturbed environments. These domesticates were sumpweed or marshelder (Figure 11.7), goosefoot or chenopodium, and sunflower. At least two additional weedy seed plants, little barley and erect knotweed, probably were not truly domesticated during the Late Archaic. Maygrass is an additional plant associated with this complex that does not appear to have been domesticated in the Archaic. The seeds of these native plants provided starches and oils in amounts that could have had dietary significance. These seeds may have been cooked in gruels or

FIGURE 11.7 Maygrass (*Phalaris caroliniana*) on the left is a native seed plant associated with the Eastern Agricultural Complex while marshelder or sumpweed (*Iva annua*) on the right was one of the first seed plants to be domesticated.

porridges in the pots and bowls people were beginning to make by the end of the Archaic. The process of domestication probably took place primarily in the Midwest and Midsouth, and people in other parts of the Eastern Woodlands did not participate in this developing pre-maize Eastern Agricultural complex (Fritz 1990). Even where Archaic peoples did adopt plant cultivation, hunting, fishing, and collecting of wild plants remained significant economic activities. Heavier reliance on food production did not develop for another millennium (Fritz 1990; Smith 1992b).

Trade, Mound Building, and Mortuary Treatments

It is also clear that significant exchange networks were established during the Archaic. Archaeologists have long known that exchange sometimes was taking place over great distances during the Late Archaic. However, more recently archaeologists have realized that there also are examples of long-distance movement of commodities during the Middle Archaic and even the Early Archaic. Notably, marine shell beads from the common Atlantic *Marginella* snail have been reported from Early Archaic levels dating between 7000 BP and 8000 BP at the Modoc Rock Shelter in Illinois (Ahler 1991).

Stone for bannerstones may have been occasionally exchanged during the Middle Archaic (Anderson and Sassaman 2004. A Middle Archaic exchange network, sometimes called the Benton Interaction Sphere, also has been documented in the Midsouth along the Tennessee River in northeastern Mississippi and northwestern Alabama. Various preforms and points, including oversized Benton points and turkey-tails made of distinctive Fort Payne chert, which is found in

cobbles in this area, have been found in caches as well as in mortuary contexts in this area (Johnson and Brookes 1989). Another example is found in the Middle to Late Archaic base camps, including **Helton phase** components at the Koster site (Cook 1976a) and Middle Archaic zones at the Black Earth site in southern Illinois (Jefferies and Lynch 1983). First, nonlocal raw materials, notably copper and galena, are found. Second, carved bone pins (see Figure 11.6) in various shapes have been decorated far beyond functional necessity. These pins are so similar among sites that their use as symbols within a broad intergroup social network seems probable. It may be that less mobility during the Middle Archaic required Archaic groups to establish some means of intergroup cooperation, and that trade and exchange provided that means (Brown 1985).

A Midwestern mortuary complex, perhaps related to the Benton exchange in the Midsouth as well as to other mortuary complexes from the Great Lakes discussed in Chapter 12, is the **Red Ocher Mortuary complex.** This complex is evident in the use of red ocher, a crumbly iron oxide, in the burials. Red Ocher burials and cremations are found in Illinois and western Indiana, Ohio, and Michigan. Bodies were placed in low artificial mounds along with large amounts of red ocher, cache blades, and distinctive turkey-tail points (Figure 11.8). Turkey-tail blades or points often were made out of a high-quality bluish chert, called Harrison County chert, found in southern Indiana. Red Ocher burials also may continue into the Early Woodland period based on the presence of pottery in some mounds (Esarey 1986).

Exchange is even better documented for the Late Archaic. For example, recovery of copper, exotic stone, and marine shell from Shell Mound Archaic burials at the Indian Knoll site in Kentucky has led to several analyses of long-distance exchange (e.g., Jefferies 1995b; Rothschild 1979; Winters 1968). Evidence for exchange of stone is also found at Poverty Point in northeast Louisiana. Thousands of tiny, highly polished stone beads, pendants, plummets, and effigies have been found, as well as a variety of stoneworking tools (Figure 11.9). Because local stone was lacking, Poverty Point people imported argillite, chert, slate, copper, galena, jasper, quartzite, sandstone, hematite, and steatite from the Appalachian Mountains, the Piedmont, the Rocky Mountains, the Ouachita Mountains, and the Great Lakes. Although it is not clear what was traded in return—perhaps perishable items—tons of rock seem to have been imported. Some of the rock was preliminarily shaped into bifaces or other standardized forms before importation, while steatite seems to have arrived already in bowl form.

As suggested in these examples the exchange of exotic materials, as well as oversized and finely crafted objects in Middle and Late Archaic contexts often

FIGURE 11.8 Examples of turkey-tail points found in Red Ocher burials.

FIGURE 11.9 Distinctive carved stone items and lapidary raw materials from the Poverty Point site.

seems to correspond to new mortuary behaviors as well as, in some places, to the construction of mounds and earthworks. During the Middle and Late Archaic formal cemeteries became common (Charles 1995). Prior to the Middle Archaic, individuals often were buried within sites. These cemeteries may imply that human populations were territorial and organized into clans. Members of these groups are believed to have used the symbols of burial to mark group membership and the cemeteries themselves to mark social boundaries (Charles and Buikstra 1983).

Elsewhere people began to construct mounds and earthworks at this time. We have already mentioned

the shift to the use of shellfish that is evident in the Shell Mound Archaic and coincident coastal shell mounds and rings. Some early shell mound sites like the Eva site in Tennessee (Lewis and Lewis 1961) and those located along the Green River in Kentucky usually are considered to represent longer-term settlements where significant middens of shell accumulated over time. Nevertheless these shell mounds may contain human burials that include burial goods such as bannerstones and marine shell beads (Claassen 1996). Rather than being simple midden features, some shell mounds and shell rings, particularly those on the coast that will be discussed in more detail in Chapter 12,

FIGURE 11.10 Students from Indiana University of Pennsylvania walking down Mound A at Watson Brake along the earthen ridge that connects mounds at this site.

may have been constructed features placed over cemeteries (Russo 1994, 1996).

There also is a growing body of evidence for earthen mounds in the lower Mississippi valley in Louisiana, where a number of mounds and mound complexes have been assigned to the Middle Archaic. For example, in northeast Louisiana, one early site is Watson Brake on the Ouachita River (Saunders et al. 1994, 2005). Here 11 mounds encircle a central area more than 300 meters (330 yds.) wide. A low ridge of alternating midden and mound fill connects the mounds, the largest of which, Mound A, is over 7 meters (23 ft.) tall (Figure 11.10). Radiocarbon dates from this site indicate that people built these mounds between 5450 BP and 4850 BP. Clay cooking objects in various shapes, **fire-cracked rock (FCR)**, and other artifactual debris suggest that people lived on these mounds, but the lack of debris in the center may mean that the area served as ritual space.

The Poverty Point site, located on Macon Ridge in northeast Louisiana, is a somewhat later example of early earthwork and mound building. Here large, concentric, C-shaped earthen ridges were built, separated from each other by ditches and in association with several mounds (see Student CD, Bonus Issues and Debates F.6, "Ridges, Isles, and the Map of Poverty Point"). Even today, after plowing has seriously reduced the ridges in height, the size of Poverty Point impresses the visitor (Gibson 2000:219). The indications of exchange at this site also are impressive, as mentioned earlier. Artifact inventories include microliths made from prepared pebble cores and clay cooking balls called Poverty Point objects (PPOs). The people of the **Poverty Point tradition** built earthworks and mounds while supporting themselves by hunting, fishing, and gathering. Many other sites are attributed to this culture, which has dates spanning the Late Archaic to the Early Woodland (ca. 3700–2500 BP).

Evidence for exchange, elaborate mortuary behavior, and monumental constructions dating to the Middle as well as the Late Archaic indicate that Archaic societies should not be viewed as uniformly organized into simple, mobile bands of closely related people foraging for resources. Instead we should recognize that in some areas people were organized tribally with some level of integration above the family level, having leaders who could organize group efforts and interactions with nonlocal groups. Another indication that some Archaic groups were tribal is the unmistakable evidence for intergroup violence in a few sites. For example, in the Green River Archaic there is evidence for decapitation, scalping, and limb dismemberment, as well as examples of stone or antler projectile points embedded in bone (Mensforth 2001). It is not clear whether the higher population levels and perhaps greater degree of group aggregation were factors in the apparent onset of intergroup violence.

Thus, we have to conclude that while Archaic societies may not have been hierarchical, their social relations were more complicated and varied than we once thought (Anderson 2004). Moreover, developments once thought to have been associated with Woodland societies, such as pottery, settled villages, farming, and mound building, all first occurred during the Archaic.

WOODLAND MOUND BUILDERS

In introducing the term "Woodland" in Chapter 10, we noted that Woodland developments on the Plains may represent contact with the peoples of the Eastern Woodlands whose lifestyles were characterized by farming and pottery making as well as by the construction of permanent settlements and burial mounds. As with the Archaic, the Woodland is now treated as a period of time beginning everywhere in the Eastern Woodlands around 3000 BP.

The less mobile lifestyle, the domestication of native seed plants, the manufacture of pottery, and the mound-building and mortuary behavior now known from some parts of the Eastern Woodlands during the Middle and Late Archaic all belie abrupt change at the Archaic–Woodland boundary. Note that the Poverty Point tradition is usually considered Late Archaic but spans the Archaic/Woodland boundary temporally. Nevertheless, the Woodland is the period in which these and other traits become widespread. At this time the peoples of the Eastern Woodlands were generally living in at least seasonally settled camps or villages and often grew some crops, although they engaged in hunting, fishing, and gathering as well. Local groups had some interaction with people elsewhere through trade in raw materials and finished items. Mortuary ceremonialism often was associated with mound building. Archaeologists once assumed that various Woodland mound-building groups were organized hierarchically into simple chiefdoms, but at present a model of tribal organization in which membership in kin groups such as clans and lineages was of importance seems more likely. Nevertheless, there is some distinction in burial treatments suggesting variation in status.

The Woodland is typically divided into Early, Middle, and Late Woodland subperiods throughout the Eastern Woodlands. In this chapter, we date the Early Woodland from approximately 3000 BP to 2200 BP and the Middle Woodland from approximately 2200 BP to 1450 BP (Table 11.1). During the Early and Middle Woodland, in addition to the wide acceptance of ceramic technology, horticulture may grow in importance, and mortuary ceremonialism, long-distance interaction networks, and mound building increase in frequency. Specific mound-building cultures including the Early Woodland **Adena** of the upper Ohio River valley and the Middle Woodland **Hopewell** of Ohio and Illinois are the best-known Woodland cultures. However, other mound-building groups, which variously demonstrate Hopewell influence, are known as well.

We date the Late Woodland between 1450 BP and 950 BP. Although once considered an insignificant interlude following the end of Hopewell interactions, this was an important time. In many places in the interior East Late Woodland, change foreshadows the agricultural intensification, settlement in town centers, and development of social hierarchies associated with the Mississippian era (Anderson and Mainfort 2002).

Early and Middle Woodland Material Culture

A major change at the Archaic Woodland boundary is from pottery being made in a few distinct centers to the general adoption of this technology throughout the Eastern Woodlands. Pottery becomes widespread through the Southeast by 2800 BP (Sassaman and Anderson 2004). Farther north pottery manufacture began in the Upper Ohio drainage and moved northward and westward. It was widespread after 3000 BP. One route of entry of ceramic technology into the Midwest probably was down the Tennessee valley into northern Kentucky and southern Illinois. Pottery vessels are efficient containers for direct heating and cooking (Sassaman 2002). Perhaps their widespread appearance coincided with the development of new techniques for cooking native seeds.

Early and Middle Woodland pottery generally was made by coiling. Vessel walls became thinner as the ceramic technology developed. Temper was variously sand, grog, grit, or limestone and became finer over time, while vessel shapes became more variable. Most notably, a wide variety of decorative treatments were introduced including both exterior and interior cord-marking, fabric impressing, as well as incising, punctating, dentate and other stamping, and various zoned motifs. Archaeologists who study ceramic assemblages also note variations in lip shape and treatment.

Variety in surface treatment, morphology, and paste has led to the recognition of a large number of regionally restricted pottery traditions. One example is the **Crab Orchard tradition** (Figure 11.11), which is found from the Early Woodland into the Middle Woodland in southern Illinois, western Kentucky, and adjacent areas. This is a distinct tradition of fabric-impressed, often flat-bottomed pottery (Butler and Jefferies 1986). On the other hand, the various Hopewell wares, very finely made and decorated ceramics that are found in sites associated with Middle Woodland Hopewell exchange and ceremonialism, are widely distributed. For example, similar design motifs to those found on the pot shown in Figure 11.12 are found in ceramics as far away as the Marksville site in Louisiana (Kidder 2002b).

Early and Middle Woodland projectile point forms vary considerably (Figure 11.13), but a few generalizations can be made. Various types of stemmed points characterize the Early Woodland. Adena points, a type associated with the Adena moundbuilders of the Upper Ohio valley, have been found as far south

FIGURE 11.11 These fragments of Crab Orchard tradition vessels found in Southern Illinois show the characteristic flat bottoms of this tradition.

FIGURE 11.12 Hopewell pot from west central Illinois; note bird design.

FIGURE 11.13 Early and Middle Woodland projectile points forms from the Eastern Woodlands.

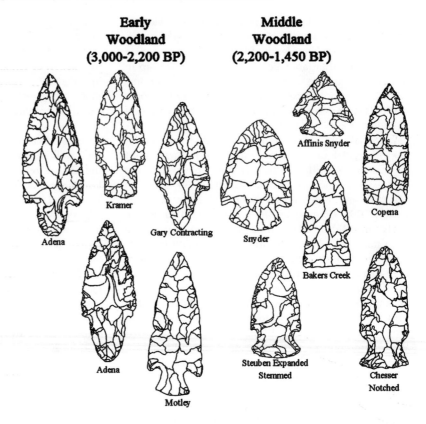

Early Woodland (3,000–2,200 BP)

Adena

Kramer

Gary Contracting

Adena

Motley

Middle Woodland (2,200–1,450 BP)

Affinis Snyder

Snyder

Copena

Bakers Creek

Steuben Expanded Stemmed

Chesser Notched

as northern Florida, but they usually are not found in the lower Mississippi valley. Middle Woodland points include trianguloid forms, expanded-stemmed lanceolate points, small thick points called spikes, and the distinctive, broad-bladed Snyders point, which is found widely in the interior East (Justice 1987).

Other aspects of lithic assemblages may be important indicators of the Middle Woodland. Both the presence of blades and high proportions of nonlocal stone are common on sites whose residents may have participated in Hopewell exchange. Studies have shown that these blades were used for a variety of domestic and ceremonial purposes (Odell 1994). Perhaps even more interesting is the wide variety of raw materials found in Middle Woodland lithic assemblages. Some of these materials have come great distances. For example, obsidian from Yellowstone was brought to Ohio during Middle Woodland times. Although it has been argued that the entire stock was transported in a single journey (de Boer 2004; Griffin et al. 1969), recent compositional analyses suggest several source quarries and alternative scenarios of transport (Hughes 2006). Cherts were often **heat treated** to improve their flaking properties as well. It appears that lithic manufacturing was very important to Middle Woodland people. For example, at the Fant site, a **Marksville**

phase site in the Yazoo Basin of northern Mississippi, more than 50 percent of the stone was nonlocal. Included were cherts from west central and southern Illinois, novaculite and quartz from the Ouachita Mountains of central and southern Arkansas, as well as a biface possibly made from Knife River flint from the Dakotas. Over 200 blades recovered from this site were made out of nonlocal Illinois cherts (Johnson and Hayes 1995).

Other items of material culture can be related to both domestic activities and ceremonial life. Utilitarian objects include many bone tools such as flakers and awls as well as lithic items such as drills and knives. Stone, shell, and copper **gorgets**, ceramic and stone smoking pipes, and finely made ground stone tools often are recovered in mortuary or other ritual contexts as we discuss later.

Subsistence and Settlement in the Early and Middle Woodland

Early Woodland lifestyles have sometimes been characterized as Archaic adaptations with pottery. However, in major river valleys where the Late Archaic archaeological record suggests large aggregated and sedentary settlements, the Early Woodland seems to represent more of breakdown in cultural patterns that developed at the end of the Archaic. In most places, people seem to have hunted, gathered, and fished, moving frequently between small encampments. Terrestrial fauna of importance include white-tailed deer, rabbit, raccoon, squirrel, and wild turkey, while fish, freshwater mussels, and other aquatic fauna were exploited as well. Exploitation of wild plants, including nuts, greens, and fruits, continued while native seed plants also are known from a number of sites in the Southeast. Major caches of seeds have been found in rockshelters in the Ozarks of northwestern Arkansas and in eastern Kentucky (Fritz 1993). At Salts Cave in Kentucky, an estimated 74 percent of the diet is attributable to cultivated and domesticated native plants during the Early Woodland (Yarnell 1974), but such an indication of heavy reliance on native cultigens has not been as clear elsewhere.

The role of plant cultivation also may have varied within the Middle Woodland, but a trend toward heavier use of native crops is well documented. In some contexts high percentages of native seeds seem to characterize the Middle though not the Early Woodland (Fritz 1993). Noting this, Bruce Smith (1992b, 1994) argued that pre-maize food-producing economies based on multiple cropping of native domesticates emerged at the onset of the Middle Woodland throughout the Eastern Woodlands. Wymer (1997) characterizes **Ohio Hopewell** populations as farmers growing native cultigens, while Yerkes (2006) believes native cultigens were simply additional resources incorporated into the seasonal foraging of people who remained hunter-gatherers. Thus, archaeologists do not agree about the actual dependence on food crops of Middle Woodland people (Wymer 1996). There also was variation within the Eastern Woodlands as to how developed pre-maize farming of native plants actually was (Gremillion 2002; Smith 1992a). Although maize was present by Middle Woodland times, it was only a minor food resource or a ceremonially important plant. The oldest directly dated maize from the Eastern Woodlands, at 2077 ±70 BP, is from the Holding site in Illinois (Riley et al. 1994). Maize is sometimes found in floral assemblages from other Middle Woodland sites, such as in the Middle Woodland component at Icehouse Bottom in east Tennessee (Chapman and Crites 1987). Even though some maize was grown, maize agriculture was not adopted at this time (see Chapter 12's case study, "A New History of Maize-Bean-Squash Agriculture in the Northeast").

Settlement variability also is evident. While most Early and Middle Woodland people may have persisted in millennia-old lifeways, living in small, seasonally mobile, egalitarian groups, large communities and centers developed in some areas. The character of settlements associated with the post-2500 BP Adena and Hopewell is much debated. The traditional assumption is that Woodland trade, mound building, and production of ritual items must have been associated both with agriculture and with human populations aggregated into large, sedentary villages. Minimally, such aggregated settlements would have provided the labor needed for construction projects and could have been organized to accomplish the variety of economic, craft, and ritual activities suggested by the archaeological record. However, evidence to support these assumptions has been lacking especially in Ohio where small hamlets are the principal type of settlement.

Recently, archaeologists working with Ohio Hopewell materials have been reconsidering a model known as the **vacant center model** (Prufer 1964), which considers mounds and earthworks as centers of seasonal or occasional ceremonial activities conducted by communities of dispersed farmers. Archaeologists have found a preponderance of small hamlets and extractive camps rather than large, aggregated communities. Some domestic refuse has been found at large earthwork centers, but much of this seems to be related to craft production or to suggest only short-term occupancy (Dancey and Pacheco 1997). Although this model is being explored primarily for Ohio Hopewell groups, it could also apply more generally to what happened in the Early and Middle Woodland (Smith 1992a). As populations came to focus more on the cultivation of floodplain plants and on other floodplain resources, they may have most often dispersed into family groups, living in small agricultural hamlets. However, the evidence on **Illinois Hopewell** settlement is ambiguous, suggesting a fairly substantial population and sites of several types in the Illinois valley. For example, the large Napoleon Hollow site (Wiant and McGimsey 1986) associated with the Elizabeth Mound group apparently was a **mortuary encampment** rather than a village, while the Apple Creek site (e.g., Struever 1968c) had a domestic orientation.

Early and Middle Woodland Mound Building, Ceremonial Life, and Interaction

The construction of mounds and earthworks is an important pan-Eastern cultural phenomenon from the end of the Archaic until the time of European contact. However, a large proportion of the known constructions can be dated to the Early and Middle Woodland. Much of this activity obviously had to do with burial of the dead, but since mounds and earthworks do not always contain burials, it is also obvious that earthen constructions had other purposes and significance. It seems clear that these constructions of earth were means of marking group identity, if only to establish where certain social groups, like clans or lineages, buried their dead. However, the elaborate layout of many mound and earthwork complexes, some of which seem to correlate with astronomical phenomena, suggest religious or ceremonial activities that would have served to integrate social groups. Both mortuary rituals and feasting (Knight 2001) probably were associated with the construction of mounds and earthworks, and there must have been symbolic meaning to these constructed landscapes that archaeologists can only begin to grasp (Brown 2006a; Lepper 2010). Understandably, archaeologists have many unanswered questions about the mound-building traditions of the Eastern Woodlands, and this is currently a very active area of archaeological research.

Between approximately 2500 BP and 2000 BP, the central and upper Ohio River valley was at the center of Adena mound building. Adena mounds are usually conical mounds of earth or stone, but their size varies, and they may or may not be surrounded by a ditch and embankment. The largest known Adena mound is the Grave Creek Mound located at Moundsville, West Virginia (Figure 11.14), which when first measured was nearly 70 feet (21 m) in height with a diameter of 295 feet (90 m) (Woodward and McDonald 2002). Beneath many Adena mounds archaeologists have found circular patterns of **postmolds**, indicating that one or more structures once stood there. Some of these structures, which are most likely mortuary facilities, may not have been roofed. Inside Adena mounds, the remains of large numbers of individuals sometimes were accumulated in repeated episodes of burial. The people used a variety of burial forms: extended burial in bark-lined pits and log tombs and cremations, performed soon after death, as well as **bundle burials**, in which decomposed remains were gathered together for secondary burial.

Adena mounds contain a diagnostic inventory of artifacts including Adena stemmed points, finely made cache blades, and Adena Plain pottery, which is grit- or limestone-tempered and relatively thin walled, plain surfaced, and undecorated. Perhaps more notable are a variety of eye-catching objects including ground stone axes and celts, pieces of hematite and barite, copper beads, bracelets, rings, and gorgets, as well as other gorgets and pendants and tubular stone and ceramic pipes. Elaborately carved stone tablets also are considered diagnostic of Adena (Figure 11.15). It is not clear whether Adena should be thought of as a separate culture or simply as a ceremonial complex and exchange system that transcended cultural boundaries.

Another example of an Early Woodland mound building complex is found in the **Tchula phase** of the lower Mississippi valley where small conical burial mounds were constructed in single episodes. Flexed or bundle burials in these mounds are thought to represent communal interments. Nevertheless, most Early Woodland burials seem to occur within villages and to consist of tightly flexed individuals placed in oval or circular burial pits along with a few grave goods.

As the third millennium BP waned, new ceremonial complexes are first apparent in Illinois and later in Ohio, where they are called Illinois and Ohio Hopewell after the Hopewell site located near Chillicothe, Ohio. It is unclear how Adena relates to Ohio Hopewell. The use of some Adena mounds seems to overlap in date with Hopewell phenomena (Cochran 1996).

The two main regional centers for Hopewell from the Midwest, Illinois and Ohio Hopewell, are both alike and different. Illinois Hopewell is known primarily from the Illinois River valley, where many burial mounds have been found on the bluffs and in the floodplain. The Gibson–Klunk mounds, located along the western bluff line of the Illinois River valley at

FIGURE 11.14 The Grave Creek Mound in Moundsville, West Virginia.

FIGURE 11.15 Carved stone tablets with elaborate designs such as these are considered diagnostic of Adena.

Kampsville, Illinois, have been particularly well studied (e.g., Braun 1979; Buikstra 1976). These mounds had central features, many of which the builders lined with logs, and grave goods including distinctive Hopewell artifacts were recovered in abundance. Although cremations were not common in these mounds, both primary burials and secondary burials of remains that had originally been buried elsewhere occurred in all parts of the mounds as well as beneath the mounds themselves. There is some status differentiation evident in the burials, but sex and age rather than heredity seem to be the primary determinants of burial treatment. Earthwork sites are rare in Illinois, but one is known from Golden Eagle, near where the Illinois River enters the Mississippi.

Ohio Hopewell sites often include both mounds and earthworks. Many Ohio mounds cover the remains of structures and contain massive quantities of artifacts. In fact, the largest quantities of Interaction Sphere objects are known from Ohio Hopewell sites. For example, a feature within one building beneath Mound 13 at Mound City, near Chillicothe, Ohio, was lined with sheets of mica and contained the cremated remains of several individuals. Besides burials and grave goods, drilled human crania and mandibles from some mounds have been interpreted as trophy skulls (Seeman 1988) or possibly relics of revered ancestors. The Ohio mounds vary in size and shape. Some mounds are loaf shaped, as the GE Mound apparently was; these may cover more than one structure

and represent a conjoining of two smaller mounds. At Marietta, along the Ohio River in southeastern Ohio, low platform mounds were constructed.

The massive geometric earthworks of the Ohio Hopewell are particularly famous structures. These earthworks are circular, square, or irregular in shape. Some encircle hilltops, many are associated with mounds, and some seem to border pathways or roads. Lepper (1996) believes that a long road once connected Chillicothe and Newark in Ohio, a distance of over 60 miles (90 km). The earthworks at Newark (Figure 11.16) are the largest known, but there are many other impressive constructions, like the Hopeton works, which is the focus of Mark Lynott's bonus case study, "The Hopeton Earthworks Project: Using New Technologies to Answer Old Questions" (Section D.7 on the Student CD). Hopewell people built these mounds with great precision and care, and we marvel at their skill. The snake effigy earthwork known as the Serpent Mound may be the best-known Ohio earthwork, but recent radiocarbon dating beneath the earthwork suggests that it may not have been built until long after Hopewell times.

DNA study is providing new insights into the composition of Hopewell communities. Bolnick and Smith (2007) recently have suggested that the Illinois Hopewell lived in **matrilocal residences** after marriage in which married couples resided with the woman's family. By comparing DNA from Illinois and Ohio Hopewell populations, they also found genetic

FIGURE 11.16 A portion of the Newark earthworks is part of a golf course today.

evidence for mating between regions, specifically for the migration of genes from Ohio to Illinois.

Participation in Woodland period interregional exchange and interaction is suggested by evidence from throughout the Eastern Woodlands. Struever (e.g., 1964) called this broad archaeological phenomenon the **Hopewell Interaction Sphere**, and this term has been widely used to describe evidence suggesting that many regional Middle Woodland traditions participated to some degree in exchange of Hopewell material culture. Artifacts and ecofacts commonly associated with Hopewell exchange include shark and alligator teeth, copper and pottery **earspools**, copper gorgets, panpipes and celts, obsidian artifacts, marine shell beads, cut sheets of mica, worked bear canines, plain and effigy **platform pipes**, pottery effigies, and Hopewell series pottery (Figure 11.17). These items often are found in burial contexts and in association with earthworks and mounds, suggesting common

ideology and leading some archaeologists to argue that Hopewell was a religious cult. Exhibit 11.1 discusses one common type of Hopewell artifact.

Although some Middle Woodland societies participated in these phenomena only in a peripheral way, there are many examples of Middle Woodland complexes suggesting Hopewell influence. Among these is the **Mann focus** represented by the GE Mound, which was a large Hopewell manifestation centered in southern Indiana. In the Southeast, the **Copena Mortuary complex** of the Tennessee River valley in northern Alabama includes about 50 burial mounds constructed over subsoil burial pits. Copena burial caves also are known (Crothers et al. 2002), and artifacts include copper reel-shaped gorgets, earspools, bracelets, celts, and beads as well as marine shell cups and beads, greenstone celts, ground galena nodules, and steatite elbow pipes (Walthall 1979). The Pinson Mounds site south of Jackson, Tennessee, is the largest

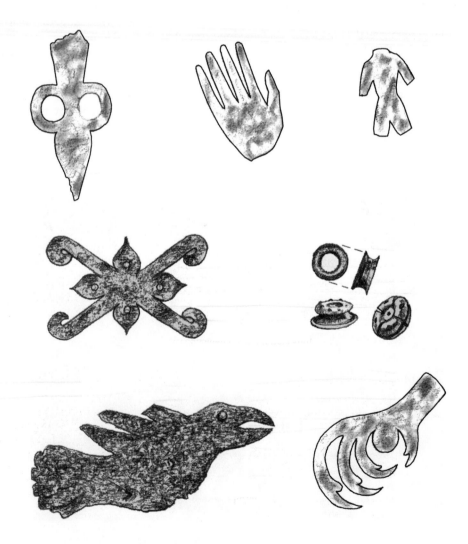

FIGURE 11.17 The Hopewell made ornaments of mica and copper in a variety of shapes as well as earspools of stone (right center).
(After Jennings 1989.)

CLUES TO THE PAST

Exhibit 11.1

Stone Platform Pipes

One diagnostic Hopewell artifact is the stone platform pipe. These pipe forms have a central bowl placed on top of a curved platform that extends to either side of the bowl. Several varieties of these pipes have been found, including ones in which the bowl is an effigy of an animal such as a bird, a bear, or a frog (Figure 11.18). These effigy pipes may be elaborately carved and finely polished; sometimes bits of copper or freshwater pearls have been set in the eyes of the effigy figures. Effigies usually faced the smoker. Other forms are spool-shaped bowls, rounded bowls, or V-shaped bases. Although these types are simpler, they also can be finely made (Figure 11.19). The platform itself contained a narrow hole for a stem, although platform pipes may have been smoked by placing the stone platform directly in the mouth rather than by adding a stem. Study of the distribution of these various types of platform pipe has suggested temporal variation in form within Hopewell (Seeman 1977). Platform pipes differ from the tubular pipes found in Adena contexts as well as from other earlier tubular and later elbow pipe forms. There also are later examples of platform pipes, but these usually differ from those found in Hopewell contexts by having flatter platforms and ridges on the platform (Gehlbach 1998).

Platform pipes were made of a variety of raw materials, but the most common material is appropriately known as Ohio pipestone. This stone is a soft buff, olive gray, or dark red limestone containing a good deal of iron. Pipestone outcrops in Ohio near the Scioto River, where many Ohio Hopewell sites are found. When originally mined, this stone is easy to work, but it hardens through exposure to air and through heating. Other raw materials were also used for pipes including sandstone, other limestone, slate, steatite, and quartzite.

The first step in making a stone pipe was to rough out the form through pecking with a hammerstone and abrading with sandstone. Partially shaped pipe blanks have been found by archaeologists, and some pipe specimens show striations from sandstone abrasion. The bowls and the smoke holes of these pipes were made with flint drills or reamers or with reeds or bone and a grinding agent like fine sand. Effigy pipes were carved with flint tools as well. This process was laborious and time-consuming. Pipes probably also were polished with the aid of animal oils and leather or fabric cloths.

Although these pipes are intriguing, they are reasonably rare in Hopewell sites, and more have been found in Ohio than in Illinois. They are nearly always found in burial as opposed to domestic contexts. Effigy platform pipes are even rarer, with only a few examples having been found outside of Ohio (Otto 1992). The largest numbers of known effigy platform pipes came from large caches of both effigy

FIGURE 11.18 Effigy platform pipes depicting various animals.

FIGURE 11.19 Plain bowl effigy pipes also tend to be finely made.

and plain platform pipes found below mounds at Mound City in Chillicothe, Ohio, and at the Tremper Mound in Scioto County, Ohio. These caches seem to have been adjacent to crematory features. Many of the pipes have been intentionally broken, a ritual practice akin to "killing" a pottery vessel by putting a hole in it.

The rarity of platform pipes and their association with burial mounds makes it clear that they were ceremonially significant items. The fact that many have been intentionally broken before burial suggests they were thought to have great power. Among Native Americans, what has been called the **smoking complex** is an important feature of ritual and ideology (Rafferty and Mann 2004; von Gernet 1992). Hopewell platform pipes certainly are linked to this complex, and the appearance of tobacco in archaeological contexts dating to the Middle Woodland is significant. Whatever else these pipes mean, they minimally indicate that smoking was a ritually important act in eastern North America nearly 2000 years ago.

Many interesting questions arise about how Hopewell societies, which are presumed to have been tribal in organization, might have produced such ritual items. In such societies full-time specialists are rare. Yet it seems obvious that even though there is variation in the quality of pipe fabrication, making these items took some artistic skill. Could anyone who was so inclined learn to make platform pipes, or were they considered so ritually powerful that only shamans or clan leaders could make or commission them? Were specialists partially supported by the lineages, or were they independent artists? Did individuals commission the making of platform pipes, perhaps to mark the status of an individual after death, or were they produced for lineages or other groups of people to use in corporate or group ritual? Finding pipes in individual burial contexts might suggest the former, while caches of pipes next to crematory features would support the latter interpretation. Archaeological investigations of the contexts of production need to be done to explore these questions (Spielmann 1998). Archaeologists also need to learn about the relationships between platform pipes and other Hopewell ritual items. These beautiful pipes, made with both technical and spiritual care great care, are of great interest to Hopewell researchers.

Middle Woodland site in the Southeast, covering approximately 400 acres (160 hectares). Saul's Mound, the tallest mound in the complex, is 72 feet (22 m) tall (see Figure 1.6), and many exotic and finely made grave goods suggesting Hopewell have been recovered from this site (Mainfort 1996).

A final example of Hopewell influence is found in the lower Mississippi valley where the long-standing local mound-building tradition continues between approximately 2150 BP and 1450 BP. Connections with Hopewell ceremonialism are obvious for the first half of this period, the Marksville phase, when mound building is most frequent. The Marksville site in Louisiana has a large C-shaped, segmented enclosure surrounding several platform and conical mounds and fronting on the bluff edge. This enclosure has a diameter of roughly 520 meters (570 yds.), but it is only one of several enclosures of mounds at the site. Mound 4 at Marksville had a mortuary platform with a central roofed vault, lined with matting. and containing the remains of several individuals. Marksville ceramics have iconography such as raptorial bird motifs, curvilinear designs, stamping, and U-shaped incisions that are like Hopewellian motifs from the Midwest. Blade tools, greenstone celts, boatstones, mica, galena, copper earspools, and plummets also are found in Marksville burials. After approximately 1750 BP, still in the Marksville Middle Woodland period, mound building becomes less frequent, ceramics are more often plain, and Hopewell exchange

items disappear. This **Issaquena phase** seems to last until Late Woodland times (ca. 1450 BP), but it is less obviously Hopewellian (Kidder 2002b).

Although Hopewell people in Ohio and Illinois were influencing people in other parts of the Eastern Woodlands, Middle Woodland phenomena arose as well from local roots. Archaeologists believe that local social imperatives were being met through trade and ritual; it does not seem that belief systems simply were being exported from the Midwestern heartlands.

The Late Woodland

The Late Woodland begins at approximately 1450 BP, when the production and exchange of Hopewell artifacts ceases and large earthwork complexes are no longer being built, and ends at 950 BP when in most of the interior Eastern Woodlands the Mississippian is evident. It is generally recognized that many Mississippian phenomena first developed at the end of the Late Woodland after around 1150 BP (AD 800), and particularly in the Midwest, an **Emergent Mississippian** period may be designated (Morse and Morse 1983). In this chapter, we have followed the more common practice of continuing Late Woodland until approximately 950 BP. Traditionally, archaeologists have understood the Late Woodland period as the time of the "**good gray cultures**" (Williams 1963). This designation reflects the idea that sandwiched between dramatic Hopewell and Mississippian developments the Late Woodland was a drab period of decline. However, during the past few decades, thanks in part to CRM-generated data, archaeologists have been rediscovering the Late Woodland as a period of variability and change. Far from being boring, Late Woodland societies may be important indicators of how and why the cultural developments of late pre-Columbian times took place (Emerson et al. 2000).

There were changes in material culture during the early Late Woodland. Ceramics were plainer than those made during the Middle Woodland; a common surface treatment was cord marking (Figure 11.20). Nevertheless, continuing earlier trends, vessel walls were thinner and temper particle size was smaller. These changes are consistent with the reduction of thermal shock, a necessary design concern if pots were being used to boil seeds (Braun 1983, 1986). The Late Woodland stone tool industry also is characterized by the disappearance of various exotic stone types as well as a reliance on utilized or minimally worked flakes rather than more formal tools for many tasks.

One Late Woodland development was the widespread adoption of the bow and arrow after 1250 BP (AD 700), marked by the predominance of small notched and unnotched triangular projectile points. These points often were made from flakes instead of directly from cores of stone. Although the bow and arrow may have been known earlier (Justice 1987), people were now making predominantly small points that archaeologists believe were arrow points. Because of its presumed efficiency as a hunting implement and as a weapon, this shift to the bow and arrow is significant. It is possible that this trend is associated with increases in population or with more nucleation of villages. There also is debate about the possible association of this change with an intensification of deer hunting and with increases in intergroup conflict and warfare (e.g., Blitz 1988; Nassaney and Pyle 1999). Examples of Late Woodland and Mississippian point types are shown in Figure 11.21.

With respect to settlement and subsistence, there seems to have been considerable variability in the changes associated with the Late Woodland. Both greater numbers of sites and larger site areas have been noted. Settlement pattern change was sometimes toward nucleation and at other times toward dispersal; no single pattern seems to have developed (Nassaney and Cobb 1991). For instance, in the Ohio valley above the Falls of the Ohio, archaeologists have found strong evidence for the nucleation of settlements, while in the lower Ohio and along the Illinois drainage, settlements may decrease in size as the Late Woodland begins. Complexes of stone walls and mounds often called "stone forts" first were made in southern Illinois and Kentucky at this time. These constructions, as well as

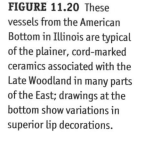

FIGURE 11.20 These vessels from the American Bottom in Illinois are typical of the plainer, cord-marked ceramics associated with the Late Woodland in many parts of the East; drawings at the bottom show variations in superior lip decorations.

the nucleated settlements in Ohio, which have moats and fortifications, may indicate defensive concerns. As we will discuss later, in the central Mississippi valley and in some parts of the Southeast, towns with mounds begin to appear at the end of Late Woodland.

Late Woodland people continued to make and use mounds during the Late Woodland. The **Intrusive Mound culture** of Ohio refers to people who often buried their dead in mounds constructed by earlier groups. Other groups, particularly in the Southeast, still were building new mounds as needed.

Some archaeologists suggest that higher population levels in the Late Woodland caused resource stress and the adoption of second-line resources like small mammals and shellfish (Jackson and Scott 2002; Peacock 2002). Intensification in the use of native seed plants as well as greater production of tropical cultigens like maize may have been a response to stress as well. However, the intensification of agricultural production was not uniform. Within the major Midwestern river valleys, archaeologists (e.g., Simon 2009; Styles and McMillan 2009) have documented intensification of the plant cultivation as evidenced by the widespread presence and large quantities of native seeds. People also used some corn and tobacco, as well as many aquatic resources, such as fish species that spawn in river backwaters. However, proportionately lower use of seed plants and greater reliance on white-tailed deer are evident in upland sites. Native seeds and eventually maize also became important to subsistence in the northern Southeast (Johannessen 1993). Nevertheless, in the southern Southeast, foraging and fishing persisted until the development of Mississippian economies.

FIGURE 11.21 Several varieties of Late Woodland and Mississippian points found in the Eastern Woodlands.

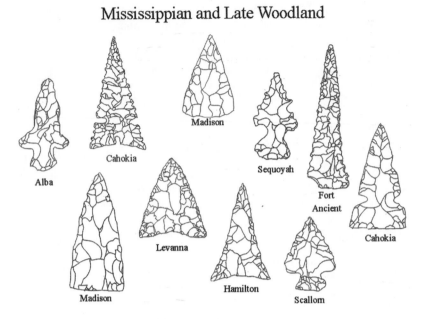

Mississippian and Late Woodland

Cahokia

Madison

Alba

Sequoyah

Fort Ancient

Levanna

Cahokia

Madison

Hamilton

Scallom

Because Late Woodland cultural phenomena defy generalization, it may be more productive to concentrate on local cultural sequences rather than broad evolutionary trajectories. One example that illustrates how the Mississippian transformation began comes from the central Mississippi River valley. Here the Late Woodland is considered to begin with the **Baytown period** (1650/1550–1250 BP), while the Terminal Late Woodland is called **Plum Bayou period** (1250–950 BP) (Rolingson and Mainfort 2002). Baytown ceramics were clay tempered and have either cord-marked or plain surface treatments, while people made several small notched, stemmed arrow points (Nassaney and Pyle 1999). Nuts and a small amount of native seeds have been found in botanical assemblages, and white-tailed deer and fish, smaller mammals, and reptiles make up faunal assemblages.

In the later Plum Bayou sites, **grog-tempered ceramics** were the most common, but bone- and shell-tempered wares also were made. Surfaces are usually plain, but people used a red slip, incised, and punctated pottery as well. Obvious arrow points including triangular Madison points were being made. Maize was a minor cultigen, while native seeds as well as nuts appear to have been significant plant foods. The diet was dominated by deer meat, but small mammals, turkey, the now-extinct **passenger pigeon**, fish, and turtles also were taken. Large towns suggestive of later Mississippian ones developed as well as mound centers. Toltec Mounds on the Arkansas River covers about 100 acres and has 18 mounds surrounded by an embankment and a ditch (Figure 11.22). Astronomical alignments apparently exist at this site. The largest mound at Toltec is about 50 feet (15 m) in height, but lower platform and burial mounds also were built there. Archaeologists recognize a hierarchy of site types for Plum Bayou including single household, multiple household, multiple household with a single mound, and centers consisting of multiple mounds (Rolingson 2002). Fragments of copper and conch shell indicating long-distance exchange also have been found in Plum Bayou sites. Although there is little evidence for powerful elites, many of the foregoing characteristics are similar to Emergent Mississippian traits to the north as well as to those of emerging polities in the lower Mississippi valley (Nassaney 1991).

In much of the Midwest, the end of the Late Woodland is marked by the widespread shift to maize agriculture during the eleventh century BP. This shift is evident both in the greater amount of maize found in sites and in changes in $^{12}C/^{13}C$ **ratio** found in human bone. Corn was present before this, but only in small amounts. What happened to make it so important in human subsistence? Apparently at some time between 1050 BP and 950 BP (AD 900–1000), perhaps in Ohio, a new variety of corn known as **Eastern Eight Row** or **Northern Flint corn** was developed. This maize variety apparently was hardier and more cold tolerant than earlier types of corn, which had ten or more rows of kernels per cob. While this type of corn successfully spread across the Great Lakes into Wisconsin during the tenth century BP, archaeobotanical studies also show that it was never important in the American Bottom (Fritz 1992; Simon 2000), where maize agriculture

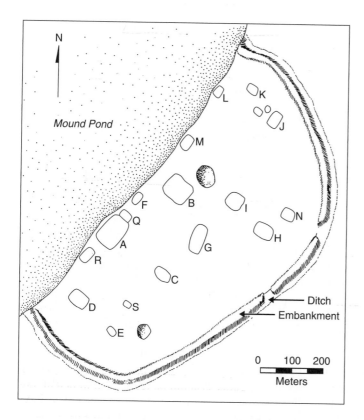

FIGURE 11.22 Plan of Toltec Mounds in Arkansas; note the embankment enclosing the mounds, which are indicated by letters and arranged in regular fashion around open areas or plazas.

first was adopted. Thus, just as there is diversity in Late Woodland adaptations, the development of Mississippian cultural phenomena cannot be attributed to the same factors everywhere.

MISSISSIPPIAN SOCIETIES

Between 1150 BP and 950 BP, cultures archaeologists call Mississippian began to develop in the major river valleys of the Southeast and southern Midwest. Mississippians were maize-bean-squash agriculturalists who also exploited fish, waterfowl, and wild plants. They were the first easterners to settle large permanent towns containing central plazas, public buildings, platform mounds, and encircling stockades. These towns, some of which were very large, apparently were centers for outlying agricultural hamlets and homesteads. Mississippians developed social hierarchies and chiefly political control, while maintaining large-scale production and long-distance exchange of raw materials and craft items. The quality of Mississippian craftsmanship is unparalleled north of Mexico. A major thematic issue in Mississippian archaeology is the nature and development of sociocultural complexity.

There is variability among societies considered Mississippian. Some of this variability is temporal,

some is regional, and some is local in scale. The emergence of Mississippian phenomena prior to 950 BP can be seen as an aspect of the terminal Late Woodland, but may be designated the Emergent Mississippian. Following this, Mississippian is divided into an Early Mississippian from 950 BP to 750 BP (AD 1000–1200), Middle Mississippian from 750 BP to 550 BP (AD 1200–1400), and Late Mississippian from 550 BP to 400 BP (AD 1400–1550). In some areas, Mississippian societies certainly persisted into the Protohistoric era. Other societies that more properly are considered Late Woodland or Late Prehistoric also existed in coastal and northern portions of the East, and these will be discussed in Chapter 12.

In general, the spread of maize agriculture and shell-tempered pottery occurred during the Early Mississippian, while complex chiefdoms linked by a shared ceremonial complex developed in several river valleys during the Middle Mississippian. Some archaeologists believe that long-standing Eastern Woodlands ideologies associated with membership in communities and lineages were replaced during Mississippian times with ideologies that elevated key individuals to positions of power. This would have meant a change from rituals honoring ancestors and establishing membership in a community to rituals reinforcing the power of chiefs who controlled agricultural surplus. It does appear that emphasis on public ritual and mound building declined even further in Late Mississippian time, while warfare and political turmoil increased. Many areas of the Midwest appear to have been abandoned by Mississippians during Late Mississippian times, although populations may have simply dispersed into the uplands, returning to older lifeways. Actual depopulation may have characterized the lower Ohio valley and adjacent areas of southern Illinois and northern Kentucky after approximately 500 BP (AD 1450) (Cobb and Butler 2002). This area has been called the **Vacant Quarter** (Williams 1980, 1990).

Mississippian Material Culture

The traditional ceramic marker of the Mississippian is shell-tempered pottery, but this type of temper wasn't used everywhere, and temper varies in some areas over time as well. Other tempers used by Mississippians include sand, grit, clay, and grog. People made a wide variety of vessel forms at this time: jars, bowls, pans, bottles, beakers and plates. Human and animal effigy vessels also became common in some areas, especially during the Late Mississippian (Figure 11.23). There was an expansion in decorative techniques such as slipping and painting as well as incising of vessels. Many Mississippian period ceramics were very finely made, but more utilitarian wares with coarser shell tempering are found as well. Finer ware types were more likely to have been decorated.

Mississippian projectile points are usually small triangular varieties, but small stemmed and side-notched points also were made, as was shown in Figure 11.21. Large hoes for cultivation purposes also were made by Mississippians, and raw materials used in their production were exchanged over some distance. For example, the Mill Creek chert of southern Illinois was used to make hoes and a variety of other items throughout the Mississippi River valley (Figure 11.24) (Cobb 2000). Many Mississippian lithic tools were simple flakes used expediently, though drills, long knife blades, and celts also were made. Nevertheless, there was a certain amount of standardization in the production of these flake tools. For example, Jay K. Johnson (1987) found that core technologies nearly identical to those identified at Cahokia in Illinois (see Box 11.1) were in use at the Carson Mound site, a site in northwestern Mississippi dating from Middle to Late Mississippian.

Ceremonially significant items, including marine shell beads and gorgets, stone palettes and figurines, copper plates, rattles, fans, and ground stone ceremonial axes, were placed in Mississippian mound and burial contexts. **Discoidals** also were made. In the Historic period, these disk-shaped stones were used in a game called **chunkey**: the stones were rolled along the ground, and players threw spears at them. These kinds of artifacts were symbols of prestige and wealth found in elite burial and ritual contexts. Besides being beautiful, they are strong evidence that Mississippian

FIGURE 11.23 Head pots similar to this one have been found in Mississippian sites.

FIGURE 11.24 Artifacts of Mill Creek chert from the central Mississippi Valley: object on the upper left is a mace; also shown are a stone sword, hoes of two varieties, and at lower left two hoe chips.

societies were ranked, and the iconography they exhibit provides important clues to beliefs.

Examination of several key artifact types as well as design motifs on artifacts from Mississippian sites particularly Cahokia in Illinois, Etowah in Georgia, Moundville in Alabama, and Spiro in Oklahoma, led archaeologists over 60 years ago to propose the **Southeastern Ceremonial complex** (Waring and Holder 1945). This complex, which is also called the **Southern Cult**, can be abbreviated as SECC. Design motifs identified included the cross, the sun circle, the bilobed arrow, the forked eye, the open eye, the barred oval, the hand and eye, and various death motifs. These designs were also found in association with various "god-animal beings" including birds, the rattlesnake, wild cats, and humans. These design elements often are combined in a single artifact (Figure 11.25). The interpretation of the SECC has been a subject of much research, discussion and debate, and important work has been done on defining styles as well as interpreting the origins and spread of these styles (Brown and Kelly 2000; King 2007).

Of course, more perishable items also were made by Mississippians. Some idea of their fabrics can be discerned from impressions in ceramics. For example, pans believed to have been used in salt reduction often have fabric-impressed surfaces (e.g., Kuttruff and Kuttruff 1996). Sometimes actual fabric is unearthed: in one burial context at Etowah in Georgia, pieces of fabric were recovered, having been preserved due to their association with copper. This fabric, which incorporated feathers, hair, yarn, and other fibers, might have been part of a garment of ceremonial significance (Sibley et al. 1996). Utilitarian bone tools such as awls and needles, as well as bone and shell ornaments, also are common.

Mississippian Households and Communities

Plaza-centered residential communities or towns with both mounds and domestic structures generally were not established until the Mississippian. Both the plazas aligned with and bounded by mounds and the platform mounds themselves are important aspects of these planned communities (Lewis et al. 1998). These plazas are not just open areas but at least in some instances constructions themselves. At Cahokia, for example, geophysical testing and coring indicates that the overlying clay deposits were stripped from the northern part of the great plaza, and then this area was reclaimed by deposits of midden mixed with clay (Dalan 1997).

Although also found in a few Middle Woodland sites (Jefferies 1994), one classic physical diagnostic for Mississippian sites is the presence of one or more platform mounds. These mounds are essentially flat-topped pyramidal structures of earth. While Woodland platforms were centers of activities but generally lacked substantial structures, Mississippian platform mounds usually served as substructures for the houses of the elite, charnel houses, council houses, sweat lodges, or other structures. Excavations into platform mounds often show that a series of buildings were used, burned, and covered in succession with layers of dirt chosen for color and composition (Figure 11.26).

One interesting Mississippian structure is the **woodhenge**, mentioned in Box 11.1. Several of these circles of large posts with possible solar alignments have been found at Cahokia. Another feature of importance in defining the Mississippian is the rectangular or square wall-trench house. It was a structure made by excavating narrow trenches and placing posts in these so-called wall trenches. Commonly, wattle-and-daub walls were then made by weaving cane between posts and plastering mud over it. Chunks of daub that were fired when houses burned are common on Mississippian sites. Structures of other types also have been identified on Mississippian sites; some were made by placing the posts in individually dug holes. House floors quite often were dug slightly into the ground, and the dirt from the excavation was mounded up along the sides of the walls. Earthlodges, known from sites in Georgia and eastern Tennessee, were circular structures that apparently were sod or earth covered, although whether these buildings were indeed completely covered with earth is unclear (Larson 1994).

Mississippian towns or at least their cores also often were bounded by stockades, palisades, and/or ditches. Compare the idealized Mississippian town plan in Figure 11.27 with the plan of the Hopeton earthworks at Newark, Ohio, shown in Bonus Case Study D.7, "The Hopeton Earthworks Project: Using New Technologies to Answer Old Questions" on the Student CD. The issue of town plan is an important subject, as exemplified by this chapter's case study by Lynne P. Sullivan, "Mouse Creek Phase Households

FIGURE 11.25 Engraved shell gorget from Spiro Mounds in Oklahoma showing multiple SECC design motifs.

FIGURE 11.26 Reconstruction of Mississippian structure wall standing inside a modern building that protects the exposed surfaces of Mound B at Wickliffe Mounds in Kentucky; note the posthole depressions on the surface of the mound and the mounds multiple layers painted on the walls of the modern building.

and Communities: Mississippian Period Towns in Southeastern Tennessee." Consult Section H of the Student CD for some of the Mississippian towns you can visit in person or on the web today.

The notion of a hierarchy of settlement types also has long been important to students of the Mississippian. The minimal unit of Mississippian society seems to have been the farmstead (e.g., Mehrer 1995; Rogers and Smith 1995). In Early and Middle Mississippian times, farmsteads often were dispersed in floodplains around towns, which in turn sometimes related to regional centers. In Late Mississippian times, settlements may have been more aggregated in response to intergroup conflict. Important research now focuses on the

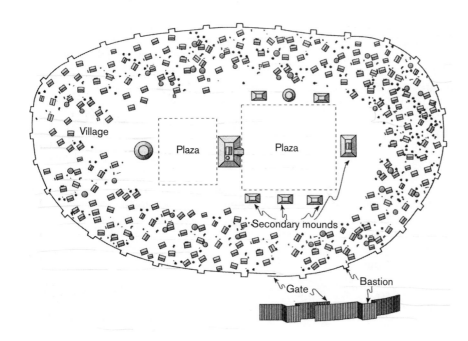

FIGURE 11.27 Idealized Mississippian town plan featuring platform mounds arranged around plazas and an enclosure encircling the houses.

relationships between political or ceremonial centers and outlying districts. Some of the largest Mississippian settlements certainly were important ceremonial and political venues. At Moundville in Alabama, one of the biggest known Mississippian sites in the Southeast, there is a large central plaza surrounded by platform and conical mounds (see Figure 2.17). Knight (1998) has argued that the plan of this site may represent a model of the social order of the chiefdom, with pairs of mounds representing different kin groups and their placement symbolizing the relative ranking of these kin groups within the polity. That is, elite kin groups might have located and constructed the monuments and burial mounds to reinforce their power and prestige.

Mississippian Subsistence and Economies

It has been argued that Mississippian populations were adapted to a specific meander belt habitat in the major river valleys of the Midwest and Southeast (Smith 1978). More recent investigators (e.g., Schoeninger and Schurr 1998) believe that Mississippian adaptations were more varied, both geographically and temporally. There is good evidence that maize was an important source of food for Mississippians. Squashes and gourds also were cultivated, as were the suite of native seed plants so important earlier. Beans are a second tropical food plant that was very important in native agriculture by the Historic period but apparently introduced only in the Late Mississippian period. At some sites, like Ocmulgee in Georgia, ridges and furrows in Mississippian fields have been found

(Riley 1994). Whether we call food production patterns at this time horticulture or agriculture, it is important not to forget that Mississippians also utilized a wide variety of wild plants and animals. White-tailed deer were very important, but so were raccoons, various species of fish, waterfowl, turkeys, several types of nuts (processed both for their meat and for their oil), wild seed plants, greens, fruits, and berries. Mississippian systems of production also involved the acquisition of raw materials to make houses, baskets, pottery, stone tools, and other implements. In addition, specialized items were produced for trade, exchange, and ritual.

There is considerable debate about how Mississippian economies actually worked. If we accept that social ranking and some form of chiefly control characterized these societies, the production and distribution of goods can be seen as important aspects of Mississippian systems. Analyses of the polity centered at Moundville in Alabama have suggested that Moundville residents were provisioned with food-stuffs from people living at smaller sites outside Moundville. Studies indicate that choice, meaty parts of deer were sent to Moundville from its outlying districts. There also seems to be evidence that craft items, often made of nonlocal raw materials, moved from Moundville to smaller settlements. For example, an area of manufacture for greenstone celts has been found at Moundville, and it is believed that these largely utilitarian items were passed out to people in outlying districts. Moundville also participated in exchange with other Southeasterners. The data show that nonlocal commodities including copper, greenstone, mica, graphite, and conch shell came from many places to Moundville. Prestige items may have been manufactured from imported materials at Moundville, or they may have arrived in completed form. Circular stone paint palettes, red slate pendants, and pottery probably were manufactured there and traded from Moundville to people outside this chiefdom (Welch 1991).

It may be that neither the provisioning of elite subsistence nor elite control of the production and exchange of prestige items suggested by this example applies elsewhere. Others have suggested that Mississippian craft production and exchange were much more decentralized (e.g., Muller 1997). For example, current evidence is that salt production occurred as a domestic activity rather than as specialist production (Muller 1986, 1997:308–332). In fact, most staple items, whether for food or raw materials, seem to have been produced in the Mississippian household by nonspecialists. Prestige goods may have been manufactured by specialists, but even at the largest sites, evidence for full-time craft specialists has been lacking (e.g., Yerkes 1983).

Recent studies have been exploring possible differences in the diets of elites and commoners in various Mississippian polities (e.g., Jackson and Scott 2003). For example, there is some evidence in faunal assemblages that elites residing in the central part of Cahokia were provisioned with deer from elsewhere. There also is some evidence that deer meat was redistributed along class lines once it had been brought to the site (e.g., Kelly 1997). Skeletal analyses have shown differences in health and diet between Mississippian elites and commoners. In eastern Tennessee, elite males, who may have had greater access to meat, seem to have been taller than male commoners and may have experienced less stress as children (Steponaitis 1986). Studies at Moundville and comparisons with several other Mississippian burial populations do not, however, indicate great differences in general health between elites and commoners (Powell 1992, 1998). It is possible that Mississippian elite used feasting to bolster their prestige, as part of a tribute system that redistributed food and products (Kelly 2001). The social context of food consumption also is important, and we may learn a great deal about Mississippian societies from the analysis of the remains of feasts as well as from domestic middens.

Mississippian Sociopolitical Systems

As the preceding discussion suggests, archaeologists generally have applied the concept of a chiefdom to Mississippian society. In this view, Mississippians lived in socially ranked societies headed by chiefs and divided into elite and commoner strata. Chiefs served as redistributors of surplus food and goods that resulted from high agricultural productivity, gaining wealth and power from this role. The larger the mound center and its apparent sphere of influence, the greater the degree of hierarchy and chiefly power envisioned (Cobb 2003).

Archaeologists have found evidence for the social differentiation expected in chiefdoms in several aspects of the Mississippian archaeological record including variation in site size, variation in house size, content and placement within sites, the presence or absence of high-quality prestige goods and exotic items, and differences in food refuse suggestive of dietary variation. One of the most productive areas of study focuses on contrasts in the treatment of the dead. For example, in Mississippian cemeteries, some individuals had greater quantities of imported materials and finely crafted objects (e.g., Goldstein 1980; Rothschild 1979), indicating probable status differences. Some Mississippian burials are in mounds and others in cemeteries or near house structures, and these different contexts may sometimes be related to whether an individual was male or female (Sullivan 2001). The richness of some mound burials is amazing, as suggested in the high-status burials from the Craig Mound at the Spiro site in eastern Oklahoma. This mound, a large saddle-shaped earthwork consisting of conjoined mounds, was partially destroyed by a famous episode of commercial looting in the 1930s (LaVere 2007). The "Great Mortuary" at the center of this mound contained a large collective burial with deposits of spectacular artifacts including copper axes, copper-covered reed baskets, ceremonial maces, large quantities of shell beads, many conch shell cups, and the wooden headdress shown in Figure 11.28 (James A. Brown 1996). Other Mississippian mortuary treatments include the secondary burial of bundles of bone in mounds and headless skeletons, some with pots at the top of the neck, such as were found at Dickson Mounds in central Illinois (see Box 14.2 for a discussion of Dickson Mounds). Initial interpretations of mortuary practices often confirmed the idea that Mississisppians were organized hierarchically and that status was ascribed or inherited at birth (e.g., Peebles and Kus 1977).

One example that is often cited as clear evidence of social hierarchy is the complex of burials contained in Mound 72 at Cahokia in Illinois (see Box 11.1). In this mound, some 260 individuals were buried in several groups. The most important burial appears to have been of an adult male who was placed on a bed of 20,000 shell beads arranged in the shape of a bird. Beneath the beads the remains of another man were found and other individuals are nearby. Burial elsewhere in the mound are no less interesting. Among these are the remains of four males whose hands and heads had been cut off, a pit containing the remains of approximately 50 young women between the ages of 18 and 25, and ten individuals placed on litters or stretchers made

FIGURE 11.28 Red cedar mask, from the Spiro site in Oklahoma, incorporating deer antlers and shell insets.

of cedar that overlie another mass burial of many individuals. Mound 72 also contained caches of projectile points, ground stone gaming disks, piles of mica, conch shells, copper sheets, and other high-value items (Fowler et al. 1999). These phenomena obviously can be interpreted as evidence of the elaborate burial rites of a paramount chief, who was buried with retainers. However, more recent analyses (Brown 2006b) have suggested that above all, the remains in Mound 72 are indicative of ritual activities, some of which may well have been communal renewal ceremonies rather than commemorations of a powerful leader.

In fact, archaeologists have begun to question the usefulness of the chiefdom model with its stress on hierarchy and political domination. This model has even come to be seen as preventing progress in understanding these societies (Pauketat 2007). Different Mississippian polities have been categorized in the literature as simple or as complex/paramount chiefdoms based on the number of hierarchical levels apparent, but new ways of looking at varying chiefdoms are also employed by archaeologists. For example, Beck (2003) maintained that rather than focus on the simple-complex dichotomy, it would be more useful to consider how power was ceded to chiefs because there are multiple ways that local communities become integrated at the regional level. Other archaeologists focus on a continuum that differentiates between political authority centered on individuals who hold prominent positions and have considerable power and wealth (**network leadership strategy**) and situations in which group solidarity rather than individual wealth and power is emphasized (**corporate leadership strategy**) (Blanton et al. 1996). In the latter case, societies are less centralized, leaders aren't necessarily wealthy because surplus is used in communal activities, and monuments, communal spaces, and ceremonies are important. Exploration of how specific Mississippian polities may fit into this kind

of conceptualization at different points in their history can be productive (King 2006). In short, archaeologists now recognize that there was much more variability in the nature and power of Mississippian polities, and they tend to focus either on specific cases or on non-hierarchical structuring in Mississippian societies.

Research on Mississippian sociopolitical organization continues to be a particularly exciting area of study, and there is much ongoing debate about the nature of particular Mississippian polities. The Mississippian society centered at Cahokia and located in the American Bottom of Illinois is the largest known and perhaps most unusual polity. There is also a detailed database on Cahokia generated by many years of research as well as extensive CRM investigations conducted over the last 30 years. Nevertheless, archaeologists do not agree about how to interpret Cahokia, as discussed in Box 11.1.

THE FORT ANCIENT TRADITION

While we can consider many Midwestern and Southeastern populations after 950 BP (AD 1000) Mississippian, Late Woodland cultural patterns continued in some parts of the Eastern Woodlands, as will be discussed in Chapter 12. The **Fort Ancient** cultural tradition of Ohio sometimes has been considered a regional variant of Mississippian despite certain obvious distinctions.

Fort Ancient developed in the central Ohio River drainage after approximately 950 BP (AD 1000) and continued in some areas for about 700 years (Drooker and Cowan 2001). People made shell-tempered ceramics that have some Mississippian stylistic elements. Fort Ancient subsistence was centered on maize and native cultigens but also included wild plants and animals. Fort Ancient settlements are primarily found in the floodplains, and villages were nucleated by 850 BP (AD 1100), but social hierarchy is less evident in this tradition than among Mississippians. Early Fort Ancient houses were small, semisubterranean rectangles associated with large storage pits, but the houses increased in size over time. Central plazas and large, possibly communal structures have been noted after 750 BP at Fort Ancient sites, as have stockades. At the Incinerator site (Sunwatch Village) near Dayton, a large central post was erected in the plaza, possibly as a means to track the sun (Figure 11.31).

In Late Fort Ancient times, settlements of the Madisonville horizon (500–260 BP) sometimes were quite large. **Stone box graves**, in which individuals were interred in coffinlike boxes of stone, are found, as well as burial mounds. The stone box graves often are located within villages, near plazas, but temporal change in this pattern also has been observed. Studies of grave goods suggest that there was little ascribed

ISSUES AND DEBATES

BOX 11.1

How Big and Powerful Was Cahokia After All?

Cahokia is an impressive place (Figure 11.29). Located east of the present city of St. Louis in the broad floodplain of the Mississippi known as the American Bottom, this ancient community still can be glimpsed amid the urban sprawl of Collinsville, Illinois. Even diminished by 200 years of American farming, road building, and occupation, this Mississippian mound center stands out among archaeological sites in North America. At the center of Cahokia is Monks Mound (Figure 1.4), North America's largest known mound, that rises about 100 feet (30 m) above the floodplain in four different terraces and covers more than 13 acres at its base. Monks Mound is so large that you might mistake it for a hill if it weren't in the middle of the floodplain. All you have to do is climb it to gain real respect for its builders. Yet Monks Mound is only the beginning of the human constructions at Cahokia. About 100 mounds, not to mention the debris of centuries of Mississippian occupation, have been found within an area of 10 square kilometers (3.9 miles²). Many of these mounds are platform mounds; others are lineal or conical mounds containing elaborate burials. Cahokia also contains plazas that have been scraped off and then leveled with new fill, the remains of a long wooden palisade that probably once enclosed the central area, large numbers of domestic as well as other structures, and several woodhenges, circular wooden structures resembling Stonehenge, that may track astronomical events. Today, the central part of Cahokia is preserved in a state park that is classified as a World Heritage Site by UNESCO. A wonderful museum with state-of-the-art

presentations tells the story of Cahokia. The visitor cannot help but come away impressed with this one-of-a-kind site. Moreover, archaeologists have found other mound groups near Cahokia that can be interpreted as part of a combined center of great importance (Figure 11.30), and some objects apparently made at Cahokia have been found at distant Mississippian sites suggesting influence over a wide area (Pauketat 2005).

Everyone agrees Cahokia is a special place, and yet archaeologists don't agree about its peak size or about the level of political and economic organization it represents. The conventional wisdom about Cahokia has been that it was a great and powerful political entity, the apical community at the top of a four-tiered hierarchy of communities controlled by Cahokia and its elites. With Cahokia as the premier mound center, slightly smaller centers, in turn, would have controlled still smaller communities with only one mound, which were themselves centers for surrounding agricultural hamlets. This complex polity could have been an incipient North American state, and with a population of 20,000 to 40,000 people, Cahokia would have been a city by ancient standards.

In this model, functionally differentiated communities within the hierarchy and separate precincts inside Cahokia produced the prestige goods and other commodities that moved around the society. The production and movement of these goods as well as labor for construction projects were controlled by the elite, whose position was validated by religious belief and symbolism. Large markets and extensive trade also characterized Cahokia, and its

FIGURE 11.29 Artist's conception of the central plaza at Cahokia; Monks Mound is in the distance.

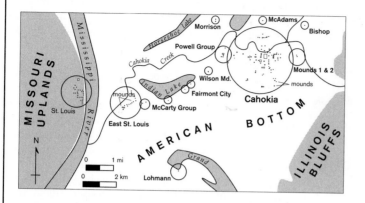

FIGURE 11.30 Mississippian mound centers in or adjacent to the American Bottom; note that Cahokia is one of several such centers.

influence was felt far and wide—perhaps even among proto-Iroquoians in what today is New York State (Dincauze and Hasenstab 1989). Perhaps Cahokia served as a gateway between the northern frontier and the Mississippian heartland of the Southeast, and derived much of its power from controlling trade on the Mississippi and other nearby rivers (Kelly 1991). This is a compelling model, which certainly accounts for the unique features of Cahokia.

However, there also are other ways of looking at Cahokia that place less emphasis on domination and hierarchy. Thanks to major CRM projects in the American Bottom during the last 30 years, we now have much very detailed information about Mississippian communities in the American Bottom. In consideration of the picture these data present, it has been argued that simpler models may fit the actual evidence more closely (Milner 1990, 1998). Rather than being a state, Cahokia can be viewed as only a very large example of a paramount chiefdom that in many respects resembled other known Mississippian polities. In this view, the regional system was fairly decentralized and other mound centers in the American Bottom could represent other potentially autonomous smaller centers headed by their own chiefs and linked by unstable political alliances. Rather than having fixed positions in an unchanging hierarchical system of settlements, different mound centers are thought to have occupied different levels of importance, in which they exerted varying levels of power over the nearly 400 years of Mississippian developments in the American Bottom.

Moreover, careful assessment of the probable numbers of structures per acre in various time periods throughout the American Bottom suggest that Cahokia's population level was much lower than some archaeologists have argued. Population actually peaked in Early Mississippian times and began to decline several centuries before the end of the Mississippian sequence in the American Bottom (Milner 1998). Cahokia itself probably had no more than 8000 inhabitants at its peak, while the population in the American Bottom as a whole might have been as large as 50,000 at one time. A kin-based social hierarchy is also central in this alternative model. High status may not be based primarily on wealth and symbols of prestige amassed by individuals but on ritual roles of clans and priests who used prestige goods in important rituals. Direct elite control of the prestige good production has not been demonstrated. Although trading was an important activity, the amount of exotic goods indicated by archaeological data was simply too small for Cahokia to have been controlling vast exchange networks.

Archaeologists studying Mississippians elsewhere also are wrestling with debates similar to those posed for Cahokia (Butler and Welch 2006; Muller 1997; Sulllivan and Mainfort 2010). There is some convergence of views toward downsizing population estimates and the scale of trade, and positing lack of a rigid hierarchy of mound centers (Pauketat and Emerson 1997). Differences of opinion remain, however, on the degree and means of domination by Cahokia and other paramount Mississippian centers. The fact is, archaeologists have much more to learn about the nature of Mississippian polities, especially the unique one represented by Cahokia (Pauketat 2005). On a positive note, these debates focus us on the central archaeological problem of how to interpret the material record. What data would you collect to help resolve the questions raised by these alternative models?

ranking among Fort Ancient populations, and the people may have been organized into a tribal confederacy rather than a hierarchical chiefdom (Drooker and Cowan 2001). On the basis of highly similar ceramics,

greater interaction among Fort Ancient populations seems probable after 500 BP (AD 1450), but breakdown of the tradition occurred after approximately 350 BP. The Shawnee may be the descendants of Fort Ancient.

FIGURE 11.31 Visitors to Sunwatch Village, a reconstruction of the Incinerator site near Dayton, Ohio, walk toward the large post at the center of the village's plaza; the original post at this spot may have provided a means to track the movement of the sun.

THE PROTOHISTORIC PERIOD AND EUROPEAN CONTACT

European presence in the Eastern Woodlands began in the seventeenth century. Some parts of the interior, such as the Ohio country, were not explored by Europeans until the eighteenth century, although the first European to visit the Ohio River valley probably was Gabriel Arthur, an English trader, captured by Indians in 1674. Nevertheless, the Protohistoric period begins when European goods such as glass beads, brass wares, and iron implements were traded from the coasts. In the Chicago area, trade beads are first evident in sites dated between AD 1620 and 1630. Besides Fort Ancient societies of Ohio, the chiefdoms of the Mississippian period sometimes persisted into the early Historic period in the Southeast. For example, Moundville and its associated sites may correspond to the **Apafalaya chiefdom** of the de Soto chronicles (Knight and Steponaitis 1998b). In contrast, Midwestern Mississippian polities apparently declined during Late Mississippian times after about 550 BP.

The Spanish were the earliest European colonizers in the Southeast, and Spain controlled much of Florida into the early nineteenth century. Ponce de Léon of "Fountain of Youth" fame made his first voyage to Florida in 1513. Other explorations and efforts at establishing colonies followed. The most important expedition was led by Hernando de Soto, who landed at Tampa Bay in late May 1539. The de Soto expedition proceeded through the Southeast for more than four years. Many men lost their lives, including de Soto himself, who died in Arkansas near the Mississippi River in 1542. About half the party made it back to New Spain in September 1543, having finally built boats and sailed down the Mississippi into the Gulf of Mexico (Hudson et al. 1989). The route of the de Soto expedition has been carefully researched and correlated with archaeological evidence. It is shown in Figure 11.32, along with the Florida expedition of Ponce de Léon. Besides the Moundville example already given, the Little Egypt site on the Coosawattee River in northwest Georgia is believed to be the main town of the Coosa chiefdom (Smith 2000), and the expedition's winter camp in 1539–1540 among the Apalachee is believed to be the Martin site near modern Tallahassee, Florida (Ewen 1989).

The French also were early seventeenth-century explorers in the Mississippi River valley. The Mississippi was partially explored by Marquette and Joliet in 1673. In 1682 La Salle made it to the Gulf, establishing a small settlement, the Arkansas Post, at the mouth of the Arkansas. Eventually the French established the Louisiana colony in the lower Mississippi valley, creating a network of settlements and military posts along the Gulf Coast and along the rivers. For a time French trade with Native peoples was extensive.

When the first Europeans arrived, the Indians of the interior parts of the Eastern Woodlands, despite their many cultural similarities, spoke languages representative of five different language families: Algonquian, Iroquoian, Siouan, Muskogean, and Caddoan. In the southern Midwest, Europeans encountered a variety of cultural groups speaking Algonquian languages and a few Siouan-speaking tribes as well. Among these people were the Shawnee of Ohio, the Mascouten of southern Michigan, the Miami of Indiana, and the Menominee and Ho-Chunk (Winnebago) of Wisconsin and the Illinois, whose territory extended southward along the Mississippi River. The Fox (Mesquakie), the Sauk, and the Kickapoo, all originally were located in Michigan or northern Ohio but were displaced early in this period to Wisconsin. Of these tribes, only the Ho-Chunk spoke a Siouan as opposed to Algonquian language, but some of the poorly understood peoples of the Ohio valley probably also were Siouan speakers.

The bulk of Southeastern tribes were Muskogean-speaking groups, such as the Alabama, Apalachee, Muskogee, Timucua, Chickasaw, Choctaw, and Creek, whose original territories were in Georgia, Alabama, Mississippi, Louisiana, northern Florida, and adjacent areas. The Natchez of the Mississippi River valley and the Tunica of Louisiana spoke languages that some have considered linguistic isolates. Southern Iroquoian speakers were the Cherokee of the southern Appalachians in northwest Georgia, southeastern Tennessee, and western South Carolina. Several groups of Cherokee towns can be recognized, and this tribe figures importantly in the later history of this part of the Southeast. Initially the Cherokee lived in nucleated towns with plazas, some of which have been excavated. Siouan-speaking tribes were found in the lower Mississippi River valley and include the Ofos, the Biloxi, and the Quapaw, as well as tribes located to the north and west. The Catawba of the

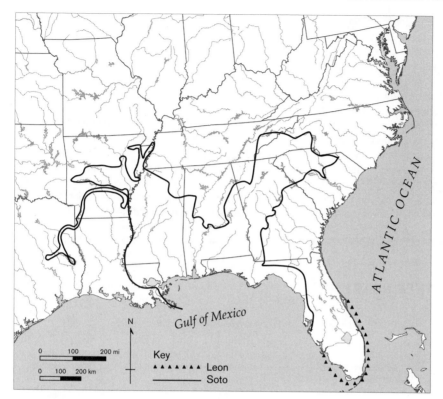

FIGURE 11.32 The routes taken by Ponce de Léon in 1513 and by Hernando de Soto between 1539 and 1543 have been carefully researched.

Carolinas and the Yuchi of Tennessee sometimes are considered linguistic isolates, although their languages are related to Siouan languages. Caddoan speakers were found only on the western margins of the Southeast, where the Caddo tribes of Arkansas and Louisiana were its main representative. The Mississippian Spiro chiefdom is the best-known Caddo antecedent (Hudson 1976).

It is important to note that the first Europeans in the Eastern Woodlands heartland entered a social context that already was rapidly changing (Brose et al. 2001). One factor was the demand for furs among native groups to the east. For example, Iroquois efforts to control the fur trade resulted in the forced dispersal of many groups in Ohio and adjacent areas during the second half of the seventeenth century (Tanner 1986). A period of general abandonment in the middle Ohio River valley during the seventeenth century is usually accepted, although the archaeological evidence concerning the end of Fort Ancient is more ambiguous (Drooker and Cowan 2001). The movements of people at this time were not just responses to European arrival or to the fur trade. Just as often they resulted from local interactions, alliance formation, and stress on local resources. In fact, removals and relocations were multidirectional, and possibly a continuation of patterns that developed in the Late Prehistoric period.

CHAPTER SUMMARY

This chapter's introduction to what archaeologists have learned about the past in the heartland of the Eastern Woodlands summarizes many important developments. The key points made in the chapter can be summarized as follows:

- For approximately 7000 years following the Paleoindian period, from 10,000 BP to 3000 BP, foraging people inhabited the interior areas of the Eastern Woodlands, but these people were not all simple, mobile hunter-gatherers living in small groups. Instead, particularly in the major river valleys, Middle and Late Archaic peoples variously experimented with more sedentary lifeways, the cultivation and domestication of native seed plants, the long-distance exchange of commodities, the manufacture of pottery containers, and even the construction of earthen and shell mounds.

- During the Early and Middle Woodland, peoples of the interior Eastern Woodlands had lifestyles characterized by pottery making, mixed economies that included cultivation of native and some tropical plants, and mound building. Long-distance exchange of raw materials and finished goods as well as some mortuary rituals variously linked people across the East especially during the Middle Woodland. However, large aggregated communities and social ranking are not usually evident.

- The Late Woodland has a reputation for being a period of decline, but it actually was highly variable and marked by the widespread adoption of the bow and arrow, higher population levels, settlement pattern change, and intensification of agricultural production in at least some cases.

- Mississippian developments at the end of pre-Columbian times were significant in many parts of the East. Mississippians were maize, bean, and squash agriculturists who built platform mounds and towns with central plazas. They were organized into chiefdoms of varying size and complexity, and they produced and exchanged prestige items displaying sophisticated craftsmanship. Mississippian ceremonialism, exchange, and iconography all were expressions of the complex and changing sociopolitical interactions that were taking place in the heartland of the East at this time.

SUGGESTIONS FOR FURTHER READING

For a review of the prehistory of eastern North America with emphasis on the mound-building cultures:

Milner, George R.
　2004 The Moundbuilders: Ancient Peoples of Eastern North America. Thames and Hudson, London.

For more information on Archaic foragers:

Emerson, Thomas E., Dale L. McElrath, and Andrew C. Fortier (editors)
　2009 *Archaic Societies: Diversity and Complexity Across the Midcontinent.* State University of New York Press, Albany.

Sassaman, Kenneth E., and David G. Anderson (editors)
　1996 *Archaeology of the Mid-Holocene Southeast.* University Press of Florida, Gainesville.

For recent perspectives on the Hopewell:

Charles, Douglas K., and Jane E. Buikstra (editors)
　2006 *Recreating Hopewell.* University Press of Florida, Gainesville.

For recent perspectives on the Late Woodland:

Emerson, Thomas E., Dale L. McElrath, and Andrew C. Fortier
　2000 *Late Woodland Societies: Tradition and Transformation Across the Midcontinent.* University of Nebraska Press, Lincoln.

For a thorough review of the evidence from Cahokia:

Milner, George R.
　1998 *The Cahokia Chiefdom: The Archaeology of a Mississippian Society.* Smithsonian Institution Press, Washington, D.C.

For a readable account of one of the chiefdoms encountered by de Soto:

Smith, Marvin T.
　2000 *Coosa: The Rise and Fall of a Mississippian Chiefdom.* University Press of Florida, Gainesville.

OTHER RESOURCES

Sections H and I of the Student CD give web links, places to visit, additional discussion questions, and other study aids. The Student CD also contains a variety of additional resources. Three bonus case studies especially relate to the materials in this chapter: Section D.2, "It Takes a Team: Interdisciplinary Research at the Koster Site,"; Section D.6, "The Dust Cave Archaeological Project: Investigating Paleoindian and Archaic Lifeways in Southeastern North America,"; and Section D.7, "The Hopeton Earthworks Project: Using New Technologies to Answer old Questions,". The Bonus Issues and Debates box, Section F.6, "Ridges, Aisles, and the Map of Poverty Point," is also relevant.

CASE STUDY

Museum collections can be just as significant resources for archaeological research as new excavations. People often envision museum collections in terms of pots, stone tools, carved figurines, and other artifacts. Of course, these are important parts of archaeological collections, but this case study shows that documents, including maps, field notes, and drawings, can be equally important. In fact, if artifact collections lack written information about context, much less can be learned from the objects themselves. In this case study, maps and other records concerning excavations done by the Works Progress Administration (WPA) during the 1930s provide a basis to explore information about Late Mississippian communities and households and also allow the investigation of some aspects of mortuary behavior. Because the sites in question are now underwater, archaeologists interested in understanding this time period in southeastern Tennessee must rely on museum collections. Fortunately, the collections in this case are well documented, and the physical evidence can be combined fruitfully with existing ethnohistorical information on Southeastern Indians. This research also shows why mapping and spatial documentation are so critical to archaeological interpretation. As you read this case study, notice the various kinds of archaeological information that are used and think about what would have been lost if the WPA excavations had been less well documented.

MOUSE CREEK PHASE HOUSEHOLDS AND COMMUNITIES

Mississippian Period Towns in Southeastern Tennessee

Lynne P. Sullivan

Imagine that you could walk into an ancient town and step into the houses and public buildings. Without even speaking to the townspeople, you would learn a lot about how they live just from looking at the kinds of things they use, and the context and arrangements of these things within and around the houses and buildings. An archaeological site that is the remains of an entire town or village contains similar information; much less of the town or village is intact, of course, and the archaeologist must make inferences. Nevertheless, the kinds of information these sites produce are invaluable for learning about many aspects of the lives of ancient peoples.

Excavating a town or village site is a daunting task because these sites typically cover several acres and contain very complex deposits. Archaeological investigations of large sites require large staffs, considerable funding, and a lot of time. But a scholar does not necessarily have to spend years in the field to study a village site. Without ever wielding a shovel, an individual researcher can reap the benefits of large excavation projects by studying existing collections. Museums curate vast numbers of professionally excavated archaeological collections, some of them the result of many years of excavation, or excavations by very large crews, at large sites. In some cases, only preliminary studies have been made of the materials. In nearly all cases, there is much more to be learned from the curated collections.

WPA ARCHAEOLOGY

The collections made by **Works Progress Administration** (WPA) crews before flooding of reservoirs by the **Tennessee Valley Authority** (TVA) offer a good example of museum collections from large village sites. The circumstances under which these collections were made also provide a glimpse into the history of archaeology in the United States. Both the WPA and TVA were part of Franklin D. Roosevelt's New Deal programs to give jobs to people who had become unemployed and to improve the quality of life during the Great Depression. WPA crews provided the labor for extensive archaeological excavations that were supervised by professional archaeologists. The large WPA excavations in the southeastern United States also helped build an infrastructure for archaeological research, as universities hired archaeologists and set up departments to administer the projects.

The Chickamauga Basin Project, on the Tennessee River near Chattanooga, was one of several WPA/TVA archaeological projects that excavated large town sites dating to the Mississippian period. Archaeological work for the Chickamauga reservoir began in early 1936 and continued through 1939. An earlier survey of the basin, conducted under the direction of William Webb of the University of Kentucky, had located some 70 sites. Thomas M. N. Lewis, who had worked with the well-known archaeologist W. C. McKern at the Milwaukee Public Museum, was hired by the University of Tennessee to run the excavation and analysis portion of the project. Lewis was the university's first archaeologist, and he worked in the newly established Division of Anthropology, a section of the Department of History. He hired young archaeologists as field supervisors, including several of Fay-Cooper Cole's University of Chicago students. Cole ran one of the first field training programs for student archaeologists in the United States. Jesse D. Jennings, one of Cole's students and later a well-known archaeologist in the Great Basin, was the main field supervisor for the Chickamauga project. Lewis also hired Madeline Kneberg, another Chicago student, to be the director of the laboratory (Sullivan 1999). At the lab in Knoxville, she oversaw materials preparation, restoration, and cataloging, as well as analysis.

Thirteen of the 70 sites located by the survey, including portions of nine prehistoric town sites, were chosen for excavation. The large WPA crews (sometimes as many as 100 workers) made it possible to excavate huge areas of these sites, and as Lewis notes in the project's manual of field and laboratory procedures, the field supervisors had to expend "much shoe leather" to keep up with the excavations. Artifacts were cleaned in the field and shipped to the Knoxville laboratory, where they were cataloged and analyzed with the assistance of several specialists from other institutions. For the Chickamauga Project alone, the lab classified over 360,000 pottery sherds and some 100,000 stone, bone, shell, and copper artifacts; workers identified almost 7000 animal bones to species, reconstructed several hundred pottery vessels, and examined all of the nearly 2000 recovered human skeletons to determine age, sex, and pathologies.

When the United States entered World War II in 1941, the **New Deal archaeology** projects were shut down and many of the staff were drafted for the war effort. Nevertheless, the information and materials collected by this project comprise the only systematic documentation of major archaeological sites that now are inundated or destroyed. The collections are especially precious because the opportunity for continued excavation no longer exists at most of the sites. However, the work that was completed laid so much of the groundwork for subsequent research in the upper Tennessee valley that the archaeological phases in the region are named for sites in the Chickamauga Basin.

Data available from the large town sites in the Chickamauga Basin include documentation of large portions of the town plans, showing spatial relationships between structures and other features; plan drawings of many structures; large and detailed data sets for studies of mortuary practices and human biology; and large numbers of intact artifacts for technological and stylistic comparative studies. These collections, which have enormous potential for continuing research, exemplify the need to care for and preserve such archaeological materials so that future scholars can use them. The Chickamauga Basin collections are suitable for a wide range of research precisely because of the systematic and standardized collecting and recording techniques used by the WPA-era archaeologists, and the preservation of within-site provenience information and large samples of various materials. The meticulous records kept by the field and laboratory archaeologists contain this information and are what make these collections valuable for continuing research.

In 1946, Tom Lewis and Madeline Kneberg published a report on the Hiwassee Island site, one of the large, excavated town sites in the Chickamauga Basin (Lewis and Kneberg 1946). They chose this site because it contained examples of several of the archaeological cultures they wished to define for this region. Earlier they had drafted, with other project supervisors, a report for the entire Chickamauga Basin Project, but the report remained an incomplete draft for over a half century. The curated project records and collections made it possible to complete and publish this important document in 1995 (Lewis and Kneberg 1995). While the report contains descriptive information about the excavated sites, and the kinds of artifacts and features found in the Chickamauga Basin, it gives little interpretation of the sites and, of course, does not include the types of analyses and interpretations possible with an additional 60-plus years of knowledge and research.

A CONTEMPORARY ANALYSIS OF TWO CHICKAMAUGA BASIN SITES

In the late 1980s, as part of my doctoral dissertation project, I analyzed several excavated village or town sites in the Chickamauga Basin. This work exemplifies the process archaeologists use to study such collections, and the kinds of questions that can be asked and addressed about ancient life in pre-Columbian towns of the Southeast. The archaeologists of the WPA era defined an archaeological complex known as the **Mouse Creek phase** based on their investigations of three large sites. We now know that the Mouse Creek phase is a Late Mississippian (500–400 BP/AD 1450–1550) complex, located mainly along the lower Hiwassee River, a tributary of the Tennessee River in southeastern Tennessee (Figure 11.33). I will examine two of the Mouse Creek phase sites, Mouse Creeks and Ledford Island, in some detail.

The archaeologists of the 1930s did not have the advantage of absolute dating techniques, such as radiocarbon dating, to help assign sites to different

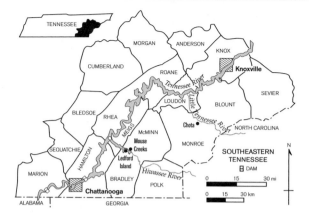

FIGURE 11.33 Location of the Mouse Creek phase sites discussed in this case study.

Mississippian period sites in the Chickamauga Basin (Table 11.4). The ethnic and biological relationships of the earlier and later Mississippian groups in the basin remain an unresolved question.

One of the first steps in studying the collections representing the Mouse Creek towns was to assemble maps of the excavations. The field workers created detailed maps of the excavated archaeological features (e.g., structure patterns, palisade lines, refuse pits), but the excavated areas were so large that many maps had to be made. To be able to look at entire excavated areas, these maps had to be assembled—similar to putting together a puzzle—so that the layouts or plans of the towns could be discerned. Maps of two of the sites, Ledford Island (Figure 11.34) and a portion of the Mouse Creeks Site (Figure 11.35), are particularly instructive for analysis of the plans of Mouse Creek phase communities.

The compiled maps provide spatial contexts for the recovered artifacts, as well as information on the arrangements of buildings and other elements of these ancient communities. To supplement this information, ground surface elevations, recorded with a surveying instrument by a WPA surveyor, were used to create topographic maps for each site. These maps show how the various features of the towns (e.g., rises, depressions, level areas) were situated on the landscape. Other maps of distributions of artifacts and certain kinds of archaeological features add more information that can be used to help interpret the town plans.

The various maps of the Ledford Island site in particular reveal rudimentary information about the overall plan and the uses of certain areas of this ancient community. The map of the excavated archaeological features shows a large area that is devoid of features (Figure 11.35). This "empty" area represents the town square or plaza. To its north is the pattern of a very large building, while the superimposed patterns of

archaeological complexes, so they classified sites and complexes solely on the basis of the kinds of things they found and the stratigraphic relationships (if any). The WPA archaeologists segregated the Mouse Creek sites from other Mississippian sites based on differences in the remains of buildings, in the pottery, and in mortuary practices. They interpreted these differences as indicating that the Mouse Creek phase represented the remains of an ethnic group or culture different from other Mississippian period sites in the region. Such interpretations were commonplace during the years before radiocarbon dating (first used for archaeological purposes in the early 1950s) because the antiquity of the archaeological record in the Americas was not known, and differences in archaeological assemblages often were attributed to migrations and/or changes in people or ethnic groups within a region, rather than to temporal differences. We now know that the Mouse Creek phase sites postdate most of the other

TABLE 11.4 Comparison of the WPA-Era and Current Chronological Sequences for Late Prehistory in the Chickamauga Basin

WPA-Era Sequence	Dates	Cultural Period	Dates	Current Sequence
Cherokee	AD1650	Historic	300 BP (AD 1650)	Cherokee
			500 BP (AD 1450)	Mouse Creek
			650 BP (AD 1300)	Dallas
Dallas/Mouse Creek			750 BP (AD 1200)	Hixon
Hiwassee Island			850 BP (AD 1100)	Hiwassee Island
	AD1400	Mississippian	1050 BP (AD 900)	Martin Farm
Hamilton		Late Woodland	1250 BP (AD 700)	Hamilton[1]

[1] Hamilton is now understood as a mortuary tradition that spans the Late Woodland and Early Mississippian periods. This tradition begins at 1250 BP, while the end date for use of Hamilton mounds is approximately 750 BP.

FIGURE 11.34 Excavation map of the Ledford Island site showing the archaeological features.

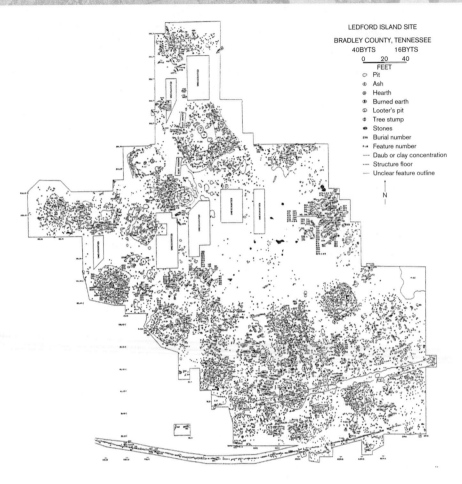

LEDFORD ISLAND SITE
BRADLEY COUNTY, TENNESSEE
40BYTS   16BYTS
0   20   40
FEET

- Pit
- Ash
- Hearth
- Burned earth
- Looter's pit
- Tree stump
- Stones
- Burial number
- Feature number
- Daub or clay concentration
- Structure floor
- Unclear feature outline

N

many smaller buildings, which were rebuilt and/or repaired several times in the same locations—surround the rest of the plaza. Near the plaza's northeastern corner is a cemetery in which were interred mostly adult males. Diagonally across the plaza is another smaller cemetery, but these skeletons were in so poor a state of preservation that for most of the individuals age and sex could not be determined. Other graves are in scattered groups throughout the town, and a line of postmolds along the southern periphery of the excavated area indicates that a wooden palisade surrounded the community.

The topographic map of the Ledford Island site especially is interesting because it shows a large depressed area in the center of the site that corresponds with the plaza. Figure 11.36 shows the topographic map superimposed on a map of artifact distributions. Artifact distributions are based on numbers of artifacts found in the upper level of soil at the site, the **plow zone**, which was disturbed by modern farmers who plowed the soil for agricultural crops. Artifact counts for each unit in the excavation grid used by the WPA

workers reflect the general pattern of artifact densities across the site. A statistical procedure called **trend surface analysis** was used to smooth the resulting contours. The artifact distributions show that the center of the site was devoid of artifacts. This clear area again coincides with the plaza, the depressed area that also is generally devoid of archaeological features. The lack of artifacts suggests that the townspeople kept this public area of their community very clean. In fact, it is possible that the area became depressed from repeated sweepings over a long period of time.

Another of the Mouse Creek phase sites, Mouse Creeks, provides more detail on the households of the townspeople. A portion of this site was not occupied as long as was the Ledford Island site, as evidenced by fewer episodes of rebuilding and repair of structures. A relatively short occupation span is of benefit to archaeologists because there is less confusion in the town plan due to overlapping and noncontemporary features. Examination of the assembled map of this site shows a line of postmolds, representing a wooden palisade that must have been an early feature of the

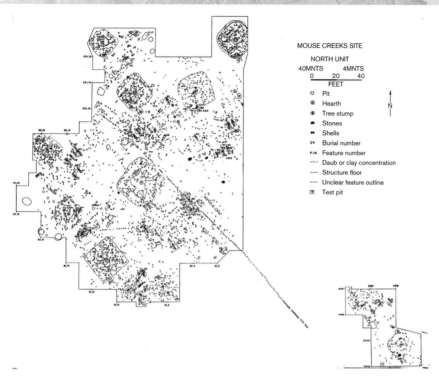

FIGURE 11.35 Excavation map of the Mouse Creeks site (north unit) showing the archaeological features.

MOUSE CREEKS SITE

NORTH UNIT

40MNTS   4MNTS

0   20   40

FEET

- ○ Pit
- ⊕ Hearth
- ⊙ Tree stump
- ▪ Stones
- ⋈ Shells
- ²⁴ Burial number
- F-14 Feature number
- ---- Daub or clay concentration
- --- Structure floor
- --- Unclear feature outline
- ⊡ Test pit

N

town because it is superimposed by other features (Figure 11.35). Perhaps the town expanded beyond the extent of this early wall, but this is difficult to determine because there is less information about the overall town plan of this site than Ledford Island. The Mouse Creeks site map does show a pattern of house basins (large square-shaped areas filled with dark-colored soil that are the remains of semisubterranean house floors), with adjacent concentrations of postmolds that are surrounded by graves. A map illustrating counts of postmolds by an excavation unit (excluding the house basins) shows that the postmold concentrations are to the southeast of each house basin (Figure 11.37). The house basins also include central hearths made of clay, surrounded by a floor area of hardened, likely trampled, clay. Short trenches, typically in the southeastern corner of each basin, are the remains of doorways. Graves of infants and young children also are found in the house basins, while those of older children and adults are placed near the postmold concentrations.

The repetition of this combination of house basins, postmold concentrations, and graves at Mouse Creeks likely reflects the remains of numerous household facilities that were the residences of the families who once occupied the town. The presence of repeated, similar architectural patterns and similar arrangements of features also indicates a cultural preference or tradition for the organization of household facilities. Each household had a large dwelling made with

log support posts, and the floor was dug into the ground. The lowered floors would have provided some additional insulation for winter months (although southeastern Tennessee has a moderate climate, winter temperatures quite often drop below freezing). The small sheltered doorways and central hearths in these buildings would have offered further protections from the elements. In contrast, the postmold concentrations adjacent to these buildings likely represent less substantial structures, possibly to provide shade from the summer sun and shelter from the region's typical, drenching rainstorms. The graves associated with these buildings likely represent "family cemeteries."

Ethnographic information from accounts written by early European explorers, traders, and settlers in the region provides clues for interpreting these archaeologically observed patterns. These accounts often mention the "summer" and "winter" houses of many native, southeastern groups. The Cherokee, who first were encountered in the eastern Tennessee region in the 1700s, had such household buildings. The Cherokee winter house was a circular structure with a central hearth. It was paired with a rectangular, less substantially built summer house, where the family gathered in good weather to cook, eat, work on various projects, store some items, and visit, or do other typical day-to-day activities. Patterns of such Cherokee households have been found archaeologically at the eighteenth-century Cherokee town of Chota in the valley of the

FIGURE 11.36 Topographic map of the Ledford Island site superimposed on a sixth-order trend surface analysis of the numbers of artifacts in the plow zone in each 10 by 10 foot (3 × 3 m) excavation unit.

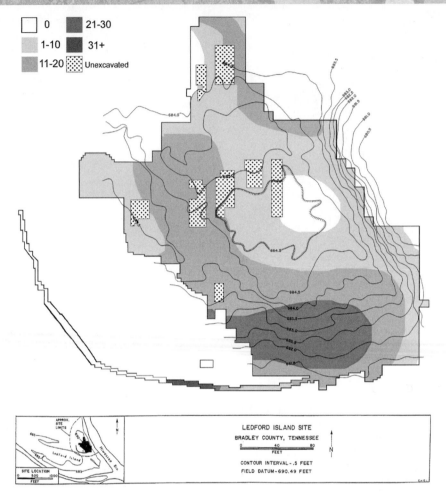

Little Tennessee River (see Figures 11.1 and 11.33). Graves were associated with the Cherokee summer houses (Schroedl 1986).

The plans of the Cherokee and Mouse Creek households are not identical (e.g., the Cherokee winter house is circular, while the Mouse Creek one is square), but there are similarities in the design of archaeologically observed and ethnographically recorded eighteenth-century Cherokee household facilities with the archaeologically observed household facilities, dating at least two centuries earlier, at Mouse Creeks. These similarities do not necessarily mean that the residents of Mouse Creeks were Cherokee, but the historical case does provide an ethnographic analogy to help interpret the observed archaeological patterns. Archaeologists often use such analogies as a basis for generating ideas to test with archaeological data, and the best analogies typically derive from historically known native groups living in the region of the prehistoric sites. We will return to this subject later.

The information about the household plans derived from the Mouse Creeks excavations also can be used to help interpret the community plan at the Ledford Island site. The apparently longer occupation span there created more complex archaeological deposits, but the understanding of the "template" of household plans, as observed at the less-complicated Mouse Creeks site, can be used to make sense of the morass of features at Ledford Island. Enough elements of household plans can be seen in the map of archaeological features at Ledford Island, including clusters of burials and postmold concentrations grouped near house basins, to allow us to infer that household facilities similar to those at Mouse Creeks also once surrounded the plaza at Ledford Island.

Thus the overall community plan at Ledford Island can be envisioned as having numerous households—each composed of winter and summer houses and a small cemetery—surrounding a large, central plaza with a very large building, architecturally similar to the smaller winter houses, and larger cemeteries flanking the plaza. A wooden palisade enclosed the community.

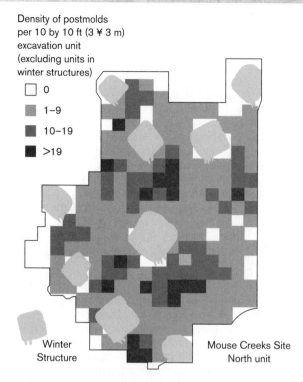

Density of postmolds
per 10 by 10 ft (3 ¥ 3 m)
excavation unit
(excluding units in
winter structures)

☐ 0

▨ 1–9

▩ 10–19

■ >19

Winter
Structure

Mouse Creeks Site
North unit

FIGURE 11.37 Postmold concentrations suggesting summer houses at Mouse Creeks.

This interpretation of the fundamental arrangement of a Mouse Creek phase community, based on compilation and visual inspection of maps and ethnographic analogies of several kinds, provides a setting for examining other aspects of the organization of this pre-Columbian society. When graves are located in residential sites, such as the Mouse Creek phase towns, mortuary practices are yet another way to learn about the social life of the community. Mortuary practices are a data set that archaeologists have found particularly useful for understanding the composition of social groups and the variety of social roles that individuals filled in ancient societies.

Studies of the social dimensions of mortuary practices rely on the principle that, in general, the treatment of an individual in death reflects the esteem he or she was accorded in life. This principle, which generally is applicable to most cultures, can be observed in many funeral rites and cemeteries of today. For example, wealthy persons often have elaborate tombs or grave markers; soldiers often are buried in special cemeteries (e.g., Arlington); and high-ranking politicians typically have specialized burial plots often associated with architecture (e.g., a presidential library). Such correlations are not perfect (consider the modern cemeteries in which all graves have identical bronze markers),

and one must remember that mortuary treatments primarily reflect how the living choose to honor or commemorate the deceased, not necessarily the actual circumstances of the deceased's social position. Even given these caveats, mortuary treatments provide useful insights to ancient cultures. The spatial arrangements and locations of graves, as well as funerary objects interred with the deceased, along with biological information such as sex and age, can be used to assess possible differences in status, and gender and age-related roles. We note parenthetically that archaeologists who study social dimensions of mortuary practices typically work with biological anthropologists, who study the physical aspects of human skeletal remains. Under the federal Native American Grave Protection and Repatriation Act, studies of human remains may require consent of affiliated descendant groups.

Cemeteries are elements of the town plan at the Ledford Island site; they are associated both with households and with the town square or plaza. This spatial distinction in itself is interesting because the households can be considered "private" residences, while the plaza clearly is a public space. Age and sex distributions of burials, as mapped at the Ledford Island site, show noteworthy patterns. As noted earlier, the cemetery on the plaza's eastern edge contained the remains mainly of adult males. In contrast, the cemeteries around the households include individuals of both sexes and all ages, except that those who died in infancy or as very young children typically were buried in the floors of the winter houses. Also, more females than males are interred near the households, in comparison to the plaza cemeteries. Other distinctions can be seen in the kinds of artifact interred with the dead. Some are associated with individuals of a particular age or sex (e.g., pots with females, pipes with males), but others also are specific to location. Several kinds of items associated with the plaza burials (e.g., large ceremonial celts or axes, large chipped stone blades made of imported chert, clusters of finely made projectile points) are not found with graves in other parts of the town. Such items can be inferred to have special meaning because they were costly to make in terms of time, craftsmanship, and/or materials. For example, the ceremonial celts are too thin actually to use for woodworking, suggesting that these items were specifically made to honor the deceased person with whom they were interred, or to reflect the honored position the person had held in society.

To interpret how these patterns may reflect principles of the organization of a single ancient society, archaeologists again turn to ethnographic analogy and studies of mortuary practices worldwide. The worldwide studies, as noted, provide general insights, while analogies from native societies of the Southeast give clues to specific cultural practices. An understanding of the typical, ethnographically recorded kinship and residence practices of Southeastern Indians especially is relevant and necessary to interpret and understand such mortuary practices, as may be applied to the pre-Columbian Mouse Creek phase communities.

Most Southeastern groups were (and some still are) matrilineal and matrilocal (Hudson 1976). By "matrilineal," anthropologists mean that kinship was reckoned though the mother's line. A child belonged to his mother's larger kin group or clan, and although the biological father did have a relationship with and influence on his children, the most important male figure in a Southeastern Indian child's life was a maternal uncle. Most Southeastern Indians lived in **extended family** (multigenerational) households that were matrilocal that is, a married couple lived in the house of the woman's family. Houses and property also passed through the female line. A married man thus lived with his in-laws; his family of origin and the children he was most responsible for educating and helping to care for (those of his sister) lived in a different house. These social constructs, based on kinship and residence, are important to keep in mind when considering the organization of Mississippian period peoples. The social dynamics accompanying these kinship and residence traditions are quite different from those of most modern-day residents of the United States.

Ethnographic information about how many of the Southeastern groups chose leaders also is relevant for considering the patterning observed at the Ledford Island site because leaders quite often were afforded distinctive mortuary treatments. Mortuary practices also can provide insights into the degree to which heredity was the means for determining leaders. Burial of children in the same manner as adult leaders suggests that heredity was a more important factor for determining leadership than personal ability, since a child would not have had the opportunity to develop leadership qualities. In the Southeast, some leadership positions tended to be inherited through certain kinship groups, such as lineages or clans. A chiefly title (some groups had a variety of chiefs) thus would be filled through a particular kin group, but the stringency of the inheritance rules for determining the holders of these positions varied considerably among groups. Some groups, such as the Natchez of current-day Mississippi, had a strictly determined, hereditary chiefly lineage. In other groups, such as the Cherokee, the senior women or clan mothers would decide which of several potentially eligible men would ascend to a chiefly office, based on each candidate's ability to lead.

The mortuary practices of the historically and archaeologically documented, eighteenth-century Cherokee are congruent with the latter scenario, and again offer particularly relevant analogies for the Mouse Creek phase. As previously mentioned, graves were associated with households of the eighteenth-century Cherokee town of Chota. Several graves also were located near the large townhouse, or public meetinghouse adjacent to the town square. These were graves of adult males, and one was known to be the resting place of Chief Oconostota. These plaza graves likely reflect acknowledgment of the interred individuals' participation in community leadership. The absence of the remains of children suggests that leadership ability, rather than inheritance, was an important factor of the status these men had acquired (see also Sullivan 2001).

The large building adjacent to the plaza and near the large plaza cemetery at the Ledford Island site appears to be analogous to the Cherokee townhouse. If the spatial patterning of the graves at Ledford Island is analogous to that at Chota, the adult males buried in the plaza cemetery can be supposed to have held positions important to the community, such as leaders or chiefs, and to have ascended to these positions largely through their ability, rather than strictly by inheritance. This interpretation is reinforced by the different kinds of objects interred with the men in the plaza and near the dwelling houses. Such objects may well represent the special status of the principal men in the community.

Another relevant aspect of eighteenth-century Cherokee society is that the townhouse, the public meetinghouse on the plaza, also served as a gathering place for the men of the community; men could go there to be away from the world of women. The households and kin groups were the realms of women, especially because the married men lived with their wives' families, the men did not own the houses, and kinship was determined through female lines. Cherokee women essentially were in charge of the households and families, including agricultural production, and they derived considerable political power and influence from these functions. In contrast, male leaders served as representatives of the entire community and were in charge of intercommunity relationships such as trading and alliances.

Until recently, many archaeologists would have suggested that the men in the Ledford Island plaza cemeteries were the sole political leaders and the "movers and shakers" in this ancient community. But such interpretations ignore the social dynamics of matrilineages and matrilocality. Given differing political roles based on gender as in the Cherokee case, interpretations of men as the sole leaders in many Mississippian societies may well misrepresent the political power and influence of women in these communities, and undermine the significance of household cemeteries (Sullivan and Harle 2010; Sullivan and Rodning 2010). Gerald Schroedl, the University of Tennessee archaeologist who supervised the excavations of the Chota site, argues that graves associated with households reflect a public acknowledgment of the ancestors linked to certain household groups (Schroedl 1986). That is, the household cemeteries honor the kin groups, in contrast to the plaza cemeteries, which honor the community. One is connected to the female realm of kin, the other with the male realm of community.

THE VALUE OF MUSEUM COLLECTIONS

Did the influential men interred in the Ledford Island plaza cemetery once sit in the large public building, sharing hunting stories, talking of great warriors, and contemplating ways in which to gain influence and obtain exotic goods at distant towns? Meanwhile, did the women, who are interred in cemeteries near their houses, speak of their dissatisfaction with the amount of deer meat in their larders and decide which man they would support (by supplying food and verbal influence) to lead a hunting party? Did they discuss, now that one of the elder chiefs had passed on, who should take his place? Did they help keep peace between communities by refusing to supply potential war parties with food? Many more questions can be asked about the patterning of architecture, artifacts, and graves at this site.

Archaeologists can only speculate about what life really was like in these ancient communities, but as we have seen, household and community plans can provide a wealth of data to shape insightful interpretations. More data sets and dimensions of analysis could be explored to answer questions about other aspects of the Mouse Creek phase communities. Archaeologists are becoming more and more aware of cultural variation and diversity across the Mississippian period Southeast. While the Mouse Creek phase communities provide examples of Mississippian period towns, they are not necessarily representative of other archaeologically known communities at other places and other times in the Southeast. Museum collections representing large communities will continue to provide data for studying and learning more about this diversity as new ideas and new analytical techniques are developed. Study of these collections is as close as we will get to stepping into the vanished towns.

DISCUSSION QUESTIONS

1. What were Mouse Creek phase communities like? What were Mouse Creek households like? Summarize what you have learned about these topics.

2. Think about the assumption that the treatment of an individual in death reflects his or her position during life. Does this make sense to you? Think of examples in addition to those given in the case study that support or contradict this assumption.

3. Consider the kinds of analogy that can be drawn to known Cherokee and other Southeastern Indian communities and households. How appropriate is it for archaeologists to turn to such information? Explain your answer.

4. Construct an argument for the value of recording and mapping during excavation and for the curation of documented archaeological collections. Use your argument to point out how uncontrolled excavation and looting can destroy opportunities to learn about the past.

CHAPTER 12

Northern and Coastal Peoples of the Eastern Woodlands

P eople often ask archaeologists a simple and obvious question, "How do you know where to dig?" Of course, archaeologists seek to understand past human culture rather than simply find the site with the neatest things from the past. Deciding where to dig has to do with what we already know as well as with what we would like to find out or with what we are required to document before planned disturbance. Archaeologists decide where to dig for a variety of reasons. While we can tell you why we are digging where we are, many factors influence decisions about where to dig.

The complicated reasons one of us (SWN) has been involved in investigating a particular site illustrates how this worked in one instance. The story begins with disastrous flooding on St. Patrick's Day in 1936, which took lives and damaged a lot of property in Pittsburgh and other parts of Western Pennsylvania. Following these floods, the U.S. Army Corps of Engineers (USACE) began an ambitious construction program along the rivers and streams that form the headwaters of the Ohio River above Pittsburgh. One of these rivers was the Conemaugh, a tributary of the Allegheny River. By 1950 plans had been made to build the Conemaugh Dam near Tunnelton in Indiana County. As a result of this dam's completion in 1952, Conemaugh River Lake was created upstream from the dam. Along the Conemaugh and its tributaries the floodplain became part of the lake. Normally much of the area is not inundated, but when rainwater or spring meltwater volumes are high, the Corps is able to hold back significant quantities of water, preventing flooding downstream.

In the mid-twentieth century a large number of flood control projects like this one were undertaken throughout the United States. Of course, because people in the past often found good reasons to live close to rivers, many archaeological sites were affected by these projects. In response, archaeologists and government officials developed programs to salvage these sites before they were destroyed. It was as part of this response that archaeologists conducted a survey of the areas that would become part of the lake. Walking the fields of the Johnston farm located along the Conemaugh in 1950, these archaeologists found artifacts that suggested a large site. Because it was thought likely to be destroyed after the construction of the Conemaugh Dam, excavations were conducted at the site in 1952, and a report about it was published in 1955 (Dragoo 1955). It turned out that the Johnston site was a large, stockaded village that subsequently has been assigned to the Johnston phase of the **Monongahela tradition**, a major late pre-Columbian cultural tradition of southwestern Pennsylvania.

In 2000, I and my colleagues at Indiana University of Pennsylvania (IUP) began a long-term research initiative designed to investigate the post AD 1000 to European contact period in several key Western Pennsylvania drainages including the Conemaugh. In this area there were a large number of recorded but poorly investigated village sites. Sites that had been excavated, like the Johnston site, had been studied before the widespread use of radiocarbon dating and other contemporary techniques. Through a series of IUP field schools and other projects, researchers have been systematically gathering new data over the past decade.

Naturally, one of the initial questions was whether, as had been anticipated in the 1950s, the Johnston site had been washed away by the waters of the Conemaugh River Lake. Since the completion of the dam there had been a number of episodes of severe flooding in Western Pennsylvania. After obtaining permission from the USACE, IUP archaeologists began looking for the site by shovel testing the known location. This work benefited the USACE because, as a federal agency, it had the responsibility to manage any cultural resources on its lands and that required knowing what sites existed in the first place.

Several initial attempts to relocate the site between 2002 and 2004, produced only sandy and silty flood deposits containing recent and ancient debris to a depth of a meter or more. This was much deeper than the depth at which the 1950s excavations had encountered features, and it suggested that the site was destroyed. Reasoning that if it were buried instead, the alluvial overburden should be shallowest away from the river bank, archaeologists tested the river terrace nearly a hundred meters away from the river in 2005. Sure enough, it became clear that the Johnston site was not gone but simply buried. Rather than scouring out this terrace, flooding has meant that sediments carried by flood waters into the Conemaugh River Lake have been dumped over the site. In a region known for its acidic soils that often lead to the rapid disappearance of organic remains, the buried Johnston site deposits contain large quantities of plant and animal remains, and there is an unusual opportunity to use modern techniques to investigate further.

So how did archaeologists know to dig at the Johnston site? Obviously there have been a variety of reasons to investigate this site. Initially it was a place that was likely to be destroyed, and one where artifacts on the surface suggested there was a site to be salvaged. Excavation produced data of regional significance. More recently, research questions about the time period of the site caused archaeologists to investigate whether it was still intact, and this research dovetailed well with the management responsibilities of the USACE. Finally, the good preservation at the site has encouraged

further excavation using modern techniques. Although the particulars may be different, the reasons archaeologists dig somewhere are likely to be a balance between research goals and the desire to record and protect information about the past rather than a simple formula about where sites are.

DEFINITION OF THE AREA

Many fascinating archaeological sites, like the Johnston site, have been investigated outside the interior portions of the Eastern Woodlands on which Chapter 11 focused (Figure 12.1). In this chapter we turn our attention to the northern and coastal portions of the Southeast and Northeast, areas for which the cultural sequences are different enough to warrant separate discussion. This means that this chapter covers regions that are particularly diverse both culturally and environmentally including the northern part of the Great Lakes area, southern Ontario and Quebec as well as the Canadian Maritimes, New England, New York, Pennsylvania and the rest of the Mid-Atlantic, the southern Atlantic coast, Florida, and the Gulf Coast from eastern Louisiana eastward. Discussing these areas together should reinforce the important point that North American cultures were highly variable, providing archaeologists with a complicated array of cultural sequences and histories not easily subsumed under the traditional Northeast and Southeast culture areas. The cultural developments covered in this chapter can be placed in the chronological framework shown in Table 12.1; note that a Mississippian period generally is absent and the Late Woodland after 950 BP often is called the Late Prehistoric.

NORTHERN AND COASTAL EASTERN WOODLANDS ENVIRONMENTS

In the northern areas discussed in this chapter, the climate is moist during all seasons, but the summers are warm and the winters are cold. In the southern Mid-Atlantic, along the southern Atlantic Coast and the Gulf Coasts the summers are hot and long and the winter is mild. There are distinct seasons, but snow and persistent freezing temperatures are rare. The southern tip of Florida has a more tropical climate, with temperatures seldom dropping below 65°F and little seasonal variation in temperature. From February through October, however, typical rainfall exceeds 50 inches (127 cm).

There are three main physiographic features of significance in the areas covered in this chapter—the Great Lakes, the Appalachian Mountain system, and the Coastal Plain—although New England can be seen as a distinct physiographic province as well. The Great

TABLE 12.1 Introduction to Northern and Coastal Eastern Woodlands Prehistory

Uncalibrated Years BP	General Periods	Northern and Coastal Eastern Woodlands					Calibrated Years BC/AD
		Gulf Coast	Florida	Atlantic Coast	New York/ New England	Great Lakes	
	Protohistoric						AD 1,650
500	Late Prehistoric		Calusa		Northern Iroquoians		AD 1,426
1,000	Early Late Woodland	Weeden Island				Princess Point Effigy mounds	AD 1,022
1,500			Weeden Island				AD 568
	Middle Woodland					First	
2,000			Swift Creek	Swift Creek		◆	0 BC
2,500	Early Woodland					Pottery	618 BC
3,000	Terminal Archaic			Susquehanna tradition	First		1,261 BC
3,500		First ◆ Pottery			◆ Pottery		1,875 BC
4,000		Gulf Formational	First				2,555 BC
4,500	Late Archaic		◆ Pottery			Maritime Archaic	3,183 BC
5,000				First ◆ Pottery			3,780 BC
5,500					Mast Forest Archaic	Lake Forest Archaic	4,344 BC
6,000							4,874 BC
6,500	Middle Archaic						5,476 BC
7,000					Gulf of Maine Archaic		5,890 BC
7,500							6,395 BC
8,000							6,911 BC
8,500							7,571 BC
9,000	Early Archaic						8,247 BC
9,500							8,788 BC
10,000				Late Paleoindian			9,445 BC
10,500							10,509 BC
11,000	Paleoindian			Clovis			10,932 BC
11,500 and prior	Pre-Clovis	?	?	?	?	?	11,394 BC and Prior

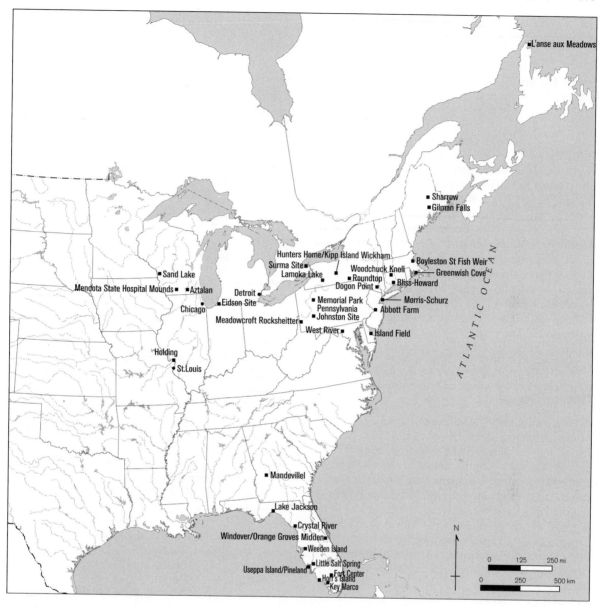

FIGURE 12.1 The Eastern Woodlands, showing the location of sites mentioned in Chapter 12.

Lakes are situated at the boundary of the Central Lowland and the Laurentian Upland physiographic provinces (Fenneman 1938) where complex glacial activity has carved deep basins in the valleys of preglacial rivers. Today, these lakes drain northeastward through the lowland valley of the St. Lawrence River. The Appalachian Mountain system trends from eastern Canada southwestward into northeastern Alabama and northwestern Georgia and marks the diffuse boundary between areas discussed in the last chapter and those covered in this one. Within the Appalachian mountain system there are a number of distinct provinces. On the west is, the Appalachian Plateau with both glaciated and unglaciated sections; the mountains themselves include the Blue Ridge Mountains of Virginia, the Adirondacks of New York State, and the Smoky Mountains, while the Piedmont an older plateau or heavily eroded **peneplain is found east of the mountains.** The boundary between the Appalachian system and the Coastal Plain often is called the **fall line,** in reference to the waterfalls that form as rivers flow over this often steep feature. The sediments of the Coastal Plain often are sandy and gravelly, reflecting deposition as the ocean moved back and forth across this extension of the continental shelf. Swamps and offshore islands characterize much of the actual coast, and southern Florida is so low-lying that most of it is swamp.

Most of the areas discussed in this chapter were forested before modern agricultural activities or extensive cutting and burning reduced the extent of forest. Truly boreal forest types that are dominated by spruce and fir are confined to areas north of the Great Lakes and some portions of Quebec and the Maritime Provinces. However, there is a broad ecotone of mixed coniferous and deciduous forest, often called the transition forest, that extends between the boreal forest and the temperate forest to the south. Within the temperate forest biome, deciduous oak hickory forest is important in southern New England and portions of the Mid-Atlantic states. Mixed forests dominated by pine occur along the coast and throughout the southern Coastal Plain and evergreens including magnolia species are mixed with some deciduous trees (Braun 1967; Gaudreau 1988; Shelford 1963). In southern Florida the various semitropical forests contain tropical hardwood species, pine, and cypress as well as salt-adapted mangroves, but extensive salt and freshwater marshes such as the Everglades also are widespread.

Climatic Change

As you may have gathered from Chapter 2, the history of environmental change is of considerable archaeological interest throughout the regions covered in this chapter. On the north the glacial advance and retreat shaped the landscape humans have inhabited. During the greatest extent of the glaciers in the Late Wisconsin (Figure 2.12), the southern margin of the ice sheet covered all of the Northern areas we are considering. Familiar coastal features also were not present or were buried under ice, while unfamiliar landforms were exposed because of the lower sea levels. Rivers extended out across a broader coastal plain. Some rivers deeply incised their valleys as they fell further as well (Bloom 1983). Lower sea levels also meant that Florida was much drier and cooler than it is today (Milanich 1994).

The northward retreat of the glaciers was associated with sea-level changes, isostatic rebound of the earth's crust as it was freed of the weight of glaciers, the drainage of glacial meltwaters, and the colonization of exposed land areas by plant and animal species. These processes made the several millennia of glacial retreat a period of extreme environmental change throughout the northern and coastal Eastern Woodlands. For each of the Great Lakes, a series of predecessor lakes can be correlated with glacial advances and retreats by geologists. Similarly, the **moraines**, where glaciers stopped for a while, and glacial lake beaches still are visible around the

Great Lakes. The earliest Great Lakes were essentially proglacial lakes made up of waters trapped between the retreating ice front to the north and the moraines or ice dams to the south. Because these various lakes could not drain northeastward through the St. Lawrence River until the glacier had retreated a considerable distance to the north, other drainage patterns through the Mississippi and Ohio valleys were established. In the upper part of the St. Lawrence valley, depressed by more than 655 feet (200 m) below its modern elevation, the Atlantic invaded the lowlands creating a vast, inland sea called the **Champlain Sea** (Figure 12.2), between ca. 12,800 BP and 10,000 BP (Kirkland and Coates 1977).

The Great Lakes were dynamic well into the Holocene, and river regimes took millennia to stabilize throughout the east (Baker 1983). Similarly complex reconfigurations developed in coastal areas such as the Gulf of Maine (Kellogg 1988), the Chesapeake Bay (Dent 1995), and Florida as sea levels rose. Gradually braided streams gave way to lower-energy rivers. Eventually meander belts and aquatic habitats similar to those of the recent past developed. Along the coast estuaries, marshes and barrier islands formed as sea levels stabilized.

Paleoecological reconstruction of biotic variables associated with these changes in glacial extent, landforms, and drainage obviously is a difficult but relevant task for archaeologists and other scholars. Detailed mapping of the changing vegetational patterns has been attempted (Bernabo and Webb 1977; Gaudreau 1988), although the most meaningful reconstructions probably are on a local scale. Pollen isopoll maps indicate that as the glaciers were shrinking, spruce forests did not become extensive. Rather, they were rapidly replaced by pine-dominated forests, which became established in a broad band stretching across the Great Lakes into New England, only to be replaced over time by the transition forest with which we are familiar. Farther south, the prairie forest ecotone was established, and oak-dominated deciduous forests quickly developed (Bernabo and Webb 1977).

Three Post-Pleistocene climatic periods have been of most interest to archaeologists working in the areas covered in this chapter. The first period is the Hypsithermal, the mid-Holocene warming and drying period that began after 9000 BP and continued until 2500 BP. The prairie forest ecotone expanded eastward at this time. In the forests of the Coastal Plain, except in the river valleys and swamps, hardwood trees became less dominant as pine was favored. There also is some evidence that the Medieval Warm period between approximately 1150 BP and 750 BP may have been significant because it expanded the land area suitable for farming in the north. A third climatic episode that may have affected peoples is the Little Ice Age (650–100 BP).

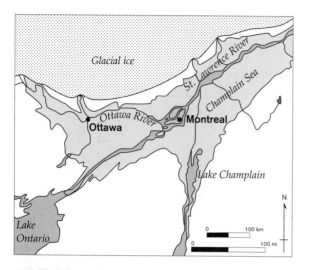

FIGURE 12.2 One of the many features of the glacial retreat in the Eastern Woodlands was the Champlain Sea, which formed in the depressed St. Lawrence lowlands and persisted until approximately 10,000 BP.

This cooler period affected growing season length in ways that may have been significant to horticultural groups living in the Northeast. However, precisely how these periods might have affected humans can be debated.

In addition, humans themselves began to alter the landscape, managing or clearing the forest to promote prey species or for farming. These more subtle changes are harder to reconstruct, but they were significant locally in both pre-Columbian and historical times.

PALEOINDIANS

As Chapter 3, made clear, there is significant Paleoindian evidence in the areas covered in this chapter that supplements what has been learned in the interior Eastern Woodlands. This evidence includes important Pre-Clovis sites, large numbers of fluted point surface finds, and key data from both the Clovis era and Late

---

Thematic Research Questions in Chapter 12

One theme of this chapter is diversity in human adaptations, but there also is a macroscale, or big picture, from which we can view the diverse cultures and histories of North America. This is certainly true for the northern and coastal areas of the Eastern Woodlands discussed in this chapter. However, you will find material directly relevant to at least four of the broad research questions discussed in Chapter 2 and listed in Table 2.1, and we touch on other themes less directly. Table 12.2 helps you locate relevant sections of this chapter for each theme. Reading these sections likely will suggest more specific questions and issues as well.

Table 12.2 Research Themes for the Northern and Coastal Eastern Woodlands

Research Question	Particularly Relevant Sections
How have humans adapted to the diverse environments of North America and to climatic change over time?	Discussions of the Archaic and Woodland cultures of the northern and coastal protions of the Eastern Woodlands including those of the Late Prehistoric
How, when, and where did food production develop in North America?	Discussion of subsistence and settlement in the Archaic and Woodland including the Late Prehistoric period
How, when, and where did sociopolitically complex, internally differentiated cultural systems develop in North America?	Discussion of the cultures of the Late Woodland and the Late Prehistoric
What ethnic identities can be identified and historically traced in North America's past?	Box 12.1, "Iroquoian Origins," and section on the Protohistoric and Contact periods
What movements of human populations can be documented in the North American past after the continent's initial settlement?	Box 12.1, "Iroquoian Origins"

Paleoindian times. Many sites probably also were drowned as the continental shelf was inundated or destroyed when landforms and drainages changed during glacial retreat. Some of our most important data on Paleoindians comes from wet sites and **sinkholes** in the limestone topography of northern Florida where preservation is excellent as well.

THE ARCHAIC

Although the Eastern Archaic was originally defined as a preceramic pattern on the basis of materials from the Lamoka Lake site in New York State (Ritchie 1932) and then designated a stage, today most archaeologists working in the areas covered in this chapter treat the Archaic as a period of time rather than a stage (but see Pleger and Stoltman 2009). Just as in the interior, the first 5000 years of the Archaic typically are subdivided into the Early Archaic, from 10,000 BP to 8000 BP, and the Middle Archaic, from 8000 BP to 5000 BP, while the Late Archaic usually is seen as spanning the period from 5000 BP to 3000 BP. These subperiod dates may vary (e.g., Ellis et al. 2009; Pleger and Stoltman 2009). Some researchers (e.g., Custer 1990, 1996; Dincauze 1990) also prefer to stress continuity between Late Paleoindian and Early Archaic peoples so that the Archaic is seen as truly starting in Middle Archaic times, when more aggregated groups began to settle into local regions.

How to subdivide the end of the Archaic can also be a point of disagreement among archaeologists. Some researchers see the beginnings of Late Archaic adaptations in the Middle Archaic, and so argue that the Late Archaic should begin earlier around 6000 BP. Other archaeologists, particularly those working in New England, the Mid-Atlantic, and the rest of the Atlantic Coast, have stressed the significance of the transition between the Archaic and Woodland, denoting a separate period called the **Transitional period** or the **Terminal Archaic**. Following Snow (1980), the Terminal Archaic can be dated between about 3700 BP and 2700 BP. Still other researchers (e.g., Custer 1984:76) have argued that it makes most sense to group the Terminal Archaic with the beginning of the Woodland period (see also Dincauze 1990). Designation of a **Gulf Formational stage** between approximately 4500 BP and 2100 BP in the Gulf Coastal Plain (e.g., Walthall 1980) has this effect as well. These kinds of debates indicate both continuing conceptualization of the Archaic as an evolutionary stage as well as the variability in regional and local sequences across the Eastern Woodlands (Emerson and McElrath 2009). In this chapter we retain the traditional tripartite division for simplicity (Table 12.1).

Archaic Material Culture

Archaic material culture in most northern and coastal regions was a great deal like that of the interior East. At the juncture between the Paleoindian period and the Archaic period, the appearance of notched points, including Hardaway, Palmer, and Kirk points, is diagnostic of the Archaic, but other differences, as listed in Table 11.3, also can be recognized. The first efforts to develop an Archaic sequence of projectile points used sites in North Carolina's Piedmont (Coe 1964), although they were refined in the interior. Following the Early Archaic bifurcates, such as the LeCroy, St. Albans, and Kanawha points, stemmed points including Stanly and Morrow Mountain in the south, and Neville, Stark, and Merrimack points (Figure 12.3) in New England (Dincauze 1976) are found.

Besides these chipped stone bifaces, heavy use of ground stone technology also is evident (Figure 12.4). Many tool forms such as adzes, celts, and gouges probably are associated with woodworking. Especially in the Early Archaic, these forms sometimes are flaked and then ground on the surface (e.g., Dent 1995:170). Pestles and various abraders also are common. In New England ground stone knives, plummets, and ground slate *ulus* or semilunar knives are found in sites, while the classic Middle Archaic ground stone implement is the spear-thrower weight, or bannerstone, that was discussed in Chapter 11 (see Figure 11.5). Of course in South Florida there is very little naturally occurring stone that can be chipped, but sandstone and shell were used for implements.

Middle Archaic people in Wisconsin, the Upper Peninsula of Michigan, and adjacent areas also began to make some items from copper as well. Extensive copper deposits are found along Lake Superior, although smaller sources are more widely distributed throughout the Northeast (Levine 1999). Many native copper mines and some copper workshop sites have been discovered (Pleger and Stoltman 2009). Copper was worked through a combination of cold hammering and heating or **annealing**.

Early-Middle Archaic people used perishable materials including fiber, wood, and bone as well. While stone objects are common, well-preserved bone is recovered less frequently, and fiber and wood have seldom been preserved. Wet sites in Florida (see later) are important exceptions (Doran 2001, 2002). Among the grave goods found in these sites are many perishable items including various antler and bone tools and ornaments, turtle shell containers, seed necklaces, shark's teeth, wooden stakes and tools, and various textiles showing several different types of twining (Andrews et al. 2001; Doran 2002). Some of these kinds of nonlithic artifacts are discussed in Exhibit 12.1.

FIGURE 12.3 Stemmed points such as these are diagnostic of the Middle Archaic in New England.

FIGURE 12.4 These ground stone implements recovered from the Beech Creek Howard site in the Bald Eagle Valley in central Pennsylvania are typical of the Archaic; the two items at the upper left are fragments of a bannerstone and a birdstone, both of which probably served as spear-thrower weights when complete.

CLUES TO THE PAST   EXHIBIT 12.1

Modified Bone, Tooth, and Antler from a Florida Wet Site

We have noted that wet sites are a great boon to archaeologists because of the inventory of perishable items they yield (see Exhibit 5.1 as well as the case study in Chapter 5). In Florida there are many wet sites because of its many rivers, marshlands, springs, and ponds as well as its extensive coastline. Among the items recovered in these sites are well-preserved fragments of animal skeletal tissues. The inventory of modified bone, tooth, and antler from the Archaic Windover site near Titusville, Florida, illustrates how useful artifact collections from wet sites can be in illuminating human lifeways (Doran 2002).

The Windover site is situated in a small pond located in the swampy eastern edge of the St. John's River valley in central eastern Florida. Construction plans for the Windover Farms development in 1982 involved demucking or scooping out of the peat deposits beneath the pond and replacing it with sand and gravel fill, but when this process was begun, workers found artifacts and human remains. Examination proved that these materials were pre-Columbian and ultimately led to avoidance of the pond and funding for excavation of the site. It should be noted that these excavations took place before the passage of NAGPRA. Today, even though Windover Pond was privately held, archaeologists likely would have approached excavation of such a sensitive site in consultation with Native people.

What was recovered from this site, which turned out to be a mortuary pond dated between 7100 BP and 7330 BP in what is designated as the Early Archaic (Doran 2002:72), was truly remarkable. The site is briefly described elsewhere in this chapter; here we highlight a part of the artifact assemblage that is among the oldest collections of modified bone in North America. Although many objects were associated with human burials, there were both utilitarian and decorative or ceremonial objects, and as a group they reveal much about technology and lifestyle at this early date (Penders 2002).

Many of the items recovered can be considered hunting implements. Included in this group were barbed and unbarbed projectile points and a bipointed fish gorge made of bone, as well as antler projectile points, atlatl weights or handles, and atlatl cups. Penders (2002) suggests that some of the atlatl weights or handles may have functioned secondarily as clubs, a possible explanation

FIGURE 12.5 An antler atlatl cup from the Windover site showing internal striations, suggesting twisting as the atlatl shaft was inserted.

for the common shattering of one end of these items. The atlatl cups, one of which is shown in Figure 12.5, are particularly interesting. The sockets on these objects were the ends of the atlatl itself into which the atlatl shaft was inserted while the tangs on the side of the cup are the atlatl hooks for the dart. Interestingly, the drilled sockets have no adhesive residue, indicating that the shafts must have fit tightly enough that adhesive wasn't needed.

Other objects are believed to have been tools used in various manufacturing activities. Antler pressure flakers with blunt tips were apparently used to work shell or chert, and antler also was used to make an apparent arrow shaft straightener. The teeth of several shark species seem to have been gravers, scrapers, or drills, and associated wood fragments suggest they were hafted to wooden handles. Heavily worn canine teeth and ulnas from medium mammals with steeply beveled lower tips may have been burnishing tools, although the teeth could have been gravers when sharp as well. Nine deer ulna specimens are more likely to have been gouges based on their size and longitudinal striation patterns. Other medium mammal bones, particularly bobcat and canid radii with their hollow interior exposed, are identified as awls by researchers. Small, thin bone needles, pins, and battens also have been recovered. These suggest that baskets, nets, cordage, and other items were being made, and indeed fragments of such fabricated materials have been found at Windover as well.

A final group of tools can be understood only as decorative or perhaps ceremonial. Included here are bird bone tubes, many of which have been incised with various rectilinear or diamond motifs (Figure 12.6). These items could have been used by shamans to smoke tobacco or to ritually suck irritants from a sick person. The split and ground shaft of a deer femur or tibia was also recovered and may have been a hairpin. Shell fragments from pond turtles, softshell turtles, and snapping turtles had numerous striations on their interior surface suggesting that they were parts of turtle shell containers or rattles. Finally, small beads made from the perforated centers of catfish vertebra or from drilling the shells of sea snails (*Marginella* cf. *apicina*) were found.

Although the size of the collection is small—only 119 items—there is rich information here. We can infer that deer and many smaller mammals, various species of birds, turtles, catfish, and sharks all were exploited in the Early Archaic. More significantly, we can conclude that hunting with atlatls was the norm and surmise that different types of bone points may have been used in acquiring different prey species. We also can conclude that people at this time were engaged in a wide variety of manufacturing activities, from tool making itself to basket and net making. The less utilitarian objects hint at the rich ideological world of these people. Associations with burials of particular ages or sexes can help us understand division of labor. For instance, atlatl weights or handles that were with burials were almost exclusively associated with males while most of the bird bone tubes were found with adult females. Archaeologists also see many items that remind them of later bone, antler, and tooth objects, allowing us to conclude that some aspects of historically documented native technology have tremendous time depth in Florida. As you can see, modified bone, antler, and teeth provide another example of how central material culture is to archaeological reconstructions of the past.

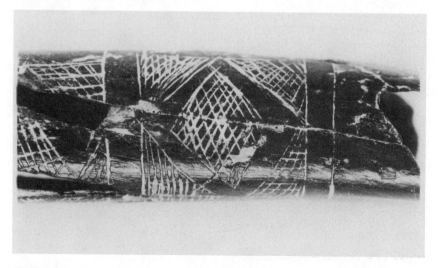

FIGURE 12.6 Close-up of a bird bone tube from the Windover site showing incised decoration.

In central Maine, southern Quebec and perhaps the Maritime Provinces a **Gulf of Maine Archaic tradition** (9500–6000 BP), characterized by the use of metamorphic rock in the creation of rods, gouges, and other ground and chipped stone artifacts, has now been recognized (Clark and Will 2006; Robinson 2006). For example, the Gilman Falls site (Sanger 1996), a quarry site on the Stillwater River north of Orono, Maine, has a Middle Archaic zone dated from 7300 BP to 6300 BP. In this zone minimally flaked pieces of phyllite, a low-grade metamorphic rock, are common, while stemmed bifaces like the Neville and Stark points of western Maine and southern New England are absent. Other tools include ground stone gouges that have full-length grooves, celts, unifacial quartz scrapers, battered cobbles, and especially ground stone rods of varying lengths.

As mentioned in Chapter 11, two broad Middle–Late Archaic cultural traditions, the Lake Forest Archaic and the Mast Forest tradition, commonly have been recognized in the Northeast culture area (Tuck 1978), and these are still associated with diagnostic point types (Figure 12.8). The relationships between these traditions are poorly delineated, and it isn't clear that they correspond to different ancient ethnicities. One debate is over whether the Lake Forest tradition predates the Mast Forest tradition, coexists with it, or is a largely geographic distinction, with Lake Forest having an interior orientation and Narrow Point/Mast Forest having a more coastal and southerly one. In the Maritime Canada and Maine, the Maritime Archaic, also mentioned in Chapter 4, apparently was contemporaneous with these other traditions (Figure 12.8).

At the end of the Late Archaic, Terminal Archaic projectile point forms found in many areas are broadbladed (Figure 12.7). For example, in the Mid-Atlantic this tradition is known as the **Susquehanna tradition**, after the Susquehanna broadpoint. Archaeological debate concerning the appearance of the Broadpoint tradition has centered on whether the appearance of broadpoints and associated elements of this tradition represent an actual migration of people into the Mid-Atlantic and Northeast from the Southeast (Cook 1976b; Turnbaugh 1975) where such forms may occur earlier in the Middle Archaic. The alternative viewpoint is that the appearance of new artifacts represents diffusions of new technology and subsistence practices.

One fascinating aspect of the Late Archaic is the appearance in assemblages of steatite bowls and fiber-tempered ceramics. Steatite bowls are common in the Appalachian Piedmont from Georgia to Massachusetts,

FIGURE 12.7 Maritime Archaic chipped and ground stone artifacts.

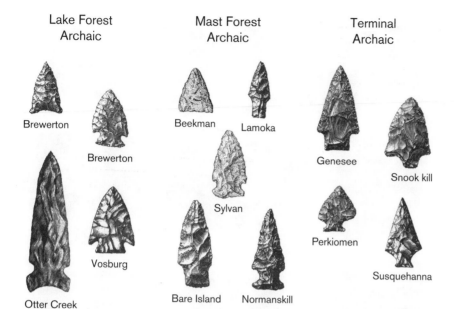

Lake Forest
Archaic

Brewerton

Brewerton

Vosburg

Otter Creek

Mast Forest
Archaic

Beekman   Lamoka

Sylvan

Bare Island   Normanskill

Terminal
Archaic

Genesee

Snook kill

Perkiomen

Susquehanna

FIGURE 12.8 Variability in characteristic projectile point forms between the Mast Forest tradition, Lake Forest tradition, and the Terminal Archaic in the Northeast and Mid-Atlantic.

where steatite can be quarried, but they are also found more widely into the interior Eastern Woodlands as mentioned in Chapter 11. People also traded steatite slabs apparently used in cooking. Vessels made of steatite tend to be shallow, thick-walled, flat-bottomed, and round to oblong, with lug handles (Figure 12.9). It is most likely that the first steatite vessels were receptacles for indirect cooking, rather than for use directly over fires.

Although archaeologists long assumed that stone vessels represented experimentation with new types of containers and thus preceded the development of pottery, Sassaman (2006) presents evidence that this technology was not important before 3700 BP. Thus, while in some areas steatite bowls precede pottery, in others pottery appears first. Regardless, the appearance of stone bowls is associated with the container revolution and possibly associated with new food preparation techniques for cooking seeds. They may also be a form of ethnic signaling (Sassaman 2005). The inclusion of steatite vessels in burial settings in southern New England around 2700 BP may indicate that they did convey social messages.

The first pottery in the Eastern Woodlands began to be manufactured during the Late Archaic in the Southeast along the Atlantic Coastal Plain in Georgia and South Carolina. Fiber-tempered pottery in the Stallings and St. Simons series are recognized beginning about 4500 BP. Besides being fiber-tempered, this pottery has either plain, punctated, or incised surfaces and is usually in bowl or open basin form. One early type, Stallings ware, is best known for its distinctive "drag and jab" punctate designs (Sassaman 2002)

FIGURE 12.9 Steatite vessel fragments; note lug handles.

(Figure 12.10). Fiber-tempered pottery was made in several parts of Florida by 4000 BP (Milanich 1994), but the Orange series pottery of the St. Johns River valley is best known. Similar pottery, including the Wheeler series pottery mentioned in Chapter 11 as well as various types made in the Gulf Coastal Plain of Mississippi and Alabama after 3500 BP, was made. In the Mid-Atlantic, a variety of ceramic types made during the Terminal Archaic have been considered "experimental wares" under the assumption that people were experimenting with ceramic technology at this time. In New York State and southern New England, the oldest pottery generally is the Vinette I type, which has been

FIGURE 12.10 Sherds of Classic Stallings ceramics, the earliest dated ceramics in Eastern North America, showing characteristic decorations.

dated as early as 3200 BP. However, in most of the northern Eastern Woodlands, pottery was not made until around 3000 BP or later.

Archaic Settlement and Subsistence

As is the case in the interior, an increase in population by Late Archaic times is inferred from the large number of sites found in northern and coastal areas when compared with Early and Middle Archaic sites. It is possible that some areas including the South Atlantic coast may

have seen little human settlement until Middle Archaic times. A classic conundrum of Northeastern archaeology focuses on the relative lack of data on the Early and Middle Archaic. The Paleoindian presence throughout the Northeast is clear. Does the small number of Early and Middle Archaic sites mean that the Northeast was depopulated as tundra and spruce parkland habitats retreated northward during the Holocene? Archaeologists no longer think so. In the first place, a number of Early and Middle Archaic sites now have been found, and the high volume of CRM archaeology is producing additional sites at a constant rate (e.g., Bergman et al. 1998; Bourque et al. 2006; Clark and Will 2006). In the second place, dramatic changes in sea level, riverine drainage regimes, and the Great Lakes during the first half of the Holocene means that many early landforms have been drowned, deeply buried, or destroyed. This certainly could explain the relative lack of Early and Middle Archaic sites on the surface. Of course, sites from the Paleoindian period have been similarly affected, but differing land-use patterns may have led to the comparatively higher frequency of Paleoindian as opposed to Early and Middle Archaic surface finds. Finally, the density of Early and Middle Archaic sites may appear to be low simply because highly diagnostic artifacts are rarer than during Paleoindian times, and assemblages harder to identify with respect to period.

During the Early and Middle Archaic people are thought to have been organized into bands of foragers who moved repeatedly on either a residential or logistical basis, perhaps coalescing seasonally into larger groups. Many known Early Archaic sites also have Paleoindian components. For example, Milanich (1994:63–64) notes that in Florida Early Archaic components are found both in well known Paleoindian sites such as Little Salt Spring (Figure 3.8) and in new areas that could be utilized as the amount of surface water increased following the Pleistocene. He argues that this patterning in site locations is what we should expect as Archaic people gradually developed new strategies in response to environmental changes.

Similar arguments might be made for other northern and coastal areas of the East that also were undergoing major environmental changes at the beginning of the Holocene. However, it should be clear that settlement and mobility strategies must be reconstructed on a regional or even local basis, and that any evolutionary progression from residential to logistical foraging (from foragers to collectors) cannot be assumed. For example in Michigan, changing mobility patterns are thought to have been just the reverse. Lower lake levels in the Early-Middle Archaic times seem to have allowed inclusion of the central uplands in logistically based foraging strategies by people living in the Saginaw and Grand River drainage basins. However, higher water levels and the associated constriction of the land mass during the Late Archaic seem to have necessitated the use of residential mobility strategies with people moving radially along tributary streams (Lovis 2009).

An important commonality in human subsistence in northern and coastal areas even during the Early and Middle Archaic is the utilization of a diverse array of aquatic and shoreline resources that were being exploited in addition to many species of mammals and birds (e.g., Whyte 1990). In Maine anadromous fish, turtles, beaver, and muskrat may have been more important than white-tailed deer and moose to Early and Middle Archaic foragers (Spiess and Mosher 2006). On Cape Cod, Middle Archaic settlement systems also suggest use of the resources of both freshwater wetlands such as glacial ponds and the estuaries at the mouths of rivers (Dunford 1999). The Boylston Street Fish Weir in Boston (Nicholas 1999: 32-33), which dates to the end of the Middle Archaic and the Late Archaic, also indicates sophisticated use of fish resources. Despite the lack of systematic data, there also is good reason to believe that Early and Middle Archaic people throughout the northern and coastal portions of the East used a variety of fruits and berries, nuts of several kinds, and many other species of plants for food, medicine, and various perishable artifacts (see AschSidell 1999; Dent and Kauffman 1985). Wet sites in Florida including Windover and Orange Grove Midden also have produced a diverse array of plant materials.

There are two other aspects of subsistence that must be highlighted when thinking about the areas covered in this chapter. First, to what extent is there evidence of early horticulture like that found in the interior during the Archaic? While the use of native or tropical cultigens never began along the Florida and Gulf coasts, horticulture eventually was adopted in some of this chapter's area. Cultivation and domestication of native plants including gourd, has generally not been found in Early and Middle Archaic contexts. However, two finds of gourd rind dated to the sixth millennium BP at the Sharrow site in Maine (Peterson and Asch-Sidell 1996) and at the Memorial Park site in north central Pennsylvania (Hart and Asch-Sidell 1997) have raised the possibility that limited cultivation of gourds began in these areas at roughly the same time as it did farther west. This chapter's case study, "A New History of Maize-Bean-Squash Agriculture in the Northeast," by John Hart addresses related issues.

There also is evidence for use of the native plants important in the Eastern Agricultural complex at a variety of Late Archaic sites in northern areas (e.g., Monaghan et al. 2006). For example, Terminal Archaic components at the Bliss–Howard and Woodchuck Knoll sites in the Connecticut River valley indicate that chenopodium was a significant subsistence item and that it was stored by people living in semipermanent villages, but it is not yet clear whether the plant had been domesticated (George and Dewar 1999). The Broome-Tech site in the Chenango River valley of southern New York State also produced a seed assemblage including plants like chenopodium, marsh elder, and false buckwheat that are part of the complex. Moreover, this seed assemblage and the wood charcoal composition, as well as high amounts of nutshell, suggest that there might have been intentional burning of the climax forest to promote both nut production and pioneer species with edible seeds (Asch-Sidell 2002). Such manipulation of the environment through fire has also been proposed for this period in the Mid-Atlantic (Stevens 1991).

A second aspect of subsistence and settlement is the exploitation of shellfish and the many shell mound sites in coastal areas of the East. It is not clear when Archaic foragers began to exploit shellfish intensively. Riverine and coastal shellfishing may not have been important until the Late Archaic. A critical factor may have been the appearance of coastal estuaries, whose saline waters are important to populations of oysters and other shellfish. On the other hand, because sea levels had not stabilized until about 5000 years ago, early sites along the coast may have been destroyed, with the result that we have an incomplete picture of the extent to which Early and Middle Archaic foragers utilized these areas. Sites like the Dogan Point site, a shell midden site in the lower Hudson River valley, indicate that at least some Middle Archaic foragers used shellfish as a resource (Claassen 1995). Here oyster shell has been dated to the sixth millennium BP (i.e., during the Middle Archaic). Similarly, at Useppa Island on Florida's Gulf Coast, Late Middle Archaic inhabitants used both quahog clams and oysters (Marquardt 1999), and at Orange Grove Midden, a wet site dating between 4000 and 6000 years ago in Florida's St. Johns River area, Purdy recovered 20 species of shellfish (Purdy 2001).

By Late Archaic times, numerous shell mound and ring sites are known along the Atlantic and Gulf Coasts. Ritchie's (1980) **Orient phase** on Long Island and in the lower Hudson River valley provides one example of intensive use of shellfish. Dent (1995) also has defined an "intensification era" from approximately 4200 to 3000 years ago in the Chesapeake Bay area. He suggests that at this time people exploited anadromous fish runs and various estuarine resources, including shellfish, exchanged lithic raw materials, and were more restricted in their settlement mobility. Large stationary populations focused on fish and shellfish appear to have lived along the South Atlantic and Gulf coasts in Late Archaic times. Horr's Island on southwestern Florida's Gulf coast is one example where four mounds and a shell ridge were constructed around several midden deposits (Russo 1994) (Figure 12.11). This site apparently was occupied year-round because it contained scallops, clams, oysters and estuary fish. Many other shell mounds, shell rings, and large sites also are known, suggesting large stationary Late Archaic populations in these coastal areas (Russo 1996; Sassaman and Anderson 2004).

Just as in the interior, there has been debate about whether these shell mounds are primarily refuse heaps or whether they have been intentionally constructed as monuments. Marquardt (2010) has argued that even shell mounds that contain obvious layering of strata can be accounted for by midden accumulation and natural processes rather than intentional construction. Other researchers, however, argue that these are architectural constructions used for feasting and other

FIGURE 12.11 Mound D at Horr's Island.

ceremonies (Kidder and Sassaman 2009). Evidence that large quantities of shell have been dumped on prepared surfaces tends to support the interpretation that rings and mounds were systematically constructed. If the shell mounds and rings of the Atlantic and Gulf coasts were constructed as part of feasts or ritual activities like burial of the dead, they do suggest more elaborate social interactions during the Late Archaic.

Archaic Mortuary Practices and Exchange

Similarly, evidence for intentional burial of the dead in formal cemeteries or mounds may also indicate the existence of more intricate social relations among Archaic peoples. There is some evidence for Early and Middle Archaic burial practices in the archaeological record from the northern and coastal Eastern Woodlands. Certainly some foragers at this time intentionally buried their dead in cemeteries. Perhaps the most dramatic finds are of mortuary pond sites in Florida. For example, at the Windover site, as early as 8000 years ago, people buried their dead in marshy pond deposits, staking the submerged bodies into the underlying peat. Excavation has revealed nearly 170 sets of human remains including brain tissue in excellent states of preservation. As described earlier in Exhibit 12.1, the preservation of bone and other artifacts in these deposits also was remarkable.

In northern New England, the **Moorehead burial complex** spans much of the Archaic between 8600 BP and 3700 BP (Robinson 1996, 2006). Burials containing gouges, adzes, celts, rods, plummets, and ground slate points have been found at several sites, and specific sites and burials may indicate changing practices over the 5000 years of the tradition. The substantial amounts of red ocher in these burials led early researchers to call the people of this tradition the "Red Paint People." How the ritual activities associated with this complex relates to the various cultural groups and traditions found in Maine and the Maritime Provinces has not been completely resolved. This complex has long been thought of as associated with the Maritime Archaic, though some researchers have argued that it is a distinct cultural phase that developed out of the Lake Forest Archaic.

Two Middle to Late Archaic burial complexes, perhaps related to the Red Ocher Mortuary complex discussed in Chapter 11, provide strong evidence for exchange and social integration across the Midwest and Upper Great Lakes as well. The **Old Copper culture** may be the more colorful of these (Robertson et al. 1999; Pleger and Stoltman 2009). As mentioned above, people in the Great Lakes area began to use copper to make implements and ornaments at this time. Most of these artifacts which include projectile points, knives, celts, awls, fishhooks, bracelets, beads,

and other items have been found in burials or in caches rather than in habitation sites. Copper artifacts are most common in the northern Midwest around the Great Lakes, but they have been found in Maryland and New Jersey as well as to the north and west of the Eastern Woodlands.

Also related to the Red Ocher mortuary complex is the **Glacial Kame Mortuary complex**, which derives its name from the practice of placing the dead in the gravel ridges or kames left by glaciation. Glacial Kame cemeteries are found in the northern Midwest and Upper Great Lakes, including portions of southern Ontario. They usually contain the tightly flexed remains of bodies that were covered with red ocher and buried in circular pits, along with drilled **sandal-sole gorgets** of marine shell, copper and shell beads, bone pins and awls, and **birdstone**s.

A key aspect of these burial complexes is the presence of prestige artifacts in widely spread sites. These sites indicate that just as in the interior Eastern Woodlands exchange networks were well established by the Late Archaic. Similarly, Poverty Point artifacts from the lower Mississippi valley have been widely found in the Gulf Coastal Plain at this time.

PEOPLES OF THE EARLY AND MIDDLE WOODLAND

The Woodland, which is often called the Ceramic period in Maine and the Maritime provinces, is the period in which the various developments of the Late and Terminal Archaic came to fruition. Many aspects of Woodland adaptations mirror those discussed for the interior Eastern Woodlands, but neither as elaborate mortuary ceremonialism nor as great a dependence on sedentary horticultural strategies characterizes the various regions covered in this chapter. Involvement in Adena and Hopewell interregional exchange is limited, and although complex, nonagricultural polities did develop in South Florida, there are very few sites and complexes considered Mississippian in these areas. However, Woodland cultural developments in the northern and coastal areas discussed here are significant in their own right, and they provide evidence of the regional cultural diversity within the Eastern Woodlands.

In this section we discuss the Early and Middle Woodland between approximately 3000 and 1500 BP, while in the next section we discuss the Late Woodland and Late Prehistoric periods. Although we refer to both the Early and the Middle Woodland, there is much less reason to make a distinction between them than in areas where Hopewell phenomena are pronounced. In Table 12.1, we have used 1950 BP (AD 0) as the boundary between Early and Middle Woodland in recognition that it is generally after this juncture that any hints of Hopewell influence appear in northern and coastal regions.

In addition, a number of researchers have argued that the distinction between the Late Archaic and the Early Woodland should not be made. Rather, the continuity of adaptations across this traditional boundary should be stressed. We have already mentioned the Gulf Formational stage dating between 4500 and 2100 BP that is used by some researchers working on the Gulf Coastal Plain (see Jackson et al. 2002 for somewhat different dates) to group the Late Archaic and Early Woodland periods together. Dincauze (1990) groups Middle Archaic through Middle Woodland people under the heading of Settlers, noting that they all were generalized hunter-gatherers with little reliance on cultigens. Similarly in the northern Great Lakes, where people generally began to make ceramics at later and varying times, the boundary between Late Archaic and Early Woodland is not clear both because people adopted ceramics at varying rates and because the adaptive contrasts of the original stage concepts are known to have been in error (Brown 1986).

Early and Middle Woodland Material Culture

There are a large number of phases and complexes for the Early and Middle Woodland defined for the northern and coastal parts of the Eastern Woodlands. Some of these cultural historical entities that are broadly diagnostic over large regions are indicated in Table 12.1. Others are too localized in their importance to be listed there, but archaeologists working in these areas find them significant. The great array of phases and complexes is testament to the process of regionalization that characterizes Woodland cultures, but also to the introduction of ceramic technology. Ceramic artifacts provided people with a new medium for cultural expression, and the inorganic nature of these artifacts has meant that they are preserved nearly as well as lithic artifacts. For this reason, archaeologists focus much attention on variation in ceramic paste, temper, decoration, and vessel form across space and time.

Nonetheless, several summary points can be made about Early and Middle Woodland ceramics. First, the adoption of ceramic technology was time transgressive, meaning that although it was made in the South Atlantic and Gulf Coastal Plain and in Florida during the Late Archaic, it was not fully adopted in the northern Eastern Woodlands until well into the Woodland period. For example, in northern Wisconsin, pottery called Nokomis and North Bay began to be made after about 1950 BP.

Second, we can contrast the Early and Middle Woodland ceramics of the Gulf Coastal Plain, Florida, and the South Atlantic Coast with those of Great Lakes, the Northeast, and the Mid-Atlantic. In the former areas, where pottery making had been developed early, fiber temper was replaced with sand and clay, and vessel forms also diversified as coiling methods replaced earlier hand-molding (Jefferies 2004). Ceramic vessels have a variety of surface treatments including incising, dentate and rocker stamping, or the application of carved wooden paddles. For example, **Deptford tradition** pottery was made in a wide area of the South Atlantic and Gulf Coastal Plains as well as in northern Florida after about 2500 BP. Deptford people often made deep, cylindrical pots that had rounded or conoidal bottoms. Particularly in the Gulf Coastal Plain they also made jars with tetrapodal supports. A very common design was check-stamping with wooden paddles. The later Swift Creek people, who lived in many of the same areas in Middle Woodland times, made pottery decorated with elaborate, often bilaterally symmetrical designs that had been carved on wooden paddles. These decorative styles are considered representative of a South Appalachian pottery tradition (Figure 12.12). Bayou La Batre ceramics known from the Early Woodland on Gulf Coastal Plain also often have dentate stamping, but other vessels were decorated by pinching or by impressing the edge of a scallop shell into the wet clay.

In the Great Lakes, the Northeast, and the Mid-Atlantic Northeast, Early and Middle Woodland ceramics most often are tempered with various types of crushed rock, and in some instances with sand or shell. Early Woodland potters made pots by coiling, and vessel forms were often conoidal. These pots usually were cord marked on both exterior and interior surfaces, reflecting use of a cord-wrapped paddle and anvil to meld and thin the coils. The earlier forms of pottery, including Vinette I (Figure 12.13), Marion thick and other Early Woodland varieties, tend to be thick walled, while by the end of the Middle Woodland, thin-walled ceramics were being made. The size

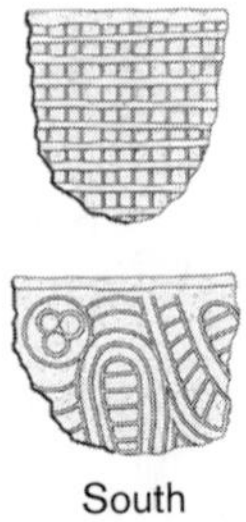

FIGURE 12.12 Linear check stamped and complicated stamped sherds designs typical of the South Appalachian Woodland pottery tradition.

South Appalachian

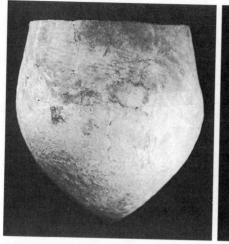

FIGURE 12.13 Vinette 1 vessels from New England are examples of the early pottery made in the northern Eastern Woodlands.

Meadowood

Lagoon

Fox Creek

Jacks Reef Pentagonal

FIGURE 12.14 The projectile points illustrated here are examples of Early and Middle Woodland points found in the Mid-Atlantic and the Northeast.

Adena

Rossville

Jacks Reef Corner Notched

Greene

of the temper particles also was reduced in some cases. Various forms of decoration, including net impressions, incising and stamping, dentates, and punctates, distinguish different Middle Woodland types of pottery within these regions.

Early and Middle Woodland people also made various straight and contracting stemmed, notched, and even triangular forms of projectile points not to mention the many indistinct forms that are encountered in sites from this time range (Figure 12.14). A variety of other chipped and ground stone tools were of course also made at this time. One interesting trend in stone tool assemblages from northern New England is a decrease in the frequency of ground stone tools like gouges, adzes, and celts. Snow (1980:298) suggests that this change may be linked with a switch from dugout to birch bark canoe technology. Early and Middle Woodland sites from the various northern and coastal regions also contain bone and shell artifacts as well as some copper and other items indicating trade.

Subsistence and Settlement Issues

Archaeological understanding of ecological and economic developments among northern and coastal people of the East during the Early and Middle Woodland has been increasing. Although Snow (1980) called this period the **Early Horticultural period** (2700–1300 BP), horticulture was adopted only to a limited degree. Most of these people continued to live mainly as hunter-gatherers, but their subsistence and settlement practices did vary by region, as did the degree to which they incorporated native and tropical cultigens into their subsistence. Unfortunately, the ethnobotanical record is spotty.

In the northern Great Lakes region and still farther north in southern Ontario people were hunter-gatherer-fishers who relied on water travel. The various northern archaeological phases may be grouped as the **Lake Forest Middle Woodland** (Fitting 1970), while Mason (1981) grouped the non-Hopewell groups of the Upper Great Lakes into the **Middle Tier Middle Woodland** (see also Brose and Hambacher 1999). Still farther north, archaeologists define the Laurel culture, mentioned briefly in Chapter 4, across a broad area of Ontario. Laurel sites are small campsites, and mobility is presumed to have been high. Data from Michigan do suggest that in the southern Great Lakes as in the interior East in general, there was experimentation with horticulture. Squash was apparently cultivated in the Saginaw valley by 2800 BP (Lovis and Monaghan 2008; Ozker 1982), while sunflower recovered at the Eidson site in southwestern Michigan was cultivated throughout the Early Woodland period (Garland and Beld 1999). Similarly, Middle Woodland Norton tradition subsistence and settlement practices in southwestern Michigan probably were similar to those found farther south where some horticultural activities were incorporated with intensive collecting of natural foodstuffs (Kingsley 1999).

Farther east there is evidence that farming appeared later than it did in the interior and that maize, bean, and squash agriculture was not established until quite late in the Mid-Atlantic and Northeast. What is much less clear is whether pre-maize farming based on native plants was a significant aspect of Early and Middle Woodland subsistence. Studies of seed size and morphology are still needed to establish when intentional cultivation began. However, the record of Eastern Agricultural complex plants and of tropical cultigens is growing (e.g., King 1999; McConaughy 2008). This chapter's case study by John P. Hart, "A New History of Maize-Bean-Squash Agriculture in the Northeast," exemplifies the kind of study that is changing our perceptions.

Along the northeastern and Mid-Atlantic coasts the intensive use of coastal and riverine resources may have inhibited the development of farming throughout the Early and Middle Woodland. One example of this process comes from Narragansett Bay in Rhode Island, where excavations at Greenwich Cove and other sites led Bernstein (1993) to argue for increasing sedentism over time without the adoption of agriculture. Other models suggest a seasonal alternation between the coast and interior river valleys during this time. Throughout New England and Mid-Atlantic, at least some larger and more permanent sites have been dated to the Early and Middle Woodland periods, but human groups may have remained seasonally mobile (Chilton 2002).

Farther south in the coastal plains and Florida it appears that pre-maize farming did not develop during the Early and Middle Woodland (Gremillion 2002). Once again the rich array of coastal and marine resources apparently was sufficient to support large semisedentary populations. However, even more important than what was available to people may have been that there was little seasonal variation in the amount of foodstuffs. One of the advantages of the native seed crops that people of the interior domesticated is that the seeds can be stored for winter use, when other sources of food are scarce. In the Atlantic and Gulf Coastal Plain and in much of Florida, such seasonal variation in foodstuffs was not an issue. For example, in reviewing the foodstuffs available to Deptford people living in Florida, Milanich (1994:116–120) notes that coastal Deptford sites, often located on live oak magnolia hammocks adjacent to salt marshes and presumed to have been occupied year-round, would have provided access to acorns, palm berries, blueberries, persimmons, wild grapes, deer, raccoons, opossums, rabbits, fresh- and saltwater turtles, ducks, sharks, rays, catfish, drum, snapper, flounder, mullet, and many other species of fish as well as oysters and clams. Many Deptford sites, whether coastal or from the interior Coastal Plain, seem to have been multiseasonal bases (Stephenson et al. 2002), an observation that again suggests the richness of the wild resource base.

Understanding the nature of these coastal forager adaptations is clearly an important research goal. While some peoples of the northern and coastal East at this time can be characterized as simple, mobile foragers, groups with access to lacustrine, riverine, and marine resources often do not fit into such a model.

In addition to relatively abundant foodstuffs and intensive use of key resources, these people also may have lived in semisedentary or sedentary villages and participated in more complex social interactions.

The Development of Mortuary Ceremonialism

Data on both exchange and mortuary ceremonialism can also be found in the Early and Middle Woodland of the northern and coastal Eastern Woodlands. In the southern Wisconsin, Early Woodland conical burial mounds have clear associations with the Red Ocher Mortuary complex that began in the Late Archaic. However, mound construction increased during the Middle Woodland when some Illinois Hopewell influence can be seen, particularly in mound groups along the upper Mississippi River. Here conical burial mounds covered rectangular burial pits or stone crypts that were reused over many years. As to the south, it appears that people were first laid in extended burial positions, but after decay, when new burials were added, their bones were bundled and placed to the side. Burial goods such a copper celts, freshwater pearls, platform pipes, obsidian implements, bear canine teeth, and pottery vessels from Illinois indicate connections with Hopewell people to the South. Several small rectangular or circular

embankments have been recorded as well, although their cultural affiliation remains unclear (Birmingham and Eisenberg 2000). Similarly, Hopewell manifestations are known from southwestern Michigan in what is called the Norton tradition, and in the Saginaw valley as well. Michigan archaeologists have debated whether these developments can be attributed to the actual migration of Hopewell people or to the diffusion of ideas and ceremonial practices (Kingsley 1999). In any case, there were also many Middle Woodland groups in Michigan that did not participate in Hopewellian practices. These include both Lake Forest Middle Woodland groups in the north and groups of the **Western Basin tradition** (1950 BP to 1450 BP) that has been defined in northern Ohio, southeastern Michigan, and southern Ontario surrounding the western end of Lake Erie.

Farther east Woodland cultures like the Adena and the Hopewell extend into extreme southwestern Pennsylvania (Dragoo 1963). Adena artifacts are sometimes found in the Mid-Atlantic and New England as well. For example, the West River site located near Annapolis, Maryland, may have had remains of a charnel house, as suggested by postmolds surrounded by a large pit containing five smaller cremation pits and three fire pits. Artifacts recovered here include blades made from nonlocal cherts, tubular pipes, gorgets, a

FIGURE 12.15 Abbott Farm series pot; note zoned-incised designs similar to Hopewell ceramics found in the Midwest (e.g., Figure 11.12).

paint cup, a grooved piece of hematite, and copper beads found with red ocher (Ford 1976). Some archaeologists identify a **Middlesex complex** or phase that encompasses materials of these kinds in the Mid-Atlantic and the Northeast (Ritchie 1980). Evidence of Hopewell influence also can be found. Elaborate Middle Woodland burials are known from the Island Field site in Delaware (Thomas 1987). Artifacts such as platform pipes, copper ear ornaments, axes, mica sheets, and projectile points made of Ohio chert, as well as mounds with central stone tombs, also have been found in burials associated with the **Squawkie Hill phase** in New York and northwestern Pennsylvania.

Although burial mounds are not common in the Mid-Atlantic, the Abbott Farm site located near Trenton, New Jersey, produced hints of Hopewell influence. The pottery from the Middle Woodland component includes shell-tempered vessels with complex zoned-incised, dentate, and stamped designs (Figure 12.15). This Abbott Farm series pottery is also found with exotic items, including possible earspools, mica sheets, caches of large argillite and jasper bifaces, conch shell fragments, and platform pipes. Other sites, like the Morris–Schurz site located along the East River in the Bronx, which contained a cache of 150 sheets of mica as well as Abbott Farm pottery and artifacts made of argillite from the Delaware valley, indicate that exchange was taking place between the area of New York City and the Delaware valley (Cantwell and Wall 2001; Kraft 2001).

The evidence for both exchange and mortuary ceremonialism during the Early and Middle Woodland is much more extensive in the South Atlantic Coastal Plain, in Florida, and in the Gulf Coastal Plain. While interregional exchange of Hopewellian items with groups from the interior is certainly evident, it also is apparent that mound building and ceremonialism among the Deptford, and later Swift Creek cultures of this area, develop from local traditions stretching back into the Archaic. For example, Late Deptford mounds (after ca. 2100 BP) in the eastern part of northwest Florida are associated with a ceremonial complex called **Yent Ceremonial complex**. The largest site is the multimound complex at the Crystal River site, but smaller sites also are known. There seems to be a dichotomy in these sites between mounds and domestic contexts, with the mounds containing copper panpipes, copper earspools, shell gorgets, shell cups, pottery made in exotic shapes, plummets, and secondary bundle burials (Stephenson et al. 2002). **Swift Creek tradition** sites, which follow Deptford sites in southern and central Georgia, have multiple mounds and are interpreted as ceremonial centers. Other Swift Creek sites lack mounds but have ring-shaped middens and central plaza-like areas. At the Swift Creek Mandeville site in Georgia, where both a platform mound and a conical burial mound have been recorded, burial pits

containing copper panpipes and earspools, clay platform pipes, prismatic blades, ceramic figurines, and mica and greenstone celts have been found.

In South Florida, Woodland earthworks, mounds, and ditches were constructed at several sites in the interior near Lake Okeechobee. For example, at Fort Center, excavations identified 14 mounds, some of which are associated with linear embankments and a circular ditch. These features may have had a drainage function, although feasting may have occurred on some of the mounds. Maize pollen dating to 450 BC was recovered from this site, and its presence is usually interpreted as evidence of the ceremonial use of maize.

CULTURES OF THE LATE WOODLAND AND LATE PREHISTORIC

Even though the end of the Hopewell Interaction Sphere probably had little impact on the daily lives of most people in the areas covered in this chapter, archaeological convention in many of these areas is to end the Middle Woodland at approximately 1500 BP. This is, however, not done by many Mid-Atlantic and New England archaeologists. In these areas, archaeologists may extend the Middle Woodland beyond what would be Hopewell times to approximately 950 BP (AD 1000), noting that major cultural shifts certainly cannot be documented before this later point in time after which the cultivation of maize, beans, and squash became more significant (e.g., Custer 1996; Snow 1980). Another approach is to dispense with general periods altogether after the Archaic and discuss regional sequences separately (e.g., Milanich 1994). In this chapter, we take the first approach and designate a Late Woodland Period, beginning at 1500 BP.

One of the main ways that the cultural story of the northern and coastal parts of the Eastern Woodlands differs from that of interior is that Mississippian polities usually did not develop. Nevertheless, many of the Woodland peoples of the northern and coastal Eastern Woodlands did make important cultural changes after approximately 950 BP. These reflect heavier emphasis on maize agriculture, settling into permanent, year-round villages, and sociopolitical developments. In addition in the South Atlantic Coastal Plain, Northern Florida and the Gulf Coastal Plain Mississippian polities did develop during this period. Thus, we subdivide the Late Woodland into an early Late Woodland period between approximately 1500 BP and 950 BP, and a Late Prehistoric period beginning at approximately AD 1000 and continuing to European contact during the sixteenth century AD. We hope this approach facilitates comparisons with developments in the interior from which people in the north and along the coasts were certainly not isolated.

Late Woodland and Late Prehistoric cultures within the areas covered by this chapter were highly diverse as the following discussion will demonstrate. Nevertheless, archaeologists have often pursued four common themes in their studies. First, people used the bow and arrow, and this is reflected in the smaller, often triangular projectile points considered diagnostic of the Late Woodland throughout the Eastern Woodlands. This technological change could be associated with more efficient and intense deer hunting, but it may also be associated with increases in intergroup conflict and warfare. In fact, particularly in the Late Prehistoric period, the evidence for intergroup conflict does increase even among non-Mississippian populations in the Eastern Woodlands as reflected both in injuries found in burial populations and in the prevalence of palisaded villages at this time (Milner 1999).

Second, variability in the composition and style of pottery continues to be a topic of great interest. Late Woodland pottery often was thinner walled, possibly to improve the cooking of native seeds and tropical cultigens. Vessel forms may indicate whether pots were used primarily for cooking or as storage containers (e.g., Chilton 1996). In addition, pottery was an important medium for social signaling that tells us much about people's identities and beliefs.

Third, many aspects of Late Woodland subsistence and settlement in northern and coastal areas are particularly fascinating to archaeologists. One aspect is the extent and the timing of the transition to agriculture that is addressed in this chapter's case study, "A New History for Maize-Beans-Squash Agriculture in the Northeast," by John Hart. However, questions related to how people organized themselves on the landscape, and whether or not they adopted horticulture, remain. Where tribal confederacies and complex polities seem to have developed without an agricultural base, archaeologists see an opportunity to understand cultural development and diversity more thoroughly.

Finally, although Hopewell mound and earthwork constructions, as well as Hopewell ceremonialism, are no longer evident, mortuary practices, ceremonial behaviors, and cosmological beliefs remain of great interest. There are many earthen and shell mounds and other constructions dated to these later periods, and in South Florida, people constructed canals as well. In the north, the Late Woodland practice of secondary burial in ossuaries, often in coastal shell middens (e.g., Kaeser 1970), suggests a sense of collective identity, while the ceremonial burial of dogs also indicates complex ideologies (e.g., Kerber 1997). These sites and features, as well as the iconography evident in artifacts, often can be linked to historically documented beliefs and ritual practices.

Given the difficulty in generalizing about this period, we will simply provide a sampling of complexes and traditions in the pages that follow, and you are encouraged to look at regional treatments for more thorough discussion of the historical sequences for the Late Woodland.

Mound Builders and Villagers of the Early Late Woodland

One example of early Late Woodland moundbuilders are the people of the **Effigy Mound culture** who inhabited portions of southern Wisconsin from the upper Mississippi valley to Lake Michigan as well as adjacent portions of Illinois, Iowa, and Minnesota. Built between approximately 1250 BP and 800 BP (AD 700–1150), these mounds were low, seldom over 5 feet (1.5 m) in height, but made in a variety of animal shapes such as panther, bear, turtle, bird, and lizard (Figure 12.16). The largest effigy mound, a bird effigy preserved on the grounds of Mendota State Hospital near Madison,

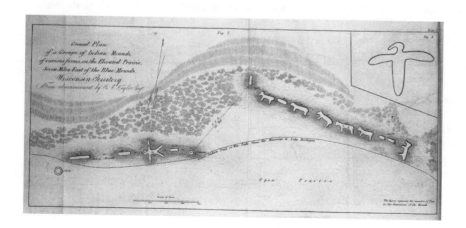

FIGURE 12.16 Historical drawing of an effigy mound group from southern Wisconsin.

has a wingspan of 624 feet (Birmingham and Eisenberg 2000:110). Effigy mounds are found in clusters, often interpreted as ceremonial centers, along with linear, conical, and oval mounds, and over 900 such centers are known from Wisconsin alone. Construction of these mounds usually began with creation of a depression, or **intaglio**, in the shape of the mound and continued with layering of differently colored soils. Mounds may contain flexed and bundle burials as well as cremations, but grave goods are relatively uncommon, and these mounds were not used repeatedly or to bury large numbers of individuals. Fireplace altars of rock are common within the mounds, as is extensive burning.

Researchers have usually have considered the people who built these mounds to be primarily mobile hunter-gatherers who ate only small quantities of cultivated plants, such as sunflower and maize, and who lived in small, probably seasonal, habitation sites (Stoltman and Christiansen 2000). Birmingham and Eisenberg (2000), however, point to recent evidence for larger villages and reliance on maize horticulture after about AD 900. These same authors argue that the mounds are not just representations of clan totems, as long believed, but also representations of the people's cosmology. In this view bird forms represent the sky and upper world, while the lower world or water is represented by various longtailed forms of panthers, turtles, and lizards. This duality is traceable to decorations on pottery, to rock art, and to contemporary Indian beliefs.

A second early Late Woodland cultural complex is the **Princess Point complex** (ca. 1450–950 BP) of southern Ontario, which is best known from the western end of Lake Ontario and the Grand River valley north of the eastern end of Lake Erie. This complex is associated with some of the earliest corn recovered in the Northeast. Evidence of corn from Princess Point sites notwithstanding, settlement strategies suggest a close association with river, lake, and other wetlands and thus the exploitation of fish. Wright (2004) suggests that the river floodplains also were important to crop production, and that a seasonal settlement strategy with movement away from floodplains for some of the year was adopted. Cemetery sites such as the Surma site at Fort Erie are attributed to the Princess Point complex, but isolated graves have been found as well. People were usually buried in a flexed position with grave goods including beads, ground slate pendants, arrowheads, whetstones, and stone pipes. Tobacco seed has also been recovered from Princess Point sites dating after about AD 800 perhaps suggesting ceremonial use of tobacco. Some exotic items in graves or otherwise suggest that exchange with people outside the area was occurring. Items recovered include marine shell from the east coast and a little native copper from Lake Superior.

Weeden Island tradition (1750/1650–950 BP) provides a final example of early Late Woodland transformations. Weeden Island is named after a site at Tampa Bay, but similar ceramics are found in sites that extend northward along the Florida coast into Alabama as well as into Georgia. Weeden Island I (before 1200 BP) ceramics had complicated stamped designs reminiscent of Swift Creek, or other highly stylized motifs and effigy forms. In Weeden Island II (after 1200 BP), new pottery types called Wakulla Check Stamped were common. In some areas, Weeden Island obviously precedes Mississippian developments, while in other sequences Late Woodland phenomena follow it (Kohler 1991; Milanich 2002). The subsistence focus for early Weeden Island I was on fish, shellfish, and other aquatic resources. Burial mounds were common and may have been the centers of lineage-based mortuary rituals. They may contain charnel houses for the processing of the dead before interment as bundle burials. It is also believed that some villages were more important than others.

In Weeden Island II, the **Wakulla culture** is recognized in northwest Florida. There are a greater number of sites; more of them are in upland areas, and settlement is less nucleated. Archaeologists have proposed that this change marks the introduction of slash-and-burn agriculture, causing frequent relocation to be close to fields. Ceramics made especially for ritual use disappear, and it has been argued that this was because corporate rituals were less frequent. People were still buried in mounds, but sometimes earlier mounds were simply reused. Over time Weeden Island II people made an increasing commitment to agriculture and eventually developed the cultural expression called **Fort Walton** Mississippian by archaeologists (Scarry 1990).

These three examples only hint at the diverse regional developments during the early Late Woodland in this chapter's areas of study. Perhaps, however, they do help dispel the idea, mentioned in Chapter 11, that nothing much important happened in the Late Woodland. In fact, it was a time of important transition and change even where Mississippian culture never developed, and this is also true of the Late Prehistoric.

Confederacies, Chiefdoms, and Others in the Late Prehistoric

By approximately AD 1000, the adoption of maize, beans, and squash agriculture and contact with Mississippian peoples of the interior were beginning to have a real impact on the Late Woodland people of the northern and coastal Eastern Woodlands. However, responses were regionally and locally diverse, indicating that diffusion of ideas and technology is only a

FIGURE 12.17 A Van Meter Trailed pot is one example of Oneota ceramics.

small part of the cultural story. Once again, we can only provide examples of the diversity suggested by the archaeological record.

Oneota, which has been called **Upper Mississippian**, was mentioned in Chapter 10 because it is found at the margins of the Midwest and Great Plains. Oneota was once thought to have developed only as Mississippians first expanded into northern Illinois and southern Wisconsin. However, better radiocarbon information now indicates that Oneota is a separate cultural tradition that emerged about 950 BP (AD 1000), at the beginning of the Late Prehistoric period, and continued until after 350 BP (AD 1600), the approximate beginning of the Protohistoric period (Brown and Sasso 2001). Oneota people made shell-tempered ceramics sometimes with distinctive decoration called trailing (Figure 12.17). Oneota lived in large villages and buried their dead in cemeteries rather than mounds. A mixed and variable subsistence base has been documented including hunting of bison and other animals, wild plant gathering, fishing, and some cultivation of maize and native

crops. Although Oneota may have depended less on maize agriculture than Mississippians of the southern Midwest, **ridged field systems** have been discovered in some Oneota sites like the Sand Lake site in western Wisconsin (Gallagher et al. 1985). There has been much debate about how intensive Oneota production was, about how large Oneota populations were, and about how climatic changes may have affected these northern agriculturalists.

Relationships between Oneota and Middle Mississippian are poorly understood, especially where these societies overlap in time and space. For example Aztalan, a mound and village complex centered on a plaza and surrounded by a palisade, is located in southern Wisconsin (Birmingham and Goldstein 2005). Its main occupation was between 850 BP and 650 BP (AD 1100–1300). Archaeologists found ceramics that remind them of Mississippian pottery from the American Bottom at Aztalan. Some have seen Aztalan as a Mississippian intrusion into the north, although grit-tempered, cord-marked, or cord-impressed ceramics typical of the local Late Woodland also are common there. This site suggests interactions between Mississippian, Oneota, and Late Woodland people, but these interactions remain poorly understood (Goldstein and Richards 1991). The complexity of such interactions is also suggested by findings of Oneota materials in the American Bottom (550–350 BP; AD 1400–1600) and elsewhere to the south after the Mississippian decline (e.g., Milner et al. 1984).

Some of the best-known archaeological cultures of the Late Woodland are those of the **Northern**

FIGURE 12.18 The long linear, bark-covered structures in this artist's conception are Iroquoian longhouses, which were inhabited by multiple families. Note the segment of the stockade shown in the lower left corner.

Iroquoian tradition, sedentary groups located in New York State, southern Ontario, and portions of Quebec who had a mixed economy based on farming and hunting and gathering. Because we can link the archaeological evidence with later ethnohistorically described villages, detailed village movement sequences have been constructed for Iroquois tribes, such as the Seneca and the Mohawk. In this approach the known village sites of a historical community are related to an earlier site believed to be the ancestral location of the same community. There are Northern Iroquoians, however, about whom we still know relatively little and for whom lineal descendants are hard to identify, including the Erie mentioned in the case study in Section D.1 of the Student CD.

Three aspects of the Northern Iroquoian tradition are particularly worthy of attention. First, the Iroquois are famous for their permanent villages containing large, multifamily longhouses, which reached their classic form by 550 BP (Figure 12.18). These bark-covered houses were up to 400 feet (120 m) in length and more than 20 feet (6 m) in width, often with storage compartments and doors at either end, and roofs shaped like an arbor. In historical times, the matrilineal Iroquois divided these structures into a series of compartments, occupied by the families of related women.

Second, since clay elbow pipes were an important item of Iroquois material culture, it is evident that Iroquoians participated in smoking complex associated with ritual and shamanistic activities in Eastern Woodlands cultures (von Gernet 1992). These pipes also were widely traded, and their presence as early as the sixth century BP far from where they had been made may indicate that the historical pattern of high male mobility and gift exchange has great time depth among the Iroquois.

Finally, warfare, in the sense of raiding and a cycle of feuds and revenge killing, unquestionably occurred among these people and was the cause of the defensive positioning, aggregation, and fortification of later Iroquoian settlements. Englebrecht (2003:112–114) argues that the clustering of communities noted from the fifth century BP onward is indicative of alliance formation between communities perpetuated through intermarriage. This process did not completely resolve competition for resources, but it eventually led to the tribal or nation entities such as Mohawk or Seneca among the Iroquois (e.g., Gramly 1977). It is in this context that the five Iroquois nations Seneca, Cayuga, Onondaga, Oneida, and Mohawk formed the famous **League of the Haudenosaunee** (People of the Longhouse). The league, which archaeologists believe was in place by about 425 BP, was both an alliance against other tribal groups and a means of reducing the warfare then pervasive. As such, it serves as a model of

other Northeastern tribal confederacies that developed in the Late Prehistoric period.

As discussed in Box 12.1, although we know a great deal about Iroquoian lifestyles, there is controversy about how the Northern Iroquoian tradition developed in the first place.

New England cultures provide another significant example of the variety of lifestyles that developed during the Late Prehistoric period. As mentioned in Box 12.1, New England Algonquian people apparently were less sedentary and perhaps less dependent on maize horticulture than the Iroquoians of the interior. Crawford and Smith (2003) define a coastal pattern in which horticulture was not significant at all for Atlantic Canada and northern New England, but the situation in southern New England is less clear. In this area historical records describing the production of crops by coastal peoples usually have not been supported by ethnobotanical evidence (however, see Largy and Morenon 2008). It may be the case that southern New Englanders did not inhabit large, sedentary villages even after they adopted maize horticulture. Instead they may have retained a long-standing pattern of seasonal movements between the coast and the interior, incorporating maize cultivation into economies still largely based on fishing and shellfishing. It may also be true that in some coastal areas, sedentary lifestyles were possible without horticulture (e.g., Bernstein 1993). Sociopolitically tribal entities do not seem to have been well defined, a situation that may have reduced tensions and prevented the kind of conflict that plagued Iroquoian societies. On the other hand, these societies were not simply egalitarian, unconnected bands of foragers. There is still room for debate about what southern New England lifestyles were actually like (e.g., Chilton 2005), but the most important point may simply be that southern New England Algonquian lifestyles do not fit common models of the association between sedentism, maize agriculture, and sociopolitical developments. For this reason alone they are highly significant.

That commitment to food production is not necessary for the development of complex, hierarchical societies is well illustrated by a fourth example of Late Prehistoric period lifestyles—the **Calusa culture** of South Florida (Widmer 2002). These people of the southwest Florida coast from south of Tampa to south of Fort Myers lived in a highly productive marine zone, but did not have access to arable land and did not grow maize. Though primarily dependent on fish and shellfish from the estuaries, they also hunted ducks, marine and terrestrial turtles, deer, and other animals. Like other South Florida groups, the Calusa made artifacts from wood, bone, and shell because of limited access to stone. This fact, coupled with the excellent

Iroquoian Origins

The distribution of Algonquian and Iroquoian language groups in the Northeast at the time of European contact raises some interesting questions. Notably, Iroquoian-speaking tribal groups occupying the interior were more or less surrounded by Algonquian-speaking groups (Figure 12.19). Moreover, differences among these tribes went beyond language. Iroquoian groups had matrilineal social structures as well as matrilocal residence patterns and lived in multifamily longhouses within compact, often fortified settlements. Their subsistence also was based on maize-bean-squash agriculture. In contrast, Algonquian groups usually were patrilineal, had **patrilocal residence**, lacked the longhouse, and often had more dispersed settlement patterns. Many Algonquians were not dependent on

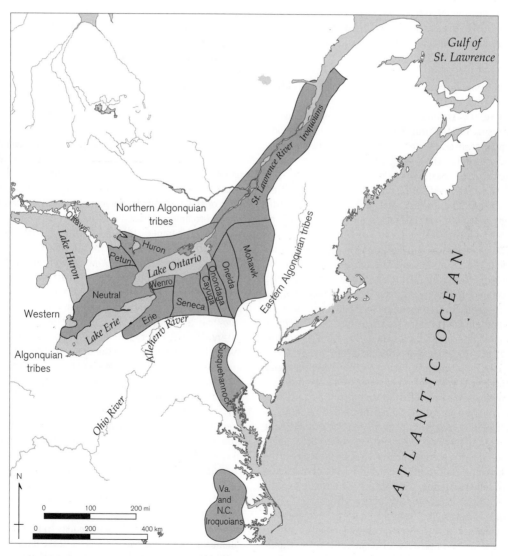

FIGURE 12.19 During early Historic times, Iroquoian-language speakers (shaded tribes) were located in the interior and surrounded by Algonquian-speaking tribes.

farming, maintaining mixed economies even when they lived in larger settlements or relying solely on hunting, fishing, and gathering. From Figure 12.19, it is easy to imagine that Iroquoians migrated northward into the Northeast, forming a wedge between the western and eastern Algonquians. Is this what happened? If so, when did it happen? What exactly were the origins of Northern Iroquoians?

This is a long-standing problem, but one that has recently generated new discussion and investigation. Early in the twentieth century, archaeologists generally assumed that Northern Iroquoians had arrived in the interior Northeast shortly before European contact. Arthur Parker (1916) situated their origins in Mississippian developments around the mouth of the Ohio River and reconstructed a multipronged migration into the current territory, using folklore and assumptions about migration common at the time. He didn't develop archaeological data in support of his migration schemes, however. As regional archaeological sequences were constructed, it became obvious that there was an Iroquoian tradition stretching back in time for at least a millennium. By the middle of the twentieth century, archaeologists were questioning the uncritical use of the concept of migration to explain culture change. The Iroquoian ceramic sequence (MacNeish 1952) established that there was considerable cultural continuity in the interior Northeast and that Iroquoians could not be understood as transplanted Mississippians. On this basis, MacNeish proposed that Iroquoians had developed culturally within the Northeast, or *in situ*.

Buttressed by the **neoevolutionism** of processual archaeology, this **"in situ hypothesis"** became the established explanation for Iroquoian origins. MacNeish had seen ceramic continuity between the Iroquoian ceramics beginning with **Owasco** about 1000 BP and the ceramics of the preceding **Point Peninsula tradition**. Linguistic glottochronological analyses estimated the date of separation of Northern Iroquoians from the Cherokee, whose Southern Iroquoian language is distinct, at somewhere between 3500 and 4000 years ago (Lounsbury 1978). On this basis it sometimes was argued that ancestral Northern Iroquoians pushed northward around the time of the Terminal Archaic (3700–2700 BP), not becoming the Iroquois until much later. In this view, the appearance of the Broadpoint tradition would represent such a migration into the Northeast. A gradual transition to agriculture and a gradual process of sedentarization attended by the development of matrilineality and matrilocality were envisioned.

Unfortunately, the "in situ hypothesis" was not necessarily evaluated any more critically than earlier migration scenarios had been. Because migration as an explanation was out of vogue within archaeology altogether, possibly anomalous data were largely ignored. In the

1990s, Snow (e.g., 1995) began arguing that existing contradictory data sufficed to warrant serious reconsideration of migration as opposed to in situ Iroquoian origins. First, Snow questioned the validity of the **Hunters Home phase** at the end of the pre-Iroquoian Point Peninsula tradition, mentioned earlier. He argued that instead of demonstrating continuity between Point Peninsula and Owasco, this phase was an amalgamation of some distinct assemblages that spanned a discontinuity between Point Peninsula and Owasco. Originally, he found a similar discontinuity between Princess Point and **Glen Meyer** complex ceramics in Ontario. An important aspect of this discontinuity is the shift among Iroquoians from ceramics made by coiling to ceramics made by molding. Snow also argued that the Point Peninsula and Princess Point groups were seasonally mobile hunter-gatherers who only supplemented their diet through horticulture, while Iroquoians were committed to growing maize. Finally, Snow argued that there is not enough linguistic diversity within Northern Iroquoian languages to argue for more than a thousand years of development from the proto-Iroquoian stage (see also Fiedel 1987).

Given these data, Snow originally proposed that the **Clemson Island culture** of north central Pennsylvania was ancestral to the Iroquoians. Supposedly, Clemson Island people moved northward, colonizing the areas that had become appropriate for maize agriculture by the beginning of the Medieval Warm period. In this view the Iroquoian complex, including longhouses, molded rather than coiled ceramics, maize agriculture, matrilineality, and matrilocal residence, arrived in New York State and Ontario already developed. New data on Princess Point from southern Ontario now indicate that maize was cultivated much earlier than previously thought. Other data also suggest more continuity between Princess Point and Iroquoian Glen Meyer phase ceramics, as well as more sedentary Princess Point communities (Crawford and Smith 1996). This could mean that the Iroquoian tradition developed in situ, but it also may mean only that migration took place earlier than originally envisioned by Snow (Fiedel 1999b; Snow 1996).

As with other issues we have raised in this book, present data are insufficient to resolve the debate about Iroquoian origins. This debate should be understood less as a search for the correct ancestral archaeological taxon than as a chance to explore significant issues in the development of sociocultural traditions. It brings into focus questions about the relationships between agriculture, settlement pattern, social organization, and ethnic identity, and it requires archaeologists to reconsider assumptions about migration and cultural development. Native tribes may also be interested in the implications (Martin 2008).

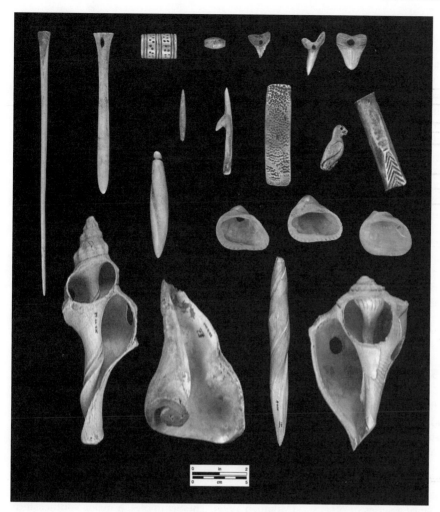

FIGURE 12.20 Artifacts of shell, bone, turtle shell, and shark teeth were made by the Calusa. The items in this photo include (left to right, top to bottom) a deer bone pin, a deer bone net shuttle, two bone beads, three perforated shark teeth, a deer bone point, a deer bone barb for a composite fish hook, a turtle bone net-mesh gauge, a bone carving of a bird, an antler socket, a whelk shell sinker, three arc shell net weights, a conch shell hammer, a whelk shell grinder, a whelk shell perforator, and a whelk shell cutting edge tool.

preservation at many coastal and wet sites, means that archaeologists have discovered many remarkable artifacts (Figure 12.20). Among these are tools related to fishing such as shell net sinkers, shell or bone mesh gauges for nets, bone and antler fishhooks and barbed harpoons, but also cutting implements, adzes, chisels, and awls made of shell or shark's teeth. Wooden objects recovered by Cushing (2000 (1896) at the end of the nineteenth century from the Key Marco site, which is actually located south of the Calusa area, have made Calusa art famous. Current evidence suggests that at least some of this material actually is older and associated with the **Glades culture** sequence of this adjacent area. Nevertheless, these materials still provide important insights into what the people of South Florida, including the Calusa, could do with wood.

After approximately 1100 BP, when population along this coast had grown considerably, the Calusa developed a complex chiefdom that persisted into the historic era (Marquardt 2004; Widmer 1988). Numerous shell middens and mounds, some of which are as high as 30 feet and hundreds of feet long, were left by the Calusa. They also constructed canals leading into shell mound complexes. For example, at the Pineland site west of Fort Myers, a central canal is bilaterally flanked by large mounds (Milanich 2004). When first explored by Cushing in 1896 this canal still was 30 feet wide, six feet deep, and two and a half miles long. Population growth, competition between chiefs, warfare between villages, intravillage alliances, and some trade and contact with other groups in Florida and southward into the Caribbean are apparent. Because the Calusa persisted into the mid-eighteenth century AD, ethnohistorical accounts can help archaeologists reconstruct much of their lifestyle.

Finally, several Mississippian cultures did influence the peoples of the Gulf and Atlantic Coastal Plains. Such "Missippianization" did not happen in the

South Atlantic Coastal Plain until after 750 BP, but in the Gulf Coastal Plain and the Northwest Florida coast, one example of a Mississippian tradition culture is the Fort Walton culture that developed out of Weeden Island between 1050 BP and 950 BP. These Mississippian people made sand-tempered pottery decorated through incising and punctuating with iconographic motifs reminiscent of the Southeastern Ceremonial complex (see Chapter 11). Their diet was based on maize and bean agriculture, although other resources were utilized as well. Fort Walton sites include farmstead and hamlet sites as well as mound centers with plazas and multiple platform mounds. For example, the Lake Jackson site is a large site located in Leon County, Florida, containing multiple mounds, one of which was approximately 82 by 91 meters (269 by 298 ft) at its base and nearly 11 meters (36 feet) high (Milanich 1994:369). Evidence at Lake Jackson for social ranking as well as chiefly control and redistribution of goods fits well within the Mississippian model outlined in Chapter 11.

THE PROTOHISTORIC AND CONTACT PERIODS

The Norse or Vikings explored the northeastern edges of the Eastern Woodland around 900 BP, briefly establishing a settlement in Newfoundland at L'Anse aux Meadows, but their impact on native lifeways is barely discernible, especially in the areas covered by this chapter (see Box 13.1). Cabot's voyage to the vicinity of Newfoundland in AD 1497 is the next important contact with Europeans, especially since a series of other Europeans including Verrazano and Gomes followed him in exploring the eastern American coast during the early 1500s. Also influential were European fishermen, who began to arrive in coastal waters each summer shortly after the explorers' voyages became known. Cartier began to explore the St. Lawrence River in the 1530s. By the end of the sixteenth century the trade in furs was stimulating additional exploration in the interior Northeast, but the Great Lakes region was not completely explored until the second half of the seventeenth century. In Florida, Ponce de Léon of "Fountain of Youth" fame made his first voyage in 1513. Other explorations and efforts at establishing colonies followed. The most important expedition was led by Hernando de Soto, who landed at Tampa Bay in late May 1539 and proceeded through the Southeast for more than four years.

At European contact, the northern and coastal parts of the Eastern Woodland were home to many Native American tribal groups. An important cultural distinction among them was between those who spoke Iroquoian languages and those who spoke Algonquian languages as outlined in Box 12.1. Generally, Algonquians lived along the coast and in the immediate interior, including the Maritime Canada, much of New England, the Delaware River drainage, New Jersey, the Delmarva Peninsula, and the Chesapeake Bay area. The Algonquin and the Nipissing of southern Ontario and Quebec also spoke Algonquian languages, as did the peoples of the Great Lakes region such as the Chippewa-Ojibwa, the Ottawa, the Sauk, the Fox and the Menominee. As discussed in Box 12.1, Iroquoians lived inland, in Ontario, the St. Lawrence drainage, New York, Pennsylvania, Virginia, and North Carolina as well. One of these groups, the Tuscaroras, moved north to New York State beginning in the early eighteenth century, after the Tuscarora Wars in North Carolina. Around 1723 they were adopted formally into the League of the Iroquois (Landy 1978).

Farther south, a number of small Algonquian-speaking groups, such as the Croatoans and Pamlico, inhabited the Atlantic Coastal Plain in North Carolina, and Siouan speaking groups like the Tutelo were found in the Virginia Piedmont. The Catawba of the Carolinas sometimes are considered linguistic isolates, although their languages are related to Siouan languages, while Cusabo is a name often given to small independent tribes living on the coast of South Carolina in the sixteenth century. Muskogean-speaking groups, such as the Guale, the Yamasee, the Timucua, and the Apalachee were found still farther south in the Atlantic and Gulf Coastal Plains and in North Florida. Non-Mississippian groups in Florida included the Calusa of the Fort Myers area and the Tequesta of the Miami area (Milanich 1995). The Seminoles, a major Southeastern tribe today, are a more recent amalgamation of Indians in Florida who speak a Muskogean language.

In most of the areas covered in this chapter, direct European contact led to Native involvement in gift exchange, and European goods such as glass beads, brass wares, and iron implements were widely traded far into the interior ahead of actual contact. There are a number of other ways in which Native peoples probably obtained European goods during this period. These include the scavenging of shipwrecks, the looting of abandoned settlements, and the taking of European clothing and belongings after hostile encounters (Pendergast 1994). Of course, once contacts became more common, existing native systems of trade and exchange were rapidly co-opted into the burgeoning global economic system. This had disastrous consequences for some Native nations, while others profited, at least for a time, as intertribal conflicts developed over the trade. For example, the Iroquois Wars between 1641 and 1701 were a series of conflicts between the Iroquois and other tribes that developed after the local beaver population had been exhausted. These conflicts resulted in the dispersal of a number of tribes (e.g., the Erie, the Huron, the Neutral) and extended westward into the Upper Great Lakes.

The most important point underscored by the archaeology of the Protohistoric period is that the sociocultural systems into which Europeans were beginning to interject themselves were dynamic systems in their own right. Like people everywhere, the inhabitants of Eastern Woodlands were enmeshed in complex economic, social, and political interactions prior to contact. Confronted with Europeans, they were not really the passive recipients of change portrayed in popular stereotypes. As a result, both Natives and Europeans shaped what happened in the colonial encounter (Axtell 2001; Brose et al. 2001).

For example, in Virginia's coastal plain, the Powhatan chiefdom amalgamated a number of Algonquian tribes. The rise of chiefs in this area was a phenomenon of the Protohistoric period rather than having much time depth. This was not a direct response to Europeans as we might imagine (Rountree and Turner 2002). Instead, aggregation took place in response to incursions by other native groups from the Piedmont onto the Virginia's inner coastal plain. Just as intergroup conflict increased among Iroquoian people in the Late Woodland, it seems to have affected people in the Chesapeake area. Military consolidation, stronger alliances, and the establishment of a hierarchy of chiefs are suggested to archaeologists by the appearance of palisaded towns, by trends in the ceramics, by the presence of high-status goods such as copper, freshwater pearls, and shell beads and gorgets, and by the appearance of large, sturdy house structures assumed to be chief's residences. For example, a surviving garment known as "Powhatan's mantle" had nearly 20,000 small *Marginella* shells sewn into it, and was probably worn by a chief (Figure 12.21).

Of course, this was the context into which the fabled Jamestown settlement was inserted by the English in 1607, after about 50 years of intermittent Spanish and English presence in the Virginia area. Initially, the interaction between the Powhatans and the English was characterized by both sides' attempts to make productive alliances. The English wanted to exploit the land for commodities that could be sold at home, while the Powhatans wanted allies against their enemies, including other tribes and the Spanish with whom they had had previous dealings. Neither party to these early contacts fully understood the other's intentions or behaviors, but each continued to play out its stratagems according to its own cultural rules.

Archaeologists have much to tell about the interaction between these people and Europeans that adds to the familiar story of European colonization and

FIGURE 12.21 The "Powhatan Mantle" probably was worn by a chief as a symbol of high status.

nation building in these areas. For example, archaeological research conducted in conjunction with the Mashantucket Pequot tribe of eastern Connecticut (e.g., McBride 1990) is providing new insights about the Pequot War in southern New England. Another topic archaeologists have helped scholars explore consists of the consequences of European contact for Native American health and population size. Although ethnologists once understood this number to be as low as 2 million and fairly constant over time, the work of historical demographers such as Sherburne F. Cook (1976) has suggested much higher numbers of people (e.g., 18,000,000 people). Specifically, it has now been widely accepted that Europeans spread diseases to which Native Americans had no immunity, leading to large-scale depopulations among Natives early in the Historic period, but understanding when and how this actually happened requires the kind of data arcaeologists provide (Dobyns 1983; Ramenofsky 1987).

CHAPTER SUMMARY

This chapter has introduced the archaeological past in the northern and coastal parts of the eastern Woodlands. Although not an exhaustive treatment, the material should make further study of archaeology in these areas understandable. The main points made in this chapter are as follows:

- The Archaic peoples of the northern and coastal Eastern Woodlands were hunter-fisher-gatherers who developed a variety of technologies to exploit diverse resources including fish, shellfish, and other aquatic resources as well as terrestrial plants and animals. Although people in only a few areas experimented with the cultivation of native seed plants, by the Late Archaic there is evidence of participation in trade networks, regional mortuary ceremonialism, and in a few areas of the South Atlantic Coastal Plain and Florida the manufacture of the first Eastern Woodlands pottery.

- The Early and Middle Woodland archaeological record indicates regional and local diversity in lifestyle, although pottery became widespread in all of the northern and coastal areas of the Eastern Woodlands. Economies were both mixed, with some use of native and tropical cultigens and primarily based on coastal and marine resources where possible. Some level of participation in Adena and Hopewell mortuary ceremonialism and associated exchange of prestige items is evident from many areas, although the local roots of mortuary and ceremonial practices also are apparent.

- The remainder of the pre-Columbian past in the northern and coastal Eastern Woodlands can be divided into an early Late Woodland from ca. 1500 BP to 950 BP and a Late Prehistoric period from ca. 950 BP to the Protohistoric and Contact periods that begin in the sixteenth centuries. Also, only some of the peoples of these areas developed mixed farming and foraging economies and sociopolitically complex groups organized into tribes, confederacies and chiefdoms, making these areas an important place to study a diversity of cultural strategies and histories.

- Although the Vikings briefly explored the Northeast coast around 900 BP, it was not until the sixteenth century AD (beginning at 450 BP) or later that Europeans seriously began to affect the native cultures of the coastal and northern eastern Woodlands through trade, alliance, and the spread of disease. Importantly, in this early part of the Columbian encounter, native societies were not passive or powerless nor Europeans necessarily dominant sociopolitically.

SUGGESTIONS FOR FURTHER READING

For insight into the mound-building cultures of Wisconsin and the Upper Great Lakes:

Birmingham, Robert A., and Leslie E. Eisenberg
　2000 *Indian Mounds of Wisconsin.* University of Wisconsin Press, Madison.

For a review of Michigan's past and insight into the archaeology of the entire Upper Great Lakes area:

Halsey, John R. (editor)
　1999 *Retrieving Michigan's Buried Past:The Archaeology of the Great Lakes State.* Cranbrook Institute of Science, Bloomfield Hills, Michigan.

For a compendium of recent studies of interest to students of Northeastern archaeology:

Levine, Mary Ann, Kenneth E. Sassaman, and Michael S. Nassaney
　1999 *The Archaeological Northeast.* Bergin & Garvey, Westport, Connecticut.

For a fascinating account of what lies beneath New York City:

Cantwell, Anne-Marie, and Diana di Zerega Wall
　2001 *Unearthing Gotham: The Archaeology of New York City.* Yale University Press, New Haven, Connecticut.

For treatment of the Iroquoian people's lifestyle using both ethnohistory and archaeology:

Engelbrecht, William
　2003 *Iroquoia: The Development of a Native World.* Syracuse University Press, Syracuse, New York.

For an interdisciplinary look at how Virginia Algonquin life was transformed in the early Contact period:

Rountree, Helen C., and E. Randolph Turner, III
　2002 *Before and After Jamestown:Virginia's Powhatans and Their Predecessors.* University Press of Florida, Gainesville.

For more on the Calusa and South Florida cultural developments:

MacMahon, Darcie A., and William H. Marquardt
　2004 *The Calusa and Their Legacy: South Florida People and Their Environments.* University Press of Florida, Gainesville.

OTHER RESOURCES

Sections H and I of the Student CD give web links, places to visit, additional discussion questions, and other study aids. The Student CD contains a variety of additional resources. The bonus case study *in Section D.1 "Interpreting the Ripley Site: A Century of Investigations" of the Student CD discusses archaeological work at a Northern Iroquoian site in New York State.*

CASE STUDY

Schoolchildren often learn that the Indians taught the Pilgrim settlers at Plymouth, Massachusetts, how to grow corn, beans, and squash by planting them together in hills to ensure sufficient food for the New England winter. This colorful story may have some basis in reality. It is clear that at European contact the Indians of southern New England did grow these crops together, and they could have taught the Pilgrims to do the same. Moreover, these plants complement each other, both as crops and as sources of food. How important was this agricultural complex to the stability and complexity of native societies? When was maize-bean-squash agriculture introduced in the Northeast? As often mentioned in this chapter, these are important questions for contemporary archaeologists. The perspective that this agricultural complex was a late development in the Northeast has been gained recently from applying new techniques to ethnobotanical and artifactual evidence preserved in archaeological collections. This case study, which tells the story of that reanalysis, indicates the potential importance of collecting and preserving plant remains. It also indicates how new techniques, applied to old evidence, may change our understanding of the past. Finally, it provides an example of how experiments may be integrated with other archaeological research. As you read, pay attention to how a variety of approaches have been used to generate new information. Did you ever think that museum collections might provide new data?

A NEW HISTORY OF MAIZE-BEAN-SQUASH AGRICULTURE IN THE NORTHEAST

John P. Hart

Most of the case studies presented in this book relate the thrill of discovery, addressing important research questions and solving seemingly intractable problems through archaeological fieldwork and analyses of materials obtained through fieldwork. The general public, students, and professional archaeologists are drawn to the process of unearthing remains of our species' history and evolution. Newspapers, magazines, television news programs, and other media often relate exciting stories on archaeological field studies that challenge our notions of the past and what it means to be human.

Every one of the archaeological field projects that you read about and participate in produces collections of artifacts and other debris of past human activities. This is the stuff of archaeology—what sets the discipline of archaeology apart from other social and behavioral sciences. The analysis of these artifact collections and their contextual documentation, such as field notes, site plans, and photographs, allows archaeologists to gain new insights into how people in the past lived, and how people's lives changed through the generations.

What happens to these collections as documents of the past once the project archaeologists complete their analyses and publish their reports gets much less public attention than the unearthing process. All these collections should, and many do, eventually make their way into museums. It is the primary job of museums to care for collections that document research, like the materials generated by archaeological excavations. Many, hopefully all, of the collections generated by the case studies you have read in this book now sit in cabinet drawers or in boxes on shelves in museums throughout North America.

But why? Once the analyses and publications for an archaeological project are complete, what use are the collections? Surely the most attractive pieces ought to be put on display, but what value can all those pottery sherds and chipped stone flakes have? They've already been analyzed, and the data are published in site reports.

There are a number of possible answers to these questions. To my mind, two are critical. First, archaeological theories, methods, and techniques are constantly changing. What represents the state of the art today may be very dated in just a few short years. Curation of collections allows archaeologists to discover new information about the past when new analytical techniques and methods, especially when combined with new theoretical approaches, can be applied to such stored materials. Often it makes more sense to reanalyze existing collections than to excavate new ones. Second, curation of collections gives archaeologists the ability to observe, examine, and compare the three-imensional objects that are depicted as two-dimensional photographs or summarily described in the tables and charts. Nothing can substitute for the examination of actual objects to generate new ideas and draw new conclusions that otherwise might never arise.

Not all important discoveries about the past, then, come about through new excavations [see, e.g., the collected papers in *Museum Anthropology* 19(3) 1995]. Analyses of existing collections, often made many decades ago, contribute important advances in our knowledge of the distant past. In this case study I relate how our knowledge of maize-bean-squash agriculture in the Northeast generally, and New York specifically, has been radically altered recently as a result of the application of new techniques and methods to museum collections.

CHANGING THE HISTORY OF MAIZE, BEAN, AND SQUASH AGRICULTURE

Maize, beans, and squash were the primary American Indian crops during the Late Prehistoric and Early Historic periods (Hurt 1987). Frequently these crops were found in what is known as a **polyculture**, an agricultural system in which plants from different species are grown together, much like a natural community of plants (Mt Pleasant 2006; Woolley and Davis 1991). Each plant in the polyculture contributes some benefit to the others, ideally resulting in higher yields per unit of land than if the crops were grown separately. This is the source of the Northern Iroquoian name for the maize-bean-squash system, the **Three Sisters**, with each sister (crop) taking care of the others (Engelbrecht 2003). The maize stalk provides a climbing pole for the bean plant; the bean plant fixes nitrogen in the soil that may be available to the maize and squash plants; the squash plant, growing low to the ground with its large leaves, acts as a mulch to discourage weed growth and maintain soil moisture (Perkl 1998).

In addition to the agronomic benefits of growing the three crops together, consuming the crops together provides nutritional benefits. Maize kernels are high in starch and calories; bean seeds provide high levels of protein, and consuming maize kernels and beans seeds together provides a complete set of amino acids (Kaplan 1963); squash seeds are high in fats and oils, and squash flesh is high in calories and various vitamins and minerals (Robinson and Decker-Walters 1996).

The agronomic and nutritional benefits of the maize-bean-squash complex, as well as its widespread use not only in northeastern North America, but in many ecological settings throughout the Western Hemisphere, make it seem like a natural system—a system that would have been adopted by American Indian groups wherever it was introduced. For many years the crops of this polyculture were thought to have been established in what is now New York, the home of the Northern Iroquoian nations, by approximately 950 BP (Ritchie 1980; Snow 1995). The crops were thought to have been adopted either in quick succession or as a unit. The establishment of the polyculture was thought to have triggered the evolution of other cultural traits that became recognizable as Northern Iroquoian soon thereafter (Hart 2001).

Intensive reliance on maize-bean-squash agriculture is one of the defining traits of the Northern Iroquoian groups of New York, surrounded as they were by speakers of Algonquian languages, many of whom relied much less heavily on agricultural produce in their subsistence systems. It had long been assumed that either the adoption of the three crops or the migration into New York (and southern Ontario) of agriculturists who grew the three crops was the catalyst for the evolution of other nonlinguistic cultural traits that came to define the Northern Iroquoians and set them apart from their Algonquian neighbors (Ritchie 1980; Snow 1995).

THE ROUNDTOP SITE

It was a major find, therefore, when in 1964 a crew from the New York State Museum, under the direction of State Archaeologist William Ritchie, found maize kernels and squash and bean seeds together in a large pit feature (Feature 35) at the Roundtop site in the Susquehanna River valley west of Binghamton, New York (Ritchie and Funk 1973). The recovery of crop remains at archaeological sites prior to the development and employment of systematic flotation processing techniques in the 1970s and 1980s was a matter of happenstance. To recover the remains of all three crops together in a single context was quite exciting. In his publications on the site, Ritchie connected the crops to a radiocarbon date of approximately 900 BP from a different context (Feature 30), which made the remains the earliest evidence of maize-bean-squash agriculture not only in New York, but in all of eastern North America. While remains of maize had been found in earlier contexts elsewhere in the East, no site had yielded beans as well as squash at such an early date, and thus not the three crops together. Over the next few decades, Roundtop was frequently cited as the earliest evidence for beans in the East (Ford 1985; Riley et al. 1990; Yarnell 1976).

At the time of the Roundtop excavations, radiocarbon dating was still a relatively new technique. Obtaining a radiocarbon date required several grams of charcoal. The charcoal that Ritchie chose for radiocarbon dating was from Feature 30, a large pit feature presumably used for storing foodstuffs, as was Feature 35, the pit in which the maize, bean, and squash remains were found. By the early 1980s archaeologists were able to use the new radiocarbon dating technique called **accelerator mass spectrometry (AMS) dating**, which can yield a date from very small amounts of charcoal. Currently as little as 2 or 3 milligrams of charcoal will suffice to obtain an AMS date. To get an idea of how little material this is, think about a typical aspirin tablet weighing 500 milligrams. Now think about one one-hundredth of that aspirin tablet: 5 milligrams is in some cases twice the amount of charred plant material needed to obtain an AMS date. This means that critical early crop remains can be dated directly. Thus AMS is a very important tool for archaeologists interested in the chronology of crops.

The collections from the Roundtop site excavations by Ritchie's crew and later excavations by Binghamton University's field school are housed in the New York State Museum. When I joined the museum's staff in 1994, I wanted to work with a collection that would introduce me to the Late Prehistoric period of the state, especially a collection from a site with information about agriculture. Roundtop fit the bill. My initial goal was to obtain direct AMS dates on the famous crop remains to substantiate their age. After some searching in the museum's collections, I was able to find maize kernels, bean seeds, and squash seeds from Feature 35 in the context Ritchie attributed to the occupation of approximately 900 BP. After confirmation of the identifications by C. Margaret Scarry, a paleoethnobotanist at the University of North Carolina at Chapel Hill, I sent maize kernels, a bean cotyledon, and part of a twig from the same context for AMS dating. To my surprise at the time, the dates came back at calibrated 650 BP (Hart 1999a). While direct dates on maize kernels from other contexts at the site were consistent with Ritchie's earlier date, beans from other contexts yielded even younger dates than those from Feature 35.

A subsequent analysis of the pottery assemblages from Features 30 and 35 revealed that the pottery from Feature 35 was dominated by sherds from pots of a type that is consistent with the 650 BP date. The pottery from Feature 30 came mostly from one large pot of a type consistent with Ritchie's date from that feature. Additional radiocarbon dates from Roundtop and analysis of pottery assemblages from other features indicated that there had been at least three temporally distinct occupations of the site. Roundtop was not the predominantly single-component site that Ritchie believed, and the maize, bean, and squash remains from Feature 35 were 250 years younger than he believed (Hart 1999a, 2000).

The presence of beans on the Roundtop site and Ritchie's belief that they dated to 900 BP or thereabouts led many archaeologists to expect that beans and maize-bean-squash agriculture would be found elsewhere in contexts in the Northeast dating to that time, and they were; but in only one other case had the bean remains been directly dated (ca. 550 BP) (Heckenberger et al. 1991). The results of the Roundtop dating project led me to question the whole history of the crops of the polyculture and to start a long-term research program, drawing primarily on museum collections, that has rewritten the history of the three crops. While my research has been directed toward the goal of a better understanding of the history of the polyculture, it has investigated each of the specific crops individually. As a result, the following summary of the research is organized by individual crops.

MAIZE (*ZEA MAYS* SSP. *MAYS*)

Genetic analyses of maize indicate that it evolved from a subspecies of teosinte (*Zea mays* ssp. *parviglumis*) in Mexico some 7000 to 9000 years ago (Matsuka et al. 2002). The earliest maize microbotanical remains (starch, phytoliths) found in Mexico are 8700 years old (Piperno et al. 2009), while the earliest maize macrobotanical remains (kernels, cob fragments) in Mexico and date to approximately 6000 years ago (Piperno and Flannery 2001). These remains came from a small cob with relatively few kernels. From this inauspicious beginning, maize has spread worldwide and is one of the world's most important grain crops. The earliest macrobotanical remains found thus far in eastern North America date to approximately 2100 years ago, based on a direct AMS date (Riley et al. 1994). These remains were recovered from the Holding site in the Illinois River valley near its confluence with the Mississippi (see Figure 11.1). While maize pollen has been identified in earlier contexts in the Southeast, the Holding macrobotanical remains had been the earliest accepted dates for maize in eastern North America. Other early direct AMS dates have been obtained on maize macrobotanical remains in Tennessee, Ohio, and southern Ontario (Crawford et al. 1997). Maize macrobotanical remains associated with wood charcoal dates of around 2300 BP at the Meadowcroft Rockshelter in Pennsylvania (Adovasio and Johnson 1981) are intriguing but remain controversial pending direct AMS dating of the remains themselves. The earliest direct date on maize macrobotanical remains in New York, in the southeastern part of the state, had been 1000 years old (Cassedy and Webb 1999). Recently an AMS date on maize from southeastern New York has been reported at 1200 years old (Knapp 2009).

As shown in Figure 12.22, the distribution of dates on and associated with macrobotanical remains across northeastern North America suggests a gradual southwest-to-northeast spread across the region. However, it was likely that this apparent trend was more a result of recovery bias than a reflection of the true history of maize across the region. For example, the Holding site produced 19 fragments of maize, but only after over 5000 liters (175 feet^3) of soil from feature

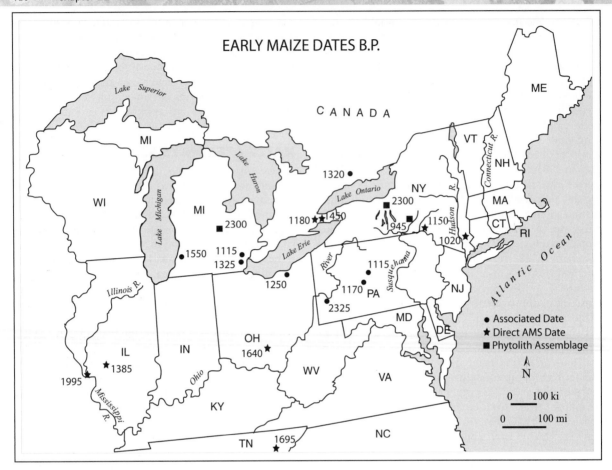

FIGURE 12.22 Early maize dates (BP) for northeastern North America.

and midden contexts had been processed through water flotation, followed by intensive identification efforts by paleoethnobotanists. No other site of Holding's age to the east has been subjected to so great a level of sampling. Thus any history of the crop inferred from the distribution of early dates is suspect.

Excavating an archaeological site is a very expensive and time-consuming endeavor, especially if one is interested in finding the earliest evidence for maize in a region. The level of sampling and flotation processing done at Holding is staggering and is unlikely to be repeated at another site anytime soon. In any event, there is no guarantee that maize macrobotanical remains would be found by another such investigation even if maize had been used at the site (Hart 1999b, 2008). The challenge then was to find another means of determining whether maize was present in New York earlier than 1000 BP. It turned out that museum collections held the key to radically changing our understanding of the history of this crop in New York.

The New York State Museum's archaeological collections contain more than 4.5 million objects. Tens of thousands of these objects are prehistoric pottery sherds. When surveying the collections, on occasion one will come across a sherd that has a layer of charred material on its inner surface. This material is referred to as cooking residue. My colleague Robert Thompson (University of Minnesota) has developed a process for extracting from cooking residues the microscopic silica bodies that plants produce as they take up water and nutrients from the soil (Hart et al. 2003). These tiny units are called opal phytoliths, and the chaffs of grasses produce a particular phytolith form called a rondel. Rondels in turn have many forms, for which Thompson has created a taxonomy. By using this taxonomy to classify 100 rondels from a cooking residue, it is possible to determine, through statistical comparison with modern samples of phytoliths from maize and other grass chaffs, what species of grass was cooked in a pot (Hart et al. 2007; Hart and Matson 2009). Coupled with direct AMS dating of the same residues, this form of analysis provides a powerful, and relatively inexpensive, means of expanding knowledge about the history of maize (and other crops).

Working with my colleague Hetty Jo Brumbach (State University of New York, Albany), I initially selected six residue samples for Thompson to analyze. These were from three sites in the northern Finger Lakes region of New York: Hunters Home, Kipp Island, and Wickham. Collections from these sites had been in the museum for five to six decades. Based on pottery types and wood charcoal radiocarbon dates obtained by the original excavators, Brumbach and I thought that the samples would date several centuries earlier than 1000 BP. Thompson was able to extract ample rondel phytolith assemblages from all the samples for statistical analysis. That analysis indicated that maize had been cooked in all the pots, along with seeds of wild rice (*Zizania aquatica*), a grass species that occurs naturally in much of eastern North America. Thompson also identified squash (*Cucurbita* sp.) and sedge (*Cyperus* sp.) phytoliths in the residues. The AMS dates on the residues from Kipp Island and Wickham were as early as the first half of the fourteenth century BP. In analyzing just six residue samples, we were able to demonstrate that maize was present in New York some 350 to 400 years earlier than the macrobotanical record suggested (Hart et al. 2003).

Subsequently we dated and analyzed an additional 18 residue samples from nine other sites. This brought the total number of samples dated and analyzed to 24 from 12 sites. These were from collections made several decades ago. In total, 18 of the residues contained rondel phytolith assemblages that were identified as maize (Hart et al. 2007; Hart and Matson 2009; Thompson et al. 2004). Of particular note is that one of the residues from the Vinette site in the Finger Lakes region was dated to calibrated 2300 BP, older than the earliest macrobotanical evidence for maize in eastern North America at the Holding site in Illinois. The remaining residues with maize phytoliths range in age from about calibrated 2000 BP to 500 BP, demonstrating a more-or-less continuous presence for maize in New York after the earliest evidence for its use. Recently, phytoliths and starch grains have been recovered from cooking residues dating to around calibrated 2300 BP in Michigan (Raviele 2010).

THE COMMON BEAN (*PHASEOLUS VULGARIS*)

Like maize, the common bean originated in Mexico, but unlike maize, there is genetic evidence to suggest

that populations in Andean South America were also brought under cultivation by ancient Native Americans (Kami et al. 1995). The earliest dates on cultivated bean in Mexico are about 2500 BP, while from South America we have 4400 BP (Kaplan and Lynch 1999). As related earlier, it has been accepted that the common bean was adopted by 1000 BP in northeastern North America. Even though bean remains were reported from 1000 BP contexts and earlier across the Northeast following Ritchie's publications of Roundtop, until the direct dating of beans from Roundtop, beans from only one other site in the Northeast had been subjected to direct dating, and the result was approximately 600 BP. After the Roundtop results, I set out with my colleague C. Margaret Scarry to directly date other beans from early contexts in the Northeast. We were able to obtain bean samples from six additional sites in Vermont, New York, and Pennsylvania from contexts reported to be as early as 1200 BP. These samples were obtained from museums and from other collection repositories. The samples from one of the Pennsylvania sites were determined by Scarry to contain no bean remains, although the others were confirmed as beans. All the bean samples yielded AMS dates at right around calibrated 650 BP, consistent with the results from Roundtop (Hart and Scarry 1999). These results, then, strongly suggest that the common bean was not a regular part of American Indian cropping systems until well over a millennium after the appearance of maize. Subsequently, none of the cooking analyzed residues produced bean phytoliths.

While we had resolved the issue on the timing of bean's appearance in the archaeological record of the far Northeast, there remained an issue of its timing across the greater Northeast, specifically in Ohio, Kentucky, Indiana, Illinois, and southern Ontario, where it was reported in numerous contexts earlier than 650 BP. My colleagues David Asch (then of the Illinois State Museum), Scarry, Gary Crawford (University of Toronto), and I assembled bean samples, in some cases with maize samples from the same contexts, from 20 more sites as far west as the lower Illinois River valley. In all cases the beans were obtained from museums or other artifact repositories. The direct AMS dates on these samples, combined with those from original samples in the Northeast, meant that there were now 51 dates from 26 sites stretching from Illinois to Vermont. None of the dates was earlier than approximately calibrated 700 BP (Hart et al. 2002). That is, the earliest date in Illinois is statistically no older than the earliest date in Vermont (Figure 12.23). Based on the macrobotanical record, then, it appears that after the common bean had been introduced to the northern portions of eastern North America, it spread

FIGURE 12.23 Early bean dates (BP) for northeastern North America.

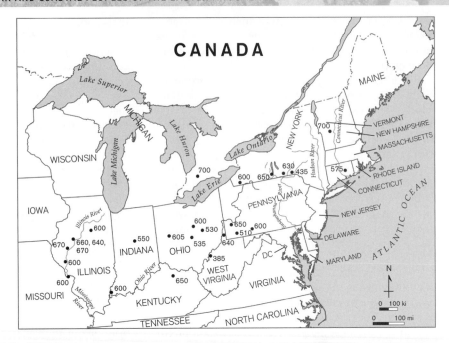

rapidly east and north, becoming an important component of agricultural systems and diets by 700 BP to 650 BP. Interestingly, beans become evident on sites from the Central Plains region a few centuries earlier than in the Northeast (Adair 2003). This suggests, but by no means conclusively proves, that beans entered the Northeast from the Plains.

SQUASH (CUCURBITA PEPO)

The third crop, squash, has a much longer history in the Northeast than maize and beans. There are two subspecies of the primary squash species present in the East prior to the crop distribution changes induced by Euro-American contact (Robinson and Decker-Walters 1996). *Cucurbita pepo* ssp. *pepo* originated in Mexico. This subspecies is represented today by many winter squash cultivars and some ornamental gourds. The second subspecies, *Cucurbita pepo* ssp. *ovifera*, originated in the Ozarks of southern Missouri and northern Arkansas and perhaps the greater Gulf Coastal Plain. Present-day cultivars include many of our summer squashes, acorn squashes, and ornamental gourds. The *ovifera* subspecies is the most likely to account for most of the squashes under cultivation by Late Prehistoric and early Historic period Indian agriculturists in the Northeast.

One thing that makes the evolution of this species so interesting is its presence on archaeological sites across the greater Northeast during the mid-Holocene,

as early as calibrated 7900 BP in Illinois (Asch and Asch 1985) and calibrated 6500 BP in Maine (Petersen and AschSidell 1996) (Figure 12.24). Based on seed size and rind thickness, it is thought that the remains represent *C. pepo* gourds. Native stands of *C. pepo* gourds produce a chemical called cucurbitacin that makes their flesh and seed coats extremely bitter (Robinson and Decker-Walters 1996). If the mid-Holocene *C. pepo* gourds shared this trait, and there is presently no reason to believe they did not, why would Indians have made use of the gourds? Why would they apparently have facilitated the spread of this species from the Gulf Coastal Plain to the far Northeast? These questions caused considerable debate in the archaeological literature.

The gourds are very small, about the size of a small adult human's fist. Each gourd contains over 100 seeds about a third to half the size of a seed from a large pumpkin. Two hypotheses for their mid-Holocene use generated the most interest: (1) dried gourds served utilitarian purposes such as fishnet floats or containers, and (2) the bitterness was removed from the seed coats and the highly nutritious seeds were eaten (Hart et al. 2004). Of course these hypotheses are not mutually exclusive, although at times they have been so treated in the archaeological literature.

There is scant evidence in the ethnohistoric record for Indians using gourds as fishnet floats in the East. While there is archaeological evidence from Florida to suggest that they were used for this

FIGURE 12.24 Early squash dates (BP) for northeastern North America.

purpose (Gilliland 1975), no archaeologist had ever reported on any experiments to determine how well the gourds would have functioned as floats. My museum colleagues Robert Daniels, an ichthyologist, and Charles Sheviak, a botanist, and I decided to test the fishnet float hypothesis (Hart et al. 2004). We first obtained two dried *C. pepo* ssp. *ovifera* gourds from southern Missouri. We extracted the seeds from one of the gourds and successfully germinated six of them. The six seedlings were raised under artificial light until each had four leaves. When there was no danger of frost, they were planted in four locations in the Albany, New York, region. Two lived long enough to produce 50 or more gourds. These were allowed to dry. Then we tested the ability of the gourds to float in water while supporting weight. We found that the gourds could support as much weight without submerging as a modern Styrofoam fishnet float of similar size.

We then attached gourds to two kinds of nets, gill nets and a seine, to determine whether they would work well as net floats (Figure 12.25). The gill nets were placed in two different ponds and left for 12 or more hours each. There was no loss in buoyancy during the trials, and the gourds suffered no obvious damage from being in the water for such long periods of time. The seine net was dragged through both calm and turbulent water in a nearby stream. The gourds kept the net open, allowing the capture of large numbers of fish of varying size. Our tests determined that *C. pepo* gourds work very well as fishnet floats—as well as modern Styrofoam floats. These results certainly added key support for the net-float hypothesis, but did not in any way disprove the seed consumption hypothesis.

Bruce Smith and C. Wesley Cowan, paleoethnobotanists who did extensive fieldwork on the natural history of *C. pepo* ssp. *ovifera* populations in the 1980s, related that they had been able to make the gourd seeds edible by boiling them for five to ten minutes (Cowan and Smith 1993). David Asch (1995) subsequently reported that he had been unable to duplicate

FIGURE 12.25 Using experimental gourd floats to seine for fish.

those results. I boiled the seeds for ten minutes and also failed to remove the seed coat bitterness (Hart et al. 2004). I subsequently undertook a series of other experiments to determine whether the seeds could be made edible (Hart 2004). Indians used wood ash dissolved in water to process a number of food items, including bitter acorns, to make them palatable. I was able to remove the bitterness from gourd seeds by boiling them in water with wood ash for one hour. I was able to speed this to 20 minutes by slightly crushing the seed coats before boiling. The bitterness was also removed by soaking slightly crushed seeds in water with wood ash for 48 hours. Soaking whole seeds in water with wood ash for a week failed to remove all of the bitterness.

The fishnet float and wood ash processing experiments have clearly demonstrated that *C. pepo* ssp. *ovifera* gourds could have been used by mid-Holocene Indians for various purposes. But they were gourds, not the fruits with edible flesh that we commonly call squash and so clearly associate with American Indian agriculture. When did these edible fruits enter Indian agricultural systems? Based on the presence of larger seeds and thicker rind fragments at archaeological sites in the Midwest, squashes were being grown by calibrated 4900 BP (King 1985). The earliest macrobotanical evidence for squash near New York is calibrated 2750 BP (Hart and Asch-Sidell 1997) in the Susquehanna Basin of Pennsylvania. The earliest evidence in New York had been the 650 BP squash seeds at Roundtop. However, as noted earlier, squash phytoliths, presumably produced by *C. pepo* ssp. *ovifera*, from a cooking residue from the Scaccia site, has been dated to calibrated 3000 BP in New York (Hart et al. 2007).

ON THE IMPORTANCE OF MUSEUM COLLECTIONS IN MODERN ARCHAEOLOGICAL RESEARCH

The ongoing museum-collections-based research program on the history of maize-bean-squash has revised our knowledge of that history considerably. No longer can we envision a process in New York, or the greater Northeast, whereby the three crops were adopted late, relative to the Midwest, as a unit or in quick succession around 1000 years ago. Rather, it is now apparent that maize and squash had much longer histories, being used by at least 2300 and 3000 years ago, respectively. Beans, on the other hand, are not evident until much later, approximately 700 to 650 years ago. Thus, the polyculture system that characterized Late Prehistoric and early Historic period American Indian agriculture in the Northeast was not in place until a few centuries before it was first observed by European explorers (Biggar 1924).

Just a few short years ago, none of these major changes in the crop histories were envisioned. The sudden occurrence of maize-bean-squash agriculture in New York about 1000 years ago was the foundation of interpretations on the "origins" of the Northern Iroquoians in New York (Hart 2001). That traditionally assumed association has now completely broken down (Hart and Brumbach 2003). Our understanding of the crops' histories now encompasses a much longer period of time, opening up new possibilities for restructuring our conceptions of how agriculture did, or did not, influence the development of various socioeconomic traits that have been used to characterize Late Prehistoric and early Historic period American Indians in the Northeast (Hart 2001). Much exciting research lies ahead as a result of these new understandings of the crops' histories.

I opened this case study with a discussion of the importance of archaeological collections. I hope that you are now convinced of the importance of preserving these collections for future research. That little of the research reviewed here could have been accomplished in such a relatively short period of time without the museum collections should amply demonstrate the importance of professionally curated collections in modern archaeological research. The collections used in this research were made decades ago. The advent of new recovery techniques over the past several decades, which ensure the recovery of a wider spectrum of the human behavioral evidence, potentially make collections made today even more valuable to future archaeologists. Having these collections curated and made available for research will ensure continued excitement of discovery about the history of our species.

DISCUSSION QUESTIONS

1. What has been the traditional perspective on when maize-bean-squash agriculture spread into the Northeast? Why does it matter that the crops in the maize-bean-squash agricultural complex now seem to have different histories?

2. How has cooking residue on pottery sherds been used to date the presence and use of maize? Does this suggest anything to you about how archaeologists should treat pottery sherds that they find in future excavations?

3. Do you think it more likely that *Cucurbita pepo ovifera* seeds were used for food, that the gourds were used as fish floats, or both? How conclusive is the experimental evidence concerning possible use? Can you think of other ways to evaluate the problem?

4. What do you think of Hart's argument that museum collections are important to future archaeological research? How does this relate to the issues discussed in "The Curation Crisis," Section F.2 of the Student CD?

CHAPTER 13

Into the Modern World

I can get better stuff than this down the street at the antique store!

That sentiment was expressed in 1993 by a member of the City Council of El Cajon, California. A local archaeologist had just shown the council a sample of artifacts collected during an excavation in the city's redevelopment area, and the council was concerned about the cost of the project. To qualify for federal funds in its planned redevelopment, the city was obliged to pay for excavation of the Corona del El Cajon Hotel site, a late nineteenth-century hotel that had burned in 1920. Shops had been built over the burned basement and abandoned yard of the hotel, and most people forgot the hotel was ever there. Archaeologists not only uncovered the basement essentially intact, but also found trash pits and privies associated with the hotel.

The council member, however, saw only an exorbitant price tag for a project that seemed to have merely produced a collection of dirty and broken bits of pottery, glass, rusty metal, animal bone, and similar items. The nearby antique store had whole dishes, complete jars, unrusted metal tools, and usable tableware that looked better and would cost much less than the artifacts the consultant had exhibited.

The council member's view is, unfortunately, a common one. Many members of the public view archaeology as an Easter egg hunt in which the object is to find the best goodies from the past. Archaeologists certainly enjoy finding spectacular objects, but that is not the goal of their research. The archaeologist seeks information about human life in the past. As we have seen in other chapters, the distant past, as measured in centuries or millennia rather than in decades or years, is of archaeological interest, but the relatively recent past, as in the case of the Corona del El Cajon Hotel excavations, often is a topic of concern as well. Objects play a part in the process of learning about past human life, but only a part. Even more important than the artifacts are the circumstances under which they are found—their **context**. Context includes the location in space and the associations with other artifacts. A bottle base, for example, can provide information about when the item was made and what it may have contained. It might be determined that a certain bottle base is from a liquor bottle made in the first decade of the twentieth century. If it was found in a privy pit along with a number of other pieces of liquor bottles, we can gain insight into the liquor consumption of historical El Cajon inhabitants. The occurrence of a quantity of liquor bottles in the privies and trash pits associated with the hotel is particularly interesting. Records indicate that when the privy was in use, El Cajon was a dry town—one in which liquor was illegal. The artifacts from the hotel excavation demonstrate the actual behavior of people who worked at or patronized the hotel rather than the behavior prescribed by the laws of the city.

The complete assemblage of bottle fragments from the layer in the privy was used to calculate an index of bottled product use that was then compared with lists from other sites to see where rural El Cajon fit. When the entire assemblage was considered, including the animal bone, ceramic sherds, and the glass, a picture of a rather elegant hotel emerged. The consultant noted that the hotel had what was, for the time, an upscale menu featuring high-quality cuts of meat, but the food apparently was served on plain ceramics. The hotel created an elegant ambiance through the use of pressed glass tableware and decorated toilet sets in the guest rooms. Layers of refuse that dated later in time document the change in the nature of the hotel from a resort to a boarding house. All this was inferred from the nature of the remains and their distribution in the ground.

Archaeological approaches to trash pits and privies stand in stark contrast to those of relic hunters and bottle collectors. Archaeologists excavate slowly, exposing and recording artifacts as they go. Records of artifact location are critical because scientists are interested in the context of each find. For the archaeologist, a broken bottle base tells as detailed a story as the whole bottle, and even small fragments of ceramics and bits of bone are collected and recorded. Bottle hunters also excavate old trash pits and privies, often illegally. Their focus is on the whole bottles and adding new specimens to their collections. Although there are a few exceptions, bottle hunters generally dig quickly, without regard to associations of materials. They do not record the location of their finds, sometimes not even noting the site from which objects were obtained. In the process of their digging for pretty specimens—the kind the city council member had expected to see—they destroy any patterning in the deposits.

To bring to a close the story of the consultant and the city council, we note that about a year later, the consultant presented his report on the excavation project. The lengthy document detailed the research goals, the historical background, the methods used, the artifacts found, and their associations, as well as the conclusions drawn from the research. A picture of life at the Corona del El Cajon Hotel was sketched that would not have been possible without the excavation. The same city council member who had talked about the antique stores earlier complimented the consultant on the high quality of his work.

Investigations of historical sites like those at Corona del El Cajon Hotel occur all over the world. In this chapter we discuss some of the research topics studied by historical archaeologists working in North America.

HISTORICAL ARCHAEOLOGY

In the preceding chapters we stopped the discussion soon after Europeans showed up. We did this both because this event marks the boundary between the Prehistoric and Historic periods, when some level of written record is available for the areas under consideration, and because once we move into the time of exploration and colonization we move into themes and issues that stretch beyond North America. This does not mean that the North America's Native peoples disappeared or that their subsequent history isn't important to archaeologists. Certainly this history is important to Native people today. It can help First Nations and tribes establish their rights. However, since the sixteenth century the indigenous peoples of North America have been drawn into global developments and affected by geopolitical forces in new and important ways. From this point onward the history of indigenous peoples is intertwined with that of other populations and cultures. As a result, the culture area approach taken in Chapters 4 through 12 no longer makes much sense.

Historical archaeology is sometimes defined as the archaeology of periods for which there are written records, but early civilizations, including the Maya, are documented in written records and these cultures are usually studied by specialists in other subfields of archaeology. Another definition is the archaeology of the modern world or the archaeology of modernization. There is some consensus that historical archaeologists study the material remains of the exploration and colonization of the world beyond Europe by Europeans. In North America this means that historical archaeologists are interested in sites that document early European settlement, in sites that record the interaction between indigenous people and Europeans, as well as in sites that record the story of the frontier, the development of early industry, the development of modern nation states and the process of urbanization. These are the topics we pursue in this chapter (Figure 13.1).

Our approach in this chapter is thematic. It is not our purpose to cover the history of North America in the Historic period. Many of you have studied this history already, and the scope of this book precludes even cursory treatment of events. Instead, presuming that you already know something about the history of the United States and Canada, our goal is to give some idea of the fascinating ways historical archaeology adds to our understanding of this part of the past. Historical

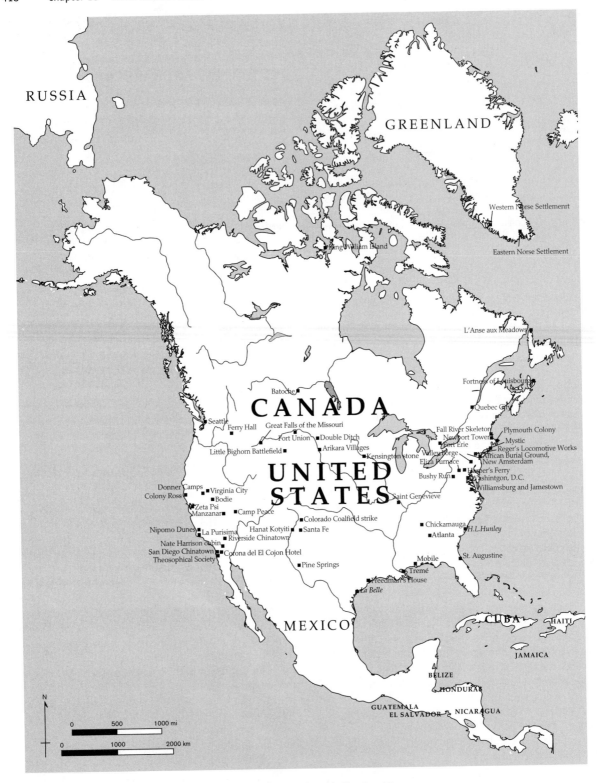

FIGURE 13.1 Locations of historical North American sites mentioned in Chapter 13.

ANTHROPOLOGICAL THEMES

Thematic Research Questions in Chapter 13

The topics of interest to historical archaeologists also relate to the broad anthropological themes we have been tracking in other chapters. You will find material directly relevant to at least three of the broad research questions discussed in Chapter 2 and listed in Table 2.1, though we also touch on other anthropological themes. Table 13.1 helps you locate relevant sections of this chapter for each theme. Reading these sections likely will suggest more specific questions and issues as well.

TABLE 13.1 Research Themes for the Historical Period

Research Question	Particularly Relevant Sections
What movements of human populations can be documented in the North American past after the continent's initial settlement?	Discussion of Contacts and Colonialism, Expansion and Settlement, and African Diaspora, as well as Box 13.1, "How Far Did the Vikings Get?" and the case study, "Community Archaeology: Understanding the Contexts of Archaeological Practice"
How did settlement by Europeans and culture contact between Native Americans and Europeans transform North American cultural and natural landscapes?	Discussions in the sections on Contact and Colonialism, Expansion and Settlement, and War and Conflict
How did the United States and Canada develop into global and industrial powers?	Discussion in sections on War and Conflict, and Modernization and Industrialism, as well as Exhibit 13.1, "Iron Furnaces"

archaeology is an exciting field because it can focus us on the everyday lives of people in the past. It doesn't discriminate against the average citizen and the disenfranchised, who often have not been the subject of written accounts. Rather, historical archaeology incorporates both the material record and written accounts and is as likely to excavate a plantation's slave quarters as the plantation mansion or workers housing as the home of industrialist, enriching understanding in significant ways. Thus, historical archaeology can tell us about the lives of people like African slaves, Natives, or immigrant laborers as well as about the lives of great historical figures. Perhaps because the recent past is more familiar, historical archaeology also engages the public in ways pre-Columbian archaeology does only rarely (Little 2007), and historical archaeologists have been at the forefront of collaborative archaeology, as this chapter's case study, "Community Archaeology: Understanding the Contexts of Archaeological Practice," by Carol McDavid and Christopher Matthews suggests.

The topics we have chosen to cover in this brief introduction to North American historical archaeology are Contact and Colonialism, Expansion and Settlement, War and Conflict, African Diaspora, and Modernization and Industrialism. Other themes might also have been chosen, but this sampling introduces the fascination of historical sites and investigations. If you have been unaware of this kind of archaeology, we hope this chapter encourages you to pursue other topics in historical archaeology.

CONTACTS AND COLONIALISM

As mentioned in Chapter 4, the earliest contact between the indigenous people of North America and the Europeans came in the Arctic with Norse voyages into the area starting in about AD 1000. Dumond (1987) equates the **Skraelings** of Norse sagas with the Dorset peoples, but objects of European origin are found in both Dorset and Thule/Inuit sites, suggesting some form of contact and possibly limited trade (Sutherland 2009). Norse colonies, the Eastern and Western Settlements, were established on the southwest coast of Greenland, and these are believed to have persisted until approximately 1450 (Arneborg and Seaver 2000). However, Norse penetration beyond Greenland is a subject of debate, as discussed in Box 13.1.

Once the Norse withdrew from Greenland, it was not until the sixteenth century AD that European

ISSUES AND DEBATES   BOX 13.1

How Far Did the Vikings Get?

The Vikings, legendary warriors and voyagers of the North, are well known and a source of pride among people of Scandinavian descent. The Viking is an icon in American culture, as exemplified in football mascots, comic books, and movies (Ward 2000). There is a long history of tales about early Viking settlement of the Americas as well. The term "Norse," which refers to the Nordic peoples who settled the Faeroe Islands, Iceland, and Greenland during medieval times, might be preferable for these early explorers of the North America. Whether we call the people Vikings or Norse, the extent of their travels in North America is still being investigated.

Many finds claim to provide evidence of a Viking presence in areas as far inland as Minnesota. An example nearer the coast, the Newport Tower in Rhode Island, has been considered a Norse religious structure. This stone building has a round second story supported on round pillars. The tower's supposed Viking origin and that of the Fall River skeleton, a human skeleton found buried with copper sheeting in Massachusetts, were immortalized in Longfellow's poem *The Skeleton in Armor*. Longfellow tells a romantic tale of a Viking and his love who settle in America to be together. The Viking builds the Newport Tower over his wife's grave, and when he dies, he is buried in his Viking armor, later to be known as the Fall River skeleton. It's a wonderful story poem; but the tower is a seventeenth-century windmill, and the skeleton represents an Indian burial from the early Historic period (Hertz 2000).

The most famous example of Viking claims that cannot be substantiated is the **Kensington stone** (Figure 13.2), found buried on a farm in Minnesota in 1898. This relic bears a runic inscription that tells of Goths and Norwegians exploring westward from Vinland

in 1362. The inscription evokes the tale of a medieval missionary expedition to Greenland, which some claim continued into the interior of North America via Hudson Bay, Lake Winnipeg, and the Red River. The Kensington stone created an immediate sensation, even though most serious scholars considered it a fraud from the beginning. Among other factors tending to negate its authenticity, the runes used are more recent than the fourteenth century. Zealous amateur historians and politicians were able to persuade the Smithsonian Institution to display the Kensington stone for a time. Nevertheless, the weight of evidence is that it is not an authentic artifact, and the Smithsonian no longer even hints that it is valid (Wallace and Fitzhugh 2000).

There is, however, some truth to tales of Viking settlement of North America. Greenland was colonized by the Norse under the leadership of Erik the Red a little more than a thousand years ago. Norse sagas known as the *Greenlander's Saga* and *Erik the Red's Saga*, long a part of the Viking oral tradition, were written down in the thirteenth century. The sagas tell of Viking voyages in the North Atlantic, and specifically of journeys to North America by Leif Eriksson, son of Erik the Red, and Thorfinn Karlsefni around 950 BP (AD 1000). The sagas identify three lands, Helluland, Markland, and Vinland. Helluland (the name refers to the area's rocky nature) is believed to have been Baffin Island, while Markland, named for the fine forests it supported, is thought to refer to southern Labrador. The location of Vinland, perhaps named for the grapevines that grew there, has been much more disputed. The sagas indicate that a settlement was established briefly in Vinland but abandoned in the face of menacing local native groups. Recent finds lead most archaeologists to believe that Newfoundland is Vinland, but because grapes do not grow this far north, the New England coast could also be Vinland. Some archaeologists note that the word *vin* may refer to pasture land, which was abundant in Newfoundland, rather than to vines or grapes (Ingstad and Ingstad 2001:103–109).

Archaeological evidence of Norse settlement was not found until excavations were done between 1961 and 1962 at L'Anse aux Meadows (Figure 13.3) at the tip of Newfoundland's northern peninsula. These established without a doubt that there were ruins of a Norse settlement here (Wallace 2000). Three multiroom halls, each flanked by at least one single-room building, are spaced along a terrace overlooking Epaves Bay, and an eighth structure, interpreted as an iron furnace hut, sits apart from these. About 50 radiocarbon dates indicate that the

FIGURE 13.2 The Kensington stone.

FIGURE 13.3 L'Anse aux Meadows.

Norse settlement was used during the eleventh century. There is a record of native use of this site at other times as well.

The Norse settlement at L'Anse aux Meadows is the only one known in North America outside Greenland, but besides this settlement, there also is good evidence of contact between Norse and Natives in the eastern Subarctic and Arctic. First, the sagas refer to Native people, calling them *skraeling*, a term used for aboriginal people in Greenland as well. Second, native art sometimes seems to depict Norsemen (Figure 13.4). Third, European metal and other objects indicate that Norsemen continued to sail to the continent until the Greenland settlements failed during the fifteenth century. Such objects are found in Dorset sites and later in Thule sites, though they remain rare. It is not clear whether the European artifacts that have been found represent direct contact or trade. They might represent scavenging after hostile encounters or shipwrecks. However, it is logical that the Norse would have used some portions of Baffin Island and northern Labrador for hunting. Archaeological traces of the Norse in Dorset sites in these areas have led some to argue that the Dorset traded ivory for Norse metal (Sutherland 2009). A Norse penny from the eleventh century AD found in the Goddard site in Maine is the most southerly find of an authentic Norse artifact (Cox 2000). This penny, which is the only Norse artifact

FIGURE 13.4 Wooden image called the Bishop of Baffin, believed to represent a Norseman.

at this site, probably was traded southward rather than brought directly by Norsemen.

How far into North America did the Vikings get? We still have more to learn, but most Norse contact and exploration seems to have been in the eastern Arctic and Subarctic. L'Anse aux Meadows probably was the most southerly base for the Norse, although they certainly explored south of that location. Isolated finds are insufficient evidence of settlement. Native trade networks can explain such finds, while only substantial remains like those at L'Anse aux Meadows will establish a true Viking presence in an area.

exploration of North American continued, and contact with Europeans did not occur in many interior areas until the nineteenth century. The quincentennial in 1992 of Columbus's voyage to the New World created considerable interest in the European explorers and the archaeological record they left behind. Columbus's encounter with the New World occurred outside the geographical area covered by this book, but there were other explorers who did travel through the areas discussed in this book. Archaeological remains for exploration are often ephemeral and difficult to recognize, although the remains of the settlements and attempted settlements have been investigated. We have discussed some of this information in the preceding chapters. Two further cases illustrates the ways in which archaeology can add important insights.

First, archaeology can provide new and important perspectives on the historical past. For example, in 1845 Sir John Franklin set out on an attempt to find the much-sought Northwest Passage. The party consisted of two ships and 129 men. The ships became icebound and were abandoned in 1848. The entire crew perished. Scattered remains were found by search parties, and later by archaeologists. Archaeological research on a site on King William Island recovered artifacts and close to 400 pieces of human bone. Analysis of the bone has been particularly interesting. Isotopic analysis of the remains indicate lead poisoning resulting from improperly soldered food cans from the crew's provisions. Lead poisoning was probably a major factor in the loss of life on the Franklin expedition. Approximately one-quarter of the human bone fragments had cut marks indicating cannibalism. This finding is consistent with reports from contemporary Inuit that some members of the expedition ate the remains of their dead associates (Keenleyside et al. 1997).

Second, through archaeology we can understand the processes of cultural change resulting from contact much more clearly. For example, study of material items recovered from Contact period Arikara sites in the Missouri River valley suggest that the adoption of European goods by the Arikara was far from simple. Direct contact with European traders began early in the 1700s, and there were many social and economic interactions that followed. However, between about 1806 and 1835, epidemics and warfare with other Indians, especially the Sioux, combined to reduce the Arikara from an independent nation to a single village incorporated with remnants of the Mandan and Hidatsa. Study of the domestic refuse from earthlodges demonstrates that items of European artifacts are first evident as early as AD 1560, but that usage of Euro-American artifacts increased dramatically in this last period of decline rather than before, when trade relationships between autonomous Arikara villages and Euro-American traders still would have been intact. Moreover, the Arikara first replace native cooking pots and stone projectile points with objects of metal, including sheet metal, which could be turned into projectile points and other tools. Before the social disruptions between 1806 and 1835, objects of European origin were primarily used to support traditional activities such as hide processing, hunting, and cooking. However, the increase of Euro-American goods in the period of disruption is in other types of objects that can be considered "nonproductive" because they have to do with personal adornment and clothing. Rogers (1993) suggests that as disease and warfare took its toll, the traditional social and political system among the Arikara broke down and people sought means of establishing social status as new relationships in consolidated villages were developed.

Complex changes and interactions also characterized the Colonial period across North America. The establishment of the British Colonies in North America is well known. Places like Jamestown, established in 1607, Plymouth (Plimoth) Colony (1620), and Williamsburg (1632) were some of the first settlements along the eastern seaboard. These and many other English colonial sites have been studied by archaeologists who have contributed knowledge on the lifeways of the early colonists and have aided in the interpretation and reconstruction of these sites (Figure 13.5). For example, paleoethnobotanical study of samples from a building at Jamestown recovered wax myrtle seeds known to have been used in the early seventeenth century to "cure" dysentery. Their presence suggests that an apothecary used the building, although it may also have been used as a brewery (Edwards 2005). The French settlement of Canada is also well known. Quebec City was established in 1608 by Samuel de Champlain. The City of Quebec has taken an active role in promoting archaeology, and ongoing excavations are actively interpreted to the public (Figure 13.6).

Although the French did not successfully settle along the Atlantic coast, they were a force in the Mississippi River valley during the seventeenth and eighteenth centuries. The Mississippi was partially explored by Marquette and Joliet in 1673. In 1682 La Salle made it to the Gulf, establishing a small settlement, the Arkansas Post, at the mouth of the Arkansas. His disastrous later expedition via the Gulf of Mexico missed the mouth of the Mississippi. It ended when he lost all his ships, and his men murdered him as he tried to go overland to find the Mississippi. Centuries later, La Salle's ship *La Belle* was found; it had sunk in Matagorda Bay, off the coast of Texas. Excavation of this ship involved constructing a large cofferdam of steel around it, and a million artifacts were recovered from this joint public/private undertaking. Conservation of these artifacts is still underway at Texas A&M University while the skeleton of one of sailors is also being intensively studied (Bruseth and Turner 2005; Roberts 1997).

Eventually the French established the Louisiana colony in the lower Mississippi valley, creating a network of settlements and military posts along the Gulf Coast and along the rivers. For a time, French trade with Native peoples was extensive. As noted earlier, France ceded Louisiana to Spain in 1763 but reacquired it in time to negotiate the Louisiana Purchase of 1803 with the Americans. Many French forts have been investigated archaeologically, as have French settlements, particularly at places like Mobile on the Gulf Coast and Saint Genevieve, the first permanent French settlement in Missouri.

Other European nations also established colonies in North America. Russians explored Alaska and the

FIGURE 13.5 Reconstructed Pilgrim village at Plimoth Plantation. Like other colonial sites, this reconstruction has benefited from archaeological investigations.

FIGURE 13.6 Archaeologists excavating beneath modern Quebec City have found important traces of the long history of human occupation at this spot.

West Coast and established fur trading outposts as far south as San Francisco, as discussed in the case study in Chapter 7, "Cultures in Contact at Colony Ross." After Henry Hudson's voyage in 1609, the Dutch established the city of New Amsterdam that eventually became New York (Cantwell and Wall 2001). However, the Spanish were particularly important in the colonial history of many areas of North America. In

September 1565, the Spanish under Pedro Menendez destroyed Fort Caroline, a French colony established in 1564 at the mouth of the St. Johns River on the Atlantic coast, and established St. Augustine. Other outposts such as Santa Elena on Parris Island also were established. The Spanish Jesuits and Franciscans built a mission system both northward along the Atlantic coast and inland (Milanich 1999). Spanish holdings in La Florida were lost to the English in 1763 after the Seven Years' War in Europe, but Spain retook Florida through a military campaign in 1781. The communities, however, remained multiethnic. Spain also acquired Louisiana from France in 1763 and held it as a colony until 1802 when King Charles IV secretly returned the territory to France.

The archaeology of St. Augustine, which remains the oldest continuously occupied non-native community in the United States, has been studied intensively (Deagan 1983), as have other aspects of the Spanish colonialism in the Southeast (Thomas 1990). One example of significant research is the comparison of human remains from before the Spanish arrived with those from the missions they established in Georgia and Florida. These data confirm that the mission Indians experienced nutritional stresses and that they probably worked quite hard, but the data do not confirm the stereotype that the Spanish conquered native populations through violence and subjugation. Instead they show that the Spanish sought to exploit native labor and land, and Native people coexisted with them for many decades (Larsen 2005).

The Spanish colonized the Southwest from the south in Mexico. By 1598 settlers had established towns, generally in the major river valleys, and Santa Fe was founded in 1610. Along with towns, the Spanish built presidios and missions. Presidios were established either where there were populations to be protected or where other Spanish interests that needed looking after. Missions, established to introduce Christianity to Native Americans, were built near populated areas (Cordell 1997). As mentioned in Chapter 9, the Pueblo Revolt in the 1680s, which briefly removed the Spanish from the area, was accompanied by population relocations and cultural change. At Cochiti in New Mexico, Hanat Kotyiti, a mesa-top pueblo established just after the revolt, has been excavated. Preucel (2000) sees evidence of revitalization of Pueblo culture at the site. Both traditional foods and ritual activities appear to have been reestablished at Hanat Kotyiti, but elements of Spanish material culture were retained as well, including religious gear. Before the end of the century, however, the Spanish had returned to power.

Franciscan missionaries, aided by soldiers, led the colonization of California starting from bases in Baja California in 1769. As mentioned in Chapter 7, the Spanish established a chain of 21 missions protected by four presidios. In addition, two towns were established for colonists. At the missions, impressive adobe brick chapels anchored compounds of adobe buildings (Figure 13.7) built with Native American labor. In the southern part of California, where water always has been a problem, the missionaries had the Indian laborers build extensive irrigation systems at several of the missions, generally of *ladrillos* (fired tiles). Jim Deetz conducted a classic excavation in the Indian barracks at La Purísima Mission (Deetz 1963), where he was able to examine the differential effects of missionization on male and female Native Americans. He concluded that traditional male activities were replaced by Spanish-derived pursuits, while female activities continued relatively unchanged. There was a lack of traditional male artifacts and an abundance of milling tools and stone bowls, items associated with traditional female activities.

Thus, Colonial period archaeology can provide significant and fascinating insights. We have provided some additional examples of colonial archaeology elsewhere in this text (e.g., see discussions in other chapters, especially Chapter 7's case study, "Cultures in Contact at Colony Ross," and the bonus case study on the Student CD, Section D.8, "Ethnicity and Class in Colonial Foodways").

EXPANSION AND SETTLEMENT

The expansion of European colonies into the interior of North America and the settlement of the west is another story you may know something about. Events surrounding settlement also provide a tremendous number of important topics for archaeological research. In both the United States and Canada, there is a long and complicated story of trade and settlement, conflicts between Indians and white, treaties, and the eventual movement of Native peoples to reservations. There also is the story of the settlers, ranchers, and homesteaders who moved into the west as permanent residents. Not all of the new settlers were of European descent: Asians and eventually African Americans also were part of this movement, and Indian nations were displaced and forcibly removed from their lands. Histories are available that give much detail about the experiences of each of these groups, but archaeology can add new information and provide new insights. Here we provide a sampling of topics archaeologists have investigated.

FIGURE 13.7 Mission La Purísima Concepción, now a California state park.

One topic of historical interest relates to the Louisiana Purchase of 1803 when the United States gained control of the Great Plains except for Texas and the Canadian portion of the Plains. Lewis and Clark's famous expedition was mounted in response to this acquisition and extended from 1804 to 1806. The recent bicentennial of this expedition stimulated archaeological investigations of sites associated with it. For example, one site investigated was the campsite at the lower portage of the Great Falls of the Missouri in Montana (Saraceni 1998). The investigations at Double Ditch Village, noted on a Lewis and Clark map, which were discussed in the case study in Chapter 10, also were stimulated by the Lewis and Clark anniversary.

Perhaps more important, after Lewis and Clark, Americans began to establish their own trading houses on the Great Plains. These enterprises were called factories and were supported by military forts. One example was Fort Union, established in 1828 at the confluence of the Yellowstone and the Missouri rivers by the American Fur Company. Not an army post, Fort Union was an important center of the Northern Plains fur trade until it was sold to the U.S. Army and razed in 1867. Extensive archaeological excavations at this site yielded large quantities of artifacts for future study and were helpful in the reconstruction of this fort, which can be visited by the public (Figure 13.8). This is just one of many fur-trading sites where archaeology has been conducted.

Another important topic related to the theme of expansion and settlement is Indian removals from the Southeast. Some Native American tribes of the Southeast had been able to survive the Colonial period, but

by the turn of the nineteenth century a tide of Euro-American settlers flooded into their lands, causing a series of conflicts like the Creek War of 1813–1814. Indians from the Midwest also relocated westward in this period, but tribes of the Southeast provide the best-known examples of removal. The Cherokee were the most acculturated to Euro-American ways, having established a democratic government and devised a written version of their traditional language. Some Cherokee were even wealthy plantation owners with property desired by Americans. The Creeks, Choctaws, Chickasaws, and Seminoles also were farmers holding coveted land. After the passage of the Indian Removal Act in 1830, most of the Indians of the Southeast were resettled west of the Mississippi. One forced relocation march, known as the **Trail of Tears**, began when federal troops routed thousands of Georgia Cherokee from their homes in 1838; nearly one-quarter of those who set out died en route. A number of Indians did escape removal, including about a thousand Cherokees, who remained in North Carolina, where the Eastern Cherokee live today (Bense 1994).

A third topic of great interest relates to mining and exploitation of mineral resources. The California gold rush of 1849 and the discovery of the Comstock lode in Nevada in 1859 brought hordes of people seeking their fortune. Their route west, the Oregon Trail, is well preserved in parts of Nevada, especially where there is actually an accumulation of tracks rather than a single trail. This dispersed trail (Figure 13.9), which covers large areas, can create headaches for land managers who have to decide which tracks are important and

FIGURE 13.8 Fort Union, the longest lasting American fur-trading outpost, operated from 1828 to 1867. Although razed after this date, it has been reconstructed as a national monument and can be visited today.

FIGURE 13.9 A section of the Oregon Trail near Boise, Idaho.

what uses are conducive to the preservation of the important remnants of the trail.

Even before the discovery of gold, however, people were attracted to California, including a group of unlucky immigrants who left Springfield, Illinois, in 1846 and became trapped by winter snows in the Sierra Nevada. This was the Donner party, who were stranded for months in makeshift camps and some hastily constructed cabins. Archaeological research has located remnants of the camps. This research continues to shed light on the ordeal of the Donner party, whose survivors are said to have resorted to cannibalism, eating parts of their fellow campmates who died. While no direct evidence of cannibalism has been found, the excavators have concluded that cannibalism did occur, probably for a brief period of time shortly before rescue. The excavations already have cleared up some misconceptions about where the encampments were, and many details of camp life were reconstructed. The most recent excavations have combined not only historical documents and archaeological data, but also informative enthnohistorical accounts from the Washoe, in whose territory the Donner party were stranded (Dixon et al. 2011).

Related directly to mining are the many ghost towns, as well as many towns that are still occupied. The historic town of Bodie in eastern California is a state park that preserves an abandoned mining town. Virginia City, in Nevada, made famous by the television series *Bonanza*, is another such town, although it has had a second life as a tourist destination. Excavation of Virginia City's Boston Saloon is discussed later in this chapter.

In Canada, the topic of the **Métis** rebellion also has received archaeological attention. If you are from the United States you may not be aware of this interesting event in Canadian history. Although the 49th parallel was set as the northern boundary of the United States in 1818, Canada was not established until 1867. The new country acquired **Rupert's Land** and the Northwest Territory in 1869 and established the various provinces in the 1870s, but Saskatchewan and Alberta were not established until 1905. The transfer to Canadian control did not happen completely peacefully. The Métis, a distinctive ethnic group of aboriginal and European fur trader descent now recognized as a Canadian First Nation, feared losing their lands and livelihood. Although they established their own provisional government under Louis Riel, the Canadians rapidly crushed this rebellion. The Métis are still fighting for land and hunting rights today. Batoche, a Métis settlement where the last battle of the rebellion occurred, has been excavated in association with Parks Canada's interpretation of this part of Canadian history (Lee 1983, 1984).

We should not forget that as Europeans settled into North America, they developed an agrarian way of life that persisted into the twentieth century. Many aspects of this lifestyle, from plantation life in the Old South to simple farmsteads across the continent to ranches in the west, are subjects of historical archaeology (Mascia 2005). Today, as urban sprawl takes over areas far beyond our cities and suburbs, these agrarian landscapes are being destroyed, making the archaeology of our agricultural past particularly significant.

As a final example of topics related to expansion and settlement, a number of interesting landscape studies can be done by historical archaeologists investigating the way in which Europeans used land, platted towns, and established farms and ranches. For example, many European settlements were planned around main streets, and many frontier towns had one long central street. Other settlers had more rigid plans for the communities they established. Mormons used a grid plan established by the Prophet Joseph Smith that emphasized equality and community by establishing equal-size lots and having houses face each other. They also used fences to bound each property and tree plantings and hedgerows to bound fields and larger parcels of land. Archaeology reveals that even in the desert, as settlement expanded away from Salt Lake, Mormon towns were hardly haphazard constructions (Leone 2010).

WAR AND CONFLICT

Conflict and violence have been themes in several earlier chapters, and wars and battle continued after the coming of Europeans. Indeed, many of the first contacts between Native North Americans and Europeans were marked by conflict. Martin Frobisher's first contact with the Inuit in 1579, for example, ended with some of Frobisher's men being kidnapped by the Inuit and Inuits being taken hostage by Frobisher (McGhee 2005:103).

There were of course many conflicts in the Colonial period throughout North America, with some of the first "Indian wars" occurring in New England in the seventeenth century. These include the Pequot War in 1637, when English colonists massacred the inhabitants of the Pequot town at Mystic, Connecticut (Hauptman 1990), establishing that a new style of warfare was practiced by Europeans. The better known King Philip's War (1675–1676) forever destroyed the multiethnic character of early colonial New England society (Drake 1999).

Despite its name, geopolitical contests between France and Great Britain in Europe eventually led to the French and Indian War in North America. This is the name Americans use for the Seven Years' War (1754–1763) or "War of the Conquest" between Great Britain and France. This war, which has been of great interest to military archaeologists, was not a war of European conquest of Indians, but instead was fought over who would control the American Northeast. One place where extensive archaeological work has been done is at the Fortress of Louisbourg in Nova Scotia (Figure 13.10). The French established this settlement, which once was a thriving commercial hub established as a base for the colonial cod fishing industry in the North Atlantic's Grand Banks. In 1758 the British

FIGURE 13.10 The reconstructions of the Fortress of Louisbourg in Nova Scotia, which fell to the British during the French and Indian War in 1858, are based in part on extensive archaeological work that exposed foundations like those shown here and recovered artifacts from this important commercial center.

besieged this fort with an army supported by 150 ships and Louisbourg fell to the British, who destroyed it. In the late twentieth century Canada began a massive project to investigate and reconstruct this town as a monument to French life in the 1740s, and today like Williamsburg in Virginia, it is a living history center that thousands of people visit each year.

Although the Treaty of 1763 established a Proclamation Line at the crest of the Appalachians, separating Indian lands to the west from British colonies to the east, colonial traders and settlers did not honor this boundary. Hostilities between Indians and the British and later the Americans continued for many years. For example, during Pontiac's War (1763–1764), many tribes joined the Ottawa chief in an attempt to remove the British from the Ohio country. One important battle was fought at Bushy Run in western Pennsylvania, where excavation and geophysical study has helped clarify the precise location of the battlefield (Johnson and Johnson 2010).

Besides the French and Indian War, the Revolutionary War, the War of 1812, and the Civil War have been key topics for historical archaeologists. Although

there is no shortage of traditional history about these wars, battlefield archaeology and archaeological research at forts, cemeteries, hospitals, farms, and the towns associated with them contribute greatly to increasing the accuracy of historical knowledge. For example, a military graveyard from the War of 1812 was found in Fort Erie, Ontario, in 1987. Excavations uncovered the remains of soldiers who had died during the American occupation of this fort, providing a detailed profile of these men and their lives (Litt et al. 1993). Archaeologists also can provide insight into more mundane aspects of life, such as what people ate, how they farmed, and what kind of structures they lived in. Such data proved particularly instructive when archaeologists working at Valley Forge in Pennsylvania, documented details about how troops were quartered there and what they ate (Figure 13.11).

Though extensively documented by historical records, the American Civil War also can be studied through archaeology. Studies of battles or military campaigns are obvious topics. For example, the defensive structures erected in 1864 at Atlanta have been archaeologically investigated (Fryman 2000), as has the

retreat of federal troops at the battle of Chickamauga in the Chattanooga area (Cornelison 2000). Much of this work is being performed as a result of CRM requirements.

Civil War shipwrecks are of great importance to understanding this war, and the **underwater archaeology** associated with them has been significant. Margolin (1994) notes that shipwrecks in the James River in Virginia are particularly important as control of the James River, with the access to Richmond it provided, was critical to both sides. However, other Civil War shipwrecks provide important time capsules from the past. One particularly interesting investigation is the raising of a Confederate submarine, the *H.L. Hunley*. Built from an iron boiler and with a nine-man crew (eight to turn cranks that powered the *Hunley* and a ninth to steer), the sub successfully attacked and sank the U.S.S. *Housatonic* on February 17, 1864. Although it signaled that it had been successful, the *Hunley* sank as

it was returning to shore. In May 1995, a team from the National Underwater Marine Agency, a private not-for-profit organization funded by best-selling author Clive Cussler, found her buried in sediment. After much careful consideration, investigators raised the *Hunley* (Figure 13.12). Remains of the crew were recovered, facial reconstructions now have given faces to these heroes of the Confederacy, and in April 2004, all the remains were reburied. Details of construction have been studied, and the artifacts provide insight into the lives of the crew.

A wide variety of other archaeological studies of Civil War era sites are being done as well (see Geier and Potter 2000; Geier and Winter 1994). Archaeological study can open a window on people left out of the story as usually told. For example, archaeological excavation of the remains of a boardinghouse operated during the various occupations of Harper's Ferry at the time of the Civil War has taught us much about the diet

FIGURE 13.12 A crane lifting the *Hunley* to the conservation lab.

and lifestyle of noncombatants trying to survive under wartime conditions (Shackel 2000).

Wars and battles with the Indians continued throughout the nineteenth century. Some recent work at the Pine Springs **Buffalo Soldiers** camp located in the Guadalupe Mountains National Park, east of El Paso, provides some interesting insights into one aspect of those conflitcts. "Buffalo Soldiers" is the name given to two regiments of African American cavalry established in 1866 and posted to various spots on the western frontier to build forts and roads, and to protect railroads, stage coaches, and settlers. The Apache were often the soldiers' adversaries in the West Texas area near the Pine Springs encampment. Survey and limited testing at Pine Springs by African American students from Howard University and by Mescalero Apache high school students reveals that the Apache used this site when the soldiers were not in residence (Figure 13.13). This project is an example of cooperation between Native Americans and African Americans in the search for the history of both groups (Davis 2005).

Another example is the archaeology done at the site of Custer's famous "last stand." This work, initiated after fire had removed the grass cover from the battlefield and left artifacts visible, has provided fresh perspective on exactly what happened in this battle. By plotting the locations of spent bullets, weaponry, other equipment, and skeletal remains, as well as by excavations, archaeologists have added to our understanding of how the combatants positioned themselves, bringing into new focus various accounts by Indians

and others of how the battle actually proceeded (Scott et al. 2000).

Still more recent wars also have left an archaeological legacy of interest. World Wars I and II were fought overseas, but the preparation for American and Canadian entry into the wars left sites that have shed light on those conflicts. At the beginning of World War II, when Japanese forces attacked Pearl Harbor, one reaction to the attack was to round up Japanese Americans and place them in internment camps. The forced relocation of these people, many of them U.S. citizens, resulted. Many families lost their homes and businesses with their internment. National Park Service archaeologist Jeff Burton has conducted archaeological studies at two of these camps, Manzanar in the high desert of eastern California and Minidoka in southern Idaho. The studies have provided information about structures, features, and artifacts from the camps, and one of the surprising findings was how much, based on the artifacts recovered, Japanese culture flourished. As Burton said in an interview, "If a group is being punished for their ethnicity, they might as well embrace it" (Archaeological Institute of America 2006).

Significant archaeology also can be done for the period after World War II. During the Cold War (approximately 1946–1989) the United States, Canada, and the countries of NATO didn't fight actual battles but they competed over who could build the most destructive weapons. The focus was on nuclear weapons of various types. Archaeologists have investigated

FIGURE 13.13 Maraina Montgomery and Chandra Harris, students at Howard University, taking a measurement at the Pine Springs Buffalo Soldier Encampment.

many aspects of this conflict, including the archaeology of the radar and ballistic missile warning systems constructed in the Arctic beginning in the 1950s to provide early warning of aircraft armed with warheads (Whorton 2002).

Cold War–related archaeology also has been conducted at and around the Nevada test site, where the United States tested its nuclear weapons from 1951 until 1992. A considerable number of CRM studies were conducted here, and the work continues. In addition to documenting pre-Columbian sites, archaeologists have been documenting the archaeology of the nuclear weapons program. From standing structures used in the testing and weapons research to Camp Peace, a spot across the highway from the boundary of the test site where protesters camped and demonstrated, archaeologists recorded the artifacts and features associated with the program. For example, one site is a furnished bomb shelter that looked like something out of a 1950s TV show, complete with a stocked kitchen and a television set. This work provides insights about a time in world history during which the possibility of nuclear war seemed quite real (Trivedi 2002).

AFRICAN DIASPORA

African Americans are another group whose story hasn't been well told in historical records. The "African Diaspora," the term for the historic movement of Africans throughout the world, was originally applied to those who were forcibly taken from Africa and brought to the New World as slaves, as well as their descendants. However, it now has been broadened to include other movements of African people.

Archaeology has much to contribute to exploring and interpreting the Diaspora. The first archaeologists to approach this topic focused on the excavation of slave cabins at plantations. Much was learned about the day-to-day life of those whose labor made the plantations work. There were surprises, too, like the recovery of shot and gun parts indicating that slaves had access to firearms. There is also evidence from both specific kinds of artifacts (e.g., quartz crystals) and particular contexts (caches and in the walls of the houses) of continuation of African religious beliefs in the Plantation context (Samford 1996).

Spurred both by growth in the field and by the discovery of sites through the CRM process, Diaspora studies now include not just slavery but also topics like the Underground Railroad that was so important to slaves escaping their status as property and heading north to the free states. Black slaves also escaped into Florida, where they became part of the Seminole Nation and fought Indian removal (Weik 2005). The establishment of free towns and the lives of African Americans in the days after the Civil War are also included. African Diaspora archaeology is a huge topic, and we have space here only to scratch the surface. This chapter's case study, "Community Archaeology:

Understanding the Contexts of Archaeological Practice" by Carol McDavid and Christopher Matthews, discusses aspects of archaeology in African American communities. In Chapter 1's discussion of New York City's African Burial Ground (Box 1.2), we provided some insight into what was learned from the excavation of a cemetery established in the early Colonial period and containing the remains of both slaves and free African Americans. Earlier in this chapter we discussed excavation of the Buffalo Soldier site of Pine Springs. Two additional examples, from the post–Civil War period, suggest the great scope of this topic.

Recent archaeological work in Virginia City, which grew to exploit the riches of the Comstock lode, has revealed remains of the Boston saloon, an establishment that served the African American members of this bustling community between 1864 and 1875. The excavations have changed stereotypical views of the western mining camp, which had been seen as primarily inhabited by white males. The discovery of 21 fragments of glass that, when reassembled, turned out to be the oldest known Tabasco bottle, suggest that African Americans on the frontier were in the forefront of experimentation with cuisines. Chemical testing of food residues confirms that ingredients consistent with the use of the commercial hot sauce were present. DNA analysis of material from a clay smoking pipe indicates use by a woman, suggesting that the view of mining camp saloons as exclusively male preserves may not be completely accurate as well. This ongoing project is expected to continue to add to our appreciation of the world of the western mining camp and to our understandings of the African American experience on the frontier .

Finally, excavations on Palomar Mountain, near San Diego, California, have uncovered the remains of a home built by Nate Harrison, a freed slave who is thought to have come to California with his master. Harrison, who died in 1920, built this cabin on the site sometime in the late 1800s, and it was well documented in photographs. When the foundations were exposed, it became apparent that Harrison had built for himself the kind of home he had known growing up. Based on the dimensions and layout, Harrison had essentially built a slave cabin (Mallios et al. 2008).

MODERNIZATION AND INDUSTRIALISM

Early American industry developed largely in the Northeast and the Mid-Atlantic, leaving a fascinating material record that archaeologists have begun to investigate. These areas were the sites of early extractive industries such as mining, oil drilling, and lumbering, and they also were the location of early manufacturing enterprises. Beginning in the eighteenth century and continuing into the nineteenth, paper mills, textile factories, pottery factories, glass factories, and ironworks were started throughout the area. Archaeology can document the actual processes and organization of production (Gordon and Malone 1994). For example, excavations in Paterson, New Jersey, provided new insights into the development of this early center of manufacturing in the United States by exploring the evolution of the Rogers Locomotive Works during the nineteenth century (Ingle 1982). In addition, the transportation industry left an early mark on these regions in the form of the canals and railroads that once crisscrossed the landscape. When excavations produce domestic refuse, archaeology also can reveal much about the lifestyles of both the owners and the laborers in these industrial enterprises. Exhibit 13.1 presents an example of the kinds of cultural resource that might be studied by archaeologists doing **industrial archaeology**.

Industrial archaeology documents technological change in American society, but also social change. The lives of workers and the social impacts of industrialization and global capitalism are just as interesting, but even less likely to have been fully recorded in historical documents. Studies of class, ethnicity, and gender issues in these contexts have been conducted by historical archaeologists. For example, the archaeology of the southern Colorado coal field strike of 1914 has been intensively studied by archaeologists. Historical documents tell us about this strike and the massacre of 25 people, including 2 women and 11 children, by Colorado state militia. However, the lives of the workers involved in this strike as opposed to the events, have not been documented, and here, archaeology can enrich the picture (Saitta 2005).

Besides industrialization, under modernization historical archaeologists consider the development of towns into cities. They examine the archaeology of these developing cities by looking at their growth, ethnic makeup, and the economics of urbanization. An interesting study of complex phenomena in an urban environment focuses on artifact types recovered from working-class households and brothels in a Washington, D.C., neighborhood between 1860 and 1920 (Seifert 1996). In the Hotel del Corona example at the beginning of this chapter, urban archaeologists demonstrated the use of alcoholic beverages at the hotel even though El Cajon, the location of the site, was incorporated as a dry town.

Another development of early cities was the establishment of ethnic enclaves. The Chinese were often forced to live in restricted areas or Chinatowns in the late nineteenth and early twentieth centuries. Several of these Chinatowns have been excavated, including ones in San Diego (Figure 13.16) and Riverside. The Woolen Mills Chinatown in San Jose was excavated as part of a

CLUES TO THE PAST

EXHIBIT 5.1

Iron Furnaces

Ruins like the one shown in Figure 13.14 still can be found throughout the Northeast. These flat-topped, almost pyramidal, cut stone structures are the remains of iron furnaces. Iron making is one of the most important examples of early industrial development in the United States. The abundance of iron ore from which iron could be obtained, coupled with the availability of limestone used in the extraction process and wood for fuel, as well as the presence of many fast-flowing streams for power, made the Northeast and the Mid-Atlantic ideal for iron production. In the eighteenth and nineteenth centuries, iron-making complexes centered on **blast furnaces** such as the Eliza Furnace proliferated. Though the ruins of the furnace stack itself may be all that remains visible aboveground, there is a great deal to be learned about these early endeavors through archaeology.

Two processes of iron extraction were brought to the Americas by European colonists. The older extraction process was to heat the ore in a charcoal fire until it was reduced to a spongy mass, or **bloom**; water-driven bellows increased the temperature of the flames. The impurities in the ore were removed through repeated heating and hammering. Bloomery forges that undertook this process were common in colonial America, but they were not as productive as blast furnaces, which by then had been developed in Europe. In a blast furnace a **flux**, usually limestone, was added with the ore to the fire to promote the separation of iron. Blast furnace technology was introduced to the Americas in the middle of the seventeenth century. An attack by Indians had ruined an earlier attempt to build a blast furnace in Virginia in 1622 (Bining 1973). In 1640 a successful ironworks was established in Saugus, Massachusetts (Gordon 1996). By the time of the American Revolution, ironworks including blast furnaces were very common throughout the Northeast and Mid-Atlantic, and these enterprises continued to be common until late in the nineteenth century.

The Eliza Furnace shown in Figure 13.14 was a charcoal blast furnace. Its construction and interior was similar to that shown in Figure 13.15. Thick outer walls of unmortared stone formed a hollow furnace stack 25 to 35 feet (7.6–10.7 m) high. The interior chamber, lined with sandstone or firebrick, was narrowest at the top, widening to about 7 feet (2.1 m) at the **bosh** and then narrowing again to a small bottom chamber called the **crucible**. Furnace stacks usually were built next to a hill, to permit access to the top of the furnace by means of a wooden charging bridge. Furnaces also were flanked with waterwheels that propelled leather bellows or, later,

FIGURE 13.14 The Eliza Furnace in Vintondale, Pennsylvania, was once at the center of an extensive iron-making operation; it is unusual because of the intact heat exchanger at its top.

blowing tubs. These bellows or blowing tubs provided the air blast needed to keep the fire burning at temperatures high enough for smelting (ca. 2600–3000°F). The air was conducted to the fire through a copper **tuyere**. Many furnaces used blasts of cold air, but hot-blast furnaces, like the Eliza Furnace, were introduced after the 1830s. In the latter type of furnace the air blast was forced through pipes that were heated over a fire or by the furnace gases themselves. The coiled pipes of the heat exchanger can still be seen at the top of the Eliza Furnace stack (see Figure 13.14). In front of the furnace was the **cast arch**, where the molten iron was tapped for use.

In operation, the furnace was filled with charcoal that was fired from the bottom and allowed to burn for several days before being charged or filled with alternate layers of charcoal, iron ore, and limestone. As the ore descended to the bosh, it became molten, and excess oxygen was removed as gas while other impurities interacted

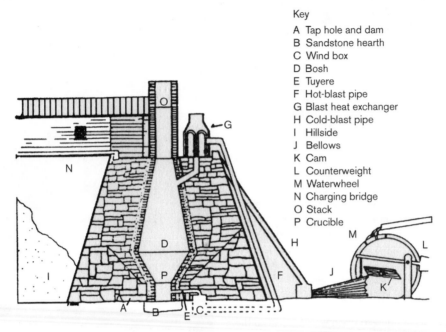

Key
A Tap hole and dam
B Sandstone hearth
C Wind box
D Bosh
E Tuyere
F Hot-blast pipe
G Blast heat exchanger
H Cold-blast pipe
I Hillside
J Bellows
K Cam
L Counterweight
M Waterwheel
N Charging bridge
O Stack
P Crucible

FIGURE 13.15 Section of a hot-blast charcoal-fired iron furnace like Eliza Furnace.

with the melting limestone. Fluid iron and **slag** collected on the furnace hearth at the bottom, but the slag was lighter and was drawn off at the **cinder notch**. The heavier iron was tapped through a hole in the dam stone normally plugged with clay. This molten iron ran into prepared molds in the sand floor of the casting shed, constructed of wood over the casting arch. The cooled bars of iron were called **pigs**. Pig iron had to be further refined at a refinery forge to burn away the carbon, which made pig iron brittle. After several reheatings and hammerings, bars of this refined or wrought iron were sent directly to blacksmiths for shaping or, eventually, to rolling and slitting mills for further cutting into nails and sheets of iron. **Blister steel**, an alloy of iron and carbon, could also be produced by keeping bars of wrought iron at red heat for up to two weeks in a pot packed with charcoal (U.S. National Park Service 1983).

Although not all these processes were necessarily accomplished at the iron furnace itself, iron furnaces were at the center of extensive iron plantations staffed by numerous people. Besides the ironmaster, who usually lived with his family in a spacious home near the furnace, there were many workers. Founders kept the furnace operating while a company clerk kept the books and managed the company store, and molders produced the pigs. Fillers charged the stack; colliers made the charcoal, and woodcutters cut the logs for charcoal. Miners mined the iron ore, usually from surface pits; teamsters transported materials, and farmers grew food to feed the workers.

If forges and rolling mills were included in the operation, even more types of workers were included in the community. A hierarchy of individuals existed, with the ironmaster and his family at the apex. The impact of this hierarchy can be glimpsed through excavations at ancillary and domestic structures. When we excavate at iron furnace complexes, we can learn about the social context of this early industry as well as the technology.

A variety of improvements were introduced into the process of iron making during the eighteenth and nineteenth centuries. One important innovation was the introduction of **coke**, a purified form of coal, as fuel. Although American furnaces did not adopt this innovation until well into the nineteenth century because of the abundant wood available, coke allowed for hotter and more rapid melting of the ore. Together with such other improvements as the replacement of bellows with blowing tubs and the conversion to hot-blast furnaces, noted earlier, these improvements led to a great increase in production at the middle of the nineteenth century that was matched only by an increase in demand as manufacturing and railroads grew. Ultimately, to meet high demand, the iron and steel industry became more centralized in urban centers such as Pittsburgh, and the small blast furnace became obsolete. Though pilfered for usable wood and metal, many furnace stacks still dot the rural landscape of the Northeast and Mid-Atlantic. These clues to the past truly remind us of other times and allow archaeologists to explore the technology and lives of earlier Americans.

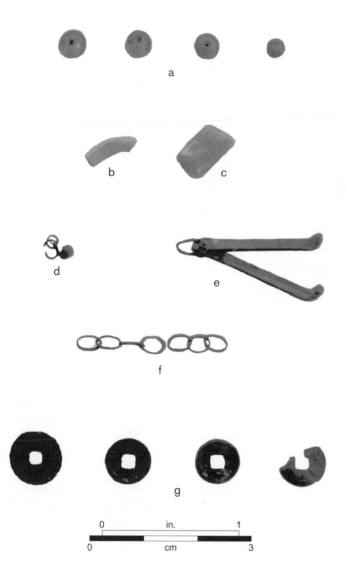

FIGURE 13.16 Artifacts from excavations in San Diego's Chinatown: (a) beads, (b) jade bracelet fragment, (c) glass bracelet fragment, (d) Chinese button, (e) cabinet key, (f) chain links, and (g) coins.

parkway development project in the late 1990s. The excavations helped demonstrate the connection of the Chinatown residents to their homeland, as indicated by the Chinese ceramics, opium tins, coins, buttons, and evidence that a great deal of fish had been imported from China. Although a wide variety of goods were recovered during the project, the items were generally inexpensive, consistent with the low wages of the laborers who were the primary residents of the Woolen Mills neighborhood (Allen and Hylkema 2000).

Although religious communes and societies had existed in North American from the Contact period (e.g., Warfel 2009), more utopian communities developed as a reaction to the commercialism of the late nineteenth and early twentieth centuries. These communities set themselves apart from the mainstream commercial society and tried to establish what they

saw as a better way of life. The ornate buildings of one such communal group, the Theosophical Society of San Diego's Point Loma, are now part of Point Loma Nazarene University, but the group's trash dump is located on City of San Diego park land. When a sewer line was planned to cross the dump, test excavations were conducted. Although local bottle hunters had been digging in the dump for decades, the archaeologists found a large number of bottle fragments and other material not taken by the relic hunters, and these artifacts provided considerable information about life in the Theosophists' community.

For example, the Theosophical Society had a boarding school, as reflected in the archaeological record by bone toothbrush handles and children's toys (doll parts, miniature dishes, marbles, and animal figurines) (Figure 13.17). Albumenized meat, a processed

FIGURE 13.17 Artifacts from the Theosophical Society dump: (a) bone toothbrush handle, (b–d) china doll parts, (e–g) toy dishes, (h, i) ceramic animals, and (j–l) marbles.

meat product, was a common offering at the Theosophist tables, as indicated by fragments of the brown jars the meat was packed in. The consumption of fresh meat does not appear to have been common, however. Beverage bottles, which include liquor bottles, made up only 6 percent of the bottled products at the Theosophical Society dump, while at the San Diego city dump from the same time period, 40 percent of the bottles had contained alcoholic beverages. Finally, numerous distinctive medicine vials indicate that the Theosophists practiced homeopathic medicine (Van Wormer and Gross 2006).

Of course you know that the American movie industry grew in California, but like most people you may not be aware that Hollywood has created an archaeological record. One archaeological project set out to examine part of that record. In 1923 Cecil B. DeMille filmed the silent epic *The Ten Commandments* in the Nipomo Dunes north of Santa Barbara. As part of this production, the filmmaker had an Egyptian city built. At the completion of the film the city was quietly dismantled and buried in a secret location in the dunes. In 1983 the site of the burial was located and an archaeological project was mounted to excavate the site. The project is ongoing, but many pieces of the set have been discovered, and these artifacts are helping to build understandings of how the early movies were filmed.

Finally, historical archaeologists have studied many of the institutions that developed in modern society including prisons, insane asylums, and poorhouses (Beisaw and Gibb 2009). Even colleges and universities have not escaped the inquiries of archaeologists. Laurie Wilkie (2010) reports on the excavations of the University of California's first fraternity—Zeta Psi. The deposits investigated dated to about 1900, and Wilkie describes the materials found, using it, along with historical documentation and oral history, to explore the early fraternity life, as well as broader themes such as masculinity and coming of age. Another university "excavation" took place at Washington State University, where a field class used the joists of the roof in a dorm that was to be demolished as collection units and collected material that had been discarded by the dorm's residents. Ferry Hall was originally built in 1892, but the building that was the focus of the class project was constructed on the site after a fire destroyed the first building in 1897. The Ferry Hall archaeological project demonstrated something of what student life was like at the beginning of the twentieth century in rural Washington (Riordan 1977).

CHAPTER SUMMARY

This chapter has just touched upon the wealth of information available on the archaeology of the Historic period. We have discussed broad themes in historical archaeology and provided some specific examples in order to give you a sense of the range and excitement of contemporary historical archaeology in North America. The most important points made in this chapter can be summarized as follows:

- North American historical archaeology is an exciting subfield that focuses on the sites and material

remains as well as the documentary record of the European expansion into the New World and the impacts of this expansion on indigenous populations. Although we have historical records of this period, archaeological investigation enriches our knowledge and understanding of these events by adding new details. Notably it tells us about the daily lives of ordinary people.

- Historical archaeologists have identified a number of themes in the study of North America's historical period, and many of these transcend the boundaries of our study area and are indeed worldwide in scope. We chose to focus on five themes: contact and colonization, expansion and settlement of the continent, war and conflict, the African Diaspora, and industrialization and modernization. These themes are of course intimately connected, so many of the archaeological projects relate to more than one of the themes.

SUGGESTIONS FOR FURTHER READING

An excellent introduction about what can be learned from historical archaeology is:

Deetz, James

    1996 In Small Things Forgotton: An Archaeology of Early American Life. Anchor Books, Doubleday, New York.

For thoughtful perspectives on a number of topics in historical archaeology:

Majewski, Teresita, and David Gaimster (editors)

    2009 International Handbook of Historical Archaeology. Springer, New York.

For discussions of issues of the African Diaspora and other topics:

Scott, Elizabeth M. (editor)

    1994 Those of Little Note: Gender, Race, and Class in Historical Archaeology. University of Arizona Press, Tucson.

For another classic discussion of the African Diaspora:

Orser, C. E., Jr.

    1998 The Archaeology of the African Diaspora. Annual Review of Anthropology 27:63–82.

For an account of the archaeology of a western mining town:

James, Ronald M.

    2012 The Virginia City: Secrets of a Western Past. University of Nebraska Press, Lincoln.

For a collection of papers on the Spanish settlement of the Southeast:

McEwan, Bonnie Gair

    1993 The Spanish Missions of La Florida. University Press of Florida, Gainsville.

For a discussion of the excavation of the first fraternity at the University of California:

Laurie A. Wilkie

    2010 The Lost Boys of Zeta Psi: A Historical Archaeology of Masculinity at a University Fraternity. University of California Press, Berkeley.

OTHER RESOURCES

The Student CD (Sections H and I) gives web links, additional discussion questions, and other study aids. The Student CD also contains a variety of additional resources. Particularly relevant resources include the bonus case study, "Ethnicity and Class in Colonial Foodways" (Section D.8).

CASE STUDY

One of the most interesting aspects of contemporary historical archaeology is that it has been at the forefront of efforts to involve the public in archaeology. If archaeologists are serious about making our work and our findings accessible to others, we must open the archaeology we are doing to the public in general and specifically to the descendants of the people we study. This means more than educating the public about what we have found and sharing our interpretations; it also means collaborating with people who are not archaeologists. Other case studies in this text have presented examples of collaboration with Native Americans (see the case studies in Chapters 5 and 7), here we look at collaboration with African American communities. In the studies described in this case study, the communities are helping set the archaeological agenda rather than participating in the excavation and research itself. You will learn what community archaeology is and how it has developed. However, as you read you should also think about how historical archaeology can be useful to descendant groups, and consider how archaeologists can find ways to encourage descendants to use archaeology for their own purposes.

COMMUNITY ARCHAEOLOGY

Understanding the Contexts of Archaeological Practice

Carol McDavid and Christopher N. Matthews

What is community archaeology? The answer to that question is as varied as the types of archaeology practiced today. A few years ago, Stephanie Moser and her colleagues (Moser et al. 2002) attempted to outline an explicit methodology for community archaeology practice. They proposed that community archaeology projects should involve local communities in decisions about research questions, field practices, project logistics, data collection and analysis, data presentation and storage, and public presentation and interpretation. One of their keys points was to note that any given project did not need to do *all* of these things—only that the community should have at least *partial* control of *some* of them.

This was a useful checklist for any potential community archaeology project, and a great place to start (the volume itself offers several good models; Marshall 2002). We would suggest that it may not go far enough—that it is, for the most part, "archaeology-centric" and more about archaeology's needs than it is about the needs of any given community. Therefore, we would include, under the heading "community archaeology," projects that are aimed at developing a critical understanding of how any *particular* archaeology can serve the needs of a *particular* community and its agendas. How do the interests of archaeology and "community" intersect—at one place, one time, for *community*-defined social and political purposes?

To explore this, we offer two detailed examples of this approach to community archaeology. We then situate our examples in the larger context of anthropological archaeology and public archaeology in this country, bringing in some additional examples. Our assumption throughout is that there is no one-size-fits-all approach with respect to community archaeology—as noted earlier, there are as many ways to practice it as there are archaeological projects, because doing it well means being able to incorporate local histories, contexts, agendas, and needs into each and every project.

Our examples are from our practice in American historical archaeology, specifically, in the field of study known as African Diaspora archaeology. Briefly, historical archaeology is aimed at understanding the modern world—usually conceived of in this country as "post-Columbus," or "post-contact," although sometimes archaeologists in other parts of the world include other text-aided archaeologies (such as medieval archaeology) in their definition of historical archaeology. For the most part, however, historical archaeologists are concerned with what happened across the world after the start of European expansion. The issues studied include colonialism (both causes and effects, especially with respect to indigenous peoples), the spread of capitalism, and global migrations and movements (whether through choice or, as often, enslavement). Our work in African Diaspora archaeology focuses on this last category, specifically on the study of African American life during and after slavery.

COMMUNITY ARCHAEOLOGY IN TEXAS, BY CAROL MCDAVID

For the past decade, I have been participating in community-wide conversations about race, class, gentrification, and historic preservation as they have emerged alongside my ongoing "dirt" archaeology research in Freedmen's Town, Houston. Following its founding by emancipated African Americans after the Civil War, Freedmen's Town became the "Mother Ward" for Houston's growing black professional class. Over time, it formed a hub where the city's black doctors, lawyers, teachers, schools, and hospitals prospered, at least until the 1930s. By the late twentieth century, because of the Jim Crow segregation, demographic shifts, a lack of zoning, and weak historic preservation ordinances, Freedmen's Town became one of the poorest neighborhoods in the city.

In the late 1990s, the Rutherford B. H. Yates Museum, a small historic house museum, started trying to save and restore what remained of the historic landscape. One part of its effort was to hire my team (the Community Archaeology Research Institute) to do both research and salvage-type archaeology on its properties. Even though a sea of gentrification-driven townhomes and lofts now dominates the neighborhood, there are pockets where historical structures remain, and we have been able to do archaeology on those properties with the help of several university field schools and an ongoing volunteer effort.

To do this work properly, we sought to understand the social and cultural context where we were working and to discover if and how archaeology could provide positive benefits to the community. To reach this sort of understanding, I have analyzed a considerable amount of data from a variety of sources, including mass media (headlines, news stories, blogs, etc.), interviews, emails, and of course my own experiences in the community. I learned how the indigenous community defines itself, and what it thinks is important (I use the term "indigenous" because this is how people tend to see themselves—as descendants of the original African American settlers). Here are some key statements from individual interviews with several community members (published in more detail in McDavid, Bruner, and Marcom 2008 and McDavid 2011).

[In the past the community was] prominent, progressive... we were self-sustaining.... We could get anything we needed... we didn't have to rely on anyone outside, we had our own doctors, lawyers, schools, and stores.... These old houses are just full of stories.... I just don't think they should go tearing them all down like that.

The narrative here is self-sufficiency and self-empowerment—expressions of freedom and independence in Freedmen's Town that is the cultural and spiritual heritage of the original community. This is, admittedly, the narrative with which I am in most sympathy.

I also examined the narratives created by newer residents, most of whom are not African American. I found that many of them enact traditional stereotypes about race, poverty, and class as they relate to both the indigenous residents and outsiders. Often they deploy these stereotypes to convince local government officials to demolish the remaining historic landscape at an even faster rate than would take place otherwise. What I have heard most frequently is that poverty equals drugs and crime, and that extreme poverty plus black people equals more drugs and crime. For example, the following is an email from one of the more vocal newer residents to a large mailing list (one of my community collaborators sent me a copy). She later formed her own civic group aimed at meeting these goals.

We need intelligent people from OUR Neighborhood [her emphasis] to... [get control of] several pieces of raw land that [were] supposed to have new single-family housing.... Right now some of this raw land is where vagrants and drug dealers hang out.... The more new housing we can get in this area, the better.

FIGURE 13.18 Home of Rutherford B. H. Yates, before and after restoration (over 80 percent of the original structure was saved, and the house is now on the National Register of Historic Places).

The "raw land" was where developers had demolished previously occupied historic houses (in the hope of building new housing) and abandoned their projects, leaving empty spaces in the neighborhood. New residents often complain to the city that the remaining historic houses are "dangerous," leading to more loss as the city refuses to give the necessary permits and recommends demolition (see Figure 13.18 for before and after images of a house that our client restored, despite the city's efforts to thwart it).

Even so, there have been numerous attempts (by indigenous residents, members of the preservation community, and our team) to work with, or at least to better understand, the perspectives of the newer residents. Unfortunately, most of these attempts have been rebuffed, and much of the public discourse about Freedmen's Town has been even more overtly negative than the attitudes expressed earlier.

To counter these ongoing narratives, we continue to document the community's own stories and uses of their neighborhood, attempting to highlight what most visitors miss. For example, most Sunday mornings the streets are clogged by churchgoers visiting their home sanctuaries. Similar public expressions of the community are found on the annual Juneteenth and Martin Luther King Day parades, or during the song worships and other ceremonies held in the historic brick intersections (Figure 13.19) (McDavid, Bruner, and Marcom 2008). These "positive" events are not always met with joy, however: on at least two occasions, newer residents called the police to complain about the "public disturbance" of gospel singing on the steps of area churches.

Based on these observations and understandings, it would be too easy to assume everyone lives behind gates and walls, and that an active, self-reliant community no longer exists. Discovering that this is not true, I now routinely ask members of the community how our research can help them. The first thing we typically hear is that people want our archaeology to help dismantle negative stereotypes about their neighborhood, and enlighten white audiences about African American history. They want our work, as supportive outsiders, to allow *other* outsiders to see the community as its indigenous residents see it—as a place where ongoing community solidarity and support are still celebrated, and where place and landscape continue to matter. These individuals understand that our work is not just about digging—they know that the fact that we are doing it, and writing about it in forums like this one, can serve their interests. Second, people tell us that they appreciate the legitimization that our work confers on their efforts to convince *others* that their community is worth saving. They use our work strategically, when *they* see the need. Third, they are enthusiastic (if a bit surprised) about our ongoing efforts to talk to white people about racism and white privilege, which we often do when we give public talks about the archaeology project (McDavid 2007).

Therefore, members of the community are pleased that our archaeological findings have indeed helped to change visitors' initial understandings about how the African American founders of Freedmen's Town lived. Earlier we noted that the neighborhood became very poor during the Jim Crow period—to

FIGURE 13.19 Celebration held by the Black United Front at the corner of Wilson and Andrews streets, Freedmen's Town, Houston (June 19, 2007).

the point that most outsiders, before visiting it, assume that it has always been impoverished and "run down." This is not the case: by the close of the nineteenth century, Freedmen's Town was the hub of an affluent black middle class. Most site visitors are surprised to learn that the founders (despite the fact that most were born in slavery) built grand Victorian mansions, as well as smaller but substantial bungalows and even smaller "shotgun" houses (see Vlach 1976 for a description of this form of American vernacular architecture).

Our excavations take place in the yards of the few remaining larger houses, where we have found many examples of Victorian-era material culture sensibility. These include fine decorated china, cut glass, jewelry, fragments of painted European wallpaper, porcelain doll parts and toy tea sets, the earliest types of electrical connections, and the like. Some of the remains materialize America's harsh color line—such as several "hot combs," a form of which is still used by African American women as a hairstyling tool. We have also found several gold-plated "pen nibs," which to us tell a compelling story about literacy and accomplishment. In addition to artifacts, we have also learned a great deal from documents (wills, diplomas, graduating class photographs, advertisements, and in one case, a list of gifts from a bridal shower!). Taken together, these archaeological, architectural, and documentary findings tell a story of achievement and substance that is at odds with typical visitor assumptions about Freedmen's Town (see Mullins 1999, 2006, for more on African American consumer culture of the same period).

Despite the community's positive response to the work itself, the Freedmen's Town work is not a community project in which the local community participates much in the actual archaeology. While they are happy when we try to involve community people (especially kids), they are just as happy for us to bring students and volunteers in from the outside, most of whom are white. They know that this will create support for their own agendas, as well as more respect for their neighborhood. Frankly, in this community, people are far too busy with their own challenges to help us do what they see as *our* jobs. But they want us to do those jobs. They want us to share what we learn, to understand and respect existing community narratives, and to support their policy and programming goals.

Archaeology is not a passive player in the work discussed here, and it would not be even if we were not sympathetic to the interests of the indigenous residents. With their help, we are learning to walk a fine line—to offer our skills, resources, and information to community people to use for their own agendas, while at the same time pursuing our own research questions.

We are learning that, given transparency and openness, these are not mutually exclusive activities.

ARCHAEOLOGY IN TREMÉ, BY CHRISTOPHER N. MATTHEWS

Community archaeology is also making increasing use of ethnographic methods in order to allow community interests to inform archaeological projects in new ways. In this sort of endeavor, archaeologists work to not only understand and address community concerns such as gentrification and racial injustice, but also to understand how archaeology itself is perceived and potentially put to use by community members on their own (Matthews 2008).

As director of the Greater New Orleans Archaeology Program (GNOAP), housed at the University of New Orleans, I undertook this sort of project in 1999. The GNOAP was based on Louisiana's regional archaeology program, which combines archaeological research in one region of the state with community outreach and education to inform and involve the public. The GNOAP was founded in 1996 to do this work in New Orleans. While the project had many accomplishments at the level of research and education, the potential opportunities of the program for making archaeology useful and important to city residents was underdeveloped when I became director in 1998. In particular, archaeology in New Orleans had not yet considered the city through the lens of one of America's most important black-majority communities, a community with some of the most evident survival of traditional African and African Diaspora cultural expressions in the material culture that remained. So, I saw an opportunity to develop a project that would draw first from an ethnographic understanding of modern and historic African American New Orleans in order to allow the archaeology itself to derive from a developed understanding of the modern community and thus explore its roots, its development, and its survival.

After researching how such a project might be accomplished (work that included research in archives, conversations with historians, preservationists, and archaeologists, and conversations with experts in African American culture in New Orleans), I was fortunate to discover the St. Augustine site, located in the Tremé section of the city. Archaeologically, the site was the former site of the Tremé Plantation house, a colonial era brickworks whose last owner gave the neighborhood its name. During the nineteenth century the plantation house was converted into a Carmelite convent whose primary purpose was to run a school for free girls of color. During the Carmelite era the still standing and functioning St. Augustine Church was erected; however, a 1920s hurricane damaged the old plantation house, which was then torn down. The lot where the house stood then became a parking area and playground, and the house that stood there was largely forgotten.

Based on the rich history of the St. Augustine site, I imagined a project that could bring to light not only new aspects of the city's past, but, with connections to both the colonial era's enslaved community and the subsequent achievements of its free people of color in the 1800s, produce a series of archaeological stories that would tie the project into the city's current African American cultural life. The project was christened "Archaeology in Tremé," and I set to work meeting with residents who could help me to better understand the meaning of an archaeological project in their neighborhood.

It was in this effort that I discovered much of what has since made the Archaeology in Tremé project a success, despite the fact that artifacts recovered from the two seasons of excavation were lost in the cleanup of the city after Hurricane Katrina. The project was successful because it allowed some of the most important aspects of the city's African American culture to be brought into view and explored. Thanks to community research and especially *community feedback*, the project was built on a foundation closely tied to how African American New Orleans connects with archaeological practice.

There are two main stories to relate. First, the most important piece of information I learned about Tremé, from its residents and advocates, was that it was the only one of the city's "historic" neighborhoods to have not *already* been designated as a **historic district**. While such designations require work from residents to achieve, the only ones that had been made in New Orleans closely followed the gentrification process, and happened only *after* the neighborhoods shifted from being majority black to majority white. This process had not occurred in Tremé.

Thus, those I spoke with about the issue were right to point out that Tremé, a majority black neighborhood, had been largely neglected by the local New Orleans preservation community. It was pointed out many times that this was especially neglectful since Tremé had *always* been black, was one of the oldest black neighborhoods in the United States, and perhaps one of its most important, having been home to important families and individuals such as Sidney Bechet and Homer Plessy.

Of course, I saw this as a great chance to toot my own horn. Here I was coming into the neighborhood to run a project explicitly about its black history and to share these results with community and the city at large. However, I soon learned that the issues behind the charges of neglect ran deeper than I originally thought. This became apparent when I learned that one of my most insightful and interesting collaborators from the community had torn down one of the project posters (Figure 13.20) and marched straight to the project's main funder, the Louisiana Endowment for the Humanities, to complain.

FIGURE 13.20 Archaeology in Tremé poster. (Produced by Lauren L. Fausterman, Marketing and Communications Department, University of New Orleans.)

This community leader and activist, who followed a strong Afrocentric way of life, had not only told me a lot about the black history of Tremé during our collaboration, but had said many times, in so many words, that the Archaeology in Tremé project would be a great benefit to the community. To learn that he was the one who complained really surprised me until I discovered his reason, at which point I also discovered what was absolutely necessary if the project was going to proceed.

His complaint was with the wording of the project's description, which stated that the project would be exploring the city's "colonial and Creole past." This was based on the St. Augustine site's connection to the city's Colonial period through the Tremé plantations, and to the city's francophone Creole population, who were in part served by the Carmelite convent and school and the St. Augustine Church. The activist demanded the posters be reprinted to read the city's "colonial Creole, and African past."

As he explained to me later, there were two problems at the root of my thinking, and of the potential of archaeology to serve the Tremé community. First, by not including "African," I had neglected to include the population he saw living in Tremé today, which had been neglected (if not displaced) throughout the city's history. Second, while many see the city's historic population of free people of color as "African American," especially those who were known then and now as Creole, their mixed-race heritage still resonates deeply and divisively within the city itself.

At issue for the activist was the need to see his community, Africans, as distinct and equally the focus of the archaeological project. While I had long seen the project this way, having failed to communicate this in public led me to at least appear neglectful in ways that Tremé residents were all too familiar with. To address this shortcoming, I developed a new approach to the project that would be not only inclusive but also responsive to the way in which I viewed the community through this process.

I turned the direction of the project, and began to explain and illustrate that that the city's "races" (white, Creole, and black) each drew from and sought a distinct heritage. Most compelling was the sense in the African American community that their heritage was simultaneously the most visible and the most vulnerable. Their heritage was the living local community and its history, as shown in the recent use of the archaeological site as a playground and festival space. This discovery was a community-driven reminder that archaeology happens *now* and begins with the surface of the ground, and is not just those discoveries found below.

The St. Augustine site ultimately proved to be a rich source of interesting material culture from the eighteenth and nineteenth centuries. From the earlier deposits, those associated with plantation house, we recovered an interesting combination of European- and Native American–made ceramics. Looking at the vessel form, we found that the Native American pots were redundant forms, and that they likely did not provide a distinct function from European-made pots that households also had. This led to the idea that the Native American pots may have been trade goods and thus a symbol of the intersecting worlds of early Louisiana's native, settler, and slave communities, whose intercultural experiences gave birth to the roots of modern New Orleans' unique diversity. Later deposits from the nineteenth century included clear signs of the emerging Creole community. Slate pencils document the school for free girls of color, two religious medallions represent the Catholic spirituality of the Carmelites, and a tobacco pipe with a Mason's compass decoration show the presence of one of the most important social organizations that free people of color used to solidify and advance their community before emancipation.

FITTING THIS INTO THE LARGER PICTURE

We think these examples introduce some ways that archaeologists practice community archaeology in the United States today; we will describe a few more examples later. Before this, we need to situate community archaeology more firmly within its disciplinary frameworks. We argue that public archaeology is a subfield of archaeology (and in Americanist practice, anthropology) and, further, we see community archaeology as but one form of public archaeology.

Within Americanist archaeology, until the early 1990s, the term "public archaeology" was used to distinguish the commercial field of CRM from its academic counterpart. This use of the term originally sprang from the idea that CRM archaeological projects are funded by the public purse and/or mandated by public legislation. Therefore, public archaeology during this period included archaeology practiced on public lands (such as national parks) as well as archaeology conducted on native (tribal) lands. It is important to note that during the beginning days of CRM, despite widespread use of the term "public archaeology," *there was little public input into the archaeological work itself.* Part of the reason was that archaeological practice was dominated by those who advocated scientific methods as the best way to do archaeology. A supposedly unbiased objectivity was the aim. From this standpoint, proper archaeology did not allow for indigenous, descendant, or local community input into excavating or interpreting archaeological sites. During this period most work with the public was overtly *educational*: the primary aim was to convince the nonarchaeological public that saving archeological sites was important. Even though we support this as a goal, this approach to archaeology did not involve the public in making decisions about archaeological sites and archaeological research. Nor did it include nonscientific data sources, such as oral history and ethnographic data, in the ways that archaeological sites were interpreted.

Changes began to emerge in the late 1980s, and the most momentous early benchmark for discipline-wide change in the United States occurred with the 1990 passage of NAGPRA (the Native American Graves Protection and Repatriation Act). This law gave Native Americans some control over the remains of their ancestors— those located on tribal lands as well as in non-Indian institutions like museums and universities. The law was limited in many ways, but the key point here is that during this period the meaning of the word "public" in "public archaeology" began to shift. It began to include diverse *living publics*. Archaeologists working with indigenous remains were, from that point, forced to take into account decendants' opinions—and their methods and interpretations began, slowly, to reflect this.

COMMUNITY CHALLENGES TO ARCHAEOLOGY

Even so, one major shortcoming of NAGPRA was the definition of "descendants" as documented, lineal descendants. This limitation continues to create challenges for Indian groups that are unrecognized as such by the federal government. In addition, NAGPRA does not apply to other types of descendant groups, such as the African American communities we discussed earlier.

The next major milestone in U.S. public archaeology emerged within historical archaeology. This occurred in 1991 when, during a CRM archaeology project being conducted prior to the construction of a new federal office building in New York City, workers discovered the remains of more than 400 free and enslaved Africans and African Americans (see Box 1.2, "Politics and Scholarship in the Investigation of New York City's African Burial Ground"). The public uproar over these remains, and the public debate about how to excavate and interpret them, established new understandings of the words "descendant," "community," and "client" within archaeology. Despite the lack of legislative mandate, the *cultural* descendants of those buried at what came to be called the New York African Burial Ground were successful in gaining control over how their ancestors' remains were excavated and interpreted (LaRoche and Blakey 1997). African American *communities* in New York City thus initiated key changes in historical archaeology, just as Indian groups had done in prehistoric archaeology.

There is still no NAGPRA for non-Indian lands, but the ethos that drove NAGPRA is now commonplace in many archaeology projects across the United States. There is, however, a major exception to this rather broad statement: most archaeology (about 80 percent) still occurs in a CRM context, which is driven by commercial agendas and motivations. It remains to be seen how, or if, meaningful public input—and by that we mean the grassroots input of ethical clients rather than the official input of commercial clients—into CRM archaeology can ever happen (King 2009). (For more on the important distinction between ethical clients and business clients, see Perry, Howson, and Bianco 2006.)

As all this was happening in the United States, similar shifts were occurring elsewhere, and a variety of postcolonial and global justice movements have played important roles in how archaeology and public archaeology are framed today. A major milestone in the global arena was the 1986 founding of the World Archaeological Congress, in part as a response to apartheid. Over the last two decades, there have been key developments within governmental, nongovernmental, and scholarly arenas, all of which have been part of an ongoing global process of reimagining how archaeological work can intersect with public interests and needs. As this has occurred, the term "public archaeology" has expanded in meaning, and it is fair to say that now most archaeologists, worldwide, think of public archaeology as *any* endeavor in which archaeologists interact with the public, and any research (practical or theoretical) that examines or analyzes the public dimensions of doing archaeology.

One interesting feature of the most recent writing is that it tends to cross the usual disciplinary lines—arguably more so than earlier public archaeologies, which tended to be situated within the typical geographic and temporal discourses (such as prehistoric archaeology, classical archaeology, and historical archaeology). In the past, for example, a typical historical archaeologist/public archaeologist might not be conversant with the public archaeology work done by an Egyptologist, or a prehistoric archaeologist, or an Africanist, because they read different journals, went to different conferences, and so on. This is not as true today, and we see this as a positive trend—not least because it has allowed particular methods and approaches common to "public" work in general to emerge.

CONTEMPORARY COMMUNITY CONTEXT RESEARCH

As noted earlier, the most basic aspect of all community-oriented research is that there is no one-size-fits-all approach. Strategies and methods that work in one geographical, political, economic, social, or cultural context may not—probably will not—work for another. Therefore, we are pleased to see community archaeology projects that include, as a major component, in-depth research about and with the community—what one might call "contemporary context" or "ethnographic" research. It is important to realize, however, that these projects are situated within *archaeology*, and are thus part of archaeology, even if they are similar in many respects (method, for example) to more traditional "ethnographic" research (see Castaneda and Matthews 2008; Mortensen and Hollowell 2009).

For example, Mark Leone and Parker Potter's classic archaeological ethnography of history and historic preservation in Annapolis, Maryland, explored, interpreted, and challenged the meaning of the past in the community where they worked (Potter 1994). Their research showed how history in Annapolis was bifurcated along consistent lines that separated the historic district from the U.S. Naval Academy, the colonial and modern eras, and the city's white and black communities. In a very different example, Julie Hollowell examined fishing villages in St. Lawrence Island, Alaska, which rely on digging up their ancestors' remains as a form of subsistence (Hollowell 2006). The ethical dilemmas raised for the archaeologists were intense, and in these types of cases it is arguably much more difficult to "support community agendas." Similar tensions were explored by Diura Van Velzen, who studied the "world of Tuscan tomb robbers" in order to understand their attitudes about subsistence digging and ownership (Van Velzen 1996).

Concern with the meaning of archaeology among living communities, and an increasingly sophisticated concern with ethical practice, has led many archaeologists working in indigenous contexts to position their work in close collaboration with tribal authorities and descendant communities (Colwell-Chanthaphonh and Ferguson 2006, 2007; Silliman 2008). Within this field, it is notable that a growing number of indigenous archaeologists are making regular contributions (Atalay 2006; Wilcox 2009). A very important recent study comes from Kerry Thompson (Thompson 2009, 2010), who, as a member of the Navajo nation, questions whether community archaeology is actually a viable goal for the Navajo. Exploring both cultural traditions that enforce an avoidance of archaeological sites as well as the practical impacts of the regulations that come with archaeology and preservation, many Navajo are skeptical of archaeology. An essential issue Thompson points to is that because legislation demands that Navajo homeowners pay for archaeological surveys prior to making any improvements on their homes, many are often forced to go without basic needs like electricity and clean water because the *total* cost becomes prohibitive. As she puts it, the concerns and ideas that drive community and indigenous archaeology can at times seem far removed from the everyday struggles of indigenous communities.

"Follow the Pots" is another innovative new study. Led by Morag Kersel and Meredith Chesson, the project is looking at various stakeholder communities in the Middle East who are involved in the antiquities trade in early Bronze Age material culture. This project broadens the scope of community archaeology from its traditional focus on forms of engagement. Kersel and Chesson are working instead to document and understand the communities that already exist in and around archaeology (archaeologists, government employees, antiquities dealers, collectors, looters, etc.), how relationships between communities are structured, and in turn how they structure both archaeological practice and the trade in antiquities. The purpose of the project is to offer "all stakeholders a voice in this dialogue [and] to cultivate greater possibilities for meaningful strategies to protect heritage resources while simultaneously developing locally nuanced and practical programs for disentangling the links between poverty and looting, and we hope fulfilling the promise of an engaged archaeology" (Kersel 2011).

Although these examples are notable because they included community research from the start of each project, this is not always possible—not least because it is sometimes difficult to convince funders that this sort of work is "real archaeology." For example, at the Bernardo Plantation in Texas (where McDavid is a co-principal investigator), oral history was funded as part of the larger research plan, but the ethnographic research was subsumed under other, more "traditional" budget categories in order to obtain funding. Something similar happened at an earlier project in Brazoria, Texas, where Kenneth L. Brown began "dirt" excavations in 1988, but research and engaging local descendant communities did not begin until 1992, as part of a master's degree project (McDavid 1997). Therefore, although it is far better when the community work occurs first (or at least alongside) excavation, it can—and often does—begin after the archaeology itself is under way.

WHAT IS A COMMUNITY *FOR* ARCHAEOLOGY?

Regardless of the timetable, or which specific strategies and methods are used, not all communities fall into easy categories, and alternatives are beginning to emerge in community archaeology research and practice. The idea of "stakeholders" is now commonplace, with stakeholders being loosely defined as any entity (person or group) that *sees itself* as having a stake in any particular site or project. In this view, stakeholder communities can include commercial developers, or "looters," or antiquity dealers—as well as descendants and local residents (often, these are the same people). In all of these self-defined and other-defined communities, context-specific tropes about power, property ownership, culture, and politics are at play. Therefore, the best community archaeology research and practice does not take any definition of community (or stakeholders, or descendants) for granted. A critical, reflexive view is essential.

Before we close, we should highlight an area where a differently defined community archaeology has emerged—this is in the growth of avocational archaeology, or archaeology practiced by nonprofessional archaeologists, often by communities themselves. Although avocational archaeologists are very active across the United States (Texas, for example, has a very active "archaeological stewards" program (the Texas Archaeological Stewardship Network), and most workers in many worthy projects are largely amateur), defining this work *as* "community archaeology" tends to be most prevalent in Great Britain. There is an active online element (http://www.britarch.ac.uk/community) as well as a long-standing and popular journal (*Current Archaeology*). Although these projects are often (though not always) field-directed by a professional archaeologists, the overall direction and workforce is often community- and/or amateur-driven.

To close, the practice of community archaeology has come of age, in the last two decades, as one important form of public archaeology. In the process, the community and public understandings that have emerged have in turn begun to contribute significant new interpretive avenues for archaeology generally, in both theory and practice. At its most basic, community archaeology is the practice of working in and with communities during the archaeological process. Although, in its original forms, this was an educational endeavor, as the subfield has developed, communities for archaeology have become far more than passive recipients of archaeological knowledge. Community archaeology is now at the vanguard of creating a multivocal, inclusive knowledge-building process, in which archaeology as it is traditionally practiced is just one of many routes to knowing the past. In fact, traditional archaeology has been displaced in some instances by alternative archaeological engagements that build on other, less considered aspects of the archaeological process, such as the authority of academic research and institutions, the politics of geography and materiality, and conflicts within cultural discourses over heritage, property, identity, and the state.

DISCUSSION QUESTIONS

1. What is community archaeology, and what are its goals? Do you think this type of archaeology is important? Why or why not?

2. How does McDavid's project in Freedmen's Town in Houston illustrate community archaeology? What challenges did she face, and what did she learn from this project?

3. How and why did Matthews's community archaeology project at the St. Augustine site in the New Orleans neighborhood of Tremé have to change in light of the community's perspective?

4. How have archaeological approaches to "public archaeology" changed? Do you agree that investigating the contemporary context for an archaeological project has positive outcomes? Why or why not?

PART THREE

The Future of North American Archaeology

CHAPTER 14

North American Archaeology for the Twenty-first Century

October is Pennsylvania Archaeology Month. Each year at this time, archaeologists hold events that help increase awareness of Pennsylvania's historic and prehistoric archaeological heritage. These events have included special museum exhibits, lectures, tours of sites and museums, displays at local malls and libraries, hands-on activities for families, and an essay contest for middle-school children. A poster announcing the month and showcasing aspects of Pennsylvania archaeology is produced each year, and distributed to schools, public venues, and archaeologists, along with details about upcoming events. Nowadays a downloadable version of the poster is also available online along with the Archaeology Month calendar and links to information on Pennsylvania's cultural resources.

One of the messages transmitted through these events is simply that there are lots of archaeological sites in Pennsylvania, a fact that still surprises too many Pennsylvanians. A second message is that the archaeological traces of Pennsylvania's past need to be conserved because they are nonrenewable. Ignorance of the existence and importance of such resources is one of the obstacles to protecting sites in Pennsylvania, as is knowledge of the ways in which sites can be destroyed. Thus, in the essay contest, children have been asked to write essays on why sites should be protected, and a frequent slogan on the posters is "Save the Past for the Future."

Both professional and avocational archaeologists volunteer their time and expertise to make these events happen. The poster printing also is funded by CRM firms, universities, and sometimes grant funds from the Pennsylvania Historical and Museum Commission. The Society for Pennsylvania Archaeology, which includes both amateur and professional archaeologists, and the Pennsylvania Archaeological Council, an organization of professional archaeologists employed in universities, CRM firms, and state agencies, take the lead on Pennsylvania Archaeology Month. Why bother? What makes this annual exercise worthwhile? The answer is simple: the future of archaeology in Pennsylvania depends on citizen support for archaeology. It is not enough for professionals in the field to know why sites should be saved, or even for students who take a course in North American archaeology to adopt the archaeological ethic of site preservation. The public at large must realize that sites of importance exist in Pennsylvania, and people must view these sites as resources worth saving.

There was a time when archaeologists were less concerned with public perceptions and less mindful of any responsibility to report their findings in a publicly accessible manner. However, one result of the growth of CRM archaeology has been to heighten the explicit awareness that what we do must be justifiable to more than a small community of scholars. Part of this involves making archaeology intelligible to the public at large. Thus, Pennsylvania's archaeology month is just one of many held in the United States and Canada that seek to educate the public about North American archaeology. It is now routine for archaeologists to give school programs, tours of their sites and public lectures (Figure 14.1), as well as for CRM mitigation projects to be required to have a portion of their budget devotion to public outreach. Ideally public education promotes a preservation ethic that ultimately will both help lower the incidence of looting and ensure that the public supports enlightened management of cultural resources. A few minutes of browsing on the Internet should turn up a wealth of information about archaeology months, weeks, or days and about public lectures, archaeology exhibits, and digs you may visit in your state or province. You may find the website for local archaeological associations as well. We have included resources of this type in Section H of the Student CD.

As we conclude our consideration of North American archaeology, it is important to consider aspects of contemporary practice such as the new emphasis on public education. This chapter takes stock of what is known about the North American past and highlights changing aspects of the field of North American archaeology.

A PERSPECTIVE ON NORTH AMERICA'S PAST

In Chapter 1 we indicated that it would not be possible to provide a complete discussion of the North American past. Even though we have covered a great deal of material in this text, there is much more that you can find out by pursuing other sources. We encourage you to investigate aspects of North American archaeology that have interested you as you've read this book. Archaeologists in many places throughout the continent can help you discover our past more deeply. Nevertheless, we hope that this book has provided a basic understanding of what is known and an idea of what archaeologists may yet find out, for we believe Confucius was right when he said, "Study the past if you would divine the future." Now that you can recognize some sites and cultures from pre-Columbian and Historic period North America, you should have a new perspective on the North American past that will remain useful in present and future circumstances.

Beyond the obvious point that there is much to know about North America's past, we hope this new perspective includes the rejection of common stereotypes about Native North Americans and their history. Most important among these inaccurate stereotypes is

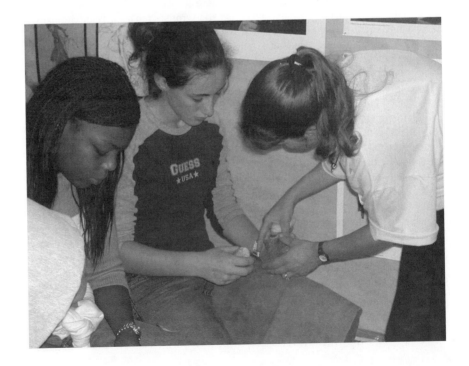

FIGURE 14.1 Archaeologist showing students how to chip stone to make a stone tool during an educational program.

the conception that North American Natives were all alike. Clearly this is grossly untrue. There was both great diversity in native cultures and great change among them over time. The cultural distance between Archaic hunters on the Great Plains and Mississippians living at Cahokia at AD 1100 was nearly as profound as that between English colonists in New England and the Algonquians they encountered. Hundreds of different ethnicities once existed, and these peoples did not have uniform customs or beliefs. Similarly, change among societies since European colonization has not been uniform. That we only partially know the story of North America's past should not be an excuse for thinking all Native people were or are alike.

A second stereotype, that Native Americans were primitive or simple, also should seem ridiculous. Exactly what is meant by the term isn't always clear, but generally "primitive" seems to refer to people living in small-scale, egalitarian, and foraging societies. It is not at all clear that such attributes make people backward or that such societies are not socioculturally sophisticated, and we hope learning about North America's past leads you to question such ideas. However, the archaeological record also makes it clear that among the native societies of pre-Columbian North America there were a number of chiefdoms characterized by agricultural production or the intensive use of marine resources, dense populations, long-distance trade and exchange, sophisticated art or craft items, social ranking, and complex ideologies. Moreover, traditional models of what to expect in complex societies don't

necessarily account for the varieties of sociocultural complexity found in North America. While these North American societies might not be the same as better known civilizations elsewhere, calling them primitive is inappropriate for many reasons. Popular ideas about how to categorize human cultures have encouraged many inaccurate stereotypes, and Native American societies provide examples that can help revise classifications based more on ignorance and prejudice than on facts.

Finally, we hope this book has dispelled the common misperception that there is nothing of archaeological importance to preserve in North America. Archaeological knowledge can be obtained in so many ways that even the smallest and most unexciting sites may contribute important information. Besides, some exciting sites are evident in ruins, and others are not highly visible on the surface. You've seen this throughout the text in case studies and other references to sites and artifacts. It is true that the archaeological record of North America's past will always be incomplete because not everything preserves, but it is also true that the thoughtless destruction and mistreatment of important cultural resources have made the record more incomplete than it would have been as a result of natural processes. Unfortunately, North American archaeological sites are routinely threatened, as discussed in Box 14.1. Not only do unscrupulous people loot and destroy sites, but new roads, shopping centers, and housing projects bulldoze them away (Figure 14.2). Legislative protections have been greatly increased in

FIGURE 14.2 Archaeological site being graded during construction near Oceanside, California. The stone mortar fragment and pestle in the foreground were noted by an archaeological monitor and collected.

How Can We Stop the Looting of Archaeological Sites?

A central value among archaeologists is that since archaeological sites, artifacts, and features are irreplaceable resources for understanding past cultures, their preservation is highly desirable. Promoting the stewardship of such resources is an ethical obligation for archaeologists. Stewardship involves managing sites responsibly and taking care of collections as well as deterring looting. Although the problem of looting has been a concern for more than a hundred years, the destruction of sites through looting may have become worse in recent years (Hollowell-Zimmer 2003). Looting is an international problem closely related to art theft and trafficking in stolen art. However, the GE Mound case described in Chapter 11 reminds us that illegal acquisition and sale of antiquities is a concern in North America as well. Another example is the extensive looting of the Slack Farm site, a Mississippian site in Kentucky where looters paid the landowner to dig, destroying many graves and structures before local complaints led to their arrest for desecration (Fagan 1995).

Encounters with collectors such as described in the opening to Chapter 6 also remind us that archaeological values are not necessarily shared universally. The issues involved are not straightforward. Some collectors argue that they preserve items that otherwise would be lost or destroyed. Archaeologists counter that out-of-context artifacts may be attractive, but they tell us much less than carefully documented items in site collections.

Who is a looter or pothunter anyway? Generally, "looting" refers to the illegal removal of artifacts and other property from sites or museums. It is clear that the some of the people who removed antiquities from the Baghdad Museum immediately after the fall of Iraq to American forces in 2003 can be called looters. Can we apply the term to someone who collects arrowheads from the surface of a plowed field without the landowner's permission? Should we confine the use of "pothunting" to digging into a site illegally? Is the intent to sell an object essential to defining the person who removed the artifact from its site as a looter? In reality, there is a wide range of activities that cause destruction of sites and information and might fall under the heading of looting or pothunting. Some of these activities result in major site destruction; thefts on a smaller scale are called "low-end looting" (Hollowell-Zimmer 2003).

Our difficulty with defining "looting" and "pothunting" precisely results from the absence of widespread agreement about what actions are appropriate, or at least acceptable, at archaeological sites and with respect to artifacts. It is difficult to stop activities that are not widely regarded as undesirable, and it is even more difficult to deter behavior we don't understand. Several recent examinations have provided insights into the culture of pothunting. For example, Early (1989) found that in Arkansas, three groups of people participate in a subculture involved in the trafficking of antiquities: (1) diggers, who actually dig into sites and remove artifacts (Figure 14.3), (2) dealers, who buy and sell the artifacts obtained by diggers, and (3) financiers, the wealthy collectors who want antiquities for their own collections. Many people involved in activities of these kinds are interested in Indian artifacts, but they do not think of undocumented and careless digging as destructive. Participants in the subculture of looting are entrepreneurial; they seek a monetary profit from their activities. Diggers may see pothunting as a possible means of getting rich akin to hitting a lottery jackpot; dealers see themselves as engaged in a business undertaking; financiers often are seeking investments and may donate unwanted materials to museums as tax write-offs.

Understanding various aspects of trafficking is important to devising strategies for curbing site destruction due to looting (Watson 2006). Various approaches might be possible. In the United States, the Archaeological Resources Protection Act (ARPA) has been designed to deter looting. This act makes it illegal to excavate or sell any archaeological resource located on federal or Indian land without a permit. Violation of ARPA can lead to a fine of $10,000 to $20,000 and/or five years in jail. ARPA does not apply to private land, but laws against interstate trafficking in stolen property can be invoked in situations like the GE Mound case. We can work for strict implementation of laws like ARPA. However, laws, even if they are consistently enforced, may not be the whole answer. Except perhaps for the most casual diggers, illegality may add intrigue to pothunting.

What else might we do to protect sites? Museums, universities, and art galleries can insist on careful documentation of ownership and **provenance** for any antiquities or collections offered them. However, most reputable institutions already do this; it's collectors who often fail to obtain such information before purchasing artifacts. Currently, antiquities offered on the Internet can be obtained without the kinds of documentation that museums routinely ask for. Thus people without any understanding of the issues involved are at risk of buying stolen property. Perhaps educational efforts by archaeologists can reduce looting and antiquities trafficking.

However, educating the public must involve more than stirring up popular interest in North America's past. Pothunters often are interested in an area's past, and many times quite knowledgeable about it. They may even have read some of the professional archaeological literature to find out where sites are and how they are

FIGURE 14.3 A particularly destructive aspect of pothunting is the focus on finding complete artifacts, which can be sold or displayed; the result is the disturbance and destruction of a great deal of material that might have provided insight into the past.

FIGURE 14.4 This sign at Pinson Mounds in Tennessee is a reminder to visitors that cultural and natural resources should be conserved for the future; of course as heritage tourism increases in sites with very high rates of visitation, even the footprints of thousands of visitors might erode surfaces and damage structures.

structured. It appears that the destruction caused by pothunting and the antiquities market is fueled by conditions beyond simple ignorance or even simple greed. Interest in the past and fascination with its traces also are involved.

The challenge is finding ways to promote a conservation ethic while still allowing the public to enjoy the traces of the past (Figure 14.4). This is a challenge for the twenty-first century.

the last 30 to 40 years, but the question of how to sensitively and responsibly manage North America's cultural resources continues to need discussion. We believe that the policy issues involved are not perceived because North America's past is not widely known. Knowledgeable citizens represent a first defense against the loss of North America's archaeological resources. We hope that the readers of this book can be counted among those who are prepared to participate in public debate about the management of cultural resources.

RECONSIDERING THEMATIC RESEARCH QUESTIONS

In Chapter 2 of this text, we acknowledged that it is easy to lose sight of the big picture when considering the complicated and varied story of North America's past. We listed eight broad thematic questions that North American archaeologists address in their work (Table 2.1). Throughout Part 2 of this book, we pointed out linkages between the topics addressed and these questions. We hope that this has given you a sense of the ways in which the North American archaeological record informs the study of broad anthropological questions. In concluding, we return to each of these themes, briefly summarizing North American contributions and research directions.

First, North American data contribute significantly to worldwide understanding of human migration at the end of the Ice Age. As we discussed in Chapter 3, the consensus about when and how the Americas were settled by humans has changed; the Clovis-First scenario is no longer an adequate explanation, either with respect to timing or with respect to what these first settlers were like. It is probable that humans did enter this continent before Clovis times, though claims of human entry before the last glacial maximum remain suspect, and the evidence is very limited. However, the Monte Verde site and others in South America, as well as evidence that Upper Paleolithic people made watercraft, help support the scant data from North America itself. This opens up the possibility of significant research on possible Pre-Clovis settlement, on various routes of entry, on similarities with early Siberian and other technologies, and on the nature of the first settlers' adaptations. In addition, as the biological characteristics of early human remains have come to light, the possibility of biologically distinct populations and multiple migrations has been raised. Osteological, dental, and genetic analyses can now be profitably undertaken. Surely, we will be learning much more about all these topics during the next few decades.

Second, humans obviously adapted to the diverse environments of North America in a variety of ways.

Simplistic notions about Native American subsistence, economics, and settlement certainly need to be discarded. The people of the North American past sometimes got most of their foods from the sea, and they used many wild plants and animals from terrestrial habitats as well. They were hunter-gatherers, horticulturists with mixed economies, and farmers who relied more intensively on the production of crops. Others, such as Northwest Coast people who constructed clam gardens, don't easily fit into any of these categories. North Americans also organized themselves in varied ways; along the West Coast and in South Florida, complex hunter-gatherer societies developed. These people were essentially sedentary, while horticulturists in southern New England remained seasonally mobile. Whether they were mobile or sedentary, throughout the continent people traded raw materials and finished products over long distances. Some of the items traded were very finely made and represent sophisticated craftsmanship. Because of the variable human strategies and lifestyles, North America can be viewed as a laboratory for investigating the many ways humans have survived over time.

Third, as flotation and ethnobotanical analysis have become more routine in archaeological research, we have come to appreciate that North America is the location for a very important part of the record of early food production. Not only can we document the use of fire and examples of encouraging and tending natural resources, but other, more direct examples of food production are evident. Archaeologists are just beginning to understand the cultivation and domestication of native plants in the Eastern Woodlands as part of the Eastern Agricultural complex. The societal implications of this early type of food production can now be explored. Certainly it is important that food production was invented independently here, just as it was in other primary centers of domestication. The timing and nature of the adoption of tropical cultigens in the Southwest, on the Great Plains, and throughout the Eastern Woodlands also is being profitably investigated by archaeologists. As indicated in Chapter 12's case study, "A New History of Maize-Bean-Squash Agriculture in the Northeast," one surprise has been that the maize-bean-squash triumvirate was not adopted as a package by easterners. Rather, each plant has its own history of acceptance. As these aspects of North America's past are rewritten by today's archaeologists, discoveries make it clear that many parts of North America represent a laboratory for testing ideas about the adoption of agriculture. We predict much more archaeological and ethnobotanical study as this is widely realized.

Fourth, discussions in many of our chapters have made clear that Native North Americans developed fascinating systems of social ranking and sociopolitical integration. This is a recurring theme of interest to archaeologists. North American complex hunter-gatherers along the West Coast, in Alaska, and in southern Florida represent particularly interesting examples of social complexity among maritime foragers. In fact, North America affords some of the best examples of this sort of lifestyle in the world, and its past should convince scholars that societies can be socioculturally complex without being agricultural. However, the topic of complexity is also important in studying agricultural polities in the Southwest and the Eastern Woodlands. Here the degree and nature of elite power, the production and exchange of prestige items, and the significance of mortuary and other ritual behavior will continue to be of great interest to archaeologists. Notably, developments such as those among the Hopewell or in Plains Village societies that appear to have been tribal seem important to understanding how humans shifted from largely egalitarian lifeways to ranked societies. The North American archaeological record suggests that anthropological ideas about sociopolitical complexity have been too narrowly defined. North America's many middle-range societies provide a field for testing ideas developed elsewhere in the world, and we think important anthropological contributions will be made by North American archaeologists in the years to come.

A fifth theme was the problem of tracing ethnic identities in the past. We hope that from reading this text you have a better sense of how archaeologists use material culture to identify ethnic groups. Because so many unknown ethnic groups existed over the millennia of the North American past, the archaeological record is potentially useful for studying the history of native groups. In fact, there are a number of recent examples of archaeological efforts to bridge archaeological interests and native perspectives on their history, particularly in the Southwest (e.g., Bernardini 2005; Gregory and Wilcox 2007). We cannot always identify historically known ethnic identities from the data we have, but material culture can be linked to ethnic identity in many instances. Several topics of growing interest archaeologically are related to efforts to trace the history of past ethnic groups. One topic has to do with how people use artifacts to signal aspects of their identity and status. A second topic is an examination of the various ways human populations can influence each other and how such influence is recognized archaeologically. Thus, the old question of Mesoamerican influence in both the Southwest and the Southeast is being explored once again.

The sixth theme is closely related to the interest in tracing ethnic identity. Archaeologists have a renewed interest in identifying human migrations based on biological and artifactual evidence. During the second half of the twentieth century, North American archaeologists tended to reject explanations based on human migration in favor of in situ evolution. Overly simplistic attributions of social change to the arrival of new groups certainly should be rejected, but the wholesale rejection of past group movements also is inappropriate. Recent discussion of possible key migrations in various areas of North America, such as the Great Basin, the Southwest, the Great Plains, and the Northeast, are healthy signs of a more sophisticated interest in this topic. Advances in genetic techniques provide new tools with which to address such problems.

Findings related to themes five and six also have led contemporary archaeologists to investigate the nature and range of pre-Columbian warfare and violence more thoroughly. Older models based on generally peaceful tribal societies may not always encompass the conflicts between ethnic groups that did exist, particularly as population levels increased over time. This is most obvious in the Southwest, where recent claims of cannibalism among the Ancestral Puebloan populations have been getting attention (see Section F.5, "Was There Cannibalism in the Prehistoric Southwest?" of the Student CD). However, intersocietal violence also has a long, though variable, record in other parts of North America (Milner 1999), and archaeologists are just beginning to explore its significance. While this does not mean that even older views of Native Americans as violent savages should be resurrected, it is clear that conflict occurred among the pre-Columbian ethnic groups of North America. New research will allow us to discard stereotypical ideas about tribal people and to adopt a more realistic understanding of the dynamic nature of past societies and their interactions.

The seventh theme noted in Chapter 2, culture contact as Europeans arrived in North America, might be understood as a special case of concern with ethnic groups and their interactions. We hope this text has made clear that for the Protohistoric and Contact periods, there is fruitful research to be done throughout North America. The complexity of Native–European interaction is very poorly known, but the story of these times is certainly not simply one of conquest by Europeans. Natives sometimes prevailed in early hostile encounters, as with the Pueblo Revolt in 1680. Regardless of ultimate outcomes, Native peoples always had their own stratagems, particularly with respect to trade and political alliances. Unfortunately, standard histories poorly document the Native side of the story. Studies that combine archaeology and ethnohistory seem to be growing in number (e.g., Ferris 2009; LaVere 1998; Smith 2000). Both scholars and Native Americans interested in tribal heritage find these studies important. Contemporary native perspectives also can add significant insight, as shown in the case study for Chapter 7, "Cultures in Contact at Colony Ross." We expect that research on early Historic period cultural interactions will grow in importance during the next few decades.

The eighth and last thematic question listed in Chapter 2 concerns the historical development of the United States and Canada into global and industrial powers. We discussed historical archaeology after the Contact and early Colonial periods in Chapter 13. Archaeology isn't less relevant to investigations of this part of the past just because documentary evidence exists, perhaps abundantly. CRM archaeology gathers evidence from historical as well as prehistoric times, and many significant insights have been gained since its inception. Among the many topics historical archaeology addresses, two seem particularly likely to receive increased attention in the immediate future. First, archaeology can provide insights about the history of African Americans, as indicated in part by the case study in Chapter 13, "Community Archaeology: Understanding the Contexts of Archaeological Practice" by McDavid and Matthews. Written accounts are seriously lacking in the details of lifestyles and circumstances for both slaves and free blacks during the eighteenth and nineteenth centuries (Delle and Levine 2004; Harrington 1996). A second area in which research seems to us to have just begun is the archaeological investigation of our industrial history. Technology is, of course, a traditional area of archaeological research, so documenting the nature of early industrial production (see Exhibit 13.1) is right up an archaeologist's alley. Thus, many aspects of industrial archaeology are likely to catch the imagination of both archaeologists and the public, and we anticipate much more industrial archaeology in decades to come.

The body of knowledge generated by North American archaeology is large and potentially important in several ways. We have tried to point out the value of this body of knowledge to understanding humans in general and to suggest possible areas for future research. Other archaeologists undoubtedly would add to our list, and probably significant topics of study will arise that no one can anticipate today. Theoretical perspectives will also change and affect the questions archaeologists ask as this century continues. For example, research in the areas of gender and individual agency seem to be growing in importance for North American archaeologists. Continued engagement with descendant populations and the growth of indigenous archaeology has already changed the field, and no doubt will continue to do so (Killion 2008; Watkins 2000). Perhaps you will help define additional research topics if you pursue North American archaeology. We are still learning about North America's past, and there is no shortage of interesting research to be done by those who pursue this field (Figure 14.5). On the other hand, you should stay tuned even if you don't formally pursue archaeology because North America contains important clues in the search for helpful answers about the human past.

FIGURE 14.5 Excavations underway at the Leetsdale site in southwestern Pennsylvania for the U.S. Army Corps of Engineers; there is a great deal still to be learned about North America's past, and archaeological studies done in the context of CRM are making important contributions to our knowledge each year.

THE CHANGING DISCIPLINE

As we think ahead about North American archaeology in the twenty-first century, besides new research directions, we can anticipate that the field itself will continue to change in a variety of interesting ways. New methods will be adopted, and preservation laws will change. Moreover, ethical concerns will need to be addressed as the social context of archaeology itself changes. It makes sense to note current trends of this type in our final chapter.

New Methods in Archaeology

Although both muscle and brain power remain important to archaeologists, contemporary archaeology relies heavily on modern technologies: from **Global Positioning System (GPS)** units (Figure 14.6) and ground-penetrating radar to the use of scanning electron microscopes and all sorts of computer-assisted mapping hardware and software. We have mentioned some of these techniques in the text and case studies, and they are reviewed as well in Sections B and C of the Student CD. It is clear that this "high-tech" trend will continue during the next few decades. Three specific areas seem most likely to impact the field in the twenty-first century.

First, geophysical survey is of increasing importance in archaeology. Techniques today include electrical resistivity measurements, use of ground-penetrating radar, and use of seismic or acoustic methods that pass various kinds of energy below the surface of the ground or water, recording the response as a means of detecting subsurface characteristics. Geophysical survey also includes more passive techniques such as magnetic survey methods that measure slight distortions in magnetic fields and metal detectors that locate objects containing metal. Such techniques allow archaeologists to learn about site structure without destroying it and to target hand excavations accordingly. The usefulness of geophysical approaches can be seen clearly in several of the case studies in this book. At this point we cannot use these techniques to locate and understand small-scale features as successfully as we can apply them to the assessment of large structural components like earthworks. However, such techniques have proliferated and improved rapidly over the last decade. We expect that they will become more effective, cheaper, and even more commonly used in the years to come.

A second tool that already is transforming the way archaeological analyses are done is GIS (Geographical Information System). This tool provides for map-based database management that is particularly useful in the analysis of the many types of spatial data archaeologists

FIGURE 14.6 Within the last decade, the use of handheld GPS units has become standard in archaeology; additional technological advances are likely to impact the field in the future.

generate. Site data can be analyzed in conjunction with environmental data in these applications, making this software useful in developing site location models. Today, many state and federal agencies use GIS software to manage site file information. With GIS, these databases become powerful tools for both management and research. Similarly, archaeologists increasingly use GIS to develop the data from archaeological excavations and surveys, linking various maps with images and descriptions of artifacts and features. The next generation of archaeologists is likely to use GIS even more. Students should develop familiarity with this kind of software as part of their college experience.

Several types of chemical and molecular analysis also are now being used in archaeology. We have mentioned research topics that benefit from the current ease with which genetic studies of mtDNA can be conducted. Genetic studies are likely to become most important in archaeological research about colonization or interrelationships among populations. Traces of blood on stone tools also can be examined to determine what species of animal left the blood. Because blood residues can survive for tens of thousands of years, the potential of this type of analysis is great. Other techniques, including a wide array of isotopic analyses, which measure chemical signatures, also can contribute to archaeological questions about diet and population history as well as dating. These are studies that can be done on bone as well as directly on many artifacts, and applications are proliferating. Of course, study of soil chemistry is another tool for understanding site use. For example, concentrations of phosphate at sites with acidic soils may confirm heavy use of animals by area residents. The possibilities for contributions by archaeological chemists are just now beginning to be understood.

Finally, as indicated in several places in this text including the case study in Chapter 12, "A New History for Maize-Bean-Squash Agriculture in the Northeast," AMS dating techniques are providing a second radiocarbon revolution within archaeology.

We can now directly date small organic objects such as beans, and even tiny portions of one-of-a-kind specimens, without destroying them. We can also get dates from residues cooked onto pots or burned into pipes, and we can date contexts with the smallest traces of organic materials. Archaeologists stand to learn a tremendous amount from the application of this technique over the next few decades; we can only imagine how forthcoming results will change our understanding of North America's past.

We expect that there are many other advances in techniques that will be used by future generations of archaeologists, and we can be confident that new techniques and new applications will be found as the twenty-first century proceeds. North American archaeologists, along with our colleagues working elsewhere in the world, are bound to benefit from these developments.

Managing and Protecting North America's Heritage

One of the most important issues archaeologists will face during the twenty-first century is the need to manage and protect the record of North America's past. How well we will succeed is not just a matter for CRM archaeologists to contemplate; all research will be limited by the nature of the record that is preserved. We discussed the importance of preserving sites in Box 14.1, but several other current issues help indicate the complexities being faced in this area.

First, as mentioned in Chapter 1, there is a real crisis in archaeological curation. Not only is there a need to preserve sites, the collections generated by archaeological research must be preserved as well (Sullivan and Childs 2003). The facilities and personnel to adequately care for the archaeological collections we now have too often are lacking, and more collections are being generated all the time. Curation is not just a matter of boxing up excavated artifacts (see Section F.2 of the Student CD). Materials must be stored so that they will remain intact, and collections must be accessible to researchers. As shown by several case studies in this volume, museum collections can be tremendously important in archaeological research, but suitable storage space is limited, and we continue to acquire more collections as research proceeds. Thus, should we be saving everything encountered, or should most items in some categories, such as fire-cracked rock or brick, be counted, weighed, and discarded? Curation is a major issue for North American archaeologists. Although we expect that a variety of creative solutions will be found over the next few decades, the archaeological community is just waking up to the crisis at hand.

A second issue that is likely to be of importance, particularly within CRM archaeology, is whether government regulations concerning cultural resources significantly impact private property rights. The Fifth Amendment to the U.S. Constitution states that no one can be deprived of property without due process or have private property taken without just compensation. On this basis today, some citizens have argued that certain environmental laws and regulations, including those that pertain to archaeological sites and historic preservation, are government "takings" for which property owners should be compensated. Of course, it is not at all clear that laws requiring the identification and assessment of cultural resources prior to development significantly limit the rights of property owners, nor are private property rights in the United States unlimited per se. Nevertheless, proponents of property rights are vocal, and key court decisions undoubtedly will affect legal interpretations with respect to environmental and cultural protection in the future. This is one of the areas in which developing public policy might be of great importance to archaeology.

Another area in which public policy is likely to continue developing has to do with the treatment of human skeletal remains and the interaction with descendant populations such as Native Americans. You have learned in this text that some interactions between archaeologists and Native Americans have been quite positive (e.g., Chapter 5's case study, "Archaeological/Anthropological–Native American Coordination: An Example of Sharing the Research on the Northwest Coast of North America"). Yet as seen in the Kennewick case (Student CD, Bonus Issue and Debate F.4), these interactions can be contentious as well. The development of better policies for dealing with such cases is in order, and we can expect this to happen over the next few years. We anticipate additional changes in laws, regulation, and practice, such as changes in NAGPRA regulations made in 2010 (Department of the Interior 2010), to develop during the twenty-first century as well.

Finally, changes in CRM practice may also result from developments in the way laws and regulations are applied. For example, one question now being actively debated within the professional community is whether the significance of a site is affected by the state of archaeological knowledge about an area or a site type. We pointed out in Chapter 2 that only sites shown to be **significant cultural resources** receive full attention within the framework of CRM. Some people have suggested that after we have fully investigated a number of sites of a particular type—for example, small lithic scatters—another site of the same type is not really as significant. At least theoretically, once we fully understand the variability that exists, gathering

Displaying the Past at Dickson Mounds

Many valuable places for learning about the past are sites at which parks and museums have been constructed to commemorate the peoples of the native past. One such place is Dickson Mounds, located in west central Illinois (see Figure 11.1). Although today this part of Illinois is rural, from the Middle Woodland through the Mississippian periods it was an area of major population concentrations. Six large centers of Illinois Hopewell people, including the Ogden–Fettie site on the museum grounds, are in the vicinity of the museum. A large Late Woodland village, known as the Myer–Dickson site, also was once located on the museum grounds, as was a Mississippian center known as the Eveland Village, and a cluster of low mounds and cemeteries from the Mississippian period. It is because of these last sites that Dickson Mounds is a museum. The story of the development of Dickson Mounds as a museum reminds us that how we interpret the past is a public as well as a scholarly concern.

Local relic hunters considered the mounds on the Dickson farm a great spot to dig for artifacts from at least the end of the nineteenth century. They disturbed the mounds just as landowners did as they farmed and built homes without attempting to preserve what lay within the earthworks. Then, in 1927 Dr. Don Dickson, a chiropractor whose family had owned the land since the 1860s, decided to excavate into one area to study the human skeletons found there. According to all accounts, Dickson was mainly curious, but his experience transformed him into one of the best-known amateur archaeologists in the Midwest. Dickson's main innovation was to leave the bones in place, carefully excavating around them with small tools and brushes. This preserved the position of the remains of individuals in the mound, opening up a whole series of questions about burial practices and culture. Dickson's method of excavation incorporated a standing invitation for family, friends, and neighbors to come by and view the work as it progressed. The onlookers asked so many questions that Dickson saw an opportunity to tell even more people about his new interest. He opened his excavations to the public, charging a small fee of 50¢ to adults to help with cost. Eventually he erected a permanent tile-block building over his excavation, which became the first Dickson Mounds exhibit hall.

To our modern sensibilities, exposed human burials may seem ghoulish, but it was never Dr. Dickson's intent to titillate morbid fancies. He wanted people to learn about the Indian past, which fascinated him. Obviously it fascinated the local public as well. Over 40,000 people came to the excavation at Dickson Mounds during the first year it was open (Harn 1995). Out of these beginnings grew a great deal of local interest in archaeology and pride in the Indian heritage of this part of Illinois. Dickson also attracted professionals, most notably Dr. Fay-Cooper Cole of the University of Chicago, who in the early 1930s ran one of the first archaeological field schools in North America near the site. So began the archaeological tradition of investigating the mounds and other sites of the area.

Despite public interest, it was not possible for Dickson to maintain the museum privately forever. Over the years, Dickson Mounds went through various administrative transfers, first becoming a state park, which Dickson and his family maintained. After Dickson's death in 1964, Dickson Mounds became part of the Illinois State Museum. The museum's exhibits, collections, and research facilities were enlarged and updated, but through it all two things stayed the same: the original burial area in which over 200 sets of human remains were displayed remained open for viewing, and members of the general public kept coming to what they saw as an educational resource. Then, beginning in the late 1980s and early 1990s, Dickson Mounds was swept into the national debate over the treatment of human skeletal material, and major change came to the facility.

At this time Native Americans across the nation were saying that the remains of their ancestors should be repatriated and reburied, not studied by anyone, and certainly not displayed. Human burials were a focal point as Native Americans found their voice and insisted on their rights. These were the years in which NAGPRA was being crafted; these were the years when archaeology and museology woke up to native concerns and issues. The Illinois museum staff, aware of national debate, recommended that the burial exhibit be closed. Initially the governor agreed, but then the public in Fulton County learned of the plan. Local residents were outraged. How could the state close "their museum"? Why should it have to listen to Indians, few of whom resided in Illinois any longer? People were unwilling for outsiders to have a say about what happened to Dickson Mounds. In an election year, the governor capitulated and reversed the decision to close the display. At this point Native American protests began in earnest; Dickson Mounds was at the center of a nationally publicized controversy. Native activists saw Dickson's educational display as an outrage. At one protest Indian demonstrators even jumped the railing of the burial exhibit and covered the bones with blankets.

Fortunately, the story of Dickson Mounds doesn't end in animosity and stalemate; a compromise was found. In 1991 a new governor decided that the burial exhibit would be closed but approved a $4 million renovation initiative for Dickson Mounds Museum. Among other improvements, completely new exhibits that better told the Native story would be undertaken. The museum closed for a year, and the human remains were given a final examination before their reburial. When the museum reopened, not only had the cemetery been sealed over once again, but in its place was a mix of exhibits telling the story of Dickson Mounds from both scientific and native perspectives (Figure 14.7).

Today's visitors to Dickson Mounds learn about the succession of cultures in the area's prehistoric past from the viewpoint of archaeological science, but the experience culminates in a dramatic, multimedia presentation called "Reflections on Three Worlds." As visitors walk down a ramp around the cemetery site, they encounter symbols, music, and voices of Native peoples introducing the Mississippian worldview. Emerging from this experience, visitors enter a photographic gallery of contemporary Native Americans that makes the point that the Indian is still very much with us today.

Many people have been happy with the compromise reached at Dickson Mounds; others complain that nonscientific perspectives are portrayed by the museum. Still

FIGURE 14.7 New exhibits at Dickson Mounds seek to tell the story of the mounds from both a scientific and a native perspective.

others may be critical of the scientific and historical focus of most of the exhibits. Many local people are probably just glad to have "their museum" back. Nevertheless, if you know the story of Dickson Mounds, and especially if you had visited the burial exhibit when it was open, you can't go there now without asking two questions. First, how should the past be publicly interpreted? Second, who should have a say about how we interpret it? These are questions that all of us who study the past must constantly consider.

redundant information at the public's expense is not warranted. The debatable question is whether such a point can be reached and if so, when that might be. A related idea under discussion is whether in some CRM projects **off-site mitigation** might be more justifiable than data recovery of redundant information. In such cases, although resources within a project right-of-way might be destroyed, information about more significant and somehow related resources might be obtained. In this manner a context for cultural resources within a project area can be established. It will be interesting to see how these debates about how to comply most responsibly with laws and regulations are resolved.

Archaeological Ethics in the Twenty-first Century

A recent discussion of the way archaeological ethics have changed over the last 30 or more years notes that archaeologists used to see ethics primarily in terms of the sites and artifacts they studied, but today they must accommodate concerns of living people as well (McGuire 2003). This provides a useful way to think about the ethics of doing archaeology today and in

the future. More information about archaeological ethics can be found at the websites of the Society for American Archaeology (http://www.saa.org) and the Canadian Archaeological Association (http://www.canadianarchaeology.com).

It is still true that the archaeologists view the archaeological record as priceless and irreplaceable, and ethical practice centers on keeping this in mind. This aspect of archaeological ethics is basic and will remain so. This is why archaeologists are concerned with saving sites and preventing the Internet sale of illegally obtained artifacts. This is why we, as a profession, must address the issue of curation. This also is why the results of archaeological research must be published, or at least accessible, both professionally and publicly. The issue of sharing archaeological knowledge, discussed only briefly in this text, is one of the important ethical dilemmas archaeologists must address in the twenty-first century (Zimmerman 2003). It has often been hard for academic researchers to produce timely reports of their research, but it also is true that CRM reports, which usually must be produced rapidly for contractual reasons, seldom reach a wide audience and often languish in what has been called the "gray literature," known to only a few. Beyond all this is the issue we raised in the opening section of this chapter, sharing knowledge with the public. Practically, archaeologists need to share archaeological knowledge through public education so that people know that it is important to fund North American archaeology through research grants or in CRM. However, what we learn about the past doesn't really belong to archaeologists in the first place, and ethical practice dictates that we make our knowledge widely available.

This is the juncture at which new understandings of the archaeological ethics surrounding living people begin to come into play. Of course, we have ethical obligations to the professional community and to our students. However, most archaeologists today also understand that our professional skills and knowledge do not necessarily give us privileged access to the archaeological record. Descendant populations are important stakeholders with respect to the past, and their concerns cannot be ignored. Laypeople with an interest in the past, such as collectors (La Belle 2003), must be considered as well. A definition of ethical conduct with respect to these other interested parties remains contested, but archaeologists will have to address this issue over the next few decades. The ethics of being an archaeologist are much more complicated than one might first think, as illustrated in Box 14.2. If you pursue archaeology, you will have to respectfully negotiate a web of obligations, so it will be helpful to begin thinking about them while still a student.

CONCLUDING THOUGHTS

We end our introduction to North American archaeology with the hope that finishing this text is more a beginning than the end of your interest in North American archaeology. There are so many fascinating things to learn about North America's past, and a number of lessons for our increasingly multicultural society. In addition, this is a dynamic field in which there are many opportunities for meaningful work. We hope you stay interested in archaeology and keep tabs on what archaeologists are learning, even if you are not inclined to pursue the field yourself. Of course you can continue to read about North American archaeology in popularly oriented publications such as *Archaeology* and *American Archaeology*, but you also can explore the field more directly.

First, there is much North American archaeology to see and visit (Figure 14.8), with information about the continent's past accessible in a wide variety of museums throughout the United States and Canada. However, archaeological sites also often have been interpreted for the public on federal, state, and private properties. These range from elaborate reconstructions with costumed interpreters such as can be found at Fort Michilimackinac (see Section D.8 of the Student CD) to sites with small visitor centers, or even just a little signage. Guides to places you can visit have been listed in several of our "Suggestions for

FIGURE 14.8 Students and professors view a display in the museum at Angel Mounds State Historic Site in southern Indiana, one of many museums, parks, and sites that the public can visit in order to learn about North America's past.

Further Reading" sections, including the one for this chapter. Section H of the Student CD lists places to visit as well.

Second, there are many volunteer and avocational opportunities to learn about local archaeology and even to participate in archaeological projects. These range from lectures to workshops to lab tours, many of them organized by museums and universities with archaeologists on staff (Figure 14.9). Your state or province also probably has an amateur society you might wish to join. The address of some amateur societies can be found under the Council of Affiliated Societies on the website of the Society for American Archaeology. Many amateur societies have their own websites, which you can find directly. Centers such as the Crow Canyon Archaeological Center in Colorado and the Center for American Archaeology in Illinois have program offerings for adults and children. A list of archaeological fieldwork opportunities worldwide is available online from the Archaeological Institute of the Americas, and you might find a North American project that will accept volunteers from this source. Organizations such as Earthwatch sometimes provide opportunities for volunteer participation in fieldwork in North America. The U.S. Department of Agriculture Forest Service has a program called Passports in Time, through which you may participate in archaeology on a volunteer basis. Websites for such opportunities are listed in Section H of the Student CD.

Third, if you are a teacher, you will be able to find a variety of resources for working with students. You can begin by looking at the Society for American Archaeology website, where the Public Education Committee posts lesson plans and other resources for teachers. A great deal of effort has gone into creating materials for teachers at the middle and junior high school levels, but these materials may be adaptable for other grade levels. The U.S. Department of the Interior Bureau of Land Management also makes available "Intrigue of the Past," a teacher's activity guide for students in the fourth through seventh grades (Smith et al. 1993). Often these resources can be supplemented with materials produced by archaeologists in your own state or province (e.g., Wolynec 2004). Teachers' workshops on archaeology may be found by searching for public programs at museums and universities.

Finally, if you have become interested enough to pursue additional coursework in archaeology and to contemplate archaeology as a career, you will probably find that the Department of Anthropology at your local university offers basic courses. Students who are considering North American archaeology as a career ideally should acquire a background in all the fields of anthropology as well as specific courses in archaeological fieldwork (Figure 14.10) and laboratory techniques (Figure 14.11) at the undergraduate level. Sometimes you can gain experience by assisting a professor with a project rather than by taking a specific course. There is

FIGURE 14.9 An archaeologist from the State Museum of Pennsylvania provides a public tour of excavations and displays on City Island, located in the Susquehanna River near Harrisburg.

FIGURE 14.10 Field training is essential for prospective archaeologists; these students were enrolled in a field school associated with Indiana University of Pennsylvania.

FIGURE 14.11 Indiana University of Pennsylvania students taking a quiz as part of their laboratory training. Undergraduate students of archaeology typically obtain training in identifying artifacts by this and other means.

currently a great deal of debate among archaeologists about how to educate the next generation of archaeologists (e.g., Bender and Smith 2000). This issue is discussed on the Student CD, Section F.7. If you have a choice of programs, it is advisable to select one that will provide some exposure to the topics indicated by the curricular principles listed in Table 14.1.

Graduate training in archaeology also can be obtained at a variety of institutions, but individuals will want to select a program based on specific interests and on the presence of congenial professors rather than program location. You will have a better sense of such matters after taking a number of undergraduate courses in archaeology.

TABLE 14.1 Principles of Curricular Reform for the Twenty-first Century
1 **Stewardship.** Archaeological resources are nonrenewable and must be fully documented.
2 **Diverse interests.** Various publics as well as archaeologists have a stake in the past, although members of these groups may approach it differently.
3 **Social relevance.** Knowledge of the past is useful in thinking critically about effective social policy for areas as diverse as the environment, social inequality, multiculturalism, and human health.
4 **Ethics and values.** Ethical considerations are central to the practice of archaeology.
5 **Written and oral communication.** Archaeologists must think logically and be able to communicate effectively both in writing and orally because archaeology depends on the support of the public.
6 **Fundamental archaeological skills.** Archaeologists must have mastered skills in excavation, analysis, report writing, and the long-term curation of artifacts.
7 **Real-world problem solving.** Analysis of case studies and internship experiences can contextualize and enhance the training of student archaeologists.

Adapted from Bender (2000:32–33).

CHAPTER SUMMARY

With this chapter we complete our archaeological introduction to the North American past. The following final points have been made:

- Study of North American archaeology provides a different perspective on what happened in North America's past and helps us discard stereotypical notions that all Native Americans were alike or that they were primitive people. It also indicates why it is important to preserve the traces of this continent's past.
- The archaeological study of North America's past has contributed important insights concerning broad anthropological themes and topics. North America is an important laboratory for understanding both the story of particular people's pasts and the story of humankind in general.

- A variety of methods, including the application of geophysical methods, the incorporation of GIS software, the development of various chemical analyses, and the application of AMS dating, promise to transform the discipline of North American archaeology during the twenty-first century.
- Contemporary North American archaeology is a complex and challenging field that is both a scholarly and a public endeavor of interest to diverse constituencies.

    There are many ways to get involved with North American archaeology, from casual visits to sites or websites to participation in excavations to acquiring degrees in the field. Materials that help readers explore these possibilities further are included in Section H of the Student CD.

SUGGESTIONS FOR FURTHER READING

For a collection of essays with new perspectives on North American archaeology:

Pauketat, Timothy R., and Diana Di Paolo Loren
  2005 *North American Archaeology.* Blackwell, Malden, Massachusetts.

For essays on the nature and theory of current archaeological practice:

Ashmore, Wendy, Dorothy T. Lippert, and Barbara J. Mills
  2010 *Voices in American Archaeology.* The Society for American Archaeology, Washington, D.C.
Sebastian, Lynne, and William D. Lipe
  2009 *Archaeology and Cultural Resource Management: Visions for the Future.* School for Advanced Research Press, Santa Fe.

For essays on archaeologists working with local communities:

Derry, Linda, and Maureen Malloy (editors)
  2003 *Archaeologists and Local Communities: Partners in Exploring the Past.* Society for American Archaeology, Washington, D.C.

For a series of essays about the complex ethics of doing archaeology today:

Zimmerman, Larry J., Karen D. Vitelli, and Julie Hollowell-Zimmer (editors)
  2003 *Ethical Issues in Archaeology.* AltaMira Press, Walnut Creek, California.

For perspectives on the relationship between indigenous people and North American archaeology:

Killion, Thomas W.
  2008 *Opening Archaeology: Repatriations Impact on Contemporary Research and Practice.* School for Advanced Research Press, Santa Fe.
Nicholas, George
  2010 *Being and Becoming Indigenous Archaeologists.* Left Coast Press, Walnut Creek, California.

OTHER RESOURCES

Sections H and I of the Student CD supply web links, places to visit, additional discussion questions, and other study aids. The Student CD contains four Bonus Issues and Debates sections that address issues raised in this chapter, "The Curation Crisis" (Section F.2),

"A Local Reaction to NAGPRA: The Kumeyaay Cultural and Repatriation Committee"(Section F.3), "Why is the Kennewick Case So Significant?"(Section F.4), and "Can Academia Train Archaeologists for the Twenty-first Century" (SectionF.7).

Glossary

Note: The Glossary contains terms found in the text and on the Student CD.

absolute dating   The determination of chronological age based on a specific time scale or calendar; compare **relative dating**.

accelerator mass spectrometry (AMS) dating   A method of obtaining radiocarbon dates that measures carbon isotopes directly, by means of a particle accelerator and a mass spectrometer, and thus can date a sample containing very little carbon.

achieved status   A position within a society and the associated rights and responsibilities that result from an individual's actions, talents, and accomplishments; compare **ascribed status**.

Adena   An Early Woodland mound-building culture or ceremonial complex centered in the central and upper Ohio River valley (ca. 2500–1900 BP); Adena mounds are conical burial mounds often surrounded by ditches and covering postholes.

Advisory Council on Historic Preservation (ACHP)   The independent federal agency that promotes historic preservation in the United States, advises the president on preservation policy, and administers the **Section 106** process.

adze   A woodworking tool that, unlike an axe, has its working edge at a right angle to the long axis of the tool's handle.

akchin   A term that refers to the mouth of an arroyo, where Hohokam and other Southwestern farmers often planted their crops to take advantage of runoff and floodwaters.

Alaska Native Claims Settlement Act (ANCSA)   U.S. law that gave Native Alaskans title to vast tracts of ancestral lands around the state through the establishment of regional native corporations; passed in 1971 and paved the way for the Alaska oil pipeline.

Aleutian tradition   A marine-based hunting and gathering cultural tradition that developed in the area of the Aleutian Islands and western Alaska beginning about 5000 BP and had a chipped stone rather than ground slate tool industry.

alluvial fan   A fanlike or cone-shaped deposit of sediment and loose rock left by a stream as it enters a valley; changes the terrain from a steep to more level slope.

Alta California   "Upper California" formed in 1804 by the Spanish north of Baja (Lower) California; the line between these colonies separated the area of the Franciscan missions in the north from the Dominican missions in the south.

altimeter   An instrument for measuring altitude with respect to sea level or another fixed level, generally by using pressure gradients.

Altithermal   The second period (7000–4500 BP) of Antevs's tripartite scheme for postglacial climate during which climate was warmer, and drier than it is at present; this term generally isn't used in the East, where archaeologists are more likely to reference the longer **Hypsithermal Interval**.

AMS dating   See **accelerator mass spectrometry (AMS) dating**.

anadromous fish   Fish species (e.g., various species of salmon) that have the ocean as their habitat but spawn and hatch in freshwater rivers.

Anasazi tradition   The archaeological tradition of the northern Southwest that was ancestral to contemporary Puebloan people; this name is disliked by many Native Americans today because of its Navajo meaning: enemy ancestor. (See also **Ancestral Pueblo**.)

465

Anathermal   The first period in Antevs's tripartite scheme for postglacial climate in the North American West, when the climate was cooler and moister than at present (9000–7000 BP).

Ancestral Pueblo   An alternative name for the archaeologically known Puebloan people of the northern Southwest. Some people argue that this term is preferable to **Anasazi** because it is not offensive to the descendants of these people.

annealing   The process of heating and cooling glass or metal to make it less brittle and more workable; used to work copper in North America.

Antelope Creek phase   A Late Prehistoric archaeological culture of the **Southern Plains Village tradition** in the Texas panhandle known for its stone slab, multiroom house structures, which may suggest influence from the Southwest.

anthropogenic sediments   Sediments introduced or created as a result of human activities as opposed to natural processes.

anthropology   The study of humans including the physical, cultural, and social aspects in the past and present. In North America, this field traditionally is divided into biological, cultural, archaeological, and linguistic subdisciplines.

Apafalaya chiefdom   A chiefdom encountered by the de Soto expedition in AD 1540; may correspond to the archaeologically known chiefdom centered at Moundville in Alabama.

arborglyphs   A carving also known as aspen art on the aspen trees of the Sierra Nevadas and the Rocky Mountains; apparently made by Basque sheepherders in the late nineteenth and early twentieth centuries.

archaeological deposits   A term that refers to the cumulative nature of human-derived sediments in an archaeological landscape; more general than **archaeological site** because it recognizes continuous variation in the intensity of the **archaeological record**.

archaeological record   The artifacts and other physical remains of past human activities that document the past and are interpreted by archaeologists.

Archaeological Resources Protection Act of 1979 (ARPA)   A U.S. law designed to prevent destruction of archaeological resources; its enforcement component imposes penalties, and its permitting component may allow recovery of cultural resources.

archaeological site   Any location at which there are material remains, including artifacts, features, or ecofacts, proving evidence of the human past.

archaeological site survey   The systematic process archaeologists use to locate, identify, and record the distribution and nature of archaeological sites on the landscape.

archaeology   The study of past human behavior and culture through the analysis of material remains.

Archaic period   A period from approximately 10,000 BP to 3000 BP that is recognized in most North American culture areas except those of the West Coast and the Arctic; the Archaic is not a general developmental stage, as originally thought.

Arctic culture area   The most northerly of the North American culture areas, defined largely by the tree line on the south; from Alaska's Yakutat Bay to the Aleutians and the Bering Sea as well as the Arctic coast east to Greenland and northern Labrador.

Arctic Small Tool tradition   A microlithic stone tool tradition associated with the first foragers to utilize North America's Arctic coast; originally called the **Denbigh Flint complex** and found in both Siberia and the North American Arctic after about 4000 BP.

artifact   Any portable object used, manufactured, or modified by humans that includes stone, ceramic, metal, wood, bone, or objects of other materials. (See also **ecofact**.)

artifact use life   The trajectory an artifact takes from manufacture to discard. Events in the use life of an artifact (e.g., breakage, repair) can alter the form of the artifact.

ascribed status   A position within a society and the associated rights and responsibilities, determined without individual initiative or choice (e.g., by being born into a particular family or being female); compare **achieved status**.

aspartic acid racemization (amino acid racemization)   A dating method based on changes in the structure of amino acids after death; results can be difficult to translate into absolute dates, but the technique is applicable to bones up to 100,000 years old.

aspect   In the **Midwestern taxonomic system**, this unit grouped one **focus** with others that were similar based on formal characteristics in material culture; in turn, aspects were grouped into **phases**, but time and space were not incorporated; rarely used today.

asphaltum   Natural asphalt such as found in seeps like the La Brea Tar Pits near Los Angeles. This natural petroleum product was used as a mastic and to caulk the plank canoes of southern California.

assemblage   A collection of artifacts and/or ecofacts from the same archaeological context (e.g., a feature, a house, a site component). Term may refer to all the materials or simply to one material class. (See also **subassemblage**.)

atlatl   A spear-thrower or throwing board that increases the thrust of a spear by increasing the length of the lever arm; made by many groups in North America and all over the world.

Augustine pattern   A cultural pattern evident in Late Prehistory in central California; intensive fishing and hunting and gathering, dense populations, burial ceremonialism, possibly associated with movement of Wintuan people into the area.

avocational archaeologists   People who lack formal education in anthropology and archaeology and are not paid for work that they do in the field.

Avonlea phase   A Late Woodland Plains bison hunting culture (1500–950 BP) that used the bow and arrow; found in southern Alberta, southern Saskatchewan, southwestern Manitoba, North Dakota, Montana, South Dakota, and northern Wyoming.

baidarka   A term derived from Russian that refers to a hunting boat made from skins and propelled by one to three paddlers using single- or double-bladed paddles; type of a kayak.

ball court   A structure with flat courts and walls reminiscent of Mesoamerican ball courts but built by the Hohokam (oval with sloping walls) and Casas Grandes people (I-shaped with straight walls) in the Southwest; integrative and ritual in nature.

band   A small mobile group of related people, usually hunter-gatherers, among whom there is relatively little social differentiation; leadership is by consensus and group membership is fluid.

bannerstone   A polished stone piece with a central drilled hole and bilateral symmetry that is presumed to have been an **atlatl** weight but is often found in Archaic burial contexts, especially in the East.

Basketmaker   In the **Pecos classification** of the Southwest, this term denoted the pithouse portion of the sequence before people built aboveground, multiroom pueblos (Basketmaker I–III); the specific definition has been modified and is used only in the Ancestral Pueblo area today.

Baytown period   The early Late Woodland period (1650/1550–1250 BP) in the central Mississippi River valley; Baytown ceramics are clay tempered and cord marked, and the people used small notched and stemmed arrow points.

bedrock milling feature   A feature for grinding of seeds, acorns, and other plant foods located within an outcrop of bedrock; mortar cups, bedrock metates, and other features related to food grinding or crushing may occur in clusters.

behavioral archaeologist   An archaeologist who has adopted an approach to archaeology formulated in the mid-1970s by Michael Schiffer and focusing on the behaviors involved in the production, manipulation, and disposal of material culture.

Beringia   The land area of northwestern North America and northeastern Asia that was exposed when the sea level dropped during the Pleistocene.

Berkeley pattern   A cultural pattern that follows the **Windmiller pattern** in central California (4000–500 BP); intensive use of coastal resources and acorn processing.

Besant phase   Bison hunting culture of the northern Great Plains beginning about 1850 BP; associated with pottery and burial mounds and in the Dakotas with the **Sonota burial complex**; considered Archaic by some archaeologists and Woodland by others.

biface   A chipped stone tool that has been worked extensively on both surfaces or faces rather than merely being retouched at the edges; bifaces can be tools themselves, serve as cores for flake production, or be **preforms** for specific tools such as **projectile points**.

big men   Individuals in some tribal societies who enjoy higher status and power owing to personal entrepreneurship and skillful use of social obligation rather than to inheritance of wealth.

bioarchaeological analysis   The analysis and interpretation of human biological remains such as skeletons found in archaeological contexts.

biological anthropology   The study of the biological aspects of humans, including human biological evolution and past and present human biological diversity.

biome   A macrolevel biological community of interacting plants and animals, as exemplified by tundra or coniferous forest.

bipoint   A bone or stone artifact that is pointed at both ends; interpreted as a type of fish gorge.

bipolar technology   A technique of percussion flaking in which a stone core is placed on an anvil and struck from above; practical for breaking up small pebbles.

birdstone   A stylized bird effigy in polished stone commonly found in Late Archaic and Early Woodland contexts in the Midwest, Great Lakes, and Northeast; commonly interpreted as an atlatl weight.

Birnirk culture   The archaeological culture that immediately preceded the **Thule culture** itself (northern Alaska, 2200–1250 BP) with a sophisticated maritime hunting technology including a distinctive flat toggling harpoon head.

Blackduck culture   An archaeological culture and ceramic style beginning about 1450 BP and continuing until European contact in the boreal forests of northern Ontario, northern Minnesota, and southern Manitoba; ancestral to Historic Ojibwa.

Black Rock period   An eastern Great Basin period from 6000 BP to 1500 BP in which the uplands, sparsely used before, began to be utilized; Elko and Gypsum Cave points mark the beginning, while Rose Springs and Eastgate points were introduced near the end.

blade   A flake at least twice as long as it is wide and more than 1.2 centimeters (0.5 in.) long, with bladelets or **microblades** being shorter; several North American archaeological cultures, including **Clovis**, developed blade industries.

blast furnace   A furnace in which iron is extracted from its ore by means of blasts of hot air in the presence of a **flux**, like limestone; more productive than a bloomery forge; common in North America between the late seventeenth and nineteenth centuries.

blister steel   An alloy of iron and carbon produced by early iron makers by keeping wrought iron packed with charcoal red hot for up to two weeks; surface texture is blistered, hence the name.

blood residue analysis   The study of traces of blood adhering to tools; differences in the hemoglobin in blood among animal species provide a means of identifying the source of a specimen, which may retain its signature characteristic for thousands of years.

bloom   The product of a bloomery forge; ore heated to a spongy state so that impurities can be hammered out of it.

blowing tubs   In iron making, a pair of tubs with water-powered pistons used to pump air into the **tuyere** of the furnace; this innovation replaced bellows as iron-making techniques developed.

Bonneville period   This period (11,000–9500 BP) in the eastern Great Basin is seen at only a few sites; stemmed points suggest a possible affiliation with the **Western Pluvial Lakes tradition**.

Borax Lake tradition   A Middle to Late Archaic tradition of the North Coast Range in California; Borax Lake points, millingstones, and manos indicating generalized foraging.

borrow pit   An excavated area, the material from which has been used as fill in another place.

bosh   The widest part in the interior of an iron furnace through which molten iron and slag descended to the **crucible**.

BP   A date designation that means "before present," or more precisely before AD 1950, the date from which calculations in radiocarbon years are made by archaeological convention.

Broadpoint tradition   A Late Archaic tradition in the Eastern Woodlands that is marked by the appearance of broad-bladed and stemmed points (e.g., Susquehanna point) after about 4000 BP; associated with the adaptive changes of the Transitional Archaic along the Atlantic Coast.

Buffalo Soldiers   Name given to two regiments of African American cavalry established by the U.S. Congress in 1866 and posted throughout the West to help protect the frontier.

bullboat   A boat made of skins by Plains Indians; shallow and saucer-shaped.

bundle burial   The gathering up, or bundling, of disarticulated, defleshed remains into a **secondary burial** context; the deceased were sometimes exposed to the elements until the soft tissue had decayed, and the bony remains reburied later.

burin   A small tool created when a blow is struck transversely to one of the edges rather than into the interior of the tool, creating a sturdy chisel-like tip, useful for working antler, ivory, and bone.

burin spall   The flake that results from making a **burin**; sometimes used as graver tips in the Arctic.

$^{12}C/^{13}C$ The ratio between two stable isotopes, carbon-12 and carbon-13, which are retained after death in bone collagen; since various food categories have different isotopic signatures, values of this ratio can indicate dietary composition.

calcined   Describing bone that has been so thoroughly burned or highly heated that all moisture and grease have been removed and the bone has been reduced to a white or blue chalky or crumbly state.

California culture area   The culture area that includes most of the modern state of California and the northern portion of Baja California, where a diverse group of Native cultures including complex coastal hunter-gatherers once existed.

California Environmental Quality Act (CEQA)   A state law enacted in 1970 for the purpose of monitoring land development in California by requiring review and permitting of proposed projects.

California Native American Burial Act   A state law passed in 1982 requiring notification of the California Native American Heritage Commission when Native American skeletal material is encountered; the most likely descendant consults on the disposition of the remains.

Calusa culture   A non-Mississippian Late Prehistoric culture of the west coast of Florida that focused its subsistence on the sea rather than agriculture; characterized by shell platform mounds and shell middens.

Campbell tradition   A cultural tradition of the Santa Barbara region in coastal California at the onset of the Pacific period; intensive use of marine and shoreline resources and various artifacts suggest that these are the ancestors of the Chumash.

Canaliño   The Late Prehistoric occupants of the Santa Barbara region and California's Channel Islands. Canaliño sites show a focus on marine resources, and the culture is thought to be similar to that of the ethnographic Chumash.

Carabelli's cusp   A small tubercle located on the lingual surface, or tongue side, of some people's upper molars, most often the right first molar; occurs in higher frequencies in European populations than in other populations.

carrying capacity   The number of organisms (human or other) that an area can support; estimated on the basis of characteristics of the natural environment and, in the case of humans, the available technology.

Cascade phase   An archaeological culture recognized in assemblages from the Snake River in Washington State and adjacent areas; leaf-shaped Cascade points date from 9000 BP to 7800 BP, after the **Windust phase**.

Cashie phase   A Late Woodland culture of North Carolina, found inland from the coast, that extends to the Historic period and has affinities with the Iroquoian societies further north; the people made quartz-tempered, stamped, incised, and plain ceramics.

cast arch   The arch at the bottom of an iron furnace, where the molten iron was tapped.

castellation   A projecting or raised section on the rim of a pot that gives the vessel a squared opening.

cataloging   The systematic recording of artifacts and other items that includes information about the items' **provenience** and a basic description; this step precedes analysis but is essential for future retrieval and research.

celt   A kind of axe or chopping implement hafted to a bone or wooden handle; sometimes celts are so finely made that ceremonial uses are suspected.

cenote   A sinkhole formed when underground water erodes away limestone, the cavern ceiling collapses, and access to the water is gained; common in regions of karstic topography; term is the Mayan word for such sinkholes that had ritual importance.

Central Plains tradition   A subdivision of **Plains Village**, grouping sites from the central Plains in Kansas, Nebraska, and western Iowa (ca. 950–500 BP).

Central Subarctic Woodland culture   Ceramic-using archaeological cultures of northern Ontario and Manitoba dating after about 2200 BP; best known is the **Laurel culture**.

Ceramic period   An alternative term for **Woodland period** used by some Plains archaeologists and also used in Maine and the Maritime provinces of Canada.

Cerbat   A regional branch of the **Patayan tradition**, which encompasses northwestern Arizona between the Coconino Plateau and the Colorado River (ca. 1250–750 BP).

Chaco Branch Anasazi   A regional branch of Ancestral Pueblo archaeological cultures centered at Chaco Canyon in northwestern New Mexico.

Chaco phenomenon   A term used by archaeologists to refer to the unique developments associated with the regional system associated with Chaco Canyon in northwestern New Mexico; characteristics include great houses, roads, and exchange items (900–650 BP).

Champlain Sea   An inland sea created in the lowlands of the St. Lawrence River as the glacier retreated; sea level rose before the valley, having been depressed by the weight of the glacier, could rebound; as a result, parts of Quebec, Ontario, New York, and Vermont were flooded.

chaparral biome   Biome consisting of the various communities of arid-adapted plants and animals found in southern California, Baja California, and portions of southern Oregon.

charmstone   A ground stone artifact in various shapes and sometimes with a drilled hole found in central California after 4000 BP; often associated with burials and believed to have been a ritual item.

check dam   A small rock feature constructed to retain water from rainfall runoff; useful in arid areas of the Southwest that receive rainfall in sudden cloudbursts but often lack permanent streams that can be diverted by more permanent irrigation features.

Chesrow complex   An early, possibly Pre-Clovis archaeological complex represented by sites in southeastern Wisconsin; modified bone and lithics dated before 11,500 BP.

chiefdom   A kin-based, ranked society in which access to resources and political power, as well as social status, are determined by hereditary proximity to the chief, who often controls the redistribution of goods and is wealthy as well as powerful.

Chihuahua tradition   A poorly understood Archaic tradition of the southeastern portions of the Southwest (ca. 7950–1700 BP).

Choris culture   The first part of the Norton tradition sequence found in northern Alaska north of the Bering Strait (3000–2500 BP); people made **feather-tempered pottery** that was cord marked, stamped, or incised and is related to pottery from northeast Asia.

Chumash   A Native American tribe that inhabited the southern coastal regions of California including several of the Northern Channel Islands; known as maritime complex hunter-gatherers both archaeologically and ethnographically.

chunkey   A game played by Southeastern Indians who rolled a stone disk with concave sides at which opposing players threw poles; the object was to hit the disk or to come close to it where it stopped.

cinder notch   A notch above the hearth of an iron furnace through which **slag** could be drawn off.

Civil Works Administration (CWA)   A federal program established as part of Franklin Roosevelt's New Deal during the Great Depression to create jobs for thousands of people who had become unemployed; some of these jobs were in archaeology.

clan   A social grouping defined by a kin connection in which descent is traced unilineally rather than through both parents; important feature of social organization in tribes.

Classic Mimbres phase   A Mogollon variant from southwestern New Mexico and southeastern Arizona (950–820 BP) known for exceptionally well-made and beautiful pottery with geometric and animal designs.

Classic period Hohokam   The culmination of the **Hohokam tradition** sequence in the southern Arizona desert (800–550 BP); compounds, multi-story pueblos, and platform mounds were characteristic.

clay cooking balls   Fired balls of clay that could be heated in a fire and placed in earth ovens for indirect cooking of food; used in places where stone was scarce, such as the coastal plains of the Southeast.

Clemson Island culture   An early Late Prehistoric designation for sites of the Susquehanna River drainage; people used cord- or fabric-impressed grit-tempered vessels, practiced maize and native plant cultivation, and constructed burial mounds.

Clovis culture   This Paleoindian culture (11,500–10,800 BP) is associated with the distinctive fluted Clovis point and the hunting of mammoths, although a wider range of resources probably was used, particularly outside the Great Plains.

Clovis-First   The idea that the Clovis fluted point makers were the first humans in the Americas, having followed large game through an **ice-free corridor** as the Ice Age waned; no longer the archaeological consensus, this scenario is still accepted by some archaeologists.

Coalescent tradition   A third **Plains Village tradition** subdivision first evident around 650 BP but continuing into the Historic period; fusion of **Central Plains Village** and **Middle Missouri traditions**.

Cochise tradition   The Archaic tradition in the southwestern Southwest (ca. 9450–2150 BP) that includes the Sulphur Springs, Chiricahua, and San Pedro phases; these people were foragers who added maize and other cultigens at the end of the sequence.

Cody complex   A Late Paleoindian archaeological complex known for finely made, unfluted, lanceolate points and the shouldered asymmetrical Cody knife; Great Plains and Southwest distribution.

Cohonina   A regional branch of the **Patayan tradition**, which developed in the area around Flagstaff, Arizona, between about 1250 BP and 750 BP.

coil-and-scrape technique   A pottery-making technique in which vessels are built up by coiling rolled lengths of clay, and then the interior and exterior surfaces are scraped and smoothed with a piece of gourd, a pottery sherd, or other expedient tool.

coiling   A method of basket making in which a bundle of strands or rods is stitched into a spiraling oval or round form; compare **twining** and **plaiting**.

coke   A purified form of coal that replaced charcoal as the fuel for iron furnaces after the mid-nineteenth century in America; hotter fires allowed for more efficient melting of iron ore.

cold-air drainage   The flow downslope of cold, dense air that tends to occur as the ground surface cools on calm nights in steep-sided mountain valleys; a layer of warmer air is found higher up the side of the valley, inhibiting the formation of frost.

cold desert biome   The desert biome of the Great Basin in the western United States, which is very arid but experiences cold winters.

Colington phase   A Late Woodland culture of coastal North Carolina that extends to the Historic period and apparently has affinities with the Algonquian societies further north; characterized by shell-tempered ceramics, ossuary burials, and Algonquian longhouses.

collar   In pottery, a raised and extended vessel mouth that begins above the neck and does not reduce the opening relative to the body diameter.

collectors   Individuals who buy, sell, and collect artifacts and art for personal enjoyment or financial gain rather than to learn about the past; such collecting only fuels the illegal acquisition of antiquities and contributes to the destruction of sites. Also used by archaeologists to refer to hunter-gatherers who establish long-term, larger base camps from which foraging parties are sent out; compare **foragers**.

colluvial fan   A fan-shaped deposit of loose sediment that accumulates at the base of a hill owing to erosion and slopewash.

Colonial period Hohokam   The second period (1175–975 BP) in the **Hohokam tradition** sequence of the southern Arizona deserts, characterized by pithouse villages and ball courts.

Comancheros   Multiethnic traders of the Southern Plains who traded in buffalo robes, meat, guns, ammunition, horses, Indian captives, and other commodities from the eighteenth to the nineteenth centuries.

community   In ecology, a group of interacting plants and animals within a habitat; usually named for the most conspicuous species.

complex hunter-gatherers   Human groups who depend on wild resources for their subsistence but have economic surplus, prestige goods, social hierarchies, hereditary leadership structures, settled villages, and other aspects of sociocultural complexity.

compliance archaeology   Archaeological investigation done in response to various **CRM** laws and regulations; this kind of archaeology does not originate with a research question but often contributes important archaeological information.

component   An archaeological unit that includes a culturally homogeneous stratigraphic or spatial unit within a site and is thought to represent a single occupation of the site; components are grouped into **phases**.

composite fishhook   A three-piece fishhook with two pieces of wood lashed together in a V shape and a bone barb attached to one leg of the V; made by Northwest Coast groups.

conical core   A type of flaked rock nodule from which **blades** have been removed from the circumference; usually with a single core platform, which may or may not be prepared, and an end opposite the platform that tapers so that the core is cone-shaped.

coniferous forest biome   Dominated by coniferous trees such as pine, spruce, fir, and hemlock, this large biome stretches across Canada south of the tundra and in the U.S. Rocky Mountains; coniferous forest also occurs in the mountains of northern Mexico.

conjunctive approach   A methodological approach suggested by Taylor in the 1940s as a critique of culture history; argues for the exploration of a full range of cultural variables rather than chronology and spatial and temporal distributions alone.

conservation archaeology   An approach that stresses the conservation of archaeological sites because they are irreplaceable, discouraging excavation except as part of the management of resources for the greatest scientific, historical, and public benefit.

container revolution   The profound changes associated with the introduction of stone and ceramic bowls at the Late Archaic–Woodland boundary in the East; possibly associated with boiling new foods like seeds to make them more palatable.

context   Refers to where an object or a feature is found as well as to what it is associated with; objects found out of context are less useful to archaeologists than objects found in place.

Copena Mortuary complex   A Middle Woodland burial complex of the Tennessee Valley in northwest Alabama that often is considered Hopewell because of the log and bark burial containers and the many Hopewell Interaction Sphere artifacts they contain.

coprolite   Human or animal feces preserved by desiccation, fossilization, or being waterlogged; provides evidence of diet.

cord-marked   Describing a surface texture created by pressing a cord-wrapped paddle into the wet surface of a clay pot before firing; this technique was used widely throughout North America.

Cordilleran ice sheet   The ice cap that expanded over the northern Rocky Mountains of Canada and the United States during the Pleistocene.

core tablet   A flake removed from the top of a core to form or rejuvenate the platform; also called a core rejuvenation flake.

corporate leadership strategy   A type of leadership in which individual displays of power, wealth, and prestige are discouraged because power is shared across sectors of society, although inequalities in ritual knowledge and control may be great; contrast with **network leadership strategy**.

cortex   The weathered outside surface of an unmodified rock; often a different color from surfaces that have been broken.

Crab Orchard tradition   The Early and Middle Woodland ceramic tradition of southern Illinois and adjacent areas characterized by cordmarked and fabric-impressed conoidal, flat-bottomed vessels; also used to denote a Middle Woodland culture in the area.

crescent   A crescent shaped stone tool associated with Paleoindian sites in California and the Great Basin.

crested blade (*lame à crêtes*)   A blade bearing bidirectional flake scars on the dorsal surface as a result of a flintknapper's preparation of a ridge to guide the blade.

CRM   See **cultural resource management**.

crucible   The narrow chamber at the bottom of an iron furnace below the **bosh**; air was conducted into the crucible via the **tuyere**.

CUHR See **cultural unaffiliated human remains**.

cultural anthropology   The study of the cultural aspects of humans, especially recent and contemporary social, technological, and ideological behaviors observed among living people.

cultural ecology   A school of anthropological thought that influenced North American archaeology in the late twentieth century; associated with the anthropologist Julian Steward, this approach focuses on the interactions between human societies and their environment.

cultural process/culture process   The mechanisms inherent in a culture that cause stability, change, or both; beginning in the 1960s, archaeologists argued that exploring these processes was their primary goal.

cultural resource management (CRM)   An applied form of archaeology undertaken in response to various laws that require archaeological investigations as part of governmental programs.

cultural resources   Sites, buildings, artifacts, and other remains that compose the nonrenewable and irreplaceable material traces of the past, including archaeological remains and historical records.

culturally modified tree (CMT)   A tree that has been used in bark stripping or other activity that scarred the surface; there is debate over how many of these trees, which are common in the forests of the West, should be preserved.

culturally unaffiliated human remains (CUHR)   Human remains for which no cultural affiliation or shared group identity with a present day Indian tribe can be determined; there is debate about how these kinds of remains should be treated under NAGPRA.

culture area   A geographical region within which there is general similarity of culture; originally developed to group ethnographically known cultures, but often extended into the archaeological past of indigenous peoples.

culture history   An archaeological approach that emphasizes the ordering of artifacts into a sequence in time and space; most important in North American archaeology in the early to mid-twentieth century, but a baseline for further study of culture.

culture stage   An archaeological construct that refers to a general level of development based on formal attributes presumed to reflect cultural evolution; the Lithic, Archaic, and Formative stages usually are not used by North American archaeologists today.

curated   A term referring to stone tools, that have been maintained by resharpening or reworked into another tool form, possibly indicating concern with the availability or quality of stone; may also refer to the care of collections, as in **curation**.

curation   The professional care of archaeological remains with the goal of best preserving specimens for future research and public education. A crisis exists with respect to the curation of archaeological collections.

Cuyamaca complex   The Late Prehistoric occupation of mountains of the San Diego region, thought to represent the ancestors of the Yuman-speaking Kumeyaay; cremation, small triangular projectile points, and ceramics are characteristics of this complex.

Darwinian archaeologist   An archaeologist who approaches archaeology by trying to explicitly apply the principles of selection and evolutionary theory to the study of archaeological phenomena.

data recovery program   In CRM archaeology, any excavation program designed to recover information about cultural resources that are likely to be destroyed by construction or other development.

datum point   The base point used as the main reference station in setting out a grid at a site or in recording site locations; controls vertical as well as horizontal information.

Death Valley I   An early Holocene complex found in and around Death Valley; generally considered to be part of the Lake Mohave complex and also included in Bedwell's Western Pluvial Lakes tradition.

debitage   The material, including chips, flakes, and other debris, produced when stone is flaked to make tools.

Denali complex   An early archaeological culture of Alaska and the western Yukon (11,000–9000 BP) with clear affinities to the **Dyuktai tradition** of Siberia; core and blade technology including microblades and wedge-shaped cores.

Denbigh Flint complex   The original complex of the **Arctic Small Tool tradition** based on materials from the bottom of the Iyatayet Creek site at Cape Denbigh but eventually found over a much wider area of the High Arctic.

dendrochronology   A dating method that compares the rings in wood to a master sequence of rings for a region; trees add rings annually, but the width of the rings depends on the climate, thus creating a sequence for comparison with archaeological specimens.

dental caries   The disease associated with tooth decay or cavities; evidence of dental caries can be used to draw conclusions regarding the health of a population.

dentalium shell   A tubular, tusk-shaped shell from the Pacific Coast, but traded into the interior of North America; used for ornamentation.

Deptford tradition   An Early and Middle Wood-land cultural tradition of South Carolina, Georgia, and northern Florida defined by distinctive checked and simple stamped vessels and possibly associated with the somewhat later **Swift Creek tradition**.

Desert Archaic   A term applied to the hunting and gathering adaptations of the Great Basin and adjacent arid areas that are now known to have been variable over time and space.

Desert culture   The name for the hunting and gathering adaptations in the Great Basin and adjacent arid areas assumed to have been basically uniform for 11,000 years into the Historic period; this idea has been abandoned as variability over time and space has become clearer.

dew claw   A vestigial or nonfunctional toe in a deer, antelope, or other animal reflecting the reduction in the number of functional toes from the five per foot of the earliest mammalian species.

diagnostic artifact   An artifact that allows archaeologists to identify a particular archaeological culture or time period; in effect it allows one to "diagnose" who made and left the item where it was found.

Dinétah phase   An archaeological phase of the upper San Juan River drainage that some archaeologists have argued represents pre–Pueblo Revolt (AD 1680) Navajo presence in the northern Southwest; other archaeologists reject assertions that the Navajo can be associated with this phase.

discoidals   A round stone with slightly concave or flat sides, apparently used in the game of **chunkey** played by Southeastern Indians.

Dismal River phase   A Protohistoric archaeological culture from southern Nebraska, central and western Kansas, and southeastern Colorado thought by many to represent proto-Apache Indians; characterized by garden plots, hunting and gathering, and large villages.

distolateral scraper   A scraper that has a steep working edge on the sides and on the ends.

domestication   The selective breeding of plants and animals to render them more beneficial to humans; domesticated species have been altered by human control of reproduction for generations.

dorsal surface   This term, used in lithic analysis, refers to the outer surface of a flake that prior to detachment was the face of the core.

Dorset tradition   A cultural tradition of the Eastern Arctic between 2500 BP and 800 BP that may have been displaced by the Thule; sea mammals, especially seals, were important for subsistence, and the people used closed-socket harpoon heads, had substantial sod winter houses, and created highly developed portable art.

Driftless area   An area in southwestern Wisconsin and northeastern Iowa that was never glaciated, though glaciers advanced around it at various points in the Ice Age; the topography here is more highly dissected than in surrounding areas.

Dyuktai tradition   A Paleolithic tradition of western Beringia dating from approximately 35,000 BP to 10,500 BP; associated with a bifacial technology generally similar to that of early sites in Alaska.

Early Agricultural period   A term for the Late Archaic in the Southwest that defines the period from the introduction of maize cultivation at approximately 3500 BP to the beginnings of the regional sequences such as Hohokam, determined on the basis of ceramics.

Early Horticultural period   The term sometimes used in New England for the Early and Middle Woodland because there is less distinction between these Woodland subperiods than elsewhere in the Eastern Woodlands; people made limited use of horticulture.

Early period   In the Plateau culture area, this refers to the archaeological period at the Pleistocene–Holocene boundary between approximately 11,500 BP and 8000 BP; Clovis and Old Cordilleran assemblages date to this period; sometimes used in the Chumash area of California (ca. 6800–2500 BP).

earspool   An ornamental earplug, usually a flat and round copper or pottery piece worn in the earlobe, sometimes big enough to stretch the earlobe greatly; common among the **Hopewell** and also the **Mississippians** of the Eastern Woodlands.

earthlodge   A common house structure on the Great Plains, considered a **Plains Village tradition** trait and still built by Historic period tribes; square or circular earth-covered dwelling with post supports and covered entrance passage.

Eastern Agricultural complex   A group of plant cultigens and domesticates of the East first cultivated in the Middle and Late Archaic; included are species of native gourds, marsh elder, chenopodium, sunflower, maygrass, little barley, and erect knotweed.

Eastern Eight-Row corn (also called Northern Flint corn)   A variety of corn developed between 1050 BP and 950 BP; this variety was more cold tolerant than earlier varieties and possibly is responsible for the spread of maize agriculture across the Great Lakes and Northeast.

ecofact   An unmodified natural item, such as part of a plant or animal, that is recovered from an archaeological site and provides information about human interaction with past environments. (See also **artifact**.)

ecotone   A community of plants and animals found at the transition between biomes or other large biotic units; characterized by a mixture of species that may attract predators, including humans.

effigy mounds   Burial mounds whose outline resembles that of an animal or, rarely, a human; these features were most common between 1250 BP and 900 BP in the upper Mississippi River valley and nearby areas; usually found in groups with linear and conical mounds.

Effigy Mound culture An early Late Woodland culture of the upper Misssissippi valley in southern Wisconsin, Iowa, Illinois and Minnesota which is characterized by complexes of effigy and other mounds and dated between approximately 1250 BP and 800 BP.

egalitarian society   A society without marked differences in wealth, power, and prestige; status differences are largely based on age, gender, or an individual's achievements.

electrical resistivity survey   A geophysical technique that measures differences in the way soils transmit an electric current, which may indicate varying retention of water and compactness between subsurface feature and nonfeature areas.

Emergent Mississippian   A term used, particularly in the Midwest, for the period from approximately 1150 BP to 950 BP when the first hints of the **Mississippian tradition** begin to be archaeologically apparent; other scholars include this time in the Late Woodland.

end scraper   A tool with a steep working edge on one end, usually made by unifacial retouch or flaking of part or all of the edge of a flake or core; perhaps most often used to scrape hides.

Environmental Impact Statement (EIS)   A document produced as a result of required assessment of the environmental effects or impacts of a proposed federal project; the impact on cultural as well as natural resources must be assessed.

estuary   A part of a river such as its mouth, a bay, a salt marsh, or a lagoon where the river meets the sea and fresh water is mixed with the salt waters of the ocean tides.

ethnicity   Membership in an ethnic group based in part on the circumstances of one's birth and in part on one's own identification with that group's cultural traits, in contrast to those of other perceived ethnic groups.

ethnoarchaeology   The ethnographic study of living people to learn how material items are used and discarded as the archaeological record is created.

ethnobotanist   A person who investigates how plants are used in various cultures; often ethnobotany is an interdisciplinary subfield within archaeology that identifies and interprets plant remains recovered from archaeological sites.

ethnohistory   A multidisciplinary field allied with archaeology that reconstructs the past history of human groups, especially nonliterate ones, based upon a combination of indigenous or foreign written sources, oral traditions, and linguistic and archaeological data.

evolutionary ecologist   An adherent of the school of thought within the evolutionary sciences that explicitly focuses on the current and historical interactions among species; some archaeologists have adopted this ecological perspective in studying the human past.

experimental archaeology   The controlled reproduction of human activities (e.g., toolmaking, structure building, pottery firing) to understand how archaeological remains were produced and used.

extended burial   A burial in which the deceased has been placed with legs extended and arms to the side; variation in placement of deceased may be culturally significant.

extended family   A family group in which at least three generations are represented in a single household or in closely situated households.

fabric-impressed ceramics   A type of pottery in which fabric has been pressed into the wet clay surface during finishing, either to help meld the coils or to roughen the surface.

Fairchance phase   A Middle Woodland phase of southwestern Pennsylvania between 1900 BP and 1550 BP that participated in the Hopewell Interaction Sphere.

fall line   The boundary between the Piedmont section of the Appalachian Mountain system and the Coastal Plain in the Southeast, often marked by waterfalls as rivers flow toward the ocean.

feather-tempered pottery   Pottery made from clay mixed with feathers; found in **Choris culture** sites in the Alaskan Arctic.

Federal Emergency Relief Administration (FERA)   The first step in the economic relief programs of Franklin Roosevelt established in 1933; its programs included the **Civil Works Administration** programs under which archaeology was done.

fiber-tempered pottery   Pottery made from clay mixed with various plant fibers; the first pottery on the Great Plains and in the Eastern Woodlands often was fiber tempered.

fire-cracked rock (FCR)   Cobbles and other pieces of rock that have been heated to the point of fracturing; common by-products of cooking in open fires and found at many sites.

flexed burial   A burial in which the deceased has been placed on its side with the legs drawn up to the chest and the arms bent; in a fetal position.

flintknapper   A person who flakes or knaps stone by striking it in order to make tools.

flotation   A process by which small **ecofacts** and **artifacts** are collected by suspending or floating the lighter materials in agitated water and collecting the heavier items that fall to the bottom; may be done in a handheld tub or with a machine.

flux   A substance used in the processing of metals; limestone was a common flux that helped remove impurities from iron ore.

focus   In the **Midwestern taxonomic system** as originally proposed, components could be grouped together into a "focus" based on formal similarities; this term is less commonly used today.

foragers   Often treated as a synonym for hunter-gatherer, this term should refer only to hunter-gatherers who live in bands that move as residential units to utilize seasonally and spatially restricted resources; compare **collectors**.

Fort Ancient tradition   A Late Prehistoric cultural tradition of the central Ohio River valley (950–250 BP); these people were settled agricultural, tribal villagers who made shell-tempered pottery with some Mississippian stylistic elements and may have been ancestral Shawnee.

Fort Walton Mississippian   A Mississippian tradition regional development or chiefdom of the Florida panhandle and adjacent areas; **Southeastern Ceremonial complex** involvement and elaborate mound building in the Middle Mississippi period.

Fremont culture   An archaeological tradition with several regional variants of the eastern Great Basin (1600–700 BP) associated with maize agriculture and baskets made through coiling, as well as pithouses and surface architecture.

Fremont dent corn   A drought- and cold-tolerant variety of corn whose kernels become indented at maturity.

frequency seriation   A form of **seriation** and relative dating that orders assemblages by the percentages or frequencies of different artifacts within them based on the idea that artifact styles first will be rare, then more important, and finally will decline in popularity.

Full-fluted horizon   A term used for Paleoindian points with deeply indented bases and lengthy flutes including Folsom, Redstone, Gainey, Barnes and Cumberland varieties; flutes on these points may have been struck by indirect percussion or pressure.

functionalism   A school of thought that sees social phenomena in terms of their function either in integrating society or in meeting the needs of the individuals that make up the society; influenced North American archaeologists in the mid-twentieth century.

Gadsden Purchase   Land purchased by the United States from Mexico in 1854 to assure U.S. possession of practicable railroad routes west; negotiated six years after the end of the Mexican War, this acquisition gave the United States much territory in the Southwest.

galena   A soft blue-gray mineral that was widely traded prehistorically; when galena is crushed, a silver glitter is produced, and the powder can provide a white pigment when oxidized; smelted into lead for shot by Mississippi Valley tribes in the Historic period.

garden hunting   The practice of trapping or otherwise procuring the animals attracted to gardens and fields; for farmers this practice allows the acquisition of meat with relatively little energy expenditure while reducing competition for planted crops.

general theory   The broadest level of archaeological theory that contributes to anthropology; theoretical frameworks that describe and attempt to explain cultural behaviors and processes that operated in the past, as opposed to **middle-range theory**.

geoarchaeologist   An archaeologist also trained in geology who evaluates sediments and stratigraphy to reconstruct the depositional history of a site or other geological questions about a site and its contents; one of the interdisciplinary methods that helps archaeologists reconstruct past environments.

Geographical Information System (GIS)   A computer program designed to retrieve, store, and manipulate geographic information; used to manage and analyze site locations, environmental attributes acquired from maps and images, and distributions within sites.

geophysical prospecting/survey   The use of geophysical techniques to investigate subsurface features without excavation; the most common instruments employed are **ground-penetrating radar (GPR)**, **magnetometers**, and **electrical resistivity survey**.

glacial   The cold part of the warm-and-cold alternation within a major period of glaciation during which ice expands. (See also **interglacial**.)

glacial kame   A mound or ridge that formed when glacial meltwater deposited poorly sorted gravels and sands; often associated with kettle holes.

Glacial Kame Mortuary complex   Late Archaic complex found in the Midwest and Upper Great Lakes and characterized by red ocher burials placed in glacial deposits; also recovered are copper and marine shell artifacts, bone pins and awls, and **birdstones**.

Glades culture   Coastal South Florida societies that were not Mississippian, although they coexisted with this tradition in time; subsistence was based mostly on marine resources including whales, sharks, crabs, rays, sailfish, and marlin.

Glen Meyer complex   An early Late Woodland complex located in southern Ontario that follows the **Princess Point complex** and has figured in arguments about the development of the Ontario Iroquoian tradition.

global positioning system (GPS)   A system of satellites that allows one's position to be calculated with great accuracy by the use of an electronic receiver; used widely by contemporary archaeologists to acquire precise locational information.

glottochronology   A method of linguistic analysis that compares two languages and estimates the time of probable divergence from a common language; somewhat controversial within linguistics but sometimes yields useful additions to archaeological data.

good gray cultures   A label for the Late Woodland of the East that characterizes these cultures as drab in comparison to Middle Woodland and Mississippian; misses the importance of the variable cultural reconfigurations and changes that occurred during this period.

gorget   A large ornament of shell, copper, wood, or stone worn suspended on a cord from the neck.

GPR   See **ground penetrating radar.**

GPS   See **global positioning system.**

graver   A chisel-like tool, often a flake with an edge worked into a sharp point, that can be used to score incisions and grooves in relatively soft material; characteristic of Paleoindian assemblages.

gray literature   Unpublished archaeological reports, most often produced as part of a **CRM** project and submitted in compliance with CRM laws and regulations; these reports often contain important information but are not readily available and the data they contain can't be utilized easily.

Great Basin culture area   The large internally drained area between the Sierra Nevada of eastern California and the Rocky Mountains in which hunter-gatherer lifeways persisted for millennia, ending only after ranching began in the late nineteenth century.

great house   A term used by Southwestern archaeologists for large, multiroom, or multistoried, aboveground structures that are bigger than average in size or in numbers of the individual rooms and kivas; interpreted as having had integrative purposes.

great kiva   An oversized pit structure or kiva in the northern Southwest that archaeologists understand to have had ritual integrative functions at the community level.

Great Salt Lake Fremont   A regional variant of the Fremont culture found around Great Salt Lake and in southern Idaho; lacking in masonry architecture that made heavier use of wild resources than other Fremont variants.

grog-tempered ceramics   Ceramics that have crushed, prefired ceramic pieces mixed with the clay before firing; usually crushed sherds from broken vessels in North America but in some parts of the world such tempering materials are specially fired and crushed.

ground-penetrating radar (GPR)   A geophysical technique that transmits waves of electromagnetic radiation into the ground and records the attributes of the reflected energy, which can reveal subsurface evidence for structures and other features.

Gulf Formational stage   A proposed cultural stage spanning the Late Archaic–Early Woodland boundary in the Southeast's Gulf Coastal Plain; not recognized by most authorities, but makes note of cultural changes that contrast with early forager lifestyles.

Gulf of Maine Archaic tradition   An Archaic tradition of Maine and the Maritime provinces in which ground stone rods, gouges, and adzes predominate; spans 9500 BP to 6000 BP, and its variations are not yet well understood.

Gypsum period   The name for the Middle Archaic in the southwestern Great Basin and Mojave Desert; millingstones as well as projectile points suggest diverse subsistence.

habitat   An area of land with physical characteristics such as minerals, soils, rainfall, and temperature that affect which plants and animals live there; habitats are modified as the plants and animals develop, use resources, deposit waste material, and eventually die.

Hakataya   A term that is essentially synonymous with **Patayan tradition** and refers to the archaeological tradition of the western Southwest after the Archaic.

haplogroup   A related group of alleles or lineage found in **mtDNA** analysis that tends to be inherited as a package; useful for tracing ancestry and relatedness.

haplogroup X   A particular **mtDNA** lineage that is found in roughly 3 percent of modern Native American populations as well as in 4 percent of European populations, raising the hypothesis that some Native Americans have a connection to Caucasian lineages.

haplotype A combination of alleles that are linked and are transmitted together on a chromosome; several haplotypes make up haplogoups and can be used to trace ancestry.

harpoon valve   A part of a composite harpoon head; two valves form a complete head, often with the addition of a stone or metal point or end blade.

Havana Hopewell   Middle Woodland, **Hopewell** culture of the Upper Mississippi River and Illinois River valleys in Illinois and adjacent Missouri and Iowa; known for distinctive zoned incised pottery.

heat treating   The practice of heating chert or flint to temperatures that allow the stone to be more effectively flaked; color changes, sharper edges, increased brittleness, and faster wear may all be results of heat treating.

Helton phase   A Middle–Late Archaic phase found at sites in Illinois and Missouri; characterized by side-notched and stemmed points, carved bone pins, and channel basin metates; there is evidence for exchange of copper, galena, and other artifacts.

heritage tourism   The industry that supports the public presentation of the past through reconstructions of sites, buildings, and events; this kind of tourism is a growing part of the economy in some areas of North America.

heterarchy   A network system in which all the elements share roughly equal positions; contrasts with hierarchies in which positions are unequal and ranked.

historic district A section of a city or landscape that is considered to have historical value because of the quality of the buildings or the significance of activities or events that took place there; historic districts may be defined by local ordinance or state and federal laws for the purpose of protecting historic buildings, sites, and other properties.

Historic period   An archaeological period that begins when written records about the past are available; in North America this is associated with contact with Europeans.

historical archaeology   A branch of archaeology that uses a mixture of archaeological and historical methods to study literate people who made written records; generally exclusive of the archaeology of ancient civilizations such as Roman or Maya.

historical particularism   An anthropological school of thought that saw cultures as unique products of specific historical developments; this approach had a strong influence on archaeologists early in the twentieth century, causing them to focus on **culture history**.

Hohokam tradition   A cultural tradition, based on irrigation farming, that developed in the southern Arizona desert area after approximately 1750 BP and persisted through several phases until at least 500 BP.

Holocene   The geologic epoch beginning at the end of the Pleistocene, or roughly the last 10,000 years; this period of relative warmth may simply be an interglacial, but it is the period of most of the human past in North America.

Hopewell   A Middle Woodland mound-building tradition with two main centers, in Ohio and in Illinois; exchange of artifacts and exotic raw materials throughout the East; large earthwork and mound complexes, but few large habitation sites.

Hopewell Interaction Sphere   The intercultural exchange of raw materials, ritual items, and shared symbolism among Middle Woodland people of the Eastern Woodlands; participation at some level is evident from Florida to Ontario, Kansas to North Carolina.

hopper mortar   A shallow mortar on which a conical basket without a bottom is affixed to contain the ground material.

horizon   As defined by Willey and Phillips (1958), an archaeological unit that links phases based on traits of material culture that appear to have spread widely during a relatively short period of time; compare **tradition**.

hot desert biome   The desert biome of southern California, Arizona, New Mexico, and many parts of northern Mexico, which is very dry and very hot in the summer and dominated by creosote bush.

households   The smallest social units that live together and cooperate economically as a family; inferred by archaeologists from structures, features, and artifacts.

Hunters Home phase   Supposedly the last Middle Woodland Phase in New York, dating between 1150 BP and 950 BP; the validity of this designation is questioned along with the **in situ hypothesis**.

Hunting phase   The archaeological unit defined as following Oak Grove in the Santa Barbara area; mortars and pestles are a part of the inventory, as are projectile points, suggesting a greater emphasis on hunting than in the **Oak Grove phase**.

hydration rim (obsidian)   A thin layer of hydrated rock, visible under polarized light, that builds up on the surface of obsidian after flaking; if environmental factors and type of obsidian are held constant, the thickness of this layer can be a measure of relative age.

Hypsithermal Interval   A Holocene warm climatic episode from about 9000 BP to 2500 BP; may be treated as the eastern equivalent of the Altithermal but more properly the name of a longer warm climatic regime with variable precipitation.

ice creeper   A flat piece of bone or ivory or, in modern times, other material, with pointed projections carved into one side; when strapped to boots, these devices provide traction on ice and snow; made by Dorset and Inuit people of the Arctic.

ice-free corridor   A strip of land east of the Rocky Mountains in Alberta where the Cordilleran and Laurentian ice sheets parted during warmer parts of the Ice Age; thought to have been a possible route for early hunters and game to enter the continental interior.

Illinois Hopewell   The variant of Hopewell culture found in the Illinois River valley; also called Havana Hopewell.

Independence phase   An early variant of the Arctic Small Tool tradition found in northern Greenland (4000–3700 BP); the first documented human occupation this far north.

index fossil   The fossil remains of an organism believed to have existed over a wide area for a relatively short period of time; can be used to correlate strata in terms of their relative age.

Indian Removal Act of 1830   The law by which Congress ordered the removal of Native people east of the Mississippi River to Indian Territory in Oklahoma; rich farmlands were confiscated for Euro-American use despite some Native resistance. (See also **Trail of Tears**.)

indigenous archaeology   Archaeology controlled by indigenous people and consistent with native values and goals.

industrial archaeology   An archaeological subfield that is focused on investigating the nature and development of industry, especially that of the early part of the Industrial Revolution.

in situ   Unmoved from the original position; describing artifacts that are the best candidates for archaeological study because context and association are known.

in situ hypothesis   The proposal that Northern Iroquoian culture originated in the Northeast from earlier cultural traditions; now being questioned based on data that could suggest in-migration into the Northeast.

intaglio   A design or pattern cut into a surface, as when effigy mound builders began by outlining the shape of the mound on the ground surface.

integrity   The condition of particular remains such as structures and features; the extent to which they have been disturbed/modified, which lowers integrity; this term is used widely in the field of historic preservation to help assess the relative importance of remains.

interglacial   The warm phase in the warm-and-cold alternation within a major period of glaciation, during which glaciers shrink in size and thickness. (See also **glacial**.)

Intrusive Mound culture   A Late Woodland archaeological culture of Ohio that postdated the mound-building Hopewell but used the Hopewell mounds to bury their own dead.

Ipiutak culture   Part of the Norton tradition that begins after 2000 BP in north Alaska; lacks pottery but is known for its elaborate art style, which shows some similarities to Siberian art styles.

isolated artifact   A single artifact, unassociated with other artifacts or features, usually recovered from the surface during archaeological survey; usually not considered by itself sufficient evidence of an archaeological site.

isostatic   A term that refers to the pressure equilibrium for layers of the earth's crust that results from gravity, layer thickness, and density; during the Pleistocene the weight of the ice sheets depressed the crust, and following it the crust began rebounding.

isotopic analysis   Analysis of the isotopic ratios preserved in human and animal bone; these chemical signatures left by different foods are an important source of information on the reconstruction of prehistoric diets (See also **$^{12}C/^{13}C$ ratio**.)

Issaquena phase   A Late Middle Woodland phase that dated between 1750 BP and 1450 BP in the lower Mississippi River valley; this phase shows less evidence of Hopewell influence than the preceding Marksville phase.

jacal   A wall construction technique using wooden stakes plastered with mud; can also refer to a building constructed in this manner and roofed with straw.

Jesuit Relations   A collection of texts about New France and its inhabitants written by various Jesuit missionaries in the seventeenth and eighteenth centuries.

Jornada Mogollon   A regional branch of the **Mogollon tradition** found in south central New Mexico, far west Texas, and northern Chihuahua, Mexico (ca. 1750–550 BP).

Kachemak stage/period   The second part of the **Kodiak tradition** (3500–1000 BP) of Pacific Alaska; maritime hunter-gatherers who made both chipped stone and ground slate tools including the *ulu*; some archaeologists consider this a separate tradition, rather than a stage of Kodiak.

Kansas City Hopewell   A Woodland cultural complex that developed in the Missouri River valley north of Kansas City after 2000 BP; pottery similar to Illinois Hopewell pottery in the Midwest; these people built mounds and practiced horticulture.

Katchina cult   A set of Pueblo spiritual beliefs and ritual practices revolving around katchinas, who mediate with the gods; possibly established 500 years ago as Mogollon and Anasazi peoples integrated in the region of the Little Colorado River.

Kayenta Branch Anasazi   A regional branch of Ancestral Pueblo archaeological cultures in northeastern Arizona (ca. 1400–650 BP).

kazigi   A large structure that served both as a ceremonial house and as a men's house among the Eskimo; apparent prehistoric examples come from some Norton tradition sites in the Bering Strait area.

Keith complex   A Late Woodland complex dating between 1350 BP and 1050 BP evident in western Kansas and Nebraska between the Platte and Arkansas rivers; characterized by Scallorn points and cord-roughened, calcite-tempered pottery.

Kennewick skeleton   A 9000-year-old skeleton recovered from the Columbia River near Kennewick, Washington, in 1996 that became the center of a major legal controversy over how **NAGPRA** should be implemented in cases of very old skeletal material.

Kensington stone   A roughly rectangular slab of stone covered in runes found in Kensington, Minnesota, in 1898; originally cited as proof that Viking explorers were in the interior of North America, this object is now considered a fraud of unknown origin.

kettle hole   A depression in the ground formed by the melting of a buried block of ice within deposits left as glaciers retreated; in formerly glaciated areas, these holes often have filled with water and become lakes.

kiva   A room used for ritual purposes by both pre-Columbian and modern Puebloan peoples in the Southwest; generally round and subterranean prehistorically, but modern examples are built aboveground and often are square.

Kodiak tradition   A cultural tradition of Kodiak Island and adjacent areas of Pacific Alaska beginning about 3500 BP; **Takli** and **Kachemak stages**.

Koniag tradition   The archaeological culture of the Late Prehistoric period on Kodiak Island and in adjacent areas that is clearly ancestral to Historic Alutiiq culture; the people were complex maritime hunters of the last thousand years.

La Jolla complex   An archaeological culture of southern California and Baja California that is part of the Millingstone horizon and is found at coastal shell midden sites.

labret   An ornament inserted into an incision in the lower lip or cheek; worn by several different peoples of the Americas.

ladrillo   A flat, fired tile, used for floors and other construction in Spanish colonial settlements.

Lake Agassiz   A proglacial lake formed by the meltwater of the Wisconsin ice sheet in the center of North America; at one time this lake was bigger than all the present-day Great Lakes combined.

Lake Creek focus   A Middle Woodland archaeological complex of the Southern Plains in the Texas and Oklahoma panhandles; shows some contact with Southwestern groups, as evidenced by the presence of Jornada Mogollon brownware.

Lake Forest Archaic   A Middle to Late Archaic archaeological tradition in the Midwest, Upper Great Lakes, and Northeast thought to be associated with adaptations to the transitional or mixed coniferous/deciduous forest; characterized by broad-bladed, side-notched points.

Lake Forest Middle Woodland   One name given to the group of non-Hopewellian Middle Woodland cultures of the northern part of the Upper Great Lakes (e.g., **Laurel**).

Lake Mohave complex   An archaeological complex that includes lozenge-shaped, stemmed points found in the Mojave and Colorado deserts of southeastern California (11,000–9000 BP); an example of the Western Pluvial Lakes tradition.

Late period   The end of the pre-Columbian sequence in the Plateau culture area from 4000 BP to AD 1720; at this time the ethnographic pattern of settlement in large pithouse villages and heavy reliance on salmon developed; sometimes used in the Chumash area of California for the time after about 1000 BP.

Late Prehistoric period   A period sometimes used by archaeologists working in the Great Plains or the Eastern Woodlands to designate cultural groups that appear archaeologically between about 900 or 1000 years ago and the Historic period.

Laurel culture   A Middle Woodland culture of the central Subarctic associated with distinctive coarsely tempered conoidal pots and burial mounds; Hopewell ceramics have been recovered from the mounds.

Laurentian ice sheet   The massive glacier that expanded over much of Canada east of the Rocky Mountains during the Pleistocene; this ice sheet met the Cordilleran during the coldest periods.

law of association   Items found together in the same stratigraphic unit are associated temporally and culturally; although exceptions are possible, this assumption is a useful working hypothesis in archaeology.

law of superposition   Layers of sediment or rock are older than layers above them and younger than those below them unless they have been disturbed by some natural or human process.

League of the Haudenosaunee   The confederacy of the five Iroquois nations in New York, the "people of the longhouse"; apparently established by about 425 BP.

level   A term archaeologists use for the vertical sections of sediment removed in excavation; a level may correspond to a natural or cultural stratum or be an arbitrary thickness.

linguistic anthropology   The study of the structure, history, and diversity of human languages as well as of the relationship between language and other aspects of culture.

Little Ice Age   A period of cold climate that began around 650 BP (AD 1300) and did not end until the middle of the nineteenth century; may be associated with cultural shifts in various parts of North America.

Little Pluvial   A period of increased effective rainfall from about 4000 BP that filled some lakes in the Great Basin.

Llano complex   An alternative name for the **Clovis culture**.

Lochnore phase   An archaeological culture of the Northern Plateau in Canada representing the beginning of the **Plateau Pithouse tradition**; these foragers utilized anadromous fish, lived in pithouses, and may have been the area's first Salishan speakers.

loess   Unconsolidated, wind-deposited sediment composed largely of silt-sized particles apparently derived from reworked glacial outwash deposits; occurs widely in the central part of the North American continent.

longhouse   A long, narrow house often inhabited by multiple families; such structures were made in various ways by different Native American groups, with the wood and bark Iroquoian longhouse of the Northeast being the most famous.

macroband   A group of related hunter-gatherer families who come together seasonally in large camps but disperse into small family bands at other times of the year.

Magnetometer   The geophysical instrument thT measures the earth's magnetic field to identify patterns in intensity and direction that may have resulted from human activities; subsurface features may be detectable in this fashion.

malacologist   A scientist who studies mollusks including snails, which can be particularly sensitive indicators of past environments.

manifest destiny   The opinion common during the nineteenth century that the United States was destined and obligated to expand its territory to the western coast. Displacement of Native populations, often considered inferior, was justified as an inevitable consequence.

Mann focus   A Hopewell culture represented by nearly 100 sites located in southwestern Indiana; named after the large habitation site, the Mann site, and known for high-quality **Hopewell Interaction Sphere** artifacts; the GE Mound is representative.

mano   A handheld grinding stone used with a **metate** to process seeds, nuts, maize, and other items.

Marginella bead   A bead made from the shell of a marine snail belonging to the genus *Marginella*; the presence of these beads in inland sites indicates long-distance exchange from coastal regions.

marine reservoir effect   The difference in radiocarbon content between marine and terrestrial organisms; marine organisms take in radiocarbon from both the atmosphere and the ocean in which they live, and in calculating radiocarbon dates on marine organisms a correction must be made for this effect.

Maritime Archaic tradition   A maritime tradition of the east coast of the Subarctic (7500–3000 BP); elaborate burials are characteristic; the people used ground slate, bone, antler, and ivory tools; Southern Branch extends into the **Northeast culture area** and Northern Branch along the Labrador coast.

Marksville phase   A Hopewell tradition phase dating from approximately 2150 BP to 1750 BP in the lower Mississippi River valley; named after the Marksville earthworks in Louisiana, where ceramics with Hopewell iconography and other Hopewell artifacts were found.

Mast Forest Archaic   Another name for the Middle–Late Archaic **Narrow Point tradition**, which emphasizes the presumed coincidence between this tradition and the oak–hickory deciduous forest of the East; "mast" refers to the nuts produced in this forest.

matrilocal residence   Describing a social norm in which married couples reside with the wife's family; this arrangement is common in societies in which descent is through the female line, or matrilineal.

meat weight estimate   An estimate of how much usable meat is represented by the bone fragments from each animal taxon in a faunal assemblage; potentially useful in determining relative dietary importance of food items.

medicine wheel   A round surface, stone feature, usually with a central stone cairn and spokes emanating from the center; these features, made on the northern Plains from the Archaic to the Late Prehistoric, apparently had ceremonial significance.

Medio period   The period in the Casas Grandes (Paquimé) sequence in which Casas Grandes reached its height (ca. 750–500 BP).

Medieval Warm period   A period of warm climate in the Northern Hemisphere that preceded the **Little Ice Age**, stretching from approximately AD 900-1300.

Medithermal   The third period of Antevs's tripartite scheme for postglacial climate in the West (after 4500 BP) during which climate has been essentially modern in character.

megafauna   The big-game animals that existed during and shortly after the Pleistocene (e.g., the mammoth and the mastodon); there is some debate concerning the role humans played in the extinction of the megafauna.

memorandum of understanding (MOU)   In CRM archaeology, a formal document between government agencies and/or other parties providing a description of each party's responsibilities in managing cultural resources.

Menlo phase   An archaeological culture in the Surprise Valley of northeastern California from approximately 6500 BP to 4500 BP; semisubterranean, multifamily houses suggesting base camps, in contrast to other more mobile Archaic adaptations in the Great Basin.

Mesa Verde Branch Anasazi   A regional branch of Ancestral Pueblo archaeological cultures from the Four Corners area; named after the cluster of famous sites at Mesa Verde in southern Colorado.

mestizo   A term of Spanish origin for people of mixed Native American and European descent.

metate   A flat or shallowly concave stone that serves as the base on which seeds, nuts, maize, and other items are ground with a **mano**.

Métis   An ethnic category for the descendants of aboriginal women and fur traders in Canada; rebelled unsuccessfully against Canadian sovereignty when **Rupert's Land** was annexed in 1870.

microblade   A small, narrow **blade** that is less than 1.2 centimeters (0.5 in.) long, made from **wedge-shaped cores** by means of pressure flaking; diagnostic of early archaeological cultures found in Alaska, western Canada, and northwestern United States, as well as Siberia.

midden   Rubbish or debris resulting from human activities; many permanent sites have specific areas where trash was disposed, and these can be archaeological gold mines because of the **artifacts** and **ecofacts** they contain.

midden ring   A ring of rubbish or occupation debris surrounding structures or other living areas in a site.

Middle Missouri tradition   A second **Plains Village tradition** subdivision centered along the Missouri River in the Dakotas; characterized by earthlodges, mixed horticulture, and bison hunting and exchange networks.

Middle period   In the Plateau culture area, this is the period from approximately 8000 BP to 4000 BP for which various hunting and gathering cultures are known, including some who built pithouses, lived in semisedentary villages and ate large amounts of salmon; sometimes used in the Chumash area of California (ca. 2500–1000 BP).

middle-range theory   Theoretical statements about how specific human behaviors correlate with observed empirical patterns such as in the archaeological record; contrasts with **general theory** about broad cultural processes to which archaeology also contributes.

Middle Tier Middle Woodland   A name sometimes given to non-Hopewellian Middle Woodland groups of the Upper Great Lakes area.

Middlesex complex   A phase designation sometimes used for Early Woodland components with Adena ceremonial objects in the Mid-Atlantic and the Northeast.

midpassage   An area enclosed by parallel rock slab walls in houses otherwise defined by elliptical rings of rock; midpassages apparently served as storage areas for **Independence**, **Pre-Dorset**, and **Dorset** people.

Midwestern taxonomic system   A method of cultural historical classification based on formal similarities and differences in material culture without reference to time and space; developed in the 1930s. (See also **component**, **focus**, **aspect**, **phase**, and **pattern**.)

Millingstone horizon   Coastal southern California sites of Archaic hunter-gatherers contain many millingstones and manos and are interpreted as indicating the addition of seed processing to older foraging lifeways.

minimum number of individuals (MNI)   The lowest number of animals that will account for the collection of bones from an animal taxon; some faunal analysts believe that this statistic provides a better estimate of dietary importance than **NISP**.

Mississippian tradition   The broad archaeological pattern that characterizes much of the Midwest and the Southeast in Late Prehistoric times; variable in nature but associated with platform mounds, agriculture, shell-tempered pottery, and chiefdoms.

mitigation   Measures taken to reduce negative impacts on the natural or cultural environment; in CRM archaeology this can include avoidance but may mean full-scale excavation of a site that otherwise would be destroyed by a construction project. (See also **off-site mitigation**.)

MNI   See **minimum number of individuals**.

Modern period   A term used by archaeologists to refer to the Protohistoric and Historic periods along the Northwest Coast.

Mogollon tradition   An archaeological tradition of the mountainous Southwest in eastern Arizona, southern New Mexico, and the Mexican states of Sonora and Chihuahua after the Archaic; not easily linked with historically known tribes.

moist temperate forest biome   The forest biome of the northern Pacific coast of North America, which receives very high rainfall and is dominated by conifers like hemlock and red cedar.

monolithic axe   An axe made from a single large piece of stone and usually not intended for actual use; associated with the **Southeastern Ceremonial complex** in the Eastern Woodlands.

Monongahela tradition   A Late Prehistoric archaeological tradition of southwestern Pennsylvania; characterized by maize-bean-squash agriculture, shell-tempered pottery, and stockaded villages.

Moorehead Burial complex   A Late Archaic mortuary complex of northern New England once associated with "Red Paint People" because of the use of red ocher in the burials; artifacts and other remains suggest affinities to the Maritime Archaic and the Terminal Archaic.

moraines   The rocks and soil or till carried and deposited by glaciers into mounds or ridges as the ice melts; end or terminal moraines mark the farthest extent of a glacier.

Moresby tradition   An early cultural tradition on the Queen Charlotte Islands in British Columbia (7500–5000 BP); characterized by microblade technology.

mortuary encampment   A special-purpose camp occupied only while rituals associated with cremating, burying, or otherwise processing the dead are conducted.

mound   An artificial pile of dirt or stone that is not the result of natural deposition processes; in pre-Columbian North America, complex mounds of various sizes and shapes were used to bury the dead, to elevate important structures, and to mark territory and ritual spaces.

Mount Mazama   A volcano in the Oregon part of the Cascade Range that erupted between 7000 BP and 6700 BP, leaving a distinctive ash layer in many areas of the West; today Crater Lake is in the collapsed caldera of this volcano.

Mouse Creek phase   A Late Mississippian phase dating from 500 BP to 400 BP (AD 1450–1550) along the Hiwassee River of eastern Tennessee; the Mouse Creeks and Ledford Island sites are representative.

mtDNA   Mitochondrial DNA, found in the mitochondria of a cell; this part of a person's genetic inheritance is an important tool in tracing lineage because it is passed on only through the maternal line.

NAGPRA   Native American Graves Protection and Repatriation Act of 1990; a federal law that requires all public institutions in the United States to inventory and possibly return human remains and culturally sensitive items to the Native American descendants.

Narrow Point tradition   Another name for the **Mast Forest Archaic**, a Middle to Late Archaic archaeological tradition possibly representing adaptation to deciduous forests south of the transition forests of the East; characterized by narrow-bladed and stemmed projectile points.

National Historic Preservation Act (NHPA)   The U.S. act at the center of federal historic preservation policy; set up the **National Register of Historic Places**, and its **Sections 106** and **110** mandate the protection and inventory of cultural resources.

National Register of Historic Places   A list of significant sites, buildings, and historic districts maintained by the secretary of the interior as required by the **National Historic Preservation Act**; these properties are eligible for grants and may be protected from development.

Neanderthal   A hominin that lived during the late Pleistocene in Europe and Southwest Asia; considered by some to be an Archaic form of *Homo sapiens* and by others to be a species separate from modern humans.

Nebo Hill phase   A Late Archaic phase known from the Missouri River valley at the Kansas–Missouri border (4500–2600 BP); characterized by lanceolate points, hilltop sites, fiber-tempered pottery, and some burial mounds suggesting Eastern affinities.

Nenana complex   A blade and biface industry found in the earliest components from sites in central Alaska (12,000–11,000 BP); Chindadn points and other chipped stone tools with general affinities to Paleoindian complexes are found, but no fluted points.

neoevolutionism   An anthropological school of thought based on the idea that human behavior and cultural change are characterized by distinct patterns and mechanisms that can be explained by evolutionary processes; developed by Leslie White.

nephrite   A hard, fibrous semiprecious stone that varies in color from green to white and is a form of jade also called greenstone; used to make adzes and other tools.

Nesikep tradition   An archaeological tradition of the Northern Plateau in British Columbia during the Middle period; the people were foragers to whom hunting of deer and elk apparently was important.

network leadership strategy A hierarchical leadership strategy in which the individual leader has a monopoly on power, dominates lesser vassals, and may acquire and display great wealth; contrast with **corporate leadership strategy**.

New Deal archaeology   Archaeological work done as part of President Franklin Roosevelt's plan to bring economic relief, recovery, and reform to the country during the Great Depression; several major excavations generated large archaeological collections.

NISP   See **number of identified specimens**.

Northeast culture area   The culture area encompassing the northern part of the Eastern Woodlands; divided in this text into the Midwest and the Great Lakes on the one hand and the Northeast proper and the Mid-Atlantic on the other.

Northern Archaic tradition   A cultural tradition that groups together a number of artifact complexes that include side-notched points, large bifaces, various scrapers, and notched pebbles found in the boreal forests of northwestern North America dating from about 6500 BP.

Northern Cordilleran complex   A term used to group materials lacking microblades but containing leaf-shaped points and blades in the western Subarctic between 10,000 BP and 7000 BP. (See also **Nenana complex** and **Old Cordilleran tradition**.)

Northern Flint corn   Another name for **Eastern Eight-Row corn**; probably developed in the Northeast between 1050 BP and 950 BP and perhaps this more cold tolerant form was responsible for the spread of maize agriculture in Late Prehistoric times.

Northern Iroquoian tradition   The cultural tradition associated with Iroquoian language speakers in the interior Northeast; includes the Iroquois tribes of New York and a number of other ethnic groups, which may be best known archaeologically.

Northwest Coast culture area   The narrow culture area that stretches along the coast of the Pacific from northern California to southern Alaska; relatively complex native cultures developed here, with economies based on spawning fish and marine resources.

Northwest Microblade tradition   A term used for early assemblages from the western Subarctic and the Northwest Coast that include microblades; other archaeologists subsume these materials under the **Paleoarctic** or the **Northern Archaic** when notched points are present.

Norton culture   A culture of the western Arctic that developed out of the **Choris culture** and was found from the Alaska Peninsula southward beginning about 2500 BP; check-stamped pottery, stone lamps, caribou hunting, and sealing were characteristic.

Norton tradition   A cultural tradition of the western Arctic from 3000 BP to 1200 BP, including the **Choris**, **Norton**, and **Ipiutak** cultures; stone tools similar to Arctic Small Tool tradition tools, but with ceramics and the oil lamp.

number of identified specimens (NISP)   The count of bone and shell fragments present in a faunal assemblage; comparison of these counts among taxa may be used to determine the nature of past subsistence; compare **minimum number of individuals**.

Numic speakers   People who speak a Numic language such as Shoshone, Paiute, or Ute; historically, Numic speakers occupied nearly the entire Great Basin.

Numic spread   The migration of Numic speakers across the Great Basin; the timing of this migration is much debated, as is the archaeological signature of Numic speakers.

Nunavut   A new Canadian territory created in 1999 in the eastern Arctic as a result of the Nunavut Land Claims Agreement in 1993; Inuit make up 85 percent of the population.

Oak Grove phase   An Archaic group in the Santa Barbara area that emphasized millingstones; followed by the **Hunting phase**.

obsidian   A naturally occurring black volcanic glass that produces some of the sharpest edges known on stone tools; traded over long distances in North America.

Ocean Bay tradition   The earliest maritime tradition along the northern Pacific coast of Alaska (ca. 7000–4500 BP); originally dominated by chipped stone implements, but ground slate tools became common in later traditions.

off-site mitigation   The mitigation of deleterious effects on cultural or other resources involving compensation for resource loss by investigating or protecting resources similar to or more important than those actually being damaged.

Ohio Hopewell   The variant of **Hopewell** found in the southern Ohio center of Hopewell.

Okvik culture   A culture associated with the earliest part of the **Thule tradition**, known for its elaborate art style that emphasizes zoned geometric patterns more than the related **Old Bering Sea culture**; developed on St. Lawrence Island of western Alaska and the Chukchi Peninsula.

Olcott   A term used to group heavily patinated material, generally from surface contexts, found in western Washington State (9000–5000 BP); characterized by leaf-shaped points (Cascade points) and pebble tools; part of the Old Cordilleran tradition.

Old Bering Sea culture   A culture associated with the earliest part of the **Thule tradition**, known for its elaborate art style that is more curvilinear than the related **Okvik** style; found on St. Lawrence Island and adjacent areas, including the Asian coast.

Old Copper culture   A Late Archaic complex of the Midwest and Upper Great Lakes characterized by burials or caches with copper artifacts that were cold-hammered or annealed before working; copper apparently came mostly from deposits along Lake Superior.

Old Cordilleran tradition   An archaeological complex including leaf-shaped points, pebble tools, and blades but lacking microblades found in sites in the Pacific Northwest; sometimes called the **Pebble Tool tradition**. (See also **Northern Cordilleran**.)

Old Women's phase   A Late Prehistoric/Protohistoric archaeological culture found in southern Alberta and Montana; characterized by bison hunting, Plains Side Notched points, and sometimes pottery.

Olivella   A genus of small marine snails from the Pacific Coast; its shells, made into ornaments, were traded into the interior prehistorically and treated as a medium of exchange.

olla   A wide-mouthed vessel with tapered sides used as cooking pot or jar.

Oneota tradition   A Late Prehistoric culture of southern Wisconsin, northern Illinois, Minnesota, and Iowa, with a mixture of Mississippian and Plains Village traits including horticulture and seasonal bison hunting, shell-tempered pottery, and mounds.

one-rod-and-bundle coiling   A type of basket construction in which a single rod is combined with a fibrous bundle (see Figure 8.15). The sewing elements pass through the bundle and wrap around the rod.

opal phytolith   A hard silica body within a plant cell that may remain within sediments after the plant has decayed; distinctive shapes allow identification of the plants that once grew in a locality, contributing to environmental reconstructions.

optically stimulated luminescence (OSL)   A method of measuring age based on time elapsed since the exposure of sediments to sunlight; sediments accumulate ionizing radiation, and optical stimulation causes them to luminesce (i.e., to produce light).

Orient phase   A phase defined for Long Island and the lower Hudson River valley in New York in which Terminal Archaic people heavily used shellfish; Orient Fishtail points are characteristic, as are cemetery burial with red ocher and grave goods.

Oshara tradition   The Archaic tradition (ca. 7450–1550 BP) of the northern Southwest including the Jay, Bajada, San Jose, Armijo, and En Medio phases; the people were foragers who added maize horticulture during the last two phases.

ossuary   A mass human burial in which the bones of many individuals are placed together in a pit or vault; generally cremation has not occurred.

overshot flaking   A difficult technique used extensively in the manufacture of Clovis points that "thins" a biface by removing a flake that travels across the face beyond the midpoint to the opposite edge.

Owasco   The name archaeologists have given to the archaeological sites that apparently precede the development of the Iroquois in New York; the validity of Owasco as a cohesive archaeological taxon has been questioned.

Pacific period   A term for the period after the Archaic on the West Coast, this designation is meant to emphasize the development of complex hunter-gatherers dependent on marine resources.

Packard complex   A Late Paleoindian or very Early Archaic complex on the Plains–Woodland border and including Agate Basin–like Plano points.

packrat midden   An accumulation of food remains and debris left by packrats (*Neotoma* spp.) that may be useful in reconstructing past environments.

paddle-and-anvil technique   A technique of pottery construction in which vessel walls are smoothed and finished by holding a stone or other anvil on the inside and paddling the outer surface into shape.

Paleoamerican   An alternate term for Paleoindian proposed by some researchers to emphasize that the biological continuity long assumed between the first settlers of the Americas and modern Indians may not have existed.

Paleoarctic tradition   A term used for early American traditions in Alaska and some adjacent areas that include microblades, wedge-shaped cores, burins, and bifaces.

Paleocoastal people   An alternative term for the early inhabitants of coastal areas; sometimes used to distinguish such people who depended on ocean and shoreline resources from the big-game hunters evoked by "Paleoindian."

Paleoeskimos   A term used for pre–**Thule tradition** people considered the ancestors of the Inuit in the eastern Arctic; some archaeologists apply the term to the **Arctic Small Tool** and **Dorset traditions**.

Paleoindian period   The beginning of the North American cultural record, which lasts from first settlement to about 10,000 years ago; no longer viewed as a formal Lithic stage, but treated as a period of time within which there was significant cultural variation.

paleolith   The term given to stone tools dated to the Paleolithic period by early North American antiquarians; these objects resembling European Lower Paleolithic tools that probably were later tool **preforms** somehow mixed into deposits of glacial age.

Paleolithic   "The Old Stone Age"; this term is used worldwide to designate the period of cultural evolution from the first stone tools (ca. 2.5 million years ago) to the end of the Pleistocene, approximately 10,000 years ago.

Paleosol   A former soil buried beneath other sediments that formed in association with ancient rather than modern climatic conditions.

Pallisades complex   The earlier of two archaeological complexes of the Northern Archaic as recognized at the Onion Portage site in Alaska; characterized by side-notched points with convex bases and, eventually, notched pebbles (6000–4500 BP).

palynology   The field of study that identifies fossil pollen and uses this information to reconstruct past environments; often an interdisciplinary specialization of importance in archaeology.

Parowan Fremont   A regional variant of the **Fremont culture** found in southwestern Utah and influenced by the **Kayenta Branch Anasazi**; Parowan people lived in settlements with pithouses and surface structures, left distinctive bone artifacts, and practiced maize agriculture.

passenger pigeon   This North American migratory pigeon, killed in great numbers because it was prized by restaurants, had become extinct by the end of the nineteenth century; passenger pigeons once traveled in huge flocks and the species may have had a population as high as 5 billion birds.

Patayan tradition   The archaeological tradition of the western Southwest after the Archaic; a number of regional cultures (e.g., **Cerbat**, **Cohonina**, **Prescott**) have been suggested.

patrilocal residence   A social norm in which married couples reside with the husband's family after marriage; common in societies in which descent is through the male line, or patrilineal.

pattern   In the **Midwestern taxonomic system**, phases were grouped into patterns based on formal attributes in material culture; the term is not used extensively today.

Pauma complex   A term applied to Archaic sites in extreme southern California; sites lack shell middens but have millingstones and a variety of flaked stone items.

Pebble Tool tradition   An alternative name for the **Old Cordilleran tradition** of the Pacific Northwest.

Pecos classification   A cultural sequence encompassing Basketmaker and Anasazi material from the Southwest, devised by Kidder in 1927 at the first Pecos Conference; still used, with modification, today in the northern Southwest.

peneplain   A gently rolling land surface that results from the advanced erosion of mountains; the Piedmont on the eastern side of the Appalachian Mountain system is such a surface.

permafrost   Permanently frozen ground underlying a surface layer that thaws and freezes seasonally; found in the Arctic tundra regions of North America.

phase   An archaeological unit consisting of several components at a number of sites defined by similar artifacts and other characteristics and found in a unique geographical area and time period; phases are thought to loosely represent cultures.

piece plotting   An excavation technique in which the three-dimensional positions of all artifacts and ecofacts are plotted; time-consuming but produces detailed information about context.

pig   In iron making, the name given to the bars of cooled iron (thought to resemble little pigs nursing from their mother's belly) formed in the sand floor in front of the **cast arch**; pig iron contains impurities such as carbon and needs further refinement.

Pinto period   The name given to the Early Archaic period in the southwestern Great Basin; comes from the triangular-bladed Pinto point form and is related to the Pinto tradition in the Southwest.

Pinto tradition   The Archaic tradition of the western Southwest from approximately 8000 BP to 1450 BP; the people were broad-based foragers who made Pinto points, various millingstones, and other tools.

Pioneer period Hohokam   The beginning (1750–1175 BP) of the **Hohokam tradition** sequence in the southern Arizona desert; characterized by wattle and daub houses in shallow pits.

pithouse   A semisubterranean structure built by various areas of North America, the lower walls were earthen or lined with rock while a wooden superstructure supported the upper walls and roof.

Pithouse-to-Pueblo transition   The change in the northern and mountainous Southwest from settlements consisting of pithouses and surface storage rooms to multiroom surface structures; occurs between 1250 BP and 950 BP as people settled into villages.

Plains culture area   The vast culture area encompassing the grasslands of North America's midcontinent that stretch from southern Canada to central Texas; bison hunting was important in this area, although many later groups also farmed in the river valleys.

Plains Village tradition   Plains cultures from about 1150 BP to Historic times in which bison hunting and horticulture were combined by people living in **earthlodge** villages in river valleys; subdivisions are Central, Middle Missouri, and Southern Plains.

Plains Woodland   The term used for cultures that began to develop on the eastern margins and in the river valleys of the Great Plains after 2500 BP as pottery was adopted and, in some cases, horticulture, and burial mounds began to be constructed.

plaiting   A method of weaving in which two or more elements are interwoven; compare **twining** and **coiling**.

Plano complex   A general term for Late Paleoindian on the Great Plains; subsumes a number of phases such as Hell Gap and Agate Basin in which unfluted lanceolate projectile points were made; points of these types sometimes are found farther east.

Plateau culture area   The interior culture area that lies between the Rocky Mountains and the mountain ranges along the Northwest Coast; native hunter-gatherers of this area relied both on salmon in the rivers and on land resources.

Plateau Pithouse tradition   A cultural tradition in the Fraser and Thomas river drainages of the Canadian Plateau that first appeared between 5500 BP and 5000 BP; believed to be associated with the northward migration of Salishan-speaking people who fished for salmon.

platform   The surface that receives the blow in flaking a piece of stone; a platform surface may be prepared or naturally occurring.

platform mounds   A mound that is flat on the top and more or less resembles a truncated pyramid; the **Hohokam** built this type of mound of rubble and refuse, but the platform type of mound is best known from the East, especially among **Mississippians**.

platform pipe   A smoking pipe with the bowl centered on top of a curved or flat platform; may be made in the form of an animal effigy and is diagnostic of the **Hopewell Interaction Sphere** in the Eastern Woodlands (see Figures 11.18 and 11.19).

Pleistocene   The geologic epoch known as the Ice Age lasting from 1.8 million years ago to 10,000 years ago; the earlier part of the Quaternary period during which glaciers alternately expanded and retreated across northern North America and Eurasia.

plow zone   The uppermost soil level composed of soil that has been disturbed by plowing; artifacts found within the plow zone also have been disturbed, making them potentially less significant than items found in undisturbed contexts.

Plum Bayou period   The terminal Late Woodland in the central Mississippi River valley (1250–950 BP); grog-tempered and some shell-tempered ceramics were made, and large towns with mounds were built, suggesting the emergence of Mississippian.

pluvial lakes   Pleistocene lakes that formed in closed basins of the West as a result of locally wetter conditions combined with colder climate worldwide.

pochteca   Long-distance traders of Mexico; sometimes claimed to have traded with North American societies.

Point Peninsula tradition   The Middle Woodland cultural tradition of New York and southern Ontario dating from 2200 BP to 1300 BP; distinct from the Hopewell tradition and possibly ancestral to the development of Iroquoian cultural phenomena in the Northeast.

polyculture   A term that refers to the practice of growing multiple crops together in one plot or field, as in maize-bean-squash agriculture.

Portage complex   The second of two Northern Archaic complexes recognized at the Onion Portage site in Alaska (4500–4400 BP).

positivism   A school of philosophy according to which objective reality can be known through empirical testing of hypotheses; influenced much of modern science, including archaeological **processualism**, but is questioned in the postmodern era.

postmodernist   A person whose philosophical position opposes the emphasis in modern thought on scientific method, stresses that reality is a social construction, and deconstructs totalizing systems of knowledge.

postmold   A hole that at one point held an upright post and now gives a negative impression of it; often the sediments filling the hole can be differentiated from those surrounding it, allowing one to plot the pattern of posts that once existed.

Post pattern   An archaeological complex of California's North Coast Ranges in the vicinity of Borax Lake (12,000–11,000 BP); characterized by Clovis points with single-shouldered points and crescents as well as evidence of generalized foraging.

postprocessualism   A series of theoretical approaches critical of **processualism**, especially its materialist and positivist aspects; stresses the social aspects of interaction in society, especially human agency, and often incorporates Marxist and feminist ideas.

pothunter   A term archaeologists use for individuals who disturb archaeological sites to gain access to artifacts without concern for investigating the culture that produced these artifacts. (See also **relic hunter**.)

Poverty Point tradition   Various Late Archaic sites including the Poverty Point site itself that were located in the lower Mississippi River valley between 3700 BP and 2500 BP spanning the Woodland transition; characterized by extensive trade, earthworks, and stoneworking.

Prairie Peninsula   An area of tail grass prairie habitat intermixed with deciduous forests that extends from the states of Missouri and Iowa into Indiana today; the extent of this Illinoian biotic province has varied with past climatic changes.

Pre-Clovis   Early North American material that is dated prior to the well-documented Clovis culture (11,500–10,800 BP); some archaeologists do not accept the identification of any materials as Pre-Clovis.

Pre-Dorset phase   An eastern Arctic expression of the **Arctic Small Tool tradition** that apparently postdates **Independence** and may be represented by the **Sarqaq culture** in Greenland.

preform   An unhafted **biface** that is roughly shaped but unfinished and unused; suitable for further working or refining into a finished tool.

Prescott   A regional branch of the **Patayan tradition** found in west central Arizona (1100–950 BP).

presidio   A Spanish period military post or garrison.

primary burial   The original interment of an individual; may be only the first step in a complicated burial program; compare **secondary burial**.

Princess Point complex   An early Late Woodland complex (ca. AD 1450–950) of southern Ontario; people grew corn but also fished and utilized other resources and may have relocated seasonally.

prismatic blade   A specialized **blade**, often triangular or trapezoidal in cross section and having several facets or flake scars on the **dorsal surface**; common in Paleoindian lithic assemblages.

probability survey   An archaeological survey in which sample portions of the area of interest are selected based on environmental or other characteristics and surveyed systematically so that the results can be used to estimate overall site distributions.

processualism   An approach to archaeology developed in the 1960s and 1970s that stressed application of the scientific method, took an ecological and systems approach to culture, and sought to explain **culture process**; criticized by the postprocessualists.

projectile point   A bifacial tool that has a haft area and may take a variety of forms; often called an arrowhead, although all projectile points are not used on arrows.

provenance   The region of origin of a raw material such as chert type or shell; also used in collections management in museums to refer to the history of ownership of an artifact or piece of art; compare **provenience**.

provenience   The exact location at which an object is found in an archaeological site; an artifact's location relative to the site's grid system; compare **provenance**.

pueblo   Spanish for town; in the **Pecos classification** Pueblo I–V encompassed the periods in which Southwesterners lived in aboveground, multiroom buildings rather than in pithouses.

quid   A mass of chewed fibers or tobacco; chewed yucca quids have been found in dry caves in the West.

radiocarbon dating   A dating technique that uses the ratio of carbon-14 to the stable carbon isotope carbon-12 as a measure of the amount of time since the death of the organism; must be calibrated to obtain calendar years.

rain shadow   A dry region that is downwind from a mountain barrier; there is little precipitation in this region because moist air masses drop their precipitation on the windward side of the mountain barrier.

rancherias   Dispersed settlements found among Native people in several areas of the Southwest and California during Historic times; contrasts with pre-Columbian nucleated pueblos.

ranked society   A society in which status, power, and access to goods and services is based on an internal system of ranking; rank is often based on the genealogical relationship of an individual or a family to a chief.

reciprocity   Exchange among persons relatively equal in social rank that establishes or reinforces social obligations between the parties.

reconnaissance   A basic form of archaeological survey designed to locate archaeological deposits (or sites) where they were previously unknown may precede more systematic or intensive **archaeological site survey**.

red ocher   A red pigment made by grinding iron-rich rocks like hematite; used around the world by hunter-gatherers and others, often mixed with oil or fat to create paint for decorating the body and numerous inanimate objects.

Red Ocher Mortuary complex   A Late Archaic and Early Woodland complex of the Midwest in which individuals were buried with large amounts of red ocher; characterized by distinctive cache blades and **turkey-tail points**.

Register of Professional Archaeologists (RPA)   An organization of archaeologists who have agreed to certain standards of research performance and ethical conduct. The RPA designation also indicates certain training and experience in archaeology.

relative dating   Determining the chronological age of a specimen based on its relative position in a stratigraphic or typological sequence, without reference to a specific time scale; compare **absolute dating**.

relic hunter   A term sometimes used for individuals who search for artifacts without regard for investigating the culture that produced these artifacts. (See also **pothunter**.)

remote sensing   A general term encompassing a variety of techniques used by archaeologists to locate subsurface features; includes **geophysical survey** techniques and aerial photography.

repatriation   The return of cultural materials and human remains to the country of origin or descendant population; for example, materials from Native American burials now are routinely returned to tribal descendants, who often rebury them.

research design   The plan of an archaeological project, including a statement of the research problem, background information, methods, and timetable; having a research design is good practice in any archaeological research and is required by granting and contracting agencies.

ridged field system   A labor-intensive technique known to have been used by Oneota and Mississippian groups in the East in which fields were raised by mounding the earth into ridges, possibly to reclaim wetlands, prevent frost damage, or control erosion.

Rio Grande Branch Anasazi   A regional branch of Ancestral Pueblo archaeological cultures in the northern Rio Grande valley of New Mexico; population aggregation took place here after the abandonment of much of the northern Southwest around 650 BP.

Riverton culture   A Late Archaic archaeological culture from the valley of the Wabash River, which flows between Illinois and Indiana; characterized by seasonal movements between base and extractive camps and by the use of freshwater mussels, microperforators, and bone and other tools.

ruderal plant   A plant that grows in disturbed land, rubbish, or waste; may be associated with gardens or fields.

Rupert's Land   A Canadian territory from 1670 to 1869 originally owned by the Hudson's Bay Company and named after Prince Rupert, the first governor of the company.

S-twist   A method of making cordage in which the fibers are twisted up to the left producing an S shape in the finished product; if visible on cord-marked pottery or in actual cordage, may be interpretable in terms of ethnicity.

Salado tradition   An enigmatic Late Prehistoric (after 600 BP) tradition in the Southwest associated with Gila polychrome pottery; some believe it represents the migration of new groups into the Hohokam area; others interpret it as indicative of the development of a religious cult.

salvage approach   An approach to archaeology that concentrates on recovery of information from a site that is about to be destroyed; this precursor to **cultural resource management** did not attempt to research questions or to long-term manage cultural resources.

San Dieguito complex   An early archaeological culture of Southern California (ca. 10,000–8500 BP); because of the lack of millingstones and the presence of large leaf-shaped points and knives, San Dieguito is assumed to represent a population of hunters of large game.

San Luis Rey complex   A Late Prehistoric complex found in southern California north of the **Cuyamaca complex** with different kinds and proportions of ceramics; seen as ancestral to the Shoshonean speakers of the area; the people practiced cremation and used small triangular points.

San Rafael Fremont   A regional variant of the **Fremont culture** that developed in southeastern Utah, influenced by the **Kayenta Anasazi**; there are surface storage structures along with pithouses and maize agriculture.

sandal-sole gorget   A gorget that archaeologists think was shaped to resemble the sole of a foot or sandal; made from marine shell often found in Late Archaic burials in the Upper Great Lakes and Midwest; these artifacts are associated with the **Glacial Kame Mortuary complex**.

Santarosae   The large island that connected the Northern Channel Islands off Santa Barbara, California, during the Pleistocene, when the sea level was lowered.

Saratoga Springs period   A time (1500–800 BP) in the southwestern Great Basin when projectile points became smaller, suggesting the introduction of the bow and arrow; as in the preceding Gypsum period, millingstones continued in use.

Sarqaq (Saqqaq) culture   A Greenlandic culture of the later **Arctic Small Tool tradition**; the people were terrestrial and marine hunters who used ground burins and burinlike tools, as well as open-socketed harpoon heads.

scientific method   The systematic investigation of phenomena by identifying a problem, developing hypotheses and test implications, making empirical observations, and reconsidering the original idea in the light of the results obtained.

scientism   The belief that there is only one method of science and that legitimate scientific conclusions can be reached only by using this method.

SECC   See **Southeastern Ceremonial Complex**.

secondary burial   A human interment that has been moved and buried again (see **bundle burial**); can be part of a continuing program of mortuary activity and preceded by **primary burial**.

Section 106   The section of the **National Historic Preservation Act** that requires federal agencies to determine if their undertakings might have any adverse effects on properties eligible for the **National Register of Historic Places**; effects must be mitigated if they are likely to occur.

Section 110   A section first added to the **National Historic Preservation Act** in 1980s amendments, requiring federal agencies to integrate historic preservation into their activities and responsibly manage the historic properties under their jurisdiction.

Sedentary period Hohokam   A subperiod in the **Hohokam tradition** sequence of the southern Arizona desert (975–800 BP); multiroom pueblos were surrounded by compound walls.

Selkirk culture   An archaeological culture of Ontario, Manitoba, and Saskatchewan from about 1050 BP to the Historic period; the people were boreal hunters and fishers, apparently ancestral to the Cree.

selvage   The narrow edge of a woven fabric that runs parallel to the **warp**.

seriation   A method for the relative dating of artifacts based on variations in style and decoration within **assemblages**; uses the theory that artifacts will most closely resemble items that are closest to them in time. (See also **frequency seriation**.)

Sevier Fremont   A regional variant of **Fremont culture** found in west central Utah and adjacent Nevada; characterized by small sites with pithouses and adobe surface rooms, Sevier gray pottery, and use of marshes with less use of maize than found among other Fremont variants.

shaft wrench   A bone tool thought to have been used to straighten arrow or spear shafts; an example is illustrated in Figure 3.16.

Shaman's teeth   A Dorset artifact consisting of a bone mouth with teeth that apparently was clasped in the shaman's mouth during ritual activities.

Shasta aspect   An expression of the Augustine pattern on California's northwest coast; this is a period of semisedentary lowland villages and seasonal upland camps. Artifacts include Gunther Barbed points, **hopper mortars**, **manos** and **metates**,

bifaces of chert, **charmstones,** and spire-lopped *Olivelia* beads.

shell midden   A type of archaeological site formed when people discard large quantities of oyster, clam, mussel, and other bivalve shells as food refuse, along with other trash.

Shell Mound Archaic   A Middle to Late Archaic series of shell middens that have accumulated into mound sites, located in the river valleys of the interior Southeast and the Midwest; shell mounds and rings located along the Atlantic and Gulf coasts and in Florida are sometimes considered related to these interior sites, but for all of them there is debate about how intentional their constructions was and about their possible ritual and intergrative significance.

shell-tempered ceramics   Ceramics in which the paste contains crushed shell inclusions; often considered a marker of **Mississippian** and other **Late Prehistoric** peoples in the Eastern Woodlands.

sherd   A broken piece of a pottery vessel; equivalent terms are potsherd and shard.

Shield Archaic tradition   A hunting and gathering tradition that developed in the boreal woodlands of the eastern Canadian Subarctic after Plano or Late Paleoindian people migrated into the area; persisted into Historic times.

Shoshonean period   Dated to after 800 BP, this period is marked by the presence of Desert Side Notched points and ceramics in the southwestern Great Basin.

shovel-shaped incisor   An incisor in which the lateral borders have a thickening or extension toward the tongue so that in cross section the tooth resembles a shovel; more common among people of Asian descent, including most Native Americans, than among other populations.

shovel test pit (STP)   A small pit excavation into areas in which the surface is obscured by vegetation or when cultural materials are believed to lie buried in sediments; used to find sites or establish the extent of buried deposits.

Sicco-type harpoon head   An open-socket harpoon head with a conspicuous central constriction that is associated with the spread of the Thule people in the Arctic.

side scraper   A tool with a steep working edge on one side, usually made by unifacial retouch or flaking of part or all of the edge of a flake or core.

significant cultural resources   Cultural resources that meet the criteria for being added to the National Register of Historic Places; a site or structure can be deemed significant even it is not actually listed.

Silvernale phase   An Oneota tradition phase (850–650 BP) from the margins of the Mississippi

River at the Wisconsin–Minnesota border; possible Mississippian-derived traits include platform mounds, village fortification, and pottery designs.

Sinagua   A regional farming tradition of the southwest found between Flagstaff and Phoenix, Arizona (ca. 1250–550 BP); this tradition has been variously grouped under other regional traditions but is now best treated separately.

sinkhole   A circular depression in the ground surface that forms when underlying rock such as limestone is dissolved by water and collapses; sinkholes may contain artifacts and other evidence of human activities.

Sinodont   A dental pattern including shovel-shaped incisors, three rooted first lower molars, and other dental traits believed to be characteristic of North Asian populations and Native Americans. (See also **Sundadont**.)

sipapu   A small hole or indentation in the floor of kivas used by the Ancestral Puebloans as well as modern-day Puebloans, symbolizing the portal through which the ancient ancestors first emerged into the present world; may be unaltered or plastered.

skeletal mass allometry   A method of making **meat weight estimates** that uses a formula for converting bone weight to meat weight; the weight of all bones assigned to a taxon is plugged into the formula, and total meat weight for the taxon is estimated.

Skraelings   The name Vikings used for the Native people of North America; considered derogatory.

skreblo   Large Siberian side scrapers often made from cortical flakes; some possible early artifacts from southern California superficially resemble these tools.

slag   A by-product of smelting iron; the impurities that can be drawn off at the cinder notch above the hearth itself, which when cool have a glassy blue-black appearance.

slip   A mixture of clay and water applied to a pottery vessel to obtain a smooth finish.

smoking complex   The group of artifacts, behaviors, and beliefs associated with ritual smoking of tobacco and other substances by the Native peoples of North America; both archaeologically and ethnographically evident.

Solutrean hypothesis   The idea that Upper Paleolithic Solutrean hunters from Europe migrated across the North Atlantic to become the first settlers of North based on similarities in lithic technology and the evidence of Pre-Clovis sites in the East.

Solutrean culture   An Upper **Paleolithic** culture of western Europe dating between 22,000 and 18,000 years ago; famous for finely made leaf-shaped bifaces.

Sonota burial complex   A Plains Middle Woodland burial pattern found along the Missouri River in northern South Dakota and southern North Dakota between 1950 BP and 1500 BP; possibly associated with the **Besant phase**.

Southeast culture area   The culture area that encompasses the southern part of the Eastern Woodlands stretching from East Texas to the Atlantic. Some of the most complex Native American chiefdoms developed among the farmers of this area.

Southeastern Ceremonial complex (SECC)   A widespread Mississippian complex between 800 BP and 600 BP, also called the **Southern cult**; recognized by motifs such as the hand and eye and the sun circle, and by finely made artifacts of stone, shell, and copper.

Southern cult   Another name for the **Southeastern Ceremonial complex (SECC)**.

Southern Plains tradition   A subdivision of the **Plains Village tradition** referring to village people of the Southern Plains in Late Prehistoric times; characterized by horticulture and bison hunting, arrow points, cord-marked pottery, and bone tools.

Southwest culture area   The culture area of the arid West encompassing most of Arizona and New Mexico as well as portions of southern Utah, Colorado, and northern Mexico; farming peoples developed relatively complex polities in this area.

Southwest Regional cult   The idea that the distinctive designs of Gila polychrome pottery that was made in the southern Southwest after 600 BP represent the spread of a pan-ethnic religious ideology associated with fertility and water control.

split-twig figurine   A figurine constructed by splitting willow twigs and wrapping the two half stems around each other to construct an animal; the figure might be pierced with another piece, suggesting use in hunting magic; found in caves in the arid West.

Squawkie Hill phase   A Middle Woodland phase in New York and western Pennsylvania associated with mounds containing central stone tombs and Hopewell Interaction Sphere objects.

state   A politically autonomous form of society with a strong centralized government, a large population, substantial settlements, a stratified class system, and a market economy; states did not develop in pre-Columbian North America.

State Historic Preservation Officer (SHPO)   The government official who has the responsibility for a U.S. state's historic preservation program; usually appointed by the governor.

steatite   A soft stone, also called soapstone, that can be carved into figurines, beads, and vessels or used in **stone boiling**; widely used by North America's pre-Columbian inhabitants.

Steed–Kisker phase   A **Central Plains Village tradition** phase from the Kansas City area in which people made shell-tempered, incised ceramics resembling those of the **Mississippians** farther east; probably a result of contact rather than actual migration.

stone boiling   Heating or cooking by dropping rocks, preheated in a fire, into a pit or basket containing liquid or food to be cooked.

stone box grave   A burial pit lined with stone slabs to form a coffinlike box; occurs in the Late Prehistoric and Mississippian societies of the Eastern Woodlands.

STP   See **shovel test pit**.

stratification   Soil or rock layers laid down in sequence; useful in associating artifacts and establishing **relative dating**.

stratified society   A society in which there are sharp class-based distinctions in wealth, access to resources, prestige, and power; often associated with the state.

stratigraphy   The description and study of stratigraphic layers; may be used to determine **relative dating** among artifacts and features in a site.

stratum   A layer of sediment or rock whose characteristics distinguish it from layers above or below it; generally the bottom strata are older than overlying ones.

Subarctic culture area   The North American culture area that stretches from the tree line southward across the continent; includes most of the Canadian coniferous forests that were inhabited by different groups of Native hunter-gatherers at European contact.

subassemblage   A collection of associated artifacts thought to represent a particular set of activities by a particular group of people; a subset of an **assemblage**.

Sundadont   A dental pattern believed to characterize South Asians but generally lacking among North Asians and Native Americans; shovel-shaped incisors, for example, are rare among sundadonts. (See also **Sinodont**.)

Susquehanna tradition   A Terminal Archaic cultural group of the coastal regions of Northeast and Mid-Atlantic; characterized by soapstone vessels, the broad-bladed Susquehanna point, and possible focus on coastal and riverine resources. (See also **Broadpoint tradition**.)

Swift Creek tradition   A Middle to Late Woodland cultural tradition of northern Florida, southeastern Alabama, and the Georgia Coastal Plain and Piedmont; defined primarily on the basis of complicated stamped pottery from shell middens and mounds.

Takli stage/period   The first of two stages of the **Kodiak tradition** in Pacific Alaska, characterized by slate points, the oil lamp, and chipped stone tools.

Taltheilei tradition   The archaeological tradition of northwestern Canada after 2600 BP; the people were caribou hunters apparently ancestral to the Historic Dené of the area.

Tchula phase   An Early Woodland phase in the central and lower Mississippi River valley, which dates to the third millennium BP; characterized by temperless pottery, sand and **grog-tempered ceramics**, and small, conical burial mounds.

temperate deciduous forest biome   The forest biome of the eastern North America, which stretches south from the coniferous forest to central Florida and contains a variety of communities in which deciduous trees dominate or are mixed with some conifers.

temperate grassland biome   The large area of grassland that spans the midsection of the North American continent from southern Canada to Texas and northeastern Mexico; also includes areas of bunchgrass between the Rocky Mountains and the West Coast.

temporal type   A class of artifacts, like index fossils in paleontology, that are defined by the consistent presence of key attributes and assumed to have been made and used only for a specific period of time.

Tennessee Valley Authority (TVA)   Established as a U.S. government corporation in 1933 to control flooding and create electric power in the Southeast; many archaeological excavations have been associated with resultant instances of site destruction and site management.

tephra   Volcanic ash and other materials that were expelled into the air during the eruption of a volcano and cooled as they were deposited.

tephrochronology   The dating and stratigraphy of volcanic ash layers (e.g., the Mount Mazama ash in the North American West).

Terminal Archaic   The period between approximately 3700 BP and 2700 BP in the Northeast and Mid-Atlantic; characterized by intensive use of riverine and coastal resources, a greater degree of sedentism, steatite bowls, and pottery. (See also **Transitional period**.)

Tertiary   The geologic period that extends from approximately 65 million to 1.8 million years ago when the Quaternary, consisting of the Pleistocene and Holocene epochs, begins.

Three Sisters   In Iroquoian tradition maize, bean, and squash, which are grown together assisting each other; the beans climb the maize stalk while they return nitrogen to the soil and the squash prevents weeds and helps the soil retain moisture.

Thule culture   The Arctic archaeological culture (pre-Inuit) that developed in northwestern Alaska, spread rapidly across the Arctic all the way to Greenland after 1050 BP, and persisted to Historic times.

Thule tradition   The archaeological manifestation of ancestral Inuit cultures in the Arctic, including the **Thule culture** itself; the people were sophisticated sea mammal hunters with an elaborate material inventory.

toggling harpoon   A type of harpoon having a head that detaches from the shaft and turns sideways, or toggles, in the prey animal; used for large sea mammals by the maritime hunters of the North.

tomol   The plank canoe of the **Chumash** of coastal southern California; made from split redwood planks sewn together and caulked to achieve watertightness, these canoes could travel on the rough ocean waters.

tradition   As defined by Willey and Phillips (1958), the archaeological unit that links phases and sites based on general attributes of material culture that persist over a long period; compare **horizon**.

traditional cultural property (TCP)   Place that has special meaning to members of an ethnic group or a community; TCPs may be eligible for the National Register of Historic Places.

Trail of Tears   A name given to the forced relocation of Southeastern Indians as a result of the Indian Removal Act of 1830; specifically the 1838 removal of the Cherokees which resulted in the deaths of many people.

Transitional period   An alternative term for the **Terminal Archaic** (ca. 3700–2700 BP) in the Northeast and Mid-Atlantic, may mark a shift toward more sedentary societies and intensive use of key resources; steatite bowls and pottery are characteristic.

tree line   The edge of the habitat at which trees are capable of growing either in the North or in the high mountains; actually a broad zone in which trees first become sparser and dwarfed and eventually give way to tundra.

trend surface analysis   The statistical procedure that takes the components of a spatially distributed variable and develops a function to highlight the main features of the distribution, making trends and patterns apparent.

Tribal Historic Preservation Officer (THPO)   A designated tribal official with responsibilities for cultural resources on tribal lands parallel to those of a **State Historic Preservation Officer (SHPO)**.

tribe   A social grouping larger than a band that has a steady subsistence base from farming, herding, or a mixed economy but is still largely egalitarian, with social institutions based on kinship and age.

tribelet   A term applied to autonomous cultural groups with hereditary leaders in California; emphasizes the small size of many of the indigenous groups; although independent, tribelets sometimes confederated.

trincheras   Terraces or walls constructed of local stone on a hillside to retain soil and moisture; found in the desert Southwest of the United States and in Mexico.

tumpline   A strap worn across the forehead or the chest to support a load carried on the back; apparently used with large burden baskets.

tundra biome   The treeless Arctic biome that stretches across North America above latitude 57° north.

turkey-tail point   A thin, leaf-shaped point with side notches that results in a small triangular base; points like this are found both in the **Red Ocher Mortuary complex** in the Midwest and in the **Western Idaho Burial complex**.

tuyere   The pipe, often made of copper, that conducted air into the interior of an iron furnace stack so that the fire remained hot.

twining   A method of basketmaking in which two or more elements are twisted around a base element (**warp**) as they are interwoven; compare **plaiting** and **coiling**.

type site   A site that is the first or the best example of a particular cultural taxon (e.g., a phase or tradition); reference to the characteristics of the type site helps define the cultural historical unit.

type specimen   A particular artifact that is the first described or the best example of an artifact type; the formal attributes of the type are based on this artifact's characteristics.

typology   A classification of material objects that systematically sorts items according to morphological, technological, functional, or other attributes; typologies may be used to construct chronologies for a region or site.

Uinta Fremont   A regional variant of the **Fremont culture** that developed in the northeastern part of Utah; characterized by small sites, lack of Utah metates, hunting, gathering, and not a great deal of maize use.

ulu   A semicircular or half-moon shaped knife made and used by various peoples in the North; known archaeologically as early as 6000 years ago in the Maritime Archaic and often made of ground slate; woman's knife among the Inuit of recent times.

umiak   An open boat, with a wooden frame covered by bearded seal or walrus hide; made by Thule and Historic Inuit people.

underwater archaeology   The investigation and study of archaeological deposits, especially shipwrecks, that are located beneath the surface of various bodies of water.

Unfluted horizon   A term used for Late Paleoindian points characterized by various lanceolate, but unfluted points and some notched forms with beveled bases; **Plano complex** points from the Great Plains would be characteristic of this horizon.

uniface   A chipped stone tool that has been worked on only one face or surface.

Upper Mississippian   A term for Late Prehistoric horticultural societies on the northern margins of the Mississippian area (e.g., Oneota) that once were thought to be Mississippian regional variants.

Upper Republican phase   A **Central Plains Village tradition** phase from western Kansas and Nebraska; characterized by square houses, bell-shaped storage pits, horticulture, and bison hunting.

Utah metate   A distinctive type of metate with a troughlike grinding surface and a shelf at one end. This type of metate is associated with the Fremont occupations of the Great Basin.

vacant center model   The proposal that Hopewell mound and earthwork centers were primarily seasonal ceremonial centers that served to cement social relations between dispersed farming hamlets rather than large habitations; the evidence is mixed.

Vacant Quarter   An area in southern Illinois, southern Indiana, northern Kentucky, and central Tennessee centered on the central Mississippi and lower Ohio River valleys, which apparently was depopulated late in prehistory, after 500 BP.

Ventana complex   The artifact assemblage from Ventana Cave in Arizona that seems to have both San Dieguito and Folsom affinities in manufacturing technique; from the Pleistocene–Holocene boundary.

ventilator   The ventilation system of a **pithouse** or **kiva**; ventilator shafts are connected to the main structure by a tunnel that lets in fresh air.

Virgin Branch Anasazi   The branch of the **Ancestral Puebloan tradition** that is located farthest west, found in northern Arizona, southern Utah, and southern Nevada (1450–650 BP).

Wakulla culture   A Late **Weeden Island tradition** manifestation of northwest Florida for which increasing reliance on agriculture can be documented; precedes **Fort Walton Mississippian**.

warp   In basketry and weaving, the elements running lengthwise; compare **weft**.

wedge-shaped core   A type of core or rock nodule commonly flaked in the making of microblades in early North American industries.

Weeden Island tradition   A Late Woodland tradition (1750/1650–950 BP) of southeast Alabama, northern Florida, and southern Georgia; characterized by complicated stamped and check-stamped ceramics, marine adaptations, mounds, and mortuary ceremonialism.

weft   In basketry and weaving, the horizontal elements perpendicular to and interlaced with the **warp**.

Wendover period   The period from 9500 BP to 6000 BP following the Bonneville period in the eastern Great Basin; sites of this period occur in a number of environmental settings and suggest a mobile way of life; millingstones are part of the assemblage.

Western Basin tradition   A Middle Woodland cultural tradition of Northern Ohio, southeastern Michigan, and southwestern Ontario apparently not linked to Hopewell.

Western Clovis   A term sometimes used to refer to fluted points found in the Far West; these points have not been found in kill sites for megafauna, as on the Plains, but have been associated with lake margin sites.

Western Idaho Burial complex   An enigmatic set of burials from western Idaho with unusual artifacts including **turkey-tail points**; large, thin bifaces, and trade items; dated between 6000 BP and 4000 BP.

Western Pluvial Lakes tradition   A tradition suggested by Bedwell for early adaptations around the pluvial lakes of California and the Great Basin at the Pleistocene–Holocene boundary; characterized by stemmed points and crescents. (See also **Western Stemmed Point tradition**.)

Western Stemmed Point tradition   A pre-Archaic, nonfluted point tradition (11,000–7000 BP) in the Great Basin and surrounding areas; characterized by large stemmed points, crescents, and other tools. (See also **Western Pluvial Lakes tradition**.)

wet site   A waterlogged archaeological site; wet sites often contain unusually well-preserved organic materials, such as wood and bone artifacts, as well as food remains.

White method   A method for calculating **meat weight estimates** in which the **MNI** for a taxon is multiplied by an average weight estimate; fails to take into account variability in body size or the possibility that entire carcasses were not utilized.

Whittlesey tradition   A Late Prehistoric cultural tradition of northeastern Ohio (950–300 BP); large, hilltop villages were surrounded by embankments, where the people practiced mixed horticulture and hunting and gathering.

Windmiller pattern   An archaeological culture found in central California, especially the Sacramento Delta, that marks the transition from the Archaic period to the Pacific; characterized by elaborate burials and exploitation of riverine and marsh resources.

Windust phase   An early period archaeological culture from the Snake River area on the Columbia Plateau in Washington State, north central Idaho, and parts of northern Oregon; the people were generalized foragers who made stemmed projectile points and other artifacts.

wing wall   A low wall that often partitions the main chamber of Ancestral Pueblo pithouses; often found in two, nonmeeting segments abutting either side of the main chamber walls.

Wisconsin glaciation   The last major episode of glacial advance in the Pleistocene of North America; from about 100,000 BP to 10,000 BP.

woodhenge   A circular arrangement of posts that may have been used for astronomical observations or for aligning buildings and mounds; more than one of these constructions apparently was built at Cahokia.

Woodland period   A cultural period recognized in areas south of the Subarctic and east of the Rockies in which agriculture, settled villages, pottery, and burial mounds usually were found; usually follows the **Archaic period** and begins 3000 to 2000 years ago.

Works Progress Administration (WPA)   A work program established in 1935 to help ease the Great Depression; the United States government employed American workers and commissioned large-scale archaeological excavations that generated important data. In 1939 the name was changed to Works Projects Administration.

World Heritage Site   A site designated by UNESCO as part of the cultural or natural heritage of all people worldwide; UNESCO maintains a list designed to promote conservation; only eight U.S. and five Canadian properties are listed.

World's Columbian Exposition   The World's Fair held in Chicago in 1893; the exhibits included large archaeological and ethnological collections; millions of Americans visited this fair, stimulating museums to develop collections in these areas.

Yent Ceremonial complex   A Deptford burial mound complex named after the Yent site in northwest Florida; mounds and burials included Middle Woodland exchange or ceremonial items like plummets, copper panpipes, earspools, and shell gorgets.

Younger Dryas A cooler period that interrupted postglacial warming trends beginning at approximately 11,000 BP; thought by some archaeologists to mark significant adaptive changes among Paleoindians.

Z-twist   A method of making cordage in which the fibers are twisted up to the right, producing a Z-shape in the finished product; if visible on cord-marked pottery or actual cordage may be interpretable in terms of ethnicity.

zooarchaeologist   An archaeologist who identifies animal remains from archaeological sites and then investigates their physiology and ecology in relation to cultural activities; this interdisciplinary specialty also is referred to as archaeozoology.

References

Abbott, David R.
2000 *Ceramics and Community Organization Among the Hohokam.* University of Arizona Press, Tucson.

Abbott, David R. (editor)
2003 *Centuries of Decline: The Hohokam Classic Period at Pueblo Grande.* University of Arizona Press, Tucson.

Ackerman, Robert E.
1984 Prehistory of the Asian Eskimo Zone. In *Arctic*, edited by David Damas, pp. 106–118. Handbook of North America Indians, Vol. 5, William C. Sturtevant, general editor, Smithsonian Institution, Washington, D.C.

Ackerman, Robert E.
1996a Spein Mountain. In *American Beginnings: The Prehistory and Palaeoecology of Beringia*, edited by Frederick H. West, pp. 456–460. University of Chicago Press, Chicago.

Ackerman, Robert E.
1996b Ground Hog Bay, Site 2. In *American Beginnings: The Prehistory and Paleoecology of Beringia*, edited by Frederick H. West, pp. 424–430. University of Chicago Press, Chicago.

Ackerman, Robert E.
1996c Lime Hills, Cave 1,. In *American Beginnings: The Prehistory and Palaeoecology of Beringia*, edited by Frederick H. West, pp. 470–477. University of Chicago Press, Chicago.

Acosta, Joseph de
1963 [1604] *The Natural and Moral History of the Indies.* Translated by Edward Grimston. Burt Franklin, New York.

Adair, Mary J.
1988 *Prehistoric Agriculture in the Central Plains.* KU Publications in Anthropology 16. The University of Kansas, Lawrence.

Adair, Mary J.
2003 Great Plains Paleoethnobotany In *People and Plants in Ancient Eastern North America*, edited by Paul E. Minnis, pp. 258–346. Smithsonian Books, Washington, D.C.

Adair, Mary J., and Richard R. Drass
2011 Patterns of Plant Use in the Prehistoric Central and Southern Plains. In *The Subsistence Economies of Indigenous North American Societies*, edited by Bruce D. Smith, pp. 307–352. Smithsonian Institution Scholarly Press, Washington, D.C.

Adams, E. Charles
1991 *The Origin and Development of the Pueblo Katsina Cult.* University of Arizona Press, Tucson.

Adovasio, James M.
1986 Prehistoric Basketry. In *Great Basin*, edited by Warren L. D'Azevedo, pp. 194–205. Handbook of North American Indians, Vol. 11, William C. Sturtevant, general editor, Smithsonian Institution, Washington, D.C.

Adovasio, James M., and William C. Johnson
1981 The Appearance of Cultigens in the Upper Ohio Valley: A View from Meadowcroft Rockshelter. *Pennsylvania Archaeologist* 51:63–80.

Adovasio, James M., with Jake Page
2002 *The First Americans: In Pursuit of Archaeology's Greatest Mystery.* Random House, New York.

Adovasio, James M., and David R. Pedlar
1994 A Tisket, a Tasket: Looking at Numic Speakers Through the "Lens" of a Basket. In *Across the West: Human Populations*, edited by D. B. Madson and D. Rhode, pp. 114–123. University of Utah Press, Salt Lake City.

Adovasio, James M., and David R. Pedlar
2004 Pre-Clovis Sites and Their Implications for Human Occupation Before the Last Glacial Maximum. In *Entering America: Northeast Asia and Beringia Before the Last Glacial Maximum*, edited by D. B. Madsen, pp. 139–158. The University of Utah Press, Salt Lake City.

Adovasio, James, David R. Pedlar, J. Donahue, and Robert Stuckenroath
1999 No Vestige of a Beginning nor Prospect for an End: Two Decades of Debate on Meadowcroft Rockshelter. In *Ice Age People of North America*, edited by Robson Bonnichsen and Karen Turnmire, pp. 416–431. Oregon State University Press for the Center for the Study of the First Americans, Corvallis.

Agenbroad, Larry D., John Johnson, Don Morris, and Thomas W. Stafford.
2003 Mammoths and Humans as Late Pleistocene Contemporaries on Santa Rosa Island, Channel Islands National Park, California. Electronic document, http://iws

.org/CISProceedings/6th_CIS_Proceedings/Agenbroad.pdf, accessed September 15, 2012.

Agger, William A., and Herbert Maschner
2009 Medieval Norse and the Bidirectional Spread of Epidemic Disease Between Europe and Northeastern America: A New Hypothesis. In *The Northern World AD 900–1400*, edited by Herbert Maschner, Owen Mason, and Robert McGhee, pp. 321–337. The University of Utah Press, Salt Lake City.

Ahler, Stanley A. (editor)
2004 *Archaeological Investigations During 2003 at Double Ditch State Historic Site, North Dakota*. Submitted to the State Historical Society of North Dakota, Bismarck.

Ahler, Stanley A., and Marvin Kay (editors)
2007 *Plains Village Archaeology: Bison-Hunting Farmers in the Central and Northern Plains*. University of Utah Press, Salt Lake City.

Ahler, Stanley A., Thomas D. Thiessen, and Michael K. Trimble
1991 *People of the Willows: The Prehistory and Early History of the Hidatso Indians*. University of North Dakota, Grand Forks.

Ahler, Steven R.
1991 Modoc Matting and Beads. *Living Museum* 53 (1):3–6.

Aikens, C. Melvin
1966 *Fremont–Promontory–Plains Relationships, Including a Report of Excavations at Injun Creek and Bear River Number 1 Sites, Northern Utah*. Anthropological Paper 32, University of Utah.

Aikens, C. Melvin
1970 *Hogup Cave*. University of Utah Anthropological Papers 93. University of Utah, Salt Lake City.

Aikens, C. Melvin
1993 *Archaeology of Oregon*. U.S. Department of the Interior, Bureau of Land Management, Oregon State Office, Portland.

Aikens, C. Melvin
1994 Adaptive Strategies and Environmental Change in the Great Basin and Its Peripheries as Determinants in the Migrations of Numic-Speaking Peoples. In *Across the West: Human Population Movement and the Expansion of the Numa*, edited by David B. Madsen and David Rhode,

pp. 35–43. University of Utah Press, Salt Lake City.

Aikens, C. Melvin, and David B. Madsen
1986 Prehistory of the Eastern Area. In *Great Basin*, edited by W. L. D'Azevedo, pp. 149–160. Handbook of North American Indians, Vol. 11, William C. Sturtevant, general editor, Smithsonian Institution, Washington, D.C.

Allen, Rebecca, and Mark Hylkema
2000 *Life Along the Gaudalupe River—An Archaeological and Historical Journey*. Friends of the Guadalupe Rover Parks and Gardens, San Jose.

Allison, James R.
2010 The End of Farming in the "Northern Periphery" of the Southwest. In *Leaving Mesa Verde: Peril and Change in the Thirteenth-Century Southwest*, edited by Timothy A. Kohler, Mark D. Varien, and Aaron M. Wright, pp. 128–155. University of Arizona Press, Tucson.

Altschul, Jeffrey H., and Thomas C. Patterson
2010 Trends in Employment and Training in American Archaeology. In *Voices in American Archaeology*, edited by Wendy Ashmore, Dorothy Lippert, and Barbara J. Mills, pp. 291–316. Society for American Archaeology, Washington, D.C.

Ames, Kenneth M.
1995 Patterns of Technological Variation Among Folsom and Midland Projectile Points. *Plains Anthropologist* 40:23–38.

Ames, Kenneth M.
2000 Review of the Archaeological Data. In *Cultural Affiliation Report*. U.S. National Park Service Center for Cultural Resources. Electronic document, http://www.cr.nps.gov/archeology/kennewick/ames.htm, accessed September 15, 2012.

Ames, Kenneth M., Don E. Dumond, Jerry R. Galm, and Rick Minor
1998 Prehistory of the Southern Plateau. In *Plateau*, edited by Deward E. Walker, Jr., pp. 103–119. Handbook of North American Indians, Vol. 12, William C. Sturtevant, general editor, Smithsonian Institution, Washington, D.C.

Ames, Kenneth M., and Herbert D. G. Maschner
1999 *Peoples of the Northwest Coast: Their Archeology and Prehistory*. Thames and Hudson, London.

Amick, Daniel
1995 Patterns of Technological Variations Among Folsom and Midland Projectile Points. *Plains Anthropologist* 40:23–38.

Amick, Daniel S., and Phillip J. Carr
1996 Changing Strategies of Lithic Technological Organization. In *Early Paleoindian Economies of Eastern North America*, edited by Kenneth E. Sassaman and David G. Anderson, pp. 163–216. JAI Press, Greenwich, Connecticut.

Anderson, David G.
1996 Models of Paleoindian and Early Archaic Settlement in the Lower Southeast. In *The Paleoindian and Early Archaic Southeast*, edited by David G. Anderson, pp. 27–57. University of Alabama Press, Tuscaloosa.

Anderson, David G.
2004 Archaic Mounds and the Archaeology of Southeastern Tribal Societies. In *Signs of Power: The Rise of Complexity in the Southeast*, edited by Jon L. Gibson and Philip J. Carr, pp. 270–299. University of Alabama Press, Tuscaloosa.

Anderson, David G., and Michael K. Faught
1998 The Distribution of Fluted Projectile Points: Update 1998. *Archaeology of Eastern North America* 26:163–187.

Anderson, David G., and Robert C. Mainfort, Jr.
2002 An Introduction to Woodland Archaeology in the Southeast. In *The Woodland Southeast*, edited by David G. Anderson and Robert C. Mainfort, Jr., pp. 1–19. University of Alabama Press, Tuscaloosa.

Anderson, David G., D. Shane Miller, Stephen J. Yerka, J. Christopher Gillam, Erik N. Johanson, Derek T. Anderson, Albert C. Goodyear, and Ashley M. Smallwood
2010 PIDBA (Paleoindian Database of the Americas) 2010: Current Status and Findings. *Archaeology of Eastern North America* 38:63–90.

Anderson, David G., and Kenneth E. Sassaman
1996 *The Paleoindian and Early Archaic Southeast*. University of Alabama Press, Tuscaloosa.

Anderson, David G., and Kenneth E. Sassaman
2004 Early and Middle Holocene Periods, 9500–3750 B.C. In

Southeast, edited by Raymond D. Fogelson, pp. 87–100. Handbook of American Indians, Vol. 14, William C. Sturtevant, general editor, Smithsonian Institution, Washington, D.C.

Anderson, Douglas D.
1968 A Stone Age Campsite at the Gateway to America. *Scientific American* 218 (6):24–33.

Anderson, Douglas D.
1984 Prehistory of North Alaska. In *Arctic*, edited by David Damas, pp. 80–93. Handbook of North American Indians, Vol. 5, William C. Sturtevant, general editor, Smithsonian Institution, Washington, D.C.

Anderson, Douglas D.
2008 Northern Archaic Tradition Forty years Later: Comments. *Arctic Anthropology* 45: 169–178.

Anderson, Duane C., Richard Shutler, Jr., and Wayne M. Wendland
1980 The Cherokee Sewer Site and the Cultures of the Atlantic Climatic Episode. In *The Cherokee Excavations: Holocene Ecology and Human Adaptations in Northwestern Iowa*, edited by Duane C. Anderson, Jr., and Holmes A. Semken, pp. 257–268. Academic Press, New York.

Andrews, R. L., J. M. Adovasio, D. C. Hyland, D. G. Harding, and J. S. Ilingworth
2001 Textiles and Cordage from the Windover Bog (8BR246). In *Enduring Records: The Environmental and Cultural Heritage of Wetlands*, edited by Barbara A. Purdy, pp. 18–37. Oxbow Books, Oxford.

Antevs, Ernst
1948 Climatic Changes and Pre-White Man: The Great Basin with Emphasis on Glacial and Postglacial Times.*Bulletin of the University of Utah* 38 (20):168–191.

Antevs, Ernst
1955 Geologic-Climatic Dating in the West. *American Antiquity* 20 (4, pt. 1):317–335.

Appelt, Martin, and Hans Christian Gulløv
2009 Tunit, Norsemen, and Inuit in Thirteenth-Century Northwest Greenland—Dorset Between the Devil and the Deep Sea. In *The Northern World AD 900–1400*, edited by Herbert Maschner, Owen Mason, and Robert McGhee, pp. 300–320.

The University of Utah Press, Salt Lake City.

Applegate, Darlene, and Robert Mainfort
2005 *Woodland Period Systematics in the Middle Ohio Valley*. University of Alabama Press, Tuscaloosa.

Archaeological Institute of America
2006 Bringing Dark Times to Light. Electronic document, http://www.archaeology.org/online/interviews/burton.html, accessed March 9, 2012.

Archambault, Joallyn
2006 Native Views of Origins. In *Environment, Origins and Population*, edited by D. Ubelaker, pp. 4–15. Handbook of North American Indians, Vol. 3, William C. Sturtevant, general editor, Smithsonian Institution, Washington, D.C.

Arneborg, Jette, and Kristen A. Seaver
2000 From Vikings to Norseman. In *Vikings: The North Atlantic Saga*, edited by William W. Fitzhugh and Elisabeth I. Ward, pp. 281–284. Smithsonian Institution Press, Washington, D.C.

Arnold, C.
2004 Arctic Harpoons. *Arctic* 42 (1):80–82.

Arnold, Jeanne E.
1992 Complex Hunter-Gatherer-Fishers of Prehistoric California: Chiefs, Specialists, and Maritime Adaptations of the Channel Islands. *American Antiquity* 57:60–84.

Arnold, Jeanne E. (editor)
2001 *The Origins of a Pacific Coast Chiefdom: The Chumash of the Channel Islands*. University of Utah Press, Salt Lake City.

Arnold, Jeanne E., and John M. O'Shea
1993 Review of *Evolution of Chumash Society: A Comparative Study of Artifacts Used for Social System Maintenance in the Santa Barbara Channel Region Before A.D. 1804*, by Chester D. King. *American Antiquity* 58:770.

Arnold, Jeanne E., and Michael R. Walsh
2010 *California's Ancient Past: From the Pacific to the Range of Light*. The SAA Press, Washington, D.C.

Arutinov, S. A., and W. W. Fitzhugh
1988 Prehistory of Siberia and the Bering Sea. In *Crossroads of Continents: Cultures of Siberia and Alaska*, edited by W. W. Fitzhugh and A. Crowell,

pp. 117–129. Smithsonian Institution Press, Washington, D.C.

Asch, David L.
1995 Aboriginal Specialty-Plant Propagation: Illinois Prehistory and an Eastern North American Post-Contact Perspective. Ph.D. dissertation, Department of Anthropology, University of Michigan, Ann Arbor.

Asch, David L., and Nancy B. Asch
1985 Prehistoric Plant Cultivation in West-Central Illinois. In *Prehistoric Food Production in North America*, edited by R. Ford, pp. 149–203. Anthropological Paper 75. Museum of Anthropology, University of Michigan, Ann Arbor.

Asch, Nancy B., Richard I. Ford, and David L. Asch
1972 *Paleoethnobotany of the Koster Site*. Report of Investigations 24. Illinois State Museum, Springfield.

Asch Sidell, Nancy
1999 Plant Use in Maine: Paleoindian to Contact Period. In *Current Northeast Paleoethnobotany*, edited by John P. Hart, pp. 191–223. New York State Museum Bulletin 494. University of the State of New York/State Department of Education, Albany.

Asch Sidell, Nancy
2002 Paleobotanical Indicators of Subsistence and Settlement Changes in Northeast. In *Northeast Subsistence and Settlement Change: A.D. 700–1300*. New York State Museum Bulletin 496. University of the State of New York/State Department of Education, Albany.

Ashley, Clifford W.
1944 *The Ashley Book of Knots*. Doubleday, Garden City, New York.

Ashmore, Wendy, Dorothy T. Lippert, and Barbara J. Mills
2010 *Voices in American Archaeology*. The Society for American Archaeology, Washington, D.C.

Association Research, Inc.
2005 Salary Survey. Electronic document, http://www.saa.org/Portals/0/SAA/membership/survey/full.pdf, accessed September 15, 2012.

Atalay, Sonya
2006 Introduction: Decolonizing Archaeology. In 'Decolonizing Archaeology—Efforts to Transform a Discipline.' *American Indian Quarterly* 30 (3):269–279.

Atwater, Caleb
1820 Description of the Antiquities Discovered in the State of Ohio and Other Western States. *Archaeologica Americana: Transactions and Collections of the American Antiquarian* 1:105–267.

Axtell, James
2001 *Natives and Newcomers: The Cultural Origins of North America.* Oxford University Press, New York.

Ayers, Jennifer
1981 Computer Summary of the Hoko River Artifacts. In *Hoko River: A 2500 Year Old Fishing Camp on the Northwest Coast of North America,* edited by Dale R. Croes and Eric Blinman, pp. 152–151. Report of Investigations 58. Washington State University, Laboratory of Anthropology, Pullman.

Bada, J. L., R. A. Schroeder, and G. F. Carter
1974 Evidence for the Antiquity of Man in North America Deduced from Aspartic Acid Racemization. *Science* 184:791–793.

Baker, Victor R.
1983 Late Pleistocene Fluvial Systems. In *Late Quaternary Environments of the United States,* Vol. 1, edited by Stephen C. Porter, pp. 115–129. University of Minnesota Press, Minneapolis.

Bamforth, Douglas B.
2002 The Paleoindian Occupation of the Medicine Creek Drainage, Southwestern Nebraska. In *Medicine Creek: Seventy Years of Archaeological Investigations,* edited by Donna C. Roper, pp. 54–83. University of Alabama Press, Tuscaloosa.

Bamforth, Douglas B.
2006 Climate, Chronology, and the Course of War in the Middle Missouri. In *The Archaeology of Warfare: Prehistories of Raiding and Conquest,* edited by Elizabeth N. Arkush and Mark W. Allen, pp. 66–100. University of Florida Press, Gainesville.

Bamforth, Douglas B.
2007 *The Allen Site: A Paleoindian Camp in Southwestern Nebraska.* University of New Mexico Press, Albuquerque.

Barlow, K. Reese
2002 Predicting Maize Agriculture Among the Fremont: An Economic Comparison of Farming and Foraging in the American Southwest. *American Antiquity* 67:65–88.

Barnosky, Anthony D., Paul L. Koch, Robert S. Feranec, Scott L. Wing, and Alan B. Shabel
2004 Assessing the Causes of Late Pleistocene Extinctions on the Continents. *Science* 306:70–75.

Barton, C. Michael, Geoffrey A. Clark, David R. Yesner, and Georges A. Pearson
2004 *The Settlement of the American Continents: A Multidisciplinary Approach to Human Biogeography.* University of Arizona Press, Tucson.

Barton, C. Michael, Steven Schmich, and Steven R. James
2004 The Ecology of Human Colonization in Pristine Landscapes. In *The Settlement of the American Continents: A Multidisciplinary Approach to Human Biogeography,* edited by C. Michael Barton, Geoffrey A. Clark, David R. Yesner, and Georges A. Pearson, pp. 138–161. University of Arizona Press, Tucson.

Basgall, M. E., and M. C. Hall
2000 Morphological and Temporal Variation in Bifurcate-Stemmed Dart Points of the Western Great Basin. *Journal of California and Great Basin Anthropology* 22:237–276.

Bass, George F.
1996 *Ships and Shipwrecks of the Americas.* Thames and Hudson, London.

Bass, William M.
1964 The Variation in Physical Types of the Prehistoric Plains Indians. *Plains Anthropologist* Memoir 1:65–145.

BBC
2004 Stone Age Columbus [Transcript]. Electronic document, http://www.bbc.co.uk/science/horizon/2002/columbustrans.shtml, accessed April 13, 2012.

Beck, Charlotte, and George T. Jones
2010 Clovis and Western Stemmed: Population Migration and the Meeting of Two Technologies in the Intermontane West. *American Antiquity* 75: 81–116.

Beck, Robin A., Jr.
2003 Consolidation and Hierarchy: Chiefdom Variability in the Mississippian Southeast. *American Antiquity* 68:641–661.

Beckett, Patrick H., and Richard S. MacNeish
1994 Archaic Chihuahua Tradition of South-Central New Mexico and

Chihuahua, Mexico. In *Archaic Hunter-Gatherer Archaeology in the American Southwest,* edited by Bradley J. Vierra, pp. 372–404. Eastern New Mexico University Contributions in Anthropology 13, Portales.

Bedwell, Stephen F.
1973 *Fort Rock Basin: Prehistory and Environment.* University of Oregon Books, Eugene.

Beisaw, April M., and James G. Gibb
2009 *Archaeology of Institutional Life.* University of Alabama Press, Tuscaloosa.

Bell, Robert E., and Robert L. Brooks
2001 Plains Village Tradition: Southern. In *Plains,* edited by Raymond J. De Mallie, pp. 207–221. Handbook of North American Indians, Vol. 13, William C. Sturtevant, general editor, Smithsonian Institution, Washington, D.C.

Bement, L. C., and B. J. Carter
2003 Clovis Bison Hunting at the Jake Bluff Site, NW Oklahoma. *Current Research in the Pleistocene* 20:5–7.

Bement, Leland C., and Brian J. Carter
2010 Jake Bluff: Clovis Bison Hunting on the Southern Plains of North America. *American Antiquity* 75:907–933.

Bender, Susan J. (editor)
2000 A Proposal to Guide Curricular reform for the Twenty-First Century. In *Teaching Archaeology for the Twenty-first Century,* edited by Susan J. Bender and George S. Smith, pp. 29–48. Society for American Archaeology, Washington, D.C.

Bender, Susan J., and George S. Smith (editors)
2000 *Teaching Archaeology in the Twenty-first Century.* Society for American Archaeology, Washington, D.C.

Bendremer, Jeffrey C.
1999 Changing Strategies in the Pre-and Post-Contact Subsistence Systems of Southern New England: Archaeological and Ethnohistorical Evidence. In *Current Northeast Paleoethnobotany,* edited by John P. Hart, pp. 133–155. New York State Museum Bulletin 494. University of the State of New York/State Department of Education, Albany.

Bennett, Matthew R., and Neil F. Glasser
1996 *Glacial Geology: Ice Sheets and Landforms.* John Wiley & Sons, Chichester.

Bennyhoff, James A., and David A. Fredrickson
1994 A Proposed Integrative Taxonomic System for Central California Archaeology. In *Toward a Taxonomic Framework for California Archaeology: Essays by James A. Bennyhoff and David A. Fredrickson*, edited by Richard E. Hughes, pp. 15–74. Contributions of the University of California Research Facility 52.

Bense, Judith A.
1994 *Archaeology of the Southeastern United States: Paleoindian to World War I*. Academic Press, San Diego.

Benson, A. B.
1987 *Kalm's Travels in North America: The English Version of 1770*. Dover, New York.

Bergman, Christopher, John Doershuk, Roger Moeller, Philip LaPorta, and Joseph Schuldenrein
1998 An Introduction to the Early and Middle Archaic Occupations at Sandts Eddy. In *The Archaic Period in Pennsylvania: Hunter-Gatherers of the Early and Middle Holocene Period*, edited by Paul A. Raber, Patricia E. Miller, and Sarah W. Neusius, pp. 45–75. Pennsylvania Historical and Museum Commissions, Harrisburg.

Berkowitz, Peggy
1997 Martin Frobisher's Quest for Gold: A Search for the Northwest Passage Quickly Turned into a Gold Hunt, and a Scandal to Rival Bre-X. *University Affairs* 38 (9). Association of Universities and Colleges of Canada. Electronic document, http://www.civilization.ca/cmc/exhibitions/hist/frobisher/aucc_e.shtml, accessed September 15, 2012.

Bernabo, J. Christopher, and Thompson Webb, III
1977 Changing Patterns in the Holocene Pollen Record of Northeastern North America: A Mapped Summary. *Quaternary Research* 8:64–96.

Bernardini, Wesley
2005 *Hopi Oral Tradition and the Archaeology of Identity*. The University of Arizona Press, Tucson.

Bernick, Katherine
1999 *Lanaak (49 XPA 78), a Wet Site on Baranof Island, Southeastern Alaska. Report of June 1999 Archaeological Investigations, State of Alaska Field Archaeology Permit 99–10*. Alaska Office of History and Archaeology, Division of Parks and Outdoor Recreation, Anchorage.

Bernstein, David
1993 *Prehistoric Subsistence on the Southern New England Coast: The Record from Narragansett Bay*. Academic Press, San Diego.

Bettinger, R. L., J. F. O'Connell, and D. H. Thomas
1991 Projectile Points as Time Markers in the Great Basin. *American Anthropologist* 93:166–173.

Bettinger, Robert L.
1998 Numic Expansion. In *Archaeology of Prehistoric Native America: An Encyclopedia*, edited by Guy Gibbon, pp. 584–592. Garland, New York.

Bettinger, Robert L., and M. A. Baumhoff
1982 Numic Spread: Great Basin Cultures in Competition. *American Antiquity* 47:485–503.

Bever, Michael R.
2006 Too Little, Too Late? The Radiocarbon Chronology of Alaska and the Peopling of the New World. *American Antiquity* 71:595–620.

Biggar, H. P.
1924 *The Voyages of Jacques Cartier*. Public Archives of Canada 11.

Binford, Lewis R.
1962 Archaeology as Anthropology. *American Antiquity* 28 (2):217–225.

Binford, Lewis R.
1978 *Nunamiut Ethnoarchaeology*. Academic Press, New York.

Binford, Lewis R.
1980 Willow Smoke and Dog's Tails: Hunter-Gatherer Settlement Systems and Archaeological Site Formation. *American Antiquity* 45 (1):4–28.

Bining, Arthur Cecil
1973 *Pennsylvania Iron Manufacture in the Eighteenth Century*. Pennsylvania Historical and Museum Commission, Harrisburg.

Binnema, Theodore
2001 *Common and Contested Ground: A Human and Environmental History of the Northwestern Plains*. University of Oklahoma Press, Norman.

Birket-Smith, K.
1959 *The Eskimos*. Methuen, London.

Birmingham, Robert A., and Leslie E. Eisenberg
2000 *Indian Mounds of Wisconsin*. The University of Wisconsin Press, Madison.

Birmingham, Robert A., and Lynne G. Goldstein
2005 *Aztalan: Mysteries of an Ancient Indian Town*. Wisconsin Historical Society Press, Madison.

Blakey, Michael L., and Lesley M. Rankin-Hill
2004 *Skeletal Biology Final Report: African Burial Ground Project. Vol. I–II*. Submitted to U.S. General Services Administration Northeastern and Caribbean Region. Howard University, Washington, D.C. electronic document, http://www.gsa.gov/portal/content/249941, accessed September 16, 2012.

Blanton, Richard E., Gary M. Feinman, Stephen A. Kowalewski, and Peter N. Peregrine
1996 A Dual-Processual Theory for the Evolution of Mesoamerican Civilization. *Current Anthropology* 37:1–14.

Blitz, John H.
1988 Adoption of the Bow in Prehistoric North America. *North American Archaeologist* 9 (2):123–145.

Bloom, Arthur L.
1983 Sea Level and Coastal Morphology of the United States Through the Late Wisconsin Maximum. In *Late Quaternary Environments of the United States*, edited by Herbert E. Wright, Jr., pp. 215–229. University of Minnesota Press, Minneapolis.

Boas, F.
1899 Property Marks of Alaskan Eskimo. *American Anthropologist* 1 (4):601–613.

Boldurian, Anthony T.
2008 Clovis Type-Site, Blackwater Draw, New Mexico: A History, 1929-2009. *North American Archaeologist* 29:65–89.

Boldurian, Anthony T., and John L. Cotter
1999 Clovis Revisited: New Perspectives on Paleoindian Adaptations from Blackwater Draw, New Mexico. *Plains Anthropologist* 36:281–295.

Bolnick, Deborah A., and David Glenn Smith
2007 Migration and Social Structure Among the Hopewell: Evidence from Ancient DNA. *American Antiquity* 72:627–644.

Bonnichsen, Robson, and Karen Turnmire
1999 *Ice Age People of North America*. Oregon State University Press for the Center for the Study of the First Americans, Corvallis.

Borden, Charles E.
1961 *Fraser River Archaeological Project*. Anthropology Papers 1. National Museum of Canada.

Bordes, F., and D. E. Crabtree
1969 The Corbiac Blade Technique and Other Experiments. *Tebiwa* 12 (2):1–21.

Bostwick, Todd W., and Christian E. Downum (editors)
1994 *Archaeology of the Pueblo Grande Platform Mound and Surrounding Features, Vol. 2: Features in the Central Precinct of the Pueblo Grande Community.* Anthropological Paper 1. Pueblo Grande Museum, Phoenix.

Bourque, Bruce J., Steven L. Cox, and Robert A. Lewis
2006 The Archaic Period of the Merrymeeting Bay Region, South Central Maine. In *The Archaic of the Far Northeast*, edited by David Sanger and M. A. P. Renouf, pp. 307–340. The University of Maine Press, Orono.

Bowers, Alfred W.
1950 *Mandan Social and Ceremonial Organization.* University of Chicago Press, Chicago.

Boyer, Jeffrey L., James L. Moore, Steven A. Lakatos, Nancy J. Akins, C. Dean Wilson, and Eric Blinman
2010 Remodeling Immigration: A Northern Rio Grande Perspective on Depopulation, Migration, and Donation-Side Models. In *Leaving Mesa Verde: Peril and Change in the Thirteenth-Century Southwest*, edited by Timothy A. Kohler, Mark D. Varien, and Aaron M. Wright, pp. 285–323. University of Arizona Press, Tucson.

Bozell, John R., Carl R. Falk, and Eileen Johnson
2011 Native American Use of Animals on the North American Great Plains. In *The Subsistence Economies of Indigenous North American Societies*, edited by Bruce D. Smith, pp. 353–385. Smithsonian Institution Scholarly Press, Washington, D.C.

Brackenridge, Henry M.
1814 *Views of Louisiana.* Privately published in Pittsburgh, reprinted 1962. Quadrangle Books, Chicago.

Bradley, Bruce A.
1991 Lithic Technology. In *Prehistoric Hunters of the High Plains*, 2nd ed., edited by G. C. Frison, pp. 369–396. Academic Press, New York.

Bradley, Bruce A.
1995 Clovis Ivory and Bone Tools. In *Le Travail et L'Usage de L'Ivoire au Paléolithique Supérieur*, edited by J. Hahn, M. Menu, Y. Taborin, P. Walter, and F. Widemann. Actes de la Table Ronde, Centro Universitario Europeo per i Beni Culturali, Ravello, Italy. Electronic document, http://www.primtech.net/ivory/ivory.html, accessed September 15, 2012.

Bradley, Bruce, and Dennis Stanford
2004 North Atlantic Ice-Edge Corridor: A Possible Paleolithic Route to the New World. *World Archaeology* 36:459–478.

Braun, David P.
1979 Illinois Hopewell Burial Practices and Social Organization: A Reexamination of the Klunk–Gibson Mound Group. In *Hopewell Archaeology: The Chillicothe Conference*, edited by David S. Brose and N'omi Greber, pp. 66–79. Kent State University Press, Kent, Ohio.

Braun, David P.
1983 Pots as Tools. In *Archaeological Hammers and Theories*, edited by James A. Moore, and Arthur S. Keene, pp. 107–134. Academic Press, New York.

Braun, David P.
1986 Coevolution of Sedentism, Pottery Technology and Horticulture in the Central Midwest, 200 B.C.–A.D. 600. In *Emergent Horticultural Economies of the Eastern Woodlands*, edited by William F. Keegan, pp. 153–181. Occasional Paper 7. Center for Archaeological Investigations, Southern Illinois University at Carbondale.

Braun, E. Lucy
1967 *Deciduous Forests of Eastern North America.* Hafner, New York.

Brecher, K. S., and W. G. Haag
1980 The Poverty Point Octagon: World's Largest Prehistoric Solstice Marker? *Bulletin of the American Astronomical Society* 12:886.

Brennan, Louis A. (editor)
1982 A Compilation of Fluted Points of Eastern North America by Count and Distribution: An AENA Project. *Archaeology of Eastern North America* 10:27–45.

Breternitz, Cory Dale (series editor)
1994 *The Pueblo Grande Project.* 7 vols. Soil Systems Publications in Archaeology 20, Phoenix.

Brewster, Melvin G.
2003 Numu Views of Numu Cultures and History: Cultural Stewardship Issues and a Punown View of Gosiute and Shoshone Archaeology in the Northeast Great Basin. Ph.D. dissertation, University of Oregon.

British Columbia Ministry of Forests, Lands, and Natural Resource Operations
2011 Kwäday Dän Ts'ìnchi. Electronic document, http://www.for.gov.bc.ca/archaeology/kwaday_dan_tsinchi/index.htm, accessed July 23, 2011.

Brody, J. J.
1977 *Mimbres Painted Pottery.* School of American Research, Santa Fe.

Brody, J. J.
1979 Pueblo Fine Arts. In *Southeast*, edited by Alfonso Ortiz, pp. 603–608. Handbook of North American Indians, Vol. 9, William C. Sturtevant, general editor, Smithsonian Institution, Washington, D.C.

Broehm, Cory J., and Troy R. Lovata
2004 Five Corner Tang Bifaces from the Silo Site, 41KA 102, a Late Archaic Mortuary Site in South Texas. *Plains Anthropologist* 49:59–77.

Brooks, Robert L.
1989 Village Farming Societies. In *From Clovis to Comanchero: Archaeological Overview of the Southern Great Plains*, edited by Jack L. Hofman, Robert L. Brooks, Joe S. Hays, Douglas W. Owsley, Richard L. Jantz, Murray K. Marks, and Mary H. Manheim, pp. 71–90. Arkansas Archeological Survey Research 35. Arkansas Archeological Survey, Fayetteville.

Brose, David S.
1994a Archaeological Investigations at the Paleo Crossing Site: A Paleoindian Occupation in Medina County, Ohio. In *The First Discovery of America: Archaeological Evidnece of the the Early Inhabitants of the Ohio Area*, edited by William Dancey, pp. 61–76. Ohio Archaeological Council, Columbus.

Brose, David S.
1994b *The South Park Village Site and the Late Prehistoric Whittlesey Tradition of Northeast Ohio.* Monographs in World Archaeology, Vol. 20. Prehistory Press, Madison.

Brose, David S., C. Wesley Cowan, and Robert C. Mainfort, Jr.
2001 *Societies in Eclipse: Archaeology of the Eastern Woodlands Indians, A.D. 1400–1700.* Smithsonian Institution Press, Washington, D.C.

Brose, David S., and Michael J. Hambacher
1999 Middle Woodland in Northern Michigan. In *Retrieving Michigan's Buried Past: The Archaeology of the Great Lakes State*, edited by John R. Halsey, pp.173–192. Cranbrook Institute of Science, Bulletin 64. Cranbrook Institute of Science, Bloomfield Hills, Michigan.

Broster, John B., and Mark R. Norton
1996 Recent Paleoindian Research in Tennessee. In *The Paleoindian and Early/Archaic Southeast*, edited by David G. Anderson and Kenneth E. Sassaman, pp. 29–57. University of Alabama Press, Tuscaloosa.

Brown, Ian W.
1990 Historic Towns of the Lower Mississippi Valley: An Archaeologist's View. In *Towns and Temples Along the Mississippi*, edited by David H. Dye and Cheryl Anne Cox, pp. 227–238. University of Alabama Press, Tuscaloosa.

Brown, James A.
1985 Long-Term Trends to Sedentism and the Emergence of Complexity in the American Midwest. In *Hunter-Gatherers: The Emergence of Cultural Complexity*, edited by T. Douglas Price and James A. Brown, pp. 201–231. Academic Press, San Diego.

Brown, James A.
1986 Early Ceramics and Culture: A Review of Interpretations. In *Early Woodland Archaeology*, edited by Kenneth B. Farnsworth and Thomas E. Emerson, pp. 598–608. Center for American Archaeology Press, Kampsville, Illinois.

Brown, James A.
1996 *The Spiro Ceremonial Center: The Archaeology of Arkansas Valley Caddoan Culture in Eastern Oklahoma*, Vol. 1. Memoirs of the Museum of Anthropology 29. University of Michigan, Ann Arbor.

Brown, James A.
2006a The Shamanic Element in Hopewellian Period Ritual. In *Recreating Hopewell*, edited by Douglas K. Charles and Jane E. Buikstra, pp. 475–488. University of Florida Press, Gainesville.

Brown, James A.
2006b Where's the Power in Moundbuilding? An Eastern Woodlands Perspective In *Leadership and Polity in Mississippian Society*, edited by Brian M. Butler and Paul D. Welch, pp. 197–213. Occasional Paper No. 33. Center for Archaeological Investigations, Southern Illinois University-Carbondale.

Brown, James A., and John Kelly
2000 Cahokia and the Southeastern Ceremonial Complex. In *Mounds, Modoc, and Mesoamerica:Papers in Honor of Melvin L. Fowler*, edited by Steven R. Ahler, pp. 469–510. Scientific Papers 28. Illinois State Museum, Springfield.

Brown, James A., and Robert F. Sasso
2001 Prelude to History of the Eastern Prairies. In *Societies in Eclipse: Archaeology of the Eastern Woodlands Indians*, edited by C. Wesley Cowan David S. Brose, and Robert C. Mainfort, Jr., pp. 205–228. Smithsonian Institution Press, Washington, D.C.

Brown, James A., and Robert K. Vierra
1983 What Happened in the Middle Archaic? Introduction to an Ecological Approach to Koster Site Archaeology. In *Archaic Hunters and Gatherers in the American Midwest*, edited by James L. Phillips and James A. Brown, pp. 165–195. Academic Press, New York.

Brown, Jennifer S. H.
2001 History of the Canadian Plains Until 1870. In *Plains*, edited byRaymond DeMallie, pp. 300–312. Handbook of North American Indians, Vol. 13, William C. Sturtevant, general editor, Smithsonian Institution, Washington, D.C.

Bruseth, James E., and Toni S. Turner
2005 *From a Watery Grave: The Discovery and Excavation of La Salle's Shipwreck, La Belle*. Texas A&M Press, College Station.

Bryan, A. L., and D. R. Touhy
1999 Prehistory of the Great Basin/Snake River Plain to About 8500 Years Ago. In *Ice Age People of North America* edited by Robson Bonnichsen and Karen Turnmire, pp. 249–263. Oregon State University Press for the Center for the Study of the First Americans, Corvallis.

Bryan, Alan L.
1991 The Fluted Point Tradition in the Americas—One of Several Adaptations to Late Pleistocene American Environments. In *Clovis: Origins and Adaptations*, edited by Robson Bonnichsen and Karen Turnmire, pp. 15–33. Oregon State University Press for the Center for the Study of the First Americans, Corvallis.

Bryson, Reid A., and F. Kenneth Hare
1974 *World Survey of Climatology*. Climates of North America 11. Elsevier Scientific, Amsterdam.

Buchanan, Briggs, Mark Collard, and Kevin Edinborough
2008 Paleoindian Demography and the Extraterrestrial Impact Hypothesis. *Proceedings of the National Academy of the Sciences* 105:11651–11654.

Buikstra, Jane E.
1976 *Hopewell in the Lower Illinois Valley: A Regional Approach to the Study of Human Biological Variability and Prehistoric Behavior*. Scientific Papers 2. Northwestern University Archaeological Program.

Buntin, John
2006 *Land Rush: Inner Cities Are Becoming Hot Places to Live. Does Government Have Any Business Telling Developers to Keep Out?* Electronic document, http://www.governing.com/topics/politics/Land.html, accessed September 15, 2012.

Bush, David R.
1999 Doing Time. *Archaeology* 52 (4):46–51.

Butler, B. Robert
1968 *A Guide to Understanding Idaho Archaeology*. Idaho State University Museum, Pocatello.

Butler, Brian M., and Richard W. Jefferies
1986 Crab Orchard and Early Woodland Culture in the Middle South. In *Early Woodland Archaeology*, edited by Kenneth B. Farnsworth and Thomas E. Emerson, pp. 523–534. Center for American Archaeology Press, Kampsville, Illinois.

Butler, Brian M., and Paul D. Welch (editors)
2006 *Leadership and Polity in Mississippian Society*. Occasional Paper No. 33, Center for Archaeological Investigations, Southern Illinois University, Carbondale.

Butzer, Karl W.
1977 *Geomorphology of the Lower Illinois Valley as a Spatial-Temporal Context for the Koster Archaic Site*. Illinois State Museum, Springfield.

Butzer, Karl W.

1978 Changing Holocene Environments at the Koster Site: A Geoarchaeological Perspective. *American Antiquity* 43:408–413.

Byerly, Ryna M., Judith R. Cooper, David J. Meltzer, Matthew E. Hill, and Jason M. LaBelle

2005 On Bonfire Shelter (Texas) as a Paleoindian Bison Jump: An Assessment Using GIS and Zooarchaeology. *American Antiquity* 70:595–626.

Caldwell, Joseph R.

1958 *Trend and Tradition in the Prehistory of the Eastern United States.* American Anthropological Association Memoir 88.

Cameron, Catherine M., and H. Wolcott Toll

2001 Deciphering the Organization of Production in Chaco Canyon. *American Antiquity* 66 :5–13.

Campbell, Sarah K.

1989 PostColumbian Culture History in the Northern Columbia Plateau: A.D. 1500–1900. Ph.D. dissertation, Department of Anthropology, University of Washington, Seattle.

Cantwell, Anne-Marie, and Diana di Zerega Wall

2001 *Unearthing Gotham: The Archaeology of New York City.* Yale University Press, New Haven, Connecticut.

Carlson, Catherine C.

1988 Where's the Salmon? A Reevaluation of the Role of Anadromous Fisheries in Aboriginal New England. In *Holocene Human Ecology in North America*, edited by George P. Nicholas, pp. 47–80. Plenum Press, New York.

Carlson, David L.

1979 Hunter-Gatherer Mobility Strategies: An Example from the Koster Site in the Lower Illinois Valley. Ph.D. dissertation, Department of Anthropology, Northwestern University, Evanston, Illinois.

Carlson, Roy L.

1990 Cultural Antecedents. In *Northwest Coast*, edited by Wayne Suttles, pp. 60–69. Handbook of North American Indians, Vol. 7, William C. Sturtevant, general editor, Smithsonian Institution, Washington, D.C.

Carlson, Roy L.

1991a Appendix B: Namu Periodization and C-14 Chronology. In *The Economic Prehistory of Namu*, by Aubrey Cannon, pp. 85–95. Publication 4. Department of Archaeology, Simon Fraser University, Burnaby, British Columbia.

Carlson, Roy L.

1991b Clovis from the Perspective of the Ice-Free Corridor. In *Clovis: Origins and Adaptations*, edited by Robson Bonnichsen and Karen Turnmire, pp. 81–90. Oregon State University Press for the Center for the Study of the First Americans, Corvallis.

Carlson, Roy L., and Luke Dalla Bona (editors)

1996 *Early Human Occupations in British Columbia.* University of British Columbia Press, Vancouver.

Carpenter, John P., Guadalupe Sánchez, and María Elisa Villalpando

2005 The Late Archaic/Early Agricultural Period in Sonora, Mexico. In *The Late Archaic Across the Borderlands: From Foraging to Farming*, edited by Bradley J. Vierra, pp. 13–40. University of Texas Press, Austin.

Carr, Kurt W., and James M. Adovasio (editors)

2002a *Ice Age Peoples of Pennsylvania*, Recent Research in Pennsylvania Archaeology 2. Pennsylvania Historical and Museum Commission, Harrisburg.

Carr, Kurt W., and James M. Adovasio

2002b Paleoindians in Pennsylvania. In *Ice Age Peoples of Pennsylvania*, edited by Kurt W. Carr and James M. Adovasio, pp. 1–50. Recent Research in Pennsylvania Archaeology 2. Pennsylvania Historical and Museum Commission, Harrisburg.

Carter, George F.

1978 American Lower Paleolithic. *Anthropological Journal of Canada* 16:2–38.

Cassedy, Daniel, and Paul Webb

1999 New Data on the Chronology of Maize Horticulture in Eastern New York and Southern New England. In *Current Northeast Paleoethnobotany*, edited by John P. Hart, pp. 85–100. New York State Museum Bulletin 494. University of the State of New York/State Department of Education, Albany.

Cassidy, Jim, L. Mark Raab, and Nina Kononenko

2004 Boats, Bones, and Biface Bias: The Early Holocene Mariners of Eel Point, San Clemente Island, California. *American Antiquity* 69:109–130.

Castaneda, Quetzil E., and Christopher N. Matthews (editors)

2008 *Ethnographic Archaeologies: Reflections on Stakeholders and Archaeological Practices.* AltaMira, Lanham, Maryland.

Chance, David H., and Jennifer V. Chance

1985 *Kettle Falls, 1978: Further Archaeological Excavations in Lake Roosevelt.* University of Idaho, Moscow.

Chapman, Carl H.

1980 *The Archaeology of Missouri*, Vol. 2. University of Missouri Press, Columbia.

Chapman, Jefferson

1975 *The Rose Island Site and the Bifurcate Point Tradition.* University of Tennessee, Department of Anthropology, Knoxville.

Chapman, Jefferson

1977 *Archaic Period Research in the Lower Little Tennessee Valley.* University of Tennessee, Department of Anthropology, Knoxville.

Chapman, Jefferson

1985 Archaeology and the Archaic Period in the Southern Ridge and Valley Province. In *Structure and Process in Southeastern Archaeology*, edited by R. S. Dickens and H. T. Ward, pp. 137–153. University of Alabama Press, Tuscaloosa.

Chapman, Jefferson, and Gary Crites

1987 Evidence for Early Maize (*Zea mays*) from the Ice House Bottom Site. *American Antiquity* 52:352–354.

Chapman, Jefferson, and Patty Jo Watson

1993 The Archaic Period and the Flotation Revolution. In *Foraging and Farming*, edited by Margaret Scarry, pp. 27–38. Plenum Press, New York.

Charles, Douglas K.

1995 Diachronic Regional Social Dynamics: Mortuary Sites in the Illinois Valley/American Bottom Region. In *Approaches to Mortuary Analysis*, edited by Lane Anderson Beck, pp. 77–99. Plenum Press, New York.

Charles, Douglas K., and Jane E. Buikstra

1983 Archaic Mortuary Sites in the Central Mississippi Drainage: Distribution, Structure, and Behavioral Implications. In *Archaic*

Hunters and Gatherers in the American Midwest, edited by James L. Phillips and James A. Brown, pp. 117–145. Academic Press, New York.

Charles, Douglas K., and Jane E. Buikstra (editors)
2006 *Recreating Hopewell*. University Press of Florida, Gainesville.

Chartkoff, Joseph L., and Kerry Kona Chartkoff'
1984 *The Archaeology of California*. Stanford University Press, Stanford, California.

Chatters, James C.
1998 Environment. In *Environment*, edited by Deward E. Walker, Jr., pp. 29–48. Handbook of North American Indians, Vol. 12, William C. Sturtevant, general editor, Smithsonian Institution, Washington, D.C.

Chatters, James C., and David L. Pokotylo
1998 Prehistory: Introduction. In *Plateau*, edited by Deward E. Walker, Jr., pp. 73–80. Handbook of North American Indians, Vol. 12, William C. Sturtevant, general editor, Smithsonian Institution, Washington, D.C.

Cheney, T. A.
1859 Ancient Monuments in Western New York. In *New York State Museum 13th Annual Report*, pp. 37–52. New York State Department of Education, Albany.

Childers, W. Morlin
1974 Preliminary Report on the Yuha Burial, California. *Anthropological Journal of Canada* 12 (1):2–9.

Chilton, Elizabeth S.
1996 *Embodiments of Choice: Native American Ceramic Diversity in the New England Interior*. Unpublished Ph.D. dissertation, University of Massachusetts, Amherst.

Chilton, Elizabeth S.
1999 Mobile Farmers of Pre-Contact Southern New England: The Archaeological and Ethnohistorical Evidence. In *Current Northeast Paleoethnobotany*, edited by John P. Hart, pp. 157–176. New York State Museum Bulletin 494. University of the State of New York/State Department of Education, Albany.

Chilton, Elizabeth S.
2002 "Towns They Have None": Diverse Subsistence and Settlement Strategies in Native New England. In *Northeast Subsistence-Settlement Change, A.D.*

700–1300, edited by John P. Hart and Christina B. Rieth, pp. 289–300. New York State Museum Bulletin 496. University of the State of New York/State Department of Education, Albany.

Chilton, Elizabeth S.
2004 Beyond "Big": Gender, Age, and Subsistence Diversity in Paleoindian Societies. In *The Settlement of the American Continents: A Multidisciplinary Approach to Human Biogeography*, edited by Geoffrey A. Clark, C. Michael Barton, David R. Yesner, and Georges A. Pearson, pp. 131–161. University of Arizona Press, Tucson.

Chilton, Elizabeth S.
2005 Farming and Sociocomplexity in the Northeast. In *North American Archaeology*, edited by Timothy R. Pauketat and Diana DiPaolo Loren, pp. 138-160. Blackwell Publishing, Malden, Massachusetts.

Churchill, S. E.
1993 Weapon Technology, Prey Size Selection, and Hunting Methods in Modern Hunter-Gatherers: Implications for Hunting in the Paleolithic and Mesolithic. In *Hunting and Animal Exploitation in the Late Paleolithic and Mesolithic of Eurasia*, edited by H. M. Bricker G. L. Peterkin, and P. Mellars, pp. 11–24. Archaeological Paper 4. American Anthropological Association.

Cinq-Mars, J., and Richard E. Morlan
1999 Bluefish Caves and Old Crow Basin: A New Rapport. In *Ice Age People of North America*, edited by Bonnichsen and Karen Turnmire, pp. 200–212. Oregon State University Press for the Center for the Study of the First Americans, Corvallis.

Claassen, Cheryl P. (editor)
1995 *Dogan Point: A Shell Matrix Site in the Lower Hudson Valley*. Occasional Publications in Northeastern Archaeology 14. Archaeological Services, Bethlehem, Connecticut.

Claassen, Cheryl P.
1996 A Consideration of the Social Organization of the Shell Mound Archaic. In *Archaeology of the Mid-Holocene Southeast*, edited by Kenneth E. Sassaman and David G. Anderson, pp. 235–258. University Press of Florida, Gainesville.

Clark, A. J.
1990 *Seeing Beneath the Soil*. Batsford, London.

Clark, Donald W.
1979 *Ocean Bay: An Early North Pacific Maritime Culture*. Mercury Series, Paper 86, Archaeological Survey of Canada. National Museum of Man, Ottawa.

Clark, Donald W.
1982 Example of Technological Change in Prehistory: The Origin of a Regional Ground Slate Industry in South-Central Coastal Alaska. *Arctic Anthropology* 19 (1):102–126.

Clark, Donald W.
1984 Prehistory of the Pacific Eskimo Region. In *Arctic*, edited by David Damas, pp. 136–148. Handbook of American Indians, Vol. 5, William C. Sturtevant, general editor, Smithsonian Institution, Washington, D.C.

Clark, Donald W.
1991 The Northern (Alaska–Yukon) Fluted Points. In *Clovis: Origins and Adaptations*, edited by Robson Bonnichsen and Karen Turnmire, pp. 35–48. Oregon State University Press for the Center for the Study of the First Americans, Corvallis.

Clark, Donald W.
1996 The Old Kiavak Site, Kodiak Island, Alaska, and the Early Kachemak Phase. *Arctic* 49 (3):211–227.

Clark, Donald W.
1998 Northwest Microblade Tradition. In *Archaeology of Prehistoric Native America: An Encyclopedia*, edited by Guy Gibbon, pp. 584–585. Garland, New York.

Clark, James A., and Richard T. Will
2006 Intersite Comparisons of Archaic Period Stone Artifacts: The Clark I Site and the Gulf of Maine Archaic Tradition. In *The Archaic of the Far Northeast*, edited by David Sanger and M. A. P. Renouf, pp. 285–306. The University of Maine Press, Orono.

Clausen, C. J., A. D. Cohen, C. Emiliani, J. A. Holman, and J. J. Stipp
1979 Little Salt Spring, Florida: A Unique Underwater Site. *Science* 203:609–614.

Cleveland, Gregory C.
1977 Experimental Replication of Butchered Artiodactyla Bone with Special Reference to Archaeological Features at 45 FR 5. In *Preliminary Archeological Investigations at the Miller Site, Strawberry Island, 1976: A Late Prehistoric Village near Burbank, Franklin County, Washington,*

edited by J. Jeffrey Flenniken Gregory C. Cleveland, David R. Huelsbeck, Robert Mierendorf, Stephan Samuels, and Fekri Hassan, pp. 30–48. Washington Archaeological Research Center Project Report 46.

Cleveland, Gregory C.
1978a Introduction. In *Annual Interim Report on the Archaeological Investigations at the Miller Site (45 FR 5) on Strawberry Island (1977), a Late Prehistoric Village near Burbank, Washington*, edited by Gregory C. Cleveland, pp. 1–10. Washington Archaeological Research Center Project Report 72.

Cleveland, Gregory C.
1978b Some Inferences About Patterned Behavioral Activities Influencing the Distribution of Artifacts and Their Soil Matrices. In *Second Annual Interim Report on the Archaeological Investigations at the Miller Site (45 FR 5) on Strawberry Island (1977), a Late Prehistoric Village near Burbank, Washington*, edited by Gregory C. Cleveland, pp. 31–60. Washington Archaeological Research Center Project Report 72.

Cleveland, Gregory, Bruce Cochran, Judith Giniger, and Hallett Hammatt
1976 *Archaeological Reconnaissance on the Mid-Columbia and Lower Snake River Reservoirs for the Walla Walla District Army Corps of Engineers.* Washington State Archaeological Research Center Project Report 27.

Cleveland, Gregory, J. Jeffrey Flenniken, David R. Huelsbeck, Robert Mierendorf, Stephan Samuels, and Fekri Hassan
1977 *Preliminary Archeological Investigations at the Miller Site, Strawberry Island, 1976: A Late Prehistoric Village near Burbank, Franklin County, Washington.* Washington Archaeological Research Center Project Report 46.

Cobb, Charles R.
2000 *Quarry to Cornfield: The Political Economy of Mississippian Hoe Production.* University of Alabama Press, Tuscaloosa.

Cobb, Charles R.
2003 Mississippian Chiefdoms: How Complex? *Annual Review of Anthropology* 32:63–84.

Cobb, Charles R., and Brian M. Butler
2002 The Vacant Quarter Revisited: Late Mississippian Abandonment

of the Lower Ohio Valley. *American Antiquity* 67 (4):625–641.

Cobb, R. M.
1987 *A Speleoarchaeological Reconnaissance of the Pickwick Basin in Colbert and Lauderdale Counties of Alabama.* Alabama State Museum of Natural History, University of Alabama. Tuscaloosa.

Cobb, R. M., B. N. Driskell, and S. C. Meeks
1995 Speleoarchaeological Reconnaissance and Test Excavations in the Pickwick Basin. In *Cultural Resources in the Pickwick Reservoir*, by C. C. Meyer, pp. 219–261. Report of Investigations 75. Report submitted to the Tennessee Valley Authority, Norris, by the Division of Archaeology, Alabama Museum of Natural History, University of Alabama, Tuscaloosa.

Cochran, Donald R.
1996 The Adena/Hopewell Convergence in East Central Indiana. In *A View from the Core: A Synthesis of Ohio Hopewell Archaeology*, edited by Paul J. Pacheco, pp. 36–52. Ohio Archaeological Council, Columbus.

Coe, Joffre L.
1964 The Formative Cultures of the Carolina Piedmont. *Transactions of the American Philosophical Society* 54 (5).

Cole, Douglas, and David Darling
1990 History of the Early Period. In *Northwest Coast*, edited by Wayne Suttles, pp. 119–134. Handbook of North American Indians, Vol. 7, William C. Sturtevant, general editor, Smithsonian Institution, Washington, D.C.

Collins, H. B.
1937 *The Archaeology of St. Lawrence Island, Alaska.* Smithsonian Miscellaneous Collections 96 (1). Smithsonian Institution, Washington, D.C.

Collins, Michael B.
1999 *Clovis Blade Technology: A Comparative Study of the Kevin Davis Cache, Texas.* University of Texas Press, Austin.

Collins, Michael B.
2005 Comparing Clovis and the Western European Upper Paleolithic: What Are the Rules of Evidence? In *Paleoamerican Origins: Beyond Clovis*, edited by Robson Bonnichsen, Bradley T.

Lepper, Dennis Stanford, and Michael R. Waters, pp. 43–50. Center of the Study of the First Americans, College Station, Texas.

Collins, Michael B.
2007 Discerning Clovis Subsistence from Stone Artifacts and Site Distributions. In *Foragers of the Terminal Pleistocene in North America*, edited by Renee B. Walker and Boyce N. Driskell, pp. 59-87. University of Nebraska Press, Lincoln.

Coltrain, Joan Brenner, Joel C. Janetski, and Shawn W. Carlyle
2007 The Stable- and Radio-Isotope Chemistry of Western Basketmaker Burials: Implications for Early Puebloan Diets and Origins. *American Antiquity:* 72: 301–321.

Colwell-Chanthaphonh, Chip, and T. J. Ferguson
2006 Memory Pieces and Footprints: Multivocality and the Meanings of Ancient Times and Ancestral Places Among the Zuni and Hopi. *American Anthropologist* 108 (1):148–162.

Colwell-Chanthaphonh, Chip, and T. J. Ferguson (editors)
2007 *Collaboration in Archaeological Practice: Engaging Descendant Communities.* AltaMira Press, Lanham, Maryland.

Conklin, Carlton S.
1962 The Dewey Knoll Site at Ripley, New York. Manuscript on file, New York State Museum, Albany.

Conklin, Carlton S.
1989 The Dewey Knoll Site at Ripley, New York. *The Iroquoian* 16:3–29.

Connolly, Thomas, Jon M. Erlandson, and Susan Norris
1995 Early Holocene Basketry from Daisy Cave, San Miguel Island, California. *American Antiquity* 60:309–318.

Cook, Sherburne F.
1976 *The Indian Population of New England in the Seventeenth Century.* University of California Press, Berkeley.

Cook, Thomas Genn
1976a Broadpoint: Culture, Phase, Horizon, Tradition or Knife? *Journal of Anthropological Research* 32:337–357.

Cook, Thomas Genn
1976b *Koster: An Artifact Analysis of Two Archaic Phases in West-Central Illinois.*

Northwestern University, Evanston, Illinois.

Cordell, Linda
1997 *Archaeology of the Southwest*, 2nd ed. Academic Press, San Diego.

Cornelison, John E., Jr.
2000 The Archaeology of Retreat: Systematic Metal Detector Survey and Information System Analysis of the Battle of Chickamauga. In *Archaeological Perspectives on the American Civil War*, edited by Clarence R. Geier and Stephen R. Potter, pp. 289–304. University Press of Florida, Gainesville.

Corr, Lorna T., Michael P. Richards, Susan Jim, Stanley H. Ambrose, Alexander Mackie, Owen Beattie, and Richard P. Evershed
2008 Probing Dietary Change of the Kwädäy Dän Ts'ìnchì Individual, an Ancient Glacier Gody from British Columbia: I. Complementary Use of Marine Lipid Biomarker and Carbon Isotope Signatures as Novel Indicators of a Marine Diet. *Journal of Archaeological Science* 35 (8):2102–2110.

Costello, Julia G., and David Hornbeck
1989 Alta California: An Overview. In *Columbian Consequences, Vol. 1: Archaeological and Historical Perspectives on the Spanish Borderlands West*, edited by David H. Thomas, pp. 303–331. Smithsonian Institution Press, Washington, D.C.

Cotter, J. L.
1937 *The Occurrence of Flints and Extinct Animals in Pluvial Deposits near Clovis, New Mexico*. Philadelphia Academy of Natural Sciences, Philadelphia.

Cotter, J. L.
1994 Foreword. In Descriptive Analyses and Taphonomical Observations of Culturally-Modified Mammoths Excavated at "The Gravel Pit," near Clovis, New Mexico in 1936, by J. J. Saunders and E. B. Daeschler. *Proceedings of the Academy of Natural Sciences of Philadelphia* 145:1–28.

Cowan, C. Wesley, and Bruce D. Smith
1993 Perspectives on a Wild Gourd in Eastern North America. *Journal of Ethnobiology* 13:17–54.

Cox, Steven L.
2000 A Norse Penny from Maine. In *Vikings: The North Atlantic Saga*, edited by William W. Fitzhugh

and Elisabeth I. Ward, pp. 206–207. Smithsonian Institution Press, Washington, D.C.

Crawford, Gary W., and David G. Smith
1996 Migration in Prehistory: Princess Point and the Northern Iroquoian Case. *American Antiquity* 61 (4):782–790.

Crawford, Gary W., and David G. Smith
2003 Paleoethnobotany in the Northeast. In *People and Plants in Ancient Eastern North America*, edited by Paul E. Minnis, pp. 172–257. Smithsonian Books, Washington, D.C.

Crawford, Gary W., David G. Smith, and Vandy E. Bowyer
1997 Dating the Entry of Corn (*Zea mays*) into the Lower Great Lakes. *American Antiquity* 62:112–119.

Cressman, Luther S., David L. Cole, Wilbur A. Davis, Thomas M. Newman, and Daniel J. Scheans
1960 Cultural Sequences at The Dalles, Oregon: A Contribution to Pacific Northwest Prehistory. *Transactions of the American Philosophical Society (Philadelphia)* 50 (10).

Croes, Dale R.
1995 *The Hoko River Archaeological Site Complex: The Wet/Dry Site (45 CA 213), 3000–1700 B.P.* Washington State University Press, Pullman.

Croes, Dale R.
1997 The North–Central Cultural Dichotomy on the Northwest Coast of North America: Its Evolution as Suggested by Wet-Site Basketry and Wooden Fish Hooks. *Antiquity* 71:594–615.

Croes, Dale R.
1999 The Hoko River Wet Site, a Joint Tribe/ University Research Effort. In *Bog Bodies, Sacred Sites and Wetland Archaeology*, edited by J. Coles B. Coles, and M. S. Jorgensen, pp. 59–66. WARP Occasional Paper 12. Short Run Press, Exeter, Devon, United Kingdom.

Croes, Dale R., and Steven Hackenberger
1988 Hoko River Archaeological Complex: Modeling Prehistoric Northwest Coast Economic Evolution. *Research in Economic Anthropology* 3:18–89.

Croes, Dale R., Katherine Kelly, and Mark Collard
2005 Cultural Historical Context of Qwu?gwes. In *Wet Site Connections*, guest edited by Dale R. Croes,

Oxbow Press (U.K.). *Journal of Wetland Archaeology* 5:141–154.

Cronon, William
1983 *Changes in the Land: Indians, Colonists, and the Ecology of New England*. Hill & Wang, New York.

Crosby, Alfred W.
1994 *Germs, Seeds and Animals: Studies in Ecological History*. M. E. Sharpe, Armonk, New York.

Crothers, George M., Charles H. Faulkner, Jan F. Simek, Patty J. Watson, and P. Willey
2002 Woodland Cave Archaeology in Eastern North America. In *The Woodland Southeast*, edited by David G. Anderson and Robert C. Mainfort, Jr., pp. 502–524. University of Alabama Press, Tuscaloosa.

Crown, Patricia L.
1994 *Ceramics and Ideology: Salado Polychrome Pottery*. University of New Mexico Press, Albuquerque.

Crown, Patricia L., and W. James Judge
1991 *Chaco and Hohokam: Prehistoric Regional Systems in the American Southwest*. School of American Research, Sante Fe.

Crumley, Carole L.
1995 Heterarchy and the Analysis of Complex Societies. In *Heterarchy and the Analysis of Complex Societies*, edited by Carole L. Crumley, Robert M. Ehrenreich, and Janet E. Levy, pp. 1–6. Archaeological Paper 6, American Anthropological Association, Arlington, Virginia.

Curran, Mary Lou
1999 Exploration, Colonization and Settling In: The Bull Brook Phase, Antecedents and Descendants. In *The Archaeological Northeast*, edited by Kenneth F. Sassaman Mary Ann Levine, and Michael S. Nassaney, pp. 3–24. Bergin & Garvey, Westport, Connecticut.

Cushing, Frank Hamilton
2000 (1896) *Exploration of Ancient Key Dweller Remains on the Gulf Coast of Florida*. University Press of Florida, Gainesville.

Custer, Jay F.
1984 *Delaware Prehistoric Archaeology*. University of Delaware Press, Newark.

Custer, Jay F.
1990 Early and Middle Archaic Cultures of Virginia: Culture Change and Continuity. In *Early and Middle Archaic*

Research in Virginia: A Synthesis, edited by T. R. Rinehart and M. E. Hodges, pp. 1–60. Archaeological Society of Virginia, Richmond.

Custer, Jay F.
1996 *Prehistoric Cultures of Eastern Pennsylvania.* Anthropological Series 7. Pennsylvania Historical Museum, Harrisburg.

Cybulski, Jerome S.
1992 *A Greenville Burial Ground.* Mercury Series, Paper 146, Archaeological Survey of Canada. Canadian Museum of Civilization, Ottawa.

Cybulski, Jerome S.
2001 *Perspectives on Northern Northwest Coast Prehistory.* Archaeological Survey of Canada Paper 160, Mercury Series, Canadian Museum of Civilization, Ottawa.

Dalan, Rinita L.
1997 The Construction of Mississippian Cahokia. In *Cahokia: Domination and Ideology in the Mississippian World*, edited by Timothy R. Pauketat and Thomas E. Emerson, pp. 89–102. University of Nebraska Press, Lincoln.

D'Aleo, Joseph S.
2002 *The Oryx Resource Guide to El Niño and La Niña.* Oryx Press, Westport, Connecticut.

Daly, Marla
1990 Mrs. Waters' Diary of Her Life on San Miguel Island, January 1–June 27, 1888. In *A Step Back in Time: Unpublished Channel Island Diaries*, edited by M. Daly, pp. 5–51. Santa Cruz Island Foundation Occasional Papers 4, Santa Barbara, California.

Damas, David
1984. Introduction. In *Arctic*, edited by David Damas, pp. 94–105. Handbook of North American Indians, Vol. 5, William C. Sturtevant, general editor, Smithsonian Institution, Washington, D.C.

Damp, Jonathan E.
2007 Zuni Emergent Agriculture: Economic Strategies and the Origins of the Zuni. In *Zuni Origins: Toward a New Synthesis of Southwestern Archaeology*, edited by David A. Gregory and David R. Wilcox, pp. 118–132. University of Arizona Press, Tucson.

Damp, Jonathan E., Stephen A. Hall, and Susan J. Smith
2002 Early Irrigation on the Colorado Plateau near Zuni Pueblo, New

Mexico. *American Antiquity* 67 (4):665–676.

Dancey, William S., and Paul J. Pacheco
1997 A Community Model of Ohio Hopewell Settlement. In *Ohio Hopewell Community Organization*, edited by William S. Dancey and Paul J. Pacheco, pp. 3–40. Kent State University Press, Kent, Ohio.

Dark, Alex
1999 The Makah Whale Hunt: Native Americans and the Environment. Electronic document, http://ww.cnie .org/NAE/cases/makah/index.html, accessed December 12, 2012.

Davis, C. Alan, and Gerald A. Smith
1981 *Newberry Cave.* San Bernardino County Museum Association, Redlands, California.

Davis, Stanley D.
1996 Hidden Falls. In *American Beginnings: The Prehistory and Palaeoecology of Beringia*, edited by Frederick H. West, pp. 413–424. University of Chicago Press, Chicago.

Davis, Stella
2005 Students Trace History of Buffalo Soldiers in the Guadalupe Mountains. Free New Mexican, August 17, 2005. Electronic document, http://www.freenewmexi-can.com/story_print.php?storyid=, accessed December 7, 2005.

D'Azevedo, Warren L.
1986 Introduction. In *Great Basin*, edited by Warren L. D'Azevedo, pp. 1–14. Handbook of North American Indians, Vol. 11, William C. Sturtevant, general editor, Smithsonian Institution, Washington, D.C.

Deagan, Kathleen
1982 Avenues of Inquiry in Historical Archaeology. In *Advances in Archaeological Method and Theory*, Vol. 5, pp. 151–177. Academic Press, Orlando, Florida.

Deagan, Kathleen
1983 *Spanish St. Augustine: The Archaeology of a Colonial Creole Community.* Academic Press, Orlando, Florida.

Dean, Jeffrey S.
1968 Chronological Analysis of Tsegi Phase Sites in Northeastern Arizona. *Laboratory of Tree-Ring Research* 3. University of Arizona Press, Tucson.

Dean, Jeffrey S. (editor)
2000 *Salado.* University of New Mexico Press, Albuquerque.

De Boer, Warren R.
2004 Little Bighorn on the Scioto: The Rocky Mountain Connection to Ohio Hopewell. *American Antiquity* 69:85–107.

Decker-Walters, Deena S.
1993 New Methods for Studying the Origins of New World Domesticates: The Squash Example. In *Foraging and Farming in the Eastern Woodlands*, edited by C. Margaret Scarry, pp. 91–97. University Press of Florida, Gainesville.

De Cunzo, Lu Ann
2004 *A Historical Archaeology of Delaware: People, Contexts and the Cultures of Agriculture.* University of Tennessee Press, Knoxville.

Deetz, James
1963 Archaeological Investigations at La Purísma Mission. *Archaeological Survey Annual Report for 1962–1963* 5:161–244.

Deetz, James
1996 *In Small Things Forgotten.* Anchor Books, Doubleday, New York.

Delcourt, Hazel R., and Paul A. Delcourt
1981 Vegetation Maps for Eastern North America: 40,000 B.P. to the Present. In *Geobotany II*, edited by Robert E. Romans, pp. 123–163. Plenum Press, New York.

Delcourt, Paul A., Hazel R. Delcourt, Patricia A. Cridelbaugh, and Jefferson Chapman
1986 Holocene Ethnobotanical and Paleoecological Record of Human Impact on Vegetation in the Little Tennessee River Valley, Tennessee. *Quaternary Research* 25:330–349.

Delle, James, and Mary Ann Levine
2004 Excavations at the Thaddeus Stevens/Lydia Hamilton Smith Site, Lancaster, PA: Archaeological Evidence for the Underground Railroad? *Northeast Historical Archaeology* 33:131–152.

Deller, D. Brian, and Christopher J. Ellis
1984 Crowfield: A Preliminary Report on a Probable Paleo-Indian Cremation in Southwestern Ontario. *Archaeology of Eastern North America* 12:41–71.

Deller, D. Brian, Christopher J. Ellis and James R. Keron
2009 Understanding Cache Variability: A Deliberately Burned Early Paleoindian Tool Assemblage from the Crowfield Site, Southwestern Ontario, Canada.

American Antiquity, Vol. 74, No. 2 (Apr., 2009), pp. 371–397.

De Mallie, Raymond J. (editor)
2001 *Plains* (Pt. 1). Handbook of North American Indians, Vol. 13, William C. Sturtevant, general editor, Smithsonian Institution, Washington, D.C.

Dent, Richard J.
2007 Seed Collecting and Fishing at the Shawnee Minisink Paleoindian Site: Everyday Life in the Late Pleistocene. In *Foragers of the Terminal Pleistocene in North America*, edited by Renee B. Walker and Boyce N. Driskell, pp. 116–131. University of Nebraska Press, Lincoln.

Dent, Richard J.
2002 Paleoindian Occupation of the Upper Delaware Valley: Revisiting Shawnee Minisink and Nearby Sites. In *Ice Age Peoples of Pennsylvania*, edited by Kurt W. Carr and James M. Adovasio, pp. 51–78. Pennsylvania Historical and Museum Commission, Harrisburg.

Dent, Richard J.
1995 *Chesapeake Prehistory: Old Traditions, New Directions*. Plenum Press, New York.

Dent, Richard J., and Barbara E. Kauffman
1985 Aboriginal Subsistence and Site Ecology as Interpreted from Microfloral and Faunal Remains. In *Shawnee–Minisink: A Stratified Paleoindian–Archaic Site in the Upper Delaware Valley of Pennsylvania*, edited by Charles W. McNett, Jr., pp. 55–79. Academic Press, Orlando, Florida.

Department of the Interior
2010 43 CFR Part 10 Native American Graves Protection and Repatriation Act Regulations—Disposition of Culturally Unidentifiable Human Remains; Final Rule, *Federal Register* 75 (49):12378–12405. Electronic document, http://edocket.access.gpo.gov/2010/pdf/2010–5283.pdf, accessed January 28, 2012.

Derenko, Miroslava V., Tomasz Grzybowski, Boris A. Malyarchuk, Jakub Czarny, Danuta Miscicka-Sliwka, and Ilia A. Zakharov
2001 The Presence of Mitochondrial Haplogroup X in Altaians from South Siberia. Letter to the editor. *American Journal of Human Genetics* 69:237–241.

Derry, Linda, and Maureen Malloy
2003 *Archaeologists and Local Communities: Partners in Exploring the Past*. Society of American Archaeology, Washington, D.C.

Detwiler, Kandace R.
2000 Gathering in the Late Paleoindian: Botanical Remains from Dust Cave, Alabama. Paper presented at the Annual Meeting of the Society for American Archaeology, Philadelphia.

Detwiler-Hollenbach, Kandace R.
2003 Nuts and More Nuts: Archaic Plant Use at Dust Cave, Alabama. Paper presented at the 60th Annual Southeastern Archaeology Conference, Charlotte, North Carolina.

Dickens, Roy S., and Linda R. Carnes
1983 Preliminary Investigations at Soapstone Ridge, DeKalb County, Georgia. *Southeastern Archaeological Conference Bulletin* 20:81–97.

Dikov, Nikolai N.
1996 The Ushki Sites, Kamchatka Peninsula. In *American Beginnings: The Prehistory and Palaeoecology of Beringia*, edited by Frederick H. West, pp. 224–250. University of Chicago Press, Chicago.

Dillehay, Thomas D.
2000 *The Settlement of the Americas: A New Prehistory*. Basic Books, New York.

Dillehay, Tom D., C. Ramírez, M. Pino, M. B. Collins, J. Rossen, J. D. Pino-Navarro
2008 Monte Verde: Seaweed, Food, Medicine, and the Peopling of South America. *Science* 320:784–786.

Dincauze, Dena F.
1976 *The Neville Site: 8000 Years at Amoskeag Falls*. Peabody Museum Monograph 4. Harvard University, Cambridge, Massachusetts.

Dincauze, Dena F.
1990 Capsule Prehistory of Southern New England. In *The Pequots in Southern New England: The Fall and Rise of an American Indian Nation*, edited by Laurence M. Hauptman and James D. Wherry, pp. 19–32. University of Oklahoma Press, Norman.

Dincauze, Dena F.
1993 Pioneering in the Pleistocene: Large Paleoindian Sites in the Northeast. In *Archaeology of Eastern North America: Papers in Honor of Stephen Williams*, edited by J. B.

Stoltman, pp. 43–60. Archaeological Report 25, Mississippi Department of Archives, Jackson.

Dincauze, Dena F., and Robert J. Hasenstab
1989 Explaining the Iroquois: Tribalization on a Prehistoric Periphery. In *Centre and Periphery: Comparative Studies in Archaeology*, edited by T. Champion, pp. 67–84. Unwin Hyman, London.

Dincauze, Dena F., and Victoria Jacobson
2001 The Birds of Summer: Lakeside Routes into Late Pleistocene New England. *Canadian Journal of Archaeology* 21:121–126.

Discovery Channel
2005 *Ice Age Columbus: Who Were the First American* [DVD], directed by Nicholas Brown. Discovery Communications.

Dixon, E. James
1999 *Bones, Boats and Bison: Archaeology of the First Colonization of Western North America*. University of New Mexico Press, Albuquerque.

Dixon, Kelly J., Julie M. Schablitsky, and Shannon A. Novak
2011 *An Archaeology of Desperation: Exploring the Donner Party's Alder Creek Camp*. University of Oklahoma Press, Norman.

Dmytryshyn, Basil, E. A. P. Crownhart-Vaughan, and Thomas Vaughan
1989 *The Russian American Colonies, 1798–1867: Three Centuries of Russian Eastward Expansion*. Oregon Historical Society, Portland.

Dobyns, Henry
1983 *Their Number Become Thinned*. University of Tennessee Press, Knoxville.

Dold, Catherine
2003 The Neighborhood Bonebed. *American Archaeology* 7 (2):32–38.

Dongoske, Kurt E., Mark Aldenderfer, and Karen Doehner
2000 *Working Together: Native Americans and Archaeologists*. Society for American Archaeology Washington, D.C.

Doolittle, William E.
2000 *Cultivated Landscapes of Native North America*. Oxford University Press, Oxford.

Doran, Glen H.
2001 The View From Windover: 15 Years After Excavation. In *Enduring Records: The Environmental and Cultural Heritage of Wetlands,*

edited by Barbara A. Purdy, pp. 9-17. Oxbow Books, Oxford.

2002 *Windover: Multidisciplinary Investigations of an Early Archaic Florida Cemetery*. University Press of Florida, Gainesville.

Dowdall, Katherine M., and Otis Parrish

2003 A Meaningful Disturbance of the Earth. *Journal of Social Archaeology* 3 (1):99–133.

Downer, A.

1997 Archaeologists–Native American Relations. In *Native Americans and Archaeologists: Stepping Stones to Common Ground*, edited by Kurt Dongoske Nina Swindler, Roger Anyon, and A. Downer, pp. 22–34. AltaMira Press, Walnut Creek, California.

Downs, James F.

1966 *The Two Worlds of the Washo: An Indian Tribe of California and Nevada*. Holt, Rinehart & Winston, New York.

Downum, Christian E., and Todd W. Bostwick

1993 *Archaeology of the Pueblo Grande Platform Mound and Surrounding Features, Vol. 1: Introduction to the Archival Project and History of Archaeological Research*. Grande Museum, Phoenix.

Dragoo, Don W.

1955 Excavations at the Johnston Site, Indiana County, Pennsylvania. *Pennsylvania Archaeologist*, 25(2): 85–147.

Dragoo, Don W.

1963 *Mounds for the Dead: An Analysis of Adena Culture*. Annals of the Carnegie Museum 37, Pittsburgh.

Drake, James D.

1999 *King Philip's War: Civil War in New England, 1675–1676*. University of Massachusetts Press, Amherst.

Driskell, Boyce N.

1994 Stratigraphy and Chronology at Dust Cave. *Journal of Alabama Archaeology* 40:18–30.

Driver, Jon

1999 Raven Skeletons from Paleoindian Contexts Charlie Lake Cave, British Columbia. *American Antiquity* 64:289–298.

Drooker, Penelope B.

2004 Pipes, Leadership, and Interregional Interaction in Protohistoric Midwestern and Northeastern North America. In *Smoking and Culture: Recent Developments in the Archaeology of Tobacco Pipes*, edited by Sean Rafferty and Rob Mann, pp. 73–124. University of Tennessee Press, Knoxville.

Drooker, Penelope B., and C. Wesley Cowan

2001 Transformation of the Fort Ancient Cultures of the Central Ohio Valley. In *Societies in Eclipse: Archaeology of the Eastern Woodlands Indians, A.D. 1400–1700*, edited by C. Wesley Cowan, David S. Brose, and Robert C. Mainfort, Jr., pp. 83–106. Smithsonian Institution Press, Washington, D.C.

Duddleson, J. Ryan

2008 Plains Woodland Pottery: A Use-Alteration Perspective. *Plains Anthropologist* 53:179–197.

Dumond, Don E.

1984a Prehistory of the Bering Sea Region. In *Arctic* edited by David Damas, pp. 94–105. Handbook of North American Indians, Vol. 5, William C. Sturtevant, general editor, Smithsonian Institution, Washington, D.C.

Dumond, Don E.

1984b Prehistory: Summary. In *Arctic*, edited by David Damas, pp. 72–79. Handbook of North American Indians, Vol. 5, William C. Sturtevant, general editor, Smithsonian Institution, Washington, D.C.

Dumond, Don E.

1987 *The Eskimos and Aleuts*, 2nd ed. Thames and Hudson, London.

Dunbar, James S., C. Andrew Hemmings, Pamela K. Vojnovski, S. David Webb, and William M. Stanton

2005 The Ryan/Harley Site 8Je1004: A Suwannee Point Site in the Wacissa River, North Florida. In *Paleoamerican Origins: Beyond Clovis*, edited by Robson Bonnichsen, Bradley T. Lepper, Dennis Stanford and Michael R. Waters, pp. 81–96. Center for the Study of the First Americans, College Station, Texas.

Dunbar, James S., and S. David Webb

1996 Bone and Ivory Tools from Submerged Paleoindian Sites in Florida. In *The Paleoindian and Early Archaic Southeast*, edited by G. Anderson and Kenneth E. Sassaman, pp. 331–353. University of Alabama Press, Tuscaloosa.

Dunford, Frederick J.

1999 Paleoenvironmental Context for the Middle Archaic Occupation of Cape Cod, Massachusetts. In *The Archaeological Northeast*, edited by Kenneth E. Sassaman Mary Ann Levine, and Michael S. Nassaney, pp. 39–54. Bergin & Garvery, Westport, Connecticut.

Dyck, Ian, and Richard E. Morlan

2001 Hunting and Gathering Tradition: Canadian Plains. In *Plains*, edited by Raymond J. De Mallie, pp. 115–130. Handbook of North American Indians, Vol. 13, William C. Sturtevant, general editor, Smithsonian Institution, Washington, D.C.

Early, Ann M.

1989 Profiteers and Public Archaeology: Antiquities Trafficking in Arkansas. In *The Ethics of Collecting Cultural Property*, edited by Phyllis Mauch Messenger, pp. 39–50. University of New Mexico Press, Albuquerque.

Echo-Hawk, Roger C.

1997 Forging a New Ancient History for Native America. In *Native Americans and Archaeologists: Stepping Stones to Common Ground*, edited by Kurt Dongoske Nina Swindler, Roger Anyon, and A. Downer, pp. 88–102. AltaMira Press, Walnut Creek, California.

Edson, O.

1875 History of Chautauqua Anterior to Its Pioneer Settlement. In *History of Chautauqua County*, edited by A. W. Young, pp. 36–49. Methews and Warren, Buffalo, New York.

Edwards, Andrew

2005 Jamestown, Virginia. In *Unlocking the Past: Celebrating Historical Archaeology in North America*, edited by Lu Ann DeCunzon and John H. Jameson, Jr., pp. 62–67. University of Florida Press, Gainesville.

Eerkens, Jelmer W.

2004 Privatization, Small-Seed Intensification, and the Origins of Pottery in the Western Great Basin. *American Antiquity* 69 (4):653–670.

Eldridge, Morely

1997 *The Significance and Management of Culturally Modified Trees: Final Report*. Prepared by Millennia Research for the Vancouver Forest Region and CMT Standards Steering Committee, Victoria, British Columbia.

Ellis, Chris J., and D. Brian Deller

1990 Paleo-Indians. In *The Archaeology of Southern Ontario to A.D. 1650*, edited by Chris J. Ellis and Neal Ferris, pp. 37–63. Ontario Archaeological Society, London.

Ellis, Chris J., and D. Brian Deller
  1997 Variability in the Archaeological Record of Northeastern Early Paleoindians: A View from Southern Ontario. *Archaeology of Eastern North America* 25:1–30.

Ellis, Christopher
  2008 The Fluted Point Tradition and the Arctic Small Tool Tradition: What's the Connection? *Journal of Anthropological Archaeology* 27:298–314.

Ellis, Christopher, Peter A. Timmins, and Holly Martelle
  2009 At the Crossroads and Periphery: The Archaic Archaeological Record of Southern Ontario. In *Archaic Societies: Diversity and Complexity Across the MidContinent*, edited by Thomas E. Emerson, Dale L. McElrath, and Andrew C. Fortier, pp. 787–837. State University of New York Press, Albany.

Elston, Robert G.
  1986 Prehistory of the Western Area. In *Great Basin*, edited by Warren L. D'Azevedo, pp. 135–148. Handbook of North American Indians, Vol. 11, William C. Sturtevant, general editor, Smithsonian Institution, Washington, D.C.

Emerson, Thomas E., and Dale L. McElrath
  2009 The Eastern Woodland Archaic and the Tyranny of Theory. In *Archaic Societies: Diversity and Complexity Across the Midcontinent*, edited by Thomas E. Emerson, Dale L. McElrath, and Andrew C. Fortier, pp. 23–38. State University of New York Press, Albany.

Emerson, Thomas E., Dale L. McElrath, and Andrew C. Fortier (editors)
  2000 *Late Woodland Societies: Tradition and Transformation Across the Midcontinent.* University of Nebraska Press, Lincoln.

Emerson, Thomas E., Dale L. McElrath, and Andrew C. Fortier (editors)
  2009 *Archaic Societies: Diversity and Complexity Across the Midcontinent.* State University of New York Press, Albany.

Engelbrecht, William
  1996 Ceramics. In *Reanalyzing the Ripley Site: Earthworks and Late Prehistory on the Lake Erie Plain*, edited by Lynne P. Sullivan, pp. 53–68. New York State Museum Bulletin 489. University of the State of New York/State Department of Education, Albany.

Engelbrecht, William
  2003 *Iroquoia: The Development of a Native World.* Syracuse University Press, Syracuse, New York.

Engelbrecht, William, and Lynne P. Sullivan
  1996 Cultural Context. In *Reanalyzing the Ripley Site: Earthworks and Late Prehistory on the Lake Erie Plain*, edited by Lynne P. Sullivan, pp. 14–27. New York State Museum Bulletin 489. University of the State of New York/State Department of Education, Albany.

Erdoes, Richard, and Alfonso Ortiz
  1997 *American Indian Myths and Legends.* Pimlico Press, London.

Erikson, Patricia Pierce, Helma Ward, and Kirk Wachendorf
  2002 *Voices of a Thousand People: The Makah Cultural and Research Center.* University of Nebraska Press, Lincoln.

Erlandson, Jon M.
  1991 Shellfish and Seeds as Optimal Resources: Early Holocene Subsistence on the Santa Barbara Coast. In *Hunter-Gatherers of Early Holocene Coastal California*, edited by Jon M. Erlandson and Roger H. Colton, pp. 89–100. Perspectives on California Archaeology 1. Institute of Archaeology, University of California Los Angeles.

Erlandson, Jon M.
  1994 *Early Hunter-Gatherers of the California Coast.* Plenum Press, New York.

Erlandson, Jon M.
  2001 The Archaeology of Aquatic Adaptations: Paradigms for a New Millennium. *Journal of Archaeological Research* 9:287–350.

Erlandson, Jon M.
  2002 Anatomically Modern Humans, Maritime Adaptations, and the Peopling of the New World. In *The First Americans: The Pleistocene Colonization of the New World*, edited by Nina Jablonski, pp. 59-92. California Academy of Sciences, San Francisco.

Erlandson, Jon M.
  2004 Anatomically Modern Humans, Maritime Voyaging, and the Pleistocene Colonization of the Americas. In *Prehistoric California*, edited by L. M. Raab and T. L. Jones, pp. 108–129. University of Utah Press, Salt Lake City.

Erlandson, Jon M., and Roger H. Colton (editors)
  1991 *Hunter-Gatherers of Early Holocene Coastal California.* Perspectives on California Archaeology 1. Institute of Archaeology, University of California, Los Angeles.

Erlandson, Jon M., and Michael A. Glassow (editors)
  1997 *Archaeology of the California Coast During the Middle Holocene.* Perspectives on California Archaeology 4. Institute of Archaeology, University of California, Los Angeles.

Erlandson, Jon M., and Terry L. Jones (editors)
  2002 *Catalysts to Complexity: Late Holocene Societies of the California Coast.* Perspectives on California Archaeology 6. Institute of Archaeology, University of California, Los Angeles.

Erlandson, Jon M., Michael H. Graham, Bruce J. Bourque, Debra Corbett, James A. Estes, and Robert Steneck
  2007 The Kelp Highway Hypothesis: Marine Ecology, the Coastal Migration Theory, and Peopling of the Americas. *Journal of Island and Coastal Archaeology* 2:161-174.

Erlandson, Jon M., Douglas J. Kennett, B. Lynn Ingram, Don A. Guthrie, D. P. Morris, Mark A. Tveskov, G. James West, and Phillip L. Walker
  1996 An Archaeological and Paleontological Chronology for Daisy Cave (CA-SMI-261), San Miguel Island, California. *Radiocarbon* 38:355–373.

Erlandson, Jon M., and Don P. Morris
  1993 Nine Thousand Years of Coastal Prehistory on Santa Rosa Island, California: A Radiocarbon Chronology for CA-SRI-1. In *Proceedings of the Fourth Conference on Research in California's National Parks.* Transactions and Proceedings Series 9, U.S. Department of the Interior.

Erlandson, Jon M., and Madonna L. Moss
  2001 Shellfish Eaters, Carrion Feeders, and the Archaeology of Aquatic Adaptations. *American Antiquity* 66 (3):412–432.

Erlandson, Jon M., Madonna L. Moss, and Matthew Des Lauriers
  2008 Life on the Edge: Early Maritime Cultures of the Pacific Coast of North America. *Quaternary Science Reviews* 27:2232-2245.

Erlandson, Jon M., and Torben C. Rick

2002 Late Holocene Cultural Developments Along the Santa Barbara Coast. In *Catalysts to Complexity: Late Holocene Societies of the California Coast*, edited by Jon M. Erlandson and Terry L. Jones, pp. 166–182. Perspectives on California Archaeology 6. Cotsen Institute of Archaeology, University of California, Los Angeles.

Erlandson, Jon. M., Torben. C. Rick, T. J. Braje, M. Casperson, B. Culleton, B. Fulfrost, T. Garcia, Daniel Guthrie, N. Jew, Douglas Kennett, Madonna L. Moss, L. Reeder, C. Skinner, J. Watts, and L. Willis
2011 Paleoindian Seafaring, Maritime Technologies, and Coastal Foraging on California's Channel Islands. *Science* 331:1181–1185.

Erlandson, Jon M., Torben C. Rick, R. L. Vellanoweth, and Douglas J. Kennett
1999 Maritime Subsistence at a 9300-Year-Old Shell Midden on Santa Rosa Island, California. *Journal of Field Archaeology* 26 (3):255–265.

Esarey, Duane
1986 Red Ochre Mound Building and Marion Phase Associations: A Fulton County, Illinois Perspective. In *Early Woodland Archaeology*, edited by Kenneth B. Farnsworth and Thomas E. Emerson, pp. 231–243. Center for American Archeology Press, Kampsville, Illinois.

Esdale, Julie A.
2008 A Current Synthesis of the Northern Archaic. *Arctic Anthropology* 45:3–38.

Espinoza-Ar, Amy
2005 Coronado's Campsite Preserved: The Conservancy Obtains an Important Addition to the Only Known Spanish Campsite in New Mexico. *American Archaeology* 9 (2):47.

Evans, Lynn L. M.
2001 *House D of the Southeast Row House: Excavations at Fort Michilimackinac, 1989–1997.* Mackinac Historic Parks, Mackinac Island, Michigan.

Ewen, Charles R.
1989 Anhaica: Discovery of Hernando de Soto's 1539–1540 Winter Camp. In *First Encounters: Spanish Explorations in the Caribbean and the United States, 1492–1570*, edited by Jerald T. Milanich and Susan Milbrath, pp. 110–118. University Press of Florida, Gainesville.

Fagan, Brian
1987 *The Great Journey: The Peopling of Ancient America.* Thames and Hudson, New York.

Fagan, Brian
1995 Black Day at Slack Farm. In *Snapshots of the Past*, edited by Brian Fagan, pp. 129–135. AltaMira, Lanham, Maryland.

Fagan, Brian
1999 *Floods, Famines and Emperors: El Niño and the Fate of Civilizations.* Basic Books, New York.

Fagan, Brian
2003 *Before California: An Archaeologist Looks at Our Earliest Inhabitants.* Rowman & Littlefield, Lanham, Maryland.

Fagan, John L.
1999 Analysis of Lithic Artifact Embedded in the Columbia Park Remains. In *Report on the Non-Destructive Examination, Description, and Analysis of the Human Remains from Columbia Park, Kennewick, Washington.* National Park Service, Archaeology Program. Electronic document, . http://www.nps.gov/archeology/kennewick/fagan.htm, accessed December 12, 2012.

Faught, Michael K.
2008 Archaeological Roots of Human Diversity in the New World: A Compilation of Accurate and Precise Radiocarbon Ages from Earliest Sites. *American Antiquity* 73:670–698.

Faulkner, Alaric, and Gretchen Faulkner
1987 *The French at Pentagoet, 1653–1674: An Archaeological Portrait of the Acadian Frontier.* Maine Historic Preservation Commission, Augusta.

Feder, Kenneth L.
2002 *Frauds, Myths and Mysteries: Science and Pseudoscience in Archaeology*, 4th ed. McGrawHill/Mayfield, Boston.

Fedje, Daryl W., and Quentin Mackie
2005 Overview of Cultural History. In *Haida Gwaii: Human History and Environment from the Time of the Loon to the Time of the Iron People*, edited by Daryl W. Fedje and Rolf W. Mathewes, pp. 154–162. University of British Columbia Press, Vancouver.

Fedje, Daryl W., and Rolf W. Mathewes
2005 Conclusion: Synthesis of Environmental and Archaeological data. In *Haida Gwaii: Human History and Environment from the Time of the Loon to the Time of the Iron People*, edited by Daryl W. Fedje and Rolf W. Mathewes, pp. 372–375. University of British Columbia Press, Vancouver.

Feest, Johanna E., and Christian F. Feest
1978 Ottawa. In *Northeast*, edited by Bruce G. Trigger, pp. 772–786. Handbook of North American Indians, Vol. 15, William C. Sturtevant, general editor, Smithsonian Institution, Washington, D.C.

Fenneman, Nevin M.
1931 *Physiography of the Western United States.* McGraw-Hill, New York.

Fenneman, Nevin M.
1938 *Physiography of Eastern United States.* Mc-Graw Hill, New York.

Fenton, William N.
1968 Editor's Introduction. In *Parker on the Iroquois*, edited by William N. Fenton, pp. 1–47. Syracuse University Press, Syracuse.

Ferg, Alan, and Karen Wilhelm
2005 *Archaeology Southwest* 19 (2). Center for Desert Archaeology, Tucson.

Ferguson, Leland
1992 *Uncommon Ground: Archaeology and Early African America, 1650–1800.* Smithsonian Institution Press, Washington, D.C.

Ferguson, T. J.
2003 Anthropological Archaeology Conducted by Tribes: Traditional Cultural Properties and Cultural Affiliation. In *Archaeology Is Anthropology*, edited by S. D. Gillespie and D. L. Nichols, pp. 137–144. American Anthropological Association Washington, D.C.

Ferring, C. R.
1989 The Aubrey Clovis Site: A Paleoindian Locality in the Upper Trinity River Basin, Texas. *Current Research in the Pleistocene* 6:9–11.

Ferris, Neal
2009 *Native-Lived Colonialism: Challenging History in the Great Lakes.* The University of Arizona Press, Tucson.

Fiedel, Stuart
1987 Algonquian Origins: A Problem in Archaeological-Linguistic Correlation. *Archaeology of Eastern North America* 15:1–11.

Fiedel, Stuart

1999a Artifact Provenance at Monte Verde: Confusion and Contradictions. Monte Verde Revisited. *Scientific American Discovering Archaeology* 15:1–11.

1999b Algonquians and Iroquoians: Taxonomy, Chronology and Archaeological Implications. In *Taming the Taxonomy: Toward a New Understanding of Great Lakes Archaeology*, edited by Ronald Williamson and Christopher Watts, pp. 193–204. East End Books, Toronto.

Fiedel, Stuart, and Gary Haynes

2004 A Premature Burial: Comments on Grayson and Meltzer's "Requiem for Overkill." *Journal of Archaeological Science* 31:121–131.

Firestone, R. B., A. West, J. P. Kennett, L. Becker, T. E. Bunch, Z. S. Revay, P. H. Schulz, T. Belgya, D. J. Kennett, J. M. Erlandson, O. J. Dickenson, A. C. Goodyear, R. S. Harris, G. A. Howard, J. B. Koosterman, P. Lechler, P. S. Mayewski, J. Montogomery, R. Preda, T. Darrah, S. S. QueHee, A. R. Smith, A. Stich, W. Topping, J. H.Wittke, and W. S. Wolbach

2007 Evidence for an Extraterretrial Impact 12,900 Years Ago That Contributed to the Megafaunal Extinctions and the Younger Dryas Cooling. *Proceedings of the National Academy of the Sciences* 104:16016–16021.

Fish, Paul, and Suzanne Fish

1999 Reflections on the Casas Grandes Regional System from the Northwestern Periphery. In *The Casas Grandes World*, edited by Curtis F. Schaafsma and Carroll L. Riley, pp. 27–42. University of Utah Press, Salt Lake City.

Fisher, Daniel C.

1984 Mastodon Butchery by North American Paleo-Indians. *Nature* 308:271–272.

Fisher, Daniel C.

1987 Mastodont Procurement by Paleoindians of the Great Lakes Region: Hunting or Scavenging? In *The Evolution of Human Hunting*, edited by M. H. Nitecki and D. V. Nitecki, pp. 309–421. Plenum Press, New York.

Fisher, Daniel C.

2004 Mastodons, Mammoths, and Humans in the North American Mid-continent. In *New Prerspectives on the First Americans*, edited by Bradley T. Lepper and Robson Bonichsen,

pp. 81–86. Center for the Study of the First Americans, College Station, Texas.

Fisher, Daniel C., Bradley T. Lepper, and P. E. Hooge

1994 Evidence for Butchery of the Burning Tree Mastodon. In *The First Discovery of America: Archaeological Evidence of the Early Inhabitants of the Ohio Area*, edited by William Dancey, pp. 43–57. Ohio Archaeological Council, Columbus.

Fitting, James E.

1970 *The Archaeology of Michigan.* Natural History Press, Garden City.

Fitzgerald, William R.

1991 An Analysis of Brass and Copper from the Ripley Site: The 1906 Sample. Manuscript on file, New York State Museum, Albany.

Fitzhugh, Ben

2003 *The Evolution of Complex Hunter Gatherers: Archaeological Evidence from the North Pacific.* Kluwer Academic-Plenum Press, New York.

Fitzhugh, William W.

1984 Paleo-Eskimo Cultures of Greenland. In *Arctic*, edited by David Damas, pp. 528–539. Handbook of North American Indians, Vol. 5, William C. Sturtevant, general editor, Smithsonian Institution, Washington, D.C.

Fitzhugh, William W., and Elisabeth I. Ward

2000 *Vikings: The North Atlantic Saga.* Smithsonian Institution Press, Washington, D.C.

Fix, Alan G.

2005 Rapid Deployment of the Five Founding Amerind mtDNA Haplogroups via Coastal and Riverine Colonization. *American Journal of Physical Anthropology* 128:430–436.

Fladmark, Knut R.

1973 The Richardson Ranch Site: A 19th Century Haida House. In *Historical Archaeology in Northwestern North America*, edited by R. M. Getty and Knut R. Fladmark, pp. 53–95. University of Calgary Archaeological Association, Calgary, Alberta.

Fladmark, Knut R.

1979 Routes: Alternative Migration Corridors for Early Man in North America. *American Antiquity* 44:55–69.

Fladmark, Knut R.

1983 Times and Places: Environmental Correlates of Mid-to-Late Wisconsin Human Population Expansion in North America. In *Early Man in the New World*, edited by R. Shutler, pp. 13–42. Sage, Beverly Hills, California.

Fladmark, Knut R., Kenneth M. Ames, and Patricia D. Sutherland

1990 Prehistory of the Northern Coast of British Columbia. In *Northwest Coast*, edited by Wayne Suttles, pp. 229–239. Handbook of North American Indians, Vol. 7, William C. Sturtevant, general editor, Smithsonian Institution, Washington, D.C.

Fladmark, Knut R., Jonathan C. Driver, and Diana Alexander

1988 The Paleoindian Component at Charlie Lake Cave (HbRf 39), British Columbia. *American Antiquity* 53(2):371–384.

Flenniken, J. Jeffrey

1977 Analysis of the Lithic Tools, 1976 Sample. In *Preliminary Archeological Investigations at the Miller Site, Strawberry Island, 1976: A Late Prehistoric Village near Burbank, Franklin County, Washington*, pp. 68–101. Washington Archaeological Research Center Project Report, Burbank.

Flenniken, J. Jeffrey

1978 Technological Analyses of the Lithic Artifacts from the Miller Site, 45 FR 5. In *Second Annual Interim Report on the Archaeological Investigations at the Miller Site (45 FR 5) on Strawberry Island (1977), a Late Prehistoric Village near Burbank, Washington*, edited by Gregory C. Cleveland, pp. 81–132. Washington Archaeological Research Center Project Report 72, Burbank.

Flenniken, J. Jeffrey

1981 *Replicative Systems Analysis: A Model Applied to the Vein Quartz Artifacts from the Hoko River Site.* Reports of Investigations 59. Laboratory of Anthropology, Washington State University, Pullman.

Flenniken, J. Jeffrey, and Anon W. Raymond

1986 Morphological Projectile Point Typology: Replication, Experimentation, and Technological Analysis. *American Antiquity* 51:603–614.

Flenniken, J. Jeffrey, and Philip J. Wilke

1989 Typology, Technology, and Chronology of Great Basin Dart

Points. *American Anthropologist* 91:149–158.

Ford, J. A.
1954 Additional Notes on the Poverty Point Site in Northern Louisiana. *American Antiquity* 19:282–285.

Ford, J. A., and C. H. Webb
1956 *Poverty Point, a Late Archaic Site in Louisiana.* Anthropological Papers 46. American Museum of Natural History, New York.

Ford, Richard I.
1981 Gardening and Farming Before A.D. 1000: Patterns of Prehistoric Cultivation North of Mexico. *Journal of Ethnobiology* 1 (1):6–27.

Ford, Richard I.
1985 Patterns of Prehistoric Plant Production in North America. In *Prehistoric Food Production in North America*, edited by Richard I. Ford, pp. 341–435. Museum of Anthropology, University of Michigan, Ann Arbor.

Ford, T. Latimer, Jr.
1976 Adena Sites on Chesapeake Bay. *Archaeology of Eastern North America* 4:63–89.

Foster, Michael S.
1994 *The Pueblo Grande Project, Vol. 1: Introduction, Research Design, and Testing Results.* Soil Systems Publications in Archaeology 20, Phoenix.

Foster, Rhonda, and Dale Croes
2002 Tribal–Archaeological Cooperative Agreement, a Holistic Cultural Resource Management Approach. *Journal of Wetland Archaeology* 2:25–38.

Foster, Rhonda, and Dale Croes
2004 Joint Tribal/College Wet Site Investigations—A Critical Need for Native American Expertise. *Journal of Wetland Archaeology* 4:125–138.

Fowler, Catherine S.
1986 Subsistence. In *Great Basin*, edited by Warren L. D'Azevedo, pp. 64–97. Handbook of North American Indians, Vol. 11, William C. Sturtevant, general editor, Smithsonian Institution, Washington, D.C.

Fowler, Don D., and David B. Madsen
1986 Prehistory of the Southeastern Area. In *Great Basin*, edited by Warren L. D'Azevedo, pp. 173–182. Handbook of North American Indians, Vol. 11 William C. Sturtevant, general

editor, Smithsonian Institution, Washington, D.C.

Fowler, Melvin L.
1959 *Summary Report of the Modoc Rock Shelter: 1952, 1953, 1955, 1956.* Illinois State Museum, Springfield.

Fowler, Melvin L., Jerome Rose, Barbara Vander Leest, and Steven A. Ahler
1999 *The Mound 72 Area: Dedicated and Sacred Space in Early Cahokia.* Illinois State Museum Society, Springfield.

Fredrickson, David A.
1973 Early Cultures of the North Coast Ranges, California. Ph.D. dissertation, University of California, Davis.

Fredrickson, David A.
1984 The North Coastal Region. In *California Archaeology*, pp. 471–527. Academic Press, Orlando, Florida.

Friends of the Ridgefield National Wildlife Refuge
2012 Cathlapotle Plankhouse Project. Electronic document, http://www.ridgefieldfriends.org/plankhouse.php, accessed February 12, 2012.

Friesen, T. Max, and Charles D. Arnold
2008 The Timing of the Thule Migration: New Dates from the Western Canadian Arctic. *American Antiquity* 73:527–538.

Frison, George C.
1974 *The Casper Site: A Hell Gap Bison Kill on the High Plains.* Academic Press, New York.

Frison, George C.
1989 Experimental Use of Clovis Weaponry and Tools on African Elephants. *American Antiquity* 54:766–784.

Frison, George C.
1991 *Prehistoric Hunters of the High Plains*, 2nd ed. Academic Press, San Diego.

Frison, George C.
1998 The Northwestern and Northern Plains Archaic. In *Archaeology of the Great Plains*, edited by W. Raymond Wood, pp. 140–172. University Press of Kansas, Lawrence.

Frison, George C.
2001 Hunting and Gathering Tradition: Northwestern and Central Plains. In *Plains*, edited by Raymond J. De Mallie, pp. 131–145. Handbook of North American Indians, Vol. 13, William C. Sturtevant, general

editor, Smithsonian Institution, Washington, D.C.

Frison, George, and Bruce Bradley
1999 *The Fenn Cache: Clovis Weapons and Tools.* One Horse Land and Cattle Company, Santa Fe.

Fritz, Gayle J.
1990 Multiple Pathways to Farming in Eastern North America. *Journal of World Prehistory* 4 (4):387–435.

Fritz, Gayle J.
1992 "Newer," "Better" Maize and the Mississippian Emergence: A Critique of Prime Mover Explanations. In *Late Prehistoric Agriculture*, edited by William Woods, pp. 19–43. Studies in Illinois Archaeology 8. Illinois Historic Preservation Agency, Springfield.

Fritz, Gayle J.
1993 Early and Middle Woodland Period Paleoethnobotany. In *Foraging and Farming in the Eastern Woodlands*, edited by Margaret Scarry, pp. 39–56. University Press of Florida, Gainesville.

Fry, Gary F.
1976 *Analysis of Prehistoric Coprolites from Utah.* Anthropological Paper 27. University of Utah, Salt Lake City.

Fryman, Robert J.
2000 Fortifying the Landscape: An Archaeological Study of Military Engineering and the Atlanta Campaign. In *Archaeological Perspectives on the American Civil War*, edited by Clarence R. Geier and Stephen R. Potter, pp. 43–55. University Press of Florida, Gainesville.

Funk, Robert E., Donald W. Fisher, and Edgar M. Reilly, Jr.
1970 Caribou and Paleo-Indian in New York State: A Presumed Association. *American Journal of Science* 268:181–186.

Gallagher, James P., Robert F. Boszhardt, Robert F. Sasso, and Katherine Stevenson
1985 Oneota Ridged Field Agriculture in Southwestern Wisconsin. *American Antiquity* 50 (3):605–612.

Galloway, Patricia
1989 *The Southeastern Ceremonial Complex: Artifacts and Analysis.* University of Nebraska Press, Lincoln.

Gamble, Lynn H.
2002 Archaeological Evidence for the Origin of the Plank Canoe in North America. *American Antiquity* 67:301–315.

Gamble, Lynn H., Phillip L. Walker, and Glenn S. Russell
2001 An Integrative Approach to Mortuary Analysis: Social and Symbolic Dimensions of Chumash Burial Practices. *American Antiquity* 66:185–212.

Gardner, James S.
1981 General Environment. In *Subarctic*, edited by June Helm, pp. 5–14. Handbook of North American Indians, Vol. 6, William C. Sturtevant, general editor, Smithsonian Institution, Washington, D.C.

Gardner, James S.
1983 Stop Me if You Heard This One Before: The Flint Run Paleoindian Complex Revisited. *Archaeology of Eastern North America* 11:48–64.

Gardner, Paul
1997 The Ecological Structure and Behavioral Implications of Mast Exploitation Strategies. In *People, Plants and Landscapes: Studies in Ethnobotany*, edited by Kristen J. Gremillion, pp. 161–178. University of Alabama Press, Tuscaloosa.

Gardner, William M.
1977 Flint Run Paleo-Indian Complex and Its Implications for Eastern North American Prehistory. In *Amerinds and Their Paleoenvironments in Northeastern North America*, edited by Walter S. Newman and Bert Salwen, pp. 257–263. Annals of the New York Academy of Sciences 288.

Gardner, William M., and Robert A. Verrey
1979 Typology and Chronology of Fluted Points from the Flint Run Area. *Pennsylvania Archaeologist* 49 (1–2):13–46.

Garland, Elizabeth B., and Scott G. Beld
1999 The Early Woodland: Ceramics, Domesticated Plants, and Burial Mounds Foretell the Shape of the Future. In *Retrieving Michigan's Buried Past: The Archaeology of the Great Lakes State*, edited by John R. Halsey, pp. 125–146. Cranbrook Institute of Science, Bulletin 64. Cranbrook Institute of Science, Bloomfield Hills, Michigan.

Gaudreau, Denise C.
1988 The Distribution of Late Quaternary Forest Regions in the Northeast: Pollen Data, Physiography and the Prehistoric

Record. In *Holocene Human Ecology in Northeastern North America*, edited by George. P. Nicholas, pp. 215–256. Plenum Press, New York.

Gehlbach, Donald
1998 Ohio's Prehistoric Pipes. D.R. Gehlbach Publisher.

Geier, Clarence R., and Stephen R. Potter
2000 *Archaeological Perspectives on the American Civil War*. University Press of Florida, Gainesville.

Geier, Clarence R., and Susan E. Winter
1994 *Look to the Earth: Historical Archaeology and the American Civil War*. University of Tennessee Press, Knoxville.

Geismar, Joan H.
1982 *The Archaeology of Social Disintegration in Skunk Hollow, a Nineteenth-Century Rural Black Community*. Academic Press, New York.

George, David R., and Robert E. Dewar
1999 Chenopodium in Connecticut Prehistory: Wild, Weedy, Cultivated or Domesticated? In *Current Northeast Paleoethnobotany*, edited by John P. Hart, pp. 121–132. New York State Museum Bulletin 494. University of the State of New York/State Department of Education, Albany.

Gibbon, Guy (editor)
1998 *Archaeology of Prehistoric Native America: An Encyclopedia*. Garland, New York.

Gibson, Jon L.
1984 *The Earthen Face of Civilization: Mapping and Testing at Poverty Point, 1983*. Office of the State Archaeologist, Baton Rouge, Louisiana.

Gibson, Jon L.
2000 *The Ancient Mounds of Poverty Point: Place of Rings*. University Press of Florida, Gainesville.

Giddings, J. L.
1964 *The Archaeology of Cape Denbigh*. Brown University Press, Providence, Rhode Island.

Gifford, Jack
1994 Smoke and Mirrors GE Gate, Part 2: "Now You See It, Now You Don't." *Central States Archaeological Journal* 41 (2):60–63.

Gilbert, M. Thomas, Dennis L. Jenkins, Anders Götherstrom, Nuria Naveran, Juan Sanchez, Michael Hofreiter, Philip F. Thomsen, Jonas Binladen, Thomas Higham, Robert M.Yohe, Robert Parr,

Linda Scott Cummings, and Eske Willerslev
2008 DNA from Pre-Clovis Human Coprolites in Oregon. *Science* 320:786–789.

Gillespie, Beryl C.
1981 Major Fauna in the Traditional Economy. In *Subarctic*, edited by June Helm, pp. 15–18. Handbook of North American Indians, Vol. 6, William C. Sturtevant, general editor, Smithsonian Institution, Washington, D.C.

Gillespie, Susan D., and Deborah L. Nichols
2003 *Archaeology Is Anthropology*. American Anthropological Association Washington, D.C.

Gilliland, Marion Spjut
1975 *The Material Culture of Key Marco, Florida*. University Press of Florida, Gainesville.

Gilman, Patricia A.
1987 Architecture as Artifact: Pit Structures and Pueblos in the American Southwest. *American Antiquity* 52:538–564.

Glassow, Michael A.
1996 *Purismeño Chumash Prehistory: Maritime Adaptation Along the Southern California Coast*. Harcourt Brace College, Fort Worth.

Goddard, Ives, and Lyle Campbell
1994 The History and Classification of American Indian Languages: What Are the Implications for the Peopling of the Americas? In *Method and Theory for Investigating the Peopling of the Americas*, edited by Robson Bonnichsen and D. Gentry Steele, pp. 189–207. Oregon State University Press for the Center for the Study of the First Americans, Corvallis.

Goebel, Ted
2004 The Search for a Clovis Progenitor in Sub-Arctic Siberia. In *Entering America: Northeast Asia and Beringia Before the Last Glacial Maximum*, edited by D. B. Madsen, pp. 311–356. The University of Utah Press, Salt Lake City.

Goebel, Ted, W. Roger Powers, and Nancy H. Bigelow
1991 The Nenana Complex of Alaska and Clovis Origins. In *Clovis: Origins and Adaptations*, edited by Robson Bonnichsen and Karen Turnmire, pp. 49–79. Oregon State University

for the Center for the Study of the First Americans, Corvallis.

Goebel, Ted, W. Roger Powers, Nancy H. Bigelow, and Andrew S. Higgs
1996 Walker Road. In *American Beginnings: The Prehistory and Palaeoecology of Beringia*, edited by Frederick H. West, pp. 356–363. University of Chicago Press, Chicago.

Goebel, Ted, Michael R. Waters, Ian Buvit, Mikhail V. Konstantinov, and Aleksander V. Konstantinov
2000 Studenoe-2 and the Origins of Microblade Technologies in the Transbaikal, Siberia. *American Antiquity* 74 (285):567–575.

Goldberg, P., and T. L. Arpin
1999 Micromorphological Analysis of Sediments from Meadowcroft Rockshelter, Pennsylvania: Implications for Radiocarbon Dating. *Journal of Field Archaeology* 26 (3):325–342.

Goldberg, P. S., and S. C. Sherwood
1994 Micromorphology of Dust Cave Sediments: Some Preliminary Results. *Journal of Alabama Archaeology* 40:57–65.

Goldman-Finn, N. S., and B. N. Driskell
1994 Introduction to Archaeological Research at Dust Cave. *Journal of Alabama Archaeology* 40:1–16.

Goldstein, Lynne G.
1980 *Mississippian Mortuary Practices: A Case Study of Two Cemeteries in the Lower Illinois Valley*. Northwestern University Archaeological Program, Evanston, Illinois.

Goldstein, Lynne G., and John D. Richards
1991 Ancient Aztalan: The Cultural and Ecological Context of a Late Prehistoric Site in the Midwest. In *Cahokia and the Hinterlands: Middle Mississippian Cultures of the Midwest*, edited by Thomas E. Emerson and R. Barry Lewis, pp. 193–206. University of Illinois Press, Urbana.

Goodman, Jeffrey
1982 *American Genesis*. Berkeley Books, New York.

Goodyear, Albert C.
1982 The Chronological Position of the Dalton Horizon in the Southeastern United States. *American Antiquity* 47:383–395.

Goodyear, Albert C.
1999 The Early Holocene Occupation of the Southeastern United States: A Geoarchaeological Summary. In *Ice Age Peoples of North America:*

Environments, Origins and Adaptations of the First Americans, edited by Robson Bonnichsen and Karen Turnmire, pp. 432–481. Oregon State University Press for the Center for the Study of the First Americans, Corvallis.

Gordon, Bryan C.
1998 Taltheilei Tradition. In *Archaeology of Prehistoric Native America: An Encyclopedia*, edited by Guy Gibbon, p. 827. Garland, New York.

Gordon, Robert
1996 *American Iron: 1607–1900*. Johns Hopkins University Press, Baltimore.

Gordon, Robert B., and Patrick M. Malone
1994 *The Texture of Industry: An Archaeological View of the Industrialization of North America*. Oxford University Press, New York.

Gorman, F.
1969 The Clovis Hunters: An Alternate View of Their Environment and Ecology. *Kiva* 35 (2):91–102.

Graham, Russell W., C. Vance Haynes, D. L. Johnson, and Marvin Kay
1981 Kimmswick: A Clovis–Mastodon Association in Eastern Missouri. *Science* 213:1115–1117.

Graham, Russell W., and Marvin Kay
1988 Taphonomic Comparisons of Cultural and Noncultural Faunal Deposits at the Kimmswick and Barnhart Sites, Jefferson County, Missouri. In *Late Pleistocene and Early Holocene Paleoecology and Archeology of the Eastern Great Lakes Region*, edited by R. S. Laub, N. G. Miller, and D. W. Steadman, pp. 227–240. Buffalo Society of Natural Sciences 53, Buffalo, New York.

Graham, Russell W., and Jim I. Mead
1987 Environmental Fluctuations and Evolution of Mammalian Faunas During the Last Deglaciation in North America. In *North America and Adjacent Oceans in the Last Deglaciation*, edited by W. F. Ruddiman and H. E. Wright, Jr., pp. 371–402. Vol. K-3, The Geology of North America. Geological Society of America, Boulder, Colorado.

Gramly, Richard M.
1977 Deerskins and Hunting Territories: Competition for a Scarce Resource. *American Antiquity* 42 (4):601–605.

Grant, Campbell
1978 Eastern Coastal Chumash. In *California*, edited by Robert F. Heizer, pp. 509–519. Handbook of North American Indians, Vol. 8. William C. Sturtevant, general editor, Smithsonian Institution, Washington, D.C.

Gray, John
2001 Young Kwaday Dan Sinchi Was Trekking High up on a Barren Glacier in His Gopher-Skin Cloak When Disaster Struck. *The Globe and Mail* 4 August:F7. Toronto.

Grayson, Donald K.
1983 *The Establishment of Human Antiquity*. Academic Press, New York.

Grayson, Donald K.
1993 *The Desert's Past: A Natural Prehistory of the Great Basin*. Smithsonian Books, Washington, D.C.

Grayson, Donald K.
1994 Chronology, Glotto-chronology, and Numic Expansion. In *Across the West: Human Population Movement and the Expansion of the Numa*, edited by D. B. Madsen and D. R. Rhode, pp. 20–23. University of Utah Press, Salt Lake City.

Grayson, Donald K.
2001 The Archaeological Record of Human Impacts on Animal Populations. *Journal of World Prehistory* 15:1–68.

Grayson, Donald K., and David J. Meltzer
2003 A Requiem for North American Overkill. *Journal of Archaeological Science* 30:585–593.

Green, F. E.
1963 The Clovis Blades: An Important Addition to the Llano Complex. *American Antiquity* 29:145–165.

Greenberg, Joseph
1987 *Language in the Americas*. Stanford University Press, Stanford, California.

Greenberg, Joseph H., Christy G. Turner, and S. L. Zegura
1986 The Settlement of the Americas: A Comparison of the Linguistic, Dental and Genetic Evidence. *Current Anthropology* 27:477–497.

Greenman, Emerson F.
1963 The Upper Paleolithic and the New World. *Current Anthropology* 4:41–66.

Gregory, David A., and David R. Wilcox (editors)

2007 *Zuni Origins: Toward a New Synthesis of Southwestern Archaeology.* The University of Arizona Press, Tucson.

Gremillion, Kristen J.
1996 The Paleoethnobotanical Record for the Mid-Holocene Southeast. In *Archaeology of the Mid-Holocene Southeast*, edited by Kenneth E. Sassaman and David G. Anderson, pp. 99–114. University Press of Florida, Gainesville.

Gremillion, Kristen J.
2002 The Development and Dispersal of Agricultural Systems in the Woodland Period Southeast. In *The Woodland Southeast*, edited by David G. Anderson and Robert C. Mainfort, Jr., pp. 483–501. University of Alabama Press, Tuscaloosa.

Gremillion, Kristen J
2004 Seed Processing and the Origins of Food Production in Eastern North America. *American Antiquity* 69 (2):215–233.

Griffin, James B., A. A. Gordus, and Gary A. Wright
1969 Identification of the Sources of Hopewellian Obsidian in the Middle West. *American Antiquity* 34:1–14.

Gross, G. Timothy
1984 *Excavations at Cougar Springs Cave (Site 5 MT 4797), a Basketmaker II Seasonal Site.* Dolores Archaeological Program Technical Report DAP 172. Bureau of Reclamation, Upper Colorado Region, Salt Lake City.

Gross, G. Timothy
1986 Technology: Facilities. In *Dolores Archaeological Program Final Synthetic Report*, edited by David A. Breternitz, Christine K. Robinson, and G. Timothy Gross, pp. 611–632. U.S. Department of the Interior, Engineering and Research Center, Denver.

Gruhn, Ruth
1994 The Pacific Coast Route of Initial Entry: An Overview. In *Method and Theory for Investigating the Peopling of the Americas*, edited by Robson Bonnichsen and D. Gentry Steele, pp. 249–256. Oregon State University Press for the Center for the Study of the First Americans, Corvallis.

Gustafson, Carl E., D. Gilbow, and Richard D. Daugherty
1979 The Manis Mastodon Site: Early Man on the Olympic Peninsula. *Canadian Journal of Archaeology* 3:157–164.

Haas, Jonathan, and Winifred Creamer
1993 Stress and Warfare Among the Kayenta Anasazi of the Thirteenth Century A.D. *Fieldiana: Anthropology* (n.s.) 21. Field Museum of Natural History, Chicago.

Hajic, Edwin R.
1990 *Koster Site Archeology. I: Stratigraphy and Landscape Evolution.* Kampsville Archeological Center Research Series 8. Kampsville, Illinois.

Halchin, Jill Y.
1985 *Excavations at Fort Michilimackinac, 1983–1985: House C of the Southeast Row House.* Archaeological Completion Report Series 11. Mackinac Island State Park Commission, Mackinac Island, Michigan.

Hall, Don Alan, and George Wisner
2000 Charting a New Era, *Mammoth Trumpet* 15 (1). Electronic document, http://www.centerfirstameri-cans.com/mammoth/issues/Volume-15/vol15_num1.pdf, accessed September 15, 2012.

Hall, Stephen A.
2000 Was the High Plains a Pine-Spruce Forest? *Rangelands* 21 (5):3–5.

Hall, Stephen A., and S. Valastro, Jr.
1995 Vegetation in the Southern Great Plains During the Last Glacial Maximum. *Quaternary Research* 44:237–245.

Halsey, John R.
1999 *Retrieving Michigan's Buried Past: The Archaeology of the Great Lakes State.* Cranbrook Institute of Science, Bloomfield Hills, Michigan.

Hamilton, Marcus J., and Briggs Buchanan
2007 Spatial Gradients in Clovis-age Radiocarbon Dates Across North America Suggest Rapid Colonization from the North. *Proceedings of the National Academy of the Sciences* 104:15625–15630.

Hamilton, Scott
1996 Over-Hunting and Local Extinctions: Socio-Economic Implications of Fur Trade Subsistence. In *Images of the Recent Past: Readings in Historical Archaeology*, edited by Charles E. Orser, Jr., pp. 416–436. AltaMira Press, Walnut Creek, California.

Hamilton, Thomas D., and Ted Goebel
1999 Late Pleistocene Peopling of Alaska. In *Ice Age People of North America*, edited by Robson Bonnichsen and Karen Turn-mire, pp. 156–199. Oregon State University Press for the Center for the Study of the First Americans, Corvallis.

Hammatt, H. H.
1970 A Paleoindian Butchering Kit. *American Antiquity* 35:141–152.

Hammond, George P., and Agapito Rey (translators)
1928 *Obregon's History of Sixteenth Century Explorations in Western North America Entitled: Chronicle, Commentary, or Relation of the Ancient and Modern Discoveries in New Spain, New Mexico, and Mexico.* Wetzel, Los Angeles.

Hanson, Gordon William
1973 The Katz Site: A Prehistoric Pithouse Settlement in the Lower Fraser Valley, British Columbia. M.A. thesis, Department of Anthropology, University of British Columbia, Vancouver. https://circle.ubc.ca/handle/2429/33046?show=full, accessed January 21, 2012.

Hanson, Jeffrey R.
1998 Late High Plains Hunters. In *Archaeology of the Great Plains*, edited by W. Raymond Wood, pp. 456–480. University Press of Kansas, Lawrence.

Hard, Robert J., and John R. Roney
2005 The Transition to Farming on the Rio Casas Grandes and in the Southern Jornada Mogollon Region. In *The Late Archaic Across the Borderlands: From Foraging to Farming*, edited by Bradley J. Vierra, pp. 141–186. University of Texas Press, Austin.

Hardesty, Donald L.
1991 Toward a Historical Archaeology of the Intermountain West. *Historical Archaeology* 25 (3):29–35.

Hargrave, Michael L., and David P. Braun
1981 Chronometry of Mechanical Performance Characteristics of Woodland Ceramics: Methods, Results, Applications. Paper presented at the 46th annual meeting of the Society for American Archaeology, San Diego.

Harn, Alan D.
1995 Two Centuries of Development at Dickson Mounds. *The Living Museum* 57 (1):12–14.

Harper, John R., James Haggarty, and Mary C. Morris
1995 *Final Report: Broughton Archipelago Clam Terrace Survey.* Prepared for Land Use Coordination Office,

British Columbia Ministry of Government Services by Coastal & Ocean Resources Inc., Sidney, British Columbia. Electronic document, http://aquaticcommons.org/1129/, accessed January 21, 2012.

Harper, Kimball T.
1986 Historical Environments. In *Great Basin*, edited by Warren L. D'Azevedo, pp. 51–63. Handbook of North American Indians, Vol. 11, William C. Sturtevant, general editor, Smithsonian Institution, Washington, D.C.

Harrington, Mark R.
1957 *A Pinto Site at Little Lake, California.* Southwest Museum Papers 17. Los Angeles.

Harrington, Mark R., and Ruth D. Simpson
1961 *Tule Springs, Nevada, with Other Evidence of Pleistocene Man in North America.* Southwest Museum Papers 18. Los Angeles.

Harrington, Spencer P. M.
1996 Bones and Bureaucrats: New York's Great Cemetery Imbroglio. In *Archaeological Ethics*, edited by Karen D. Vitelli, pp. 221–236. AltaMira Press, Walnut Creek, California.

Hart, John P.
1999a Dating Roundtop's Domesticates: Implications for Northeastern Late Prehistory. In *Current Northeast Paleoethnobotany*, edited by John P. Hart, pp. 47–68. University of the State of New York/State Department of Education, Albany.

Hart, John P.
1999b Maize Agriculture Evolution in the Eastern Woodlands of North America: A Darwinian Perspective. *Journal of Archaeological Method and Theory* 6:137–180.

Hart, John P.
2000 New Dates on Classic New York State Sites: Just How Old Are Those Longhouses? *Northeast Anthropology* 60:1–22.

Hart, John P.
2001 Maize, Matrilocality, Migration and Northern Iroquoian Evolution. *Journal of Archaeological Method and Theory* 8:151–182.

Hart, John P.
2004 Can *Cucurbita pepo* Gourd Seeds Be Made Edible? *Journal of Archaeological Science* 31:1631–1633.

Hart, John P.
2008 Evolving the Three Sisters: The Changing Histories of Maize,

Bean, and Squash in New York and the Greater Northeast. In *Current Northeast Paleoethnobotany II*, edited by John P. Hart, pp. 87–99. The University of the State of New York, Albany.

Hart, John P., David L. Asch, C. Margaret Scarry, and Gary W. Crawford
2002 The Age of the Common Bean (*Phaseolus vulgaris* L.) in the Northern Eastern Woodlands of North America. *Antiquity* 76:377–385.

Hart, John P., and Nancy Asch-Sidell
1996 Prehistoric Agricultural Systems in the West Branch of the Susquehanna River Basin: A.D. 800 to A.D. 1350. *Northeast Anthropology* 52:1–30.

Hart, John P., and Nancy Asch-Sidell
1997 Additional Evidence for Early Cucurbit Use in the Northern Eastern Woodlands East of the Allegheny Front. *American Antiquity* 62:523–537.

Hart, John P., and Hetty Jo Brumbach
2003 The Death of Owasco. *American Antiquity* 68:737–752.

Hart, John P., Hetty Jo Brumbach, and Robert Lusteck
2007 Extending the Phytolith Evidence for Early Maize (*Zea mays* ssp. mays) and Squash (*Cucurbita* sp.) in Central New York. *American Antiquity* 72:563–583.

Hart, John P., Robert A. Daniels, and Charles A. Sheviak
2004 Do *Cucurbita pepo* Gourds Float Fish Nets? *American Antiquity* 69:141–148.

Hart, John P., and R. G. Matson
2009 The Use of Multiple Discriminate Analysis in Classifying Prehistoric Phytolith Assemblages Recovered from Cooking Residues. *Journal of Archaeological Science* 36:74–83.

Hart, John P., and C. Margaret Scarry
1999 The Age of Common Beans (*Phaseolus vulgaris*) in the Northeastern United States. *American Antiquity* 64:653–658.

Hart, John P., Robert G. Thompson, and Hetty Jo Brumbach
2003 Phytolith Evidence for Early Maize (*Zea mays*) in the Northern Finger Lakes Region of New York. *American Antiquity* 68:619–640.

Hasenstab, Robert J.
1999 Fishing, Farming and Finding the Village Sites. In *The Archaeological Northeast*, edited by Mary Ann Levine, Kenneth E. Sassaman, and Mischael S.

Nassaney, pp. 139–153. Bergin & Garvey, Westport, Connecticut.

Hauptman, Laurence M.
1990 The Pequot War and Its Legacies. In *The Pequots in Southern New England: The Rise and Fall of an American Indian Nation*, edited by Laurence M. Hauptman and James D. Wherry, pp. 69–80. University of Oklahoma Press, Norman.

Haury, Emil W.
1950 *Stratigraphy and Archaeology of Ventana Cave* (second printing 1975). University of Arizona Press, Tucson.

Haury, Emil W.
1976 *The Hohokam: Desert Farmers and Craftsmen.* University of Arizona Press, Tucson.

Hayden, Brian
1982 Interaction Parameters and the Demise of Paleo-Indian Craftsmanship. *Plains Anthropologist* 27:109–123.

Hayden, Brian
1997 *The Pithouses of Keatley Creek: Complex Hunter-Gatherers on the Northwest Plateau.* Harcourt Brace College, Fort Worth, Texas.

Hayden, Brian, and June M. Ryder
1991 Prehistoric Cultural Collapse in the Lillooet Area. *American Antiquity* 56:50–65.

Hayden, Brian, and Rick Schulting
1997 The Plateau Interaction Sphere and Late Prehistoric Cultural Complexity. *American Antiquity* 62:51–85.

Hayes, Alden C.
1964 *The Archaeological Survey of Wetherill Mesa.* National Park Service. Washington, D.C.

Haynes, C. Vance, Jr.
1993 Clovis–Folsom Geochronology and Climatic Change. In *From Kostenki to Clovis: Upper Paleolithic–Paleo-Indian Adaptations*, edited by O. Soffer and N. D. Praslov, pp. 219–236. Plenum Press, New York.

Haynes, C. Vance, Jr.
1995 Geochronology of Paleoenvironmental Change, Clovis Type Site, Blackwater Draw, New Mexico. *Geoarchaeology* 10:317–388.

Haynes, C. Vance, Jr., and George Agogino
1986 Geochronology of Sandia Cave. *Smithsonian Contributions to Anthropology* 32:1–32.

Haynes, C. Vance, Jr., and E. T. Hemmings

1968 Mammoth-Bone Shaft-Wrench from Murray Springs, Arizona. *Science* 159:186–187.

Heckenberger, Michael J., James B. Petersen, and Nancy Asch-Sidell
1991 Early Evidence of Maize Agriculture in the Connecticut River Valley of Vermont. *Archaeology of Eastern North America* 20:125–150.

Hegmon, Michelle
2003 Setting Theoretical Egos Aside: Issues and Theory in North American Archaeology. *American Antiquity* 68 (2):213–243.

Hegmon, Michelle
2005 Beyond the Mold: Questions of Inequality in Southwest Villages. In *North American Archaeology*, edited by Timothy R. Pauketat and Diana Di Paolo Loren, pp. 213–234. Blackwell, Malden, Massachusetts.

Heldman, Donald P., and Roger T. Grange, Jr.
1981 *Excavations at Fort Michilimackinac, 1978–1979: The Rue de la Babillarde.* Mackinac Island State Park Commission, Mackinac Island, Michigan.

Helm, June
1981 Introduction. In *Subarctic*, edited by June Helm, pp. 1–4. Handbook of North American Indians, Vol. 6, William C. Sturtevant, general editor, Smithsonian Institution, Washington, D.C.

Hemmings, E. Thomas
1984 Investigations at Grave Creek Mound 1975–76: A Sequence for Mound and Moat Construction. *West Virginia Archaeologist* 36 (2):3–39.

Henning, Dale R.
2005 The Evolution of the Plains Village Tradition. In *North American Archaeology*, edited by Timothy R. Pauketat and Diana Di Paolo Loren, pp. 161–186. Blackwell, Malden, Massachusetts.

Henning, Dale R.
2007 Continuity and Change in the Eastern Plains, A.D.800–1700: An Examination of Exchange Patterns. In *Plains Village Archaeology: Bison-Hunting Farmers in the Central and Northern Plains,* edited by Stanley A. Ahler and Marvin Kay, pp. 67–82. University of Utah Press, Salt Lake City.

Hertz, Johannes
2000 The Newport Tower. In *Vikings: The North Atlantic Saga*, edited by William W. Fitzhugh and Elisabeth I. Ward, p. 376. Smithsonian Institution Press, Washington, D.C.

Hester, J. J.
1972 *Blackwater Locality No. 1: A Stratified Early Man Site in Eastern New Mexico.* Fort Burgwin Research Center Publication 8. Ranchos de Taos, New Mexico.

Hester, Thomas R., Harry J. Schafer, and Kenneth L. Feder
2008 *Field Methods in Archaeology.* Left Coast Press, Walnut Creek, California.

Heye, George C.
1921 Certain Artifacts from San Miguel Island. Museum of the American Indian Notes and Monographs Vol. 4, No. 7. Heye Foundation, New York.

Hicks, Brent A.
2004 *Marmes Rockshelter: A Final Report on 11,000 Years of Cultural Use.* Washington State University Press, Pullman.

Hildebrant, William R., and Kelly R. McGuire
2002 The Ascendance of Hunting During the California Middle Archaic: An Evolutionary Perspective. *American Antiquity* 67:231–256.

Hill, Jane H.
2007 The Zuni Language in Southwestern Areal Context. In *Zuni Origins: Toward a New Synthesis of Southwestern Archaeology*, edited by David A. Gregory and David R. Wilcox, pp. 22-38. University of Arizona Press, Tucson.

Hill, Matthew E., Jr.
2007 A Moveable Feast: Variation in Faunal Resource Use Among Central and Western North American Paleoindian Sites. *American Antiquity* 72 (417–438).

Hill, Rebecca
2001 Review of *Man Corn: Cannibalism and Violence in the Prehistoric American Southwest*, by Christy G. Turner and Jacqueline A. Turner. *Anthena Review* 2 (2). Electronic document, http://www.athenapub .com/revhub1.htm, accessed June 26, 2012.

Hillerman, Tony
1988 *A Thief of Time.* Harper & Row, New York.

Hoard, Robert J., and William E. Banks (editors)
2006 *Kansas Archaeology.* University Press of Kansas, Lawrence.

Hoard, Robert J., and Henry W. Chaney
2010 Olivella Shells From Kansas Archaeological Sites. *Plains Anthropologist* 55:293–298.

Hodder, Ian
1985 Postprocessual Archaeology. In *Advances in Archaeological Method and Theory*, Vol. 8, edited by Michael Schiffer, pp. 1–26. Academic Press, New York.

Hodder, Ian
1991 *Reading the Past: Current Approaches to Interpretation in Archaeology*, 2nd ed. Cambridge University Press, Cambridge.

Hoff, Ricky
1980 Fishhooks. In *Hoko River: A 2,500 Year Old Fishing Camp on the Northwest Coast of North America*, edited by Dale R. Croes and Eric Blinman, pp. 160–188. Reports of Investigations 58. Laboratory of Anthropology, Washington State University, Pullman.

Hofman, Jack L.
1989 Hunters and Gatherers in the Southern Great Plains. In *From Clovis to Comanchero: Archeological Overview of the Southern Great Plains*, edited by Jack L. Hofman, Robert L. Brooks, Joe S. Hays, Douglas W. Owsley, Richard L. Jantz, Murray K. Marks, and Mary H. Manheim, pp. 25–60. Arkansas Archeological Survey Research Series 35. Arkansas Archeological Survey, Fayetteville.

Hofman, Jack L., and Robert L. Brooks
1989 Prehistoric Culture History: Woodland Complexes in the Southern Great Plain. In *From Clovis to Comanchero: Archeological Overview of the Southern Great Plains*, edited by Jack L. Hofman, Robert L. Brooks, Joe S. Hays, Douglas W. Owsley, Richard L. Jantz, Murray K. Marks, and Mary H. Manheim, pp. 61–71. Arkansas Archeological Survey Research Series 35. Arkansas Archeological Survey, Fayetteville.

Hofman, Jack L., and Russell W. Graham
1998 *The Paleo-Indian Cultures of the Great Plains.* Archaeology of the Great Plains. University Press of Kansas, Lawrence.

Holen, Steven R., and David W. May
2002 The La Sena and Shaffert Mammoth Sites: History of Investigations, 1987–1998. In *Medicine Creek: Seventy Years of Archaeological Investigations*, edited by Donna C. Roper, pp. 20–36.

University of Alabama Press, Tuscaloosa.

Holliday, V. T.
1987 A Reexamination of Late-Pleistocene Boreal Forest Reconstructions for the Southern High Plains. *Quaternary Research* 28:238–244.

Holliday, V. T.
1997 *Paleoindian Geoarchaeology of the Southern High Plains.* University of Texas Press, Austin.

Holliday, Vance T., and David J. Meltzer
2010 The 12.9-ka ET Impact Hypothesis and North American Paleoindians. *Current Anthropology* 51:575–607.

Hollinger, R. Eric, Stephen Ousley, and Charles Utermohle
2009 The Thule Migration: A New Look at the Archaeology and Biology of the Point Barrow Region Populations. In *The Northern World AD 900–1400*, edited by Herbert Maschner, Owen Mason, and Robert McGhee, pp. 131–154. The University of Utah Press, Salt Lake City.

Hollowell, Julie
2006 Moral Arguments on Subsistence Digging. In *The Ethics of Archaeology. Philosophical Perspectives on Archaeological Practice*, edited by C. Scarre and G. Scarre, pp. 69–93. Cambridge University Press, Cambridge.

Hollowell-Zimmer, Julie
2003 Digging in the Dirt: Ethics and "Low-End Looting." In *Ethical Issues in Archaeology*, edited by Larry J. Zimmerman, Karen D. Vitelli, and Julie Hollowell-Zimmer, pp. 45–56. AltaMira Press, Walnut Creek, California.

Holmes, Charles E.
1996 Broken Mammmoth. In *American Beginnings: The Prehistory and Palaeoecology of Beringia*, edited by Frederick H. West, pp. 312–317. University of Chicago Press, Chicago.

Holmes, Charles E., Richard Vander Hoek, and Thomas E. Dilley
1996 Swan Point. In *American Beginnings: The Prehistory and Palaeoecology of Beringia*, edited by Frederick H. West, pp. 319–323. University of Chicago Press, Chicago.

Holmes, William H.
1903 *Aboriginal Pottery of the Eastern United States.* Twentieth Annual Report of the Bureau of American Ethnology, Washington, D.C.

Holmes, William H.
1914 Areas of American Culture Characterization Outlined as an Aid in the Study of the Antiquities. *American Anthropologist* 16 (3):413–446.

Homsey, L.
2004 The Form, Function, and Organization of Anthropogenic Deposits at Dust Cave, Alabama. Unpublished Ph.D. dissertation, Department of Anthropology, University of Pittsburgh, Pittsburgh, Pennsylvania.

Hopkins, David M.
1967 *The Bering Land Bridge.* Stanford University Press, Stanford, California.

Hopkins, David M.
1973 Sea Level History in Beringia During the Last 250,000 Years. *Quaternary Research* 3:520–540.

Houart, Gail L.
1971 *Koster: A Stratified Archaic Site in the Illinois Valley.* Illinois State Museum, Springfield.

Howard, Edgar B.
1935 Evidence of Early Man in North America. *The Museum Journal* 244 (2–3):61–157.

Howard, Joel C.
2003. Pressing Matters: Archaeology Students Dig for Printing History. *The Daily Cougar* (University of Houston) 18 November:1. Houston, Texas.

Huckell, Bruce B.
1982 The Denver Elephant Project: A Report on Experimentation with Thrusting Spears. *Plains Anthropologist* 27:217–224.

Huckell, Bruce B.
1995 *Of Marshes and Maize: Preceramic Agricultural Settlements in the Cienega Valley, Southeastern Arizona.* University of Arizona, Tucson.

Huckell, Bruce B.
1996 The Archaic Prehistory of the North American Southwest. *Journal of World Prehistory* 10:305–373.

Huckell, Bruce B.
1998 Ventana Cave. In *Archaeology of Prehistoric Native America: An Encyclopedia*, edited by Guy Gibbon, pp. 864–865. Garland, New York.

Huckell, Bruce B., and J. David Kilby (compilers)
2004 *Readings in Late Pleistocene North America and Early Paleoindians: Selections from American Antiquity.*

Society for American Archaeology, Washington, D.C.

Huddleston, Lee Eldridge
1967 *Origins of the American Indians: European Concepts, 1492–1729.* University of Texas Press, Austin.

Hudson, Charles
1976 *The Southeastern Indians.* University of Tennessee Press, Knoxville.

Hudson, Charles, Chester B. Depratter, and Marvin T. Smith
1989 Hernando de Soto's Expedition Through the Southern United States. In *First Encounters: Spanish Explorations in the Caribbean and the United States, 1492–1570*, edited by Jerald T. Milanich and Susan Milbrath, pp. 77–98. University Press of Florida, Gainesville.

Huelsbeck, David R.
1989 Food Consumption, Resource Exploitation, and Relationships Within and Between Households at Ozette. In *Households and Communities: Proceedings of the 21st Annual Conference*, edited by S. MacEachern, D. Archer and R. Gavin, pp. 157–167. University of Calgary Archaeological Association, Calgary, Alberta.

Huelsbeck, David R.
1994 The Utilization of Whales at Ozette. In *Ozette Archaeological Project Research Reports, Vol. 2: Fauna*, edited by Stephan R. Samuels, pp. 265–303. Reports of Investigation No. 66, Department of Anthropology, Washington State University, Pullman, and the National Park Service, Seattle.

Hughes, Richard E.
2006 The Sources of Hopewell Obsidian: Forty Years After Griffin. In *Recreating Hopewell*, edited by Douglas K. Charles and Jane E. Buikstra, pp. 361–375. University of Florida Press, Gainesville.

Humboldt State University
2004 *CA-HUM-513/H, The Nursery Site.* Electronic document, http://sorrel.humboldt.edu/~archlab, accessed June 3, 2006.

Hurt, R. Douglas
1987 *Indian Agriculture in America: Prehistory to Present.* University Press of Kansas, Lawrence.

Ijzereef, F. Gerard
1989 Social Differentiation from Animal Bone Studies. In *Diet and Crafts in Towns*, edited by D. Serjeantson and

T. Waldron, pp. 41–53. BAR British Series 199. British Archaeological Reports, Oxford.

Ikawa-Smith, Fumiko
2004 Humans Along the Pacific Margin of Northeast Asia Before the Last Glacial Maximum: Evidence for Their Presence and Adaptations. In *Entering America: Northeast Asia and Beringia Before the Last Glacial Maximum*, edited by D. B. Madsen, pp. 285–309. The University of Utah Press, Salt Lake City.

Ingle, Marjorie
1982 Industrial Site Building: Implications from the 1978–79 Investigations at the Rogers Locomotive Works, Paterson, New Jersey. In *Archaeology of Urban America: The Search for Pattern and Process*, edited by Roy S. Dickens, Jr., pp. 237–256. Academic Press, New York.

Ingstad, Helge, and Anne Stine Ingstad
2001 *The Viking Discovery of America: The Excavation of a Norse Settlement in L'Anse aux Meadows, Newfoundland*. Checkmark Books, New York.

Irwin-Williams, Cynthia
1979b Post-Pleistocene Archaeology, 7000–2000 B.C. In *Southwest*, edited by Alfonso Ortiz, pp. 31–42. Handbook of North American Indians, Vol. 9, William C. Sturtevant, general editor, Smithsonian Institution, Washington, D.C.

Irwin-Williams, Cynthia, and C. V. Haynes, Jr.
1970 Climatic Change and Early Population Dynamics in the Southwestern United States. *Quaternary Research* 1:59–71.

Isabella, Jude
2011 The Edible Seascape. *Archaeology* 64(5):30–33.

Jackson, H. Edwin, Melissa L. Higgins, and Robert E. Reams
2002 Woodland Cultural and Chronological Trends on the Southern Gulf Coastal Plain: Recent Research in the Pine Hills of Southeastern Mississippi. In *The Woodland Southeast*, edited by David G. Anderson and Robert C. Mainfort, Jr., pp. 228–248. The University of Alabama Press, Tuscaloosa.

Jackson, H. Edwin, and Susan L. Scott
2002 Woodland Faunal Exploitation in the Midsouth. In *The Woodland Southeast*, edited by David G. Anderson and Robert C. Mainfort, Jr., pp. 461–482. University of Alabama Press, Tuscaloosa.

Jackson, H. Edwin, and Susan L. Scott
2003 Patterns of Elite Faunal Utilization at Moundville, Alabama. *American Antiquity* 62:464-487.

Jackson, Robert H., and Edward Castillo
1995 *Indians, Franciscans, and Spanish Colonization: The Impact of the Mission System on California Indians*. University of New Mexico Press, Albuquerque.

Jacobsen, William H.
1986 Washoe Language. In *Great Basin*, edited by Warren L. D'Azevedo, pp. 107–112. Handbook of North American Indians, Vol. 11, William C. Sturtevant, general editor, Smithsonian Institution, Washington, D.C.

James, Ronald M.
2012 *The Virginia City: Secrets of a Western Past*. University of Nebraska Press, Lincoln.

James, Steven
1994 Hohokam Hunting and Fishing Patterns at Pueblo Grande: Results of the Archaeofaunal Analysis. In *The Pueblo Grande Project, Vol. 5: Environment and Subsistence*, edited by Scott Kwiatkowski, pp. 249–318. Soil Systems Publications in Archaeology 20, Phoenix.

Jameson, John H., Jr.
1997 *Presenting Archaeology to the Public: Digging for Truths*. AltaMira Press, Walnut Creek, California.

Jantz, Richard F., and Douglas Owsley
2001 Variation Among Early North American Crania. *American Journal of Physical Anthropology* 114:146–155.

Jefferies, Richard W.
1987 *The Archaeology of Carrier Mills: 10,000 Years in the Saline Valley of Illinois*. Southern Illinois University Press, Carbondale.

Jefferies, Richard W.
1994 The Swift Creek Site and Woodland Platform Mounds in the Southeastern United States. In *Ocmulgee Archaeology: 1936–1986*, edited by David J. Hally, pp. 71–83. University of Georgia Press, Athens.

Jefferies, Richard W.
1995a The Status of Archaic Period Research in the Midwestern United States. *Archaeology of Eastern North America* 23:119–144.

Jefferies, Richard W.
1995b Late Middle Archaic Exchange and Interaction in the North American Midcontinent. In *Native American Interactions: Multiscalar Analyses and Interpretations in the Eastern Woodlands*, edited by Michael S. Nassaney and Kenneth E. Sassaman, pp. 73–99. The University of Alabama Press, Knoxville.

Jefferies, Richard W.
2004 Regional Cultures, 700 BC–AD1000. In *Southeast*, edited by Raymond D. Fogelson, pp. 115–127. Handbook of North American Indians, Vol. 14, William C. Sturtevant, general editor, Smithsonian Institution, Washington, D.C.

Jefferies, Richard W.
2008 *Holocene Hunter-Gatherers of the Lower Ohio River Valley*. The University of Alabama Press, Tuscaloosa.

Jefferies, Richard W., and B. Mark Lynch
1983 Dimensions of Middle Archaic Cultural Adaptation at the Black Earth Site, Saline County, Illinois. In *Archaic Hunters and Gatherers in the American Midwest*, edited by James L. Phillips and James A. Brown, pp. 299–322. Academic Press, New York.

Jefferson, Thomas
1787 Excavation of a Virginia Burial Mound in 1784. In *The Archaeologist at Work: A Source Book in Archaeological Method and Interpretation*, edited by R. F. Heizer, pp. 218–221. Harper & Brothers, New York, 1959.

Jenkins, Dennis L., Craig E. Skinner, Jennifer Thatcher, and Keenan Hoar
1999 Obsidian Characterization and Hydration Results of the Fort Rock Basin Prehistory Project. Paper presented at the Northwest Anthropological Conference, Newport, Oregon.

Jennings, Jesse D.
1957 *Danger Cave*. Anthropological Paper 27. University of Utah, Salt Lake City.

Jennings, Jesse D.
1964 The Desert West. In *Prehistoric Man in the New World*, edited by Jesse D. Jennings and Edward Norbeck, pp. 149–174. University of Chicago Press, Chicago.

Jennings, Jesse D.
1973 The Short Useful Life of a Simple Hypothesis. *Tebiwa* 13 (1):1–9.

Jennings, Jesse D.
1978 *Prehistory of Utah and the Eastern Great Basin*. Anthropological Paper 98, University of Utah.

Jennings, Jesse D.
1986 Introduction: Prehistory. In *Great Basin*, edited by Warren L. D'Azervedo, pp. 113–119. Handbook of North American Indians, Vol. 11, William C. Sturtevant, general editor, Smithsonian Institution, Washington, D.C.

Jennings, Jesse D.
1989 *Prehistory of North America*, 3rd ed. Mayfield, Mountain View, California.

Jett, Stephen J., and Peter B. Moyle
1986 Exotic Origins of Fishes Depicted on Prehistoric Mimbres Pottery from New Mexico. *American Antiquity* 51:688–720.

Johannessen, Sissel
1993 Farmers of the Late Woodland. In *Foraging and Farming in the Eastern Woodlands*, edited by Margaret Scarry, pp. 57–77. University Press of Florida, Gainesville.

Johnsen, D. Bruce
2004 A Culturally Correct Proposal to Privatize the British Columbia Salmon Fishery. (November). *George Mason University School of Law Working Papers Series*. Working Paper 8. http://law.bepress.com/gmu

Johnson, Alfred E.
2001 Plains Woodland Tradition. In *Plains*, edited by Raymond J. De Mallie, pp. 159–172. Handbook of North American Indians, Vol. 13, William C. Sturtevant, general editor, Smithsonian Institution, Washington, D.C.

Johnson, Ann Mary, and Alfred E. Johnson
1998 The Plains Woodland. In *Archaeology of the Great Plains*, edited by Raymond Wood, pp. 201–234. University Press of Kansas, Lawrence.

Johnson, Eileen (editor)
1977 *Paleoindian Lifeways*. The Museum Journal 17. West Texas Museum Association, Lubbock.

Johnson, Eileen
1987 *Lubbock Lake: Late Quaternary Studies on the Southern High Plains*. Texas A&M University Press, College Station.

Johnson, Eileen
1991 Late Pleistocene Cultural Occupation on the Southern Plains. In *Clovis: Origins and Adaptations*, edited by Robson Bonnichsen and Karen Turnmire, pp. 215–236. Oregon State University Press for the Center for the Study of the First Americans, Corvallis.

Johnson, Eileen
2005 Late-Wisconsinan Mammoth Procurement in the North American Grasslands. In *Paleoamerican Origins: Beyond Clovis*, edited by Robson Bonnichsen, Bradley T. Lepper, Dennis Stanford, and Michael R. Waters, pp. 161–182. Center for the Study of the First Americans, College Station, Texas.

Johnson, Jay K.
1987 Cahokia Core Technology in Mississippi: The View from the South. In *The Organization of Core Technology*, edited by Jay K. Johnson and Carol A. Morrow, pp. 187–205. Westview Press, Boulder, Colorado.

Johnson, Jay K., and Samuel K. Brookes
1989 Benton Points, Turkey Tails, and Cache Blades: Middle Archaic Exchange in the Midsouth. *Southeastern Archaeology* 8:134–145.

Johnson, Jay K., and Fair L. Hayes
1995 Shifting Patterns of Long-Distance Contact During the Middle Woodland Period in the Northern Yazoo Basin, Mississippi. In *Native American Interactions: Multiscalar Aanalyses and Interpretations in the Eastern Woodlands*, edited by Michael S. Nassaney and Kenneth E. Sassaman, pp. 100–121. University of Tennessee Press, Knoxville.

Johnson, John R., Thomas Stafford, Jr., Henry Ajie, and Don P. Morris
2002 Arlington Springs Revisited. In *Proceedings of the 5th California Islands Conference*, edited by D. Browne, K. Mitchell and H. Chaney, pp. 541–545. Santa Barbara Museum of Natural History, Santa Barbara, California.

Johnson, William J., and Donald W. Johnson
2010 Bushy Run Battlefield-Looking for Forbes Road. Electronic document, http://www.archaeology-geophysics.com/PDF%20papers/Looking%20for%20Forbes%20Road%20paper.pdf,accessed September 15, 2012.

Jones, Debra L., and Susan Guise Sheridan
1994 Reconstruction of Hohokam Diet Utilizing Trace-Element Variation. In *The Pueblo Grande Project, Vol. 6: The Bioethnography of a Classic Period Hohokam Population*, edited by Dennis P. Van Gerven and Susan Guise Sheridan, pp. 75–85. Soil Systems Publications in Archaeology 20, Phoenix.

Jones, George T., Charlotte Beck, Eric E. Jones, and Richard E. Hughes
2003 Lithic Source Use and Paleoarchaic Foraging Territories in the Great Basin. *American Antiquity* 68 (1):5–38.

Jones, Terry L., and Kathryn A. Klar (editor)
2007 *California Prehistory: Colonization, Culture, and Complexity*. Alta Mira, Lanham, Maryland.

Jones, Terry L., Richard T. Fitzgerald, Douglas J. Kinnett, Charles H. Miksicek, John L. Fagan, John Sharp, and Jon M. Erlandson
2002 The Cross Creek Site (CA-SLO1797) and Its Implications for New World Colonization. *American Antiquity* 67:213–230.

Jordan, Richard H., and Richard A. Knecht
1988 Archaeological Research on Western Kodiak Island, Alaska: The Development of Koniag Culture. In *Late Prehistoric Development of Alaska's Native People*, edited by R. D. Shaw, R. K. Harritt, and D. E. Dumond, pp. 185–214. Plenum Press, New York.

Joyce, Arthur A.
1988 Early/Middle Holocene Environments in the Middle Atlantic Region: A Revised Reconstruction. In *Holocene Human Ecology in Northeastern North America*, edited by George P. Nicholas. Plenum Press, New York.

Judge, W. James
1991 Chaco: Current Views of Prehistory and the Regional System. In *Chaco and Hohokam: Prehistoric Regional Systems in the American Southwest*, edited by Patricia L. Crown and W. James Judge, pp. 11–30. School of American Research, Santa Fe.

Justice, Noel D.
1987 *Stone Age Spear and Arrow Points of the Midcontinental and Eastern United States*. Indiana University Press, Bloomington.

Justice, Noel D.
2002 *Stone Age Spear and Arrow Points of California and the Great Basin*. Indiana University Press, Bloomington.

Kaeser, Edward
1970 Archery Range Ossuary, Pelham Bay Park, Bronx County, New York. *Pennsylvania Archaeologist* 40:9–34.

Kami, J., V. B. Velásquez, D. G. Debouck, and P. Gepts
1995 Identification of Presumed Ancestral DNA Sequences of Phaseolin in *Phaseolus vulgaris*. *Proceedings of the National Academy of Sciences (Philadelphia)* 92:1101–1104.

Kamp, Kathryn
1998 *Life in the Pueblo: Understanding the Past Through Archaeology.* Waveland Press, Prospect Heights, Illinois.

Kane, Allen E.
1986a Prehistory of the Dolores River Valley. In *Dolores Archaeological Program Final Synthetic Report*, edited by David A. Breternitz, Christine K. Robinson and G. Timothy Gross, pp. 353–435. U.S. Department of the Interior, Engineering and Research Center, Denver.

Kane, Allen E.
1986b Social Organization and Cultural Process in Dolores Anasazi Communities, A.D. 600–900. In *Dolores Archaeological Program Final Synthetic Report*, edited by David A. Breternitz, Christine K. Robinson and G. Timothy Gross. U.S. Department of the Interior, Engineering and Research Center, Denver.

Kantner, John
2004 *Ancient Puebloan Southwest.* Cambridge University Press, Cambridge.

Kaplan, Lawrence
1963 Archaeology and the Domestication in American *Phaseolus* (beans). *Economic Botany* 19:358–368.

Kaplan, Lawrence, and Thomas F. Lynch
1999 *Phaseolus* (Fabaceae) in Archaeology: AMS Radiocarbon Dates and Their Significance for Pre-Columbian Agriculture. *Economic Botany* 53:261–272.

Kay, Marvin
1998a The Central and Southern Plains Archaic. In *Archaeology of the Great Plains*, edited by W. Raymond Wood, pp. 173–200. University Press of Kansas, Lawrence.

Kay, Marvin
1998b The Great Plains. In *Archaeology of the Great Plains*, edited by Raymond Wood, pp. 16–47. University Press of Kansas, Lawrence.

Keefer, D. K., S. D. deFrance, M. E. Moseley, J. B. Richardson III, D. R. Satterlee, and A. Day-Lewis
1998 Early Maritime Economy and El Niño Events at Quebrada Tacahuay, Peru. *Science* 281:1833–1835.

Keenleyside, Anne, Margaret Bertulli, and Henry Fricke
1997 The Final Days of the Franklin Expedition: New Skeletal Evidence. *Arctic* 50:36–46.

Keenlyside, David L.
1991 Paleoindian Occupations of the Maritimes Region of Canada. In *Clovis: Origins and Adaptations*, edited by Robson Bonnichsen and Karen Turnmire, pp. 163–174. Corvallis: Oregon State University Press for the Center for the Study of First Americans, Corvallis.

Kellogg, Douglas C.
1988 Problems in the Use of Sea-Level Data for Archaeological Reconstructions. In *Holocene Human Ecology in Northeastern North America*, edited by G. P. Nicholas, pp. 81–104. Plenum Press, New York.

Kelly, John
1991 Cahokia and Its Role as a Gateway Center in Interregional Exchange. In *Cahokia and the Hinterlands*, edited by Timothy R. Pauketat and Thomas E. Emerson, pp. 61–80. University of Illinois Press, Urbana.

Kelly, Kenneth G.
2005 Historical Archaeology. In *Handbook of Archaeological Methods*, edited by Herbert D. G. Maschner and Christopher Chippindale, pp. 1108–1137. AltaMira Press, Lanham, Maryland.

Kelly, Lucretia S.
1997 Patterns of Faunal Exploitation at Cahokia. In *Cahokia: Domination and Ideology in the Mississippian World*, edited by Timothy R. Pauketat and Thomas E. Emerson, pp. 69–88. University of Nebraska Press, Lincoln.

Kelly, Lucretia S.
2001 A Case of Ritual Feasting at the Cahokia Site. In *Feasts: Archaeological and Ethnographic Perspectives on Food, Politics, and Power*, edited by Michael Dietler and Brian Hayden, pp. 334–367. Smithsonian Institution Press, Washington, D.C.

Kelly, Robert L.
1995 *The Foraging Spectrum: Diversity in Hunter-Gatherer Lifeways.* Smithsonian Books, Washington, D.C.

Kelly, Robert L.
2003 Maybe We Do Know When People First Came to North America and What Does It Mean If We Do? *Quaternary Research* 109–110:133–145.

Kelly, Robert L., and David Hurst Thomas
2011 *Archaeology*, 6th ed. Wadsworth Cengage Learning, Belmont, California.

Kelly, Robert L., and Lawrence C. Todd
1988 Coming into the Country: Early Paleoindian Hunting and Mobility. *American Antiquity* 53 (2):231–244.

Kelso, Gerald
1970 Hogup Cave, Utah: Comparative Pollen Analysis of Human Coprolites and Cave Fill. In *Hogup Cave*, edited by C. Melvin Aikins, pp. 251–262. Anthropological Paper 93, University of Utah.

Kendrick, Gregory D.
1982 *The River of Sorrows: The History of the Lower Dolores River Valley.* U.S. Department of the Interior, National Park Service, Rocky Mountain Regional Office, Denver.

Kennedy, Roger G.
1994 *Hidden Cities: The Discovery and Loss of Ancient North American Civilization.* Penguin Books, New York.

Kennett, Douglas J., and James P. Kennett
2000 Competitive and Cooperative Responses to Climatic Instability in Coastal Southern California. *American Antiquity* 65:379–395.

Kennett, Douglas J., James P. Kennett, James West, Jon M. Erlandson, John R. Johnson, Ingrid L. Hendy, Alan West, and Terry L. Jones
2008 Wildfire and Abrupt Ecosystem Disruption on California's Northern Channel Islands at the Ållerød-Younger Dryas Boundary (13.0–12.9 ka). *Quaternary Science Reviews* 27:2530–2545.

Kent, Barry C.
1984 *Susquehanna's Indians.* Harrisburg: Pennsylvania Historical and Museum Commission.

Kerber, Jordon E.
1997 *Lambert Farm: Public Archaeology and Canine Burials along Narragansett*

Bay. Harcourt Brace College, Fort Worth.

Kersel, Morag M.

2011 When Communities Collide: Competing Claims for Archaeological Objects in the Market Place. Dynamics of Inclusion in Public Archaeology, Special issue, *Archaeologies* 7(3) 518–537.

Kidder, Alfred V.

1924 An Introduction to the Study of Southwestern Archaeology with a Preliminary Account of the Excavations at Pecos. *Papers of the Southwestern Expedition* 1.

Kidder, Tristram R.

2002a Mapping Poverty Point. *American Antiquity* 67 (89–101).

Kidder, Tristram R.

2002b Woodland Period Archaeology of the Lower Mississippi Valley. In *The Woodland Southeast*, edited by David G. Anderson and Robert C. Mainfort, Jr., pp. 66–90. University of Alabama Press, Tuscaloosa.

Kidder, Tristram R., and Kenneth E. Sassaman

2009 The View From the Southeast. In *Archaic Societies: Diversity and Complexity Across the MidContinent*, edited by Thomas E. Emerson, Dale L. McElrath, and Andrew C. Fortier, pp. 667–694. State University of New York Press, Albany.

Killion, Thomas W.

2008 *Opening Archaeology: Repatriations Impact on Contemporary Research and Practice*. School for Advanced Research Press, Santa Fe.

King, Adam

2006 Leadership Strategies and the Nature of Mississippian Chiefdoms in Northern Georgia. In *Leadership and Polity in Mississippian Society*, edited by Brian M. Butler and Paul D. Welch, pp. 73–90. Occasional Paper No. 33, Center for Archaeological Investigations, Southern Illinois University, Carbondale.

King, Adam (editor)

2007 *Southeastern Ceremonial Complex: Chronology, Content, Context*. The University of Alabama Press, Tuscaloosa.

King, Chester D.

1976 Chumash Inter-Village Economic Exchange. In *Native Californians: A Theoretical Retrospective*, edited by Lowell John Bean and Thomas

C. Blackburn, pp. 289–318. Ballena Press, Menlo Park, California.

King, Chester D.

1990 *The Evolution of Chumash Society: A Comparative Study of Artifacts Used in Social System Maintenance in the Santa Barbara Channel Region Before A.D. 1804*. Garland, New York.

King, Frances B.

1985 Early Cultivated Cucurbits in Eastern North America. In *Prehistoric Food Production in Eastern North America*, edited by Richard I. Ford, pp. 73–98. Museum of Anthropology, University of Michigan, Ann Arbor.

King, Frances B.

2004 Changing Evidence for Prehistoric Plant Use in Pennsylvania. In *Current Northeast Paleoethnobotany*, edited by John P. Hart, pp. 11–26. New York State Museum Bulletin 494. University of the State of New York/State Department of Education, Albany.

King, James E.

1981 Late Quaternary Vegetational History of Illinois. *Ecological Monographs* 51 (1):43–62.

King, James E., and William H. Allen

1977 A Holocene Vegetation Record from the Mississippi River Valley, Southeastern Missouri. *Quaternary Research* 8:307–323.

King, Thomas F.

2008 *Cultural Resource Laws and Practice*, 3rd ed. AltaMira Press, Lanham, Maryland.

King, Thomas F.

2009 *Our Unprotected Heritage: Whitewashing the Destruction of Our Cultural and Natural Environment*. Left Coast Press, Walnut Creek, California.

Kingsley, Robert G.

1999 The Middle Woodland Period in Southern Michigan. In *Retrieving Michigan's Buried Past: The Archaeology of the Great Lakes State*, edited by John R. Halsey, pp. 148–172. Cranbrook Institute of Science, Bloomfield Hills, Michigan.

Kinkade, M. Dale, William W. Elmendorf, Bruce Rigsby, and Haruo Aoki

1998 Languages. In *Plateau*, edited by Deward E. Walker, Jr., pp. 49–72. Handbook of North American Indians, Vol. 12, William C. Sturtevant, general editor, Smithsonian Institution, Washington, D.C.

Kirk, Ruth, and Richard D. Daugherty

1978 *Exploring Washington Archaeology*. University of Washington Press, Seattle.

Kirk, Ruth, and Richard D. Daugherty

2007 *Archaeology in Washington*. University of Washington Press, Seattle.

Kirkland, James T., and Donald R. Coates

1977 The Champlain Sea and Quaternary Deposits in the St. Lawrence Lowland, New York. In *Amerinds and Their Paleoenvironments in Northeastern North America*, edited by Walter S. Newman and Bert Salwen, pp. 498–507. Annals of the New York Academy of Sciences, Vol. 288.

Klippel, Walter E., and Darcy F. Morey

1986 Contextual and Nutritional Analysis of Freshwater Gastropods from Middle Archaic Deposits at the Hayes Site, Middle Tennessee. *American Antiquity* 51:799–813.

Knapp, Timothy D.

2009 An Unbounded Future? Ceramic Types, Cultures, and Scale in Late Prehistoric Research. In *Iroquoian Archaeology and Analytic Scale*, edited by Laurie E. Miroff and Timothy D. Knapp, pp. 101–129. University of Tennessee Press, Knoxville.

Knath, Eigel

1966/1967 The Ruins of Musk-ox Way. *Folk* 8–9:191–219.

Knight, Vernon James

1998 Moundville as Diagrammatic Ceremonial Center In *Archaeology of the Moundville Chiefdom*, edited by Vernon James Knight and Vincas P. Steponaitis, pp. 44–62. Smithsonian Institution Press, Washington, D.C.

Knight, Vernon James

2001 Feasting and the Emergence of Platform Mound Ceremonialism in Eastern North America In *Feasts: Archaeological and Ethnographic Perspectives on Food, Politics, and Power*, edited by Michael Dietler and Brian Hayden, pp. 311–333. Smithsonian Institution Press, Washington, D.C.

Knight, Vernon James, and Vincas P. Steponaitis

1998a *Archaeology of the Moundville Chiefdom*. Smithsonian Institution Press, Washington, D.C.

Knight, Vernon James, and Vincas P. Steponaitis

1998b A New History of Moundville. In *Archaeology of the Moundville*

Chiefdom, edited by Vernon James Knight and Vincas P. Steponaitis, pp. 1–25. Smithsonian Institution Press, Washington, D.C.

Koch, Amy, and John R. Bozell
2003 Environmental and Cultural Variation in the Nebraska Sand Hills. In *Islands on the Plains: Ecological, Social and Ritual Use of Landscapes*, edited by Marcel Kornfeld and Alan J. Osborn, pp. 167–190. University of Utah Press, Salt Lake City.

Kohler, Timothy A.
1991 The Demise of Weeden Island, and Post–Weeden Island Cultural Stability, in Non-Mississippianized Northern Florida. In *Stability, Transformation and Variation: The Late Woodland Southeast*, edited by Michael S. Nassaney and Charles R. Cobb, pp. 91–110. Plenum Press, New York.

Kohler, Timothy A.
1992 Field Houses, Villages and the Tragedy of the Commons in the Early Northern Anasazi Southwest. *American Antiquity* 57:617–635.

Koldehoff, Brad
1983 Paleo-Indian Chert Utilization and Site Distribution in Southwestern Illinois. *Wisconsin Archaeologist* 64 (3–4):201–238.

Koldehoff, Brad, and John A. Walthall
2009 Dalton and the Early Holocene Midcontinent: Setting the Stage. In *Archaic Societies: Diversity and Complexity Across the Midcontinent*, edited by Thomas E. Emerson, Dale L. McElrath, and Andrew C. Fortier, pp. 137–151. State University of New York Press, Albany.

Kooyman, Brian, Margaret E. Newman, Christine Cluney, Murray Lobb, Shayne Tolman, Paul McNeil, and L.V. Hills
2001 *Identification of Horse Exploitation by Clovis Hunters Based on Protein Analysis* 66 (4):686–691.

Kopperl, Robert E
2003 Cultural Complexity and Resource Intensification on Kodiak Island, Alaska. Ph.D. dissertation, Department of Anthropology, University of Washington, Seattle.

Kornfeld, Marcel
2007 Are Paleoindians of the Great Plains and Rockies Subsistence Specialists? In *Foragers of the Terminal Pleistocene in North America*, edited by Renee B. Walker and Boyce N.

Driskell, pp. 32–58. University of Nebraska Press, Lincoln.

Koski, Randolph A., McKee. Edwin H., David H. Thomas
1973 Pigment Composition of Prehistoric Pictographs of Gatecliff Shelter, Central Nevada. *American Museum Novitates*, 2521. Electronic document, http://hdl.handle.net/2246/2727, accessed September 15,2012.

Kraft, Herbert C.
1986 *The Lenape: Archaeology, History and Ethnography*. New Jersey Historical Society, Newark.

Kraft, Herbert C.
2001 *The Lenape-Delaware Indian Heritage: 10,000 B.C.–A.D. 2000*. Lenape Books, Elizabeth, New Jersey.

Krass, Dorothy Schlottbauer
2000 What Is the Archaeology Curriculum? In *Teaching Archaeology in the Twenty-first Century*, edited by Susan J. Bender and George S. Smith, pp. 9–16. The Society for American Archaeology, Washington, D.C.

Krause, Richard A.
2001 Plains Village Tradition: Coalescent. In *Plains*, edited by Raymond J. De Mallie, pp. 196–206. Handbook of North American Indians, Vol. 13, William C. Sturtevant, general editor, Smithsonian Institution, Washington, D.C.

Krauss, Michael E., and Victor K. Golla
1981 Northern Athapaskan Languages. In *Subarctic*, edited by June Helm, pp. 67–85. Handbook of North American Indians, Vol. 6, William C. Sturtevant, general editor, Smithsonian Institution, Washington, D.C.

Krech, Shepard, III
1999 *The Ecological Indian: Myth and History*. W.W. Norton, New York.

Kroeber, Alfred L.
1916 Zuñi Potsherds. *Anthropological Papers of the American Museum of Natural History* 18 (1):7–37. American Museum of Natural History, New York.

Kroeber, Alfred L.
1925 *Handbook of the Indians of California*. Bureau of American Ethnology, Bulletin 78. Washington, D.C.

Kroeber, Alfred L.
1963 *Cultural and Natural Areas of Native North America*, 4th ed.

University of California Press, Berkeley.

Kuckelman, Kristin, Ricky R. Lightfoot, and Debra L. Martin
2002 The Bioarchaeology and Taphonomy of Violence at Castle Rock and Sand Canyon Pueblos, Southwestern Colorado. *American Antiquity* 67:486–513.

Kuehn, Steven R.
2007 Late Paleoindian Subsistence Strategies in the Western Great Lakes Region: Evidence for Generalized Foraging from Northern Wisconsin. In *Foragers of the Terminal Pleistocene in North America*, edited by Renee B. Walker and Boyce N. Driskell, pp. 32–58. Unversity of Nebraska Press, Lincoln.

Kunz, Michael L., and Richard E. Reanier
1996 Mesa Site, Iteriak Creek. In *American Beginnings: The Prehistory and Palaeoecology of Beringia*, edited by Frederick H. West, pp. 497–504. University of Chicago Press, Chicago.

Kuttruff, Jenna Tedrick, and Carl Kuttruff
1996 Mississippian Textile Evidence on Fabric-Impressed Ceramics from Mound Bottom, Tennessee. In *A Most Indispensable Art: Native Fiber Industries from Eastern North America*, edited by James B. Petersen, pp. 160–173. University of Tennessee Press, Knoxville.

Kuzmin, Yaroslav V., and Susan G. Keates
2005 Dates Are Not Just Data: Paleolithic Settlement Patterns in Siberia Derived From Radiocarbon Records. *American Antiquity* 70:733–789.

Kvamme, Kenneth L.
2003 Geophysical Surveys as Landscape Archaeology. *American Antiquity* 68 (3):435–457.

Kvamme, Kenneth L.
2004 *Geophysical Findings at Double Ditch State Historic Site (32BL8) North Dakota, 2003*. Department of Anthropology, University of Arkansas. Submitted to PaleoCultural Research Group, Flagstaff, Arizona.

Kwiatkowski, Scott
1994 *The Pueblo Grande Project, Vol. 5: Environment and Subsistence*. Soil Systems Publications in Archaeology 20, Phoenix.

La Belle, Jason M.
  2003 Coffee Cans and Folsom Points: Why We Cannot Continue to Ignore the Artifact Collectors. In *Ethical Issues in Archaeology*, edited by Larry J. Zimmerman, Karen D. Vitelli and Julie Hollowell-Zimmer, pp. 114–127. AltaMira Press, Walnut Creek, California.

Lahren, L., and R. Bonnichsen
  1974 Bone Foreshafts from a Clovis Burial in Southwestern Montana. *Science* 186:147–149.

Lambert, Patricia M.
  2002 The Archaeology of War: A North American Perspective. *Journal of Archeological Research* 10:207–241.

Landy, David.
  1978 Tuscarora Among the Iroquois. In *Northeast*, edited by Bruce G. Trigger, pp. 518–524. Handbook of North American Indians, Vol. 15, William C. Sturtevant, general editor. Smithsonian Institution, Washington, D.C.

Lantis, Margaret
  1984 Aluet. In *Arctic*, edited by David Damas, pp. 161–184. Handbook of North American Indians, Vol. 5, William C. Sturtevant, general editor, Smithsonian Institution, Washington, D.C.

Largy, Tonya, and E. Pierre Morenon
  2008 Maize Agriculture in Coastal Rhode Island: Imaginative, Illusive, or Intensive? In *Current Northeast Paleoethnobotany II*, edited by John Hart, pp. 73–85. New York State Museum Bulletin 512. University of the State of New York/State Department of Education, Albany.

LaRoche, Cheryl J., and Michael Blakey
  1997 Seizing Intellectual Power: The Dialogue at the New York African Burial Ground. *In the Realm of Politics: Prospects for Public Participation in African-American Archaeology and Plantation Archaeology*. Special issue, *Historical Archaeology* 31 (3):84–106.

Larsen, Clark Spencer
  2005 Bioarchaeology of the Spanish Missions. In *Unlocking the Past: Celebrating Historical Archaeology in North America*, edited by Lu Ann DeCunzon and John H. Jameson, Jr., pp. 25–29. University of Florida Press, Gainesville.

Larson, Lewis
  1994 The Case for Earth Lodges in the Southeast. In *Ocmulgee Archaeology:

1936–1986, edited by David J. Hally, pp. 105–115. University of Georgia Press, Athens.

Larson, M. L.
  1997 Housepits and Mobile Hunter-Gatherers: A Consideration of the Wyoming Evidence. *Plains Anthropologist* 42 (161):353–369.

Laub, Richard S.
  2002 The Paleoindian Presence in the Northeast: A View from the Hiscock Site. In *Ice Age People of Pennsylvania*, edited by Kurt W. Carr and James M. Adovasio, pp. 105–122. Pennsylvania Historical and Museum Commission, Harrisburg.

Laub, Richard S., Mary F. DeRemer, Catharine A. Dufort, and William L. Parsons
  1988 The Hiscock Site: A Rich Late Quaternary Locality in Western New York State. In *Late Pleistocene and Early Holocene Paleoecology and Archaeology of the Eastern Great Lakes Region*, edited by Richard S. Laub, Norton G. Miller, and David W. Steadman, pp. 67–81. Bulletin of the Buffalo Society of Natural Sciences, Buffalo, New York.

Laughlin, W. S.
  1980 *Aleuts: Survivors of the Bering Land Bridge*. Rinehart & Winston, New York.

LaVere, David
  1998 *The Caddo Chiefdoms: Caddo Economics and Politics, 700–1835*. University of Nebraka Press, Lincoln and London.

LaVere, David
  2007 *Looting Spiro Mounds: An American King Tut's Tomb*. University of Oklahoma Press, Norman.

LaVarenne, François Pierre
  2001 *The French Cook*. English Translation (1653) by I.D.G. Southover Press, East Sussex, United Kingdom.

Layton, R.
  1989 *Conflict in Archaeology of Living Traditons*. One World Archaeology Series. Unwin Hyman, London.

Leader-Post [Regina, Saskatchewan]
  2008 Iceman's DNA Linked to Coastal Aboriginals. April 26. Posted on Canada.com. Electronic document, http://www.canada.com/reginaleaderpost/news/story.html?id=e9d68150–22ab-4b53-bcef-c0514231148e, accessed July 25, 2011.

Least Heat-Moon, William
  1984 *Blue Highways*. Fawcett Crest, New York.

LeBlanc, Steven A.
  1983 *The Mimbres People: Ancient Pueblo Potters of the American Southwest*. Thames and Hudson, London.

LeBlanc, Steven A.
  1999 *Prehistoric Warfare in the American Southwest*. University of Utah Press, Salt Lake City.

Lee, E.
  1983 *Archaeological Investigations at Batoche National Historic Site, 1982*. Research Bulletin 219, Parks Canada, Ottawa.

Lee, E.
  1984 *Archaeological Research at Batoche N.H.S-1983 Field Season*. Research Bulletin 219, Parks Canada, Ottawa.

Lee, T. E.
  1956 Position and Meaning of a Radiocarbon Sample from the Sheguiandah Site, Ontario. *American Antiquity* 22:79.

Lehmer, Donald J.
  1971 *Introduction to Middle Missouri Archaeology*. Anthropological Paper 1. U.S. National Park Service, Washington, D.C.

Lekson, Stephen H.
  1987 *Great Pueblo Architecture of Chaco Canyon, New Mexico*. University of New Mexico Press, Albuquerque.

Lekson, Stephen H.
  1999 *The Chaco Meridian: Centers of Political Power in the Ancient Southwest*. AltaMira Press, Walnut Creek, California.

Lekson, Stephen H.
  2005 Chaco and Paquimé: Complexity, History, Landscape. In *North American Archaeology*, edited by Timothy R. Pauketat and Diana Di Paolo Loren, pp. 235–272. Blackwell, Malden, Massachusetts.

Lekson, Stephen H.
  2008 *A History of the Ancient Southwest*. School for Advanced Research, Santa Fe.

Leone, Mark P.
  2010 Mormon Fences, Selections from "Archaeology as the Science of Technology: Mormon Town Plans and Fences." In *Critical Historical Archaeology*, pp. 109-122. Left Coast Press, Walnut Creek, California.

Leone, Mark P., P. B. Potter, and Paul A. Shackel
  1987 Toward a Critical Archaeology. *Current Anthropology* 28:282–302.

Leonhardy, Frank C., and David G. Rice

1970 A Proposed Cultural Typology for the Lower Snake River Region, Southeastern Washington. *Northwest Anthropological Research Notes* 4:1–29.

Lepper, Bradley T.
1996 The Newark Earthworks and the Geometric Enclosures of the Scioto Valley: Connections and Conjectures. In *A View from the Core: A Synthesis of Ohio Hopewell Archaeology*, edited by Paul J. Pacheco, pp. 224–241. Ohio Archaeological Council, Columbus.

Lepper, Bradley T.
1999 Pleistocene Peoples of Midcontinental North America. In *Ice Age People of North America: Environments, Origins and Adaptations of the First Americans*, edited by Robson Bonnichsen and Karen Turnmire, pp. 362–394. Oregon State University Press for the Center for the Study of the First Americans, Corvallis.

Lepper, Bradley T.
2010 The Ceremonial Landscape of the Newark Earthworks and the Raccoon Creek Valley. In *Hopewell Settlemnet Patterns, Subsistence and Symbolic Landscapes*, edited by A. Martin Byers and DeeAnne Wymer, pp. 97–127. University of Florida Press, Gainesville.

Lepper, Bradley T., and David J. Meltzer
1991 Late Pleistocene Human Occupation of the Eastern United States. In *Clovis: Origins and Adaptations*, edited by Robson Bonnichsen and Karen Turnmire, pp. 175–184. Oregon State University Press for the Center for the Study of the First Americans, Corvallis.

Levine, Mary Ann
1990 Accommodating Age: Radiocarbon Results and Fluted Point Sites in Northeastern North America. *Archaeology of Eastern North America* 18:33–63.

Levine, Mary Ann
1997 The Tyranny Continues: Ethnographic Analogy and Eastern Paleo-Indians. In *Caribou and Reindeer Hunters of the Northern Hemisphere*, edited by Lawrence J. Jackson and Paul T. Thacker, pp. 221–244. Avebury Press, Aldershot, United Kingdom.

Levine, Mary Ann
1999 Native Copper in the Northeast; An Overview of Potential Sources Available to Indigenous People. In *The Archaeological Northeast*, edited by Mary Ann Levine, Kenneth E. Sassaman and Michael S. Nassaney, pp. 183–199. Bergin & Garvey, Westport, Connecticut.

Levine, Mary Ann, Kenneth E. Sassaman, and Michael S. Nassaney
1999 *The Archaeological Northeast*. Bergin & Garvey, Westport, Connecticut.

Lewis, R. Barry, Charles Stout, and Cameron B. Wesson
1998 The Design of Mississippian Towns. In *Mississippian Towns and Sacred Spaces: Searching for an Architectural Grammar*, edited by R. Barry Lewis and Charles Stout, pp. 1–21. University of Alabama Press, Tuscaloosa.

Lewis, Thomas M. N., and Madeline Kneberg
1946 *Hiwassee Island: An Archaeological Account of Four Tennessee Indian Peoples*. University of Tennessee Press, Knoxville.

Lewis, Thomas. M. N., and Madeline Kneberg
1995 *The Prehistory of the Chickamauga Basin in Tennessee*, compiled and edited by Lynne P. Sullivan. 2 vols. University of Tennessee Press, Knoxville.

Lewis, Thomas M. N., and Madeline. K. Lewis
1961 *Eva, an Archaic Site*. University of Tennessee Press, Knoxville.

Lightfoot, Kent G.
1997 Cultural Construction of Coastal Landscapes: A Middle Holocene Perspective from San Francisco Bay. In *Archaeology of the California Coast During the Middle Holocene*, edited by Jon M. Erlandson and Michael Glassow, pp. 129–141. UCLA Institute of Archaeology, Los Angeles.

Lightfoot, Kent G., and Edward M. Luby
2002 Late Holocene in the San Francisco Bay Area: Temporal Trends in the Use and Abandonment of Shell Mounds in the East Bay. In *Catalysts to Complexity: Late Holocene Societies of the California Coast*, edited by Jon M. Erlandson and Terry L. Jones, pp. 263–281. Cotsen Institute of Archaeology, Los Angeles.

Lightfoot, Kent G., Antoinette Martinez, and Ann M. Schiff
1998 Daily Practice and Material Culture in Pluralistic Social Settings: An Archaeological Study of Culture Change and Persistence from Fort Ross, California. *American Antiquity* 63 (2):199–222.

Lightfoot, Kent G., Otis Parrish, Roberta A. Jewett, E. Breck Parkman, and Daniel F. Murley
2001 The Metini Village Project: Collaborative Research in the Fort Ross State Historic Park. *Society for California Archaeology Newsletter* 35 (2):23–26.

Lightfoot, Kent G., Thomas A. Wake, and Ann M. Schiff
1991 *The Archaeology and Ethnohistory of Fort Ross, California, Vol. 1: Introduction*. Contributions of the University of California Archaeological Research Facility 49. Archaeological Research Facility, Berkeley, California.

Lipe, William D.
2010 Lost in Transit: The Central Mesa Verde Archaeological Complex. In *Leaving Mesa Verde: Peril and Change in the Thirteenth-Century Southwest*, edited by Timothy A. Kohler, Mark D. Varien, and Aaron M. Wright, pp. 262–284. University of Arizona Press, Tucson.

Litt, Paul, Ronald F. Williamson, and Joseph W. A. Whitmore
1993 *Death at Snake Hill: Secrets from a War of 1812 Cemetery*. Ontario Heritage Foundation Local History Series No. 3. Dundurn Press, Toronto.

Little, Barbara J.
2007 *Historical Archaeology: Why the Past Matters*. Left Coast Press, Walnut Creek, California.

Litwinionek, Luc, Eileen Johnson, and Vance T. Holliday
2003 The Playas of the Southern High Plains: An Archipelago of Human Occupation for 12,000 Years on the North American Grasslands. In *Islands on the Plains: Ecological, Social and Ritual Use of Landscapes*, edited by Marcel Kornfeld and Alan J. Osborn, pp. 21–43. University of Utah Press, Salt Lake City.

Logan, Brad
2006 Kansas City Hopewell: Middle Woodland on the Western Frontier. In *Recreating Hopewell*, edited by Douglas K. Charles and Jane E. Buikstra, pp. 339–358. University Press of Florida, Gainesville.

Loubser, Johannes H. N.
2003 *Archaeology: The Comic*. AltaMira Press, Walnut Creek, California.

Lounsbury, F. G.
1978 Iroquoian Languages. In *Northeast*, edited by Bruce G. Trigger, pp. 334–343. Handbook of North American Indians, Vol. 15, William C. Sturtevant, general editor, Smithsonian Institution, Washington, D.C.

Lovis, William A.
1986 Environmental Periodicity, Buffering, and the Archaic Adaptations of the Saginaw Valley of Michigan. In *Foraging, Collecting and Harvesting: Archaic Period Subsistence and Settlement in the Eastern Woodlands*, edited by Sarah W. Neusius, pp. 117–143. Southern Illinois University at Carbondale, Center for Archaeological Investigations, Carbondale.

Lovis, William A.
2009 Hunter-Gatherer Adaptations and Alternative Perspectives on the Michigan Archaic: Research Problems in Context. In *Archaic Societies: Diversity and Complexity Across the Midcontinent*, edited by Thomas E. Emerson, Dale L. McElrath, Andrew C. Fortier, pp. 725-754. State University of New York Press, Albany.

Lovis, William A., and G. William Monaghan
2008 Chronology and Evolution of the Green Point Flood Plain and Associated *Cucurbita pepo*. In *Current Northeast Paleoethnobotany II*, edited by John Hart, pp. 141–150. New York State Museum Bulletin 512. University of the State of New York/State Department of Education, Albany.

Loy, Thomas H., and E. James Dixon
1998 Blood Residues on Fluted Points from Eastern Beringia. *American Antiquity* 63:21–46.

Lundelius, E. L., Jr.
1972 Vertebrate Remains from the Gray Sand. In *Blackwater Locality No. 1: A Stratified Early Man Site in Eastern New Mexico*, edited by J. J. Hester, pp. 148–163. Fort Burgwin Research Center Publication 8, Ranchos de Taos, New Mexico.

Lurie, Rochelle
1982 Economic Models of Stone Tool Manufacture and Use: The Koster Site Middle Archaic. Ph.D. dissertation, Department of Anthropology, Northwestern University, Evanston, Illinois.

Lydolph, Paul E.
1985 *The Climate of the Earth*. Rowman & Littlefield, Lanham, Maryland.

Lyman, R. Lee
1980 Freshwater Bivalve Molluscs and Southern Plateau Prehistory: A Discussion and Description of Three Genera. *Northwest Science* 54 (2):121–136.

Lyman, R. Lee, and Michael J. O'Brien
2003 *W. C. McKern and the Midwestern Taxonomic Method*. University of Alabama Press, Tuscaloosa.

Lynott, Mark J.
2004 Earthwork Construction and the Organization of Hopewell Society. *Hopewell Archeology* 6 (1):24–31.

Lynott, Mark J., and John Weymouth
2002 Preliminary Report, 2001 Investigations, Hopeton Earthworks. *Hopewell Archeology* 5 (1):1–7.

Lynott, Mark J., and Alison Wylie
1995 *Ethics in American Archaeology*. Society for American Archaeology Press, Washington, D.C.

Lyon, E. A.
1996 *A New Deal for Southeastern Archaeology*. University of Alabama Press, Tuscaloosa.

Mabry, Jonathan B.
2005 Changing Knowledge and Ideas About the First Farmers in Southeastern Arizona. In *The Late Archaic Across the Borderlands: From Foraging to Farming*, edited by Bradley J. Vierra, pp. 41–83. University of Texas Press, Austin.

MacDonald, George F.
1968 *Debert: A Paleo-Indian Site in Central Nova Scotia*. Anthropological Paper 16. National Museum of Canada, Ottawa.

MacDonald, George F.
1989 *Kitwanga Fort Report*. Mercury Series, Directorate Paper. Canadian Museum of Civilization, Hull, Quebec.

MacMahon, Darcie A., and William H. Marquardt
2004 *The Calusa and Their Legacy: South Florida People and Their Environments*. University Press of Florida, Gainesville.

MacNeish, Richard S.
1952 Iroquois Pottery Types: A Technique for the Study of Iroquois Prehistory. *Anthropological Series* 31 (44):711–722.

Madsen, D. B.

1986 Prehistoric Ceramics. In *Great Basin*, edited by Warren L. D'Azevedo, pp. 206–214. Handbook of North American Indians, Vol. 11, William C. Sturtevant, general editor, Smithsonian Institution, Washington, D.C.

Madsen, David B.
1979 The Fremont and the Sevier: Defining Prehistoric Agriculturists North of the Anasazi. *American Antiquity* 44:711–722.

Madsen, David B.
2004 Colonization of the Americas Before the Last Glacial Maximum: Issues and Problems. In *Entering America: Northeast Asia and Beringia Before the Last Glacial Maximum*, pp. 1–26. The University of Utah Press, Salt Lake City.

Madsen, David B., and D. Rhode
1994 A Tisket, a Tasket: Looking at Numic Speakers Through the "Lens" of a Basket. In *Across the West: Human Population Movement and the Expansion of the Numa*, pp. 114–123. University of Utah Press, Salt Lake City.

Mainfort, Robert C.
1996 Pinson Mounds and the Middle Woodland Period in the Midsouth and Lower Mississippi Valley. In *A View from the Core a Synthesis of Ohio Hopewell Archaeology*, edited by Paul J. Pacheco, pp. 370–391. Ohio Archaeological Council, Columbus.

Majewski, Teresita, and David Gaimster (editors)
2009 *International Handbook of Historical Archaeology*. Springer, New York.

Malhi, R., B. Kemp, J. Eshelman, J. Cybulski, D. Smith, S. Cousins, and H. Harry
2007 Mitochondrial Haplogroup M Discovered in Prehistoric Americans. *Journal of Archaoelogical Services* 34:642–648.

Mallios, Seth, Matthew Tennyson, Hillary Sweeney, Jaime Lennox, Brenda Cabello, Erika Kleinhans, and David Caterino
2008 *Archaeological Excavations at the Nate Harrison Site in San Diego County, California: An Interim Technical Report for the 2007 Field Season*. San Diego State University, San Diego, California.

Malouf, Carling I., and John Findlay
1986 Euro-American Impact Before 1870. In *Great Basin*,

edited by Warren L. D'Azevedo, pp. 499–516. Handbook of North American Indians, Vol. 11, William C. Sturtevant, general editor, Smithsonian Institution, Washington, D.C.

Mandel, Rolfe D., Trina L. Arpin, and Paul Goldberg
2003 *Stratigraphy, Lithology and Pedology of the South Wall at Hopeton Earthworks, South-Central Ohio.* University of Kansas, Lawrence.

Mandryk, Carole A. S.
2004 Invented Traditions and the Ultimate American Origin Myth: In the Beginning.... There Was an Ice-Free Corridor. In *The Settlement of the American Continents: A Multidisciplinary Approach to Human Biogeography*, edited by C. Michael Barton, Geoffrey A. Clark, David R. Yesner, and Georges A. Pearson, pp. 113–120. University of Arizona Press, Tucson.

Mann, Daniel H., Aron L. Crowell, T. D. Hamilton, and Bruce P. Finney
1998 Holocene Geologic and Climatic History Around the Gulf of Alaska. *Arctic Anthropology* 35 (1):112–131.

Marcus, Jacob Rader
1959 *American Jewry—Documents—Eighteenth Century: Primarily Hitherto Unpublished Manuscripts.* Hebrew Union College Press, Cincinnati, Ohio.

Marcus, Jacob Rader
1970 *The Colonial American Jew, 1492–1776,* Vols. I–III. Wayne State University Press, Detroit, Michigan.

Margolin, Samuel G.
1994 Endangered Legacy: Virginia's Civil War Naval Heritage. In *Look to the Earth: Historical Archaeology and the American Civil War*, edited by Clarence R. Geier, Jr. and Susan E. Winter, pp. 76-98. University of Tennessee Press, Knoxville.

Marlar, Richard A., Banks L. Leonard, Brian R. Billman, Patricia M. Lambert, and Jennifer E. Marlar
2000 Biochemical Evidence of Cannibalism at a Prehistoric Puebloan Site in Southwestern Colorado. *Nature* 407:74–78.

Marquardt, William H. (editor)
1999 *The Archaeology of Useppa Island.* Institute of Archaeological and Paleoenvironmental Studies, Monograph 3. University of Florida, Gainesville.

Marquardt, William H.
2004 Calusa. In *Southeast*, edited by Raymond D. Fogelson, pp. 204–212. Handbook of North American Indians, Vol. 14, William C. Sturtevant, general editor, Smithsonian Institution, Washington, D.C.

Marquardt, William H.
2010 Shell Mounds in the Southeast: Middens, Monuments, Temple Mounds, Rings, or Works? *American Antiquity* 75:551–570.

Marquardt, William H., and Patty Jo Watson
1983 The Shell Mound Archaic of Western Kentucky. In *Archaic Hunters and Gatherers in the American Midwest*, edited by James L. Phillips and James A. Brown, pp. 323–339. Academic Press, New York.

Marquardt, William H. and Patty Jo Watson
2005 *Archaeology of the Middle Green River Region, Kentucky.* Institute of Archaeology and Paleoenvironmental Studies, University of Florida, Gainesville.

Marshall, Yvonne (editor)
2002 Community Archaeology. Special Issue, *World Archaeology* 34 (2): 211–403.

Martin, Paul S.
1973 The Discovery of America. *Science* 179:969–974.

Martin, Paul S.
1979 Prehistory: Mogollon. In *Southwest*, edited by Alfonso Ortiz, pp. 61–74. Handbook of North American Indians, Vol. 9, William C. Sturtevant, general editor, Smithsonian Institution, Washington, D.C.

Martin, Paul S., and Richard G. Klein
1984 *Quaternary Extinctions: A Prehistoric Revolution.* University of Arizona Press, Tucson.

Martin, Paul S., John B. Rinaldo, Elaine A. Buhm, Hugh C. Cutler, and Roger Grange, Jr.
1952 Mogollon Cultural Continuity and Change: The Stratigraphic Analysis of Tularosa and Cordova Caves. *Fieldiana: Anthropology* 40.

Martin, Scott W. J.
2008 Languages Past and Present: Archaeological Approaches to the Appearance of Northern Iroquoian Speakers in the Lower Great lakes Region of North America. *American Antiquity* 73:441–463.

Martin, Susan R.
1999 *Wonderful Power: The Story of Ancient Copper Working in the Lake Superior Basin.* Wayne State University Press, Detroit, Michigan.

Martin, Terrance J.
1981 Animal Remains from the Gros Cap Site: An Evaluation of Fish Scales Versus Fish Bones in Assessing the Species Composition of an Archaeological Assemblage. *Michigan Archaeologist* 27 (3–4):77–86.

Martin, Terrell L.
2007 Early Woodland Black Sand Occupation in the Lower Missouri Valley, Western Missouri. *Plains Anthropologist* 52:43–61.

Martindale, Andrew R. C., and Susan Marsden
2003 Defining the Middle Period (3500 BP to 1500 BP) in Tsimshian History Through a Comparison of Archaeological and Oral Records. *BC Studies* 138:13–50.

Marwitt, John P.
1986 Fremont Cultures. In *Great Basin*, edited by Warren L. D'Azevedo, pp. 161–172. Handbook of North American Indians, Vol. 11, William C. Sturtevant, general editor, Smithsonian Institution, Washington, D.C.

Maschner, Herbert D. G.
1997 The Evolution of Northwest Coast Warfare. In *Troubled Times: Violence and Warfare in the Past*, edited by Debra L. Martin and David W. Frayer, pp. 175–178. Gordon & Breach, Amsterdam.

Mascia, Sara
2005 The Archaeology of Agricultural Life. In *Unlocking the Past: Celebrating Historical Archaeology in North America*, edited by Lu Ann DeCunzo and John H. Jameson, Jr., 119–133. University of Florida Press, Gainesville.

Maslowski, R. F.
1981 *Great Lakes Archaeology.* Academic Press, New York.

Maslowski, R. F.
1996 Cordage Twist and Ethnicity. In *A Most Indispensable Art: Native Fiber Industries from Eastern North America*, edited by J. B. Petersen, pp. 88–99. University of Tennessee Press, Knoxville.

Mason, Owen K.
2009 Flight from the Bering Strait: Did Siberian Punuk/Thule Military Cadres Conquer Northwest Alaska? In *The Northern World AD 900–1400,*

edited by Herbert Maschner, Owen Mason, and Robert McGhee, pp. 76–128. The University of Utah Press, Salt Lake City.

Mason, Ronald J.
1962 The Paleo-Indian Tradition in Eastern North America. *Current Anthropology* 3 (3):227–278.

Mason, Ronald J.
1981 *Great Lakes Archaeology.* Academic Press, New York.

Masse, W. Bruce
1991 The Quest for Subsistence Sufficiency and Civilization in the Sonoran Desert. In *Chaco and Hohokam: Prehistoric Regional Systems in the American Southwest*, edited by Patricia L. Crown and W. James Judge, pp. 195–223. School of American Research, Santa Fe.

Mathien, Frances Joan
2001 The Organization of Turquoise Production and Consumption by the Prehistoric Chacoans. *American Antiquity* 66 (1):103–118.

Matson, R. G.
1976 *The Glenrose Cannery Site.* National Museum of Man, Ottawa.

Matson, R. G.
2007 The Archaic Origins of the Zuni: Preliminary Explorations. In *Zuni Origins: Toward a New Synthesis of Southwestern Archaeology*, edited by David A. Gregory and David R. Wilcox, pp. 97–117. University of Arizona Press, Tucson.

Matson, R. G., and Gary Coupland
1995 *The Prehistory of the Northwest Coast.* Academic Press, San Diego.

Matsuoka, Y., Y. Vigoroux, M. M. Goodman, J. Sanchez, E. Buckler, and J. Doebley
2002 A Single Domestication for Maize Shown by Multilocus Microsatellite Genotyping. *Proceedings of the National Academy of Sciences* 99:6080–6084.

Matthews, Christopher N.
2008 The Location of Archaeology. In *Ethnographic Archaeologies: Reflections on Stakeholders and Archaeological Practices*, edited by Q. Castaneda and C. N. Matthews, pp. 157–182. AltaMira Press, Lanham, Maryland.

Maxwell, Moreau S.
1984 Pre-Dorset and Dorset Prehistory of Canada. In *Arctic*, edited by David Damas, pp. 359–368. Handbook of North American Indians, Vol. 5,

William C. Sturtevant, general editor, Smithsonian Institution, Washington, D.C.

Maxwell, Moreau S.
1985 *Prehistory of the Eastern Arctic.* Academic Press, Orlando, Florida.

McAvoy, J., and L. McAvoy
1997 *Archaeological Investigations of Site 44 SX 202, Cactus Hill, Sussex County, Virginia.* Nottoway River Survey Archaeological Research, Sandston, Virginia.

McBride, Kevin A.
1990 The Historical Archaeology of the Mashantucket Pequots, 1637–1900: A Preliminary Analysis. In *The Pequots in Southern New England: The Fall and Rise of an American Indian Nation*, edited by Laurence M. Hauptman and James D. Wherry, pp. 96–116. University of Oklahoma Press, Norman.

McBride, Kim A., and W. Steven McBride
1996 From Colonization to the 20th Century. In *Kentucky Archaeology*, edited by R. Barry Lewis, pp. 183–211. University of Kentucky, Lexington.

McCarthy, Helen, Robert A. Hicks, and Clinton M. Blount
1985 A Functional Analysis of Western Mono Food Processing in the Southern Sierra Nevada. In *Cultural Resources of the Crane Valley Hydroelectric Project Area, Madera County, California*, pp. 303–356. Infotec Research and Theodoratus Cultural Research for Pacific Gas & Electric Company, San Francisco.

McCartney, Allen P.
1998 Aleutian Tradition. In *Archaeology of Prehistoric Native America: An Encyclopedia*, edited by Guy Gibbon, pp. 12–13. Garland, New York.

McConaughy, Mark A.
2008 Current Issues in Paleoethnobotanical Research from Pennsylvania and Vicinity. In *Current Northeast Paleoethnobotany II*, edited by John Hart, pp. 9–27. New York State Museum Bulletin 512. University of the State of New York/State Department of Education, Albany.

McDavid, Carol
1997 Descendants, Decisions, and Power: The Public Interpretation of the Archaeology of the Levi Jordan Plantation. *In the Realm of Politics: Prospects for Public Participation in*

African-American Archaeology, special issue, *Historical Archaeology* 31 (3):114–131.

McDavid, Carol
2007 Beyond Strategy and Good Intentions: Archaeology, Race, and White Privilege. In *An Archaeology of Civic Engagement*, edited by B. Little and P. Shackel, pp. 67–88. AltaMira, Lanham, Maryland.

McDavid, Carol
2011 When Is "Gone" Gone? Archaeology, Gentrification, and Competing Narratives About Freedmen's Town, Houston. *Archaeologies of Poverty*, special issue, *Historical Archaeology* 45 (3)74–88.

McDavid, Carol, David Bruner, and Robert Marcom
2008 Urban Archaeology and the Pressures of Gentrification: Claiming, Naming, and Negotiating "Freedom" in Freedmen's Town, Houston. *Bulletin of the Texas Archaeological Society* 79:37–52.

McDonald, Jerry N.
2000 An Outline of the Pre-Clovis Archeology of SV-2, Saltville, Virginia, with Special Attention to a Bone Tool Dated 14,510 yr BP. *Jeffersonia* 9:1–59. Virginia Museum of Natural History, Martinsville.

McElrath, Dale L., Thomas E. Emerson, and Andrew C. Fortier
2000 Social Evolution or Social Response? A Fresh Look at the "Good Gray Cultures" After Four Decades of Midwest Research. In *Late Woodland Societies: Tradition and Transformation Across the Midcontinent*, edited by Thomas E. Emerson, Dale L. McElrath, and Andrew C. Fortier, pp. 3–36. University of Nebraska Press, Lincoln.

McElrath, Dale L., Andrew C. Fortier, and Thomas E. Emerson
2009 An Introduction to the Archaic Societies of the Midcontinent. In *Archaic Societies: Diversity and Complexity Across the Midcontinent*, edited by Thomas E. Emerson, Dale L. McElrath and Andrew C. Fortier, pp. 23–38. State University of New York Press, Albany.

McEwan, Bonnie Gair
1993 *The Spanish Missions of La Florida.* University Press of Florida, Gainesville.

McGahey, Samuel O.

1996 Paleoindian and Early Archaic Data from Mississippi. In *The Paleoindian and Early Archaic Southeast*, edited by David G. Anderson and Kenneth E. Sassaman, pp. 354–384. University of Alabama Press, Tuscaloosa.

McGhee, Robert

1984 Thule Prehistory of Canada. In *Arctic*, edited by David Damas, pp. 369–376. Handbook of North American Indians, Vol. 5, William C. Sturtevant, general editor, Smithsonian Institution, Washington, D.C.

McGhee, Robert

1996 *Ancient People of the Arctic*. University of British Columbia Press, Vancouver, British Columbia.

McGhee, Robert

2005 *The Last Imaginary Place: A Human History of the Arctic World*. Oxford University Press, Oxford.

McGhee, Robert

2009 When and Why Did the Inuit Move to the Eastern Arctic? In *The Northern World AD 900–1400*, edited by Herbert Maschner, Owen Mason and Robert McGhee, pp. 155–163. The University of Utah Press, Salt Lake City.

McGimsey, Charles R., III, and Hester A. Davis

2000 The Old Order Changeth; or, Now That Archaeology Is in the Deep End of the Pool, Let's Not Just Tread Water. In *Teaching Archaeology in the Twenty-first Century*, edited by Susan J. Bender and George S. Smith. Society for American Archaeology, Washington, D.C.

McGuire, Randall H.

2003 Foreword. In *Ethical Issues in Archaeology*, edited by Larry J. Zimmerman, Karen D. Vitelli and Julie Hollowell-Zimmer, pp. 115–127. AltaMira Press, Walnut Creek, California.

McGuire, Randall H., and Michael B. Schiffer

1982 *Hohokam and Patayan: Prehistory of Southwestern Arizona*. Academic Press, New York.

McKern, Will Carleton

1939 The Midwestern Taxonomic Method as an Aid to Archaeological Culture Study. *American Antiquity* 4:301–313.

McKibbin, Jean

1976 *The Frugal Colonial Housewife, by Susannah Carter [1772]*. Dolphin Books, Garden City, New York.

McNeil, Paul, L.V. Hills, Brian Kooyman, and M. Shayne Tolman

2004 Late Pleistocene Geology and Fauna of the Wally's Beach Site (DhPg-8) Alberta, Canada. In *Archaeology on the Edge: New Perspectives from the Northern Plains*, edited by Brian Kooyman and Jane H. Kelley, pp. 79–94. Canadian Archaeological Association Occasional Paper No. 4. University of Calgary Press, Calgary, Alberta.

Medford, Edna Greene (editor)

2004 *History Final Report: The African Burial Ground Project*. Submitted to the U.S. General Services Administration, Northwestern Caribbean Region. Electronic document, http://www.gsa.gov/portal/content/249941, accessed September 16, 2012. Meeks, S. C.

1994 Lithic Artifacts from Dust Cave. *Journal of Alabama Archaeology* 40:79–106.

Meeks, S. C.

1998 The Use and Function of Late Middle Archaic Projectile Points in the Midsouth. Unpublished M.A. thesis, Department of Anthropology, University of Alabama, Tuscaloosa.

Mehrer, Mark W.

1995 *Cahokia's Countryside: Household Archaeology, Settlement Patterns and Social Power*. Northern Illinois University Press, Dekalb.

Mehringer, Peter J., Jr.

1986 Prehistoric Environments. In *Great Basin* edited by Warren L. D'Azevedo, pp. 31–50. Handbook of North American Indians, Vol. 11, William C. Sturtevant, general editor, Smithsonian Institution, Washington, D.C.

Meighan, C. W.

2000 Overview of the Archaeology of San Clemente Island, California. *Pacific Coast Archaeological Society Quarterly* 36 (1):1–17.

Meltzer, David

1984–1985 On Stone Procurement and Settlement Mobility in Eastern Fluted Point Groups. *North American Archaeologist* 6:1–27.

Meltzer, David

1988 Late Pleistocene Human Adaptations in Eastern North America. *North American Archaeologist* 6:1–27.

Meltzer, David

1989 Stone Exchanged Among Eastern North American Paleoindians? In *Eastern Paleoindian Lithic Resource Use*, edited by Christopher J. Ellis and Jonathan C. Lothrop, pp. 11–39. Westview Press, Boulder, Colorado.

Meltzer, David

1991a Altithermal Archaeology and Paleoecology at Mustang Springs on the Southern High Plains of Texas. *American Antiquity* 56:236–267.

Meltzer, David

1991b On "Paradigms" and "Paradigm Bias" in Controversies over Human Antiquity in America. In *The First Americans: Search and Research*, edited by Tom D. Dillehay and David J. Meltzer, pp. 13–49. CRC Press, Boca Raton, Florida.

Meltzer, David

1993 *Search for the First Americans*. St. Remy Press and Smithsonian Institution, Montreal and Washington, D.C.

Meltzer, David

2004 Modeling the Initial Colonization of the Americas: Issues of Scale, Demography, and Landscape Learning. In *The Settlement of the American Continents: A Multidisciplinary Approach to Human Biogeography*, edited by C. Michael Barton, Geoffrey A. Clark, David R. Yesner, and Georges A. Pearson, pp. 123–137. University of Arizona Press, Tucson.

Meltzer, David J.

2006 *Folsom: New Archaeological Investigations of a Classic Paleoindian Bison Kill*. University of California Press, Berkeley.

Meltzer, David J.

2009 *First Peoples in a New World: Colonizing Ice Age America*. University of California Press, Berkeley.

Meltzer, David J., and Vance T. Holliday

2010 Would North American Paleoindians Have Noticed Younger Dryas Age Climate Changes? *Journal of World Prehistory* 23:1–41.

Meltzer, David J., and Bruce D. Smith

1986 Paleoindian and Early Archaic Subsistence Strategies in the Eastern North America. In *Foraging, Collecting and Harvesting: Archaic*

Period Subsistence and Settlement in the Eastern Woodlands, edited by Sarah W. Neusius, pp. 3–31. Center for Archaeological Investigations, Southern Illinois University at Carbondale, Carbondale.

Mensforth, Robert P.
2001 Warfare and Trophy Taking in the Archaic Period. In *Archaic Transitions in Ohio and Kentucky Prehistory*, edited by Olaf H. Prufer, Sara E. Pedde and Richard S. Meindl, pp. 110–138. Kent State University Press, Kent, Ohio.

Meyers, J. Thomas
1970 *Chert Resources of the Lower Illinois Valley.* Illinois State Museum, Springfield.

Mickelson, D. M., Lee Clayton, D. S. Fullerton, and H. W. Borns, Jr.
1983 The Late Wisconsin Glacial Record of the Laurentide Ice Sheet in the United States. In *Late Quaternary Environments of the United States*, edited by Stephen C. Porter, pp. 3–37. University of Minnesota Press, Minneapolis.

Mierendorf, Robert R.
1983 Stratigraphy at the Miller Site, 45 FR 5, a Prehistoric Village on Strawberry Island. In *The 1978 and 1979 Excavations at Strawberry Island in the McNary Reservoir*, edited by Randall F. Schalk, pp. 39–74. Laboratory of Archaeology and History Project, Report 19. Washington State University, Pullman.

Milanich, Jerald T.
1994 *Archaeology of Pre-Columbian Florida.* University of Florida, Gainesville.

Milanich, Jerald T.
1995 *Florida Indians and the Invasion from Europe.* University Press of Florida, Gainesville.

Milanich, Jerald T.
1999 *Laboring in the Fields of the Lord: Spanish Missions and Southeastern Indians.* Smithsonian Institution Press, Washington, D.C.

Milanich, Jerald T.
2002 Weeden Island Cultures. In *The Woodland Southeast*, edited by David G. Anderson and Robert C. Mainfort, Jr., pp. 353–372. University of Alabama Press, Tuscaloosa.

Milanich, Jerald T.
2004 Prehistory of Florida After 500 BC. In *Southeast*, edited by Raymond D. Fogelson, pp. 191-203.

Handbook of American Indians, Vol. 14, William C. Sturtevant, general editor, Smithsonian Institution, Washington, D.C.

Miller, Jo Anne
1994 Pueblo Grande Flotation, Macrobotanical, and Wood Charcoal Analyses. In *The Pueblo Grande Project, Vol. 5: Environment and Subsistence*, edited by Scott Kwiatkowski, pp. 127–204. Soil Systems Publications in Archaeology 20, Phoenix.

Miller, Wick R.
1986 Numic Languages In *Great Basin*, edited by Warren L. D'Azevedo, pp. 98–106. Handbook of North American Indians, Vol. 11, William C. Sturtevant, general editor, Smithsonian Institution, Washington, D.C.

Milliken, Randall
1995 *A Time of Little Choice: The Disintegration of Tribal Culture in the San Francisco Bay Area, 1769–1810.* Ballena Press, Menlo Park.

Milner, George R.
1990 The Late Prehistoric Cahokia Cultural System of the Mississippi River Valley: Foundations, Florescence and Fragmentation. *Journal of World Prehistory* 4:1–43.

Milner, George R.
1998 *The Cahokia Chiefdom: The Archaeology of a Mississippian Society.* Smithsonian Institution Press, Washington, D.C.

Milner, George R.
1999 Warfare in Prehistoric and Early Historic Eastern North America. *Journal of Archaeological Research* 7 (2):105–151.

Milner, George R.
2004 *The Moundbuilders: Ancient Peoples of Eastern North America.* Thames and Hudson, London.

Milner, George R., Thomas E. Emerson, Mark W. Mehrer, Joyce A. Williams, and Duane Esarey
1984 Mississippian and Oneota Periods. In *American Bottom Archaeology: A Summary of the FAI-270 Project Contribution to the Culture History of the Mississippi River Valley*, edited by Charles J. Bareis and James W. Porter. University of Illinois Press, Urbana.

Minnis, Paul E.
2003 Great Plains Paleoethnobotany. In *People and Plants in Ancient Eastern North America*, pp. 258–346. Smithsonian Books, Washington, D.C.

Minnis, Paul E., and Wayne J. Elisens
2000 *Biodiversity and Native America.* University of Oklahoma Press, Norman.

Mitchell, Donald C.
2001 *Take My Land, Take My Life: The Story of Congress's Historic Settlement of Alaska Native Land Claims, 1960–1971.* University of Alaska Press, Fairbanks.

Mitchell, Douglas R. (editor)
1994a *The Pueblo Grande Project, Vol. 2: Feature Descriptions, Chronology, and Site Structure.* Soil Systems Publications in Archaeology 20, Phoenix.

Mitchell, Douglas R. (editor)
1994b *The Pueblo Grande Project, Vol. 7: An Analysis of Classic Period Mortuary Patterns.* Soil Systems Publications in Archaeology 20, Phoenix.

Mochanov, Yuri A., and Svetlana Fedoseeva
1996a Aldansk: Aldan River Valley, Sakha Republic. In *American Beginnings: The Prehistory and Palaeoecology of Beringia*, edited by Frederick H. West, pp. 157–214. University of Chicago Press, Chicago.

Monaghan, G. William, William A. Lovis, and Kathryn C. Egan-Bruhy
2006 Earliest *Cucurbita* from the Great Lakes, Northern USA. *Quaternary Research* 65:216–222.

Montgomery, J. L., and J. Dickenson
1992 Additional Blades from Blackwater Draw Locality No. 1, Portales, New Mexico. *Current Research in the Pleistocene* 9:32–33.

Montgomery, R. G., W. Smith, and J. O. Brew
1949 Franciscan Awatovi: The Excavation and Conjectural Reconstruction of a 17th Century Spanish Mission Establishment at a Hopi Indian Town in Northeastern Arizona. In *Papers of the Peabody Museum of American Archaeology and Ethnology.* Harvard University, Cambridge, Massachusetts.

Moore, Clarence B.
1899 Certain Aboriginal Remains of the Alabama River. *Journal of the Academy of Natural Sciences of Philadelphia* 11:288–347.

Moore, Clarence B.
1905 Certain Aboriginal Remains of the Black Warrior River. *Journal of*

the *Academy of Natural Sciences of Philadelphia* 13:125–347.

Moore, Clarence B.
1913 Some Aboriginal Sites in Louisiana and Arkansas. *Journal of the Academy of Natural Sciences of Philadelphia* 16:7–99.

Moratto, Michael J.
1984 *California Archaeology*. Academic Press, New York. Reprinted in 2004 by Coyote Press, Salinas, California.

Morlan, Richard E.
1973 *The Later Prehistory of the Middle Porcupine Drainage, Northern Yukon Territory*. National Museum of Man, Ottawa.

Morlan, Richard E.
1986 Pleistocene Archaeology in the Old Crow Basin: A Critical Reappraisal. In *New Evidence for the Pleistocene Peopling of the Americas*, edited by Alan L. Bryan, pp. 27–48. Center for the Study of Early Man, Orono, Maine.

Morse, Dan F., and Phyllis A. Morse
1983 *Archaeology of the Central Mississippi Valley*. Academic Press, New York.

Morse-Kahn, Deborah
2003 *Archaeology Parks of the Upper Midwest*. Roberts Rinehart, Lanham, Maryland.

Mortensen, Lena, and Julie Hollowell (editors)
2009 *Ethnographies and Archaeologies: Iterations of the Past*. University Press of Florida, Gainesville.

Moser, Stephanie, Darren Glazier, James E. Phillips, Lamya Nasser el Nemr, Susan Richardson, Andrew Conner, and Michael Seymour
2002 Transforming Archaeology Through Practice: Strategies for Collaborative Archaeology and the Community Archaeology Project at Quseir, Egypt. *World Archaeology* 34:220–248.

Mosimann, J. E., and P. S. Martin
1975 Simulating Overkill by Paleoindians. *American Scientist* 60:304–313.

Moss, Madonna L.
2011 *Northwest Coast: Archaeology as Deep History*. Society for American Archaeology, Washington, D.C.

Moss, Madonna L., and Jon M. Erlandson
1992 Forts, Refuge Rocks, and Defensive Sites: The Antiquity of Warfare Along the North Pacific Coast of North America. *Arctic Anthropology* 29(2): 73–90.

Moulton, G. E.
1983 *The Journals of the Lewis and Clark Expedition*. Atlas of the Lewis & Clark Expedition 1. University of Nebraska Press, Lincoln.

Mt Pleasant, Jane
2006 The Science Behind the Three Sisters Mound System: An Agronomic Assessment of an Indigenous Agricultural System in the Northeast. In *Histories of Maize: Multidisciplinary Approaches to the Prehistory, Biogeography, Domestication, and Evolution of Maize*, edited by J. E. Staller, R. H. Tykot, and B. F. Benz, pp. 529–538. Academic Press, Burlington, Vermont.

Mudie, Petra J., Greer, Sheila, Judith Brakel, James H. Dickson, Clara Schinkel, Ruth Peterson-Welsh, Margaret Stevens, Nancy J. Turner, Mary Shadow, Rosalie Washington
2005 Forensic Palynology and Ethnobotany of *Salicornia* Species (Chenopodiaceae) in Northwest Canada and Alaska. *Canadian Journal of Botany* 83:111–123.

Mueller, Chuck
2005 Ancient Tools at High Desert Site Go Back 135,000 Years. *San Bernadino County Sun* 24 November. Electronic document, http://www.sbsun.com/news/ci_3247286, accessed December 7, 2005.

Muller, Jon
1986 Pans and a Grain of Salt: Mississippian Specialization Revisited. *American Antiquity* 51 (2):405–409.

Muller, Jon
1989 The Southern Cult. In *The Southeastern Ceremonial Complex: Artifacts and Analysis*, edited by Patricia Galloway, pp. 11–26. University of Nebraska Press, Lincoln.

Muller, Jon
1996 Cyrus Thomas, Nineteenth Century Synthesis and Antithesis. Paper presented at the Symposium History of Archaeology: Synthesizing American Archaeology, 61st Annual Meeting of the Society for American Archaeology, New Orleans.

Muller, Jon
1997 *Mississippian Political Economy*. Plenum Press, New York.

Mullins, Paul R.

1999 *Race and Affluence: An Archaeology of African America and Consumer Culture*. Kluwer Academic/Plenum, New York.

Mullins, Paul R.
2006 Racializing the Commonplace Landscape: An Archaeology of Urban Renewal Along the Color Line. *World Archaeology* 38 (1):60–71.

Munson, Cheryl Ann, Marjorie Melvin Jones, and Robert E. Fry
1995 The GE Mound: An ARPA Case Study. *American Antiquity* 60 (1):131–159.

Munson, Patrick J.
1969 Comments on Binford's "Smudge Pits and Hide Smoking: The Use of Analogy in Archaeological Reasoning." *American Antiquity* 34 (1):83–85.

Munson, Patrick J.
1990 Folsom Fluted Projectile Points East of the Great Plains and Their Biogeographical Correlates. *North American Archaeologist* 11 (3):255–272.

Nash, Stephen Edward
1999 *Time, Trees and Prehistory: Tree-Ring Dating and the Development of North American Archaeology*. University of Utah Press, Salt Lake City.

Nash, Stephen Edward
2000 *It's About Time: A History of Archaeological Dating in North America*. University of Utah Press, Salt Lake City.

Nassaney, Michael S.
1991 Spatial–Temporal Dimensions of Social Integration During the Coles Creek Period in Central Arkansas. In *Stability, Transformation and Variation: The Late Woodland Southeast*, edited by Michael S. Nassaney and Charles R. Cobb, pp. 177–220. Plenum Press, New York.

Nassaney, Michael S., and Charles R. Cobb
1991 Patterns and Processes of Late Woodland Development in the Greater Southeastern United States. In *Stability, Transformation and Variation: The Late Woodland Southeast*, edited by Michael S. Nassaney and Charles R. Cobb, pp. 285–322. Plenum Press, New York.

Nassaney, Michael S., and Kendra Pyle
1999 The Adoption of the Bow and Arrow in Eastern North America: A View from Central Arkansas. *American Antiquity* 64 (2):243–263.

Neitzel, Jill

1991 Hohokam Material Culture and Behavior: The Dimensions of Organizational Change. In *Exploring the Hohokam: Prehistoric Desert Peoples of the American Southwest*, edited by George Gumerman, pp. 177–230. University of New Mexico Press, Albuquerque.

Nelson, Margaret

1999 *Mimbres During the Twelfth Century; Abandonment, Continuity and Reorganization.* University of Arizona Press, Tucson.

Nelson, Nels

1916 Chronology of the Tano Ruins, New Mexico. *American Anthropologist* 18 (2):150–180.

Nepstad-Thornberry, Curtis, Linda Scott Cummings, and Kathryn Puseman

2002 A Model for Upper Republican Subsistence and Nutrition in the Medicine Creek Locality: A New Look at Extant Data. In *Medicine Creek: Seventy Years of Archaeological Investigations*, edited by Donna C. Roper, pp. 197–211. University of Alabama Press, Tuscaloosa.

Neuman, Robert

2010 North American Indian Tent Encampments: Tipi Rings, Wooden Wall Anchors, and Windbreaks. *Plains Anthropologist* 55:241–250.

Neumann, Thomas W., Robert M. Sanford, and Karen G. Harry

2010 *Cultural Resources Archaeology: An Introduction*, 2nd ed. AltaMira Press, Lanham, Maryland.

Neusius, Phillip D.

1996 Lithic Assemblage Variability in the Parker Collection. In *Reanalyzing the Ripley Site: Earthworks and Late Prehistory on the Lake Erie Plain*, edited by Lynne P. Sullivan, pp. 69–77. New York State Museum Bulletin 489. University of the State of New York/State Department of Education, Albany.

Neusius, Sarah Ward

1982 Early-Middle Archaic Subsistence Strategies: Changes in Faunal Exploitation at the Koster Site. Ph.D. dissertation, Department of Anthropology, Northwestern University, Evanston, Illinois.

Neusius, Sarah W.

1986a The Dolores Archaeological Program Faunal Data Base: Resource Availability and Resource Mix. In *Dolores Archaeological Program Final Synthetic Report*, edited by David A. Breternitz, Christine K. Robinson, and G. Timothy Gross, pp. 199–303. U.S. Department of the Interior, Engineering and Research Center, Denver.

Neusius, Sarah W.

1986b Generalized and Specialized Resource Utilization During the Archaic Period: Implications of the Koster Site Faunal Record. In *Foraging, Collecting, and Harvesting: Archaic Period Subsistence and Settlement in the Eastern Woodlands*, edited by Sarah W. Neusius. Occasional Paper 6. Center for Archaeological Investigations, Southern Illinois University at Carbondale, Carbondale.

Neusius, Sarah W.

1988 Faunal Exploitation During the McPhee Phase: The Evidence from the McPhee Community Cluster. In *Anasazi Communities at Dolores IV: McPhee Village*, edited by Allen E. Kane and Christine K. Robinson, pp. 1209–1291. U.S. Department of the Interior, Engineering and Research Center, Denver.

Neusius, Sarah W.

1996 Faunal Analysis and the Parker Collection. In *Reanalyzing the Ripley Site: Earthworks and Late Prehistory on the Lake Erie Plain*, edited by Lynne P. Sullivan, pp. 78–89. New York State Museum Bulletin 489. University of the State of New York/State Department of Education, Albany.

Neusius, Sarah W.

2008 Game Procurement Among Temperate Horticulturists: The Case for Garden Hunting by the Dolores Anasazi. In *Case Studies in Environmental Archaeology*, 2nd ed., edited by Elizabeth Reitz, C. Margaret Scarry, and Sylvia Scudder, pp. 297–314. Springer, New York.

Neusius, Sarah W., and Melissa Gould

1988 Faunal Remains from Grass Mesa Village: Implications for Dolores Anasazi Adaptations. In *Anasazi Communities at Dolores III: Grass Mesa Village*, edited by William D. Lipe, James N. Morris, and Timothy A. Kohler, pp. 1049–1135. U.S. Department of the Interior, Engineering and Research Center, Denver.

Neusius, Sarah W., Lynne P. Sullivan, Phillip D. Neusius, and Claire McHale Milner

1998 Fortified Village or Mortuary Site? Exploring the Use of the Ripley Site. In *Ancient Earthen Enclosures of the Eastern Woodlands*, edited by Robert C. Mainfort and Lynne P. Sullivan, Jr., pp. 202–230. University Press of Florida, Gainesville.

Neves, W., and M. Hubbe

2005 Cranial Morphology of Early Americans from Lagoa Santa, Brazil: Implications for the Settlement of the New World. *Proceedings of the National Academy of the Sciences* 102:18309–18314.

Newby, Paige, James Bradley, Arthur Spiess, Bryan Shuman, and Philip Leduc

2005 A Paleoindian Response to Younger Dryas Climate Change. *Quaternay Science Reviews* 24:141–154.

Newell, Gillian E., and Emiliano Gallaga

2003 *Surveying the Archaeology of Northwestern Mexico*. University of Utah Press, Salt Lake City.

Nials, Fred L., David A. Gregory, and Donald A. Graybill

1989 Salt River Streamflow and Hohokam Irrigation Systems. In *The 1982–1984 Excavations at Las Colinas: Environment and Subsistence*, edited by Donald A. Graybill, David A. Gregory, Fred L. Nials, Suzanne K. Fish, Robert E. Gasser, Charles H. Miksicek, and Christine R. Szuter, pp. 59–76. Arizona State Museum Archaeological Series 162(5), Tucson.

Nicholas, George

1999 A Light but Lasting Footprint: Human Influences on the Northeastern Landscape. In *The Archaeological Northeast*, edited by Mary Ann Levine, Kenneth E. Sassaman, and Michael S. Nassaney, pp. 25-38. Bergin and Garvey, Westport, Connecticut.

Nicholas, George

2010 *Being and Becoming Indigenous Archaeologists*. Left Coast Press, Walnut Creek, California.

Nickel, Robert

2007 Cultigens and Cultural Traditions in the Middle Missouri. In *Plains Village Archaeology: Bison-Hunting Farmers in the Central and Northern Plains*, edited by Stanley A. Ahler and Marvin Kay, pp. 126-136.

University of Utah Press, Salt Lake City.

O'Brien, Michael J., and R. Lee Lyman
1999 *Seriation, Stratigraphy and Index Fossils: The Backbone of Archaeological Dating.* Kluwer Academic/Plenum Press, New York.

O'Brien, Michael J., and W. Raymond Wood
1998 *The Prehistory of Missouri.* University of Missouri Press, Columbia.

O'Brien, Patricia
1994 The Central Lowland Plains: An Overview. In *Plains Indians, A.D. 500–1500: The Archaeological Past of Historic Groups*, edited by Karl H. Schlesier, pp. 199–223. University of Oklahoma Press, Norman.

O'Connell, James
1975 *The Prehistory of Surprise Valley.* Ballena Press Anthropological Papers 4, Ramona, California.

Odell, George
1994 The Role of Stone Bladelets in Middle Woodland Society. *American Antiquity* 59 :102–120.

Odell, George
2002 *La Harpe's Post: A Tale of French–Wichita Contact on the Eastern Plains.* University of Alabama Press, Tuscaloosa.

Odell, George, and Frank Cowan
1986 Experiments with Spears and Arrows on Animal Targets. *Journal of Field Archaeology* 13:195–212.

Olson, Deborah
1983 A Descriptive Analysis of the Faunal Remains from the Miller Site, Franklin County, Washington. M.A. thesis, Department of Anthropology, Washington State University, Pullman.

Orr, Kenneth G., and James A. Brown
1974 *Zimmerman Site: A Report of Excavations at the Grand Village of Kaskaskia, LaSalle County, Illinois.* Illinois State Museum, Springfield.

Orr, Phil C.
1962 The Arlington Springs Site, Santa Rosa Island, California. *American Antiquity* 27:417–419.

Orr, Phil C.
1968 *Prehistory of Santa Rosa Island.* Santa Barbara Museum of Natural History, Santa Barbara, California.

Orser, Charles E., Jr.
1996 Introduction: Images of the Recent Past. In *Readings in Historical Archaeology*, edited by Charles E.

Orser, pp. 9–13. AltaMira Press, Walnut Creek, California.

Orser, Charles E., Jr.
1998 The Archaeology of the African Diaspora.*Annual Review of Anthropology* 27:63–82.

Ortiz, Alfonso (editor)
1979 *Southwest.* Handbook of North American Indians, Vol. 10, William C. Sturtevant, general editor, Smithsonian Institution, Washington, D.C.

Ortman, Scott G.
2010 Evidence of a Mesa Verde Homeland for the Tewa Pueblos. In *Leaving Mesa Verde: Peril and Change in the Thirteenth-Century Southwest*, edited by Timothy A. Kohler, Mark D. Varien, and Aaron M. Wright, pp. 222–261. University of Arizona Press, Tucson.

Osborne, Douglas
1957 *Excavations in the McNary Reservoir Basin near Umatilla, Oregon.* Bureau of American Ethnology Bulletin 166, River Basin Survey Paper 8.

Osborne, Douglas, and Robert H. Crabtree
1961 Two Sites in the Upper McNary Reservoir. *Tebiwa* 4 (2):19–36.

O'Shea, John M.
1988 Social Organization and Mortuary Behavior in the Late Woodland Period in Michigan. In *Interpretations of Culture Change in the Eastern Woodlands During the Late Woodland Period*, edited by Richard W. Yerkes, pp. 68–85. Department of Anthropology, Ohio State University, Columbus.

Ossenberg, Nancy S.
1974 Origins and Relationships of Woodland Peoples: The Evidence of Cranial Morphology. In *Aspects of Upper Great Lakes Anthropology*, edited by Eldon Johnson, pp. 15–39. Minnesota Historical Society, St. Paul.

Otto, Martha Potter
1992 A Prehistoric Menagerie: Ohio Hopewell Effigy Pipes. In *Proceedings of the 1989 Smoking Pipe Conference: Selected Papers*, edited by Charles F. Hayes, III, Connie Cox Bodner, and Martha Sempowski, pp. 1–14. Rochester Museum and Science Center, Rochester, New York.

Overstreet, D. F., and T. W. Stafford, Jr.
1997 Additions to a Revised Chronology for Cultural

and Non-cultural Mammoth and Mastodon Fossils in the Southwestern Lake Michigan Basin. *Current Research in the Pleistocene* 14:70–71.

Overstreet, David F.
2004 Pre-Clovis Occupation in Southeastern Wisconsin. In *New Perspectives on the First Americans*, edited by Bradley T. Lepper and Robson Bonnichsen, pp. 41–48. Center for the Study of the First Americans, College Station, Texas.

Overstreet, David F.
2005 Late-Glacial Ice-Marginal Adaptation in Southeastern Wisconsin. In *Paleoamerican Origins:Beyond Clovis*, edited by Robson Bonnichsen, Bradley T. Lepper, Dennis Stanford and Michael R. Waters, pp. 183–195. Center for the Study of the First Americans, College Station, Texas.

Ozker, Doreen
1982 *An Early Woodland Community at the Schultz Site, 20SA2, in the Saginaw Valley and the Nature of the Early Woodland Adaptation in the Great Lakes Region.* Anthropological Paper 70. Museum of Anthropology, University of Michigan Ann Arbor.

Pacheco, Paul J.
1996 *A View from the Core: A Synthesis of Ohio Hopewell Archaeology.* Ohio Archaeological Council, Columbus.

Parker, Arthur C.
1907 *An Erie Indian Village and Burial Site at Ripley, Chautauqua County, N.Y.* New York State Museum Bulletin 117. State Department of Education, Albany

Parker, Arthur C.
1916 The Origin of the Iroquois as Suggested by Their Archaeology. *American Anthropologist* 18:479–507.

Parker, Arthur C.
1922 *The Archaeological History of New York.* New York State Museum Bulletins 237 and 238. University of the State of New York. Albany.

Parker, John
1976 *The Journals of Jonathan Carver and Related Documents, 1766–1770.* Minnesota Historical Society Press, St. Paul.

Parker, Kathryn E.
1996 Three Corn Kernels and a Hill of Beans: The Evidence for Prehistoric Horticulture in Michigan. In *Investigating the Archaeological Record of the Great Lakes State*, edited by

Margaret B. Holman, Janet G. Brashler, and Kathryn E. Parker, pp. 307–339. New Issue Press, Western Michigan University Press, Kalamazoo.

Parkman, E. Breck
1996/1997 Fort and Settlement: Interpreting the Past at Fort Ross State Historic Park. *California History* 75 (4):354–369.

Parmalee, Paul W., Andreas A. Paloumpis, and Nancy Wilson
1972 *Animals Utilized by Woodland Peoples Occupying the Apple Creek Site, Illinois*. Illinois State Museum, Springfield.

Parrish, Otis, Daniel Murley, Roberta A. Jewett, and Kent G. Lightfoot
2000 The Science of Archaeology and the Response from Within Native California: The Archaeology and Ethnohistory of Metini Village in the Fort Ross State Historic Park. *Proceedings of the Society for California Archaeology* 13:84–87.

Patterson, Thomas C.
1995 *Toward a Social History of Archaeology in the United States*. Harcourt Brace College, Fort Worth, Texas.

Pauketat, Timothy R.
2005 The Forgotten History of the Mississippians. In *North American Archaeology*, edited by Timothy R. Pauketat and Diana Di Paolo Loren. Blackwell, Malden, Massachusetts.

Pauketat, Timothy R.
2007 *Chiefdoms and Other Archaeological Delusions*. AltaMira Press, Lanham, Maryland.

Pauketat, Timothy R., and Diana Di Paolo Loren (editors)
2005 *North American Archaeology*. Blackwell, Malden, Massachusetts.

Pauketat, Timothy R., and Thomas E. Emerson
1997 Conclusion: Cahokia and the Four Winds. In *Cahokia: Domination and Ideology in the Mississippian World*, edited by Timothy R. Pauketat and Thomas E. Emerson, pp. 269–278. University of Nebraska Press, Lincoln.

Pavesic, Max G.
1985 Cache Blades and Turkey Tails: Piecing Together the Western Idaho Archaic Burial Complex. In *Stone Tool Analysis: Essays in Honor of Don E. Crabtree*, edited by Mark G. Plew, James C. Woods, and Max G.

Pavesic, pp. 55–89. University of New Mexico Press, Albuquerque.

Peacock, Evan
2002 Shellfish Use During the Woodland Period in the Middle South. In *The Woodland Southeast*, edited by David G. Anderson and Robert C. Mainfort, Jr., pp. 444–460. University of Alabama Press, Tuscaloosa.

Pearsall, Deborah M.
2000 *Paleoethnobotany: A Handbook of Procedures*. Academic Press, New York.

Peebles, Christopher S., and Susan Kus
1977 Some Archaeological Correlates of Ranked Societies. *American Antiquity* 42:421–448.

Pendergast, James F.
1994 The Introduction of European Goods into the Native Community in the Sixteenth Century. In *Proceedings of the 1992 People-to-People Conference: Selected Papers*, edited by Charles F. Hayes III, Connie Cox Bodner and Lorraine P. Saunders, pp. 7–18. Rochester Museum and Science Center, Rochester, New York.

Perkl, Bradley E.
1998 *Cucurbita pepo* from King Coulee, Southeastern Minnesota. *American Antiquity* 63:279–288.

Perry, Warren R., Jean Howson, and Barbara A. Bianco
2006 Chapter 15: Summary and Conclusions. In *New York African Burial Ground Archaeology Final Report: Volume 1*. Howard University, Washington, D.C. Electronic document, http://www.africanburial-ground.gov/ABG_FinalReports.htm, accessed March 24, 2012.

Petersen, James B.
1996 Fiber Industries from Northern New England: Ethnicity and Technological Traditions During the Woodland Period. In *A Most Indispensable Art: Native Fiber Industries from Eastern North America*, edited by J. B. Petersen, pp. 100–119. University of Tennessee Press, Knoxville.

Petersen, James B., and Nancy Asch-Sidell
1996 Mid-Holocene Evidence of *Cucurbita* sp. from Central Maine. *American Antiquity* 61:685–698.

Petersen, James B., R. N. Bartone, and B. J. Cox
2002 The Late Paleoindian Period in Northeastern North America: A

View from Varney Farm. In *Ice Age Peoples of Pennsylvania*, edited by Kurt W. Carr and James M. Adovasio. Pennsylvania Historical and Museum Commission, Harrisburg.

Petersen, Kenneth L.
1986 *Climatic Reconstruction for the Dolores Project*. U.S. Department of the Interior, Engineering and Research Center, Denver.

Petersen, Kenneth L., and Vickie L. Clay
1987 Characteristics and Archaeological Implications of Cold Air Drainage in the Dolores Project Area. In *Dolores Archaeological Program Supporting Studies: Settlement and Environment*, edited by Kenneth L. Peterson and Janet D. Orcutt, pp. 311–324. U.S. Department of the Interior, Engineering and Research Center, Denver.

Petersen, Kenneth L., Meredith H. Mathews, and Sarah W. Neusius
1986 *Environmental Archaeology*. U.S. Department of Interior, Engineering and Research Center. Denver.

Phillips, James L., and James A. Brown
1983 *Archaic Hunters and Gatherers in the American Midwest*. Academic Press, New York.

Pielou, E. C.
1991 *After the Ice Age: The Return of Life to Glaciated North America*. University of Chicago Press, Chicago.

Pilling, Arnold R.
1982 Detroit: Urbanism Moves West: Palisaded Fur-Trade Center to Diversified Manufacturing City. *North American Archaeologist* 3:225–242.

Pilling, Arnold R., and Dean L. Anderson
1999 Euro-American Archaeology in Michigan: The British Period. In *Retrieving Michigan's Buried Past: The Archaeology of the Great Lakes State*, edited by John R. Halsey, pp. 312–316. Cranbrook Institute of Science, Bloomfield Hills, Michigan.

Pilon, Jean-Luc
1996 The North American Subarctic. In *The Oxford Companion to Archaeology*, edited by Brian M. Fagan, Charlotte Beck, George Michaels, Chris Scarre, and Neil Asher Silberman, pp. 516–517. Oxford University Press, New York.

Pilon, Jean-Luc
1998 Central Subarctic Woodland Culture. In *Archaeology of Prehistoric*

Native America, edited by Guy Gibbon, pp. 133–135. Garland, New York.

Pinson, Ariane O.
2011 The Clovis Occupation of the Dietz Site (35lk1529), Lake County, Oregon, and Its Bearing on the Adaptive Diversity of Clovis Foragers. *American Antiquity* 76:285–313.

Piperno, Dolores R., and Kent V. Flannery
2001 The Earliest Archaeological Maize (*Zea mays* L.) from Highland Mexico: New Accelerator Mass Spectrometry Dates and Their Implications. *Proceedings of the National Academy of Sciences* 98:2101–2103.

Piperno, Dolores R., Anthony J. Ranere, Irene Holstb, José Iriarte, and Ruth Dickau
2009 Starch Grain and Phytolith Evidence for Early Ninth Millennium B.P. Maize from the Central Balsas River Valley, Mexico. *Proceedings of the National Academy of Sciences* 106:5019–5024.

Pitulko, V., P. Nikolsky, E. Girya, E. Basillyan, V. Tumskoy, S. Koulakov, S. Astakhov, E. Pavlova, and M. Anisimov
2004 The Yana RHS Site: Humans in the Arctic Before the Last Glacial Maximum. *Science* 303:52–56.

Pleger, Thomas C., and James B. Stoltman
2009 The Archaic Tradition in Wisconsin. In *Archaic Societies: Diversity and Complexity Across the MidContinent*, edited by Thomas E. Emerson, Dale L. McElrath, and Andrew C. Fortier, pp. 697–723. State University of New York Press, Albany.

Pokotylo, David L., and Donald Mitchell
1998 Prehistory of the Northern Plateau. In *Plateau*, edited by Deward E. Walker, Jr., pp. 81–102. Handbook of North American Indians, Vol. 12, William C. Sturtevant, general editor, Smithsonian Institution, Washington, D.C.

Polhemus, Richard R.
2002 Introduction. In *The Tennessee, Green, and Lower Ohio Rivers Expeditions of Clarence Bloomfield Moore*, edited by Richard R. Polhemus, pp. 1–27. University of Alabama Press, Tuscaloosa.

Porcasi, J. F., T. L. Jones, and L. M. Raab
2000 Trans-Holocene Marine Mammal Exploitation on San Clemente Island: A Tragedy of the Commons Revisited. *Journal of Anthropological Archaeology* 19:200–220.

Porcasi, Paul, Judith F. Porcasi, and Colin O'Neill
1999 Early Holocene Coastlines of the California Bight: The Channel Islands as First Visited by Humans. *Pacific Coast Archaeological Society Quarterly* 3 (2–3):2–24.

Porter, Joy
2001 *To Be Indian: The Life of Iroquois-Seneca Arthur Caswell Parker*. University of Oklahoma Press, Norman.

Pott, Kenneth R.
1999 Underwater Archaeology in Michigan. In *Retrieving Michigan's Buried Past: The Archaeology of the Great Lakes State*, edited by John R. Halsey, pp. 312–316. Cranbrook Institute of Science, Bloomfield Hills, Michigan.

Potter, James M.
1997 Communal Ritual and Faunal Remains: An Example from the Dolores Anasazi. *Journal of Field Archaeology* 24 (3):353–364.

Potter, Parker B., Jr.
1994 *Public Archaeology in Annapolis: A Critical Approach to History in Maryland's Ancient City*. Smithsonian Institution Press, Washington, D.C.

Pourade, Richard F.
1960 *The History of San Diego: The Explorers*. Union-Tribune, San Diego.

Powell, Eric A.
2004 Early Dates, Real Tools? *Archaeology Online News*, November 17, 2004. Electronic document, http://www.archaeology.org/online/news/topper.html, accessed December 12, 2012.

Powell, Mary Lucas
1992 In the Best of Health? Disease and Trauma Among the Mississippian Elite. In *Lords of the Southeast: Social Inequality and the Native Elites of Southeastern North America*. Archaeological Papers of the American Anthropological Association 3.

Powell, Mary Lucas
1998 Of Time and the River: Perspectives on Health During the Moundville Chiefdom. In *Archaeology of the Moundville Chiefdom*, edited by Vernon

James Knight, Jr., and Vioncas P. Steponaitis, pp. 102–119. Smithsonian Institution Press, Washington, D.C.

Prentiss, William C., and Ian Kuijt (editors)
2004 *Complex Hunter-Gatherers: Evolution and Organization of Prehistoric Communities on the Plateau of Northwestern North America*. University of Utah Press, Salt Lake City.

Preston, Douglas
2002 Introduction. In *In Search of Ice Age Americans*, edited by Kenneth Tankersley, pp. 8–30. Gibbs Smith, Layton, Utah.

Preucel, Robert W.
1991 *Processual and Postprocessual Archaeologists: Multiple Ways of Knowing the Past*. Occasional Paper 10. Center for Archaeological Investigations, Southern Illinois University at Carbondale, Carbondale.

Preucel, Robert W.
2000 Living on the Mesa Hanat Kotyiti, A Post-Revolt Cochiti Community in Northern New Mexico. *Expedition* 42 (1):8–18.

Prufer, Olaf H.
1964 The Hopewell Complex of Ohio. In *Hopewellian Studies*, edited by Joseph R. Caldwell and Robert L. Hall, pp. 85–106. Illinois State Museum Scientific Papers Vol. XII, Springfield.

Pullar, Gordon L.
1992 Ethnic Identity, Cultural Pride, and Generations of Baggage: A Personal Experience. *Arctic Anthropology* 28 (2):182–191.

Purdy, Barbara A.
2001 Archaeological Investigations of Water-Saturated Deposits in Volusia County, Florida: Groves Orange Midden on Lake Monroe. In *Enduring Records: The Environmental and Cultural Heritage of Wetlands*. Oxbow Books, Oxford, United Kingdom.

Quaife, Milo
1921 *Alexander Henry's Travels and Adventures*. Lakeside Press, Chicago.

Raab, L. M., K. Bradford, and A. Yatsko
1994 Advances in Southern Channel Islands Archaeology: 1983–1993. *Journal of California and Great Basin Anthropology* 16:243–270.

Raab, L. M., and Daniel O. Larson
1997 Medieval Climatic Anomaly and Punctuated Cultural Evolution

in Coastal Southern California. *American Antiquity* 40 (1):319–336.

Raab, L. M., and A. Yatsko
2000 Prehistoric Human Ecology of Quinquina: Archaeological Resources Management, Research Design and Maritime Cultural Evolution on San Clemente Island, California. Draft manuscript on file, Natural Resources Office, North Island Naval Air Station, San Diego.

Raab, L. M., A. Yatsko, W. J. Howard, and J. Cassidy
2004 Mariners to Messiahs: New Perspectives on Maritime Prehistory from San Clemente Island, California. Manuscript on file, Natural Resources Office, North Island Naval Air Station, San Diego.

Rafferty, Sean M., and Rob Mann
2004 *Smoking and Culture: The Archaeology of Tobacco Pipes in Eastern North America*. University of Tennessee Press, Knoxville.

Ramenofsky, Ann F.
1987 *Vectors of Death: The Archaeology of European Contact*. University of New Mexico Press, Albuquerque.

Ramos, Maria, and David Duganne
2000 Exploring Public Perceptions and Attitudes About Archaeology. Electronic document, http://www.saa.org/Portals/0/SAA/pubedu/nrptdraft4.pdf, accessed June 27, 2012.

Randall, Asa R.
2002 Technofunctional Variation in Early Side-Notched Hafted Bifaces: A View from the Middle Tennessee River Valley in Northwest Alabama. Unpublished M.A. thesis, University of Florida, Gainesville.

Rasmussen, Morten, Yingrui Li, Stinus Lindgreen, Jakob Skou Pedersen, Anders Albrechtsen, Ida Moltke, Mait Metspalu, Ene Metspalu, Toomas Kivisild, Ramneek Gupta, Marcelo Bertalan, Kasper Nielsen, M. Thomas P. Gilbert, Yong Wang, Maanasa Raghavan, Paula F. Campos, Hanne Munkholm Kamp, Andrew S. Wilson, Andrew Gledhill, Silvana Tridico, Michael Bunce, Eline D. Lorenzen, Jonas Binladen, Xiaosen Guo, Jing Zhao, Xiuqing Zhang, Hao Zhang, Zhuo Li, Minfeng Chen, Ludovic Orlando, Karsten Kristiansen, Mads Bak, Niels Tommerup, Christian Bendixen, Tracey L. Pierre, Bjarne Grønnow, Morten

Meldgaard, Claus Andreasen, Sardana A. Fedorova, Ludmila P. Osipova, Thomas F. G. Higham, Christopher Bronk Ramsey, Thomas V. O. Hansen, Finn C. Nielsen, Michael H. Crawford, Søren Brunak, Thomas Sicheritz-Pontén, Richard Villems, Rasmus Nielsen, Anders Krogh, Jun Wang, and Eske Willerslev
2010 Ancient Human Genome Sequence of an Extinct Paleo-Eskimo. *Nature* 463:757–763.

Raven, Christopher
1984 Northeastern California. In *California Archaeology*, edited by Michael J. Moratto, pp. 431–469. Academic Press, Orlando, Florida.

Ravesloot, J. C.
1988 *Mortuary Practices and Social Differentiation at Casas Grandes, Chihuahua, Mexico*. Anthropological Papers 49. University of Arizona, Tucson.

Raviele, Maria E.
2010 Assessing Carbonized Archaeological Cooking Residues: Evaluation of Maize Phytolith Taphonomy and Density Through Experimental Residue Analysis. Ph.D. dissertation, Michigan State University, Ann Arbor.

Rawlings, Tiffany A., and Jonathan C. Driver
2010 Paleodiet of Domestic Turkey, Shields Pueblo (5MT3807), Colorado: Isotopic Analysis and Its Implications for Care of a Household Domesticate. *Journal of Archaeological Science* 37:2433–2441.

Reid, Jefferson, and Stephanie Whittlesey
1997 *The Archaeology of Ancient Arizona*. University of Arizona Press, Tucson.

Reid, Kenneth
1984 *Nebo Hill: Late Archaic Prehistory on the Southern Prairie Peninsula*. Publications in Anthropology 15. University of Kansas, Lawrence.

Reimer, P. J., Baillie, M. G. L., Bard, E., Bayliss, A., Beck, J. W., Blackwell, P. G., Bronk Ramsey, C., Buck, C. E., Burr, G. S., Edwards, R. L., Friedrich, M., Grootes, P. M., Guilderson, T. P., Hajdas, I., Heaton, T. J., Hogg, A. G., Hughen, K. A., Kaiser, K. F., Kromer, B., McCormac, F. G., Manning, S. W., Reimer, R. W., Richards, D. A., Southon, J. R., Talamo, S., Turney, C. S. M., van der Plicht, J., and Weyhenmeyer, C. E.
2009 IntCal09 and Marine09 Radiocarbon Age Calibration

Curves, 0–50,000 Years cal BP. *Radiocarbon* 51(4), 1111–1150.

Reitz, Elizabeth J., Irvy R. Quitmyer, H. Stephen Hale, Sylvia J. Scudder, and Elizabeth S. Wing
1987 Application of Allometry to Zooarchaeology. *American Antiquity* 52 (2):304–317.

Reitz, Elizabeth J., and Elizabeth S. Wing
1999 *Zooarchaeology*. Cambridge University Press, Cambridge.

Renaud, E. B.
1931 Prehistoric Flaked Points from Colorado and Neighboring Districts. *Proceedings of the Colorado Museum of Natural History (Denver)* 10 (2):1–21.

Renouf, M. A. P., and Trevor Bell
2009 Contraction and Expansion in Newfoundland Prehistory, AD 900–1500. In *The Northern World AD 900–1400*, edited by Herbert Maschner, Owen Mason, and Robert McGhee, pp. 263–278. The University of Utah Press, Salt Lake City.

Rhodes, Richard A., and Evelyn M. Todd
1981 Subarctic Algonquian Languages. In *Subarctic*, edited by June Helm, pp. 52–66. Handbook of North American Indians, Vol. 6, William C. Sturtevant, general editor, Smithsonian Institution, Washington, D.C.

Richards, Michael P., Sheila Greer, Lorna T. Corr, Owen Beattie, Alexander Mackie, Richard P. Evershed, Al von Finster, and John Southon
2007 Radiocarbon Dating and Stable Dietary Isotope Analysis of Kwaday Dan Ts'inchí. *American Antiquity* 72:719–733.

Rick, Torben C.
2007 *The Archaeology and Historical Ecology of Late Holocene San Miguel Island*. Cotsen Institute of Archaeology, University of California, Los Angeles.

Rick, Torben C., and Jon M. Erlandson
2011 Kelp Forests, Coastal Migrations, and the Younger Dryas: Late Pleistocene and Earliest Holocene Human Settlement, Subsistence, and Ecology on California's Channel Islands. In *Archaeology of the Younger Dryas: Case Studies from Around the World*, edited by E. Meten, in press.

Rick, Torben C., Jon M. Erlandson, and René Vellanoweth
2001 Paleocoastal Marine Fishing on the Pacific Coast of the Americas:

Perspectives from Daisy Cave, California. *American Antiquity* 66 (4):595–614.

Riggs, Charles R.

2005 Late Ancestral Pueblo or Ancestral Pueblo? An Architectural Perspective on Identity. *Kiva* 70:323–348.

Riley, Thomas J.

1994 Ocmulgee and the Question of Mississippian Agronomic Practices. In *Ocmulgee Archaeology: 1936–1986*, edited by David J. Hally, pp. 96–104. University of Georgia Press, Athens.

Riley, Thomas J., Richard Edging, and Jack Rosen

1990 Cultigens in Prehistoric Eastern North America: Changing Paradigms. *Current Anthropology* 31:525–542.

Riley, Thomas J., Gregory R. Waltz, Charles J. Bareis, Andrew C. Fortier, and Kathryn E. Parker

1994 Accelerator Mass Spectrometry (AMS) Dates Confirm Early *Zea mays* in the Mississippi River Valley. *American Antiquity* 59:490–497.

Riordan, Timothy B.

1977 The Ferry Hall Attic Site: An Example of the Above-Ground Archaeology. *Northwest Anthropological Research Notes* 11 (2):143–145.

Ritchie, William A.

1932 The Lamoka Lake Site. *Researches and Transactions of the New York State Archaeological Association* 7 (4):79–134.

Ritchie, William A.

1980 *The Archaeology of New York State*, rev. ed. Harbor Hill Books, Harrison, New York.

Ritchie, William A.

1989 *A Typology and Nomenclature for New York Projectile Points.* New York State Bulletin 384. University of the State of New York/State Department of Education, Albany.

Ritchie, William A., and Robert E. Funk

1973 *Aboriginal Settlement Patterns in the Northeast.* Memoir 20. New York Museum & Science Service, University of the State of New York, Albany.

Ritterbush, Lauren W.

2007 Oneota Interaction and Impact in the Central Plains. In *Plains Village Archaeology: Bison-Hunting Farmers in the Central and Northern Plains*, edited by Stanley A. Ahler and

Marvin Kay, pp. 181-192. University of Utah Press, Salt Lake City.

Roberts, David

1997 Sieur de La Salle's Fateful Landfall. *Smithsonian Magazine*, April.

Roberts, Heidi, Richard V. N. Ahlstrom, and Barbara Roth

2004 *From Campus to Corporation: The Emergence of Contract Archaeology in the Southwestern United State.* Society for American Archaeology Washington, D.C.

Robertson, James A., William A. Lovis, and John R. Halsey

1999 The Late Archaic: Hunter-Gatherers in an Uncertain Environment. In *Retrieving Michigan's Buried Past*, edited by John R Halsey, pp. 95–124. Cranbrook Institute of Science, Bloomfield, Michigan.

Robinson, Brian S.

1996 A Regional Analysis of the Moorehead Burial Tradition: 8500–3700 B.P. *Archaeology of Eastern North America* 24:95–148.

Robinson, Brian S., Jennifer C. Ort, William A. Eldridge, Adrian L. Burke, and Bertrand G. Pelletier

2009 Paleoindian Aggregation and Social Context at Bull Brook. *American Antiquity* 74:423–447.

Robinson, Brian S.

2006 Burial Ritual, Technology, and Cultural Landscape in the Far Northeast: 8600–3700 B.P. In *The Archaic of the Far Northeast*, edited by David Sanger and M. A. P. Renouf, pp. 341–381. The University of Maine Press, Orono.

Robinson, R. W., and D. S. Decker-Walters

1996 *Cucurbits.* CAB International, New York.

Rogers, J. Daniel

1993 The Social and Material Implications of Culture Contact on the Northern Plains. In *Ethnohistory and Archaeology: Approaches to Postcontact Change in the Americas*, edited by J. Daniel Rogers and Samuel M. Wilson, pp. 73–88. Plenum Press, New York.

Rogers, J. Daniel, and Bruce D. Smith

1995 *Mississippian Communities and Households.* University of Alabama Press, Tuscaloosa.

Rogers, Malcolm J.

1929 Stone Art of the San Dieguito Plateau. *American Anthropologist* 31:454–467.

Rogers, Malcolm J.

1939 *Early Lithic Industries of the Lower Basin of the Colorado River and Adjacent Desert Areas.* San Diego Museum of Man Papers No. 3.

Rohn, A. H., and A. M. Emerson

1984 *Great Bend Sites at Marion, Kansas.* Publications in Anthropology 1. Wichita State University, Kansas.

Rolingson, Martha A.

2002 Plum Bayou Culture of the Arkansas–White River Basin. In *The Woodland Southeast*, edited by David G. Anderson and Robert C. Mainfort, Jr., pp. 44–65. University of Alabama Press, Tuscaloosa.

Rolingson, Martha A., and Robert C. Mainfort, Jr.

2002 Woodland Period Archaeology of the Central Mississippi Valley. In *The Woodland Southeast*, edited by David G. Anderson and Robert C. Mainfort, Jr., pp. 20–43. University of Alabama Press, Tuscaloosa.

Roll, Tom E., and Steven Hackenberger

1998 Prehistory of the Eastern Plateau. In *Plateau*, edited by Jr. Deward E. Walker, pp. 121–137. Handbook of North American Indians, Vol. 12, William C. Sturtevant, general editor, Smithsonian Institution, Washington, D.C.

Roper, Donna C.

2007 The Origins and Expansion of the Central Plains Tradition. In *Plains Village Archaeology: Bison Hunting Farmers in the Central and Northern Plains*, edited by Stanley A. Ahler and Marvin Kay, pp. 53–63. The University of Utah Press, Salt Lake City.

Roper, Donna C., and Elizabeth P. Pauls (editors)

2005 *Plains Earthlodges: Ethnographic and Archaeological Perspectives.* University of Alabama Press, Tuscaloosa.

Rose, Mark

1999 The Topper Site: Pre-Clovis Surprise. *Archaeology* 52 (4). Electronic document, http://www.archaeology.org/9907/news-briefs/clovis.html., accessed September 16, 2012.

Roseman, Charles C., and Timothy D. Weaver

2004 Multivariate Apportionment of Global Human Craniometric

Diversity. *American Journal of Physical Anthropology* 125:257–263.

Rothschild, Nan A.
1979 Mortuary Behavior and Social Organization at Indian Knoll and Dickson Mounds. *American Antiquity* 44 (4):658–675.

Rountree, Helen C., and E. Randolph Turner, III
2002 *Before and After Jamestown: Virginia's Powhatans and Their Predecessors*. University Press of Florida, Gainesville.

Rousselot, J. L., W. W. Fitzhugh, and A. Crowell
1988 Maritime Economies of the North Pacific Rim. In *Crossroads of Continents: Cultures of Siberia and Alaska*, edited by W. W. Fitzhugh and A. Crowell, pp. 151–172. Smithsonian Institution Press, Washington, D.C.

Rozaire, Charles
1978 Archaeological Investigations on San Miguel Island, California. Unpublished report, Los Angeles County Museum of Natural History.

Rozoy, J. G.
1978 *Les derniers chasseurs: l'Epipaléolithique en France et en Belgique. Essai de synthèse*. Special Bulletin of Societé Archéologique Champenoise 2. Imprimerie de Compiègne, Reims, France.

Ruby, Bret J.
1997 Current Research at Hopewell Culture National Historical Park. *Hopewell Archeology* 2 (1):1–6.

Russo, Michael
1994 Why We Don't Believe in Archaic Ceremonial Mounds and Why We Should: The Case from Florida. *Southeastern Archaeology* 13:93–108.

Russo, Michael
1996 Southeastern Archaic Mounds. In *Archaeology of the Mid-Holocene Southeast*, edited by Kenneth E. Sassaman, pp. 259–287. University Press of Florida, Gainesville.

Saitta, Dean J.
2005 Labor and Class in the American West. In *North American Archaeology*, edited by Timothy R. Pauketat and Diana Di Paolo Loren, pp. 259–285. Blackwell, Malden, Massachusetts.

Samford, Patricia
1996 The Archeology of African-American Slavery and Material Culture. *The William and Mary Quarterly* 53:87–114.

Sanders, Stanley
1999 The High Lava Plains. Electronic document, http://spot.pcc.edu/~mhutson/malheur/HighLavaPlains.html.

Sandweiss, D. H., H. McInnis, R. L. Burger, A. Cano, B. Ojeda, R. Paredes, M. Del Carmen Sandweiss, and M. Glascock
1998 Quebrada Jaguay: Early South American Maritime Adaptations. *Science* 281:1830–1833.

Sanger, David
1996 Gilman Falls Site: Implications for the Early and Middle Archaic of the Maritime Peninsula. *Canadian Journal of Archaeology* 20:7–28.

Saraceni, Jessica E.
1998 Searching for Lewis and Clark. *Archaeology* 51 (1). Electronic document, http://www.archaeology.org/9801/newsbriefs/lewis.html, accessed December 12, 2012.

Sassaman, Kenneth E.
1993 *Early Pottery in the Southeast: Tradition and Innovation in Cooking Technology*. University of Alabama Press, Tuscaloosa.

Sassaman, Kenneth E.
1996 Technological Innovations in Economic and Social Contexts. In *Archaeology of the Mid-Holocene Southeast*, edited by Kenneth E. Sassaman and David G. Anderson, pp. 57–74. University Press of Florida, Gainesville.

Sassaman, Kenneth E.
1997 Refining Soapstone Vessel Chronology in the Southeast. *Early Georgia* 25 (1):1–20.

Sassaman, Kenneth E.
1999 A Southeastern Perspective on Soapstone Vessel Technology in the Northeast. In *The Archaeological Northeast*, edited by Mary Ann Levine, Kenneth E. Sassaman and Michael S. Nassaney, pp. 75–95. Bergin & Garvey, Westport, Connecticut.

Sassaman, Kenneth E.
2002 Woodland Ceramic Beginnings. In *The Woodland Southeast*, edited by David G. Anderson and Robert C. Mainfort, Jr., pp. 298–420. University of Alabama Press, Tuscaloosa.

Sassaman, Kenneth E.
2005 Structure and Practice in the Archaic Southeast. In *North American Archaeology*, edited by Timothy R.

Pauketat and Diana DiPaolo Loren, pp. 79–102. Blackwell, Oxford.

Sassaman, Kenneth E.
2006 Dating and Explaining Soapstone Vessels: A Comment on Truncer. *American Antiquity* 71 (1):141–156.

Sassaman, Kenneth E., and David G. Anderson
1996 *Archaeology of the Mid-Holocene Southeast*. University Press of Florida, Gainesville.

Sassaman, Kenneth E., and David G. Anderson
2004 Late Holocene Period, 3750 to 650 B.C. In *Southeast*, edited by Raymond D. Fogelson, pp. 101–114. Handbook of North American Indians, Vol. 14, William C. Sturtevant, eneral ditor. Smithsonian Institution, Washington, D.C.

Saunders, J. J.
1977 Lehner Ranch Revisited. In *Paleoindian Lifeways*, edited by E. Johnson, pp. 48–64. The Museum Journal 17. West Texas Museum Association, Lubbock.

Saunders, J. J.
1980 A Model for Man–Mammoth Relationships in Late Pleistocene North America. In *The Ice-Free Corridor and Peopling of the New World*, edited by N. W. Rutter and C. E. Schweger, pp. 87–98. Canadian Journal of Anthropology 1, Edmonton, Alberta.

Saunders, J. J., G. A. Agogino, A. T. Boldurian, and C. V. Haynes, Jr.
1991 A Mammoth-Ivory Burnisher-Billet from the Clovis Level, Blackwater Locality No. 1, New Mexico. *Plains Anthropologist* 36:359–364.

Saunders, J. J., C. V. Haynes, Jr., D. J. Stanford, and G. A. Agogino
1990 A Mammoth-Ivory Semifabricate from Blackwater Locality No. 1, New Mexico. *American Antiquity* 55:112–119.

Saunders, Joe W., Thurman Allen, and Roger T. Saucier
1994 Four Archaic? Mound Complexes in Northeast Louisiana. *Southeastern Archaeology* 13:134–153.

Saunders, Joe W., Rolfe D. Mandel, C. Garth Sampson, Charles M. Allen, E. Thurman Allen, Daniel A. Bush, James K. Feathers, Kristen J. Gremillion, C. T. Hallmark, H. Edwin Jackson, Jay K. Johnson, Reca Jones, Roger T. Saucier, Gary L. Stringer, and Malcom F. Vidrine
2005 Watson Brake, a Middle Archaic Mound Complex in Northeast

Louisiana. *American Antiquity* 70 (4):631–668.

Saunders, Lorraine P.
1992 A Consideration of Local Origins for Epidemic Disease in Certain Native American Populations. In *Proceedings of the 1992 People-to-People Conference: Selected Papers*, edited by Charles F. Hayes, Connie Cox Bodner, and Lorraine P. Saunders, pp. 105–114. Rochester Museum and Science Center, Rochester, New York.

Scarry, C. Margaret
2003 Patterns of Wild Plant Utilization in the Prehistoric Eastern Woodlands. In *People and Plants in Ancient Eastern North America*, edited by Paul E. Minnis, pp. 50–104. Smithsonian Books, Washington, D.C.

Scarry, John F.
1990 Mississippian Emergence in the Fort Walton Area: The Evolution of the Cayson and Lake Jackson Phases. In *The Mississippian Emergence*, edited by Bruce D. Smith, pp. 227–250. Smithsonian Institution Press, Washington, D.C.

Schaafsma, Curtis F.
1996 Ethnic Identity and Protohistoric Archaeological Sites in Northwestern New Mexico: Implications for Reconstructions of Navajo and Ute History. In *The Archaeology of Navajo Origins*, edited by Ronald H. Towner, pp. 19–46. University of Utah Press, Salt Lake City.

Schaafsma, Curtis F., and Carroll L. Riley
1999 *The Casas Grandes World*. University of Utah Press, Salt Lake City.

Schalk, Randall F.
1978 Some Observations on Migratory Fish in the Plateau. In *Second Annual Interim Report on the Archaeological Investigations at the Miller Site (45 FR 5) on Strawberry Island (1977), a Late Prehistoric Village near Burbank, Washington*, edited by Gregory C. Cleveland, pp. 61–80. Project Report 72. Washington Archaeological Research Center, Pullman.

Schalk, Randall F. (editor)
1983 *The 1978 and 1979 Excavations at Strawberry Island in the McNary Reservoir*. Project Report 19. Washington State University, Laboratory of Archaeology and History, Pullman.

Schalk, Randall F., and Deborah Olsen
1983 The Faunal Assemblages. In *The 1978 and 1979 Excavations at Strawberry Island in the McNary Reservoir*, edited by Randall F. Schalk, pp. 75–110. Project Report 19. Washington State University, Laboratory of Archaeology and History, Pullman.

Schiffer, Michael B.
1975 An Alternative to Morse's Dalton Settlement Pattern Hypothesis. *Plains Anthropologist* 20:253–266.

Schiffer, Michael B.
1976 *Behavioral Archaeology*. Academic Press, New York.

Schlanger, Sarah H.
1986 Population Studies. In *Dolores Archaeological Program Final Synthetic Report*, edited by David A. Breternitz, Christine K. Robinson, and G. Timothy Gross, pp. 493–524. U.S. Department of the Interior, Engineering and Research Center, Denver.

Schlanger, Sarah H.
1988 Patterns of Population Movement and Long-Term Population Growth in Southwestern Colorado. *American Antiquity* 53:773–793.

Schlesier, Karl H.
1994 *Plains Indians, A.D. 500–1500: The Archaeological Past of Historic Groups*. University of Oklahoma Press, Norman.

Schoeninger, Margaret J., and Mark R. Schurr
1998 Human Subsistence at Moundville: The Stable-Isotope Data. In *Archaeology of the Moundville Chiefdom*, edited by Vernon James Knight, Jr., and Vincas P. Steponaitis, pp. 120–132. Smithsonian Institution Press, Washington, D.C.

Schroedl, Gerald F.
1973 *The Archaeological Occurrence of Bison in the Southern Plateau*. Report of Investigations 51. Washington State University, Laboratory of Anthropology, Pullman.

Schroedl, Gerald F. (editor)
1986 *Overhill Cherokee Archaeology at Chota-Tanasee*. Report of Investigations 38. Department of Anthropology, University of Tennessee, Knoxville.

Schuldenrein, Joseph
1998a Changing Career Paths and the Training of Professional Archaeologists: Observations from the Barnard College Forum, Part I. *SAA Bulletin* 16 (1).

Schuldenrein, Joseph
1998b Changing Career Paths and the Training of Professional Archaeologists: Observations from the Barnard College Forum, Part II. *SAA Bulletin* 16 (3).

Schulting, Rick
1994 The Hair of the Dog: the Identification of a Coast Salish Dog-Hair Blanket from Yale, British Columbia. *Canadian Journal of Archaeology* 18:57–76.

Schurr, T. G., S. W. Ballinger, Y. Gan, J. A. Hodge, D. A. Merriwether, and D. N. Lawrence
1990 Amerindian Mitochondrial DNAs Have Rare Asian Mutations at High Frequencies, Suggesting They Derived from Four Primary Maternal Lineages. *American Journal of Human Genetics* 46:613–623.

Schurr, Theodore G.
2004 The Peopling of the New World: Perspectives from Molecular Anthropology. *Annual Review of Anthropology* 33:551–583.

Schurr, Theodore G.
2005 Tracking Genes Through Time and Space: Changing Perspectives on New World Origins. In *Paleoamerican Origins: Beyond Clovis*, edited by Robson Bonnichsen, Bradley T. Lepper, Dennis Stanford, and Michael R. Waters, pp. 221–242. Center for the Study of the First Americans, College Station, Texas.

Scott, Douglas D., Richard A. Fox, Melissa A. Connor, and Dick Harmon
2000 *Archaeological Perspectives on the Battle of the Little Bighorn*. University of Oklahoma Press, Norman.

Scott, Elizabeth M.
1985 *French Subsistence at Fort Michilimackinac, 1715–1781: The Clergy and the Traders*. Archaeological Completion Report Series 9. Mackinac Island State Park Commission, Mackinac Island, Michigan.

Scott, Elizabeth M.
1991 "Such Diet as Befitted His Station as Clerk": The Archaeology of Subsistence and Cultural Diversity at Fort Michilimackinac, 1761–1781. Unpublished Ph.D. dissertation, Department of Anthropology University of Minnesota.

Scott, Elizabeth M. (editor)
1994 *Those of Little Note: Gender, Race, and Class in Historical Archaeology*.

University of Arizona Press, Tucson.

Scott, Elizabeth M.
1996 Who Ate What? Archaeological Food Remains and Cultural Diversity. In *Case Studies in Environmental Archaeology*, edited by E. J. Reitz, L. A. Newsom, and S. Scudder, pp. 339–256. Plenum Press, New York.

Scott, Elizabeth M.
2001 Faunal Remains from House D of the Southeast Row House, British Period (1760–1781). In *House D of the Southeast Row House: Excavations at Fort Michilimackinac, 1989–1997*, by L. L. M. Evans, Appendix 1. Archaeological Completion Report Series 17. Mackinac Island State Historic Parks, Mackinac Island, Michigan.

Scott, Elizabeth M.
2002 Interpreting Ethnicity from Archaeological Faunal Remains. Paper presented at the 2002 Conference of the Society for Historical and Underwater Archaeology, Mobile, Alabama, January 10.

Sebastian, Lynne
1992 *The Chaco Anasazi: Sociopolitical Evolution of the Prehistoric Southwest.* Cambridge, Cambridge University Press.

Sebastian, Lynne, and William D. Lipe
2009 *Archaeology and Cultural Resource Management: Visions for the Future.* School for Advanced Research Press, Santa Fe.

Seeman, Mark F.
1977 Stylistic Variation in Middle Woodland Pipe Styles: The Chronological Implications. *Mid-Continental Journal of Archaeology* 2 (1):47–66.

Seeman, Mark F.
1988 Ohio Hopewell Trophy-Skull Artifacts as Evidence for Competition in Middle Woodland Societies Circa 50 B.C.–A.D. 350. *American Antiquity* 53 (3):565–577.

Seeman, Mark F.
1994 Intercluster Lithic Patterning at Nobles Pond: A Case for "Disembedded" Procurement Among Early Paleoindian Societies. *American Antiquity* 59 (3):565–577.

Seeman, Mark F.
1995 When Words Are Not Enough: Hopewell Interregionalism and the Use of Material Symbols at the GE Mound. In *Native American Interactions: Multiscalar Analyses and Interpretations in the Eastern Woodlands*, edited by Michael S. Nassaney and Kenneth E. Sassaman, pp. 122–143. University of Tennessee Press, Knoxville.

Seifert, Donna
1996 Mrs. Starr's Profession. In *Images of the Recent Past: Readings in Historical Archaeology*, edited by Charles E. Orser, Jr., pp. 191–211. AltaMira Press, Walnut Creek, California.

Serjeantson, Dale
1989 Introduction. In *Diets and Crafts in Towns*, edited by D. Serjeantson and T. Waldron, pp. 1–12. B.A.R., Oxford, United Kingdom.

Service, Elman R.
1962 *Primitive Social Organization: An Evolutionary Perspective.* Random House, New York.

Shackel, Paul A.
2000 "Four Years of Hell": Domestic Life in Harpers Ferry During the Civil War. In *Archaeological Perspectives on the American Civil War*, edited by Clarence R. Geier and Stephen R. Potter, pp. 217–228. University Press of Florida. Gainesville.

Shelford, Victor E
1963 *The Ecology of North America.* University of Illinois Press, Urbana.

Sherwood, Sarah C.
2001 The Geoarchaeology of Dust Cave: The Depositional History of a Late Paleoindian Through Middle Archaic Site in the Middle Tennessee River Valley. Unpublished Ph.D. dissertation, Department of Anthropology, University of Tennessee, Knoxville.

Sherwood, Sarah C., Boyce N. Driskell, Asa R. Randall, and Scott C. Meeks
2004 Chronology and Stratigraphy at Dust Cave. *American Antiquity* 69 (3):533–554.

Shipley, William F.
1978 Native Languages of California. In *California*, edited by R. F. Heizer, pp. 80–90. Handbook of North American Indians, Vol. 8, William C. Sturtevant, general editor, Smithsonian Institution, Washington, D.C.

Shott, Michael J., and Henry T. Wright
1999 The Paleo-Indians: Michigan's First People. In *Retrieving Michigan's Buried Past: The Archaeology of the Great Lakes State*, edited by John R. Halsey, pp. 59–70. Cranbrook Institute of Science, Bloomfield, Michigan.

Sibley, Lucy R., Kathryn A. Jakes, and Lewis H. Larson
1996 Inferring Behavior and Function from an Etowah Fabric Incorporating Feathers. In *A Most Indispensable Art: Native Fiber Industries from Eastern North America*, edited by J. B. Petersen, pp. 73–87. University of Tennessee Press, Knoxville.

Silliman, Stephen W. (editor)
2008 *Collaborating at the Trowel's Edge: Teaching and Learning in Indigenous Archaeology, Amerind Studies in Archaeology.* University of Arizona Press, Tucson.

Silver, Timothy
1990 *A New Face on the Countryside: Indians, Colonists and Slaves in South Atlantic Forests, 1500–1800.* Cambridge University Press, Cambridge.

Silverberg, Robert
1968 *Mound Builders of Ancient America.* New York Graphic Society, New York.

Simmons, Amelia
1984 [1796] *The First American Cookbook,a facsimile of American Cookery [1796].* Dover, New York.

Simms, Steven R.
2008 *Ancient Peoples of the Great Basin and Colorado Plateau.* Left Coast Press, Walnut Creek, California.

Simon, James J. K., and Amy F. Steffian
1994 Cannibalism or Complex Mortuary Behavior? An Analysis of Patterned Variability in the Treatment of Human Remains from the Kachemak Tradition of Kodiak Island. In *Reckoning with the Dead: The Larsen Bay Repatriation and the Smithsonian Institution*, edited by T. L. Bray and T. W. Killion, pp. 75–100. Smithsonian Institution Press, Washington, D.C.

Simon, Mary L.
2000 Regional Variation in Plant Use Strategies in the Midwest During the Late Woodland. In *Late Woodland Societies: Tradition and Transformation Across the Midcontinent*, edited by Thomas E. Emerson, Dale L. McElrath, and Andrew C. Fortier, pp. 37–75. University of Nebraska Press, Lincoln.

Simon, Mary L.
2009 A Regional and Chronological Synthesis of Archaic Period Plant Use in the Midcontinent. In *Archaic Societies: Diversity and Complexity Across the Midcontinent*, edited by Thomas E. Emerson, Dale L. McElrath, and Andrew C. Fortier, pp. 81–114. State University of New York Press, Albany.

Simons, Donald B., Michael J. Shott, and Henry T. Wright
1984 The Gainey Site: Variability in a Great Lakes Paleo-Indian Assemblage. *Archaeology of Eastern North America* 12:266–279.

Singleton, Theresa
1995 The Archaeology of Slave Life. In *Images of the Recent Past: Readings in Historical Archaeology*, edited by Charles E. Orser, Jr., pp. 141–165. AltaMira Press, Walnut Creek, California.

Slaughter, B. H.
1975 Ecological Interpretation of the Brown Sand Wedge Local Fauna. In *Late Pleistocene Environments of the Southern High Plains*, edited by F. Wendorf and J. J. Hester, pp. 179–192. Fort Burgwin Research Center Publication, Ranchos de Taos, New Mexico.

Smith, Bruce D.
1978 Variation in Mississippian Settlement Patterns. In *Mississippian Settlement Patterns*, edited by Bruce D. Smith, pp. 479–503. Academic Press, New York.

Smith, Bruce D.
1986 The Archaeology of the Southeastern United States: From Dalton to DeSoto, 10,500–500 B.P. *Advances in World Archaeology* 5:1–92.

Smith, Bruce D.
1992a The Floodplain Weed Theory of Plant Domestication in Eastern North America. In *Rivers of Change: Essays on Early Agriculture in Eastern North America*, edited by Bruce D. Smith, pp. 19–33. Smithsonian Institution Press, Washington, D.C.

Smith, Bruce D.
1992b Prehistoric Plant Husbandry in Eastern North America. In *Rivers of Change: Essays on Early Agriculture in Eastern North America*, edited by Bruce D. Smith, pp. 281–300. Smithsonian Institution Press, Washington, D.C.

Smith, Bruce D.
1994 The Origins of Agriculture in the Americas. *Evolutionary Anthropology* 3:174–184.

Smith, Bruce D.
2001 Low-Level Food Production. *Journal of Archaeological Research* 9(1): 1–43.

Smith, Bruce D., C. Wesley Cowan, and Michael P. Hoffman
1992 Is It an Indigene or a Foreigner? In *Rivers of Change: Essays on Early Agriculture in Eastern North America*, edited by Bruce D. Smith, pp. 67–100. Smithsonian Institution Press, Washington, D.C.

Smith, Geoffrey M.
2010 Footprints Across the Black Rock: Temporal Variability in Prehistoric Foraging Territories and Toolstone Procurement Strategies in the Western Great Basin. *American Antiquity* 75 :865–885.

Smith, Marvin T.
2000 *Coosa: The Rise and Fall of a Mississippian Chiefdom*. University Press of Florida, Gainesville.

Smith, Shelley J., Jeanne M. Moe, Kelly A. Letts, and Danielle M. Paterson
1993 *Intrigue of the Past: A Teacher's Activity Guide for Fourth Through Seventh Grades*. U.S. Department of the Interior, Bureau of Land Management, Washington, D.C.

Snead, James E.
2001 *Ruins and Rivals: The Making of Southwest Archaeology*. University of Arizona Press, Tucson.

Snow, Dean R.
1980 *The Archaeology of New England*. Academic Press, New York.

Snow, Dean R.
1994 *The Iroquois*. Blackwell, Malden, Massachusetts.

Snow, Dean R.
1995 Migration in Prehistory: The Northern Iroquoian Case. *American Antiquity* 60 (1):59–79.

Snow, Dean R.
1996 More on Migration in Prehistory: Accommodating New Evidence in the Northern Iroquoian Case. *American Antiquity* 61 (4):791–796.

Snow, Dean R.
2000 Introduction. In *Teaching Archaeology in the Twenty-first Century*, edited by Susan J. Bender and George S. Smith, pp. v–vi. Society for American Archaeology, Washington, D.C.

Sobolik, Kristin D.
2003 *Archaeobiology*. The Archaeologist's Toolkit 5, Larry J. Zimmerman and William Green, series editors. AltaMira Press, Walnut Creek, California.

Spector, Janet D.
1993 *What This Awl Means: Feminist Archaeology at a Wahpeton Dakota Village*. Minnesota Historical Society Press, St. Paul.

Spence, Michael W., Robert H. Pihl, and Carl R. Murphy
1990 Cultural Complexes of the Early and Middle Woodland Periods. In *The Archaeology of Southern Ontario*, edited by C. J. Ellis and Neal Ferris, pp. 37–63. Ontario Archaeological Society, London Chapter, London.

Spielmann, Katherine A.
1991 Coercion or Cooperation? Plains–Pueblo Interaction in the Protohistoric Period. In *Farmers, Hunters, and Colonists: Interaction Between the Southwest and the Southern Plains*, edited by Katherine A. Spielmann, pp. 36–50. University of Arizona Press, Tucson.

Spielmann, Katherine A.
1998 Ritual Craft Specialist in Middle Range Societies. In *Craft and Social Identity*, edited by Cathy Lynne Costin and Rita P. Wright, pp. 153–159. Archaeological Papers of the American Anthropological Association 8.

Spier, Robert F. G.
1970 *From the Hand of Man: Primitive and Preindustrial Technologies*. Houghton Mifflin, Boston.

Spiess, Arthur, and John Mosher
2006 Archaic Period Hunting and Fishing Around the Gulf of Maine. In *The Archaic of the Far Northeast*, edited by David Sanger and M. A. P. Renouf, pp. 383–408. The University of Maine Press, Orono.

Spiess, Arthur, Deborah Wilson, and James Bradley
1998 Paleoindian Occupation in the New England–Maritimes Region: Beyond Cultural Ecology. *Archaeology of Eastern North America* 26:201–264.

Squier, Ephraim G.
1851 *Antiquities of the State of New York*. George Derby, Buffalo, New York.

Squier, Ephraim G., and E. H. Davis
1848 *Ancient Monuments of the Mississippi Valley*. Smithsonian

Contributions to Knowledge, Vol. 1. Smithsonian Institution, Washington, D.C.

Stager, John K., and Robert J. McSkimming
1984 Physical Environment. In *Arctic*, edited by David Damas, pp. 27–35. Handbook of North American Indians, Vol. 5, William C. Sturtevant, general editor, Smithsonian Institution, Washington, D.C.

Stanford, Dennis
1991 Clovis Origins and Adaptations: An Introductory Perspective. In *Clovis: Origins and Adaptations*, edited by Robson Bonnichsen and Karen Turnmire, pp. 1–13. Oregon State University Press for the Center for the Study of First Americans, Corvallis.

Stanford, Dennis
1996 Foreshaft Sockets as Possible Clovis Hafting Devices. *Current Research in the Pleistocene* 13:44–46.

Stanford, Dennis
1999 Paleoindian Archaeology and Late Pleistocene Environments in the Plains and Southwestern United States. In *Ice Age People of North America: Environments, Origins and Adaptations of the First Americans*, edited by Robson Bonnichsen and Karen Turnmire, pp. 281–339. Oregon State University Press for the Center for the Study of the First Americans, Corvallis.

Stanford, Dennis, and Bruce Bradley
2002 Ocean Trails and Prairie Paths: Thoughts About Clovis Origins. In *The First Americans: The Pleistocene Colonization of the New World*, edited by Nina Jablonski, pp. 255–271. Memoirs of the California Academy of Sciences 27, San Francisco.

Stanford, Dennis, and M. A. Jodry
1988 The Drake Clovis Cache. *Current Research in the Pleistocene* 5:21–22.

Stanley, Dwight A., Gary M. Page, and Richard Shutler, Jr.
1970 The Cocanour Site: A Western Nevada Pinto Phase Site with Two Excavated "House Rings." In *Five Papers on the Archaeology of the Desert West*, pp. 1–15. Nevada State Museum Anthropological Paper No. 15.

Stapp, D., and M. Burney
2002 *Tribal Cultural Resource Management: The Full Circle to Stewardship (Heritage Resources Management Series, Vol. 4)*. AltaMira Press, Walnut Creek, California.

Steele, D. Gentry, and Joseph F. Powell
1994 Paleobiological Evidence for the Peopling of the Americas: A Morphometric View. In *Method and Theory for Investigating the Peopling of the Americas*, edited by Robson Bonnichsen and D. Gentry Steele, pp. 249–256. Oregon State University Press for the Center for the Study of the First Americans, Corvallis.

Steele, D. Gentry, and Joseph F. Powell
2002 Facing the Past: A View of the North American Human Fossil Record. In *The First Americans: The Pleistocene Colonization of the New World*, edited by Nina Jablonski, pp. 93–122. Memoirs of the California Academy of Sciences, San Francisco.

Steffian, Amy F., Elizabeth Pontti-Eufemio, and Patrick G. Saltonstall
2002 Early Sites and Microblade Technologies from the Kodiak Archipelago. *Anthropological Papers of the University of Alaska* 2 (1):1–38.

Steffian, Amy F., and Patrick Saltonstall
2001 Markers of Identity: Labrets and Social Evolution on Kodiak Archipelago. *Alaska Journal of Anthropology* 1 (1):1–27.

Stein, Julie, and William Farrand
1999 *Sediments in Archaeological Context*. University of Utah Press, Salt Lake City.

Stein, Julie K.
1992 *Deciphering a Shell Midden*. Academic Press, San Diego.

Stein, Julie K.
2000 *Exploring Coast Salish Prehistory: The Archaeology of San Juan Island*. Burke Museum of Natural History and Culture, Seattle.

Steinen, Karl T.
2006 Kolomoki: Cycling, Settlement Patterns, and Cultural Change in a late Middle Woodland Society. In *Recreating Hopewell*, edited by Douglas K. Charles and Jane E. Buikstra, pp. 178–189. University of Florida Press, Gainesville.

Stephenson, Keith, Judith A. Bense, and Frankie Snow
2002 Aspects of Deptford and Swift Creek of the South Atlantic and Gulf Coastal Plains. In *The Woodland Southeast*, edited by David G. Anderson and Robert C. Mainfort, Jr., pp. 318–351. University of Alabama Press, Tuscaloosa.

Steponaitis, Vincas P.
1986 Prehistoric Archaeology in the Southeastern United States, 1970–1985. *Annual Review of Anthropology* 15:363–404.

Stepp, David
1997 California Lake Site Rich in Fluted Projectile Points. *Mammoth Trumpet* 12 (2):10–12.

Stevens, J. Sanderson
1991 A Story of Plants, Fire and People: The Paleoecology and Subsistence of the Late Archaic and Early Woodland in Virginia. In *Late Archaic and Early Woodland Research in Virginia: A Synthesis*, edited by Theodore R. Reinhart and Mary Ellen Hodges, pp. 185–220. Archaeological Society of Virginia, Courtland.

Steward, Julian H.
1938 *Basin-Plateau Aboriginal Sociopolitical Groups*. Bureau of American Ethnology Bulletin 120, Washington, D. C. (Reprinted by the University of Utah Press, Salt Lake City.)

Steward, Julian H.
1955 *Theory of Culture Change: The Methodology of Multilinear Evolution*. University of Illinois Press, Urbana.

Stewart, Hilary
1977 *Indian Fishing: Early Methods on the Northwest Coast*. University of Michigan Press, Seattle.

Stewart, R. Michael
1990 Clemson Island Studies in Pennsylvania: A Perspective. *Pennsylvania Archaeologist* 60 (1):79–107.

Stewart, R. Michael
1994 *Prehistoric Farmers of the Susquehanna Valley: Clemson Island Culture and the St. Anthony Site*. Occasional Publications in Northeastern Anthropology 13. Archaeological Services, Bethlehem, Connecticut.

Stewart-Abernathy, Leslie C., and Barbara L. Ruff
1989 A Good Man in Israel: Zooarchaeology and Assimilation in Antebellum Washington, Arkansas. *Historical Archaeology* 23 (2):96–112.

Stoltman, James B.
1978 Temporal Models in Prehistory: An Example from Eastern North America. *Current Anthropology* 19:703–746.

Stoltman, James B., and George W. Christiansen
2000 The Late Woodland Stage in the Driftless Area of the Upper Mississippi Valley. In *Late Woodland Societies: Tradition and Transformation Across the Midcontinent*, edited by Thomas E. Emerson, Dale L. McElrath, and Andrew C. Fortier, pp. 497–524. University of Nebraska Press, Lincoln.

Stone, Peter G., and Philippe G. Planel
1999 Introduction. In *The Constructed Past: Experimental Archaeology, Education, and the Public*, edited by Peter G. Stone and Philippe G. Planel, pp. 1–14. Routledge, London.

Stone, Richard
2004 A Surprising Survival Story in the Siberian Arctic. *Science* 303:33.

Storck, Peter L.
1984 Glacial Lake Algonquin and Early Paleo-Indian Settlement Patterns in Southcentral Ontario. *Archaeology of Eastern North America* 12:286–298.

Storck, Peter L.
1991 Imperialists Without a State: The Cultural Dynamics of Early Paleoindian Colonization as Seen from the Great Lakes Region. In *Clovis: Origins and Adaptations*, edited by Robson Bonnichsen and Karen Turnmire, pp. 153–162. Oregon State University Press for the Center for the Study of the First Americans, Corvallis.

Straus, Lawrence G.
2000 Solutrean Settlement of North America: A Review of Reality. *American Antiquity* 65:219–226.

Straus, Lawrence Guy, David J. Meltzer, and Ted Goebel
2005 Ice Age Atlantis? Exploring the Solutrean-Clovis 'Connection.' *World Archaeology* 37 (4):507–532.

Strong, Emory M.
1959 *Stone Age on the Columbia River.* Binfords and Mort, Portland, Oregon.

Struever, Stuart
1964 The Hopewell Interaction Sphere in Riverine–Western Great Lakes Culture History. In *Hopewellian Studies*, edited by Joseph R. Caldwell and Robert L. Hall, pp. 85–106. Scientific Papers Vol. XII. Illinois State Museum, Springfield.

Struever, Stuart
1968a Flotation Techniques for the Recovery of Small-Scale Archaeological Remains. *American Antiquity* 33:353–362.

Struever, Stuart
1968b Problems, Methods, and Organization: A Disparity in the Growth of Archaeology. In *Anthropological Archeology in the Americas*, edited by Betty V. Meggers, pp. 131–151. Anthropological Society of Washington, Washington, D.C.

Struever, Stuart
1968c Woodland Subsistence-Settlement Systems in the Lower Illinois Valley. In *New Perspectives in Archaeology*, edited by Sally R. Binford and Lewis R. Binford, pp. 285–312. Aldine, Chicago.

Struever, Stuart, and Felicia Antonelli Holton
1979 *Koster: Americans in Search of Their Prehistoric Past.* Anchor Press/Doubleday, New York.

Stryd, Arnoud R.
1998 Nesikep Tradition. In *Archaeology of Prehistoric Native America: An Encyclopedia*, edited by Guy Gibbon, pp. 560–561. Garland, New York.

Stryd, Arnoud R., and Michael K. Rousseau
1996 The Early Prehistory of the Mid-Fraser–Thompson River Area. In *Early Human Occupations in British Columbia*, edited by Roy L. Carlson and Luke Dalla Bona, pp. 177–204. University of British Columbia Press, Vancouver.

Styles, Bonnie W.
1986 Aquatic Exploitation in the Lower Illinois River Valley: The Role of Paleoecological Change. In *Foraging, Collecting and Harvesting: Archaic Period Subsistence and Settlement in the Eastern Woodlands*, edited by Sarah W. Neusius, pp. 145–174. Center for Archaeological Investigations, Southern Illinois University at Carbondale, Carbondale.

Styles, Bonnie W.
2000 Late Woodland Faunal Exploitation in the Midwestern United States. In *Late Woodland Societies: Tradition and Transformation Across the Midcontinent*, edited by Thomas E. Emerson, Dale L. McElrath, and Andrew C. Fortier, pp. 77–94. University of Nebraska Press, Lincoln.

Styles, Bonnie W., and Walter E. Klippel
1996 Mid-Holocene Faunal Exploitation in the Southeastern United States. In *Archaeology of the Mid-Holocene Southeast*, edited by Kenneth E. Sassaman and David G. Anderson, pp. 115–133. University Press of Florida, Gainesville.

Styles, Bonnie W., and R. Bruce McMillan
2009 Archaic Faunal Exploitation in the Prairie Peninsula and Surrounding Regions of the Midcontinent. In *Archaic Societies: Diversity and Complexity Across the Midcontinent*, edited by Thomas E. Emerson, Dale L. McElrath, and Andrew C. Fortier, pp. 39–80. State University of New York Press, Albany.

Styles, Thomas R.
1985 *Holocene and Late Pleistocene Geology of the Napoleon Hollow Site in the Lower Illinois Valley.* Kampsville Archeological Center Research Series 5, Kampsville, Illinois.

Sullivan, Lynne P.
1992 Arthur C. Parker's Contributions to New York State Archaeology. *Bulletin, Journal of the New York State Archaeological Association* 104:3–8.

Sullivan, Lynne P. (editor)
1996 *Reanalyzing the Ripley Site: Earthworks and Late Prehistory on the Lake Erie Plain.* University of the State of New York/State Department of Education, Albany.

Sullivan, Lynne P.
1999 Madeline D. Kneberg Lewis: Leading Lady of Tennessee Archaeology. In *Grit-Tempered: Early Women Archaeologists in the Southeastern United States*, edited by Nancy M. White, Lynne P. Sullivan, and Rochelle Marrinan, pp. 57–91. University Press of Florida, Gainesville.

Sullivan, Lynne P.
2001 Those Men in the Mounds: Gender, Politics, and Mortuary Practices in Late Prehistoric Eastern Tennessee. In *Gender in the Archaeology of the Mid-South*, edited by Jane Eastman and Christopher Rodning, pp. 101–126. University Press of Florida, Gainesville.

Sullivan, Lynne P., and S. Terry Childs
2003 *Curating Archaeological Collections: From the Field to the Repository.* Archaeologist's Toolkit 6. AltaMira Press, Walnut Creek, California.

Sullivan, Lynne P., and Michaelyn S. Harle
2010 Mortuary Practices and Cultural Identity at the Turn of

the Sixteenth Century in Eastern Tennessee. In *Mississippian Mortuary Practices: Beyond Hierarchy and the Representationist Perspective*, edited by L. P. Sullivan and Robert C. Mainfort, Jr., pp. 234–249. University Press of Florida, Gainesville.

Sullivan, Lynne P., Eleazer D. Hunt, and Richard G. Wilkinson
1996 History of Investigations. In *Reanalyzing the Ripley Site: Earthworks and Late Prehistory on the Lake Erie Plain*, edited by Lynne P. Sullivan, pp. 28–51. University of the State of New York/State Department of Education, Albany.

Sullivan, Lynne P. and Robert C. Mainfort, Jr. (editors)
2010 *Mississippian Mortuary Practices: Beyond Hierarchy and the Representationist Perspective*. University Press of Florida, Gainesville.

Sullivan, Lynne P., Sarah W. Neusius, and Phillip D. Neusius
1995 Earthworks and Mortuary Sites on Lake Erie: Believe It or Not at the Ripley Site. *Mid-Continental Journal of Archaeology* 20 (2):115–142.

Sullivan, Lynne P., and Christopher B. Rodning
2010 Residential Burial, Gender Roles, and Political Development in Late Prehistoric and Early Cherokee Cultures of the Southern Appalachians. In *Residential Burial: A Multi-Regional Exploration*, edited by Ron Adams and Stacie King, pp. 79–97. American Anthropological Association Washington, D.C.

Surovell, Todd
2003 Simulating Coastal Migration in New World Colonization. *Current Anthropology* 44:580–591.

Sutherland, Patricia D.
2009 The Question of Contact Between Dorset Paleo-Eskimos and Early Europeans in the Eastern Arctic. In *The Northern World AD 900–1400*, edited by Herbert Maschner, Owen Mason, and Robert McGhee, pp. 279–299. The University of Utah Press, Salt Lake City.

Suttles, Wayne
1990a Environment. In *Northwest Coast*, edited by Wayne Suttles, pp. 16–29. Handbook of North American Indians, Vol. 7, William C. Sturtevant, general editor, Smithsonian Institution, Washington, D.C.

Suttles, Wayne
1990b History of Research: Early Sources. In *Northwest Coast*, edited by Wayne Suttles, pp. 70–72. Handbook of North American Indians, Vol. 7, William C. Sturtevant, general editor, Smithsonian Institution, Washington, D.C.

Suttles, Wayne
1990c Introduction. In *Northwest Coast*, edited by Wayne Suttles, pp. 1–15. Handbook of North American Indians, Vol. 7, William C. Sturtevant, general editor, Smithsonian Institution, Washington, D.C.

Suttles, Wayne (editor)
1990d *Northwest Coast*. Handbook of North American Indians, Vol. 7, William C. Sturtevant, general editor. Smithsonian Institution, Washington, D.C.

Sutton, Mark Q.
1980 Some Aspects of Kitanemuk Prehistory. *Journal of California and Great Basin Anthropology* 2:214–225.

Sutton, Mark Q.
1986 Warfare and Expansion: An Ethnohistoric Perspective on the Numic Spread. *Journal of California and Great Basin Anthropology* 8 (1):65–82.

Sutton, Mark Q.
2009 People and Language: Defining the Takic Expansion into Southern California. *Pacific Coast Archaeological Society Quarterly* 41(2&3):31–93.

Sutton, Mark Q., and Brooke S. Arkush
2007 *Archaeological Laboratory Methods: An Introduction*, 4th ed. Kendall/Hunt, Dubuque, Iowa.

Swagerty, William R.
2001 History of the United States Plains Until 1850. In *Plains*, edited by Raymond J. De Mallie, pp. 256–279. Handbook of North American Indians, Vol. 13, William C. Sturtevant, general editor, Smithsonian Institution, Washington, D.C.

Swanton, John R.
1946 *The Indians of the Southeastern United States*. Smithsonian Institution Press, Washington, D.C.

Syms, E. L.
1985 Fitting People in the Late Prehistory of the Northeastern Plains. In *Archaeology, Ecology and Ethnohistory of the Prairie–Plains Forest Border Zone of Minnesota and Manitoba*, edited by J. Spector and E. Johnson, pp. 73–107. J and L Reprint, Lincoln.

Szuter, Christine R., and Frank E. Bayham
1989 Sedentism and Animal Procurement Among Desert horticulturalists of the North American Southwest. In *Farmers as Hunters: The Implications of Sedentism*, edited by Susan Kent, pp. 80–95. Cambridge University Press, Cambridge.

Tamm, Erika, Toomas Kivisild, Maere Reidla, Mait Metspalu, David Glenn Smith, Connie J. Mulligan, Claudio M. Bravi, Olga Rickards, Cristina Martinez-Labarga, Elsa K. Khusnutdinova, Sardana A. Fedorova , Maria V. Golubenko, Vadim A. Stepanov, Marina A. Gubina, Sergey I. Zhadanov, Ludmila P. Ossipova, Larisa Damba, Mikhail I. Voevoda, Jose E. Dipierri, Richard Villems, Ripan S. Malhi
2007 Beringian Standstill and Spread of native American Founders. *PLoS One* 2(9):e 829.

Tankersley, Kenneth
1988 A Close Look at the Big Picture: Early Paleoindian Lithic Procurement in the Midwestern United States. In *Eastern Paleoindian Lithic Resource Use*, edited by Christopher J. Ellis and Jon C. Lothrop, pp. 259–292. Westview Press, Boulder, Colorado.

Tankersley, Kenneth
1994 Clovis Mastic and Its Hafting Implications. *Journal of Archaeological Science* 21:117–124.

Tanner, Helen Hornbeck
1986 *Atlas of Great Lakes Indian History*. University of Oklahoma Press, Norman.

Taylor, R. E., L. A. Payen, C. A. Prior, P. J. Slota, Jr., R. Gillespie, J. A. J. Gowlett, R. E. M. Hedges, A. J. T. Jull, T. H. Zabel, D. J. Donahue, and R. Berger
1985 Major Revisions in the Pleistocene Age Assignments for North American Human Skeletons by C-14 Accelerator Mass Spectrometry: None Older Than 11,000 C-14 Years B.P. *American Antiquity* 50:136–140.

Taylor, Walter W.
1948 *A Study of Archeology*. American Anthropological Association Memoir 69. American Anthropological Association, Menasha, Wisconsin.

Taylor, William E., Jr., and George Swinton
1967 Prehistoric Dorset Art. *Beaver* 298:32–47.

Teague, Lynn S.

1993 Prehistory and the Traditions of the O'Odham and Hopi. *Kiva* 58 (4):435–455.

Teller, J. T., and Lee Clayton
1983 *Glacial Lake Agassiz.* Special Paper 26. Geological Association of Canada.

Thiessen, Thomas D. (editor)
1993 *The Phase I Archeological Research Program for the Knife River Indian Villages National Historic Site.* Four parts. Occasional Studies in Anthropology 27. Midwest Archeological Center, U.S. National Park Service, Lincoln, Nebraska.

Thiessen, Thomas D.
1999 *Emergency Archeology in the Upper Missouri River Basin: The Role of the Missouri Basin Project and the Midwest Archeological Center in the Interagency Archeological Salvage Program, 1946–1975.* Midwest Archeological Center, U.S. National Park Service, Lincoln, Nebraska.

Thiessen, Thomas D., W. Raymond Wood, and A. Wesley Jones
1979 The Sitting Rabbit 1907 Map of the Missouri River in North Dakota. *Plains Anthropologist* 24:145–167.

Thomas, Cyrus
1894 *Report of the Mound Explorations of the Bureau of Ethnology.* Bureau of American Ethnology. Washington, D.C.

Thomas, David Hurst
1973 An Empirical Test for Steward's Model of Great Basin Settlement Patterns. *American Antiquity* 38 (2):155–176.

Thomas, David Hurst
1974 An Archaeological Perspective on Shoshonean Bands. *American Anthropologist* 76 (1):11–23.

Thomas, David Hurst
1981 How to Classify the Projectile Points from Monitor Valley, Nevada. *Journal of California and Great Basin Anthropology* 3 (1):7–43.

Thomas, David Hurst
1983a The Archaeology of Monitor Valley: 1. Epistemology. *Anthropological Papers of the American Museum of Natural History* Epistemology 58 (1):1–194.

Thomas, David Hurst
1983b The Archaeology of Monitor Valley: 2. Gatecliff Shelter. *Anthropological Papers of the American Museum of Natural History* Gatecliff Shelter 59 (1):1–552.

Thomas, David Hurst
1985 The Archaeology of Hidden Cave, Nevada. *Anthropological Papers of the American Museum of Natural History* 61 (1):1–430.

Thomas, David Hurst
1986a Contemporary Hunter-Gatherer Archaeology in America. In *American Archaeology: Past and Present*, edited by D. J. Meltzer, D. D. Fowler and J. A. Sabloff, pp. 237–276. Smithsonian Institution Press, Washington, D.C.

Thomas, David Hurst
1986b Points on Points: A Reply to Flenniken and Raymond. *American Antiquity* 51 (3):619–627.

Thomas, David Hurst
1987 Historic and Prehistoric Land-Use Patterns at Reese River. *Nevada Historical Society Quarterly* 30 (2):111–117.

Thomas, David Hurst
1988 The Archaeology of Monitor Valley: 3. Survey and Additional Excavations. *Anthropological Papers of the American Museum of Natural History* 66 (2):131–633.

Thomas, David Hurst
1989 Diversity in Hunter-Gatherer Cultural Geography. In *Diversity in Archeology*, edited by Robert D. Leonard and George T. Jones, pp. 85–91. Cambridge University Press, Cambridge.

Thomas, David Hurst
1990 The Spanish Missions of La Florida. In *Columbian Consequences, Vol. 2: Archaeological and Historical Perspectives on the Spanish Borderlands West*, edited by David Hurst Thomas, pp. 357–397. Smithsonian Institution Press, Washington, D.C.

Thomas, David Hurst
1998 *Archaeology*, 3rd ed. Harcourt Brace College, Fort Worth, Texas.

Thomas, David Hurst
1999 *Exploring Ancient Native America: An Archaeological Guide.* Routledge, New York.

Thomas, David Hurst, and Robert L. Bettinger
1976 Prehistoric Piñon Ecotone Settlements of the Upper Reese River Valley, Central Nevada. *Anthropological Papers of the American Museum of Natural History* 53 (3):262–366.

Thomas, David Hurst, and Robert L. Kelly

2006 *Archaeology*, 4th ed. Thomson/Wadsworth, Belmont, California.

Thomas, Trudy
1983 The Visual Symbolism of Gatecliff Shelter. In The Archaeology of Monitor Valley: 2. Gatecliff Shelter. *Anthropological Papers of the American Museum of Natural History* Gatecliff Shelter 59 (1):332–352

Thompson, Kerry F.
2009 Forum Comment: Government Cultural Resource Management Versus Navajo People. *Heritage Management* 2:241–251.

Thompson, Kerry F.
2010 Is Community Archaeology a Viable Goal for the Navajo Nation? Presented at the *Wenner-Gren Workshop on the Dynamics of Inclusion in Public Archaeology.* African Burial Ground National Monument, New York City.

Thompson, Laurence C., and M. Dale Kinkade
1990 Languages. In *Northwest Coast*, edited by Wayne Suttles, pp. 30–51. Handbook of North American Indians, Vol. 7, William C. Sturtevant, general editor, Smithsonian Institution, Washington, D.C.

Thompson, Raymond H.
2000 The Crisis in Archeological Collection Management. *CRM* 23 (5):4–6.

Thompson, Robert G., John P. Hart, Hetty Jo Brumbach, and Robert Lusteck
2004 Phytolith Evidence for Twentieth-Century B.P. Maize in Northern Iroquoia. *Northeast Anthropology* 68:25–40.

Thoms, Alston V.
1989 The Northern Roots of Hunter-Gatherer Intensification: Camas and the Pacific Northwest. Ph.D. dissertation, Department of Anthropology, Washington State University, Pullman.

Thurman, Karen
2001 The Wooden Canvas: Documenting Aspen Art Carvings in Southwest Colorado. *Heritage Matters*, November.

Thwaites, Reuben G.
1959 *The Jesuit Relations and Allied Documents.* 73 vols. Burrows Brothers, Cleveland.

Tiffany, Joseph A.
2007 Examining the Origins of the Middle Missouri Tradition. In

Plains Village Archaeology: Bison-Hunting Farmers in the Central and Northern Plains, edited by Stanley A. Ahler and Marvin Kay, pp. 3-14. University of Utah Press, Salt Lake City.

Tikhmenev, P. A.
1978 *A History of the Russian-American Company.* University of Washington Press, Seattle.

Todd, Lawrence, David C. Jones, Robert S. Walker, Paul C. Burnett, and Jeffrey Eighmy
2001 Late Archaic Bison Hunters in Northern Colorado: 1997–1999. Excavations at the Kaplan–Hoover Bison Bonebed 5(LR3953). *Plains Anthropologist* 46 (176):125–147.

Tolkien, J. R. R.
1966 *The Hobbit.* Houghton Mifflin, Boston.

Toll, H. Wolcott
2001 Making and Breaking Pots in the Chaco World. *American Antiquity* 66 (2):56–78.

Toner, Mike
2010 The Clovis Comet Controversy. *American Archaeology* 143:12–18.

Towner, Ronald H.
1996 *The Archaeology of Navajo Origins.* University of Utah Press, Salt Lake City.

Townsend, Joan B.
1980 Ranked Societies of the Alaska Pacific Rim. In *Alaska Native Culture and History,* edited by Y. Kotani and W. B. Workman, pp. 123–156. Senri Ethnological Studies 4. National Museum of Ethnology, Osaka, Japan.

Trigger, Bruce G. (editor)
1978 *Northeast.* Handbook of North American Indians, Vol. 15, William C. Sturtevant, general editor, Smithsonian Institution, Washington, D.C.

Trigger, Bruce G.
2006 *A History of Archaeological Thought,* 2nd ed. Cambridge University Press, Cambridge.

Trivedi, Bijal P.
2002 *Archaeologists Explore Cold War Nuclear Test Site.* Electronic document, http://news.nationalgeographic.com/news/2002/07/0708_020710_TVnucleararchae.html.

Tuck, James A.
1971 An Archaic Cemetery at Port au Choix, Newfoundland. *American Antiquity* 36 343–358.

Tuck, James A.
1978 Regional Cultural Development, 3000–300 B.C. In *Northeast,* edited by Bruce G. Trigger, pp. 28–43. Handbook of North American Indians, Vol. 15, William C. Sturtevant, general editor, Smithsonian Institution, Washington, D.C.

Tuck, James A.
1998 Maritime Archaic Tradition. In *Archaeology of Prehistoric Native America: An Encyclopedia,* edited by Guy Gibbon, pp. 494–496. Garland, New York.

Tunnell, C.
1978 *The Gibson Lithic Cache from West Texas.* Texas Historical Commission, Office of the State Archaeologist, Austin.

Turnbaugh, William A.
1975 Toward an Explanation of the Broadpoint Dispersal in Eastern North American Prehistory. *Journal of Anthropological Research* 31 (1):51–68.

Turner, Christy G.
1983 Dental Evidence for the Peopling of the Americas. In *Early Man in the New World,* edited by Richard Shutler, Jr., pp. 13–42. Sage, Beverly Hills, California.

Turner, Christy G.
1994 Relating Eurasian and Native American Populations Through Dental Morphology. In *Method and Theory for Investigating the Peopling of the Americas,* edited by Robson Bonnichsen and D. Gentry Steele, pp. 131–140. Oregon State University Press for the Center for the Study of the First Americans, Corvallis.

Turner, Christy G., and Jacqueline A. Turner
1999 *Man Corn: Cannibalism and Violence in the Prehistoric American Southwest.* University of Utah Press, Salt Lake City.

Tveskov, Mark, and Thomas Connley
1997 The Paulina Lake Site: An Early Holocene Occupation at Newberry Crater, Central Oregon. Research Division, State Museum of Anthropology, University of Oregon. Electronic document, http://oregon.uoregon.edu/~osma/Paulina.html.

Ubelaker, Douglas H. (editor)
2006 *Environment, Origins, and Population.* Handbook of North American Indians, Vol. 3, William C. Sturtevant, general editor, Smithsonian Institution, Washington, D.C.

Umatilla Chamber of Commerce
2004 History. Electronic document, http:// www.umatilla.org/chamber-umatilla-history.htm.

U.S. National Park Service
1983 Hopewell Furnace National Historic Sites, Pennsylvania. In *Handbook 124.* Division of Publications, National Park Service, U.S. Department of Interior, Washington, D.C.

U.S. National Park Service
2004 Fort Vancouver National Historic Site: Archaeology. Electronic document, http://www.nps.gov/fova/historyculture/archaeology-and-collections-a.htm, Accessed March 24, 2012.

Van Gerven, Dennis P., and Susan Guise Sheridan
1994 *The Pueblo Grande Project, Vol. 6: The Bioethnography of a Classic Period Hohokam Population.* Soil Systems Publications in Archaeology 20. Phoenix.

Van Pool, Christine S.
2003 The Shaman-Priests of the Casas Grandes Region, Chihuahua, Mexico. *American Antiquity* 68 (4):696–718.

Van Velzen, Diura Thoden
1996. The World of Tuscan Tomb Robbers: Living with the Local Community and the Ancestors. *International Journal of Cultural Property* 5:111–126.

Van West, Carla R.
1996 Agricultural Potential and Carrying Capacity in Southwestern Colorado, AD 901–1300. In *The Prehistoric Pueblo World, AD 1150–1350,* edited by Michael A. Adler, pp. 214–227. University of Arizona Press, Tucson.

Van Wormer, Stephen R., and G. Timothy Gross
2006 Archaeological Identification of an Idiosyncratic Lifestyle: Excavation and Analysis of the Theosophical Society Dump, San Diego (CA-SDI-10,5311H), California. *Historical Archaeology* 40 (1):119–137.

Van Wormer, Stephen R., and William R. Manly
1994 *A Sense of Time and Place: SDI-13,031H Archaeological Mitigation*

Report, Main Street Redevelopment Project, El Cajon. William Manly Consulting, San Diego.

Varenne, François Pierre
2001 The French Cook. Southover Press, East Sussex, United Kingdom.

Varien, Mark D., William D. Lipe, Michael A. Adler, Ian M. Thompson, and Bruce A. Bradley
1996 Southwestern Colorado and Southeastern Utah Settlement Patterns: AD 1100–1300. In The Prehistoric Pueblo World, AD 1150–1350, edited by Michael A. Adler, pp. 86–113. University of Arizona Press, Tucson.

Vaughn, Sheila J., and Claude N. Warren
1987 Toward a Definition of Pinto Points. Journal of California and Great Basin Anthropology 9:199–213.

Vehik, Susan C.
2001 Hunting and Gathering Tradition: Southern Plains. In Plains, edited by Raymond J. De Mallie, pp. 131–145. Handbook of North American Indians, Vol. 13, William C. Sturtevant, general editor, Smithsonian Institution, Washington, D.C.

Vellanoweth, R. L., M. Lambright, J. M. Erlandson, and and T. C. Rick
2003 Early New World Perishable Technologies: Sea Grass Cordage, Shell Beads, and a Bone Tool from Cave of the Chimneys, San Miguel Island. California Journal of Archaeological Science 30:1161–1173.

Vellanoweth, René L., Torben C. Rick, and Jon M. Erlandson
2000 Middle and Late Holocene Maritime Adaptations on Northeastern San Miguel Island, California. In Proceedings of the 5th California Islands Conference, edited by D. Browne, K. Mitchell and H. Chaney, pp. 607–614. Santa Barbara Museum of Natural History, Santa Barbara, California.

Verrengia, Joseph B.
2000 LabTests Show Evidenceof Cannibalism by Ancient Indians of the Southwest. Associated Press, September 7. Electronic document, http://www.lexisnexis.com/hottopics/lnacademic/, accessed September 16, 2012.

Vickery, Kent D., and James C. Lifton
1994 A Proposed Revision of the Classification of Midwestern Paleoindian, Early Archaic and Middle Archaic Projectile Points. In The First Discovery of America: Archaeological Evidence of the Early Inhabitants of the Ohio Area, edited by William Dancey, pp. 177–210. Ohio Archaeological Council, Columbus.

Vierra, Bradley J.
1994 Introduction: What Is the Archaic? In Archaic Hunter-Gatherer Archaeology in the American Southwest, edited by Bradley J. Vierra. Eastern New Mexico University Contributions in Anthropology 13, Portales, New Mexico.

Vierra, Bradley J.
2005 The Late Archaic Across the Borderlands: From Foraging to Farming. University of Texas Press, Austin.

Vivian, R. Gwinn
1990 The Chacoan Prehistory of the San Juan Basin. Academic Press, San Diego.

Vlach, John
1976 The Shotgun House: An African Architectural Legacy. Pioneer America 8:47–70.

Von Däniken, Erich
1970 Chariots of the Gods. Bantam Books, New York.

von Gernet, Alexander D.
1992 Hallucinogens and the Origins of the Iroquoian Pipe/Tobacco/Smoking Complex. In Proceedings of the 1989 Smoking Pipe Conference: Selected Papers, edited by Charles F. Hayes III, Connie Cox Bodner and Martha Sempowski, pp. 171–185. Rochester Museum and Science Center, Rochester, New York.

Wagner, Gail E.
2003 Eastern Woodlands Anthropogenic Ecology. In People and Plants in Ancient Eastern North America, edited by Paul E. Minnis, pp. 126–171. Smithsonian Books, Washington, D.C.

Waguespack, Nicole M., and Todd A. Surovell
2003 Clovis Hunting Strategies, or How to Make Out on Plentiful Resources. American Antiquity 68 (2):333–352.

Waguespack, Nicole M., and Todd A. Surovell
2003 Clovis Hunting Strategy, or How to Make Out on Plentiful Resources. American Antiquity 143:12–18.

Walde, Dale
2006 Avonlea and Athabaskan Migrations: A Reconsideration. Plains Anthropologist 51:185–197.

Walker, Deward E., Jr.
1998a Plateau. Handbook of North American Indians, Vol. 12, William C. Sturtevant, general editor, Smithsonian Institution, Washington, D.C.

Walker, Deward E., Jr.
1998b Introduction. In Plateau, edited by Deward E. Walker, Jr., pp. 1–7. Handbook of North American Indians, Vol. 12, William C. Sturtevant, general editor, Smithsonian Institution, Washington, D.C.

Walker, Deward E., Jr., and Roderick Sprague
1988 History Until 1846. In Plateau, edited by Deward E. Walker, Jr., pp. 138–148. Handbook of North American Indians, Vol. 12, William C. Sturtevant, general editor, Smithsonian Institution, Washington, D.C.

Walker, Ernest G.
1992 The Gowen Sites: Cultural Responses to Climatic Warming on the Northern Plains (7500–5000 BP). Mercury Series, Paper 145, Archaeological Survey of Canada. Canadian Museum of Civilization, Quebec.

Walker, Renee B.
1997 Late-Paleoindian Faunal Remains from Dust Cave, Alabama. Current Research in the Pleistocene 14:85–87.

Walker, Renee B.
1998 The Late Paleoindian Through Middle Archaic Faunal Remains from Dust Cave, Alabama. Unpublished Ph.D. dissertation, Department of Anthropology University of Tennessee, Knoxville.

Walker, Renee B.
2000 Subsistence Strategies at Dust Cave: Changes from the Late Paleoindian Through Middle Archaic Occupations. Report of Investigations 78. Office of Archaeological Services, University of Alabama.

Walker, Renee B.
2007 Hunting in the Late Paleoindian Period: Faunal Remains from Dust Cave, Alabama. In Foragers of the Terminal Pleistocene in North America, edited by Renee B. Walker and Boyce N. Driskell, pp. 90–115.

Unversity of Nebraska Press, Lincoln.

Walker, R. B., K. Detwiler, S. C. Meeks, and B. N. Driskell
2001 Berries, Bones and Blades: Reconstructing Late Paleoindian Subsistence Economies at Dust Cave, Alabama. *Mid-Continental Journal of Archaeology* 26 (2):169–197.

Walker, Renee B., Darcy F. Morey, and John H. Relethford
2005 Early and Mid-Holocene Dogs in Southeastern North America: Examples from Dust Cave. *Southeastern Archaeology* 24 (1):83–92.

Walker, Renee B., and Paul W. Parmalee
2004 A Noteworthy Cache of Goose Humeri from Late Paleoindian Levels at Dust Cave, Northwestern Alabama. *Journal of Alabama Archaeology* 50 (1):18–35.

Wallace, Birgitta
2000 The Viking Settlement at L'Anse aux Meadows. In *Vikings: The North Atlantic Saga*, edited by William W. Fitzhugh and Elisabeth I. Ward, pp. 208–216. Smithsonian Institution Press, Washington, D.C.

Wallace, Birgitta, and William W. Fitzhugh
2000 Stumbles and Pitfalls in the Search for Viking America. In *Vikings: The North Atlantic Saga*, edited by William W. Fitzhugh and Elisabeth I. Ward, pp. 374–384. Smithsonian Institution Press, Washington, D.C.

Wallace, William J.
1955 A Suggested Chronology for Southern California Coastal Archaeology. *Southwestern Journal of Archaeology* 11:214–230.

Walthall, John A.
1979 Hopewell and the Southern Heartland. In *Hopewell Archaeology: The Chillicothe Conference*, edited by David S. Brose and N'omi Greber, pp. 200–208. Kent State University Press, Kent, Ohio.

Walthall, John A.
1980 *Prehistoric Indians of the Southeast: Archaeology of Alabama and the Middle South*. University of Alabama Press, Tuscaloosa.

Walthall, John A.
1991 *French Colonial Archaeology: The Illinois Country and the Western Great Lakes*. University of Illinois Press, Urbana.

Ward, Elisabeth I.
2000 Reflections on an Icon: Vikings in American Culture. In *Vikings: The North Atlantic Saga*, edited by William W. Fitzhugh and Elisabeth I. Ward, pp. 365–373. Smithsonian Institution Press, Washington, D.C.

Warfel, Stephen G.
2009 Ideology, Idealism, and Reality: Investigating the Ephrata Commune. In *The Archaeology of Institutional Life*, edited by April M. Beisaw and James G. Gibb, pp. 137–150. University of Alabama Press, Tuscaloosa.

Waring, Antonio J., and Preston Holder
1945 A Prehistoric Ceremonial Complex in the Southeastern United States. *American Anthropologist* 47 (1):1–34.

Warren, Claude N.
1968 Cultural Tradition and Ecological Adaptation on the Southern California Coast. *Eastern New Mexico University Contributions in Anthropology* 1 (3):1–14.

Warren, Claude N.
1984 The Desert Region. In *California Archaeology* edited by Michael J. Moratto, pp. 339–430. Academic Press, Orlando, Florida.

Warren, Claude N.
2002 Time, Form, and Variability: Lake Mojave and Pinto Periods in Mojave Desert Prehistory. In *Essays in California Archaeology: A Memorial to Franklin Fenenga*, edited by William J. Wallace and Francis A. Ridell, pp. 129–141. Contributions of the University of California Archaeological Research Facility 60.

Warren, Claude N., and Robert H. Crabtree
1986 Prehistory of the Southwestern Area. In *Great Basin*, edited by Warren L. D'Azevedo, pp. 183–193. Handbook of North American Indians, Vol. 11, William C. Sturtevant, general editor, Smithsonian Institution, Washington, D.C.

Warren, Claude N., Martha Knack, and Elizabeth von Till Warren
1980 *A Cultural Resource Overview for the Amargosa–Mojave Basin Planning Units*. California Bureau of Land Management, Riverside.

Waters, Michael R. and Thomas W. Stafford
2007 Redefining the Age of Clovis: Implications for the Peopling of the New World. *Science* 315: 1122-26.

Waters, Michael R., Charlotte D. Pevny, and David L. Carlson
2011 *Clovis Lithic Technology: Investigation of a Stratified Workshop at the Gault Site, Texas*. Texas A&M Press, College Station, TX.

Watkins, Joe E.
2000 *Indigenous Archaeology: American Values and Scientific Practice*. AltaMira Press, Walnut Creek, California.

Watkins, Joe E.
2003 Beyond the Margin: American Indians, First Nations and Archaeology in North America. *American Antiquity* 68 (2):273–285.

Watson, Peter
2006 Convicted Dealers: What We Can Learn. In *Archaeology, Cultural Heritage, and the Antiquities Trade*, edited by Neil Brodie, Morag M. Kersel, Christina Luke, and Kathryn Walker Tubb, pp 93–97. University Press of Florida, Gainesville.

Webb, C. H.
1977 *The Poverty Point Culture*. Geoscience Publications, Geoscience and Man 17. Department of Geography and Anthropology, Louisiana State University, Baton Rouge.

Webb, S. David, Jerald T. Milanich, Roger Alexon, and James S. Dunbar
1984 A *Bison antiquus* Kill Site, Wacissa River, Jefferson County, Florida. *American Antiquity* 49 (2):384–392.

Wedel, Waldo R.
1986 *Central Plains Prehistory: Holocene Environments and Culture Change in the Republican River Basin*. University of Nebrasks Press, Lincoln.

Wedel, Waldo R.
2001 Plains Village Tradition: Central. In *Plains*, edited by Raymond J. DeMallie, pp. 186–195. Handbook of North American Indians, Vol. 13, William C. Sturtevant, general editor, Smithsonian Institution, Washington, D.C.

Wedel, Waldo R., and George C. Frison
2001 Environment and Subsistence. In *Plains*, edited by Raymond J. DeMallie, pp. 44–60. Handbook of North American Indians, Vol. 13, William C. Sturtevant, general editor, Smithsonian Institution, Washington, D.C.

Weik, Terrance M.
2005 Black Seminole Freedom Fighters on the Florida Frontier. In *Unlocking the Past: Celebrating Historical*

Archaeology in North America, edited by Lu Ann De Cunzo and John H. Jameson, Jr., pp. 36-44. SHA Public Outreach and Education Project and University of Florida Press, Gainesville.

Welch, Paul D.
1991 *Moundville's Economy*. University of Alabama Press, Tuscaloosa.

Wendorf, F., and J. J. Hester
1975 *Late Pleistocene Environments of the Southern High Plains*. Fort Burgwin Research Center, Ranchos de Taos, New Mexico.

West, Frederick H.
1996a Beringia and New World Origins. II: The Archaeological Evidence. In *American Beginnings: The Prehistory and Palaeoecology of Beringia*, edited by Frederick H. West, pp. 536–559. University of Chicago Press, Chicago.

West, Frederick H.
1996eb Donnelly Ridge. In *American Beginnings: The Prehistory and Palaeoecology of Beringia*, edited by Frederick H. West, pp. 302–307. University of Chicago Press Chicago.

Whalen, Michael E., and Paul E. Minnis
2001a Architecture and Authority in the Casas Grandes Area, Chihuahua, Mexico. *American Antiquity* 66:651–668.

Whalen, Michael E., and Paul E. Minnis
2001b *Casas Grandes and Its Hinterland: Prehistoric Regional Organization in Northwest Mexico*. University of Arizona Press, Tucson.

Whalen, Michael E., and Paul E. Minnis
2003 The Distant and the Local in the Origin of Casas Grandes, Chihuahua, Mexico. *American Antiquity* 68:314–332.

Whalen, Michel E., and Paul E. Minnis
2009 *The Neighbors of Casas Grandes: Excavating Medio Period Communities of Northwest Chihuahua, Mexico*. University of Arizona Press, Tucson.

Wheat, Joe Ben
1972 *The Olsen–Chubbock Site: A Paleoindian Bison Kill*. American Antiquity Memoir 26.

Wheat, Margaret M.
1967 *Survival Arts of the Primitive Paiutes*. University of Nevada Press, Reno.

White, T. E.
1953 A Method of Calculating the Dietary Percentage of Various Food Animals Utilized by Aboriginal Peoples. *American Antiquity* 18 (4):396–398.

White, Tim D.
1992 *Prehistoric Cannibalism at Mancos 5MTUMR-2346*. Princeton University Press, Princeton, New Jersey.

Whitridge, Peter J.
1999 The Construction of Social Difference in a Prehistoric Inuit Whaling Community. Ph.D. dissertation, Department of Anthropology Arizona State University, Tempe.

Whitze, Alexandra
2001 Researchers Divided over Whether Anasazi Were Cannibals. *Dallas Morning News*, 1 June. Electronic document, http://news.nationalgeographic.com/news/2001/06/0601_wireanasazi.html.

Whorton, Mandy
2002 Evaluating and Managing Cold War Era Historic Properties: The Cultural Significance of US Air Force Defensive Radar Systems. In *Matériel Culture: The Archaeology of Twentieth-Century Conflict*, edited by John Schofield, William Gray Johnson and Colleen M. Beck, pp. 216–226. Routledge, New York.

Whyte, Thomas R.
1990 A Review of Evidence of Human Subsistence During the Early and Middle Archaic Periods of Virginia. In *Early and Middle Archaic Research in Virginia: A Synthesis*, edited by T. R. Rinehart and M. E. Hodges, pp. 119–131. Archaeological Society of Virginia, Richmond.

Wiant, Michael D., Edwin R. Hajic, and Thomas R. Styles
1983 Napoleon Hollow and Koster Site Stratigraphy. In *Archaic Hunters and Gatherers in the American Midwest*, edited by James L. Phillips and James A. Brown, pp. 147–164. Academic Press, New York.

Wiant, Michael D., and Charles R. McGimsey
1986 *Woodland Period Occupations of the Napoleon Hollow Site in the Lower Illinois Valley*. Center for American Archeology, Kampsville, Illinois.

Widga, Chris
2004 Early Archaic Subsistence in the Central Plains: The Spring Creek (25FT31). *Plains Anthropologist* 49:25–58.

Widmer, Randolph J.

1988 *The Evolution of the Calusa: A Nonagricultural Chiefdom on the Southwest Florida Coast*. The University of Alabama Press, Tuscaloosa.

Widmer, Randolph J.
2002 The Woodland Archaeology of South Florida. In *The Woodland Southeast*, edited by David G. Anderson and Robert C. Mainfort, Jr., pp. 373–397. University of Alabama Press, Tuscaloosa.

Wilcox, David R., David A. Gregory, and J. Brett Hill
2007 Zuni in the Puebloan and Southwestern Worlds. In *Zuni Origins: Toward a New Synthesis of Southwestern Archaeology*, edited by David A. Gregory and David R. Wilcox, pp. 165–209. University of Arizona Press, Tucson.

Wilcox, David R., and Bruce W. Masse (editors)
1981 The View from the Hopi Mesas. In *The Protohistoric Period in the North American Southwest AD 1450–1700*, pp. 321–335. Arizona State University Anthropological Research Papers 24.

Wilcox, Michael
2009 *The Pueblo Revolt and the Mythology of Conquest: An Indigenous Archaeology of Contact*. University of California Press, Berkeley.

Wilcox, Michael
2010 NAGPRA and Indigenous Peoples: the Social Context and Controversies, and the Transformation of American Archaeology. In *Voices in American Archaeology*, edited by Wendy Ashmore, Dorothy Lippert, and Barbara J. Mills, pp. 178–192. Society for American Archaeology, Washington, D.C.

Wilford, John Noble
2004 The Oldest Americans May Prove Even Older. *New York Times* 29 June. New York.

Wilke, Philip J.
1978 *Late Prehistoric Human Ecology at Lake Cahuilla, Coachella Valley, California*. University of California Archaeological Research Facility Contribution 38.

Wilke, Philip J.
1988 Bow Staves Harvested from Juniper Trees by Indians of Nevada. *Journal of California and Great Basin Anthropology* 10 (1):3–31.

Wilkie, Laurie A.
2010 *The Lost Boys of Zeta Psi: A Historical Archaeology of Masculinity at a University Fraternity.* University of California Press, Berkeley.

Will, G. F., and H. J. Spinden
1906 The Mandans: A Study of Their Culture, Archaeology, and Language. *Papers of the Peabody Museum of American Archaeology and Ethnology* 3 (4):81–219.

Willey, Gordon R.
1966 *An Introduction to American Archeology, Vol. 1: North and Middle America.* Prentice-Hall, Englewood Cliffs, New Jersey.

Willey, Gordon R., and Jeremy A. Sabloff
1993 *A History of American Archaeology,* 3rd ed. W. H. Freeman, San Francisco.

Willey, Gordon R., and Philip Phillips
1958 *Method and Theory in American Archaeology.* University of Chicago Press, Chicago.

Willey, P.
1990 *Prehistoric Warfare on the Great Plains: Skeletal Analysis of the Crow Creek Massacre Victims.* Garland, New York.

Williams, Stephen
1963 The Eastern United States. In *Early Indian Framers and Villages and Communities,* edited by William Hag, pp. 267–325. National Park Service, Washington, D.C.

Williams, Stephen
1980 The Armorel Phase: A Very Late Complex in the Lower Mississippi Valley. *Southeastern Archaeological Conference Bulletin* 22:105–110.

Williams, Stephen
1990 The Vacant Quarter and Other Late Events in the Lower Valley. In *Towns and Temples Along the Mississippi,* edited by D. H. Dye and C. A. Cox, pp. 170–180. University of Alabama Press, Tuscaloosa.

Williams, Stephen
1991 *Fantastic Archaeology: The Wild Side of North American Prehistory.* University of Pennsylvania Press, Philadelphia.

Willig, Judith A.
1991 Clovis Technology and Adaptation in Far Western North America: Regional Pattern and Environmental Context. In *Clovis: Origins and Adaptations,* edited by

Robson Bonnichsen and Karen Turnmire, pp. 91–118. Oregon State University Press for the Center for the Study of the First Americans, Corvallis.

Wilmsen, Edwin N.
1974 *Lindenmeier: A Pleistocene Hunting Society.* Harper & Row, New York.

Wilshusen, Richard H.
1989 Unstuffing the Estufa: Ritual Floor Features in Anasazi Pit Structures and Pueblo Kivas. In *The Architecture of Social Integration in Prehistoric Pueblos,* edited by William D. Lipe and Michelle Hegmon, pp. 89–142. Occasional Papers of the Crow Canyon Archaeological Center 1. Crow Canyon Archaeological Center, Cortez, Colorado.

Wilshusen, Richard H., and Eric Blinman
1992 Pueblo I Village Formation: A Reevaluation of Sites Recorded by Earl Morris on Ute Mountain Tribal Lands. *Kiva* 57:251–269.

Wilson, C. Dean, and Richard H. Wilshusen
1995 Reformatting the Social Landscape in the Late Pueblo I–Early Pueblo II Period: The Cedar Hill Data in Regional Context. In *The Cedar Hill Special Treatment Project: Late Pueblo I, Early Navajo and Historic Occupations in Northwestern New Mexico,* edited by Richard H. Wilshusen, pp. 43–80. LaPlata Archeaological Consultants, Dolores, Colorado.

Wilson, Michael C., and James A. Bums
1999 Searching for the Earliest Canadians: Wide Corridors, Narrow Doorways, Small Windows. In *Ice Age People of North America,* edited by Robson Bonnichsen and Karen Turnmire, pp. 214–239. Oregon State University Press for the Center for the Study of the First Americans, Corvallis.

Winham, R. Peter, and F. A. Calabrese
1998 The Middle Missouri Tradition. In *Archaeology of the Great Plains,* edited by Raymond Wood, pp. 269–307. University Press of Kansas, Lawrence.

Winter, J. C., and P. Hogan
1992 The Dinétah Phase of Northwestern New Mexico: Settlement and Subsistence. In *Current Research on the Late Prehistory and Early History of New Mexico,*

edited by B. J. Vierra, pp. 299–312. New Mexico Archaeological Council, Albuquerque.

Winters, Howard
1968 Value Systems and Trade Cycles of the Late Archaic in the Midwest. In *New Perspectives in Archaeology,* edited by Sally R. Binford and Lewis R. Binford, pp. 175–221. Aldine, Chicago.

Wiseman, James
2001a Declaration of Independence. *Archaeology* 54 (4):10–12.

Wiseman, James
2001b Point: Archaeology as an Academic Discipline. *SAA Archaeological Record* 2 (3):8–10.

Wissler, Clark
1914 Material Cultures of the North American Indians. *American Anthropologist* 16 (3):447–505.

Wissler, Clark
1926 *The Relation of Nature to Man in Aboriginal North America.* Oxford University Press, New York.

Witthoft, John
1952 A Paleo-Indian Site in Eastern Pennsylvania: An Early Hunting Culture. *Proceedings of the American Philosophical Society (Philadelphia)* 96:464–495.

Wolf, Eric
1982 *Europe and the People Without History.* University of California Press, Berkeley.

Wolynec, Renata B.
2004 *Project Archaeology: Pennsylvania: An Educational Standards-Based Curriculum for Grades Four Through Eight, 2002-2003.* Pennsylvania Archaeological Council and Pennsylvania Historical and Museum Commission, Harrisburg.

Wolynec, Renata B.
1977 The Systematic Analysis of Features from the Koster Site, a Stratified Archaic Site. Ph.D. dissertation, Department of Anthropology, Northwestern University Evanston, Illinois.

Wood, W. Raymond
1969 Two House Sites in the Central Plains: An Experiment in Archaeology. *Plains Anthropologist* 14 (44, pt. 2):Memoir 6.

Wood, W. Raymond
1971 *Biesterfeldt: A Post-Contact Coalescent Site on the Northeastern Plains.* Smithsonian Contributions

to Anthropology 15. Smithsonian Institution, Washington, D.C.

Wood, W. Raymond (editor)

1998 *Archaeology on the Great Plains.* University Press of Kansas, Lawrence.

Wood, Raymond

2001 Plains Village Tradition: Middle Missouri. In *Plains,* edited by Raymond J. De Mallie, pp. 186–195. Handbook of North American Indians, Vol. 13, William C. Sturtevant, general editor, Smithsonian Institution, Washington, D.C.

Woodbury, Anthony C.

1984 Eskimo and Aleut Languages. In *Arctic,* edited by David Damas, pp. 49–63. Handbook of North American Indians, Vol. 5, William C. Sturtevant, general editor, Smithsonian Institution, Washington, D.C.

Woodward, Susan L., and Jerry N. McDonald

2002 *Indian Mounds of the Middle Ohio Valley: A Guide to Mounds and Earthworks of the Adena, Hopewell, Cole and Fort Ancient People.* McDonald and Woodward, Blacksburg, Virginia.

Wooley, Christopher B., and James C. Haggarty

1995 Archaeological Site Protection: An Integral Component of the Exxon Valdez Shoreline Cleanup. In *Exxon Valdez Oil Spill: Fate and Effects in Alaskan Waters, ASTM STP 1219,* edited by Peter G. Wells, James N. Butler, and Jane S. Hughes., pp. 933–949. American Society for Testing and Materials, Philadelphia.

Woolley, Jonathan, and Jeremy H. C. Davis

1991 The Agronomy of Intercropping with Beans. In *Common Beans: Research for Crop Improvement,* edited by A. vonSchoonhoven and O. Voysest, pp. 707–735. CAB International, Wallington, Oxon, United Kingdom.

Workman, William B.

1998 Northern Archaic Tradition. In *Archaeology of Prehistoric Native America: An Encyclopedia,* edited by Guy Gibbon, pp. 567–569. Garland, New York.

Wormington, H. Marie, and Dorothy Ellis

1967 *Pleistocene Studies in Southern Nevada.* Nevada State Museum Anthropological Paper 13.

Wright, H. T., and R. B. Roosa

1966 The Barnes Site: A Fluted Point Assemblage from the Great Lakes Region. *American Antiquity* 31:850–860.

Wright, Herbert E., Jr.

2006 Climate and Biota of Eastern North America. In *Environment, Origins, and Population,* edited by Douglas H. Ubelaker, pp. 99–109. Handbook of North American Indians, Vol. 3, William C. Sturtevant, general editor, Smithsonian Institution, Washington, D.C.

Wright, James V.

1981 Prehistory of the Canadian Shield. In *Subarctic,* edited by June Helm, pp. 86–96. Handbook of North American Indians, Vol. 6, William C. Sturtevant, general editor, Smithsonian Institution, Washington, D.C.

Wright, James V.

1995 *A History of the Native Peoples of Canada,* Vol. 1. Mercury Series, Paper 152. Archaeological Survey of Canada. Canadian Museum of Civilization, Ottawa.

Wright, James V.

1998 Shield Culture. In *Archaeology of Prehistoric Native America: An Encyclopedia,* edited by Guy Gibbon, pp. 760–761. Garland, New York.

Wright, James V.

1999 *A History of the Native Peoples of Canada,* Vol. II. Mercury Series, Paper 152, Archaeological Survey of Canada. Canadian Museum of Civilization, Ottawa.

Wright, James V.

2001 *A History of the Native People of Canada.* Electronic document, http://www.civilization.ca/cmc/exhibitions/archeo/hnpc/npint00e.shtml, accessed September 16, 2012.

Wright, James V.

2004 *A History of the Native Peoples of Canada,* Vol III, Part 1(AD 500-European Contact). Mercury Series, Paper 152, Archaeological Survey of Canada. Canadian Museum of Civilization, Ottawa.

Wycoff, Don G.

1985 The Packard Complex: Early Archaic Pre-Dalton Occupations on the Prairie–Woodlands Border. *Southeastern Archaeology* 4 (1):1–26.

Wycoff, Don G.

1999 The Burnham Site and Pleistocene Human Occupations of the Southern Plains of the United States. In *Ice Age People of North America: Environments, Origins and Adaptations of the First Americans,* edited by Robson Bonnichsen and Karen Turnmire, pp. 340–361. Oregon State University Press for the Center for the Study of the First Americans, Corvallis.

Wymer, Dee Anne

1996 The Ohio Hopewell Econiche: Human–Land Interaction in the Core Area. In *A View from the Core: A Synthesis of Ohio Hopewell Archaeology,* edited by Paul J. Pacheco, pp. 36–52. Ohio Archaeological Council, Columbus.

Wymer, Dee Anne

1997 Paleoethnobotany in the Licking River Valley, Ohio: Implications for Understanding Ohio Hopewell. In *Ohio Hopewell Community Organization,* edited by William S. Dancey and Paul J. Pacheco, pp. 153–171. Kent State University Press, Kent, Ohio.

Yansa, Catherine

2007 Lake Records of Northern Plains Paleoindian and Early Archaic Environments: The "Park Oasis" Hypothesis. *Plains Anthropologist* 52:109–144.

Yarnell, Richard A.

1974 Plant Food and Cultivation of the Salts Cavers. In *Archaeology of the Mammoth Cave Area,* edited by Patty Jo Watson, pp. 113–122. Academic Press, Orlando, Florida.

Yarnell, Richard A.

1976 Early Plant Husbandry in Eastern North America. In *Cultural Change and Continuity: Essays in Honor of James Bennet Griffin,* edited by Charles Cleland, pp. 265–274. Academic Press, New York.

Yerkes, Richard W.

1983 Microwear, Microdrills and Mississippian Craft Specialization. *American Antiquity* 48 (3):499–518.

Yerkes, Richard W.

2006 Middle Woodland Settlements and Social Organization in the Central Ohio Valley: Were the Hopewell Really Farmers? In *Recreating Hopewell,* edited by

Douglas K. Charles and Jane E. Buikstra, pp. 50–61. University of Florida Press, Gainesville.

Yesner, David R.
2007 Faunal Extinction, Hunter-Gatherer Foraging Strategies, and Subsistence Diversity Among Eastern Beringian Paleoindians. In *Foragers of the Terminal Pleistocene in North America*, edited by Renee B. Walker and Boyce N. Driskell, pp. 15–31. Unviersity of Nebraska Press, Lincoln.

Zawacki, April Allison, and Glenn Hausfater
1969 *Early Vegetation of the Lower Illinois Valley.* Illinois State Museum. Springfield.

Zeder, Melinda A.
1997 *The American Archaeologist: A Profile.* AltaMira Press, Walnut Creek, California.

Zellar, Terry
1987 Arthur C. Parker: A Pioneer in American Museums. *Curator* 30 (10):41–62.

Zellar, Terry
1989 Arthur Parker and the Educational Mission of American Museums. *Curator* 32 (2):104–122.

Zhang, Linhai, Charles R. Brown, David Culley, Barbara Baker, Elizabeth Kunibe, Hazel Denney, Cassandra Smith, Neuee Ward, Tia Beavert, Julie Coburn, J. J. Pavek, Nora Dauenhauer, and Richard Dauenhauer
2010 Inferred Origin of Several Native American Potatoes from the Pacific Northwest and Southeast Alaska Using SSR Markers. *Euphytica* 174:15–29.

Zimmerman, Larry J.
2003 *Presenting the Past.* Archaeologist's Toolkit 7. AltaMira Press, Walnut Creek, California.

Zimmerman, Larry J., Karen D. Vitelli, and Julie Hollowell-Zimmer (editors)
2003 *Ethical Issues in Archaeology.* AltaMira Press, Walnut Creek, California.

Credits

If not listed below by figure number, figures were generated for this publication by Oxford University Press.

1.1 Beverly A. Chiarulli; 1.4 By permission of Cahokia Mounds State Historic Site; 1.5 Sarah W. Neusius; 1.6 Phillip D. Neusius; 1.8 Courtesy James Judge; 1.9 Vincas P. Steponaitis; 1.10 Photograph by Sandy Tradlener, by permission of Crow Canyon Archaeological Center; 1.11 Sarah W. Neusius; 1.12 G. Timothy Gross; 1.13 Virginia Caramana; 1.14 Sarah W. Neusius; 1.15 Beverly A. Chiarulli; 1.16 Courtesy Soil Systems, Inc; 1.17 Courtesy Soil Systems, Inc.; 1.18 Courtesy Soil Systems, Inc; 1.19 Courtesy Soil Systems, Inc.

2.3 Alvin Walter; 2.4 Marcia Adams; 2.5 Sarah W. Neusius; 2.6 Sarah W. Neusius; 2.7 Marcia Adams; 2.8 G. Timothy Gross; 2.11 Sarah W. Neusius; 2.13 Courtesy Julie Stein; 2.15 Courtesy Robert Kelly; 2.16 Originally published in Jefferies, 1987, reproduced by permission of the Board of Trustees, Southern Illinois University; 2.17 Sarah W. Neusius.

3.2 All Rights Reserved Image Archives Denver Museum of Nature and Science; 3.3 Virginia W. Caramana; 3.4 From *Archaeology of the Great Plains*, edited by the W. Raymond Wood, published by the University Press of Kansas © 1998, used by permission of the publisher, and reprinted from *Prehistoric Hunters of the High Plains* Second Edition by George C. Frison, p. 160, © 1991 with the permission from Elsevier; 3.5 Redrawn with permission from Martin SCIENCE 179:969 (1973). Copyright 1973 AAAS;

3.6 Sarah W. Neusius; 3.7 From Carr and Adovasio 2002, published by the Pennsylvania Historical and Museum Commission, 2002; 3.8 Drawn by Simon S.S. Driver, from *Ancient North America: The Archaeology of a Continent*, by Brian Fagan, Thames and Hudson, London and New York; 3.9 Photo by Ruth Kirk; 3.11 Frederick A. West; 3.12 Redrawn and modified after Dixon 1999, p. 168; 3.14a and 3.14b Illustrations by Valerie Waldorf; 3.16 From Meltzer, 1993, courtesy David Meltzer; 3.17 Arizona State Museum, University of Arizona, E. B. Sayles, photographer, Image 3145; 3.18 From Carr and Adovasio 2002, published by the Pennsylvania Historical and Museum Commission; 3.19 Photograph by Michael R. Waters, courtesy David Carlson; 3.20 Courtesy Jon Erlandson 3.21 From Erlandson et al., SCIENCE 331:1181–1185. Reprinted with permission from AAAS.; 3.22 From Erlandson et al., SCIENCE 331:1181–1185. Reprinted with permission from AAAS.; 3.23 Courtesy Jon Erlandson.

4.3 Illustrated by Eric O. Mose; 4.4 Shield Archaic Culture artifacts © Canadian Museum of Civilization, catalogue no. CD94-679-004, image no. S87-1289; 4.5 Adapted from Clark, 1984 by permission of the University of Alaska and the University of Wisconsin Madison; 4.7 From Dumond 1987, photo by Don E. Dumond, items held by the University of Oregon Museum of Natural and Cultural History; 4.8 From Clark, 1984, Figure 5 by permission of the University of Alaska and the University of Wisconsin Madison; 4.9 From Rousselot et al. 1988, Figure 195, by permission of William Fitzhugh; 4.10 From Dumond, 1987, drawing by Carol Steichen Dumond by permission of Don E. Dumond, objects in the collections of the U.S. Fish and Wildlife Service; 4.11 From Dumond, 1987, drawing by Carol Steichen Dumond, items held by the University of Oregon Museum of Natural and Cultural History; 4.12 From Dumond, 1987, drawing by Carol Steichen Dumond; 4.13 From McGhee 1978, Color Plate II, courtesy Robert McGhee; 4.14 From Dumond, 1987, line drawing by Carol Steichen Dumond after Knuth 1966/67; 4.15 From Maxwell, 1985, Figure 5.2, with permission from Elsevier; 4.16 From Dumond, 1987, Figures 57–61 photo by Don E. Dumond, objects in the collections of the Canadian Museum of Civilization; 4.17 From McGhee, 1978, Plate 10 courtesy Robert McGhee; 4.18a Floating or flying bear, ivory © Canadian Museum of Civilization, catalogue no. PgHb1:13692, photo Ross Taylor, image no. S90-2623; 4.18b Pair of swans, ivory © Canadian Museum of Civilization, catalogue no. JlGu-2:156, photo Ross Taylor, image no. S90-3058; 4.18c Miniature mask, antler © Canadian Museum of Civilization, catalogue no. PgHb-7:523, photo Ross Taylor, image no. S90-2633; 4.18d Shaman's teeth, ivory © Canadian Museum of Civilization, catalogue no. NhHd-1:1121, photo Ross Taylor, image no. S90-3192; 4.18e "Killed" human figure © Canadian Museum of Civilization, catalogue no. RaJu-1:109, photo by Ross Taylor, image no. S90-2944; 4.19 Douglas D. Anderson; 4.20 From Dumond 1987, photo by Don E. Dumond, items held by the University of Oregon Museum of Natural and Cultural History; 4.21 From Dumond, Chapter 3 In Jennings, 1983, Figure 3.7; 4.22 adapted from Willey 1966 Figs 7.8 and 7.12; 4.23 From Arutinov and Fitzhugh, 1988, Figure 137 by permission of William Fithugh; 4.24 From Maxwell, 1985, Figure 8.3a © 1985, by permission of Elsevier; 4.25 Ceramic pot © Canadian Museum of Civilization, catalogue no. EdKh.1, photo Jean-Luc Pilon, image no. S2000-5685; 4.26 Courtesy Ben Fitzhugh; 4.27 Courtesy Ben Fitzhugh; 4.28 Courtesy Ben Fitzhugh; 4.29 Courtesy Ben Fitzhugh.

5.2 From Stewart 1977, courtesy Hilary Stewart; 5.3 Bob Whitlam, courtesy of the Washington State Department of Archaeology and Historic Preservation; 5.4 Frederick Hadleigh West; 5.5 Courtesy Knut Fladmark; 5.6 Figure 18, p. 90, Ames and Maschner 1999; 5.7 Courtesy Kenneth M. Ames and Canadian Museum of Civilization; 5.8 Courtesy Kenneth M. Ames; 5.9 Photo by Ruth Kirk from Kirk and Daugherty 1978, p. 101 left side; 5.10 From

MacDonald, George, 1983, *Prehistoric Art of the Northwest Coast*, Fig. 6.16, by permission of Archaeology Press, Simon Fraser University; 5.11 University of British Columbia Museum; 5.12 Courtesy of Dale R. Croes, illustration by Nancy Romaine, Royal British Columbia Museum; 5.13 From Hoff 1980, Figs. 58, 59, 63 and 64; 5.14 Image OrHi 105047, Oregon Historical Society; 5.15 From Ayers 1980, Figure 49; 5.17 Photograph by Ruth Kirk, from Kirk and Daugherty 1978, p. 100; 5.18 From Suttles, 1990b, Fig. 1, by permission of the *Handbook of North American Indians*; 5.19 Figure 84, Ames and Maschner, 1999; 5.20 Photograph by Ruth Kirk from Kirk and Daugherty 1978, p. 104; 5.21 Photograph by Harvey S. Rice from Kirk and Daugherty 1978, p. 102; 5.22 Model of Kitwanga Fort © Canadian Museum of Civilization, CVH vol. 77, S24, Image no. D2006-05010; 5.23 Courtesy of the Qwu?gwes Cultural Studies Project; 5.24 Courtesy of the Qwu?gwes Cultural Studies Project; 5.25 Courtesy of the Qwu?gwes Cultural Studies Project; 5.26 Courtesy of the Qwu?gwes Cultural Studies Project.

6.2 Courtesy Mike Rousseau; 6.3 G. Timothy Gross; 6.4 Reproduced from Ames et al. 1998, figure 2, p. 105 (after Leonhardy and Rice, 1970) by permission of the *Handbook of North American Indians*; 6.5 After Butler, 1968, Fig. 13; 6.6 Courtesy Knut Fladmark and the Canadian Museum of Civilization; 6.7 Courtesy of Max Pavesic; 6.8 Drawing by Roald Fryxell for Kirk and Daugherty; 6.9 Courtesy Mike Rousseau; 6.10 Courtesy Knut Fladmark; 6.11 Courtesy Knut Fladmark; 6.12 Drawing by Chris Walsh Heady from Kirk and Daugherty 1978, p. 73; 6.13 Reproduced from Schalk 1983, Figure 6.6; 6.14 Reproduced from Osborne 1957, Fig. 2; 6.15 Reproduced by permission of the Society for American Archaeology from *American Antiquity* 62(1) 1997; 6.16 Photo by Brian Hayden; 6.17 From Osborne, 1957, Plates 29 and 30; 6.19 G. Timothy Gross; 6.20 G. Timothy Gross; 6.21 From Schalk 1983, Figs 6.2 and 6.3.

7.2 G. Timothy Gross; 7.3 From Chartkoff and Chartkoff, 1984, Figure 30, courtesy Joseph Chartkoff; 7.4 From Chartkoff and Chartkoff, 1984, Figure 49, courtesy Joseph Chartkoff; 7.5 G. Timothy Gross courtesy of the San Diego Museum of Man; 7.6 G. Timothy Gross, artifacts from the Cleveland National Forest, courtesy of the San Diego Archaeological Center; 7.7 From Chartkoff and Chartkoff 1984, Figure 33, courtesy Joseph Chartkoff; 7.8 *Toward a*

Bulletin 60, Figure 104; 12.10 Courtesy Ken Sassaman; 12.11 Courtesy Mike Russo; 12.12 Reprinted from Bense, 1994, Figures 6.4, 6.5, 6.6, and 6.7 © 1994, with permission of Elsevier; 12.13 Reprinted from *The Archaeology of New England* by Dean R. Snow, p. 123, © 1980 with permission of Elsevier; 12.14 Reprinted from Ritchie 1989, Bulletin 384, New York State Museum, printed by permission of the New York State Museum, Albany, NY; 12.15 Reproduced by permission of the New Jersey State Museum; 12.16 Wisconsin Historical Society, Image #5173; 12.17 Reprinted from the *Archaeology of Missouri, Volume II* by Carl H. Chapman, by permission of the University of Missouri, © 1980 by the Curators of the University of Missouri; 12.18 Drawing by Ivan Kochsis, Courtesy of Museum of Ontario Archaeology, London; 12.19 After Trigger, 1978, p. ix, by permission of the *Handbook of North American Indians*; 12:20 Courtesy of Florida Museum of Natural History, photo by Jeff Gaeg, graphic by Pat Payne; 12.21 Ashmolean Museum, Oxford University, Image AN1685.B.205; 12.22 Courtesy John Hart; 12.23 Courtesy John Hart; 12.24 Courtesy John Hart; 12.25 Courtesy John Hart.

13.2 Courtesy of Smithsonian National Museum of Natural History; 13.3 Courtesy of Smithsonian National Museum of Natural History; 13.4 "Bishop of Baffin," wooden carving © Canadian Museum of Civilization, catalogue no. KeDq-7:325, Image no. S94-6299; 13.5 Sarah W. Neusius; 13.6 Sarah W. Neusius; 13.7 G. Timothy Gross; 13.8 Sarah W. Neusius; 13.9 Photo by Virgil M. Young, Boise, Idaho; 13.10 Sarah W. Neusius; 13.11 Sarah W. Neusius; 13.12 Courtesy the Friends of the Hunley; 13.13 Courtesy Eleanor King, photo by Alina Epstein; 13.14 Phillip D. Neusius; 13.16 From Van Wormer et al. 1998 Fig. 62, Courtesy of Affinis Environmental Services; 13.17 G. Timothy Gross; 13.18 Courtesy Carol McDavid; 13.19 Courtesy Carol McDavid, photo by Debra Blacklock-Sloan; 13.20 Courtesy Christopher N. Matthews.

14.1 Beverly A. Chiarulli; 14.2 Photo by Andy Gilletti, courtesy Affinis Environmental Services; 14.3 From Loubser, Johannes H. N. 2003 by permission of AltaMira Press; 14.4 Sarah W. Neusius; 14.5 Beverly A. Chiarulli; 14.6 Sarah W. Neusius; 14.7 Lobby Exhibit, Dickson Mounds Museum, by permission of the Illinois State Museum; 14.8 Sarah W. Neusius; 14.9 Beverly A. Chiarulli; 14.10 Courtesy New York State Museum, Albany, NY A1990.04 Photo 7:6; 14.11 Sarah W. Neusius.

A.1 Plate XIX in Squier and Davis, 1848; A.2 Harvard University, Peabody Museum Photo 2004.24.1365.1; A.3 Courtesy National Anthropological Archives, Smithsonian Institution, Negative # 92-5784; A.5 Photo Courtesy of SIUC Media and Communications Resources; A.6 Courtesy Office of Public Affairs, Southern Methodist University; A.7 Sarah W. Neusius; A.8 Beverly A. Chiarulli.

B.1 Beverly A. Chiarulli; B.2 Beverly A. Chiarulli; B.3 Courtesy New York State Museum, A1992.04, Photo 1:5; B.4 Sarah W. Neusius; B.5 Sarah W. Neusius; B.6 G. Timothy Gross; B.7 Sarah W. Neusius; B.8 Sarah W. Neusius; B.9 Courtesy New York State Museum Albany, NY, A1992.04, Photo 1:21; B.10 Beverly A. Chiarulli, B.11 G. Timothy Gross.

C.1 Sarah W. Neusius; C.2 Redrawn based on student notebooks from excavations at the C.W. Harris site, San Diego County, CA; C.3 From Meltzer, 1993 courtesy David J. Meltzer; C.4 Reproduced from p. 6, Stokes and Smiley, 1968 by permission of the University of Chicago Press; C.5 Sarah W. Neusius; C.6 Virginia Caramana.

D1.2 Courtesy New York State Museum, A1990.04, photo 1:5; D1.3 Courtesy New York State Museum; D1.4 Courtesy New York State Museum, A1992.04, Photo 49:6; D1.5 Courtesy New York State Museum; D2.1 Photo by D. Baston, courtesy of the Center for American Archaeology; D2.3 Photo by D. Baston, courtesy of the Center for American Archeology; D2.4 Photo by D. Baston, courtesy of the Center for American Archeology; D2.5 Photo by D. Baston, courtesy of the Center for American Archeology; D3.1 Courtesy Anthony Boldurian; D3.2 Joanna Boldurian; D3.3 Figure 24, p. 57, Boldurian and Cotter, 1999 by permission of the University of Pennsylvania Museum of Archaeology and Anthropology; D3.4 Figure 25, p. 59, Figure 26b, p. 61 and Figure 33b, p. 71, Boldurian and Cotter, 1999 by permission of the University of Pennsylvania Museum of Archaeology and Anthropology; D3.5 From Lahren and Bonnichsen, SCIENCE 186:147 (1974). Reprinted with permission from AAAS.; D3.6 Figure 46, p. 96, Boldurian and Cotter, 1999 by permission of the University of Pennsylvania Museum of Archaeology and Anthropology; D3.7 Joanna Boldurian; D4.1 G. Timothy Gross; D4.2 Erin M. King; D4.3 Erin M. King; D4.4 Reproduced by permission of the Society for American Archaeology from American Antiquity 69(1), 2004; D5.1 Dolores Archaeological Program slide, curated at the Anasazi Heritage Center, Dolores, CO; D5.2 Dolores Archaeological Program slide, curated at the Anasazi Heritage Center, Dolores, CO; D5.3 Dolores Archaeological Program slide, curated at the Anasazi Heritage Center, Dolores, CO; D5.4 Figure 5.11, p. 405 in Kane, 1986a, image curated at the Anasazi Heritage Center, Dolores, CO; D5.5 Figure 5.13, p. 407 in Kane, 1986a, image curated at the Anasazi Heritage Center, Dolores, CO; D5.6 Figure 5.17, p. 413 in Kane, 1986a, image curated at the Anasazi Heritage Center, Dolores, CO; D6.1 Reprinted by permission from *Southeastern Archaeology*, Vol. 24(1); D6.2 Courtesy Renee B. Walker; D6.3 Reproduced from Walker et al. 2001 by permission of AltaMira Press; D6.4 Courtesy Renee B. Walker; D6.5 Courtesy Renee B. Walker; D6.6 Courtesy Renee B. Walker; D6.7 Illustration by Jennifer L. Kirkmeyer, courtesy Boyce N. Driskell; D6.8 Illustration by Jennifer L. Kirkmeyer, courtesy Boyce N. Driskell; D6.9 Courtesy Renee B. Walker; D6.10 Courtesy Renee B. Walker; D7.1 Plate XVII in Squier and Davis, 1848; D7.2 Courtesy Mark Lynott; D7.3 Courtesy Mark Lynott; D7.4 Courtesy Mark Lynott; D8.1 Donald P. Heldman, courtesy Elizabeth M. Scott; D8.2 Donald P. Heldman, courtesy Elizabeth M. Scott; D8.3 Courtesy Elizabeth M. Scott; D8.4 Courtesy Elizabeth M. Scott; D8.5 Courtesy Elizabeth M. Scott; D8.6 Courtesy Elizabeth M. Scott.

E1.1 Courtesy of the University of Rochester, Department of Rare Books and Special Collections; E2.1 Courtesy Linda Mayro.

F2.1 G. Timothy Gross, courtesy San Diego Archaeological Center; F4.1 Keith Kasnot, National Geographic Image Collection, #675694; F6.1 Reproduced by permission of the Society for American Archaeology from *American Antiquity* 67(1) 2002; F6.2 Reproduced by permission of the Society for American Archaeology from *American Antiquity* 67(1) 2002; F6.3 Reproduced by permission of the Society for American Archaeology from *American Antiquity* 67(1) 2002.

Index

Page numbers followed by *t* and *f* refer to tables and figures, respectively.